# *Law School Publications*

## *of*

## WEST PUBLISHING COMPANY
### St. Paul 2, Minnesota

***

### ACCOUNTING

Shannon's Accounting and the Law, 604 pages, 1957.

Shannon's Legal Accounting, 366 pages, 1951.

### ADMINISTRATIVE LAW

Davis' Cases, 592 pages, 1959.

Davis Text, 617 pages, 1959.

Davis' Cases, Text and Problems, 609 pages, 1960.

Merrill's Cases, 720 pages, 1954.

### ADMIRALTY

Robinson's Text, 1025 pages, 1939.

Sprague and Healy's Cases, 859 pages, 1950.

### AGENCY

Seavey and Hall's Cases, 431 pages 1956.

Seavey's Studies, 451 pages, 1949.

Steffen's Cases, 2nd Ed., 902 pages, 1952.

Tiffany's Text, 2nd Ed., 485 pages, 1924.

### BANKRUPTCY

MacLachlan's Text, 500 pages, 1956.

Nadler's Cases on Creditor-Debtor Relations, 698 pages, 1956.

Nadler's Supp., 233 pages, 1959.

Sturges' Cases on Debtors' Estates, 4th Ed., 1291 pages, 1949.

See Creditors' Rights.

### BILLS AND NOTES

Aigler's Cases, 2nd Ed., 566 pages, 1955.

Britton's Text, 1245 pages, 1943.

Moore's Cases, 2nd Ed., 409 pp., 1940.

Smith & Moore's Cases, 4th Ed. 1070 pages, 1941.

### CIVIL PROCEDURE

McBaine's Cases, Introduction, 399 pages, 1950.

### CODE PLEADING

Clark's Cases on Modern Pleading, 1042 pages, 1952.

Clark's Text, 2nd Ed., 874 pages, 1947.

Cleary's Cases on Pleading, 2d Ed., 434 pages, 1958.

Stayton's Cases, Texas Pleading, 851 pages, 1953.

### COMMON LAW PLEADING

McBaine's Cases, Introduction to Civil Procedure, 399 pages, 1950.

Shipman's Text, 3rd Ed., 644 pages, 1923.

Stayton's Cases (Texas), 1952.

### COMMUNITY PROPERTY

Burby's Cases, 4th Ed., 342 pages, 1955.

Huie's Texas Cases on Marital Rights, 781 pages, 1955.

Verrall's Cases, California Community Property, 320 pages, 1960.

### CONFLICT OF LAWS

Ehrenzweig's Text, 367 pages, 1959.

Goodrich's Text, 3rd Ed., 662 pages, 1949.

Lorenzen's Cases, 6th Ed., 918 pages, 1951.

Selected Readings, 1151 pages, 1956.

Stumberg's Cases, 497 pages, 1956.

## CONSTITUTIONAL LAW

Dodd's Cases, 5th Ed., 1438 pages, 1954.

Dodd's Cases, 5th Ed., Shorter Ed., 969 pages, 1954.

Dodd's Supplement, 1960.

Forrester's Cases, 879 pages, 1959.

Forrester's Supplement, 1960.

Rottschaefer's Text, 982 pages, 1939.

Rottschaefer's Cases, 975 pages, 1948.

## CONTRACTS

Corbin's Cases, 3rd Ed., 1381 pages, 1947. 1953 Supplement, 36 pages.

Corbin's Text, Student Edition, 1224 pages, 1952.

Fuller's Cases, 994 pages, 1947.

Simpson's Cases, 592 pages, 1956.

Simpson's Text, 692 pages, 1954.

## CORPORATIONS

Richard's Cases, Rev. 3rd Ed., 1067 pages, 1940.

Stevens & Larson's Cases, 2nd Ed., 741 pages, 1955.

Stevens' Text, 2nd Ed., 1125 pages, 1949.

## CREDIT TRANSACTIONS

Maxwell & Riesenfeld's California Cases on Security Transactions, 371 pages, 1957.

Sturges' Cases, 4th Ed., 599 pages, 1955.

## CREDITORS' RIGHTS

Nadler's Cases on Creditor and Debtor Relations, 698 pages, 1956.

Nadler's Supp., 233 pages, 1959.

Sturges' Cases Debtors' Estates, 4th Ed., 1291 pages, 1949.

## CRIMINAL LAW

Hall & Glueck's Cases, 2d Ed., 699 pages, 1958.

Miller's Text, 649 pages, 1934.

Stumberg's Texas Cases, 505 pages, 1954.

## DAMAGES

Crane's Cases, 3rd Ed., 337 pages, 1955.

McCormick's Text, 811 pages, 1935.

## DICTIONARIES

Black's, one volume.

Bouvier's, two volumes.

## DOMESTIC RELATIONS

Compton's Cases, 638 pages, 1951.

Madden's Text, 748 pp., 1931.

## DRUGS AND DRUGGISTS

Arthur's Text, 4th Ed., 399 pp., 1955.

## ENGINEERING LAW

Simpson & Dillavou's Text, 4th Ed., 506 pages, 1958.

## EQUITY

Cook's Cases, 4th Ed., 1192 pp., 1948.

McClintock's Text, 2nd Ed., 643 pages, 1948.

Van Hecke's Cases on Equitable Remedies, 651 pages, 1959.

## EVIDENCE

McCormick's Cases, 3rd Ed., 663 pages, 1956.

McCormick's Text, 774 pages, 1954.

Selected Writings, 1232 pages, 1957.

## FEDERAL ANTI-TRUST LAWS

Oppenheim's Cases, 1188 pages, 1959.

## FEDERAL JURISDICTION AND PROCEDURE

Bunn's U. S. Courts, Text, 5th Ed., 408 pages, 1949.

Forrester's Dobie & Ladd Cases, 968 pages, 1950.

## FEDERAL TAXATION

Bruton and Bradley's Cases, 808 pages, 1955.

## FRAUD AND MISTAKE

Keeton's Cases, 514 pages, 1954.

## FUTURE INTERESTS

Gulliver's Cases, 624 pages, 1959.

Powell's Cases, 2nd Ed., 1068 pages, 1937.

Simes Text, 495 pages, 1951.

## INSURANCE

Keeton's Basic Insurance Law, 655 pages, 1960.

Vance's Text, 3rd Ed., 1290 pages, 1951.

Vance's Cases, 4th Ed., 994 pages, 1952.

## INTERNATIONAL LAW

Hudson's Cases, 3rd Ed., 770 pages, 1951.

Wilson's Text, 3rd Ed., 623 pages, 1939.

## INTRODUCTION TO LAW
Bowman's Text, 307 pages, 1929.
Smith's Text, 2nd Ed., 468 pages, 1939.
See Legal Method

## JUDICIAL REMEDIES
Cribbet's Cases, 762 pages, 1954.

## JURISPRUDENCE
Simpson and Stone's Cases Law and Society, Book I, Law and Society in Evolution, 692 pages, 1948. Book II, Law in Modern Democratic Society, 902 pages, 1949. Book III, Law, Totalitarianism and Democracy, 796 pages, 1949.
Wu's Cases, 719 pages, 1958.

## LABOR LAW
Handler & Hays' Cases, 3rd Ed., 824 pages, 1959.
Handler & Hays' Supp., 58 pages, 1960.

## LANDLORD AND TENANT
Jacobs' Cases, 2nd Ed., 815 pages, 1941.

## LEGAL ACCOUNTING
See Accounting.

## LEGAL BIBLIOGRAPHY
How to Find the Law, 5th Ed., 207 pages, 1957.

## LEGAL ETHICS
Pirsig's Cases on the Legal Profession, 211 pages, 1957.

## LEGAL HISTORY
Radin's Text, 612 pages, 1936.

## LEGAL METHOD
Fryer and Benson's Legal Method and Legal System, 1 volume Ed., 843 pages, 1950.

## LEGISLATION
Nutting and Elliott's Cases, 2nd Ed., 402 pages, 1955.

## MARITAL RIGHTS
Huie's Texas Cases, 781 pages, 1955.

## MILITARY LAW
Schiller's Cases, 590 pages, 1952.

## MORTGAGES
Osborne's Cases Property Security, 2nd Ed., 725 pages, 1954.
Osborne's Text, 1117 pages, 1951.
Sturges' Cases Credit Transactions, 4th Ed., 599 pages, 1955.

## MUNICIPAL CORPORATIONS
Stason and Kauper's Cases, 3rd Ed., 692 pages, 1959.

## NATURAL RESOURCES
Martz's Cases, 1124 pages, 1951.

## OIL AND GAS
Huie, Walker and Woodward's Cases, 848 pages, 1960.
Kulp's Cases, 3rd Ed., 910 pages, 1947. Supplement, 1953.
Summer's Cases, 781 pages, 1952.

## PARTNERSHIP
Crane's Text, 2d Ed., 655 pages, 1952.
Gilmore's Cases, 3rd Ed., 501 pages, 1949.
Reuschlein's Cases on Partnership & Unincorporated Business, 660 pages, 1952.

## PERSONAL PROPERTY
Aigler, Smith and Tefft's Cases on Property, 2 Vols., 1339 pages, 1960.

## PERSONAL PROPERTY—Continued

Bigelow's Cases, 3rd Ed., 500 pages, 1942.

Fryer's Readings, 3rd Ed., 1184 pages, 1938.

## PLEADING

See Code Pleading.

See Common Law Pleading.

## PRESS, LAW OF

Hale's Text, 3rd Ed., 691 pages, 1948.

## PROPERTY SECURITY

Osborne's Cases, 2nd Ed., 725 pages, 1954.

See also Mortgages.

## PUBLIC UTILITIES

Auerbach & Nathanson's Cases on Federal Regulation of Transportation, 1223 pages, 1953.

## QUIZZERS

Ballantine's Problems.

Burby's Law Refreshers.

Owen's Quizzer.

Smith's How to Answer Law Examinations.

Smith's Law Reviews.

## REAL PROPERTY

Aigler, Bigelow & Powell's Cases on Property, 2nd Ed., Two Vols., 1686 pages, 1951.

Aigler, Smith & Tefft's Cases on Property, 2 Vols., 1339 pages, 1960.

Bigelow's Cases on Rights in Land, 3rd Ed., 1024 pages, 1945.

Burby's Text, 2nd Ed., 758 pages, 1954.

Horack and Nolan's Land Use Controls, 240 pages, 1955.

Jacobs' Cases Landlord and Tenant, 2nd Ed., 815 pages, 1941.

## REAL PROPERTY—Continued

Moynihan's Introduction, 154 pp., 1940.

Smith's Survey, 398 pages, 1956.

## REMEDIES

Wright's Cases, 498 pages, 1955.

## RESTITUTION

Keeton's Cases, (Fraud and Mistake) 514 pages, 1954.

Thurston's Cases, 964 pages, 1940.

## RIGHTS IN LAND

Aigler, Smith and Tefft's Cases on Property, 2 Vols., 1339 pages, 1960.

## SALES

McCurdy's Cases, 727 pages, 1959.

Vold's Text, 2nd Ed., 611 pages, 1959.

Vold's Cases, 3rd Ed., 1960.

## STATUTES

Selected Statutes, 5th Ed., 373 pages, 1944.

See Legislation.

## SURETYSHIP AND GUARANTY

Osborne's Cases, 65 pages, 1955.

Simpson's Text, 569 pages, 1950.

Simpson's Cases, 538 pages, 1942.

Sturges' Cases Credit Transactions, 4th Ed., 599 pages, 1955.

## TAXATION

Bruton and Bradley's Cases, 808 pages, 1955.

## TITLES

Aigler, Bigelow & Tefft's Cases on Property, 2 Vols., 1339 pages, 1960.

## TORTS

Green, Malone, Pedrick & Rahl's Cases on Injuries to Relations, about 500 pages, 1959.

Green, Malone, Pedrick & Rahl's Cases, 2nd Ed., 855 pages, 1957.

Hepburn's Cases, 3rd Ed., 540 pages, 1954.

Prosser's Text, 2nd Ed., 952 pp., 1955.

Seavey, Keeton and Keeton's Cases, 768 pages, 1957.

**TRADE REGULATION**

See Federal Anti-Trust Laws.
See also Unfair Trade Practices.

**TRIAL PRACTICE**

McBaine's Cases, **3rd Ed.**, 1063 pages, 1952.

Stayton's Cases, **Texas Civil and Criminal Trial**, 794 pages, 1953.

Stayton's Cases, **Texas Appellate Procedure**, 796 pages, 1952.

**TRUSTS**

Bogert's **Text**, 3rd **Ed.**, 804 pages, 1952.

**TRUSTS—Continued**

Powell's Cases, Trusts and Wills, **639** pages, 1960.

Smith's Survey, 167 pages, 1949.

**UNFAIR TRADE PRACTICES**

Oppenheim's Cases, 1534 pages, 1950.

Oppenheim's Supplement, 389 pages, 1960.

**WILLS**

Atkinson's Text, 2nd Ed., 975 pages, 1953.

Turrentine's Cases, 419 pages, 1954.

# CORBIN ON CONTRACTS

## One Volume Edition

By

**ARTHUR LINTON CORBIN**

Emeritus Professor of Law

Yale Law School

Author of

Corbin's Cases on Contracts

Corbin on Contracts in Eight Volumes

Special Advisor on Contracts, American Law Institute

ST. PAUL, MINN.

WEST PUBLISHING CO.

1952

# PREFACE

IN THE preparation of this volume, consisting in large part of excerpts from the author's large general treatise on the subject, much of the text has of necessity been omitted. This has included some entire Chapters; all of the Chapters dealing with the Remedies by way of Damages, Restitution, and Specific Performance; and all of Part VIII dealing with Illegal Bargains with the exception of a short introductory Chapter. In general, omissions of entire Sections have been indicated in the footnotes.

The omission of almost all of the citations of cases, with the discussion of their facts, although likewise inevitable, is much more serious. Where the tentative "working rules" and opinions expressed by the author are thought to be doubtful, the general treatise should be consulted. In order to make this consultation easy, the Sections printed in this volume have the same numbers as in the treatise. Furthermore, footnote numbers have also been retained, even where the footnotes themselves could not be printed. By this means, it is made possible for the student to make use of the detailed index of the large treatise, in which there are references to both Section numbers and footnote numbers. The student should be aware, as is the author of this volume, of the dangers involved in the uncritical acceptance of any other person's generalizations. The capacity to advise clients and to convince the courts can be acquired only by making one's own independent analysis and comparison of facts and decisions and juristic reasoning.

ARTHUR L. CORBIN

Yale University, 1952

VII

# TABLE OF CONTENTS

## PART 3. INTERPRETATION—PAROL EVIDENCE—MISTAKE

## PART 4. CONSTRUCTION AND LEGAL OPERATION OF CONTRACT—CONDITIONS OF LEGAL DUTY

## PART 5. RIGHTS OF THIRD PARTIES—ASSIGNMENT— JOINT AND SEVERAL CONTRACTS

### TOPIC A. THIRD PARTY BENEFICIARIES

# THE LAW OF CONTRACTS

## INTRODUCTORY

### CHAPTER 1

### PRELIMINARY DEFINITIONS

## § 1. The Main Purpose of Contract Law is the Realization of Reasonable Expectations Induced by Promises

The underlying purpose of law and government is human happiness and contentment, to be brought about by the satisfaction of human desires in the highest practicable degree. It has been found that this end can best be attained, in cases where there are conflicting human interests and desires, by establishing a judicial and administrative system that acts with a reasonable degree of uniformity. It is impossible that this uniformity should be absolute and perfect; the judges and other officers who are the agents of society in the process of reconciling interests and in distributing satisfaction of desires are mere human beings, with all of the ordinary human limitations; and the cases arising before these judges and other officers have a diversity that continually increases with the development of our modern civilization.

That portion of the field of law that is classified and described as the law of contracts attempts the realization of reasonable expectations that have been induced by the making of a promise. Doubtless, this is not the only purpose by which men have been motivated in creating the law of contracts; but it is believed to be the main underlying purpose, and it is believed that an understanding of many of the existing rules and a determination of their effectiveness require a lively consciousness of this underlying purpose.

The law does not attempt the realization of every expectation that has been induced by a promise; the expectation must be a reasonable one. Under no system of law that has ever existed are all promises enforceable. The expectation must be one that most people would have; and the promise must be one that most people would perform. This necessarily leads to a complexity in the law, to the construction of the various rules determining the circumstances under which a promise is said to be enforceable and those under which its performance will be excused.

It must not be supposed that contract problems have been solved by the dictum that expectations must be "reasonable." Reasonableness is no more absolute in character than is justice or morality. Like them it is an expression of the customs and mores of men—the customs and mores that are themselves complex, variable with time and place, inconsistent and contradictory. Nevertheless, the term is useful, giving direction to judicial research, and producing workable results. The reasonably prudent man, reasonable care and diligence, reasonable expectations, are terms that are not to be abandoned, at least until we can demonstrate that others will work better.

Not all promises are enforceable even though the expectations of the promisee and third parties are reasonable. Law is a human institution; and the machinery for its administration is human machinery. This means that there are imperfections and uncertainties and variation and inconsistency. Sometimes a promise will not be enforced by one of the customary remedies, even though another remedy may be granted. Thus, there are cases in which a judgment for damages is obtainable, but a decree for specific performance is not; in other cases a decree for specific performance is obtainable even though the remedy in damages is not. A promise may become unenforceable by reason of the mere passage of time, in accordance with some statute of limitation; and this may be the case however reasonable it may be for the promisee still to expect performance.

It cannot truthfully be said that the law operates uniformly with respect to the promises of the rich and the poor, the employer and the employee. Sometimes the rich can escape enforcement by reason of their ability to employ the ablest counsel or to prolong litigation. More often, however, the poor can escape enforcement when the rich can not. Judges as well as juries moderate the operation of the law in favor of the poor as against the rich; in our country, it is the comparatively poor who determine what the law is. As between an employer and his employees, the contract may, as a practical matter, be substantially unenforceable against the latter. Battles have been fought for the system called "collective bargaining"; but from the employer's standpoint a collective bargain has often been found to be an illusion.

By the foregoing, it is not meant that injustice prevails or that there is no law. For all human kind, justice is relative, not absolute. In spite of the long tradition that "justice" is absolute and eternal, the tradition has always been incorrect. *Fiat justitia ruat coelum* is a phrase impressive mainly because of its being in Latin and not understandable. When the skies begin to fall, Justice removes the blindfold from her eyes and tilts the scales.

## § 2. Legal Obligation Defined

It is commonly said that a contract cannot exist even though there have been expressions of mutual assent, unless there is also a legal obligation. This is often defined in purely figurative language. An obligation is "a legal bond or tie." It is a *vinculum juris*. It is indeed hard to avoid the use of figurative language like this; and for merely literary purposes, it is not desirable to avoid it. Nevertheless, an obligation is neither a rope nor a chain.

In English legal history, the term "obligation" has been used in a variety of senses. At times it has meant a formal document, such as a sealed bond. Again, it has meant the entire group of jural relations created by certain facts, usually expressions of agreement. The tendency has been to narrow its usage, so that it has come to be an almost exact synonym of the term "legal *duty*." This is a term that should be used solely as a correlative of the term legal *right*. If a duty (obligation) exists, it is a duty to some person who has a right against the one subject to the duty. If a legal right exists, it is a right against some person who is under a duty to the one having the right. These two correlative terms express a legal relation between the two persons, this rela tion consisting of certain specific facts of a kind such as have in the past caused organized society to give remedies against the duty bearer in favor of the right holder.  This is what is meant by *vinculum juris,* and by "control" that the holder of the right has over the bearer of the duty.  Past judicial and legislative history enables us to look at the specific facts and predict that A can get judgment against B if the latter does not perform as he promised (do his duty).  Legal relations are merely existing facts of life viewed in the light of a past uniformity of societal action, that enable us to predict similar action in the future with respect to two or more persons.

### § 3. Definition of the Term "Contract"

This term has been defined in a good many different ways. Definitions have been constructed by almost all writers on law and in many thousands of judicial opinions.[1]  The fact that these definitions are not in agreement has led occasionally to a little confusion;  but the harm is not so great as might be expected. Diversity of definition does at times lead to a confused analysis, obscure reasoning, and to unnecessary misunderstanding and litigation.  This is, of course, socially harmful;  and it occasionally leads to an unjust decision and to uncertainty in the law.  It is a very common error to suppose that legal terms, such as contract, have one absolute and eternally correct definition.  The fact is that all such terms have many usages, among which every one is free to select.  One usage is to be preferred over another only in so far as it serves our necessity and convenience.

A study of its common usage will show that the term "contract" has been made to denote three different kinds of things in various combinations:  (1) the series of operative acts of the parties expressing their assent, or some part of these acts;  (2) a physical document executed by the parties as an operative fact in itself and as lasting evidence of their having performed other necessary acts expressing their intentions;  (3) the legal relations resulting from the operative acts of the parties, always including the relation of right in one party and duty in the other.

---

1.  Compare the following definitions.  "The most popular description of a contract that can be given is also the most exact one ; namely, that it is a promise or set of promises which the law will enforce. The specific mark of a contract is the creation of a right, not to a thing, but to another man's conduct in the future."  "Every agreement and promise enforceable by law is a contract."  Wald's Pollock, Contracts (3d Ed.) pp. 1, 2.

A contract is "an agreement enforceable at law, made between two or more persons, by which rights are acquired by one or more to acts or forbearances on the part of the other or others."  Anson, Contracts (2d Am.Ed., Huffcut) p. 11. "The act alone is the contract, the resulting contractual relation is quite a different thing."  Holland, Jurisprudence (10th Ed.) p. 251. See also Bentham's classification, Works, III, 191.

A very common definition is that a contract is a promise enforceable at law directly or indirectly. This has the advantage of brevity, and it is perhaps as useful a definition as any that has been thus far suggested. It places emphasis upon one of the operative acts, an expression of assent. This is restricted to an expression that is promissory in character. By restricting it further to a promise that is enforceable at law, it brings into the definition the element of legal operation and effect. Such a definition as this does not inform us as to what kind of facts will be operative to create legal rights and duties; it merely gives us a mode of describing such operative facts after we have found by other means that they do have legal operation.

A contractual transaction is not always as simple as the foregoing definition would indicate. The two contracting parties may make mutual promises, and either one of the parties may make more than one promise. Promissory expressions that are thus grouped together by the parties as a single transaction are ordinarily described as a single contract, frequently leading, however, to difficult questions of "divisibility." In such a case the contract is defined as a group of promises.[2]

In another very common form of definition, the term "promise" is not used. Instead, a contract is said to be an agreement enforceable at law.[3] This puts the emphasis upon the expressions of both the contracting parties, the word "agreement" being used to denote the expressions of both, whereas the word "promise" denotes merely an expression by the promisor alone. This definition also, however, includes the element of legal relation; and, like the previous definition, it makes no attempt to tell us of what kinds of expressions the agreement must consist and by what other facts they must be accompanied, in order that legal enforcement will follow. Neither definition makes any attempt to specify the kind of remedy or sanction that will be applied and that constitutes enforcement by the law. To define contract as an "agreement" seems to exclude "unilateral" contracts to be hereafter analyzed and illustrated. There are in-

---

**2.** The definition of the American Law Institute Contracts Restatement, § 1, is as follows: "A contract is a promise or a set of promises for the breach of which the law gives a remedy, or the performance of which the law in some way recognizes as a duty."

It should be observed that no definition can ever be the one and only "correct" definition. It is a matter of usage and convenience. Usages differ; but convenience requires that in a document like the Restatement of Contract Law the usage should be consistent. It would be a very damaging error to assume that the term "contract" is used in other documents—for instance, the Constitution of the United States—in the identical limited sense that is here adopted for the convenience of restating the law. The Constitution includes among "contracts" wholly executed transactions, while the Restatement does not.

deed various types of contracts made by the act of one party alone, requiring neither assent nor consideration by the other. The word "agreement" is not clearly descriptive of such a contract.

The Uniform Commercial Code, § 1—201 (1950 draft) declares that "Contract means the total obligation in law which results from the parties' agreement as affected by this Act and any other applicable rules of law." This definition points to the sum-total of the legal relations created by the acts of agreement; but it also includes those operative acts of promise or of offer and acceptance since the definition is limited to those obligations that "result from" such operative acts.

In a treatise on contract law, as well as in the decision of litigated cases, the essential problem is not one of definition; and if a solution appears to have been derived from a definition, there can always be found an "inarticulate major premise" based on opinions as to societal policy—the prevailing mores of men in their business dealings and other social relations. Therefore, to determine whether a "contract" has been made and what are the resulting legal relations is a matter for the entire treatise, not for an introductory chapter. Instead of simplicity and uniformity, we shall find complexity and variation. In the huge societies of today, transactions are continually escaping from old forms and patterns; and opinions as to social policy and the general welfare are affected by the conflicts among large groups struggling for a greater share in the objects of desire. New classifications are continually required; and old generalizations must be continually limited or replaced. For the expression and communication of these, rules must be stated in words that can be defined; but the definitions are merely "working definitions" that are useful only in so far as they aid in conveying our thoughts to others, and the rules are merely tentative "working rules" that become confusing and harmful the moment that they cease to work.

## § 4.  Barter and Gift Distinguished from Contract

Practically all of the commonly accepted definitions of contract exclude those transactions that may be properly described as a barter. A mutual, present and fully effective exchange of lands or chattels creates no contractual duty. If A has apples to sell and B has money, A may offer the apples to B for the money. B may accept by delivering to A the possession of the money. Such a transaction is a barter. The character of the commodities exchanged is not material. Such a transaction creates new physical relations, and in an organized society it creates new legal relations. These new relations arise by the voluntary action and consent of the two parties; but there is created no special right in one party by which to compel a subsequent performance by the other. If contract should be defined as consisting of the operative acts of offer and acceptance by the parties, a bartering transaction would be a contract. If the term "contract" is used to denote a formal document executed by the parties, evidencing their mutual assent, there are many bartering transactions in which such a document that could properly be described as a contract is drawn up. A documentary bill of sale would often be a contract in this sense.

In the case of a fully effective exchange of lands or chattels, however, there may be no promise made that is ever enforceable at law or that is capable of breach. Such a fully effective exchange, without including any enforceable promise by either party, creates numerous legal relations. These, however, should be described, and are customarily described, as property relations, and not as contractual relations. This is because they are relations not merely between the two parties themselves, but between each of those parties and all other persons who are subject to law. The two parties are said to have received rights *in rem,* a term that is useful, even though likely to mislead some into thinking that such a right is a physical relation to the *res.* The legal relations created are not special relations between A and B; they involve all persons alike and exist in total independence of the voluntary action or consent of the third persons involved. If, after the completed barter of apples for money, A should forceably deprive B of the apples sold and conveyed to him, he is breaking no promise and is committing no different wrong from that committed by X, if he should do the same; and he is subject to no different penalties. B could maintain no action against A for breach of contract, although he could maintain an action in tort for A's wrongful conversion of the goods.

What has been said above in relation to barter can, in most respects, be said with equal truth in relation to an executed gift. If A has lands or chattels and executes a gift to B, which B accepts, there are acts of offer and acceptance, and there is mutual assent; but there are no contractual rights and duties. As in the case of a barter, the only rights involved are property rights, or rights *in rem.* The only duties created are those general duties binding upon non-participating persons as well as upon A. The executed gift creates new legal relations, and these arise from the voluntary acts of offer and acceptance; but there is no promise and there is no contractual right or duty.

A contract, as this term is used herein, differs from a gift, a barter, or other conveyance of property, in two ways: In contract, one of the operative facts is the making of a promise, whereas all of the others may take place without any promise. Secondly, they differ in their legal operation, a contract always

7

creating a special right *in personam,* a right in the promisee against the promisor, with the correlative special duty in the promisor to the promisee of rendering the performance promised. The legal relations created by a gift, a barter, or any other conveyance, pure and simple, do not include any special rights and duties between the two parties involved; the legal relations created are relations *in rem;* that is, they are manifold relations with all other persons who are subject to law.

It must be observed, however, that conveyances of land or chattels may be accompanied by contractual promises as a part of the same transaction. When this is the case there is both a contract and a conveyance. Thus, if A has apples or automobiles or land to sell and B has no money with which to buy, a barter of the property for the money is not possible; but A may be willing to make a conveyance of his property to B in return for B's promise to pay money in the future. If B agrees to this, makes his promise to pay, and receives a conveyance of the property, B comes under new relations *in rem* with all other members of ordinary society, while at the same time he becomes bound by a special duty *in personam* to A—a duty the like of which B owes to no other person whatever. A's correlative right against B is a contract right. B's rights, with respect to the subject matter of the conveyance, are property rights.

Furthermore, it is very common indeed for one who makes a transfer of land or chattels to accompany the transfer with a warranty of title or of quality or with some other promise. In such a case, there is a contract as well as a conveyance, and the transferee gets both property rights and contract rights.

## § 5. Formal and Informal Contracts

Contracts have commonly been classified in several ways that must here be given some consideration. The descriptive terms in common use must be considered and defined. One such classification is expressed by the terms formal contract and informal contract; a second classification is into unilateral contracts and bilateral contracts; a third classification is into void, voidable, and unenforceable contracts.

A formal contract is one, the legal operation of which is dependent upon the form in which it is made, the mode of expression, and not upon the sufficiency of the consideration that is given in return for it, or upon any change of position by the promisee in reliance upon it. An informal contract, on the other hand, is one the legal operation of which does not depend upon the form in which it is made or the mode of expression; most of such contracts depend for their legal validity upon the presence of a sufficient consideration given in return for the promise, but others are enforceable without any consideration given in return,

8

for various reasons, all of which must be discussed in great detail hereafter in dealing with the subject of consideration and with other reasons for enforcement of promises. Informal contracts have very commonly been called "simple" contracts also; and certain kinds of formal contracts have been described as "specialties".

Among the contracts that are commonly classified as formal in character are contracts under seal, recognizances, and negotiable instruments. To the discussion of contracts under seal, an entire chapter must hereafter be devoted. The law applicable to negotiable instruments is so special in character and so extensive in amount, that it is commonly treated as an independent subject; it could not be stated and explained with any fulness in less than one large volume. Attention is called throughout this work, however, to many of the instances in which the law of negotiable instruments is different from that which is applicable in the case of other kinds of contracts. A recognizance is usually, if not always, a formal acknowledgment of indebtedness, made in the presence of a court, or before a magistrate who is authorized to take such acknowledgment, or by means of a document filed with a clerk of court as a part of the record of a pending litigation.[4] In some jurisdictions the term may have still other uses. In early English history the recognizance seems to have played a much more important part than it does at present in the United States. The taking of recognizances was authorized by certain statutes, one of which was known as the Statute of Merchants. The mayors of certain towns in which various staple commodities were bought and sold were authorized to take such recognizances. A recognizance so taken was often called a Statute Merchant or a Statute Staple. In legal effect it conclusively established the existence of the indebtedness, and it enabled the creditor very easily to obtain legal remedies for the collection of his debt.[5]

4. An example of a recognizance in a criminal case is to be found in State of Maine v. Chandler, 8 A. 553, 79 Me. 172 (1887). The court said: "It is an obligation of record founded upon contract, and entered into by the recognizors upon certain conditions, upon the breach of which the recognizance became forfeited, and an absolute debt of record, in the nature of a judgment, was created, and upon which scire facias properly lies for the recovery of the forfeiture."

5. Concerning recognizances the American Law Institute, Contracts Restatement, § 9, says: "A recognizance is an acknowledgment in court by the recognizor that he is bound to make a certain payment unless a specified condition is performed.

"Recognizances are in use chiefly to secure (1) the attendance in court at a future day of the recognizor, or (2) the prosecution of an action, or (3) the payment of bail."

## § 6. Voidable Contracts

In the case of a voidable contract, there is usually both a power to avoid and a power to validate. The agreement is, to some extent, legally operative;[6] but there are differences in what its legal operation may be. Where A induces the agreement of B by fraud, as long as it remains wholly executory by both parties it can hardly be said that B is under a legal duty. In an action by A on B's promise, all that B needs to do is to plead and prove the fact of fraud; and if A's own complaint had shown the fraud and absence of ratification, B could have successfully demurred. It is not necessary to B's defense that he should have done an act of avoidance before the action is brought or before filing his plea.

Thus, in an action by the vendor against the purchaser to recover the purchase price of land, the defendant pleaded that the agreement was induced by fraudulent representations on the part of the plaintiff. He pleaded no act of avoidance by him prior to the bringing of the suit or prior to the filing of his plea. The contract was wholly executory, there having been no conveyance or payment or delivery of possession. The court held that the plea stated a good defense. The agreement had created no duty in the defendant to pay the price; and his failure to pay was not a breach of contract. The court said: "In the case of an executory contract, a refusal to perform any obligation thereunder and the defense of an action brought thereon are all that the defrauded party can do by way of asserting his right to disaffirm the contract; and, unless his silence or delay has operated to the prejudice of the other party, he may first assert his right when his adversary first asserts his claim by action." [7] If a conveyance had already been made to the purchaser or if he had been put in possession of the land, in order to avoid the contract it would have been necessary for him to tender a reconveyance or to surrender the possession.

The same distinction exists in the case of contracts that are said to be voidable on the ground of infancy. As long as such an agreement is wholly executory on both sides, the infant is under no enforceable duty whatever. When sued for an alleged breach, all the infant needs to do is to plead his infancy as a defense. It

---

**6.** "It was resolved that in all cases when the deed is voidable, and so remains at the time of the pleading (as if an infant seals and delivers a deed, or a man of full age by duress) in these and the like cases, the obligor cannot plead *non est factum*, for it is his deed at the time of the action brought." Whelpdale's Case (1605) 5 Coke, 119 a; Wald's Pollock, Contracts (3d Ed.) p. 7; Windscheid, Pandekten, I, §§ 70, 82.

**7.** **N.J.**—Roberts v. James, 85 A. 244, 83 N.J.L. 492, Ann.Cas.1914B, 859 (1912).

See in accord:
Eng.—Aaron's Reefs v. Twiss, [1896] A.C. 273.

is not necessary that he should have done any act of avoidance prior to his making the plea. Here, too, according to the commonly existing law of infancy, if the infant had received a part performance and still retains it at the time of suit, it would be necessary for him to give it up; its continued retention after becoming of age soon operates as a ratification.

In none of these cases is the agreement wholly void of legal operation. It may or it may not create a legal duty in the party having the power of avoidance; but it certainly is fully operative as against the other party to the agreement, except in those cases where he, too, may have a power of avoidance.[8] In all such cases, whatever legal relations the agreement in fact creates are voidable by one of the parties; and the agreement may be made fully operative as against both of the parties, by the exercise of a power of validation. There is a power to validate, as well as a power to avoid; and most such contracts as are commonly said to be voidable can be described with equal accuracy as validatable.[9]

### § 7. Void Contracts

· The meaning that is most commonly intended to be conveyed by the word "void" is total absence of legal effect. It may sometimes be confused with the word "voidable"; but the error involved is nearly certain to be an error as to the legal operation of facts and not one of mere terminology. One who says that an agreement or a promise is "void" usually supposes that it has no legal operation whatever, being in many cases quite unaware that a number of important legal relations have been created.

In the term "void contract," there is a self-contradiction. This is because the term "contract" is always defined so as to include some element of enforceability. There is no such weakness, however, in the term "void agreement." This is because the term "agreement" is commonly used to mean nothing more than the expressions of the parties, their acts of offer and acceptance, without any reference whatever to any resulting legal relation. The same is true of the term "void promise," since the word promise is used to denote a mere promissory expression without any implication that it either is or is not legally enforceable or otherwise operative.

8. Both parties might be infants.

9. The definition of the American Law Institute Contracts Restatement, § 13, is as follows: "A voidable contract is one where one or more parties thereto have the power, by a manifestation of election to do so, to avoid the legal relations created by the contract; or by ratification of the contract to make it valid and enforceable."

Many promises are made that are not contracts and are not capable of becoming enforceable by any act of acceptance or by any action in reliance. A promise that creates no legal relation of any kind may properly be called a void promise. Likewise, there are many expressions of mutual agreement that make no change in the legal relations of the parties; they may properly be said to be void agreements. Most bargains that are described as "illegal" are not wholly void of legal effect; but an agreement by two parties for the doing of acts that both know to be a felony would have no legal operation and be "void," although the acts themselves, when performed, would have very important effects indeed. If the expressions of two parties purporting to be acts of offer and acceptance are materially different in meaning and the facts are not such as to create an estoppel against either one, there is neither a contract nor an agreement. Not only is it inaccurate to say that the contract is void; it is equally inaccurate to say that there is a void agreement. In such a case the individual expressions of the two parties, the offer and the acceptance, are not entirely void of legal effect. Each one of them may be a legally operative offer creating in the other party a power of acceptance. The transaction is merely one of offer and counter-offer.

In cases where the transaction of the parties is in fact a mutual agreement, but is legally void, and also in cases where there is no contract for the reason that there are no mutual expressions of assent, the parties may nevertheless follow the transaction by action that is itself legally operative. A party may make a conveyance of land, even though there was no contract making it his duty to make the conveyance. The agreement may have been void, but the conveyance is not. A party may render service to another, both of them erroneously thinking that an agreement has been reached and a contract has been made. In such a case the rendition of the service is a legally operative act, even though there was no contract and there was a misunderstanding instead of an agreement.

## § 8.  Unenforceable Contracts

If a contract is defined as either a promise or an agreement that is enforceable at law, the term unenforceable contract would seem to be as self-contradictory as is the term void contract. But the law affords a variety of remedies for the enforcement of a contract. Some of these are non-judicial in character, while others may be described as judicial remedies. In addition to the usual direct means of enforcement of a promise, there are also various indirect means of enforcement. There are certain

12

agreements with respect to which the most commonly used direct means of enforcement are not available, but which cannot properly be called either void or voidable. They have some effect upon the legal relations of the parties, and they are enforceable by various indirect and non-judicial remedies. It is agreements of this sort that have commonly been grouped together under the heading of unenforceable contracts.[10] The term has rendered some useful service and it will not be abandoned here; but it should be observed that there are important differences in the legal relations that are created by the various agreements that are called unenforceable contracts.

A perfectly valid contract may become unenforceable by virtue of the statute of limitations—a statute which provides that one or more of the direct judicial remedies shall not be available unless asked for within a specified period of time.[11] The expiration of the period fixed by the statute, however, does not make such a contract void. If a promisee holds goods in pledge or a mortgage on land as collateral security for the performance of a promise, the barring of direct judicial remedies by the statute of limitations will not prevent him from using this collateral security as a means of enforcement.[12] Furthermore, the original contract, even though direct remedies are barred by the statute, is still operative to create in the promisor a power of binding himself by a new directly enforceable duty, by a mere expression of his own will, without any act of assent by the other and without any new consideration. A contract cannot properly be said to have become void if it is still operative to create such a power of validation. Neither can such a contract properly be described as voidable after its direct enforcement has been barred by the statute, because the promisor has no power of avoidance whatever. He cannot destroy the rights of the other party or create new rights or privileges in himself.

A contract may be unenforceable, also, by reason of the statute that is commonly called the statute of frauds. If there is no

---

10. The definition of the American Law Institute Restatement of Contracts, sec. 14, is as follows: "An unenforceable contract is one which the law does not enforce by legal proceedings, but recognizes in some indirect or collateral way as creating a duty of performance, though there has been no ratification."

11. The first statute of limitations, passed in the 21st year of James I, provided that the action of debt should not be maintainable after the lapse of six years. In form, this was not applicable to other legal writs; much less was it applicable to a bill in equity. It has often been a matter of litigation to determine whether a statute limiting actions of contract is applicable to a quasi contractual action.

12. Weems v. Carter, 30 F.2d 202 (C. C.A.4th, 1929).

written memorandum sufficient to satisfy the requirements of that statute, the direct judicial remedies at common law are not available to the plaintiff if the defendant chooses to take advantage of the statute. The oral agreement, however, is far from being without legal operation. Either party has the legal power to make the contract directly enforceable as against himself, by signing a proper written memorandum; but he cannot by such a process make the contract enforceable in his own favor. In the subsequent chapters dealing with the statute of frauds will be found a full discussion of the legal operation of an oral contract that is made directly unenforceable by the statute.[13]

### § 9. Agreement Defined

What is meant by the term agreement? How does it differ from such terms as contract and obligation? Like all other legal terms, it, too, has been used in a variety of senses. No doubt, it is frequently used as an exact synonym of the term contract. It seems desirable, however, to narrow its meaning so that it expresses nothing more than mutual assent, nothing more than the terms offer and acceptance. To say that there is an agreement generally means that two or more persons have expressed themselves in harmony. Of course these harmonious expressions can be with regard to any subject in life. Two persons may be in agreement that Napoleon was a great general, or that Smith is the best man for President, or that the weather is disagreeable. In the law of contracts, however, the term agreement is commonly used to mean the expressions of two or more persons respecting a subject-matter of a kind that in the past has stimulated official action on the part of organized society. In the law of contracts we mean by the term agreement a transaction between two parties that ordinarily leads to contract.[14]

Agreement consists of mutual expressions; it does not consist of harmonious intentions or states of mind. It may well be that intentions and states of mind are themselves nothing but chemical reactions or electrical discharges in some part of the nervous system. It may be that some day we may be able to observe a state of mind in the same way that we observe chemical processes and electrical discharges. At present, however, what we observe for judicial purposes is the conduct of the parties. We observe this conduct and we describe it as the expression of a state of mind. It is by the conduct of two parties, by their bodily manifestations, that we must determine the existence of what is called agreement. This is what is meant by the anciently-honored term "meeting of the minds." This is what is meant by mutual assent.

As we proceed through this treatise it will appear over and over again that one may be "bound" by a contract in ways that he did not intend, foresee, or understand. The juristic effect (the resulting legal relations) of a man's expressions in word or act may be very different from what he supposed it would be. The legal effects that are produced by an "agreement" depend upon past legislative and judicial history, of which men must necessarily be largely ignorant. They may depend also upon surrounding factors that are unknown to the parties and upon subsequently occurring circumstances that could not at the time of agreement be known to anybody. Courts often declare that they "can not make contracts for the parties," a statement that is quite true; but it is of much greater importance to realize that the courts must determine the requirements of justice and that the legal effects thus given to expressions of agreement are seldom exactly what one or both of the agreeing parties supposed or expected.

By the foregoing it is not meant that courts are indifferent to the actual intentions and expectations of men or to the legal effects that one or both contracting parties thought that they were producing. But in the law of contracts, as in all other legal fields, "justice" is not attained by giving the parties unlimited freedom or power, by enforcing every result that either one of them expected and intended, or by never enforcing a result unless both of them expected and intended it.

The Uniform Commercial Code, § 1—201 (1950 draft) declares that "Agreement means the bargain in fact as found in the language of the parties or in course of dealing or usage of trade, or course of performance or by implication from other circumstances."

The word "agree" is often used by contractors and even by draftsmen of statutes with a meaning that is identical with that of "promise." Thus, one may say "I agree to pay one hundred dollars," or "I agree to receive a horse in full satisfaction of the debt." This usage is too common to be eliminated. When the word "agree" or "agreement" is used, the context may show that the intended meaning is something other than mutual expressions of assent.

## § 10. "Bargain" as a Contractual Expression

Without doubt, the word "bargain" is often used as substantially synonymous with agreement and contract. In this work, however, it is used with the connotation of a definite exchange of equivalents, of a quid pro quo. This is believed to be in accord with prevailing usage. As so used, a bargain is one kind of agreement. There are many agreements that are not bargains;

and there are many contracts that involve no bargain.[15]  But a bargain is always an agreement for an exchange.[16]

The exchange agreed upon may be a promise for a promise—the ordinary bilateral contract; it may be a promise by one party in exchange for some executed performance by the other—the ordinary unilateral contract; it may also be an exchange of two commodities—a barter.  There may also be a bargain for an exchange in a double sense, for an exchange of promises and for an exchange of the promised performances.  In the case of aleatory bilateral agreements, this double exchange does not exist; the two promised performances are not regarded or agreed by the parties to be equivalents.[17]  In no case are the premiums to be paid for a policy of insurance or for a surety bond regarded as the agreed equivalent of the amount promised conditionally by the insurer or the surety.

There are many agreements that are not bargains just as there are many contracts that are not bargains.  Two parties may express mutual agreement in the case of a sealed promise to make a gift.  There is agreement, and there may be contract, in such a case; but there is no bargain.  Also, a promise may become binding by reason of action by the promisee in reliance upon it, even though such action was not bargained for and neither party has agreed upon it as the equivalent of the promise.

Just as there are agreements that are not contracts, so also there are bargains that create no contract.  One may bargain for and actually receive many an agreed equivalent that is insufficient consideration for a promise; such a bargain makes no contract.

## § 11.  Offer Defined

An offer is an expression by one party of his assent to certain definite terms, provided that the other party involved in the bar-

15.  For illustrations of contracts that involve no exchange of equivalents and no "bargain" see Chapter 10, Contracts Under Seal, and Chapters 8, 9, Informal Contracts Without Assent or Consideration.  Illustrative sections in Restatement, Contracts, are sections 86–90, 95–110.

That there may be a bargain by an exchange of promises, without any intention that the promised performances are also to be exchanged, see Aleatory Contracts, Chapter 38 herein, and Contracts Restatement, §§ 291–293.  Most bilateral contracts involve a bargain for an exchange of the promised perform-ances as well as for an exchange of promises.  See section 266 and following sections of the Contracts Restatement.  Most unilateral contracts involve a bargain for the exchange of a promise for a performance that is not promised.

16.  Restatement, Contracts, § 4: "A bargain is an agreement of two or more persons to exchange promises or to exchange a promise for a performance."  It may also be an agreed exchange of two performances, as in case of a "barter."

17.  See Chapter 38, Aleatory Contracts.

gaining transaction will likewise express his assent to the identically same terms. An offer looks forward to an agreement—to mutual expressions of assent.

Can it properly be said that an offer—a mere expression of assent to certain terms by one party—before any acceptance or similar expression of assent by the other party, has any legal operation whatever? There are some cases in which it can properly be said that such an expression of assent has no legal operation. There are certain persons who may be quite capable of expressing assent to certain terms, and yet in whom the law recognizes no capacity to make a contract. Various limitations on such legal capacity are discussed elsewhere. Furthermore, there are expressions of assent looking forward to a similar expression of agreement by another party, and yet no effect will be given to these expressions by the law, because it has not been customary to do so. Two friends may mutually agree to meet at luncheon or to play golf together, without in any way affecting their legal relations. The differences between such social engagements and a business agreement that constitutes a contract will be discussed in a subsequent Section. It should be observed here, however, that, as the term "offer" has been defined above, it may or it may not be a legally operative fact.

The definition of offer that has been proposed above is an attempt at a factual description, without any reference whatever to the legal operation of the facts so described. There are two kinds of questions that are presented to the courts for their solution. First. What were the facts that occurred or existed? This question must be answered by making a historical investigation, by receiving oral testimony and other evidence, and drawing inferences therefrom. Secondly. What is the legal operation and effect of the facts that are found to have existed? Assuming that an offer is made as a part of a business transaction and that it is made by a person possessed of full contractual capacity, what change in legal relations is brought about by the making of an offer? It is believed that the best short description of this change is that an offer creates a power of acceptance in the offeree.[18] It will not be disputed by any one that, after an offer is made, a voluntary expression of assent by the offeree is all that is necessary to create what we call contract. This is what is meant, and it is all that is meant, by saying that an offer creates a power of acceptance in the offeree. The exercise of

---

18. With respect to the resulting legal relations, offer and acceptance may be defined thus: An *offer* is an act on the part of one person whereby he gives to another the legal power of creating the obligation called contract. An *acceptance* is the exercise of the power conferred by the offer, by the performance of some other act or acts. Both offer and acceptance must be acts expressing assent.

this power by the offeree will create a new and very important change in the legal relations of the parties. But the power to bring about this important change by the act of acceptance is itself an important juristic fact, and it is the legal result of the offer standing quite alone. For this reason, it seems to be reasonable and convenient to say that the offer may be an operative fact creating a new legal relation—the relation of power in the offeree to create new changes in legal relations, with the correlative liability in the offeror that such a change will take place without any further action or expression on his own part.

What kind of act creates a power of acceptance and is therefore an offer? It must be an expression of will or intention. It must be an act that leads the offeree reasonably to believe that a power to create a contract is conferred upon him.[19] This applies to the content of the power as well as to the fact of its existence. It is on this ground that we must exclude invitations to deal or acts of mere preliminary negotiation, and acts evidently done in jest or without intent to create legal relations. All these are acts that do not lead others reasonably to believe that they are empowered "to close the contract." So long as it is reasonably apparent that some further act of the offeror is necessary, the offeree has no power to create contractual relations by an act of his own, and there is as yet no offer.

An expression of willingness to make a contract is not operative as an offer unless it is made in such a manner as justifies another person in thinking that it is directed to him for his acceptance. An oral statement of such willingness made to a third person who has no authority to communicate it is not operative as an offer; and a written statement to the same effect is not an offer, even though without any authorized delivery and without negligence it becomes known to a person who tries to accept. So also the mere passing of a resolution by a board of directors or by a town council, uncommunicated by them or by anyone with authority, creates no power of acceptance in one who learns of it in some fortuitous manner.[20] A legislative enactment promising exemption from taxation, addressed to no specifically named party, is almost certain to be held not to be an offer of a contract.[21]

In order to be legally operative and to create a power of acceptance, it is necessary that the offer shall contain all the terms of the contract to be made. It is not enough for one party to say what he himself will promise to do; he must also say what he

19. In Frederics, Inc. v. Felton Beauty Supply Co., 198 S.E. 324, 58 Ga.App. 320 (1938), the sending of a complete documentary contract signed by the Vice President of a corporation justified the other party in believing it was an offer empowering him to consummate the contract by signing it himself and mailing it back.

will do it for, that is, what the other party must do in exchange. If A says to B: "I will sell and convey Blackacre to you," and B replies: "I will pay you $5,000," no contract has been made as yet. In order to make a bilateral contract, the offer must state the terms of both the promises to be made; one party offers to exchange his specified promise for a similarly specified promise by the other party. By acceptance, the other party not only makes the requested return promise, he also assents to the exchange of the two specified promises as offered.

## § 12. Simultaneous Expressions of Assent

It is quite possible for two persons to reach an agreement and to express that fact in words or other conduct, without going through the specific process of an offer made by one, followed by a separate and independent acceptance by the other. For example, the terms of an agreement between two persons, A and B, might be prepared in advance by a third person, C, and communicated by him in completed form to A and B. Thereupon, A and B stand in each other's presence and repeat in unison, "We mutually agree in accordance with the terms prepared for us by C." It is believed that in such a case the mutual expressions of A and B would have operative effect as a contract, even though it is impossible to point out one of them as having made the offer and the other as having made the acceptance. No instance of a contract made in this manner has ever come under the observation of the present writer. Offer followed by acceptance is the substantially universal method. This is true of written contracts as well as of those made by word of mouth. In the case of a written contract, one of the parties always signs the document first and then presents it to the other party for his signature. This is an offer by the first party; and acceptance consists of the signature and delivery of the document by the second party.[22]

Where a written contract is prepared in duplicate, it is quite conceivable that the two documents are, first, signed simultaneously by the two parties, then exchanged between them, and finally again signed simultaneously. The parties may well be regarded as making simultaneous identical offers and simultaneous acceptances. The offers are in duplicate, and the acceptances are in duplicate, as well as the completed documentary contracts. The first exchange of the two documents, each signed by one party only, consummated no contract; it was a mere crossing of identical offers. But each party would have power

---

22. If the document presented by one party appears to be complete and to be duly executed by an officer authorized to make contracts, the other party has power to accept by attaching his own signature and returning the document by mail. Frederics, Inc. v. Felton Beauty Supply Co., 198 S.E. 324, 58 Ga.App. 320 (1938).

to close the deal and consummate the contract by signing the document passed to him, unless it was actually understood that there should be no contract until both had signed in duplicate. In the latter case, if the last two signatures are simultaneous, it is impossible to say which party is offeror and which is offeree. Valid contracts are not unknown in which there are duplicate copies, each of which is signed by one party only.[23]

## § 13. What is a Promise

The term "promise" must continually be used in any statement of the law of contracts. The act constituting an offer and the act constituting an acceptance thereof may each consist in a promise. One of the most common definitions of the term "contract" itself is that it is a promise directly or indirectly enforceable at law. A definition of the term "promise" is, therefore, suggested as follows: A promise is an expression of intention that the promisor will conduct himself in a specified way or bring about a specified result in the future, communicated in such manner to a promisee that he may justly expect performance and may reasonably rely thereon.[26]

It should be observed that the express words used in making a promise do not always specify conduct on the part of the promisor himself as the object of expectation by the promisee. Thus, if A promises B that C will not disclose a trade secret, the ultimate object of desire on B's part is conduct on the part of C, and is not in terms conduct on the part of the promisor A.[27] It is believed, however, that A is promising and that B is being led to expect conduct on the part of A that will be sufficient to induce the desired non-disclosure on the part of C. If conduct on A's part sufficient to attain this purpose turns out to be impossible, then it is full indemnification by A that is expected.

26. The definition accepted by the American Law Institute, Restatement, Contracts, § 2, is as follows:

"(1) A promise is an undertaking, however expressed, either that something shall happen, or that something shall not happen, in the future.

"(2) Words which in terms promise the happening or failure to happen of something not within human control, or the existence or non-existence of a present or past state of facts, are to be interpreted as a promise or undertaking to be answerable for such proximate damage as may be caused by the failure to happen or the happening of the specified event, or by the existence or non-existence of the asserted state of facts."

It is believed that this definition is not substantially in conflict with that proposed in the text above.

27. See Tode v. Gross, 28 N.E. 469, 127 N.Y. 480, 13 L.R.A. 652, 24 Am. St.Rep. 475 (1891); also Sinclair Refining Co. v. Jenkins Petroleum Process Co., 99 F.2d 9 (C.C.A.1st, 1938), where the defendant contracted to induce its employes to make applications for patents and to assign them to the plaintiff.

In order to constitute a promise, the expression of intention by the promisor is not required to be in words. It may be made by the use of sign language or by any other conduct that under the existing circumstances has a promissory meaning. Promises may be tacit, implied, or inferred, as well as express. A man will be held to have made a promise if he has reason to know that his words or other conduct may reasonably cause another to believe that a promise is being made and such belief actually results, even though he does not himself intend to convey such a meaning.[28]

## § 14. Promise and Warranty

A promise may be expressed in the form of a warranty, and that which appears to be the object of desire and expectation on the part of the promisee may be something over which the promisor has absolutely no power or control. Thus, as a part of a contract that A is making with B, A may warrant that a horse is sound and free from vice, or that a steel rail is free from internal and invisible flaws, or that the ship "Peerless" arrived in Amsterdam day before yesterday. Warranties of this kind may turn out, on proper interpretation, not to be promises at all, but to be mere representations of fact, the truth of which is a condition precedent to the duty of the other party.[29] If proper interpretation, however, shows them to be promises, it is believed that what is being promised and what the promisee is being led to expect on the part of the promisor, is indemnification against loss, in case the facts turn out to be not as represented. It is not that the promisor will instantly make the vicious horse gentle, or the

---

28. Restatement, Contracts, § 5: ". . . a promise in a contract must be stated in such words either oral or written, or must be inferred wholly or partly from such conduct, as justifies the promisee in understanding that the promisor intended to make a promise."

See Chapter 25 dealing with Implication.

29. Warranties in insurance contracts are usually representations of fact, the truthfulness of which is a condition precedent to the insurer's duty to pay. Even though they are in promissory form, as they sometimes are, they are not likely to be interpreted as promises for breach of which an action will lie. It is not always easy to determine whether words in a contract are intended to constitute a promise creating a duty in one of the parties, or are intended to make some fact or event a condition precedent to the other party's duty. They may have both effects at once, one party undertaking a duty and the other party's reciprocal duty being made conditional. It is not every "warranty" contained in an insurance policy that will be given the effect that was intended by the insurer.

Warranties in the law of Sales, express and implied, are dealt with in the Uniform Commercial Code—Sales, §§ 2—312 to 318 (1950 draft).

steel rail flawless, or cause the Peerless to have been in Amsterdam when she was in the Bay of Biscay.[30]

## § 15. Expressions of Intention, Hope, or Desire

A promise is an expression of intention, but it is not every expression of intention that can properly be called a promise. An expression of intention is not a promise unless it is communicated to one or more persons under such circumstances that they will expect performance and may reasonably act in reliance upon the expression. In an early English case, the father of a young lady made the general statement that he intended to give £100 to the man who should thereafter marry the daughter with her father's consent. It was held that this statement was not a promise, and that a young man who acted in reliance upon it and fulfilled the conditions could not get judgment for the payment of the money.[31]  So also, a statement of intention may be made under such circumstances of excitement or may be accompanied by such evidence that it is mere bluster or bragging, that no one would be justified in understanding it to be a promise to be relied upon.[32]  The line of distinction between promises and such non-promissory statements of intention is in many cases difficult to draw. It must be drawn by making what seems to be a reasonable interpretation of the expressions of the parties in the light of the surrounding facts—an interpretation that must be made by a jury, or by a judge acting in the jury's place.[33]  No doubt the

---

31.  An averment that the defendant "asserted and published" that he would pay £100 is not a sufficient averment of a promise to pay it. Weeks v. Tybald, Noy, 11 (1605). There is no doubt, however, that an assertion or publication of an intention may be made under such circumstances as to be reasonably understood as a promise. In such a case a promise has been made; and the plaintiff should aver that the defendant "promised."

32.  "If it was the real understanding of the parties that the defendant was to procure an actual purchaser with such splendid profits to the plaintiff from so small an investment, there was a contract which should be given effect. To create an obligation such must have been the understanding. If what was said was mere talk, boasting by the broker of what could be accomplished, hopeful talk as to land prospects, without a genuine intention that the defendant was bound to produce a purchaser at the price fixed, there was no contract. The proofs will tell." Smith v. Vosika, 208 N.W. 1, 166 Minn. 18 (1926).

33.  In Anderson v. Backlund, 199 N.W. 90, 159 Minn. 423 (1924), a tenant stocked the land with cattle in reliance on the landlord's assurance as to water as follows: "Never mind the water, John, I will see there will be plenty of water because it never failed in Minnesota yet." This made no contract, because by reasonable interpretation the words were mere prediction and encouragement, not promise. The indefiniteness of the words tends to this conclusion. The result would probably have been different if the landlord had said: "I will drive a producing well", or "I will construct and fill a reservoir" of a specified capacity.

fact that an expression of intention if interpreted as a promise would be improvident is influential in the process of interpretation.

A person may express his intention to do something in the future without promising to do it.[34] There is nothing contradictory or inconsistent in the following statement: I fully expect and intend to leave you a thousand dollars in my will, but I do not promise to do it. A statement of intention is the mere expression of a state of mind, put in such a form as neither to invite nor to justify action in reliance by another person. A promise is also the expression of a state of mind, but put in such a form as to invite reliance by another person, making it reasonable and customary to throw the risk of loss arising from nonperformance upon the one making the promise. One can make a promise without actually having the intention of performing it, just as one can express an intention without promising; but if he uses words of promise and at the same time clearly expresses an intention not to perform it, the promissory words have no meaning or effect.

It may be difficult to determine whether a legislative act is an offered promise or a mere expression of an intention and a policy. Thus, a railway tax law provided "that the rate of taxation fixed by this act or any other law of this state shall not apply to any railway company hereafter building and operating a line of railroad . . . until the same has been operated for the full period of ten years, unless the gross earnings shall equal $4,000 per mile." It was held that this was not an offer to contract; and Mr. Justice Holmes said: "The broad ground in a case like this is that, in view of the subject matter, the legislature is not making promises, but framing a scheme of public revenue and public improvement. In announcing its policy, and providing for carrying it out, it may open a chance for benefits to those who comply with its conditions, but it does not address them, and therefore, it makes no promise to them. It simply indicates a course of conduct to be pursued until circumstances or its views of policy change." It was, therefore, held that a company that had constructed a railroad in reliance on the words of the taxation statute had no contract rights and that the state was free to tax such a company without impairing the "obligation of a contract." [35]

---

**35.**   **U.S.**—Wisconsin & M. R. Co. v. Powers, 24 S.Ct. 107, 191 U.S. 379, 48 L.Ed. 229 (1903). It may be suggested that while the interpretation given by the court seems not unreasonable to a disinterested party, it would not seem so reasonable to one who had built a railroad and rendered the desired service in reliance on the statutory assurance. It may be sound policy to deprive legislatures of the power to bind the state by promises of future exemption from taxation.

The fact that the legislative enactment is not addressed to a specifically named party, even though it may invite action in reliance upon it, is a factor indicating that a promissory offer is not being made.[36]

## § 16. Illusory Promises

There are certain forms of expression that have been described as "illusory promises." As this term itself implies, an illusory promise is not a promise at all as that term has been herein defined. If the expression appears to have the form of a promise, this appearance is an illusion. Suppose, for example, that X guarantees payment of P's note in return for C's written promise to forbear from suing P as long as C wishes to forbear. In this case C's words may create the illusion of a promise, but, in fact, he has made no promise. The fundamental element of promise seems to be an expression of intention by the promisor that his future conduct shall be in accordance with his present expression, irrespective of what his will may be when the time for performance arrives. In the supposed case, the words used by C are not such as may reasonably be relied upon by P. The clear meaning of C's expression is that his future conduct is to be in accordance with his own future will, just as it would have been, had he said nothing at all.[37]

## § 17. Implied Assumpsit

Sometimes a promise is said to be "implied in law," such a promise being distinguished from a promise that is implied in fact. This distinction and these terms have a long history in Anglo-American law. A promise that is implied in fact is merely a tacit promise, one that is inferred in whole or in part from expressions other than words on the part of a promisor. It is a question of fact whether or not in a particular case a promise should be so inferred. When a promise is said to be "implied in law," it is meant that neither the words nor the other conduct of the party involved are promissory in form or justify any inference of a promise. The term is used to indicate that the party in question is under a legally enforceable duty, just as he would have been if he had in fact made a promise.

For some centuries in our legal history, promises were enforced by the use of the common law writ of assumpsit, this word

---

37. For cases in which an illusory promise can be found, see:

N.Y.—Strong v. Sheffield, 39 N.E. 330, 144 N.Y. 392 (1895), "I will hold it [the note of a third person, without pressing for payment] until such time as I want my money".

Eng.—Great Northern R. R. v. Witham, L. R. 9 C. P. 16 (1873), "I am instructed to inform you that my directors have accepted your tender, dated, etc., to supply this company at Doncaster station any quantity they may order during the period ending October 31."

having the literal meaning "he promised." For a number of reasons the action at common law that was initiated by the use of this writ, was a very convenient one, by the use of which justice was satisfactorily attained. Other forms of action were less satisfactory. A pressure arose to allow the use of the action of assumpsit for the collection of non-contractual money debts, debts arising out of transactions that included no promise whatever, either express or tacit. The courts yielded to this pressure, and justified themselves by saying that in these cases a promise was implied in law. The legal duties that were enforced by the use of this fictitious promise have in recent years come to be described as quasi-contractual.

## § 18.   Express and Implied Contracts [38]

Contractual duty is imposed by reason of a promissory expression. As to this, there is no difference between an express contract and an implied contract; all contracts are express contracts.[39] But there are different modes of expressing assent. Expression may be by the tongue, the eye, the hand, or by all of them at once. It may be by language, by words in any language, by words written or spoken. Yet there is also "sign language" which may consist of signs that are mere translations from a language of words, or of signs that convey ideas independently of any word language. A contract made by sign language is an express contract.

The language used to express assent, whether of words or of other signs and symbols, may be one invented by the parties themselves for their own private communications, or indeed for one communication only. They may use code words instead of English words, their own code, or the Morse code, or the Western Union telegraphic code. They may twist ordinary English words into code words, so that man signifies dog and tree signifies a thousand bushels of wheat. A contract made by a code communication is an express contract. Throwing up one's hat is usually an expression of joy; but it may be made to express assent to an agreement to sell land for ten thousand dollars.

From the above, it appears also that all contracts are implied contracts; for the meaning to be given to any and all of these modes of expression is found by a process of implication and inference. There are implications in English words as well as in other signs and symbols; and what your words imply is also what your words express.[40] Assent may be expressed by acts that have no antecedent agreed meaning, although no meaning can be attributed to them except in relation to the previous usage and

40.  Great Lakes & St. Lawrence
Transp. Co. v. Scranton Coal Co.,
239 F. 603 (C.C.A.7th, 1917).

conduct of men. The inference to be drawn from the acts is determined by what the actor and other men have used them to express.[41]

The distinction between an express and an implied contract, therefore, is of little importance, if it can be said to exist at all. The matter that is of importance is the degree of effectiveness of the expression used. Clarity of expression determines the reasonableness of understanding and eases the court's problem in case of dispute. The character of the evidence to be presented to the court depends upon the mode of expression used: [42] and the more variant and obscure the mode, the more difficult the court's problem. Nowhere is accomplished artistry worth more than in the drafting of an important contract. It may be an exaggeration to say that nowhere is it less often to be found.

When an expression of agreement is put into words that are frequently used with more than one meaning, it is difficult, and sometimes impossible, to decide that an express contract exists. Likewise, when conduct other than words is such as persons frequently perform with different meanings, it is difficult, and sometimes impossible, to decide that an implied contract exists.

It is now well understood that a contract may be unilateral; that is, that only one of the parties makes a promise, the consideration for which is some non-promissory performance rendered by the other or for which no consideration is necessary. In such cases, it is nearly always the promisor who makes an offer of his promise and requests action or forbearance in return. If such is the offer that has been made, it is usually unreasonable to infer that the offeree has made a promise that he will render the requested performance. Generally, therefore, the implication of a return promise is directly bound up with the interpretation of the terms of the offer. If the offeror has not asked for a promise, the normal result is that he doesn't get one; but if the offeror does ask for a promise and the conduct of the offeree makes him believe reasonably that the requested promise has been made, the court will generally find that it has been made, by implication if not expressly. This will be true, whether the plaintiff is trying to prove that the defendant made such an implied promise in order to maintain action for its enforcement,[43] or whether the plaintiff is trying to show that he himself made

41. That a mutual contract to marry can be made tacitly, by a course of conduct not including any express promissory words, see Homan v. Earle, 53 N.Y. 267 (1873), stating in detail the conduct of the defendant from which a promise was inferred.

43. U.S.—Sylvan Crest Sand & Gravel Co. v. U. S., 150 F.2d 642 (C. C.A.2d, 1945); Mills-Morris Co. v. Champion Spark Plug Co., 7 F.2d 38 (C.C.A.6th, 1925).

such an implied promise in order to establish a consideration for the express promise of the defendant.[44]

Parties who have made an express contract to be in effect for one year (or any other stated time) frequently proceed with performance after expiration of the year without making any new express agreement, of extension or otherwise. From such continued action a court may infer that the parties have agreed in fact to renew the one-year contract for another similar period. Illustrations can be found in leaseholds, employment transactions, and contracts for a continuing supply of some commodity.[45]

## § 19. Contract and Quasi Contract Distinguished

A distinction has long been suggested between contracts implied in fact and contracts implied in law. A contract that is implied in fact has just been discussed in the preceding sections; it is one sort of an express contract. Something very different is meant by the term "contract implied in law"; it is an obligation that is created by the law without regard to expressions of assent by either words or acts. Some confusion was caused by the use of the term "implied contract" to refer to such different kinds of obligation; and the tendency is now strong to substitute the term "quasi contract" in place of the term "contract implied in law." [47]

The term "quasi contract" is directly derived from the Roman law, in which obligations were classified as arising *ex contractu* or *quasi ex contractu* and *ex delicto* or *quasi ex delicto*. The term has the merit of helping to avoid the older confusion by reason of its unaccustomed and foreign form. It has the demerit of being wholly non-descriptive and also of actually continuing a similar confusion. The term *quasi* is introduced as a weasel word, that sucks all the meaning of the word that follows it; but this is a fact that the reader seldom realizes.

A quasi contractual obligation is one that is created by the law for reasons of justice, without any expression of assent and sometimes even against a clear expression of dissent. If this is true, it would be better not to use the word "contract" at all. Contracts are formed by expressions of assent; quasi contracts quite otherwise. The legal relations between contractors are dependent upon the interpretation of their expressions of assent; in quasi contract the relations of the parties are not dependent on such interpretation.

It must be admitted, or indeed asserted, that considerations of equity and morality play a large part in the process of finding a promise by inference of fact as well as in constructing a quasi contract without any such inference at all. The exact terms of the promise that is "implied" must frequently be determined by

27

what equity and morality appear to require after the parties have come into conflict.[48]   Like most other boundary lines in legal classification, that between contract and quasi contract is "wavering and blurred."   Nevertheless, the classification is logically sound, necessary and useful.

Any successful attempt to explain and classify quasi contracts would fill many pages.[49]   This is not a work that purports to make such explanation or classification; but at various points, especially in dealing with remedies for breach, many rights and remedies that are commonly called quasi contractual will be considered.   For present purposes, it will be enough to give a few illustrations.

Mistakenly believing that he owns Blackacre, A pays the taxes and makes permanent improvements thereon, without the knowledge or assent of the real owner B.   When B is requested to reimburse A, he positively refuses.   Nevertheless, the law will in some such cases make it B's duty to reimburse A.   B's obligation is called quasi contract.[50]

B finds or steals A's money and refuses restitution; he is under a quasi contractual duty to make such restitution.[51]

Under compulsion of law, or in order to protect his own interest in property, A makes payment of money that it was B's legal duty to pay.   In spite of any express refusal, B is under a quasi contractual duty to reimburse A.[52]

---

**48.**   In Parev Products Co. v. Rokeach, 124 F.2d 147 (C.C.A.2d, 1941), Judge C. E. Clark said: "Should, therefore, a covenant be implied under all the present circumstances?   When we turn to the precedents we are met at once with the confusion of statement whether a covenant can be implied only if it was clearly 'intended' by the parties, or whether such a covenant can rest on principles of equity.   Expressions can be found which insist on 'intention,' . . .   One may perhaps conclude that in large measure this confusion arises out of the reluctance of courts to admit that they were to a considerable extent 'remaking' a contract in situations where it seemed necessary and appropriate so to do.   'Intention of the parties' is a good formula by which to square doctrine with result.   That this is true has long been an open secret."   Of course, where intent, though obscure, is nevertheless discernible, it must be followed; but a certain sophistication must be recognized—if we are to approach the matter frankly—where we are dealing with changed circumstances, fifteen years later, with respect to a contract which does not touch this exact point and which has at most only points of departure for more or less pressing analogies."

**49.**   See Restatement, "Restitution" (1937), and works on "Quasi Contracts" by Keener (1893) and Woodward (1913); also Corbin, Quasi Contractual Obligations, 21 Yale L. J. 533 (1912).

**51.**   The common count in assumpsit for "money had and received" was sustained in such cases as these.   In general, some form of assumpsit was sustainable as an alternative remedy for a tort by which the wrongdoer enriched himself at the expense of the plaintiff.   See Corbin, Waiver of Tort, 19 Yale L.J. 221 (1910).

A finds B's house afire and his cattle starving and renders service and incurs expense in saving and feeding them. In some states, B is under a quasi contractual duty of reimbursement.[53]

Why should such cases as these be classified as contracts at all, even with such qualifying modifiers as "quasi" or "implied in law"? The chief reason that they came to be so classified, both in Roman law and in the English common law, is that no other suitable and really descriptive classification was available, and it was desired to make use of the remedial forms of action by which contracts were enforced. Public welfare required that an enforceable duty should exist without regard to assent or dissent; and the sanctions and remedies of contract law were convenient and effective. In English law, the writ of assumpsit was at hand and was appropriate to serve the purpose. While the word "assumpsit" means literally "he promised", it was easy for the courts to create the fiction of a promise in these cases, to say that the law implied a promise, and then to refuse all opportunity to the defendant to deny it. The action of debt was older than assumpsit; and in very many instances a debt existed without being either created or accompanied by a promise to pay it. To avoid the much abused defense called "wager of law" that was available in actions of debt, the courts permitted the creditor to sue in assumpsit, an action in which that defense was not available, saying that a debt implies an assumpsit.[55] This made it easily possible for the courts to expand the use of assumpsit to include new cases where obligation had not previously been recognized, making this one of the most important growing points in the evolution and expansion of law. So, under the head of quasi contract are included numerous odds and ends of obligation, without other pigeon holes in which to place them, even though they have little in common with consensual agreement and may have great differences among themselves.[56]

In certain cases, a restitutionary remedy is available as an alternative to money damages, both for breach of an express contract and for a tort. The measure of recovery in cases of this kind is generally the amount of the unjust enrichment of the defendant. Since this is generally the measure of recovery also in cases of restitution for mistake, duress, and certain voluntary benefits, this alternative remedy is very frequently described as quasi contractual in character. At common law, the same forms

---

55.   Eng.—Slade's Case, 4 Coke, 92b (1602).

56.   The following cases illustrate and explain the difference between true contract and quasi contract:

Conn.—Fischer v. Kennedy, 138 A. 503, 106 Conn. 484 (1927); Gregory

v. Lee, 30 A. 53, 64 Conn. 407, 25 L.R.A. 618 (1894).

N.H.—Sceva v. True, 53 N.H. 627 (1873).

Pa.—Hertzog v. Hertzog, 29 Pa. 465 (1857).

Eng.—Moses v. Macferlan, 2 Burr. 1005 (1760), by Lord Mansfield.

of action were available, these being the various varieties of assumpsit. The remedy of restitution, as an alternative of damages for breach of contract, is considered in Chapters 61 and 62.

## § 20.  Express Assumpsit and Implied Assumpsit

The writ of assumpsit was developed in the common law courts for the enforcement of promises that were not previously enforceable in the actions of covenant and debt. Covenant lay only on promises under seal. Debt, in its later history, lay only when the defendant could be shown to owe some definite sum of money. Many promises, however, in reliance on which the promisee has materially changed his position, neither create a money debt nor are under seal. As the demand for the enforcement of such promises arose, a remedy was invented to meet it. This remedy was afforded by the writ of assumpsit, created by making only a slight variation in the wording of the older writ of trespass on the case. This variation consisted merely in an allegation in Latin that the defendant promised (*super se assumpsit*) and that the plaintiff had relied thereon to his injury.

In the course of time, this writ was applied to the enforcement of promises actually made, whether express or implied in fact from conduct other than words, and also to the enforcement of obligations described heretofore as quasi contracts. The writ was sustained in all cases in which the court was willing to hold that the law would imply an assumpsit; and in Slade's Case [57] the court held that whenever a debt existed the law would imply an assumpsit. The result of this holding was that the action of debt was largely replaced by assumpsit; and the subsequent growth of contract law took place mainly in the cases in which assumpsit was used as the form of action. Such terms as "special assumpsit", "express assumpsit", "implied assumpsit", and "indebitatus assumpsit" came into use; but this does not indicate that they were different forms of action or that separate writs were invented for them. Since the action would be sustained if the plaintiff proved an express promise, or a promise inferred from acts other than verbal expression, or a money debt, or any quasi contractual obligation that the court was willing to recognize, it became unnecessary to draw sharp lines among them or to distinguish clearly between contracts implied in fact and quasi contracts. The use of the form of action called assumpsit required the making of no such distinction; and in many reported cases it does not appear whether the court found that the defendant had promised or merely that the defendant had so conducted himself that he ought to be compelled to pay money by which he would otherwise be unjustly enriched.

The common counts in assumpsit are merely abbreviated and stereotyped statements that the defendant is indebted to the

---

57.  4 Coke, 92b (1602).

30

plaintiff for a variety of commonly recurring reasons, such as money had and received, money lent, work and labor done, and goods sold and delivered. They are allegations of indebtedness, and the action may be properly described as indebitatus assumpsit. It was not required that the indebtedness should be an agreed amount or one that had already been computed and liquidated. Counts asking judgment for a reasonable amount for work done or for goods sold were described by the Latin phrases *quantum meruit* and *quantum valebat*.

The common counts could be used for the enforcement of express promises if they were such as to create a money debt, as well as for the enforcement of implied promises and quasi contracts. It cannot be said that the line between express assumpsit and the common indebitatus counts is also the distinguishing line between express promises and implied promises or between actual promises and quasi contracts. There was no reason why a quasi contract should not be enforced in an action of "special" assumpsit—an action on the special case—rather than in "general" assumpsit in which the case is stated in one or more of the common counts.[58]

## § 21. Unilateral Contracts Distinguished from Bilateral

The differences between a unilateral contract and a bilateral contract, as those terms are now commonly used, lie both in the operative acts of the parties and also in the legal relations created thereby. A unilateral contract consists of a promise or group of promises made by one of the contracting parties only, usually assented to by the other or by some one acting on his behalf. There are many cases in which such an assent is not required.[59] A bilateral contract consists of mutual promises, made in exchange for each other by each of the two contracting parties. In the case of a unilateral contract, there is only one promisor; and the legal result is that he is the only party who is under an enforceable legal duty. The other party to this contract is the one to whom the promise is made, and he is the only one in whom the contract creates an enforceable legal right. In a bilateral contract both parties are promisors and both parties are promisees; and the legal effect of such a contract is that there are mutual rights and mutual duties. The distinction between these two classes of contracts is of importance in the analysis of a contractual transaction and in determining its validity and its exact legal operation. A failure to recognize this distinction has in innumerable instances led to the making of such an erroneous statement as, "Both parties must be bound, or neither is bound"; and occasionally it has led to an unjust and erroneous decision.[60]

60. Courts very frequently use the term "unilateral" to refer to a    promise that is without consideration especially in those cases where

It is, of course, true that, as in the case of other legal expressions, the terms unilateral and bilateral have been used in senses other than those here adopted. Some courts and law writers, adopting a definition other than that here given and assuming that the definition so adopted is the one correct, absolute, and eternal definition, have declared that in the nature of things there can be no such thing as a unilateral contract. It has been said that a unilateral contract is a legal solecism.[61] A very learned writer has declared that a unilateral contract is as impossible in its nature as "a unilateral elephant" or "unilateral twins."[62] It is not infrequently said that, until an offer has been accepted, the contract is unilateral and cannot be enforced; it is obvious that in such a case the term "contract" should not be used at all.[63]

It is very commonly stated that it takes two to make a contract. In the great majority of cases, that is, in the case of "bargains," this is a true statement; but there are exceptions. In a subsequent chapter there will be found a discussion of certain classes of promises that are enforceable, without any consideration being given for them and without any expression of assent by the promisee. These are special classes, however; they cannot be considered at this point. The term unilateral contract as defined herein does not mean that there is only one party to the contract. It does mean, however, that the promise or promises have been made by one party alone. In the great majority of cases, however, the promise of this party will not be an enforceable contract unless a sufficient consideration has been given in return for it, or unless there has been some expression of assent to the delivery of a document containing the promise. In most cases, therefore, even though a contract may properly be described as unilateral, it takes two persons to make it. The action of a second party, usually the promisee, is in most cases necessary, in order to make a promise binding; and, unless the promise that is made is enforceable at law, we do not call it a contract at all. In all cases of "bargain", one party offers his promise in exchange for a specified consideration; and in order to "close the deal" and make a "contract" that consideration must be given. If this consideration is action or forbearance instead

mutual promises have been given, but one of them is illusory; as where A offers a promise to carry all the milk that B may care to ship, at fixed rates, and B accepts the offer and promises to pay those rates for all milk shipped by him with A. This usage should be abandoned. Both A and B have made seeming promises, but neither one has resulted in either a right or a duty. There is no obligation, unilateral or otherwise. A has made an offer and perhaps B still has a power of acceptance. This one new relation might be described as unilateral; but the same may be said of any offer, and it is not customary to do so.

62. John S. Ewart, reviewing Anson on Contracts, 33 Harv.L.R. 626.

of a promise, the resulting contract is "unilateral"; it nevertheless takes two to make it.

Of course more than two individuals may participate in a contractual transaction. When such is the case, the persons involved are usually divided into two separate groups, each of which is contracting with the other group. For very many purposes, such a contract may be treated just as if it had been made by two individuals, and not by two groups of individuals; and the contract may be properly described as either bilateral or unilateral, in accordance with the promises that have been made. It must not be forgotten, however, that, as the number of participating individuals increases, the various legal relations among them will increase by geometrical progression. Many issues of law may arise amongst these individuals that could not possibly arise in the case of a contract made by two individuals only. This makes necessary a full discussion later on of those contracts that are commonly described as joint or joint and several. New and as yet unsolved problems have arisen out of the process called "collective bargaining" between great employing corporations and their employees who may be numbered in the hundreds of thousands.

No doubt it is quite possible for three or more persons to participate in one contractual transaction, without being segregated into two groups only. This would make possible such classifications as "trilateral" contracts and "quadrilateral" contracts. Thus far, no one has found it necessary to make use of such a classification in making a statement of contract law.

The distinction between unilateral and bilateral contracts will continually appear in the chapters dealing with offer and acceptance and with consideration. It may be useful at this point, however, to give some illustrations of a unilateral bargain and of unilateral contracts that are not "bargains". Observe that in such a contract there is only one promisor, and that he may be either the offeror or the offeree—the party who first proposes the making of such a contract or the party to whom it is proposed and who is to accept the proposal.

(1) A makes a promise in writing to pay to B $100 and signs, seals and delivers the document. This is a unilateral contract that creates a duty in A and a correlative right in B, just as soon as B, or some one acting in his behalf, receives delivery of the document. The promisor is the offeror. The transaction is not a "bargain"; nothing is exchanged for the promise.

(2) A delivers to B his promissory note or his I O U in return for $100, then lent to A by B. A is the only promisor, the only one under a contractual duty; and the contract is unilateral.[64]

Cash is bargained for and received in exchange for the written promise.

(3) A accepts a bill of exchange drawn upon him by B in favor of C. This creates a right in C and a duty in A; and the contract is unilateral. The promisor is the offeree.

(4) A offers a reward of $100 to any one who will return a lost article. B returns the article with the intent to accept the offer. A unilateral contract has thus been made.[65] The offeror is the only promisor.

(5) A writes to B, "Ship me 2 cars XX flour via B. & O., at once, price $10 per bbl. C.O.D." B ships at once as requested.

(6) A sends his brother to B with the following letter of credit, "Let Harry have $100 and I will guarantee repayment in 30 days." B advances $100 as requested.

(7) A promises B to pay him a salary at the rate of $10,000 a year for B's services as superintendent. B may recover at the specified rate for such service as he thereafter renders, but the hiring is a hiring at will. B has made no promise to continue in service. If, by implication, a promise by B is found that his service shall be of a certain kind or quality, the contract is to that extent bilateral.

It has been said that unilateral contracts are made either by an offer of a promise for an act or by an offer of an act for a promise. This means, although the descriptive words are not exact, that the single duty may rest on the offeror, the right being in the offeree, or vice versa. The words are inexact, because the making of a promise is itself an act. All offers are acts and all acceptances are acts, whether the resulting legal relations are property as in the case of a barter, or constitute a contractual obligation, either unilateral or bilateral. In example (1) above, the offeror makes a promise and undertakes a duty, but he requests no act whatever as an equivalent. The only act on the part of the offeree is such an act of acceptance of the physical document as may be necessary to constitute a legally effective delivery by the offeror. The duty is on the offeror.

Example (2) is a case where it does not clearly appear which one made the offer. If A offered his I O U to be accepted by a transfer of money, it was an offer of a promise for an act. If B offered a transfer of the money in return for the I O U, the only promise was made by the offeree and it was the offeror who gave the bargained-for equivalent (the money).[66]

In example (3), C makes the offer when he presents the bill to A for acceptance. He thereby confers upon A the legal power of binding himself alone to pay a sum of money. In presenting the bill C does an act, but he is not offering this act as the legal equivalent and agreed return for A's promise. There is no offer of an act for a promise; but the act of the offeror was necessary before the offeree could undertake the duty. The acceptance of such a bill may, however, be only one act in a large and complex transaction, in which mutual promises are made.

A bilateral contract is made in exactly the same way as is a unilateral bargain or a barter. The offeror does an act conferring a power upon the offeree, and the offeree does the act that constitutes the exercise of the power. The legal result, however, is a relation consisting of mutual rights and duties, special and personal in character. The following are examples of bilateral contracts:

(8) A says to B, "I promise to serve you as bookkeeper for one month in return for your promise to pay me $100." B replies, "I accept."

(9) A writes to B, "I promise to convey Blackacre to you on June 1st in return for your promise to pay me $1,000 at that time. You may accept by cable, using the one word 'Blackacre'." B sends the cable despatch "Blackacre", as requested.

In case (8) the acts of offer and acceptance are oral promissory words. In case (9) the offer is the act of writing and the further acts whereby this writing is sent to the offeree. The acceptance consists of acts by B, whereby he directs the cable company to transmit the word "Blackacre." These acts by B would not customarily amount to a promise to pay $1,000; but in this case they do become such a promise because A will so interpret them and B knows it. In the same way any other act, in itself meaningless, may be specified and may thereby become a return promise.

It is not always an easy matter to determine whether a contract is in fact unilateral or bilateral. Frequently, this determination will have very important results, especially where the offeror has attempted to revoke his offer, as explained elsewhere. The form of words used by the parties is not at all conclusive, when examined out of their setting and with the aid of nothing but a dictionary. The meaning of words, as used by the parties to a contract, cannot be determined with mathematical certainty; and the judge who is most certain to do injustice is the pedant who holds contractors to meticulous accuracy in the usage of words and in the construction of sentences.[67]

---

67. In Hollidge v. Gussow, Kahn & Co., 67 F.2d 459 (C.C.A.1st, 1933), a dealer sent a written order to a publisher "for 160,000 copies of the K. Courier (an advertising leaflet) divided into 8 issues of 20,000 per issue." Delivery, one issue per month. "Price $940 per issue, $7,- 520 complete for 8 issues." Contents and material "subject to okay." "Subject to approval of your credit dep't." There was no proof of any oral or written acceptance, but there were conferences and one issue was printed and delivered. The dealer then

It can hardly be said that courts are often pedantic in this matter, though it is possible that professors of law may be. The distinction between unilateral and bilateral has not yet been very thoroughly grasped by the multitude of lawyers, a fact which has led again and again to the erroneous statement that one cannot be bound unless the other is bound. The judges, therefore, are not in general too likely to hold that a proposed contract is unilateral when the parties meant it to be bilateral.[68]

Suppose A writes to B, "I will pay you $5,000 for Blackacre," and B replies, "I accept your offer." This seems to be bilateral, and it is too late for A to revoke. A clearly makes a promise to pay money; and, according to the ordinary understanding of mankind, he requests B to make a return promise to convey the land. But if A has asked an actual conveyance of Blackacre as the equivalent of his promise, B can accept only by executing a deed of conveyance, not by saying "I promise to convey."

became bankrupt. Did the publisher have a claim for lost profits on the next 7 issues? It was held, rightly, that the "order" was an offer to make one contract, not eight separate ones, and that if the contract was to be unilateral the publisher bound the dealer irrevocably by making a substantial beginning of the requested performances for 8 months. The dealer was bound by a unilateral contract to pay $7,520, conditional on the monthly publications. Restatement, Contracts, § 45, was held applicable. In a case like this, it would be equally reasonable to find that the publisher had made a return promise by implication to publish the 8 issues. Had the publisher failed to continue publication, the dealer should have had a claim for damages.

# PART I

# FORMATION OF CONTRACT

---

## TOPIC A

## OFFER AND ACCEPTANCE

---

### CHAPTER 2

### OFFERS; CREATION AND DURATION OF POWER OF ACCEPTANCE

---

## § 22. Preliminary Negotiation

The history of any contractual transaction is merely the narration of a series of events. It is always of advantage to consider these events in their chronological order, determining their legal operation one by one as they have occurred. In case there is litigation, the problem before the court always is to determine what kind of a judgment or decree to render and what action to command. When a lawyer is consulted in regard to the case, it is his function to predict and to advise his client as to what the judicial decree will be, in case there is litigation, and what action will be commanded. To determine these matters, it is helpful to consider the whole transaction step by step as it may have occurred, separating those facts that are immaterial from those that are material, and the facts that are merely evidential from those that are legally operative.

A bargaining transaction usually begins with what may be described as preliminary negotiation. This may include mere general discussion of a very indefinite character. There may be requests for estimates or bids.[1] There may be the puffing of wares by advertising their qualities and stating their prices. This may be done in newspapers or by handbills or in magnificently illustrated catalogs. Much of this preliminary negotiation may be totally inoperative to affect the legal relations of the parties involved. Its purpose may be merely to acquaint another person with a certain fact and to excite in him a bargaining desire; but inoperative preliminary negotiation may or may not lead to the making of a legally operative offer.

The term "preliminary negotiation," however, may be used to include all those communications and other events in a bargaining transaction that are antecedent to acceptance, that is, antecedent to the completion of the contract. In this sense, every offer that is made is a part of the negotiation that is preliminary to the making of a contract. There may, indeed, be more than one offer. In the preliminary haggling process, there are frequently offers and counter-offers, each one of which has a certain legal operation, but none of which is transformed into a

1. A letter to jobbers, stating the terms on which Iver Johnson revolvers would be sold, was held not to be an offer, but an invitation to submit offers on certain terms. Mont-gomery Ward & Co. v. Johnson, 95 N.E. 290, 209 Mass. 89 (1911).

See the succeeding sections for the discussion of further cases.

contract, for lack of acceptance on the part of the offeree. In determining whether or not a bargaining transaction actually results in the making of a contract, it is frequently necessary to consider all of the preliminary negotiations, all of the offers and counter-offers, interpreting the various expressions of the parties, in order to form a judgment as to whether they ever finally expressed themselves as in agreement on completed and definite terms.

If by "preliminary negotiation" we mean preliminary to a contract, we include in the term all operative offers and counter-offers that are antecedent to effective acceptance. The term may also be used to include only those communications that are antecedent to any power of acceptance and are themselves without any legal operation. In the latter case we include no operative offer whatever.[2]

In the process of negotiation a party may use words that standing alone would normally be understood to be words of "contract," at the same time limiting them in such a way as to show that a subsequent expression of assent on his part is required. In such case the expression is neither an operative offer nor an operative acceptance; it is preliminary negotiation. Thus, a written proposal stating many terms may be made "subject to agreement" on another specified matter; or it may be said: "I reserve final determination for tomorrow." Words such as these will in nearly all cases be held to show that an operative assent has not yet been given.[3]

In a much cited case, the plaintiff offered to sell his interest in a patent to the defendant on stated terms. The latter was willing to buy, but only on condition that a trusted third person, one Abernethie who was not present, should approve the deal. The report states: "It was then proposed that, as the parties were all present and might find it troublesome to meet again, an agreement should then be drawn up and signed, which, if Abernethie approved of the invention, should be the agreement, but if Abernethie did not approve, should not be one." Later, the plaintiff brought suit, setting forth this written instrument as a contract. The defendant pleaded that Abernethie did not approve. The court held, quite justly, that oral testimony of the conversation was not excluded by the "parol evidence rule," giving as a reason that until Abernethie expressed approval no contract had been made. This reasoning is believed to be erroneous. Abernethie was not one of the contracting parties, and his expression of approval of the invention was not to be the acceptance of the plaintiff's offer. No further expression of assent by either party was contemplated; and Abernethie was not an agent of the defendant empowered to accept an offer. Neither party had power of revocation. This was merely a case in which the plaintiff

39

gave his promise to sell in exchange for the defendant's conditional promise to buy, the condition being an act of a third party. The parties were irrevocably bound in exactly the same way that they would have been bound if the condition had been expressed in the signed writing.[4]

Preliminary negotiation, including offers and counter offers, may take place after the making of one contract but prior to the making of another. The negotiation may be with reference to a possible rescission of a contract already made or the variation thereof by the substitution of new terms. If such negotiation never arrives at an acceptance of a definite offer, the original contract still stands and may be enforced.[5]

Preliminary actions and communications, even though not in themselves legally operative as an offer of a bargain, may nevertheless be highly important in determining whether a contract has subsequently been consummated and what are its terms. Such communications may be incorporated into the offer that is finally accepted; and in any case they form part of the background against which the final expressions of agreement must be interpreted and understood. Even if those final expressions are put in the form of a written document, now often described as a written "integration", purporting to be the final and complete expression of all terms agreed on, a just interpretation of that integration can not be made without considering the actions and communications of the parties in the preliminary bargaining process. It is the intentions and meanings of the parties that are being "integrated," and it is those meanings and intentions that justice requires the court to determine and make effective.

## § 23. Preliminary Communications Compared to Offers—Interpretation

The determination of whether a certain communication by one party to another is an operative offer, and not merely an inoperative step in the preliminary negotiation, is a matter of interpretation in the light of all the surrounding circumstances.[6] Since two cases are never identical in the exact words used, in the existing relations and history of the parties, in the circumstances surrounding the communication, the decision made in one of them can never be regarded as a conclusive precedent for the other. Nevertheless it may be a suggestive and enlightening precedent.[7] Even in making this limited use of it, however, it must be remembered that the printed report of the case practically never gives us its entire setting, and that in the delicate process of interpretation the decisive factor may have been something that is not in print. It is the sum-total of factors that leads

---

4. The case is Pym v. Campbell, 6 El. & Bl. 370 (1856).

to a decision; and without knowing all of them it is not possible to know with assurance just what the court was interpreting and just why it arrived at its conclusion.

The interpretation of words and actions is in part an effort to ascertain the meaning given to those words and actions by the speaker and actor. To an equal extent it is an effort to ascertain the meaning given to those words and actions by another person to whom they are communicated. Before determining what legal operation shall be given to the words and actions, it is necessary also to determine whether either party actually knew or had reason to know the meaning given by the other party. Sometimes this last determination can not be made without knowing the meaning that would be given to the words and actions by other men; at other times it is determined with good assurance by the express admissions of one party or by the communications made to him by the other.[8]

## § 24. Request for an Offer is Not an Offer—Auctions

In the process of negotiation it is not uncommon for one party to request the other to make an offer. When such a request is made, the subject matter is usually already specific and most of the terms are already understood. In these cases the request must not itself be taken to be the operative offer, even though it is expressed in what may appear to be offering words. Thus at an auction specific goods are "offered for sale," for immediate delivery and on advertised terms of cash or credit. Yet in the ordinary case the buyers are being requested to submit bids and are not being empowered to accept an offer to sell. The bid is an offer, not an acceptance.[9] The bidder is requested to name a definite price that he is willing to pay, and thus to state the terms of a bargain and make an offer that will create a power of acceptance in the auctioneer.

Frequently the same situation exists in the case of an advertisement for bids on some building or other construction, public or private, or on the furnishing of supplies. The advertisement is not an offer; it is a request for offers.[10] This is true even

9. Payne v. Cave, 3 T.R. 148 (1789).

10. Pa.—Leskie v. Haseltine, 25 A. 886, 155 Pa. 98 (1893).

Eng.—Spencer v. Harding, L.R. 5 C. P. 561 (1870).

Even though a statute requires the letting of a contract to the lowest bidder, there is no contract with the lowest bidder if the only acceptance is of a higher bid. Kelly v. Board of Freeholders, 101 A. 422, 90 N.J.L. 411 (1917).

It must be borne in mind that an advertisement may be so worded that readers are reasonable in understanding it to be an offer to sell or to buy. In Crummer & Co. v. Nuveen, 147 F.2d 3, 157 A.L.R. 739 (C.C.A.7th, 1945), a published notice by a County Board to bondholders was held to be an offer to buy at par, all bonds tendered and not a mere request to submit bonds for acceptance by the Board.

though it may be common practice to accept the best bid made. Such an advertisement may not even request an offer; it may request merely a reply that will further the negotiation in the direction of an offer. Even if it requests an offer, it may not induce one. There may be no reply at all; or the reply may be a mere quotation of price or an expression not yet indicating a readiness to close the deal.[11]

Sometimes the expressions of a travelling salesman or soliciting agent amount to no more than an invitation to submit an offer. He may be authorized neither to make an offer nor to accept one. In such a case, an order for goods given by the solicited customer is a mere offer, even though it clearly states all the terms and even though it is on a printed form supplied by the solicitor's own principal. It is revocable in spite of an express provision that it shall "not be subject to countermand." [12] The fact that the order is solicited and its terms largely dictated by the solicitor or his principal may have an important effect upon the mode of acceptance. An acceptance by the solicitor "subject to the approval of the home office" is no acceptance at all; but it does not prevent the principal from having power to accept. The circumstances may be such as to justify the customer in believing that his offer has been accepted, if the principal merely remains silent.[13] And the terms of the order signed by the customer may be such as to empower the principal to bind him without sending any notice of acceptance, a notation

---

11.   Eng.—Harvey v. Facey, [1893] A.C. 552.

In Williams v. Favret, 161 F.2d 822 (C.C.A.5th, 1947), in preparation for making a bid for government construction a general contractor asked the plaintiff—a sub-contractor—to submit a quotation for the electrical work. The plaintiff submitted such a quotation, expressly adding the following: "If our estimate used wire us collect prior to June 6 or else same is withdrawn." The general contractor (defendant) wired on June 6 "We used your bid for wiring on barracks and dispensary Gulfport." Another bidder on the general contract had similarly wired the plaintiff. After being awarded the general contract as the lowest bidder, the defendant made a sub-contract for the electrical work with a person other than the plaintiff; this resulted in the present action for damages. In spite of a vigorous dissent, it is believed

that the court's decision that the defendant had committed no breach of contract was correct. If the plaintiff's "quotation" of a price was in fact an offer, the defendant's "use" of it in making his own bid was not an acceptance. It was not so in express terms; and such an implication is not reasonable. The defendant's "use" of the estimate in making his own bid did no more than to prevent its being "withdrawn." Such action in reliance, in view of the plaintiff's express words, might well be held to make an offer irrevocable, in accordance with Restatement, Contracts, § 90. Doubtless it should also have weight in interpreting the plaintiff's submission of an estimate as a firm offer and not a mere "quotation" of a price.

12.   See Challenge Wind & Feed Mill Co. v. Kerr, 53 N.W. 555, 93 Mich. 328 (1892).

of approval on the written order or some other overt action or forbearance being sufficient.[14] In these cases, the solicitor submits a form of offer: this is inoperative and preliminary. The customer signs an order, thereby making an offer; in this order he can specify or limit the power of acceptance as he sees fit. Finally, the dealer represented by the solicitor must express his acceptance, the method complying with terms of the offer and the usual rules governing acceptance.

## § 25. Offer by Publication or Advertisement

It is quite possible to make a definite and operative offer to buy or to sell goods by advertisement, in a newspaper, by a handbill, or on a placard in a store window.[15] It is not customary to do this, however; and the presumption is the other way. Neither the advertiser nor the reader of his notice understands that the latter is empowered to close the deal without further expression by the former. Such advertisements are understood to be mere requests to consider and examine and negotiate; and no one can reasonably regard them otherwise unless the circumstances are exceptional and the words used are very plain and clear.[16]

On the other hand it is very common, where one desires to excite many people to action, to offer a reward for such action by general publication in some form. Such offers must be reasonably interpreted, according to their terms and the surrounding circumstances; but action in accordance with such an interpretation will close a contract. There are many cases of offers of a reward for the capture of a person charged with crime, for desired information, for the return of a lost article, and for the winning of a prize contest.[17] The contracts so made are almost always unilateral.

Although a dealer's advertisements of his goods, in circulars and periodicals or by radio, are seldom to be interpreted as in themselves offers creating a power of acceptance, the descriptive statements made therein as to quality of the goods may sometimes be reasonably understood to be warranties that become a part of a contract for sale of such goods that is subsequently entered into with a buyer.[18] This is not so if the advertised statements would be taken by a reasonable person to be mere "puffing" or expressions of opinion. The question depends

15. In Carlill v. Carbolic Smoke Ball Co. [1893] 1 Q. B. 256, the words were plain and clear, and a deposit was placed in a bank as evidence of "good faith." The advertisement was of a reward of £100 to any one who caught the influenza after using a smoke ball.

17. See:

U.S.—Shuey v. U. S., 92 U.S. 73, 23 L.Ed. 697 (1875), reward for capture of murderer of Lincoln, also for information leading to capture.

upon the usual principles of interpretation and upon the expressions of the parties in their negotiations subsequent to the advertisement.

## § 26.  Quotation of Prices

A quotation of prices is not an offer; for a mere quotation of price leaves unexpressed many terms that are necessary to the making of a contract. A quotation is usually a price per unit of quantity, as when corporate stock is quoted at $85 per share, hogs at $4.50 per hundred pounds, cotton at 12 cents per pound, or flour at $9 per barrel. Such a quotation leaves unstated the amount to be sold, the time and place of delivery, the terms of payment, and other matters usually agreed upon before closing a deal. As will appear below, the use of the word "quote" does not in itself prove that these other terms have not been already agreed upon, tacitly or otherwise;[19] but one who asserts a contract must show that they have been so agreed upon. A quotation of price, standing alone, is not an offer.[20]

## § 28.  Catalogs and Circulars

Dealers in goods, whether wholesale or retail, are in the habit of sending out catalogs, price lists, and circulars, advertising their wares, quoting prices, and soliciting business. Generally they are happy to receive orders so induced, and generally they accept them and supply the goods. Sometimes, however, the quantity ordered is too great, or the goods are out of stock, or a mistaken price has been given, or a rival attempts to take an unfair advantage; these cases test the operation of the document that was circulated. The result commonly reached is that it was not an operative offer and that there is no contract.[23] Unless the words used are unusually clear to the contrary, the circular is a mere preliminary invitation to trade that creates no power. Operative offers have been found in circulars promising a reward[24] and in school and university catalogs.[25]

20.   Nebraska Seed Co. v. Harsh, 152 N.W. 310, 98 Neb. 89, L.R.A. 1915F, 824 (1915), may be regarded as a close case.

23.   In Montgomery Ward & Co. v. Johnson, 95 N.E. 290, 209 Mass. 89 (1911), the defendant sent out a circular letter to jobbers, stating the terms on which revolvers would be sold. The plaintiff at once ordered a specified quantity. The court held that there was no contract, saying, "An invitation to prospective buyers to negotiate for a license, and to trade with the defendant, even when confined to a definite class, imposes no obligation on the sender of accepting any offer which thereafter might be received. The order of the prospective buyer does not ripen into a contract of sale until the defendant's acceptance, and then only as to goods specifically ordered."

24.   Eng.—Carlill v. Carbolic Smoke Ball Co., [1893] 1 Q.B. 256; Williams v. Carwardine, 4 B. & Ald. 621 (1833).

25.   Mo.—Niedermeyer v. Curators of State University, 61 Mo.App. 654 (1895).

## § 29. Partial Agreements—"Contract to Make a Contract"

Communications that include mutual expressions of agreement may fail to consummate a contract for the reason that they are not complete, some essential term not having been included.[26] Frequently agreements are arrived at piecemeal, different terms and items being discussed and agreed upon separately. As long as the parties know that there is an essential term not yet agreed on, there is no contract; the preliminary agreements on specific items are mere preliminary negotiation building up the terms of the final offer that may or may not be made.[27] Even though one of the parties may believe that the negotiation has been concluded, all items agreed upon, and the contract closed, there is still no contract unless he is reasonable in his belief and the other party ought to have known that he would so believe.

The same result exists in cases where a complete and operative offer is made, but is not unconditionally accepted. The reply may be a partial or a conditional acceptance, in which case certain terms of the offer are agreed upon while others are not. The parties may proceed with their negotiations as to these others, without any new and distinct reference to the terms already assented to. There is no contract until agreement is reached on all terms, the preliminary and partial agreements being expressly or impliedly incorporated into the final offer and acceptance.[28]

Further illustrations are to be found in the cases of a so-called contract to make a contract. It is quite possible for parties to make an enforceable contract binding them to prepare and execute a subsequent documentary agreement.[29] In order that such may be the effect, it is necessary that agreement shall have been expressed on all essential terms that are to be incorporated in the document. That document is understood to be a mere memorial of the agreement already reached. If the document or contract that the parties agree to make is to contain any material term that is not already agreed on, no contract has yet been made; and the so-called "contract to make a contract" is not a contract at all.[30]

We must not jump too readily to the conclusion that a contract has not been made from the fact of apparent incompleteness. People do business in a very informal fashion, using abbreviated and elliptical language. A transaction is complete when the parties mean it to be complete. It is a mere matter of interpretation of their expressions to each other, a question of fact. An expression is no less effective that it is found by the method of implication. The parties may not give verbal expression to

28.   See Purrington v. Grimm, 76 A. 158, 83 Vt. 466 (1910), where it was held that such a complete agreement was finally reached and a contract made.

such vitally important matters as price, place and time of delivery, time of payment, amount of goods, and yet they may actually have agreed upon them. This may be shown by their antecedent expressions, their past action and custom, and other circumstances.[31]

Even though certain matters are expressly left to be agreed upon in the future, they may not be regarded by the parties as essential to their present agreement. Furthermore, the terms left for future settlement may be within definite and prescribed limits. The exact price may be left for future negotiation within a specified maximum and a specified minimum. In such a case it may be intended that the buyer shall have a binding option to buy at the maximum, or the seller shall have one to sell at the stated minimum, or both may have such options.[32] An agreement to grant a license in a "standard form" to be thereafter adopted by the patentee granting it becomes an enforceable contract as soon as the patentee adopts such a form.[33] There may be a valid contract even though one of the parties must still submit specifications as to assortment of sizes or qualities.[34]

So where a lease provided that the lessee should have an option to purchase "for the sum of $18,000 on terms to be agreed upon," it is obvious that the time of payment and the security for deferred payments are not yet settled; and yet the court held that a contract had been consummated and decreed specific performance.[35] The lessee had an option to buy for cash unless the lessor should specify other reasonable terms.

The court will be more ready to find that the apparently incomplete agreement was in fact complete and required the payment and acceptance of a "reasonable" price or a performance on "reasonable" terms, in case the parties have already rendered some substantial performance or have taken other material action in reliance upon their existing expressions of agreement. The fact that they have so acted is itself a circumstance bearing upon the question of completeness of their agreement.[36] The court may be more ready to reach such a result in case the remedy asked and given is the equitable remedy of specific performance than in a case where the remedy to be given is a judgment for money damages.

Two persons may fully agree upon the terms of a contract, knowing that there are other matters on which they have not agreed and on which they expect further negotiation. Such an expectation does not prevent the agreement already made from being an enforceable contract. This may be true even though

32.　**U.S.**—Wood County Grocer Co. v. Frazer, 284 F. 691 (C.C.A. 8th, 1922).

they expressly provide in their agreement that the new matters, when agreed upon, shall be incorporated into a written lease or other formal document along with the contract already made.[38]

## § 30. Formal Document Contemplated by the Parties

One of the most common illustrations of preliminary negotiation that is totally inoperative is one where the parties consider the details of a proposed agreement, perhaps settling them one by one, with the understanding during this process that the agreement is to be embodied in a formal written document and that neither party is to be bound until he executes this document. Often it is a difficult question of fact whether the parties have this understanding; and there are very many decisions holding both ways. These decisions should not be regarded as conflicting, even though it may be hard to reconcile some of them on the facts that are reported to us in the appellate reports. It is a question of fact that the courts are deciding, not a question of law; and the facts of each case are numerous and not identical with those of any other case. In very many cases the question may properly be left to a jury.[39]

The courts are quite agreed upon general principles. The parties have power to contract as they please. They can bind themselves orally or by informal letters or telegrams if they like. On the other hand, they can maintain complete immunity from all obligation, even though they have expressed agreement orally or informally upon every detail of a complex transaction. The matter is merely one of expressed intention.[40] If their expressions convince the court that they intended to be bound without a formal document, their contract is consummated, and the expected formal document will be nothing more than a memorial of that contract. In very many cases the court has been convinced that such was the intention and has held the parties bound by a contract even though no document has been executed.[41] On the other hand, the court may be convinced that the parties did not mean to be bound until the formal document is executed, in which case there is no contract until its execution by both parties. There are many other cases holding that such was the intention and that no contract was made.[42]

Usage and custom may be decisive of the issue. The greater the complexity and importance of the transaction, the more

---

38. **U.S.**—Beech Aircraft Corporation v. Ross, 155 F.2d 615 (C.C.A. 10th, 1946), express provision for subsequent revision of prices "by mutual agreement"; T. H. Flood & Co. v. Bates, 283 F. 364 (C.C.A.7th, 1922).

41. Rossiter v. Miller, 3 App.Cas. 1124 (1878); Brogden v. Metropolitan Ry. Co., 2 App.Cas. 666 (1877 H.L.).

likely it is that the informal communications are intended to be preliminary only. The fact that the parties contemplate the execution of a document is some evidence, not in itself conclusive, that they intend not to be bound until it is executed.[43]

It is not uncommon for a party to express agreement upon one or more terms, either orally or by letter, "subject to the execution of a satisfactory contract." Normally, this means that the formal document is to be the only binding expression of agreement.[44] The phrase "subject to" is not wholly conclusive as to this. It depends on the matter to which the obligation is to be "subject." If this matter is the signature of a party or other expression of his will, presumably no contract has yet been made. But if the matter is some event or some act of a third person, the parties may now be bound irrevocably, though their obligation may be a conditional one. Such would be the case if they agree upon the sale of an article subject only to an expression of opinion by X as to its quality or value.

The subsequent conduct and interpretation of the parties themselves may be decisive of the question as to whether a contract has been made even though a document was contemplated and has never been executed.[45] They may both have already begun performance and may have made statements that are strongly evidential. Of course, the subsequent conduct of the parties may constitute a tacit contract on the terms previously agreed upon, even though the understanding had at first been that the execution of a formal document was necessary.[46]

In making the factual interpretation that the application of the rules of this section requires, the following classification of cases, in which the parties contemplate the reduction of their terms of agreement to a more formal document, may be found helpful: (1) At one extreme, the parties may say specifically that they intend not to be bound until the formal writing is executed. (2) Next, there are cases in which they clearly point out one or more specific matters on which they must yet agree before negotiations are concluded. (3) There are many cases in which the parties express definite agreement on all necessary terms, and say nothing as to other relevant matters that are not essential but that other people often include in similar contracts. (4) At the opposite extreme are cases like those of the third class, with the addition that the parties expressly state that they intend their present expressions to be a binding agreement or contract; such an express statement should be conclusive on the question of their "intention."

If the facts of a case properly fall within either the third or the fourth class above, a valid contract has been made. This is true, even though one or both of the parties may be aware that the formal writing will when prepared contain such additional provisions as they may then agree upon. However formal and complete a written contract may be, it is always competent for the parties to vary the terms or to add new ones by mutual agreement.[47a] The existence of such a possibility as this has no effect upon the validity of any contract, formal or informal.

## § 31. What Constitutes a Written Contract—There may be a Series of Communications [48]

The term "written contract" has no single and uniform meaning, no one "correct" meaning. In this it is no different from all other terms that are in common use in any language and in any country. The meaning that is intended to be conveyed by such a term, when used by a party to a transaction or by a legislature in a statute, must be determined by the usual processes of interpretation in the light of all the relevant surrounding circumstances. The same is true as to the meaning that is in fact conveyed to one who hears or reads it. When such meanings, so determined, are at variance it depends upon our opinions of policy and justice whether legal effect shall be given to any one of them or to none. Often the choice will depend primarily upon the purpose with which the term is used, whether by a contractor or by a legislature. The considerations affecting the determination are very different, when the issue is as to the existence of a prerequisite to obligation, from those that are decisive when the application of the so-called "parol evidence rule" or of some specific "statute of limitations" is in question.

If a written draft of an agreement is prepared, submitted to both parties, and each of them expresses his unconditional assent thereto, there is a written contract. So far as the common law is concerned, the making of a valid contract requires no writing whatever; and even if there is a writing, there need be no signatures unless the parties have made them necessary at the time they express their assent and as a condition modifying that assent.[49] Even if two parties have expressly agreed that they shall not be bound by contract until a written document has been signed and delivered, this does not deprive them of the power to bind themselves by a subsequent oral contract. All that is necessary to eliminate the agreement requiring a writing is to make a new agreement not to require one or to make a new

---

47a.   A very instructive case falling within class 3 above is Rossiter v. Miller, 3 App.Cas. 1124 (H.L. 1878). A formal contract was drafted by solicitors, as was contemplated, and the defendant refused to sign it.

In Frank Bowman Co. v. Lecato, 292 F. 73 (C.C.A.4th, 1923), offer and acceptance were abbreviated cables. Each party then submitted a draft of a formal contract that the other party refused to sign.

agreement clearly expressing the intention to be legally bound when it is made. Of course, the first agreement that a writing shall be necessary is a fact to be given some evidential weight in interpreting the subsequent expressions of the parties; it is not lightly to be discarded in determining whether the parties have later agreed to be bound without a writing.

An unsigned agreement all the terms of which are embodied in a writing, unconditionally assented to by both parties, is a written contract. It is true that the fact that they have expressed unconditional assent must be proved by testimony of their unwritten expressions; it is not evidenced by the writing itself. But the same is true of a writing that has been signed by both parties. Writing does not make a contract, not even if the writing bears both signatures. The fact that a man has signed an apparently complete expression of the terms of a contract is indeed strong evidence that he is thereby expressing his unconditional assent. In the absence of all other evidence to the contrary, it is almost enough; but if there is other evidence to the contrary, the signature itself is not conclusive. Even if the writing is both signed and sealed, there is no contract without delivery; and delivery, which is itself an expression of intention to give the document immediate binding effect, must always be proved by evidence extrinsic of the document itself. The necessity of such extrinsic evidence does not prevent the document from being a contract under seal; no more does the necessity of extrinsic evidence of unconditional assent prevent an unsigned document from being a written contract.[50]

In the process of making a contract, either orally or in writing, the parties may express their assent piecemeal, agreeing upon individual terms as the negotiation proceeds. These expressions are merely tentative and are inoperative in themselves; there is no contract until the parties close their negotiation and express assent to all the terms of the transaction together.[54] In giving expression to such a final assent, however, the parties frequently do not restate the various terms that they have previously tentatively agreed upon. Those terms may be either formally or tacitly incorporated by reference. This is especially likely to be true when the negotiation has been conducted by letter or telegram. In such cases, in determining the existence of a contract and its terms, the entire correspondence must be searched and interpreted. There must be found a final closing of the deal, each party indicating by an overt expression that the process of negotiation is complete and that he now assents to all the terms already tentatively adopted. The correspondence must show what those terms are; and the fact that they were so adopted by both parties must be established. Here, the proof of the contract consists chiefly in a series of documents, more or less informal in character, no one of which would be legally operative standing alone. This proof is written proof; and the contract may properly be described as a written contract, even though there are several writings that the parties have never physically attached to each other.[55]

When the contracting parties are found to have intended to reduce their agreement to a single complete writing and not to be bound by their antecedent communications, it will usually be found also that they intend not to be bound until the writing has been signed by every one of them.[56] They may express the contrary intention, however; and if they do so, the lack of one or more signatures does not prevent consummation of a contract. They may bind themselves without any signatures whatever. One party may make a signed written offer, expecting no more than an oral acceptance; or there may be a signed written acceptance of an oral offer.[57] Further, it may be clearly understood that all those who sign shall be bound by contract, even though others to whom the document is presented may fail to sign or assent.[58] Thus, in a composition with creditors, it may be expressly provided that all creditors who sign shall be bound, even though others do not; or they may make their obligation conditional upon the signatures of a specified proportion, in number of creditors or in total amount of indebtedness.

A signature may be operative without respect to its position on the document, although it is customary to sign at the end of the writing and beneath the written provisions. There must be satisfactory evidence that the signature was affixed with intent to authenticate and express assent to the entire document.[60]

One who signs his name to a writing that purports to be a contract does an act that is strong evidence that he intends to make himself a party thereto, bound as a promisor and entitled as a promisee. Even if he does not so intend, the principles of estoppel may bind him notwithstanding. It should not be so held, however, if the other parties know or have reason to know that such is not the intention. If one signs the contract and accompanies his signature by such descriptive words as "agent" or "trustee," he may be held to have bound himself personally as a party to the contract.[61] It should not be so held if the other parties knew better or if the instrument as a whole indicates the contrary.

The question as to the existence of a completely integrated written contract is involved in all cases applying the "parol evidence rule" and is very often poorly handled there. There is no contract at all, in spite of the existence of a signed formal writing, if the parties say at the time that it is not so intended; and there is no completely written contract if the parties intentionally misstate the consideration, or leave out a part of it, in order to deceive third persons or for any other reason.[62]

### § 33.   Printed Terms on Billheads and Letterheads

Men and corporations engaged in business often have printed matter on their billheads and letterheads, the purpose of which is to limit in various ways their liabilities and obligations under contracts made by the use of these papers.  A common printed line is to the effect that "all contracts are subject to strikes, accidents, and causes beyond our control."  The purpose of this appears to be that all contractual promises shall be conditional upon the non-occurrence of the events specified; it does not in itself prevent the creation of a power of acceptance.  Another common statement, so printed, is to the effect that "all contracts and orders are subject to the approval of the home office." [73] The purpose of this is that the negotiating agent shall have no power to bind his principal, and that expressions of agreement on the paper shall therefore be no more than an offer to be accepted or rejected by the principal at his pleasure.

Such provisions as these are effective to attain their purpose only in case they are actually called to the attention of the other party to the negotiation or are so laid before him that he may be reasonably, and is in fact, believed to have been made aware of them.[74]  It is a question of fact, to be determined as are other such questions, whether the other party was really aware of the printed provision or was reasonably believed to have been so aware.  If the provision is in small type on the edge of the paper, comparatively inconspicuous, and no reference is made to it in the negotiation or in the specially written parts of the document, it will generally be held not to be a part of the agreement or to affect it in any way.[75]

The question whether the collateral printed terms are inconsistent with the written ones is a question of interpretation of language; and it is for the court to decide rather than the jury, just as in other cases of interpretation of language.[76]

Even if the printed provision is in large type and is expressly brought to the attention of the other party, it is not a desirable way to insert a term in the agreement.  If a contract is negotiated in writing, even by a series of informal letters, all important provisions should be incorporated in the communication that is specially prepared for the transaction.  Of course, it is enough to insert a few express words, distinctly referring to the printed form.[77]  Indeed, it is possible to incorporate in this way many printed forms consisting of numerous paragraphs.  In no case should the words of reference fail to identify with certainty the printed matter that is so incorporated.

## § 34.  Intention to Affect Legal Relations—Social Engagements and Jests

It is sometimes said that, in order to make an enforceable contract, it is necessary that the parties should have consciously intended to affect their legal relations.  Social engagements are said not to constitute contracts, because the parties had no such intention.  These statements are, to a considerable extent, erroneous.  There seems to be no serious doubt that a mutual agreement to trade a horse for a cow would be an enforceable contract, even though it is made by two ignorant persons who never heard of a legal relation and who do not know that society offers any kind of a remedy for the enforcement of such an agreement.[81]  However, although the statement that there can be no enforceable contract unless the parties intended to affect their legal relations cannot be supported, it is even farther from the truth to say that their expressions of intention as to their legal relations are immaterial.  Transactions that are ordinarily called social engagements will be enforceable contracts if the parties sufficiently express an intention that they shall be so enforceable.  Likewise, business agreements that under ordinary circumstances would be regarded as enforceable contracts are prevented from being thus enforceable if the parties expressly declare that they do not intend to affect their legal relations and are depending solely upon the sanctions of honor and morality.[82]  In order to make an enforceable contract, it is not necessary that the parties should consciously advert to legal relations, but it is necessary that they should not express an intention to exclude legal relations.[83]  The following statements may be of assistance in distinguishing between non-enforceable social engagements and contractual agreements.  1.  If the subject matter and terms of a transaction are such as customarily have affected legal relations and there is nothing to indicate that the one now asserting their existence had reason to know that the other party

---

**82.**  In Rose and Frank v. Crompton, [1925] A.C. 445, [1923] 2 K.B. 261, 129 L.T. 610, the defendants were British manufacturers who had long been doing business with the plaintiffs, an American firm.  They executed an agreement in writing appointing the plaintiffs to be exclusive selling agents in the United States, making many detailed arrangements for the doing of business on a large scale, and containing many mutual promises.  The document then proceeded, "This arrangement is not entered into nor is this memo written as a formal or legal agreement and shall not be subject to legal jurisdiction in the law courts either of the United States or England."  A dispute afterwards arose and an action was brought.  The English court held that the provision just quoted had the effect of preventing any legal sanction and that the written agreement was not a contract.  It held further, however, that in so far as orders had been sent in under this agreement and accepted by the defendant, there was a binding informal contract for the execution of the order.

intended not to affect his legal relations, then the transaction will be operative legally.[84] 2. If the subject matter and terms are not such as customarily have affected legal relations, the transaction is not legally operative unless the expressions of the parties indicate an intention to make it so.[85]

Expressions in promissory form that are intended only as a jest or a banter and that either are in fact so understood or would be so understood by a reasonable person are not operative as either an offer or an acceptance.[88] It is otherwise, however, if the jesting element is so well concealed that the expression is reasonably understood to mean what it appears to mean.[89] The same may be said with respect to statements made as mere bluster and braggadocio.[90]

In a case where the corporate records were so drawn as to indicate a sale of oil on credit, but the surrounding circumstances showed that the sale was merely a sham made to deceive the Mexican Government, it was held that there was no contract.[91]

It is only when we ask whether the expressions of agreement will affect the action of society, will be operative to create legal relations, that we must begin to differentiate between different kinds of subject-matter and different kinds of expressions. It is true that the judicial and executive officers have not in the past been interested in many kinds of subject-matter on which agreements are made, and have not been stimulated to action by such agreements—that is, these agreements do not create legal relations. The term "social engagements" has been applied to some of the agreements of this sort. The line of division between what is "social" on the one hand and what is legally operative on the other, between agreements that make contracts and those that do not, can be determined only by inductive study and comparison of what the courts have done in the past. Case by case, they have drawn a line, although like other lines, it is drawn with a wide and imperfect brush, not with a draftsman's pen. Being drawn by many hands, there are gaps in places and there are conflicting lines in other places.

## § 35. Duration of Power of Acceptance Created by an Offer

Courts and writers often speak of the "duration of an offer"; also of the "termination of an offer"; but if an offer is an expression of assent, as we have defined it here, they do not mean the time occupied by that expression or the time when that expression is complete. Instead, they are thinking of the legal operation of the offer—of the power of acceptance created in the offeree. They do not care how long the offeror took to express himself; instead, they want to know how long the offeree has within which he can accept and whether the time limit has arrived. We shall speak here, therefore, of the duration of the power of acceptance and of the termination of that power.

At the time that he makes his offer, the offeror has full control of its terms, of the person who shall have power to accept, of the mode of acceptance, and of the length of time during which the power of acceptance shall last. When he makes the offer he may specify in it the time within which acceptance must occur; if he does so, the power of acceptance is limited accordingly.[92]

The offeror's limitation of the time is not operative if it is not communicated to the offeree so that he knows or should know of it;[93] but if so communicated it operates with certainty. It makes no difference that the time specified is much less than a reasonable time. The offeror is the creator of the power; and it dies, just as it was born, by the will of its creator. He need make no offer at all; and he may so word his seeming offer that it is impossible of acceptance. A offers to sell property to B for a sum of money, saying "this must be accepted not later than yesterday." There is no offer at all, and no power of acceptance. A says to B, "I offer you all my land in Alaska for $500, on condition that you accept within an hour." At the end of an hour B's power of acceptance is gone; it makes no difference that B has spent much money and effort in an attempt to discover the character and value of A's holdings or that the time limit was highly unreasonable.[94]

Occasionally, it may be difficult to interpret the words of an offer and to determine whether or not the offeror has in fact fixed a time limit. Thus he may write, "please reply by return of post," or "reply by return of wagon," or "waiting your reply by return."[95] Does he mean by expressions such as these that the power to accept shall last only until the next post leaves, or until the same wagon starts back? This question cannot be answered here; the answer depends upon the context and all the circumstances. It is nothing more than a sort of directing guide to say that the meaning given to such expressions is that which would be given to them by a reasonable man in the exact position of the offeree. Since the offeror has chosen his own words, the court will in case of doubt adopt the meaning that is more favorable to the offeree;[96] but if a reasonable man in the offeree's position would have known that the meaning was doubtful, his power should usually be restricted to the shorter time. The factors by which a "reasonable time" is determined, to be discussed below,

**92.** **Wis.**—Atlee v. Bartholomew, 33 N.W. 110, 69 Wis. 43, 5 Am.St. Rep. 103 (1887), an acceptance by telephone at 3:45 P.M. of an offer saying "must know by 2:30 today" was too late.

"At any time" does not mean forever. Starkweather v. Gleason, 109 N.E. 635, 221 Mass. 552 (1915).

**95.** **U.S.**—Eliason v. Henshaw, 4 Wheat. 225, 4 L.Ed. 556 (U.S.1819).

will usually be decisive in cases where the words of the offeror do not clearly set a time limit for acceptance.

It is not unusual for a seller or promoter, in order to induce the purchase of stock, bonds, or other property, to promise the buyer to repurchase the subject matter if the buyer shall "at any time" become dissatisfied with his bargain. This is an irrevocable offer; but the buyer's power to accept it does not last forever, although the words "at any time" appear to include a long if indefinite period. They should be held to make a "reasonable time" long enough to give the buyer an opportunity to learn the value of his purchase by experience with its productiveness of income and with the market.[97]

### § 36.    Reasonable Time for Acceptance

If the offeror has not communicated a specific time limit with sufficient definiteness, the power of acceptance by the offeree continues for a reasonable time.[1] This is the time that a reasonable man in the exact position of the offeree would believe to be satisfactory to the offeror. It is not the time that the offeree would like to have, in order to watch the market or to adjust his other affairs or to make estimates and calculations, however reasonable it may be for him to desire the necessary time. All of these are factors to be considered; they may have a bearing on the question of reasonableness. Various factors having such a bearing will be considered below.

What is a reasonable time in any case is a question of fact, to be determined by a consideration of all the circumstances existing when the offer and the attempted acceptance are made. There is no rule or principle of law by the use of which a decision can be reached deductively. When it is said, as it often is, that when the facts from which the inference is to be drawn are not in dispute the question is one of law for the court,[2] what is meant is that the court will itself draw the inference and decide the question, instead of submitting it to a jury. In respect to this, it is no different from all other questions and inferences of fact.

The actual but uncommunicated intention of the offeror may well be decisive of what is a reasonable time in certain cases. It will not be considered in determining whether the belief and action of the offeree were reasonable. Being unknown to him, he could not consider it. The time taken by him may be quite reasonable, even though longer than was intended by the offeror. Uncommunicated intention will never have the effect of decreasing the time that otherwise seems reasonable.

On the other hand, it may well be held to have the effect of lengthening the time. The time actually taken by the offeree may properly be held to be reasonable, if the offeror intended the power to last so long, even though on the facts known to him it was not at all reasonable for the offeree to think that he was accepting in time. A reasonable time may be longer than the offeror intended, but it can never be less. The primary, and perhaps the sole, purpose of limiting the power of acceptance to a reasonable time, is the protection of the offeror against results that he does not expect or foresee. If those results are caused by his own action, the law will compel him to abide by them for the protection of others; hence, an offeror may sometimes be bound by an acceptance that he did not expect. But he needs no protection against an acceptance that he in fact hoped for and meant to invite, even though he did not expressly state as long a time as he intended.

In a well-known early New York case, an offer was sent from San Domingo to New York on December 17. An unconditional acceptance was mailed on the following March 31. It might properly be held that this acceptance was too late, the time taken being unreasonable. But the offeror in San Domingo mailed letters during the month of April, stating that the offer was still open. These letters were never received by the offeree, because he died before their delivery. The court held, and properly, that a contract was consummated.[4]

When two negotiating parties are in each other's presence, and one makes an offer to the other without indicating any time for acceptance, the inference that will ordinarily be drawn by the other party is that an answer is expected at once. If the immediate reply is not an acceptance, the offeror has the instant opportunity to continue the negotiation and to express his will. He may keep his offer open as made, or vary it, or wholly revoke it; and the validity of an acceptance subsequently made will depend upon the words and conduct of the offeror. If, when the first reply is not an acceptance, the offeror turns away in silence, the proper inference is that the offer is no longer open to acceptance.

The foregoing would seem to be properly applicable to a negotiation by telephone when offeror and offeree are themselves speaking. The important point is that they have means of instant expression and communication. The fact that they can not see each other is important only as it excludes those means of communication that are visual in character. If the offeror "rings off" as soon as he finds that the first reply to his offer is not an acceptance, the normal inference is that the power to accept it is terminated.

4.   N.Y.—Mactier v. Frith, 6 Wend.
103, 21 Am.Dec. 262 (N.Y.1830).

If the parties do not have means of instant communication, the normal inference to be drawn is that instant reply is not required; a reasonable time for acceptance is somewhat longer.[5] This applies where the means of communication is the post, the telegraph, or special messenger. In every case alike, the inference to be drawn is subject to be controlled by other circumstances, by previous custom, and by the expressed will of the offeror.

The power of acceptance will last much longer than it otherwise would in case the conduct of the offeror reasonably leads the offeree to believe that the offer is still open. An offer is operative as long as the offeror says that it shall be; likewise it is operative as long as his conduct leads the offeree to believe that it is. If after having made an offer to do specified work for a stated price, the offeror is told to go ahead with the work, his going ahead as requested will bind him to complete it at the stated price, even though some months may have elapsed since his offer was made. His proceeding as requested, with reason to know that the offeree still regards his bid as operative justifies the offeree in so regarding it.[6]

The particular case just stated is quite capable of a different analysis. The request by the offeree to go ahead with the work may be regarded as the making of a new offer, adopting by tacit reference the provisions of the offer previously made by the workman; going ahead as requested, without comment or objection, would operate as an acceptance of the new offer. It is clear that in the absence of antecedent conduct of the original offeror leading the offeree to believe the offer to be still open, an attempted acceptance after expiration of a reasonable time would be effective only as a return offer and not as an acceptance.

If the subject matter of an offer to buy or sell is one that has a fluctuating value in the market, this fact tends strongly to shorten the time that will be held reasonable for acceptance.[7] A purchase and sale, whether for cash or on credit, is always a speculation in future values. To allow the offeree to accept after taking time to watch the market, is similar to allowing him to bet on a sure thing. It is not reasonable for him to believe that the offeror is willing for him to do this.[8] This is applicable to such commodities as shares of corporate stock, oil, cotton, or

---

7. In Minnesota Linseed Oil Co. **v.** Collier White Lead Co., 4 Dill. 431, Fed.Cas.No. 9,635 (C.C.Minn.1876) the court said: "It seems clear that the intention of the plaintiff, in making the offer by telegraph, to sell an article which fluctuates so much in price, must have been upon the understanding that the acceptance, if at all, should be immediate, and as soon after the receipt of the offer as would give a fair opportunity for consideration. The delay here was too long, and manifestly unjust to the plaintiff, for it afforded the defendant an opportunity to take advantage of a change in the market, and accept or refuse the offer as would best subserve its interests."

wheat, although with respect to all of them there are periods in which market prices are relatively stable. If no fluctuation has occurred, the time taken for acceptance is more likely to be held reasonable.

Land is a subject matter less likely to fluctuate in the market, and a correspondingly longer time will be reasonable for acceptance.[9] There are boom times, even in land, and also times of rapidly falling values; in such times the time that will be held reasonable is much shorter. With land as with chattels, the actual situation is the one to consider; if values have fluctuated acceptance will be too late after a relatively shorter time, if they have not fluctuated a longer time is more likely to be held reasonable.

The purpose of the offeror, to be attained by the making and performance of the contract, will affect the time allowed for acceptance, if it is or should be known to the offeree. In such case there is no power to accept after it is too late to attain that purpose. An offer of a reward for the capture of a specific criminal cannot be accepted by capturing him after the statute of limitations has barred prosecution for his offense; it may be reasonable to assume that the offer remains open as long as such prosecution is possible.[10] An offer of a reward for the arrest and conviction of persons who may hereafter commit a specified crime may be held to have lapsed after the deterrent effect of publication of the offer has ceased.[11]

The discontinuance of the publication of the offer is a fact of importance; but it does not cause the immediate termination of the power to accept. If the proposal contemplates a contract the performance of which is to begin by a particular date, a reasonable time for acceptance would not extend beyond that date.[12] If the proposed contract is to be unilateral, the acceptance to consist of full performance itself, a reasonable time for acceptance will necessarily include the time reasonably necessary for completing the requested performance; but this does not show how soon the rendition of the performance must begin. There is a reasonable time for beginning the performance; and this must be determined by a consideration of the same factors as in other kinds of contracts. In cases of this type the beginning of the requested performance will nearly always operate as an acceptance that is sufficient to prevent revocation of the offer. The offeror's contractual duty, however, will be conditional on substantial completion of the performance that he requested. Sometimes, but not necessarily, the beginning of the performance by the offeree will justify an inference that he promises to complete the performance; the bargain is then bilateral.

A public offer of a reward for information will, unless restricted in terms, create a power of acceptance in any one who becomes aware of the offer if no one else has already given the requested information. As soon as the information has been given to the offeror, the power of acceptance by any other person is at once terminated.[13] This is true even though he does not know that another has already given the information. As any reasonable person knows, the service of the second informer, and of any later one, is of no value; and it is obvious that the offeror is not promising to pay many times over for the same information. In this respect an offer of a reward for information differs from an offer of a reward for a service that can be rendered more than once and that has value to the offeror, however many times repeated. So, an offer to pay a hundred dollars to any one who catches the influenza after using the offeror's patent preventive can be accepted by many individuals, each of whom has a right to the sum offered if he succeeds in catching the influenza as specified.[14] In this case the conditional promise of the reward is offered in return for using the nostrum (not for catching the influenza) and almost every new user is accompanied by a new sale.

The fact that the offeror uses a particular method of communicating his offer does not in itself control either the mode of acceptance or the time within which it must occur; but the fact that the offeror uses the telegraph or other rapid method of communication is a fact of importance in the direction of the conclusion that a reasonable time is short. As will appear hereafter, the mode of communicating an offer may have important effects upon the power of acceptance in respect of the mode in which the acceptance is communicated.

## § 37.   Effect of Delay in the Delivery of an Offer

When two persons are negotiating at a distance, and not by telephone, it is possible that there will be some unexpected delay in the delivery of the offer to the offeree. A letter may be delayed in the mail; and a private messenger may fall ill on the way or be negligent and forgetful, or depart intentionally from the performance of his service. In the case of private business offers, it is usually held that there is no power of acceptance until the offer is received by the offeree; and the question arises as to whether the delay will limit the time within which he can accept or will even prevent any power of acceptance from existing at all.

If, at the time the offer is received, the time specified for acceptance has not yet expired, or the time that would have been reasonable had the offer been received without delay has not yet expired, there is no doubt that the offeree has a power of acceptance. If such time for acceptance has expired already and the offeree knows or has reason to know it, the courts are likely to hold that he gets no power of acceptance at all. If the offeree neither knows nor has reason to know that the time has expired, he has a power to accept.  The offeror must be held to have taken the risks of delay in the delivery of his offer, in so far as those risks can not be minimized or avoided by reasonable prudence and understanding on the part of the offeree.  If the latter is not warned by the terms of the offer and has no other reason to know of the delay, his power of acceptance will continue from the time of receipt just as if no delay had occurred. In most cases the offeree will have some indication of the delay from the date of the letter, the postmarks, the condition of the envelope, or statements of the messenger.  All such indications must be considered.[15]

In a well-known English case, an offer to sell wool was mailed to the offeree, incorrectly addressing him at Bromsgrove, Leicestershire, instead of Bromsgrove, Worcestershire.  This caused a delay of two days in the mails.  An acceptance, mailed immediately upon receipt of the offer was held to consummate a contract, even though the offer said "receiving your answer in course of post" and the offeror had sold his wool before the answer in fact arrived.[16]

A similar case was decided in the same way by the United States Supreme Court.  An offer to insure against loss by fire was mailed on December 2 to the plaintiff at an incorrect address; it was not received by him until December 20.  He accepted on the terms proposed and mailed his acceptance on December 21.  The insured dwelling was burned on December 22, before the letter of acceptance was delivered.  The contract to insure was held consummated.[17]  This decision should be approved, even though the offeree had reason to know of the delay, since there had been no change in insurance rates or in the risks of loss by fire.

### § 38.  Offers Are Usually Revocable

When one party makes an offer to contract with another he creates a power of acceptance in that other; but also, except in the cases that are hereafter discussed, he retains a power of revocation and withdrawal.  The method of exercising this power varies; usually it is by giving notice to the offeree.[18]  By exercising this power to revoke—by an effective revocation, the offeree's power of acceptance is terminated.[19]  After an acceptance has become effective, there is no power in either party to revoke or withdraw.

16.  Eng.—Adams v. Lindsell, 1 B. & Ald. 681 (1818). If the date, the postmark, or other facts, had given warning to the offeree of the delay, and he should have known that the offeror would not regard the delayed answer as being "in course of post," the decision should have been the other way.

17.  Tayloe v. Merchants' Fire Ins. Co., 9 How. 390, 13 L.Ed. 187 (U.S.1850).

Even though the offeror states when he makes the offer that the offeree shall have a definitely stated time in which to accept, or states that the offer will remain open for a definite time, the offer is nevertheless revocable at the will of the offeror.[20] An offer of this kind seems to be what some business men mean by a "firm offer". There is an implied promise not to revoke; but if the parties think that it is effective to deprive the offeror of the power to revoke, they are mistaken.[21]

Not infrequently, especially in the case of a written offer, it is expressly stated that it shall "not be subject to countermand." By this, no doubt the offeror understands that he is promising not to revoke the offer for the prescribed period, or for a reasonable time; and both parties may believe that the offer is thereby made irrevocable. Nevertheless, there still remains a power to revoke.[22] The express or implied promise not to revoke is not enforceable, unless it is under seal, or a consideration is given in exchange, or the offeree has changed his position in reliance upon it. The effect of these factors in making an offer irrevocable is discussed hereafter.

A statement by the offeror that his offer will remain open for a specified time is not wholly inoperative, even though it does not deprive him of the power to revoke. Its effect is to determine exactly the duration of the power of acceptance, in the absence of some new terminating factor such as a notice of revocation or a rejection. It makes no difference whether the stated time is unreasonably long or unreasonably short; it is nevertheless controlling, so that an acceptance after the expiration of the stated time is too late and an acceptance prior to such expiration is in time even though the contract is now very disadvantageous to the offeror.

As a matter of course, the offeror's power of revocation ceases at the instant that an acceptance by the offeree becomes effective. As will appear later, the mailing of a letter of acceptance will frequently consummate a contract at once, depriving the offeror of all power to revoke even though his notice of revocation is already despatched by mail, telegram, or private messenger. Even though an offer is revocable, an acceptance within the allotted time and before revocation makes a contract.[23]

**20.** Dickinson v. Dodds, 2 Ch.D. 463 (1876).

In Boston & M. R. Co. v. Bartlett, 3 Cush. 224 (Mass.1849) there was a written offer to sell, at any time within 30 days. The court said: "The counsel for the defendants is most surely in the right, in saying that the writing when made was without consideration, and did not therefore form a contract. It was then but an offer to contract, and the parties making the offer most undoubtedly might have withdrawn it at any time before acceptance. But when the offer was accepted, the minds of the parties met, and the contract was complete."

An order for goods may be either an offer to buy or the acceptance of an offer to sell. In the latter case, it consummates the contract; and no power of revocation or withdrawal remains in either party. If it is an offer to buy and has not yet been accepted by the seller, the order can be revoked in the same manner as other offers.[24] This is true even though the order states in terms that it is not subject to countermand.

There are continuing offers that create power in the offeree to make a series of separate contracts by a series of independent acceptances. After one such proper acceptance, the power of revocation ceases as to it; but a notice of revocation will terminate the offeree's power to make any further contract by a later acceptance.[25] So, a continuing offer to supply goods at stated prices cannot be revoked after an order for a specific quantity, as to that quantity; but a revocation deprives the offeree of power to bind the offeror by any subsequent orders.[26]

A promise of guaranty, when it is a mere offer by the guarantor, is revocable like other offers.[27] This is true whether the offer of guaranty provides for acceptance by a return promise, by appointing someone to a position of trust, or by the giving of credit in the form of goods or money or acceptances to some third person. It becomes irrevocable after the indicated acceptance has been given. A letter of credit or promise to guarantee the repayment of advances to be made to a third person is ordinarily an offer that can be accepted by the making of an advance, a unilateral contract being the result. As to the advance once made, the offer of guaranty is no longer revocable; if the offer is a divisible one creating power to make a series of separate unilateral contracts, a notice of revocation is effective as to advances not yet made.[28] Reasonable interpretation of the words of the parties may show that their contract is really bilateral as a whole and not divisible into parts; in this case the first act of acceptance makes the contract and binds both parties. It is possible also that the offer contemplates a binding and irrevocable option, to be consummated by the giving of a single order or the making of a single payment or the advancement of a single amount upon the credit of the offeror. The contract so consummated may be either unilateral or bilateral;[29] but there is no

**26.**   **Wis.**—Hopkins v. Racine Malleable & Wrought Iron Co., 119 N.W. 301, 137 Wis. 583 (1909).

**27.**   See Consolidated Portrait & Frame Co. v. Barnett, 51 So. 936, 165 Ala. 655 (1910).

**28.**   See Offord v. Davies, 12 C.B. (N.S.) 748 (1862).

**29.**   There was such an irrevocable option in Vickrey v. Maier, 129 P. 273, 164 Cal. 384 (1913).

In the case of Great Northern R. Co. v. Witham, L.R. 9 C.P. 16 (1873), the first order for goods under the standing offer (not inclosing cash in payment) made a separate bilateral contract for the purchase and sale

promise of further orders or payments or advancements, and yet the standing offer is irrevocable.

## § 39.  Notice of Revocation Necessary

An offeror has full power over the terms of his offer.  He can create in the offeree a power of acceptance that is as limited, or as difficult of exercise, as he pleases; and he can reserve in himself a power of revocation to be exercised in any way that he sees fit.  In order to do this, all that is necessary is that the offeree shall be informed of the limitation, or of the reservation, at any time before the offer is accepted.  If the offer is in writing, the limitation, or the reservation, should be expressed in the writing itself, so that knowledge of the whole comes to the offeror at the same time.  It is not necessary, however, that such limitation, or reservation, be put into the same writing or into any writing at all.  It will be equally effective if orally communicated to the offeree.  The statute of frauds and some other statutes require certain kinds of contracts to be in writing;  but none of these statutes makes any requirement as to the form in which an offer shall be made.  The terms of any offer may be all in writing, or all orally expressed, or partly written and partly oral.

After an offer has once been made, however, in any manner that is sufficient to make it irrevocable, it cannot be either varied or revoked by the offeror, by any communication either oral or in writing.  A so-called "binding option" is an illustration of this. The offeree's power of acceptance cannot be varied by the offeror, either as to the mode of exercising it or as to the substance of the contract to be made.  And, of course, the offeror cannot make an irrevocable offer revocable by merely saying afterwards that it shall be so.  This would be a contradiction in terms; the so-called irrevocable offer would not be irrevocable.

If the offer as originally made was a revocable offer, then it is subject to variation or destruction as the offeror may desire.  By a subsequent communication, he can wholly terminate the power of acceptance.  Likewise, he can limit the mode of acceptance— as, for example, by requiring an acceptance in writing instead of an oral one or by requiring it to be within an hour instead of within a longer time originally applicable.  And further, he can create in himself a power of revocation in a manner that would not previously have been effective.  Thus, one who has made a written offer to sell land for a sum of money, with the written statement that it shall remain open for a month, can effectively change it at anytime before acceptance by an oral communication raising the price, or requiring acceptance within a week, or

of the goods so ordered.  It did not make the offer irrevocable as to new orders, although this was a question that the court did not have to decide.  The court talked of the contract as if it were unilateral.

creating a power in himself to revoke by a sale to a third person without notice to the offeree.[30]   Any communicated change in the terms of an offer operates as a revocation of that offer.[31]

An offeror may expressly provide in his offer that it shall be revocable at will and without notice.   An offer with such a provision creates a flimsy power of acceptance in the offeree.   It seems probable that the courts would hold in such a case that an acceptance will consummate a contract if made before the offeror has in some way given overt expression to his intention to revoke.   It is not enough for him merely to assert, after the acceptance has been made, that he has revoked in accordance with the reserved power.

A purported offer that reserves the power to withdraw at will even after an acceptance should not be described as an offer at all, but as an invitation to submit an offer.

One who has made an offer to sell property has no power to revoke it merely by making a sale of the property to a third person.[32]   Such a power can be expressly reserved; but the offeree must know of the reservation.   A sale to a third person may make it hard for the offeror to perform as offered; but the offeree has power of acceptance even after the property has already been sold, if he is ignorant of such sale.   As appears in subsequent discussion, knowledge of the offeree that the offeror has contracted to sell to another terminates his power of acceptance.

If there has been no express provision as to the mode of revocation, either in the terms of the offer as originally made or by some other communication to the offeree, a power of revocation exists none the less.   The decisions have established the rule in such cases, however, that revocation is not effective unless it has been communicated to the offeree.   It is not enough merely to mail a notice of revocation, properly addressed to the offeree; his power of acceptance will remain unaffected until the letter has been received by him.[33]   It has not yet been determined whether, in order to be effective, the letter of revocation must have been actually read by him.   It is here suggested, however, that it should be held effective as soon as the offeree has had a reasonable opportunity to open and read the letter after it has been put into his hands or has been delivered at his business or home address.

It was once held that a change of mind by the offeror, totally uncommunicated, would prevent any subsequent acceptance from making a contract.   This holding may have been due to the very commonly expressed opinion that the assent of the two parties must be simultaneously expressed, an opinion long since discarded; or it may have grown out of the generally held notion that there must be a meeting of minds at a moment of time and that there is no such meeting if the mind of the offeror has changed. In a well-known English case, the defendant offered to sell 266 hhd. of tobacco at a stated price if the plaintiff would give notice of his acceptance before four o'clock that day. The plaintiff gave such notice before four o'clock, but the defendant had changed his mind and refused to sell. The report says nothing whatever as to any notice to the plaintiff of such change of mind. The court held that no contract was made.[34] There are very many later cases that are definitely in conflict with this; and they must be regarded as establishing the existing law.[35] In a few cases, specious and unnecessary attempts have been made to distinguish the case. It is clear today that the consummation of a contract does not require two actually consenting minds at one moment of time; it is equally unnecessary that there should be simultaneous expressions of consent. Unless a power of revocation without notice is expressly reserved as above explained, a message of revocation is not effective to terminate the power of acceptance until it is received.

In this respect a revocation of offer differs from an acceptance of offer; and it is reasonable that they should differ. An offeror invites an acceptance by the offeree and, because of the custom of men, has reason to know that the offeree will regard his expression of acceptance as closing the deal and as justifying immediate steps toward performance or other action in reliance. The offeree, on the other hand, has never invited a revocation of the offer and usually has no reason to expect one.[36] This is again considered in discussing acceptance by post.

### § 40. Revocation Otherwise Than by Direct Notice

An offeree's power of acceptance can be terminated otherwise than by a direct notice or communication sent to him by the offeror, containing express words of revocation. The purpose of requiring a communicated revocation is to prevent the offeree from accepting the offer and thereafter changing his position in reliance upon the offeror's promise. Other facts besides a notice from the offeror may make it unreasonable for the offeree to accept and rely; and he should be held to the standard of a reasonable man.

In a much discussed English case, one Dodds made an offer in writing to Dickinson to sell property for £800, saying: "This offer to be left over until Friday, 9 o'clock A.M." On Thursday, Dodds executed a formal contract to sell the property to one Allan; and on that same day Dickinson was told of this by his own associate and agent, one Berry. The report says that Berry told Dickinson that "Dodds had been offering or agreeing to sell the

---

34. Eng.—Cooke v. Oxley, 3 T.R. 653 (1790, K.B.).

property to Thomas Allan." This information at once spurred Dickinson into action. Before Friday at 9 o'clock, he had handed a written acceptance to Dodds' mother-in-law, and had caused Berry to deliver a written acceptance to Dodds in person. The court held that no contract was consummated by Dickinson's acceptance; and it dismissed his bill in which he asked for specific performance, for an injunction against a conveyance to Allan, and for damages.[37]

Lord Justice James said that Dickinson "knew that Dodds was no longer minded to sell the property to him as plainly and clearly as if Dodds had told him in so many words, 'I withdraw the offer.'" If this statement is true, the decision should be supported. But the statement is not true, if all that Dickinson learned was that Dodds had been "offering" to sell the property to another man. It is not unusual for an owner to make several offers to sell specific property, even though he may know that there is a possibility that more than one will accept and that he will be caught in more than one binding contract. In his desire to find at least one purchaser, he takes that chance. It seems, therefore, that knowledge by an offeree that a later offer has been made to another is not knowledge that the offeror no longer wishes to sell to him.

The quoted statement appears to be true, however, if Dickinson was informed that Dodds had bound himself by a contract with Allan, a contract that was not in terms conditional on Dickinson's failure to accept in time. It may not be unusual for a man to make two offers; but it is very unusual for him to make two contracts to sell the same property to different men. Therefore knowledge that one such contract has been made is enough to inform a reasonable man that the offeror no longer desires to make a second contract. The same is true of knowledge of other action by the offeror that clearly indicates a desire not to keep an offer open. In the absence of knowledge such action (e. g. a sale to another person) does not revoke the offer.[38]

In cases like this, the offeree must have "knowledge"; it is not enough that he has heard a "rumor." But Dickinson had "knowledge" of whatever Berry told him; for Berry was Dickinson's own agent and what Berry told him was true. If the information given the offeree is not true, of course, his power of acceptance continues; even if it is true, his power continues if he did not in fact believe it and was not unreasonable in refusing to believe it.

The American Law Institute has accepted the rule of revocation, as applied in Dickinson v. Dodds, but has stated it in so limited a form that it applies only to offers for the sale of property.[2]

37.　Eng.—Dickinson v. Dodds, 2 Ch. D. 463 (1876).

This form of "restatement" was due to the criticism to which the English decision has been subjected, while at the same time it was felt that the actual court decisions thus far rendered require recognition of the rule as stated. The present writer believes that the rule will not be thus restricted in the later decisions of the courts. Indeed, the Institute does not state that it is not applicable to offers other than for the sale of property; and it should not be inferred that the Institute meant to deny that it is applicable to them. The Restatement of the law does not purport to contain all the law that now is, much less all the law that is to be. It does not crystallize or embalm the body of the law or attempt to prevent its subsequent judicial growth and evolution. Such an attempt, if made, would be footless and headless.[43]

### § 41. Revocation of General Offer by Publication

When an offer has been made by publication, to a large number of unidentified persons, a power of acceptance is created in all those who read it. This power can be terminated by a personal notice of revocation, as in the case of an offer to one specific person; but it is impracticable for the offeror to find and to notify all those among the total millions of men who may have seen his offer. It might have been held, nevertheless, that no other method of revocation would be effective, and that the difficult position in which the offeror finds himself is one that he has brought upon himself—or, as it was once often said, is due to "his own folly." The Supreme Court of the United States, however, had such sympathy with the offeror, who in the case before the Court was the United States, that it saved the offeror from the unfortunate position. The court held that an offer by publication can be revoked by publication and that the power of acceptance is terminated even though some offeree never hears of the revocation and completes the acceptance as originally invited.

The facts of the case were as follows: President Andrew Johnson issued a proclamation offering a reward of $25,000 for the apprehension of John H. Surratt, believed to be implicated in the murder of Abraham Lincoln. Later he issued a similar proclamation revoking the offer. One Ste. Marie, a zouave in the service of the Papal Government knew of the original offer, recognized Surratt in the same service, and caused his arrest. This service was rendered by him after the proclamation of revocation was published but wholly without knowledge of it. The court held, as one of the reasons for refusing judgment for the reward, that the revocation was effective.[44] The rule thus applied in fa-

44.  **U.S.**—Shuey **v.** United States,        Pollock says of this case: "it seems
92 U.S. 73, 23 L.Ed. 697 (1875).        a rather strong piece of judicial

vor of the government has been applied in some other cases to published offers of reward made by private persons.[45]

Cases are sure to arise requiring a determination of how long the publication of the revocation must continue and how wide must be its distribution. Surely, an offer that has been posted on a bulletin board for a year and seen by passing thousands cannot be revoked instantly by tacking on the same board a notice of revocation that has been seen by nobody.[46] Some have suggested that the revocation should be effective when it has been given "equal publicity" with that given to the offer.[47] In the Supreme Court case above, we are not told what President Johnson did to cause the widespread publication of his first proclamation, or whether the second proclamation was issued in the same manner. It is highly improbable that the second proclamation actually received as great publicity. It had not the news interest of the first one.[48]

## § 42. Irrevocable Offers—Meaning of "Irrevocable"

One who has made an offer to contract with another can, without question, change his mind. Even if he has promised not to do so and has been paid for his promise, still he can change his mind. Also, he can communicate that fact to the offeree if the latter is within reach of the post, the telephone, or the radio. But it is quite another question whether he can, either by changing his mind or by communicating that fact to the offeree, undo what he has already done and destroy the power that by his offer he has created in the offeree. As has already been seen, he can do this in the case of an ordinary offer; but there are cases in which he has created a power of acceptance and is himself powerless to terminate it and to escape from his own liability to become bound. There are irrevocable offers. Our problem now is to state what offers are irrevocable, what factors make them so, and what is meant by irrevocability.[49]

legislation." Wald's Pollock, Contracts (3d Ed.) p. 23. To the writer it seems no stronger than are the decisions on any other rule of the law.

48. Some of the reasoning of the court is not easy to approve. Consider the following: "True, it is found that then, and at all times until the arrest was actually made, he was ignorant of the withdrawal; but that is an immaterial fact. The offer of the reward not having been made to him directly, but by means of a published proclamation, he should have known that it could be revoked in the manner in which it was made." Why a Papal zouave "should have known" anything about American law is difficult to see, especially when the rule involved was one that no court had yet laid down.

49. In earlier times, an irrevocable offer was declared to be a "legal impossibility." "It is indispensable to the making of a contract that the wills of the contracting parties do, in legal contemplation, concur at the moment of making it. An offer, therefore, which the party making it has no power to revoke, is a legal

An offer may be irrevocable in the sense that revocation is physically impracticable or even entirely impossible; that is, the acts necessary to operate as a revocation can not physically be done. The offeror may be legally privileged to do these acts, and the performance of them would effectuate a revocation and terminate the power of acceptance, while at the same time they are not within his physical capacity. In other words, the offeror has both the privilege and the legal power to revoke, but is unable physically to do it. For example, one who has made an offer by mail to another is suddenly cut off by a flood from all communication with the outside world. Any ordinary offer may become irrevocable in this manner, unless a power of revocation without notice has been reserved. Many an offeror, desiring to revoke, has found to his cost that the offeree is too far away; or that the wires are down, the mails too slow, and the offeree without a radio set.

Secondly, an offer may be irrevocable in the sense that the offeror has made a binding promise not to revoke it and will have to pay damages if he does revoke. If this is all that is meant, the offeror can actually revoke but is under a legal duty not to do so; he has the legal power to terminate the offeree's power of acceptance, but is not legally privileged to exercise this power. As we proceed with the discussion, cases of this kind will be presented and analyzed.

Thirdly, an offer may be irrevocable in the sense that by no act can the offeror terminate the offeree's power. Even though he can and does communicate to the offeree his desire to revoke, such communication is legally inoperative as a revocation; the offeree, in spite of a notice received, retains his power to con-

---

impossibility." Langdell, Summary of the Law of Contracts, sec. 178, also sec. 4. See also, Wormser, The True Conception of Unilateral Contracts (1916) 26 Yale Law Journal, 137, note; Lee, Contract, Jenks Digest of Eng. Civ. Law, sec. 195; Ashley, Contracts, sec. 13.

Observe that in Langdell's quoted statement he adds the phrase "in legal contemplation." This is pregnant with the admission that the wills of the parties do not have to concur *in fact*. And it is obvious that if the concurrence of wills can be supplied by a fiction "in contemplation of law," the fiction can be discarded and the law can "contemplate" the truth, that concurrence of wills is not necessary.

In Adams v. Lindsell, 1 B. & Ald. 681

(1818), it was said: "The defendants must be *considered in law* as making, during every instant of the time their letter was travelling, the same identical offer to the plaintiffs." It is obvious fiction to say that the offeror continuously repeats his offer; but it is no fiction that the power of the offeree continues even though the offeror has changed his mind, that the offeree's act of acceptance will induce society to compel performance. See also Boston & M. R. Co. v. Bartlett, 3 Cush. 244 (Mass.1849); Nyulasy v. Rowan, 17 Vict.L.R. 663 (1891). If an offer were at every instant revocable, these decisions would be wrong, and Cooke v. Oxley, 3 T.R. 653 (1790) would not have been overthrown.

summate and to enforce the contract as the offer originally contemplated. This is irrevocability in its strictest sense, the total absence of legal power. The offeror may be physically able to make the communication or to do other acts; but they simply won't work legally.

We shall now consider some of the factors that make an offer irrevocable in one or both of the last two senses.

### § 43. Options Created by a Conditional Contract or Covenant

An offer can be made irrevocable in two ways, and probably only two; these are by contract and by statute. As has already been seen, an ordinary offer between private individuals is always revocable by the offeror. It is irrevocable only when he has promised not to revoke it, or has promised the offered exchange of performances on condition of acceptance within a period of time, and that promise is binding by reason of a seal, a consideration given in exchange, or subsequent action in reliance upon it.[50] Such a binding promise is itself a contract, as that term is commonly defined. In such cases, also the offeree is said to have a "binding option." [51]

Option contracts are considered in detail in Chapter 11 in this treatise; but it is important to observe here that a binding option is a standing offer as well as a contract. It involves a binding promise, and is therefore a contract, usually unilateral in character; but the giving of an "option" is also the making of an offer of some exchange and creates a power of acceptance in the holder of the option, just as in the case of revocable offers. If, in return for ten dollars paid by B, A gives to B an option to buy Blackacre for $5,000 at any time within thirty days on condition of notice to be mailed within that time, a unilateral contract has been made. This is a promise to convey the land, on the express condition of notice of acceptance within thirty days and on the constructive condition of tender of $5,000 within a reasonable time after such notice. The equivalent given in exchange for this conditional promise is ten dollars. The advantage that B gets in return for his ten dollars is that he has a power of acceptance for thirty days, to be exercised by the mailing of a letter. This is a conditional contract to convey Blackacre, and not a collateral contract to hold an offer open.

Does A have any power of revocation, whereby he can terminate B's power of acceptance? In the first place, it is clear that if A gives a revocation to B, this constitutes a breach of his contract by repudiation. The promise of A, paid for by B, certainly creates in B a right that A shall not repudiate. Further, it creates in B a right that A shall not transfer the land to a third person, a right that is enforceable specifically by an injunction so long as a conveyance has not been made, and by a judgment for damages in any case. Even a conveyance to a third person, actually made, with notice of revocation received by B, does not deprive B of a power of acceptance. If the third person had actual or constructive notice of B's option, and B gives the specified notice within thirty days, B can get a decree for specific performance, operative against both A and the third person.[52] In spite of conveyance, B still had power to accept. If the third person, however, received the conveyance without notice of B's option, then equity will not deprive him of his advantageous position; he is an innocent purchaser for value, with equally good rights of his own. Even in this case, A's revocation and conveyance to an innocent purchaser do not terminate B's power to accept; they merely deprive B of one form of remedy, the form that would work injustice to an innocent third person. His remedy in damages for A's breach of a consummated contract to convey is available.

## § 44.  Contract to Keep an Offer Open

Instead of making, in the beginning, a binding promise to convey on specified conditions, it is possible for one to make an offer of a contract with specified terms, and then to make, at the same time or later, a collateral contract not to revoke the offer. Here we have two separate transactions, an offer that creates a power of acceptance, and a contract that certainly makes it the offeror's legal duty not to revoke. The question now is: does that collateral contract also create in the offeree an immunity from revocation—does it deprive the offeror of the power to revoke as well as of the legal privilege to do so?

Such transactions as the above are different in form from the conditional contract discussed in the preceding section; but the jural relations that they create are the same. The collateral promise not to revoke the offer may be made enforceable by sealing and delivery, or by a consideration given in exchange, or by subsequent action in reliance. For example, A offers to sell Blackacre to B for $5,000. The next day, in return for ten dollars paid, A promises B not to revoke the offer for thirty days. These two transactions, an offer to sell and a subsequently made contract not to revoke, have the same legal operation as would the single conditional contract previously discussed. By the contract not to revoke, the offer that was theretofore revocable is made irrevocable. B's revocable option to buy has become a binding option.

An obstacle to specific performance in equity has been supposed to exist in case the option (let us suppose an option to buy) is made binding by a contract to hold an offer open instead of being created by a conditional covenant or simple contract to convey. In the latter case there is a completed obligation to convey, and this may be enforced. In the former case there is no such obligation, and none can now be made by an acceptance because the option contract has been broken and the offer has been revoked. This obstacle can be avoided by the simple expedient of not seeing it. The asserted impossibility of doing an act has many a time been disproved by doing it. If by definition the thing is impossible, change the definition. The objection can be met by the easy method of declaring the offer irrevocable and the contract not to revoke unbreakable. That this can be done has already been shown above. There is nothing foreign to our law in the idea of an irrevocable power, and the legal relation resulting from an offer is a legal power. Equity can specifically enforce the offeror's promise not to revoke by the simple process of declaring the revocation inoperative. The power to accept being still alive, the offeree may exercise it and thus create the obligation to convey, all fit and ready for specific enforcement.

## § 46. Offers Made Irrevocable by Statute

There are certain offers that have been made irrevocable by statute. One illustration may be found in bids for the construction of a building or other public work, made to the state, a city, or some other governmental corporation. If a statute declares that such a bid shall be irrevocable for some period, there is no power of revocation by the bidder.[54] There are a few statutes making a "firm" offer irrevocable if it is in writing and states that it shall remain open for a definite time, or for a reasonable time.[55]

By such statutes in this country we do in a limited class of cases what the codes and legal systems of many other countries do with respect to all offers, both public and private. The code provisions are not exactly uniform; but they provide for irrevocability under the circumstances and conditions that are specified.[56]

The statute, and the terms of a bid that is regulated thereby, may provide for the making of a deposit that is to be forfeited

---

54. **Md.**—City of Baltimore v. J. L. Robinson Const. Co., 91 A. 682, 123 Md. 660, L.R.A.1915A, 225, Ann.Cas. 1916C, 425 (1914), city could accept bid for public work in spite of attempted revocation.

55. N.Y.Laws 1941, c. 328: "When hereafter an offer to enter into a contract is made in a writing signed by the offeror, which states that the offer is irrevocable during a period set forth or until a time fixed, the offer shall not be revocable during such period or until such time because of the absence of consideration for the assurance of irrevocability. When such a writing states that the offer is irrevocable but does not state any period or time of irrevocability, it shall be construed to state 'that the offer is irrevocable for a reasonable time."

A provision to the same effect is contained in the Uniform Commercial Code—Sales, Sec. 2-205 (1950 draft).

by the bidder in case he withdraws his bid and refuses to execute a written contract. If this deposit is held to be liquidated damages and not a penalty, then it limits the damages that the bidder must pay.[57] This does not mean that the bidder is legally privileged to withdraw his bid; it means only that the damages payable for a wrongful withdrawal are fixed in advance by agreement of the parties. There are cases in which a promise will be specifically enforced, in spite of a provision for liquidated damages;[58] but this is seldom true of a promise to do extensive construction work.

## § 48. Irrevocable Offers under Seal

The sealing and delivery of a writing have no legal effect unless the writing contains a promise; but they cause a promise to be an enforceable contract, without the necessity of a consideration or of any action in reliance. This is the common law, handed down and approved for centuries; in a considerable number of states it has been affected by statutes limiting or abolishing the legal efficacy of a seal.[63] It is indeed a rare offer in writing that does not contain some kind of a promise, either express or implied; by the common law, sealing and delivery make that promise binding and the power of acceptance as safe from any revocation as would the payment of a consideration. Usually, the offer contains a promise to render the performance that is offered in exchange for some return performance, conditional on the rendition of that return within a specified time.[64] On delivery of such a promise under seal, there exists at once a conditional unilateral contract to perform as stated. The offeree is not bound by anything; he has a binding option, an irrevocable offer.

On refusal of the offeror to perform, because of his attempted revocation, the offeree can get judgment for damages. If the offeror's sealed promise was to make a conveyance of land, the better doctrine is that the offeree has a right to a decree for specific performance in the absence of other factors making such a decree inequitable. Some courts have thought that the absence of a consideration for the option is a sufficient reason for refusing specific enforcement, sealing and delivery not having the meritorious appeal that consideration has.[65] It is believed that this is erroneous; the better decisions hold otherwise.[66] In such cases, the decree is not one that compels the offeror to give something for nothing. Even though it is only a seal that makes the offer irrevocable, there is an agreed exchange that the offeree will be compelled to make in return for the land. The promise to convey is conditional upon the giving of this return performance.

**63.**  See Chapter 10, Contracts Under Seal.

If it is not so grossly inadequate as to shock the chancellor's conscience, specific enforcement seems to be equitable and just.

## § 49.  Revocation after Part Performance by the Offeree

There are very many cases in which acceptance is to consist of the rendition of the performance for which the offeror offers his promise.  This is often described as "the offer of a promise for an act"; and the resulting contract when the acceptance is complete is unilateral.[70]  As will again appear, in the chapter dealing with contracts without assent or consideration, a promise may become a binding contract by reason of a change of position by the offeree in reliance upon it.  There can be no possible doubt of this, if the change of position is the very performance requested by the offeror; it is then the agreed equivalent for which his promise is exchanged and constitutes consideration therefor.

One question before us in the present section is whether an offer becomes irrevocable as soon as the offeree begins, or has rendered some substantial part of, the performance for which the offeror is bargaining.  A second question, closely related but not identical, is whether an offer becomes irrevocable as soon as the offeree has changed his position in reliance upon it, such change being one that the offeror had reason to foresee but not constituting a part of the performance for which he bargains and for which his offered promise was made.

As to the first of these questions, decisions are now so numerous and so nearly uniform in result as to leave small doubt as to the general rule of law that must be stated.  Where one party makes a promissory offer in such form that it can be accepted by the rendition of the performance that is requested in exchange, without any express return promise or notice of acceptance in words, the offeror is bound by a contract just as soon as the offeree has rendered a substantial part of that requested performance.[71]  Indeed, the American Law Institute has stated the rule that he is bound by contract, and the offer irrevocable as previously discussed herein, just as soon as the offeree has tendered the requested performance or has actually rendered a part of it.

The cases that justify the above doctrine, in at least one of its forms, have been decided in the very teeth of two other doctrines that have been repeated many times as representing the common law.  The first of these is that both parties to a contract must be bound by it or neither is bound.  Even the judges who have repeated this misleading doctrine have themselves often enforced

---

**71.**  **U.S.**—Hollidge v. Gussow, Kahn & Co., 67 F.2d 459 (C.C.A.1st, 1933) equally reasonable here to find a return promise making a bilateral contract; A. B. Dick Co. v. Fuller, 213 F. 98 (D.C.N.Y.1914), promise to pay for invention of stencil by an employee, irrevocable when latter "began work in reliance upon it".

a unilateral contract, although they may not have described it as unilateral and were not aware that the decision was inconsistent with the stated doctrine. The doctrine must either be abandoned or be expressly limited to the class of cases in which it is true. The second doctrine is to the effect that, in the case of an offer of a promise for an act or series of acts, there is no contract until the acts constituting the acceptance are entirely completed. If the decisions now to be discussed are to be supported—and they must be—this second doctrine must be wholly abandoned.

In order to help promote the construction of a street railway, the defendant executed his note for $2,000, payable to the Traction Company thirty days after completion of the railway to a specified street. This was given to a bank to hold in escrow and to deliver after completion of the railway as specified. No time was fixed within which the completion must occur. About four months after the note was executed, the Traction Company paid $1500 for a franchise. Some months later construction work was begun in a desultory manner. About two years after execution of the note, its maker notified the Traction Company that he revoked and would not pay. The company thereafter proceeded with the work to completion. It was held that the revocation was wholly ineffective, after part performance by the company. The offeree still retained its power to complete the requested performance.[72]

In another case, the defendant wrote to her daughter, then living in Missouri, that if she would give up her home and come to Maine and there care for the defendant for the rest of her life on the defendant's farm, the defendant would permit the daughter to live on that farm and have its income and would further leave the farm to the daughter at death. After the daughter had come to Maine and begun caring for her mother, the latter revoked the offer and conveyed the farm to another child. The court held the revocation to be wrongful, and decreed that the farm be held in trust for the daughter. Here, the court expressly acknowledged that the contract was "unilateral," that the daughter made no return promise; but the part performance made the offer irrevocable.[73]

Oftentimes, in order to encourage employees to remain with him, an employer promises them a "bonus" if they are still in his employ at the end of a year. He is especially likely to do this in

72. Cal.—Los Angeles Traction Co. v. Wilshire, 67 P. 1086, 135 Cal. 654 (1902).

73. Me.—Brackenbury v. Hodgkin, 102 A. 106, 116 Me. 399 (1917). Of course, the final decree would make provision for the mother's support. The daughter would not get the farm in full without rendering the full equivalent.

cases where the employment is at will and the employee is not bound by any contract to remain at work. In such cases, the employer's promise is an offer to pay the added sum of money in return for continuing to work for a whole year. Does the employer still have the power to revoke this offer after the employee has remained in service for almost the whole year, or for some lesser period? The courts have held that he is not privileged to revoke then, although a revocation is so far effective as to deprive the employee of any power to complete his acceptance.[74] In this respect, and in the remedies that are available, such a revocation is like any other wrongful discharge. In no such case can the employee continue at work against the employer's will, and by completing the full period make the employer a debtor for the full salary. The discharged employee has only a right to damages, measured by the full sum promised less what he can earn by reasonable effort elsewhere after the discharge. This should be the measure of damages in case of the promised bonus. In all these cases, however, the discharged employee has the alternative remedy of quantum meruit.

In one case, the defendant offered a reward for the arrest and conviction of some criminals. The plaintiff arrested them and induced their confession, but they were not convicted because the defendant wished to use their testimony in other cases and so had the indictments dismissed. It was held that the plaintiff was entitled to the reward.[75]

Where a reward has been offered for the finding and return of lost property, the offer is not revocable after part performance in reliance upon it, even though the offeror gives notice before there has been actual return of the property. Even in such a case, the finder has a lien to secure payment of the reward.[76]

A charitable subscription is not revocable, by either death or notice, if the promisee has partly performed the condition of the subscription in reliance on the promise before the supposed revocation occurs.[77] One who has offered a prize to the winner of a contest under stated rules cannot revoke his offer or change the rules thereof as against those who have already partly complied with its terms.[78] In cases of this sort there is little possibility of finding that the contract is bilateral, but it has become irrevocable.

**74.** **N.C.**—Roberts v. Mays Mills, 114 S.E. 530, 184 N.C. 406, 28 A.L.R. 338 (1922).

**Wis.**—Zwolanek v. Baker Mfg. Co., 137 N.W. 769, 150 Wis. 517, 44 L.R. A., N.S., 1214, Ann.Cas.1914A, 793 (1912).

**78.** In Wachtel v. National Alfalfa Journal Co., 176 N.W. 801, 190 Iowa 1293 (1920), the defendant opened a circulation contest, offering prizes to those winning the most votes by securing subscriptions, but later discontinued the contest when the plaintiff was the leader therein. The plaintiff was held entitled to damages for breach of contract.

In some of the cases, the court denies effect to a revocation for the reason that the offeror was acting "in bad faith." [79] But the only ground for asserting his bad faith is that the offeree has already acted in reliance on the offered promise. After such action, the court thinks it is unreasonable for the offeror to revoke. No doubt, the greater the action of the offeree and the greater the resulting benefit to the offeror, the more inequitable and unfair his revocation becomes. In general, it is not thought to be bad faith to revoke any offer before it has been accepted, even though the purpose is to avoid contracting with the offeree; but in the cases now under discussion, part performance by the offeree makes a subsequent revocation by the offeror a breach of contract.

## § 50.  Real Estate Brokerage and Other Agency Cases

There has been an immense amount of litigation with respect to the commissions of land brokers and other agents. This is due in part to the character of the business itself, vendors and purchasers often feeling that the commission charged is disproportionate to the service rendered. In large part, however, it is due to the fact that the terms of agreement between principal and broker are often expressed in vague form with no clear provision as to matters that become subjects of dispute. Much must be supplied from usages of the business that are none too well known or too definitely proved. Gaps must be filled by that uncertain process called "implication," a mixture of determining the meanings of the parties by interpretation of their words and actions and of doing justice according to the mores and practices of the community. The legal relations of the parties must vary with the variation of the operative facts of the particular transactions, their complexity and variation being increased by the fact that at least three parties are always involved—a seller, a purchaser, and a broker.

In some cases the transaction between the principal and his agent is a bilateral contract. In the past, because of inadequate analysis and unfamiliarity with the "unilateral" contract, a transaction was often erroneously supposed to be thus bilateral. An owner who puts his land in the hands of a broker for sale usually promises to pay a commission for the service; the broker seldom promises in return that he will produce a purchaser, although he may promise, expressly or impliedly that he will make diligent effort.[80] If the parties have thus made mutual promises, the transaction no longer has the status of an unaccepted offer; and neither party has a power of revocation. Any power of contracting with a third party in the principal's name that may have been given to the agent can be withdrawn by the principal, even though he may have contracted not to withdraw it; but this is not the revocation of an offer made to the agent. It is possible also, even though principal and agent have made a bilateral contract, for the principal to reserve a power of termination either by notice or by effecting a sale through other channels.[81] With such reserved powers the present section is not concerned; it must be left to treatises on the law of agency.

The cases with which we are now dealing include those in which an owner merely puts his land in the broker's hands, promising him a commission for the service of producing an able and willing purchaser, the broker making no return promise that he can or will produce such a purchaser. Such a transaction as this is an offer of a unilateral contract, an offered promise by the owner creating in the broker a power of accepting by actual rendition of the requested service. Such an offer as this may become irrevocable even before the service is fully rendered. Under what circumstances is the power, or the privilege, of revocation lost, and to what extent?

An owner who merely "lists" his property with a land broker for sale or rent may thereby make no promise or offer of any kind. His communication to the broker may be no more than an invitation for the submission of proposals that the owner may or may not accept. In such a case, the owner is legally privileged to reject any proposal so made; and upon such a rejection he is under no duty to pay the broker for services rendered, either a broker's customary commission or quantum meruit.[82] This may accord with the reasonable interpretation of the communications between owner and broker, even though the owner states a "net" price at which he is willing to sell.[83] It is not wise to attempt to state a rule of law for determining whether such an interpretation is or is not the reasonable one.[84]

The most commonly recurring case is one in which the owner employs a broker to find a purchaser able and willing to buy, on terms stated in advance by the owner, and in which the owner promises to pay a specified commission for the service. This is an offer by the owner, the broker's power of acceptance to be exercised by the actual rendition of the requested service. Here the only contemplated contract between the owner and the broker is a unilateral contract—a promise to pay a commission for services rendered.[87] Such an offer as this is revocable by the owner by notice before the broker has rendered any part of the requested service;[88] possibly also before he has rendered a "substantial" part of the service. A sale by the owner to a third party, with no notice thereof to the broker, is certainly not operative as a revocation.[89]

In a good many cases of this kind it has been held that the owner is no longer privileged to revoke his offered promise after the broker has taken substantial steps in the process of rendering the requested service, by advertising the property for sale, soliciting prospective buyers, showing the property, or otherwise; in such a case the revocation and discharge of the broker is held to be a breach of contract.[90]  In some of these cases the court's theory is that the contract has become bilateral, although the facts as stated indicate no promise by the broker for breach of which the owner could have maintained an action.  Often, however, the court merely holds that part performance by the broker has made the owner's promise binding.

The amount recoverable is not the full amount of the promised commission unless the agent proves that he would have fully performed according to the owner's offer and this would have entailed no additional expense.[91]  If he cannot convince a jury that he would have found a buyer but for the owner's discharge, he can recover nothing; the owner's promise to pay was conditional on substantial performance as specified.[92]

The beginning of the requested service makes the owner's offer irrevocable in the sense that it is now a breach of contract to revoke it; it is not irrevocable in the sense that the agent can still proceed with performance in spite of further expense and by finding a buyer become entitled to the full commission as a money debt.  Some cases seem to have gone almost this far, however.  But the law of agency is such that the agent's power to bring the principal into contract relations with third persons can be terminated by the principal even though it is a breach of contractual duty to terminate it.  Although not legally privileged to do this, the owner has power to do it.  After being notified not to proceed with efforts to sell, the agent's power (in the absence of an estoppel) to bind his principal to a third person is destroyed.  It does not necessarily follow from this that the agent's power to complete the acceptance of the owner's offer to himself is also terminated.  Indeed, if the completion of the requested services does not include the making of a contract between the principal and a third person—and it does not if the condition was merely the finding of a willing buyer—the agent still has power to complete the acceptance and to earn the full

90.   See:

U.S.—Tahir Erk v. Glenn L. Martin Co., 116 F.2d 865 (C.C.A. 4th, 1941); Calkins v. F. W. Woolworth Co., 27 F.2d 314 (C.C.A.8th, 1928) certiorari denied 49 S.Ct. 80, 278 U.S. 645, 73 L.Ed. 558 (1929).

Ark.—Blumenthal & Co. v. Bridges, 120 S.W. 974, 91 Ark. 212, 24 L.R. A.,N.S., 279 (1909).

92.   If the promise to pay commission was clearly conditional on the consummation of performance by a fixed time, the agent's power ceases at that time in spite of his rendition of substantial part performance theretofore.  See Zeimer v. Antisell, 17 P. 642, 75 Cal. 509 (1888).

commission if no additional expense is involved in such completion.

In the cases as they are reported, it is often impossible to tell whether the court thinks that the agent promised to render services or not. Occasionally it is said that the contract becomes bilateral as soon as the agent has rendered part performance.[93] If the action were one brought by the owner for damages for the agent's failure to make diligent effort, it is far from certain that the court would be ready to find a promise by the agent.

Even though the owner has made a bilateral contract with his broker, empowering the latter to consummate a contract of sale and binding the former to pay a commission for the service, the actual understanding of the parties or the relevant usages of the business may be such that the owner remains legally privileged to find his own purchaser and sell the property. In such a case, the owner has no power to terminate his contract with the broker except by making his own independent sale and giving notice thereof to the broker; but he has made no promise to his broker, expressly or by implication, that he will not make his own sale. A mere refusal to consummate a sale by the broker and to pay the agreed commission would be a breach of contract.[94]

Again, the terms of the contract between the owner and the broker may be such that the latter does not have an "exclusive agency". The broker may have reason to know that the owner reserves the privilege of employing additional agents and consummating a sale through them. In this, as in the case just stated previously, the owner has made no promise not to consummate an independent sale.[95] In neither case, however, is the question one of revocability of an offer made by the owner to his broker. There was a contract between them, one not revocable by the owner; and the question is merely as to the terms and conditions of the owner's promise, one to be determined by the usual processes of interpretation and construction.

## § 51.  Effect of Action in Reliance That is Not Part Performance

There are cases holding that action by the offeree in reliance on the offered promise does not make it irrevocable if such action is not part performance of the exchange requested by the offeror. Expense incurred in preparation to render the requested performance or in investigating whether or not it is desirable to accept the offer are, under these holdings, not sufficient to prevent effective revocation or to make a revocation wrongful.[99] It seems likely that these cases will sooner or later be disapproved, in as much as the courts are now holding that a promise is made enforceable by substantial and definite action in reliance, if that action is such as the promisor had reason to foresee as the result of his promise.[1] Surely, one who offers a promise in return for a requested performance in exchange has reason to foresee that his offer may cause expenditure in preparation to render the requested performance. In many such cases, the offer should be held to have become irrevocable, as that term is explained herein. In order to make a promise binding, action in reliance does not have to be part of a requested consideration; indeed, promises to make a gift, no consideration of any kind being contemplated, may become enforceable by reason of action in reliance upon them.[2]

If the action by the offeree is not part performance of the requested consideration and also is not such action as the offeror had reason to foresee as the result of his offer, it will not make the offer irrevocable in any sense. One who submits a bid for supplying materials requests and has reason to foresee an acceptance, by part performance it may be; but usually he should not be held to foresee that the offeree would make a contract with a third person at a price that is determined by the terms of the bid, before the bid itself has been accepted and without notifying the bidder that his bid is going to be so used. Even if he knows that his bid will be used as a basis for bidding on some larger contract, it should still be revocable by notice given while the offeree's bid on the larger contract is still revocable at will.[3]

## § 52. Fiction of an Implied Promise Making the Contract Bilateral

Realizing that it is inequitable to allow an offeror to revoke after part performance by the offeree, but supposing that neither party can be bound unless both parties are bound, courts have been very ready to find that the rendering of part performance is an acceptance that implies a promise to perform the balance.[4]

---

2.   Restatement, Contracts, § 90.

See Chapters 8 and 9, Informal Contracts Without Assent or Consideration.

3.   U.S.—James Baird Co. v. Gimbel Bros., 64 F.2d 344 (C.C.A.2d, 1933). The direct contrary was held in Farnsworth & Co. v. Albert, 79 F. Supp. 27 (D.C.La.1948), but the law there applied was the law of Louisiana, much of which derives from French and Roman law. Also, the bidder had reason to know that his bid might be used by the offeree in making his larger bid on a construction contract. That larger bid, so made in reliance, had been accepted before any withdrawal by the defendant of his bid on the plastering. See Harris v. Lillis, 24 So.2d 689 (La.App.1946). Also contra is Northwestern Engineering Co. v. Ellerman, 10 N.W. 2d 879, 69 S.D. 397 (1943).

It is on the reasoning stated in the text that the decision in Petterson v. Pattberg, 161 N.E. 428, 248 N.Y. 86 (1928), is to be supported if it can be approved at all.

4.   See:

Cal.—Los Angeles Traction Co. v. Wilshire, 67 P. 1086, 135 Cal. 654 (1902).

The contract so made is then described as bilateral, so that subsequent notice of revocation is too late to be effective. If the implication of a return promise by the offeree is reasonable and in accord with the terms of the offer, the reasoning and decision of the court are not open to criticism.[5] But it may be that the implication of such a promise is a pure fiction and solely for the purpose of holding revocation to be ineffective. To indulge in such a fiction when it is contrary to the fact is wholly unjustifiable unless the result of it is one that ought to be reached without it. In the present instance the result is desirable and correct; but it is the part performance or other action in reliance that makes the offer irrevocable and not the fictitious promise of the offeree to render the requested performance.

## § 53. *When a Standing Offer of a Series of Separate Contracts is Irrevocable

There is one sort of case in which the offer is not made irrevocable either by a part performance or by an express notice of acceptance. This is the case in which an offer has been made in such terms as to create a power to make a series of separate contracts by a series of separate acceptances. The closing of one of these separate contracts by one acceptance leaves the offer still revocable as to any subsequent acceptance. Thus, if a party offers to guarantee the repayment of such loans as the offeree may make from time to time to a third party, or the payment by a third party for such goods as the offeree may thereafter sell to him, or the payment of such drafts as the offeree may discount for a third person, the making of one loan or one credit sale or one discount is final as regards that one performance but does not prevent revocation by notice before any further act of acceptance.[6] One separate contract of the contemplated series has been made and is irrevocable; but notice of revocation prevents the consummation of any other contract in the series.

Just as in the case of an offer for a single acceptance, these offers may be made irrevocable; they will create a binding option if a consideration is given for the offeror's promise to do the series of acts. The offer may itself specify that the making of

Kan.—Braniff v. Baier, 165 P. 816, 101 Kan. 117, L.R.A.1917E, 1036 (1917).

Mo.—American Publishing & Engraving Co. v. Walker, 87 Mo.App. 503 (1901).

5. U.S.—Hollidge v. Gussow, Kahn & Co., 67 F.2d 459 (C.C.A.1st, 1933),
is a case accepting the theory that an offer may be made irrevocable by beginning the requested performance.

6. Great Northern R. Co. v. Witham, L.R. 9 C.P. 16 (1873), semble; Offord v. Davies, 12 C.B. (N.S.) 748 (1862), guaranty of bills to be discounted as presented.

one loan, or the giving credit on one bill of goods, or the discounting of one bill of exchange, will be a consideration making the offer irrevocable as to further transactions. Thus, if a guarantor writes: "In consideration of your discounting the bill for $1000 that my son presented to you today, I will guarantee the repayment of all bills drawn by him and accepted by you in the next six months," the discounting of the specified bill is enough to prevent revocation as to subsequent bills drawn by the son. Also, if a dealer writes: "In return for your buying twelve carloads of glass flasks, I promise to sell to you at the same price as many more carloads as you may care to order during the year." On assenting to a contract for the twelve carloads, the buyer gets an irrevocable option on any reasonable number of other carloads.[7]

It is a question of interpretation, sometimes difficult, whether the offer contemplates a single transaction with one acceptance, involving a series of performances, or contemplates a series of independent transactions concluded by a series of separate acceptances. If the performances are so interrelated that the cost and the risks overlap, the former interpretation will generally be the more reasonable one.[8]

### § 54.  Effect of Death or Insanity on Power of Acceptance

It is very generally said that the death of the offeror terminates the offeree's power of acceptance even though the offeree has no knowledge of such death.[9] Such general statements arose out of the earlier notion that a contract cannot be made without an actual meeting of minds at a single moment of time, a notion that has long been abandoned. The rule has also been supposed to follow by some logical necessity from the dictum that it takes two persons to make a contract. It is not contrary to that dictum to deny that death terminates power to accept; the offer was made by a living man and is accepted by another living man. One and one make two. The rule has also been explained on the ground that the surviving offeree intended to contract with the deceased offeror and can not be forced into relations with a personal representative, a different person. This explanation is not applicable in case the surviving offeree is the one who is insisting on the validity of the contract. It is somewhat more plausible if it is the surviving offeree who is defending against the contract. He accepted in reliance on the promise and credit of a specific living person, and the shift to those of a personal representative may be materially disadvantageous. In practically all cases, however, the accepting offeree is sufficiently

7.   Minn.—Koehler & Hinrichs Mercantile Co. v. Illinois Glass Co., 173 N.W. 703, 143 Minn. 344 (1919).

84

protected by the rule that makes any contractor's duty constructively conditional on the ability of the other party to render substantially in full the agreed exchange for which the offeree bargained. If the offeror's personal representative can sufficiently assure the performance of this condition, there is little reason for refusing to enforce the contract against the offeree. He is in the very position that he would occupy if the offeror's death had occurred the moment after acceptance instead of just before it. In either case, if the personal representative is unwilling or unable to render the agreed exchange substantially in full, the promises made by the offeree will not be enforced against him.

If the offer that was made is an irrevocable offer, having either the form or effect of a binding option contract, the right and power of the option holder are assignable without the offeror's consent; and they are not terminated by the death of the offeror.[10] Likewise, it should be held that if the offer is so made that it can be accepted by the performance of a series of acts, the beginning of those acts before death of the offeror prevents the death from terminating the power of the offeree. By such action he has made the offer irrevocable.[11]

It has even been held, and justly, that the doing of the requested acts after the death of the offeror, but in ignorance thereof, consummates a contract. Thus, where through an agent an offeror orders the shipment of goods to the agent, and the offeree ships the goods in ignorance that the offeror has died, the offeree can collect the price from the offeror's estate.[12] So, also, where one has given his promise to guarantee payment for goods to be sold, money to be lent, or service to be rendered to another, the sale or loan or service in ignorance of the promisor's death has been held to enable the promisee to enforce the promise of guaranty against the guarantor's estate.[13] Some cases have held the contrary, however;[14] and also it has been held that the offeree can not accept after he has knowledge that the offeror is dead.[15]

If the offer is one that is accepted by a mere expression of assent, as by the mailing of a letter of acceptance, there is no very serious objection to refusing to give effect to such an acceptance, occurring after the offeror's death, as long as the offeree has not materially changed his position in reliance on the contract and without knowledge of the death. Furthermore, there are cases in which the offeror's death will make performance impossible, and in which such would be the case even though the death occurs after acceptance has taken place. Thus, if A offers to render his own personal service to B, A's death makes performance impossible and operates as a discharge of contractual duties, whether B's acceptance occurred before or after A's death. If A's promised performance is not one that is personal to himself, his death does not operate as a discharge. If B had accepted before A's death, the contract is binding upon both B and A's personal representative. There is no necessary reason to deny a similar effect to an acceptance by B in ignorance of A's prior death. Thus, if A promises to pay money asking for a promise by B to deliver goods or to render services that do not require A's personal cooperation, acceptance by B in ignorance of A's prior death could be held to consummate a contract binding on B and A's representative. Probably, this result would not be reached, however, if B learns of A's death before making any material change of position.

The death of the offeree, before acceptance, has also been held to terminate power, so that a subsequent acceptance by the offeree's representative is ineffective.[16] There is not much reason to criticise this result, since the representative has knowledge of the death and there can be no change of position with unforeseen injury. Here too, if the offer was a binding option contract or has become so by the offeree's action before his death, and if the contract is not one that has become impossible of performance by reason of the death, the offeree's personal representatives can accept the offer and consummate a contract.[17]

It has been held that the insanity of the offeror, supervening after making his offer, terminates the power of acceptance.[18] This is even more doubtful than the rule as to the offeror's death. Insanity is far less easily determinable as a fact than is death, either by the contracting parties themselves or by a court. Some kinds and degrees of insanity have been held not to make an agreement void, or even voidable, even though the insanity existed before the offer was made; and in these cases supervening insanity of the same kind and degree should not terminate the power of acceptance. It seems reasonable to say that supervening insanity should have no greater effect than it would have if it existed prior to the making of the offer.[19]

# CHAPTER 3

# ACCEPTANCE AND REJECTION OF OFFER

### § 55. Two Parties Necessary for a Contract, a Promisor and a Promisee

As has been stated earlier, a contract does not necessarily involve reciprocal promises or reciprocal duties; it may be "unilateral," in that only one party makes a promise, with the result that he alone is under a legal duty and the other party alone has a legally enforceable right. It does indeed take two to make a "bargain"; there must be mutual assent to the exchange of performances. It takes only one to make a promise; but there must be another one to whom the promise is made. For any executory contract, there must be at least two parties, a promisor and a promisee.

It has often been said that a man cannot contract with himself.[1] This is a mere truism if we have first defined contract as requiring the existence of legal rights and duties. If we define a legal relation as a relation existing between human individuals, it is obvious that there must be at least two persons for such a relation to exist. The statement, however, truism though it is, may be so used as to lead to unfortunate and incorrect results. It may be supposed, for example, that an agreement is entirely inoperative if it purports to be made by a partnership or other unincorporated association with a member of such association. There is no reason why such an agreement should not operate as a valid and enforceable contract between the individual member and the other members of the association that purports to make the agreement. For the purpose of giving a judicial remedy and for other practical purposes, there is nothing to prevent a court from treating the association of individuals as if it were an independent unit. The adopting of such procedure as this does not result in holding that the association is a corporation, and that the legal relations of its members are to be determined by the law of corporations.

An individual whose name appears on both sides of a contract transaction is not contracting with himself; he is merely contracting with the others. He gets no rights against himself and owes himself no duties; neither law nor equity ever recog-

---

1. "It is a first principle that, in whatever different capacities a person may act, he can never contract with himself, nor maintain an action against himself. He can in no form be both obligor and obligee." Eastman v. Wright, 6 Pick. 316 (Mass.1828); Gorham's Adm'r v. Meacham's Adm'r, 22 A. 572, 63 Vt. 231, 13 L.R.A. 676 (1891).

nized such relations. His rights and duties with respect to the others are determined just as their rights and duties are determined. Suppose that A and B execute a contract whereby they promise to sell land to A and C; in such case A will have an enforceable right against B that he shall make the conveyance that he promised. B will have a similar right against A. And C, as a third party beneficiary, will have rights against both A and B.[2]

### § 56. In a Bargaining Transaction, Only the Offeree Has Power to Accept

In making an offer of a bargain, the offeror controls not only all the terms of the agreement but also the person or persons in whom a power of acceptance is created. An offer may be made by A to one specific person B; in such case B is the sole person who can accept A's offer. The power of acceptance is not assignable by B to any third person; nor can any third person who learns of A's offer substitute himself for B as the second party to the contract.[3] This is true even though the offer is one that requires no personal performance by B and no financial responsibility is to be assumed by him; it is true even though A is not acquainted with B and would be equally willing to contract with C instead. In such case A may be content with the substitution and may proceed with performance without objection; but C's attempt to accept in place of B operates as a new offer to A and not as an acceptance. A can accept this new offer by words or conduct as in the case of other offers; generally it would not be necessary for A to send a reply to C, since C's communication purports to be an acceptance and assumes that no reply is required. Nevertheless, there is no contract made until A has in some sufficient manner expressed his assent to C's proposal.

The rule stated above is based in part upon the fact that in many cases it actually makes a difference to A who the other party to the contract shall be; in even larger measure it may be based upon the once prevailing notion that "contract" involved a strictly personal relation, so personal indeed that contract rights were thought to be impossible of assignment. Even after

2.   In Welling v. Crosland, 123 S.E. 776, 129 S.C. 127 (1923), A and B contracted to sell land to A and 19 others, each of these buyers promising severally to pay separate sums. It was held that A and B could get a decree for specific performance by the 19 others. "It is true that A was a party to the trust agreement, one of the syndicate. How this fact may relieve the other members from their obligations we cannot conceive. They were aware of it when they entered into the agreement, and as it has turned out, the entry of A was a benefit to them rather than otherwise, for he bears his proportion of the purchase price, to that extent relieving the others."

3.   Cal.—Grieve v. Mullaly, 293 P. 619, 211 Cal. 77 (1930).

the decline and final demise of that notion, the non-assignability of the power of acceptance created by a revocable offer persists. It persists, also, in spite of the fact that in nearly all cases B can accept A's offer and at once thereafter assign his contract rights and delegate the performance of his own duties to C without A's assent.[4]

There are many contracts requiring personal performance by B; but even in these, B's rights against A are assignable. In no case has B the power to rid himself of his duties by assigning them to C, even though their performance is not personal and can be delegated. This leads to the observation that when B attempts to assign his power of acceptance or when C attempts to substitute himself as acceptor, their action is usually to be interpreted as an attempt to substitute C for B in all respects as party to the contract with A. They mean not only that C shall have the rights against A but also that performance shall be by C in place of B and that the duty to render that performance shall be in C alone, with no duty whatever in B. Such a result as this cannot be brought about, even today, by the process of assignment without A's assent; nor can it be brought about by substituting C for B as offeree.[5]

There are some offers by A that do not provide that B shall render any personal performance or undertake any legal duty whatever. The proposed contract is to be unilateral, as where A promises B a sum of money for the rescue of A's child or for procuring a buyer for Blackacre. In such a case, B can accept A's offer by causing C to rescue the child or to procure the buyer, and at the same time he can assign to C his right to the money. It may be that the law will so develop that in cases like this the offeree can assign the power to accept; but thus far it has not been suggested by the courts.[6]

---

**4.** See, for example, Carluccio v. 607 Hudson St. H. Co., 57 A.2d 452, 141 N.J.Eq. 449 (1948). The assignee was denied specific performance for inequitable conduct.

In Polhamus v. Roberts, 175 P.2d 196, 50 N.M. 236, 170 A.L.R. 991 (1946), an owner made an offer to lease property to A. The latter accepted, requiring however that the lease should be executed in the name of B. This was not an effective acceptance. This would be correct even though A would have had power to assign the lease to B if he had himself first accepted and bound himself in accordance with the terms of the lease.

**5.** One to whom an offer is made cannot substitute in his place a corporation of which he is president. Strauss & Co. v. Berman, 147 A. 85, 297 Pa. 432 (1929).

An offer of guaranty to J. M. & Co., a partnership, cannot be accepted by J. M. & Co. a corporation later formed, even though its incorporators and stockholders are identical with the partners. Jordan Marsh Co. v. Beals, 87 N.E. 471, 201 Mass. 163 (1909).

## § 57.  Assignment of Power by an Option Holder—Irrevocable Offers

In the case of an irrevocable offer, made irrevocable by the giving of consideration or by a seal, the power of acceptance can be assigned without the assent of the offeror.  In these cases the offeree has what is called a "binding option," and the transaction has already created a contract.  The holder of the option has contract rights; and usually he is as yet under no duties, the option contract being unilateral.  The transaction also involves an offer to the holder of the option, who has an irrevocable power of acceptance.  The courts have treated such a transaction as a unit, with the result that the option holder's power, as well as his rights, is assignable without the assent of the other party.[9]

Just as in the case of other contracts, however, if the exercise of the option involves the undertaking of a legal duty by the option holder, the rights of any assignee will be conditional upon the undertaking of that duty by the contemplated party.  Likewise, if the contract made by the exercise of the option is one that requires a personal performance by the option holder, the rights of the assignee will be conditional on such personal performance.  Thus, if A gives to B a binding option to buy land for a sum of money in cash, B can assign the option to C and the latter can compel conveyance by A on proper tender of the cash; no credit is involved and it is immaterial who pays the money.  On the other hand, if the option given to B is to buy land for B's note for $1,000 and for B's services as an attorney, B can assign his option to C, but C's right to a conveyance will be conditional on giving B's note and the readiness of B to act as attorney.  C cannot compel performance by A if he tenders his own note and services in place of B's.

## § 58.  Motive with which Acceptor Renders Performance

Ordinarily the motive that induces one to offer a reward is his desire to procure the performance that he requests.  Ordinarily, also, the motive that induces someone to render the requested performance is his desire for the reward that he knows has been offered.  Even in the case of the offeror, however, his desire for the performance may not be his sole motive; and in the case of an acceptor, the requested service may be rendered from motives wholly other than a desire for the offered reward.

In a well-known English case a reward was offered for information leading to the arrest of a criminal.  After having been severely beaten by the criminal in question, one Mary Ann Williams gave the requested information.  In one report of this case,

9.   Minn.—Koehler & H. Mercantile Co. v. Illinois Glass Co., 173 N.W. 703, 143 Minn. 344 (1919) semble; McMillan v. Ames, 22 N.W. 612, 33 Minn. 257 (1885).

it does not appear whether or not Mary knew of the offer when she gave the information; but it does appear that she gave it for other reasons than a desire for the reward. She believed that she was about to die; and she gave the information in order to ease her conscience, and perhaps to get even with the man who had beaten her or to avoid discomforts in the after life. The court said that her motives were immaterial and held that she was entitled to the reward.[10] In another report of the case, counsel are said to have admitted that Mary "must have known of it as it was placarded all over Hereford where she lived".

We shall not here attack this decision, although some courts have stated a contrary opinion [11] and some persons who have rendered the requested service from other motives than a desire for the offered reward may forbear to seek the reward or even refuse it when tendered.[12] Generally, however, a bargaining contract is explained as the result of mutual expressions of agreement or as requiring the intentional acceptance of an offer. Like other definitions and rules, these are rationalizations from the decided cases. They are useful; but they are not consistent with all past court decisions and they do not necessarily control future decisions. Contracts are not always consummated by the machinery of offer and acceptance. If two persons repeat in unison, and in each other's presence, the terms of a contract prepared for them by a third person, they make a valid contract. So also, if two persons simultaneously sign duplicate copies of a contract prepared for them by a third person. In these cases, no doubt they are consciously expressing mutual assent to the same terms; and usually the motive of each is his desire for what the other gives or promises.

In another English case,[13] a dealer published an advertisement promising to pay £100 to anyone who should use his carbolic smoke ball according to directions for two weeks and thereafter catch the influenza. The plaintiff did as requested and caught the influenza. Judgment was rendered for the £100. Without doubt the paramount motive of the offeror was the desire to make sales and receive money. Probably the paramount motive of the plaintiff, the offeree, was to gain immunity from a disease. If the plaintiff attained this chief object of desire, he would receive no money at all. That these were the motives of offeror and offeree did not prevent the formation of a valid unilateral contract.

Whatever the motive or motives may be, it is generally asserted that there must be an expression of intention to agree upon definite terms. Even this, however, is not always true. If

10.   Williams v. Carwardine, 4 B. & Adol. 621 (1833).

13.   **Eng.**—Carlill v. Carbolic Smoke Ball Co., (1893) Q.B. 256.

one person tenders delivery of a unilateral promise under seal, there is a contract if the promisee receives the document; he need not know its contents. Also when a debtor makes a new promise to pay a barred debt, this promise is a binding contract without any expression of assent by the creditor.[14]

In any case, it is certain that in rendering a requested performance it is not necessary that the sole motive of the offeree shall be his desire for the offered reward. It need not even be his principal or prevailing motive. The motivating causes of human action are always complex and are frequently not clearly thought out or expressed by the actor himself. This being true, it is desirable that not much weight should be given to the motives of an offeree and that no dogmatic requirement should be embodied in a stated rule of law.

## § 59.  Knowledge of Offer as a Pre-requisite to Acceptance

Probably most contracts are bilateral in character—a promise is exchanged for a return promise. Unless one party offers such an exchange and requests another party to make the return promise, no such return promise will be made. As a practical matter, communication of the offer is necessary.

In unilateral contracts also, if the offeror makes a promise for a performance to be rendered by a specific person, it is very seldom that the performance will be rendered by that person unless he knows that he is requested and that he is promised compensation. Here, too, as a practical matter, communication of the offer is necessary.

But there is one class of unilateral contracts of which as much cannot be said. There are many offers of reward published broadcast for the rendition of a service by any person who may be fortunate enough to be able to do it. Thus, rewards are publicly offered for the discovery and return of lost articles, for the construction of a machine and flying in it across an ocean, for the capture and conviction of some person charged with crime. In these cases, it may happen that some person is engaged in rendering the exact performance requested, either before the offer is published or before he has himself heard of it. Sometimes, he has completed the performance in entire ignorance of the offer; and it has been held in a number of cases that the offeror's promise of compensation is not enforceable by one who has done this.[15] There is no power of acceptance by one to whom the offer is wholly unknown.

This is quite logical and is consistent with the assumption that "contract" requires conscious assent to terms proposed by an-

14.  See Restatement, Contracts, §§ 85–94.

other. It is probable, indeed, that the chief reason for enforcing a promise is that it has induced the promisee to act in reliance upon it. One who has rendered a service without knowledge of an offered promise has not so acted. But the chief reason is not necessarily the only reason for enforcing a promise; and if it seems good to the courts to enforce a promise when the promisor has received the desired equivalent, even though the one rendering it knew nothing of the promise and rendered the service from other motives, there is no sufficient reason for refusing to call that enforceable promise a contract.

There are cases in which the courts have taken this latter view and have enforced the promise, even though the person rendering the required service did so in ignorance of the promise.[16] Most, but not all, of these have been cases in which the promise was made by some public corporation such as a state or a city; and they have been explained on the theory that the published promise of reward was a public grant and not within the field of contract.[17] But whether it is within this field depends solely upon the way in which we choose to delimit the field. Whether the promise of reward is public or private, it may equally well be called a "grant"; and in either case the result is that we have an enforceable promise. The recovery is the amount or value of the performance promised, not the value of the performance rendered by the plaintiff and received by the defendant. The remedy is the customary contract remedy.

Moreover, to call the offer of a state or municipality a "grant," by statute or ordinance, is to describe it in a way that is different from that in which it is commonly regarded. Often, the offer of reward is made by the proclamation of some public officer and not by an act of legislation. But whether made in one way or the other, it is generally regarded and recognized for what it is— a promise to pay for service, made as many other public contracts are made, and made in the same way that private persons and associations make their contracts.

Some courts have thought that where two offers, identical in terms, cross in the mail—as where A writes B offering to sell Blackacre for $5,000, and at the same time B writes A offering to pay $5,000 for Blackacre—there is no contract.[18] Such a holding is also logical and consistent with the theory that contract exists only when one party has been induced to accept and rely upon the promise of another. There are very few examples of identical offers that have crossed in the mails; and the question must be regarded as still unsettled.[19]

It may be that a little confusion would ensue if crossed offers were to be held to make a contract. In any case, it is certain that each such offer creates a power of acceptance in the other party and that an acceptance by either one closes the deal and makes the contract that each of them offered to make.[20]

## § 60. Knowledge of the Offer after Part Performance Already Rendered

It has been vigorously argued that, where a reward is offered in return for specified acts, it is necessary to a valid acceptance that the acceptor should have knowledge of the offer during the whole time that he was performing the requested acts, and that a part performance without knowledge followed by a completion of performance with knowledge makes no contract. This view has been adopted by the American Law Institute.[21]

Nevertheless, it is believed that the rule will not give satisfaction; and if it does not, there is no necessity that the courts shall follow it. If it is followed by the courts, then the offer is impossible of acceptance by the one who has rendered part performance without knowledge of the offer; and it is likewise impossible of acceptance by anyone if the part performance already rendered cannot be repeated. The normal person who learns of an offer of reward after he has already partly performed will proceed with the performance in reliance on the offer and with expectation of the reward. Thus, he has assented to the offer, he has acted in reliance upon it, and the promisor has received the entire benefit that he promised to pay for. The offeror does not prescribe the rendition of the entire service as the mode of expressing assent to his offer; he merely promises the reward as compensation for the entire service. If the offeree's part performance rendered after he knows of the offer is not regarded as an "acceptance," it should be held to satisfy the requirements of the rule in Restatement, Contracts, § 90, wherein certain promises are declared to be binding contracts in the absence of both mutual assent and consideration. In the present instance it is not necessary to appeal to that rule.

It may be that, if the acceptor renders the first part performance with the expressed intention of rendering it as a gift to the promisor, a different result should be reached; but in the reward cases now being considered this is practically never the case. Often the part performance is rendered without any intention to make a gift to anybody and with the hope of a reward and the intention to claim it if one shall be offered. When so many have believed that the promise should be enforceable by one who renders the entire service without knowledge of the offer, it seems quite unreasonable to refuse enforcement to one who renders only a part without such knowledge and completes the performance with intention to accept.

Even if the part performance rendered without knowledge is of such character that it can be repeated, it seems foolish to require the acceptor to repeat it in order to earn the reward. If A offers $1000 to anyone who will scale a wall and bring down a person threatened with death by fire, shall one who has already scaled the wall climb down and scale it again in order to earn the reward? If A offers a sum of money for the ploughing of a field, shall B, who has already ploughed part of it by mistake, plough that part over again when he learns of the offer? There seems to be no established rule of law that the entire performance by one party shall be consciously given by him in exchange for the promise of the other, although there is a rule that a promise is not enforceable unless the promisor gets substantial performance of that which he asks in return.

It should be borne in mind that preparation to perform is not identical with the requested performance. If one offers a reward for the return of a lost article, the fact that the party returning it had found it prior to the making of the offer, or prior to his knowledge of it, is immaterial. There is a contract if he renders the specific service requested (the return) with knowledge of the offer. The same result should be reached even though the part performance rendered without knowledge is a part of the very performance requested by the offeror and for which he promises the reward.

## § 61.  Acceptance "Subject to Approval" by a Third Party

There is no contract if an offer to sell land is accepted "subject to" approval of title by the offeree or his attorneys.[22] The meaning usually attributed to such words as "subject to" is that a promise that is so limited is a conditional promise, one that is different from that for which the offeror bargained. An acceptance "subject to a formal contract" or "subject to a proper contract to be prepared by our solicitors" has been held in a number of cases not to be an operative acceptance.[23]

If "subject to the approval of title by my solicitor" means only that my duty to pay shall be conditional on your transferring to me the marketable title that you promise in your offer, the acceptance may properly be held to be unconditional. But the quoted words do not appear to have so limited a meaning. Instead, they indicate that the acceptance is conditional on the opinion of "my solicitor" on the question of title.[24]

A transaction that consists of an unconditional offer followed by a conditional acceptance must be distinguished from one in which neither party has yet made an operative offer. In the process of negotiation an agreement may be expressed on certain matters, both parties knowing that on other matters of importance agreement has not been reached; in such a case, the expected contract is still "subject to" expressions of agreement by both parties.[25]

96

It must also be borne in mind that an acceptance subject to the assent or "permit" of a third party is not a conditional acceptance if the offer was in identical terms subject to that very assent or "permit." [26] It is quite possible for the parties to make a valid contract in which the rights and duties of each are conditional on the happening of some event not within their control, such as the expression of opinion by a third party. For such a result it must be shown that the parties intend that negotiation between themselves is closed, leaving no power of revocation or withdrawal in either one. This being shown, the acceptance is not a "conditional acceptance" varying from the offer; but the rights and duties created by such a contract are conditional rights and duties.

On the other hand, if an offeror or one who solicits offers expressly provides that he will not be bound by a contract until "approval at the home office" or until the expression of approval by an attorney or engineer, there will be no contract until that approval takes place, unless there are subsequent expressions of agreement to be bound without it. An acceptance that ignores such a requirement by the offeror can be no more than a counter-offer. One who has made such a requirement should not be permitted to trick the other party into a contract by "waiving" it, as long as the other party reasonably believes that his own expression of assent is revocable until it occurs.

## § 62. Acceptance by Overt Act

Can an offer ever be accepted in any other way than by an "overt act"? Before discussing this question, it should be noted that some promises may become binding without any acceptance at all; they are promises that are not offered as a part of any bargaining exchange. Suppose that A signs and seals a written promise to pay money to B, puts this in a closed envelope and delivers it to C to hold for B and to deliver to B at a convenient time. An irrevocable unilateral contract is thereby consummated, even though B knows nothing of the transaction and has never authorized C to act for him, and even though no one but A himself knows what is in the envelope. To make A's promise binding, delivery of the envelope to C was necessary. Some courts have held effective delivery cannot be made without an expression of C's assent to take possession; but this assent is not an assent, either on B's behalf or on his own, to the terms of an offer, and it is not the acceptance of an offer of a contract.

Further, a new promise to pay a debt that has been barred by statute of limitations or has been discharged in bankruptcy is binding just as soon as it is communicated to the promisee. No expression of assent by the latter is necessary.[27] The promisor has made no bargaining offer.

Unilateral contracts involving no bargaining element require no expression of assent called an acceptance. In bargaining contracts such an expression is required; and, in these instances, expression nearly always requires overt action. There may be a few cases in which silence alone—total inaction—is an expression of assent that is legally operative as an acceptance, because of the antecedent conduct of the parties and the surrounding circumstances. The problem of silence as an acceptance is dealt with elsewhere.

Acceptance by words, whether written or oral, is acceptance by overt action. The words "I accept your offer", spoken by the offeree, are overt action by him. It will be seen, therefore, that acceptance is by overt act, without regard to whether the resulting contract is bilateral or unilateral, whether the acceptance is promissory or non-promissory. Ordinarily, the making of a promise is by overt action.

Nevertheless, it is important to consider different types of overt action, their significance as expressions of assent, and their effect on the legal relations of the parties.

In the beginning, it must be made clear that in the cases often described as an "offer of a promise for an act" the act that is requested may constitute the making of a promise, and the resulting contract may be bilateral. If an offer is made by A to sell to B a parcel of land for $5,000, at the same time specifying that B may accept by hanging out a flag so that A can see it as he goes by, the offer is one empowering B to make a bilateral contract, not a unilateral one. A offers his promise of a conveyance in exchange for B's promise to pay $5,000. The hanging out of the flag is, to be sure, an "act"; but also it is sign language by the use of which B makes and communicates to A his promise to pay $5,000. Except for the promissory significance of the act of hanging out the flag, A would never offer his promise of a conveyance for it.[28]

If, on the other hand, A desires that a flag be hung on a certain flagpole and offers his promise to pay $10 to B for hanging the flag there, the act of hanging the flag constitutes B's acceptance, just as in the case above; but now it is not sign language and B makes no promise. In the present case, the act of hanging out the flag is not only the act for which A offers to exchange his own promise, but also the act for which he promises to exchange his ten dollars. In the first case, A offered to exchange his own promise for a similar promise by B; but the conveyance of the land was to be exchanged for $5,000. There was an exchange of promises, and also an exchange of performances.

Without doubt, many cases can be found in the reports illustrating the offer of a promise for an act, in which the act is promissory and the resulting contract bilateral. It must suffice here to make reference to a very few. A carrier promised to receive 10,000 staves and transport them to Mobile, at a specified freight rate, if the owner would place them on a certain wharf and have them ready on arrival of the carrier's ship.[29] Here, the specified acceptance was to consist of the act of piling the staves on the wharf, after which the carrier's offer became irrevocable; but the piling of the staves there was not all that was eventually to be done by the offeree—he was later to do the very important act of paying the agreed freight. At some point in his accepting action, the offeree made a promise to pay the freight. If he did not do this, no contract was ever made.

There are numerous cases in which one offers to transfer ownership of chattels and authorizes the offeree to take possession on certain terms. The taking possession by the offeree is an acceptance by an act, and it is also a promise to comply with the specified terms.[31].

Often it is not easy to determine whether or not the act of acceptance is promissory in character. This is merely another way of saying that it is often difficult to interpret the offer; for the power of acceptance is created by the offer, and the acceptance must comply with its expressed terms. Let us consider in detail the following case:

The defendant wrote a letter to her son-in-law, the plaintiff, promising that if he would move from Missouri to Maine and would care for the defendant during her life, he should have the ownership of the home place after the defendant's death and the use of it during her life. The plaintiff moved as requested and cared for the defendant for a few weeks. Trouble ensued, caused, as the court finds, by the unreasonable demands and bad disposition of the defendant, whereupon she conveyed the premises to her son—a co-defendant. The plaintiff filed a bill in equity to compel a reconveyance from the son to his mother, to restrain the prosecution of a statutory ejectment suit brought by the son, and to obtain a decree that the mother should hold the land in trust for the plaintiff. The relief asked was granted in full.[32]

The court says: "The offer was the basis, not of a bilateral contract, requiring a reciprocal promise, a promise for a promise,

---

**29.** Mott v. Jackson, 55 So. 528, 172 Ala. 448 (1911). In the actual case, it may well be that in the oral conversation between the shipper and the carrier, the former promised to ship the staves and to pay the freight, the latter promising in exchange to carry to Mobile if the staves were on the wharf ready for loading. In such case, the act of piling the staves on the wharf was not an acceptance at all; it was merely a condition of the carrier's duty. But no such promise by the shipper was alleged by the plaintiff.

**32.** Me.—Brackenbury v. Hodgkin, 102 A. 106, 116 Me. 399 (1917).

but of a unilateral contract requiring an act for a promise. . . . The plaintiff here accepted the offer by moving from Missouri to the mother's farm in Lewiston and entering upon the performance of the specified acts. . . . The existence of a completed and valid contract is clear."

In this case the defendant was the offeror, and by her letter she created in the plaintiff the power to form a contract between them by accepting. What was this power and how was it to be exercised? The defendant has clearly offered to undertake the duty of allowing the plaintiff to enjoy the use of certain lands during her life and of conveying to him the fee therein at her death. Did she in return ask the plaintiff to promise to support her until her death? No such promise was asked for in express terms, nor was such a promise expressly made. Nevertheless, it would not be unreasonable to find an implication of such a promise both in the offer and in the acceptance. In such case, the contract would be bilateral, for each of the parties would be undertaking to perform certain acts in the future. The contract would include mutual rights and mutual duties. The act of the plaintiff in moving to Maine might have been understood by both parties as an expression of an intention to undertake the duty of supporting the defendant during her life; that is, this act would be a promissory act. If such was the fact, the decision is justifiable; for the contract was fully completed,—the requested promissory acceptance had been given, and the offeror had knowledge of it.[33]

The court says, however, that the contract was unilateral. This means that the plaintiff was requested to make no promise, either by words or by other action. He undertook no duty for breach of which he would be bound to pay damages. He could have abandoned the place in Maine and ceased to support the defendant, without committing any breach of contract. It does not follow from this, however, that the defendant was not bound, and still had the power and privilege of revoking her offer.

Since the court was willing to hold that the defendant's offer became irrevocable after the plaintiff rendered the substantial part performance of moving from Missouri to Maine, this made it unnecessary to decide whether or not the plaintiff had by his action promised to render complete performance for the defendant's life. In either case, the plaintiff was entitled to the remedy that he sought. But if the parties had been reversed, the plaintiff having wilfully abandoned performance, before giving to the defendant a judgment for damages it would have been necessary to find that the plaintiff had, by implication, promised to render all the requested service.[34]

34.   In Hollidge v. Gussow, K. & Co., 67 F.2d 459 (C.C.A.1st, 1933), the de-   fendant made a written order for 160,000 copies of an advertising pa-

Whether the expressions of the parties be interpreted as making either a bilateral or a unilateral contract, in either case the defendant's duty to convey the land should be held to be conditional upon performance in full by the plaintiff; and the defendant's duty to permit continued occupancy by the plaintiff should be held to be conditional upon the plaintiff's continuing to render the support requested. If the plaintiff promised to perform, the defendant's duty is constructively conditional on substantial performance of that promise; if the plaintiff did not promise to perform, the defendant's duty is constructively conditional upon the substantial performance of the requested service. In the actual case, therefore, the final decree should have been a conditional decree, making proper provision for the continued support of the defendant. If, even because of the defendant's own wilful breach, it had become impracticable to carry out the purposes of the agreement, the decree should have been restricted to compensatory damages only, or should have required the land to be held in trust for the plaintiff subject to proper provision for the defendant's continued support for life.

It is sometimes said, in cases like the foregoing, that the contract is consummated as soon as the first substantial act has been done as requested by the offeree.[35] This is reasonable and just; and our contract theories should be moulded in harmony therewith. If the facts justify it, a promise to complete the requested performance can be found by implication, and the contract is bilateral.[36] If the facts do not justify such an implication, then a unilateral contract exists in which the defendant's duty is conditional upon continued performance by the plaintiff.[37] In cases

per, in 8 monthly issues of 20,000 each. The court held that this order was made irrevocable by the publisher's delivery of the first issue. The publisher was held entitled to damages for the defendant's failure to take the other 7 issues. A promise by the publisher to deliver them might easily have been implied, and no doubt would have been if the publisher had been the one committing the breach.

**36.** An excellent illustration is found in Wood & Brooks Co. v. D. E. Hewitt Lbr. Co., 109 S.E. 242, 89 W.Va. 254, 19 A.L.R. 467 (1921). The plaintiff sent an order for 500,000 feet of lumber on fully stated terms, saying "If you cannot deliver as ordered please advise us immediately." The defendant made no reply; but within the time

limited for performance it shipped 160,000 feet and notified plaintiff as to inspection. There were additional circumstances. The jury was held justified in finding that the defendant had impliedly promised to fill the order as given.

If one offers his promise to pay for specified construction or for service over a period of time, the beginning of the work so that it is known by the offeror may be a sufficient acceptance to bind both parties by mutual promises.

**N.Y.**—White v. Corlies, 46 N.Y. 467 (1871), semble.

**Wis.**—Albright v. Stegeman Motor Car Co., 170 N.W. 951, 168 Wis. 557, 19 A.L.R. 463 (1919).

**37.** The offer might be clearly so worded as to require this interpre-

of this sort, the parties may not be at all clear in their own minds as to the legal relations that they desire to create; and the court must determine their legal relations, not because the parties have clearly assented to them but because they have done certain acts that ought to result in such relations.

Although the beginning of the action requested by the offeror may make his offer irrevocable, the substantial completion of the requested action is necessary before the offeror's promise is immediately enforceable. If the offeree performs in part and then delays completion beyond a reasonable time, he cannot enforce the offeror's promise. If a buyer orders the shipment of six hogsheads of rum at once, the shipment of three hogsheads is not an acceptance.[38] In determining how soon the offeror is discharged by the offeree's failure to complete the requested acts, the terms of the offer must be interpreted with the same regard to usage and to customary practices as in the case of any other kind of contract. If the offeror has not expressed an intention to the contrary, it may be reasonable for the offeree to ship the goods in separate parcels and at different times. In the absence of a clear requirement that the requested action shall be completed within a definite time, completion within a reasonable time is enough.

One who makes an offer to sell land for a stated price "if paid within 15 days" thereby promises to deliver his deed of conveyance concurrently with payment. For this reason an operative acceptance is possible without an actual delivery of the money. If within the 15 days the buyer appears and gives notice of his acceptance and readiness to procure the money by drawing his check on a sufficient bank account, but the vendor is not then able to deliver the required deed within the 15 days, a contract has been consummated without actual payment.[39] It should perhaps be regarded as bilateral.

## § 63.   Unilateral Contract—Acceptance by Beginning Requested Performance

The American Law Institute has approved the rule that when a promise is offered in exchange for specified action or forbearance the promise becomes binding and irrevocable as soon as part of the requested performance has been actually rendered or a proper tender of performance has been made. It says: "If an offer for a unilateral contract is made, and part of the consideration requested in the offer is given or tendered by the of-

tation. In the case above discussed, the defendant might have written: "I ask you to leave Missouri and move to Maine. You need make no promises of any kind to me. In consideration of your moving here as I have requested, I promise to leave the land to you at my death, on condition that you have lived upon it and supported me until that time."

feree in response thereto, the offeror is bound by a contract, the duty of immediate performance of which is conditional on the full consideration being given or tendered within the time stated in the offer, or, if no time is stated therein, within a reasonable time." [40]

In order to make this rule applicable it must be a part of the requested consideration that is given or tendered; it is not enough that the offeree has begun the preliminary preparations for performance. It is not always easy to find an exact dividing line between the performance requested and preparations to perform it. It may not be necessary to draw the line in most cases; for, as the Institute recognizes, a promise may become binding and irrevocable by reason of substantial action by the promisee in reliance upon it.[41] Preparations to render a requested performance may be substantial and expressive; and the promisor may have ample reason to foresee that they will be made.

The reason for the rule above laid down is, not that part performance or tender is the "equivalent" of full performance, but that honorable men do not repudiate their promises after part performance has been given or tendered. The Institute says "it is obviously unjust to allow so late withdrawal." In countries where the Civil Law prevails, an offered promise is irrevocable, for either the expressly stated or a reasonable time, even without any part performance or tender; and our own business men are becoming accustomed to making a "firm offer" (meaning irrevocable for some period).[42] In the United States there is sufficient judicial authority to support the rule stated by the Institute.

Holding that the offered promise has become binding and irrevocable involves no injustice to the promisor. Although bound by contract, his duty to render the performance that he has promised is conditional on completion of the consideration as he requested in his offer. This is exactly as it would have been if the bargain had been bilateral. "There can be no actionable duty on the part of the offeror until he has received all that he demanded, or until the condition is excused by his own prevention of performance by refusing a tender." [43]

**40.** Restatement, Contracts, § 45. "Revocation of Offer for Unilateral Contract; Effect of Part Performance or Tender."

**41.** Restatement, Contracts, § 90, "Promise Reasonably Inducing Definite and Substantial Action." This is discussed at length herein in Chapter 8, Contracts without Mutual Assent or Consideration.

In Comment *b*, to section 45, quoted above, it is said: "Moreover, merely acting in justifiable reliance on an offer may in some cases serve as sufficient reason for making a promise binding."

## § 64.    Acceptance of a Published Offer of a Reward for Action

Published offers of a reward for some desired action are nearly always offers of a unilateral contract. The offeror makes a promise in exchange for which he asks for action or forbearance, not for a promise to act or to forbear. Usually, he does not specify the particular acts by which the desired result is to be attained; it is the attainment of the result for which he promises to pay. As in the case of other offerors, he can limit the power of acceptance exactly as he sees fit.[44] He can require the specific mode of producing the result, as well as the result itself; in the absence of such a requirement, the particular mode used is not material, but success in producing the result is essential.

The limits on the power of acceptance—the result that must be attained and the required mode of attaining it—are ascertained by interpretation of the terms of the published offer. This interpretation requires common sense instead of pedantry; it must be reasonable, so as to accord with the understanding of ordinary men to whom the offer is addressed and whose action is invited. The words of the offer are seldom so clear and detailed as to exclude all variation in interpretation and in the exact form of acceptance.

Thus, rewards are frequently offered for the "arrest and conviction" of some specified person charged with crime. In the absence of expressions showing a contrary intention, this will be interpreted so that acceptance is possible by one who does not himself do the physical acts constituting the "arrest." It is obvious that acceptance does not require the acceptor to perform in person an act or group of acts called "conviction." Arrest can be made vicariously by one whom the offeree employs for the purpose; and conviction is a result that can be brought about only by court procedure and the action of public officers. It may even be sufficient to give information to the public officers whose official duty it is to arrest and to prosecute, if as a result thereof the arrest and successful prosecution follow.[45] A different interpretation of the offer has been made where two separate rewards were offered, one being for the "apprehension" of the fugitive and the other being for "information" leading to his apprehension.[46]

---

44. An offer of a prize to the one forming the most words out of the letters included in the word "determination," in accordance with stated rules, is an offer of a unilateral contract. To be a valid acceptance, the performance must comply with the stated rules. The submission of a list of 4,137 words, of which only 1,457 were formed as required by the rules, is not a valid acceptance, even though no other competitor submitted as large a list of correctly formed words. Scott v. People's Monthly Co., 228 N.W. 263, 209 Iowa 503, 67 A.L.R. 413 (1929).

46. U.S.—Shuey v. United States, 92 U.S. 73, 23 L.Ed. 697 (Ct.Cl.1875).

Plenty of difficulty will be found in determining what is meant by "information" and whether the communications by the claimant have in fact caused the arrest and conviction. The claimant may have supplied but a single clue, one that would have been insufficient without the addition of other clues supplied by other men. The information supplied will not be sufficient if the arrest and conviction would, without it, have occurred exactly as they did occur. But it may be sufficient even though, standing alone, it would not have produced the arrest and conviction. The relation of cause and effect must be established.[47] The claimant's communication must be what is generally called, perhaps unhappily, the "proximate cause." However unhappy this expression may be, and whatever may be the difficulties of applying it, we cannot avoid the problem itself, or escape the labor and difficulty of decision, by merely adopting another form of words.

It is not sufficient to give information to some private citizen who is under no public duty to act upon it.[48] If he is not induced thereby to act, the result for which the reward was offered is not produced and the condition of the offer not performed. If the citizen is induced thereby to act, and the desired result follows, the action of that citizen is almost certain to be regarded as such an intervening cause as to exclude the claimant. It would be otherwise if that other citizen purports to act as the agent and in behalf of the claimant who gave him the clue. In the absence of some fiduciary relation, the citizen is free to act in his own behalf and to earn the reward by complying with the terms of the offer.

A reward for "information" is not earned by making a communication of facts that are already known to the offeror or to the public officers whose duty it is to perform the action and to produce the result for which the "information" is desired.[49]

In very many of the reward cases, the requested service has been rendered by more than one person, no one of whom has done enough to entitle him to the whole reward. If they have consciously collaborated in their performance, so that they have produced the requested result as a "joint enterprise," they are jointly entitled to the reward.[50] Frequently, however, they have acted without collaboration, each one supplying some necessary piece of information or doing some one of the requested acts, the result being produced by the sum total of their independent acts. It has been held that in such a case no one is entitled to the reward or to any part of it.[51] In some such cases, however, the offeror actually regards himself as bound and pays the money. The litigation, if any, is then as to the proper subdivision of the reward, the action being in the nature of an interpleader, whether brought by the offeror or by some of the claimants. In these cases, the courts have divided the reward in proportion to the service rendered, roughly estimated.[52] If the claimants are found not entitled to the reward, either jointly or severally, the money is retained by the offeror himself, even though it may have been paid into court.[53]

In view of the actual custom in these cases, courts may well forbear to apply the supposed rules of mutual assent with narrow severity. Even in case the offeror fights all the claimants, a division of the reward among them is just and equitable, without regard to their collaboration or having acted in a "joint enterprise." This is because they have produced the requested result and each has been induced to render his part of the service by the promise of reward.[54]

Where a reward is offered for the finding and return of a sum of money or other lost property, and only a part of it is found and returned, there are cases holding that the claimant is entitled to a pro tanto share of the reward.[55] This seems just and reasonable unless the offer is so worded as to make it clear that the apportionment of the reward is contrary to the offeror's intention, and if the performance requested is readily divisible and the ratio of benefit received by a part performance is determinable. Apportionment was refused where a reward was offered for the capture of two persons and the claimant captured only one of them.[56]

## § 65. When the Words "I Accept Your Offer" would be Ineffective

An offer or proposal may be so worded that the offeree gets no power to accept by the words, written or spoken, "I accept your offer." Where one party wrote to another offering to supply specified goods at certain prices for the period of twelve months in such quantities as the latter might order from time to time,—a reply by the offeree saying "I accept your offer as made" did not make a contract.[62] This is not for lack of mutual expressions of assent, but because the form of the offer is such as to make the offeree's expression insufficient as a consideration. By using the quoted words the offeree has made no promise to buy any quantity and has given no other consideration. Yet the proposal by the first party was an operative offer and remains so for a year unless sooner revoked. The offeree can effectively accept at any time within the year by ordering some specific quantity, thereby consummating a bilateral contract to sell and to pay for that quantity.

In another case, the defendant signed a writing headed "Hopkins Gate Contract," saying, "The Racine Iron Company hereby agrees with Floyd Hopkins to furnish, at any time hereafter during the life of the patent, castings for the patent farm gate of

---

53.   Kan.—Taft v. Hyatt, 180 P. 213, 105 Kan. 35 (1919).

said Hopkins . . . for forty cents per set." [63] This was a standing offer, but it was not itself a contract. Nor could it be accepted by Hopkins by merely signing the document himself, or by saying "I accept your offer." An order for a specific number of castings would be an effective acceptance and would consummate a bilateral contract to make and to pay for the number of castings ordered. The order for definite goods is an acceptance that is invited; and it is a sufficient consideration for the reason that it is a promise to pay the specified price.

Again, if an employer offers employment at specified wages and on stated conditions to continue for an indefinite period and to be terminable at the will of either party, a mere statement "I accept your offer" creates no binding contract. This is because neither party has yet made a promise that can be enforced or that purports to bind him to render any performance whatever. By express provision, performance is still to be subject to his will; and a refusal to render any performance at all would be no breach of duty.

Nevertheless, the employer's offer creates a real power of acceptance, one that exists before any verbal acceptance and that continues to exist after such an acceptance. The words "I accept your offer" are certainly not a rejection.

The employee may be fully authorized by the employer's proposal to proceed with performance without any further assent by the employer; and if he does so proceed, the employer will be bound to pay the specified wages for service rendered. If this is true, the employee had power to accept by action, though not by the words "I accept your offer." If the offer was one to pay fifty dollars per week, the provision for termination at will might be meant to reserve the privilege of termination only at the end of a weekly period. In such case, actually beginning work may reasonably be held to create a bilateral contract for one week's service and pay.[64] If the provision is not so interpreted, then acceptance by rendering service makes only a unilateral contract to pay for service actually rendered before notice of revocation.[65]

### § 66. Acceptance by Forbearance from Action

An acceptance may be by forbearance to act as well as by action, if it is forbearance that is requested by the offer. Thus, if an officer of a bank offers to guarantee a depositor against loss if he will leave his deposit with the bank, the acceptance of the offer and the requested consideration are merely the depositor's forbearance to withdraw the deposit. The depositor makes no

63.   Wis.—Hopkins v. Racine M. & W. Iron Co., 119 N.W. 301, 137 Wis. 583 (1909).

return promise, and is privileged to withdraw the deposit at any time; but in the absence of any notice of revocation the guarantor is bound to indemnify the depositor against loss as long as any part of his money remains on deposit.[66] The same result was reached where a publisher promised to pay a distributor a weekly sum as long as the distributor forbore to handle a rival publication.[67]

In the field of suretyship and guaranty, where a creditor is pressing for payment and some form of legal action is threatened or is imminent, it is not at all uncommon for the debtor to obtain the indorsement of a third party on his note or a written guaranty by a third party, for the purpose of inducing the creditor to forbear from action. In very many such cases, it is reasonable for the creditor to understand that he is being asked for forbearance in fact and not for a promise of such forbearance. If he does reasonably so understand the presentation of the indorsed note or the written guaranty creates in the creditor a power of acceptance by actual forbearance as expressly or impliedly requested, without making any promise to forbear or giving any notice that he accepts. The actual forbearance is itself an expression of acceptance by the creditor and is the requested consideration for the promise of the indorser or guarantor. If no time of forbearance is specified, forbearance for a reasonable time is sufficient to bind the indorser or guarantor.[68] And it is believed that if the question is whether the promisor has power to revoke the offer the "reasonable time" necessary to make his offer irrevocable may be considerably shorter than the reasonable time required before the indorser or guarantor can be considered in default and subject to immediate action by the creditor. The request for forbearance need not be put into words; the creditor may be quite reasonable in inferring such a request from the mere fact that an indorsed note or guaranty is presented to him".[69]

## § 67.  When Notice of Acceptance is Necessary

It has been sometimes argued that notice of acceptance is always necessary, except when the offeror clearly indicates otherwise, and that "notice" means knowledge brought home to the offeror. This was thought to be applicable especially in the case of contracts made by correspondence. Thus, it was said by Bramwell, L. J: "It is necessary, as a rule, to constitute the contract that there should be a communication of acceptance

---

66.  Va.—Looney v. Belcher, 192 S.E. 891, 169 Va. 160 (1937).

The grantee of mortgaged land offered his promise to pay the debt if the mortgagee would not fore-close. The mortgagee thereupon forbore to foreclose for ten years. There was a sufficient acceptance by the mortgagee. Carter v. Burns, 61 S.W.2d 933, 332 Mo. 1128 (1933).

to the proposer. As a consequence of or involved in the first proposition, if the acceptance is written or verbal—i. e., is by letter or message, as a rule, it must reach the proposer or there is no communication and so no acceptance of the offer." [72]

It is not easy to discover where Bramwell found his "rule" that there must be communication, or why it is a "consequence" of that rule that "communication" necessarily means "receipt." It looks very much like the assumption of a major premise and a begging of the question as a means of proving a desired conclusion. Such a rule as he assumes does not come down out of the sky; it must be found, if at all, in our judicial and legislative history. The fact is that such a general requirement is not to be found.[73] Such a rule can indeed be found applied in certain types of cases; and it is necessary to classify the cases and to determine boundary lines and reasons for adhering to them.

In the first place, there is no question that the offeror can require notice of acceptance in any form that he pleases. He can require that it shall be in any language and transmitted in any manner. He may require notice to be given by a nod of the head, by flags, by wig-wag, by a smoke signal on a high hill. He may require that it be by letter, telegraph or radio, and that there shall be no contract unless and until he is himself made conscious of it.[74]

Secondly, the offeror can specify a mode of making an acceptance of his offer, without making that method exclusive of all others. If the mode that he specifies is one that may not bring home to him the knowledge that his offer has been accepted, then such knowledge by him is not a requisite. The offeror can specify a mode of acceptance without any knowledge of the law of contract and without thinking in terms of offer and acceptance at all. This will be considered below.

Thirdly, if the offeror specifies no mode of acceptance, the law requires no more than that the mode adopted shall be in accord with the usage and custom of men in similar cases.[75] If proof of such usage and custom is wanting or is uncertain, the court must consider probable convenience and results and then help by its decision to establish a custom for the future and a rule of law.

In cases of this third class, it has been suggested that notice need not be given if the proposed contract is unilateral and must be given if it is bilateral. This is not a safe classification. Where

72. Household Fire & C. Acc. Ins. Co. v. Grant, 4 Ex.D. 216 (C.A. 1879). A majority of the court disagreed with him.

74. Mass.—Lewis v. Browning, 130 Mass. 173 (1881).

75. It is usage and custom that justify giving notice of acceptance by mail or telegraph. See § 78.

the offeror makes a promise and requests some non-promissory action in return, the performance of that action will generally be enough without the giving of any notice to the offeror; but if the offeror offers some performance and requests a promise in return, the necessity of a notice of acceptance is usually the same as if the contract were to be a bilateral one. It is generally true that in cases in which the offer cannot be accepted without the making of a return promise, custom and the law require some notice of acceptance.[76]

The most reasonable rule, applicable in cases of the third class, seems to be that if the offer is of such a kind that the offeror needs to know of the acceptance in order to determine his subsequent action, and the offeree has reason to know this, a notice of acceptance must be given. If the offeree is asked to make a promise, it is not enough for him to express assent secretly, or to tell his wife or his neighbor that he accepts, or to take the train expecting to go to the offeror's place of business,[77] or to begin work in preparation to perform that which he is asked to promise to perform.[78] One who asks for a promise is asking for an expressed assurance for the purpose of guiding his future conduct.

One who offers to pay or to become guarantor for the debt of another, in order to induce forbearance to enforce payment, and specifies with reasonable clearness that he expects a promise of such forbearance within a specified or a reasonable time, merely beginning to forbear is not operative as an acceptance.[79] The requested promise must be made within the required time.

Even if the offeree is not asked to make a promise, the facts may be such as to show clearly the need of the offeror to know that acceptance has taken place in order to plan for the future. This is often the case where the offeror is a debtor who is seeking a discharge by a substituted contract, a release, or an accord and satisfaction. One against whom a claim for unliquidated damages is being made offers to substitute his definite promise of a sum of money, or of services, in return for immediate discharge; acceptance requires notice sent to the offeror.[80] Here, acceptance

77. Kan.—Trounstine v. Sellers, 11 P. 441, 35 Kan. 447 (1886).

78. N.Y.—White v. Corlies, 46 N.Y. 467 (1871).

79. See:

N.Y.—Strong v. Sheffield, 39 N.E. 330, 144 N.Y. 392 (1895).

Eng.—Gaunt v. Hill, 1 Starkie 10 (1815).

80. Such a case is Trounstine v. Sellers, 11 P. 441, 35 Kan. 447 (1886). Goods had been sent by Trounstine to a local merchant, with respect to which some misunderstanding arose. The merchant wrote proposing to return the goods in settlement, paying for the part already disposed of. Intending to accept this offer, Trounstine started on a trip that would eventually take him to the merchant's place of busi-

is not a promise; it is a mere expression of assent that operates to discharge his claim to unliquidated damages. But the offeror needs to know that he is discharged and free from duty, just as much as he would need to know that he has acquired new rights by means of a promise made to him.

Whenever the case is such as to require a notice of acceptance, it is not enough for the offeree to express mental assent, or even to do some overt act that is not known to the offeror and is not one that constitutes a customary method of giving notice. If the overt act is one that clearly expresses an intention to accept the specific offer and is in fact known by the offeror, there is an effective acceptance. This is because the offeror has actual knowledge.[81]

So a builder cannot accept an offer of a building contract by merely buying materials and starting work on them in his shop.[83] But it would probably be enough if he had begun unloading such materials in the offeror's presence at the place of performance.[84]

A subscription for shares probably cannot be accepted merely by passing a vote of the board of directors and entering the vote on the minutes of the corporation.[85] It may be that the vote and record thereof would make the subscriber a participating and voting shareholder; but he expects to be informed that he has become one.

For similar reasons, it has been held that the vote of an official board to accept a bid is not operative as an acceptance; it must be officially communicated.[86] The vote of a school board, or other official board, electing to a position one who has made application for the appointment, has been held to be revocable by the board prior to the sending of an official notice to the applicant.[87] This is justifiable if the election is regarded as the acceptance of an offer; but it may be regarded otherwise and may be held to be an irrevocable act.

## § 68. Notice as a Requisite of Guaranty and Letters of Credit

Any attempt to review and criticise the innumerable cases in the field of suretyship and guaranty must be left to monographic treatises on that special topic. The confusion and conflict in that

ness. Before his arrival there, the merchant had mortgaged his entire stock, including the goods in question. To accept the merchant's offer, it was necessary to send some notice to him, although the notice, if sent, would not have been a promise. It would have been a discharge of the merchant and the acquisition of new rights by Trounstine.

83. **N.Y.**—White v. Corlies, 46 N.Y. 467 (1871).

85. In re London & Northern Bank, [1900] 1 Ch. 220. And see Household Fire & C. Acc. Ins. Co. v. Grant, 4 Ex.D. 216 (1879), holding that it is enough that the company mailed a notice of allotment of shares, even though the letter was never delivered to the offeror.

field seem to be due in large part to a similar confusion in the general doctrines applicable to all agreements.

It is beyond question that in many thousands of cases an offer to become guarantor for another has been made in such terms as to induce the offeree to advance money, goods, or services on credit without first sending any notice of acceptance to the offeror. Later, when demand is made for him to pay the debt of another in accordance with his promise, the guarantor complains of this lack of notice and asserts that his offer was not accepted as the law requires.

With respect to this, there is nothing peculiar to the relation of suretyship that requires the application of rules different from those applicable in other contracts. One who offers to be surety or guarantor [89] for another can prescribe or suggest the mode of acceptance, just as in other cases. He can prescribe the giving of notice, by mail or otherwise, if he likes. In very numerous cases, however, he makes no such suggestion; and if the offeree acts as requested, the offer should be held to be accepted.

In a well known case,[90] Frank Eaton wrote from Nova Scotia to Bishop in Illinois: "If Harry needs more money, let him have it, or assist him to get it, and I will see that it is paid." In reliance on this and at Harry's request, Bishop indorsed Harry's note to Stark. This action by Bishop was an operative acceptance that instantly bound Frank Eaton as surety. A telegraphic revocation would have been too late, even though Bishop had not yet written or mailed any notice to Frank that he had complied with the latter's request. A unilateral contract had been consummated by an offered promise requesting action, followed by the offeree's action as requested. Frank Eaton's legal duty as surety for Harry may, indeed, be conditional on various events, including a notice or two, to occur subsequently; but it is not the occurrence of these events that constitutes acceptance of the offer.[91]

The foregoing reasoning has received much judicial approval;[92] and it is adopted by the American Law Institute.[93] Many of the

---

90. Mass.—Bishop v. Eaton, 37 N.E. 665, 161 Mass. 496, 42 Am.St.Rep. 437 (1894). Approved in Lascelles v. Clark, 90 N.E. 875, 204 Mass. 362 (1910).

93. Restatement, Contracts, § 56, reads: "Where forbearance or an act other than a promise is the consideration for a promise, no notification that the act or forbearance has been given is necessary to complete the contract. But if the of-

feror has no adequate means of ascertaining with reasonable promptness and certainty that the act or forbearance has been given, and the offeree should know this, the contract is discharged unless within a reasonable time after performance of the act or forbearance, the offeree exercises reasonable diligence to notify the offeror thereof."

The illustrations that are added to this section seem to be based upon Bishop v. Eaton, supra.

cases that say that a notice of acceptance is required confuse notice as the required form of acceptance of an offer with a later notice as a condition precedent to the surety's duty to make payment of the debt.

An offer to become surety for another may request some promise in return, either by the creditor or by the principal obligor. If it does this, a notice that the requested promise is given must be made in order to accept the offer.[94] Mere action in reliance on the surety's offer would not be enough. In such a case, the offeror may wish to establish a continuing "line of credit" for the principal; or he may wish to be assured of a profitable continuing suretyship business for himself.

### § 69. Notice as a Condition Distinguished from Notice as an Acceptance

As indicated in the preceding section the giving of a notice may be a condition in an already consummated contract, even though no notice of acceptance is necessary to consummate it. Most contracts create conditional duties to render some performance in the future; but they are none the less valid contracts for being conditional. A binding and irrevocable obligation may exist long before it is the promisor's duty to pay over the counter— before he is under a duty of immediate performance. A fire insurance policy, duly delivered, is a valid contract, even though the insurer's duty to pay is conditional upon the occurrence of a fire and upon the giving of notice that a fire has occurred. Notice of some fact may be made a condition precedent to a duty of rendering immediate performance, either by express terms of the contract or by construction of law. This is not a notice of acceptance that makes the contract. So, the duty of a surety is certainly conditional upon non-payment at maturity by the principal; and it may also be held to be conditional upon a notice that the credit has been given and another notice that there has been a default.[99] In the present chapter, we are dealing with notice as a necessary part of an operative acceptance, not with notice as a condition precedent to a duty of immediate performance.

### § 70. Offer of a Promise, Requesting Non-promissory Action in Return

The most common form of a unilateral contract is that in which the offeror makes a promise and asks some performance by the offeree in return, clearly indicating that the requested performance is the entire agreed exchange both for his promise and for the performance that he promises. Thus A requests B to ship him specified goods by a named carrier, promising to pay the price that B has previously listed. The actual shipment by B as directed will ordinarily transfer ownership of the goods to A, so that the transaction is an executed sale on credit. The contract is then unilateral, unless by custom or by some expression in A's offer there is a warranty of quality or other implied promise by B to render further performance in addition to the shipment. In either case the act of shipment is an operative acceptance.[1] The same situation exists where a buyer promises to pay for goods in return for delivery by the seller.[2] In cases like these, it has often been held that the offeree may accept by mailing a letter containing a promise to supply the goods—an "acceptance of the order," and that a revocation after such acceptance is too late, even though the goods are not yet shipped.[3] It must not be assumed too readily that an order for goods is an offer of a promise in return for title to the goods to be conveyed by the act of shipment or otherwise. The offeror frequently wishes a return promise, as the offeree understands. The language used may be elliptical, and understood to be so.

General offers of a reward or money payment are frequently made by publication, requesting or inviting the doing of some non-promissory act such as the return of a lost article, the giving of information, the arrest of a fugitive,[4] the use of a medicine,[5] the winning of a contest,[6] the advance of goods or money to a third person.[7] In these cases, the act is both the acceptance and

---

**1.** In Port Huron Machinery Co. **v.** Wohlers, 221 N.W. 843, 207 Iowa 826 (1928), the defendant signed a written order directing the plaintiff to ship immediately certain farm machinery and promising to pay a specified price therefor. The plaintiff immediately shipped the goods and the next day received a telegram from the defendant cancelling the order. The court held that a contract was made and that the cancellation was ineffective.

**4.** The requested act may be either the actual arrest of the fugitive or the giving of information that leads to his arrest. Such offers are frequently worded rather indefinitely; they should be interpreted reasonably. Often, acceptance may be either by actual arrest or by the giving of information.

See:

U.S.—Shuey v. United States, 92 U.S. 73, 23 L.Ed. 697 (1875), one sum offered for "apprehension" and a different sum for "information"; McClaughry v. King, 147 F. 463, 7 L.R. A., N.S., 216, 8 Ann.Cas. 856 (C.C.A. 8th, 1906), arrest required.

Tex.—Choice v. Dallas, 210 S.W. 753 (Civ.App.1919).

**5.** The proprietor of a medicine published an offer to pay £100 to anyone who should use his medicine as directed and thereafter catch the influenza. In reliance on this, the plaintiff used the medicine and caught the influenza. The use of the medicine was an operative acceptance, consummating a unilateral contract. No notice was necessary. Carlill v. Carbolic Smoke Ball Co., [1893] 1 Q.B. 256.

**7.** In Rome v. Gaunt, 140 N.E. 242, 246 Mass. 82 (1923), the defendant wrote a letter to a Woolen Mill promising to "finance your purchases of wool not to exceed $20,000 at any one time, in return for the cash discount of 2% which we understand you can obtain from your wool dealers." The Mill showed this to the plaintiff, a wool dealer, and he sold wool to the Mill on credit. The defendant later learned of this sale. It was held that there was a valid contract of guaranty.

the only subject of agreed exchange to be received by the offeror. Unless otherwise specified in the offer, no notice of acceptance by the offeree is necessary; his act is enough.[8]

Another example of a unilateral contract in the form of an offered promise to pay for service to be rendered, is the case of an agreement to employ a person for an indefinite period at a stated salary per day or month or year. In a good many such cases, it has been held that the employee has made no promise of any kind; he accepts the offer by merely continuing to render the specified service, and becomes entitled to the promised salary in proportion to the work actually done.[9] By such an interpretation of the expressions of the parties as this, the transaction is a "hiring at will." [10] The employee is privileged to stop work at any time; the employer is bound by his promise to pay for service rendered, but has the power of revocation as to service not yet rendered.

In other similar cases, however, the court has drawn the inference of mutual promises to serve and to pay for at least one full period, the length of which is the period by which the stated salary is measured.[11]

There are cases in which an employer has promised a "bonus," some form of benefit in addition to agreed wages or salary, on condition that the employee or employees remain in service for a stated period. In such cases the offered promise is almost always so made as to make it unnecessary for the employee to give any notice of his assent. It is sufficient that he continues in the employment as requested. It is certain that after so continuing in performance, the employer cannot withdraw or repudiate his promise without liability either in damages or for a proportionate part of the bonus promised.[12] A unilateral contract exists.

Many contracts between a real estate agent and his principal are unilateral in character. The principal promises to pay a commission for finding a purchaser willing to pay a stated price; the agent does not promise to find such a purchaser, but has a right to the commission if he finds one.[13] A unilateral contract exists as soon as the principal's offer has become irrevocable by reason of the agent's action in reliance upon it. In some cases the principal may request and the agent may give a return promise to make diligent effort, or to advertise the property, thus making a bilateral contract. In any case, whether the contract is unilateral or bilateral, the owner may make his duty to pay the commission conditional on final consummation of a contract of sale or even on actual receipt of the price.[14]

It must not be assumed too readily that one who makes an offer to pay for specified service does not ask for a promise of such service. Frequently, and perhaps usually, the starting of the requested service by the offeree justifies the inference that he is also promising to complete the service.[15] If there is such an implied promise in return, the contract is bilateral and both parties are bound to perform. Transactions of this kind must be interpreted with common sense and in accordance with the actual usages of men.

## § 71.  Offer of an "Act" for a Promise

In most unilateral contracts, the promise is made by the one making the offer, the acceptance of which is by action or forbearance on the part of the offeree, as in the cases just discussed above. In some cases, however, the only binding promise is made by the offeree, the consideration for that promise being service rendered by the offeror or property transferred by the offeror. An offer of this kind has been described, somewhat unhappily, as the offer of an act for a promise. This is not so unhappy a description if the offer consists of services actually rendered, for compensation to be paid by the offeree. The acceptance of the benefit of the services is a promise to pay for them, if at the time of accepting the benefit the offeree has a reasonable opportunity to reject it and knows that compensation is expected. In some cases, at the time he accepts the benefit of the services, the offeree makes an express promise to pay for them. Whether the offeree's promise is express or implied, the contract then being made is unilateral if no return promise by the offeror can be found.[16]

---

15.    An offer to leave property by will in return for personal care and service for the rest of the promisor's life may contemplate a return promise to render the care and service as well as the rendition of the service itself. See Davis v. Jacoby, 34 P.2d 1026, 1 Cal.2d 370 (1934), a promissory acceptance found by implication; Brackenbury v. Hodgkin, 102 A. 106, 116 Me. 399 (1917), offer irrevocable after part performance, promise could have been implied.

An order for 160,000 copies of an advertising leaflet, to consist of 8 monthly issues of 20,000 each was held to become irrevocable as an offer after one issue had been delivered. The court could easily have found an implied promise by the publisher to furnish the other 7 issues; and it probably would have done so if the publisher had been the one committing the breach. Hollidge v. Gussow, K. & Co., 67 F.2d 459 (C.C.A.1st, 1933).

A written order for 500,000 feet of lumber by the plaintiff, on stated terms, contained this: "If you cannot deliver as ordered, please advise us immediately." The defendant made no reply; some months later and within the time specified for performance he notified the plaintiff that some carloads were ready. Later he shipped and the plaintiff received 160,000 feet. These facts, with others, justified the jury in inferring a promise by the defendant to fill the entire order. Wood & Brooks Co. v. D. E. Hewitt Lbr. Co., 109 S.E. 242, 89 W.Va. 254, 19 A.L. R. 467 (1921).

16.    Cases enforcing such an express or implied promise are:

N.Y.—Gellert v. Dick, 13 N.E.2d 603, 277 N.Y. 123 (1938).

In cases of this sort, a defendant who has been enriched by the plaintiff's services, knowing that the plaintiff rendered them with expectation of pay may be held bound to pay reasonable compensation on a quasi-contractual theory.[17] However, it is just as easy to find a promise to pay such compensation by implication in fact as it is to hold that the law creates such a duty without regard to assent. If the same result is reached by either process, it is unnecessary for the court to determine which one is adopted and applied.

A real estate broker may without request on the part of the principal find and bring him a willing and able purchaser, informing the principal that he will expect a commission if a sale is made. The broker's work is then all done and he makes no promise. No doubt the principal can then make a sale to the purchaser introduced by the broker without binding himself to pay a commission. This is because the services have been thrust upon him; he is privileged not to accept the offer and he is not disabled from making a sale without accepting the offer. Nevertheless, he has the power to accept the offer and to bind himself, this power to be exercised by making the sale and by expressing assent to the broker's proposal.[18]

The case is not substantially different where the broker has rendered his service at the request of one who assumed without authority to act as the agent of the principal, although in holding the principal bound by his acceptance of the services the courts will now use the language of agency; they will speak of his being bound by "ratification." But this ratification is identical with the acceptance of an offer; and on such ratification, the resulting contract is unilateral exactly as above. The broker has made no promise and his services are all done before the principal makes any promise. This may be a case of past consideration; but if so we must make the best of it.

There are many instances of domestic services that have been rendered by one expecting payment for them, as the recipient knows, but by one who has made no promise to render them. The rendition of such services is an offer; and a promise to pay for them is implied from the acceptance of the services by the offeree.[19] When such services are rendered by a close relative, or by one who lives in ordinary family relations with the defendant, the court often finds that the defendant was reasonable in thinking that they were rendered without expectation of pay

S.D.—Edson v. Poppe, 124 N.W. 441, 24 S.D. 466, 26 L.R.A.,N.S., 534 (1910).

Wash.—Muir v. Kane, 104 P. 153, 55 Wash. 131, 26 L.R.A.,N.S., 519, 19 Ann.Cas. 1180 (1909).

Other cases have refused to enforce such a promise on the ground that the consideration is wholly past.

and that an implication of a promise to pay is not justified. This issue has been litigated in numberless cases. If an implied promise to pay is found to have been made, the contract is nearly always unilateral. There may, in some cases, have been a promise by the one rendering the service that he will continue to render it for some future period; in these, the contract is bilateral.

A unilateral contract is made if one proposes the transfer of his property interest in a specific chattel, expressly excluding any warranty and all possible collateral promises, in return for the offeree's promise to pay a price, and the offeree duly accepts. Thus, if A sends a book to B, offering to sell it at a price, and B keeps the book, either expressly or impliedly promising to pay the price, a contract is consummated by B's acceptance.[20] It is a unilateral contract, unless we can find by inference a tacit promise by A of some performance in the future. No doubt such tacit promises are generally inferable. A dealer in horses may offer to sell one to X saying: "This horse is yours as he stands, without warranty or other promise, in return for your promise to pay me $100 in thirty days." If X makes the requested promise the contract is made; and it is unilateral in character. It is an executed sale on credit without warranty. The consideration for X's promise is the property in the horse. The offer is so worded as to empower X to transfer the property to himself by his own act of acceptance, the very same act by which he binds himself to pay the price. The consideration for X's promise to pay is not past; it is the simultaneous transfer of ownership, that takes place with the making of the promise.

A property interest in a party wall can be offered by actually building it; and a tacit promise to pay for it may be inferred from silence with knowledge that it is being built.[21]

### § 72.  Silence as a Mode of Acceptance

It is an old maxim that silence gives consent; but this is not a rule of law. It is certain that, if the only facts are that A makes an offer to B and B remains silent, there is no contract.[22] This is true whether the offer is made orally or by mail or telegraph. Silence may indicate that the offeree did not hear or receive or understand the offer; or it may indicate that he preferred to give no thought to the offer and to waste no time and effort in making a reply, whether orally or by a writing. In such cases, the offeror is not reasonable in giving to the offeree's mere silence an interpretation that he accepts. So, if a party sends a book

---

20.   **Mass.**—Hobbs v. Massasoit Whip Co., 33 N.E. 495, 158 Mass. 194 (1893).

**Mo.**—Austin v. Burge, 137 S.W. 618, 156 Mo.App. 286 (1911).

**N.H.**—Fogg v. Portsmouth Atheneum, 44 N.H. 115, 82 Am.Dec. 191 (1862).

or paper or other goods to another, with a letter saying that he is offering it for sale at a specified price, the party to whom it is sent is not bound by a contract to pay for it if he does nothing and says nothing. If a party to an existing contract proposes a modification thereof, the mere silence of the other party leaves the contract as before without modification.[23] European opinion appears to agree with the Anglo-American law, as indeed it should where the usages of business men and their understandings and expectations are substantially alike.[24]

## § 73. Can Offeror Make Silence Operate as Acceptance?

It should here be plainly set forth that an offeror has no power to cause the silence of the offeree to operate as an acceptance when the offeree does not intend it to do so.[27] The offeree's own conduct may be such as to make his silence operative against him; and the offeror's conduct may be such as to make the offeree's silence a sufficient acceptance binding upon the offeror. But an offeror can not, merely by saying that the offeree's silence will be taken as an acceptance, cause it to be operative as such. He can not force the offeree to take his pen in hand, or to spend a two-cent stamp, or to open his mouth, under penalty of being bound by a contract if he does not. It is substantially the same case as where an offeror attempts to give the meaning of an acceptance to some other ordinary act of the offeree that the latter wishes to do without giving it such a meaning. If A offers his land to B for a price, saying that B may signify his acceptance by eating his breakfast or by hanging out his flag on Washington's birthday or by attending church on Sunday, he does not thereby make such action by B operative as an acceptance against B's will. If B shows that he had no intent to accept, and that he ate his breakfast merely because he was hungry, or hung out his flag because it was his patriotic custom, or went to church to hear the sermon, no contract has been made even though A truly believed that B meant to accept.

It is a different question, however, whether an offeror can make the offeree's mere silence operative as an acceptance as against himself when the offeree desires that it should so operate. In a few cases, the offeror has written to the offeree that if he wishes to accept he can do so merely by remaining silent, without troubling to send notice of any kind or doing any other act. In two such cases, the offeree made up his mind to accept and remained silent as the specified mode of accepting; yet the court held that no contract had been made.[28]

In one aspect, this seems to be not unreasonable. The opposite rule, in such cases, would enable the offeree to await the event,

28.  N.H.—Prescott v. Jones, 41 A.     Eng.—Felthouse v. Bindley, 11 C.B.N.
352, 69 N.H. 305 (1898).          S. 868 (1862).

and to deny the fact of acceptance if the contract now appears to be to his disadvantage, or to assert the fact of acceptance if appearances are to the contrary. This argument, however, proves too much; for it applies with equal force, to any positive act that might reasonably be performed even though no offer has been made, and that has no more probative force to establish assent than to establish some other fact. Whether or not it would be so applied may be regarded as doubtful. A strong argument in favor of holding the acceptance good is that the offeror has only himself to blame if the terms of his offer put him at the mercy of the offeree, and that he should not be permitted to escape liability when he has induced the offeree to believe that there is a contract and to act in reliance thereon.[29] The weight of these opposing arguments can not be determined with certainty; but it will be a rare case where the offeree has not done some overt act which indicates his intention to accept, and in such case the courts will undoubtedly hold that the acceptance is good.[30]

## § 75.  Silence Plus Additional Circumstances

There are many cases in which, because of the past relations of the parties or of accompanying circumstances, the silence of the offeree after receipt of an offer has been held to constitute acceptance and to create a contract. These are all cases in which the conduct of the party denying a contract has been such as to lead the other reasonably to believe that silence, without communication, would be sufficient. Usually it has been the offeror who asserts that the offeree has accepted by silence and who is suing the offeree for breach; [36] but the question may arise with the parties reversed, the offeree asserting that he was justified in believing that his silence would be a sufficient acceptance.

Thus, where a party ships goods to another at the latter's standing request, the receipt and retention of the goods without any notice of refusal to accept them have been held to sustain a verdict that there was an acceptance and a promise to pay.[37] Where a periodical is sent by mail under circumstances such that the sendee knows that it is being offered at the subscription price, the receipt and reading of the periodical have been held to be an acceptance.[38] A different result should be reached if the

---

29. The American Law Institute has adopted this rule in spite of the two decisions to the contrary. See Restatement, Contracts, § 72(1b).

36. Such a case is Wood & Brooks Co. v. Hewitt Lbr. Co., 109 S.E. 242, 89 W.Va. 254, 19 A.L.R. 467 (1921).

37. Hobbs v. Massasoit Whip Co., 33 N.E. 495, 158 Mass. 194 (1893).

The same result has been reached where a piano was in the offeree's possession on trial, with a promise to return it if not accepted. F. O. Evans Piano Co. v. Tully, 76 So. 833, 116 Miss. 267, L.R.A.1918B, 870 (1917), noted in 27 Yale L.J. 561.

38. Austin v. Burge, 137 S.W. 618, 156 Mo.App. 286 (1911).    •

sendee has made no use of the periodical and has merely failed to refuse it at the post office or to notify the sender of his rejection.

In like manner, where goods are shipped on different terms from those proposed by the buyer, the acceptance and user of the goods without notice of dissent is an acceptance of the terms of the seller's counter-offer.[39]

One who sees a party wall being built by his neighbor on their common boundary line, knowing that the neighbor expects to be reimbursed one half the cost, is bound to pay therefor if he afterwards makes use of the wall, even though his mere silence might not be sufficient evidence of a promise to pay.[40] It is clear that a party will not be permitted to receive and enjoy benefits that he knows are being offered to him at a price without paying for them, if he had an opportunity to reject them when they were offered without any expense or material inconvenience. Silence may here consummate his acceptance because the facts fairly call upon him to speak.

Frequently, services are rendered under circumstances such that the party benefited thereby knows the terms on which they are being offered. If he receives the benefit of the services in silence, when he had a reasonable opportunity to express his rejection of the offer, he is assenting to the terms proposed and thus accepts the offer.[41]

It is not uncommon for a company to send out a travelling salesman to solicit orders, without power to contract, expressly providing that all orders are subject to acceptance at the home office. In such cases, it seems reasonable for the party whose order was solicited to expect word from the soliciting company within a reasonable time if his order is not accepted. There are well considered cases holding that acceptance may be inferred from silence, especially when supported by the previous custom of the parties or a general trade usage.[42] Other cases have held that the circumstances were not such as to justify an inference of assent to the order.[43]

## § 76. Multiple Acceptances

An offer may be so made as to empower a single offeree to accept many times, or to empower many offerees to accept. In the former case, the resulting series of contracts between the two parties may be either unilateral or bilateral, and may be wholly independent of each other or may be related in some way to each other. In the latter case, the contracts resulting from separate acceptances by different offerees will usually be quite separate and independent contracts.[47]

---

40. Day v. Caton, 119 Mass. 513, 20 Am.Rep. 347 (1876).

47. Illustrations exist in cases holding that one making a charitable

Continuing guaranties are common illustrations of the former. "In consideration of your discounting bills of exchange for Davies and Company, we hereby guarantee for the period of one year the prompt payment of all such bills to the extent of $3,000." The discounting of each bill as it is presented is a separate acceptance of this offer, each one creating a new unilateral contract with the guarantor. After each discount, the offer would be made irrevocable as to that particular bill; but it would remain revocable by notice with respect to subsequent bills.[48]

A letter of credit may be addressed to a single offeree, or to any bank or banker, or to whom it may concern. "To the X Filling Station: If A should ask you to sell him gasoline from time to time during the next twelve months, please supply him on thirty days credit. I guarantee payment of his debts so contracted, not exceeding a total of $200."[49] This can be accepted by X by selling gasoline to A many times, but can be accepted by no one else. Here, too, the resulting contracts would all be unilateral and independent of each other. Such a letter of credit, however, may be addressed to any and all filling stations, or to any one of a particular line of stations, just as a traveller's letter of credit is usually addressed to a large number of specified correspondents. Such an offer can be revoked by notice received by the offeree before it is acted upon by him.[50]

There are also standing offers to manufacture and sell specified kinds of goods at stated prices, in quantities to be fixed by the buyer. "The Racine Company hereby agrees with F. Hopkins to furnish, during the life of the patent, castings for the patented Hopkins gate, for forty cents per set." A succession of orders sent in by Hopkins for specified reasonable numbers of sets of castings would make a series of separate bilateral contracts.[51]

---

subscription is contracting with all the other subscribers, or that all who make entry into a racing contest contract with all the others that they will obey the rules of the race, or that an agent in contracting with his principal may also be contracting with all other similar agents.

**48.** Eng.—Offord v. Davies, 12 C. B. (N.S.) 748 (1862).

**49.** Ala.—Consolidated Portrait & Frame Co. v. Barnett, 51 So. 936, 165 Ala. 655 (1910).

**50.** The Uniform Commercial Code —Letters of Credit, § 4—105 (1950 draft) provides that a letter of credit shall be irrevocable from the moment of its receipt by the beneficiary, even though no consideration was given for its issuance. The adoption of such a provision would seem to require a different decision from that in the above text.

**51.** Wis.—Hopkins v. Racine M. & W. Iron Co., 119 N.W. 301, 137 Wis. 583 (1909).

Eng.—Great Northern R. Co. v. Witham, L.R. 9 C.P. 16 (1873).

## § 77. Alternative Modes of Acceptance

As already indicated, an offeror can limit the power of acceptance very narrowly. He can prescribe in the terms of the offer itself one specific mode of acceptance. But instead of being thus limited, the offer may prescribe no mode of acceptance whatever. There must be enough to indicate that the offeror intends to create a power of acceptance, but this is quite possible in the absence of any suggestion whatever as to the mode of acceptance. In this case the offeree can accept in any manner that is reasonable under the circumstances.

An even larger power of acceptance may be created by the offeror. He may suggest and authorize an acceptance in one or more particular modes, without making them exclusive. In such case, compliance with the suggested mode will close the contract, however unreasonable or unusual the mode may be; but so also will compliance with any other reasonable mode. In this case, the offeree has all the power that he would have if the mode of acceptance had been exactly prescribed; and in addition thereto, all the power that he would have if no mode of acceptance had been mentioned at all.

The foregoing rules of acceptance are applicable to all kinds of contracts alike, unilateral and bilateral; but in their application certain distinctions are to be observed and some difficulties must be overcome. It is not always easy to determine what mode of acceptance the offeror has required or suggested; a reasonable construction must be put upon his words or other conduct. If the offeror has prescribed no mode of acceptance and if the offeree has not adopted some mode suggested by the offeror, it must be determined whether or not the mode actually adopted is to be deemed reasonable.

It is obvious that there may be alternative modes of acceptance of a single offer; and it may be added that in some instances the legal relations created by these varying modes will not be identical. Thus, if a buyer sends an order for goods, there are many cases in which the offeree can accept either by shipping the goods at once or by mailing a letter of acceptance.[53] By the former method, the property in the specific goods may pass at once; and the contract may be unilateral. By the latter method, a bilateral contract is made; and there is no passing of property in any specific goods.

Of course, when he orders the goods, the buyer can specify one exclusive mode of acceptance. He can require immediate shipment as the only form; or he can require immediate acceptance by wire. But the ordinary order for goods, in accordance with some catalog or list or solicitation, does neither of these things; and it may be quite reasonable to accept by shipment, by writing, or by telegram or telephone.

An employer may offer a promise of employment at specified wages in such a manner as to empower the offeree to accept either by actually beginning work or by promising to go to work.[54] Beginning work in response to the offer would nearly always justify the inference of a promise to complete it. Actual shipment of part of the goods ordered, if in accordance with an instalment order or with custom or course of dealing, may justify the inference of a promise that the balance will be shipped.[55] If the order is for shipment in one lot, shipment of less may operate as an acceptance and a breach at the same time,[56] but it may also be no more than a return offer to sell the part shipped or a performance in accordance with an urgent request and for the accommodation of the buyer.[57]

Ordinarily, one who makes an offer to sell property for a price contemplates a bilateral contract and expects a notice of acceptance. This is true even though the offer is in the form of an irrevocable option to buy. Nevertheless, in such a case the offeree can accept by making a tender of the price without other notice. If the offeror accepts the tender, the resulting payment may constitute full performance by the buyer and the resulting contract is unilateral. If the offeror rejects the tender, he is guilty of a breach of contract for which the buyer can maintain suit for damages or specific performance.[58]

## § 78.  Acceptance by Post

As has already been stated, an offeror can specify any mode of acceptance that he pleases. By his offer he creates the power of acceptance; and he can limit it as he desires. Without regard to the mode in which he communicates his offer, he can require acceptance by telegraph, telephone, or letter; and he can require that it shall be received instead of merely started.[61] But in order to limit the power of acceptance, he must either communicate the limitation to the offeree before the latter accepts, or else make his offer in such manner and terms that the offeree has reason to know that his power is so limited.

Where the parties are negotiating at a distance from each other, the most common method of making an offer is by sending it by mail; and more often than not the offeror has specified no particular mode of acceptance. In such a case, it is now the prevailing rule that the offeree has power to accept and close the contract by mailing a letter of acceptance, properly stamped and addressed,[62] within a reasonable time. The contract is re-

62.   **N.J.**—Potts v. Whitehead, 20 N. J.Eq. 55 (1869).
Restatement, Contracts, § 67, reads: "An acceptance sent by mail or otherwise from a distance is not operative when despatched, unless it is properly addressed and any other precaution taken which is ordinarily observed to insure safe transmission of similar messages."

garded as made at the time and place that the letter of acceptance is put into the possession of the post office department.[63]

Various reasons have been given for so holding; and for a long time some learned theorists and judges denied that such was the rule and even that the courts had power to make it the rule. The objections have now mostly died away; and no one doubts that the courts can make such a rule, because they have in fact made it. In as much as the rule seems to be causing no great dissatisfaction, it may now be supposed that the courts are not likely to unmake it.

The reason that is most often given for the rule is that the offeror, by sending his offer by mail, has made the post his agent to receive and carry the acceptance. Sometimes it is said that the post is the common agent of both parties.[64] It requires only slight consideration to perceive that this reasoning is defective. The term "agent" is generally used to refer only to some human person with power to act on his principal's behalf. The "post" is not a person, although there are many persons in the postal service; and it is by no act of any such person that the making of the contract is consummated. A letter box on the corner is neither a person nor an agent; and yet the acceptance is effective when the letter of acceptance is dropped into that box.[65] It is the offeree himself (or some person authorized by him) who drops the letter in the box. It is he who has the power and who exercises it by his action. The "box" has no power and does no act. It is true that a postman may thereafter remove the letter from the box; but the contract has already been made and the removal has no legal operation. All this is equally true in case the letter is mailed by dropping it through the proper slit inside of a post office building.

Sometimes it is said that the mailing of the letter of acceptance makes the contract for the reason that by the act of mailing the offeree puts the letter irrevocably out of his own possession and control. The present post office regulations provide, however, that the sender of a letter can recall it. He can stop delivery by telegraphing ahead and can cause the return of the letter to himself. This is discussed in a later section.

A better explanation of the existing rule seems to be that in such cases the mailing of a letter has long been a customary and expected way of accepting the offer. It is ordinary business usage. More than this, however, is needed to explain why the letter is operative on mailing rather than on receipt by the offeror. Even though it is business usage to send an offer by mail, it creates no power of acceptance until it is received. Indeed,

64.  **Eng.**—It was so argued in Household Fire & C. Acc. Ins. Co. v. Grant, 4 Ex.D. 216 (1879).

most notices sent by mail are not operative unless actually received.

The additional reasons for holding that a different rule applies to an acceptance and that it is operative on mailing may be suggested as follows: When an offer is by mail and the acceptance also is by mail, the contract must date either from the mailing of the acceptance or from its receipt. In either case, one of the parties will be bound by the contract without being actually aware of that fact. If we hold the offeror bound on the mailing of the acceptance, he may change his position in ignorance of the acceptance; even though he waits a reasonable time before acting, he may still remain unaware that he is bound by contract because the letter of acceptance is delayed, or is actually lost or destroyed, in the mails. Therefore this rule is going to cause loss and inconvenience to the offeror in some cases. But if we adopt the alternative rule that the letter of acceptance is not operative until receipt, it is the offeree who is subjected to the danger of loss and inconvenience. He can not know that his letter has been received and that he is bound by contract until a new communication is received by him. His letter of acceptance may never have been received and so no letter of notification is sent to him; or it may have been received, and the letter of notification may be delayed or entirely lost in the mails. One of the parties must carry the risk of loss and inconvenience.[66] We need a definite and uniform rule as to this. We can choose either rule; but we must choose one. We can put the risk on either party; but we must not leave it in doubt. The party not carrying the risk can then act promptly and with confidence in reliance on the contract; the party carrying the risk can insure against it if he so desires. The business community could no doubt adjust itself to either rule; but the rule throwing the risk on the offeror has the merit of closing the deal more quickly and enabling performance more promptly. It must be remembered that in the vast majority of cases the acceptance is neither lost nor delayed; and promptness of action is of importance in all of them. Also it is the offeror who has invited the acceptance.[67]

A third possibility has been suggested, but little considered. This is that the mailing of the acceptance shall consummate a conditional contract, one that at once becomes irrevocable by either party but that is conditional upon actual receipt of the letter within a reasonable time by the offeror. To this rule, also, the business community could no doubt adjust itself; but it has no such advantages in the allocation of risk as to justify advocating its adoption at the present time.[68]

If the offer has not itself been sent by mail, the theory that the post is the common agent of the parties breaks down. Also, there is so much the less reason for holding that the offeror has authorized an acceptance by mail.[69] As in all other cases, he may have expressly authorized such an acceptance. In some well-reasoned cases, it has been held that the power to accept by mailing a letter may rest upon facts other than an express or implied authorization. Even though the offer was not made by mail and there was no authorization, the existing circumstances may be such as to make it reasonable for the offeree to accept by mail and to give the offeror reason to know that the acceptance will be so made. Such may be usage and business practice. In such case, the acceptance is operative on mailing.[70]

The fact that an offer is sent by wire is not itself evidence of an authorization to accept by mail—indeed it tends to show that a more speedy form of acceptance is desired. Yet the nature of the proposed contract, the time of the expected performance, the absence of price fluctuation, and other factors may be sufficient to warrant a decision that an acceptance by mail is operative on mailing.[71]

An offeror can always so word his offer and so limit the power of acceptance as to make the receipt of the acceptance necessary to the creation of a contract. Indeed, if he merely says "Notice of your acceptance must be given within 30 days," this may be held to mean that the notice must be received within that time. It would be different if he says, "Please reply by return of post." The latter specifies a mode of communication but does not make receipt necessary. Where an already completed contract contained a provision creating an option to be exercised by the giving of notice within a stated time, it has been held that it is not enough that the notice was mailed within that time.[72] Here, the question is one of interpretation of language. Probably, when parties use the word "notice," they usually mean a communication received.

So, also, where in an already completed contract, a power of revocation or termination by notice is reserved, the notice is not operative until actually received.[73]

If the circumstances are such that the acceptance is operative at starting it by mail or telegraph, the fact that it is delayed on the way [74] or even that it is lost and never received [75] does not affect the validity of the contract already made. This presup-

69.   Scottish American Mortg. Co. v. Davis, 74 S.W. 17, 96 Tex. 504, 97 Am.St.Rep. 932 (1903), held that acceptance by mail was not authorized since the offer was not by mail, and that a mailed acceptance could therefore be recalled.

70.   **Eng.**—Henthorn v. Fraser [1892] 2 Ch. 27, offer delivered in person; Household Fire & C. Acc. Ins. Co. v. Grant, 4 Ex.D. 216 (1879), offer put in the hands of offeree's soliciting agent.
Restatement, Contracts, §§ 64, 66.

71.   **Okl.**—Farmers' Produce Co. v. McAlester Storage & Com. Co., 150 P. 483, 48 Okl. 488, L.R.A.1916A, 1297 (1915).

poses that such loss or delay is not caused by the fault of the offeree. Of course, in these cases there is likely to be injury or inconvenience; but it is the risk of this that someone has to carry; that one is the offeror unless he has so made his offer as to prevent it.

## § 79. Acceptance by Telephone

In a few cases the courts have dealt with the making of a contract by telephone. Restatement, Contracts, § 65, states, "Acceptance given by telephone is governed by the principles applicable to oral acceptance where the parties are in the presence of each other". There is no comment; and no illustrations are given. The question before the courts has been as to the place at which the contract should be regarded as having been made. This has been held to be the place at which the offeree speaks the words of acceptance into the telephone transmitter.[76]

When an acceptance is made orally in the presence of the offeror, there is no appreciable lapse of time between the act of speaking and the hearing of the sounds. Nevertheless, if the offeree knows or has reason to know that the offeror does not actually hear or understand his words of acceptance, a contract is not consummated. Undoubtedly the same is true in the case of an acceptance by telephone; and under some circumstances the offeree has more reason to doubt the effectiveness of his communication by telephone than in the case of an acceptance face to face.

## § 80. Withdrawal of a Letter of Acceptance from the Mails

The postal regulations have for a long period made it possible for the sender of a letter to intercept it and prevent its delivery to the addressee. This has caused some doubt to be expressed as to whether an acceptance can ever be operative upon the mere mailing of the letter, since the delivery to the post office has not put it entirely beyond the sender's control.

It is believed that no such doubt should exist. The question should not turn upon the total loss of power to control, but rather upon the reasonableness of regarding this as a proper method of accepting an offer. First, if the offeror expressly says that acceptance may be by the mailing of a letter, the offeree certainly has power to accept as thus authorized. The withdrawal of the letter, with the consent of the post office, would not make the acceptance inoperative, although it might prevent the offeror from ever knowing that his offer had been accepted. Secondly, if the offeror specifies that acceptance must be made by a communication received by him, or by some mode other than the

---

76. Bank of Yolo v. Sperry Flour
Co., 74 P. 855, 141 Cal. 314 (1903).

mere mailing of a letter, there is no contract until the prescribed method has been followed. If the offeree intercepts his letter of acceptance, no contract has been made; and there is no contract upon the mailing of the letter, whether he intercepts it or not. Thirdly, if the offeror has specified nothing whatever, then the acceptance should be operative on mailing if according to ordinary custom and business usage, the offeree is reasonable in regarding the agreement as consummated when the letter is mailed. In view of common practices, in view of the difficulties involved in the process of interception of a letter, and in view of the decisions and printed discussions dealing with acceptance by post, it is believed that the fact that a letter can be lawfully intercepted by the sender should not prevent the acceptance from being operative on mailing. If the offer was made under such circumstances that the offeror should know that the offeree might reasonably regard this as a proper method of closing the deal, and the offeree does so regard it, and makes use of it, the contract is consummated even though the letter of acceptance is intercepted and not delivered.[77]

## § 81.    Acceptance by Telegraph—When Operative

In the United States, the telegraph is not part of the postal system; instead, the service is rendered by public service corporations. Communication by telegraph is comparatively so speedy and there is such general confidence in its reliability that often the telegraph is used instead of the mail as a means of making and accepting offers. These facts have caused the rules applicable to acceptance by telegraph to be very similar to those applicable to acceptance by post.

The offeror can, by proper expression of his will, either totally exclude the telegraph or make its use an absolute requirement. He can make it one of several alternative methods; and he can provide that a telegraphed acceptance shall be operative only on receipt by him.[80] But he may do none of these things; and yet the telegraph may in fact be used by the offeree.

If the offeror expressly or by reasonable implication authorizes the use of the telegraph to accept, a properly started and directed telegram of acceptance is operative on putting the message in the hands of the telegraph company. Just as a letter must be stamped, so must the telegraphic charges be paid or credit agreed on by the company. The fact that the telegram might possibly be recalled or delayed or lost does not prevent its operation as an acceptance.[81]

If the offer is itself by telegraph this is a fact that tends toward an inference of authorization to use the same method in accepting; also, it tends toward a finding that the offeree is reasonable in accepting by telegraph and in supposing that starting the telegram makes the contract.[82]

If the court finds that the offeree is thus reasonable and that the offeror had reason to expect as much, the acceptance is operative at starting.[83] Such a finding by the court, however, is not a necessary result of the fact that the offer was by telegram. All other surrounding circumstances should be considered. If the offeree knows facts indicating that his accepting telegram will be delayed, it may be quite unreasonable for him to adopt this method, or at least to act on the assumption that he can close the contract by leaving his message at the telegraph office.

If the offer is not by telegraph and the offeror says nothing as to the mode of acceptance, acceptance by telegraph may nevertheless be a proper mode. If all the other requirements of an acceptance are fulfilled, acceptance by telegraph will be operative at least as soon as the telegram is received.[84] It is quite possible, indeed, that the telegraphic acceptance will be operative on starting. The method may be entirely reasonable, in accord with business usage of the time and place, and one that the offeror had reason to expect, so that acceptance should be effective on starting the telegram.[85] In some cases, however, it has been held that the acceptance is not operative until the telegram is received.[86] It is true that in such a case there is little reason for saying that the telegraph is the common agent of both parties or that the offeror has authorized its use and has agreed to carry the risk of delay or nondelivery. Since these arguments are not conclusive in cases of acceptance by post, they need not be regarded as conclusive in cases of acceptance by telegraph. In at least one case, it has been held that an acceptance by mail may be operative on mailing even though the offer was by telegraph.[87] Without doubt, it would much more often be reasonable to accept by telegraph an offer that came by mail than to accept by mail an offer that came by telegraph. The use of the telegraph by an offeror is some indication that speed of communication is desired.

## § 82. Acceptance Must be Unconditional

A communicated offer creates a power to accept the offer that is made and only that offer. An expression of assent that changes the terms of the offer in any material respect may be operative as a counter-offer; but it is not an acceptance and

---

**82.** **U.S.**—Minnesota Linseed Oil Co. v. Collier White Lead Co., 4 Dill. 431, Fed.Cas. No. 9,635 (C.C.Minn. 1876).

**Conn.**—L. & E. Wertheimer v. Wehle-Hartford Co., 9 A.2d 279, 126 Conn. 30, 125 A.L.R. 985 (1939).

**87.** **Okl.**—Farmers' Produce Co. v. McAlester Storage & Com. Co., 150 P. 483, 48 Okl. 488, L.R.A., 1916A, 1297 (1915).

consummates no contract.[88]  An expression that purports to be an acceptance, but is so expressed as to be operative as an acceptance only on a condition that is not so specified in the offer, is not an acceptance at all.  It may be described as "a conditional acceptance"; but this does not mean that it is operative as an acceptance or even that it will become so operative if the condition afterwards occurs.  It is operative only as a counter-offer; and unless the offeror expresses unconditional assent to it, there will never be a contract.[89]

One offers to sell Blackacre to another for a stated price, saying that the offer will remain open until Christmas.  The other replies: "I accept your offer now, at the price named, on condition that the price of cotton shall rise to twelve cents by Christmas."  This makes no contract, either now or hereafter, even though cotton reaches the specified price.  This counter-offer creates an immediate power of acceptance in the original offeror; he need not wait for the price of cotton to rise.

The question whether a communication by an offeree is a conditional acceptance or counter-offer is not always easy to answer.  It must be determined by the same common-sense process of interpretation that must be applied in so many other cases.[90]  In an old case that has been much discussed,[91] one who had been offered certain brandy in which both parties had an interest, at a price, replied as follows: "I shall delay coming to any determination till I again hear from you. . . .  The prospect of war between France and Spain may defeat the object of this speculation [one previously agreed upon], in which case I will at once decide to take the adventure to my own account."  This was held not to be an acceptance on condition and not to prevent the offeree from making a valid acceptance later.[92]  Nor was it a counter offer creating a power of acceptance in the other party.

An offeror who orders the shipment to him of a specified bill of goods may so word his order as to require acceptance by shipment of the entire order.  If he does so, a shipment of a part of the order, or of partly different goods, is not an operative acceptance.[93]  The offer, as in all other cases, must be interpreted in the light of past custom and usage; and it may appear that the offeree is empowered to accept by piecemeal shipments.  There have been a good many cases so holding.

## § 83.  An Acceptance may be Unconditional Even Though the Acceptor Makes a Conditional Promise

It should be noted that a proposal fails to be an operative offer unless it specifies, directly or by reference, all the terms of the

91.  N.Y.—Mactier's Adm'rs v. Frith,
6 Wend. 103, 21 Am.Dec. 262 (N.Y.
1830).

131

contract to be made. If the contemplated agreement is to be bilateral, the proposal must state the terms of each promise in full. The offeror must not only state the terms of the promise that he is himself willing to make; he must also state the consideration for which he is willing to exchange it.[96] If the offeree changes any term of either promise or changes the consideration that the offer proposes for any promise, he is not accepting the offer. The offeror and offeree, alike, must express agreement as to every term of the contract. The offeror does this in the offer; the offeree must do it in his acceptance.

To say that the acceptance must be unconditional is not to say that the promises assented to must be unconditional promises. If the offeror proposes an exchange of conditional promises, the offeree must assent unconditionally to that exact exchange. Thus, where A offers to buy a patent at a named price, on condition that X shall express approval of the patent, and B promises to sell it at that price and subject to the same condition, they have made a valid and irrevocable contract. This is so, even though if X fails to approve neither A nor B will be under any duty of paying or transferring. The failure of X to approve shows no defect in the expressions of assent—the offer and the acceptance. A and B were exactly agreed; and they exactly expressed their agreement. A gave his conditional promise to pay in exchange for B's promise to assign the patent subject to the very same condition. Both parties assented to the exchange of these very promises.

The result is the same even though one of the exchanged promises is conditional and the other promise is not. All that is necessary is that both parties shall assent to this exact exchange. Suppose that A offers to sell his automobile to B for $1,000, delivery and payment by June 1. Liking the appearance of the car, B replies: "I will buy the car and pay $1,000 according to your offer, but only on condition that my engineer X shall inspect the car and say that it is worth the price." A has offered his promise for no such return promise as this; there is no contract. But B has made a counter offer of his conditional promise to buy, an offer that A now has power to accept. He thereupon replies: "I assent to your modification and agree to sell on your terms." A contract has been made.

The parties now reduce their agreement to a signed writing as follows: "It is mutually agreed, (1) that A will sell his automobile to B for $1,000, delivery and payment by June 1, and (2) that B will accept the car and pay the price by that date, if after an inspection Engineer X says that in his opinion the car is worth the price.

　　　　　　　　　　　　　　　　　　　[Signed]　A.
　　　　　　　　　　　　　　　　　　　　　　　　B."

This is a valid written contract, creating the same rights and duties as did the previously made oral contract of which it is an exact written integration. The promises of both parties are conditional. A's promise to sell and deliver is constructively conditional on concurrent payment of $1,000. B's promise to pay is likewise conditional on concurrent delivery of the car and also expressly conditional on inspection and approval by X. The express condition can be waived by B if he so desires. If X refuses to inspect, and even if he inspects and states that the car is not worth $1,000, B can still make it A's duty to deliver by tendering $1,000 by June 1.[97]

If, in the foregoing case, either party should give notice repudiating the contract, and thereafter but before June 1 Engineer X should inspect the car and say it was worth $1,000, the other party could enforce the contract against the repudiator. Also, if one of the parties without excuse causes Engineer X to refuse to inspect, his action is a breach. If a party to a contract which is conditional on the granting of a "permit" causes the granting authority to refuse the "permit", an action for damages for breach of contract is maintainable.[98]

### § 84.  Acceptance Not Conditional, Even Though Grumbling or Accompanied by a Request or by a New Offer

An expression of acceptance is not prevented from being exact and unconditional by the fact that it is "grumbling," [1] or that the offeree makes some simultaneous "request"; [2] but it must appear that the "grumble" does not go so far as to make it doubtful that the expression is really one of assent, and that the offeree has assented to the offer even though the offeror shall refuse to comply with the "request." The following would be a valid acceptance: "I accept your offer as made; but I still insist that you are driving a very hard bargain." This has been described as a "grumbling assent." A plain acceptance of an offer to sell goods is not invalidated by adding, "Please ship tomorrow if possible." [3] Nor is it invalidated by a request that the contract already made shall be reduced to writing; [4] but the fact that a formal document is contemplated is some evidence of an intention not to be bound until the document is executed.

An acceptance is not invalidated by the fact that the offeree, in the same letter, makes an offer to buy additional goods, if it is

**97.**    See Pym v. Campbell, 6 El. & Bl. 370 (Q.B.1856), where the facts were similar to those stated above.

**2.**    **U.S.**—Netherwood v. Raymer, 253 F. 515 (D.C.Wis. 1918), affirmed 257 F. 284 (C.C.A.1919).

**Vt.**—Ackerman v. Carpenter, 29 A.2d 922, 113 Vt. 77 (1943).

**4.**    **N.C.**—Billings v. Wilby, 96 S.E. 50, 175 N.C. 571 (1918).

**Vt.**—Ackerman v. Carpenter, 29 A.2d 922, 113 Vt. 77 (1943).

clear that this new offer is wholly independent of the acceptance.[5] It is possible that this may be made clear even though the new offer is one the acceptance of which will make a new contract that is a substitute for the first one and will operate as a discharge.[6]

### § 86.  Attempts by the Offeree to Restate in His Acceptance the Terms of the Offer

If the purported acceptance attempts to restate the terms of the offer, such restatement must be accurate in every material respect.[8] It is not a variation if the offeree merely puts into words that which was already reasonably implied in the terms of the offer.[9] But the very form of words used by the offeror is material if the offeror so intended and so indicated in his offer; an acceptance using a different form makes no contract.[10] A variation in the substance of the offered terms is material, even though the variation is slight.[11]

The acceptance of an offer to sell land making no specifications or limitations as to title is not made conditional by including a provision requiring "marketable title." [12] By judicial decision and conveyancing custom, unless otherwise specified in the offer, the vendor impliedly promises "marketable title" and the conveyance of such title is an implied condition of the purchaser's duty. But an acceptance "subject to the approval of title by our attorneys" is not an operative acceptance, the specified condition being materially different from any that would be implied.[13] There are many cases in which an offeree has failed to make a valid acceptance by including some provision as to quality of title that is other than mere "marketable title." [14]

### § 87.  Attempts by the Offeree to State in His Acceptance the Legal Operation of the Agreement

There is a material difference between an acceptance that is conditional upon the inclusion of a term that is already contained in the offer by implication, and one that is conditional upon the

---

**5.** In Purrington v. Grimm, 76 A. 158, 83 Vt. 466 (1910), in a letter accepting an offer to sell goods, the buyer added: "Please send also a tapping bit and a reamer." The court held that this request did not make the acceptance conditional. It was merely a new offer to buy two additional items for a different price.

**10.** U.S.—Phoenix Iron & Steel Co. v. Wilkoff Co., 253 F. 165, 165 C.C. A. 65, 1 A.L.R. 1497 (C.C.A.6th, 1918).

In Poel v. Brunswick-Balke-Collender Co., 110 N.E. 619, 216 N.Y. 310 (1915), reargument denied 111 N.E. 1098, 216 N.Y. 771, the offeror promised delivery at stated times, and the offeree specified that delivery at those times should be "guaranteed." The latter form would much more certainly make delivery on time "of the essence" than would ordinary words of promise.

recognition of certain rights in the offeree these being rights that would in fact be created by an unconditional acceptance. Thus, if A offers to sell goods to B for $100 cash, an acceptance by B is not ineffective or conditional if worded thus, "I accept and will pay $100 cash on delivery." In the absence of proof of a different usage, A's offer to sell "for cash" means "for cash on delivery." If B's acceptance had been, "I accept on condition that I shall be privileged to resell the goods," the express condition is of a different kind and yet the result is probably the same—the acceptance is effective. When one buys goods of another, one of the legal effects of the sale is that the buyer is legally privileged to resell them, in the absence of an express agreement to the contrary. The acceptance, although conditional in form, would not be understood as adding anything new to the offer.

In expressing agreement, the parties usually think and speak in terms of action and other facts, not in terms of the resulting legal relations. Usually, then, they must take their chance as to what the courts will subsequently hold their legal relations to be. If the offeree departs from the words of action and fact, as used by the offeror, and accepts in terms of the resulting legal relations (as of course he may do if he wishes), he shows that he requires agreement on legal effects as well as on the action promised and that he does not assent to the taking of a chance on the matter.[16]

The expression in words of that which is already implied in the terms of the offer is not a variation therefrom; but the attempt to express, in advance, the legal operation of the words used in the offer may be a material variation. It is more than mere interpretation of those words. This is a matter as to which the subsequent conduct of the parties is usually decisive. The acceptance should not be held to be conditional if the offeror himself did not so treat it; and after action has been taken in the

16. On this ground the decision rendered in Phoenix Iron & Steel Co. v. Wilkoff Co., 253 F. 165, 1 A.L.R. 1497 (C.C.A.6th, 1918), may be sustained. The court said: "A decision that an absolute acceptance of an option followed in the same writing by a request or demand of something not within the option, and to which the optionee is not entitled, creates a contract, is not an authority for holding that one is created when the acceptance is on its face qualified by being made conditional on its being agreed that the optionee shall have a right not mentioned in the option if he would have had such right by virtue of law had he absolutely accepted the option, on the ground that in such a case the acceptance, though such is its character on its face, is in reality an absolute acceptance."

The court found, however, that the acceptance was conditional on inspection of the goods "before shipment," whereas by the law of sales the buyer had a right of inspection "before payment." Even so, the difference was not great; and the question remained whether the parties did not eliminate it by their subsequent action.

belief that agreement has been reached, a court should not over-weigh minor differences in form.

## § 88.  Mode of Acceptance can be Prescribed by the Offeror

In the making of any bargain, the party making the "offer" is proposing an exchange of equivalents.  To do this, he must state both sides of the bargain; he must indicate clearly that which he does or promises to do and also that which the offeree must do or promise to do.  Unless he does this, the offeree gets no power of acceptance.  To determine what these proposed equivalents are, we must interpret the words and acts of the offeror.  In order to accept the offer—to make the bargain and close the deal—the offeree must give the exact equivalent for which the offeror bargains.  If it is in any material respect different, there is no contract.  If the offeror asks for a promise in return, that very promise must be made; but he may or may not prescribe the words or acts by which that promise is expressed.

The offeror creates the power of acceptance; and he has full control over the character and extent of the power that he creates.  He can prescribe a single and exclusive mode of acceptance.  It makes no difference how unreasonable or difficult the prescribed mode may be, if the offeror clearly expresses, in the terms of the communicated offer itself, his intention to exclude all other modes of acceptance.  The more unreasonable the method appears, the less likely it will be that a court will interpret his offer as requiring it and the more clear and definite must be the expression of his intention in words.  Cases could be collected in great number holding that an attempt to accept was inoperative because it was not in the mode prescribed.  The offer may prescribe acceptance "by return mail," by telegraph, by doing a series of specific acts, by producing a stated result, by causing the receipt of a letter of notification.[17]

The offeror may suggest a mode of communication or other mode of acceptance without prescribing it as the exclusive mode. If he does this the suggested mode will be sufficient; but other modes that are reasonable under the circumstances will also be sufficient.  If no method is either suggested or prescribed, the acceptance must be in a manner that is reasonable, in consideration of the subject matter of the offer and the common usages of men.[18]

When one party solicits and receives an order or other expression of agreement from another, clearly specifying that there is to be no contract until ratification or assent by some officer or representative of the solicitor, the solicitation is not itself an offer; it is a request for an offer.[19]  The order that is given upon such a request is an offer, not an acceptance.  The soliciting party is not specifying a mode of acceptance when he specifies assent or ratification "at the home office" as a prerequisite.  The party complying with the request, by giving the order or otherwise, is making an offer; and in so doing he may or he may not prescribe the mode in which his offer shall be accepted. Under such circumstances as these, he seldom prescribes any mode, although he may expressly or tacitly assent to a mode suggested by the soliciting agent. It may be, therefore, that an uncommunicated assent "at the home office" will be sufficient; indeed, it may be that silence and absence of any notice that his order is rejected may be sufficient.[20]

## § 89. Counter Offers and Their Effect

In the process of negotiation concerning a specific subject matter, there may be offers and counter offers. One party proposes an agreement on terms that he states; the other replies proposing an agreement on terms that are different. Such a counter proposal is not identical with a rejection of the first offer, although it may have a similar legal operation in part. In order to deserve the name "counter offer," it must be so expressed as to be legally operative as an offer to the party making the prior proposal. It is not a counter offer unless it is itself an offer, fully complying with all the requirements that have been previously discussed. This does not mean that all of its terms must be fully expressed in a single communication; often they can be determined only by reference to many previous communications between the two parties. In this, a counter offer differs in no respect from original offers. But there is no counter offer, and no power of acceptance in the other party, unless there is a definite expression of willingness to contract on definitely ascertainable terms.

If the party who made the prior offer expresses his assent to the terms of the counter offer, a contract is thereby made on those terms.[23] The fact that the prior offer became inoperative is now immaterial; and the terms of that offer are also immaterial except in so far as they are incorporated by reference in the counter offer itself. Very frequently, they must be adverted to in order to determine what the counter offer is. Often, the acceptance of a counter offer is evidenced by the action of the offeree in proceeding with performance rather than by words.[24] Silence will not be an acceptance except under circumstances which would make it so operative in the case of an original offer.[25] If the original offeror proceeds with performance in consequence of the counter offer, he can maintain no action for breach of the terms that he had originally proposed.[26]

The terms "counter offer" and "conditional acceptance" are really no more than different forms of describing the same thing.

26.   **U.S.**—Iselin v. U. S., 46 S.Ct.
458, 271 U.S. 136, 70 L.Ed. 872
(1925).

They are the same in legal operation. Whether the word "offer" is used or not, a communication that expresses an acceptance of a previous offer on certain conditions or with specified variations empowers the original offeror to consummate the contract by an expression of his assent to the new conditions and variations. That is exactly what a counter offer does. Both alike, called by either name, terminate the power of acceptance of the previous offer. They might properly be discussed under a single heading, instead of under two headings as is done here.

## § 90. Power to Accept an Offer is Terminated by a Counter Offer or Conditional Acceptance

In addition to its effect in creating a power of acceptance, a counter offer ordinarily terminates the power to accept the previously made offer to which it is a "counter," or reply, in the negotiation.[27] The reasons given for this seem none too strong; but the rule has been established without meeting serious criticism. A counter offer has often been said to be a "rejection" of the prior offer; but this seems untrue in fact and should not be given as a reason for the rule just stated. A counter offer is usually only a step in the higgling process, the purpose of which is to obtain the most advantageous terms.

A counter offer differs from a rejection not only in its form and meaning but also in its legal effect. They may be alike in terminating the power to accept an offer previously made, as the courts have chosen to hold; but a counter offer creates a new power of acceptance, and a mere rejection does not.

It seems that there is some sort of feeling that an offeree should have but one chance, to accept or not to accept; he should take it or leave it. To the present writer, this does not carry much conviction. If the original offeror has been induced to contract with a third person, or otherwise to change his position, we have the basis for a better argument.

A question has been raised as to when a counter offer becomes operative to terminate the power of accepting the prior offer. As an offer it creates no power of acceptance until it is received, just as in the case of other offers. It is believed also that it should not terminate the power to accept a prior offer until it has been received; not until then can it produce any effect upon the original offeror's action or state of mind. So a counter offer, or even a flat rejection, started in the mail and on the way, should not invalidate an acceptance, by wire or other mode of communication, if the latter is received as soon as or prior to the counter offer or rejection. But since acceptances by mail or telegraph are in

27. **U.S.**—Beaumont v. Prieto, 39 S.Ct. 383, 249 U.S. 554, 63 L.Ed. 770 (1919); Staley Mfg. Co. v. Northern Coops., 168 F.2d 892 (C.C. A.8th, 1948); Hoffstot v. Dickinson, 166 F.2d 36 (C.C.A.4th, 1948).

certain cases held to be operative from the time they are started, the courts should protect the original offeror from being misled to his injury. If he receives a counter offer or rejection, and is led thereby to make a material change of position before receipt of the acceptance, the latter should be held to be inoperative as an acceptance, even though it was started before the counter offer was received. The acceptance in such a case might reasonably be given the effect of a renewed offer of the same contract.[28]

### § 92. Power of Acceptance Not Terminated by a Counter Offer if Either Offeror or Offeree so Prescribes

The power of accepting an offer is created by the act and will of the offeror. It is believed that, as its creator, he should be able to extend its existence as long as he desires. If he has led the offeree to believe that it will exist for a stated time, or for a reasonable time, he cannot terminate the power at an earlier time unless he causes notice of his revocation to be received by the offeree prior to acceptance, or unless he has expressly reserved the power to revoke without such notice. This rule of law is for the protection of the offeree. But the rules of law, heretofore discussed, to the effect that the power of acceptance is terminated by a counter offer or a rejection are solely for the protection of the offeror. The offeror can, in the beginning, cause the power to accept his offer to continue for a time that would otherwise be regarded as very unreasonable. Likewise, he can extend the legal operation of his offer by renewing it from time to time. There seems to be no good reason why he should not be able to prevent the offeree's power of acceptance from being terminated by a counter offer or rejection. Suppose that in making an offer he says: "This offer shall continue to be open for your acceptance until I notify you to the contrary, even though you may reject it daily or send me numerous counter proposals." This should be given the effect that is intended.

Likewise, the offeree may well be held to have the power to prevent his counter offer (or even a rejection) from terminating his power of acceptance. Suppose he should say: "I am still con·sidering your offer; but meantime, I am now willing to buy the property you offer if you will reduce your price by $500." There is no reason why this should lead the offeror into a change of

28. The American Law Institute has adopted a rule with which the above text is in harmony. Restatement, Contracts, § 39, is as follows: "Rejection by mail or telegram does not destroy the power of acceptance until received by the offeror, but limits the power so that a letter or telegram of acceptance started after the sending of the rejection is only a counter-offer unless the acceptance is received by the offeror before he receives the rejection." A decision in substantial harmony with this is E. Frederics Inc. v. Felton Beauty Sup. Co., 198 S.E. 324, 58 Ga.App. 320 (1938).

position, or why it should operate to terminate the power of accepting the original offer still under consideration.[31]  The same result should obtain if the offeree says: "As at present advised, I must reject your offer; but circumstances may change, and I may later consider your offer again."

No one doubts that one who has made an offer can disregard or refuse the counter offer, and by a return communication make his original offer once more fully operative.[32]  There seems to be no sufficient reason for holding that he has no power to produce this continuing result by his expression of such an intention in advance.

### § 93.   Inquiries and Separate Offers Distinguished from Counter Offers

Just as "requests" and "suggestions" do not turn an otherwise absolute acceptance into a conditional one, so too they do not constitute counter offers.  One reason for this is that they are not themselves offers of any kind.  The offeree writes: "Is this your lowest price?" or "If I doubled the amount, I suppose you would make the price lower"; [33] or "You may send me 800 tons as offered by you, but I trust that you will make it 1200 tons at 68 shillings." [34]  In these cases, there is no counter offer.  In the first two there is a mere request for information as to possible lower prices, no power of acceptance being created in the original offeror.  They do not affect the power to accept the offer previously made.  In the last case, there is a valid acceptance of the offer of 800 tons; and the contract thereby consummated is not affected by the fact that the acceptor makes an additional offer to buy 400 more tons at 68 s. if the seller will accept settlement at that rate for the first 800 tons also.

An offer is not a "counter offer" if it is so expressed as to show that it deals with a different subject matter, so that the contract that is proposed is not a substitute for the one proposed by the prior offer.  A offers to sell Blackacre to B, and the latter replies, "I am considering your offer; meantime I offer to sell Whiteacre

---

31.   No decision on this point has been found; but the American Law Institute has adopted a rule in harmony with the above text.  Restatement, Contracts, § 38, reads: "A counter-offer by the offeree, relating to the same matter as the original offer, is a rejection of the original offer, unless the offeror in his offer, or the offeree in his counter-offer states that in spite of the counter-offer the original offer shall not be terminated."

33.   Va.—First Nat. Exch. Bank of Roanoke v. Roanoke Oil Co., 192 S.E. 764, 169 Va. 99 (1937), inquiry as to a possible better offer.

Eng.—Stevenson, Jaques, & Co. v. McLean, 5 Q.B.D. 346 (1880), offeree inquired whether the seller would allow a period of credit.

34.   See Tinn v. Hoffmann & Co., 29 L.T. (N.S.) 271 (1873).

to you for $5,000." B has made no counter offer, as that term is used by the courts and in this treatise. The same would be true if B had replied, "I accept your offer of Blackacre. I now offer to sell it back to you, along with my adjoining farm Whiteacre, for the sum of $10,000."

## § 94. Effect of Rejection of an Offer

The power of acceptance created by an ordinary offer is terminated by a communicated rejection. This is true even though a definite time was given by the offeror for considering his offer and the rejection is before that time has expired. When the offeror receives a notice of rejection, he is very likely to change his position in reliance thereon; one aspect of this is that he will not think it necessary to send a notice of revocation, in those cases in which he has power to revoke. This has led to the rule that a definite rejection terminates the offeree's power to accept.

This effect should not be given to a rejection, if it is contrary to the offeror's own expressed intention and desire. In making an offer, the offeror has control of its terms and the time and mode of acceptance; he can create such a power of acceptance as he pleases. The rule that a rejection terminates power is solely for the protection of the offeror; and there seems to be no sufficient reason for terminating the power of acceptance against his will. Suppose that an offer is made thus: this offer will be left open for acceptance for 30 days, without regard to any rejection, conditional acceptance, or counter offer. After a rejection by the offeree, he would still have power to accept during the unexpired portion of the 30 days.[35] The offeror's own statement would tend to make the offeree less ready to give due deliberation before putting up rejections and counter offers as trial balloons.

A rejection is a definite statement that it is the offeree's intention not to accept the offer. There is no rejection if the offeree merely writes: "Is this the best offer that you will make?" or, "Please wire whether you would allow an additional month's credit";[36] or, "I am holding your offer under advisement to see whether war will break out."[37] A statement that "at present I

---

35. The American Law Institute supports this rule with respect to counter-offers, and seems to mean to do so as to rejections also, since a counter-offer is said to be a "rejection." Restatement, Contracts, § 38, reads thus: "A counter-offer by the offeree, relating to the same matter as the original offer, is a rejection of the original offer, unless the offeror in his offer, or the offeree in his counter-offer states that in spite of the counter-offer the original offer shall not be terminated." Comment *b* states: "An offeror may state in his offer that it shall continue for a stated time in any event and that meanwhile he will be glad to receive counter-offers." The phrase "in any event" is broad enough to include a rejection.

must reject your offer, but will continue to consider it" should not be held to be a rejection.

At an auction sale it is not a rejection of a bid for the auctioneer to delay the fall of the hammer and to ask for higher bids. If a higher bid is actually made, however, the first bidder would be reasonable in supposing that his bid is no longer operative, whether on a theory of rejection or for other reasons.

When bids are solicited and are sent in for simultaneous opening, or for consideration all together, a bidder should usually be held reasonable in supposing that his bid is rejected as soon as one of the competing bids is accepted. But a mere notice of acceptance may not have any operation in this latter case, for the reason that a formal written contract is contemplated; and it has been held that each bid remains open for acceptance for a reasonable time so long as no contract with a competing bidder has actually been consummated.[38]

In order to terminate the power of acceptance, a rejection must be communicated to the offeror; it is not operative on mailing, or on starting a messenger, or on saying to a secretary: "draw a letter of rejection at once, sign it in my name, and mail it." The rule as to the effect of a rejection is for the protection of the offeror; and it should go no further than is necessary to attain this purpose. If a rejection is mailed and thereafter the offeree sends a telegram: "I accept your offer; disregard letter of rejection mailed this morning," the acceptance should be held to be effective and the rejection ineffective in case the telegram is received before the letter is received.

On the other hand, if after mailing a rejection the offeree changes his mind and mails a letter of acceptance, there should be held to be no contract in case the letter of rejection is received first.[39] This is so, in spite of the rule that an acceptance by post is effective on mailing, and even though the acceptance is mailed before the rejection is received by the offeror. The offeree, in such a case, has reason to know that the rejection is likely to be received first and to cause the offeror to change both his mind and his position.

---

**39.** This is supported by the American Law Institute, Restatement, Contracts, § 39, which reads: "Rejection by mail or telegram does not destroy the power of acceptance until received by the offeror, but limits the power so that a letter or telegram of acceptance started after the sending of the rejection is only a counter-offer unless the acceptance is received by the offeror before he receives the rejection." No doubt a similar result should obtain even though a letter of acceptance is posted first and is followed by a telegram of rejection that is received ahead of the letter.

# CHAPTER 4

# INDEFINITENESS AND MISTAKE IN EXPRESSION

## § 95. Vagueness and Indefiniteness of Terms [1]

A court cannot enforce a contract unless it can determine what it is. It is not enough that the parties think that they have made a contract; they must have expressed their intentions in a manner that is capable of understanding. It is not even enough that they have actually agreed, if their expressions are not such that the court can determine what the terms of that agreement are. Vagueness of expression, indefiniteness and uncertainty as to any of the essential terms of an agreement, may prevent the creation of an enforceable contract.[2]

Generalizations like the foregoing no doubt render some service in the administration of the law; but they may result in serious injustice unless they are applied with common sense in the light of much experience. Vagueness, indefiniteness, and uncertainty are matters of degree, with no absolute standard for comparison. It must be remembered that all modes of human expression are defective and inadequate. Every student of language knows this to be true of words. Every good dictionary shows that most important words have several, or even many, meanings; and these meanings themselves must be expressed in other words that are equally difficult of definition. Other modes of expression have like uncertainty; actions may, as the old adage avers, speak louder than words, but it is often not true that they express intention with greater definiteness and certainty.

143

A promise that is too uncertain in terms for possible enforcement is an illusory promise; but to determine whether or not it is an "illusion" one must consider the degree and effect of its uncertainty and indefiniteness.[3]

Vagueness and indefiniteness of language may be such as to indicate clearly that the parties do not themselves understand that they are contracting. In such cases they are merely engaged in the inoperative process of preliminary negotiation.[4]

In considering expressions of agreement, the court must not hold the parties to some impossible, or ideal, or unusual standard. It must take language as it is and people as they are. All agreements have some degree of indefiniteness and some degree of uncertainty. In spite of its defects, language renders a practical service. In spite of ignorance as to the language they speak and write, with resulting error and misunderstanding, people must be held to the promises they make. The court must not be overly fearful of error; it must not be pedantic or meticulous in interpretation of expressions.

Although courts have often said that they do not make contracts for the parties,[5] it is nevertheless true that in the process of interpretation and construction both court and jury must make findings in doubtful cases and cannot avoid the occasional enforcement of a contract some of the terms and effects of which were not in the minds of the parties.

If the parties have concluded a transaction in which it appears that they intend to make a contract, the court should not frustrate their intention if it is possible to reach a fair and just result, even though this requires a choice among conflicting meanings and the filling of some gaps that the parties have left.[6] Their expressions should be interpreted *ut res magis valeat*.[7] The application of such a rule as this is believed to come nearer to attaining the purpose of the contracting parties than any other, to give more business satisfaction and to make contract a workable instrument.[8] As between merchants, their usages and customary modes of expression and of doing business must be taken into account; their expressions often leave conscious gaps to be filled in this manner.[9]

An order for 20,000 woolen cardigans was accepted "subject to government restrictions as to sales and war clause." This was assented to by the buyer; and 3,000 cardigans were delivered,

6.    There is an excellent discussion of this problem in Mantell v. International Plastic Harmonica Corp., 55 A.2d 250, 141 N.J. Eq. 379, 173 A.L.R. 1185 (1947), where an agreement between the producer of a new invention and a distributor left the price to be paid by the latter subject to later determination in large degree by the producer.

1,200 being paid for. Thereupon the seller, without any justifying reason arising from war, refused further delivery. The court held that, even though both parties believed that a contract existed and had rendered performances under it, no contract had been consummated for the reason that no "war clause" had ever been agreed upon.[10] The evidence showed no "usual" or "customary" war clause to which the words might refer. The court's reasoning should not be accepted.[11] The order and the conditional acceptance made no contract; but no sufficient reason appears for refusing to make reasonable "implications" in order to make effective what the parties themselves believed, after a large performance had taken place.

An agreement that is evidenced by a signed written document may not state all the terms that are agreed upon. Even though the writing may not itself clearly state price, subject matter, or conditions, other evidence may be sufficient to fill the gaps and to remove doubts. The writing may incorporate other documents by reference or may indicate a method by which to determine the unstated terms that were actually agreed on.[12]

### § 96. Time of Performance Indefinite—Promises of "Permanent" Employment

It is characteristic of men to make offers and agreements without specifying a time for acceptance or a time for the rendition of performance; and yet it may be clear that they intend to create a power of acceptance and a valid contract. In such cases it is evident that they do not regard any specific point of time as essential; and usually acceptance is given or performance rendered without the occurrence of any dispute. When such a dispute does arise, it is necessary for the court to decide whether the power of acceptance was to last forever, or if not for how long; also, to decide whether the time for performance was left to the discretion of the one promising to render it. The result generally reached is that the time is neither unlimited nor discretionary. Acceptance must be within a "reasonable time" and the promised performance must be rendered within a "reasonable time." [15]

Parties often make a bilateral agreement for the sale of goods at a specified price or for the rendition of services at specified wages, fixing a time for delivery of the goods or rendition of the services but not fixing a date for making the money payment. In such cases the gap is so readily supplied from general usage or the previous course of dealing that no uncertainty is perceived and both parties are bound. In the absence of agreement or course of dealing to the contrary, the price is payable on delivery, and wages are payable at the end of a period of actual service, a period that is indicated either by the terms of agreement or by custom.

Simple agreements for the sale of goods are frequently made without expressing in words any time for either delivery or payment. Seldom will it be held that this makes it too uncertain for enforcement. Usage and custom will generally furnish a basis for determining whether the transaction is a cash sale or a credit sale, including the length of the credit period; and the finding is most likely to be that delivery is promised within a reasonable time.[16] Under a contract to sell goods still to be manufactured, a reasonable time for delivery must take into account such factors affecting performance as the seller's factory capacity, the extent of prior orders to be filled, and the availability of labor and materials.[17]

It appears, therefore, that a contract is usually not too indefinite for enforcement merely because it fixes no time for an agreed performance. If that performance is something that is simple and can readily be rendered at any one or more of many moments of time, the court will infer that the parties have agreed upon performance within a reasonable time. Of course, this standard is itself indefinite; what is reasonable is a question of fact and a matter on which opinions will differ. Nevertheless, it is a standard that is practically workable and one that results in satisfactory solutions.

In certain kinds of contracts, this reasoning may not be applicable. Thus, where one party promises to make a loan of money to another, the promise is hardly enforceable unless the length of the period of credit is agreed on.[18] The borrower would probably not be satisfied with a loan repayable "on demand"; and usually there would be no data upon which to determine a reasonable time. If such data exist, indicating the probable intention of the parties, the evidence thereof should be received.[19]

## § 97. Indefiniteness of Price—Money as a Commodity

In the process of negotiating an agreement, a term that is most frequently left indefinite and to be settled by future agreement, or by some other specified method, is the price in money—the compensatory exchange for the subject matter of purchase. This is true both of agreements for the rendition of service and of those for the purchase and sale of goods.[30] If the parties provide a practicable, objective method for determining this price or compensation, not leaving it to the future will of the parties themselves, there is no such indefiniteness or uncertainty as will prevent the agreement from being an enforceable contract. The same is true if they agree upon payment of a "reasonable" price or compensation. There are many cases, however, in which it is clear that the parties have not agreed upon a "reasonable price," and also have not prescribed a practicable method of determination. Where this is true, the agreement is too indefinite and uncertain for enforcement.[31] The court should be slow to come to this conclusion if it is convinced that the parties themselves meant to make a "contract" and to bind themselves to render a future performance. Many a gap in terms can be filled, and should be, with a result that is consistent with what the parties said and that is more just to both than would be a refusal of enforcement.[32]

The "subject matter" of an agreement for the sale of goods is two-fold—the goods and the price; the price is as much the subject matter of agreement, and as important a part, as are the goods. The "subject matter" of a contract for the rendition of services is both the labor and the wages. These agreements are for the exchange of two performances, agreed to be of equal value, quid pro quo. When parties agree upon an exchange of goods or services for money, they are putting an agreed valuation, in terms of money, upon the goods or services; but, whether they realize it or not, they are also putting an agreed valuation upon the money in terms of goods or services. There have been long periods of time during which people have thought of the dollar, or the pound, or the franc, as if it were a mere "unit" incapable of fluctuation. Two world wars, with their astronomical expenditure and waste and the resulting "inflation," have taught most of us better. These so-called "units" are indeed a convenient "medium of exchange"—of exchanging goods and services for other goods and services; but this "medium" of exchange is itself a subject of exchange, one that will determine the amount of other goods and services that the receiver of the money may in the future enjoy. If, therefore, the court can not determine how much money the parties have agreed to exchange for specified goods, the agreement is no more enforceable as a contract than it would be if the court can not determine the amount or kind of goods to be exchanged. It is true, however, that parties are much more likely to leave the "price" of goods or services open and unstated than to leave so the amount of the goods or services; and the apparent gap can be more readily and justly filled by recourse to the "market" for the goods or services, or to the parties' own "course of dealing," or to a multitude of factors called "reasonableness."

---

32.   A. M. Webb & Co. v. Miller Co., 176 F.2d 678 (C.A.3d, 1949), 157 F.2d 865 (C.C.A.3d, 1946); Shayeb v. Holland, 73 N.E.2d 731, 321 Mass. 429 (1947), lessee's option to buy the land specifically enforced, though no price was named, the court finding "reasonable price" by implication. The decision in the latter of these two cases was based largely on the fact that the lessee had made valuable improvements as the lease expressly permitted. The case is an excellent one.

In the following cases, the agreement as to price was held too indefinite for enforcement: a promise to divide profits "upon a very liberal basis"; [33] to pay "good wages" to a teacher; [34] to pay "not exceeding $300 per week"; [35] to pay "a fair share of my profits" in addition to a specified salary; [36] to pay an amount "commensurate with the earnings of the company" in addition to salary; [37] to pay "a satisfactory amount." [38] In cases like these, however, it must be borne in mind that after a part performance has been received, a just compensation must be paid even if the agreement is indefinite as to price. There are cases in which the court has been much more willing to find the meaning "reasonable compensation" in language that seems fully as indefinite as in the cases just cited.[39]

## § 98.   Agreed Methods of Determining the Price or Amount

An agreement is not unenforceable for lack of definiteness of price or amount if the parties specify a practicable method by which the amount can be determined by the court without any new expression by the parties themselves.[44] An agreement to sell shares of stock that is commonly bought and sold on a stock exchange is enforceable if the price is agreed to be the "market price" at a certain time on that exchange. If there is a "market price" for the goods or services that are the subject of agreement, it is sufficient that the agreement is for payment at the market price.[45] Sometimes, however, there is no market or "market price" that can be established by proof; but "market" is a very flexible term and may cover a wide extent of territory and include many small shops or wide highways.

It is sufficient if the agreement provides that the price shall be the amount that arbitrators or that X, a specific third person, shall fix as a fair price.[46] The agreed price is sufficiently definite if it is "the rate that A paid to B" for similar goods or services.[47] If it is a specified proportion of the amount for which the buyer shall thereafter sell the goods to a third person, there is some doubt on the score of indefiniteness.[48] If the goods are delivered and are in fact resold at a price, the indefiniteness is removed; but if the seller refuses to deliver and the buyer makes no contract for resale to a third person it may be difficult to determine the price to be paid. Even in the latter case, however, it may be possible to determine with a sufficient degree of accuracy the amount that the buyer could have obtained on resale by the use of ordinary skill and diligence.

## § 99.   Reasonable Price—Quasi Contract Remedy after Performance

An agreement to pay a "fair price" for land or goods or services may be regarded as identical with a promise to pay a "reasonable price." If such is the accepted meaning, the agreement is sufficiently definite for enforcement.  It is obvious that a contract to pay a reasonable price, or reasonable compensation for service, leaves plenty of opportunity for difference of opinion and dispute.  It can not properly be assumed that only one price or wage is reasonable under the particular circumstances of any case.  Reasonableness is a matter of opinion; and opinions differ, even though they are equally honest and well informed.  A promise to pay a reasonable price or wages is, in its legal effect, a promise to pay a sum that a court or jury may determine in case of dispute.  This practically always entails the payment of costs of suit, also, although the court should use some discretion.  Interest, as damages for delay in payment, may in many cases be justly held to begin only after the amount due has been liquidated by a verdict or finding of fact;  but no hard and fast rule to this effect should be laid down.

How much is reasonable in any particular case is a question of fact, not one of law.  There is no rule of law by which the amount can be deductively determined.  Like other inferences of fact, however, the evidence from which it must be drawn may be so clear and convincing as to justify the court in withdrawing it from the jury.  It is then generally said that the question is "one of law for the court."

After goods have actually been delivered and accepted, or services actually rendered and received, the defendant is bound to make reasonable compensation therefor, whether the agreement under which the benefit was received was too indefinite for enforcement or not.  It then becomes unnecessary to determine whether the defendant in reality promised to pay a reasonable price.  If he did so promise, the court is enforcing his express promise.  If he did not, the duty to pay is described as quasi contract;  but it is identical in result.[54]

In case no performance has been received by the defendant, a quasi contractual recovery is not available;  and if the court gives a remedy for breach it must be because it finds the agreement of the parties sufficiently definite for enforcement.

## § 100.  Uncertainty of Subject Matter to be Exchanged for Price

It is not always the price in money that is left uncertain in an agreement; sometimes it is that for which the price is to be paid. If no method is agreed upon for rendering this subject matter sufficiently definite for enforcement, the agreement must nearly always fail of legal effect;[55] it is not customary for courts to fill the gap by finding that a "reasonable" amount of goods or land or labor has been agreed upon as the exchange for the money.  It should not be said, however, that such a finding may not be just and true in some cases.[56]

If the agreement expresses the subject matter of exchange in such a way that it can be identified or definitely determined by the court, it is enough for enforcement.  If a method of identification and determination is agreed upon, such that its application produces a reasonable degree of definiteness, the same is true.[57]  If for $5,000, paid or promised, A promises to convey to B any motor car in A's stock, there is a valid contract.  Of course, it is a condition precedent to A's duty of immediate transfer that B shall make his selection, but the uncertainty will be removed by the method agreed upon, that is, the exercise of B's power of selection.[58]

A promise by A, for a sufficient consideration, to deliver to B all the coal that B needs to run his factory for a year, is not invalid even though this leaves to B the option of not running his factory at all or of running it at such a rate as he honestly believes it is most beneficial to run it.[59]  An employment agreement by which A is hired to keep B's books is not rendered unenforceable by the fact that B may vary his books and the method of keeping them.  Contracts for the sale of the "entire output" of a mine, factory, farm, or other business are not too indefinite for enforcement, even though the producer has a freedom of choice in determining that output.[60]

## § 101.   Effect of Subsequent Action by the Parties

Even though the parties have expressed an agreement in terms so vague and indefinite as to be incapable of interpretation with a reasonable degree of certainty, they may cure this defect by their subsequent conduct and by their own practical interpretation.[65]  If the parties have used such indefinite language as to leave it uncertain whether or not they intend to close the deal and make a contract, subsequently proceeding with or accepting performance under it may remove the uncertainty.  If the expressions used leave the subject matter, or the price or the time or any other element of the performance incapable of determination, the rendition of a part or all of the performance may make clear the meaning that should be given to those expressions.[66]

Even if the subsequent conduct of the parties does not make clear the meaning of their original expressions, it may be such as to create a new and definite tacit contract.  This new tacit contract may be enforceable in itself without regard to whether it is identical with the earlier expressions of agreement.  If it is

59.    Ill.—Minnesota   Lbr.   Co.   v.
Whitebreast Coal Co., 43 N.E. 774,
160 Ill. 85, 31 L.R.A. 529 (1896).

identical, well and good; if it is not identical, it is nevertheless enforceable, and the earlier inconsistent agreement is discharged by a substituted agreement. Just as parties may replace a definite verbal contract with another and different verbal contract, so may they replace one with another and different tacit contract.[67] Actual performances under a general indefinite arrangement may amount to no more than a series of separate transactions, valid in themselves, but not clearing up the indefiniteness as to time, price, or amount so as to make the general arrangement an enforceable contract.[68]

There are many cases in which an agreement fixes no time limit and provides that it shall be terminable at the will of either party. This is not an enforceable contract when made. Nevertheless, if performance as specified is rendered under it, a valid obligation to pay the specified compensation is created.[71] The rendition of the service is the exercise of a power and creates a contract, that may be either unilateral or bilateral. Previously, it is clear, there was no contract and nothing to be made clear and definite by any process of interpretation.

## § 102. Subsequent Action may Create a Quasi Contract

Even if the subsequent action of the parties fails to clarify an indefinite agreement sufficiently to make it enforceable, it may nevertheless confer such an uncompensated benefit upon one of the parties as to put him under a non-contractual obligation of paying the reasonable value of such benefit. This obligation is not contractual, because it is essentially different from any actual agreement of the parties. It is limited to the duty of making payment at a reasonable rate for value actually received.

## § 103. Mistake—Difficulty and Complexity of the Subject

The subject of mistake is one of the most difficult in the law. This is because men make so many mistakes, of so many different kinds, with so many varying effects. To err is indeed human. It would be a very damaging mistake to suppose that we know just what to do and say as to every mistake, or that we can lay down safe and easy rules and generalizations based upon our judicial experience. Nevertheless, it is by this experience that the future must be guided; and to guide the future requires some kind of classification and generalization, broad or narrow, by which each new case can perhaps be placed and determined.

Because of this complexity and difficulty, it is necessary to devote a separate chapter to the subject of Mistake. At this point, there will be stated only enough to prevent a reader of the chapter dealing with Offer and Acceptance and Mutual Assent from being misled, and to give him some tentative direction as to such supposed requirements as a "meeting of the minds" and as to "objective" and "subjective" theories of contract. Even the doing of this much requires some repetition. The citation and discussion of specific cases will mainly be postponed to the subsequent Chapters 27–29 on Mistake. In those chapters will be found a discussion of the many varieties of mistake and of the several remedies that are available.

In the process of coming to an agreement, mistakes are frequently made, either by one or by both of the parties. If both are mistaken, the mistakes that they make are seldom identical. Accurate analysis will show that this is true, even in those cases where the court declares that the mistake was "mutual."

One party may be mistaken as to what the other party said— the words and other expressions that he used. Or, he may be mistaken as to what the other party intended to convey; although he knows the exact words and expressions used, he gives to these words and expressions a meaning different from that which the other party gave to them. The meanings given by the two parties may not only be different from each other, one of them or both of them may be different from that which would be given by some third person, or by a reasonably prudent and intelligent third person.

Again, although no mistake is made as to either the words used or the meaning given to them, there may be a mistake as to some factor that was influential in inducing assent. One party may be mistaken as to the identity or the solvency of the other party, or as to the correct addition of certain figures used in determining the amount of a bid, or as to market values.

Again, one party may know, or have reason to know, the fact that the other party is laboring under a mistake. He may know or have reason to know the meaning that is given to words and expressions by the other party. He may be negligent in choosing his own words and expressions, or in failing to know the meaning given to words and expressions by the other party.

Finally, the mistake may be discovered and notice given before there has been any material change of position; or the change of position may have occurred before discovery or notice.

The operative effect of the mistake and the kind of relief to be given will depend upon factors such as those listed above.

### § 104.  Mistake as to the Words Used, or as to the Meaning Given to Words and Expressions

In coming to an agreement, the expressions of the parties may be wholly oral, in which case mistakes may arise out of faulty enunciation or faulty hearing. If a seller offers to sell a horse for $165, and the offeree hears the offer as $65, the words "I accept your offer" will not consummate a contract.[74] No one would doubt this result if the words of acceptance had been "I accept your offer at $65." Defective enunciation can be avoided; but few people are so well trained in expression as to avoid it and it is seldom that they can be charged with "negligence" because of it. Defective hearing also can sometimes be avoided, and no doubt careful persons will generally avoid mistakes by realizing that they may not have heard distinctly and correctly; but even more seldom will they be charged with "negligence" for not avoiding mistakes due to the inaccurate hearing of words. It is always a mere question of fact, however, whether the words were not correctly heard and also whether one of the parties did not have reason to know what the words were and how they were heard.

In the case of a contract that has been reduced to writing, there is less probability of a mistake as to the words in fact used and a greater probability that the mistake, if made, will be held to be negligent. Most such mistakes are made by reason of signing a document without reading it, or after a hasty and inaccurate reading.[75] In one case, however, an agent drew up a written building contract in duplicate, causing the builder to promise to erect the building for $33,500 and the owner to promise to pay $23,000 for erecting it.[76] If either party was negligent in this case, the two parties were equally negligent.

A much more common form of mistake is as to the meaning of words and expressions. Both parties know with accuracy the words used but understand them differently. Either party may inadvertently or ignorantly use words that by common usage do not express his meaning and intention. Either party may inadvertently or ignorantly give to another's words a meaning that the other did not intend or that may not accord with common usage. In such a case there is a misunderstanding of the terms used in making a contract, a misunderstanding that prevents a "meeting of the minds", that is, prevents a true agreement. Nevertheless, there may be a valid contract in spite of such a lack of true agreement.

When two parties have reduced their agreement to writing, using the words that each of them consciously intends to use, it is often not a sufficient ground for declaring that the agreement is

---

74.   Ill.—Rupley v. Daggett, 74 Ill. 351 (1874).

Mass.—Neel v. Lang, 127 N.E. 512, 236 Mass. 61 (1920).

75.   In the chapter on Mistake there is a section dealing at some length with cases of this kind.

76.   Mass.—Vickery v. Ritchie, 88 N. E. 835, 202 Mass. 247, 26 L.R.A.,N. S., 810 (1909).

void or subject to cancellation by the court that the parties subsequently gave different meanings to the agreed language, or even that they gave different meanings thereto at the time that the agreement was expressed. If the meaning that either one of them gave to the words was the only reasonable one under the existing circumstances, the other party is bound by that meaning and there is a contract accordingly.[78] If one of the parties gave a meaning to the language that is not the only reasonable one under the circumstances, and the other expressed his assent knowing that the first party was giving it this meaning, that is the meaning that the court should adopt, and there is a contract accordingly. But if the parties had materially different meanings, and neither one knew or had reason to know the meaning of the other, there is no contract.[79]

Raffles v. Wichelhaus is a well-known English case that has been very much discussed. A buyer and a seller made what appeared to be an agreement for the purchase and sale of a stated amount of Surat cotton to arrive by the ship Peerless from Bombay. It happened that there were two ships then at Bombay, both named the Peerless. The buyer knew of only one of these ships; and depended on the arrival of the cotton on that ship in October. The seller knew only of the other ship, the one on which he shipped the cotton; and he asserted a breach of contract when the buyer refused to receive the cotton on its arrival in December. The court held that no contract existed and that the plaintiff had no right to damages.[83]

The decision in this case is clearly correct; and it would be the same if the parties had been reversed. No convincing reason was shown for charging either party with the loss or for penalizing one for the benefit of the other. The possibility of dividing the loss has not been recognized at common law. In this case the parties used identical words, equally well descriptive of the two ships; but by those words they meant different things, a fact that neither one of them had reason to know. Each one used his words with reasonable prudence and according to the common usage of men.

### § 105. Mistake in Transmission of Messages

A misunderstanding as to the terms of an agreement has frequently been caused by an error in the transmission of a tele-

**79.** Some of the better known cases so holding are:

**Cal.**—Rovegno v. Defferari, 40 Cal. 459 (1871).

**Mass.**—Kyle v. Kavanagh, 103 Mass. 356, 4 Am.Rep. 560 (1869).

**Eng.**—Raffles v. Wichelhaus, 2 Hurl. & C. 906 (1864).

It is believed that Restatement, Contracts, § 71, is substantially in harmony with the sections on Mistake in the present treatise.

gram. A telegraphic offer that has been correctly written out by the offeror is handed to the telegraph clerk. Because of the negligence of such a clerk, the terms of the offer are changed so that a materially different offer is delivered to the offeree.

If the offeree knows or has reason to know that such a change has occurred, he has no power to bind the offeror by an acceptance of the offer as delivered. The change may be such as to make it unintelligible to a reasonable man; or it may be such that the proposal is one that no reasonable man would make. Thus, the price at which goods are offered for sale may be so greatly reduced that a reasonable man would suspect error. The offeree is not permitted to "snap up" such an offer.[87]

The troublesome case is the one in which the change is such that the offeree has no reason to know that it has been made. The offer as delivered is one that he reasonably believes to be the one that the offeror intends to make. In one case, lath were offered for sale at $2.10 per thousand. The telegraph clerk left off the 10; and the offer as delivered read $2 per thousand. The court held that acceptance made a contract at $2, binding the offeror to deliver.[88] This is supported by a considerable number of cases in the United States;[89] but there are very well-considered cases to the contrary.[90]

The reason for such a conflict in decision is that there are two innocent sufferers from the fault of another, and the courts have felt it necessary to choose one of them to bear the entire loss. The truth is that usually there is no convincing reason for making such a choice. Sometimes it is said that one of the parties has "assumed the risk" of telegraphic mistake, this one being either the one who sent the telegram in question, or the one who first used the telegraph, or the one who suggested that it be used.[91] More often than not, such a statement as this is a mere statement of the result reached rather than the reason for reaching it. Again, it may be said that the sender of the telegram has chosen the telegraph company as his agent, thus making it appear that some general rule of agency can be deductively applied. While it is true that the sender of a telegram knows that it must be translated by the clerks into a telegraphic code and back into words, with some possibility of error in the process, this is hardly enough to establish a relation of agency. Assuredly, the sender does not hold out the telegraph clerk as his agent with power to contract in his behalf. Nor is the clerk his servant. The telegraph company is a public servant, much like the post office (if not identical with it as in England), under com-

88. Me.—Ayer v. Western Union
Tel. Co., 10 A. 495, 79 Me. 493, 1
Am.St.Rep. 353 (1887).

pulsion to serve all comers and to bear the responsibility that accompanies public service.[92]

Perhaps a reason for choosing the sender of the telegram instead of the receiver to take the first impact of the loss can be found in actual business practices and mores or in business convenience.[93]  In some of the cases, it has appeared as a fact that the sender felt bound to supply the goods at the mistaken price, or at least that he made a settlement with the receiver of the telegram and then brought suit against the telegraph company. Even though the court held that the sender of the telegram was not bound by the incorrectly delivered offer, in one case it was further held that the settlement was a reasonable effort to avoid losses and that the telegraph company had reason to foresee that such a settlement would be made.[94]

### § 106.  Objective and Subjective Theories

There has been a good deal of discussion with respect to two so-called theories of contract, known as the "objective theory" and the "subjective theory."  By the first, it is argued that a valid contract is created by agreement in expression, the subjective intention of the parties being immaterial.  By the second, it is argued that a contract is not created unless there is agreement in intention, properly expressed.  The law of contract can not be explained by either of these theories standing alone.

The cases demonstrate plainly enough that a person may be held bound in accordance with his expressions as understood by others, even though his own intention and meaning were different.[98]  This has led courts and writers to adopt the so-called "objective" theory, and to say that parties are bound by what they say and not by what they think, or even to say that they are bound in accordance with the meaning that reasonable third parties would give to their expressions without regard to the meaning given by either of the parties themselves.  The actual decisions do not justify a statement that goes so far.[99]

In earlier times a so-called "will theory" of contract was generally held.  Contract is made by the voluntary agreement of men and not by the state.  A man is not bound by a contractual duty unless he willed it so.  Out of some theory like this came such terms as "meeting of the minds", or the equivalent phrases in Latin aggregatio mentium and consensus ad idem.  When these phrases, applied with logical severity, produce a result that

---

98.   Illustrative cases are:
Cal.—Brant v. California Dairies, 48 P.2d 13, 4 Cal.2d 128 (1935).

Mass.—Mansfield v. Hodgdon, 17 N. E. 544, 147 Mass. 304 (1888).

Mo.—Embry v. Hargadine-McKittrick D. G. Co., 105 S.W. 777, 127 Mo. App. 383 (1907).

does not square with business mores and the prevailing ideas of justice, they must be disregarded as inapplicable and untrue. Nevertheless, they are in very common use and we can not altogether throw them aside.

In the process of making a contract, the actual and proved intent of either of the parties should not be disregarded, unless he knowingly or negligently has misled another person to his injury. If no other person has been so misled, it should make no difference what expressions would have been chosen by other reasonable or intelligent users of language or what meaning the expressions actually used would have conveyed to such third persons. Of course, the actual intent of the one party and the actual understanding of the other are matters of fact that may be difficult of proof; and in the process of making this proof the expressions that would be used and the meanings that would be given by other reasonable men may be decisive. A more detailed consideration of this may be found in the chapter on Interpretation.

### § 107.  Mutual Assent—"Meeting of the Minds"

It takes two to make a "bargain," although there are many "unilateral" contracts that can be made without any expression of assent by the promisee. The great majority of contracts are bargaining contracts, the purpose of which is to effect an exchange of promises or of other performances. To attain this purpose, there must be mutual expressions of assent to the exchange. These expressions must be in agreement; but it is not necessary that they shall consist of identical words or identical acts. Their words and acts are called "expressions" because they are external symbols of the thoughts and intentions of one party, symbols that convey these thoughts and intentions to the mind of the other party. The symbols so used by one party may be ill-chosen, or the experience and intelligence of the other party may be so variant from that of the first that the understanding of the second is materially different from that of the first. When this is the case, it can not be said that there has been a "meeting of the minds" or that the parties are in "agreement," in the sense in which those terms are usually understood.

It has already been shown, and it will appear at many places in this treatise, that a "meeting of the minds" is not an unvarying prerequisite to an enforceable contract. But if it is made clear that there has in fact been no such "meeting of the minds," the court will not hold a party bound by a contract varying from his own understanding unless his words and conduct were such that he had reason to know that the other party would be and was in fact misled. This is discussed, in a manner that is not altogether consistent with very frequently recurring statements, in the chapter on Interpretation. In determining whether a party had reason to know the other party's understanding, he must be judged in relation to the usage and understanding of other people; but in determining whether a party did in fact know the other party's understanding, much more direct and cogent evidence (such as statements made to him and by him) may be available.

There is no actual "meeting of the minds," even though the terms of the bargain are reduced to writing and signed by both parties, if one of them did not in fact read or understand the written terms; yet he is bound in case the other party had no reason to know that he did not read or understand. In modern business life there are innumerable "standardized" contract forms, such as are found in insurance, transportation, sales of goods, and distribution agencies, prepared by one party for his recurrent use in many transactions. They may contain many provisions, often in fine print, the purpose of which is to limit his own obligations and to avoid risks that he would otherwise have to bear. He may present this to the other party, often much less well informed or advised, on the basis of "accept this or get nothing," well knowing that the other party does not know or understand. In these cases, the requirement of an actual "meeting of the minds" may well be made effective against the party in the superior position. Even if the other party knew and understood, provisions have sometimes been refused enforcement as "unconscionable."

Prevailing opinion as to justice and sound policy may require more than this, leading to legislative regulation of business transactions. In some lines, as in insurance and transportation, the "standardized" contract is in a form prepared by the legislature or by a public commission and presented to both contracting parties on the basis of "use this or make no contract," or even on the more stringent basis of "use this." In such cases the traditional "freedom of contract" is much restricted. The same thing is true in the field of "collective bargaining" between groups of men known as labor unions and corporations, with respect to the legal relations of the individual members of the two groups. As yet government submits no "standardized" form; but a settlement between "Big Steel" and a nation-wide Union sets a standard that smaller units find it difficult not to follow.

### § 108.  Auction Sales—Offers to Sell and to Buy

The public auction sale has long been an established institution with customs and usages generally well known in the community. These customs and usages vary in different regions; and they vary also in relation to the subject matter of the sale. The customs of a regularly established auction mart must be considered in determining the effect of a transaction there; the customs of a horse market may differ from those of auction sales of cotton, tobacco, or household goods. Also, statutory provisions are not infrequently found, as for example in the Uniform Sales Act.[1] Except when otherwise provided by statute, one who puts up goods at auction can by proper notice determine the legal effect of his acts;[2] and one who makes a bid can do the same. General rules stated in this section, therefore, must be understood as widely prevailing but not necessarily universal.

When an auctioneer presents an article for sale at auction and asks for bids, he is ordinarily not making an operative offer and creates no power of acceptance. Instead, he is asking for offers to be made to him; and the bids made in response thereto are themselves offers that can be revoked by the bidders prior to an acceptance by the auctioneer.[3] This is true even though the seller or his representative has issued advertisements or made other statements that the article will be sold to the highest bidder, or is offered for sale to the highest bidder. Such statements are merely preliminary negotiation, not intended and not reasonably understood to be intended to affect legal relations. When such is the case, the seller or his representative is as free to reject the bids, highest to lowest, as are the bidders to withdraw them.[4] The seller may at any time withdraw the article from sale, if he has not already accepted a bid. He need give no reasons; indeed, he rejects all bids by merely failing to accept them—by doing nothing at all. It is not necessary for him to say that "the privilege is reserved to reject any and all bids."[5] Such a statement is merely evidence that the goods are not being offered "without reserve."

The acceptance of a bid at auction is commonly signified by the fall of the hammer or by the auctioneer's announcement "Sold." All that is necessary is that the auctioneer shall express his intention to accept the bid, in any mode that is clear to the bidder or that he has reason to know and understand. After such an acceptance, the sale is consummated. Neither party can withdraw and the auctioneer has no power to accept a higher or different bid.[9] This is not affected by a reservation of the "right to reject any and all bids;" but it is otherwise if there is an express reservation of the power to "rescind the sale" within a stated time after the auction.[10] This is the power to terminate a contract, not to reject an offer.

**3.** Payne v. Cave, 3 Term R. 148 (1789), is the leading English case on this subject.

# TOPIC B

# CONSIDERATION

## CHAPTER 5

### REASONS FOR ENFORCEMENT OF PROMISES; ACTS, FORBEARANCES AND PROMISES GIVEN IN EXCHANGE

## § 109.  Is a Definition of Consideration Practicable?

Immense effort has been made to discover the "origin" of the concept of consideration, to construct the "correct" definition of consideration, and to express in words the true consideration "doctrine" by means of which the enforceability of informal promises can be determined.  The present writer believes that there never was any specific and definite "origin" to be discovered, that no particular definition can (or ever could) be described as the only "correct" one, and that there has never been a simple and uniform "doctrine" by which enforceability can be deductively determined.  Nevertheless, the use of the term can not be avoided; but, in making use of it, it is necessary to consider the purpose for which it is used and to make sure that justice is not being defeated by using it in accordance with some narrow and limited definition.

In the early history of English law, informal promises may not have been enforced at all.  It is not to be dogmatically asserted that they were not.  Records of the administration of the law are too scanty.  The difficulties of travel and communication were such that scores of local communities knew little of each other, developed separate customs, and had individual rulers and lords who were quite independent in most matters.  It may well be that disputes over broken promises were decided by vociferation or by battle or were left undecided.  It is not improbable, however, that such disputes were frequently taken to the local lord, or to the priest, or to some locally respected ancient.  In any case, there seems to have been no general or "common" law of contract.  The concept of law as "common" law appears not to have been developed until the kings had overcome the barons, the parliament had been developed, and the king's courts had become generally available throughout the entire country to those seeking justice. It is true that there were the "laws" of King Alfred; but they were few and rudimentary, and they were never in force throughout England. There was also the "Danelaw," a term that speaks of a territory where the Danes laid down the law but does not speak of the law that they laid down. The Saxons long looked back with yearning to the laws of the good king Edward the Confessor; but this must have meant little more than that they hated to be ruled by William the Bastard and his sons.

In spite of the absence of "common" law, and particularly a common law of informal contract, it is not impossible that broken promises were followed by consequences in the nature of a societal sanction, that these consequences had some degree of uniformity in various communities, and that there may have been recognized reasons for enforcing some informal promises and for not enforcing others. Among these reasons may have been "consideration," described no doubt in another language and by other terms. It is not improbable that among these reasons were *quid pro quo,* something given as an agreed exchange, benefits received by the promisor, detriments incurred by the promisee, action by the promisee in reasonable reliance.

What makes this seem not improbable is the fact that all these have been held to be good reasons for enforcing an informal promise since England began to create and enforce a common law of contract and since the time when court records and law "reports" began to be made and preserved.

Knowledge of what the early law and custom were has much lively historical interest and would have some practical value, also, to courts and lawyers and clients. We must be content, however, without this knowledge, and must discover our contract law and our doctrine of "consideration" from the reports and records of recent times, containing as they do the customs, the decisions, the doctrines, and the reasoning of the men who have been the ministers of justice.

The reports and records of recent times! Courts and jurisdictions scattered over all the continents and the seven seas! Cases by the million! Libraries so labyrinthine as to require a guide! The leaves of the books like the leaves of the trees! Who can now read all the reports of cases dealing with the law of consideration for informal promises, stating the reasons deemed sufficient for enforcing such promises, laying down the doctrines and constructing the definitions? Certainly not the writer of this volume. He has merely read enough of them to feel well assured that the reasons for enforcing informal promises are many, that the doctrine of consideration is many doctrines, that no definition can rightly be set up as the one and only correct definition, and that the law of contract is an evolutionary product that has changed with time and circumstance and that must ever continue so to change.

If the foregoing is true, should not the chapter on "consideration" stop at this point? Not unless all chapters on all topics of the law should stop at such a point. This topic is no different from other topics, except in age and the number of its illustrations and case applications. If it is useful to study the history of any topic and to compare and correlate its cases, it is useful here. If it is elsewhere possible to construct useful working rules that professors may teach and lawyers may use to direct their clients and judges may use to point the way to justice, it is possible here.

Here, as elsewhere, a sufficient reason for comparative historical study of cases in great number is the fact that such study frees the teacher and the lawyer and the judge from the illusion of certainty; and from the delusion that law is absolute and eternal, that doctrines can be used mechanically, and that there are correct and unchangeable definitions. Having thus been freed from illusion and delusion, the study must be continued until it demonstrates that useful working rules and definitions can be found and stated; that such rules and definitions, if well constructed, are useful guides to justice even though they are not absolute and eternal. Here, as elsewhere, it is our function to construct working rules and definitions. The process and the result are made no different by the admission that the rules and definitions are not absolute but relative, not eternal but changeable. They will be useful if they are based on judicial history down to date, if they clearly indicate the facts and transactions to which they apply, and if they are in accord with the prevailing judicial action of modern time. At the least, we can review and classify the facts that have been held to be (or not to be) a "sufficient consideration" to make an informal promise enforceable. If we find a high degree of uniformity and agreement, rules can be stated and definitions attempted. We can consider the rules and definitions of the past, show the extent to which they have worked, and indicate the variation and progress that require a new restatement.

## § 110.   Not All Promises are Legally Enforceable

The mere fact that one man promises something to another creates no legal duty and makes no legal remedy available in case of non-performance. To be enforceable, the promise must be accompanied by some other factor. This seems to be true of all systems of law. The question now to be discussed is what is this other factor. What fact or facts must accompany a promise to make it enforceable at law?[1] Are these facts many or few? Can they be briefly defined and described?

Some promises are enforceable because of the form in which they are made and the symbols by which they are accompanied. A promise might be enforceable because the promisor "pledged his faith," or called on God to witness, or made the sign of the cross. Even today, certain promises are enforceable if they are accompanied by a "solemn" recognition of obligation in court or before some magistrate; this is known as a recognizance. The English court was once not far from holding that a promise was binding if it was expressed by the mystery of writing; Lord Mansfield held that a written promise was binding without any consideration,[2] but the House of Lords overruled him.[3] The principal formal contract in our existing law, binding because of its form alone, is the contract under seal. A separate chapter will be devoted to this kind of formal contract. Modern legislation has gone far in reducing its importance, even approaching its abolition.

For several centuries, it has been customary to say that by the common law no informal promise is enforceable if it is without consideration. The origin of this requirement has been said to be a "mystery." Continental jurists and students, familiar with the Roman law and the European systems based upon it, have had difficulty in understanding it and have complained at the absence of authoritative definition and codified doctrinal statement. They often appear to assume that consideration is capable of exact definition and that the doctrine could be put into a simple codified form. Our own scholars have seemed to make the same assumption; they have constructed definitions and doctrines. The same is true of the judges and their court opinions. Almost always the assumption is implicit, if not explicit, that there is a rule or doctrine that can be and must be applied deductively and dogmatically. But this assumption is a shining example of what Holmes called the "illusion of certainty." The rules and doctrines and definitions constructed by the learned judges and the doctors of law do not agree. By no single one of them can the innumerable judicial decisions be reconciled or explained. It is very doubtful whether a man could, in a single life time, make such a careful study of the facts of the cases as to be able to say whether or not any single definition or statement of doctrine is in accord with the "weight of authority."

Be it noted that it is not enough merely to make a count of dicta—to determine which definition or worded rule has been repeated most often. The problem is to determine whether the decision was actually an application of and in harmony with the worded doctrine. In each case we must know the facts on which the court passed judgment. A careful study of the facts of cases, as they are reported, will show that decisions are frequently not determined by doctrines and even that they are sometimes

---

**2.**   **Eng.**—Pillans v. Van Mierop, 3 Burr. 1663 (1765).

**3.**   Rann v. Hughes, 7 T.R. 350, note; 4 Bro.P.C. 27 (1778).

inconsistent with the very doctrines upon which they purport to be based.

It can always be said, to be sure, that certain decisions are erroneous, that the reasoning is fallacious, and that the statements of doctrine are incorrect. The present writer will be found saying this, along with others. But with respect to our present subject, with respect to the definition of such a shop-worn term as consideration, the decisions are too numerous and too various to justify any confident statement that all that are not in harmony with some one definition or stated rule are erroneous.

Therefore, when the statement is made that no informal promise is enforceable if it is without consideration, it must be understood as a statement that no informal promise is enforceable unless it is accompanied by one of those factors that have been held, more or less generally, to be sufficient to make a promise enforceable. As thus understood, is the statement much better than to say that an informal promise is legally enforceable when the facts are such as to make it legally enforceable? Is it shocking to put a definition or rule of law in such a naked form as to show that it completely begs the question? It should not be so; for what often seems to be our favorite method of legal argument is to beg the question in complicated and repetitious terms. It should console us for our frailty that a conclusion is not necessarily wrong because it was arrived at by merely assuming or asserting it—by begging the question. Decisions are very generally more satisfactory than the reasoning by which they are justified. But we must examine the decisions as well as the reasoning and must know the facts creating the issue that was decided.

A promise is not binding without consideration. A promise is not binding unless it is accompanied by one of those factors that have been held (or *will be* held) to make it binding. Our first problem, then, is not to make a definition or to state a rule, but to examine cases and find what are those factors that have been held to make a promise enforceable, and what other factors have been held to be insufficient for that purpose. In this search, we shall find that when a court holds that a certain factor justifies the enforcement of a promise, it calls it a "sufficient consideration"; and when it holds that it does not justify enforcement, it calls it either no consideration or an insufficient one. If our search further shows that this judicial process has resulted in including a good many different kinds of factors under the term "sufficient consideration," there is no reason for surprise and there should be no grief or disappointment.[4] Our search is not

---

4.　The following case shows that some reasons for enforcing a promise were recognized in the 16th century that would be disregarded now; the term "consideration" does not appear in the report. The plaintiff sold goods to J. N. upon the guaranty of J. S. and an action on

for the purpose of justifying a definition or proving a rule; it is to learn what promises have been enforced in the past in order to know (if we may) what promises will be enforced in the future. If the courts do not (and will not) enforce all promises, we need to know what promises they will enforce and why, and to know what promises they will not enforce and why. This is the object of our study of the subject "consideration" for a promise. In each new case, the question for the court is "should this promise be enforced." Its problem is not merely to determine mechanically, or logically, whether it falls within Professor Wiseacre's statement of the doctrine of consideration or complies with some commonly repeated definition. This is not to say that the Professor's statement, or Restatement, or the learned judge's dictum, can be safely disregarded.

the case was brought on this guaranty against the executor of J. S. The report contains the following: "The plaintiff alleges that the latter left assets to his executors to pay all debts and legacies, and to satisfy them also. The question was whether or not this action lay against the executors. And it was adjudged by all the justices that he recover in this action, for two reasons: One, that he had no other remedy at common law than this action; the other, because the plaintiff had delivered the goods upon the promise of the testator and there is no reason that his soul should be in jeopardy and that he should suffer prejudice by his promise when there was sufficient with which to pay the plaintiff. And so judgment was given." Anonymous, Y.B. 12 Hen. VIII, 11, 3 (1521).

Holdsworth, "Modern History of the Doctrine of Consideration", reprinted in Selected Readings on Contracts, 61, says: "Consideration thus acquired its technical meaning in the common law mainly in relation to the action of assumpsit. It became the compendious word used to express the conditions under which that action would lie, and therefore the condition precedent for the validity of all those contracts which could only be enforced by that action."

Further on Holdsworth tells us that the "doctrine" has been affected by "quid pro quo" necessary to the maintenance of the action of debt and by notions originating in the Court of Chancery. He then says: "The result is that, though the main principles of the doctrine of consideration have been developed as logical deductions from the conditions for success in the action of assumpsit, other influences have made themselves felt; and, in the eighteenth and early nineteenth centuries, some of them seemed likely to give the doctrine a shape very different from the shape which it was taking in the sixteenth and seventeenth centuries, when it was being developed mainly from its procedural basis in assumpsit. During the nineteenth century a return was made to this procedural basis. But the result has been that the final shape of the doctrine has not been settled till quite modern times."

In the fluxing social and economic conditions left by two world wars, one is much less likely to assume the permanence of any rule or doctrine. After indicating so clearly the evolutionary growth of the "doctrine of consideration" why should Holdsworth suggest that its evolution is now over and that the doctrine has received its "final shape"?

It must be admitted that our factual search can be only partial and incomplete. No single writer can possibly examine the many thousands of cases in which the decision has dealt with some phase of consideration for a promise. This constitutes a very special reason for the probability of error; and it constitutes a most conclusive reason against dogmatism and over-confidence.

A very limited search of the cases and their facts will show that the factors that have been held to be legally operative to make a promise enforceable can be classified according to their relation in time with the making of the promise. Courts have given such operation (1) to facts long antecedent to the promise; (2) to facts that are substantially contemporaneous with it; and (3) to subsequently occurring facts generally consisting of action in reliance on the promise. We must discover what kinds of facts in each of these categories will make a promise enforceable. A much less important problem will be to determine which of them should be called a "consideration."

## § 111.  Should the Requirement of Consideration be Abandoned?

Perhaps the question here put is substantially the same as, Should all promises be enforced. If it is the same, there is little use in putting it. By no system of law have all promises been enforced. By the Roman law and systems derived therefrom, a promise is not enforceable without some sufficient *causa*. The problem of what constitutes a sufficient causa with them is very similar to our problem of what is a sufficient consideration, although the factors that will be held to be sufficient are not identical. In both great legal systems alike, the problem is to determine what promises should be enforced and what ones should not, what are sufficient reasons for enforcement, what are the accompanying factors that justify enforcement. In the Roman law, these factors were called sufficient "causa"; there must have been a reason for making the promise that was also deemed to be a sufficient reason for enforcing it.[5] So far as the present writer can learn, no one knows all of those reasons that constituted sufficient *causa*. Reasons are innumerable; and the courts, like our own, must have varied a good deal in their reasoning and their decisions.[6] It appears, also, that the factors

---

5.  Buckland, in his work on Roman Law, CXLV, p. 409, says of contract: "It involved a concurrence of two wills as to future conduct of one or both of the parties. Such a concurrence, to be capable of proof, must be in some way expressed. The law might hold that any expression sufficed, that the moment agreement was provable

there was a contract. Roman law did not take this position; it started from the point of view that an agreement was not enforceable unless there was some reason why it should be. At first, like other systems, it found this reason in Form."

6.  That "causa" at Roman Law may be even less capable of defini-

constituting sufficient *causa* varied with time. Then as now, there was an evolution of law, because there was an evolution of life and custom and belief as to human welfare. So far as human history has gone, the fact is that we do not wish to enforce all promises and the courts have not enforced all promises. Therefore, we must continue to determine the factors that make promises enforceable; and our legal history will compel us to do this under some such title as "consideration." Doubtless, this would not be denied by those who have suggested the abandonment of the "doctrine." It may well be that they had in mind some specific form of doctrine that, like the present author, they knew did not explain all the cases.[7] The American Law Institute has adopted a definition of "consideration" that limits it to something that is bargained for and given in exchange for a promise; but

tion than is consideration, see Buckland, Roman Law, 425; Lorenzen, Causa & Consideration, 28 Yale L. J. 621.

7. Holdsworth, "Modern History of Consideration," reprinted in Selected Readings on Contracts, 61, says: "It may be questioned whether in its present form its weaknesses do not outweigh its advantages. . . . In fact, the doctrine of consideration in its present form is something of an anachronism. The substantive law has long ago broken away from the leading strings of the forms of action, and the law of actions has become merely adjective law. But our theory of contract is still governed by a doctrine which is historically developed with great logical precision from the procedural requirements of the form of action by which simple contracts were enforced."

This statement assumes that the doctrine has a "present form," one that is developed "with great logical precision." The statement may be true of certain great law writers, one of whom is Holdsworth. It is not true of the applied law in the courts of the United States. As Holdsworth says, the "substantive law" has not remained tied by the old "leading strings," except when administered by judges whose limited historical knowledge blinds them to evolutionary process; and the "doctrine of consideration" is itself sub-

stantive law. The statement would be monstrously true of the Restatement of Contracts, if it did not itself free the courts from the "leading string" of its own definition (sec. 75) by specifically stating that many informal promises are enforceable without any consideration as so defined (see secs. 85–92). Holdsworth himself, following Markby (Elements of Law, 3rd ed. 310–317), agrees that the doctrine, in the narrow and "logically precise" form that he adopts, should not be "the only test of the validity of a simple contract."

The late Professor Ashley said: "Technical requirements, such as the accidental and unnecessary doctrine of consideration are likely to disappear, bringing the law in accord with the modern sense of justice." With this we cannot agree, because it is certain that the modern sense of justice does not approve of enforcing every promise— not even every promise made with intent to create an obligation. There is much revolt against the enforcement of a sealed promise if without other consideration. We now demand that acts or facts other than the act of promising shall exist, before we recognize obligation. These acts or facts are the considerations or causes that induce us to exert societal force at the request of a promisee.

immediately it devotes ten sections to inform us what other factors will make a promise enforceable. The term "consideration" can be totally abandoned as well as limited; we should then instantly be obliged to consider, under other descriptions, the factors that will make a promise enforceable.

If "consideration" is regarded only as something that evidences "serious intent" or intention to be legally bound, it might reasonably be argued that such an intention may be sufficiently evidenced in other ways. The reduction of a promise to writing might be regarded as sufficient evidence. But a promisor may be legally bound by his promise even though he did not make it "seriously" and even though he intended not to be bound at all. The existence of some kinds of consideration may evidence an intention to be legally bound or a serious intention to keep the promise; but that is not the only reason that the promise is enforceable and it is not a necessary reason for enforceability. However variable and widely or narrowly inclusive the usage of the term "consideration" may be, we shall have to struggle along with it in the process of differentiating between enforceable and non-enforceable promises.

## § 112. Is Consideration Evidence of Intention to be Bound?

This question has sometimes been answered in the affirmative, with the thought, it may be, that the reason that the law enforces a contract is that the contractor willed it so, that he made his promise with "serious" intent or with intention to be legally bound. Serious intent is not a very definite concept; and it is not identical with intention to be legally bound. The cases show, however, that neither of them is necessary to enforcement; although it may be that both of them commonly exist. In order to be bound by a contract, it is not necessary that the promisor should know the law of contract or even that there is any such law. Practical jokers and intentional defrauders have often been held to be legally bound by a promise that they did not intend to perform, that they were not "serious" or honest in making, and that they did not believe to be enforceable.

The chief purpose underlying the law of contract is not to carry out the will of the promisor, although that may be one of many purposes. It is believed that the chief purpose of enforcement is the avoidance of disappointment and loss to the promisee.[8] It is the reasonable expectation of the promisee (or beneficiary) that the law chiefly takes into account. The purposes underlying the law of contract are no doubt numerous and complex. If it is obvious that the promisor was not serious and had no will to be

---

**8.**　Either to the promisee or to the beneficiary of the promised performance—either the one who bought and paid for the promise or one who has reasonably relied on it.

bound, it is probably true that the court will require specific and convincing evidence that the promisee's expectation of performance and his reliance on the promise were reasonable. But if such convincing evidence is given, the promise will be enforced against a non-serious and unwilling promisor. The existence of what we call sufficient consideration is very generally evidence that the expectation of performance was reasonable and that refusal to enforce would not satisfy the community. As will be seen throughout this chapter, other factors under other names may also constitute such evidence.

### § 113. Meaning of "Nudum Pactum"

It was once much more common than now to express legal doctrine in the form of a Latin phrase or maxim, taken from either classical or medieval Roman law. Sometimes such Latin maxims are in forms different from their originals and are given a markedly different use and meaning. One example of this is the phrase "nudum pactum." In Roman law, it seems to have described an agreement that was not invested with the form that was necessary to enforceability. In the common law, it came to be used to describe an informal promise that was not enforceable for lack of a sufficient consideration. The phrase is no longer in fashion and should be abandoned.[9]

### § 114. Is an Informal Promise without Consideration Wholly Void?

An informal promise without consideration, in any of the senses of that term, creates no legal duty and is not enforceable.[10] But this statement is not correct if we limit the definition of consideration so as to require it to be a bargained-for equivalent given in exchange for the promise. There are many informal promises that are enforceable, even though there is no consideration as thus defined. In every case, however, an informal promise is never enforceable if it stands utterly alone. To be enforceable, there must be some accompanying factor of the past (generally called "past consideration"), or there must be some subsequent changes of position in reliance on the promise. Without any such accompanying factor, an informal promise to make a gift is not binding.

Nevertheless, an informal promise to make a gift can not be said to have no legal operation whatever. If it could have none, it ought not to be enforceable even if there are other accompanying factors. But we know that when the proper factors are added the promise is itself enforceable. In such a case, the promise is as necessary to enforceability as are the other factors; it is one of the legally operative facts.

Furthermore, there is one other effect of an informal promise to make a gift. If the promise is executed and the promised performance is actually rendered, the promisee can safely receive it without any liability to the payment of compensation. That the performance was rendered in pursuance of a promise to render it as a gift sufficiently rebuts an inference that the recipient impliedly promises to pay; and it also will usually prevent any quasi-contractual duty to make restitution. The promise gives character to the rendered performance as a gift, a character that without the promise it might not have. This is true, whether the promise is to make a gift of services, money, goods, or land.[11]

The requirement of consideration is one that can not be avoided by an express waiver on the part of the promisor, either when the promise is made or later.[12] Such a waiver merely turns the promise into a promise to make a gift. Of course, when sued on such a promise, the defendant can confess judgment or let judgment be entered against him by default, and the judgment itself will be enforceable just like other judgments. It is the judgment that is enforceable, not the antecedent promise. Such action by the defendant operates as a gift of a legal right against him. He could, also, perform his gratuitous promise without being sued, thereby executing a gift of the performance that he renders.

It is not necessary, at this point, to cite cases in which the courts have refused to enforce an informal promise without consideration. Frequently, however, it has been held that a promise to a creditor to pay a debt owed him by a third person is not enforceable, if made after the debt has been incurred and in return for no forbearance or other consideration.[13] The same is true of a promise made to a debtor to pay what he owes to the creditor; neither the debtor (promisee) nor the creditor (beneficiary) can enforce it.[14]

### § 115.  Reasons for Making a Promise and Reasons for Giving Consideration

In discussing the subject of consideration, both in deciding a specific case and in forming a general theory, it may be useful to try to answer the following questions: 1. Why was the promise made?  2. Why was the supposed consideration given? Both are questions of causation. What was the inducing cause of a person's action? The answer is sufficiently difficult in the law of contract, as it is in the law of tort; and it is not made easier by delving into metaphysics or psychology.

First, why was the promise made?  (1) It may have been to obtain certain action or forbearance of economic advantage to the promisor; for example, a conveyance of land or chattels, a carriage of goods to market, a forbearance to compete in business. These are the objects of desire by the promisor; and in order to get them or a promise of them, he makes his own promise. No doubt the great majority of promises enforceable at law are made for this reason. There is a desire for economic advantage; and usually this advantage can be obtained only by promising to pay for it. It is this desire that forms subjectively his motive for promising; the advantageous action or forbearance of the other person, however, is his "motive" or inducement in an objective sense.

(2) It may have been to obtain certain action or forbearance of no economic advantage to the promisor, but which will nevertheless give him feelings of satisfaction; for example, a donation by another to a university or to a church, a service to the poor and needy, a public exhibition of fireworks, a forbearance to drink intoxicants. Here, as in (1), there is the same subjective desire that will be satisfied by an objective action or forbearance. Such action, however, does not involve economic advantage to the promisor.

(3) It may have been to obtain no action or forbearance by another, but solely because of past action or forbearance; for example, a past loan of money that has been outlawed, a past friendly service rendered by one now in financial difficulty, an existing relationship by blood or marriage.

(4) It may have been to obtain a feeling of satisfaction, there being no action or forbearance by another, either past or future, as where one promises to make a Christmas gift.[15]

Some of the foregoing promises would be legally enforceable and others not. In all there was some motivating cause; but in (1) and (2) there was a desire for objective conduct of another person and in (3) and (4) there was not.

Secondly, why was the consideration given? (1) It may have been to obtain the promise of the other party, such promissory expression by him being the object of desire. A more remote but equally important object may have been to obtain the performance promised by the other party. One who bargains for or otherwise induces a promise usually desires both promise and performance, although he might be content with one without the other.

(2) It may have been in reliance on a promise already made, and hence not to induce the promise to be made. (a) The promise may have been conditional upon such action by the promisee; and if so, he performs this action not to induce the making of the promise but to induce the performance of the promise. (b) The promise may not have been thus conditional. If so, the action by the promisee is not to induce either the promise on its performance, but is taken by him for other reasons, partly perhaps because the performance that was promised will recoup expenditures incidental to his action or will prevent losses that

he would otherwise have prevented himself. In these cases the action taken in reliance may have been either slight or substantial, there may or may not have been reason for the promisee to believe that his action was desired by the promisor, and it may or may not have been such as a reasonable man in the promisor's place would have foreseen.

(3) It may have been given for any one of numberless other reasons; as for example, (a) by mistake, (b) as a gift, or (c) for some equivalent, quite independent of the promise, received from the promisor or from a third person.

(4) It may have been given for a combination of reasons including parts or all of (1), (2) and (3).

The term consideration has been narrowly defined so as to include only a few of the foregoing performances. It has been broadly defined so as to include more of them. Nowhere has it been defined so as to include all of them; and never has it been held that each and all of them will be sufficient to make the promise enforceable. Nevertheless, wherever the line is drawn, the drawing of the line is not possible without considering motives and inducing causes—without answering to some extent the two questions: Why was the promise made? and why was the supposed consideration given?

### § 116. Must Consideration be Something Requested or Bargained for?

The question here put has very often been answered in the affirmative. Our leading writers and jurists have so answered it. This will be more fully discussed in the sections dealing with the effect of action in reliance upon a promise. The term contract has already been defined herein as being somewhat more inclusive than the term bargain. There are enforceable promises that are not a part of any bargain; and there are promissory bargains that are not legally enforceable. And if a promise is enforceable, we say that there is a contract.

Now, if we can have a binding informal promise without any bargain, it would seem that the consideration for it is something that is not bargained for or else that such a promise is binding without any consideration at all. Yet it has been said times innumerable that no informal promise is binding without consideration; and, in writing their opinions, it is the universal practice of judges to use the word "consideration" to describe the factor that is held to make the promise enforceable. Often enough, this factor is not something that was requested or bargained for by the promisor.

The American Law Institute has seen fit to define consideration as anything that is bargained for by the promisor and given by the promisee in exchange for the promise, and as nothing else. This made it necessary to add other sections stating that certain informal promises are binding without a bargain and without any consideration. Undoubtedly this is a possible (and not unreasonable) method of stating our existing law; but it is not the usual way of the lawyers and judges for the last few centuries. The Institute's way may be an improvement over the old way; and it may be that the profession will abandon its customary talk and adopt it. If it does, we shall have to define consideration as something requested by the promisor in return for his promise and given in exchange by the other party; but we shall then have to state in other terms the other kinds of things that make an informal promise enforceable.[16]

It is certain that in commercial transactions there is usually an agreed exchange of equivalents. Each of the parties is bargaining for something—either a bird in the hand or a bird in the bush. If either party does nothing but make a promise, the other party is bargaining for a bird in the bush—for a future performance that is promised. These birds—these subjects of agreed exchange—whether delivered or merely promised, are the considerations, the subjects of exchange, the inducing causes of the agreement. In almost all such instances, the requested bird is a sufficient consideration to satisfy the requirements of law, and the promise given in exchange is binding. The few special cases where it is not sufficient will be discussed separately in later sections.

### § 117. Is Consideration a "Quid Pro Quo"?

A *quid pro quo* is the antithesis of something for nothing.[18] It expresses the idea of a bargain—an exchange of this for that. It is a concept and an expression that were much more greatly used in the action of debt than in any of the other common law actions. In this action the plaintiff alleged that the defendant had received something under such circumstances that he owed its return to the plaintiff, either specifically or its value in money. Eventually, the action of debt came to be used solely for the recovery of a definite sum of money owed to the plaintiff because of the receipt by the defendant of something of value. This something was the *quid* for which the defendant was legally indebted in money.

There are many money debts that are not based on assent at all, and that do not involve the making of any promise. These non-promissory debts have come to be called quasi-contracts. The American Law Institute has published a volume entitled "Restitution," stating the law of noncontractual money debts.

Most money debts are created by a promise to pay for money or goods or services received by the defendant. They are very frequently unilateral contracts—a promise by the defendant for a performance fully rendered by the plaintiff; witness a promissory note for money lent.

## § 118.  Motive and Inducement—Must Consideration be the "Inducing Cause" of the Promise?

It is often repeated that "motive" is not the same thing as consideration,[25] or the equivalent of it; but the discussions seldom if ever attempt to explain what is meant by the term "motive."  If motive is a desire for some object or to attain some end—a state of mind—it can not be identified with consideration in any of the senses in which the latter term is used.  If "motive" is the object that is desired or the end to be attained, it can often be identified with consideration.  In most business transactions, a party who makes a promise is almost always induced thereto by the fact that he desires some action or forbearance by the

---

25.   In Thomas v. Thomas, 2 Q.B. 851 (1842), the defendant, an executor, had promised the testator's widow to carry out the wish of the deceased to give her a house.  It was argued by counsel for the defendant that this promise was not made binding by the fact that the widow had promised to make repairs and to pay £1 yearly toward the ground rent.  Counsel said that it was "a mere gift cum onere," and further: "What is meant by the consideration for a promise but the cause or inducement for making it? . . . The rent and repairs cannot be said to have been the cause or motive which induced the executors to make this agreement."  But Patteson, J., replied to this: "It would be giving to causa too large a construction if we were to adopt the view urged for the defendant; it would be confounding consideration with motive.  Motive is not the same thing with consideration.  Consideration means something which is of some value in the eye of the law, moving from the plaintiff; it may be some benefit to the defendant, or some detriment to the plaintiff; but at all events it must be moving from the plaintiff.  Now that which is suggested as the consideration here, a pious respect for the wishes of the testator, does not in any way move from the plaintiff; it moves from the testa-

tor; therefore, legally speaking, it forms no part of the consideration."

Of this statement by Patteson, J., it may be noted that he thinks (1) that "value in the eye of the law" is not identical with value in the market place; (2) that consideration must move from the plaintiff— certainly not the law today; and (3) that "a pious respect for the wishes of the testator" was something that "moves from the testator," whereas it was nothing but a state of mind of the defendant, the man who made the promise.  It is clear, however, that the case was well decided, and also that the motivating cause or inducement of the promise was not identical with the factors that were held to be a sufficient "consideration."

The opinion in this case has led to many repetitions of the statement that "motive" and "consideration" are not identical.  See Hoffer v. Eastland Nat. Bank, 169 S.W.2d 275 (Tex.Civ.App.1943).

Restatement, Contracts, § 84(a): "Consideration is not insufficient because of the fact (a) that obtaining it was not the motive or a material cause inducing the promisor to make the promise."  And yet the Institute says in § 75 that nothing is ever consideration, either sufficient or insufficient, unless it is bargained for by the promisor as the exchange for his promise.

other party in exchange.　There is a desiring state of mind and also an object of desire.　The consideration for the promise is this desired action or forbearance given in exchange and, objectively speaking, is the "motive" for which the promise is made; it is the inducing cause of the promise.[26]

Contractual transactions, however, are not limited to "business transactions"; and the foregoing statement as to motivation is not always true even of business transactions.　As in the case just discussed in the footnote, there may be a sufficient consideration that is quite different from that which constituted the actual motivating cause of the promise.[27]

This is all quite consistent with the view of Mr. Justice Holmes; and yet he thought, and in various cases held, that consideration must be one side of an agreed exchange and must constitute at least "the conventional motive or inducement."[28]　Others, also, have held this view, either influenced by Holmes himself, or on independent grounds.[29]　This will be discussed more fully in the sections dealing with action in reliance on a promise.

The American Law Institute has not adopted the exact language of Holmes.　It does not say that it must be "given and accepted as the conventional motive or inducement of the promise."　But its language, when analyzed, seems to amount to the same thing; for it defines consideration as that which "is bargained for and given in exchange for the promise."　It lists the following as the subjects of bargain and exchange: "an act other than a promise; a forbearance; the creation, modification or destruction of a legal relation; a return promise."[30]　If something is "bargained for" by the promisor, it is evidently "his conventional motive or inducement."

Neither Holmes nor the Institute requires that consideration shall be the sole inducement or motivating cause of the promise, or even that it shall be the prevailing or chief inducement.　But it must be enough of an inducement that it is in fact bargained for.

Both Holmes and the Institute recognize that not every inducement that is bargained for will be held to be a sufficient consideration to make a promise enforceable.　Certain exceptions are made and must be stated.　The Institute also recognizes explicitly that there are other factors, not things bargained for and not within its definition, that will make a promise enforceable.[31]　In a court opinion, Holmes also has recognized this.[32]

30.　Restatement, Contracts, § 75.

31.　Id.　§§ 85–93.

32.　In Martin v. Meles, 60 N.E. 397, 179 Mass. 114 (1901), Holmes said: "Of course the mere fact that a promisee relies upon a promise made without other consideration does not impart validity to what before was void.　There must be some ground for saying that the acts done in reliance upon the promise were contemplated by the form

## § 119.  Must Consideration be Something That is Regarded as Such by Both Parties?

Some of our leading jurists have said that nothing can be consideration for a promise unless it is regarded as such by both parties.[35]  Those who make this assertion apparently have adopted the definition that consideration is a bargained-for equivalent given in exchange for the promise.  If we accept this definition we can accept the statement.  If the promisor bargains for something, that is what he regards as the equivalent of his promise;  and if the promisee gives it in exchange for the promise, he must regard the promise as the equivalent of what he gives.  So both parties regard it as consideration, even though they may not know the law of contract and may never have heard the word consideration.

On the other hand, if we do not accept this definition, the statement can not be accepted.  There are many factors that will make a promise enforceable that are not bargained for and are not given in exchange for the promise.  If we include them within the term consideration, then the factors that are so included need not be regarded as such by either party.  If a new promise is made to pay a debt barred by statute of limitations, that past debt is held to be a sufficient reason for enforcing the new promise.  This is so, even though neither party thinks of the past debt in that light.  Of course, it is the existence of that debt that helps to cause the debtor to make the new promise.

Likewise, if a promisee acts in reasonable reliance upon a promise, that promise may be held enforceable even though the

of the transaction either impliedly or in terms as the conventional inducement, motive and equivalent for the promise.  But courts have gone very great lengths in discovering the implication of such an equivalence, sometimes perhaps having found it in matters which would seem to be no more than conditions or natural consequences of the promise."

35.  Mr. Justice Holmes has already been quoted, in Wisconsin & Mich. R. Co. v. Powers, 24 S.Ct. 107, 191 U.S. 379, 48 L.Ed. 229 (1903), as saying that "by the express or implied terms of the supposed contract, the promise and the consideration must purport to be the motive each for the other, in whole or at least in part."  The opinion is quoted and approved in Banning Co. v. California, 36 S.Ct. 338, 341, 240 U.S. 142, 153, 60 L.Ed. 569 (1915).

In McGovern v. New York, 138 N.E. 26, 234 N.Y. 377, 25 A.L.R. 1442 (1923), Mr. Justice Cardozo said: " 'Nothing is consideration,' it has been held, 'that is not regarded as such by both parties.'  Philpot v. Gruninger, 14 Wall. 570, 577, 20 L.Ed. 743 ;  Fire Ins. Ass'n v. Wickham, 141 U.S. 564, 579, 12 S.Ct. 84, 35 L.Ed. 860 ;  De Cicco v. Schweizer, 221 N.Y. 431, 438, 117 N.E. 807 (1917).  The fortuitous presence in a transaction of some possibility of detriment, latent but unthought of, is not enough.  Promisor and promisee must have dealt with it as the inducement to the promise.  Holmes, Com.Law, 292 ; Wis. & Mich. R. Co. v. Powers, 191 U.S. 379, 386, 24 S.Ct. 107, 48 L.Ed. 229 ;  1 Wil.Cont. § 139, p. 309.' "

promisor did not in fact know of such action and so did not regard it as consideration or as anything else. Even the promisee who acts in reliance may not regard his action as any reason for enforcing the promise; he may perform the action because he believes that the promise will be kept, without the necessity of any enforcement.

Whether consideration is so defined as to include or to exclude such factors as these, we can safely say that their operative effect is not dependent upon the manner in which both parties, or either party, regarded them.

## § 121.  Benefit to the Promisor as Consideration

There is no doubt that most enforceable promises are made by the promisor for the purpose of getting in return something that he regards as beneficial to him. He promises to pay money in order to induce another to work for him or sell goods to him or transfer title to land. There is no doubt, also, that these beneficial subjects of exchange are a sufficient consideration for a promise. Nevertheless, the element of benefit to the promisor is not necessary to the sufficiency of consideration.[37] Of course, "benefit," like other words, is used to convey a variety of meanings. The most common usage is to make the word express the idea of economic advantage. Most contractual promises are parts of a commercial transaction and in such transactions the motive of each party is a desire for economic gain—for something having economic value to him. But there are innumerable transactions, even including many that are called commercial, in which the promisor receives nothing of economic advantage; he receives no "benefit" that is measurable with money or even with other objects of desire.

The promise of an accommodation surety is a very common illustration; he promises to answer for the debt of another in order to induce the promisee to lend money or to sell goods "on credit" to the principal obligor.[38] In this transaction, there is benefit in the sense of economic gain to the principal; but the surety receives nothing and gets no economic gain or benefit. In some such cases, the surety may obtain an indirect gain because of the use to which the principal will put the money or the goods; but the enforceability of a surety's promise does not depend upon such indirect benefit any more than upon a direct one.

It is true that in all cases, of every kind, there is some motivating reason for making a promise; the surety desires that the promisee shall lend or convey to the principal. Thus, he bargains for and gets in return a benefit to the principal. Is this also a "benefit" to himself, in the common usage of that term? It is believed not. Grandfather promises to give his little granddaughter an allowance of twenty five cents a week; he desires to see her eyes light up at the promise itself and to get vicarious pleasure out of her joy in buying a ribbon. Grandfather has an object of desire and gets it—one that he much prefers to the possession of a quarter of a dollar. But this is not a "benefit" in the economic sense. Nor is it a "benefit" in the sense known and used by lawyers and judges; for there is no doubt that the object of his desire, benefit though it may be in some reasonable sense, is not a sufficient consideration for his promise; the promise to pay the allowance can not be enforced at law.

A few other illustrations must suffice. Many a gratuitous bailee has promised to care for or to deliver some object confided to his care. At the request of the bailor, he receives money and promises to deliver it to a third party. Here, the promisor is given possession of money, a thing of value; but to him it is merely a burden and can not properly be regarded as of economic advantage or "benefit," and so his promise is universally regarded as "gratuitous." Nevertheless, the promise is enforceable; the promisor must render the promised service.[39] There are many instances in which a person promises to pay money to another, the consideration being the rendering of service or the conveyance of property to a third person who may himself make no promise whatever.[40] It is the promisor's desire to make a gift of the service or the property to the third person. There is sufficient consideration in these cases and the promise is enforceable, even though the promisor has no economic interest in either the labor or the property and gets no benefit to himself. The surrender of a claim against a third person is sufficient consideration even though the benefit is solely to the third person.[41]

## § 122. Detriment to the Promisee as Consideration

It has often been said that no consideration is legally sufficient unless it is either a benefit to the promisor or a detriment to the promisee.[45] We have just dealt with the concept of benefit. It is not so easy to dispose of the concept of "detriment"; yet it is believed that "detriment" as an absolute requirement also must go. The American Law Institute has abandoned it, for it says: "Gain or advantage to the promisor or loss or disadvantage to the promisee, or the relative values of a promise and the consideration for it, do not affect the sufficiency of consideration." [46]

Some of our ablest and most learned scholars have searched the past, looking for "origins" of the doctrine of consideration.[47] During some centuries after the Norman conquest, our law of

45. The definition given in Currie v. Misa, 10 Exch. 162 (1875), is often used by American courts, with or without quotation marks. A valuable consideration may consist either in some right, interest, profit, or benefit, accruing to the one party, or some forbearance, detriment, loss, or responsibility given, suffered, or undertaken by the other.

contract was developed chiefly in the common law actions of debt and assumpsit. The history of these actions is most enlightening; and the results of the studies of Holmes, Ames, and many others have aided greatly in our understanding of the law and its growth. If it is supposed, however, that the tracing of these forms of action back to their origin has resulted in the discovery of a doctrine that existed from time immemorial, that determined the decisions of courts, and that is still to be stated as the existing law, the supposition is quite erroneous. In using these forms of action, the courts were not applying a ready-made doctrine of consideration. In the long series of decisions through the centuries, the courts were trying to determine what promises should be enforced and why. In each new case new reasons were advanced for enforcing the promise sued upon; the courts weighed these reasons in the light of such legal history as they knew and in the light of their other experience, and determined the sufficiency of the reasons. Many of the reasons that induced the making of a promise were held to be sufficient reasons for its enforcement; others were held to be insufficient. Sometimes, reasons were held to be sufficient for enforcement of a promise, even though they had nothing whatever to do with the making of the promise. It is by this process that the "doctrine" of consideration has been built up; and it is still building. The long series of factors that were held to be a sufficient "consideration," and the smaller series of factors that were held to be insufficient, can be analyzed and classified. It is by this analysis and classification that doctrines are discovered and stated, and that tentative predictions as to the future can be made. But the series of factors is never closed; the rules and doctrines are always in process of construction and change; and the tentative predictions must occasionally fail.

It was chiefly in the action of assumpsit that the scholars, particularly Dean Ames, found the element of detriment to the promisee. The form called assumpsit has been believed to be derived from the earlier action of trespass, aided by the Statute of Westminster II which caused the development of the intermediate offspring of trespass called trespass on the special case (or just "case," for short). It may be that there is an error of some importance in this belief; but it is not necessary to determine this, for our present purposes. It is certainly true that assumpsit was regarded as an action for damages for a wrongful injury. Assumpsit could not be maintained unless harm to the plaintiff was shown. The gist of the action consisted of the promise made by the defendant, his non-performance constituting a breach, and resulting harm to the plaintiff. It is in this element of "harm" to the plaintiff that one germ of consideration has been found, leading to the doctrine that consideration consists of detriment to the promisee and that without such detriment there is no sufficient consideration.

It should be observed, first, that the element of harm for which the action of assumpsit was maintained was harm that resulted from the breach (the mis-performance of the promisor), not harm that was incurred as an inducement of the promise. It was not a detriment given in exchange for the promise, but a detriment that was caused by non-performance of the promise. Furthermore, the harm for which the plaintiff sought compensation was always harm that consisted of an affirmative loss—a subtraction from the plaintiff's property or personal capacity and integrity. In contract actions of the present day, the "harm" for which the plaintiff sues is principally the non-receipt of the promised performance; it is not a subtraction from the plaintiff's estate or person, but a disappointment in not receiving a promised addition. "Consequential" losses may, however, be included, just as in "assumpsit." In the early history of assumpsit, therefore, we do not find either the doctrine that a promise is not binding unless some performance that is detrimental to the promisee is given in exchange for it, or the contract rule of damages that the plaintiff can get judgment for the value of the promised performance.

"Economically detrimental!" Is the "detriment" of which the books so often speak necessarily an economic detriment—one that has value in the market and can be measured with money? Without doubt, the word "detriment" is used with varying meanings, and often without having in mind any clear and definite meaning. Probably, the idea of economic loss is the generally prevailing one that is meant to be expressed. Neither court opinions nor treatises have given us any other definition.

It is true that most of the considerations that have been given constitute a detrimental economic change in the promisee's life. It is true, also, that most detrimental economic changes are a sufficient consideration when bargained for and given in exchange for a promise. There are a good many cases, however, in which a consideration that was held to be sufficient can not reasonably be regarded as involving any economic loss. Let us consider some of these.

In a leading English case decided a century ago, the defendant guaranteed the payment of three bills of exchange amounting to £9,666, in return for the plaintiff's surrender of a certain writing signed by the defendant and also having the form of a guaranty. The defendant pleaded that the document so surrendered was "void and of no value." The court held that even if this were true the consideration was sufficient. It was the object of the promisor's desire and was bargained for by him. On appeal to the Exchequer Chamber, Lord Abinger, C. B., said: "the actual surrender of the possession of the paper to the defendant was a sufficient consideration without reference to its contents." [48] If it be said that the surrender of a piece of paper is a detriment in the nature of an economic loss, even though the writing on it is of no consequence, this amounts to an admission that actual economic loss is not required.

More than 250 years earlier, it had been held that a promise by the defendant to pay rent due from another person was made binding by a consideration consisting only of the showing to the defendant the documentary lease stating that the claimed rent was payable. The report says: "for when a thing is to be done by the plaintiff, be it never so small, this is a sufficient consideration." [49] Can it truthfully be said that any act of the plaintiff, "be it never so small," is also an economic loss or detriment?

A promise to pay the debt of another was held to be made binding by a consideration consisting only of the promisee's taking an oath that the claim was honest.[50] It was said by Emery, J., of the Supreme Court of Maine: "A cent or a pepper corn, in legal estimation, would constitute a valuable consideration." [51] And Sir George Jessel, M. R. said that according to English law "a creditor might accept anything in satisfaction of a debt except a less amount of money. He might take a horse or a canary or a tomtit if he chose and that was accord and satisfaction." [52] So also it would be a sufficient consideration for any promise, according to generally accepted statements.[53]

That consideration need not be a detriment to the promisee is further shown by the modern cases holding that consideration can be given by a third person and does not need to move from the promisee at all.[54] The American Law Institute has accepted this, and states that "Consideration may be given to the promisor or to some other person. It may be given by the promisee or by some other person." [55]

When consideration is defined as a detriment to the promisee, this does not mean that the contract must be a detriment to him. A contract does not have to be a losing contract in order to be enforceable. Whatever may be the meaning that is given to the term detriment, it is applied only with respect to that which is called consideration and not at all to that which is promised in return therefor or to the net market value of the contract to either party

48.   Eng.—Haigh v. Brooks, 10 Adol. & El. 309 (1840).

49.   Eng.—Sir Anthony Sturlyn v. Albany, Cro.Eliz. 67 (1587).

50.   Eng.—Knight v. Rushworth, Cro.Eliz. 469 (1596).

A similar case is Brooks v. Ball, 18 Johns. 337 (N.Y., 1820).

55.   Restatement, Contracts, § 75(2).

## § 123. Must Consideration be a "Legal Detriment"?

It has been asserted by many writers and judges that to constitute a sufficient consideration the detriment incurred by the promisee must be a "legal detriment." It need not involve actual loss; but it must be a detriment "in the eye of the law." Also, it will not be sufficient, even though it is an actual loss, unless it is a "legal detriment." Thus, the Circuit Court of Appeals has said: "The detriment need not be real; it need involve no actual loss to the promisee. The word, as used in the definition, means legal detriment as distinguished from detriment in fact." [56] Such statements as this, common as they are, are a flat abandonment of any requirement of economic loss or detriment as a fact.

Such statements not only abandon the requirement of actual detriment; they tell us nothing at all as to the nature of this "detriment" that is said to be required. To say that it must be a "legal detriment" says no more than that the detriment must be one that the law recognizes as sufficient, a prime illustration of begging the question. What kind of consideration will make a promise binding? Why, it must be a consideration that is legally sufficient. Obviously, a true statement; also, obviously, one that gives not the slightest help in determining whether a consideration that is before us is a sufficient one.

The very common statement that consideration must be a "legal detriment," or that it must have "value in the eye of the law," was induced by the discovery that courts were holding considerations to be sufficient even though they were not "detriments" in fact and had no "value" in the market place, and were holding other considerations to be insufficient even though they were such detriments and had such value. We must abandon the term "legal detriment" because it does not serve the desired purpose; we must separate the good from the bad considerations on some basis other than "detriment" or "market place value."

## § 125. One Consideration Exchanged for Several Promises

A single and undivided consideration may be bargained for and given as the agreed equivalent of one promise or of two promises or of many promises. The fact that there are many promises given in exchange for the one consideration does not make it insufficient as to any of them.[66] If it would be sufficient to support each of the promises taken separately, it is sufficient for all of them.[67] This is true whether the two or more prom-

---

**67.** Restatement, Contracts, § 83, reads: "Consideration is sufficient for as many promises as are bargained for and given in exchange for it if it would be sufficient cient    "(a) for each one of them if that alone were bargained for, or

"(b) for at least one of them, and its insufficiency as consideration for any of the others is due solely

ises are made by the same person or by different persons. It may not be true, however, if the so-called consideration is not a bargained-for exchange, but is either some past consideration or some subsequent action in reliance. This will be explained in the discussion of those topics.

If an employee renders service in exchange for a promise of specified wages and also for a promise of a bonus if the service continues for a specified period, the service is sufficient consideration for both promises of the employer.[68] If excavation work is done in return for a promise by A to pay ten cents a yard and also for a second promise of B to pay five cents a yard additional, the work is sufficient to support the promises of both A and B.[69] Very generally, there is only a single consideration given for the promises of a principal obligor and his surety, as where a loan of money is made to P in return for P's note and for a collateral guaranty by S.

## § 126. Two Considerations, One being Bad or Not Proved

If two considerations are given for a promise, one of them being legally sufficient to support a promise and the other not sufficient, the promise is enforceable. It is enough that there is one sufficient consideration.[72] The promise may not be enforceable, however, if the insufficient consideration is also illegal. One who gives an illegal consideration for a promise is not given a remedy to enforce it, on grounds of public policy. The reason for this, if there is another and lawful consideration, is public policy, not lack of consideration. This will be discussed in a subsequent section.

A sharp distinction must be made between mere legal insufficiency of a part of the consideration that is in fact given and a partial failure of a performance that was promised. The latter has nothing to do with the sufficiency of the consideration that was exchanged for a promise. It is a partial failure to render the performance that was the agreed exchange for the performance that was promised in exchange. Such a partial failure may be so substantial in character as to justify refusal to perform the return promise. This is dealt with in chapters on Performance and Discharge of Contract.

## § 127. Adequacy of the Consideration

That which is bargained-for by the promisor and given in exchange for the promise by the promisee is not made insufficient as a consideration by the fact that its value in the market is not equal to that which is promised. Consideration in fact bargained for is not required to be adequate in the sense of equality in

to the fact that it is itself a promise for which the return promise

would not be a sufficient consideration."

value.[74] Very generally, we speak of "value" as if it were definite and exact, an easily ascertainable amount of money. In fact, it is always variable, always a matter on which opinions may differ, and frequently one that is very difficult to estimate. The value of any subject matter is the amount of money that it can be exchanged for in the market. Yet, in this statement, the term "market" is as uncertain and indefinite as the term value.

If there are willing buyers and sellers, there is a market; and it is their willingness that determines value. When two parties agree upon an exchange of this for that, they constitute a part of the market. We have a free market, under our common law, for the reason that the courts have left it free. They do not require that one person shall pay as much as others may be willing to pay, or that one person shall receive for what he sells as little as others may be willing to receive for a like article. The contracting parties make their own contracts, agree upon their own exchanges, and fix their own values. Inadequacy of consideration may be so gross as to be evidence of fraud, mistake, or undue influence; but in the absence of these it will seldom affect the enforceability of a promise.[75]

A few of the more striking cases will be cited from the reports. Parting with a document, the contents of which can in fact render no service, has been held to be a sufficient consideration for a promise to pay a large sum of money.[76] Services or property are sufficient consideration for a promise to pay much more money than anyone else would pay for them.[77] Forbearance to put a lien on the defendant's property is sufficient consideration for the owner's promise to pay a debt due from a third person,

---

74. The rule stated in this sentence would probably be regarded as a "safe" rule for counsellors in the process of making a contract that is sure to withstand litigation as discussed by K. N. Llewellyn, "The Modern Approach to Counselling and Advocacy," 46 Col. L.Rev. 167 (1946). But he rightly says that it is an unsafe rule to say that "the adequacy of consideration will not be inquired into by the courts," or that *any* bargained-for detriment" is a sufficient consideration. As the succeeding sections will show, bargains in which a good-faith equivalence exists are the better insurable risks.

75. Restatement, Contracts, § 81, reads: "Except as this rule is qualified by secs. 76, 78–80, gain or advantage to the promisor or loss or disadvantage to the promisee, or the relative values of a promise and the consideration for it, do not affect the sufficiency of consideration." Approved in Benward v. Automobile Ins. Co., 60 F. Supp. 995 (D.C.N.Y.1945), affirmed 155 F.2d 521 (C.C.A.). The exceptions noted are dealt with herein in other sections.

76. N.C.—Wilkinson v. Oliveira, 1 Bing., N.C. 490 (1835), worthless letter.

Ohio—Judy v. Louderman, 29 N.E. 181, 48 Ohio St. 562 (1891).

Eng.—Haigh v. Brooks, 10 Adol. & Ellis, 309 (1839), promise to pay nearly £10,000 in return for the surrender of a written guaranty that may have been unenforceable.

even though the lien if actually filed would have been discharged by paying a much smaller sum.[78]

Often, very high compensation is promised for services rendered to one who is sick or disabled; these are enforced without regard to the market value of the services rendered.[79]  The naming of a child as requested is a sufficient consideration for a promise of support and education or a promise to pay a sum of money however large.[80]  A promise to make an endowment of $5,000 was held sufficiently supported by a return promise to catalogue the fund in memory of the donor.[81]

The gross inadequacy of the consideration, as measured by the opinions of other men, may tend to support the conclusion that the parties did not actually agree upon an exchange, that the "peppercorn" was not in fact bargained for by the promisor. If it was not bargained for, it was not a consideration, according to the definition that makes agreed bargain the test.  Persons sometimes say that they have bargained, when their other conduct shows that they have not; and they sometimes actually bargain for something when their written or oral statement is that they have bargained for something else.  Courts must first determine the fact of bargain and agreed exchange before they can properly apply the rules of consideration as a bargained exchange.

The rule that adequacy of consideration is not required, and that the value of the consideration is to be left solely to the free bargaining process of the parties, leads in extreme cases to seeming absurdities.  When the consideration is only a "peppercorn" or a "tomtit" or a worthless piece of paper, the requirement of a consideration appeared to Holmes to be as much of a mere formality as is a seal.[82]  In such extreme cases, a tendency may be observed to refuse to apply the rule; [83] but it is a tendency that has not been carried very far.  Such cases can sometimes be explained on the ground that the court feels that there was no bargain in fact and that the stated consideration was a mere pretense.

A mere expression of assent to an offer to confer a benefit is not a consideration for the offered promise, for the reason that it is not bargained for even though it is requested.  Even if the assent were bargained for and given in exchange for the promise, it is very unlikely that it would be held to be a sufficient consideration.  The same is true of the acceptance of an executed gift.[84] The case is different if the offered benefit or gift involves something more than benefit, the assent or acceptance causing the

---

**80.   Mass.**—Gardner v. Denison, 105 N.E. 359, 217 Mass. 492, 51 L.R.A., N.S., 1108 (1914).

offeree to incur obligations, responsibilities, or burdensome risks.[85]

As is insisted herein, in many places, there are many promises that are enforced at law, even though there is nothing that is bargained for or given in exchange. In all such cases, there is some factor that is practically always called the "consideration"; and it constitutes a reason for enforcement by the court. Since, in these cases, this reason is not something that is bargained for by the promisor and is not valued by the bargaining process, its value and importance must be determined by the court. In these cases, the "consideration" (if, along with the courts, we call it such) must be substantial in character; an inconsequential tomtit will not do.

The consideration for which a man bargains may not be his sole, or even his chief, reason for making his promise; and the court may enforce the promise with a good conscience, even though in its estimation the subject matter given in exchange has little value. But when the promisor has received nothing in exchange and the court is depending on some other reason for enforcement, it must be a good reason in the opinion of the court itself.

One holding an auction advertised that a new automobile would be given to the person whose name should be drawn from a box containing the names of those attending. The fact that the plaintiff came to the auction, although she made no bid, was held to be a sufficient consideration.[92] Here, as in the case of lotteries and horse-race betting, many large aleatory promises were exchanged for many small actions, because the offeror knew that although he induced a large crowd to attend he would have to deliver only one automobile.

A very small consideration is sufficient to support the promise of an option-giver, for a different reason. Suppose that A pays 25 cents in return for B's promise to sell and convey Blackacre for the price of $10,000 at any time within 30 days. The sum of 25 cents is not "inadequate" as an exchange for B's promise, although it would be exceedingly inadequate as an exchange for Blackacre.[93] But it is not being exchanged for Blackacre, or even for a promise to convey Blackacre; it is being exchanged for a promise to exchange Blackacre for $10,000. B has bought a power to compel the exchange of Blackacre for $10,000, a power continuing 30 days; for this power he has paid 25 cents, a small sum. We can not say that it is an "inadequate" price to pay for such a power until we know the "market" for it—the opinions of other dealers as to its value in money. There may or may not be such a "market". It is true, however, under our existing law, that B's promise to A is enforceable even though it is proved that other dealers in land would gladly have paid $1,000 for the "option" that A got for 25 cents. Nor is B's promise made unenforceable by the fact that the other dealers would gladly have paid $50,000 for Blackacre.

## § 128.　Unconscionable Bargains

Agreements for the exchange of different currencies or for the loan of a sum of money at a high rate of interest may be so extreme as to appear unconscionable according to the mores and business practices of the time and place. When such is the case, a chancellor would certainly refuse equitable remedies. This is illustrated by the "equity of redemption" in the law of mortgages that was held to exist in the teeth of express words to the contrary in a contract; also, by equity's refusal to enforce other contract penalties and forfeitures. The courts of common law did not create a rule against unconscionability and did not purport to refuse to sustain a common law action to enforce an unconscionable agreement. It is difficult to believe, however, that the judges of today, practically all of them "chancellors" as well as "judges", can fail to be influenced by equitable doctrines in the granting of any of the remedies that are available. There is sufficient flexibility in the concepts of fraud, duress, misrepresentation, and undue influence, not to mention differences in economic bargaining power, to enable the courts to avoid enforcement of a bargain that is shown to be unconscionable by reason of gross inadequacy of consideration accompanied by other relevant factors.[94] Courts have often avoided the enforcement of unconscionable provisions in long printed standardized contracts, in part by the process of "interpretation" against the party using them, and in part by the method used by Lord Nelson at Copenhagen.

## § 129.　A Sum of Money as Consideration for a Promise to Pay a Larger Sum

One apparent exception to the rule of adequacy discussed in a preceding section is the case of a promise to pay a sum of money in return for a smaller sum of money. The giving of $10 is not a sufficient consideration for a promise of the immediate repayment of $20.[95] There are few cases of this sort; and they can probably be explained on the ground that there was in fact no bargain. They may be justifiably rested, however, upon the fact that the two sums exchanged have values that are fixed by law, values that can not vary with the opinions of men. The two values bear a mathematically certain relation to each other.

95.　So held in Schnell v. Nell, 17 Ind. 29, 79 Am.Dec. 453 (1861), where the defendant, for stated reasons not themselves sufficient, promised in consideration of one cent to pay sums amounting to $600. In this case, it was not contended that the one cent was money lent and that the excess of $599.99 was interest for its use. "The consideration of one cent is plainly in this case merely nominal and intended to be so."

Cases in which this is not true are not within the supposed exception.

In an ordinary contract for a loan of money, the debtor promises to repay a sum larger than the amount advanced; but the repayment is to be made at a later date and the difference is interest for the use of the money lent. The value of this use is as much a matter for the agreement of the parties as is the value of a chattel. Therefore, in the absence of a usury statute, a contract that requires the payment of a very high rate of interest will be enforced, up to the point at which "unconscionability" becomes an operative factor.[96]

If the two sums of money to be exchanged are in different currencies, not having a mathematically certain relation to each other, the ordinary rule applies. Usually, there is no relation that is fixed by law in the relative values of pounds and dollars, or of francs and rubles. A contract for the exchange of such foreign currencies is not invalidated by the fact that it is not in accord with the generally prevailing rate of exchange. At the present time, gold has been withdrawn from active circulation and it has been forbidden by federal law to reckon a gold dollar as having different value from a paper dollar. Before the passing of this statute, paper dollars were subject to market depreciation in terms of gold, so that a promise to pay $20 in paper for $10 in gold was enforceable.[97] Likewise, certain coins have an exceptional scarcity value in the market in terms of the dollar as a mere measure of value; a promise to pay $3,000 in exchange for one silver dollar minted in 1804 would be enforced. The rare coins have market values that are changeable and uncertain; and the recognition of this fact has not been forbidden by statute.

### § 130. Nominal Consideration—Effect of a Written Acknowledgment

The requirement of a sufficient consideration for a promise is not satisfied by a pretense that there is a consideration when in fact there is none. A nominal consideration is not a sufficient one, if we mean by nominal that the stated consideration is a pretense and not a reality.[98] This is true whether the statement indicates that the consideration is large or small. Since the law does not require the consideration to be adequate, written promises are often stated to be "in consideration of one dollar." Here, we have a case of "nominal" consideration, if the statement is untrue. The smallness of the consideration may not make it insufficient to support the promise if it was in fact bargained for and given in exchange. One dollar given or promised is a sufficient consideration except for a promise of a larger amount of money.[99] But it is not a sufficient consideration when there is no dollar given or promised.[1] In holding the nominal consideration of one dollar to be insufficient, courts have not always taken the

189

trouble to determine whether or not it was in fact given or promised. Some of them may have disregarded it because of its relative smallness, although this is not consistent with the rule that is generally laid down.[2] An option contract is not invalid for insufficient consideration, even if the amount actually paid for it is only one dollar or a few dollars;[3] but in these cases the small sum is not shown to be an inadequate exchange for the option.

If in fact there was no consideration for a promise, it is not made enforceable by the fact that there is a written recital of consideration or by an acknowledgment that a consideration has been given and received.[4] The facts can be proved by other testimony, in direct contradiction of the recital or acknowledgment. Of course, the recital or acknowledgment is admissible in evidence as an admission of the fact by any party who executed the document.

Many written contracts recite that a promise made therein is "in consideration of one dollar and other valuable considerations." Such a recital as this does not prevent anybody from proving that the dollar was neither given nor promised, or from proving that there were in fact no "other valuable considerations." [8]

## § 131.  Is Consideration Required to be Valuable?  Love and Affection

It is a very common statement that a consideration must be "valuable" in order to be sufficient to sustain a promise. The statement is quite true as long as we define consideration as something that is bargained for and given in exchange for a promise. In order to have "value," a thing must be an object of human desire; it must be a thing that is bargained for and for which men will give other things in exchange. But men actually bargain for things that are not recognized by the law as a sufficient consideration; they are not sufficient even though they are valuable. Thus, we are prevented from saying that anything that is valuable is also a sufficient consideration. This has led some courts to say that in order to be sufficient a consideration must be valuable "in the eye of the law." [9] As so modified, it can not be admitted that the statement renders any service at all. It is no more than to say that a consideration is not legally sufficient unless the law regards it as sufficient.

To say that consideration must be valuable is not to say that it must be as valuable in the market as is that which is promised in exchange for it.[10] Nor is it to say that it must have value in any particular degree. It must merely be valuable in the sense that it is something that is bargained for in fact. One may promise his own price; and the law will enforce the promise.

The requirement of value, therefore, is one that excludes those things that are not the subjects of bargain and exchange by men.

It may, perhaps properly be regarded as excluding "love and affection." And yet, to the writer, it seems that love and affection are sometimes, even though rarely, bargained for. Whether such a bargain ever attains the desired end may be doubted. At all events, a promise to pay money in consideration of love and affection to be given in return is not an enforceable promise, even though the promisee gives proof that the desired love and affection were given in exchange. It is a matter of course that the fact that a promisor already has love and affection for the promisee is not a sufficient consideration for his promise to make a gift. It may very well be the motivating reason for the making of many a promise, and it may sometimes be held to be a sufficient "causa" in Roman and Continental law; but it is not given in exchange for the promise and by our law it is not a sufficient reason for enforcement of the promise of which it is the motivating cause.

### § 132.    Change in Legal Relations as a Consideration

Not infrequently it has been said that no consideration is sufficient unless it involves the "surrender of a legal right."[14] The statement can hardly be justified, whatever definition may be constructed for the terms "surrender" and "legal right." Men may bargain for acts and forbearances that involve no change in existing legal relations; and they can bargain for some specified change in legal relations without specifying the acts or forbearances by which the change may be effected. In either case there is sufficient consideration.

Most of the acts for which men bargain do, in fact, change some legal relation of the actor with others. If the promisor bargains for the act itself, as he generally does, it is not necessary that either party should know what are the changes in legal relations that the act will effectuate. They need not even know what a legal relation is. The contracting parties are usually aware, however, in at least a dim and half-conscious fashion, that legal relations will be changed and that it is this change for which the promisor really is bargaining. In the purchase of an automobile on credit, the buyer bargains and gives his promise "for the automobile." But what does he mean by this? In the first place, he means a change in physical possession; but, even more positively, he means a change of "ownership"—he wants the automobile to become "his" automobile. By this, he means that he is bargaining for a change in those legal relations that are called "property." Indeed, that is a term that the buyer is likely to use himself; he wants the automobile to become "his property." No further analysis of ownership or property is likely to be made by either party.

When the seller executes the bill of sale, or when he delivers possession, ownership passes to the buyer. The previously existing property relations of the seller with all other persons are now extinguished and similar property relations are created between the buyer and all other persons. If these property relations are called "rights," as they frequently are, it may properly be said that the promisee (seller) has surrendered his rights. If a more detailed analysis of property is made, into rights, powers, privileges, and immunities, then the seller has extinguished all of these and has created similar ones in the buyer.

Of course, the surrender of a right, or the extinguishment of any other beneficial legal relation, is a sufficient consideration when bargained for by the promisor.[15] This is true even though the right that is surrendered is future and conditional,[16] or is unenforceable by reason of the statute of frauds.[17] The discharge of rights created by a bilateral contract that has not been fully performed by either party is sufficient consideration.[18] The discharge of a debt owed by a third person is sufficient, even though such discharge can not benefit the promisor.[19] Where a creditor agrees to release one partner from a partnership debt in return for his retirement from the firm and the assumption of the debt by the continuing partners, there is sufficient consideration for the creditor's promise.[20]

The surrender and extinguishment of a legal power is a sufficient consideration, just as is the forbearance to exercise it without its surrender. Examples of this are the surrender of the power of accepting an offer, effected by rejecting it,[21] and the surrender of a power of attorney or power as an agent, effected by giving up the documentary appointment or by resignation.[22] One who has an option between two alternative performances has the power to discharge his duty by either performance. The surrender of this option, thereby extinguishing the power of discharge by rendering one of the performances is a sufficient consideration.[23]

If a promisor bargains for a forbearance to act, it is much less likely that the giving of the consideration effects any change in legal relations. When uncle promises nephew $5,000 in consideration of the latter's forbearance to smoke until he is twenty-one, the requested forbearance is sufficient consideration even though it involves no change in any existing legal relation.[24] It has been said that the boy surrenders his "right to smoke"; but

---

22. Forbearance to exercise a power, without actually surrendering it, is also sufficient.

See:

Cal.—Flint v. Giguiere, 195 P. 85, 50 Cal.App. 314 (1921), same.

Tenn.—White v. McMath & Johnston, 156 S.W. 470, 127 Tenn. 713, 44 L.R.

A., N.S., 1115 (1913), forbearance to accept the offer of a third person.

In these cases, the court does not distinguish between the extinguishment of the power and mere forbearance to use it.

24. See Hamer v. Sidway, 27 N.E. 256, 124 N.Y. 538, 12 L.R.A. 463, 21 Am.St.Rep. 693 (1891).

whatever is meant by this phrase, he surrenders none of it. At every moment of the period of forbearance, he retains the legal privilege of smoking, just as completely as he had it before the uncle made his offer. The boy extinguishes no privilege; he merely forbears to smoke, thus forbearing to act in a way that at all times it is his legal privilege to act. The boy's forbearance to smoke is a sufficient consideration, even though his legal relations are unchanged.

Other examples of a forbearance that is a sufficient consideration, even though no legal relation of anybody is changed are: forbearance to bring a suit against the defendant or a third person;[25] forbearance by a wife to request her husband to make her the beneficiary of an insurance policy;[26] forbearance to sell property or to accept an offer made by some third person;[27] forbearance to file a mechanic's lien.[28]

A change in legal relations is not a necessary part of sufficient consideration; but such a change may be bargained for by the promisor and if the requested change is thereupon brought about by the promisee, the consideration is sufficient. Here, the promisor does not bargain for any particular act; it is results that he wants and for which he bargains. It will be sufficient if the promisee brings about those results by any action, whether his own or that of third persons. Thus, if one promises to pay $5,000 for title in fee simple to Blackacre, it is immaterial whether the promisee creates such ownership in the promisor by livery of seisin, by a deed of conveyance executed by himself, or by a similar deed of a third person.

A promisor may bargain for the creation of a legal right, without specifying the act by which it is created; or he may bargain for a specified act that will create it. The same is true with respect to any other legal relation. The promisor may bargain for a power,[29] a privilege, or an immunity; or he may bargain for a specified act that will create them. In each case the acceptance must be in accordance with the offer that is made.

A promisor generally bargains for acts or forbearances that he describes, rather than for a change in legal relations that they may produce. Even then, he may make his own promise conditional not only on the rendering of the acts or forbearances but also on their being effective to produce the change in legal relations. It is clear that he may bargain for acts alone, for change in legal relations alone, for both at once, or for either one on other specified conditions.

## § 133. Lack of Consideration Distinguished from "Failure of Consideration"

When a promise is given by one party to another, without anything being bargained for or given in exchange for it, the promise is without consideration. The promise may be a binding unilateral contract anyway, by reason of its being made before a court or under seal, or because of subsequent action or forbearance by the promisee. But if none of these other factors exists, the promise is not enforceable.

In innumerable cases, however, a promise has been declared to be unenforceable because there has been a "failure of the consideration." This does not mean lack of consideration; nor does it often mean that the promise, now unenforceable, was never a valid contract. It does mean, on the other hand, that a performance for which the promisor bargained has not been rendered; in many cases, though not in all, that failure is a good legal excuse for his refusal to perform his own promise, and it may be a good reason for compelling restitution if he has already performed.

Suppose, first, that A offers his promise to B to deliver goods (or transfer title to land or to render a specified service) in exchange for actual payment by B of $2,000 within 30 days. This promise at once creates in B a power of acceptance; but it is as yet not a contract by reason of lack of consideration. If 30 days go by without a tender of the money by B, the promise of A is still not binding and for exactly the same reason as before—the lack of consideration. In addition, B's power of acceptance has expired by time limitation; but lack of consideration did not prevent the creation of B's power, nor is it "failure" of consideration that causes its end.

Suppose, secondly, that A offers his promise to B to deliver goods in exchange for B's promise to pay $2,000 therefor within 30 days. In this case B must exercise his power of acceptance by communicating a return promise within a reasonable time. If he does so, a valid bilateral contract at once is made. A's promise no longer lacks consideration; the requested consideration is B's promise to pay, and A has received it. Nevertheless, A's binding promise may become unenforceable in the future by reason of B's refusal or inability to pay. This refusal or inability is described as "failure of consideration." In this case it is a failure to render the promised performance. The consideration for A's promise was B's promise to pay; while the "consideration" that fails is the performance of B's promise (the money payment).

## § 134. Marriage is Sufficient Consideration

Marriage may be bargained for in return for a promise; and it is a sufficient consideration.[36] Usually the return promise is to make some kind of a marriage settlement; but it may be to render any other kind of performance. The marriage bargained for may be a marriage with the promisor or marriage with a third person. It is a sufficient consideration without regard to the wealth or disposition of the spouse who is being married. There is no need to try to determine whether the marriage is a beneficial or a detrimental one. In either case, it is a very important change in the legal relations of the one giving the consideration.

A promise to marry is likewise a sufficient consideration for a return promise; witness the many breach of promise suits under the common law.[39]

### § 135.   Forbearances and Promises to Forbear as a Consideration—Forbearance to Exercise a Privilege

It may be that the consideration for which a promisor bargains is usually affirmative action by the promisee or by some third person; but forbearance to act is also an object of desire and is actually bargained for in great numbers of cases. When so bargained for, the fact that it is forbearance rather than action makes it not the least less likely that it is a sufficient consideration. It is useful, nevertheless, to set forth a good many of the kinds of forbearances that have been held to be sufficient.

That action in reliance on a promise, even though not bargained for by the promisor, may make the promise binding will be discussed in a later section. There, too, it will appear that forbearance in reliance may have the same effect as does affirmative action.[40]

In practically all cases in which an actual forbearance would be a sufficient consideration, a promise of such forbearance would be equally sufficient.[41] The slight exceptions will not be considered at this point. If the consideration is forbearance, with no promise to forbear, the contract is a unilateral contract. At what moment in the process of forbearing the offer becomes irrevocable and the promise conditionally binding has been discussed in the chapter on offer and acceptance. It is certain that this moment may be antecedent to the completion of the requested forbearance.

During the period immediately after World War I, when the cost of living was rapidly increasing, the teachers of the town of Wallingford petitioned the town for an increase in their salaries to the extent of $300. This was in October, after the teachers were already at work under separate written contracts with the town which determined the work to be done and the salary to be paid and further provided that the teacher could terminate the contract at any time by giving thirty days' notice. At the time of the petition, the town school committee was informed that some of the teachers had received offers of positions elsewhere at higher pay. The committee voted to increase the teachers' salaries to the extent of $150 each. This vote was communicated to the teachers, with the result that they all continued to teach in Wallingford. There was a constitutional provision in Connecticut forbidding town officers to make gifts of public money; and the town treasurer refused to pay orders drawn upon him for the $150 increases in salary. The Supreme Court held that the town was bound by contract to pay to the teachers the amount of the increase and that the town treasurer must pay the orders.[42]

There is no doubt that this decision of the Connecticut court should be sustained. The vote of the town school committee to increase the salaries was an offer of a promise to the teachers, in order to induce them to remain in their positions and to forbear to resign. This was communicated to the teachers, and it produced the desired result on their part. In order to accept the offer, it was not necessary for them to give any notice of acceptance to the school committee. The terms of the offer did not require any notice of acceptance. The mode of acceptance reasonably to be understood and the consideration that was impliedly requested of them was their continuing to work as teachers and their forbearance to exercise their option of resigning.

Without actually so deciding, the court appears to have thought that the town's promise to pay the increased salaries would not be enforceable unless the teachers, in return, promised the town that they would not resign. The court says: "It is said that, while there was forbearance on the part of the teachers in this matter, there was no promise to forbear and, therefore, no real consideration for the promise of increased pay. But actual forbearance is evidence of an agreement to forbear, and in the absence of proof to the contrary is often held to be incompatible with any other condition." It may well be that the court was correct in finding that there was an implied promise on the part of the teachers to forbear to exercise their option of resigning during the remainder of the school year. Unless the town asked the teachers for such a promise, however, it was not at all necessary for them to make it, in order to accept the offer of the town and to make binding the promise of the increased salary. The facts stated in the report indicate that all that was impliedly requested by the town was actual continuance to teach and actual forbearance to resign. This requested consideration the teachers gave, making a valid and enforceable unilateral contract. The teachers forbore to exercise their contract privilege of resigning by giving thirty days' notice; but it does not appear that they surrendered it. By a reasonable interpretation of the transaction, if one of the teachers had given a thirty days' notice of his desire to resign, this act would merely have terminated his right to salary after the expiration of the thirty days; it would not

42.    **Conn.**—State ex rel. Marsh **v.** Lum, 111 A. 190, 95 Conn. 199 (1920).

have been a breach of contract by him. Until the expiration of the thirty-day period of notice, the teacher would have had a right to the payment of his salary at the increased rate.

It should be observed further that, in continuing to teach and forbearing to resign, the teachers were not merely doing that which they were required to do under their original teaching contracts. It is true that it was their pre-existing and their continuing duty under their written contracts to teach throughout the remainder of the school year as long as they did not give the thirty-day notice of resignation. The option provision merely gave them the power of terminating their contractual duty by giving a notice, and this power was not exercised by any of them. The new and sufficient consideration given by them for the promise of increase in salary was not merely their continuing to do their pre-existing duty as teachers; it was also their actual forbearance to exercise their reserved power of termination. This was a forbearance that they were under no duty whatever to give to the town. It was of value to the town; and in order to get it, the town promised to pay an increase of $150.

It follows from the foregoing that the payment of the $150 increase was in no respect a gift to the teachers; and the constitutional provision forbidding the making of gifts in no way justified the town treasurer in refusing to pay.[43]

## § 136.   Forbearance to Exercise a Legal Power as Consideration

If a man drinks or swears, within the bounds of custom, he is exercising one of his legal privileges; but he is not thereby exercising a legal power, he is changing no existing legal relations. One who has a legal power does not always have the legal privilege of using it. One exercises a power wrongfully when he commits a tort or a crime or is guilty of a breach of contract. One who forbears to exercise some legal power that he has is usually also forbearing to exercise his legal privilege. His forbearance, in such cases, is all the more certainly a sufficient consideration for the reason that he is forbearing to exercise a power as well as a privilege. The element of this forbearance that the promisor may bargain for, either exclusively or in part, may be forbearance to use the power. If an offer has been made to B by A, B has power to accept; and if C promises B $100 for not accepting A's offer, C is bargaining for B's forbearance to use his power to accept. There is sufficient consideration for C's promise.[49]   The

---

49.   In White v. McMath & Johnston, 156 S.W. 470, 127 Tenn. 713, 44 L.R.A., N.S., 1115 (1913), a landowner had made an offer to sell his land to the plaintiffs. The defendant wished to buy the same land but could not induce the owner to deal with him while the plaintiffs were still considering the offer made to them. The defendant thereupon promised to pay the plaintiffs $240 for a consideration expressed as follows: "The consideration for the payment of said sum is the relin-

following are further examples of forbearance to exercise a legal power as sufficient consideration: forbearance to terminate a contract or a tenancy by giving notice in accordance with a reserved power;[50] forbearance to revoke an offer for a specified time; [51] forbearance to exercise a power of creating a mechanic's

quishment by said McMath and Johnston of their right to purchase said land at said prices, and leaving me, W. C. White, free to conduct negotiations on my own account with said owners." This consideration was held to be sufficient and the promise was enforced. The character of this consideration is deserving of some analysis.

Suppose first that the plaintiffs, without making any promise to the defendant, merely forebore at his request to accept the landowner's offer to sell. In this case they never lost the power of accepting the offer until the landowner himself withdrew it. Further, making no promise to the defendant, they were at all times legally privileged to accept the landowner's offer. They gave up, therefore, neither their power nor their privilege of accepting that offer. Nevertheless, their forbearance to exercise the power of acceptance would be a sufficient consideration.

Suppose secondly, the plaintiffs promised the defendant not to accept the offer. The contract would now be bilateral and the plaintiffs would be under an enforceable duty to the defendant. The promise thus made by the plaintiffs would also be a sufficient consideration. They would still have the power of accepting the landowner's offer, but they would be under a legal duty to the defendant not to exercise it.

Suppose, thirdly, that in return for the defendant's promise the plaintiffs had written to the landowner rejecting his offer. This would make a valid unilateral contract, binding the defendant to pay the money promised. The plaintiffs make no promise to the defendant but they do an act which extinguishes their power of accepting the offer of the landowner. That

power was of value to them and its extinguishment by the rejection is ample consideration for a return promise.

Suppose, fourthly, that in return for the defendant's promise the plaintiffs had assigned to the defendant their power of accepting the offer made by the landowner. The courts have nearly always said that the power of accepting an offer cannot be assigned. If this statement is correct, there would be no sufficient consideration for the defendant's promise. If the statement is incorrect such an assignment would be ample consideration. There is no doubt that the power of acceptance created by what is called an "option contract" is assignable by the holders of the option. If in the present instance the plaintiffs had had such an option, they had the power of assigning it to the defendant. It does not appear, however, that they possessed such an option.

Suppose, fifthly, that the defendant had promised $240 if the plaintiffs would forbear to make a counter offer to the landowner. In this case the requested forbearance to make an offer, or a promise so to forbear, would be a sufficient consideration. The plaintiffs were legally privileged to make a counter offer. The forbearance to exercise this privilege or their extinguishment of their privilege by making a binding promise to the defendant, would equally constitute a sufficient consideration whether they made such a promise or merely forbore; in either case alike, they still retained the power of making a counter offer and of contracting with the landowner. Their forbearance to exercise this power would be a sufficient consideration for a return promise even though they at all times continued to possess the power.

lien;[52] forbearance to exercise a mortgagor's power to redeem after a foreclosure suit;[53] forbearance to make an offer or a bid at auction;[54] forbearance to withdraw a bank deposit.

## § 137.   Is Forbearance, without a Promise to Forbear, Sufficient?

The nature and the making of a unilateral contract have been discussed in an earlier chapter.  Such contracts are now pretty well understood by the bench and bar;  but it was not always so, and the term "unilateral contract" was often used to mean a promise without consideration and not enforceable.  As heretofore stated, the fact is that the unilateral contract was the only kind of simple contract that was known to the common law of England, for some centuries before bilateral contracts were recognized.  The existence of a contract debt required an executed quid pro quo.  After bilateral agreements consisting of mutual promises came to be enforced, they eventually occupied a very large place in the legal mind.  It became a common statement in the last century that "both parties must be bound or neither is bound."  This led to a number of decisions in respect to forbearance as a consideration that are quite erroneous.  They held that forbearance alone would not be sufficient, and that the return promise would not be binding unless there was a promise to forbear and not merely forbearance in fact.[55]

A clear distinction should be made between a case in which the promisor bargains for and receives the actual forbearance that he desires, asking for and receiving no promise, and that in which he does not bargain for forbearance but actually receives it because the promisee forbears in reliance on the promise.  Some cases make this distinction and hold that the forbearance is not a sufficient consideration, not because it was not promised, but because it was not bargained for and given in exchange for the promise.[56]  Such a decision as this may possibly be justified on its facts.  The doctrine that action or forbearance in reliance on a promise will make it enforceable is now well established, though its zone of application has rather indefinite boundaries.  But these cases clearly recognize that forbearance without being promised is a sufficient consideration if the promisor actually bargained for such forbearance without its being promised.

There are plenty of cases holding that forbearance if expressly or impliedly bargained for is a sufficient consideration;[57]  and

---

54.   Pa.—Bailey v. Marshall, 34 A. 326, 174 Pa. 602 (1896).

57.   In Strong v. Sheffield, 39 N.E. 330, 144 N.Y. 392 (1895), the court said: "There is no doubt that an agreement by the creditor to forbear the collection of a debt presently due is a good consideration for an absolute or conditional promise of a third person to pay the debt, or for any obligation he may assume in respect thereto. Nor is it essential that the creditor should bind himself at the time to forbear

the contrary decisions and dicta must be disregarded. Also, there are now many cases holding that forbearance in reliance may make a promise enforceable even though it was neither promised nor bargained for.[58]  Services given at request are a sufficient acceptance of and consideration for a promise to pay for them, even though the employee makes no return promise to render the services or to continue the employment for any definite time;[59] and there is no less reason for holding a requested forbearance to be sufficient.

As in the case of other unilateral contracts, actual forbearance to sue does not involve the surrender of any right or privilege; at any moment during the process of forbearance, the promisee is privileged to cease forbearing and to bring his suit. And if he had any right to be enforced against the defendant, that right remains enforceable in the suit that he brings, so far as the present transaction is concerned. This fact has often been raised as an objection by the defendant when sued upon his new promise given for the forbearance. In one early English case,[60] the report reads: "It was moved in arrest of judgment, that here is not any consideration, for the defendant hath not any means to compel the plaintiff for to surcease his suit, for there is not any cross promise set forth in the declaration; and although that he doth surcease his suit, yet he may begin the same again." In spite of the objection, the plaintiff had judgment. In another case [61] the defendant objected that the plaintiff's "action still remains"; and the court adjudged for the plaintiff: ". . . the Court held an action of debt would well lie against the testator for the fifty shillings, being a sum of money due upon a contract in which he received quid pro quo; for the forbearing of a suit is as beneficial in saving, as some other things would have been in gaining."

It is clear that if a promisor bargains for a promise of forbearance, and is given none or only an illusory one, the fact that forbearance afterwards actually takes place is not an acceptance of his offer. This may justify some decisions.[63] In one case, a

collection or to give time. If he is requested by his debtor to extend the time, and a third person undertakes in consideration of forbearance being given to become liable as surety or otherwise, and the creditor does in fact forbear in reliance upon the undertaking, although he enters into no enforcible agreement to do so, his acquiescence in the request, and an actual forbearance in consequence thereof for a reasonable time, furnishes a good consideration for the collateral undertaking. In other words, a request followed by performance is sufficient, and mutual promises at the time are not essential, unless it was the understanding that the promisor was not to be bound, except on condition that the other party entered into an immediate and reciprocal obligation to do the thing requested."

63.  It clearly justifies the decision in Gaunt v. Hill, 1 Starkie 10 (1815), where in order to save his brother from debtor's prison he

wife indorsed her husband's note for a debt previously contracted; the creditor promised her in return that he would forbear to press her husband on the note "until I want my money." These words of the creditor constituted a mere illusory promise, not a real one; and the wife's indorsement promise to pay the note was held to be without sufficient consideration and unenforceable. This was the holding, even though the creditor had in fact forborne to press the husband for a year and a half.[64]

## § 138.    Forbearance for an Unspecified Time

If a promisor bargains for a promise of forbearance for a specified time, that promise must be given in acceptance. If a promisor bargains for actual forbearance (without a promise) for a specified time, his promise is conditional on continued forbearance for that time, although during its progress his offer is irrevocable. Very often, however, a promise is given by a surety in order to induce forbearance by the creditor, without specifying that such forbearance must be promised or that it must continue for any specified time. In such cases, forbearance by the creditor for a reasonable time is an acceptance of the offer and is a sufficient consideration for the surety's promise.[65] In like manner, a promise to forbear for a reasonable time is a sufficient consideration if it is given as bargained for.[66]

## § 139.    Forbearance from Suit or Other Legal Remedy or Defense

One of the most common kinds of forbearances that are bargained for by a promisor is forbearance to bring suit or forbearance to make use of some legal remedy. This is also one of the most common kinds of action in reliance on a promise, even though the promisor did not bargain for it. Of course, such forbearance as this is sufficient consideration, if the claim on which suit or other legal action was threatened was valid and enforceable.[67] Such forbearance as this is sufficient consideration for a promise of a third person, even though the claim is not one that

wrote: "I wish to know if you will give him a full discharge if I will pay one moiety of his debt. . . .if you will accept this call upon me tomorrow morning." The creditor waited a week and then wrote that "I shall not proceed against your brother." The mere forbearance was not what was requested; and the promise, if it was one, came too late.

64.    Strong v. Sheffield, 39 N.E. 330, 144 N.Y. 392 (1895), the court saying: "The consideration is to be tested by the agreement, and not by what was done under it. It was a case of mutual promises, and so intended." Perhaps a more accurate interpretation of the creditor's words would show that his promise was not illusory. Furthermore, the defendant appears to have been content with the promise as made, and she actually received for a year and a half the forbearance that she desired. Her indorsement might well have been enforced.

was asserted against him and the forbearance was of no advantage to him.[68]

If the plaintiff promised to forbear to sue his debtor in return for the promise of some performance by a third person, there is a valid bilateral contract. The plaintiff is then under an enforceable duty to the third person to forbear to sue the debtor for such time as the plaintiff specified in his promise; and the debtor will be a third-party beneficiary of the contract and can make use of it affirmatively and defensively in accordance with the prevailing law of third-party beneficiaries.[69]

An extension of time given by a creditor to his debtor is a sufficient consideration for a third person's promise.[70] Frequently this promise is a promise to pay the debt in the form of an indorsement or a guaranty. The "extension of time" is ordinarily a promise of forbearance instead of a forbearance without a promise. Such a promise would make the new agreement bilateral, even though it would also extinguish the debtor's duty to pay prior to the end of the extended period. It would also create a duty in the creditor not to bring suit.

It makes no difference in what court the suit was to be brought or had been brought. The forbearance at request to bring a suit, or to proceed further with a suit already brought, may be a sufficient consideration whether the suit was for some legal remedy or was in equity or probate or other court.[71]

## § 140. Forbearance to Press an Invalid Claim

Claims made by one person against another are frequently disputed and may be invalid. The claimant may not have the right or the defense that he thinks he has. Of course, if his claim is valid and correct, his forbearance to press it is sufficient consideration for a return promise;[73] this has been discussed in the preceding sections. But forbearance to press a claim, or a promise of such forbearance, may be a sufficient consideration even though the claim is wholly ill-founded. It may be ill-founded because the facts are not what he supposes them to be, or because the existing facts do not have the legal operation that he supposes them to have. In either case, his forbearance may be a sufficient consideration, although under certain circumstances it is not. The fact that the claim is ill-founded is not in itself enough to prevent forbearance from being a sufficient consideration for a promise.[74]

Forbearance to bring a suit, or to proceed with one already brought, or to press a claim in any other way, is not a sufficient consideration if the forbearance is with knowledge that the claim is ill-founded and void. This is on grounds of public policy, not because the forbearance is not beneficial to the promisor or detrimental to the promisee. Presumably, an ill-founded suit will be lost; and forbearance to bring it would generally not be detrimental to the claimant; this is true whether he knew that it was ill-founded or not.  There may occasionally be some benefit to be derived from pursuing an ill-founded claim—indeed, the suit might be won, or the claim might be admitted and paid; therefore the forbearance may be a detriment even though the claim is made in bad faith.  It is certainly a benefit to the promisor to be relieved of the necessity of defending a suit.  But the existence of such detriment to the promisee and benefit to the promisor does not make the promise enforceable or cause the forbearance to be held a sufficient consideration.  Forbearance to press an ill-founded claim, known to be ill-founded and made in bad faith, is not a sufficient consideration.[75]  The reason for this is that, if it were recognized as sufficient, ill-founded claims would be infinitely increased in number and the offense that is known as blackmail would become a profitable racket.  If a claim is ill-founded because it is based on a transaction known to be illegal, there are added reasons for holding that forbearance or dismissal is not a sufficient consideration.[76]

In a good many court opinions, it is stated that forbearance to press a claim (or a promise to forbear) is not sufficient consideration unless the claim was doubtful, that is, unless the claimant had some reasonable ground for belief in the justice of the claim.[78]  All agree that the claim must be made in good faith.  No doubt the absence of any reasonable ground for belief in its validity is some evidence that the claim was not made in good faith; but it would not be conclusive evidence.  Many courts are satisfied if the claimant had an honest belief in his claim, without regard to whether he had any reasonable basis for it.[79]  As a practical matter, the difference between the two stated doctrines may not be great.

In some cases it has been held that forbearance to press a claim that is barred by statute of limitations or one that is unenforceable by reason of the statute of frauds is not sufficient as a consideration.[83]  These cases should not be followed.  A barred debt is a sufficient basis for a promise to pay it, made by the debtor himself.  This indicates that efforts at collection made by the creditor are quite justifiable and might be successful.  Forbearance to make these efforts should be held to be a sufficient consideration for a promise by the debtor, even though he promises something different from payment of the debt itself, or for a promise by a third person.[84]  Likewise, the statute of frauds never makes an oral promise absolutely inoperative; and the obligee of such a promise is fully justified in pressing for collection.  There is always a possibility of collection, by finding written evidence

75.    U.S.—In re Greene, 45 F.2d 428
(D.C.N.Y., 1930), "imaginary claim".

or otherwise. Forbearance should be held sufficient as a consideration.

The reasoning in regard to forbearance as a consideration is applicable in all compromise agreements. There may be forbearance and a binding promise even though there is no compromise; but in all compromise agreements there is forbearance to press a claim or a promise of such forbearance. The promise to pay or to do something more than the promisor admits to be due and something less than the promisee claims is supported by the promisee's forbearance to press for the whole of his claim or for his promise of such forbearance. A compromise contract is not invalidated by the fact that the claim was unfounded, if it was believed in by the party making the claim. After the compromise is agreed on, whether as yet performed or not, the merits of the original claim become immaterial. Such contracts are nearly always sustained.[87]

## § 141. Doubt as to the Law Applicable to Undisputed Facts

Usually, the facts on which a claim is based are in dispute; and usually, also, there is no possibility of proving with mathematical certainty what the facts were. Sometimes, however, the facts are not themselves doubtful or disputed, the doubt or dispute being as to the actual legal operation of facts that are admitted by both parties. It is believed that little difference should be made between doubtful facts and doubtful law—between a dispute as to what the facts are and a dispute as to the legal operation of agreed facts. As Justice Holmes once said in a much quoted passage, the certainty of law is an illusion. Besides, "the law" can be determined only by what legislators have said and judges have decided in the past; and these sayings and decisions are as much a matter of "fact" as are the mailing of a letter, the speed of a car, or the words that A spoke to B on the fourth of July.[92]

The fact that a lower court has decided against the claim, or that a court has held adversely to it in a suit to which the claimant was not a party, does not make forbearance insufficient.[93] Forbearance to appeal or to litigate the question anew, as the claimant is privileged to do, is a sufficient consideration if the claim was such that forbearance to press it by suit would originally have been sufficient.

Nevertheless, some legal rules and doctrines are more definitely established and worded than others. Thus, for several centuries the promise of a married woman was held to be wholly void. Later, the courts of equity undermined this rule in certain classes of cases; but until this occurred, followed by reform legislation, the common law rule as to the contracts of married women must have been known to most persons making a business agreement. One who threatened suit on a married woman's promise would generally be making a claim that he knew to be void.  In such a case, the forbearance to press the claim would not be sufficient consideration;  and one who asserted that he made his claim in good faith would seldom be believed.  He would hardly have any reasonable ground for his belief.[94]

If the rule of law that is applicable to undisputed facts is not well established, there can be no doubt that forbearance to press a claim based on those facts should be held to be a sufficient consideration if the claimant was acting in good faith in the belief, either that the courts would sustain his claim or that he had a fair chance that they would do so.[95]

## § 142.   Bilateral Contracts—A Promise as Consideration for a Return Promise

A promise is a sufficient consideration for a return promise. This has been true for at least four centuries, ever since bilateral contracts were recognized.[96]  There are certain exceptions to the rule;  these will be discussed in following sections.

What is the reason that constitutes the basis of this rule?  In spite of many statements to the contrary, it is clear that a promise is not a sufficient consideration either because it is a "detriment" to the man who makes it or because it imposes a legal duty upon him.  We can not know that it creates a legal duty until we first know that the bilateral agreement is an enforceable contract.  To say that a promise is a sufficient consideration because it is binding, or because it creates a duty, or because it causes its maker to be subject to suit, is an obvious case of begging the question.  In a purely bilateral contract, a promise for a promise, each promise is the consideration for the other.  If each promise

---

94.  The claim made in Loyd v. Lee, 1 Strange 94 (1718), was on a note executed by a married woman ; and the decision can be justified as in the text above.

95.  In Cook v. Wright, 1 Best & S. 559 (1861, Q.B.), an assessment for street improvements was made by a public commission against Wright, the resident agent for Mrs. Bennett, the non-resident owner.  Wright did not believe himself bound to pay the assessment, under the existing legislation ; but the commissioners believed that he was, and another agent in a like case had submitted after being sued.  Wright gave his personal notes for the sum claimed, in return for the forbearance of the commissioners to sue.  These notes were enforced, even though the court knew that Wright had not been legally bound by the assessment.  In his opinion, it was said by Blackburn, J.: "We agree that unless there was a reasonable claim on the one side, which it was bona fide intended to pursue, there would be no ground for a compromise ; but we cannot agree that (except as a test of the reality of the claim in fact) the issuing of a writ is essential to the validity of the compromise.  The position of the parties must necessarily be altered in every case of compromise, so that, if the question is afterward opened up, they cannot be replaced as they were before the compromise."

is a sufficient consideration because it is binding on its maker, then in some occult way we are aware that each promise is binding before we know that there is a sufficient consideration for it.

It has often been said that a promise is a sufficient consideration because it is a "detriment" to its maker, and that it is a detriment because it subjects its maker to a legal duty and to a suit. This begs the question as has just been explained, at the same time lugging in the concept of "detriment." It is true that the making of a promise might be regarded as a "detriment" to the one who makes it, merely because the mouthing of the words requires effort or the writing of the words uses up ink and paper. It seems to be true, also, that if a promisor should clearly bargain for the mere oral expression "God save the king," or for the writing of such words as "Now is the time for all good men to come to the aid of the country," the speaking or the writing of the words would be a sufficient consideration for his promise. Such a transaction as this is a unilateral contract, if it is found to be a real "bargain" and not a "merry jest."

When one offers his promise to render service or to deliver goods in return for a promise to pay $500, is he bargaining for mere words, as in the above illustration? An affirmative answer is possible but hardly reasonable; in the present state of commerce and of education, it is believed that the offeror bargains not for the mere promissory words but for both the words and the performance that they promise. Both are the objects of his desire, the assuring words being the immediate object and the actual performance the ultimate object.

It is no doubt true also, in the present state of commerce and education, that the offeror expects the return promise to be legally enforceable. He may even make it clear, in express words, that he is bargaining for such enforceability, for legally effective promissory words as well as for the performance that they promise. The case in which he does this must be very rare. In some cases he does not even expect legal enforceability, and knows that he does not get it. He may willingly exchange his own promise for a return promise that is not enforceable, as when with knowledge of the law of infancy he bargains to deliver goods for an infant's promise to pay for them. In such a case, he neither bargains for nor gets a legally enforceable promise. What he does bargain for is the infant's words of promise and for the money that they promise. He is willing to make this bargain because he believes that the infant will keep his promise. He takes a risk, indeed, but it is not much greater than in other cases. Such an offeror is legally bound, even if the infant is not; but his risk of having to give something for nothing is somewhat reduced by another factor. As long as delivery has not yet been made, his duty to deliver is conditional on the infant's continuing ability and willingness to pay the price. If the infant becomes insolvent, the seller may stop delivery; if the infant repudiates, the seller is discharged from obligation. In these cases, there is the same "failure of consideration" as if the buyer had been of mature age.

It is not necessary, however, to continue this speculation as to the offeror's intention, or to determine whether he is bargaining for an oral expression or a written one, or for a legal obligation. The speculation that has occurred was made necessary only by the fact that learned scholars sought for the "secret" of consideration, for its "true meaning", for its "real essence". Many if not all of us thought for a time that it was found in the concept of detriment to the promisee. Assuming, as we were wont to do, that rules of law come first and decisions after, that courts have always been bound to follow the antecedent rule however much their steps may have erroneously wandered, we now further believed that no promise can be enforceable unless the promisee incurred a "detriment." This belief forced us to find somehow a detriment in the making of a promise; for we could not deny that a promise is sufficient to make a return promise enforceable.

The course of events and the current of decisions have compelled us to abandon this theory of "detriment to the promisee" as the solution of the "mystery of consideration", as the one and only basis of enforceability of promises. There was no "secret," although there was much to discover. There were only the ever-growing multitude of transactions of men, the flood of decisions by innumerable judges, the evolution of our social practices and mores, the rolling river of life.

Detriment to the promisee is only one of the factors leading to enforcement of a promise; it is still an important one. But the "detriment" need not be suffered by the promisee; and promises may be enforceable without the suffering of any "detriment" by anybody. We need no longer say that a promise is a sufficient consideration for a return promise because the making of it is a detriment, or because it is binding, or because its making requires muscular effort. Bilateral promissory agreements became enforceable because people made them and relied upon them and performed them. Our economy has long been a credit economy; it is largely by the keeping of promises that we live and prosper, and by the breaking of which we suffer and die.

This is not to say that every promise is enough to make a return promise enforceable, is a sufficient "consideration." We can no more say that than we can say that every executed performance is a sufficient consideration for a return promise. In most cases both of them are sufficient; and it is necessary to deal with the factors that prevent them from being so.

In order to be enforceable, the two promises of a bilateral contract do not have to be made at the same time; indeed, it is almost impossible for them to be so made. The offeror makes his promise as a part of his offer to exchange it for a specified promise of the offeree; and the latter makes his return promise as a part of his expression of acceptance. It is true that the offeror is not bound by his promise until acceptance, so that the two promises become binding simultaneously. This, however, is the legal effect of the offeror's promise, not his act of making it.

### § 143. Is the Sufficiency of a Promise as Consideration Dependent on the Sufficiency of the Promised Performance as One?

It is not every action or forbearance that is recognized by the law as a sufficient consideration for a promise, even though the promisor clearly bargains for it in fact. Sometimes men bargain for things that are not legitimate objects of desire; they also bargain for things that are legitimate but that are not regarded as a good reason for holding a man to his promise. As a general rule, with very few exceptions, a promise is a sufficient consideration for a return promise if the performance that is promised would be a sufficient consideration.[97] Also, it is a general rule, with perhaps only one exception, that a promise is not a sufficient consideration if the performance that is promised would not be one.[98]

The only exceptions to the first of these two rules that have occurred to the writer are the following: (1) A promise can be so vague and indefinite in its expression that it cannot be enforced and is therefore not a sufficient consideration. An actual performance rendered, however, can not be vague and indefinite

---

**97.** In Thorpe v. Thorpe, 12 Mod. 455 (1701), Holt, C.J., said: "A is possessed of Black Acre, to which B has no manner of right, and A desires B to release him all his right to Black Acre, and promises him, in consideration thereof, to pay so much money, surely this is a good consideration and a good promise, for it puts B to the trouble of making a release. Then where the doing a thing will be a good consideration, a promise to do that thing will be so too." See, also, 2 Street, Foundations of Legal Liability, 110 (1906); Williston, Consideration in Bilateral Contracts, 27 Harv.L.Rev. 518 (1914).

"So far as regards the matter of the consideration, as being executed or executory it may be observed that whatever matter, if executed, is sufficient to form a good executed consideration; if promised, is sufficient to form a good executory consideration: so that the distinction of executed and executory consideration has no bearing upon the question of the sufficiency of any particular matter to form a consideration." Leake, Contracts (1st Ed.) p. 314; Id. (2d Ed.) pp. 612, 613.

**98.** Restatement, Contracts, § 78, recognizes this rule and declares it to be applicable even to a promise to render one of two or more alternatives: "A promise is insufficient consideration if the promisor knows or has reason to know at the time of making the promise that it can be performed by some act or forbearance which would be insufficient consideration for a unilateral contract."

and it needs no enforcement.  Therefore, sometimes a bilateral agreement that is unenforceable against either promisor by reason of the vagueness of one of the promises has been held to become enforceable as a unilateral contract when the party making the vague promise renders a definite and complete performance.[99]  The acceptance of this performance as satisfactory by the other party might be regarded as a new expression of assent and a repetition of his former promise, thus making a new contract;  and it might be said, also, that the definite performance rendered was never promised at all, the vague words not constituting a promise.  If this be approved as sound, then we have no exception to the stated rule.  Frequently, however, both the courts and the parties think that a promise was made, in spite of vagueness of expression, and that the rendition of the definite performance is merely additional evidence of what was in fact promised.  The present writer prefers to say that there is no promise made until there is an expression that is capable of being understood.  On this theory, the performance is a sufficient consideration;  but there was no antecedent promise made.[1]

(2)  The second exception is a real one.  A promise may be void for some special reason, such as illegality, even though the promised performance is lawful.  Certain Sunday laws declare void any business contract made on Sunday.  So, a promise made on Sunday, to render service on Monday, would not be a sufficient consideration;  whereas the Monday service would be quite sufficient.  This exception has little importance, however;  for the return promise that was made on Sunday would also be void, and a new express or implied promise would have to be found on Monday as the agreed exchange for the performance then rendered.

(3)  A third exception is one in which A promises a payment in return for a promise of B to perform his already existing duty.  Here the defect in the contract originates in B's promise;  most courts have held that it is not a sufficient consideration and that A's promise is void.  A's promise being void, it is, in its turn, not a sufficient consideration for B's promise.  Yet, if A had paid cash, instead of promising to pay it, B would have been bound by his return promise and there would be a valid unilateral contract.  It appears, therefore, that A's promise is not a sufficient consideration although the performance that he promises would be sufficient.[2]

A survey of the cases leads clearly to the conclusion that, with respect to sufficiency as a consideration, promise and the performance promised stand together;  if the rendition of a per-

**2.**  Hay v. Fortier, 102 A. 294, 116 Me. 455 (1917), is a case that illustrates this exception.

formance is a sufficient consideration for a promise that is given in exchange for it, then the promise to render that performance is likewise sufficient. We need not forget the exceptions merely because they are few and insignificant; but we should not forget that they are indeed few and insignificant. We may find that there is no sound reason for their survival. The general statement is consistent with common sense and practical convenience. According to our present social and business mores, a man's word should be as good as his deed in determining the enforceability of a return promise; and surely his deed should be as good as his mere word.[10] It supports and is supported by the belief that when men exchange reciprocal promises each one is bargaining not only for the other's promise but also for the performance that he promises. Each knows that there is some risk that the performance will not be rendered; and each may be aware that one party's risk is greater than the other's (as in an aleatory contract); but even so, each one bargains for and hopes to get the performance that is promised him.

## § 144.  An Implied Promise as a Consideration

Implied promises have been discussed in an earlier chapter.[11] It was there argued that an implied promise is also an express promise, the implication being necessarily derived from some kind of expression by the promisor; an express promise can be made by other conduct as well as by words.

Promises are discovered by "implication," either for the purpose of enforcing the implied promise itself,[12] or for the purpose of finding a sufficient consideration for another promise that is enforced. It is the latter purpose in which we have an interest at this point. If a promisor bargains for another promise in return and gets it, he is bound. It makes no difference that the return promise is implied from conduct or from language that is not in the form of express promissory words. That is, it makes no difference with respect to the question of sufficiency of consideration. It may make a vital difference with respect to the question whether the offer has been accepted in accordance with

12.  In Sylvan Crest Sand & Gravel Co. v. U. S., 150 F.2d 642 (C.C.A. 2d, 1945), where the contract provided for cancellation by the United States at any time, the court sustained an action against the government, finding by implication a promise to take and pay for the trap rock and to give shipping directions or to give notice of cancellation within a reasonable time. "Beyond question the plaintiff made a promise to deliver rock at a stated price; and if the United States were suing for its breach the question would be whether the 'acceptance' by the United States operated as a sufficient consideration to make the plaintiff's promise binding. Since the United States is the defendant the question is whether it made any promise that has been broken."

its terms.   An implied promise is not prevented from being a sufficient consideration by the fact that it is implied from conduct or from words that are not in express promissory form.[13]

## § 145.   An Illusory Promise is Not Sufficient Consideration

If what appears to be a promise is an illusion, there is no promise; like the mirage of the desert with its vision of flowing water which yet lets the traveller die of thirst, there is nothing there. By the phrase "illusory promise" is meant words in promissory form that promise nothing; they do not purport to put any limitation on the freedom of the alleged promisor, but leave his future action subject to his own future will, just as it would have been had he said no words at all.

If A asks B to promise some future performance and B makes no answer, B has made no promise.   This is true, even though when the future time arrives B may then be willing to perform as requested and may actually so perform.   If, under these circumstances, A thinks that B has made a promise, he is under an illusion.   The same is true if instead of making no answer B had replied, "I predict that when the time comes I shall be willing to do what you ask."   A prediction of future willingness is not an expression of present willingness and is not a promise.   To see a promise in it is to be under an illusion.   We reach the same result if B's reply to A is, "I promise to do as you ask if I please to do so when the time arrives."   In form this is a conditional promise, but the condition is the pleasure or future will of the promisor himself.   The words used do not purport to effect any limitation upon the promisor's future freedom of choice.   They do not lead the promisee to have an expectation of performance because of a present expression of will.   He may hope that a future willingness will exist; but he has no more reasonable basis for such a hope than if B had merely made a prediction or had said nothing at all.   As a promise, B's words are mere illusion. Such an illusory promise is neither enforceable against the one making it, nor is it operative as a consideration for a return promise.[21]

21.   See Great Northern R. Co. v. Witham, L.R. 9 C.P. 16 (1873), in which Witham offered to supply "such quantities . . . as your storekeeper may order from time to time" at stated prices.   The Railway company wrote that Witham's offer was accepted.   But such an acceptance was only a promise to buy such quantities as they might thereafter order.   Their promise was illusory and was not a consideration sufficient to bind Witham and make his offer irrevocable.   It should be further observed, however, that Witham's offer asked for no such acceptance.   It asked for "orders."   The court did not doubt that an order for a specific amount, before notice of revocation, would make a valid contract.   The contract thus made would be bilateral in character, unless the order was accompanied by full payment in cash.

This is true even though the other promisor in fact bargains for a mere illusory promise in return and gets it. A man may bargain for mere words, without regard to their meaning or effect as a promise.[22] If he does so, and the words are expressed as requested, there may be a valid contract; but it is unilateral, not bilateral. Thus, if A offers his promise to pay $100 in return for B's shouting "God save the king," or saying "abracadabra," it may be that B has power to make a valid unilateral contract by accepting as requested. Likewise, if A offers his promise to pay $100 in return for B's saying "I will deliver to you 50 bushels of wheat if I wish to do so," B's saying these words may consummate a valid unilateral contract. But in the cases where the courts have refused to enforce a promise because the return promise was illusory, they evidently believed that the defendant did not bargain for the mere writing or speaking of the words, but thought that he was getting an expression of assurance that future performance would depend upon present statement and not upon future will or desire. If the promisor bargains for some sort of real promise, and receives only an illusion, there is no contract for the reason that the offer has not been accepted as well as for the reason that there is no sufficient consideration.[23] If the promisor chooses the very words that he requests the other party to use in accepting and those words are an "illusory promise," a valid unilateral contract can properly be held to exist.

As matter of course, no action will lie against the party making the illusory promise.[24] Having made no promise it is not possible for him to be guilty of a breach. Generally, the suit is against the party who really made a promise and the problem is as to the existence of sufficient consideration. This is dealt with under the heading of Option Contracts. The fact that one party has an unlimited option as to one or more performances does not prevent him from enforcing a promise of the other party if he gave a sufficient consideration for that promise that is not affected by his option.[25]

Where a dealer offers to supply on stated terms such quantities of goods as the offeree may choose to order during the next year and the offeree expresses assent thereto, there is no contract because the offeree has made no promise and has given no other consideration for the dealer's promise. Nevertheless, the transaction is operative as a standing offer to sell; and if the offeree, before any revocation, sends in an order for a definite amount of goods, a bilateral contract for such goods is effected.[26] However "illusory" his former expression of assent may be as a promise, his present order is an enforceable promise to buy and pay for the goods ordered, in accordance with the dealer's communicated terms.

## § 146.   Voidable or Unenforceable Promises as a Consideration

It has been said, thousands of times, that both parties to a contract must be bound or neither is bound.  It has been shown already that there are innumerable unilateral contracts, as to which this statement is quite untrue.  The law of contract is not limited to agreements that create reciprocal legal duties.  What the law generally requires is a sufficient consideration;  this may be fully performed in the very act of acceptance, so that the acceptor is never bound by legal duty to do or to forbear to do anything.

The statement comes nearer to the truth in the case of bilateral contracts, promise exchanged for promise.  Usually, both promises become binding simultaneously at the moment of acceptance of the offer.  If, at that moment, something prevents one of the promises from being legally enforceable, it is frequently assumed that the return promise is void for lack of sufficient consideration.[28]  There are some notable exceptions to the stated rule, if it really exists, in which one party may be bound by his promise even though the other party is not.[29]  It is difficult to find any support for the supposed rule, other than mere dicta of judges and writers, made perhaps with nothing but "illusory" promises in mind.

One of these exceptions is a bilateral contract between an infant and an adult.  By the common law, the adult is bound by his promise even though the infant is not bound by his.[30]  It is usually said that the infant's promise is voidable but not void;  but even where by statute or otherwise an infant's promise is declared to be void, the infant can generally enforce the return promise of the adult.  While the contract remains wholly bilateral and unperformed, the only consideration for the adult's promise is the void or voidable promise of the infant.  According to the generally prevailing law of infancy, if he is sued on his promise before having received any part performance, all that he needs to do is to plead infancy as a defense.  He does not have to show that he in some way avoided the contract prior to the suit.  Even when one is sued on a promise that he never made, he must plead the fact in defense or judgment will go against him.  The infant's position seems to be not much different from this, so far as being "bound" is concerned.  Some of the legal relations are indeed different.  The infant has a power of ratification on becoming of age.  It is not necessary to make a complete analysis here;  at any rate, it is clear that the infant's promise, void, voidable, or ratifiable, is a sufficient consideration.  The same is true of the promise of an insane person.[31]

30.   Eng.—Holt v. Ward Clarencieux, 2 Strange 937 (1732, K.B.), mutual promises of marriage made by a girl of fifteen and a man of full age;  Forrester's Case, 1 Sid. 41 (1662).

Another type of exception is a promise voidable for fraud, duress, or illegality. If one party to a bilateral contract is induced to make it by fraudulent representations by the other party, he has the power of avoidance and also the power to ratify. The promise of the defrauder is enforceable, while that of the injured party is not. It is true that a suit to enforce the defrauder's promise, brought with knowledge of the fraud, operates as a ratification; but even prior to the suit, the defrauder was bound, while the defrauded party was not. There was no absence of a sufficient consideration.[32]

In the case of a bilateral contract requiring an illegal performance, the illegality being due to facts known to one of the parties but not to the other, the innocent party can often maintain an action for breach of contract by the guilty one, although the latter could not enforce the promise of the former.[33] Attempts have been made to explain these cases on some theory other than contract, but the fact remains that the innocent party has been given damages for breach of contract, the court not being handicapped by any narrow definition of consideration or any limited theory of contract.

Another type of exception is the case of a bilateral contract that is within the statute of frauds and has been reduced to writing and signed by one party only. The contract is unenforceable against the one who has not signed; but his unenforceable promise is a sufficient consideration, so that he can enforce the signed promise of the other party.[34]

The promises of a sovereign government, including those of the United States and of the individual states, cannot be enforced in the courts unless there is definite legislation authorizing such action. The fact that the promise of the government is unenforceable does not render it an insufficient consideration for the promise of the other party to the contract.[35]

### § 148. Aleatory and Conditional Promises as Consideration for a Return Promise

A promise is not made insufficient as a consideration for a return promise by the fact that it is conditional, even though the condition is one that is purely fortuitous and may never happen at all.[49] A promise that is subject to such a fortuitous condition

---

**35.** Section 147. Non-binding Promises as Consideration—Rule in Restatement, Contracts, § 80, is here omitted. It contains a criticism of the Restatement rule.

**49.** Restatement, Contracts § 77: "except as qualified by secs. 78–80, any promise whether absolute or conditional is a sufficient consideration." The exceptions referred to need not here be explained.

Observe that in the present section we are dealing with the sufficiency of an aleatory promise as a consideration for a return promise, and not with the sufficiency of

is called an "aleatory" promise. It is a chance-taking promise, but is not necessarily an illegal wager even under various statutes directed against gambling. Insurance and commercial contracts for the carrying of existing risks are in most instances lawful.

Most offered promises are conditional on an expression of acceptance; but when acceptance has taken place the condition is performed and the promise is no longer thus conditional. Even after acceptance, in the case of bilateral contracts, at least half of the promises constituting the contract are conditional on something. Frequently one promise is conditional upon performance or tender of performance of the return promise. Thus the promise of an employer to pay wages is generally conditional on the rendering of the service promised in return by the workman. The promise of a buyer of land or chattels to pay the price is generally conditional on conveyance, or tender thereof, of the land or the chattels. Of course, the fact that a promise to pay is conditional in this manner does not render it an insufficient consideration; it is not an aleatory promise.

An employee's promise to render specified service if and when requested by the employer is a sufficient consideration for the employer's promise to pay a regular salary per month for life. The employee's promise to serve is conditional on request by the employer; but the option is in the employer, not the employee. Such is the effect of this bilateral agreement, even though it is made on the employee's reaching a retirement age and the employer contemplates requesting little or no service; he must continue to pay the agreed salary for life, though he requests and receives no service.[50]

A promise may be conditional on some event that is certain to occur at some time, but one over which neither party has any control. A promise to pay money upon the death of X is such a promise; it is a sufficient consideration for a promise that is given in exchange.

A promise is not insufficient as a consideration, even though it cannot be performed without first obtaining the assent of some third person, and even though the third person is under no obligation whatever to give his assent. The promise may be expressly or impliedly conditional upon such assent being given. If such is the case, the failure to secure such assent would not itself be a breach of the promise; nor would failure to render the promised performance in the absence of assent be a breach, for the reason that a condition precedent has not occurred. In

the consideration that is given for an aleatory promise. Such consideration may indeed be very small, as appears in the cases put in the earlier section on Adequacy of Consideration.

spite of this, the conditional promise is a sufficient consideration for another promise given in return.[51] If, on the other hand, the promise was not expressly or impliedly conditional upon the giving of assent by a third person, but it is an undertaking by the promisor to render a performance that will be impossible for him to render unless he secures the assent of a third person, his unconditional promise to render the performance includes by implication a promise that he will secure the third person's assent.[52] In this case his failure to do so would in itself be a breach of his contract and his promise is certainly a sufficient consideration for a promise given in return.

A contract is not invalidated by the fact that a promisor makes his duty to render performance conditional on the non-occurrence of "strikes, fires, and other circumstances over which we have no control." [53] This is a very common provision in contracts for the manufacture and delivery of goods by a stated time. The provision is rather indefinite and requires the exercise of discretion by the court in determining what constitutes such a strike or fire or other circumstance as will prevent liability for failure to perform.

A promise is not rendered insufficient as a consideration by being made expressly conditional upon some voluntary act of the promisor himself, in case the forbearance to do that act would itself be a sufficient consideration if it were bargained for. Thus, where A promised to charter a ship to B at a stated rate, if A should thereafter buy the ship; B promised in return to pay the stated rate if the ship should be delivered to his use. This was held to be a valid bilateral contract.[54] A's promise bound him either to charter the ship to B or not to buy it.

If a seeming promise is made conditional upon an event that can not occur at all, as the promisor knows, no real promise has been made. This is one form of the so-called "illusory promise"; it is not a sufficient consideration for another promise. If, on the other hand, the promise is conditional upon an event that may possibly occur, it is not illusory; and it is not made an insufficient consideration by the fact that the probability that the event will occur is very slight.[55]

Ordinary bets on a horse race or an election may be illegal by statute; but each promise is not prevented from being a sufficient consideration by the fact that it may never have to be paid.[56] Each party to the bet hopes and believes that he will win and that

54.   Scott v. Moragues Lbr. Co., 80 So. 394, 202 Ala. 312 (1918).

55.   The American Law Institute, Contracts Restatement, § 84(f),

"Consideration is not insufficient because of the fact that it is a promise, performance of which is conditional on either a future or past event, if when the promise

he will have to pay nothing. The event that is the subject of the bet must either happen or not happen; and it is known in advance that the winner will not have to pay. Yet this fact does not make the winner's promise an insufficient consideration. This is true even though the subject of the bet is a past event, provided that its happening or not happening is not known to the parties at the time of the agreement. It is true, that in such a case the bet seems to be actually won at the time it is made; but to the parties it seems that each is taking the same sort of a chance as if the event were of the future.

Suppose that the good ship Jeannette has sailed for Arctic seas, and that she has not been heard from. The owner procures a marine insurance policy, giving his promissory note for the premium in return for the insurer's promise to pay the value of the ship if sunk between date of sailing and date of policy. This is a valid bilateral contract. If the ship has not foundered, the owner must still pay his note; and it is no defense to the insurer that the ship had foundered and that he was a sure loser.[57] In cases like this, there may always be some difficulty in proving the event; so that each party may be regarded as having some chance of being the winner.

Other illustrations of aleatory contracts are as follows: A buyer of land thinks he has received fewer acres than was represented. It is then agreed that the seller will return to the buyer $16 for each acre of deficiency that a survey shows, and that the buyer will pay to the seller $16 for each acre of excess as shown by the survey. This is a valid contract, even though it seems certain in advance that one promisor will not have to pay anything.[58] Nor is the contract invalidated by the fact that each party feels sure that he knows his ground, and that the survey shows that one of them was right. Of course, they could not know with mathematical certainty what the new survey would show.

Again, suppose that A has a share in a trading adventure. Wishing to hedge thereon and reduce his responsibilities, he agrees with B that he will pay over to B one half of the profits if any, in return for B's promise to pay to A one half of the losses if any. This is a valid contract.[59]

A dispute having arisen over title to land, the parties agreed to submit the matter to arbitration. A promised that if the arbiter decided against him he would take no action to recover the

is made there is any possibility, or there would seem to a reasonable man in the position of the promisor to be any possibility, that the promise can be performed only by some act or forbearance which would be sufficient consideration."

59. **N.Y.**—Coleman v. Eyre, 45 N.Y. 38 (1871).

land; and B promised that if the arbiter decided against him he would at once surrender possession. B lost the decision; and A was given judgment for damages for B's refusal to vacate.[60]

A physician promised to render necessary medical services to B for life, in return for B's promise to bequeath the sum of $100,-000 to the physician. B's promise was binding, even though B might need slight medical service or even none at all.[61]

Suretyship and guaranty contracts are aleatory in character. In one case, A guaranteed the payment of bills of exchange accepted by X for £162, in return for B's guaranty of a bill of £300 for goods bought by Y.[66] If X pays according to his acceptance, B remains bound to pay £300 even though A has to pay nothing. If both X and Y default, A must pay £162 and B must pay £300.

### § 149. Promises Conditional upon Events within the Promisor's Own Power

One who in words promises to render a future performance, if he so wills and desires when the future time arrives, has made no real promise at all. If a promise is expressly made conditional upon something that the parties know can not occur, no real promise has been made. It has been thought, also, that promissory words are illusory if they are in form a promise that is conditional on some fact or event that is wholly under the promisor's control and his bringing it about is left wholly to his own will and discretion.[67] This is not true, however, if the words used do not leave an unlimited option to the one using them.[68] It is true only if the words used do not in fact purport to limit future action in any way. Thus, if A promises to charter a specified ship to B on certain terms if A shall thereafter buy the ship, these words leave A clearly privileged not to buy the ship and in such event also privileged not to charter it to B; but it is equally clear that the words do not leave A privileged to buy the ship and then not charter it to B. A contract on such terms is valid and enforceable.[69]

It is very clear indeed that promissory words are not nullified by making the promise conditional on some event within the promisor's own power, if at the same time he impliedly promises to make reasonable effort to bring the event about or to use good faith and honest judgment in determining whether or not it has in fact occurred.[71] When words are put in promissory form,

66. Christie v. Borelly, 29 L.J.C.P. 153 (1860).

69. Scott v. Moragues Lbr. Co., 80 So. 394, 202 Ala. 312 (1918). The promisor has an option between chartering to B and not buying the vessel at all. This is a limited option and is a restriction on the future conduct of A. If A will not charter to B, he must not buy. If he buys, he must charter, and B must pay therefor.

courts are loath to give them an interpretation that makes them empty in fact and misleading to others.

A promise to pay "when able" to do so, or to pay a specified sum "at my convenience," has been held not illusory and to be enforceable.[72] The fact of ability to pay and the fact of convenience can be determined by objective tests, even though their application must depend upon many related and varying factors. Such a promise to pay is not conditional upon the promisor's own wish and desire, but upon an economic situation that can be objectively determined by a court.

When it appears to a court's satisfaction that the parties have believed themselves to be making a contract, to be affecting their legal relations with each other, sound practical policy requires that their mutual expressions should be given an interpretation that will effectuate their belief and intention.[73] The courts have often made such a statement, and none seems to have doubted its soundness. There is no reason for surprise in the fact that its applications show differences in breadth of understanding, in willingness to fill gaps, in independence of narrowly expressed rules. It is quite true that courts should not and do not make contracts for the parties; but they should and generally do use common sense in interpreting and giving effect to serious transactions.

## § 151.  Condition Distinguished From Consideration

The term "condition" is discussed in a later chapter. For our present purposes. it is enough to define a condition as as operative fact or event that is necessary to the existence of some legal relation. If A promises to pay B a sum of money on his wedding day, B's marriage is a condition precedent to A's duty to pay. In this case, B's marrying may be the consideration for A's promise as well as a condition of A's duty to pay. If A offered his promise to B as part of a bargain, requesting B to get married in return for his promise, then B's marrying is the acceptance of A's offer and the consideration for A's promise. It is also an event that is necessary to the existence of a legal duty in A to pay the promised amount.

On the other hand, A may have promised the money as a mere gift, motivated solely by love and affection. If so, B's marriage is not a consideration for A's promise; but just as before A has made it a condition of his promise of a gift. The fact that A's promise is thus conditional does not make it a binding promise. It is merely a promise of a gift *cum onere*.[81] Marriage is a valuable and sufficient consideration if bargained for as such; otherwise, it is not. Even if it is not bargained for and is not called a "consideration," it might nevertheless be held to make the promise of a gift binding and enforceable. It is a serious change of position by the promisee, in reliance on A's promise, a change that the terms of A's promise show A had ample reason to foresee. In many of the cases in which gift promises of land were enforced, the promise was conditional upon moving to and residing on the land.[82] The performance of the condition is sometimes described as a "consideration." In other cases, it is not. In many other gift cases, the promise was not made on condition; but the action in reliance occurred anyway. If the condition is such that its performance requires substantial effort or expense by the plaintiff, its performance should be and has been held to make the promise enforceable.[83] In such a case, the courts have said that the performance of the condition is a sufficient consideration for the promise, without making a nice discrimination between performance of a condition that is also a consideration and performance of a condition that is only action in reliance on the promise.[84]

Suppose, next, that A promises to pay a sum of money to B as soon as A shall get married to C. Here, there is no possibility that A's marriage can be the consideration for A's promise; but it is a condition precedent to his duty to pay B, just as B's marriage was in the previous illustration. A's promise will not be binding unless something else is given as a consideration, or there is other action by B in reliance on A's promise, or the promise is under seal.

A few other illustrations follow. In consideration of a premium of $50 paid in cash, an insurance company promises to pay B the amount of his loss if his house shall burn. Here, the fire is a condition, but not the consideration.

A lends money to B, receiving in exchange B's note and a written guaranty of payment by S. Here, nonpayment by B at maturity is a condition precedent to the duty of S to pay the debt. By the law of some states, a notice of B's default is also a condition precedent. But neither of these is a consideration.

A and B sign a building contract, B promising to build and A promising to make instalment payments on receipt of architect's certificates. The architect's certificate is a condition of A's duty to make any payment; but it is not a consideration.

Oftentimes, the contracting parties use the term "condition" to describe what is also the consideration. Thus, A promises to pay B $1,000 "on condition that B shall convey Blackacre by warranty deed to C." The conveyance is here both the consideration and a condition of A's duty, although the word "consideration" is not used.[85] There are many cases in which it is hard to determine whether or not a certain fact or event is a condition of a promisor's duty; and sometimes it is hard to determine what was the consideration for a promise.

# CHAPTER 6

## CONSIDERATION—MUTUALITY OF OBLIGATION—RE-QUIREMENT BARGAINS—EFFECT OF OPTION

---

## § 152. Mutuality of Obligation

For the existence of a valid contract, is there a general requirement that there must be "mutuality of obligation"? Before this question can be answered in either way, a discussion is necessary of what is meant by the phrase "mutuality of obligation." That such mutuality is necessary is one of the most commonly repeated statements known to the law of contract. Both parties to a contract must be bound or neither is bound. The contract is void for lack of mutuality. Thus the law is stated.

The concept of "mutuality" is an appealing one; and it has played an important part in the making of decisions as well as in the writing of opinions. In criticising the term and its use by the courts, therefore, we must not be too ready to disregard what lies behind it. Even though there is vagueness and inconsistency and error in the use of the phrase, it will continue to have an appealing sound and to influence decisions. Mu-

221

tuality seems to connote equality, fairness, justice.[1]  So we have the concept appearing in several different connections. We have (1) mutuality of assent, widely asserted as a requirement, but actually often disregarded; (2) mutuality of consideration, although if only one promise is made we need to search for only one consideration; (3) mutuality of remedy, many times given as a requirement for granting the remedy of specific enforcement, but with so many exceptions that they occupy substantially the whole field; (4) mutuality of obligation.

So appealing has been this last phrase that the term "unilateral contract," seeming to be its opposite, almost came to mean a one-sided unenforceable promise.  A valid contract had to be "mutual"; if not mutual, it was "unilateral" and void.  But the judges are now following the leading text writers in using the term "unilateral contract" to mean one that consists of a single binding promise.  Such a promise can be binding if it is under seal or if an executed consideration has been exchanged for it. In cases like these, it is not necessary that there should be two reciprocal promises or that the parties should be mutually bound by enforceable duties to each other.[2]

Mutuality of obligation should be used solely to express the idea that each party is under a legal duty to the other;  each has made a promise and each is an obligor.  This is the meaning with which the term is commonly used.  There are cases, however, in which it is otherwise defined.  In order to save the supposed requirement of "mutuality," it is sometimes declared that it means nothing more than that there must be a sufficient consideration. Even though one of the parties has made no promise and is bound by no duty, the contract has sufficient mutuality if he has given an executed consideration.[3]  Thus, the validity of a unilateral contract is recognized, at the same time appearing not to run counter to the requirement of mutuality.  While the result reached in these cases is sound, such a method of rationalizing it merely perpetuates confusion of thought.  There are now plenty of cases that clearly recognize the validity of a unilateral contract.[4]  Courts now often say correctly that it is consideration that is necessary, not mutuality of obligation.[5]

There are many cases giving lack of mutuality as the reason for holding that no contract was made, in which the plaintiff made no promise of any kind.[6]  In some of these, it might have

1.　The supposed requirement of "mutuality" is not that the promised performances must be of equal value in the general market, or that each promise made by one party shall have its own reciprocal promise made by the other party. Warren v. Ray County Coal Co.,

207 S.W. 883, 200 Mo.App. 442 (1919).

2.　See Restatement, Contracts, §§ 12, 75, 76, and 85–94.  The Restatement is approved in Jackson v. Pepper Gas Co., 133 S.W.2d 91, 280 Ky. 226, 126 A.L.R. 1370 (1939).

been possible to find a return promise by a process of implication;[7] but if the basis of such an implication is too slight and no other consideration was given for the defendant's promise, of course the decision that no contract was made is correct. It is quite correct also to say that mutuality of obligation is lacking, and equally correct to say that even a single obligation is lacking. It may be a satisfactory reason for holding the defendant's promise unenforceable that there was no consideration; merely saying that there was no mutuality is wholly unsatisfactory.

In most option contracts, the option holder makes no promise, but pays cash or gives some other executed consideration. The option giver's promise is enforceable, in spite of lack of mutuality of obligation.[8]

In very many cases in which one party makes an offered promise, but receives no return promise, the offer is made in such a way that it can be accepted piecemeal by rendering a requested performance, thus making a valid unilateral contract on the offered terms.[9] If A promises to buy all the goods that B may make and deliver, on specified terms, a letter by B saying that he accepts, but making no promise either to make any goods or to forbear to make for others, is no acceptance. B gives no consideration for A's promise. Yet the actual delivery of goods by B, as specified, will cause A's promise to take and pay for that quantity to be enforceable.[10] Unless the part performance is so rendered as to justify the implication of a promise to render the entire performance proposed in the offer, such part performance leaves the offer revocable at the will of the offeror as to all but the part performance.[11]

In these cases, the court often says that, although the agreement was void for lack of mutuality, it is made binding by performance—even by part performance, so far as concerns the part actually performed. Since such offers are usually made in such terms as to give the offeree the power to accept either by making a promise or by rendering actual performance, the acceptance by such actual performance consummates a valid unilateral contract. But if the offer requires a promissory acceptance, then these cases can usually be justified on the theory that the rendering of actual performance is a counter offer, at the rates specified in the first offer, and that the receipt of such performance is an acceptance by the original offeror. Often, it is not necessary to determine which theory is applied, since the facts are such as to make both of them applicable. But if the offer is so made as to exclude acceptance by performance, or if the performance by the offeree is rendered without the knowledge of the offeror, the facts should be carefully analyzed to see which theory is applicable if either one is so.

### § 153. Promise to Pay a Bonus or Pension Conditional on Continued Service

A promise by an employer to pay a bonus or a pension to an employee in case the latter continues to serve for a stated period is not enforceable when made;[12] but the employee can accept the offer by continuing to serve as requested, even though he makes no promise.[13] There is no mutuality of obligation; but there is sufficient consideration in the form of service rendered. Indeed, the employer's offered promise becomes irrevocable by him as soon as the employee has rendered any substantial service in the process of accepting; and this is true in spite of the fact that the employee may be privileged to quit the service at any time.

Even though an offered promise is a promise of a single performance and creates no power to make a series of separate obligations by piecemeal and repeated acceptances, the offer may become irrevocable and binding by reason of a part performance by the offeree. A part performance of the bargained-for consideration, forming a part of the expected process of acceptance, is now held to make the offer irrevocable although the duty of the offeror is conditional upon completion by the offeree. The bonus cases just referred to are of this kind. Although the bonus is not fully earned until the service has continued for the full time, after a substantial part of the service has been rendered the offer of the bonus cannot be withdrawn without a breach of contract. Also, if a bank promises to make a loan, on collateral security to be given and approved, its promise may become enforceable by the actual delivery and receipt of the security, even though the promisee has never made a promise to borrow any particular sum and no bilateral contract exists.[14]

### § 154. Unilateral and Bilateral Agency Contracts

Contracts between principal and agent, like other employment contracts, may be either bilateral or unilateral. The principal may promise either a salary or commissions or both; and the agent may promise in return to render specified services for some stated period. In these cases, there is "mutuality of obligation"; the consideration for each promise is the return promise. A real estate agent, with whom property is placed for sale, seldom promises that he will find a purchaser at the price desired by the principal; but he may, either expressly or impliedly, promise that he will diligently advertise and solicit. Here, too, there is "mutuality of obligation," the contract being bilateral. The

---

13.   **Ohio** —Sigman v. Rudolph Wurlitzer Co., 11 N.E.2d 878, 57 Ohio App. 4 (1937), pension system.

14.   **N.D.**—Murphy v. Hanna, 164 N. W. 32, 37 N.D. 156 (1917).

validity of such a contract is not affected by the fact that the principal promises to pay nothing for the agent's diligent efforts; his promise is to pay for the production of a purchaser on the terms fixed.[15] Nor is it affected by the fact that the agent makes no promise to find a purchaser, the very result for which the commission is promised. Two promises may be exchanged for each other, even though the two promised performances are not exchanged at all, and are not regarded by the parties as of equivalent value. The principal has agreed to exchange his money for finding a purchaser, not for diligently looking for one.

Many contracts between principal and agent are purely unilateral, there being no "mutuality of obligation." As in the case just discussed, the principal promises to pay a commission for the finding of a purchaser, for the actual selling or buying of stock or bonds or commodities, or for some other completed result; but the agent or broker may make no return promise at all, not even a promise of diligent effort. In a case like this, the principal's promise is not binding when it is first made, unless it is under seal;[16] but it becomes irrevocable as soon as the agent has performed some substantial action in the process of attempting to earn the commission, and it becomes immediately enforceable when the requested result is attained and the time set for payment has come. Here, the agent has never made any promise; but he has acted at request and in reliance on the principal's promise. There is never any "mutuality of obligation"; but there is a valid unilateral obligation as soon as the agent's services are recognized as a sufficient executed consideration to create it.[17]

## § 156. Promise to Buy All of One's Needs or Requirements or Total Consumption

A promise to buy of another person or company all of some commodity or service that the promisor may thereafter need or require in his business is not an illusory promise; and such a promise is a sufficient consideration for a return promise.[22] It is true that the amount to be delivered or paid for can not be determined at the time the contract is made; but the terms of the promise give a sufficiently definite objective standard to enable a court to determine the amount when the time comes for enforcement. It is not a promise to buy all that the buyer wishes or may thereafter choose to order; the amount is not left to the will of the promisor himself.

The word "require" is not here used in the sense of request or order; instead, it is the equivalent of need or use. The promisor's duty is conditional upon the existence of an objective need for the commodity or service, and the promisor may have a high degree of control over the happening of this condition; but this does not render the promise illusory and empty of content. It states a limitation upon the promisor's future liberty of action; he no longer has an unlimited option.

It makes no difference how great or small this limitation is— at least, until it approaches near to the vanishing point. The extent of the limitation affects the value of the promise and the size of the performance that is promised, but not its sufficiency as a consideration.

It is true that by such a promise as this, the promisor may not undertake to continue a business on its present scale or even to run the business at all.[23] It is true that the amount that will be needed or required will vary with the scale on which the business is run. Much, therefore, is left to the judgment of the promisor, even to his will and desire; but not everything is thus left. The promise contains one very definite element that specifically limits the promisor's future liberty of action; he definitely promises that he will buy of no one else. If he needs or requires or uses any of the named commodity, he must buy it of the one specified.[24]

Promises of this type have various forms; and the extent of the limitation they impose varies accordingly. The following are examples of valid bilateral contracts: (1) A promises to sell on stated terms, and B promises to buy, all the coal that may be used by certain vessels then owned by B.[25] Here, B is privileged to withdraw his vessels from service and buy no coal at all. He is privileged, also, to install oil burning boilers or a gas engine, and buy no coal. But no coal for their use may be bought of anyone other than A; if the vessels use coal, it must be coal purchased of him.

(2) A promises to sell on stated terms, and B promises to buy, all the ice that he may use or resell up to the amount of one hundred tons per day.[26] Here B's promise is a smaller limitation on his liberty than in the preceding case. If he uses and sells no ice, he is not bound to buy any. If he uses only 20 tons per day, he must buy the twenty tons from A. If he uses 150 tons per day, he must buy 100 tons from A; but he is privileged to buy the extra 50 tons elsewhere. By this contract, B acquires an

---

23. In some cases, the court has found an implied promise to remain in the business during the specified period.

25. **N.Y.**—Wells v. Alexandre, 29 N. E. 142, 130 N.Y. 642 (1891).

26. **U.S.**—Mills-Morris Co. v. Champion Spark Plug Co., 7 F.2d 38 (C.C. A.6th, 1925) all the spark plugs re-

quired in the normal course of plaintiff's business; Loudenback Fertilizer Co. v. Tenn. Phosphate Co., 121 F. 298, 61 L.R.A. 402 (C.C.A. 5th, 1903).

**N.Y.**—Nassau Supply Co. v. Ice Service Co., 169 N.E. 383, 252 N.Y. 277 (1929); Asahel Wheeler Co. v. Mendleson, 167 N.Y.S. 435, 180 App. Div. 9 (1917).

"option" to buy 100 tons of ice per day, his promise not to buy of anyone else up to that amount being the consideration.[27]

(3) A promises to sell on stated terms all the ice that B may order during the next three months; and B promises to buy of A all that he may use or resell during that time up to the amount of 100 tons per day. Here B's promise is identical with that made by him in case (2); but A's promise is a larger one than before. There is no limit, except that of reasonableness under the circumstances, on B's power to order ice and to make it A's duty to deliver. In case (2), the limit was 100 tons per day. But if B's promise is a sufficient consideration for a small promise exchanged for it, it is equally sufficient for a larger promise. The parties make their own bargain.

Again, the seller may promise to supply all that the buyer may need, not exceeding a certain maximum; and the buyer may promise to take all that he may need, not to be less than a certain minimum. This lessens the buyer's right by giving the seller an option above the maximum, but it enlarges the buyer's duty by depriving him of any option below the minimum.[28]

In these cases, it is not necessary that the buyer should already have an established business as a going concern, with determinable needs and requirements.[29] If within the specified limits B promises to buy exclusively of A, he is giving a sufficient consideration for A's promise. The existence of an established business is a factor to be given weight in the interpretation of A's return promise; in no case does he promise to sell an infinitely large quantity, even though there is no express limitation.[30] Here is a case in which the court will fill a gap, finding its evidence in the customs of men, both in the sale of such commodities and in the wording of their agreements. Without saying so, men intend to deal within the limits of what is practicable and reasonable.[31]

Some courts have assumed that, because of a supposed requirement of mutuality, a requirement contract is valid only in a case where the agreement is made in connection with an established business, having needs capable of reasonably definite pre-estimate, and have held that the agreement is unenforceable where the buyer is a jobber or dealer and buys for resale only and is in

---

**28.** In Wood County Grocer Co. v. Frazer, 284 F. 691 (C.C.A.8th, 1922), a contract was held valid, although it provided a maximum price and a minimum price, and that "in case party of the first part should find it necessary to ask party of the second part to pay more than the minimum price herein shown, then said price shall be optional with the party of the second part and he need not accept shipment of sugar." It appears that here the seller had a limited option not to sell at less than the named maximum price; and the buyer had a limited option not to buy at more than the named minimum. Beyond that, neither party had any option. The seller could compel purchase at the minimum price; the buyer could compel sale at the maximum price.

such a position as to make it uncertain whether or not he will need any of the commodity at all.[32] This is believed to be erroneous.

In all these cases, B's promise is a very limited one. If the suit is by A against B, it is necessary for A to show that B has broken his promise, that the condition precedent has occurred, that B has acted beyond the limits of his legal privileges indicated by his promise.[33]

### § 157. Promise to Supply Goods as Promisee May Order

In what purports to be a bilateral contract, one party sometimes promises to supply another, on specified terms, with all the goods or services that the other may order from time to time within a stated period. A mere statement by the other party that he assents to this, or "accepts" it, is not a promise to order any goods or to pay anything. There is no consideration of any sort for the seller's promise; and he is not bound by it.[34] This remains true, even though the parties think that a contract has been made and expressly label their agreement a "contract."[35] In cases like this, there may be no good reason for implying any kind of promise by the offeree. Indeed, the proposal and promise of the seller has the form of an invitation for orders; and the mode of making an operative acceptance is to send in an order for a specific amount. By such an order, if there has been no previous notice of revocation, a contract is consummated binding both parties.[36] The standing offer is one of those that empowers the offeree to accept more than once and to create a series of separate obligations. The sending in of one order and the filling of it by the seller do not make the offer irrevocable as to additional amounts if the parties have not so agreed.[37]

In a well-known English case, a dealer wrote to a corporation offering to supply it, at stated prices, with such quantities of specified goods "as your storekeeper may order from time to time." The corporation replied, saying that they accepted his offer as made. By this attempted acceptance, the corporation made no promise to buy any amount and so gave no consideration. Later on, however, they sent in orders for specified amounts, thereby promising to pay at the rates offered.[38] By each of these orders, a valid bilateral contract was consummated. It should be observed that the offer was so worded that it could

36.   Cal.—Keller v. Ybarru, 3 Cal. 147 (1853).

Mich.—Cooper v. Lansing Wheel Co., 54 N.W. 39, 94 Mich. 272, 34 Am.St. Rep. 341 (1892), the agreement might have been interpreted as a bilateral contract for the plaintiff's entire supply of wheels.

Eng.—Great Northern R. Co. v. Witham, L.R. 9 C.P. 16 (1873).

38.   Eng.—Great Northern R. Co. v. Witham, L. R. 9 C. P. 16 (1873).

be accepted only by giving an order for goods; so that the first letter was not an acceptance of any kind.

A promise to supply on stated terms all the goods or services that the promisee may thereafter order is not itself an illusory promise. Instead, it is a very definite promise that creates a large power in the promisee. It is an enforceable promise if the promisee gives any sufficient consideration for it. The consideration may be anything that the promisor bargains for and that is given in exchange for it. (1) Thus, if A promises to supply on stated terms all the goods that B may choose to order within a year, and in return therefor B pays $100 to A, a valid unilateral option contract has been made. B has made no promise and there is no mutuality of obligation; but B has given a sufficient consideration and A's offered promise is not revocable.[40] An order by B for goods on the terms stated will create a valid bilateral contract, in spite of a previous notice of revocation by A.

(2) Again, if A offers the same promise as above in exchange for B's giving a first order for a specified amount, and B accepts by giving that order, a valid bilateral option contract has been made. A is irrevocably bound by his promise; and B is bound to pay for the first order of goods. B is not bound to order any further goods; but he has an irrevocable power to bind A to fill further orders on the stated terms.[41]

(3) If A makes the same promise as above in order to induce B to promise that he will thereafter buy such goods exclusively of A, and B accepts by giving that promise, a valid bilateral option contract has been made.[42] B has made no promise to order any goods of A; but he has promised not to buy of anybody else, and this promise is a sufficient consideration. Of course, A's large promise is a sufficient consideration for B's negative promise. If B buys of a third person, A can get damages and frequently an injunction. If A attempts to revoke and refuses to fill an order, B can get damages and under some circumstances a decree for specific performance.

Other examples of valid option contracts, similar to the foregoing are: (4) A promises to fill all B's orders for coal for one year, at stated prices, in return for B's promise to buy of A a minimum of 100 tons. (5) A promises to sell on stated terms to B all the ice B may order up to 100 tons per day for a year, in

41. In Koehler & Heinrichs Mercantile Co. v. Illinois Glass Co., 173 N.W. 703, 143 Minn. 344 (1919), in return for a promise by the offeree to take and pay for 12 carloads of flasks, the defendant promised to deliver the 12 carloads and promised, also, to deliver such an additional number of carloads as the offeree might choose to order during the year.

return for B's promise to buy of A all ice used by him up to 100 tons per day.[43]

If for any of the foregoing promises by A, there is no consideration given by B other than a written statement that he accepts A's offer, there is no contract. B is not bound, because he has made only the illusory promise "I will buy of you if I wish to give you an order." A is not bound, because B's illusory promise is neither an acceptance nor a sufficient consideration.

## § 158.   Promise to Sell Producer's Total Output

A promise to buy of another all of a commodity that the promisor may need or require or consume in his business is not an illusory promise, even though it leaves a good deal of liberty to the promisor. It contains enough of a limitation to be a real promise and to be a sufficient consideration for a return promise. The same is true of a promise by a producer to sell his entire output or production to another.[44] The one is a total consumption contract, with some freedom left to the consumer. The other is a total production contract, with some freedom left to the producer. At the very least, the promisor binds himself not to sell any of his output to any third person. He has the limited option between selling to the promisee and not producing at all.

In cases like this the contract is not aleatory, because the promise of each is conditional upon the same event. Suppose a contract for the sale at a stated rate of "all the pineapples he may grow"; the condition is uncertain, but the performances promised are equally uncertain. No pineapples, no pay. Some pineapples, some pay. Many pineapples, much pay. A uniform ratio is maintained between goods delivered and amount to be paid. The performance of the condition is at the option of the seller, and the buyer has no option whatever; but this fact does not make the contract aleatory.

The promisor may or may not promise in addition that he will maintain his production at some stated level, or that he will continue to run the mine or factory or farm with diligence.[45] Such subsidiary promises add materially to the limitation on the promisor's freedom of action and may add value to the promise given. No such subsidiary promise and no such added value are necessary to the sufficiency of the promise as a consideration for a return promise.[46] Even though the promisor retains the privilege of closing down the works and of producing and delivering nothing, he has given a sufficient consideration in promising to sell his entire output, whatever it may be, to the promisee and none to others.

The promisor may strengthen his promise by undertaking to produce and deliver a stated minimum quantity or he may weaken it by limiting his undertaking to some stated maximum.[47]

In the latter case, he is promising not his entire output whatever it may be, but his output up to the stated maximum. Beyond that amount he has made no promise at all. There may be both a minimum and a maximum, so that the promisor has no option below the minimum, a limited option between the minimum and the maximum, and unlimited freedom beyond the maximum. The exact terms of the promise are to be found by the usual processes of interpretation; the court must be ready to find promises by reasonable implication as well as in express words.[48]

The commodity the entire output of which the producer promises to sell may be a mere by-product of his producing plant.[49] Its sufficiency as consideration and the validity of the contract are not affected by this fact; but it makes it less likely that the seller has promised, by implication or otherwise that he will produce a minimum amount or that he will continue to carry on the work of production for a stated time. Ordinarily, he would wish to make his duty to sell a mere by-product conditional upon the exigencies of the main business; he would not bind himself to let the tail wag the dog.[50]

## § 159. Promises to Buy or Sell, Conditional on Future Prices

The fact that the parties make the price to be paid for a commodity dependent upon future contingencies does not invalidate their agreement if an objective method is provided for determining what the price shall be. The contract is not invalidated by the fact that the buyer is given the option of buying elsewhere if he can get the goods at a price lower than the amount specified in the contract.[51] Here, the buyer's option is not between buying all of the seller and not buying any at all; it is between buying all of the seller and not buying any at a price equal to or higher than the seller's price.

If the seller promises to lower the price to meet prices subsequently made by competitors, there may be no option in either party as to the price to be paid.[52] It is merely determined by the subsequent action of competitors of the seller. The seller may not promise to meet such prices; but he may be given the option of doing so. If he meets such prices, the buyer must buy of the seller or not at all; if he does not meet such prices, the buyer has the privilege of buying elsewhere. Such promises are not illusory and the contract is valid.[53]

53. In Jessup & Moore Paper Co. v. Bryant Paper Co., 129 A. 559, 283 Pa. 434 (1925), the plaintiff agreed to sell, and the defendant to buy, 150 to 200 tons per month of bleached soda pulp, during the year 1921, with the following provision for fixing the price to be paid: "On the last day of each month . . . the Jessup & Moore Paper Co., the sellers, will fix their price for their pulp for each [succeeding] calendar month. Upon receipt of notice of this

A contract may provide for the purchase and sale of some commodity, naming both a maximum and a minimum price, and providing that if the parties cannot subsequently agree on a price the seller shall have an option to sell at the named minimum and the buyer shall have an option to buy at the named maximum. Such a bilateral agreement is a valid contract, each party's promise being a sufficient consideration for the other promise.[54]

## § 160. Effect of Promisor's Option on the Sufficiency of his Promise as Consideration

On the basis of what has appeared in preceding sections, it is now possible to say that a promise is not rendered insufficient as a consideration for a return promise by the fact that promisor is expressly given some option, or choice, between performances, provided that this option is not wholly unlimited. In what has been described as an illusory promise, the alleged promisor's option is unlimited, exactly as it would have been had he never used the promissory words at all. In the promises heretofore described as not illusory and stated to be a sufficient consideration, the promisor had a limited option.[55]

price, if unsatisfactory to the Bryant Paper Company, the buyers shall then submit to the sellers a bona fide offer from a pulp manufacturer, admitted by both the sellers and buyers to be responsible, to furnish the [buyers] 100 to 200 tons of bleached soda pulp during the ensuing month, at a lower price. If the buyers do not submit such offer from a pulp manufacturer, the price named by the sellers shall be binding on both parties during the month involved. If, however, the buyers submit such offer, the sellers shall have the right to substitute the price so submitted instead of the price fixed by the sellers, and, if so substituted, both parties shall be bound thereby. If not accepted by the sellers, the buyers shall be at liberty to accept the proposal of such other pulp manufacturer for the ensuing month's supply, and shall not be bound, during that period, to accept deliveries from" the sellers.

54. In Wood County Grocer Co. v. Frazer, 284 F. 691 (C.C.A.8th,

1922) there was an agreement for purchase and sale of 2,000 bags of beet sugar, at not less than $16.12 nor more than $22.12 per bag, the buyer promising to accept the sugar in any event at the minimum price and the seller to deliver in any event at the maximum price. This was held valid, although the buyer had an option not to take the sugar at any price above $16.12 and the seller had an option to charge as much as $22.12 and an option not to deliver if buyer refused to pay that price.

55. As a matter of course, a promise is not rendered insufficient as a consideration by the fact that an option or choice is given to *the promisee*. The transactions commonly referred to as "options" are of this kind. Often, the promisee pays cash for such an "option"; but, even if he gives a return promise instead of cash and the transaction is "bilateral," there is no question that the option giver's promise is a sufficient consideration.

If a promisor undertakes to perform one of two alternatives, he has a very limited option—a choice between two, a choice only one better than Hobson's. His promise is a sufficient consideration for a return promise, unless for some special reason, not related to the option itself, one of the alternatives would not be a sufficient consideration. The greater the number of alternatives that by the terms of the promise are left open to the promisor, the less is the limitation upon his own future will; but the promise still remains a sufficient consideration. It remains so until the limitation becomes non-existent, or, it may be, practically negligible.

If A promises to sell to B either his motor car or his team of mules, in return for B's promise to pay $300, there is a valid bilateral contract. If A promises to select one out of his herd of a thousand steers and sell it to B, in return for B's promise to pay $80, there is a valid bilateral contract. In the latter case, A has a thousand objects of choice; in the former, only two.[56] If A promises to charter the good ship Sea Gull to B at a stated rental, if he buys her from the present owner, and B promises to pay the rental, there is a valid bilateral contract.[57] A's field of choice is very wide indeed; but it is not unlimited. His choice is not the unlimited one between buying the Sea Gull and not-buying her; because if he buys he must charter her to B. His choice is between not-buying the Sea Gull, on the one hand, and buying-and-chartering her to B, on the other. Of course, "not-buying the Sea Gull" includes an almost infinite number of possibilities—almost, but not quite. A's promise excludes him from the following important objects of choice: buying the Sea Gull and using her himself; buying her and chartering her to X. It is this exclusion that makes A's promise a sufficient consideration. In this case, A has not made a promise to perform one out of many alternatives, any one of which is the agreed equivalent of B's promised payment. There is only one of the many possible choices that is the agreed equivalent of B's money; this is buying-and-chartering the Sea Gull. If A chooses any one of his many other alternatives, B has to pay nothing. The agreed exchange is between the chartering (actual delivery) and the paying. This shows that the contract is not "aleatory;" the two promises are conditional on the same event and must be performed together or not at all.

A promise is never rendered insufficient as a consideration for a return promise by the reservation of an option between performances, if every one of those performances involves effort, expense, or change of position—that is, if every one of them

57. **Ala.**—Scott v. Moragues Lbr.
Co., 80 So. 394, 202 Ala. 312 (1918).

would be a sufficient consideration if it were bargained for separately.[58]

In drawing a contract containing a power to cancel or other option in a promisor, special care should be taken to see that the contract expresses a clear and undoubted consideration given by this promisor for any return promise. If the promise with an option is the only consideration given for a return promise, make sure that the option is limited in some substantial way and is made to appear so; make sure that the promise is not illusory, but promises something substantial in any event. Let there be some executed payment or other executed performance in fact made and not merely recited. If there is an "option to cancel," draw the provision so that the exercise of the option will not affect the option holder's executed performance and will not result in his getting something for nothing or in the other party's losing everything that he expected to gain by the transaction.

## § 161.   Promises Including an "Option to Cancel"

The "option to cancel" is a common method of producing a result very similar to that produced by making a promise conditional on personal satisfaction. One contractor attempts by this means to retain in as large a degree as possible his own economic freedom of choice, observing results as performance of the contract proceeds and cancelling the contract if these results are not satisfactory to him. The legal power created by this "option to cancel" is not generally made conditional upon dissatisfaction with the results; it is a power to cancel if the contractor so wills and desires. His option between cancelling and not cancelling is unlimited. The retention of such power is not in itself illegal; but in some cases it has been held to invalidate the contract on the ground that it prevents mutuality of obligation.[59]

In some cases, the court seems to have thought that the reservation of a power to cancel in one party is substantially the same as if he had made an illusory promise. In most cases, however, it is far otherwise; and in every case there is some difference. The power to cancel that is reserved is invariably a power to cancel the whole contract, including both promises alike. Where one promise is illusory and the other is not, it looks as if the one promised performance must be rendered whether the other is or not. This is not so in the case of a power to cancel. If the power is exercised, both parties are freed from their promissory duties; if it is not exercised, neither one is freed. It does not appear to involve an attempt to get something for nothing; and there is no such result whether the power is exercised or not.

This being so, the contract should not be regarded as unfair for its supposed lack of "mutuality." No court or writer has maintained that the validity of a contract depends upon an objective equality of advantages or values. Each promise made by one party does not have to be matched by an equivalent promise made by the other. Each right or power or privilege possessed by one party does not have to have its exact counterpart in the other.[60] Several types of cases will be considered in the succeeding sections.

Whether a promise with a power to cancel is held to be a sufficient consideration for a return promise or not, it is certain that no action for breach can be maintained against the promisor if he has exercised his power to cancel and has otherwise properly performed.[61] It is quite unnecessary to say in such a case that the contract is invalid for lack of mutuality; the real reason for denying a remedy is that the promisor had the power to cancel and used it in due season. The same is true in any case where the court finds that the defendant made no promise whatever, or has committed no breach of any promise that he made.[62] It should be observed, however, that a power to cancel may be reserved in such limited form as not to affect duties of performance that have arisen prior to the cancellation. The extent of the reserved power depends upon the expressions in the agreement and the reasonable implications to be drawn therefrom.[63]

## § 162.   Power of Revoking an Offer is a Power to Cancel

When A makes an offer to B, the latter gets a power of acceptance with an unlimited option between using it and not using it. Also A, the offeror, has a power; it is usually called the power to revoke, but it might as well be called a power to "cancel." There is no contract as yet, no contractual rights and duties; so this power is not a power to cancel a contract. It is like such a power, however, in this—that its exercise results in the extinguishment of legal relations then existing. The "cancellation" of a contract extinguishes rights and duties; the "cancellation" (or revocation) of an offer extinguishes the power of acceptance. Some offers are entirely irrevocable; but in the case

---

63. See Sylvan Crest S. & G. Co. v. U. S., 150 F.2d 642 (C.C.A.2d, 1945), where the United States reserved a power to cancel at any time and yet the court held that the defendant committed a breach of contract where it permitted and expected the plaintiff to be ready to perform its part for two years without either ordering deliveries or giving notice of cancellation. The government "short form contract" was what it purported to be, with gaps to be filled by reasonable implication; and the court was justified in finding an implied promise to give shipping orders within a reasonable time unless it gave notice of cancellation.

of ordinary offers the offeror has an unlimited option between revoking and not revoking. The question of whether or not this unlimited option invalidates a contract does not arise, because there is as yet no contract for another reason—lack of acceptance by the other party.

That the existence of an unlimited option to revoke or cancel, as described in the preceding paragraph, does not necessarily invalidate a contract is indicated in the following case: B offers $200 for a binding option for 30 days on land owned by A. A refuses such an option, believing that he may find a desirable purchaser himself. Thereupon B says, "Make me a written thirty-day offer, revocable at your pleasure, at the price of $5,-000, and tomorrow I will pay you $100 for so doing." A assents to this, and delivers to B the written offer, "For thirty days I offer Blackacre to B for $5,000, this offer to be revocable at my pleasure at any time before acceptance." B's return promise to pay $100 to-morrow is thereby made binding. There is a valid contract, A's act being operative as a consideration in spite of his retaining an unlimited "option to cancel." The written document is beneficial to B in that it gives him a power of acceptance; it would have been worth more had it also given him an immunity from revocation, but B thought the revocable power itself worth $100. Neither A's power to "cancel" in this case, nor his exercise thereof, is intended to affect B's duty to pay $100. Its exercise will in no way benefit B; instead it will deprive him of the benefit of a thirty-day power. But it does not wholly destroy all the value of A's act, since that act created in B, for one moment at least, a power of accepting and binding A to convey Blackacre.

The power that was reserved in the foregoing case was a power to cancel the offer to sell; it was not a power to cancel the entire contract. The contract that was made may perhaps be regarded as unilateral, a promise to pay $100 for the act of delivering the written offer; but it is to be observed that this act is itself an express promise—a promise to sell Blackacre for $5000. A notice of revocation of this offer makes A's promise to sell wholly unenforceable; but it does not affect B's duty to pay A $100. That this hypothetical case is not merely fanciful is shown by the actual case now to be stated.

In a Connecticut case,[64] the plaintiff promised to buy and the defendant promised to sell and to ship within three months from date a certain amount of plate glass at an agreed price. At the end of the defendant's letter accepting the plaintiff's order, there

64.　Gurfein v. Werbelovsky, 118 A. 32, 97 Conn. 703 (1922). See comment in 32 Yale Law Journal, 496.

was the following sentence: "You have the option to cancel the above order before shipment." The plaintiff never exercised the option so given to him, but the defendant later repudiated the contract and refused to ship the glass either during the three months or later. The court rightly held that a valid contract was made by the parties, in spite of the option to cancel that was given to the buyer. The buyer's option was not an option to cancel at any time; in order to be effective, his cancellation would have to be before shipment of the goods by the seller, and this means that notice of such cancellation would have to reach the seller before it could be effective. Shipment of the goods by the seller would have utterly extinguished the buyer's power to cancel. It follows from this that the buyer's promise to buy the glass was not wholly illusory; it amounted to a good deal more than a mere promissory expression to buy the goods and to take them if he should thereafter so desire. The buyer put himself, to a very considerable degree, in the power of the seller, and, therefore, his promise to buy, even though it included the reserved power to cancel, was a sufficient consideration for the defendant's promise to deliver. The ruling made by the court carries out the express intention of both parties. It is strictly in accord with the accepted definitions of consideration and it accords with public policy in making legally effective a business transaction made in good faith and relied upon by the parties thereto.

### § 163.  Effect of Power to Cancel at Any Time without a Specified Period of Notice

If a promisor reserves the power to cancel at any time without notice, his promise seems to be unenforceable, at least as long as there has been no performance by the other party to the agreement. While still wholly executory, the promisor is not bound for the reason that he can cancel without notice by merely willing to do so; and the other party's promise is not binding for lack of consideration. In every case of this kind, however, the agreement should be scrutinized carefully to see whether the promisor did not give some consideration that was not affected by his power to cancel, and also whether there has not been a part performance that makes up for the defects of the consideration.[66]

If A promises to pay $100 a week for service and B promises to serve for one year beginning June 1 if he then so pleases, there is no contract; B's promise is no promise. The same is true if B says, "I promise to serve for one year beginning June 1, but I reserve the privilege of not serving." If the law should hold this to be a valid contract, enforceable against A even though B does not render service, it would be compelling A to pay money for nothing given in return. As made above, however, A's promise is clearly conditional on the actual rendition of service by B. There is no contract for the reason that B has neither made a promise nor begun to serve. If, with no revocation by A, service is begun by B on June 1, a valid contract then comes into existence.[67]

Is the case materially different if B's promise is, "I promise to serve for one year beginning June 1, but I reserve the option to cancel by giving notice before that date"? Both technically and practically there is a difference, because the terms of B's promise no longer leave his option unlimited. His option is between serving and giving notice, and not as in the first case above between serving and not serving. The cost to B of one of these alternatives—the giving of notice—may be slight. Nevertheless, it would be sufficient to satisfy the requirement of a consideration if agreed upon as such. The writing and mailing of a letter is more than a peppercorn. Promises to pay large sums of money for a consideration no greater than this have been enforced.[68] The fact that in those cases the letter or document was the agreed consideration, and in the present case it is not, is an important difference; but it is one that bears in favor of the validity of the present supposed contract. If the promise of the letter is the agreed consideration, the damages recoverable for breach would be merely the value of the letter, frequently a very slight sum. In the present case the consideration is B's promise to serve for a year conditional on his not giving notice before June 1. For breach of this promise, assuming no notice given, A's damages would be the net value of the promised service, a substantial amount.[69] It is true that if B exercises his option to cancel, A will be deprived of his expected beneficial service; at the same time he will be relieved of his duty to pay, so that he will not be giving something for nothing. In the cases

68. **Eng.**—Haigh v. Brooks, 10 Adol. & El. 309, 323 (1840, Exch.); Wilkinson v. Oliveira, 1 Bing.N.C. 490 (1835).

69. In Sylvan Crest S. & G. Co. **v.** U. S., 150 F.2d 642 (C.C.A.2d, 1945), a substantially similar case, the court sustained an action for damages against the United States, finding in spite of an option to cancel at any time an implied promise by the United States either to take and pay for trap rock and to give shipping instructions or to give notice of cancellation within a reasonable time. The court's argument is in harmony with the text above. The suit, however, was against the party having the option to cancel. The implication of a promise to pay, conditional on not giving notice of cancellation within a reasonable time, demonstrates the existence of a valid bilateral contract. Failure to give notice of cancellation for two years, while the plaintiff was ready and willing to begin deliveries, and failure to give instructions to ship, operated as breach of a substantial promise by the United States. Also, this promise was a sufficient consideration for the plaintiff's promise to deliver rock, one not rendered insufficient or illusory by the reserved power to cancel.

cited, the promisor was compelled to pay a large sum for next to nothing. The present case is, therefore, much like the case of Scott v. Moragues Lumber Co.,[70] where Scott promised to charter a vessel to the Lumber Co. if he should buy it, and the latter promised to pay rental therefor if delivered to him. All that Scott needed to do to escape liability in that case was to forbear to buy, a forbearance that would cost him not even the trouble and expense of mailing a notice and would benefit the Lumber Co. not at all. Such a forbearance would, however, prevent Scott from making the possible gains accruing from ownership. In the present hypothetical case, B's promise is so worded as to assume a risk that Scott did not run, the risk of inability to give the notice of cancellation before June 1. There is no risk that Scott will be unable to forbear to buy the ship.

By giving the notice of cancellation, B not only goes to some trouble and expense; he also loses his right to payment by A. We must not, however, attempt to use this as a consideration on which to base the validity of the contract; because, until we can determine that the contract is in fact valid, we cannot know that B has any right that will be lost by cancellation. We can prove nothing by begging the question.

In such a contract as the one just discussed, the party having power to cancel has an option between alternatives—between performing and giving notice. But this is not an "alternative contract" in the sense that the other party bargains for either of the two alternatives; he does not have to pay anything for the notice. The giving of the notice relieves him from obligation as well as the notice-giver himself. This makes such a contract a reasonable one under ordinary circumstances; it is certainly not unconscionable.[71]

In spite of the foregoing argument, the courts have often assumed that the reservation of a power to cancel, unconditional except on the giving of notice at any time, makes a promise so nearly illusory as to be an insufficient consideration for a return promise. The cases that are criticised herein for invalidating a contract for lack of mutuality will nearly always be found to have more serious faults than that of disregarding the argument just made above.

If the power to cancel by giving notice is reserved for a limited period, or until the other party has shipped goods or has ordered a specified quantity or taken other action in performance of his return promise,[72] there is added reason for holding that the reservation does not make the promise illusory. Suppose that one promises a college to leave it $10,000 by will, for the purpose

70.    80 So. 394, 202 Ala. 312 (1918).

72.    This is the case of Gurfein v.

Werbelovsky, 118 A. 32, 97 Conn. 703 (1922), discussed in the preceding section.

of aiding in a campaign to raise a million dollars for a new building, at the same time reserving the power to revoke at any time prior to his death by notice in writing to the college president. This is not an illusory promise, in spite of the reserved power to revoke. There is no doubt that if the college raises the money and builds the building, an action will lie against the promisor's administrator for $10,000 if the promisor has not given the specified notice. The expected action of the college in reliance on the promise is enough to make it binding according to its own terms. This shows that such a promise as this is a material limitation upon the promisor's freedom of action, and that it should also be held to be itself a sufficient consideration for any return promise that may be given in exchange for it. It is not the same as a promise to pay $10,000 to the college if the promisor wishes to do so in the future. Such a promise is an illusion; failure of the promisor to bequeath the money to the college would sufficiently evidence the absence of a will to do so, and no action would lie against the administrator.

In a Virginia case,[73] the parties signed a written agreement whereby the plaintiff promised to sell from 400 to 600 tons of fertilizer and the defendant promised to take and pay for it, in instalments as ordered by him during a specified period. The agreement contained the following provision in behalf of the plaintiff: "We reserve the right to cancel this contract at any time we may deem proper, but in the event of such cancellation the provisions of this contract shall govern the closing of all business begun thereunder." Under this agreement the defendant never ordered or requested the shipment of any fertilizer whatever and wholly refused to take or pay for any. The court held that there was no valid contract, for the reason that the plaintiff gave no sufficient consideration for the defendant's promise to buy. The agreement was bilateral in form; and the specified consideration for the defendant's promise to buy was the plaintiff's promise to sell and deliver. This was thought to be an illusory promise, however, for the reason that, in the light of the reservation quoted above, it did not purport to limit the plaintiff's freedom of will in the slightest degree.

The court's analysis of the agreement should not be approved. First, the reasonable implication is that the power to cancel should be exercisable only by giving notice to the buyer. Secondly, the power itself was not applicable to any "business begun thereunder." Surely the sending in of an order for a specific amount by the buyer would be the beginning of such "business." By the sending of such an order, before notice of cancellation, the

73.　Va.—American Agri. Chem. Co.
v. Kennedy & Crawford, 48 S.E.
868, 103 Va. 171 (1904).

seller should be held bound to fill the order.  If this is correct, the plaintiff seller was in the position of one who has made a continuing offer, revocable only by notice;  and the defendant received something having legal operation and something of value in return for his promise to buy.  It was not an illusory promise: "I will sell you fertilizer if I wish to."  It was a promise to deliver at a specified price conditional on not giving notice of cancellation before an order for shipment was given.  This had substance enough to induce the defendant to bargain for it;  and the bargain is not unconscionable since the defendant will in no case have to pay money without getting its agreed equivalent in fertilizer.

The court further held that the fact that the plaintiff made preparations for performing in accordance with this agreement, by way of manufacturing the fertilizer, putting it in sacks, and offering it to the defendant did not supply the element of consideration or make the promise of the defendant binding.  On this point, also, the decision is subject to criticism.  The defendant had ample "reason to foresee" the action taken by the plaintiff in reliance on the agreement.  True, the plaintiff had reserved a limited power to cancel;  but it never used it and the bargain was not made with the expectation that it would be used.  Instead, the plaintiff manufactured enough fertilizer to supply the defendant.  Doubtless, it could divert this fertilizer to the supply of its other customers, but only at a loss of profits that it would otherwise have made.[74]  Inasmuch as action in reliance will often be enough to cause enforcement of a promise for which there is no agreed exchange, the action in reliance here is more than ample to justify compelling the defendant to keep his promise to exchange his money for the agreed fertilizer.

### § 164.  Power to Cancel by Giving a Notice for Some Specified Period

Frequently, the provision is that one party shall have the power to cancel by notice given for some stated period, such as "notice for thirty days," or "terminable on one week's notice." When this is the case, the contract should never be held to be

---

**74.**  This appears to satisfy reasonably well the requirements of Restatement, Contracts, § 90, discussed herein at §§ 193–209.  It is true that this "action in reliance" on the defendant's promise was not the agreed equivalent or "consideration" for that promise.  The "consideration" was the plaintiff's conditional promise to sell;  and the agreed equivalent of the defendant's money was the fertilizer to be delivered.

The court rightly says that "the promise *of the defendants* to purchase from the plaintiff was not a continuing offer, which when accepted, was mutually binding upon both parties."  But it should have said, also, that the conditional promise *of the plaintiff* to sell to the defendant created in the defendant as much power as would a continuing offer to sell and was a sufficient consideration for the defendant's promise to buy.

rendered invalid thereby for lack of "mutuality" or for lack of consideration. The decisions mostly agree with this.[76] The party in whom the power has been reserved has made a real promise, one that in terms purports to control his action during the specified period of notice. For performances continuing during that period, he must pay at the agreed rate. His cancellation is effective only at the end of the period; thereafter he will not have to pay, but neither will he receive performance. The longer that he postpones his notice of cancellation, the longer the contract will continue to control both parties.

If an agency contract provides that the agent shall have power to terminate by giving thirty days' notice and that the employer shall have power to terminate only for good cause shown, there is a valid bilateral contract. If the employer discharges the agent without good cause, the agent can get judgment for damages.[77] The agent's promise to render service is not made illusory by the power to cancel on thirty days' notice; and it is a sufficient consideration for the employer's return promise.

### § 165. Power to Cancel for Cause or on Some Condition Other Than Promisor's Own Will

A promise to pay if the promisor is satisfied with the performance rendered by the other has already been shown to be a sufficient consideration. The same is true of a promise in which the promisor reserves the power to cancel for good cause or on some condition that is not wholly controlled by the will of the promisor himself.[78] Even if the promisor is himself to be the judge of the cause or the condition, he must use good faith and an honest judgment. The power to cancel certainly does not render the promise illusory if the power is itself conditional upon some voluntary act of the other party.[79]

### § 166. Power to Cancel on Some Specified Nonperformance of Duty by the Other Party

Very often it is provided that one party shall have a power to cancel in case of some specified breach of duty by the other. This is more often called a "right to rescind" or a privilege of termination. The words may be that the contract shall be "null and void" in case of such breach or non-performance. The only difference between the last form and the preceding ones is that the non-performance seems itself to terminate, while in the preceding forms there is no termination until the first party, by notice or otherwise, exercises his power. Even in the "null and void" case, however, the first party need not take advantage of his freedom. He has power to waive the condition, remaining bound himself and leaving the other party still empowered to complete his performance and earn his full compensation, less damages if there has been a breach.

All of these cases alike differ from that in which one party reserves a power to cancel at will or on contingencies other than the other's non-performance of his promise. In the cases here put, the power to cancel, or "right to rescind" or to terminate, is provided by agreement as one of the remedies available for breach. They do not hold that the contract is in fact cancelled or rescinded or discharged as a whole. Even when it is said that the contract shall be "null and void" on the other party's non-performance, the words seldom mean what they seem to mean. Usually, it is clear that on such non-performance, the first party is legally privileged to stop performing; the first party's duty is conditional on performance by the other. It is his legal duty, and not the entire contract, that becomes "null and void" or terminated. The reservation of this kind of a power is never regarded as destroying "mutuality" or invalidating the contract.[83]

Where a power to cancel is reserved at the will of one party, or on the happening of some condition other than a breach by the other party, the intention practically always is that the exercise of the power shall discharge both parties alike, leaving no claim to damages for a breach. It is this kind of reservation that is sometimes thought, often erroneously, to nullify the agreement from the beginning by preventing "mutuality" or causing the consideration to be insufficient.

An employer who has reserved the power to terminate an agency contract "for dishonesty, incompetency, negligence, inattention, or irresponsibility" has made a real promise, not a merely illusory one. If he discharges the agent for no good cause that satisfies the quoted provision, the agent can get judgment for substantial damages.[84] This being so, it is obvious that the employer's promise is sufficient consideration for a return promise made by the agent.

### § 167.  Power to Cancel may be Given to Each of the Parties

Frequently, the power to cancel or terminate is given to both parties alike.[85] In such a case, of course no enforcement is possible against either party before actual performance has begun, if he properly exercises his reserved power. But the agreement is not void; a part or a full performance rendered by one party before termination by the other will enable him to get judgment for the agreed compensation for such performance. The other party can not escape liability on the ground of lack of mutuality. This situation continues as long as neither party has exercised his reserved power.

The validity of the contract is to be determined in exactly the same way as in the case of an option in one party only. Each promise, and its attendant option, must be considered separately and its sufficiency as a consideration must be determined. That

243

each party has an option merely requires going over the ground twice.

In a number of cases, it has been said that if one of the parties reserves a power to terminate the contract, it will be interpreted as giving a similar power to the other party.[86] It may be that this interpretation is justified in some particular cases; but such an implication is not a necessary one and is not required by any general rule or doctrine of the law. It is quite erroneous to suppose that there is any rule of "mutuality" that requires such an implication.

### § 168. Effect of Exercising Power to Cancel after Part Performance

The extent of a reserved power to cancel, and the effect of its exercise, depend upon the terms of the contract creating the power. As matter of course, the contract should be so drawn as to provide for these matters in clear terms. The fact that a part performance has already taken place does not, ordinarily, nullify the power to cancel; but, on the other hand, the exercise of the power does not, ordinarily, terminate the duty of making compensation for the part performance.[88] An agent, whose agency has thus been terminated, is entitled to his commission on orders already turned in by him, and to the agreed compensation for services already rendered.[89]

In an "output" contract, termination by exercise of a reserved power will, ordinarily, leave the buyer bound to pay for goods produced prior to the termination.[90] If the party, who has himself reserved a power to cancel, has properly performed without exercising his power, he can enforce return promises; if the other party repudiates the contract, he has no right to the restitution of a money deposit held by the first as liquidated damages for his repudiation.[91]

The foregoing affords additional reasons for not jumping to the conclusion that the reservation of a power to cancel invalidates a contract by nullifying the consideration or creating a supposed lack of "mutuality." As matter of course, the reserved power to cancel may be varied or wholly nullified by a subsequent agreement, oral or written. An oral assurance that the power will not be exercised may be made enforceable by the establishment of a place of business or other material change of position in reasonable reliance thereon.[92]

---

91.   **N.D.**—Gile v. Inter-State Motor Car Co., 145 N.W. 732, 27 N.D. 108 (1914). The decision in Goodyear v. H. J. Koehler Sporting Goods Co., 143 N.Y.Supp. 1046, 159 App. D. 116 (1913), is contra to this; but the dissenting opinion should be accepted.

92.   **N.C.**—Erskine v. Chevrolet Motors Co., 117 S.E. 706, 185 N.C. 479, 32 A.L.R. 196 (1923).

# CHAPTER 7

## CONSIDERATION—EFFECT OF PRE-EXISTING DUTY

## § 171. Performance of a Pre-existing Duty as Consideration— Meaning of the Term

Most acts and forbearances, or promises of future performance, are a sufficient consideration for a promise if they are bargained for by the maker of that promise and are given in exchange for it. One of the most important exceptions consists of those performances that are required of the performer, exactly as rendered by him, by a pre-existing legal duty. The same is true of a promise to render such a performance. The very frequently stated rule is that neither the performance of duty nor the promise to render a performance already required by duty is a sufficient consideration for a return promise.

245

There has been a growing doubt as to the soundness of this doctrine as a matter of social policy. This has been evidenced in ways that will hereafter appear. In certain classes of cases, this doubt has influenced courts to refuse to apply the rule, or to ignore it, in their actual decisions. Like other legal rules, this rule is in process of growth and change, the process being more active here than in most instances. The result of this is that a court should no longer accept this rule as fully established. It should never use it as the major premise of a decision, at least without giving careful thought to the circumstances of the particular case, to the moral deserts of the parties, and to the social feelings and interests that are involved. It is certain that the rule, stated in general and all-inclusive terms, is no longer so well-settled that a court must apply it though the heavens fall.

The present writer does not know the origin of this rule or the reasons that led courts to adopt it in the first place. Doubtless, some part has been played by the notion that "duty" should be performed without reward. Doubtless, also, there have been tough cases in which the promisor has been subjected to a hold-up game, so that he made his new promise under some degree of economic duress. It is certainly possible that a contractor may purposely bid low in order to get the contract, and then to refuse to perform, after it is too late to obtain another contractor without loss and inconvenience, in order to induce a promise of more pay. The strict enforcement of the supposed general rule would tend to remove this temptation from bidders, since they would know that a promise so induced would not be legally enforceable. But the application of the rule has not been so strict and uniform as to make the non-enforcement of the new promise certain. It has become clear that the moral and economic elements in any case that involves the rule should be weighed by the court, and that the fact of pre-existing legal duty should not be in itself decisive. It would be foolish to say this, in the light of the frequent repetition and application of the rule, but for the fact that the statement finds support in many actual decisions, in critical articles and law treatises, and in the new Restatement of Contract law by the American Law Institute. When general rules have never been applied with uniformity and appear to be breaking down into a number of other rules that take new factors into consideration, it behooves both writers and courts to weigh the matter anew and to be ready to reach new results.

One is under a legal duty when some performance is required of him and some form of societal compulsion is applicable against him. Compulsion does not necessarily mean the application of force to his person, although this is certainly a sufficient sanction for legal duty; it also includes any other form of societal sanction or penalty that is made applicable for the purpose of

inducing performance.  A judicial decree for specific performance is such a sanction, even though the case may be one in which
the decree will not involve application of force to the person;
a judgment for damages or for restitution is such a sanction,
even though the defendant may be judgment proof and no money
or goods ever be taken from him.

A duty is "pre-existing," within the meaning of the present
topic, when it exists by reason of some transaction that is antecedent to the promise for which consideration is being sought and
of which enforcement is asked.  If A promises to build a house in
return for B's promise to pay a sum of money, this transaction
creates a duty in A;  it did not exist antecedently to the making of
B's promise in return.  But if, after this transaction has occurred, there is a subsequent one whereby B induces A to build
the identical house in return for a second promise of new compensation, made either by B or by X, the consideration for this new
promise is nothing but the performance by A of his already existing duty created by the first transaction.

Furthermore, a pre-existing duty does not defeat consideration unless it is a still-existing duty.  If a duty has been effectively discharged, the performance thereafter of that which had
previously been required, is not the performance of duty;  and its
sufficiency as a consideration is not affected by the fact that it
had once been legally required.

## § 172.  Performance of Duty as Detriment or Benefit

In this treatise the attempt to define consideration in terms of
benefit to the promisor or detriment to the promisee has been in
large part abandoned;  but it may be desirable, nevertheless, to
discuss those concepts in their relation to the present subject.
When a master promises more pay for the same service, or a
servant promises more service for the same pay, or a landowner
promises a greater price for the same building to be constructed,
there is always a bargain in fact.  The promisor bargains for the
desired performance and gives his promise in exchange for
it.  Why, then, does the fact that the promisee was under
a pre-existing and unrescinded duty to render that performance
affect the validity of the agreement?  It has been said that the
reason is that the rendition of this performance is neither a benefit to the promisor nor a detriment to the promisee—no benefit
to the promisor because he was already entitled to it without
bargaining anew, and no detriment to the promisee because in
rendering it he was merely discharging and relieving himself
from a burdensome duty.[1]  This explanation involves either an

---

1.   In Vanderbilt v. Schreyer, 91 N.
Y. 392 (1883), the court argued as
follows: "It being clear that Vanderbilt had no legal right to require, as a condition to the fulfillment of his contract, the performance of an act not required by the
contract, it is difficult to see what

error of fact or an error of logic. It is error of fact to suppose that one gets no benefit when he gets only that to which he had an existing right. A bird in the hand is worth much more than a bird in the bush; [2] and that is why the promisor bargains to pay more in order to get it. It is likewise error of fact to suppose that performance of duty is no detriment to the promisee. If this performance is the payment of money, it is money that he might have paid to other persons with greater advantage to himself (and even without doing any legal wrong whatever); if it is the rendition of service, it is the spending of time and effort that might more advantageously have been spent elsewhere. It is true that failure to render the performance would have left the promisee liable in damages for breach of his duty; but it should be obvious that the damages that he could be compelled to pay would have no definite relation to the extent of the advantage that he might have derived from using his time and money otherwise.

If it be granted that there are benefit and detriment in fact, but asserted that there is no "legal benefit" or "legal detriment," then the error becomes one of logic. The addition of the adjective "legal" subtly begs the question. It is merely saying that performance of duty is not a legally operative consideration because it is not a consideration that is legally operative. The question remains, Why should it not be legally operative, as in the case of other bargained-for equivalents? Why is it not a "legal benefit" or a "legal detriment"? The answer must be made to turn, not on terms of factual benefit or detriment, but upon terms of public policy and general welfare. Performance of duty will not be recognized as sufficient consideration for a promise if such recognition would be injurious to the general welfare.

benefit he has bestowed or what inconvenience he has suffered in return for the undertaking assumed by the defendant. He promises to do only that which he was before legally bound to perform. Even though it lay in his power to refuse to perform his contract, he could do this only upon paying the other party the damages occasioned by his nonperformance, and that in contemplation of law would be equivalent to performance. He had no legal or moral right to refuse to perform the obligation of the contract into which he had upon a good consideration voluntarily entered."

Pollock, Contracts, ed. 9, p. 198, says: "Andrew's performance of his binding promise to Peter does not appear capable of being a consideration for a new promise by John to Andrew; not because it cannot be beneficial to John, for this it may very well be, but because in contemplation of law the performance is no detriment to Andrew, but on the contrary is beneficial to him, inasmuch as it discharges him of an existing obligation. Therefore the necessary element of detriment to the promisee is wanting." There is no more reason for distinguishing between a detriment *in fact* and a detriment "in contemplation of law" than for distinguishing between a benefit *in fact* and a benefit "in contemplation of law."

Where the duty that is performed as a consideration for a promise is a duty to a third person, there has never been any doubt that the performance is beneficial to the promisor. It is something to which he has no pre-existing right, something that he may never get; he bargains for it and gets it in exchange for his promise.[3]

It is the increasing recognition of the truth of the above conclusions that has largely been the cause of the present tendency to abandon benefit and detriment as tests of the sufficiency of a consideration. It is not that benefit to the promisor or detriment to the promisee is of no importance; the existence of either one tends strongly toward the enforcement of a promise and the finding that consideration is sufficient. It is merely that the absence of these factors is not decisive in all cases and that a promise may be enforceable and the consideration for it may be sufficient without either one of them.

## § 173.    Different Classes of Duties and Sources from Which They Arise

The pre-existing duty that may be held to affect the sufficiency of consideration may be of various classes and may arise out of a variety of facts. The effect upon such sufficiency varies so considerably that some of these classes must be discussed separately. Thus, the pre-existing duty may have been contractual or quasi-contractual in character, and therefore owed to some specific person or persons, or it may have been a duty owed to all persons alike so that its breach constitutes a tort or a crime. Among the latter, in particular, are found many of the duties of

---

**3.** In DeCicco v. Schweizer, 117 N.E. 807, 221 N.Y. 431 (1917), it is perfectly clear that the performance by Count Gulinelli in marrying Blanche was of some benefit to the defendant. Mr. Schweizer received all those benefits that are to be derived from alliance with a noble Italian family. Such an alliance carries with it social prestige, even though some not enjoying such an alliance may be inclined to scoff and others actually having such an alliance may not be enjoying it. This social prestige means power to influence the action of others in business affairs as well as in social life. The action of the Count has money value, and the fact that this value cannot be determined with certainty is not material.

The existence of actual benefit to C from the performance by A is well shown in McDevitt v. Stokes, 192 S. W. 681, 174 Ky. 515 (1917). Here, the defendant (C) promised the driver (A) of a race horse owned by B that, in return for his driving in an important race, he would receive $1,000 if he won the race. A was already under contract with B to drive the horse in this race. He drove with skill and was the winner. The defendant was the owner of the sire, the dam, and two full brothers of the horse to be driven by A. As such owner, he received a prize of $300 from the racing association; and, in addition, the value of the four horses owned by him was increased by $25,000, as was admitted by demurrer.

public officers. And further, in the case of contractual duties, the contract that created the duty may have been made by the same two parties who make the new agreement that is sought to be enforced, or it may have been made by the present promisee and a third party. This latter distinction may be expressed by saying that the pre-existing duty may be one that is owing to the present promisor whose promise is sought to be enforced, or it may be one that is owing to some third person.

Illustrations bringing out this last distinction are as follows: (1) A is bound by contract with B to build a certain house. Later, A performs this duty to B in exchange for a new promise by B to pay additional compensation. This may be referred to hereafter as a "two party case." (2) A is bound by contract with B to build a certain house. Later, A performs this duty to B in exchange for a new promise by C to pay additional compensation. This is a "three party case." It is conceivable that C's promise in case (2) should be held enforceable, while that of B in case (1) should not, even though the consideration given by A in the two cases is identical.

A third case that is substantially the same as case (1), and one that will also be dealt with as a two party case, may be supposed as follows: A is bound by contract with X to build a certain house. By an effective assignment, X transfers his right to B, so that A's duty is now owed to B. Later, A performs this duty to B in exchange for a new promise by B to pay additional compensation.

### § 174. Discharge of Duty Distinguished from Creation of Duty

For purposes of clear analysis, if for no other reason, a distinction must be drawn between the discharge of an existing duty and the creation of a new duty. In question form the distinction may be put thus: (1) Does performance in part or in full, as required by an existing duty to another person discharge that duty? (2) Does performance as required by an existing duty to another person constitute a sufficient consideration for a new promise by that other person or by a third person?

As to the first of these two questions, it is plain to be seen that full and exact performance of a duty will discharge that duty. The only doubtful question is whether the rendering of only part performance of the duty can operate as a discharge of the whole. It is clear that it can not do this without the consent of the obligee to whom the duty is owed.[4] But suppose that the part performance is offered on the terms that it shall be accepted as a full discharge, and it is so accepted by the obligee! Is the duty then discharged as a whole? It was more than once stated by Lord Chief Justice Coke that a part can not operate as a discharge of the whole, even if the obligee so agrees.[5] A debt of £20 can not be discharged by a payment of £10. And no doubt he would have said that a duty to render 20 days' labor could not be discharged by working 10 of those very days.

While the statements made by Coke in the two cited cases were mere dicta, they led finally to a direct decision by the House of Lords in accordance with them. The famous case of Foakes v. Beer,[6] decided in 1884, was a case of this sort. John W. Foakes was indebted to Julia Beer on a judgment for the sum of £2090, 19s. It was thereupon agreed by Julia Beer that she would accept in full satisfaction of the debt £500 in cash and the balance of £1590, 19s in semiannual instalments of £150 each. Foakes paid the full sum of £2090, 19s, exactly as Julia Beer required, and so regarded his judgment debt discharged. But Julia Beer then bethought herself that she had also had a right to interest on the judgment; and she proceeded to ask for execution on the judgment for the unpaid interest. The House of Lords held that in spite of the agreement of Beer and the full payment of the principal by Foakes, the duty to pay interest was not discharged and the judgment might properly be executed. The payment of £2090, 19s did not operate to discharge the duty of Foakes to pay that sum with interest, even though Beer had agreed that it should.

Without doubt, a proper interpretation of the facts of this case indicates that Beer impliedly promised that she would take no further action on the judgment; and the court discussed the case as if it were a question whether payment of less than the full sum due could be a sufficient consideration for Beer's promise. But it should be observed that Foakes was not bringing suit for breach of such a promise by Beer. Instead, Beer was enforcing the judgment obligation of Foakes. The question was whether the pre-existing judgment debt was discharged; and the court held that it was not.

In a much earlier case in which the facts were closely parallel to those of Foakes v. Beer, the court had held that a part payment was a sufficient consideration for a promise by the creditor, even though it would not discharge the full debt.[7] A creditor had obtained a judgment for a debt of £5. The debtor thereupon paid £4 to the creditor in exchange for the latter's promise to acknowledge satisfaction of the judgment in full. This promise the creditor broke and the judgment remained enforceable as to the balance unpaid. The debtor brought an action of assumpsit for damages for breach of the creditor's promise. The court gave judgment for the plaintiff, holding that even though £4 would not satisfy a £5 debt, the payment of the

6.  L.R. 9 App.Cas. 605 (1884).        7.  Eng.—Reynolds v. Pinhowe, Cro. Eliz. 429 (1595).

£4 was a sufficient consideration for the creditor's promise to make an effective acknowledgment of satisfaction.

This earlier case, and other similar ones, were not cited to the House of Lords in Foakes v. Beer. Had they been cited, it may well be that a different decision would have resulted. The House of Lords might, indeed, have adhered to the distinction between discharge of duty and the creation of duty; but in fact the distinction was not referred to and the question discussed was the question whether part payment could be a sufficient consideration for a return promise.

In spite of adherence to this distinction by Lord Coke and other early judges, it is believed that it is of no substantial value and that the House of Lords was quite justified in disregarding it. If part payment is a sufficient consideration for the promise to accept it as full satisfaction, the payment and the promise together should be held to operate as full satisfaction and discharge. To hold otherwise would be to cause circuity of action most undesirable in character. If the debt is still undischarged, the creditor can proceed, as in Foakes v. Beer, to collect the balance. But if the part payment is a sufficient consideration for the creditor's promise, the debtor can maintain suit for breach and in that suit can collect as damages every cent that the creditor has collected in breach of his promise. The two proceedings would exactly counterbalance each other; and the expense thereof and the time of the court would be totally wasted. Indeed, to avoid such wasteful circuity, it has long been held that a binding promise never to sue on a claim is operative as a discharge of that claim; and therefore the House of Lords was practically correct in regarding the problem in Foakes v. Beer as one of sufficiency of consideration for a promise. But it might better have snuffed out the false distinction by holding that the payment made was a sufficient consideration for Beer's implied promise and was operative as a discharge of the whole judgment debt.

## § 175. Performance of Duty to the Present Promisor as a Consideration

In most of the actual decisions, the court has held that there is no sufficient consideration if all that is given and received for the promise is the performance of a pre-existing duty to the one who makes the promise.[8] Here is a specific illustration. A owes

8. As the discussion in preceding sections shows, the writer believes that there is no good reason for distinguishing, at this point, between actual performance of duty and a promise to perform the duty —between unilateral and bilateral agreements. Therefore, in discussing "performance of duty" as a consideration, it will be intended to include also *promises* of performance of duty," except where the text expressly indicates the contrary intention.

a debt to B of $100, overdue and unpaid. A thereupon pays $50 to B in exchange for B's promise to receive it in full satisfaction of the debt: B is not bound by his promise, for A has given nothing as consideration other than the performance of half of his pre-existing duty to B.[9] There are very respectable cases holding the contrary, giving a variety of reasons for so doing.[10] Some of the cases on each side, and their reasons, will be discussed in the sections that follow. The payment by A, in part or in full, of his debt to B is not a sufficient consideration for a promise by B of any new performance, such as a promise to extend the time for payment of the balance or a promise to render some new service to A.[11]

Of course the part payment of a debt, or other mere part performance of an existing and enforceable duty, does not operate as a discharge of the whole if the creditor does not in fact assent to receive it as such; and evidence to show that he did not is not excluded by the fact that he signed a receipt for the money "in full payment."[12] Nor can a promise in consideration of such a part performance be enforced if no such promise is established.

In New York a comparatively recent statute has been enacted that should be held to abolish the whole pre-existing duty doctrine with respect to cases in which the modifying agreement of the parties is in writing, whether this agreement has been executed or is still wholly executory. The statute provides that such a modifying agreement shall not be invalidated by the absence of consideration.[16]

In many of these conflicting cases, specific factors can be found by reason of which reasonable distinctions can be drawn;

---

**9.** Foakes v. Beer, 9 App.Cas. 605, decided by the House of Lords in 1884, is the case most often cited in support.

**10.** The leading case is Munroe v. Perkins, 9 Pick. 298, 20 Am.Dec. 475 (Mass.1830). In substantial accord with it are the following:

**N.H.**—Frye v. Hubbell, 68 A. 325, 74 N.H. 358, 17 L.R.A. 1197 (1907).

**N.Y.**—Lattimore v. Harsen, 14 Johns. 330 (1817).

**16.** N.Y.Pers.Prop.Law, § 33, and Real Prop.Law, § 282, were amended by Laws 1936, c. 281, by adding the following: "An agreement hereafter made to change or modify, or to discharge in whole or in part, any

contract, obligation, or lease, or any mortgage or other security interest in personal or real property, shall not be invalid because of the absence of consideration, provided that the agreement changing, modifying, or discharging such contract, obligation, lease, mortgage, or security interest, shall be in writing and signed by the party against whom it is sought to enforce the change, modification or discharge." See also a later amendment, N.Y. Laws 1941, c. 329.

The Uniform Commercial Code—Sales, § 2—209 (1950 draft) provides: "(1) An agreement modifying a contract within this Article needs no consideration to be binding."

sub-classifications are possible, and perhaps desirable, with separate rules to be applied. The American Law Institute has, in the present instance, made no such distinctions or sub-classifications. It has accepted the majority rule, substantially as used in court opinions. If the consideration is merely the performance of a legal duty that is neither doubtful nor honestly disputed, it is declared to be insufficient if the duty is one that is owed "to the promisor." [17]

Where an employee is bound by contract to perform service at an agreed wage, the rendition of that service as agreed is not a sufficient consideration for a promise by the employer to pay increased wages.[18] Likewise, if an employer is bound to pay a salary for specified services, the payment of that salary is not a sufficient consideration for a promise by the employee to render additional services.[19] If the employment agreement is for no definite period, or is "at will," a new agreement modifying the salary to be paid or the work to be done is not invalid for lack of sufficient consideration. There is continued performance not required by the first agreement.[20] The same is true where one party, having a power of termination, forbears to exercise it in return for a new promise.[21]

## § 176. Performance of Duty to a Third Person as a Consideration

Performance of a pre-existing duty owed to the present promisor is generally held not to be a sufficient consideration; and the American Law Institute states this as the prevailing rule, even though some cases are and ought to be decided otherwise. But suppose that the pre-existing duty is owed to a third person and not to the promisor. Is the performance of this kind of duty a sufficient consideration for a promise? The American Law Institute has stated that it is sufficient.[26] This should be supported for two reasons: (1) the promisor gets the exact consideration for which he bargains, one to which he previously had no right and one that he might never have received; (2) there are no sound reasons of social policy for not applying in this case the ordinary rules as to sufficiency of consideration. The performance is bargained for, it is beneficial to the promisor, the promisee has forborne to seek a rescission or discharge from the third person to whom the duty was owed, and there is almost never any probability that the promisee has been in position to use or has in fact used any economic coercion to induce the mak-

26.   Restatement, Contracts, § 84(d): "Consideration is not insufficient because of the fact (d) that the party giving the consideration is then bound by a contractual or quasi-contractual duty to a third person to perform the act or forbearance given or promised as consideration."

ing of the promise. There is now a strong tendency for the courts to support these statements and to enforce the promise. The reasons that may be advanced to support the rule that is applied in the two-party cases, weak enough as they often are in those cases, are scarcely applicable at all in three-party cases.

If an actual count of cases is made, from earlier centuries down to date, the greater number have been decided against the promisee.[27] The performance of his duty to a third person was held not to be a sufficient consideration. Nevertheless, this should not now be called the "weight of authority." To the numerous cases to the contrary, holding such performance a sufficient consideration,[28] must be added much critical juristic opinion, the Restatement by the American Law Institute, and the fact that many recent decisions are on this side. In spite of past decisions, no state or federal court need hesitate to give judgment against the promisor if the "merits of the case" seem to require it.[29]

A surety is under a legal duty to pay the creditor, just as is the principal debtor. Suppose that a person, who is not himself indebted but who is interested in the welfare of the principal, asks the surety to pay the debt and promises to reimburse him for doing so. Payment of the debt by the surety is only the performance of his legal duty; but it has been held to be a sufficient consideration for the promise.[30] If it is the principal debtor himself, or a co-surety, who asks the surety to pay, his promise of reimbursement is now sufficiently supported by his own legal duty to contribute, or indemnify; but even when this duty may not have existed, the surety's payment of the debt was held to be a sufficient consideration for the promise to reimburse.[31]

The same situation exists where a contractor is hesitating to proceed with performance because of doubt whether he will get his pay, and is induced to proceed by a promise of a third person to guarantee payment.[32] Some cases have held the guaranty to be unenforceable, where the doubt was not on grounds that legally justified the hesitation.[33]

27.   U.S.—Nat. Electric Signaling Co. v. Fessenden, 207 F. 915 (C.C.A. 1st, 1913).

Ala.—Johnson's Adm'r v. Sellers' Adm'r, 33 Ala. 265 (1858).

Kan.—Schuler v. Myton, 29 P. 163, 48 Kan. 282 (1892).

Ky.—McDevitt v. Stokes, 192 S.W. 681, 174 Ky. 515 (1917).

N.Y.—Arend v. Smith, 45 N.E. 872, 151 N.Y. 502 (1897); Robinson v. Jewett, 22 N.E. 224, 116 N.Y. 40 (1889); Vanderbilt v. Schreyer, 91 N.Y. 392 (1883).

28.   Mass.—Abbott v. Doane, 40 N. E. 197, 163 Mass. 433, 34 L.R.A. 33, 47 Am.St.Rep. 465 (1895).

N.Y.—DeCicco v. Schweizer, 117 N.E. 807, 221 N.Y. 431 (1917).

Eng.—Scotson v. Pegg, 6 H. & N. 295 (1861); Shadwell v. Shadwell, 30 L. J.C.P. 145 (1860); Bagge v. Slade, 3 Bulst. 162 (1614).

33.   N.Y.—Vanderbilt v. Schreyer, 91 N.Y. 392 (1883); Teele v. Mayer, 173 App.Div. 869, 160 N.Y.S. 116 (1916).

Suppose that A is bound by a contract with B to erect a building for an agreed price, and that for some reason A is thinking of breaking the contract. Thereafter, A proceeds with performance at the request of C and in exchange for C's promise of added compensation. It was held in some cases that C's promise is not enforceable.[34] This can be justified if A's conduct has been substantially fraudulent;[35] but it should not be followed if A entered into the building contract in good faith and later contemplated throwing up the job because of losses in performance. It is clear that if circumstances of hardship may justify a court in enforcing a promise of added compensation made by B, they all the more certainly do so if the promise is by C.[36]

The same reasoning is applicable to contracts for all other kinds of service; but there are cases holding that the third person's promise is not enforceable.[37]

### § 177. The Case of DeCicco v. Schweizer, a Marriage Settlement Promise

In an interesting New York case,[38] a written document was prepared containing the following: "Whereas, Miss Blanche Schweizer, daughter of Joseph Schweizer . . . is now affianced to and is to be married to Count Oberto Gulinelli. Now, in consideration of all that is herein set forth, the said Joseph Schweizer promises . . . to pay annually to his said daughter Blanche . . . the sum of two thousand five hundred dollars."

This was delivered to the Count, and four days later the marriage took place. For ten years the payment was made; and suit was brought to recover the eleventh annual instalment. The plaintiff sued as assignee of both the daughter Blanche and her husband. The court held that there was sufficient consideration for the defendant's promise.

In spite of some inconsistency in the opinion of the court, examination of the facts will show that Count Gulinelli was the promisee and that the consideration for Schweizer's promise was the marriage itself. It also appears that the Count and Blanche

---

35.  In Lingenfelder v. Wainwright Brewing Co., 15 S.W. 844, 103 Mo. 578 (1890), the promise was by B and was not enforced; but A's conduct was thoroughly unjustifiable.

38.  **N.Y.—DeCicco v. Schweizer,** 117 N.E. 807, 221 N.Y. 431 (1917).

An earlier English case is substantially like DeCicco v. Schweizer in its facts and was decided the same way. Shadwell v. Shadwell, 9 C.B.

N.S. 159, 30 L.J.C.P. 145 (1860). To the writer, it seems pretty clear that in these two cases, neither party was bargaining with the promisee. In both, the happy engagement had already been made. The promises were those of the bride's father and the groom's uncle, motivated by a generous desire to make an annual gift. In both, there was the same action by the promisee in reasonable reliance.

were engaged to be married and the wedding day set before Schweizer's promise was made.  Blanche was the named payee, but was not the promisee.[39]  But, whether father made his promise to the Count, or to Blanche, or to the two of them jointly, all that either one of them did, or both together, was to perform a ceremony that each was under a legal duty to the other to do.  It is the performance of this duty that the court holds to be a sufficient consideration for Schweizer's promise.  It is the performance of a legal duty owed to one other than the promisor himself.

The court did not overrule earlier New York cases to the contrary;[40] it made an attempt to distinguish them, on the ground that they were cases of "a promise by A to B to induce him not to break his contract with C," whereas this is a case of "a promise by A, not merely to B, but to B and C jointly, to induce them not to rescind or modify a contract which they are free to abandon."  Such a distinction would seem to require an assumption that if the defendant offered his promise to both the Count and the daughter instead of to the Count alone, this in some way causes it to be no longer the duty of each to carry out the engagement contract.  They are said to be "free to abandon," seeming to mean thereby that their marriage is no longer the performance of a pre-existing duty in each.  This line of reasoning, it is submitted, is unsound.

Neither Blanche nor the Count was "free to abandon," or privileged not to marry.  Each of them, however, was legally privileged to propose a rescission of the engagement contract, or to accept such a proposal if made by the other; and the forbearance to exercise this privilege is, without doubt, a sufficient consideration.  But this is equally true of every three-party case that the courts have ever decided.  The forbearance to offer a rescission by any party to a contract is a sufficient consideration for a promise of a third party, whether the other party to the contract is willing to accept the offer or not, and even though he would reject it if made.

### § 178.  Actual Performance of Duty is as Good a Consideration as is a Promise to Perform Duty

There is no good reason for distinguishing between performance of the duty and a new promise to perform it, on the part of the one who owes the duty to a third person.  They should alike be held to be a sufficient consideration.  It has been argued by able men that the bilateral agreement is a valid contract, while the unilateral one is not—that performance by A of his duty to B is not a sufficient consideration for a promise by C, while a promise by A to C to perform his duty owed to B is sufficient.  One should hesitate before holding that a promise of performance is a better consideration than the performance itself would be; in the present instance such a holding is certainly erroneous.

The reason that was given to sustain the argued conclusion is that performance of duty cannot be a "detriment" to the performer, but that a new promise made by A to C to perform A's existing duty to B is a detriment to A because it binds him by a duty to a new promisee. Even though A's promises to B and to C can be discharged by a single performance, the theory is that it is a detriment to be under a new duty to render an identical performance.

This argument is unsound for the same reason that the like argument is unsound when made to apply the detriment theory of consideration to bilateral contracts in general: it begs the question. If a promise has to be known to be binding before we can tell whether or not it is a sufficient consideration for a return promise, the enforceability of most bilateral agreements must remain a mystery forever. For this reason, the argued distinction between the bilateral and the unilateral agreement falls to the ground. A promise by A to C to perform his pre-existing duty to B cannot be shown to be a sufficient consideration for the reason that it creates a duty in A to a new party.

Nevertheless, bilateral agreements are known to be enforceable contracts, since the courts enforce them. And we have a theory of consideration that is applicable to them; the courts hold that a promise is a sufficient consideration for a return promise without first knowing that it is binding. Is not this theory applicable to a bilateral agreement between A and C in which A promises merely to perform his pre-existing duty to B? The answer to this question is yes, unless the courts think that the fact that A's promise is merely to perform his duty is a good reason for not applying it. This fact is still generally thought to be a good reason for not applying it to the two-party case—a bilateral agreement between A and B. It is the goodness of this reason that must be determined, in both kinds of cases alike. It cannot be dodged in the three-party case by the hocus-pocus known as "detriment because it is binding."

### § 179. Two Separate and Independent Contracts for One Performance

When A is under contract with B to render a specified performance and later makes a new contract with C to render this identical performance, the two contracts are quite separate and independent. The fact that A can discharge them both by a single performance is an interesting fact, but has no bearing upon the validity of the two contracts. This is true whether the two contracts are unilateral or are bilateral, or are one of each.

Let us suppose a case based upon one taken from the reports.[43] A has contracted with B to drive the latter's mare, Grace, in the "Futurity." Later, C procures A's new promise to drive Grace in this race by paying to A $1,000 cash in advance. There can be no question that this is a valid and enforceable unilateral contract. C's cash is ample consideration for A's promise. This being true, if A now fails to drive in the race as promised, he is bound to pay damages to both B and C. The right of B and the right of C are wholly independent of each other, however; likewise, A's correlative duty to B is wholly independent of and separate from his correlative duty to C. The fact that A might have satisfied his duty to B and his separate duty to C by performing one and the same act is quite immaterial and shows no identity in the legal relations. A's new promise to C is an operative fact that lays a train of new consequences. It causes nonperformance of the promised act to have new legal effect. The resulting duty to compensate C is not the same as his secondary duty to compensate B; these two duties cannot even be performed by making one payment.

Furthermore, if A and B now unite in rescinding their original agreement, this discharges A's duty to B, but it does not discharge A's duty to C; neither is this rescission in itself a breach of A's duty to C. A's new contract with C, absolutely binding though it was, did not deprive A of either the power or the privilege, of joining with B in a rescission. It deprived him merely of the privilege, in relation to C, of not driving Grace. Such a rescission, absolutely valid though it was, leaves A's duty to C just as it was before; and A's subsequent failure to drive in the race will still create in C a secondary right to damages. All these facts go to show that A's promise to C has an operative effect different from that of his promise to B.

In many cases of this sort A's duty to B will be substantially different from his duty to C in another respect. His duty to B may be expressly or constructively conditional upon some performance by B. A's duty to B to drive in the race may be conditional upon B's payment of salary then due and his furnishing of board and lodging. The new duty to C may not be subject to these conditions. However, even if A should make his new duty to C expressly subject to the same conditions—payment of salary by B, etc.,—the reasons given above are amply sufficient to show that it is a duty different from that owed to B. The fact is that a duty is a legal relation between two persons, and such a relation between A and B is not a relation between A and C.

Such being the legal relations of the parties in the case of a unilateral contract between A and C, where A has promised and

43.  Ky.—McDevitt v. Stokes, 192 S.
W. 681, 174 Ky. 515 (1917).

C has paid, there is no impossibility in creating similar legal relations where the new agreement between A and C is bilateral. A's new duty to C, if created by the law, will be beneficial to C and detrimental to A, just as in the case of other bilateral contracts. Also, A's promise to C will be just as valuable and effective per se, as in the case of other bilateral contracts. The fact that A may now receive a greater compensation than he would have received had C made no contract is immaterial. B and C both receive exactly what they desired: each of them obtains a separate promissory act from A; each also obtains from A's promised performance exactly the benefit that he expected; and if we hold that the new agreement is valid, each obtains an enforceable legal right against A. On the other hand, A has done wrong to no man, and the public interest has been fully protected.

The new duty of A to C where C has paid A $1,000 for his new promise to drive Grace in the "Futurity" is not a duty not to rescind his pre-existing contract with B. The same is true where the new contract between A and C is bilateral. After A has promised C that he will drive Grace in the "Futurity," he remains privileged, just as before, to accept an offer of rescission made by him or by B. Such a rescission by A will be no breach of his promise to C. In spite of such a recission, it is still quite possible for A to drive Grace. The only ways in which A can break his contract with C are to fail to drive Grace when the day arrives, or to send to C an unconditional anticipatory repudiation. The rescission of the contract with B is neither of these. This is true even in cases like DeCicco v. Schweizer; for a mutual rescission by the Count and the daughter would be no breach of a promise by the Count to the father. Blanche and the Count might still appear before a magistrate and be married, and this would fulfil perfectly the Count's promise.

It should be noted here that A's new promise to C requires a new consideration for enforceability; it is not supported by his pre-existing duty to B to render the same performance. In this respect the three-party case differs from the two-party case. If A makes a new promise to B to perform his existing duty to B, this promise is binding without any new consideration being given for it.

The same could, of course, have been held with respect to A's new promise to C; it, too, could have been held to be supported by his pre-existing duty to B to render the same performance. But in no case have the courts so held. The reasons that have been thought sufficient for enabling B to enforce the new promise to him without any new consideration are not sufficient to enable C to do the like.

## § 180.    Performance of Public or Official Duty

The performance of his official duty by a public officer is not a sufficient consideration for a promise of an extra compensation or reward. This differs from the case of an ordinary contractual duty in that the public are more directly interested in the officer's performance, and also that public officers may be more likely to scamp their jobs in the hope of extorting special compensation from individuals. This principle has been held applicable to sheriffs, constables, and other police officers,[44] to guardians,[45] and even to corporate officers.[46]

Governmental offers of a reward may be made in such a way, either by legislative act or by an authorized official, that they may be accepted and the reward earned by the police or other public officers.[47] In such cases, the public policy involved is determined by the representatives of the public duly empowered for the purpose.

If a reward is offered for a specified service, a public officer may accept and earn the reward if any part of the service is not included within his official duties.[48] That which is outside of his duty is a sufficient consideration. The fact that part of the requested consideration is already within the officer's duty does not render him incompetent to accept. The notions of public policy underlying the general rule are not so strong and well-established as to have such a result. The fact is that rewards are often paid to public officers in cases in which the officer is not legally entitled.

## § 182.    Is a Contractual Duty Always Alternative?

It has been suggested by learned writers, perhaps as a method of supporting decisions in which the promise of additional compensation is enforced, that the legal duty created by a contract is always in the alternative, being a duty either to perform specifically or to pay damages. If this were a sound theory of legal duty, it would eliminate the problem of pre-existing duty and it would require the disapproval of most if not all of the majority decisions. If one has an option between two performances, the giving up of this option, or the exercise of it in one way rather than the other, is a sufficient consideration for a return promise. If one has the privilege of performing in one way rather than another, or the power of creating such a privilege by rendering some other performance, the forbearance to exercise the privilege or the power is a sufficient consideration. Thus, if A is bound to deliver to B either a touring car or a motor truck, the option being in A, the abandonment of this option and the delivery of the car instead of the truck is a sufficient consideration for a promise of additional compensation, whether this promise is made by B or by a third person. So also, if A has promised not to com-

261

pete with B in business, with the provision that he can regain the privilege of competition by paying the sum of $5000, A's continued forbearance to compete and to regain the privilege of competition by making the necessary payment is a sufficient consideration. In such cases, the consideration given by A is not merely the performance of duty.

Therefore, if a contractor always has the lawful alternative between specific performance and the payment of unliquidated damages, his rendition of the former and forbearance to choose the latter would be sufficient consideration.[51] But it can not be admitted that a contractor has such a lawful alternative, unless all alternatives are lawful. Does the criminal have a lawful alternative between obedience to the law and paying the penalty, between not shooting his victim and electrocution of himself? Does the tort-feasor have a lawful alternative between not converting his neighbor's goods and paying their adjudged value at the end of a damage suit? There are, indeed, statutes providing that for the doing of certain acts a specified payment must be made, some of which are interpreted as being for revenue purposes only and not prohibitory; but these are exceptional. Usually a penalty is said to imply a prohibition. If the statute is solely for revenue, there would be no wrong in inciting another to do the acts in question; indeed, such an incitement might be regarded as an advantage to the state. But we are not privileged to induce another person to break his contract with a third person. The causing of such a breach is itself a tort;[52] and in the tort action it is no defense that the contract breaker will be liable in damages to compensate for his breach.

A duty is a legal relation that exists whenever certain action or forbearance is expected of an individual, and in default of it the representatives of organized society will act in some predetermined manner injurious to the defaulting individual. In any case there is a possibility that this societal action will not in fact take place; for the default may not be discovered, or no one may care to start a proceeding against the defaulter, or he may by evasion or by force prevent any action. This possibility exists in the case of a secondary duty to pay damages or to make restitution, as well as in the case of a primary duty to perform specifically. Such a possibility, therefore, does not prove the nonexistence of a duty in a particular case, for it is to be found in all cases.

51.    Thus in Munroe v. Perkins, 26 Mass. (9 Pick.) 298 (1830), the Court said: "The plaintiff having refused to perform that contract, as he might do, subjecting himself to such damages as the other parties might show they were entitled to recover, he afterward went on upon the faith of the new promise and finished the work. This was a sufficient consideration."

## § 183. Policy of Recognizing Performance of Duty as a Sufficient Consideration.

There are plenty of court opinions in which it is declared that the performance of duty ought not or can not be recognized as a sufficient consideration; but in practically none of these is there found a discussion of the reasons for the rule and the policy on which it is based. The matter is often dismissed with the mere statement of the supposed rule, or perhaps with the additional statement that such a performance is not a detriment to the promisee or a benefit to the promisor. The inaccuracy of this latter assertion has already been discussed.

The conflict that exists in the statement of the law and in its actual application indicates that there is much doubt whether the supposed rule is in accord with sound policy or with prevailing sentiment. Doubtless there is some feeling that while the laborer is worthy of his hire, he is not worthy of additional pay beyond what he agreed to work for. There is a very strong countervailing sentiment to the effect that the promisor ought to keep his promise, having got from the promisee exactly what he bargained for. The decision of a case has frequently turned on which of these feelings happens to be uppermost in the mind of the court. The rule in Foakes v. Beer was influenced in large part by the purely mathematical notion that 10 can not be equal to 20 and therefore can not operate as satisfaction. At the same time, grave dissatisfaction with the rule of Foakes v. Beer is expressed by a majority even of the courts that feel bound to apply it.

Frequently no better reason can be given for the existence of a rule, instead of a different one, than that it has been so decided or that it accords with the "weight of authority." That is not a bad reason; it may be a sufficient one. A much better reason for supporting a stated rule is that it accords with the opinions and practices of men, the mores that prevail in the community. However, these too may be in doubt; and they are themselves subject to change. In such case, we need to know whether the rule promotes or is in accord with the general social and economic welfare.

It is perhaps generally believed that a rule approving as a sufficient consideration either a performance in accordance with a pre-existing duty, or the promise of such a performance, would operate to encourage the non-fulfilment of duties and the making of threats of non-fulfilment. Thus, it is conceivable that if policemen are allowed to enforce payment of a reward offered for the performance of official duty, or for promises of such performance, they will be tempted to postpone the performance of duty until some additional reward is offered. So too an unscrupulous contractor might threaten to break his contract or might improperly postpone performance for the purpose of inducing an offer of a greater compensation. If this general welfare argument is sound, it justifies the rule of law in its generally stated form; and it applies equally to unilateral and to bilateral contracts.

It must be admitted that the above argument has some weight. No doubt it should be regarded as conclusive in cases of policemen and other officials with public duties.[53] It would have much weight, also, in cases where the pre-existing duty is a contractual one and is a duty owed by the promisee to the present promisor.[54] There may be some danger that dishonest contractors will attempt to blackmail the other party to the contract into promising a higher compensation. There is far less danger, however, that such blackmailing efforts will be directed against third persons who are strangers to the contract; and even where there is such a conscious and successful effort, it is much more difficult to see that anyone is wronged. Of course, if the effort to get a promise of compensation from a third party results in a breach of the pre-existing duty to a second party, this is a wrong not to be encouraged.

It would not be particularly difficult to classify cases of this sort along strictly moral lines, to separate the sheep from the goats, and to enforce the new promise in favor of an honest contractor while refusing to enforce it in favor of the blackmailer or the dishonest. There is reason to believe that a considerable part of the apparent conflict in the decisions can be explained on this ground. Such a distinction can not often be made in cases of public officials where the non-fulfilment of the pre-existing duty would be a tort or other public injury; and yet there are some cases holding that public officers can collect promised extra rewards. The distinction can often be drawn very properly in cases where there are only two parties involved and the previous duty was owed to the present promisor.[55]

---

53. **Mass.**—Pool v. Boston, 59 Mass. (5 Cush.) 219 (1849).

**Tenn.**—Stamper v. Temple, 25 Tenn. 113, 6 Humph. 113 (1845).

54. **Mo.**—Lingenfelder v. Wainwright Brewing Co., 15 S.W. 844, 103 Mo. 578 (1890).

**Eng.**—Stilk v. Myrick, 2 Camp. 317 (1809).

55. Thus, in Munroe v. Perkins, 26 Mass. (9 Pick.) 298 (1830), the plaintiff had done his best and had reached a point where his lack of credit was preventing further per-

formance. It is not too much to say that the moral sense of the community would be shocked by allowing the defendant to break his new promise. On the other hand, in Lingenfelder v. Wainwright Brewing Co., 15 S.W. 578, 103 Mo. 578 (1890), the promise was extorted from the defendant by threats and other inexcusable conduct. This distinction seems to be adopted in effect in King v. Duluth & M. Ry. Co., 63 N.W. 1105, 61 Minn. 482 (1895), in the following dictum: "But where the party refusing to complete his contract does so by

The distinction is very easily drawn in three-party cases where the previous duty is a contractual duty to a third person. Indeed, it is believed that a great number of such cases fall on the enforceable side, and the sheep would be far more numerous than the goats. In many of these cases it would be shocking to the conscience and in conflict with the prevailing mores of society to refuse to enforce the new promise.

## § 184.  Effect of Increased Difficulty, Expense, or Hardship

It was once the generally stated rule that impossibility of performance of a contractual duty was no defense. If this ever was the actually applied rule, it has long since ceased to be so. Not only this, it has come about that the term "impossibility" has been made to cover a wide range of situations, including what would be more accurately described as impracticability by reason of danger, difficulty, or expense. If a contractual duty has been terminated by reason of such forms of impracticability, a subsequent performance is as a matter of course a sufficient consideration for a promise of increased compensation.[56] In such a case the promisee renders a performance that he is no longer under a duty to render.

But there are many degrees of danger, difficulty, and expense; and even under liberal modern practice, some of them do not operate to terminate the contractual duty. It is not every unexpected difficulty or unforeseen expense that justifies a contractor in failing to perform. Nevertheless, if the difficulty and expense are such that they would not have been foreseen by a reasonably prudent man and have not been allowed for in making the bargain, their occurrence excites sympathy for the unfortunate contractor. In such cases he is not regarded as a bad man for asking increased compensation, a fact that is often recognized by the other party to the contract and that induces him to make a new promise. If the only consideration for this promise, however, is the performance that was required by the previous contract, we still have a case falling directly within the present topic, in spite of our sympathy induced by the unexpected difficulty.

Inasmuch as the only reason for refusing to recognize performance of a pre-existing duty as a sufficient consideration is the fact that such recognition would encourage contractors to play a "hold up" game, it is quite possible and is probably desirable to draw a line of distinction between cases in which the "hold

reason of some unforeseen and substantial difficulties in the performance of the contract, which were not known or anticipated by the parties when the contract was entered into, and which cast upon him the additional burden not contemplated by the parties, and the opposite party promises him extra pay or benefits if he will complete his contract, and he so promises, the promise to pay is supported by a valid consideration."

up" game is being played and cases where it is not. In the latter cases the performance of the pre-existing and undischarged duty may be recognized as a sufficient consideration for a promise; and the occurrence of unexpected difficulty or expense may be accepted as sufficient evidence that the promisee is a citizen of merit and not to be classified with highwaymen. There are some cases in which this distinction has been expressly recognized and adopted; and in still other cases in which the new promise was enforced, the facts were of this character.[57] It must be admitted that "moral" distinctions of this kind are frequently hard to apply in specific cases. When is the contractor playing a "hold-up game?" Perhaps a fair answer to this question is that he is not playing such a game if the other party thinks that he is not and willingly promises additional compensation without protest, and can not establish the existence of deceit and false representation.

In the well-known case of Munroe v. Perkins,[58] the plaintiff was a worthy building contractor who had made a losing contract to construct a hotel and who did not have sufficient resources to continue performance. He made no threats and did not repudiate his duty; but he could not proceed with construction because he had no money and was refused credit at the bank. Both labor and materials were unobtainable. The defendant, knowing these facts, induced the plaintiff to proceed with performance and enabled him to obtain the necessary credit at the bank by assuring him in the presence of bank officers that he would be paid the actual cost of construction. Of course, the plaintiff was performing no more than his contractual duty; but he was not a bad man and he was given judgment on the new promise. The court did not suggest the distinction that is here being made and did not

---

57. See the following dictum by Judge Swan in United States, use of Pierce Steel Pile Corp. v. Miller, 81 F.2d 8 (C.C.A.2d, 1936): "If, as they contend, Pierce was already bound to drive the piling to solid rock at the unit prices specified in the letter of April 4th, a second promise to do the same work furnished no consideration for Miller's promise to pay the higher prices set forth in the letter of May 14th. Am. Law Institute, Restatement, Contracts, sec. 78; 1 Williston, Contracts, sec. 130; Stilk v. Myrick, 2 Camp. 317; Vanderbilt v. Schreyer, 91 N.Y. 392. Although this rule is generally recognized, its application has frequently been avoided by finding some form of consideration when the situation was such that performance would entail unexpected hardship and the contractor's request for additional compensation was not coercive or morally blameworthy. See Schwartzreich v. Bauman-Basch, Inc., 231 N.Y. 196, 131 N.E. 887; Sasso v. K. G. & G. Realty & Const. Co., 98 Conn. 571, 120 A. 158; Linz v. Schuck, 106 Md. 220, 67 A. 286; Michaud v. MacGregor, 61 Minn. 198, 63 N.W. 479; King v. Duluth, M. & N. R. Co., 61 Minn. 482, 63 N.W. 1105; Meech v. City of Buffalo, 29 N.Y. 198; Osborne v. O'Reilly, 42 N.J.Eq. 467, 9 A. 209, 33 Yale L.J. 78." A still later case is United States v. Lange, 35 F. Supp. 17, D.C.Md. (1940), affirmed 120 F.2d 886.

58. 9 Pick. 298 (Mass.1830).

base its decision upon the fact that the plaintiff was meritorious; but this fact could hardly fail to be of influence in the result. The reasons that were very briefly given by the court were that the plaintiff might have repudiated his duty and substituted a mere duty to pay damages, and secondly that the new transaction amounted to a "waiver" or rescission of the former contract. As is shown in succeeding sections, neither of these reasons can be supported; but the decision can nevertheless be sustained.

In another case, the plaintiff contracted to build a cellar for an agreed price. A quicksand, unknown to both parties, was encountered, requiring great additional expense. The defendant induced the plaintiff to complete the work by promising to pay its actual cost. The court held this promise binding.[59] In this case, the finding of the quicksand did not in itself terminate the plaintiff's legal duty to build the cellar. That performance was neither impossible nor impracticable. In cases like this, however, the agreement must be carefully scrutinized to see whether the plaintiff's duty was not conditional on some supposed state of facts, so that the risk of quicksands is still carried by the owner; also whether the owner did not misrepresent existing conditions. Frequently it may appear that the contractor has performed more that his contract duty required.

The unexpected difficulty and expense may be caused by war conditions. Where the plaintiff notified the defendant of his intention to discontinue the work of building a dam for this reason, the defendant promised to pay such an amount as would prevent actual loss. The dam was thereupon completed; and the new promise was enforced.[60]

The unforeseen difficulty and expense may be due to many other causes, such as strikes and threats by workmen [61] or increased wage costs due to pressure from government officers.[62] Of course, if the party who promises extra pay has himself unjustly caused the increased difficulty and expense, this may operate as a discharge of the contractor from duty; performance is then a sufficient consideration, since there is no pre-existing duty to be performed.[63]

The mere fact that a contractor has made a losing contract, or that he has encountered difficulties and costs that were reasonably to be foreseen, is generally held not to be a sufficient reason for his asking for more pay or for enforcing a promise of more pay by the other party.[64] These are risks that either

59.   Linz v. Schuck, 67 A. 286, 106 Md. 220, 11 L.R.A. 789, 129 Am.St. Rep. 481, 14 Ann.Cas. 498 (1907). 185 Cal. 366 (1929), increased costs of labor and material of frequently recurring kind.

64.   **Cal.**—Western Lithograph Co. v. Vanomar Producers, 197 P. 103, **Minn.**—King v. Duluth M. & N. R. Co., 63 N.W. 1105, 61 Minn. 482

were, or ought reasonably to have been, within the contemplation of the parties when making the contract.

## § 186. Effect of an Agreement to Rescind the Pre-existing Contract

In a number of modern cases the court has thought it possible to avoid the effect of the pre-existing duty rule by finding that there was an agreement for the rescission of the previous contract. Such rescission having operated to discharge the previous duty, the performance when rendered by the promisee is a sufficient consideration for the promise given in exchange. In several of these cases the court failed to observe that it was arguing in a circle, making the validity of the new agreement depend upon the rescission while the validity of the rescission depended upon the new agreement.

It is quite true that the mutual rights and duties existing under a bilateral contract can be discharged by a mutual agreement of rescission. When such a rescission has taken place, neither party has any further right or duty under the rescinded contract. If that contract was a contract of employment, the servant is out of a job and free to take a different one, and the master is out of a servant and free to hire a new one in his place. In such a case as this, the two parties have exactly the same power to make a new contract as they would have had if there had been no previous transaction between them. A new agreement for exactly the same service at either a greater or a less compensation will not be invalidated by the fact that the servant was previously bound to render such service. The rescission terminated that previous duty; so that at the time the new agreement is made there is no already existing duty to affect its validity. This is true whether the new agreement is unilateral or bilateral in form—whether the master's promise of compensation at the altered rate is given in exchange for the servant's new promise of the identical service or for his actual rendition of that service.

It has been erroneously supposed that the result is the same even though the "rescission" is made simultaneously with and is incorporated in the new agreement for the modified compensation.[72] Here is to be found the vicious argument in a circle. The

(1895), a contractor should expect frozen ground in Minnesota in winter.

72. It is expressly so stated in Schwartzreich v. Bauman-Basch Inc., 131 N.E. 887, 231 N.Y. 196, reargument denied 132 N.E. 905, 231 N.Y. 602 (1921); and it is the theory actually applied in the following cases:

Conn.—Sasso v. K. G. & G. Realty & Const. Co., 120 A. 158, 98 Conn. 571 (1923).

Mass.—Munroe v. Perkins, 9 Pick. 298 (1830).

trouble is that in such a case there is no rescission at all. Suppose, for example, a bilateral employment contract for a year's service at $90 per week. The servant, being dissatisfied, asks for more pay; and the master promises $100 per week for the identical service. This promise of the master cannot be sustained on the theory that there has been a rescission of the former contract, without wholly nullifying the supposed rule that performance as required by pre-existing duty is not a sufficient consideration for a promise. And this is true whether at the time the promise of increased compensation is made the parties say or do not say that they rescind the previous contract. The new and modifying agreement purports to change only a single term of the previous contract, and it purports to change nothing else. The new agreement may be expressed in various forms; but its real meaning and legal operation remain the same. Consider the following modes of expressing the new agreement:

(1) Servant says, "I offer a modification of our contract by substituting $100 for $90." Master replies, "I assent thereto."

(2) Servant says, "I promise to render the identical service if you will promise $100 in place of $90." Master replies, "I so promise."

(3) Servant says, "I offer to rescind our contract and to substitute instead a new contract for the same service at $100 per week." Master replies, "I accept your offer."

It is clear that the meaning and the effect of these three agreements are exactly the same, and that the fact that the word "rescind" is used in case number (3) does not affect the matter in the least. It is just as if the master had said to the servant, "I release you but I do not release you," and servant had said to the master, "I release you from your duty to pay me $90 on condition that you bind yourself to pay me $100 instead." The new agreement does nothing more and is intended to do nothing more than to modify the compensation, to substitute $100 for $90; and this is exactly what every new agreement to pay more for the performance of an existing duty is intended to do.[73]

Why are able judges so easily convinced that a simultaneous "rescission" eliminates the difficulty created by a pre-existing duty? It is because they think that justice requires its elimination and the enforcement of the promise of more pay. It carries out the intention of the parties. This fact should make us pause before we apply the old rule in cases still to come. There may still be good reasons for applying that rule. Enforcement of the new promise may be the consummation of fraud or economic duress; the contractor may have planned it that way. In such a case, performance of the pre-existing duty should not be held to be sufficient consideration, for reasons of policy. In the absence of any such reason, it is believed that the new promise may properly be enforced. It may be that express words of "rescission" tend to strengthen the conclusion that the promisor was willingly recognizing a moral obligation. Moreover, various courts have recognized the power of a creditor to discharge his debtor by a gift process. If, in a case of the present sort, it is clear that the party who promises additional compensation means to make a gift, with no element of fraud or duress, there is no strong reason why the court should not enforce the new promise.[74] In such a case, however, it is better not to make a specious argument that old rules are still being applied and that old precedents are being followed.

### § 187. Payment of a Disputed Debt as Consideration—Compromises

The payment of money that one does not owe, or the rendition of any other performance that one is not bound to render, is a sufficient consideration for a return promise. But the mere fact that a creditor's claim is disputed by the debtor, in whole or in part, and in good faith, does not mean that he does not owe the debt as claimed or that he is not under a duty to pay it. If the creditor's claim is in fact correct, and he reduces it to judgment, he can also obtain damages for the wrongful refusal and delay of the debtor. It is no defense against such damages that the debtor thought in good faith that the debt had been paid or for any other reason was not due. The debtor is bound to perform his duty without suit; and he is penalized in damages and costs for not doing so.

Nevertheless, where a claim is disputed in good faith, payment or other performance by the debtor is held to be sufficient consideration for a return promise.[75] This seems clearly to be an exception to the rule that performance of a pre-existing duty is not a sufficient consideration. It has been thought not to be an exception, for the reason that one is privileged to litigate such disputes, and that one is not bound to pay until the determination of the dispute by a court; this seems erroneous for the reasons given above. The sound reason for holding that payment or other performance is a sufficient consideration is that compromises of disputed claims ought to be and in fact are favored and supported by the courts. Reduction of litigation by mutual agreement of litigants is much to the public interest; and in order to attain this desired end, it is necessary to sustain the compromise agreement without regard to whether the claim was correct or incorrect. If it was incorrect, the alleged debtor has paid more than he was bound to pay; but he cannot get it back. If the claim was correct, the debtor was legally bound to perform as he did; and the creditor has received less than he was justly entitled to, but he can collect no more.

Indeed, there are many cases holding that if a creditor is making one undivided claim, only a part of which is disputed by the debtor, the payment by the debtor of the part that he admits to be due is a sufficient consideration for a promise by the creditor.[76] A reason often given for this is that the debtor is bound to pay no part of an undivided claim so long as any part of it is honestly disputed, so that in paying even that part of the claim that he admits to be correct he is doing more than he is then bound by legal duty to do. This argument seems erroneous, however, unless his admission that the sum actually paid by him was due was an incorrect admission. Indeed, there are many other cases holding that such a payment is not a sufficient consideration for a promise to give up the balance of the claim.[77] In cases of this sort, the new transaction can scarcely be described as a compromise; it is rather a total victory by the debtor and a total surrender by the creditor, so far as concerns the matter actually disputed. But even if it is not a compromise, and even though the debtor has merely performed a legal duty, the debtor's payment or other performance should be held to be a sufficient consideration. The policy underlying the general rule represented by the decision in Foakes v. Beer, that payment of part of an admitted debt cannot be a sufficient consideration, is too doubtful to be permitted to apply in cases that are not on all fours with that case. Where part of a claim is disputed in good faith, the case would better be classified among the compromises, as the courts have very often in fact done.

## § 188. Unliquidated Claims

There are claims to the payment of money, the amount of which is indefinite and uncertain and is capable of being made definite and certain only by agreement of the parties or by the finding of a court. Illustrations are claims for damages for a tort or for a breach of contract. In these cases an agreement between the parties fixing the amount to be paid in settlement is a valid contract. There may have been no dispute as to the sum to be paid, but there was doubt; and the agreement has reduced doubt to certainty. Also, the payment of any definite amount, accepted in full settlement, constitutes an accord and satisfaction; and such a payment is sufficient consideration for a return promise.[78]

These cases may be explained on the ground that there was as yet no duty to make immediate payment of any definite sum. But even if the duty to pay unliquidated damages should be recognized, with a penalty in the shape of interest or other damages for delay in making the settlement, still it is undisputed law that the payment of a definite sum is a sufficient consideration for a promise, without regard to whether the sum paid is more or less than a court would have awarded or is more or less than the injury suffered by the claimant can be shown to have been. Even granting that there is a legal duty to make immediate compensation for a wrongful injury, the uncertainties that are involved make it sound policy to give validity to agreements of compromise or agreements that reduce the amount to certainty, whether such agreements are fully executed or remain executory. If the terms of a contract are such as to leave the amount payable for goods or services uncertain in amount, by reason of indefiniteness in modes of measurement or otherwise, a mutual agreement by which the uncertainty is removed by fixing a specific amount or by substituting a definite method of measurement is not invalid by reason of pre-existing legal duty. Whether it is unilateral or bilateral in form, there is a sufficient consideration to support the substituted contract.[79]

### § 190. Compositions with Creditors—the Rule of Foakes v. Beer Not Applicable

Part payment by a debtor of his already overdue debt is not operative as a full satisfaction, even though the creditor so agrees, and is not a sufficient consideration for a promise. This rule has never been held to prevent the enforcement of a composition agreement with two or more creditors. There are several reasons for this, wholly apart from the fact that the rule in Foakes v. Beer has not given general satisfaction.

Of course, when two or more creditors make mutual promises to each other that they will give up in part or in whole their claims against a debtor, there is a valid contract among the creditors and the debtor is a donee beneficiary of this contract. Now that it is the well-settled rule in the United States that a contract is enforceable in favor of a donee beneficiary, this is a sufficient reason for holding that an ordinary composition agreement is enforceable in favor of the debtor.[87] But such compositions have been enforced for centuries, even in jurisdictions that had not yet accepted the rule in favor of beneficiaries.

In ordinary compositions, the promises of the creditors to accept a part as a full discharge are made to the debtor as well as to each other. If so, the debtor is a promisee as well as a beneficiary. But it is to be observed that if the validity of the composition is dependent upon the fact that the creditors make mutual promises the consideration is one that moves from third parties and not from the debtor himself. It was long believed by many that consideration must move from the promisee, and not from some third person in his behalf. But there remains no further justification for this belief since the modern development in favor of third party beneficiaries. If a beneficiary can enforce a contract even though he neither was a promisee therein nor gave the consideration, it is obvious that he should be in no worse position if he is in fact the promisee. Therefore, the modern rule is that consideration need not move from the promisee; and this rule is applicable to compositions with two or more creditors.[88]

Again, however, it is to be observed that compositions were enforced in favor of a debtor even in jurisdictions that ordinarily required consideration to move from the promisee. If the only consideration that moves from him is the payment of a part of his debt, we should then have another exception to the supposed rule that performance of duty is not a sufficient consideration. It is possible, however, to find another consideration that moves from the debtor himself. Composition agreements are universally made with the understanding that the participating creditors shall be treated alike, with no preference of one over another. Such a preference, secretly made and without a creditor's assent, is a fraud upon him making the composition voidable by him. It is clear, therefore, that the debtor ordinarily promises by implication that he will treat all alike, thereby giving up a rather important privilege that he had at common law. A debtor is legally privileged to prefer one creditor over another as long as he makes no composition agreement to the contrary, except so far as this is limited by bankruptcy statutes. The exercise of this privilege would often be of great advantage to a debtor; and it would always be to the disadvantage of non-preferred creditors by reducing the assets available to them. Therefore, if the debtor is himself a party to the composition agreement and does not expressly retain the privilege of making special settlements and preferences, he gives up a valuable legal privilege in return for the promises of the creditors to accept part as settlement of the whole. There is no reason for refusing to recognize this as sufficient consideration.

### § 191. A New Promise by the Debtor may be Valid Even Though the Return Promise of the Creditor is Not

In bilateral contracts, it has been thought that both promises must be binding or neither is binding—that if for any reason one of the exchanged promises is not binding it cannot be operative as a consideration for the return promise. The validity of this notion has been discussed elsewhere.[89] It would seem to follow from this supposed rule that if a debtor and a creditor make a bilateral agreement, the debtor promising to pay part or all of his debt and the creditor promising something in return, the agreement is void as a whole and neither promise is enforceable.

It is true that the creditor is not bound by his promise; but in spite of this it will be observed that the debtor is bound by his. There are cases actually so holding, and correctly, although they give different reasons for the result.[90]

A promise by a debtor or other obligor to perform his already existing legal duty is binding without any new consideration whatever; and the fact that the creditor gives some inoperative consideration is immaterial. The duty itself—the past debt—is said to be a sufficient consideration. Of course this is not true if we define consideration as a bargained-for equivalent. But even though we adopt this narrow definition, we must remember that the courts have not yet generally adopted it; and when they have said that the past debt is a sufficient consideration they have meant and they will continue to mean that the past debt is a sufficient reason for enforcing the new promise.

The unpaid debt is held to be a sufficient reason for enforcing a new promise to pay it, even though it has become unenforceable by reason of a statute of limitations or a discharge in bankruptcy. The new promise "waives" the bar and renews the duty. And if a barred or discharged debt is a sufficient reason for enforcing a new promise to pay it, *a fortiori* a debt that has not been barred or discharged is a sufficient reason.[91] Thus, a new promise by a debtor, made before the debt has been barred by a statute of limitations, operates as a new starting point of obligation and is enforceable even after expiration of the period allowed for enforcing the former contract.

It has also been held that the debtor's promise is made binding by actual performance of the creditor's promise, even though the creditor's unenforceable promise is not a sufficient consideration. Thus where a creditor promised forbearance until April 1 in return for the debtor's promise to pay the debt on or before that date, and the creditor actually forbore for the full period, it was held that thereafter the creditor could maintain suit on the debtor's new promise.[92] Of course, he could have sued on the debtor's original contract also, unless it had been barred by statute of limitations or otherwise; but it was not necessary for him to do so.

The foregoing is one of the rare cases, possibly the only one, in which actual performance is a sufficient consideration even though a promise of that very same performance is not. The unilateral contract is binding even though the bilateral contract is not. Forbearance by the creditor has no defect as a consideration, being something that he was not previously bound to give; and it makes no difference that the debtor's return

92. Me.—Hay v. Fortier, 102 A. 294, 116 Me. 455 (1917).

promise was merely to perform his pre-existing duty. There is no law that prevents a man from buying two enforceable promises of the same performance, giving a sufficient consideration for each one. Thus, one who has already contracted for a new motor car at the price of $2000 has a right to delivery of the car without tendering his old car as an addition to the price, and he will not be bound by a promise to throw in the old car. But if he in fact delivers the old car for a second promise that the new car will be delivered, he has given a sufficient consideration for this new promise.

### § 192.  Performance of Something Additional to What the Pre-existing Duty Required

In the present connection, it is to be remembered that the law does not require that every part and parcel of a bargained-for consideration shall be of a kind that would be operative to make a return promise binding; it is enough that any part of it is of such a kind. Therefore, if the bargained-for performance rendered by the promisee includes something that is not within the requirements of his pre-existing duty, the law of consideration is satisfied. It makes no difference that the agreed consideration consists almost wholly of a performance that is already required and that this performance is the main object of the promisor's desire. It is enough that some small additional performance is bargained for and given.[94]

Thus, if a creditor promises to give an extension of time, this promise is not enforceable if the only consideration is the debtor's payment of a part of his overdue debt or the debtor's promise to pay his debt on or before the end of the extension.[95] Such performance is already required by the debtor's existing contractual duty to the creditor. But if the debtor gives his pocket knife in addition as a part of the consideration for the creditor's promise of extension, the promise is enforceable. So also, if the debtor promises to pay interest at an increased rate; or promises to pay the identical rate that he is already bound to pay, if his new promise is to pay such interest for the full period of extension.[96] In the latter case the debtor had the valuable power of stopping the running of interest by making a tender of the amount due at the time of tender; after the new agreement of extension for a definite period, he no longer has that power, and

94.  Restatement, Contracts, § 84 (c): "Consideration is not insufficient because of the fact that the party giving the consideration is then bound by a duty owed to the promisor or to the public, or by any duty imposed by the law of torts or crimes, to render some performance similar to that given or promised, if the act or forbearance given or promised as consideration differs in any way from what was previously due."

the creditor has a definite investment at the agreed rate for the full extended period.

Again, the creditor's new promise is binding if the debtor gives in return not only his promise to pay part or all of the debt but also some new collateral security, such as the signature of a third party as surety or a mortgage on land or chattels.[97]

For exactly the same reasons, the giving of something different from what was previously due, even though of slight value, accepted by the creditor as a full settlement of the debt, is operative as an accord and satisfaction. Thus, it was said by Lord Coke: "it appears to the judges that by no possibility can a lesser sum be a satisfaction to the plaintiff for a greater sum; but the gift of a horse, hawk or robe, etc., in satisfaction is good . . in the case at bar it was resolved that the payment and acceptance of parcel before the day in satisfaction of the whole would be a good satisfaction in regard of circumstance of time; for peradventure parcel of it before the day would be more beneficial to him than the whole at the day; and the value of the satisfaction is not material. So if I am bound in £20 to pay £10 at Westminster and you request me to pay £5 at the day at York, and you will accept it in full satisfaction of the whole £10, it is a good satisfaction for the whole; for the expenses to pay it at York is sufficient satisfaction." [98]

In another case a debtor was insolvent and was contemplating applying for a discharge in bankruptcy. A creditor promised to receive thirty cents on the dollar as full satisfaction and thereby induced the debtor not to make the expected application. The court held that the part payment and the additional forbearance operated as a complete discharge.[99] It seems very probable that the debtor's forbearance was not so much an object of the creditor's desire that it formed a part of the bargained-for exchange; but it took place in justifiable reliance on the creditor's promise, as the creditor had reason to expect.

Continuation in service by one who is not already bound by contract to continue is a sufficient consideration for a promise to pay a "bonus" for so continuing.[1] A bonus so promised is not a gift; it is a raise in wages in return for new service.

---

98. **Eng.**—Pinnel's Case, 5 Coke 117a (1602). Coke's argument seems to have come from Brian, C. J., in a Year Book case nearly a century before.

# TOPIC C

## INFORMAL CONTRACTS WITHOUT MUTUAL ASSENT OR CONSIDERATION

### CHAPTER 8

### RELIANCE ON A PROMISE AS GROUND FOR ENFORCEMENT

## § 193. Reasons for This Classification and Analysis

For the purposes of this treatise and for the purposes of most contract litigation, contracts are binding promises. Most contracts are "bargains" whereby two parties express mutual assent to an exchange of equivalents—an exchange of a promise for a return promise or an exchange of a promise for a return performance that includes no promise. This fact led to the much repeated statement that both mutual assent and consideration are prerequisites to the creation of a valid informal contract. All contracts were divided into two great classes: "simple contracts" (informal) and "specialties" (formal).

This classification and analysis of the transactions of men was never adequate. Specialties, being promises under seal or recognizances before a magistrate, could be binding without any consideration or expression of assent by the promisee; but in addition there have always been many informal promises that are enforceable without any expression of assent by the promisee and without any consideration in the sense of an equivalent given in exchange. These informal contracts are not "bargains" and are not made by the process of offer and acceptance. They are "unilateral" and not "bilateral" contracts.

Informal promises, neither under seal nor in the form of a recognizance, have been enforced for a variety of reasons. The most important of these is, indeed, the giving of a "consideration" for the promise, something bargained for by the promisor. Promise and consideration constitute an exchange of equivalents by mutual agreement; it takes two persons to make such a bargain. But sufficient reasons for enforcing an informal promise have also been found in transactions and other events wholly antecedent to the promise, transactions and events that have a causal relation to the making of the promise but were not offered in exchange for it and did not take place either as a "consideration" for the promise or in reliance upon it. Sufficient reasons have likewise been found in matters wholly subsequent to the promise, matters caused by the promise and in reliance upon it but neither asked for nor given as a "consideration" in exchange for it.

The common statement that no informal promise is enforceable in the absence of a "consideration" could be and was supported by giving to that term a coverage wide enough to include both the antecedent factors and the subsequent reliance, wholly disregarding the absence of an agreed equivalency or exchange. When subsequent action in reliance was held to make a promise enforceable it was called a "consideration"; when antecedent factors were held to make a promise enforceable they were and still are called "past consideration."

From the time of its origin in English legal history down to the present time, the "doctrine of consideration" has never had clearly defined boundaries; nor has the term "consideration" itself ever had a usage that was uniform and consistent, or a clear definition that has been uniformly stated and applied. None of the English courts ever started with either a doctrine or a definition. This is true of the courts of common law, as they developed and used the actions of debt and assumpsit; it is equally true of the court of Chancery and of all the other systems of courts that from time to time have existed in England and America.

The American Law Institute, however, has stated a doctrine (or a number of rules) and has constructed a definition.[1] These are

---

1. Restatement, Contracts, §§ 75–84. It is a "restatement" only in the same sense that any statement of existing law by a new author is

stated as if they are now definite and certain and generally prevailing, whether they were in earlier times or not. The doctrine and the definition are limited in such a way that the Institute was immediately compelled to construct a number of additional rules stating when an informal promise will be enforceable without any consideration at all.[a]  Courts should not overlook this fact, or fail to examine these additional rules, in quoting or applying the Institute's statement of the consideration doctrine.[3]  It was not heretofore the custom of courts to follow the Institute's usage and to say that informal promises may be enforceable without consideration.  Instead, they made their own statements and definitions flexible enough to include practically all the known reasons for enforcing an informal promise.  The acknowledged capacity of the common law for evolutionary growth has always enabled the courts to recognize new reasons for enforcing informal promises.  It remains within their power and duty to do this, with conservative judgment and extreme care just as before, even though they accept the work of the Institute and strictly follow its language;  but instead of expanding the field of "consideration" to make it serve their purpose, they will be more likely to add new cases to those in which informal promises have been enforced without "consideration."

This variation in method and in language can be made a distinct improvement in the administration of justice, since it directs the court's attention, not merely to the determination of the sufficiency of consideration by a supposedly deductive logical process, but also to the weighing of the social and economic reasons for enforcing the promise that was made in the case before the court.  The phrase "supposedly deductive" is here used intentionally, since courts have always weighed the social and economic reasons, either consciously or sub-consciously, and have made the law develop with the times in a manner that would be quite impossible if the judicial process were merely one of deductive logic.  The Institute does not say in express terms that its list of informal promises that are enforceable without consideration is not a complete and closed list;  but such is the fact, as the very form of its stated rules makes apparent.

**a** restatement. It certainly does not look like older statements, or restatements; and it is different from any of them in substantial matters.

**2.** Id. §§ 85–94.

**3.** E. I. DuPont DeNemours Co. v. Claiborne-Reno Co., 64 F.2d 224 (C.C.A.8th, 1933), is a case in which the court seems to have fallen into this error, holding that there was no sufficient consideration as defined by the Institute, and passing no judgment whatever as to whether the action in reliance on the promise made that promise enforceable in accordance with section 90 of the Restatement.

In this treatise, therefore, the analysis of the American Law Institute is accepted and followed, but without limiting enforceable promises to those that are included within the Institute's stated rules.   The present Topic deals with informal promises for which there was no bargained-for exchange but which may be enforceable because of antecedent factors that caused them to be made or because of subsequent action that they caused to be taken in reliance.

### § 194.  Effect of Subsequent Action in Reliance on a Promise

At this point, we begin to consider the informal promises that are enforceable without any consideration in the sense of something that is bargained for and given in exchange.   The very first question to be answered is, What kinds of action or forbearance in reliance on a promise will make that promise enforceable.

It is now quite clear that an informal promise may be enforceable by reason of action in reliance upon it, even though that action was not bargained for by the promisor and was not performed as an agreed exchange for the promise.   This is demonstrated by the decisions of the courts of common law from the very beginnings of the action of assumpsit, by the decrees of courts of equity making a very flexible use of the doctrine of "estoppel," [4] and by the judgments of the modern courts using the formless and all-inclusive "civil action."

Mr. Justice Holmes once said: "Of course the mere fact that a promisee relies upon a promise made without other consideration does not impart validity to what before was void.   There must be some ground for saying that the acts done in reliance upon the promise were contemplated by the form of the transaction either impliedly or in terms as the conventional motive, inducement, and equivalent for the promise." [5]   This was immediately followed, however, by a qualifying sentence: "But the courts have gone very great lengths in discovering the implication of such an equivalence, sometimes, perhaps even having found it in matters which would seem to be no more than conditions or natural consequences of the promise."

4.   In the following cases, not being actions for damages, a gratuitous promise was held binding by reason of changes of position in reliance on it:  Central London P. Trust v. High Trees House [1947] 1 K.B. 130, tenant continued to occupy and to do business in reliance on landlord's promise of rent reduction.

Re Wm. Porter & Co. [1937] 2 All Eng. 361 (Ch.D.), company continued in business in reliance on director's assent to give up his right to fees amounting to £2,670.

5.   **Mass.**—Martin v. Meles, 60 N.E. 397, 179 Mass. 114 (1901). This statement is substantially identical with one made earlier by him in his work on the Common Law. It was obiter dictum in the case before him; for in that case he found sufficient consideration and enforced the subscription promise.

The American Law Institute has abandoned the first part of Holmes's statement; and in place of his accompanying qualification has stated the following definite rule of law: "A promise which the promisor should reasonably expect to induce action or forbearance of a definite and substantial character on the part of the promisee and which does induce such action or forbearance is binding if injustice can be avoided only by enforcement of the promise." [6]

It is the belief of the present writer that the court decisions compel the inclusion of some such rule as that adopted by the Institute, and that the generally prevailing law never was inconsistent with it. It is true that Mr. Justice Holmes's rule and definition had judicial approval in a good many opinions other than his own; but, from the beginning of the use of the term consideration, many things have been included among sufficient considerations that are not within either Holmes's definition or that adopted by the Institute. The courts have included "past considerations" that could not possibly have been given in exchange for the later promise, and many actions and forbearances subsequent to the promise that were not in fact bargained for.[7] It is true that in most cases in which a promise has

---

6.   Restatement, Contracts, § 90.
The Institute gives the following illustrations under § 90: (1) A mortgagor makes improvements on his land in reliance upon the mortgagee's promise not to foreclose for a specified time.

(2) A promisee resigns a profitable employment in reliance upon a promise to give him an annuity for life, the promisee also becoming disqualified from again obtaining good employment.

(3) A promisee goes to college at the request of the promisor and attends for several years in reliance upon the promisor's promise to give him $5,000 at completion of his course.

7.   In the following cases, where the promise of a gift of land was followed by possession and the making of improvements the promise was held to be enforceable by various remedies, and the court declared that the action of the donee was a "valuable consideration":

U.S.—King v. Thompson, 9 Pet. 204 (1835).

Iowa—Pranger v. Pranger, 164 N.W. 607, 182 Iowa 639 (1907).

Me.—Bigelow v. Bigelow, 49 A. 49, 95 Me. 17 (1901).

Md.—Haines v. Haines, 4 Md.Ch. 133 (1853).

N.Y.—Freeman v. Freeman, 43 N.Y. 34, 3 Am.Rep. 657 (1870), "a consideration in equity." Young v. Overbaugh, 39 N.E. 712, 145 N.Y. 158 (1895).

Eng.—Crosbie v. McDoual, 13 Ves.Jr. 148 (1806).

U.S.—King v. Thompson, 9 Pet. 204 (U.S.1835): "To constitute a valuable consideration, it is not necessary that money should be paid: but if, as in this case, it be expended on the property, on the faith of the contract, it constitutes a valuable consideration." Yet in this case, the parties and the court continually refer to the promise as being one to make a "gift" of the land. The same is true of Haines v. Haines, 4 Md.Ch. 133 (1853), in which the language above quoted is repeated and approved.

been enforced there was an agreed exchange of promise and consideration. Such is the custom of men in making promises. We do not overlook this fact when we assert that it is not the exclusive custom and that courts have always found other sufficient reasons for enforcing an informal promise.

A promise by a debtor or other obligor, made to the creditor or obligee, to perform the obligation or not to plead the statute of limitations as a defense, is binding after the promisee in reliance thereon has forborne to sue until the period of limitation has barred his original action.[8] The promise by an obligor to perform his existing legal duty is a binding promise as soon as it is made, being supported by the existing co-extensive legal duty. Subsequent action or forbearance in reliance on the promise constitutes merely an added reason for enforcement. A promise not to plead the statute of limitations, however, is not co-extensive with an existing duty and must rest on the subsequent reliance. The fact that the promisor is said to be "estopped" to plead the statute in breach of his promise is merely a traditional way of saying that the promise will now be enforced, even though it was not enforceable when made.

## § 195.  Action in Reliance Doctrine Is Consistent with Both Historical Development and Current Definitions

Holding that action in reliance makes a promise enforceable is consistent with the most common of all the definitions of consideration. When judges say that consideration must be either a detriment to the promisee or a benefit to the promisor, they seldom require in terms that it must be a consciously exchanged equivalent for the promise. They do not stop to determine whether or not it was such an equivalent; and in some of the cases it was not.[9]

Another of the most commonly used definitions of consideration is the following: "Consideration is something done, forborne, or suffered, or promised to be done, forborne, or suffered by the promisee in respect of the promise." [10] What is the mean-

In Hardesty v. Richardson, 44 Md. 617, 22 Am.Rep. 57 (1876), the promise of the defendant to convey land as a gift was found not to have been on condition that the plaintiff should take possession and make improvements; yet specific performance was decreed. It was enough that the plaintiff had thus acted in reliance on the promise. The court said, "This constitutes a good equitable consideration."

In Seavey v. Drake, 62 N.H. 393

(1882), Smith, J. said: "The expenditure in money or labor in the improvement of the land induced by the donor's promise to give the land to the party making the expenditure, constitutes, in equity, a consideration for the promise, and the promise will be enforced."

10.  This is used by Sir William Anson in his work on Contracts and is taken chiefly from an opinion in the case of Currie v. Misa, L.R. 10 Exch. 162 (1875).

ing of the phrase "in respect of the promise?"  If it is used to mean "in return for the promise," or "as an agreed exchange for the promise," the simple words to express it exactly ought to have been used.  Surely, one who acts in reliance on a promise is acting "in respect of the promise."  The definition is flexible enough to include the actions and forbearances with which we are now dealing.

In the early history of English law, the doctrine of consideration had no part and there was no definition to be found.  The action of debt seems to have required the receipt of a quid pro quo;  but that action was not regarded as one for the enforcement of a promise.  A debt was very often held to exist in the absence of any promise, either express or implied.  In later times, for the purpose of substituting the action of assumpsit for the older action of debt, the English court held that when a debt was proved to exist, an assumpsit (a promise) would be implied by the law.[11]

The action of assumpsit, a variation of the action of trespass on the special case, was the first action used and intended for the enforcement of informal promises.  The breach of a promise was regarded as a sort of deceit;  and the remedy was compensatory damages for the injury caused by the promisee's action in reasonable reliance.[12]  This was one of the germs from which the doctrine of consideration sprung;  and from that day to this the courts have been familiar with the idea of reliance on a promise as a reason for enforcement.  There is certainly no historical inconsistency in the rule stated by the American Law Institute in section 90.

### § 196.  Reliance on a Promise Is a Consequence and Not an Inducement, an Effect and Not a Cause

When a court enforces a promise because of some "past consideration," that consideration may have induced and caused the making of the promise;  but it was not given in exchange for it.  The promise certainly did not induce the giving of that consideration.  In the case of action in reliance, the relation of the two factors is just the contrary: the promise comes first and induces the subsequent action in reliance;  that subsequent action is an effect and not a cause of the promise.  The two kinds of cases are alike in one respect only;  there was no bargain, no agreed exchange of equivalents.

While Mr. Justice Holmes said that consideration must be the "conventional motive, inducement and equivalent for the prom-

---

11.  **Eng.**—Slade's Case, 4 Coke 92 b;  Yelv. 21;  Moore K.B. 433, 667 (1602).

12.  See Ames, History of Assumpsit, 2 Harv.L.R. 1, 53 (1889).

ise," his use of the word "conventional" shows that he knew that it did not have to be the actual motive, the real inducement, or the market equivalent. The Restatement by the Institute shows that it fully agrees with this. It is equally clear that both Holmes and the Institute knew that action in reliance is a "natural consequence" of a promise and not an inducing cause; and both knew that courts have enforced promises because of such natural consequences.

No attempt is made in this treatise to explain the Roman and Continental concept of "causa;" it is undoubtedly as complex and as variable as is consideration itself. But it would appear, superficially at least, that "past consideration" would fall readily within the concept of "causa" and that action in subsequent reliance would not. Whether by "causa," they mean inducement of the promise or a sufficient reason for enforcement of the promise, this writer knows not. Very likely it includes both, just as our courts have made "consideration" include both. It may well be, also, that "causa" includes so many antecedent reasons for making a promise that it would make enforceable every promise on which it would be reasonable to rely. If such is the case, it would be unnecessary for the Roman and Continental jurists to develop an action in reliance doctrine.

## § 197. Gratuitous Notes Given to Strengthen Bank Assets

There are many cases in which a promissory note is given to a bank, without consideration, by an officer or stockholder, or by some other interested person, for the purpose of strengthening its apparent assets. In reliance upon this, the bank is permitted to do business. In many instances, the promisee bank or its trustee or assignee has been able to enforce payment of the note.[13] The accompanying circumstances vary. Sometimes the bank becomes insolvent, or would become so if the note is held to be void. Sometimes the note was knowingly given in order to conceal the condition of the bank from bank examiners. In all alike, however, there has been action in reliance on the note; action by the promisee bank, by bank examiners, by depositors and other creditors. The members of the last named class may not know of the note's existence; but if it had not been given they might not have become creditors to the existing extent.

13.   U.S.—D'Oench, Duhme & Co. v. Federal Dep. Ins. Corp., 62 S.Ct. 676, 315 U.S. 447, 86 L.Ed. 956, rehearing denied 62 S.Ct. 910, 315 U.S. 830, 86 L.Ed. 1224 (1942), note given to conceal bank's weakness, assigned to plaintiff as security for a loan (a case showing that there some "federal general common law"); Deitrick v. Greaney, 60 S. Ct. 480, 309 U.S. 190, 84 L.Ed. 694, rehearing denied 60 S.Ct. 611, 309 U.S. 697, 84 L.Ed. 1036 (1940), note executed by a bank director to conceal an illegal purchase of its own stock by the bank; Rinaldi v. Young, 92 F.2d 229, 67 App.D.C. 305 (1937).

There are cases holding that the bank can not recover on a note of the sort here being discussed, if the bank is not insolvent and the shareholders and creditors are not shown to have changed their position in reliance on the note.[14] It may well be that in such cases the application of the reliance doctrine and the enforcement of the promise are not necessary to avoid injustice. In still other cases recovery has been denied, even though the action was brought by a receiver for the benefit of bank creditors.[15]

Whether there has been fraudulent intent or not, it would be scandalous not to enforce payment of the note, if otherwise any depositor or other creditor would be a loser. Justification for such enforcement can be phrased in terms of "estoppel" or in terms of the action in reliance by various parties. In any case, there has been no consideration in the sense of a bargained-for equivalent.[16] In some cases the court has been content to rest its decision against the promisor on a mere appeal to the prevailing beliefs as to public policy.[17]

## § 198. Charitable Subscription Promises

A long and constantly increasing line of decisions in the United States has established the binding character of most subscription agreements for educational, religious, and other charitable purposes. Such a subscription promise can seldom be justly regarded as part of a bargaining agreement that provides for the exchange of an agreed equivalent by the promisee. It is clearly understood that such a subscription is a donation; and yet promises of this kind are now almost universally enforced.

This may well be regarded as a reversal of the adage that "taught law is tough law." It is not so tough in the face of a generally felt public interest. Yet it is often tough in one respect: it continues to be taught even after, in actual application by the courts, it has been largely abandoned. The teacher and law writer, having developed, with hard historical labor, a "theory" of consideration, continues to support the theory and to note with regret and disapproval the cases that are in substantial conflict with it, while perhaps giving it lip service and creating an appearance of harmony by the use of fiction and implication.[18] The wealth of repetitious discussion of this topic makes

18. This is indicated in the long line of articles and student notes in the numerous law magazines. Some of these are the following: 13 Corn.L.Q. 270, 12 id. 467, 8 id. 57; 34 Harv.L.Rev. 220, 15 id. 312, 12 id. 506; 13 Iowa L.Rev. 332; 27 Mich.L.Rev. 88, 23 id. 910, 22 id. 260; 12 Minn.L.Rev. 643, 6 id. 167; 76 U. of Pa. L.Rev. 749, 62 id. 296; 11 Va.L.Rev. 643, 9 id. 458; 3 Wis.L.Rev. 275; 37 Yale L.J. 823, 34 id. 99. Numerous others can be found. This flood of critical discussion is due partly to the fact that one or two cases, such as Presbyterian Church of Albany v. Cooper, 20 N.E. 352, 112 N.Y. 517 (1889), have been so widely used in casebook instruction.

it unnecessary and undesirable to give it extended space here. But the principal grounds on which the courts have enforced charitable subscriptions will be stated.

The reason most commonly given for enforcing charitable subscriptions is that the promisee has given a sufficient considertion by acting in reliance on the subscription.[19] Usually this action is the carrying out of the purposes for which the subscription was made. Buildings are built, contracts are let, professorships are established. The subscriber desired the action either specifically or in kind, and had reason to foresee that it would be taken. Such cases support the doctrine that action in reliance may make a promise binding, whether such action is called a consideration or not. Sometimes the specific action that followed in reliance on the subscription was contemplated by him when he made his promise; in other cases the subscription was in aid of the general undertakings of the promisee and the action in reliance was merely the continuance of its existing functions.[20]

In some cases, additional reasons have been given for the enforcement of the subscription promise. Thus, it has been held that the acceptance of the subscription by the trustees of the charity implies a promise on their part to execute the work contemplated and to carry out the purposes for which the subscription was made.[21] The implied promise of the trustees is said to be a sufficient consideration for the subscriber's promise. By such an implied promise, the trustees may sometimes be assuming duties that were not already incumbent upon them as trustees, but this does not necessarily show that the transaction was a bargaining transaction.

Subscriptions are frequently made expressly conditional on the raising of some specified additional amount. This has in some cases been regarded as a request by the subscriber, with a decision that efforts to perform the condition are also an agreed consideration.[24] No doubt, this would usually be a strained interpretation; the raising of the specified amount is a mere condition of the promised gift and not a bargained-for considera-

20. Re Estate of Griswold, 202 N.W. 609, 113 Neb. 256, 38 A.L.R. 858 (1925).

21. "The promisor wished to have a memorial to perpetuate her name. She imposed a condition that the 'gift' should 'be known as the Mary Yates Johnston Memorial Fund.' The moment that the college accepted $1,000 as a payment on account, there was an assumption of a duty to do whatever acts were customary, or reasonably necessary, to maintain the memorial fairly and justly in the spirit of its creation. The college could not accept the money and hold itself free thereafter from personal responsibility to give effect to the condition." Allegheny College v. National C. Co. Bank, 159 N.E. 173, 246 N.Y. 369, 57 A.L.R. 980 (1927).

tion.  But the efforts of representatives of the donee might in some cases be properly regarded as such action in reliance on a subscription as to make it binding.  Certain cases holding the subscription binding on other grounds have refused to regard the expenditures of the promisee in conducting the campaign as themselves a consideration.[25]  Of course, they are not bargained for by the subscriber; but they may be incurred in reliance on his promise.

In still other cases, it has been held that the promises of the subscribers mutually support each other.[26]  On this theory the subscription contract is a bilateral contract between subscribers of which the charitable organization is a donee beneficiary.  But the promises of the subscribers are nearly always to the beneficiary, and not to each other.  There is no bargain in fact between the subscribers.[27]  Certain cases holding that mutual subscriptions cannot create an enforceable right in the donee were based upon the doctrine, now generally abandoned, that beneficiaries cannot enforce a contract to which they are not parties and for which they give no consideration.[28]

In the absence of a return promise by the promisee, the subscriptions are very commonly held to be mere revocable offers that become irrevocable only when action has been taken in reliance upon them.[29]  Either the death of the subscriber or a notice of his revocation, before any change of position in reliance, prevents the subscription promise from becoming a contract with the promisee.  This accords with the generally prevailing theories of contract, unless the promisee accepts the subscription by making a return promise, either express or implied, thus consummating a bilateral contract; or unless the transaction can reasonably be interpreted as a bilateral contract between subscribers of which the promisee is a donee beneficiary.

Mutual subscriptions for a business purpose as contrasted with a charitable purpose can usually be distinguished on the ground that they are in reality bargaining transactions.[30]  The promisee in such cases, whether he is another subscriber or is a committee acting for the subscribers, usually does something that may reasonably be regarded as an equivalent given in exchange for the subscriber's promise.  Even in these cases, however, it may at times require a liberal use of fiction in order to arrive at such an interpretation; and the promises may well be held enforceable on the ground of action taken in reasonable reliance upon them.

28.    Mass.—Cottage St. M. E. Ch. v. Kendall, 121 Mass. 528, 23 Am. Rep. 286 (1877).

N.Y.—Presbyterian Church of Albany v. Cooper, 20 N.E. 352, 112 N.Y. 517, 3 L.R.A. 468, 8 Am.St.Rep. 767 (1889).

## § 200. Limits of the Action in Reliance Doctrine

The fact that a mutually agreed equivalent is given for a promise makes the promise enforceable, without regard to market values of that supposed equivalent. It is of equal value (equivalent), so far as the law is concerned, for the reason that the two parties have made the exchange; and the "value" of a thing is what you can get for it. There is a small twilight zone of doubt as the agreed equivalent approaches zero in the general market.[32]

If action or forbearance in reliance on a promise be accepted as a sufficient reason for enforcing the promise, as it surely must be, even though we are no longer to describe it as a "consideration," no such definite statement as the above can be made as to the extent of the action or forbearance that is necessary to make it sufficient for the purpose. Some helpful statements can be made. The supposed definiteness and certainty of any rule of law is partly an illusion; and it is always a matter of degree. The degree of uncertainty in the action in reliance doctrine is far from being the greatest among our existing rules of law.

First, it can be said with assurance that the action or forbearance must amount to a substantial change of position. The abandonment of a peppercorn or the turning over of the hand will not be enough. A generous promise of a gift of $100 will not be made enforceable by the fact that the promisee walks a few blocks to the bank in the reasonable belief that the promise will there be performed.[33] Of course, in every case the question will arise, What is substantial. It cannot be answered by a formula. It is a matter of fact, to be determined by court and jury, under appellate supervision as in other cases. Not only is it matter of fact; it has no absolute standard of measurement. Beyond doubt, it is relative to the other circumstances and especially to the content of the promise and the cost to the promisor of his promised performance. As the history of this doctrine has shown, it is closely related to, or a part of, the even more elastic and uncertain doctrines of estoppel.

In determining whether or not the action in reliance is substantial, a court should face its responsibility with open eyes, knowing that here, at least, the just answer cannot be arrived at by any deductive logic or by a mechanical jurisprudence. It will always require an experienced judgment, a knowledge of the ways and feelings of men and of the social mores of the time. The writer is willing to suggest that the relative economic needs and capacities of the parties and the needs and interests of the promisor's dependents and creditors should be taken into consideration, particularly in determining the form of remedy and the extent of the recovery.[34] The more free and flexible the court is willing to be in determining the extent of the recovery, the more variation is made possible in applying such a requirement as that the action in reliance must be "substantial."

Secondly, it can be said with equal assurance that the action or forbearance must either have been actually foreseen by the promisor, or must be of such a kind as a reasonable person in his position would have foreseen when making the promise. This, too, raises a question of fact for court and jury; but it is a question with which they are already familiar. There are existing standards, created in such fields of law as negligence and the interpretation of agreements, in the application of which the courts have already acquired much experience.

Thirdly, an actual promise must have been made and this promise must itself have induced the action or forbearance in reliance on it.[35] In this world of complexity, it is indeed perilous to attempt to determine the inducing cause of anything, especially the inducing cause of a human being's act or forbearance. Perilous or not, we attempt it daily and often believe that life and death depend upon our success therein. The courts cannot avoid this question, so long as courts of justice exist. The question is with them so constantly that they are hardened to the peril, even if not quite unconscious of it.

Section 90 of the Contracts Restatement includes all of the foregoing requirements. It adds others that make it a careful and conservative statement, though not quite a timid one. It says that the action or forbearance must be "definite" as well as substantial. All action is definite after it occurs; so, the Institute must have meant that the promisor must have had reason to foresee the definite action or forbearance that in fact followed. Without doubt, the more keen and accurate the foresight of the promisor was or ought to have been, the stronger is the case for enforcement. Probably, however, the standards to be applied are those that have been developed in the fields of negligence and estoppel. The action or forbearance need not be such that the promisor or anyone else could have foreseen the exact time and place of its occurrence. Definiteness, too, is a matter of degree, as the writers of the Restatement knew. We may therefore mildly approve of the requirement that the action must be "definite," without speculating much as to its exact meaning.[36]

The rule constructed by the Law Institute in section 90 of the Restatement is limited to cases in which the action or forbear-

---

**34.** In Re Estate of Griswold, 202 N.W. 609, 113 Neb. 256, 38 A.L.R. 858 (1925), the claims of heirs and creditors were suggested in argument, but apparently it was not in evidence how much of the promisor's estate would be left after payment of his charitable subscription.

ance in reliance is "on the part of the promisee." This may be as far as it was safe to go on the basis of cases already decided. But in new cases, the courts need not feel themselves to be equally restricted. Generally, it will be the promisee himself who acts in reliance; so that there is less reason to foresee action by others. But if a promise is made by A to B for the benefit of C, it will often be action by C that A has reason to foresee; and it seems reasonably clear that action or forbearance by a named or intended beneficiary of the promise should be included in the stated rule.[37] In one case, also, the promise to the donee was specifically enforced largely because a third person, in reliance on the promise, had erected a building on the land as an added gift to the donee.[38] If the promisor actually foresees, or has reason to foresee, such action by a third person, it may be quite unjust to refuse to perform the promise.

Finally, the Restatement justifies enforcement of the promise only "if injustice can be avoided only by enforcement of the promise." This raises the perilous question, What is justice, without giving any rules or standards for its answer. Here, too, the courts are accustomed to the peril. But, if all the other requirements of the stated rule are satisfied, does not justice always require enforcement of the promise? So far as the Restatement itself informs us, the answer is Yes. The quoted clause has the merit, however, of invoking Justice and reminding the court that this particular rule cannot be applied by a mechanical process. Indeed, by its very existence, the clause is a suggestion that sometimes the answer should be No.

It may be suggested further that, in applying any action in reliance doctrine, the court should consider the merits and defects of all the possible remedies that are available. Enforcement of a promise does not necessarily mean Specific Performance. It does not necessarily mean Damages for breach. Moreover the amount allowed as Damages may be determined by the plaintiff's expenditures or change of position in reliance as well as by the value to him of the promised performance. Restitution is also an "enforcing" remedy, although it is often said to be based upon some kind of a rescission. In determining what justice requires, the court must remember all of its powers, derived from equity, law merchant, and other sources, as well as the common law. Its decree should be molded accordingly.

A limitation on the reliance doctrine that has been given judicial approval may be stated as follows: If a promisor offers his

---

**38.** In Roberts-Horsfield v. Gedicks, 118 A. 275, 94 N.J.Eq. 82 (1922), a promise of a gift of land was specifically enforced in favor of the promisee because she had taken possession and because her aunt, who was the donor's wife, had built a house on the land as an additional gift to the promisee.

promise as part of a bargain for and in consideration of a specified equivalent, the promisee can not make the promise binding by acting in reliance upon it in a manner that constitutes no part of that specified equivalent. So, it has been held that an offer to sell materials at a stated price, "for prompt acceptance after the general contract has been awarded" was not made irrevocable by the fact that the offeree made a bid for the general contract in reliance on the offered prices.[39]

A promisor who offers his promise, expressing with reasonable clearness that he expects a definite promise in return, will seldom be held bound by the promisee's beginning the action or forbearance that he is asked to promise, without the knowledge of the offeror and without making the desired promise.[40] Here there is no acceptance as the terms of the offer requires; and the action or forbearance in reliance is not reasonable without making the requested promise. On the other hand, after knowledge of the action or forbearance that is progressing, acquiescence may cure the defect. Also, the offer may have been in such terms that it can be accepted by mere action or forbearance, thus completing an actual bargain.

### § 202. Difficulty of Determining when Subsequent Action in Reliance Was in Fact Bargained for

There are many cases in the reports in which it is not possible to determine whether the promise was enforced because an agreed equivalent was exchanged for it or because the promisee acted in reliance upon it. No such distinction is discussed by the court and the facts as reported do not show whether or not the action in reliance was bargained for by the promisor. There is no necessity for making the distinction if the action in reliance is a sufficient reason for enforcing the promise even if it was not bargained for. But a consideration that is exchanged for a promise may be sufficient for enforcement even though it does not constitute a substantial change of position and has little value in relation to the performance that is promised in return. In cases of this latter sort, it is necessary to know whether or not the promisee's action in reliance on the promise was exchanged for it by mutual agreement.

In practically all cases in which a consideration is given in exchange, it consists of some kind of action or forbearance, by the promisee in reliance on the promise.[42] The fact that it was performed in reliance does not show that it was not bargained for. Action by the promisee that was the agreed exchange for

39. N.Y.—James Baird Co. v. Gimbel Bros., 64 F.2d 344 (C.C.A.2d, 1933).

the promise was, of course, foreseen by the promisor. He asked for it and got it.

In ordinary business transactions, a promise is given for a consideration for the reason that the consideration is of economic benefit to the promisor. The fact that the promisee's action in reliance is such an economic benefit is some evidence that the promise was given in exchange for it. But men bargain for considerations that are not economic benefits; and the fact that the promisee's action in reliance was of no benefit to the promisor is far from conclusive evidence that he did not give his promise in exchange for it.

## § 203.  Cases Where the Promisee's Action in Reliance Was Desired by the Promisor, but Was Not of Benefit to Him

In a great many cases, the defendant desired and requested the action or forbearance by the plaintiff and gave his promise in order to induce it, but that action or forbearance was of no economic or other direct benefit to the defendant. In these cases, the defendant desired it because it would be beneficial to the plaintiff himself; and in making the promise both the plaintiff and he regarded him as a generous benefactor.[43]

The action or forbearance taken by the promisee in such cases, as in practically all other reliance cases, is quite sufficient as a consideration if it is in fact bargained for and given in exchange for the promise. Also, it is quite possible for a promisor to bargain for action that is beneficial to the actor and not to himself. In such case, it is a sufficient consideration without regard to benefit to himself or detriment to the promisee. It is sufficient, even though the transaction is all detriment to the promisor and all benefit to the promisee, although such would seldom be the fact.

In cases like this, the promise is nearly always enforced as a contract, and the action or forbearance is called a consideration for the promise. Neither judges nor writers often express any doubt, although there are a few cases in which enforcement was refused because of supposed absence of any bargaining exchange, even though the action of the promisee was desired and intentionally induced by the promisor.[44] The facts of these cases are so closely similar to the others in which the promise was enforced that they often seem to be wrongly decided, a fact that indicates that the bargaining element is not so important as the fact that the action in reliance was reasonably induced by the promise and was foreseen by the promisor.

44.    Ala.—Kirksey v. Kirksey, 8 Ala.
131 (1845).

The following is an illustrative case that has been often cited and is familiar to several generations of law students. The bill of exceptions thus stated the facts: "That the plaintiff took a trip to Europe in 1878 and that said trip was taken by said plaintiff, and the money spent on said trip was spent by the said plaintiff, at the instance and request of said Combs, and upon a promise from him that he would reimburse and pay to the plaintiff all the money expended by him in said trip; and that the trip was so taken and the money so expended, by the said plaintiff, but that the said trip had no connection with the business of said Combs; and that said Combs spoke to the witness of his conduct, in being willing to pay his nephew's expenses, as liberal and generous on his part."[45]

If this is to be called a bargain, it certainly was not a business bargain. If the rule stated in section 90 of the Contracts Restatement be accepted, it is unnecessary to struggle with the definition of bargain and with the application to such facts. There is no question that in most such cases the promise of the uncle to his nephew should be enforced. The action taken by the nephew was expensive, though gratifying and worth its cost; he was actually requested by the promisor to take it; he took it in reliance on the promise and might not have taken it otherwise. The court thought that this was different from "a promise to make another a present;" and it is true that there are gift promises that are not made to induce specific action. Yet it seems none the less a promise of a gift because it was conditional on travel abroad. The promises to give land that have been specifically enforced in equity have not been regarded as any the less a promise of a gift by reason of the fact that they were conditional on the donee's coming to live on the land.[46]

## § 204. The Doctrine Described as Promissory Estoppel

One of the earlier attempts at a doctrine of enforceability because of action in reliance was to state a rule that a promise might become enforceable by reason of "promissory estoppel." The use of this phrase made some headway, because it satisfied the need of the courts for a justification of their enforcement of certain promises in the absence of any bargain or agreed exchange.[47] Nevertheless, the phrase is objectionable. The word estoppel is so widely and loosely used as almost to defy definition; yet, in the main, it has been applied to cases of misrepresentation of facts and not to promises.[48] The American Law Insti-

45. Md.—Devecmon v. Shaw, 14 A. 464, 69 Md. 199, 9 Am.St.Rep. 422 (1888).

47. See the discussion of this subject by Cardozo in Allegheny College v. National Chautauqua County Bank, 246 N.Y. 369, 159 N.E. 173, 57 A.L. R. 980 (1927).

tute was well advised in not adopting this phrase and in stating its rule in terms of action or forbearance in reliance on the promise.

## § 205.   Adjustment of the Remedy to Suit the Individual Case—Equitable Remedies

It has sometimes been suggested that action in reliance on a promise (but not its agreed equivalent) is a sufficient reason for specific enforcement in equity but not for giving a judgment for damages at law.   It is true that cases are very numerous in which equity has decreed specific performance on such grounds. Equitable estoppel was, as the name implies, the creation of courts of equity.   But the latter doctrine came to be used in bolstering up defenses in actions at law; and courts of law could not have been far behind the Chancery when they sustained an action of assumpsit by reason of action in reliance on a promise.

Now that law and equity are generally administered by a single system of courts of law, the doctrines and remedies of both are available if properly presented and applied for.   Since equitable decrees were more flexible than judgments at law and could be molded to suit the justice of a particular case, there are cases in which the action in reliance doctrine will justify the award of an equitable remedy when it does not justify a judgment for damages.

The equitable remedy does not have to be specific enforcement of the promise.   Equity had power to award damages in lieu of specific enforcement; it could award a restitutionary remedy measured by benefits received instead of following the usual rules for measuring damages; and it could moderate the damages awarded by restricting them to the amount by which the plaintiff was actually out of pocket, without attempting to compel the defendant to pay over the full value of his promised performance.   The fact is that the courts of common law had as much power over their money judgments as did the court of Chancery.   They could and did award restitution in many kinds of cases; and in practical result they exercised as great control over the amount of money awarded as damages for breach.

There is no reason why the courts of the present day should not "make the remedy fit the crime" and make the amount of a judgment for damages depend upon the special circumstances and the merits of the claims of all existing claimants.   In doing this, they can properly justify their action by an appeal to their equitable powers inherited from the Chancellor; but it is believed that such an appeal is unnecessary.   The courts are still courts of justice; and justice, though not dependent on the length of the Chancellor's foot, has always been dependent on the circumstances of the individual case.   This is especially true

294

with respect to the form and extent of the remedy to be applied.[49]

So then, the modern court can decree specific performance, if that seems the best remedy, making its decree conditional on some performance by the plaintiff or on the various allowances and reductions that equity may require. It can require the defendant to make restitution of the specific thing received by him, or restitution of the money value of what he has received.[50] It can measure this money value by determining the net addition to his economic resources—his "unjust enrichment," or by determining the market equivalent of the labor and materials received by him—"quantum meruit." Instead of restitution in any of its forms the court can give judgment for damages measured by the value of the promised performance—the usual remedy for breach of contract, or measured by the actual outlay incurred by the plaintiff in past performance without including any expected profit that full performance of the defendant's promise would have brought him.[51] In its origin, the action of assumpsit measured the damages by the extent of the injury suffered by the plaintiff in reliance on the undertaking of the defendant, not by the value of the performance promised by the defendant or the profit that was expected by the plaintiff to be derived from that performance. The growth of the law and the statutory creation of new courts of general jurisdiction have not deprived the courts of these historical remedial powers. With a lively consciousness of what these powers are, the modern court should grant its various remedies with discrimination, taking care to make the remedy suit the individual case before it.[52]

The remedy given to a plaintiff who sues for breach of a promise on which he reasonably relied, but for which he gave no bargained-for equivalent, can be made dependent on the extent of the action or forbearance in reliance, while at the same time making the value of the performance promised by the defendant the maximum that is recoverable. As in other cases, the

51. In Goodman v. Dicker, 169 F. 2d 684, 83 U.S.App.D.C. 353 (1948), the defendant promised to give to the plaintiff a dealer's franchise to sell radios. After the plaintiff had justifiably incurred expenses in preparation to act as such dealer, the defendant repudiated his promise. The dealer was given judgment for the amount of his expenses, but nothing as damages for expected profits. The court speaks in terms of "estoppel" and does not refer to the Restatement, Contracts, § 90.

52. In King v. Thompson, 34 U.S. (9 Pet.) 204 (1835), the donee took possession and made improvements costing $4000 on land worth $2500. The court said that the expenditure was a valuable consideration, but refused specific performance because of indefiniteness of terms. It decreed a lien on the premises for the value of the improvements. In fact, the amount of the lien was in excess of the existing market value of the entire property.

burden of proof is on the plaintiff. Frequently, the proof will justify allowance of the maximum, just as in the case of a promise for which consideration was given. Sometimes, the action in reliance includes the assumption of obligations extending far into the future. In the case of a charitable subscription, the donee's action in reliance will usually be found to be much greater than the amount of any single subscription; and, if payment of the full amount is enforced, it will have to be used for the very purposes for which it was promised. These are factors tending to justify the full recovery that courts have thus far always awarded. In other cases, the action in reliance may be of a kind that can hardly be measured, as where the promisee forbears to collect a debt in reliance on the defendant's promise to pay it. Had he not forborne, would he have collected? Sometimes, this cannot be determined; at other times a reasonably definite opinion can be formed. In still other cases, the action in reliance may have cost very little, and that little can be measured.[53] In these, the damages awarded might well be adjusted to that cost. Not infrequently, the action in reliance on the promise is the marriage of the promisee, a change of position that cannot be valued in terms of money. This should strongly support specific enforcement or the award of damages measured by the full money value of the promised performance.

Where, in reliance on the defendant's promise to obtain insurance, the plaintiff has forborne to insure himself, shall the court hold that the defendant has made himself an insurer?[54] In these cases, the market value of the promised service is very little; and the trouble avoided by the plaintiff is likewise slight. The defendant's neglect may have extended over a very short time; the plaintiff might have been equally neglectful had there been no promise. Surely these factors should be considered in awarding a remedy.

In one case, the amount suffered by the plaintiff as a result of non-performance was identical with the amount that the defendant was already morally obligated to pay and would have had to pay had he kept his promise.[55] There can be no doubt that judgment for the full amount is justified.

Cases are very numerous in which a promise to transfer land as a gift has been specifically enforced because of action by the

---

54. In Brawn v. Lyford, 69 A. 544, 103 Me. 362 (1907), Comfort v. Mc-Corkle, 268 N.Y.S. 192, 149 Misc. 826 (1933), and Thorne v. Deas, 4 Johns. 84 (N.Y.1809), the answer was no. But, in Siegel v. Spear & Co., 138 N.E. 414, 234 N.Y. 479 (1923), and Lusk-Harbison-Jones v. Universal Credit Co., 145 So. 623, 164 Miss. 693 (1933), under somewhat different circumstances, the answer was Yes.

55. N.H.—Carr v. Maine Central R. Co., 102 A. 532, 78 N.H. 502 (1917).

promisee in reliance on the promise.[56]   This action usually includes the taking of possession and the making of permanent improvements; but other changes of position have induced the same result.   Not infrequently, the court of equity has said that the action in reliance is a sufficient consideration, although the parties had never agreed upon it as the equivalent of the promise to convey the land.[57]   In many of these cases, the plaintiff's action in reliance was action that the promisor had expressly made a condition of his gift,[58] as where he says, "if you will move to this place and put it in repair, I will give it to you." This is a promise of a gift *cum onere*; it is not a bargain for a quid pro quo.

Cases are also to be found in which the court refused to decree specific performance of the gift promise, for the reason that the change of position and the expenditures were slight in relation to the value of the land.[59]   Indeed, one of the commonly expressed reasons for specific enforcement is that the action in reliance has been substantial and is of a kind that is very difficult of estimation.

The question does not turn solely upon the relation between the amount of money expended and the value of the land or the value of its use and occupation.   Many imponderables should be taken into consideration.   The promisee's equity surely increases with the length of time that the place has been occupied as a home.[60]

---

56.   **U.S.**—Neale v. Neales, 76 U.S. (9 Wall.) 1, 19 L.Ed. 590 (1869), possession, improvements, and marriage.

**Kan.**—Greiner v. Greiner, 293 P. 759, 131 Kan. 760 (1930), following A. L. I. Contracts Restatement, § 90; Dyer v. School Dist., 92 P. 1122, 76 Kan. 889 (1907), oral promise to give land for school followed by building and use.

**N.Y.**—Messiah Home v. Rogers, 106 N.E. 59, 212 N.Y. 315 (1914), specific performance as against a subsequent mortgagee with notice; Young v. Overbaugh, 39 N.E. 712, 145 N.Y. 158 (1895); Freeman v. Freeman, 43 N.Y. 34, 3 Am.Rep. 657 (1870).

57.   Dean Pound, Consideration in Equity, Wigmore Cel. Essays, 441, says of Crosbie v. McDoual, 13 Ves. Jr. 148 (1806), "In that case a testator, after providing an annuity

and a legacy for the donee, told her that he would provide her a house free of expense and entered into negotiations for the purchase of one.   Accordingly, and in reliance thereon, the donee thereafter made expenditures and incurred liabilities to third persons. The promise to provide the house was specifically enforced against the representatives of the deceased donor.   It will be noted that here, as in most of these cases, not only had the donee acted on the gift, but the contest was between a donee and the representatives of a deceased donor.   Evidently there was no common-law contract.   But Lord Erskine assumed that there was.   He did not suggest any difference between law and equity in this regard. . . .   After reciting what the donee did on the faith of the promise, he says: 'That forms a consideration in the law.'"

In determining whether action in reliance on a promise, in any particular case, is sufficient to make that promise enforceable, it may be helpful to suggest a number of questions to be answered. First, was the action in reliance actually bargained for by the promisor and given by the promisee in exchange for the promise? If the answer to this is yes, we have a case of true consideration, even as that is narrowly defined by the American Law Institute. But if the answer is no, the following additional questions are suggested:

1. Was the action of the promisee actually *induced*, in part or in whole, by the promise?

2. Was that action or forbearance substantial, constituting a material change of position by the promisee?

3. Did the promisor desire or request it, even though not offering his promise in exchange for it?[63]

4. Did the promisor have reason to foresee such action or forbearance as a probable result of his promise?

5. Was the promised performance costly or difficult?

6. What ratio does the cost or value of the action in reliance bear to that of the promised performance?

7. In the light of the answers to the foregoing questions, what remedy, if any, will be just and equitable? Should it be full money Damages, measured by the value of the promised performance and the foreseeable injury resulting from non-performance; or Restitution, measured by the promisor's own unjust enrichment; or Reimbursement of the expenditures and losses incurred by the promisee; [64] or Specific Performance?

The granting of any remedy, the enforceability of the promise, and the form and extent of the particular remedy granted should depend, and may properly be made to depend by the court, upon the answers to the above questions. It is not here asserted that the answers will infallibly lead to a definite decision in all cases, or that there are no other questions that will be useful in determining a just solution.

## § 207. Promises by a Gratuitous Bailee

Among the earliest cases in which an action of assumpsit for damages was sustained are those against a bailee of chattels who promised to render service without compensation. A distinction was drawn between mere nonfeasance and some kind of injurious misfeasance. If the promisor never took possession of the chattel and so did nothing at all, no action would lie against him; [79] but having taken possession or having actually begun performance, if he failed to return or injured the chattel negligently he was held liable in damages.[80]   Sometimes it is argued that the promisee has given a consideration by surrendering possession of the chattel;  but it seems clear that this is nothing but a change of position in reliance on the promise and not a bargained-for equivalent.   Again, it is argued that the promisor's negligent or wilful misfeasance is a tort;  and frequently this may be true.   But these decisions have generally rested on breach of promise by the defendant and the change of position by the plaintiff in reliance on the promise.   There seems to be no good ground for denying the soundness of this reasoning.   Of course, if the possession is requested by the promisor and is given in exchange for the promise, it is a sufficient consideration, even though such possession is short and of little value.[81]

One who promises gratuitously to collect a note or bill that is entrusted to him is liable in damages for his negligent failure resulting in loss.[82]   One who makes a like promise to invest funds received from another is liable for their loss through negligent investment.[83]   One who promises to carry money entrusted to him and to deliver it in payment of a debt has been held liable in damages for not performing, even though the money itself is intact.[84]   Such cases as these ought to be, and have been, regarded as cases in contract and not in tort.   It must be so in any case in which the action is for the bailee's failure to render a promised performance that the non-contractual duties of a bailee would not have included.

## § 208.   Gratuitous Promise to Procure Insurance

There are cases holding that a gratuitous promise to procure insurance on the plaintiff's property is made enforceable by the plaintiff's forbearance, in reliance on the promise, to procure

80.  Ala.—Dabbs v. Letson, 98 So. 4, 210 Ala. 306 (1923).

Eng.—Baxter & Co. v. Jones, 6 Ont. L.R. 360 (1903), gratuitous agent liable for misfeasance; Coggs v. Bernard, 2 Ld.Raym. 909 (1703), negligent loss of liquor being carried gratuitously; Powtuary v. Walton, 1 Roll.Abr. 10, pl. 5 (1598), negligent injury to a horse by a farrier.

81.  In Bainbridge v. Firmstone, 8 Adol. & El. 743 (1838), the defendant requested and was allowed to take possession of some boilers in order that he might weigh them. This was held to be a sufficient consideration for a promise to put them back in place.

84.   In Carr v. Maine Cent. R. Co., 102 A. 532, 78 N.H. 502 (1917), the defendant had overcharged the plaintiff and promised to procure the consent of the Interstate Commerce Commission to a rebate.  In reliance thereon, the plaintiff gave some documents to the defendant and forbore to apply for consent himself until it was too late to get consent.  The court sustained an action on the case for damages, saying that it "sounds in tort" for negligence. But the only negligence was a neglect to keep a promise. There was no neglect to care for or to return the documents.

such insurance himself.[85]  In other cases, the contrary has been held.[86]  It can scarcely be supposed in such cases as these that the plaintiff's forbearance was bargained for by the defendant, even though he expressly invited it.  The apparent conflict can be in some degree explained by the fact that, if the promise is held binding, the promisor becomes himself an insurer and his liability may be very heavy.  Of course, the plaintiff's loss, through not being insured, is equally heavy.  There seems to be no alternative but to throw the whole loss on one or on the other, on the kind promisor who promised a small service for nothing and then forgot, or on the promisee who relied on a promise for which he gave nothing but who might himself have neglected to insure promptly if the defendant had made no promise.

One who promises gratuitously to take out insurance for the plaintiff and then negligently obtains a policy that does not cover the risk that the promised insurance was to cover is held liable in damages for the resultant loss.[87]  This may be called misfeasance rather than nonfeasance;  but the defendant was not a bailee and his neglect caused no injury to person or property.

85.  **Miss.**—Lusk-Harbison-Jones Inc. **v.** Universal Credit Co., 145 So. 623, 164 Miss. 693 (1933), citing Contracts Restatement, § 90.

In Siegel v. Spear & Co., 138 N.E. 414, 234 N.Y. 479 (1923), the plaintiff had bought goods of defendant on instalment, defendant holding a chattel mortgage.  Plaintiff wished to store the furniture during the summer, and defendant promised to store it free of charge and to have it insured for plaintiff's benefit.  It was destroyed by fire, without insurance.  The court gave judgment for damages for breach of contract, distinguishing Thorne v. Deas and Brawn v. Lyford infra.  In this case, the defendant had an interest in the property, with a reason for desiring possession of the goods and insurance thereon.  Although there does not seem to have been a bargain for the plaintiff's surrender of possession and forbearance to insure, the fact that he delivered possession in reliance on the promise made it more reasonable for him to trust the defendant to insure.  A similar case is Schroeder v. Mauzy, 118 P. 459, 16 Cal.App. 443 (1911).

86.  **Me.**—Brawn v. Lyford, 69 A. 544, 103 Me. 362 (1907).

# CHAPTER 9

## PAST CONSIDERATION

## § 210. Past Consideration—Meaning of the Term

In the law of contracts, the central and the inevitable problem is that of enforceability of promises. There are plenty of subsidiary and collateral problems; the primary question is, When will a promise be enforced. In the first place, it is to be observed that mere promissory words are not enough. This seems to have been true in Roman jurisprudence, also. A bare promise—*nudum pactum*—was not enforceable; there had to be some formalities or other accompanying factors, making the transaction a *pactum vestitum*. Anglo-American culture, jurisprudence, and language are to a large extent based upon that of Rome. Many doctrines have been drawn from the Roman law, and many Roman legal terms found an abiding place with us. *Nudum pactum* is one of these terms. But it must not be supposed that either a doctrine or a term has the same meaning and application in its new environment. The factors that caused a promise to be enforceable at Roman law and made it a *pactum vestitum* are not identical with the ones that in our system clothe a promise with enforceability. The sufficient *causa* of the Romans is not identical with our sufficient consideration.

The factors that will lend enforceability to an informal promise, in our system of law can be roughly divided into three classes: past, present, and future. More exactly, these classes may be described thus: (1) facts occurring prior to the making of the promise and not with any purpose of inducing the promise in exchange; (2) acts and forbearances given in exchange for the promise and bargained for by the promisor; (3) acts and forbearances occurring subsequent to the promise and not bargained for by the promisor. It is the first of these classes that is the subject of the discussion at this point. Happenings of the past, not bargained for by a promisor, are far less likely to be held to make his promise enforceable than are those for which he bargains. Not infrequently, however, such happenings induce the making of a subsequent promise; and in such case they are commonly described as "past consideration" for the promise. Furthermore, in important classes of cases, that "past consideration" is held to be a sufficient reason for enforcing the promise that is induced thereby.[1]

Irrespective of the definition or usage as to the word "consideration," it is necessary for us to spend much effort in determining and stating what sorts of past events will be operative to make a subsequent promise enforceable. In large classes of cases the courts are continuing to hold that they will so operate. The necessities of courts, lawyers, and clients require us to state what facts will make a promise binding and not merely what facts we are willing to describe by the term "consideration."

In all cases where a promise is enforced because of past events, it is not supposed that any of those events constitute an agreed equivalent for the promise or for the performance that is promised. The promisor is making his promise because those events occurred, but he is not making his promise in order to get them. There is no "bargaining"; no saying that if you will do this for me I will do that for you. One who insists on defining "consideration" as some action or forbearance exchanged for a promise by the bargaining process can therefore not call any of these motivating past events by the name consideration. This is the explanation why more than one learned author has said that a "past consideration" is no consideration. Nevertheless, the term "past consideration" is so firmly established in our judicial language that its use will perforce continue. Whether we thus use the term or reject it, we must in any event consider and state in the form of legal rules those classes of unbargained for events of the past that will be held to make a subsequent promise enforceable.

A promise is never held to be made enforceable by reason of past events unless those events have such a relation to the promise as to constitute its inducing cause. They need not be the sole inducement of the promise; but they must at least be one of the major inducing factors. The events of the past are uncounted; comparatively few of them are known to any promisor; and, even of those that are known to him, few indeed can truly be said to be an inducing factor in the making of any subsequent promise.

In our search for the "past considerations" that are operative, therefore, we need look only among those that are inducing factors, causing promises to be made. Many of these inducing factors are quite insufficient. It is neither necessary nor possible for us to state all such factors as are not sufficient although we shall consider some of them. It will be difficult enough to make a list of the "past considerations" that have been held to be operative.

### § 211. An Existing Indebtedness or Obligation Supports a New Co-extensive Promise

A past debt, still existing and enforceable, is a sufficient basis for the enforcement of a new promise by the debtor to pay it.[2] This is true, whether the past debt is contractual or quasi-contractual in character. Indeed, it was held in an ancient and leading case[3] that where a legally enforceable debt exists the law will imply an assumpsit, even in the absence of any express or other actual promise by the debtor to pay it. This holding was no doubt for the purpose of enabling a creditor to sue in assumpsit instead of in the action of debt, thereby depriving the debtor of the ancient defense known as "wager of law," a defense that had come to be fraudulently used. That defense was

---

3.    Slade's Case, 4 Coke, 92 b; Yelv.
21; Moore K.B. 433, 667 (1602).

available in the action of debt, but not in assumpsit; and its elimination forced the debtor to present his defense, if he had any, to a jury.[4]

It is obvious that if a past, but still enforceable, debt is a sufficient reason for implying a fictitious promise and enforcing that, it must be at least equally sufficient for the enforcement of an express promise (or one that is implied in fact) by the debtor. The law would indeed be strangely inconsistent if this were not so; for it is universally held that a past debt that has been barred by the statute of limitations is a sufficient basis for a new promise.

If the debt is itself still enforceable, it may be thought that the new express promise is of no importance; but such is not the case. This express promise not only once served to knock out "wager of law"; it also now serves to start anew the running of the statutory period of limitation. This is true, whether the past debt has already been barred or is not yet barred.[5] In either case, the creditor now has the full statutory period in which to sue, beginning with the date of the new promise. This being so, it shows that this new promise has legal operation—it makes a judicial remedy available to the promisee when one would otherwise not be available. This is what other contractual promises do; it is the principal test of what is meant by legal duty and by contract.

One who is already bound to pay for services rendered at his request can be sued upon his subsequent express promise to pay the debt.[7] If a debtor gives to his creditor a promissory demand note for the amount of his debt, this note is an enforceable contract.[8] Such a note, executed as a gift and in the absence of any pre-existing debt, would not be enforceable.[9]

A promissory note for the exact amount of a pre-existing debt of the maker is enforceable without any new consideration, even though it is given in substitution for a previous note that has been made void by an innocent alteration by the holder.[10] Further, the new note may operate as a ratification of that which was previously voidable for fraud or as a waiver of performance of some condition precedent.[11]

When it is said in all these cases that the existing debt is a "sufficient consideration" for the new promise to pay it, what is meant is that the past transaction is a sufficient reason for enforcing the new promise. The past facts that were then sufficient to create a legal duty are now still sufficient to support an express promise. This became common law, not as an exception to an antecedent doctrine of consideration, but as a component part of the amorphous doctrine of consideration in its process of making.

An existing debt is also a sufficient reason for the debtor's giving a mortgage or other security to the creditor;[15] but an executed mortgage or a delivered security is operative to create a property interest in the creditor by reason of execution and delivery alone.  There is no promise by the debtor that needs enforcement.  If the mortgage or other security is merely promised, and is not yet executed, the promise is not made enforceable by the mere fact that a debt exists.

## § 212.  Promises in Excess of the Existing Debt or Duty

While an existing debt or legal duty is a sufficient reason for enforcing a promise to pay that debt, or any part of it, or to perform the duty, it is not a sufficient reason for enforcing a promise to do anything else.[16]  The new promise must be co-extensive with the existing debt or other duty, or must be to render a performance that is wholly and exactly included within that debt or duty.  Thus an existing overdue debt of $100 is a sufficient basis to sustain the debtor's promise to pay $100 to the creditor, or to pay $80 or any other sum less than $100; but it is not a sufficient basis for a promise to pay $101.  Further, it is believed that if A is under a legal duty to B to deliver to B two specific machines, this is enough to support A's promise to deliver either one or both of those machines to B; but no case of this exact sort has been discovered in the reports.[17]

An existing duty to pay a sum of money is not sufficient to make enforceable the debtor's promise to discharge it in labor or goods; and a duty to deliver a machine or to render service will not support a promise to pay a sum of money instead, or to deliver a different machine or to render different service.  In cases of this type, however, it must be remembered that a promise by the obligee to receive labor or goods in lieu of money due him, or to receive any different performance in lieu of that required by the previous duty, is a sufficient consideration for the debtor's new promise.  Such a new bilateral agreement between obligor and obligee is a valid accord executory that is enforceable like any other bilateral contract.[18]

When services have been rendered at request, there is frequently an implied promise to pay reasonable compensation therefor.  A subsequent express promise of the obligor to pay a definite sum is evidence of what such "reasonable compensation" is; but it will not be enforced if it is found to be in excess of what was reasonably implied in the first transaction.[19]

16.   In Earle v. Oliver, 2 Exch. 71 (1848), Parke, J., said: "But it does not follow that, though a promise revives the debt in such cases, any of those debts will be sufficient consideration to support a promise to do a collateral thing as to supply goods, or to perform work and labor."

One who has sold a horse at an agreed price without warranty is not bound by a warranty that he makes subsequently without new consideration. The new warranty is not supported by the past consideration (the price paid by the buyer) unless it was already expressed or implied in the original transaction.[20]

## § 213.   Existing Debt of a Third Person Will Not Support a Promise

The promise of one person to pay a pre-existing debt owed to the promisee by a third person is not enforceable in the absence of a consideration or of such action by the promisee in reliance on the promise as to take the place of a consideration. The third person's pre-existing debt is not a sufficient "past consideration" to support the defendant's promise to pay it.[24] A special illustration of this is the promise of an executor to pay out of his own pocket a debt that had been owed by his testator. The fact that the debt is still chargeable against the estate represented by the executor is not a sufficient reason for enforcing the executor's promise.[25] The executor's existing duty is merely to distribute the assets according to law; no doubt this duty would be sufficient to support the executor's promise to pay a claimant his proper share of the assets at the time required by the law for their distribution. Promises like the foregoing, to pay the debt of another person, living or dead, are required to be in writing by the statute of frauds; but the fact that such a promise is in writing, signed but not sealed, is not enough to make it enforceable.

In the great field of suretyship, it is beyond question that the debt or obligation of the principal obligor is not a sufficient basis for the enforcement of the promise of the surety or guarantor. If the promises of the principal and the surety are made simultaneously, they may be supported by a single consideration; the loan of money by the creditor to the principal is a sufficient consideration for the promises of both principal and surety. But for the promise of any surety that is made subsequently to the advancement of the money to the principal, there must be a new consideration.[26] The fact that the loan has been made and the principal is indebted is not a sufficient reason for enforcement of the surety's subsequent promise.

## § 214.   New Promise to Perform an Obligation Barred by Statute of Limitations

In all jurisdictions there are statutes limiting the time within which civil actions must be brought. If, within the statutory period applicable to a particular claim, an action for its enforcement is not begun, the claim is said to be barred by "statute of

20.   Eng.—Roscorla v. Thomas, 3 Q.
   B. 234 (1842).

limitations." There is a vast amount of law as to the operation of these statutes, relating to the time when the statutory period begins to run, to the effect of part payments and new promises and acknowledgments, and to other matters. We are concerned here only with the enforceability of a new promise by the obligor, made after the statute has barred the legal remedy.

If a debtor makes a new promise to his creditor to pay his existing debt, no bar having yet arisen, this promise is enforceable, being sufficiently supported by the existing legal duty of the promisor. This has been previously discussed. In such a case, the creditor's remedy on the new promise is not barred by statutory limitation until the lapse of the full period counting from the time of breach of this new promise. Such a promise extends the time for enforcement.[30] Likewise, if a debtor makes a new promise to his creditor to pay a debt that has already become unenforceable by operation of a statute of limitations, this promise is enforceable in accordance with its own terms without any new consideration. It is supported by the "past consideration." Though the debtor was protected by a legal bar, he is regarded as still under a moral obligation to pay the barred debt.[31]

The debtor's other creditors cannot effectively object to his thus reviving the remedy on a barred debt; after such revival, the particular creditor can file his claim and share with other creditors under a general assignment for the benefit of creditors.[32]

Often it is said that the remedy is barred, but not the "debt." Certain it is that the law regards the past transaction as still having some legal operation. It is still sufficient to support the creditor's rights in collateral securities, real or chattel, and also his right against a guarantor or other kind of surety if the facts happen to be such that the statutory protection is not applicable to the surety as well as the principal debtor.[33] Certain, also, it is that in spite of the statutory bar the past transaction is still operative to create in the debtor the legal power of making a binding promise without consideration.

A theory once commonly accepted on which the legal result is explained is that the new promise is the waiver of a defense, that the new promise itself creates no new legal duty, and that we are not required to rest upon a moral obligation or a "past consideration" theory.[34] This "waiver" theory is no longer regarded as satisfactory. Even if we call the new promise a "waiver of defense," it is clear that it renews the legal remedy, that this remedy remains available for an extended period of limitation, and that the extent of the obligation that has now been made enforceable is determined by the terms of the new promise. All this is the result, without any consideration given in exchange for the new promise; and the reason that this is the result is that there was a "past consideration" to support the new promise. We might just as well say that the new promise is enforceable as a contract.[35]

In any case, attention must be called to the fact that the power of the debtor to bind himself without new consideration for his promise is limited. He can revive the old obligation, if one previously existed, but can create no larger or different one. If he is turning a moral obligation into a legal one, the newly promised performance must be one that was included within the moral obligation. If without new consideration he is ratifying a previous transaction that created what we are pleased to call a "voidable" obligation—voidable on such grounds as infancy, fraud, duress and mistake—the legal duty created by the ratification cannot include a performance that was not included within the "voidable" obligation. This is what lies behind the expression "waiver of a defense." But any one who creates a brand new obligation for a new consideration is also waiving a defense, the difference being that there is no limit on the nature and size of the performance that he binds himself to render. In the "past consideration" cases, there is such a limit. A new consideration will support any promise; a "past consideration" will support only a promise to do that which the community already believes ought to be done.[36]

### § 215. The New Promise may be Limited in Amount or may be Conditional

When one is contracting on the basis of new consideration, he can limit his duties as he sees fit. The same is true where he is promising on the basis of a "past consideration." Although a man ought to pay his barred debts, he is protected on grounds of public policy against direct judicial enforcement. He need not dispense with this protection at all; and, if he is willing to do away with it, he can do this in part only, instead of in whole, and he can limit his promise by providing for new conditions precedent to duty. Thus, one who owes a barred debt of $100 and says to his creditor, "I will pay you five dollars and no more," is now legally bound to pay only five dollars.[38] If he promises to pay the $100 in weekly instalments of five dollars each, no action lies for the full debt until after twenty weeks.[39] If he pays five dollars, saying at the same time that he will pay no more, no new obligation is created.[40]

---

39.   **Mass.**—Gillingham v. Brown, 60 N.E. 122, 178 Mass. 417, 55 L. R.A. 320 (1901).

40.   **Conn.**—Hale v. Morse, 49 Conn. 481 (1882).

**N.H.**—Barker v. Heath, 67 A. 222, 74 N.H. 270 (1907), semble.

The new promise may be made conditional on any new performance or event.[41] Frequently, a debtor promises to pay the debt as soon as he is financially able to do so. This makes his "ability" to pay a condition precedent to a right of action; and it must be alleged and proved by the creditor.[42] What constitutes ability to pay is indeed a variable quantity; and often, in the light of surrounding circumstances, a promise so worded has been interpreted as a promise to pay within a reasonable time.[43] The following are illustrations of other conditions that have been specified by the debtor: to pay "as soon as I sell the mill;" [44] "after one more year of successful business;" [45] on condition that an attachment should be vacated; [46] to pay a stated sum on condition of assent to it as full satisfaction; [47] to deliver certain shares of stock or other property on condition of acceptance in satisfaction.[48]

## § 216.   New Promise may be Implied from an Acknowledgment of a Debt as Existing

The new promise to pay can be made in any form of expression, by word or act, that is capable of understanding and proof. It is very generally held that an acknowledgment that a sum of money is actually due, if made without any accompanying denial of willingness, justifies the inference of a promise to pay.[49] To justify such an inference, the acknowledgment must be of a present indebtedness; an admission that there was once a debt and that it has never been paid, is not quite enough in the absence of accompanying factors evidencing present willingness to pay or a present sense of obligation.[50]

There was once some variation in the way in which the statute was regarded, some courts regarding it as a statute of presumption and others as a statute of repose. By the former, the expiration of the statutory period was believed to raise a presumption that the debt has been paid; by the latter, there was no such presumption, the purpose of the statute being to prevent the making of stale claims as to the merits of which the evidence may have disappeared, and for the relief of debtors. By the former view, a definite admission that the debt had never been paid defeated the presumption and was said to "toll the statute." By the latter view, which is now the prevailing one, such an admission is not enough; there must in addition be an expression of willingness to give up the protection of the statute.

## § 217.   Revival of Remedy by Part Payment

The making of a part payment on account of a larger claim then identified and not denied,[57] justifies the inference of a prom-

41.   U.S.—Bell v. Morrison, 1 Pet.
351 (1828).

ise to pay the balance and revives an enforceable right to that balance.[58] This is true whether the payment is made to be applied toward either the principal debt or interest thereon. If the payment is made before the statutory period has fully expired, the implied promise starts a new period running in place of the partly expired one. The new period begins from the day of payment.[59] The debtor can, by any appropriate expression, prevent the inference of a promise to pay the balance.[60] Such is the case if he says, "I pay you this but will pay no more."

To justify the inference of a promise to pay the balance, the payment made must be the voluntary act of the debtor or his authorized agent; otherwise, he is neither acknowledging nor promising.[61] A sale of securities and the use of the proceeds in reduction of the debt do not affect the duty of the debtor to pay the balance, if such sale and application are solely by authority of a court or are in accordance with a power given to the creditor by the debtor as a part of the original transaction that has become barred.[62] A sale of securities and an application of the proceeds in reduction of the debt, by virtue of a new authority given by the debtor himself, are the same as a part payment made by the debtor and have the same effect in renewing the remedy.[63]

Where the amount due is doubtful or disputed, the payment of a definite sum by the debtor, offered by him as full settlement, is not an admission that any balance is still due.[64] Instead, the acceptance of the money, so offered, operates as an accord and satisfaction.

### § 219. The Cause of Action Consists of Both Old Debt and New Promise

In the past, some puzzling questions arose as to the time when the new cause of action first arose. For most purposes, it is when the new promise is made. But the fact that this seems to be the logical conclusion does not prevent a court from looking back to the basis on which the new promise rests. If the old contract was a negotiable instrument, an assignee who became such after the making of the new promise on which he must depend was allowed to sue in his own name.[77] This merely anticipated the modern law that permits an assignee of a non-negotiable claim to sue in his own name.

In all "past consideration" cases, the new promise is a necessary factor in the plaintiff's cause of action. Either the old transaction created no enforceable obligation, or something that

---

77. See:
Md.—Lamar v. Manro, 10 G. & J. (Md.) 50 (1838).

Mass.—Way v. Sperry, 6 Cush. 238, 52 Am.Dec. 779 (1850); Little v. Blunt, 9 Pick. 488 (1830).

has occurred since has barred its enforcement. The action, therefore, should not be described either as being "on the old promise" or as being on the new one; it is "on" both of them, since they are equally necessary.[78] Doubtless, it is better to allege the whole story in the original complaint; but the plaintiff should not be penalized if he follows an old form in which the plaintiff first alleges the original contract, and to a plea of the statute of limitations (or other bar) replies by alleging the new promise.[79]

If the plaintiff pleads and proves nothing but the old contract, he must lose his case as against a proper plea of the statutory bar. If he pleads and proves nothing but the new promise, without alleging or proving the antecedent transaction that induced the new promise, again he must lose his case, as against an ordinary plea of the general issue. Any such new promise must have something else to support it; either a "past consideration," a bargained-for equivalent, or subsequent action in reliance. Why, then, should we pick out any one of the necessary operative facts and say that the action is "on" it alone?

In all jurisdictions, the revived cause of action is itself subject to be barred by a statute of limitations; and the statutory period begins to run from the time that the new promise, express or implied, is made, if it is a promise that is immediately performable.[80] If it is a promise to pay at some future date, or on the performance of some condition, no action of any kind is maintainable until the specified date or the performance of the condition; in this case, the new statutory period is counted only from the breach of the new promise.[81] The statutory period that is applicable against the new right of action depends upon the character and form of the new promise and the provisions of the various statutes. It is not determined by the character and form of the original transaction. If the new promise is under seal, the period is that which the statute makes applicable to sealed instruments.[82] If the new promise is merely implied from an acknowledgment or a part payment, the period is that which the statute provides for implied contracts; and this is true, even though the original transaction was a contract under seal.[83] If the new promise is in writing and the old contract was not, the statute applicable to written contracts will be applied.[84]

If a new promise to pay is made by the debtor before the period of limitation has expired, the creditor is not at all dependent upon this new promise, in case he brings his suit before the end of that period. His original cause of action is still a good one. It has sometimes been thought that in such case the action must

79.    **Ala.**—Wolffe v. Eberlein, 74 Ala.
99, 49 Am.Rep. 809 (1883).

be "on the old promise"; whereas it must be "on the new promise" if that promise is made after action barred.[85] Such a distinction is quite erroneous. In either case, the new promise is sufficiently supported by the "past consideration"; but in the latter case it is a necessary part of the only cause of action that the creditor has, while in the former case it is not.

## § 220. New Promise to Pay a Barred Judgment or Specialty Debt

When a claim has been reduced to judgment for the payment of money, the antecedent claim is said to be merged in the judgment; and the obligation is a debt. Sometimes and for certain purposes, it has been held that a judgment debt is a "contract." In this treatise and in the Restatement of the American Law Institute, the term contract is defined more narrowly, so as not to include the judgment of a court or the obligation that it creates. It must not be supposed, however, that the more narrow definition is the only correct one; and it would be an outrage to limit the term contract as used in a statute or a constitution in accordance with a narrow definition constructed for the sake of certainty and convenience in a treatise.

The kinds of obligations to which a statute of limitations applies must be determined by the statute itself. There are statutes that bar the enforcement of judgment debts; and there are methods available to a judgment creditor to prevent the bar from operating against him. Is a judgment debt so different in character from other debts as to prevent it from being a sufficient "past consideration," either before it is barred by statute or afterwards, for a new promise by the debtor to pay the money due?

The question was not always asked in this form. It sometimes has been this: Can the debtor revive the remedies on a judgment that has been barred by statute? Put in this form, a majority of the decisions have been in the negative.[86] The most effective remedy for enforcement of a judgment is a writ of execution.[87] After the judgment is barred by statute of limitations or in bankruptcy, the remedy by writ of execution is certainly not available. Probably, there is no authority for holding that the debtor has power, by waiving the statutory bar or by new promise to pay, to make the writ of execution again available for immediate enforcement. Only a court can render judgment, or authorize such a remedy.

Another available remedy is to bring a new action, asking for another judgment that can in its turn be enforced. At common law, this new action could have been "debt on the judgment." After the bar of the statute, this remedy too is unavailable. It was held in some cases that a new promise by the debtor to pay

312

the judgment debt so effectively removed the statutory bar that an action of debt on the judgment could again be maintained.[88] This, too, was thought by many to be improper for the same reasons that were applicable to the writ of execution. The judgment of a court could again be made effective and enforceable only by the court itself, not by the debtor. To those holding this view, a contract may be revived by the contracting debtor; but a judgment is not a contract.[89]

The sustaining of such an action as "debt on the judgment" should now be regarded as being nothing more than a recognition that the past judgment and the debtor's new promise together create an enforceable obligation, one that is now enforceable by appropriate court procedure. If the common law form of debt is still available as a remedy, it should be held to be applicable here. Under many modern codes, it has been abolished. In such case, the ordinary civil action should be sustained. The sustaining of such an action, even though it be described as "debt on judgment," does not mean that we are giving power to the debtor to do that which only a court should have power to do; it means only that the existing facts are sufficient reason for the recognition and enforcement of a duty to pay a sum of money. But for the statute of limitations, the facts would have been sufficient without a new promise; in spite of the statute, they are sufficient with a new promise. All that the plaintiff should need to do is to allege the new promise and the antecedent reason for its enforcement—the "past consideration," which in this case is the judgment debt.

For reasons similar to those given in the case of a judgment, it was sometimes held that the obligation of a barred specialty debt could not be revived by a parol promise.[90] These reasons similarly should be disapproved. The reasons for enforcing new promises to pay simple contract debts, barred by the statute of limitations or discharged in bankruptcy, are equally cogent in the cases of judgments and specialty debts. It is not necessary to hold that the old judgment is revived so as to be enforceable just as before. All that is necessary is to hold that it is a sufficient reason for enforcing a new promise to pay it, in part or in full. Many cases have so held;[91] and these should be followed in order to make the law reasonable and consistent as well as just.

The statutory period within which suit must be brought for the enforcement of the obligation, created, in part at least, by the new parol promise, is not the period applicable to judgments

---

88.   Two such cases are Carshore v. Huyck, 6 Barb. (N.Y.) 583 (1849), and Olcott v. Scales, 3 Vt. 173, 21 Am.Dec. 585 (1831).

91.   **Ala.**—Wolffe v. Eberlein, 74 Ala. 99, 49 Am.Rep. 809 (1883). **N.Y.**—Carshore v. Huyck, 6 Barb. 583 (1849).

or specialties, but the one declared by the statute to be applicable to informal contracts.[92] Both logic and convenience tend to this result, although there might be little practical harm in permitting suit for the longer period.

In this, as in other similar cases, the extent of the recovery should be determined by the terms of the new promise. If it is a promise to pay a part only, or to pay only on the occurrence of some condition precedent, the enforceable duty should be limited accordingly.

In the form of a civil action under the modern codes, the plaintiff should allege all the operative facts, and the question as to debt on judgment or assumpsit on New Promise ought not arise. Even so, if the complaint alleges only the judgment, and the defendant pleads limitation, a replication should not be held to be a variance or departure merely because it alleges a new promise. A complete cause of action is stated in complaint and replication; and it is a single cause of action.

### § 222.  New Promise to Pay a Debt Discharged in Bankruptcy

A new promise by a debtor, made after his discharge in bankruptcy, to pay his creditor a balance left unpaid by the distribution of assets in the bankruptcy proceeding, is an enforceable promise.[97] No new consideration is necessary; the promise is supported by the transaction that created the discharged debt— a "past consideration." Such a new promise is binding, even though made before the court has entered its decree of discharge, provided that it is made after the filing of the bankruptcy petition or the adjudication of bankruptcy.[98] Under any bankruptcy statute, all claims existing at a date that is indicated in the statute will be discharged by the subsequent decree. A new promise by the debtor, made before that date, would suffer the same fate as would the original claim itself;[99] but a promise made after that date cannot be proved in the proceeding and is not included in the discharge.

A few of the earlier cases held that a new promise by the debtor was not binding, distinguishing between bankruptcy and statute of limitations in that the former discharged the debt while the latter merely barred the remedy.[1] This distinction did not survive, for the reason that there are equally strong grounds for enforcing the new promise in the two cases. The creditor has not been paid; and he has been deprived of his remedy by com-

---

**97.**    U.S.—Zavelo v. Reeves, 33 S.Ct. 365, 227 U.S. 625, 57 L.Ed. 676 (1913); Mutual Reserve Fund Life Ass'n v. Beatty, 93 F. 747 (C.C.A. 9th, 1899).

N.Y.—Herrington v. Davitt, 115 N.E. 476, 220 N.Y. 162 (1917); Dusenbury v. Hoyt, 53 N.Y. 521, 13 Am. Rep. 543 (1873); Shippey v. Henderson, 14 Johns. 178, 7 Am.Dec. 458 (1817).

pulsion of law.  In the one case as in the other there is still a moral obligation to pay the unpaid balance, sufficient to support an express promise by the debtor if he is willing to recognize its existence.[2]  The consideration that was given for the bankrupt debtor's original promise is still operative as a "past consideration" for the debtor's subsequent promise to pay.  And if the original promise was made binding by some factor other than a consideration, such as a statute, a seal, or action in reliance, that factor likewise remains a sufficient support for the debtor's new promise.

As in other "past consideration" cases, the past performance will not support a new promise to render a performance different from that originally required.[4]  It must be a promise to render the same performance or a fractional part of it.  A "waiver of a defense" restores a former duty but does not create a new one;  and even though we may agree that a new legal obligation is being created by the new promise, the "past consideration" is not regarded as a sufficient reason for creating an obligation to render a different performance.

The new obligation is created by and dependent on the new promise.  If the new promise is itself limited or conditional, no action lies against the debtor unless the condition has been performed.[5]  A promise to pay ten per cent of the barred debt renews one tenth of the debt.[6]  A promise to pay the debt "as soon as I sell the mill" is enforceable after the mill is sold and not before.[7]  When the condition is performed or occurs, however, the promise becomes enforceable, being sufficiently supported by the "past consideration." [8]  But an antecedent debt of $100 will not support a subsequent promise to pay $110, even though it is neither barred nor discharged;  it cannot be expected to be more efficacious after it has become unenforceable.

If a debt has been discharged by the voluntary action of creditors in assenting to a composition, under which they receive only a part of the sums due them, the courts hold that a new promise by the debtor to pay the balance is not enforceable.[9]  This is not applicable, however, to a composition entered into by the creditors as a part of a bankruptcy proceeding.  The discharge granted in bankruptcy is by order of court;  the creditors have no choice but to yield to it.  This is held to be no less true, even though the creditors have been given the opportunity to agree upon a composition in the course of the proceeding.  After such a composition, there remains as much of a moral obligation to pay the balance of a debt as is the case after any discharge in bankruptcy without a composition agreement;  a new promise to pay that balance is binding without any new consideration.[10]

4.    See Earle v. Oliver, 2 Exch. (W. H. & G.) 71 (1848).

The past obligation is sufficient support for the new promise even though it was subject to a condition not yet performed when the new promise was made. Thus, a new promise by a principal debtor to reimburse his surety, in case the surety is thereafter compelled to pay the creditor, is sufficiently supported by the principal's equitable duty to make such reimbursement, even though this duty is contingent and not immediate.[12] The new promise, of course, is subject to the same condition precedent and is co-extensive with its supporting duty. The old conditional duty will not support a new unconditional one; but it will support one requiring the same performance on the same condition and even though it is subject to additional conditions.

### § 223.  Must the New Promise be in Writing?

In most of the states, by statute, the new promise to pay a barred debt is not enforceable unless it is in writing.[14] As in the case of the original statute of frauds, this writing may be sufficient even though it is informal and is in need of much explanatory evidence.[15] In the absence of such a statutory requirement, the new promise need not be in writing to be enforceable; it is not a promise to pay the debt of another person  Neither is it required to be in the same form as was the original contract enforcement of which is now barred.

The statute requiring the new promise to be in writing in these cases is held not to be applicable if there is a new and sufficient consideration given in exchange for it.[16] The purpose of the statute is merely to make unenforceable those gratuitous oral promises that are based solely upon the past debt itself. It is to protect obligors from being deprived of the protection of the statute of limitations by perjured testimony that he "waived" the statute or that he made a new gratuitous oral promise to pay the debt. It should be remembered that an honest debtor pays his debts when able, even when barred by statute of limitations. And it may be suggested that a new consideration for a promise can be established by perjury about as easily as can the promise itself.

### § 224.  New Promise by an Indorser after a Technical Discharge

Where an obligation has been discharged or its enforcement barred by some act or neglect of the creditor, by reason of a rule of law for the protection of the obligor, but where the promisor received the value that he bargained for and has not suffered actual injury, a new promise to perform as originally bound is enforceable without a new consideration. The past transaction and its resulting benefit are sufficient reason for enforcement. It is not necessary to determine whether or not there was a moral obligation to perform existing before the new promise was made.

So, an indorser or other surety, who has been discharged by the creditor's failure to give notice of default or to sue the principal or to perform some other condition required by a rule of law, is bound by a new promise to pay.[17] The same is true where the surety was discharged by a binding extension of time given to the principal debtor.[18] A new promise to pay a note that has been discharged by an alteration on its face by the payee has been enforced.[19] Where a debt to a corporation was unenforceable because the corporation was doing business without complying with state law, the debtor's new promise to pay, made after compliance with the law was held enforceable.[20]

There are many contracts in which the promise of one of the parties is expressly conditional on some specified fact or event. If this express condition does not occur, the promisor is not bound; but often the condition can be waived. If the condition is not some performance that constitutes a material part of the agreed equivalent of the promisor's performance, the promisor can bind himself by a new promise or expression of waiver, either before or after the failure of the condition to occur.[21] If, on the other hand, the condition is a return performance constituting a material part of the agreed equivalent of the promisor's performance, he cannot afterwards eliminate this condition precedent and bind himself by an expression of waiver or a new promise without a new consideration.

### § 225. Promise to Refund an Over-payment Made under Compulsion of a Judgment

If a debtor pays by mistake more than is actually due, the payee is under a legal duty to repay, a duty that fully supports an express promise to repay. If, however, the claim has been reduced to judgment, the amount so adjudged is legally due without regard to errors that were not successfully shown in court.[24] Yet, even though the judgment creditor owes no duty to repay an excess, it has been held that if he promises to repay it, his promise is enforceable.[25] This promise is supported only by a moral obligation that is well recognized by community opinion.

### § 226. New Promise after an Effective Voluntary Discharge

A past transaction is held not to be a sufficient reason for enforcing a subsequent promise, even though the promisor received benefits and even though he was once legally bound, if the obligation was voluntarily discharged by the creditor without mistake or other invalidating factor.[26] This is true even though the discharge was in part or in whole an executed gift. One who

317

gives away property has no power to recall it after performance; and the same is true of an executed gift discharge. Therefore, the new promise of a discharged debtor, to render the unperformed part of his previous duty, is not enforceable in the absence of new consideration if the discharge was by a release under seal (or a writing that is equally operative),[27] by a voluntary composition agreement,[28] by a novation,[29] or by an accord and satisfaction.[30] After such a voluntary discharge, it may well be that the community would generally not recognize the existence of any moral obligation; but it seems not to be necessary to consider the point.

As a matter of course, an obligor who has been discharged by rendering performance in full has no power to bind himself to perform over again by making a new promise without consideration.[31] Such a new promise would be regarded in exactly the same light as if it were made in the absence of any antecedent transaction or obligation.

It has been held in New York that if a creditor assents to a voluntary composition discharging the debtor without payment in full, as a part of which the debtor expressly declares that a moral obligation to pay the unpaid balance shall continue to exist, a new promise made later on to pay this balance will be enforceable. The "past consideration" and reserved moral obligation support the new promise.[32] This seems just and reasonable and in harmony with the law applied in other cases dealing with "past consideration."

## § 227. New Promise to Perform a Contract Voidable for Infancy

At common law the contracts of an infant are said to be voidable, but not void. That they are not void is made clear by the fact that the infant can almost always enforce them against the other party. In most cases it is equally true, however, that the contract cannot be enforced against the infant if he cares to take advantage of his infancy as a defense. By the common law an infant has power upon reaching the age of 21 to validate his contracts made during infancy. A new promise by him to perform in accordance with his previously made agreement is binding without any new consideration.[33] The reason for this enforceability must be found in the past transaction—in the infant's unenforceable promise and the consideration that was then given for it. This is one more example of "past consideration." In some states, there is a statute requiring the ratifying promise to

**32.  N.Y.**—Straus v. Cunningham, 144 N.Y.S. 1014, 159 App.Div. 718, (1913);  Taylor v. Hotchkiss, 80

N.Y.S. 1042 (App.Div.1903), affirmed 71 N.E. 1140, 179 N.Y. 546 (1904).

be in writing; but this does not affect the nature of the consideration.

The "past consideration" in these cases is not sufficient to support a promise of ratification unless it would have been sufficient to support the return promise then made by the infant, except for the fact of his infancy.[34] If the infant's promise was void for lack of consideration, and not merely voidable on the ground of infancy, a ratifying promise at majority will not be enforceable.

In some jurisdictions, it has been held that the ratifying promise is not binding unless the contract originally made was one that was beneficial to the infant. This is not the generally prevailing rule. If the consideration originally given was sufficient to support a return promise by an adult, it is also sufficient to support the ratifying promise.[35] It was very early held that even though the infant's promise was that of a surety to answer for the debt or default of another, a ratification after majority is binding.[36]

Just as in other "past consideration" cases, a mere promise of ratification is not enforceable except so far as it is coextensive with the past undertaking of the infant. A new promise to render a performance different from or in excess of that required by the original promise will not be enforced unless there is new consideration.

Just as in the case of contracts barred by statute of limitations, there was once much discussion as to whether the promisee's action must or should be brought on the original agreement or on the ratifying promise.[37] It now seems quite clear that this was a waste of energy. In the absence of a ratification after majority, which may be either express or implied from the continued enjoyment of benefits, the promisee does not have an enforceable claim. Likewise, no action is sustainable upon the ratifying promise unless there was a past agreement that would have been valid except for infancy. The past transaction and the new promise are both necessary; and both must be alleged and proved by the plaintiff in order to win his case. It is both proper and desirable for him to allege them both in his original declaration; but if he wishes he may merely allege the original contract, making no reference to infancy, and in his replication to a plea of infancy allege the ratifying promise.

As in the case of other promises dependent upon "past consideration," the extent of the promisor's obligation depends upon the terms of the new promise. The ratifying promise may be limited to only a specified part of the debt, it may be a promise to pay at a definite future date or in instalments, and it may be conditional on any event that the promisor then specifies. In such cases, the promisee's claim is not enforceable until the conditions have been performed and the specified time has arrived.[39]

## § 228.  Contracts Voidable for Fraud, Duress, or Mistake

An executory promise that has been induced by fraud or duress, or in certain kinds of cases by mistake, are unenforceable against the promisor.  In these cases, the contract is said to be voidable.  In order to avoid it, the facts may be such as to require the promisor to return something that he has received.  With the method by which the power of avoidance must be exercised, we are not now concerned.[41]  Instead, we are considering ratification by a new promise.  If in any of these cases, with full knowledge of the fraud or mistake and after any duress has ceased to exist, the party affected thereby makes a new promise to perform in accordance with the original agreement, no new consideration is required for this promise.[42]  The "past consideration" found in the former transaction is sufficient to support the later promise if it would, when given, have been sufficient to support the original promise but for the fraud, duress, or mistake.

We need not stop to speculate, in these cases, whether or not the community recognizes the existence of a moral obligation sufficient to support the subsequent promise.  In many such cases, it would generally be denied.  The past transaction, with its advantages such as they are, is a sufficient reason for enforcing a new promise, without regard to whether there was any moral duty.

## § 229.  Ratification by Principal of Unauthorized Contract by an Agent

If one party, without any sufficient authority, makes a contract on behalf of another party as principal, the latter is not bound thereby.  Nevertheless, the principal has a power of ratification.  By such a ratification he binds himself to perform the promises theretofore made in his behalf; his new promise requires no new consideration.  By the exercise of his power of ratification, however, the principal usually obtains new rights or advantages that he would not have without it.  It is not necessary that this should be the case, however, in order that the principal's ratifying promise should be binding.  The other party to the unauthorized contract may have fully performed his part before the defendant makes his ratifying promise, and the performance so rendered may be in no way beneficial to the defendant; and yet the ratifying promise of the principal will be en-

39.  **N.H.**—Edgerly v. Shaw, 25 N.H. 514, 57 Am.Dec. 349 (1852).

forced.[43] In such a case, the only ground for enforcing the principal's new promise is the "past consideration."

### § 230. The Use and Value of the Moral Obligation Doctrine

About a century and a half ago, Lord Mansfield held that an informal promise is enforceable if the performance promised is one that the promisor is already under a moral duty to the promisee to render.[44] In such a general form as this, the rule is no longer generally accepted. In a few states it is not infrequently repeated. In no state is the idea underlying it wholly abandoned. All "past consideration" cases, or nearly all, are cases in which enforcement depends upon recognition of some existing moral obligation; this is made apparent by the language of the courts in great numbers of cases.[45]

The rule laid down by Lord Mansfield, and still repeated today in some kinds of cases, operates as an escape from more hardened and definitely worded rules of law. By making a direct appeal to the mores of the time, it permits an easy and satisfying evolution of the law of promises by judicial action. Informal promises without consideration are not enforceable—perhaps thus saith the law. But a moral obligation is a sufficient consideration—thus may say the court. The term "consideration" has always had a shifting, variable content. By such means, every rule of law has growth and change, even including the supposedly unchangeable law of the Medes and Persians.

Like other stated rules, this rule is composed of words. Like other rules, also, this one makes an appearance of definiteness and exactitude, seeming to permit and to require the decision of cases by a process of deductive logic alone. A moral obligation is a sufficient consideration—as if anyone can and must recognize moral obligation on sight. It is because of this that the broadly stated rule of Lord Mansfield is so generally disapproved,

---

**14.** In Hawkes and Wife v. Saunders, Cowper 289 (1782), Lord Mansfield said: "Where a man is under a legal or equitable obligation to pay, the law implies a promise, though none was ever actually made. *A fortiori*, a legal or equitable *duty*, is a sufficient consideration for an actual promise. Where a man is under a moral obligation, which no court of law or equity can enforce, and promises, the honesty and rectitude of the thing is a consideration."
Lord Mansfield was trained in the civil law systems of Scotland and of Rome. He saw the merits of the Roman doctrine of *causa*, and no doubt also saw that the reasons underlying that doctrine have frequently had great influence in the judicial growth of the Anglo-American systems of common law and equity.

**45.** U.S.—Old American Life Ins. Co. v. Biggers, 172 F.2d 495 (C. A.Okl.1949), see Oklahoma statute.

Ala.—Webb v. McGowin, 168 So. 199, 232 Ala. 374 (1936), heroic act benefiting promisor.

even in courts where it is frequently appealed to. In many cases where moral obligation is asserted, the court feels that the promise ought not to be enforced; instead of going into the perilous and uncertain field of morality and denying the existence of moral obligation, it is easier to deny the rule. But on the other hand, in cases where the promise is one that would have been kept by ordinary citizens, and the court feels that enforcement is just, an appeal to the rule of moral obligation reaches a satisfying result and averts criticism. It is a common assumption that moral obligation is clear and certain; and it is part of our mores that what morality requires must be done. Therefore, in those classes of cases in which community opinion speaks in no uncertain tones, a promise is enforced if the promisor was already under a moral obligation to render the promised performance. In these cases, we can say with the courts that the moral obligation is a sufficient consideration; or we can say with the American Law Institute that no consideration is required. In other cases, where community opinion is divided and speaks doubtfully, the judicial arm of society withholds enforcement; and we can explain the result by saying (1) that there was no consideration for the promise, or (2) that a moral obligation is not a sufficient consideration, or (3) that no moral obligation exists.[46] In cases within the very large doubtful zone, the third of these explanations is avoided, because the court knows that it does not know, and because of the controversy that would ensue.

From the foregoing, it seems obvious that a treatise on the law of promises must classify the cases and construct descriptive rules, determining as well as possible when a "past consideration" is sufficient to induce enforcement and when it is not; or, avoiding the term consideration, determining when a past transaction is a sufficient reason for enforcing a subsequent promise; or, using the term "moral obligation," determining when the courts have recognized antecedent moral obligation as a sufficient reason for enforcing a subsequent promise.

Our problem is not that of determining whether a moral obligation is created by the promise itself, although standing alone and unconnected with other facts it is believed that it does not. Courts have never enforced promises that stand thus alone and unconnected. This, at least, can be stated as a fact, on the basis of which a definite rule of future court action can be laid down.

Nor will the present writer attempt to determine when moral obligation exists, or to state any universal or even any general test of its existence. The effort here is limited to the much more humble task of reporting and classifying the work of many judges, stating rules of their past action as an aid in advising and predicting future action. It is certain that the advice will not always be taken and that the prediction will not always be correct.   Just as in the past, court action will vary with the multitude of human impulses, especially with changing tides of community opinion.   There will have to be new classification and new rules.   Such is the evolutionary process of law and of mankind.

It has been said that the recognition of moral obligation as a sufficient consideration "would annihilate the necessity for any consideration at all, inasmuch as the mere fact of giving a promise creates a moral obligation to perform it."[47]   This is erroneous in two respects: First, the doctrine deals with a moral obligation created by facts antecedent to the making of the express promise, not with that which the promise itself may be regarded as creating.   Secondly, it seems very clear that many promises are made under such circumstances that the community would recognize no resulting moral obligation of keeping them.[48]   There is an approved maxim to the effect that a bad promise is better broken than kept.

### § 231.   Moral Obligation Apart from Economic Benefit to the Promisor with Subsequent Reliance by the Promisee

The consensus of community opinion will frequently assert the existence of a moral obligation to divide one's worldly goods with another, or to furnish him with care and support, or to give compensation for service rendered, even in cases where there was no antecedent transaction between the parties themselves by virtue of which any legal duty could arise and where the first party has received no pecuniary benefits whatever from the second.   In cases like this, the nearly universal holding is that the existing moral obligation is not a sufficient basis for the enforcement of an express promise to render the performance that it requires.[49]   The general statement is that it is not a sufficient "consideration" for the express promise.

A very little thought should be convincing that the existence of a moral obligation is not a matter of mathematical or logical certainty, and also that a clear consensus of community opinion often cannot be proved by evidence, although it may or may not exist.   The difficulties and differences of opinion involved in the determination of such a question are probably much greater

---

47.   **Eng.**—Lord Denman in East-wood v. Kenyon, 11 Adol. & El. 438 (1840).

48.   These criticisms are approved in Ferguson v. Harris, 17 S.E. 782, 39 S.C. 323, 39 Am.St.Rep. 731 (1893), and Muir v. Kane, 104 P.

153, 55 Wash. 131, 26 L.R.A.,N.S., 519, 19 Ann.Cas. 1180 (1909).

49.   **Conn.**—Cook v. Bradley, 7 Conn. 57, 18 Am.Dec. 79 (1828), necessaries furnished to the defendant's poor father.

R.I.—Shepard v. Rhodes, 7 R.I. 470, 84 Am.Dec. 573 (1863).

than those involved in determining the existence of "legal" obligation. This may tend to explain the attitude of the majority of courts on the subject; and it may justify the generally stated rule, in spite of the fact that most legal rules and legal duties are grounded in the prevailing mores of a people and in nothing else.

Some examples of such a moral obligation may be stated. (1) The defendant's adult son, returning home after a journey, fell desperately ill on the way. A good Samaritan, the plaintiff, took him in and gave him support, nursing, and medical care, until his death. Later, the defendant promised to reimburse the plaintiff for his service and expenses. The promise was held not enforceable.[50]

(2) Two partners, A and B, were close friends and associates. When A was on his death bed, he was promised by B that the latter would look after the business interests of A's widow. This promise was held unenforceable, even though it was alleged that B's breach of the promise caused the widow to lose her property.[51]

(3) One who had lived in immoral relations with a woman, with resulting injury to her much greater than that suffered by him, promised her on separating that he would pay her an annuity. After paying it for some time, he promised to pay, and she promised to accept, a specified sum in full satisfaction. His promise was not enforceable.[52]

(4) If the father of an illegitimate child is legally bound to support it, his promise to furnish such support or to pay for support rendered is itself enforceable without any consideration. But, in states where he is under no such legal obligation, it has frequently been held that his express promise to furnish such support is not made enforceable by the fact that he is under a moral obligation to furnish it. This is true with respect to a promise to reimburse the mother or a third person for support already supplied,[53] and with respect to a promise to such persons to furnish support in the future.[54] Such decisions will seldom be made now, because the legal obligation of the father, without any promise, is so generally recognized.[55] Furthermore, courts have been astute to find some sufficient consideration in these cases; [56] as soon as a moral obligation of this sort comes to be generally recognized in a community, it is rapidly turned into a legal obligation without the necessity of a promise.

50. Mass.—Mills v. Wyman, 3 Pick. 207 (1826).

51. Minn.—Rask v. Norman, 109 N. W. 704, 141 Minn. 198, 17 A.L.R. 1296 (1918).

52. U.S.—Re Greene, 45 F.2d 428 (D. C.N.Y.1930).

(5) The moral obligation of a husband to carry out the wishes of his deceased wife, even though based on affection and on long and faithful service in the accumulation of property, is not sufficient to make his express promise enforceable.[57]

(6) The promise of a son to pay the debts of his father, whether before or after the latter's death, and before or after the latter's discharge in bankruptcy, is not enforceable if without consideration.[58] The existence of a moral obligation in these cases would generally be doubted; but even if found to exist, it would not support the express promise. The same is true of a promise by a widow to pay the debt of her deceased husband.[59]

(7) One who was saved from death or severe injury by the unselfish intervention of another, who suffered disabling injury thereby, promised to pay an annuity to the latter for life. This promise was enforced, the court opinions indicating that few would doubt the existence of a moral obligation.[60] The contrary was held on facts similar but not identical, the court's opinion being less convincing.[61] In these cases, the transaction that induced the subsequent promise involved economic as well as physical detriment to the one and like benefit to the other.

(8) A bare promise without consideration and also without any preexisting moral obligation that can operate as a "past consideration" does not in itself create such a moral obligation as will support a subsequent promise. So a renewal note is no better than the prior one that it was given to renew; if the prior note was void, so is the subsequent one.[62]

Although the foregoing represents the great weight of authority with respect to a general doctrine that a moral obligation is a sufficient basis for the enforcement of an express promise to perform it, there are a few jurisdictions in which such a doctrine has been stated and approved. Even in these jurisdictions, however, the cases in which promises have been enforced because based on a moral obligation do not include many that would not have been enforced in jurisdictions refusing to state the doctrine in such broad general terms; and in every jurisdiction there are "past considerations" that are held sufficient to support an express promise, for the reason that they appeal to the community sense of moral obligation.[63]

## § 232. Love, Friendship, Blood Relationship

Love and affection and friendship are not subjects of barter and sale. No promise is made enforceable because it was in-

57.   **Ind.**—Schnell v. Nell, 17 Ind. 29, 79 Am.Dec. 453 (1861).

60.   **Ala.**—Webb v. McGowin, 168 So. 199, 232 Ala. 374 (1936).

61.   **N.C.**—Harrington v. Taylor, 36 S.E.2d 227, 225 N.C. 690 (1946).

duced by any of these or by the fact of blood relationship. This is true whether it is the love of the promisor for the promisee or the love of the promisee for the promisor.[64] It is true, even if the promise is given in order to induce, and actually does induce, feelings of love and affection in the promisee for the promisor. Even if it is bargained for as a consideration, it is not a legally sufficient one.

Even in the States recognizing, either by statute or by court decision, that a moral obligation may be sufficient support for an express promise, it would probably always be held that the mere existence of love, affection, or blood relationship is not enough to establish the existence of such a moral obligation.[66] Their courts have said that the moral obligation must be one arising out of a transaction involving economic benefit or detriment;[67] but there is nothing to prevent them from extending their doctrine to other cases in which community sentiment is clear.

### § 233. Past Service Rendered at Request of One Who Later Promises to Pay Therefor

In the early history of the common law action of assumpsit, there were a good many cases in which this action was sustained upon an express promise to pay for a past service that had been rendered by the plaintiff at the defendant's request.[68] There is some, though not very much, modern authority to the same effect.[69]

In many of these cases, the question seems not to have been raised whether the defendant's request was made under such circumstances that the plaintiff was then justified in inferring a promise to pay reasonable compensation for the requested service. If such a promise was reasonably to be implied at the time of the request, no subsequent express promise would now be necessary for its enforcement. The service was not only requested, it was bargained for by the defendant and given by the plaintiff in exchange for the defendant's implied promise of reasonable compensation. The evidence on which the inference of a promise is based will vary in its cogency; and no doubt a court must often welcome the defendant's own recognition of obligation in the form of a subsequent express promise.

---

68.   Eng.—Gale v. Golsbury, stated in 3 Dyer 272 b; Sidenham v. Worlington, 2 Leon. 224 (1585); Marsh v. Rainsford, 2 Leon. 111 (1588); Beaucamp v. Neggin, Cro.Eliz. 282 (34 Eliz.), for money paid to a third person at defendant's request; Riggs v. Bullingham, Cro.Eliz. 715 (1599); Barker v. Halifax, Cro.Eliz. 741 (1600); Bosden v. Thinne, Yelv. 40 (1603); Lampleigh v. Brathwait, Hob. 105, 1 Sm.L.C. 67 (1615); Townsend v. Hunt, Cro.Car. 408 (1635).

There are cases, however, in which the subsequent promise was enforced, even though the court, expressly recognized that no promise whatever should be inferred from the defendant's request, under the circumstances then existing.[70] In these cases, there was no agreed exchange of promise for service, and no consideration as that is defined by the American Law Institute. The legal duty of the defendant, therefore, is created by a promise without consideration, the reason for its enforcement being found in the past service at the promisor's request. In some of these cases, at least, the request was as essential as was the service itself, especially where the service was not beneficial in any pecuniary way to the defendant; the absence of a request was often given as a reason for refusing to enforce a subsequent promise to pay.[71]

If at time of the request the defendant impliedly promised to pay reasonable compensation, the legally enforceable duty thereby created is sufficient to support a co-extensive express promise subsequently made. The service rendered was, in some cases, the payment of a definite sum of money; and the subsequent express promise was to make reimbursement of that sum. If the service was such as not to have a liquidated value, and the defendant subsequently promises to pay a definite amount, the promise may properly be regarded as evidence of reasonable value, and so no more than co-extensive. If it is shown to be greater than the reasonable value, as to that excess it is not enforceable.[72] Sometimes, however, no effort seems to have been made to determine whether or not the past services were worth as much as the amount subsequently promised.[73]

Services are often rendered by one person to another, especially when residing together as members of a family, with the mutual understanding that they are not to be paid for. This may be true even though in various instances the services are expressly requested by the person benefited. In such cases there is no implied or constructive promise to pay. If subsequently, the person benefited makes an express promise to pay, that promise will not be made enforceable by the fact that the services were rendered at the request of the promisor.[74]

---

**70.** In Bosden v. Thinne, Yelv. 40 (1603), the plaintiff, at the defendant's request, had become surety for the price of wine bought by a third person; and the court admits that no promise was to be inferred from the request.
A similar case in exact accord is Bradford v. Roulston, 8 Irish C.L. 468 (1858), stated supra.

**74. Iowa.**—Allen v. Bryson, 25 N.W. 820, 67 Iowa 591, 56 Am.Rep. 538 (1885).

**Mass.**—Moore v. Elmer, 61 N.E. 259, 180 Mass. 15 (1901); Shepherd v. Young, 8 Gray 152, 69 Am.Dec. 242 (1857).

Sometimes persons are requested to submit plans or drawings for consideration by the one so requesting, the understanding being that they will be paid for if actually used. In such a case, there seems to be no implied promise to pay in the absence of actual use; but there may be an implied promise to consider the plans submitted and to form an honest judgment as to their merit. Where the plans have not been adopted, for reasons unconnected with their merit, a subsequent promise to reimburse the amount of the expenses incurred in making the plans has been held to be enforceable.[75] Such a decision seems reasonable, even if not within commonly stated rules.

## § 234. Past Services Beneficial to Defendant but Not Requested by Him

When some performance has been rendered by one person at the request of another, a subsequent express promise by that other to pay compensation has in some cases been enforced. It has frequently been doubted, however, whether such should be the decision unless there was an implied promise of compensation at the time the request was made. The theory behind these doubts is that contract requires "bargain"—that there must be an agreed exchange of promise for the performance. While it has steadily become more clear that contract is broader than bargain, it is also clear that if a performance is rendered by one person without any request by another, it is very unlikely that this other person will be under a legal duty to pay compensation. It has been the general assumption, also, that in such cases the law will not enforce a subsequent express promise to pay compensation. There have been a good many cases expressly so holding.[76] At the same time, there are too many decisions to the contrary to be disregarded, either as evidence of the law of specific jurisdictions or as evidence of such a generally prevailing conviction as to lead to similar decisions in other jurisdictions. There is, and always has been, active competition between these rules for acceptance by the judicial community as "the common law."

It is certain that if there is a field in which a past unrequested performance will support a subsequent express promise, it is a comparatively narrow one. It cannot have such an effect if it was in no respect received by or beneficial to the one making the subsequent promise. Suppose that Samaritan feeds and clothes needy Stranger. Later, Generous Observer promises to

---

**76.   Ariz.**—Wulff v. Lindsay, 71 P. 963, 8 Ariz. 168 (1903), services of land broker.

**Eng.**—Eastwood v. Kenyon, 11 Adol. & El. 438 (1840), a case that is often said to have established the English law; Hayes v. Warren, 2 Strange, 933 (1732); Jeremy v. Goochman, Cro.Eliz. 442 (1596); Hunt v. Bate, Dyer, 272 (1568).

reimburse Samaritan. There are no cases indicating that Observer will be held bound by his promise.[77] The case is very different from one in which the later promise of compensation is made by the benefited Stranger.

Secondly, it is equally clear that if the past unrequested performance was rendered as a gift, a subsequent promise of compensation made by the donee will not be enforced.[78] Such is the case, even though the gift performance was rendered as such at the request of the recipient.

Thirdly, there are certain kinds of cases in which the law requires that an unrequested beneficial performance must be paid for, even though the recipient makes no promise to pay and even flatly refuses payment. In these cases, the duty to pay is non-contractual, often called quasi-contractual. The legal duty is not based upon promise or assent. No attempt will be made here to explain when it is that the law creates such non-contractual duties to pay. The Roman law described some such cases by the phrase *negotiorum gestio*. The following is one illustration: a farmer's bull has strayed and is in danger of being totally lost or destroyed. A stranger impounds the bull, feeds him, and saves him for the farmer. By the Roman law, the farmer is bound to pay reasonable compensation for the benefit received. He may be bound by the Anglo-American law, also, if we search the cases in equity as well as in indebitatus assumpsit. If he is so bound quasi-contractually, that legal duty is a sufficient basis for the farmer's express promise to pay compensation. This is a kind of "past consideration" that has already been discussed.

But the Anglo-American law of quasi-contract has not been very fully developed. It may not be certain that the farmer would have to pay compensation for the service. In an actual case, he felt a moral obligation and expressly promised to pay. The Vermont court held that the promise was binding.[79] The past benefit received, though not requested, was a sufficient basis for his express promise.

One form of unilateral contract has been commonly described as an offer of an act for a promise, meaning that the offer is made by the rendition of service, and followed by an acceptance by promising to pay. It is seldom if ever suggested that in a contract, so made, the promise is to pay for a "past considera-

77.    Mass.—Mills v. Wyman, 3 Pick. (Mass.) 207 (1825), here the needy Stranger was the adult son of the promisor.

79.    Vt.—Boothe v. Fitzpatrick, 36 Vt. 681 (1864).

Chase v. Corcoran, 106 Mass. 286 (1871), is a case in which the court enforced a quasi-contractual duty to make compensation, without any promise being made. A boat in danger of destruction was saved and repaired.

tion" rendered without request.[86]   In some such cases, there may be an accepting promise made by implication before the completion of the service.   Sometimes the contract is truly bilateral, the offeror impliedly promising to complete the service started, and the offeree promising to pay therefor.   But in other cases, it is highly probable that the services are completed before any promise by the offeree is made, either expressly or impliedly.   If the promise follows promptly after completion of the service, no question is likely to be raised.   Suppose that one man gives valuable information to another, expecting payment, and the other at once promises compensation.   Should the decision turn on whether the promise was made before the promisor knew what the information was? [87]

A new and valuable idea or plan for advertising purposes may be communicated to a large dealer by a perfect stranger with the expressed hope that it will be used and compensation paid. The use of it by the dealer raises the implication of a promise to pay, one that may be binding.[88]   It seems clear that the information has been fully communicated before the user by the offeree, with its implied promise;  but the legal privilege of making such use was clearly conditional on the making of a promise to pay. Although the offeror's act was completed long before the return promise, it was legally operative to create the privilege of user simultaneously with the return promise to pay.   This is certainly sufficient as a consideration for the promise.

## § 235.   Past Performance under an Existing Contract does Not Support a Promise of New Compensation

When a valid contract has been made binding one party to render a promised performance for a specified consideration, his rendition of that performance exactly as required by his existing duty is not a sufficient consideration for a promise of more pay by the other party.[89]   The fact that the consideration originally

---

86.   A land broker was denied recovery of his commission on this ground in Warner & Co. v. Brua, 168 N.E. 571, 33 Ohio App. 84 (1929). This should not be followed.   Owens v. Baker, 193 N.E. 778, 48 Ohio App. 347 (1933), appears to be contra.

87.   In Gellert v. Dick, 13 N.E.2d 603, 277 N.Y. 123 (1938), a complaint was sustained because it alleged that "it was agreed between the plaintiff and the defendants at the time of the conveying of said information that  .  .  .  they would pay to the plaintiff a reasonable

commission."   The court held that this alleged a bargain and agreed exchange, not a "past consideration."   Two   judges   dissented. There was no antecedent request for the information.

88.   See:

Ind.—Liggett & M. Tobacco Co. v. Meyer, 194 N.E. 206, 101 Ind.App. 420 (1935).

89.   Such is the general rule, as stated elsewhere in this chapter; but there are cases holding that a promise to pay additional compen-

agreed on was not adequate, measured by the general market, and that the contract was a losing one, does not alter this rule.[90] It cannot be said with any assurance that such facts put a moral obligation on the other party to increase the compensation. Most people in ordinary business would agree that the promisor is morally as well as legally bound to render his promised performance on the terms as originally agreed.

If the foregoing is true, it appears to be equally certain that a new promise of additional compensation should not be enforceable if it is made after the first party has already rendered his promised performance. In such a case, the promisor bargains for nothing and receives nothing in exchange for his promise. He has already received everything before he makes the new promise. The element of agreed exchange, or bargain, is lacking. In addition, the promisee has done nothing in reliance on the new promise, so that the action in reliance doctrine is also inapplicable. There are many cases holding the new promise to be not enforceable.[91]

So, it is held that a promise of added compensation is not binding if it is made after full performance of a building contract by the builder,[92] or after an agent or workman has completed his promised service,[93] or after goods have been delivered in accordance with a contract of sale.[94] After a chattel has been delivered as required by contract, a new promise warranting its soundness or quality is not binding in the absence of new consideration for it. The past delivery of the chattel, without warranty, was complete fulfilment of the contract and the full equivalent of the price paid; that price was not given as a consideration for the warranty promise and is held not to be a sufficient reason for enforcing it.[95] After an agreed sale of a business, a promise by the seller not to compete, made later as an afterthought, is not supported and made enforceable by the past payment of the price by the buyer.[96] When goods have been delivered or services rendered on credit as required by contract,

sation is enforceable if the contractor encounters unforeseen difficulties and costs that could not reasonably be foreseen when the contract was made. The new promise in such cases is the recognition of an already existing moral obligation; and it is made before the return performance is actually rendered.

Conn.—Blakeslee v. Board of Water Com'rs, 139 A. 106, 106 Conn. 642, 55 A.L.R. 1319 (1927).

Md.—Linz v. Schuck, 67 A. 286, 106 Md. 220, 11 L.R.A.,N.S., 789, 124 Am.St.Rep. 481 (1907).

95.   Ind.—Summers v. Vaughan, 35 Ind. 323, 9 Am.Rep. 741 (1871).

Me.—Brawn v. Lyford, 69 A. 544, 103 Me. 362 (1907).

Eng.—Roscorla v. Thomas, 3 Q.B. 234 (1842); Andrew v. Boughey, Dyer, f. 75, p. 23 (6 Edw. 6).

96.   Ark.—Kimbro v. Wells, 165 S. W. 645, 112 Ark. 126 (1914).

such past performance is not sufficient to support a later promise by a third person to guarantee payment by the buyer.[97]   When land has been conveyed exactly as agreed, the price paid in exchange therefor will not support a new promise by the vendor to make up a supposed deficiency, to pay taxes, or to insure.[98]

Where the consideration formerly paid was grossly inadequate, the courts will be astute to find some additional element of fraud, mistake, or undue influence, on the basis of which a legal duty sufficient to support an express promise may be found.[99]   If no such element is found, however, and no legal duty already exists, the case will be very rare in which the community would generally recognize a moral obligation to pay additional compensation.[1]

## § 237.   Ratification of a Contract Made by a Married Woman

At common law, a married woman was held to have no capacity to bind herself by contract.  This grew out of the mores of ancient times in which wives were treated as practically the slaves of their husbands.  The general theory was such that the courts said that the woman's contract was "absolutely void," differentiating it from the contract of an infant, which was described as "voidable."  This led to the question whether the woman's new promise, made after acquiring capacity to contract by widowhood or divorce, to perform what she had previously promised was binding.

It was held in England that forbearance to bring suit on the married woman's promise was not a sufficient consideration for her new promise, since that previous promise was legally void, as the community must have known it to be.[7]   Modern courts have no quarrel with this decision; but nothing was said about moral obligation or past consideration.  In a much later case, this was made a ground of distinction; and the woman's moral obligation to perform her original promise was held to be a sufficient reason for enforcement of her new ratifying promise.[8]   The distinction between "void" and "voidable," however, had much influence in leading most of the courts of the United States to

7.   In Loyd v. Lee, 1 Str. 94 (1718), the court held that the forbearance to sue on a promissory note given by a married woman was not a sufficient consideration for her promise to pay it, made after she became a widow.  The reason given was that the note was "absolutely void."  The report does not state, however, why the note was void; and a distinction might well be taken between a note that was void solely because of coverture and one that was void for lack of consideration.  In the latter case there would not be such a moral obligation as would support the new promise.  A distinction such as this was taken in Lee v. Muggeridge, 5 Taunt. 36 (1813).

8.   Eng.—Lee v. Muggeridge, 5 Taunt. 36 (1813).

a different decision. They were further influenced by the unwillingness of a considerable majority of them to hold that an antecedent moral obligation is a sufficient "past consideration" for a promise. The more generally applied American rule, therefore, has been that a ratifying promise made by a woman after acquiring capacity by reason of widowhood or divorce is not enforceable unless there is a new and sufficient consideration.[9]

Statutes have very generally, though not everywhere and in all cases, given to married women the same capacity to make contracts that they would have if unmarried; so that the problem of ratification has become of comparatively little importance. It may be said, however, that the distinction between "void" and "voidable" is not in itself a sufficient reason for refusing enforcement of the new promise. The actual usage and application of the two terms are overlapping and confused. The prevailing notions of general welfare and policy may once have been such as to justify refusal to enforce the ratifying promise by a woman, while enforcing such a promise in the cases of infancy, fraud, statute of limitations and bankruptcy. A time arrived when these notions became less convincing and finally became almost wholly non-existent. The reasons for the older rule of law having ceased to exist, the rule itself would no doubt have been entirely swept away by judicial action, except for the fact that the legislatures gave married women contracting capacity and made subsequent ratification unnecessary.

In some cases, doubt was expressed as to whether a married woman was under any moral obligation to perform her contractual promises.[10] When the common law denied her any contracting capacity, enabled her husband to acquire full ownership of her personal property, and gave to him complete control of the income of her real property, it certainly made performance by her an extremely difficult matter. Also, in some cases, the husband was legally bound to pay the bill. These facts may well explain why a ratifying promise was generally held unenforceable. In a number of jurisdictions, however, if there was a consideration given in exchange for the married woman's promise, it was held to be sufficient reason to enforce a ratifying promise, a moral obligation to keep her promise being thought to exist.[11]

## § 239. The Rule Stated by the Reporters of Wennall v. Adney

In an often quoted note by the reporters of an English case,[23] it is said: "An express promise, therefore, as it should seem, can

11.   N.Y.—Goulding v. Davidson, 26 N.Y. 604 (1863).

Eng.—Lee v. Muggeridge, 5 Taunt. 36 (1813), promise by married woman to repay money advanced at her request to her son.

23.   Eng.—Wennall v. Adney, 3 Bosanquet & Puller 249 (1802).

only revive a precedent good consideration which might have been enforced at law through the medium of an implied promise, had it not been suspended by some positive rule of law; but can give no original right of action if the obligation on which it is founded never could have been enforced at law, though not barred by any legal maxim or statute provision."

The wording of this note is subject to criticism from many angles. It is never a "consideration" that is enforced or revived. It is the new promise that is enforced and that can be said to "revive" a previously existing duty. Further, the new promise is often enforced even though there was no previously enforceable duty of any kind, whether "through the medium of an implied promise" or otherwise. Also, it is enforced in cases where the previously enforceable duty was not enforceable by virtue of any "implied promise;" it might, indeed, have been itself created by an express promise. Again, it is enforced in cases where no antecedent duty, since barred by statute or maxim, was ever recognized. Thus, it appears that the quoted statement is not sufficiently inclusive; there are express promises that are enforceable, even though some of the stated requirements do not exist.

On the other hand, the quoted statement may induce the belief that wherever a duty would have been recognized and enforced but for some "legal maxim," a new express promise will be enforced. So understood, the statement includes too many new promises. For example, if A promises to make a Christmas gift of $100. to B, it may be said that the promise is unenforceable by virtue of the "legal maxim" that requires a sufficient consideration. But a new express promise by A to B to perform his previous promise is no more enforceable than was the original promise. The rule that an informal promise without consideration is not enforceable is as much a "legal maxim" as is the rule that an infant's promise is not enforceable.

There are many cases, including those involving the ratification of promises by infants, in which a past transaction (generally creating some moral obligation) has been held to be a sufficient reason for enforcing a new promise, even though previously there never had been an enforceable legal obligation.[24] It is true that the new promise often recreates an obligation that was once enforceable; but also it often creates a legal obligation when one never before existed.[25]

25. Chief Justice Gibson stated the matter more soundly in Kennedy v. Ware, 1 Pa. 445, 44 Am.Dec. 145 (1845), when he said that the moral obligation doctrine was intended for cases in which "the promisor has received actual benefit, but is protected from liability by some statute or stubborn rule of law." This does not require that there should once have been a legal obligation that has since been barred.

334

Statutes against usury may expressly declare the contract of the borrower to be void; yet a new promise to repay the money lent is enforceable. The statute does not "suspend" a previous obligation; it prevents one from being created by the express contract. Nor is it the statute that prevents the law from implying a promise; no promise is reasonably to be implied that is different in terms from those of an express promise that covers the whole ground.[26] It is true that the law may at times disregard an express promise and create a non-contract duty that is different; but this is not by a process of inference or implication.

When a debt is discharged in bankruptcy, it is a statute that bars the previous remedy; but the existing facts would never have justified the implication of a promise had there been no bankruptcy law. The debtor's express promise would have controlled.

The enforceability of the new promise cannot be made to depend upon the distinction between void and voidable, if we make that distinction itself depend upon whether or not the obligor has power of ratification. Begging the question never proves anything and never guides a court to the proper decision.

The learned reporters, Bosanquet and Puller, did not themselves beg the question. Instead, they used the very method that we must now use and must continue to use. They made a comparative inductive study of the past decisions and drafted a generalization therefrom. The very form in which they drew it shows that it was a tentative rule; "as it should seem" are the words by which they introduce it. It was their Restatement, based upon such experience as they had; and it has been a working rule that has considerably influenced further growth of the law.[27] It helped to prevent the repetition of the loose doctrine that a moral obligation is always a sufficient consideration; but it could not stop the social forces that underlie that doctrine. It, too, is a working rule that works, within limits. It is necessary now, just as it was with the learned reporters and all their predecessors, to restate the rules of law in the light of

26. In Goulding v. Davidson, 26 N. Y. 604 (1863), the court justly criticises the rule drafted by the two reporters, saying: "This remark is strictly true as to a promise founded on the contract alone; but the case of usurious loans, which the borrower will be held to pay upon a subsequent promise, shows that when, behind the void contract, there is a sufficient consideration, it will sustain the subsequent promise.

27. The rule of the reporters was quoted with approval in the leading case of Eastwood v. Kenyon, 11 Adol. & El. 438 (1840).

further collected experience. Sometimes, and perhaps here, the best we can do is to review that experience, without attempting any general and all-inclusive restatement.[28]

28. The American Law Institute in its Restatement, Contracts, secs. 85–89, drafts several limited rules as to cases in which a new promise, induced by some "past consideration" will be enforced. These, too, are good working rules. But if the Institute means to assert that they include all the cases in which such new promises have been enforced in the past, and that in the future no such promises should be enforced unless they are included within these "restated" rules, its assertion is erroneous.

# TOPIC D

# FORMAL CONTRACTS

---

## CHAPTER 10

### CONTRACTS UNDER SEAL—RECOGNIZANCES

---

## § 240. Formality and Mystery in Contract Law—Seals

The organization of human society is in constant evolution. In order to get the safety and comfort that are attainable by living and acting in a large group, men develop some degree of uniformity of conduct. This uniformity can, in its earlier stages, be described as "folkways," more or less unconscious in character. Later, men become conscious of this uniformity, accept it as necessary and beneficial, and in various ways penalize nonconformity. We then have a system of opinion and conduct that may be described as the "mores," expressed, as time goes on, in the form of rules of morality and rules of law. These, too, are in constant process of variation.

In all systems of law that are known to mankind, one of the most important parts is the group of rules governing the performance and enforcement of promises. Men must indeed be able to foresee and rely upon the conduct of others even in the absence of voluntary promises made by them; this is evidenced by the rules that we call the law of torts and the law of crimes. But another immense field of human conduct is the field of contract.

Men make promises, leading others to expect special types of conduct on the part of the particular promisor; and the survival and comfort of any group of men have been found to require the keeping of promises—at least, the keeping of the most of them under most circumstances. The keeping of promises is in the folkways and mores of mankind; and in the vast majority of cases they are kept and performed without thought of breach or necessity of enforcement. The sanction of no trust in the future is sufficient.

Not all promises, however, are required by the mores to be kept and performed; and our rules of contract law do not so require. Society, acting through its courts and other officers, does not always apply its enforcing power against a promise breaker. In order that we may rely with assurance and safety, we must know when the power of society will be so applied. We must know the factors that are operative to induce societal enforcement. These factors are many and complex. They change with time and place. Knowledge of them is not a simple matter.

One of the vitally important factors is the form in which a promise is made and expressed. In the early history of a legal system, this factor overweighs all others. The formalities of all kinds of procedure loom large in the eyes of ignorance and inexperience. In the course of time, their relative importance diminishes; but even now they play a considerable role and they render a useful service.

In earlier centuries, men who feared ghosts were asked to swear by the ghosts of their ancestors. In making promises, those who feared and worshiped an awful Deity pledged their faith, or called God to witness, or made the sign of the cross. The small boys of today no doubt feel the weight of an awful sanction when they say "I cross my heart to die."

It is in part, at least, as a survival of these awe-inspiring ceremonies, that we have today a few instances of the formal contract—the transaction whose operative effect depends upon the form of its execution or the ceremony of its making. The principal one of these is the contract under seal.[1] Another that deserves a short discussion is the recognizance.

The present author has made no attempt to determine the origin or to trace the history of seals, public or private, except so far as is necessary to the statement of our existing law. Some account by earlier writers will be quoted in the footnote below.[2]

---

1. See Frederick E. Crane, "The Magic of the Private Seal," 15 Col. L.R. 24 (1915), also in Selected Readings in the Law of Contracts.

2. Deed (Defined in Termes de la Ley, 149–152). Translated in the first American edition from the London edition of 1721.

"Deed is a writing sealed and delivered, to prove and testify the agreement of the party whose deed it is to the thing contained in the

## § 241. What is a Seal—Its Attachment or Adoption

For some period in its history, a seal appears to have consisted of a bit of wax or other adhesive substance, attached to the

deed; as a deed of feoffment is a proof of the livery of seisin, for the land passes by the livery of seisin; but when the deed and the delivery are joined together, that is a proof of the livery, and that the feoffor is contented that the feoffee shall have the land.

"All deeds are either indented, whereof there are two, three, or more parts, as the case requires; of which the feoffor, grantor, or lessor hath one; the feoffee, grantee, or lessee another; and peradventure some other body a third, etc. Or else they are poll deeds, single, and but one, which the feoffee, grantee, or lessee hath, etc. And every deed consists of three principal points, (without which it is no perfect deed to bind the parties) namely, writing, sealing, and delivery.

"1. By writing is shewed the parties' names to the deed, their dwelling places, their degrees, the thing granted, upon what considerations, the estate limited, the time when it was granted, and whether simply or upon condition, with other such like circumstances. But whether the parties to the deed write in the end their names, or set to their marks, (as it is commonly used) it matters not at all, (as I think) for that is not meant, where it is said, that every deed ought to have writing.

"2. Sealing is a farther testimony of their consents to what is contained in the deed; as it appears in these words, In witness whereof, etc., or to such effect, always put in the latter end of deeds, without which words the deed is insufficient.

"And because we are about sealing and signing of deeds, it shall not be much amiss here to shew you, for antiquity's sake, the manner of signing and subscribing deeds

in our ancestors the Saxons' time, a fashion differing from that we use now, in this, that they to their deeds subscribe their names, (commonly adding the sign of the cross), and in the end did set down a great number of witnesses, not using at that time any kind of seal; and we at this day, for more surety, both subscribe our names, (though that be not very necessary) and put to our seals, and use the help of witnesses besides.

"That the former fashion continued absolute until the time of the conquest by the Normans, whose manners by little and little at the length prevailed amongst us; for the first sealed charter in England, is thought to be that of king Edward the Confessor, to the abbey of Westminster, who being educated in Normandy, brought into the realm that and some other of their fashions with him. And after the coming of William the Conqueror, the Normans liking their own country custom, (as naturally all nations do) rejected the manner that they found here, and retained their own, as Ingulphus the abbot of Croiland, who came in with the conquest witnesses, saying: "The Normans do change the making of writings (which were wont to be firmed in England with crosses of gold, and other holy signs) into an impression of wax, and reject also the manner of the English writing." Howbeit, this was not done all at once, but it increased and came forward by certain degrees; so that first and for a season the king only or a few other of the nobility, used to seal; then the noblemen, for the most part, and none other. Which thing a man may see in the history of Battle-Abby, where Richard Lucie, chief justice of England, in the time of king Henry II, is reported have blamed a mean subject for

parchment or paper on which was written the promise or terms of agreement.[3] It was melted or otherwise softened and pressed firmly upon the document so that it would stick there, at the

that he used a private seal, whereas that pertained (as he said) to the king and nobility only.

"At which time also, as J. Rosse notes it, they used to engrave in their seals their own pictures and counterfeits, covered with a long coat over their armours. But after this, the gentlemen of the better sort took up the fashion, and because they were not all warriors, they made seals engraven with their several coats or shields of arms, for difference sake, as the same author reports. At length about the time of Edward III seals became very common; so that not only such as bear arms used to seal, but other men also fashioned to themselves signets of their own devices, some taking the letters of their own names, some flowers, some knots and flourishes, some birds and beasts, and some other things, as we now yet daily see used.

"Some other manners of sealings besides these have been heard of among us; as namely, that of king Edward III, by which he gave to Norman the Hunter,

> The hop and the hop town,
> With all the bounds upside
> down:
> And in witness that it was
> sooth,
> He bit the wax with his fore
> tooth.

"The like to this was shewed me by one of my friends in a loose paper, but not very anciently written, and therefore he willed me to esteem of it as I thought good. It was as follows:

" 'I, William, King, give to thee Plowden Royden, my hop and hop lands, with all the bounds up and down, from heaven to earth, from earth to hell for thee and thine to dwell, from me and mine, to thee and thine, for a bow and a broad arrow, when I come to hunt upon yarrow. In witness that this is sooth, I bite this wax with my tooth, in the presence of Magge, Maud, and Margery, and my third son Henry.'

"Also that of Alberick de Vere, containing the donation of Hatfield, to which he affixed a short black-hafted knife like an old half-penny whittle, instead of a seal: with divers such like.

"But some peradventure will think, that these were received in common use and custom, and that they were not the devices and pleasures of a few singuler persons: such are no less deceived than they that deem every charter and writing, that hath no seal annexed, to be as ancient as the conquest; whereas indeed sealing was not commonly used till the time of king Edward III, as hath been already said.

"3. Delivery, though it be set last, is not the least; for after a deed is written and sealed, if it be not delivered, all the rest is to no purpose.

"And this delivery ought to be done by the party himself, or his sufficient warrant; and so it will bind him whosoever wrote or sealed the same: and by this last act the deed is made perfect, according to the intent and effect of it; and therefore, in deeds, the delivery is to be proved, etc.

"Thus you see, writing and sealing, without delivery, is nothing to purpose: sealing and delivery, where there is no writing, work nothing: and writing and delivery without sealing, make no deed. Therefore they all ought jointly to concur to make a perfect deed."

Accounts of the origin and development of seals may be found in Wigmore, Evidence, ed. 3, vol. 7, § 2161; and Jeaffreson, A Book About Lawyers, vol. 1, pp. 21–24 (1867 ed.).

same time being given some significant form of motto or device. That it had to consist of wax is asserted by Lord Coke who said, "Sigillum est cera impressa, quia cera sine impressione non est sigillum." [4] The fact that this is an excellent example of begging the question, pompously concealed by putting it into a dead language, should not cause us to overlook the fact that Coke's statement may have been true. Indeed, Coke had so great an influence over English law that by merely stating it in Latin he could make it true for a century or more.

Coke's chief emphasis, however, lies in his assertion that the wax must bear an impression. Very often, this impression was made by pressing on the softened wax with a signet ring so made as to leave a legible device stamped upon the wax, a device that was made comparatively durable by the hardening of the wax. [5] This device might be the coat of arms, or shield, of the obligor. It might be other things as well. The old lexicographer reports that the king could give efficacy to the wax by biting it with his "foretooth." Possibly it would have been a very bold man, in the time of Edward III, who would have attempted to follow the royal example; but now that kings are not so awe-inspiring, the method could no doubt be safely used.

Customs come and customs go. Sealing with wax came in; and sealing with wax has gone out. Only a few centuries ago, writing itself was a mystery to the common citizen. The preparation of a written parchment, the dropping of the melted wax, the impression of a noble device by means of a costly ring of gold and precious stones, the solemn act of delivery to the obligee: it is no wonder that church and state lent their enforcing sanctions to so formidable an array of acts. They were formalities to be sure; but formalities were once of heavy import; and the fact that the word itself now meets disrespect and ridicule shows the extent to which custom changes with time.

In early American history, the art of writing became known to all; but coats of arms and rings of gold and jewels were rare indeed. Common citizens acquired title to land and executed deeds of conveyance. Documentary forms were printed, with blank spaces for names and places and description. A dotted line indicated the place for signature; and at its end was printed the word "seal", or the letters "L.S." (locus sigilli), to indicate the place where wax was to be dropped and impressed. [6] In many

4.  3 Inst. 169; quoted by Kent in Warren v. Lynch, 5 Johns. 239 (N.Y., 1810).

5.  That sealing with a signet ring was practiced in early Biblical times, see Genesis, 38, 18; Esther, VIII, 8, 10.

6.  Held sufficient in Loraw v. Nissley, 27 A. 242, 156 Pa. 329 (1893), even though there was no witnessing clause that referred to a seal.

thousands of cases, no wax was attached. Sometimes the grantor put a scrawl with his pen around the word "seal" or the printed letters "L.S." Should such documents be denied the intended effect for the lack of "cera impressa"? There were indeed cases holding that these documents were not sealed instruments; sometimes, however, in order that the plaintiff might win his case rather than lose it. The simple form of action called "assumpsit" could not be used to enforce a sealed contract; to sustain the plaintiff's action in that form, the court might hold that the document bearing no wax was not "under seal." [7]

Since matters of remedy and procedure are determined by the law of the forum and not by the law of the place where a contract is made, an action on an instrument bearing the word "seal" in parentheses has been held barred by the statute of limitations applicable to unsealed contracts if by the law of the forum such an instrument is regarded as not "under seal," even though in the State of execution it is regarded as "under seal" with a longer period of limitations allowed.[8] It seems clear, however, that the question whether what is on the face of an instrument makes it an instrument "under seal" is one of substantive law and not of remedy or procedure.[9]

That such deeds of conveyance, long relied on and in common use, should be held invalid was not to be endured. Statutes were passed validating them, and providing that a pen scrawl, the word "seal" written or printed, the letters of mystery "L. S.," should be effective as a seal.[10] Even without the aid of statute, some of the courts were wise enough to recognize new custom and to hold that documents so executed should have their intended validity as deeds of conveyance or as sealed contracts.[11]

In executing a formal contract, the local custom and the local statute must be known and followed. It may be said that in general a document will be held to be under seal if it appears on the face of it that the party executing it intended it to be so. Among the forms of seal that are in use in most of the states are wax, a gummed wafer,[12] an impression in the paper itself,[13]

7. So held in Warren v. Lynch, 5 Johns. 239 (1810, N.Y.). On the other hand, an action of "covenant" would not lie on such an instrument. Andrews v. Herriot, 4 Cow. 508 (1925, N.Y.).

The law of New York as to sealed instruments, both statutory and judicial, has had a very chequered career. See Crane, "The Magic of the Private Seal," 15 Col.L.R. 24, Selected Readings in Contracts, 598 (1915); Lloyd, "Consideration

and the Seal in New York," 46 Col.L.R. 1 (1946). The N. Y. Civil Practice Act, § 342, now provides: "Except as otherwise expressly provided by statute, the presence or absence of a seal upon a written instrument hereafter executed shall be without legal effect."

12. These wafers vary in size, are generally red in color, and may have a perfectly plain surface. In the case of corporations, the red wafer and the paper beneath it

the word "seal," [14] the letters "L.S." (signifying "locus sigilli"),[15] a pen scrawl.[16] Sometimes it has been held that the newer of these forms are not effective as a seal unless there is a witnessing clause stating that the document is under seal.[17] It has been held also, that a document is under seal if there is a witnessing clause that says that it is, even though there is nothing attached to or impressed in the paper itself.[18] This goes farther than other courts will go. The New York court held that it is not enough that an instrument says that it is sealed, or that the parties intended it to be a sealed instrument; there must be something on the document itself—a word, a scrawl, a wafer, or an impression—that is put there, or adopted after it is put there, with intent that it shall operate as a seal.[19]

It has been sometimes thought that one purpose of a seal is to identify the party executing the instrument, thereby authenticating it as his very "act and deed." A waxen seal impressed by the device borne by a signet ring does in fact serve such a purpose. So too did the imprint of the king's foretooth, as would also a thumb print. But, even in early days, many seals that were held to be effective could serve no such purpose. An instrument could be effectively sealed by using the seal of another person; and many persons executing a document together could adopt a single seal as the seal of each and all.[20] Of course, wax or wafer bearing no device can identify nobody; and the same is true of the printed or typed "seal" and "L.S."

The fact that a document bears a seal on its face is not proof that the seal was attached or adopted by the signer or named obligor. The seal may be of such a character that its presence is evidential of attachment or adoption, the weight of such evidence varying with the circumstances. It may be enough to establish the fact prima facie; but it is always a fact to be proved; and relevant testimony of all kinds is admissible to disprove it.[21] One man can not bind another by attaching a seal without authority any more than he can bind him by forging his signature.

### § 243. Signature as Part of a Sealed Instrument

If an instrument is properly sealed and delivered by the party to be bound by it, the fact that it does not bear his signature does not affect its validity and legal operation. This was expressly held in several decisions at common law.[27] This is easily understandable when we bear in mind the fact that for centuries after sealed instruments were in effective use comparatively few people could write. Sealing and delivery were the operative facts.

are often given an impression bearing the corporate name and the word "seal." The wafer may bear other devices; and it has been held that an ordinary revenue stamp may be affixed as a seal. Van Bokkelen v. Taylor, 62 N.Y. 105 (1875).

Now that practically every one can write and can sign his name, the signature of the obligor is universally expected; and few persons would accept and act in reliance on a document that is not signed.

## § 244. What Constitutes Delivery of a Sealed Instrument

A contract under seal or other sealed instrument does not become operative as such until the party executing it does some overt act indicating that he intends it to be immediately operative. This act is called "delivery." In the great majority of cases, delivery takes place by the obligor's putting the instrument into the possession of the obligee or of some third person as agent of the obligee. There are cases, however, in which it was held that an effective delivery had taken place in spite of the fact that the document had not come into the possession of the obligee or his agent. In all of them the obligor had done an act indicating an intention that the sealed instrument should be immediately effective.

A leading case decided in the House of Lords supplies a good illustration of this.[28] The plaintiff employed an agent to obtain a policy of insurance on a ship. The agent obeyed instructions and caused the defendants to execute the policy. The defendants charged the premium to the agent personally; and he collected the amount of it from the plaintiff. The policy itself, however, remained in the office of the secretary of the defendants. A month later, the defendants demanded payment of the premium by the agent, who failed to pay. Several months later the ship was lost. The court held that the insurance policy was operative and enforceable. The defendants had signed and sealed the instrument and set it aside for manual delivery when called for. Also, they had treated the premium as paid by charging it to the personal account of the agent. The plaintiff had reason to believe that he was insured against loss. The court held that, although no manual delivery to another person had taken place, the defendants had manifested an intention to make the instrument at once operative and that this satisfied the requirement of "delivery."

Cases like the foregoing indicate that the operative fact is overt action by the obligor expressing an intention to make the sealed document at once operative and justifying the obligee in relying upon it.[29] The fact that this overt action is usually a manual delivery of the instrument has caused the courts to say that it is not operative until it is "delivered." They do not abandon the word when they hold that another mode of expression is effective; instead, they merely stretch the word "delivery" so as to include facts other than a manual transfer of possession.[30]

---

28.  Eng.—Xenos v. Wickham, L.R.
2 H.L. 296 (1867).

The manual transfer of possession of a document to another person as a mere custodian or agent for the one making the transfer is not an operative delivery. Such a custodian or agent holds subject to the instructions of his principal. A subsequent delivery by the custodian or agent is operative if made in accordance with the principal's instructions and not otherwise.[31]

Signing and sealing an instrument are not sufficient to make it operative; nor does it necessarily become operative on the day that it is dated. The final operative act is "delivery," as that term is explained above. This has been held since very early times.[32] The obligor's intention to make delivery may be expressed otherwise than by words; but otherwise colorless acts may be given operative meaning by the words that accompany them.[33] Mere intention alone, not overtly expressed, is not enough to effect a "delivery." [34]

The delivery of a document incomplete in some essential part is not effective. It was often held that the filling of the material blanks after delivery of a deed did not make it effective.[35] A new delivery after the filling of the blanks is, of course, an effective delivery.[36] Even without a new delivery, the conduct of the obligor or grantor may be such as to make the instrument effective by estoppel, in the hands of an innocent holder for value.[37]

### § 247. Delivery "In Escrow", or as an Escrow [47]

It was stated in the preceding section that delivery may be made to a third person, other than the grantee or promisee. We are now to deal with cases in which the delivery is made to a third person (not merely as a custodian or agent for the one so delivering) with instructions to deliver the instrument to the grantee or promisee only on the performance of some specified condition. This is now generally described as a delivery "in escrow."

What is an escrow and what is its legal operation? Literally the word means merely a writing,[48] without regard to signing, sealing, or delivery. In Anglo-American law, however, it has been most frequently used in connection with writings under seal. In the period of the Year Books the question most litigated was put in this form: Is the writing the grantor's "deed" or is it merely an "escrow"? It would appear in the light of this antithesis that an escrow is not a deed at all; and numberless statements to that effect have been handed down to us.[49]

When we consider, however, the cases in which the term escrow has been used, and observe the varieties of legal operation that have been given to writings in the various stages of their career, it will be observed that the courts do not make that legal operation depend upon the term of description used. Instead, they determine the legal operation first, and then choose a descriptive term that seems to justify it. The document may be operative in one way and not in another; in holding it to be operative in the one way, a court will call it a deed, and in holding it to be inoperative in the other way will call it an escrow.

It has been supposed that a distinction could be taken between a delivery to a depositary *as the deed* of the grantor to be delivered over on condition, and a delivery *as an escrow* to take effect as a deed on the performance of a condition. It was supposed that the former was a deed and that if the grantee should get possession by any means, he could maintain action thereon and the grantor could not plead *non est factum;* but otherwise in the latter case.[50] This was properly disapproved by Kent,[51] and is not a sound distinction. The document is the grantor's deed in either case, its future legal operation being alike dependent on fulfillment of the condition.[52]

An escrow is a written document, delivered to a person other than the grantee or obligee named therein, in its final and completed form, the depositary being instructed to hold it, for the benefit of the grantee or obligee and not merely as a custodian for the grantor,[53] and to deliver it to the grantee or obligee on the fulfillment of some condition not specified in the document itself. Such a document is often a deed of conveyance, a contract under seal, a bond, a note, or a release. The character of the instrument as an escrow is fixed by the provision for performance of a condition, and the word "escrow" is not at all necessary.[54]

### § 249.  Legal Operation of a Delivery in Escrow before Performance of the Condition

Where a document has been delivered as an escrow the parties almost always contemplate a second delivery in the future, and a second delivery is in fact generally made by the depositary. Out of this fact arose the idea that a conditional delivery or a delivery as an escrow could not be made to the grantee himself, because in such case it is evident that no second delivery is contemplated. Hence also arose the notion that the document does not "take effect" until the second delivery, inasmuch as it is expressly made clear that there are certain "effects" that it shall not have at the first delivery. The document is said not to be a contract; or if it be a deed of conveyance it is said that title does not pass. Such loose general statements are due to a failure to analyze such concepts as "title" and "contract" and to observe that legal effects are complex and not simple. The confusion of mind and of statement is no less today than in the time of the Year Books.

The ordinary function of an escrow or of a conditional delivery of a document is to give security to both parties to an existing transaction. The grantor or promisor wishes to retain a certain property interest or not to assume immediate duties and liabilities, and at the same time to be assured of getting certain values in return. The grantee or promisee wishes ample security that if he gives those return values, he will actually be invested with the property that he covets or with the contract rights for which he bargains. In order that each party shall have this security it is necessary for society to take notice of the escrow transaction and to indicate that societal action will be in large measure determined thereby. That is what is meant by "legal relations," by saying that a document "takes effect" or is legally "operative," and by such terms as "property interest" and "contract rights."

The courts did not hesitate to make the escrow subserve the economic function for which it was designed. They gave it exactly the effects that the parties desired. They made it irrevocable and binding from the time of the first delivery; they made it immediately enforceable, however, only in futuro and conditionally. On subsequent fulfillment of the condition, they gave it immediate and full enforcement without any second delivery.

First, it is undisputed that after delivery as an escrow the grantor or promisor has no power of revocation.[65] The grantee or promisee is in a position of legal immunity or safety. This shows that the transaction has no longer the status of an unaccepted offer. The delivery of the document to the grantee will be specifically compelled after fulfillment of the condition, even though before its fulfillment the grantor has instructed the depositary not to deliver it; [66] and the document is operative, even though the grantor has made a conveyance to a third person,[67] or has regained possession of the document and destroyed it.[68]

Secondly, no new delivery by the depositary to the grantee is necessary to invest the latter with all the legal relations intended by the parties as the final consummation of the transaction. Upon fulfillment of conditions the grantee will be regarded as owner as completely as if the document had been delivered formally into his hands.[69] If the escrow is a promissory document, action will lie thereon, if all conditions are fulfilled, without any delivery into the hands of the promisee.[70] Even though a second delivery by or on behalf of the grantor or obligor has become impossible by reason of death or coverture before the fulfillment of the conditions, upon such fulfillment the document will be made fully operative.[71] To effect this result, the doctrine of "relation back" was appealed to, Chancellor Kent saying that "justice requires a resort to a fiction."[72] It can and should be described in more realistic fashion, recognizing that the property interest is divided between grantor and grantee, and that contract rights may be future and conditional in this case as in others.

Thirdly, it has been and should be held, in cases where a deed of conveyance is delivered as an escrow, or to the grantee on condition, that the grantee has a property interest before any second delivery, an interest that is subject to execution by his creditors [73] and one that includes a power of making conveyances to others.[74] Doubtless these in some measure depend upon the character of the conditions upon which the escrow was delivered. Possession, with its complex jural relations, may be vested in either party as they may agree.[75] If possession is still in the grantor, he will usually be the one entitled to rents and profits.[76] If the subject matter is land, the grantee has an interest that will descend to his heir.[77] It is beyond the scope of this article to consider in detail this division of the property interest or to discuss apparent conflicts in the decisions.

The vitally important and operative fact is not a second delivery of the document, whether a conveyance or a contract; it is the fulfillment of the condition. As stated above, such fulfillment makes the document fully operative without any new delivery; and it is likewise true that a new delivery without fulfillment of the condition is not operative at all except in cases where subsequent reliance by an innocent purchaser may create an estoppel.[78] Of course, the party who delivers an instrument in escrow has power to waive the condition on which it was to become fully operative and can validate a wrongful delivery by the escrow holder by a ratification thereof.[79]

## § 252.  Consideration Not Necessary for a Sealed Promise

The most important difference between a formal and an informal contract at common law lies in the fact that a formal contract can be made operative by sealing and delivery. Neither a consideration, as now defined, nor subsequent action in reliance is necessary in order to make the sealed promise enforceable.[97] Formal contracts, including those under seal, were recognized and enforced by the common law for some centuries before the doctrine of consideration was invented. That doctrine was evolved in the process of recognizing informal contracts, and was the result of the effort to determine what informal promises should be made legally enforceable.

One who has made a promise under seal is often said to be estopped to deny that a consideration was given for his promise. It is said that the seal "imports a consideration," or that it raises

---

79. In Sections 250 and 251 of the complete Treatise will be found a discussion of the "Effect of Deliv- ery to the Promisee Himself, Subject to an Oral Condition" and "What is a Conditional Delivery."

a "conclusive presumption" of a consideration for the promise. For two centuries, at least, in early English law this could not have been true, if the word "consideration" is taken in the sense in which it is now generally used. The succeeding paragraphs will show that it is equally untrue today.[98] Except as otherwise provided by statute, a sealed promise is binding without any consideration; proof that no consideration was given does not show that it is not a binding contract and does not prevent enforcement. If the promisor offers evidence that there was no consideration for the purposes of showing that he is not bound, he must fail of his purpose. It is only in this sense that he may be said to be "estopped" to prove that there was no consideration; [99] this is merely one of the bad uses to which the much abused term "estoppel" is put. It is only in this sense that there is a "presumption" of consideration, a usage that is even worse; for why should a court "presume" the existence of something that is wholly unnecessary and immaterial.

The statement that a seal "imports a consideration" was probably first made by one who used the word "consideration" in the sense of deliberation, a sense that still accords with common usage of English. It may well have been true, once upon a time, that one who sealed and delivered a writing did so only after careful thought and mature deliberation.[1] While that remained

---

**98.** "Specialties—Those formal common-law contracts under seal—were enforced in the absence of an allegation of consideration, not because it was conclusively presumed that they were founded on a consideration, but because consideration was not an essential element to such contracts. Contracts under seal were enforceable at common law because of the formality of their execution, and such contracts were fully recognized and enforced long before the doctrine of consideration appeared in the law." Lacey v. Hutchinson, 64 S.E. 105, 5 Ga.App. 865 (1909), holding, however, that the rule is not applicable to a sealed instrument of a sort unknown to early common law.

**1.** In Sharington v. Strotton, 1 Plowden 298 (7 & 8 Eliz.K.B.), one Andrew Baynton covenanted under seal to stand seized of certain lands to the use of his brother Edward and of others of the same blood, in consideration of his desire that the lands might continue in possession of his blood relatives and of the good will and brotherly love that he bore to Edward and the others. It was argued for the plaintiff that there was no sufficient consideration to validate the conveyance under the statute of uses. Bromley and an apprentice of the Middle Temple argued for the defendant that the following considerations were sufficient to support the covenant to stand seized: (1) affection for the provision of the heirs male of the covenantor; (2) the continuance of the land in his name and blood; (3) brotherly love. In support, they advanced quaint arguments based upon nature, upon scripture, and upon public policy. The court held that these three considerations were sufficient. It was argued further for the defendant that the covenant was itself effective without consideration. Counsel's language is thus reported: "You shall have an action of debt upon this deed, and the con-true, it may well be that sealing and delivery imported (that is, was evidential of) careful consideration and deliberation; but it was of no import whatever in justifying an inference that an agreed equivalent was given in exchange for the promise.

Often, a contract under seal contains an express acknowledgment that a stated consideration has been received; and the obligor is said to be "estopped" by his acknowledgment to deny its truth. Since the sealed promise is a binding contract at common law even though no consideration was given for it, the express acknowledgment is unnecessary to enforcement; and proof of its untruth would not establish invalidity.[2] There is no estoppel preventing the promisor from showing that the acknowledgment is untrue, that a consideration was expressly or impliedly promised, and that it has not been received. If the promised consideration has not been given, the appropriate actions are maintainable to enforce performance or to get damages for its nonperformance. For such a purpose, the sealed acknowledgment does not prevent proof of nonpayment.[3]

Furthermore, the fact that a promise is under seal does not prevent it from being expressly or constructively conditional. It may be conditional upon performance of the agreed consideration. The acknowledgment that this consideration has been received does not prevent proof to the contrary, when the purpose is to show that a condition of the promisor's duty has not been performed, a condition the performance of which is the agreed equivalent of the obligor's promised performance. This proof is not to show that the promise is not binding and irrevocable; its purpose is only to show that the binding promise was expressly or constructively conditional and that the duty of immediate performance would not arise until the condition is performed.

This was not always so at common law. In an action on a sealed promise it was said that "failure of consideration," as well as mere want of consideration, was no defense.[4] These cases

---

sideration is not examinable, for in the deed there is a consideration, viz. the will of the party that made the deed." And again: "Where it is by deed, the cause or consideration is not enquirable nor is it to be weighed, but the party ought only to answer to the deed, and if he confesses it to be his deed, he shall be bound, for every deed imports in itself a consideration, viz. the will of him that made it."

2.   Where by statute a seal has been made only presumptive evidence of a consideration, it has been held

that a sealed option acknowledging the receipt of one dollar could not be invalidated by proof that the dollar had not been paid. Cochran v. Taylor, 7 N.E.2d 89, 273 N.Y. 172 (1937). The decision is correct if the words of the statute are to be taken literally; but it is otherwise if the intent of the legislature was to deprive the seal of its former effect to make a promise enforceable even though made without consideration. Such statutes have generally been interpreted so as to have this latter effect.

even held that fraud was no defense, so that such problems were thrown into equity, where the presently existing law was established. We must remember, however, that "failure of consideration" was once not a good defense in an action on any bilateral contract. The doctrine of implied and constructive conditions was the creation of the nineteenth century.

A promise under seal is binding without any consideration; but this does not mean that the performance promised is not being exchanged for an agreed equivalent. One can bind himself by a sealed promise to give something for nothing; but in vast numbers of cases the parties to a sealed contract intend no such result and make no such agreement. Instead, they mean to effect an exchange of equivalents, just as in the case of informal contracts. If one of the parties will not, or can not, render the performance constituting his side of this exchange, must the other party nevertheless render his performance for nothing by reason of the fact that the contract is under seal? To ask the question is to answer it in the negative.[5]

Suppose that A seals and delivers to B the following instrument: "I O U $100 for money lent, the receipt whereof is hereby acknowledged." Having received the instrument, B intentionally or forgetfully fails to give A any money whatever. When sued on this obligation, can not A prove that no money was actually advanced to him? It may well be that possession of such a document makes out a prima facie case for B. The court might even throw the burden of proving the fact upon the defendant A. But it should never tell A that his offered evidence is immaterial or that he is "estopped" to introduce it. The wording of the instrument shows that A intended to make a unilateral contract; his was the only promise. But it also shows that he intended to exchange his sealed promise for $100 in cash lent; and his duty to pay B is constructively conditional upon the receipt of the cash. The fact that his promise is sealed does not prevent its being thus conditional or prevent proof of the truth. Justice is not as blind as that.

Suppose that two parties execute a sealed building contract, in which A promises to pay $10,000 to B on a specified date and B promises to complete the building by that date. Is A bound to pay even though B does not build? Can B refuse performance and still get judgment for $10,000? Here the agreement under seal is bilateral; and neither promise is expressly conditional on performance by the other. But the duty of each is constructively conditional. The law requires neither party to give something for nothing, not even though both of them have signed, sealed, and delivered.

351

## § 254. Statutory Changes Affecting Sealed Contracts

In a great many states, the common law of sealed instruments has been changed in important respects by legislative action. Some of these changes have been made by those who knew little of common law history and did not well understand the existing legal rules as to formal and informal contracts. They magnified the advantages of the doctrine of consideration and thought it very unjust that a man should be held bound by his promise because of an empty "formality" like a seal. It will not here be attempted to review in detail the statutes of the various states. Two of the more common types of legislation will be discussed.

Half of our states have passed a statute purporting to abolish private seals and to make them wholly inoperative when used.[14] Under such a statute, a written promise under seal has no greater or different legal operation than has a written promise not under seal. Presumably a release under seal has no greater or different effect than has a written unsealed release. Sometimes there is a supplementary statute providing that a written release shall be legally effective, irrespective of absence of consideration for it. Sometimes, also, it is enacted that a promise in writing shall be enforceable unless the promisor proves affirmatively that there was no consideration for it.

A second sort of statute provides that a seal shall be only "presumptive evidence" of a consideration.[15] Under such a statute the burden of going forward with evidence to show the absence of consideration is on the defendant promisor. In default of such evidence by the promisor, judgment will be rendered enforcing the promise, even though the plaintiff neither alleges nor offers proof of a consideration. A statute of this kind may apply only to executory promises and not to releases.[16]

Without doubt the main purpose of such a statute as this is to make a sealed promise unenforceable if there is in fact no consideration for it.[17] But it is to be noted that the statute does not expressly say anything of the kind. Instead of limiting the legal effect of a seal, it gives a new and additional effect to it. The draftsmen of such a statute as this mistakenly supposed, just as many judges have done, that at common law a promise under seal was enforceable for the reason that the seal "imports" a consideration or is "conclusive evidence" of a consideration. Therefore, in order to lessen the importance and effect of the seal, they enacted that it should be not "conclusive" but only "presumptive evidence" of a consideration. This statute gives a new evidential effect to the seal without depriving it of its common law function of making a gratuitous promise enforceable.

The New Jersey court observed the truth of the foregoing, and held that the statute did not invalidate a sealed instrument without consideration if the parties intended it to be operative without any consideration.[18] By a later statute (Pamph. L. 1900, 366), it was further provided that in actions upon a sealed instrument the defendant may plead and prove absence or failure of consideration with the same effect as if the instrument were not sealed.[19]

A statute purporting to abolish seals entirely would seem to make the existence of a contract under seal impossible, and therefore to make inapplicable a statute of limitations fixing a special period of time within which an action on a contract under seal must be brought. This effect would not be produced by a statute that merely declares that a seal shall be only presumptive evidence of a consideration. Such a statute recognizes the fact that a contract under seal is distinct from an informal contract, so that a special statute of limitations would still be applicable. It may perhaps still accord with public policy to allow an action for breach of a covenant in a deed of conveyance for a longer period than that applicable to an informal contract.

## § 256. Unilateral and Bilateral Sealed Contracts

If a deed poll is a unilateral contract it need not be sealed and delivered by the obligee named as such therein; it is the obligation of the obligor alone to the obligee, on which the latter maintains suit. But a deed poll may on its face purport also to contain a reciprocal promise by an obligee.[35] In order to make the instrument operative as his sealed contract also, it is necessary that he should seal and deliver. Nevertheless, it can be proved by parol that he did in fact execute the instrument; and often it seems to be assumed without much proof.[36] A mere expression of assent by parol on the part of such an obligee is ample proof that he made the purported reciprocal promise; but it is

18. **N.J.**—Aller v. Aller, 40 N.J.L. 446 (1878). Judgment was given enforcing a father's gratuitous promise under seal to pay his daughter $312 as a gift.

In New York by express statutory provision, and in New Jersey by judicial construction, the legislation does not apply to releases or to executed contracts and conveyances.

35. If A signs, seals and delivers his promise to pay B $100, the instrument containing nothing else, we have a unilateral contract under seal. Since B is the only party on whom the instrument confers a right, there is no necessity for execution in duplicate.

A sealed instrument that contains reciprocal promises (or reciprocal conveyances) is still sometimes called an *indenture*. This is no doubt due to the fact that formerly such instruments were written in duplicate on a single sheet and then cut into two independent parts with an irregularly indented (serrated) edge on each part. The genuineness of either part can therefore be tested by producing the duplicate "indenture" and fitting the serrated edges together, just as we do in the case of a Yale lock and key.

not the same as sealing and delivery unless the expression of assent is directed toward the execution of the document as well as
to making the promise. An obligee who has made the reciprocal
promise in this manner, without sealing or delivery by him,
could be sued in assumpsit for breach of his promise but not in
covenant as on a sealed contract.[37] We have, in such a case, a
bilateral contract consisting of the sealed promise of A exchanged
for the informal promise of B. There should be no difficulty in
recognizing this possibility, even in a state where seals are given
their common law effects; and the two mutual promises should
be enforced by appropriate procedures. Under modern systems
of procedure, this involves no difficulty.

### § 257.  Contracts in Writing—Effect of Reducing an Agreement to Writing without a Seal

At common law, a contract is not turned into a specialty by
the mere fact that it is in writing and signed by the party to be
charged. Writing differs from word of mouth; and it may properly be described as a "form." But a written contract is not a
"formal" contract in the sense that its form is operative to make
it enforceable without consideration.[38] The statute of frauds
declares that certain kinds of contracts shall not be enforceable
by action, unless they are evidenced by a note or memorandum in
writing and signed; but the statute does not make such a contract enforceable if there is a signed writing without either seal
or consideration.

Other statutes, with specifically limited coverage, may be
found in most of the States providing that certain contracts shall
not be enforceable unless executed in the form of a signed writing.[39] Examples are new promises made without consideration
ratifying a contract made in infancy, or renewing an obligation
barred by statute of limitations or discharged in bankruptcy.

If a contract has been fully reduced to writing, so that it is
said to be "integrated," executed with the expressed intention to
displace and make inoperative all antecedent parol understandings and expressions of agreement, this fact makes the so-called
"parol evidence rule" applicable.[40] For this one purpose, informal contracts are classified as written and unwritten (or
integrated and unintegrated). But the fact is that if two parties
are proved to have made a contract by word of mouth, expressly
providing therein that all antecedent written and oral understandings are displaced and made inoperative, such antecedent

---

38.   So held in the leading case of
Rann v. Hughes, 7 T.R. 350 (1778,
H.L.), overruling earlier cases that
seemed to hold otherwise.

See § 31 for a discussion of what
constitutes a "written contract."

understandings, written as well as oral, are made just as inoperative as if the new agreement were in writing.

A statute, called the "Uniform Written Obligations Act," has been proposed, primarily to create a method by which a person may effectively bind himself by a gratuitous promise, especially in states that have abolished seals and thereby destroyed the ancient common law method. Pennsylvania [41] is the only state that has adopted this statute. It seems beyond question that some such method should be available. Often there are reasonable grounds for desiring and using such a power; and the existence of such a power is not against the public interest. It may be that persons whose claims are based upon a promise having sufficient consideration, or who have materially changed their position in reliance on a gratuitous promise, should have priority over those whose claims are based on a formal writing without consideration or change of position. This is a problem that must be worked out separately. They can be given such priority, if it is thought desirable, without wholly invalidating the other kind of contractual claim. This problem has some complexity. The proposed Uniform Act does not attempt to deal with it. In addition, the wording of the proposed Uniform Act can, without doubt, be improved upon.

## § 258. Bonds and Recognizances

At common law, a bond was a writing, sealed and delivered, binding the obligor to pay a sum of money. If not under seal it was not a "bond."[42] There are debenture bonds, being merely sealed promises to pay money and creating ordinary debts; and penal bonds, in which the obligor is "held and firmly bound," but in which his duty to pay is made expressly dependent upon the nonperformance of some condition. Where seals have been abolished, the absence of a seal does not prevent a document from being so described and enforced. Also, where seals have not been abolished, the absence of a seal from a document which otherwise purports to be a "bond" does not prevent its enforcement as an informal contract.[43]

In a penal bond, after a statement that the obligor is "held and firmly bound in the penal sum of ——— dollars," appears such words as the following: "the condition of this obligation is that if John Doe shall duly appear in court [or, if the obligor shall duly prosecute his appeal; or, if the principal shall truly account for

---

41. The Act as adopted in Pennsylvania, 33 P.S. § 6, is as follows: "A written release or promise, hereafter made and signed by the person releasing or promising, shall not be invalid or unenforceable for lack of consideration, if the writing also contains an additional express statement, in any form of language, that the signer intends to be legally bound."

all moneys entrusted to him; or, other specified performance] then it shall be void, otherwise to be and remain in full force and effect." Words such as these make it appear that the bond creates an immediate indebtedness, subject to be defeated and discharged by a condition subsequent. In its actual effect, however, such is not the case. Such a bond is a valid contract as soon as executed, creating what may properly be described as a primary obligation; but it does not create an immediately enforceable indebtedness. In the case stated above, the appearance of John Doe in court will discharge the obligation of the bond, to which therefore it may properly be called a condition subsequent. But there is no breach of contract by the obligor, and no action will lie against him, unless and until John Doe has failed to appear within the time allowed. His failure to appear is a condition precedent to the obligor's duty to make payment and is a necessary element in a cause of action.[44] The enforcement of penalties and forfeitures, in excess of the harm suffered, is now abhorrent to the law; and it is only in cases in which the harm is not capable of being measured and liquidated in money that the penalty of a bond will be enforced. In other cases, the plaintiff's recovery will not exceed the amount of the injury that he proves. It is necessary for the obligee in the bond to prove that the performance on which the bond was to be void has not been rendered and the extent of his loss caused by such nonperformance. This is discussed more at length, with the authorities, in the chapter on Remedies.[45]

Statutes requiring or otherwise providing for the giving of a bond with surety should generally be held to be substantially complied with if the principal and surety appear personally in court and there make a proper recognizance to the effect that they are held and firmly bound as the statute requires. Such an oral or written acknowledgment, made and recorded in the court, creates exactly the same obligation and affords exactly the same security as would a written bond with the same wording, signed, sealed, and delivered by the parties.[46] The legislative use of the word "bond" may be such as to include a written or unwritten recognizance.

A recognizance is an acknowledgment of indebtedness, made before a court or other magistrate empowered to receive such acknowledgments.[47] It is made for the purpose of creating a binding obligation, thereby giving security for the rendition of some performance, such as the appearance in court of one charged with crime or the furnishing of support to a dependent or the prosecution of a civil action. The debt so acknowledged is therefore usually conditioned to be void if the accused duly appears or the support is furnished or the action brought and properly carried through. There seems to be no reason why an ordinary unconditional debt can not be created by a unilateral recognizance; but recognizances are usually like penal bonds in being conditional.

In early days in England, the recognizance was an oral acknowledgment; and, in the absence of a statutory requirement otherwise, it may still be oral.[48] There were statutes providing for such recognizances before magistrates such as the mayor of a town or fair in which staples or other merchandise was bought and sold. Reference was often made to such a recognizance as a "statute merchant" or a "statute staple." At the present time provisions for the taking of recognizances usually require that the acknowledgment be in writing filed with the court or magistrate or that it shall be properly recorded in its record books.[49] It has sometimes been called a "contract of record."[50]

# TOPIC E

## OPTION CONTRACTS

---

### CHAPTER 11

### VARIETIES OF OPTIONS—THE LEGAL RELATIONS OF THE PARTIES

---

## § 259. Option Contracts Create a Privilege of Choice between Alternatives and a Power to Affect Legal Relations Thereby

There are various kinds of options; in all of them the option-holder has a choice, a power of electing between alternatives.[1] Usually this choice or power of electing is possessed by only one party; but it is possible for both parties to a transaction to have an option. Thus, in the case of any subsisting, unaccepted offer, not yet become a contract, an option is possessed by both parties; the offeree may accept or reject at his option; the offeror has the option of withdrawing his offer before acceptance.

In this case, the exercise of his power by either party at once extinguishes the power of the other.

There are consummated contracts also in which each party has an option; in these too the terms may be such that the exercise of one power will extinguish the other, but sometimes they are not related to each other in this manner.

In most cases, any person who has made a promise in a contract might be said to have an option between performance of his duty and committing a breach of it. His choice of the second alternative is unlawful, however; and the current judicial reme-

---

1. The word "option" is derived from "opto," to choose. The Century Dictionary defines it as, "(1) Choice, wish, preference, election; (2) the power or liberty of choosing, the opportunity of electing, or selecting, an alternative, or one of several lines of conduct."

358

dies are available to prevent and to compensate. He has the legal power to commit a breach but not the legal privilege.[2] There are, indeed, some cases in which there is no possibility of not performing as promised; but, even in these cases, the promisor can express an unconditional repudiation and thus be guilty of a breach.

Again, there are certain option contracts that are made illegal by statutes the object of which is the prevention of gambling in stocks and commodities.[3] These statutes do not make the exercise of his power of choice by an option-holder illegal; they forbid the making of the agreement by which one is given such a power of choice. These statutes have raised some difficult questions and have caused the courts to draw fine distinctions. These questions as to legality will not be dealt with at this point.

Alternative contracts are option contracts, sometimes the promisor having the option of rendering either one of two alternative performances, and sometimes the option between the two being in the promisee. In the one case, the promisor has the power to discharge his duty in either one of two ways;[4] in the other, the promisee has the power to determine which of two performances it shall be the promisor's duty to render.[5] That a promisor has an option between alternatives does not mean that he is privileged not to perform either of them.

In public auctions and in the letting of contracts by means of competitive bidding, the one soliciting the bids usually has the privilege of rejecting all of them. It is possible, however, for him to bind himself by contract to accept the highest bid or the lowest bid, as the case may be. The language sometimes used in

2. The word "option" may be used to connote legal privilege as well as legal power, the choice of either of the alternatives being lawful. This is no doubt the current usage. If so, it is best not to say that one has an option between performance and breach of his contract.

3. See Riordan v. McCabe, 173 N. E. 660, 341 Ill. 506, 83 A.L.R. 512 (1930), and note in 83 A.L.R. 522.

See Century Dictionary defining "option": "(4) On stock, or other exchanges, a privilege, secured by the payment of a certain premium, or consideration, either (1) of calling for the delivery, or (2) of making delivery, of a certain specified amount of some particular stock or produce, at a specified price, and within specified limits of time. The first kind of option is usually designated a *call*, and the second a *put;* but both are sometimes called *futures*."

In its process of full definition, the Century uses all of the following words: privilege, power, liberty, opportunity. These are certainly not synonyms.

4. Debenture bonds often provide that the obligor shall have the option of calling them at a stated price and within stated periods. This creates in the debtor a power to discharge his debt otherwise than by payment at full maturity. See Catholic Order of Foresters v. North Dakota, 271 N.W. 670, 67 N. D. 228, 109 A.L.R. 979 (1937).

auction sales is that the seller binds himself to sell to the highest bidder "without reserve." [6]  To make such a promise binding there must be either a seal or a consideration; it is not enough that the goods are advertised as being offered for sale to the highest bidder.  A seller who thus binds himself by contract gives to each prospective bidder a binding and irrevocable option, a power to consummate the sale by making a bid, conditional on there being no higher bid.

In this chapter we shall consider in some detail the making, the legal operation, and the enforcement of various kinds of lawful option contracts.  This will involve some overlapping with other chapters dealing with irrevocable offers, consideration, and remedies.

### § 260.  Option Contracts may be either Unilateral or Bilateral

An option contract can be either unilateral or bilateral, as those terms are defined in this treatise.  If A pays B $100 cash in return for B's promise to convey Blackacre to A for $5,000 if paid within thirty days, they have made a unilateral option contract.  A has an irrevocable option to buy, good for thirty days; he has made no promise of any kind, being equally privileged to buy or not to buy—his option or freedom of choice is wholly unlimited.[7]  Nevertheless, B's promise is binding because he has been paid $100 for it.

On the other hand, suppose that instead of paying cash A had given to B his promissory note for $100, or his oral promise to pay that sum, in return for B's promise to convey Blackacre to A for $5,000, if paid within thirty days.  The contract thus made is bilateral, each party having made a binding promise.[8]  A has the identical option that he had before; and, as before, it is not revocable by B for thirty days.

### § 261.  Forms of Words Used—"Refusal," "First Right to Buy"

The words in an agreement by which one of the parties is given an option are variable; it requires no set form, and the word "option" need not be used.  It is enough if one party promises a performance on some condition to be performed by the other, but one that the latter does not promise to perform.  If he promises to perform it, he has no option; and if the condition is one that consists of something other than his own action, again he has no option.

The parties are likely to use such phrases as "the right to buy," [9] "the privilege of increasing quantity as much as they may

8.   Vickrey v. Maier, stated and discussed in a succeeding section, is an example of such a bilateral option contract.

desire"; [10] "the option to purchase." They seldom use the word "power," although it is the word that best describes the relation of the option holder to the option giver.[11]

There are certain other terms in common use that may have a different meaning and effect, such as "the refusal," "the first refusal," "the right of pre-emption," "the first right to buy." As in all cases, these must be interpreted in the light of their context and of all surrounding facts. If, in return for $10 paid, A agrees that B shall have "the refusal" of Blackacre for thirty days at $2,000, this is an option contract creating in B the power of creating a right to an immediate conveyance by giving notice within thirty days and by tendering $2,000.[12] If, in return for $10 paid, A merely agrees that if he should wish to sell B shall have the first refusal at $2,000, there is a valid unilateral contract, but it creates no power of acceptance in B, and B has no option.[13] This contract creates in B a right that A shall make no sale of Blackacre without first offering to sell it to B for $2,000.[14] Before making a sale to others, it is A's duty to give B an option.[15] Usage may support us in calling this contract an "option contract;" but if so, it is obvious that those words are being used to describe two very different contracts, one of which creates a power while the other does not. The interpretation and effect are similar, if B is given "the first right to buy" at $2,000. If A afterwards expresses his willingness to sell at the specified price, B at once gets an option and power to consummate the contract.[16] The fact that the owner receives an offer to buy a larger tract, including that covered by the pre-emptive right, and is willing to accept the offer, does not bind him to offer either the larger tract or the smaller one to the holder of such right; nor does it deprive such holder of his right that the limited tract shall not be sold to another without first offering it to him.[17]

A contract that one party shall have the "preference as a purchaser" is specifically enforceable against both the promisor and a purchaser from him with notice, even though no price is named.[18] This makes it the promisor's duty not to sell at any price without first offering the property at that price to the promisee. This is not an option; but the promisor must give the promisee an option before selling. Nor is the promisor's duty terminated by merely making an offer to the promisee to sell to him at a price that is higher than the price at which a sale is subsequently made. The promisee's refusal to buy at that higher price does not extinguish his right to have the preference over other buyers at any lower price.[19]

10. Minn.—Koehler & Hinrichs
Merc. Co. v. Illinois Glass Co., 173
N.W. 703, 143 Minn. 344 (1919).

The condition that is to be performed by the option holder must be agreed upon and expressed with such a degree of certainty as to enable a court to determine what it is and whether or not it has been properly performed. Otherwise the transaction is no more than an agreement to agree, to contract on terms still to be agreed upon.[20] So, it has been held that an agreement saying only that "if the premises are for sale at any time, the lessee shall have the refusal of them" is too uncertain for enforcement. The amount to be paid for the land is not stated and must still be agreed upon.[21] The quoted language may, however, bear the interpretation that the lessor promises that the lessee shall have the refusal of the premises, at the price that may be offered in good faith by a third party, before such offer shall be accepted. Under this interpretation, the contract creates no option to buy; but it gives to the promisee the right that before the owner shall sell to any third party, the lessee shall have an option to buy at the price offered to or offered by that third party.

Consider the following case: One Vickrey subscribed and paid for certain shares in the Maier Packing Co. Later, a written agreement was executed by Vickrey and Simon Maier as follows: Vickrey "agrees that before offering said stock for sale, he will first notify first parties (Maier) and give them the first right to buy the same at the price offered by any bona fide intending purchaser. In consideration of which, said first parties agree and obligate themselves to pay or cause to be paid to second party (Vickrey) a dividend of six per cent per annum on said stock, and that at any time after six months from date hereof, on ninety days notice, they will purchase said stock at the price paid therefor . . . but the party of the second part shall not be obligated to sell said stock at the price paid therefor." Vickrey gave the proper notice of his acceptance within the time specified, and demanded payment from Maier of the price that Vickrey had originally paid for the shares. The court held the contract binding and reversed a judgment for defendant entered in the trial court.[22]

In this case, V had an option to sell to M at the same price previously paid by V. The promise of M to buy it at that price was an irrevocable offer, creating in V a power of acceptance. There was sufficient consideration to make that promise binding and irrevocable, this consideration being the promise of V not to sell to a third party without first offering the shares to M at the price offered by the third party. The contract did not create in M an option to buy. He had no power of acceptance at any price,

22.   Cal.—Vickrey v. Maier, 129 P. 273, 164 Cal. 384 (1913).

by the exercise of which he could compel V to transfer the shares; but he had a legal right that V should give him such an option, before selling to anyone else.[23]

Consider also the following case: The owner of land promised a railroad company that for a period of five years he would accept no offer to purchase made by the Peoria and P. U. R. Co. without first giving written notice thereof to the promisee and giving it the option to purchase for a period of fifteen days at the offered price. This contract created no option in either party. If the named railroad should make an offer the owner of the land was privileged not to accept it, and also not to make any offer to the promisee. But the owner was bound by duty not to accept the offer of the Peoria company without first giving a fifteen day option at the same price to the promisee. In breach of this duty, the owner accepted an offer made by the Peoria company, without giving an option to the promisee. The court held that the promisee was entitled to a decree for specific performance.[24]

## § 262.  Form of Promise Made—Promise to Keep Offer Open

An option contract can be made in either of two ways. First, for example, A can promise under seal, or for a sufficient consideration, to sell and convey property to B for a stated price at B's option, on condition of either notice or actual payment within 30 days. This is a conditional contract to sell;[25] it does not have the form of an offer. Secondly, A can make a formal offer to sell his property to B at a stated price; and, either at the same time or thereafter, A promises B, for a sufficient consideration or under seal, to keep the offer open for 30 days.[26] Here, we have two transactions instead of one—an ordinary offer to sell and a contract not to revoke or to make performance impossible by conveying to a third person.

It has been supposed that these two forms of option agreements are different in their legal operation as well as in their form. The present writer is convinced that their legal operation is identical. The first is in form a contract and not an offer; and yet it creates a power in B that is identical with that created by the offer in the second. By the second, B is given an enforceable right that A shall not revoke or repudiate that is identical with the one that is created in the first. In both, a notice of revocation served on B by A would be a breach of contractual duty, and a cause of action; while in neither one would it deprive B of his power to accept by giving notice or tendering payment as agreed. Such an acceptance after revocation would create a right and duty of immediate performance, enforceable by the usual contract reme-

24.  Ill.—Toledo, P. & W. R. R. v. Brown, 31 N.E.2d 767, 375 Ill. 438 (1941).

dies of damages, restitution, and specific performance. In both cases alike, B's right to specific performance could be blocked by A, by transferring the property to an innocent purchaser for value; this would be so both before and after B gives notice of his acceptance, and without regard to any notice of revocation given by A. Further, even though B knows of a conveyance by A to an innocent purchaser for value, his notice of acceptance given to A would have exactly the same effect in both cases; in neither case would he need to give it in order to maintain an action for damages.

By some courts it has been thought that, in cases of the above second class, the offer can be revoked in spite of the collateral contract that the offer shall be held open for a specified time.[27] Such a revocation is, of course, a breach of the collateral contract; but that contract has been broken and the primary offer is in fact revoked. On this theory, if the holder of an option to buy is notified that the offer is revoked, his subsequent attempt at acceptance is inoperative and no contract of purchase and sale is consummated. The option holder can sue for damages for breach of the promise to hold the offer open; but he cannot get either a judgment for damages or a decree for specific performance as to the wrongfully revoked offer to sell.

In the results actually reached, the above theory is not accepted. The collateral contract to hold the offer open has the effect of holding it open, the result being that the subsequent acceptance consummates a contract of sale, one for the breach of which a judgment for damages will be entered or a decree for specific performance obtained.[28] No doubt this is enforcing a contract that at the moment of acceptance the offeror did not intend to make—mutual assent at that moment was lacking. The courts merely hold that mutual assent at that moment is not required, that the power of accepting the offer still exists in spite of a revocation, that the contract to hold the offer open is self-executing and keeps it open willy-nilly. The result is just; and inconsistent theories can be dropped.[29]

### § 263. Options under Seal or for a Consideration

A unilateral option contract, irrevocable by the option giver, can be made in several ways: First, it can be made by a written promise under seal, delivered to the promisee or his representative.[30] A promise so made is a binding contract at once, enforceable by the same remedies and on the same conditions as are other sealed contracts. A notice of revocation given to the promisee is not effective to destroy the latter's power of accept-

---

30.    N.C.—Thomason v. Bescher, 97 S.E. 653, 176 N.C. 622 (1918).

ance or his contractual rights.[31] The fact that no consideration was given for the option does not make it unenforceable, either at law or in equity.[32]

Secondly, such a contract can be made by a promise for which a consideration is given.[33] This consideration is not made insufficient by the fact that it is a small one. Adequacy of consideration, as judged by general market standards, is no more required here than in other cases. One dollar, actually paid or promised, is sufficient to make the offered promise irrevocable, just as sealing and delivery would.[34] Cases refusing specific enforcement on the ground of inadequacy of this consideration must be disapproved; a matter that is of more importance is the character and value of the performance to be rendered by the promisee after acceptance. If, however, the consideration is nominal in fact as well as in amount—that is, it is merely named and is in fact neither given nor promised, then there is no consideration at all, and the option giver has power of revocation as in the case of other revocable offers.[35]

Thirdly, an option contract can be made binding and irrevocable by subsequent action in reliance upon it, even though such action is neither requested nor given in exchange for the option promise.[36] This is discussed in the chapter dealing with consideration and with action in reliance as an operative substitute for consideration. An option promise is no different from other promises in this respect; but it is surmised that cases will be rare in which the option holder will be reasonably induced to change his position in reliance upon an option promise that is neither under seal nor made binding by a consideration, or in which the option giver has reason to expect such change of position. Nevertheless, if A offers to sell land to B for a stated price and promises that B may have a week in which to have his engineers make expensive experiments as to the use and value of the land, the making of such experiments before notice of revocation should be held to make the promise binding.[37]

32. An action for damages will lie even though there was notice of revocation before acceptance. Mc-Millan v. Ames, 22 N.W. 612, 33 Minn. 257 (1885).

Likewise, a decree for specific performance is obtainable. Cochran v. Taylor, 7 N.E.2d 89, 273 N.Y. 172 (1937).

33. Frequently, an option to buy land is given in consideration of a sum of money that is to be regarded as a part of the total purchase price in case the option holder later elects to buy. Whether or not it is to be so regarded is a question of interpretation of the words of the option giver. Sometimes those words are not very clear on the point. See:

N.C.—Winders v. Keenan, 77 S.E. 687, 161 N.C. 628 (1913).

Vt.—Ackerman v. Carpenter, 29 A.2d 922, 113 Vt. 77 (1943).

37. In Wilson v. Spry, 223 S.W. 564, 145 Ark. 21 (1920), the holder of an option to buy timber lands made a "cruise" of the lands at a

The cases in which a revocable offer becomes irrevocable by reason of the rendering of a part of the requested performance by the offeree have already been discussed.[38] If the part performance justifies the inference that the offeree has promised to complete the performance, making the contract bilateral, there is no longer any option; but those cases in which the offer has become irrevocable by reason of part performance, and yet no promise to complete is inferred, are true illustrations of an option contract. The offeror is bound, his duty being conditional on proper completion by the offeree; but the offeree is not bound to complete the performance—he has the option to cease performance if he is willing to throw away what he has already done.

Where a promise or agreement that is in form contractual is in fact not binding for lack of either a seal, a consideration, or action in reliance upon it, it is a mere revocable offer, not an option contract. The offeree has a power of acceptance and has an option between accepting and not accepting. After a proper acceptance has taken place, this option is gone; and a contract has been made,[39] one that may or may not be an option contract. So, if the only consideration is an illusory promise, there is no contract and no binding option, although there may still be an operative offer and a power of acceptance.[40]

In most cases, the consideration given for an option is not merely nominal. Frequently, the payment made for an option to buy or to sell some property is a very substantial amount.[41] In the cases where the option agreement is merely a subsidiary part of a larger transaction, as where a lessee is by the terms of the leasing contract given an option to buy or to renew the lease, the consideration for the option is seldom a definitely determinable portion of what the option holder gives to the other party. It is not at all necessary for the parties to agree upon such a division of the total consideration given by the option holder; it is not necessary for either the parties or the court to make a separate valuation of the option in order that it should be enforceable.[42]

cost of $25 per day in order to estimate the amount and value of the timber. Further, he promised the option giver to do this; and the court regards his promise as a consideration for the option. The fact that the holder of an "option" to renew a lease employed an architect to draw plans did not prevent the lessor's death from operating as a revocation, where the option contained no promise that it should extend for any period of time. Bard v. Kent, 122 P.2d 8, 19 Cal.2d 449, 139 A.L.R. 1032 (1942).

38.　See §§ 49–51, Irrevocable Offers.

39.　Cal.—Walter G. Reese Co. v. House, 124 P. 442, 162 Cal. 740 (1912).

40.　Great Northern R. Co. v. Witham, L. R. 9 C. P. 16 (1873), is such a case.

41.　U.S.—The Coca-Cola Bottling Co. v. The Coca-Cola Co., 269 F. 796 (D.C.Del.1920).

## § 264. Form of the Acceptance and of the Contract made Thereby

Although an option contract is itself binding—that is, it is a contract before the option holder makes his choice and exercises his power [43]—nevertheless, the exercise of the power changes the legal relations of the parties. We shall now consider the character of the act by which the power is exercised and the nature of the contractual relations that exist thereafter.

The power of the option holder is generally called a power of acceptance, the antecedent transaction being regarded as the offer of a promise of some performance. In order to simplify the discussion, let us consider a simple option to buy, whereby in consideration of $100 paid, A promises B to convey Blackacre for $5,000 at B's option, to be exercised within 30 days. This is a binding unilateral contract, since it is a promise exchanged for a sufficient cash consideration. It is also commonly called an offer to sell the land to B for $5,000. This usage is not at all objectionable, if we realize that an offered promise may also be a binding promise. It certainly creates a power in B to be exercised, in the case stated, by giving notice of consent to buy. And on the giving of such notice within the time limit, the legal result is almost identical with that of the acceptance of an ordinary revocable offer to sell.[44] When a lease creates in a tenant an option to renew for an extended period, the giving of the required notice at once operates as an extension of the lease; the execution of a new documentary lease is not necessary.[45]

The option giver may provide in express terms that notice of acceptance shall be in writing; [46] and, indeed, if the subject matter is land, the acceptance must be in writing and signed in order to constitute a sufficient memorandum as against the party accepting. But if there is no such provision in the option document, acceptance may be by an oral notice; [47] and even though the transaction is within the statute of frauds, the fact that the acceptance is oral does not prevent enforcement against the giver of an option evidenced by his signed writing.[48]

As already stated, A's promise is from the very beginning a binding contract, his duty to convey being conditional on notice by B within 30 days. The sending of such a notice by B is not merely the acceptance of an offer; it is also the performance of a condition precedent to A's duty of immediate performance. In a subsequent chapter dealing with conditions and conditional contracts, it will be amply shown that an agreement is not pre-

---

46. See Ackerman v. Carpenter, 29 A.2d 922, 113 Vt. 77 (1943), the express provision being as follows: "by due notice in writing within the time specified, and the failure to serve such notice within the time specified shall terminate this option without further action." The court held that a proper notice had been properly served.

vented from being a binding contract by the fact that there are conditions precedent to be performed.[49]

From the foregoing, it appears that the promise of A to sell for $5,000 is both an offer and a contract, and that the notice given by B is both an acceptance of the offer and the performance of a condition precedent to A's duty of immediate conveyance of the land. Even if A's promise to sell were not already irrevocable and a contract, the giving of notice by B within 30 days would still be a condition precedent to A's duty. Most offers are conditional on some kind of notice of acceptance. The difference is that in the case of the ordinary offer, it is the fulfilment of the condition called acceptance that makes the offer irrevocable. While in the above example of an option contract it was the payment of $100 that made it irrevocable. There is no usage whatever in which a promise is called a contract until something has made it irrevocable. In the case of an ordinary offer, therefore, the notice of assent is a condition precedent to irrevocability and to the formation of contractual obligation, as well as a condition precedent to A's duty of immediate conveyance. In the above example of an option contract, the notice is only a condition precedent to the latter, not to the former.

There is, therefore, a difference between the legal effect of a notice of acceptance of a revocable offer and the effect of the notice given by B in exercising his contractual option. The former notice has the greater effect of the two—it makes the only contract that there is. The latter notice does not make a new contract—it merely pushes an already existing contractual obligation one step further along its way, turning the duty of A that was conditional on notice into a duty that is no longer so conditional.

Whether we call the notice given by B the acceptance of an offer or the performance of a condition, we must subject to analysis the character of the contract as it exists afterwards. In the simple option contract above, the giving of notice by B causes the existing unilateral contract to become a bilateral contract.[50] His notice is not only the performance of a condition of A's promissory duty to convey; it is also the making of his own promise to pay $5,000 for the land. Even if A's promise had previously been only a revocable offer, B's notice of acceptance would have made a bilateral contract to sell and to buy; but, then, there would have been no antecedent unilateral contract at all. The legal relations existing subsequently to the notice would be identical in the two cases; but the legal relations existing antecedently to the notice were not identical.

In the bilateral contract existing after notice by B, each party now being bound by a promise, the duty of each is still a conditional duty. A's duty of immediate conveyance by deed is conditional upon tender of $5,000 by B within a reasonable time; and

B's duty to make immediate payment of $5,000 is conditional upon tender of a deed of conveyance of marketable title. These acts are made conditions of the two duties, not by the express words of either party, but by usage and the prevailing judicial notions of what is just. In this treatise, such conditions are called constructive conditions. The condition of notice within 30 days, however, is an express condition, because it is made such by A's own promissory language.

Just as in the case of all other offers, the offeror can prescribe any mode of acceptance that he pleases and he can make his offered promise conditional upon any facts and performances that he sees fit. The simple option to buy, above stated, might be worded as follows: "In consideration of $100 paid, A promises B to convey Blackacre on payment of $5,000 within 30 days." In the absence of evidence showing that this language is elliptical the form of acceptance and the condition of A's duty are the actual tender of $5,000 within 30 days. Nothing is said about a notice of acceptance; and the giving of such a notice would have no effect, unless the contrary intention can be found by reading between the lines and by drawing inferences from surrounding factors.[51]

51. The remainder of this chapter, Sections 265–274 of the general Treatise, is here omitted. These sections deal in detail with special kinds of option contracts, such as Option to Terminate or Disaffirm; Options to Sell, to Buy, or to Lease; Options in Service and Agency Contracts; Double Options. Other matters considered are Specific Enforcement, Power of Assignment, Option Holder's Interest in Land, and Time of the Essence.

# PART II

# STATUTE OF FRAUDS *

---

## CHAPTER 12

### HISTORY AND LEGAL OPERATION OF THE STATUTE

---

## § 275. Introductory

In the earlier history of the common law of England oral promises appear not to have been generally enforced by the king's courts. No statement as to what the local courts and communities may have done in such cases can safely be made without an extended investigation by a trained historical scholar. The ecclesiastical courts may have enforced oral promises accompanied by a pledge of religious faith or an appeal to God. Of the common law writs issued by the king's courts, the writ of covenant was much earlier than the writ of assumpsit, the former not being applicable to ordinary oral promises. The action of debt was also much earlier than assumpsit; but the theory underlying debt was not that a promise was being enforced, but that, because of the receipt by the debtor of something valuable, he owed its return or its equivalent to the creditor. Undoubtedly debt was available in many cases in which the debtor had orally promised to pay; but it was also available in cases in which no promise whatever had been made. By the Statute of Merchants, a formal acknowledgment of indebtedness or obligation made before certain specified officers, such as the mayor of a town where there was a market for staple commodities, was enforceable, the recognizance before the officer often being referred to as a Statute Merchant or a Statute Staple.

---

* In the general Treatise, the treatment of this subject fills the entire Volume 2, with citation of some thousands of cases and with detailed discussion. In the present volume, not many pages can be devoted to the subject and few cases can be cited.

It appears, therefore, that although oral promises were enforced under certain circumstances, it was the attendant circumstances rather than the promise itself that was the basis of legal obligation. Not until the development of the action of assumpsit in the 14th century did oral promises assume the aspect of enforceability at common law, and even then there had to be one of those accompanying circumstances that came to be known as "consideration." With the development of assumpsit, however, the enforcement of oral promises by the king's courts became the ordinary thing, and legal enforcement could be obtained on the strength of the oral testimony of witnesses. This caused the perpetration of fraud to be rather easy for those who were able to suborn perjured testimony; and in 1677 (29 Chas. II) the Parliament enacted a Statute for the Prevention of Frauds and Perjuries. This statute contained twenty five sections and provisions.[1] In sections 4 and 17, the heroic method was adopted of declaring that certain types of oral promises should not be enforceable at all. It was a limitation upon our power to make enforceable contracts.

The purpose of sections 4 and 17 was to prevent the foisting of an obligation of specified classes by perjury upon one who had never assented to assume it. The requirement of a signed writing

1. In addition to contracts, these sections dealt with conveyances, wills, trusts, judgment and execution. It was partly drafted by Sir Heneage Finch (Lord Nottingham), but was criticised and amended by a committee of judges and others, Lord Chief Justice North having a large hand, it appears, in the drafting of sections 4 and 17. Sections 4 and 17 of the English Statute of Frauds as enacted in 1677 (29 Chas. II) are as follows:

Section 4. And be it further enacted that from and after the said 24th day of June no action shall be brought whereby to charge any executor or administrator upon any special promise to answer damages out of his own estate; or whereby to charge the defendant upon any special promise to answer for the debt, default, or miscarriages of another person; or to charge any person upon any agreement made upon consideration of marriage; or upon any contract or sale of lands, tenements, or hereditaments, or any interest in or concerning them; or upon any agreement that is not to be performed within the space of one year from the making thereof; unless the agreement upon which such action shall be brought, or some memorandum or note thereof shall be in writing, and signed by the party to be charged therewith, or some other person thereunto by him lawfully authorized.

Section 17. And be it further enacted by the authority aforesaid, that from and after the said 24th of June no contract for the sale of any goods, wares, or merchandises, for the price of ten pounds sterling or upwards, shall be allowed to be good, except the buyer shall accept part of the goods so sold, and actually receive the same, or give something in earnest to bind the bargain, or in part payment, or that some note or memorandum in writing of the said bargain be made and signed by the parties to be charged by such contract, or their agents thereunto lawfully authorized.

no doubt tends to attain this end; but the method is far from infallible. For example, a memorandum does not cease to satisfy the statutory requirement even though it is lost or destroyed. Its existence and contents are permitted to be proved by oral testimony; this may be perjured. Under other circumstances, proof by oral testimony is permitted by the courts. The two sections make no effort to prevent the perpetration of fraud by forgery of a written memorandum; but doubtless it is more difficult to avoid detection in forgery than in perjury.

Such gain in the prevention of fraud as is attained by the statute is attained at the expense of permitting persons who have in fact made oral promises to break those promises with impunity and to cause disappointment and loss to honest men. It is this fact that has caused the courts to interpret the statute so narrowly as to exclude many promises from its operation on what may seem to be flimsy grounds. The courts cannot bear to permit the dishonest breaking of a promise when they are convinced that the promise was in fact made. The statute of frauds is regarded as a technical defense that often goes counter to the merits.[2]

2. In many cases the courts have worked indefatigably to prevent a defendant from using the statute to defeat the enforcement of his promise. In Bader v. Hiscox, 174 N.W. 565, 188 Iowa 986, 10 A.L.R. 316 (1919), the plaintiff had been seduced by the defendant's son and had brought civil and criminal proceedings. The defendant promised to convey land to plaintiff if she would marry the son and dismiss the proceedings. The plaintiff fully performed her part, and the court enforced the defendant's oral promise. To do this, the court avoided the marriage clause of the statute by holding that marriage was not the consideration because it was not the "end to be attained" but was a mere necessary "incident"; it avoided the land clause by holding that full performance of the consideration by the plaintiff took the case out of the statute; and it avoided the clause dealing with defaults of another by the bare assertion that "the defendant did not undertake to answer for the debt or default of his son. . . . The obligation assumed by him was primary and upon his own credit." This seems to have been a meritorious decision in a case where to apply the statute would have done grave injustice. The antecedent decisions were such as to enable the court to hurdle three different clauses of the statute, all three of which seem applicable to the defendant's promise.

"The fact that the courts have seen fit to take out of its operation so many cases where the danger of perjury is just as great as in the cases left within it, perhaps evinces a judicial feeling that the protection to public morality and individual honesty afforded by the statute is a fanciful and remote benefit; while, on the other hand, it is obvious that the enforcement of contracts honestly made is one of the immediate ends of the administration of law, and this whether the contract be written or not." Street, Foundations of Legal Liability, 189.

"Courts are very slow to apply the statute of frauds where by so doing instead of preventing a fraud its application will have the effect to work a fraud." Piper v. Fosher, 23 N.E. 269, 121 Ind. 407 (1889).

The statute has been set up as a defense in many thousands of cases; and it has been interpreted so strictly and applied so narrowly that its meaning as applied can now be determined only by a comparative study of the cases, not merely by the simpler methods of statutory interpretation. As Buckley, L. J., said: "It is now two centuries too late to ascertain the meaning of section 4 by applying one's own mind independently to the interpretation of its language. Our task is a much more humble one; it is to see how that section has been expounded in decisions and how the decisions apply to the present case." [3] No doubt the same could be said of almost any written constitution or statute, but usually with a lesser degree of truth.

In the case of the common law rules, new and disturbing elements continually appear, turning old rules that once were a sound basis of prediction into empty and lifeless formulae or worse. Ordinarily the change occurs slowly; and acute lawyers who know the life around them as well as mere verbal formulae can take the changes into account in making their advisory predictions for clients. Statutory rules in the beginning usually create an illusion of certainty; with experience the illusion vanishes. Safe prediction as to the exact operation of the statute must await actual experience in its application. It is always true that along the boundaries of its application the statutory rule varies and is recreated exactly the same as a common law rule, and for the very same reasons. This is not judicial usurpation; it is merely inevitable necessity.

The statute of frauds has now been a part of the law of the land for more than one quarter of a millenium. It has been interpreted and applied by the courts in tens of thousands of cases. Surely there have been experience and time enough to create uniformity and to make prediction a pleasure. It is safer, however, merely to say that they have sufficed to destroy the illusion. The legislative words usually are, "No action shall be brought whereby to charge." If this was meant to prevent the "bringing" of actions, how great the disappointment! The bulky

"From the purview of it, declaring that no action shall be brought in the cases therein enumerated, the true intent of the statute was to prevent the fraudulent imputation of a contract, rather than the fraudulent denial of one." Henderson v. Hudson, 1 Munf. 510 (Va. 1810). It not only does not prevent the latter, it aids and abets in effectuating it. This could hardly have been the "true intent" although it is the true effect.

3. Eng.—Hanau v. Ehrlich, [1911] 2 K.B. 1056.

In Reeve v. Jennings, [1910] 2 K.B. 522, Lord Coleridge said: "The statute of frauds has been much buffeted about by decisions, but its life is not quite extinct." In the case before him he held that the statute made the promise unenforceable.

contents of the reports and the digests suggest that an action has in fact been brought in almost every instance where a "special promise" of the prescribed classes has been made and has not been performed, as well as in great numbers of cases where the alleged promise has not been made at all. In the latter cases the statute may have been an added safeguard for the innocent against the dishonest; in the former cases it offers a possible refuge for contract breakers. If the statute was intended as a basis for predicting the behavior of plaintiffs and their lawyers, the best that we can say of the legislature is that it "meant well." Of course, it is possible to assert that but for the statute many more cases would have been brought, especially fraudulent ones; no one can prove what would have been had there been no statute. It is at least as probable that but for the statute there would have been fewer broken promises and less litigation.

If the legislature intended to lay a basis not for predicting the behavior of plaintiffs but for predicting the decisions of judges when actions are brought on the special promises described in the statute, the disappointment is also very great. There is much conflict and lack of uniformity. Two conflicting tendencies have been evident for the whole two hundred and seventy years. One of these is to regard the statute as a great and noble preventive of fraud and to apply it against the plaintiff with a good conscience even in cases where no doubt exists that the defendant made the promise with which he is charged. The other and much more frequent one is to enforce promises that a jury would find to have been in fact made, and if necessary to this end to narrow the operation of the statute. This narrowing of application was sometimes accompanied by general words of encomium for the great statute; but in recent years the courts nearly always say nothing on the subject except what may be necessary to the business actually in hand, the enforcement of the promise. The narrowing process has been in part one of supposed interpretation of language and in part one of permitting the jury to determine the application of the statute by a general verdict under instructions that do not in fact hamper the jury in its effort to do "justice."

The statutory clause forbidding an action on a promise that "is not to be performed within the space of one year" has been so interpreted as not to apply to contracts where either party can and does perform his own part within one year although the other cannot,[4] or to contracts that can on any remote contingency be

<hr/>

4.   **Ariz.**—Diamond v. Jacquith, 125 P. 712, 14 Ariz. 119, L.R.A.1916D, 880 (1912).

  **Mo.**—Bird v. Bilby, 215 S.W. 909, 202 Mo.App. 212 (1919).

  **Vt.**—Pierce v. Paine's Est., 28 Vt. 34 (1855).

  **Eng.**—Donellan v. Read, 3 B. & Ad. 899 (1832).

performed within a year but that in fact have been in course of performance for a great many years before bringing suit.[5]  In many hundreds of cases a defendant has been held on his oral promise to answer for the debt of another by instructing the jury that the defendant is bound if "sole credit" was given to him and none to the third person.[6]  Under such an instruction, if the jury believes that the promise was made and relied upon, a verdict is rendered for the plaintiff and sustained on appeal.

There has been a slight tendency to regard the statute of frauds as based upon "paramount moral considerations" leading to the result that a court should give it a broad instead of a narrow

5.    U.S.—Warner v. Texas & P. R. Co., 17 S.Ct. 147, 164 U.S. 418, 41 L.Ed. 495 (1896), contract enforced after 13 years; Quirk v. Bank of Commerce & Trust Co., 244 F. 682 (C.C.A.6th, 1917), service for life.

Ky.—Myers v. Saltry, 173 S.W. 1138, 163 Ky. 481, Ann.Cas.1916E, 1134 (1915) motion denied 175 S.W. 626, 164 Ky. 350, to rear and educate a child.

In Adams v. Union Cinemas, [1939] 3 All Eng. 136 (C.A.), the plaintiff sued for damages for breach of an oral employment contract. The defendant pleaded the statute of frauds and that the employment was for two years. The defendant had promised to reduce the contract to writing, both parties expecting that the two year term would be included. The court found that the only existing contract was an oral one, for an indefinite period that would last only until a writing was executed. This would appear to be an excellent way of avoiding the application of the statute. MacKinnon, L. J., said that the trial judge "took the view that he was not compelled to hold that it was within the statute, and the question before us is whether, there being no real doubt as to what happened, and no conceivable danger of perjury or subornation of perjury, we are compelled to hold that this action must be dismissed because the claim is brought under an agreement which is not to be performed within the space of one year . . . One difficulty in the way of Stable, J., was that the plaintiff and his advisers, perhaps by inadvertence or by too sanguine an expectation, thought the defendants would not be so ungentlemanly as to plead the statute." The plaintiff had made a statement of claim to the effect that the agreement was to employ him for two years; but the court found that the oral agreement was in fact only to continue until the execution of a writing, and this would be for an indefinite period.

Du Parcq, L. J., said: "The much abused statute of frauds has no operation in this case." Also, that he would hate to have to explain the case to an "intelligent foreigner" who would ask: "Why is it that counsel for the defendants was much more anxious even than counsel for the plaintiff to show that his client had entered into an agreement to employ the plaintiff for a longer time and at a larger salary? Is it because of undue generosity on their part?"

6.    Me.—Hines & Smith Co. v. Green, 118 A. 296, 121 Me. 478 (1922).

Md.—Myer v. Grafflin, 31 Md. 350, 100 Am.Dec. 66 (1869).

Mass.—Hammond Coal Co. v. Lewis, 143 N.E. 309, 248 Mass. 499 (1924).

Eng.—Darnell v. Tratt, 2 C. & P. 82 (1825); Simpson v. Penton, 2 Cr. & M. 430 (1834).

application and should also refuse to enforce a foreign contract if the requirements of the statute of the forum are not satisfied.[7] It is believed that such a view is far from sound, and that our courts in general do not hold or apply such a view.[8]

It is believed by many that, even as narrowly interpreted and applied, the statute perpetrates more injustice than it prevents; and its entire repeal has been advocated.[9] Perhaps there is

7.  2 Wharton, Conflict of Laws (3d ed. 1905) Sec. 690.

Kan.—Barbour v. Campbell, 168 P. 879, 101 Kan. 616 (1917).

Ohio.—Heaton v. Eldridge, 46 N.E. 638, 56 Ohio St. 87, 36 L.R.A. 817, 60 Am.St.Rep. 737 (1897).

Cf.:

Ohio —Detroit & Cleveland Nav. Co. v. Hade, 140 N.E. 180, 106 Ohio St. 464 (1922).

8.  "It would seem that a contract which has been entered into in a foreign state or country where written evidence is not required should be enforced elsewhere. Moral considerations of a paramount character, sufficient to warrant a disregard of private rights, not being involved, the application of the local statute should be restricted to contracts made within the state." Lorenzen, Statute of Frauds, 32 Yale L.J. 311, 337 (1923).

9.  Criticisms adverse to the statute may be found as follows: by Mr. Justice Stephen, with the apparent approval of Sir F. Pollock, in 1 L.Q.R. 1 (1885); a sarcastic editorial note by Goodhart "celebrating" the 250th anniversary of the statute in 43 L.Q.R. 1 (1927); 6 Holdsworth, Hist. of Eng. Law, 379–397, "these clauses have outlived their usefulness"; editorial note by Pollock in 29 L.Q.R. 247 (1913) "piece of antiquated legislation;" F. M. Burdick, "A Statute for Promoting Fraud," 16 Col.L.R. 273; E. C. Firth, "A Doubt on the Statute of Frauds," 9 L.Q.R. 366 (1893).

"It is only in respect of very special kinds of contracts that written evidence can wisely be demanded by the law. In the case of all ordinary mercantile agreements such a requirement does more harm than good; and the law would do well in accepting the principle that a man's word is as good as his bond. The statute of frauds, by which most of these rules of exclusive evidence have been established, is an instrument for the encouragement of frauds rather than for the suppression of them." Salmond, Jurisprudence (6th ed. 1920) 447.

"I have sometimes in more formal moods said to myself that no contract should be enforceable unless it was a written contract; in other words, that the valid formation of the contract should be conditioned on its being reduced to writing. That would be nice in theory. But a little reflection has told me that not only every day bargains but many most important contracts are made and done by word of mouth." . . . "The Statute does not require the contract to be in writing, either at the date when it was concluded or afterwards. What it requires is a note or memorandum signed by the party to be charged or his agent made at any time before action." . . . (Of Williston's chapters on the statute) "I confess I found it, however ably and brilliantly done, somewhat depressing. There is no principle involved. It is all devoted to construing badly drawn and ill-planned sections of a statute which was an extemporaneous excrescence on the Common Law, imposed, as it were, from without as recently as the third part of the 17th Century." Lord Wright, reviewing Williston on Contracts in 55 Law Q.Rev. 189, 204, 205.

greater confidence at present in the capacity of courts and juries to determine the truth by means of oral testimony than there was in the time of Charles II. The rules as to the competency of witnesses and the admissibility of testimony have been made much more liberal. Perjury on the witness stand may be less common than it once was.[10]

"He rests his defence on the statute of frauds, which probably generates as many frauds as it prevents." Lamborn v. Watson, 6 Har. & J. 252, 255, 14 Am.Dec. 275 (Md.1824).

"The whole argument is grounded on the interpretation of the statute of frauds, that unfortunate statute, the misguided application of which has been the cause of so many frauds. Like any other statute, it is to be read with common sense and understanding." Bacon, V.C., Morgan v. Worthington, 38 L.T. (N.S.) 443, 445 (1878).

In Hillhouse v. Jennings, 38 S.E. 599, 60 S.C. 373 (1900), the court said: "Hard cases arise when this provision of our law is applied; but this court does not make the law, but it does enforce it in sorrow over its rigor in some instances." The South Carolina court has avoided some of its sorrow by largely nullifying the statutory provision affecting promises to answer for the debt of another person. It sustains a verdict for the plaintiff on the oral promise of a landlord to guarantee payment of money lent to his tenant.

S.C.—Farmers' Bank v. Eledge, 120 S.E. 362, 126 S.C. 517 (1923); Gaines v. Durham, 117 S.E. 732, 124 S.C. 435 (1923).

See the review by the trial judge in Charles R. Ablett Co. v. Sencer, 224 N.Y.S. 251, 130 Misc. 416 (1927).

10. "The statute of frauds was in its nature reactionary. It radically interfered with the lines of natural growth in contract law. It made form a necessary element in many of our most common transactions and thus ran counter to a deep principle of growth in this department of law.

"The statute of frauds is therefore essentially and necessarily, in some of its features at least, a temporary phenomenon in the evolution of contract law. Born of a desire to prevent the imposition of liability by means of perjured testimony, the need for it must decrease as the means of discovering and punishing perjury are increased. This danger has undoubtedly been greatly lessened by alterations made during the last fifty years in the law of evidence." II Street, Foundations of Legal Liability, 196.

Thayer, Prelim. Treatise on Evid., 180, says: "There is reason to surmise that a leading motive in the enactment of that comprehensive but strange and very un-English piece of legislation, the statute of frauds, was found in the uncertainty that hung over everything at a period when the law of proof was so unsettled. It will be remembered that it was then a very critical time; that the attaint as an operative thing had vanished, while the law of new trials was in its infancy, and the rules of our present law of evidence but little developed."

Thayer further says, id. 430: "It must be remembered what such a fear at that period meant. Not yet had any distinct system of rules for excluding evidence come into existence. The power of judges to set aside verdicts as being against the evidence had begun to be exercised, but had not got far. The attaint was still the regular way of controlling the jury and this had practically lost its hold. The jury still held its old character and function, might decide on its own knowledge alone,

On the other hand many judges have extolled the merits of the statute in glowing terms.[11] And the legislatures of practically

and if it heard evidence, might reject it all. This power of the jury and its exemption from fine and imprisonment for deciding against the evidence were vindicated in Bushell's Case, Vaughan, 135, in 1670.

"The statute of frauds, six years later, relieved against this state of things by requiring in a great many cases that there should be a writing or some specific act or formality, before an action could be brought or a claim established . . . After the statute of frauds—a very extraordinary enactment to have been passed by an English-speaking community in any age, so comprehensive is it and so far reaching— no jury could find a contract of the sort named in sec. 4, unless there were a writing; or one named in sec. 17, unless there were either a writing or one of the facts there specified; no jury could find a devise of real estate without a signature and witnesses, as required in sec. 5, or a will of personalty without writing, except under circumstances indicated in secs. 19 to 23. To the most important dealings of men the statute of frauds gave new security. It is not probable that so wide reaching an act could have been passed if jury trial had been on the footing which it holds today. And in construing the statute it was entirely natural that different ideas should prevail in the equity and the common law courts."

11. As might be expected, Lord Kenyon was all for a strict application. In Chater v. Beckett, 7 T.R. 201 (1797) he said: "I lament extremely that exceptions were ever introduced in construing the statute of frauds; it is a very beneficial statute; and if the courts had at first abided by the strict letter of the act it would have prevented a multitude of suits that

have since been brought." The justice of his "lament" would be more evident if he could tell us that this "multitude of suits" were brought fraudulently and supported by perjury instead of being brought by an honest man for breach of a contract actually made. In Dunphy v. Ryan, 6 S.Ct. 486, 116 U.S. 491, 29 L.Ed. 703 (1885), Woods, J., said: "The statute of frauds is founded in wisdom and has been justified by long experience." But he adds: "Courts of equity, to prevent the statute from becoming an instrument of fraud, have in many instances relaxed its provisions."

In Woollam v. Hearn, 7 Ves.Jr. 211 (1802), Sir William Grant said: "Thinking, as I do, that the statute has been already too much broken in upon by supposed equitable exceptions, I shall not go farther in receiving or giving effect to parol evidence than I am forced by precedent." But more than a century later, the Privy Council held in direct conflict with his decision and did not even mention the case. United States v. Motor Trucks, Ltd. [1924] A.C. 196.

"No statute has been so much, and, in my opinion, so justly eulogized for its wisdom as the statute of frauds. This branch of it tends to repress evil practices which would otherwise spring up to the insecurity of all. But for the salutary influence of this statute, thousands would tumble into ruin by having their estates taken from them to answer for the debts, defaults, and miscarriages of others. So far therefore from believing that this branch of the statute of frauds has a tendency to produce injustice and wrong, I think it the only bulwark of security to shield men from those evils which the statute was intended to remedy." Leland v. Creyon, 1 McCord, 100, 105, 10 Am. Dec. 654 (S.C.1821).

every State in the United States have re-enacted the provisions of section 4; [12] while about two-thirds of the States did the same as to section 17, and its provisions are included in the Uniform Sales Act. Further, the policy of the statute has been extended to new classes of cases. Thus, there are statutes providing that an oral promise renewing the obligation of a barred debt is not enforceable,[13] that a real estate agent cannot enforce a promise to pay his commission unless he has a written memorandum, and that an infant's contract cannot be validated except by a writing. In some States, a new promise to pay a debt that has been discharged in bankruptcy is unenforceable unless in writing.[14] In others a writing is required for the enforcement of any contract to devise or bequeath property by will.[15] By statute in New York, it is provided that a modification or a discharge of an existing contract shall not be invalid for lack of consideration in case the modification or discharge is by a signed writing.[16]

See also, Jesse W. Lilienthal, "Judicial Repeal of the Statute of Frauds," 9 Harv.L.R. 455 (1896), criticising the part performance doctrine.

12.   The English statute of frauds is in force in New Mexico by virtue of judicial decision. See Childers v. Talbott, 16 P. 275, 4 N.M. 168 (1888). It is in force in Maryland by virtue of Article 5 of the Declaration of Rights in the Constitution of Maryland. See Lewis v. Tapman, 44 A. 459, 90 Md. 294, 302, 47 L.R.A. 385 (1900).

13.   These statutes, however, are ordinarily held not to be applicable to a new promise of the debtor that is given in return for a new and sufficient consideration. It applies only to voluntary promises of the debtor that have no basis other than the past debt itself. See Strong v. Sunset Copper Co., 114 P.2d 526, 9 Wash.2d 214, 135 A.L. R. 423 (1941).

14.   Ark.—Polk v. Stephens, 176 S. W. 689, 118 Ark. 438 (1915).

Ga.—Beasley v. Padgett, 110 S.E. 739, 28 Ga.App. 268 (1922).

Me.—Ames v. Storer, 14 A. 67, 80 Me. 243 (1888).

Mass.—Nathan v. Leland, 79 N.E. 793, 193 Mass. 576 (1907).

N.J.—Holt v. Akarman, 86 A. 408, 84 N.J.L. 371 (1913).

N.Y.—Tompkins v. Hazen, 58 N.E. 762, 165 N.Y. 18 (1900).

15.   There are such statutes in Arizona, California, Massachusetts, Ohio, and New York.

See:

Ariz.—Brought v. Howard, 249 P. 76, 30 Ariz. 522, 48 A.L.R. 1347 (1926).

Cal.—O'Brien v. O'Brien, 241 P. 861, 197 Cal. 577 (1925).

Mass.—Barlow v. Barlow, 124 N.E. 285, 233 Mass. 468 (1919).

Ohio—Ayres v. Cook, 43 N.E.2d 287, 140 Ohio St. 281 (1942), affirming 46 N.E.2d 629 (Ohio App.1941).

Under Conn. G.S.1930, Sec. 1632, no action can be maintained for any charges or repairs made by any repairman or automobile mechanic exceeding the sum of $50 unless the same is authorized in writing by the owner or possessor for any expenditure in excess of that sum. Blue Ribbon Garage Inc. v. Klein, 148 A. 370, 110 Conn. 449 (1930); Di Biase v. Garnsey, 133 A. 669, 104 Conn. 447 (1926).

16.   N.Y.Laws 1936, c. 281. By a later statute, N.Y.Laws 1941, c. 329, it was provided that a written contract cannot be modified by a subsequent oral agreement if it

One factor that may not infrequently cause a court to voice approval of the statute is that it seems to afford an easy solution of a difficult case. Where there is a serious doubt and conflicting evidence as to whether the asserted agreement was made and as to its specific terms, it may bring an admirable sense of relief to the judge to let the statute bear the brunt of the decision. Very many cases are found in which the court has seemed to apply the statute with vigor and approval, but in which its review of the evidence shows that the decision might well have been the same had there been no statute to apply.[17]

With these conflicting tendencies and opinions, it is difficult to find a basis for a confident judgment as to the balance of good or ill caused by the statute.[18] It is clear that it tends to prevent the perpetration of fraud by perjury, and so may have af-

contains an express provision against such oral modification.

17. General Overseas Corp. v. Republic P. I. Corp., 74 F.Supp. 698 (D.C.N.Y.1947), is an excellent illustration. The trial court, Rifkind, J., gives a full review of the facts, the testimony as to the oral agreement, and the many letters and telegrams. From this review, it might be thought that the court was applying the statute with meticulous detail. The last full page of opinion, however, is devoted to showing that the trial judge does not believe the oral testimony of the plaintiff. Instead, he is convinced that the plaintiff himself refused to sign the final integration, accurately prepared. Even if there had been no statute, the plaintiff would have lost his case.

18. Street, Foundations of Legal Liability, Vol. 2, p. 170, says: "With the policy of the statute we are not at this juncture particularly concerned. It cannot escape observation, however, that the method of reaching the evil arrived at was very indirect and ran curiously counter to the previous development of English contract law. The almost infinite amount of litigation which has resulted from the enactment known as the statute of frauds shows that it was poorly

drafted and altogether failed to pursue natural lines of cleavage in our law. . . . But notwithstanding all the difficulties of interpretation which the statute has presented, and notwithstanding the oblique and wholly unscientific way in which the statute cuts into the symmetry of our contract law, it is safe to say that no enactment has ever received more universal commendation. It may be conceded that much of the encomium showered upon it has been misplaced and in many cases perfunctory; since the courts have been most eulogistic when compelled to apologize for the gross injustice which the application of the statute has sometimes occasioned. On the whole it has apparently vindicated its right to be, and there is probably no jurisdiction applying the common law in any form where the provisions of this statute, especially section four, are not in some way in force. Subsequent legislation as well as judicial sense has therefore in the main approved it."

In James v. Smith, [1891] 1 Ch. 384, 6, Kekewich, J., said: "It is no part of my judicial duty to say whether on the whole the statute of frauds has been a beneficial or mischievous statute, as to which I am, of course, aware there have been many opinions." This is quite correct; but the actual be-

forded a considerable amount of protection to the innocent. On the other hand, it causes injustice in those many cases where it is successfully used as a technical defense against a meritorious claim based on an oral contract the terms of which are undoubted. It can hardly be doubted that the statute renders some service by operating *in terrorem* to cause important contracts to be put into writing. Indeed, many laymen have the erroneous notion that an agreement is never binding until it is written and signed.

Reduction to writing undoubtedly tends to prevent not only fraud and perjury but also the disputes and litigation that arise by reason of treacherous memory and the absence of witnesses. Perhaps the courts have already reached the best solution possible: Let the statute continue to render its *in terrorem* service; but at the same time interpret it strictly and apply it as seldom as possible in a litigated case.[19] An amendment to the statute would probably be desirable providing that it shall not be effective as a defense except to a party who is willing to submit himself to examination in court on the merits of the case and who under oath denies making the promise as alleged.[20]

Such good as the statute renders in preventing the making of perjured claims and in causing important agreements to be reduced to writing is attained at a very great cost of two different sorts: First, it denies enforcement to many honest plaintiffs; secondly, it has introduced an immense complexity into the law and has been in part the cause of an immense amount of litigation as to whether a promise is within the statute or can by any remote possibility be taken out of it. This latter fact is fully

lief of a learned judge as to the matter is almost certain to affect his interpretation and application of the statute in a particular case.

19. In Townsley v. Sumrall, 2 Pet. 170, 7 L.Ed. 386 (U.S.1829), Mr. Justice Story, speaking for the court, said: "In cases not absolutely closed by authority, this court has already expressed a strong inclination not to extend the operation of the statute of frauds, so as to embrace original and distinct promises, made by different persons at the same time upon the same general consideration." The court held that the plaintiff, who had purchased a bill of exchange from the drawer at the defendant's request and in reliance on the defendant's promise to accept the bill when presented, could maintain action on this oral promise.

"Enactments, also, which impose forms and solemnities on contracts, on pain of invalidity, are construed so as to be as little restrictive as possible of the natural liberty of contracting. It was in allusion to the statute of frauds that Lord Nottingham said that all acts which restrain the common law, that is, apparently, which impose restrictions unknown to the common law, ought themselves to be restrained in exposition: Ash v. Abdy, Swant. 664." Maxwell, "The Interpretation of Statutes" (5 Engl. ed.) 469–470.

20. See Iowa Code (1924) § 11288: "The oral evidence of the maker against whom the unwritten contract is sought to be enforced shall be competent to establish the same."

evidenced by the space necessary to be devoted to the subject in this volume and by the vast number of cases to be cited.[21]

At present, the chief support of the statute is to be found in the juristic habit of courts and lawyers for two hundred and seventy years. While both courts and lawyers constantly search for ways of avoiding the application of the statute, it is nevertheless one of the main sources to which they go for the tests of enforceability. Being in express, statutory form, it promotes that "illusion of certainty" on which the stability of all legal systems so largely depends. Even the present treatise, attempting to portray the illusion of certainty as the illusion that it is, attempts also to state a system of tentative, guiding doctrines that will render service in both the decision and the prevention of future disputes and that are therefore not wholly an illusion. The total repeal of the statute would involve such a wrench to the mental habits of bench and bar that it is very unlikely to occur.[22]

A law student, at the end of his first year, should be able to answer the following questions:

1. What are the five classes of contracts included in Section 4?

2. What are the requirements, as expressed in the words of Section 4, for the enforcement of a contract?

3. To what extent is a contract legally operative if it does not fulfil these requirements?

4. What judicial remedies may be available even if the statutory requirements are not fulfilled?

5. What class of contracts is included within Section 17 (or within the provisions of the Uniform Sales Act or of the Uniform Commercial Code)?

6. What are the alternative requirements, as expressed in Section 17 (or in the Sales Act or the Code) for the enforcement of a contract?

---

21. Smith, Contracts, 75, commenting upon Lord Nottingham's statement that every line of the statute was worth a subsidy, observes: "Every line has cost a subsidy, for it is universally admitted that no enactment of any Legislature ever became the subject of so much litigation."

"This provision comes to us from the original statute of frauds, 29 Car. II, of which it has been said by an enthusiast that every line was worth a subsidy, and by a cynic that every line has cost a subsidy to interpret. The latter statement has been gaining force as the in-genuity of greed has, through centuries, been strained to escape this apparently plain provision, until its application is now surrounded by such a cloud of decisions as to defy exhaustive examination." McCord v. Edward Hines L. Co., 102 N.W. 334, 124 Wis. 509 (1905).

22. A defense of the statute, as being sound and beneficial in policy and in operation, has been made by Llewellyn, "What Price Contract," 40 Yale L.J. 704, 747 (1931). His discussion, however, is brief and undocumented.

7. Is a contract that does not fulfil the requirements legally "void" or "voidable"?

8. Was the statute enacted for the purpose of preventing the making or the performance or the enforcement of oral contracts? What is its purpose? What is its actual effect?

## § 276.  Meaning of the Term "Within the Statute"

According to prevailing judicial language, a contract is said to be "within the statute" if its provisions are such that its operation and enforceability depend upon compliance with the requirements of the statute; it is said to be "not within the statute" if its operation and enforceability do not depend upon such compliance. According to this usage, a contract may be "within the statute" even though it is completely in writing and duly signed and delivered, so that the requirements of the statute are fully satisfied.

Not infrequently, however, when the court finds that there is a sufficient memorandum satisfying the requirements of the statute and making the contract enforceable, it will be said that the memorandum is sufficient to "take the case out of the statute." In other cases, where there has been such a part performance that the courts choose to enforce the contract in the absence of any memorandum in writing, it may be said that the part performance "takes the case out of the statute." Such language as this merely means that the court will enforce the contract either because the requirements of the statute are satisfied or because justice requires enforcement in spite of the statute.

This language will be avoided in this treatise. A contract is either within the statute or not within it. If it is within the statute, there is nothing that can take it out. The statute of frauds describes six different classes of contracts for which it makes certain requirements for enforcement; and a particular contract either is included within one or more of those six classes or it is not so included. If it is so included, the requirements of the statute either are complied with or they are not. If so complied with, the statute does not prevent enforcement; but the contract is nevertheless included within the six classes described in the statute and is not taken out of them. If the requirements are not so complied with, there are other facts that may prevent the application of the statute and make the contract enforceable. It is mere camouflage to say that these facts take the case out of the statute. The fact that it is beneficial camouflage need not blind us to its real character.

Attention should be called to the fact that the provisions of a contract may be such that it falls within more than one of the six classes described in the statute. It may be a contract for the sale of land and at the same time be made in consideration of marriage or be one that is not to be performed within one year. Again, it may be a contract for the sale of both land and goods, or it may be one for the sale of goods that is not to be performed within one year.[23] The fact that a contract falls within two of the classes rather than only one of them does not affect the express statutory requirements for enforcement if the two classes in question are both within Section 4 of the statute. The statute makes identical requirements for the enforcement of contracts falling within that section, irrespective of the particular one of the five classes described therein within which it is included. But the requirements made in Section 17 of the statute are not identical with those made in Section 4. Therefore, if a particular contract happens to fall within both sections of the statute, its enforceability is affected by the requirements of both sections.

Thus, the mere fact of a part payment will fully satisfy the requirements of Section 17, and make an oral contract for the sale of goods enforceable. But a part payment does not satisfy the requirements of Section 4; and therefore, if an oral contract for the sale of goods is also one that is not to be performed within one year, a part payment will not make it enforceable.[24]

Without doubt there are some cases in which the court's attention has been so centered upon one clause of the statute that it has failed to observe that the contract also fell within a second clause. In a few cases, also, the court has thought that only one of the clauses was meant to be applicable at a time, or that since contracts for the sale of goods were specifically dealt with in Section 17 they were not meant to be affected by the provisions of Section 4. There is not much reason for this, however; but it can be used if the court wishes to put this kind of a limit upon the operation of the statute. So far as it has been considered by the courts, it has usually been disapproved. It has been held that the clause of Section 4 referring to contracts not to be performed within one year is applicable to contracts for the sale of goods that are not to be performed within that period.[25]

---

23. David Taylor Co. v. Fansteel Products Co., 255 N.Y.S. 270, 234 App.Div. 548 (1932), affirmed 185 N. E. 718, 261 N.Y. 514, acceptance and receipt of part of goods sold does not satisfy the one-year clause.

To similar effect:

U.S.—White v. So. Kraft Corp., 132 F.2d 381 (C.C.A.8th, 1942); Simpson-Fell Oil Co. v. Pierce Petroleum Corp., 32 F.2d 576 (C.C.A.8th, 1929).

Del.—Bryant v. Credit Service, 175 A. 923, 6 W.W.Harr. 360 (Del. Super.Ct.1934).

Eng.—Prested Miners, etc., Co. v. Garner, [1910] 2 K.B. 776, affirmed [1911] 1 K.B. 425.

24. Del.—Bryant v. Credit Service, 175 A. 923, 6 W.W.Harr. 360, (1934).

Mass.—Sarkisian v. Teele, 88 N.E. 333, 201 Mass. 596 (1909).

## § 278.   The Statute of Frauds is Not Part of the Common Law

All treatises on the law of contracts deal with the statute of frauds, almost as if it were a part of the common law of the land; yet it is not a part of the common law in the same sense as are the doctrine of consideration and the rules as to mutual assent. Court decisions of one State are regularly cited as authority in the courts of other States; yet the statutes that are being interpreted and applied may have substantial differences. Accuracy always requires a knowledge of the specific statute in every case that is cited as authority. There is not one statute of frauds; there are many statutes of frauds.

Nevertheless, it is possible for a treatise to discuss profitably the law relating to such a statute or statutes. In such a discussion, it is necessary either to assume the existence of a statute in some specific form, or to treat statutes comparatively and call attention to their differences in form and effect. The American Law Institute adopted the former alternative, set out in advance the terms of a statute to be used as a basis, and then proceeded to lay down general rules for its interpretation and application.[31] This it could do for the reason that the provisions of the original English statute of frauds have been retained in nearly their exact form in so many American jurisdictions. In other instances the provisions of the English statute have been adopted with minor changes in form that do not affect interpretation and application. To this extent, therefore, there is common *statutory* law which has been the basis for a great mass of judicial common law, made by the judges in exactly the same way that they have made the doctrine of consideration and the rules of offer and acceptance.

In a treatise like this, it is possible to present critically this judicial common law and the common statutory law. It is even possible in some measure to call attention to existing statutory variations and to differentiate the court decisions that interpret and apply them. There is an obvious physical limit to the extent to which this can be done; and every reader of court decisions or of treatises must be alert to discover whether statutory variations have been overlooked or misunderstood.

---

25.   **Del.**—Bryant v. Credit Service, 175 A. 923, 6 W.W.Harr. 360 (1934).

**Eng.**—Prested Miners Gas Indicating Elec. Lamp Co. v. Garner, [1910] 2 K.B. 776, affirmed [1911] 1 K.B. 425.

The oral contract is not enforceable, even though there has been a part payment and an acceptance and receipt of part of the goods. See Atwood's Adm'r v. Fox, 30 Mo. 499 (1860); and Saunders v. Kastenbine, 45 Ky. 17 (1845). The latter case is certainly to be disregarded, since by its own terms the contract could have been performed within one year.

31.   Restatement, Contracts, Chapter 8.

## § 279. The Legal Operation of the Statute of Frauds

Attention should first be called to the fact that the operation of the statute is no longer to be determined as a matter of mere independent interpretation of the statutory words. Its operation must now be determined with reference to the two and a half centuries of cases applying it. Like the United States Constitution, the statute of frauds is the product not only of those who drafted and enacted it, but also of those who have interpreted and applied it. This has often been recognized by the courts. Thus, an English judge said: "It is now two centuries too late to ascertain the meaning of section 4 by applying one's own mind independently to the interpretation of its language. Our task is a much more humble one; it is to see how that section has been expounded in decisions and how the decisions apply to the present case." [32] Fifty years earlier an American judge had said: "This being the interpretation of the statute, by the decisions, are we not bound by it, even although, it may be true, that the statute, taken by its letter, is susceptible of a different interpretation, perhaps requiring a different interpretation? We think so. These decisions started with the statute, they traveled with the statute, they have reached us with the statute. Having thus run with the statute in so long a journey—almost through centuries— they ought, at length, to be considered as having grown to the statute, and as now making a part of it." [33]

Many inconsistent and conflicting statements are to be found, in treatises and in the opinions of the courts, as to the operation of the statute of frauds upon the legal relations of the contracting parties. This is due partly to differences in the form of words in which the various statutes have been cast by the legislature, and more largely to the fact that distinctions between rules of substantive law and remedies and rules of procedure and evidence are so indistinct and elusive. How the statute operates can be clearly presented only by showing that operation in great detail. This is attempted in the succeeding sections; but a brief introductory statement of conclusions may be useful at this point.

The statute as usually enacted does not lay down a rule as to the admissibility of evidence, although it undoubtedly affects the relevancy of offered testimony in many cases.[34] It is not a rule governing the formal procedure of courts or officers. It affects

32. Eng.—Buckley, L. J., in Hanau v. Ehrlich, [1911] 2 K.B. 1056.

33. Ga.—Durham v. Taylor, 29 Ga. 166 (1859).

34. "The statute is not a mere rule of evidence, but a limitation of judicial authority to afford a remedy."

Mass.—Glass v. Hulbert, 102 Mass 24, 3 Am.Rep. 418 (1869).

Pa.—Safe Deposit & Trust Co. v Diamond Coal Co., 83 A. 54, 234 Pa 100, L.R.A.1917A, 596 (1912).

See further § 288.

the legal relations of the contracting parties and should be called a rule of substantive law; legal rights and duties are incapable of definition without reference to societal remedies.[35]  The statute may also properly be described as a rule of remedial law.  By clear and appropriate words, a legislature can make its statute anything it pleases—a rule of evidence as well as a rule of substantive law; and it can make its statute operate substantively so far as to deny any legal operation whatever to an oral contract.  It may be that in a few instances, the operation of the statute in these respects turns upon the special form of words adopted; but it is clear that the use of such words as "void" and "rule of evidence" in stating the effect of the statute that is being applied is almost always erroneous.

A contract where the parties have not complied with the requirements of the statute is neither void nor voidable;[36] it has much effect upon the legal relations of the contracting parties with each other and with third persons.  It can be properly described as unenforceable, however, inasmuch as the ordinary legal remedies are unavailable.  If the defense of the statute is properly made, a judgment for damages for breach of the contract cannot be obtained; and neither can a decree for specific performance [37] unless there has been fraud, mistake, or substantial part performance or action in reliance on the contract.  It has been

35.  See Corbin, Rights & Duties, 33 Yale L.J. 501 (1924).  Also, the sections hereafter dealing with Conflict of Laws and Substance and Procedure.

36.  **Conn.**—Costello v. Costello, 59 A.2d 520, 134 Conn. 536 (1948); Wolfe v. Wallingford Bank & T. Co., 1 A.2d 146, 124 Conn. 507, 117 A.L.R. 932 (1938).

**Ky.**—Clay v. Carter, 11 S.W.2d 91, 226 Ky. 453 (1928).

**Mass.**—Sennott v. Cobb's Pedigreed Chicks, 84 N.E.2d 466, 324 Mass. 9 (1949).

**Miss.**—Washington v. Soria, 19 So. 485, 73 Miss. 665, 55 Am.St.Rep. 555 (1896).

**Pa.**—Sferra v. Urling, 195 A. 422, 328 Pa. 161 (1937).

**Eng.**—Brittain v. Rossiter, 11 Q.B.D. 123 (1879).

After making an oral contract for the sale of land, an attempted revocation by one of the parties is inoperative as a revocation.  A memorandum thereafter executed will make the contract enforceable. Holland v. Hand, 176 A. 430, 317 Pa. 70 (1935).

In Carrington v. Roots, 2 M. & W. 248, 256 (1837, Exch.), Baron Parke said: "If it was an agreement for the sale of an interest in land, it was not binding, by virtue of the 4th section. . . . I think the right interpretation of that section is this,—that an agreement which cannot be enforced on either side is, as a contract, void altogether." In Reade v. Lamb, 6 Exch. 130, 132 (1851), Pollock, C. B. agreed with this and said: "there is no distinction between the 4th and 17th sections." In Leroux v. Brown, 12 C.B. 801 (1852), however, the court held that the statute laid down only a rule of procedure and not of substance.  The American cases require the modification of all these views.

held that a statutory criminal process, provided for the enforcement of certain types of contracts, is not available; [38] and the contract cannot be indirectly enforced by the use of tort remedies, by alleging that refusal to perform the contract or to execute a sufficient memorandum is tortious,[39] or by suing the seller of goods in trover because he has repudiated the oral contract and sold the goods to a third person.[40]

In the foregoing ways the statute may make a contract "invalid"; but there are many other ways in which the "validity" of the contract is recognized. "Valid" is a term with a shifting content; but it is often used with the notion that the "living thought" within its "skin" is unchangeable and certain. A contract is "valid" insofar as it has legal operation and "invalid" insofar as it has not.[41]

A contract within the statute of frauds is valid and operative, even though the requirements of the statute are not complied with, in the following respects: (1) After a full performance by both parties, it determines their legal relations to the same extent that it would if the statutory requirements had been satisfied. (2) In certain cases a part performance will make the oral contract enforceable by equitable remedies, and full performance by one party may make common law remedies available against the other. (3) It creates legal relations between the contractors and third persons in many respects identical with those created by completely valid contracts. (4) It often creates a privilege of taking certain action that otherwise would have been tortious and forbidden. (5) It often operates as a defense in a quasi-contractual action, the defendant being ready and willing to perform

---

**41.** This makes it useless to collect long lists of cases saying that the contract is "void," others that the statute does not affect "validity" but "relates to the remedy only," and others that the statute merely lays down a rule of evidence. For such a list, see 37 C.J. S., Statute of Frauds, § 223, pp. 721, 722.

In Amsinck v. American Insurance Co., 129 Mass. 185 (1880), the court said: "But the oral contract to purchase was not void or illegal by reason of the statute of frauds. Indeed, the statute presupposes an existing lawful contract; it affects the remedy only as between the parties, and not the validity of the contract itself; and where the contract has actually been performed, even as between the parties themselves, it stands unaffected by the statute. It is therefore to be 'treated as a valid subsisting contract when it comes in question between other parties for purposes other than a recovery upon it.'" The court was quite correct in holding that the oral contract of sale created an insurable interest; but it should not be said that the statute does not affect the "validity" of the contract, because validity cannot be separated from remedy. A contract is not totally invalid if there are any remedies, direct or indirect, or if its existence will affect court action with respect to the parties. But insofar as the principal enforcing remedies known to the law are denied by the statute, the contract has been made pro tanto invalid.

as agreed. (6) If security is given for its performance, whether in the form of a mortgage on land or chattels, a pledge of goods or choses in action, or personal suretyship, that security is enforced just as if the primary contract were completely valid—this being a recognition of that primary contract and frequently a very effective, if indirect, way of enforcing it.[42] (7) It is admissible in evidence in a dozen instances to establish other operative facts. (8) It creates in the party to be charged a legal power of making it completely operative against himself by signing a sufficient memorandum. But for the contract, such unilateral action by him, there being no mutual expression of assent, seal, or consideration, would be inoperative. By such unilateral action the contract is validatable as against the party using the power.[43] (9) A party to the oral contract has no power of avoidance; in spite of a definite repudiation, it is still enforceable against him if a sufficient memorandum is afterwards obtained.[44] (10) And lastly, if a debtor owes two debts, one of which is unenforceable by reason of the statute, and makes a payment without directing its application, the creditor can apply it to the debt that is within the statute.[45] In the sections that follow, these general assertions will be supported.*

### §§ 280–300.　General Statements as to Legal Operation of the Statute

The statute of frauds was applicable in courts of equity as well as in courts of common law; and as enacted in the several States it is applicable in all the modern courts. Nevertheless the courts of equity often specifically enforced oral contracts, even though the courts of common law would not have enforced them in an action for money damages. Since the original statute and most of the statutes as enacted in the United States require no more than a "note or memorandum" signed by "the party to

---

* For reasons of space alone, the supporting sections here referred to must be omitted. This includes all of Sections 280–300.

The remaining treatment herein is restricted to a brief discussion of the specific clauses of the statute and to their interpretation and application in a limited number of cases. Almost the whole of the remaining chapters in Volume 2 must be looked for in the general Treatise. Chapters 13 and 14 are omitted in their entirety, even though this excludes such important subjects as Oral Contracts to Vary or Rescind earlier written contracts, Divisibility and the partial enforcement of oral contracts, Manner of Raising the Defense, Remedies of Restitution and Reformation. For the two chapters dealing with these topics, only a few suggestive and challenging statements will be substituted. The remaining Chapters 15–23, while not omitted as a whole, will be reduced to a minimum.

The student must not suppose that the brief discussion in this volume will render him competent to answer more than a small part of the questions in which the statute of frauds is involved.

be charged," a party who has not himself signed and against whom the contract could not be enforced can enforce it against the party whose signature is attached. In such a case, however, enforcement will be dependent on substantially full performance by the non-signing party. An oral promise, even though not enforceable by action, is a sufficient consideration for a written and signed promise.

Refusal to sign a proper written memorandum is not "fraud"; nor is it "fraud" even though there was an express oral promise to sign, however unreasonable or dishonorable the refusal may be. It may be possible, however, to prove that the execution of a sufficient written memorandum was fraudulently prevented.

The statute of frauds, as enacted by the several States, varies to some extent both in form of words and in the specific requirements that must be satisfied for enforceability. The requirements in a State in which a suit is brought may not be the same as those of a State in which the contract was made or the State in which it was to be performed. The court will then have a puzzling question as to which statute to apply. This is not a simple question; its answer requires study of the subject known as Conflict of Laws. Some courts have thought, erroneously, that the answer can be found by determining whether the statute lays down a rule of "substantive law" or a rule of "procedure." A brief discussion of the problem is given in Sections 293 and 294 of the general Treatise.

# CHAPTER 13

## STATUTE OF FRAUDS—ORAL VARIATION OR RESCISSION; CONTRACTS PARTLY WITHIN

### §§ 301–316. Oral Variation or Rescission; Contracts Partly Within the Statute

The statement is very frequently made that a written contract that is within the statute of frauds can not be modified by a parol agreement. This statement is inaccurate. If the new agreement, as modified, is one that is not itself within the statute, it is enforceable according to its own terms; it is operative, not only as a new contract but also as a discharge of and substitution for the former written one. If the new agreement, as modified, is within the statute and there is no such note or memorandum as satisfies the statutory requirements, the new agreement is not enforceable by action; in such case, the former written contract remains enforceable as long as the conduct of the party attempting to enforce it is not operative as an estoppel.

Even if a contract is in writing, whether it is required by the statute to be in writing or is not so required, it can be rescinded by parol agreement as long as it is wholly executory. If, however, it is a contract for the conveyance of land and the conveyance has been made, a reconveyance can not be effected by a parol agreement.

The following are illustrative cases:

(1) A contract of employment for a period of two years is put into writing as required by the statute. The parties can effectively rescind it by parol agreement; also they can modify it by substituting a parol agreement reducing the period of employment to six months.

2. S contracts in writing with C to be surety for the debt of P. This contract can be rescinded by S and C by a parol agreement. Also, they can modify it by a parol agreement whereby C lends money direct to S to enable the latter to make a separate loan to P.

3. V makes a written bilateral contract for the sale of land to P. Most courts hold that they can rescind this contract by parol agreement. After V has made conveyance of the land to P, a mere parol rescission does not operate as a reconveyance.

4. Seller makes a written bilateral contract for the sale of goods to Buyer at the price of $1000. They can rescind this

by parol agreement; also, they can modify it by a parol agreement substituting different goods at the price of $40.

5.   V makes a written contract for the sale of land to P, the latter's duty to pay being made expressly conditional on tender of a perfect title by May 1.  V allows May 1 to go by without making such tender because P orally tells him that performance on time is not necessary.  The contract is enforceable by V against P after May 1.

A contract may consist of two or more promises.  One of these may be such that if it stood alone it would not be within the statute.  If this promise has its own separate and apportioned consideration, it may be enforceable in the absence of any writing, even though the remaining promises are within the statute and not enforceable.  Such a contract is often described as being divisible and only partly within the statute.  If the promises are not thus divisible or if the promises are otherwise so related as to be interdependent, no promise is enforceable unless the requirements of the statute are satisfied as to all of them.  Cases of great complexity occur, making analysis difficult and causing conflict in decisions.  Their discussion must be left to the general Treatise.

# CHAPTER 14

## STATUTE OF FRAUDS—MANNER OF RAISING DEFENSE; REMEDIES OF RESTITUTION AND REFORMATION

### §§ 317–320.  Manner of Raising the Defense of the Statute

In order for a party to make use of the statute to prevent the enforcement of an oral contract, he must in some manner call the court's attention to the fact that the contract is within the statute and that he claims the benefit of it.  There are several ways in which courts have permitted this to be done.  1. It is everywhere sufficient to plead the defense of the statute in express terms; in some jurisdictions this is the only effective way.  2.  In many states the defense may be made by expressly denying the making of the contract as alleged (plead the general issue) and then objecting to the admission of oral testimony by the other party.  3. Some courts hold that, if the party asserting the contract fails to allege that a sufficient writing was executed, the defense of the statute can be made by demurrer.

If the defense is not made in one of these ways, it is said to be waived and the oral contract can be proved and enforced. In no case should enforcement of an oral contract be refused on grounds of the statute as against a party who admits in court that the contract was actually made as alleged.  The purpose of the statute is not to enable contractors to repudiate contracts that they have in fact made; it is only to prevent the fraudulent enforcement of asserted contracts that were in fact not made.

### §§ 321–334.  Restitution as a Remedy against a Party Who Repudiates

After a party has rendered some performance under an oral contract and the other party has received benefits thereby, the latter will not be permitted to repudiate the contract and to retain the benefits without making compensation.  The law creates a duty to make restitution of the money value of such benefits; and if restitution in this form is not adequate a decree for the specific restitution of property received may be available. If the performance rendered and received consists of money payments, repayment will be adjudged; if it consists of goods or services their value in money must be paid; if it consists of

393

land conveyed, its value in money can be recovered or a specific reconveyance will be compelled if justice so requires; if it consists of improvements on land by a purchaser, the repudiating vendor must pay for the improvements. For the purpose of proving the value of a performance so rendered and received, the terms of the oral contract are admissible in evidence.

If a performance under an oral contract has been rendered by the party who repudiates it and claims the benefit of the statute, there is a conflict as to whether he has a right to restitution. Many courts hold that he has no such right as long as the other party is ready and willing to perform the oral contract. In cases of this kind difficult questions have arisen that can not be considered here. Sometimes refusal of restitution may operate as an unjust penalty.

## §§ 335–345.  Reformation for Mistake—Equitable Remedies

Fraud, accident, and mistake form one of the large subdivisions of former equity jurisdiction. The law that was thus established and the remedies that were granted are all embedded in our prevailing system of law. On the grounds indicated by these terms, contract transactions may be declared rescinded, documents may be cancelled, and correction and reformation may be decreed. The subject of Mistake is considered at some length later in this treatise. In the present chapter we shall deal only with the extent to which the statute of frauds affects the application of the law and the remedies that are available, with respect to contracts that are within the statute and to writings that have been induced or affected by fraud, accident, or mistake.

The great purpose of the statute is to prevent the enforcement, by means of false and perjured testimony, of alleged contracts that were not in fact made. To that end it purports to deny enforcement unless the contract or some note or memorandum thereof is in writing and signed. But the statute does not in the least purport to require that such a signed writing shall be enforced or given effect without regard to fraud, accident, or mistake in its inducement or its form. If a contract has been materially affected by factors such as these, all courts alike will refuse enforcement, will declare it to be void or voidable, and will nullify written instruments by decreeing "rescission" or "cancellation." For these purposes and remedies, it makes no difference whatever whether the contract is one that is within the statute of frauds or not.

Courts go much further, however, than merely to refuse enforcement or declare nullity. In great numbers of cases they have granted the remedy called Reformation and have then actively enforced the contract as thus "reformed." It is quite possible that the fraud, accident, or mistake may be such that it has prevented any actual agreement by the parties. Writings may be invalid or erroneous, not only because they do not truly represent an agreement actually made, but also because there was no actual agreement to be represented. In the latter case Reformation is not a proper remedy; there is no agreement by which an erroneous writing can be corrected and to which it can be made to conform. But very often the parties have in fact agreed, and a writing is executed that, by reason of fraud, accident, or mistake, differs materially in its terms and its legal effect. Thus, although the parties agreed upon a sale of 100 acres of land, the deed of conveyance may include either more or less than 100 acres; the description in the deed may apply to a wholly different tract. The parties may have agreed by telephone on the sale of bank shares at $1160 per share, and the written confirmation may erroneously state the price to be $1060.

Many are the kinds of errors that have been made. They have been caused fraudulently and intentionally by one party, by the misunderstanding of an attorney or draftsman, by the mechanical error of a typist, by mutual ignorance of the facts or of the meaning and effect of words, or in various other ways. If facts like these are satisfactorily proved, should the court correct the error and enforce the agreement in fact made? This is the remedy that has been described as Reformation, even though the erroneous writing may not be physically altered and no new signature may be attached by either party. In cases such as this, the agreement that is made effective by Reformation and is enforced is not one that has been correctly reduced to writing; and yet it is being enforced in spite of the statute of frauds. The courts have believed that, even though the error was not caused by fraud, it is fraudulent for a party to refuse correction and to insist upon taking advantage of the error. Thus the spirit and purpose of the statute are given effect, although its letter may be disregarded.

There are cases in which the court has refused to reform and enforce, thinking that the statute must be literally obeyed and that rescission and restitution are all that justice requires. In general, however, the courts have shown increasing liberality in granting the remedy. In all cases, they require that the terms of the unwritten agreement shall be proved by clear and convincing evidence. In no case is the mere absence of a sufficient writing enough to induce enforcement; the insufficiency must be clearly shown to have been caused by fraud, accident, or mistake.[a]

a. Authorities sustaining reformation:

U.S.—McDonald v. Yungbluth, 46 F. 836 (C.C.Ohio, 1891).

Conn.—Spirt v. Albert, 146 A. 717, 109 Conn. 292 (1929).

Mich.—Lane v. Neifert, 215 N.W. 302, 240 Mich. 475 (1927).

Minn.—Olson v. Erickson, 44 N.W. 317, 42 Minn. 440 (1890).

Eng.—U. S. v. Motor Trucks, [1924] A.C. 196.

Restatement, Contracts, § 509.
Compare and criticize:

Idaho—Allen v. Kitchen, 100 P. 1052, 16 Idaho 133, L.R.A.1917A, 563.

Mass.—Glass v. Hulbert, 3 Am.Rep. 418, 102 Mass. 24 (1869).

N.Y.—Friedman & Co. v. Newman, 174 N.E. 703, 255 N.Y. 340, 73 A. L.R. 95 (1931).

# CHAPTER 15

## STATUTE OF FRAUDS—DEBTS OF ANOTHER— SURETYSHIP AND GUARANTY

---

### § 346.   Promises of an Executor or Administrator

The first provision of section 4 is that "no action shall be brought whereby to charge any executor or administrator upon any special promise to answer damages out of his own estate." It would be difficult to determine the meaning of these words standing alone. A promise "to answer damages"; but damages for what? The cases applying this provision are not numerous; but so far as they exist they have made this provision merely a special illustration of the second provision.[20] The promises that are within this clause are promises of an executor or administrator to answer for the debt, default, or miscarriages of the decedent whose estate is being administered or for obligations of the estate arising at his death. The debtor himself being dead, there is a temptation to collect the deficit from the executor or administrator personally if the debtor's estate is insufficient. A promise by the executor or administrator to pay out of his own pocket such a deficit, or to pay the whole debt, is within the statute.[21] Such is the case even though the promise is conditional, as where he promises to pay the claim if an arbitrator finds it to be a valid one.[22] An executor or administrator has no power to create a new claim against the decedent or his estate.[23] He can

---

20.   Two cases in which this clause is best discussed and other cases best reviewed are Brown v. Quinton, 122 P. 116, 86 Kan. 658, Ann. Cas.1913C, 392 (1912), and Smolka v. James T. Chandler, 20 A.2d 131, 2 Terry 255, 134 A.L.R. 629 (Del. 1941), "the phraseology of the statute 'to answer damages' is equivalent in meaning to pay debts."

bind himself personally to pay the debt of the estate; but, with the exceptions hereafter noted, the statute requires a writing. In all cases of contracts made by an executor, the judgment is against the executor personally,[24] although he may be able to charge the estate with the sum paid.

Such a case differs from ordinary suretyship only in this, that there is no living third person who is the principal debtor. This may perhaps be the reason why the draftsman of the statute thought a separate clause was necessary to give the desired protection. The promise of an executor or administrator is not a promise to answer for the debt of another person. When a debtor is dead no one is under any obligation to pay his creditors except the executor or administrator; and this person's obligation to the creditors is merely to administer the assets according to law. If there is a deficit after full administration, no one on earth owes the creditors any duty to pay it. A promise to pay such a deficit, therefore, is not a promise of a surety. Nevertheless, there was once a person who owed the full amount, and it is customary to speak of the debt as a debt of his "estate"; hence, a promise of an executor to pay the debt is treated as if it were the promise of a surety to answer for the debt of another person, and the rules for determining the application of the statute in suretyship cases are substantially identical with those determining the application of the clause concerning executors and administrators.[25]

In general, the same factors that are sufficient to keep a promise from being one to answer for the debt or default of another are likewise sufficient to keep an executor's promise from being within the first clause of the statute. In neither case is it within the statute if the promise is to pay out of a fund put in the promisor's hands for this very purpose. Indeed, the words of the first clause are expressly "to answer damages out of his own estate." Therefore, a promise by an executor to pay a debt of the decedent out of the funds of the estate is enforceable without any writing.[26] It is merely a promise to do that which as executor he is already bound to do.[27] An executor who promises to pay one creditor of the "estate" more than his just share of the assets is promising to commit a breach of trust, and the promise is void. If he promises to pay one creditor his exact share of the assets when properly determined, he is promising to do that which it is already his legal duty to do. Such a promise is not within the statute.

In like manner, the promise of an executor may be made for some consideration of such benefit to him personally that it forms his leading object in making the contract.[28] In this case, no writing is necessary to bind him, even though the performance that he promises will incidentally discharge an obligation of the decedent or his estate.

### § 347. Promises of Guaranty and Suretyship—"Special Promise"—"Debt, Default, or Miscarriages"

The second provision of section 4 is that "no action shall be brought . . . whereby to charge the defendant upon any special promise to answer for the debt, default, or miscarriages of another person." This provision is substantially inclusive of the first provision in that section that has just been considered.

The only significance of the adjective "special" in this phrase is to restrict the statutory provision to promises in fact made. The statute applies to express promises and to tacit promises that are expressed by conduct other than words. It does not apply in cases where duties are created by the law without any promissory assent.[37] In these latter cases, the courts have frequently said that the law "implies" a promise and that there is an "implied assumpsit." The original purpose of this was to expand the use of the common law form of action called assumpsit so that it could be used in the enforcement of both contractual and non-contractual debts. This led to the use of the term "special assumpsit" as opposed to "indebitatus assumpsit," the latter sometimes called "general assumpsit" and including the common indebitatus counts. A good deal of confusion has arisen between promises "implied in fact" and promises "implied in law," the latter term being one that should be wholly abandoned. The statutory provision does not apply to fictitious "promises implied in law"; but it does apply to promises in fact made, whether they are put into words or are expressed by other acts or symbols.

It is not necessary here to attempt an exact definition of the word "debt," inasmuch as the three terms "debt, default, or miscarriages" have been held to include all legal obligations under which a person can come, contractual or non-contractual, requiring a money payment or any other kind of performance. At times the word "debt" has been used restrictively as applying only to an obligation to pay a definite sum of money. Generally its use is much wider, so as to be practically synonymous with such terms as legal duty and legal obligation. It has always been used to include both consensual and non-consensual obligations. The wider usage is the one adopted in applying the statute of frauds.[38]

A person may be indebted without being in default or having committed a miscarriage of duty. These two terms were added to the statute so as to make perfectly clear that it includes promises to answer for another person's breaches of duty of all kinds as well as for his unmatured debts. Thus the following promises are all within the statute: to pay an existing but unmatured debt; to pay an existing matured debt; to pay damages, liquidated or unliquidated, that already have been or may be in the future caused by a breach of contract or by a tort;[39] to deliver goods that another is under obligation to deliver;[40] to see that X returns a horse that he has borrowed;[41] to guarantee a vendor's warranty of soundness;[42] to promise that a soldier will not desert;[43] to guarantee a seller's implied warranty of title [44] or a lessor's covenant of quiet enjoyment.[45]

In one case the term "miscarriages" was held to have a broader signification than "default"; and it was made to include the failure of a newly organized corporation to succeed in business.[46] This case must certainly be disapproved. Miscarriage, like default, means failure to perform as required by some legal duty, whether contractual or otherwise.

### § 348.  Collateral or Original

It is often said that a promise is within the statute if it is "collateral," but not so if it is "original"; and it is sometimes supposed that these terms afford a test for determining the application of the statute. This is not the case, however, since the ordinary usage of the two terms—especially the term "original"—is not such as to make them clearly serviceable. Not all promises that can be correctly described as "collateral" are within the statute and some "original" promises are within it. This is made apparent in the other sections herein dealing with the guaranty clause of the statute; and it is to these other sections that one must go to find the various tests of the application of the statute.[47]

If the terms are of any service, they can be so only as terms descriptive of a result arrived at on grounds quite independent of the terms themselves. They could be restricted so as to mean by "original" that the promise is for any reason not within the guaranty clause of the statute, and by "collateral" that it is within that clause.

### § 349.  Obligation of Another Person, Present or Future

A promise is not within this clause of the statute unless there is an obligation of some third person to the promisee, either already existing or subsequently existing. The third person must at some time be under a legal duty of performance to the promisee, a duty that will be discharged by the performance of the new promisor. That legal duty need not be unconditional or immediate. It may be created prior to the new promise, simultaneously with it, or subsequently. It may be a duty created by consent or by law independently of consent. It may be contractual, quasi-contractual, or in the field of tort. In all of the following cases if S makes a promise to C to do that which will discharge the duty of P, and makes his promise for the benefit of P and not solely or primarily for his own benefit, S is P's surety and his promise is within the statute: (1) P owes C an already overdue money debt; (2) C advances $100 to P simultaneously with S's promise, taking P's note payable in 30 days; (3) P is already employed by C and is in duty bound to repay sums to be collected by P in the future; (4) C promises S to sell goods to P on credit on P's request, and later does so, taking P's promise to repay after inheriting money from X. In each and every case, however, P must in fact be or become under a legal duty to C, and the performance promised by S must be agreed upon by C as a discharge of that duty; if there is no such duty the case is not within the statute.[48]

The following promises are not within the suretyship clause of the statute, for the reason that no one but the promisor is bound to render the promised performance to the promisee: a promise to indemnify a person against loss in a business undertaking or other adventure, even though the losses to the promisee may be caused by non-payment of debts that third persons may incur to him;[52] a promise to a shareholder "guaranteeing" him against loss by depreciation of his shares or that certain dividends will be paid by the corporation;[53] a promise to indemnify an officer for making a tortious levy on the goods of the wrong person;[54] a promise to indemnify the promisee against loss by reason of bringing or defending a suit[55] or by reason of an entry or other action that is believed to be lawful but may turn out to be otherwise.[56]

## § 356. Principal Debtor's Obligation Voidable or Unenforceable

A promise is not within the statute unless there is an obligation of a third person to the promisee that will be discharged in whole or in part by the promised performance. Therefore if the claim of C against P is absolutely void, a promise of S to pay it would not be within the statute.[92] But the term "obligation," as here applied, includes obligations that are voidable or unenforceable, so long as they are not also wholly void. Therefore the statute includes promises to answer for the debt of another even though that other is an infant and could lawfully avoid payment.[93] Cases to the contrary exist but are in the minority.[94] The same is true of a debt voidable for fraud or duress; but a promise to pay such a debt might be held to be conditional upon non-avoidance by the debtor. Where the principal debtor's promise is unenforceable by reason of non-compliance with the statute of frauds, a promise of another person to answer therefor is within the statute; the promise is not void but is legally operative in many ways, as is shown elsewhere herein.

## § 357.  Promise Must be to the Creditor or Obligee

To fall within the statute, a promise must be made to a creditor or obligee to whom the third person is then or later becomes under obligation.[95]  A promise to a debtor to pay or otherwise answer for his debt or default to a third person is not within the statute.[96]  Thus, where Eastwood was indebted to Blackburn on a promissory note, and Kenyon promised Eastwood to pay Blackburn the sum due, Kenyon's promise was enforceable even though not in writing.[97]  Where Davis was indebted to a bank, and Faulkner promised Davis to pay the bank, Faulkner's promise was not within the statute.[98]  Not only can the promisee maintain suit upon the oral promise, but the creditor can also, suing as a creditor beneficiary of the contract.[99]

In many of these cases the defendant has promised not only the debtor but the creditor also.  This does not change the application of the statute.[1]  The promise to the creditor merely reinforces the promisor's duty that would exist anyway by reason of the contract with the debtor;  and the promisor is himself the principal and ultimate obligor.

## § 358.  Form of the Promise

The application of the statute should not be made to depend upon the form of words used by the promisor.  If the consideration moves directly to another person, for which that person becomes indebted to the promisee, and if that person is bound to exonerate the promisor, as the promisee knows, the relationship is that of creditor, principal debtor, and surety, and it is the sort of case intended to be included within the statute of frauds. Wherever the relation between the two obligors is that of principal and surety and this fact is known to the creditor, the case is within the statute.  Supposed distinctions between a "surety" and a "guarantor" are not material in this connection.  It is true that there are different kinds of guaranty and suretyship promises, differences that are woven into the terms of the promise and that may exist irrespective of whether the word "guaranty" or the word "suretyship" is used.  The surety may guarantee, warrant, assure, promise, insure, or indemnify, with the same meaning and the same legal effect in each case.[14]  Differences necessarily lie, however, in the performances that he is promising.  He may promise a payment of money on a certain day, or such a payment thirty days after default by P, or he may guarantee that judgment against P can be collected, or he may promise to insure or to indemnify C against loss by reason of a loan to P. The legal duty of S in each case will be measured by the extent

---

97.  **Eng.**—Eastwood v. Kenyon, 11 A. & E. 438 (1840).

98.  **N.C.**—Davis v. Faulkner, 119 S.E. 819, 186 N.C. 438 (1923).

and character and conditions of the performance promised. In all the cases put, however, S is a surety and his promise is within the statute. There will be differences also in the purposes for which S makes his promise to C and in the kind of consideration that C gives for the promise; these may be sufficient to take S's promise out of the statute as will appear in discussing the "leading object" rule.

In each of the following cases, assuming that at S's request C sells goods to P on credit, the particular form of words in which S's promise is couched does not take the promise out of the statute: (1) "If P doesn't pay, I will"; (2) "I will pay the bill";[15] (3) "I will see you paid";[16] (4) "I will guarantee payment";[17] (5) "I will be your surety";[18] (6) "I will indemnify you against loss";[19] (7) "I will insure payment to you"; (8) "I will pay if P becomes insolvent"; (9) "I will be your surety that the debt can be collected."

In each of these cases P is the principal debtor because he promised C to pay, because he gets the whole beneficial consideration from C and C knows it, and because P is bound to exonerate S. In (1), the promise is expressly conditional on nonpayment by P; each one of the others is likewise conditional in legal effect, and was so intended by the parties even though they did not so state in express terms.

The fact that the principal debtor's obligation is a conditional one, or that the promise to answer for it is conditional on something besides the principal's nonperformance, does not take the promise out of the guaranty clause of the statute.[20] Further, a promise to pay a part of the debt of another is as much within the statute as is a promise to pay all of his debt.[21]

A promise to sign a document that will make the signer a surety for the debt of another to the promisee is within the statute.[22] The following promises are illustrations: to indorse another's note;[23] to sign a note as accommodation maker;[24] to accept a bill for accommodation;[25] to sign a bond as surety.[26]

## § 364. Promised Performance must Operate to Discharge the Debtor

A promise to answer for the debt or default of another is a promise to discharge the debt or other obligation. It makes no difference whether the promised performance is similar to or different from that owed by the principal debtor; a promise to discharge another person's money debt by delivering an automobile to the creditor would be within the statute.[65] It would be answer-

---

15. **Eng.**—Butcher v. Andrews, Comb. 473, Salk. 23 (1698); Marriot v. Lister, 2 Wils. 141 (1762).

ing for the debt. But a promise the performance of which will not operate as a discharge of the debt either in whole or in part is not within the statute.[66] The following promises have been held not within the statute: a promise to forbear to pay moneys due to the principal debtor until the creditor could issue garnishment papers;[67] to get one T. P. M. to sign as surety for the debt;[68] to pay £50 if the creditor would forbear to sue the debtor for a month;[69] a warranty that the principal debtor is solvent[70] or is not an infant;[71] to induce the principal debtor to execute a chattel mortgage as security.[72] If a promise is to pay a sum measured by the debt of a third person, but the promised payment is not to discharge that debt, the promisor is not a surety and his promise is not within the statute.[73]

In these cases performance by the promisor would in no part discharge the obligation of the principal debtor; and the promisor would be equally bound to perform his promise even though the principal debtor commits no default whatever.

### § 365. Novations Not within the Statute

To fall within the statute, the promise must be one the performance of which will discharge the obligation of another. Therefore, if the promise itself is accepted by the creditor in immediate discharge of and in substitution for the third person's obligation, the promise is not within the statute. In such case the contract is called a novation. There is nothing in the words of the statute itself to indicate clearly that a novation promise by which one pays the debt of another was not intended to be included; but the cases appear to be unanimous in holding that it is not.[74] The promise must be one to answer for an obligation that has existence after the promise is made, although it may also have had a previous existence or may not exist until long after the promise is made. A creditor cannot take the guarantor's promise out of the statute by discharging the principal debtor after the making of the guaranty.[75] Instead, he would thereby discharge the guarantor also.

For a novation to exist, the third person's duty to the creditor must be discharged at the time the new promise is made, although this need not be known to the person so discharged. The discharge depends only upon the assent of the creditor to receive the new promise in substitution for and discharge of the old one.[76] No consideration from the discharged debtor to the new promisor is necessary.[77]

---

74.    **Ala.**—La Duke **v.** Barbee, 73 So. 472, 198 Ala. 234 (1916); Smith Bros. v. Miller, 44 So. 399, 152 Ala. 485 (1907); Aultman v. Fletcher, 18 So. 215, 110 Ala. 452 (1895).

**N.Y.**—Booth **v.** Eighmie, 60 N.Y. 238 (1875); Meriden Britannia Co. v. Zingsen, 48 N.Y. 247, 8 Am.Rep. 549 (1872); Milovsky v. Shapiro, 172 N. Y.S. 346 (1918).

# CHAPTER 16

## DEBTS OF ANOTHER—LEADING OBJECT RULE—INDEMNITY CONTRACTS

---

## § 366. "Leading Object" Rule—Benefit to the Promisor

This rule has been stated as follows: "When the leading object of the promise or agreement is to become guarantor or surety to the promisee for a debt for which a third party is and continues to be primarily liable, the agreement, whether made before or after or at the time with the promise of the principal, is within the statute, and not binding unless evidenced by writing. On the other hand, when the leading object of the promisor is to subserve some interest or purpose of his own, notwithstanding the effect is to pay or discharge the debt of another, his promise is not within the statute."[1] The substance of this rule has been expressed in various other forms and it has received wide application and approval.[2] It is obvious that any such rule must involve fine distinctions in degree of benefit and difficult questions as to purpose

---

1. **U.S.**—Davis v. Patrick, 12 S.Ct. 58, 141 U.S. 479, 35 L.Ed. 826 (1891); Emerson v. Slater, 22 How. 28, 16 L.Ed. 360 (1859).

2. An often quoted form of statement is found in Emerson v. Slater, 22 How. 28, 16 L.Ed. 360 (U.S.1859). "But whenever the main purpose and object of the promisor is not to answer for another, but to sub-serve some pecuniary or business purpose of his own, involving either a benefit to himself, or damage to the other contracting party, his promise is not within the statute, although it may be in form a promise to pay the debt of another, and although the performance of it may incidentally have the effect of extinguishing that liability."

and motive. Sometimes it is not easy to determine the "leading object," as the courts have found.

Among the questions that may arise are the following: Must the promisee as well as the promisor be aware of the "leading object" and participate in the promisor's purpose?[3] Must the "leading object" of the promisor also constitute his "sole" object of desire? Must the purpose of the promisor be a "business purpose" as opposed to a social or philanthropic one? Must his interest be a "pecuniary interest" rather than a sentimental one? Is it material that the indebted third party gets some benefit also, either from the making of the new promise or from its performance? How substantial and immediate must be the benefit to the promisor? Does the promisor have a right of exoneration by the third party? On performance by the promisor does he have a right of indemnity against the indebted third party, or does he assume the position of an assignee of the creditor's right? To these questions a short and dogmatic answer cannot be given.

The "leading object" rule in its various forms has been subjected to more or less criticism.[4] The best answer to this criticism is to be found in the vast number of cases in which it has been applied. It involves difficult questions of fact; but nevertheless it is believed that this rule has a sound logical and practical basis. There is a difference between cases where the promisor makes his promise for the benefit and accommodation of another and cases where he makes it for his own benefit and concern.[5] In the former cases he is a surety, having to some degree a fiduciary relation with the third person; in the latter cases he is a stranger to the third person and does not belong to the class deserving the protection of the statute. In the former cases he has the equitable rights of exoneration and indemnity; in the latter cases he has not, his right against the third person being that of an assignee only. This will be developed more fully below, after first presenting the forms in which the rule has appeared and the cases in which it has been applied.

It is very clear that if the creditor and the promisor are contracting on such terms as to show that they intend the promisor to become an assignee of the creditor's right against the debtor, the promise to the creditor is not within the statute. The promisor is not promising to answer for the debt of another; he is promising to buy the debt of another. Often, however, the purpose of the promisor is merely to acquire the beneficial consideration that the creditor gives for his promise, without intending either to discharge the debtor or to become an assignee of the debt. In such cases, when the promisor actually pays, the facts will usually make it seem just to put him in the position of the creditor as an assignee of his right against the debtor. Whenever this is true, the promise to pay should be held to be not within the statute.

As has already been observed in a previous section,[8] the defendant's promise is not within the statute if the promised performance will not discharge the debt of another in whole or in part. When a promise is made to pay for some consideration of benefit to the promisor, there is always a possibility that the payment is not intended to affect any other person's obligation. If such was the intent, the promise is not to answer for the debt of another. The "leading object" rule, however, operates to take thousands of promises out of the statute, even though the promised performance was intended and will actually operate to terminate another's duty to the creditor, in spite of occasional statements to the contrary.[9] Not enough consideration has been given to the fact that in these cases the promisor may become an assignee in the creditor's exact place, thus showing that he is a debtor and not a surety for another debtor. In general the parties seem not to contemplate this possibility very clearly, although they clearly intend no gift to the third person.

In discussing this subject the contrasting words that will be used herein are "surety" and "debtor." If the facts are such as to take the case out of the statute, the promisor will be called a "debtor"; if otherwise, he will be called a "surety." The two terms themselves, however, cannot be used as the basis of distinction in applying the statute. It is not enough to say that a promise is not within the statute because the promisor is a "debtor," any more than it is enough to say that it is not within the statute because the promise is an "original" one and not "collateral." The basic distinctions must be found in the actual situation of the parties to the transaction. The following sections are a discussion of various combinations of facts in which the courts have applied the statute, determining whether there was or was not a beneficial consideration of such a character as to constitute the promisor's "leading object" so as to make him a "debtor" instead of a "surety" and his promise "original" instead of "collateral."

### § 367. "Leading Object" is Not Identical with "Consideration"

It should be noted in the beginning that a consideration may be sufficient to satisfy the requirements of the common law of contracts without being sufficient to satisfy the "leading object" rule and take the promise out of the statute of frauds. A promise is not out of the statute merely because there is a consideration for it.[10] It might better be said that a promise is never within the statute unless there is a consideration for it, since the requirement of a consideration for an informal promise was part of the law of contracts long before the passage of the statute, and the statute was not passed for the purpose of making unenforceable promises that were already unenforceable.[11] The statute is applicable to promises to answer for the debt of another for which there is some sufficient consideration. It appears, however, that certain kinds of consideration will prevent a promise from being one "to answer for the debt of another" and will make the promisor a debtor on his own account. The problem, therefore, is to determine what kinds of consideration will make a promisor a debtor on his own account and what kinds will not. This will form the subject matter of a number of following sections.

### § 368.   Illustrations of Beneficial Consideration Constituting the "Leading Object"—Protection of Property Interest

There are several very frequently recurring situations in which the promisor is held to be a debtor and not a surety. He may have been bound by some previous duty of his own and may be bargaining for forbearance or other relief in return for his promise.[12] Although not bound by a personal duty, he may have been under a liability to the loss of some of his property by virtue of a lien or mortgage held by the promisee or by virtue of some other power over his property interests held by the promisee.

If the promisor has a property interest to protect and the plaintiff has either a lien thereon or the power to create one, a forbearance to enforce the lien or to use the power is of direct benefit to the defendant. If to protect his interest he promises to discharge the debt, for which the lien was security, in consideration of forbearance to enforce the lien, the promise is not that of a surety and is not within the statute.[13] So a promise by the owner of an equity of redemption to pay a mortgage debt with which his land is charged, but for which he was not personally bound, in consideration of the mortgagee's forbearance to foreclose, is not within the statute.[14]

The actual existence of a lien is not necessary in order to hold that the promisor is a debtor and not a surety. The promisee's forbearance to attach the promisor's goods or to attack the validity of the title claimed by the promisor may be enough to satisfy the "leading object" rule.[15] So also may be a forbearance to levy execution or to make a bid at an execution sale of property that the promisor wishes to buy free and clear, or on which he wishes to make an unhampered attachment or levy himself.[16] Forbearance by the promisee to bring action against the estate of a deceased person may be a sufficient "leading object" for a promise to pay the promisee's claim by the beneficiaries of the estate whose shares would be decreased by the promisee's action.[17]

In these cases the promise is not taken out of the statute merely because the promisor has a "property" interest to protect. While "property" has long been a term to conjure with, in this

13.   **U.S.**—Cincinnati Traction Co. v. Cole, 258 F. 169 (C.C.A.6th, 1919); Choate v. Hoogstraat, 105 F. 713 (C.C.A.7th, 1901).

instance there is no magic possessed by it that is not equally possessed by other types of "leading objects" and benefits received.

The "leading object" that is sufficient to take a promise out of the statute must be found in the consideration for the promise and not in the promise itself or in the result of its performance. The promise is itself a promise to a creditor to pay a debt due to him from a third party; if it is not such a promise, it is certainly not within the statute. The performance of the promise will clearly benefit the creditor; and it will benefit the debtor too by discharging his duty to that creditor (although as appears later, it may be merely the substitution of a new creditor in the one who is making payment). The *promisor* is not in the least benefited by the performance of his own promise. In order to take his promise out of the statute, he must be bargaining for a consideration that is beneficial to himself and that constitutes his primary object of desire.

Thus in Bailey v. Marshall,[18] the defendant promised to pay Pennock's debt to the plaintiff. The consideration for which he bargained was the plaintiff's forbearance to bid at the sale in competition with the defendant; but it was not beneficial to Pennock at all. Indeed, it was likely to be quite injurious to Pennock in causing his property to sell at a low price, so injurious that such contracts have been held to be fraudulent and illegal. The benefit to the defendant, therefore, was not only his leading object, it was his *sole* object.

## § 369. Promises to Pay Debts Due Subcontractors

In building contract cases several parties are involved. The owner wishes to get the building and it is the duty of the contractor to complete it. Materialmen and laborers have contract rights against the contractor for goods sold and labor done. If the contractor fails to pay the materialman, the latter is usually privileged to hold up further deliveries, and the contractor owes a debt for goods already delivered and damages for breach. The contractor may have abandoned the whole contract; and if so, the materialman may have no power to charge him in debt for any further deliveries. Or the contractor may be still on the job and desirous of further deliveries.

(1) In any case where the building contractor is not indebted for the goods or labor for which the defendant promises to pay, it is clear that the promise is not within the statute. The building contractor may not be indebted for them for any one of several reasons. He may never have contracted to pay for them at all; as, for example, where he asked the plaintiff for credit and was refused, whereupon the goods were sold, or work done under

18.　34 A. 326, 174 Pa. 602 (1896).

a contract made solely and directly with the defendant.[21]　Secondly, he may have contracted with the plaintiff for the goods or labor, but may not be indebted for them because he had himself broken and repudiated his contract before they were supplied and the plaintiff thereafter contracted solely with the defendant.[22]　And thirdly, he may not be indebted for the goods or labor because the plaintiff himself has repudiated the contract to supply them on his credit and thereafter has contracted solely with the defendant.[23]　If, in order to get his building completed or for any other purpose, the owner himself buys outright from the materialman the further goods necessary, promising therefor only the market prices, with no reference whatever to the contractor's past debt, the owner is not a surety and his promise is not within the statute.[24]

(2)　The owner may buy outright the further goods or service, and promise in return to pay their market price and also the past debt of the contractor.　In such case the owner's promise is certainly divisible and is enforceable as to the agreed price of the new goods supplied to him.[25]　Many cases have held that the owner's oral promise to pay the contractor's past debt is also enforceable, since the owner gets the newly supplied goods, and gets them in return for his promise of a sum composed of two parts— the market price and the past debt.[26]　A few cases are contra and deny enforcement of the oral promise to pay the past debt.[27]

(3)　If the contractor is still on the job, the owner may ask the materialman to continue to supply goods to the contractor for use on the building, promising in return to pay for such new goods, or even promising to pay their market price and also the past debt.　In this case, the contractor is indebted for the new goods as well as for the goods supplied previously; but it is generally held that the owner's promise is not within the statute, on the ground that the delivery of the new goods to the contractor for incorporation into the building was directly beneficial to the owner and formed his "leading object." [28]　In such cases it is quite possible for the owner to make this contract solely for his own benefit and as a stranger to the contractor; he may even intend to become an assignee of the materialman.　If the owner does this he is merely buying the creditor's claim and he is not a surety.　In other cases, however, his purpose is to help the contractor perform the contract by becoming a surety for him.　In some cases it may be difficult to determine what his purpose was;

---

28.　**U.S.**—Davis v. Patrick, 12 S.Ct. 58, 141 U.S. 479, 35 L.Ed. 826 (1891), defendant was a creditor of a mining company and promised to pay the past and future wages of the plaintiff as superintendent if he would remain in charge and protect the defendant's interests; Cincinnati Traction Co. v. Cole, 258 F. 169 (C.C.A.6th, 1919), decided on other grounds also.

and in them the doubt should be resolved against the owner, provided that at his request and in consideration of his promise the promisee delivered goods or rendered service actually beneficial in a pecuniary way to the promisor.

## § 370.  Further Illustrations of "Leading Object"

There are many other types of beneficial consideration in return for which the defendant has been willing to promise to pay the debt of another and which have been held sufficient to make the defendant a debtor instead of a surety. It may be land, goods, or money conveyed directly to the promisor;[36] payment by the plaintiff of a debt due to the promisor or the doing of that which will secure payment thereof;[37] the performance or discharge of an obligation owed by the promisor to some third person;[38] the granting to the defendant of a valuable contract;[39] or any other consideration that in fact induces the defendant to promise to pay for it for his own benefit.[40]

## § 384.  Contracts of Indemnity

The conflict that exists in regard to promises of indemnity is in part due to differences in definition of the word "indemnity" and to mental confusion arising out of the complexity of legal relations in cases involving at least three parties and often more than three. The statute itself does not contain the word "indemnity"; it does not say "any special promise to indemnify another." A promise of indemnity is within the statute only in case it is held to be a promise to answer for the debt or default of another person. When will it be so held?

In the first place, it is clear that a promise of indemnity is not within the statute if there is no duty owed by a third person to the promisee that would be discharged by the performance of the new promisor or the performance of which would discharge the new promisor. Thus, if A says to B: "If you will buy 100 shares of X stock, I will indemnify you against loss," A's promise is not within the statute, since there is no third person who owes anything to B, the promisee.[89] The same reason applies to promises to indemnify an officer who seizes goods at the promisor's request,[90] or one who brings or defends a suit in which the promisor has some interest,[91] or one who is induced to make an entry or a user that may turn out to be tortious.[92] A promise to a debtor or other obligor to pay his debt or save him harmless from his obligation is a promise of indemnity not within the statute.[93]

Secondly, it is equally clear that a promise of indemnity is within the statute if it is made to a creditor of some third person and for that person's benefit and accommodation, and if performance by either the third person or the new promisor will discharge the duty of the other to the creditor. In such a case

411

the word indemnify may be used in about the sense of "guarantee" or "be surety for." Such use of the term is not bad English, although it ought to be avoided in law. Thus, if S says to C: "Lend money to P and I will indemnify you against loss," the promise of S is a promise to answer for P's debt to C and is within the statute.[94]

### § 385. Oral Contract to Indemnify a Surety

There is one type of case that presents special difficulties and that has resulted in much conflict of decision. This is a promise to indemnify one who is a surety, a guarantor, or bail for a third person. The following are illustrations: A says to S, (1) "Indorse P's note to C as surety and I will indemnify you;" (2) "Guarantee P's debt to C and I will save you harmless"; (3) Lend P your credit in the purchase of goods from C and I will see that you lose nothing." In cases like these the clear weight of authority is that A's promise is not within the statute;[95] but a good many decisions have been contra,[96] and some law writers agree with them.[97]

The majority decisions already cited are supported by many cases holding that one who becomes a surety on the oral promise of a co-surety to indemnify him can enforce that promise.[98] In this case it is true that the promisor is usually bound to the creditor to pay the whole debt, although his duty to a co-surety is merely to pay his pro rata share; but it is also true that the promisee is a surety for another person who owes to such promisee the duty of exoneration and indemnity. Direct support is also found in most of the cases dealing with promises to indemnify bail. These are discussed separately below.

### § 387. Promises to Indemnify Bail

A bail bondsman is a surety; and a promise to indemnify him against loss by reason of his going bail is in almost all respects like a promise to indemnify other kinds of sureties.[22] Indeed, there is no difference whatever in the case of a bail bondsman in

95. **U.S.**—Townsley v. Sumrall, 27 U.S. (2 Pet.) 170, 7 L.Ed. 386 (1829).

**Eng.**—Thomas v. Cook, 8 B. & C. 728 (1828); Reader v. Kingham, 13 C.B. N.S. 344 (1862); Wildes v. Dudlow, L.R. 19 Eq. 198 (1874); Harburg India Rubber Comb Co. v. Martin, [1902] 1 K.B. 778, semble; Guild & Co. v. Conrad, [1894] 2 Q.B. 885; In re Bolton, 8 T.L.R. 668 (1892).

97. Williston, Contracts, § 482; Arnold, Outline of Sur. and Guar. (1927).

Holding the view supported herein, see Stearns, Suretyship (1922) § 33; Costigan, Cases on Contracts, 1254, note 18; Bishop, Contracts, § 1216; Corbin's Anson on Contracts (1930) § 97; 2 Street, Foundations Leg. Liab., 186; Burdick, Suretyship and the Statute of Frauds, 20 Col. L.Rev. 154 (1920); Steinmetz, Guaranty and Indemnity and Credit Insurance, 44 Am.L.Rev. 736 (1910); 25 R.C.L. 524, § 109. And see Browne, Statute of Frauds, § 162.

a civil case, although a bail bond in a civil case is not so common as it once was in the days of imprisonment for debt. All the decisions are to the effect that a promise to indemnify S if he will go bail for P in a civil case brought against P by C is not within the statute. This is true even though we assume that in such cases P is bound to exonerate and to reimburse S, just as in other cases of suretyship.

The same result is reached in the case of a bail bondsman in criminal cases. A promise to indemnify the bondsman is not within the statute.[23] This may be supported, however, on a ground not applicable to civil bail cases. It has been held, though not universally, that if S bails out P in a criminal case, S has no right that P shall exonerate or reimburse him in case of P's default in appearance; this is on the ground that P is in S's custody and the public welfare requires that S should have the utmost interest in surrendering P back into custody of officers of the law for trial.[24] The policy of this rule may be regarded as doubtful, particularly in cases where a cash deposit is accepted as the equivalent of a personal bond of a surety. But in any jurisdiction holding that the bail bondsman has no right against the person for whom he goes bail it is certain that a promise to indemnify the bail bondsman is not within the statute.[25]

## § 388.　Insurance Promises are Not within the Statute

There are different kinds of insurance; and no doubt the term is sometimes used loosely enough to include suretyship. Better usage, however, would exclude suretyship and would make the statute inapplicable to cases that are called insurance. In the case of "liability insurance" the insurer cannot be a surety, for his promise is to one who may in the future become an obligor in default; the promise is therefore to an obligor to pay his debt to a third person, and it falls within the rule applicable in such cases. One who insures another against loss by tornado is not answering for the debt or default of another person, for there is no other person. But the promise of one who insures against losses caused to the promisee by the tort or other breach of duty of indeterminate third persons would be within the statute were it not for the fact that the insurer is a total stranger to those third persons and the contract is not made in the least for their benefit. The insurer is not a surety and the reasoning of the preceding section is applicable.[26] In such cases the promise is solely for the benefit of the promisee; and the performance of the promise does not discharge the defaulting third person. Even if performance by the insurer should discharge the third person's duty

26.　Minn.—Quinn-Shepherdson Co.
v. United States Fidelity & G. Co.,
172 N.W. 693, 142 Minn. 428 (1919).

to the promisee, there is nothing in the relations of the parties to prevent the insurer from taking an assignment from the promisee and getting full judgment, even though in excess of the amount paid, against the defaulter.[27] This kind of insurance is called "credit insurance"; and the insurer's promise should be held not within the statute, for the reason that the relations between the insurer and the indeterminate third parties that may become indebted are not those of surety and principal. The insurance contract is not made at the request or for the benefit and accommodation of such third persons, and there is a consideration of benefit to the promisor that constitutes the sole object for which he gives the promise.[28]

A contract of reinsurance is a contract with the original insurer to fulfill its obligations with its policy holders. The promisee is an obligor, not a creditor, and the promise is not one of suretyship or within the statute of frauds.[29]

## § 389.  Del Credere Agency

It is very common for a factor or other agent selling goods or making other contracts for his principal to insure the principal against loss caused by nonpayment by third persons or other failure of performance by them. The reasoning of the preceding two sections is clearly applicable here; and it is uniformly held that the promise of the del credere agent is not within the statute.[30] Such an agent is contracting solely for his own benefit; his leading object is to make larger commissions as an agent; he is a stranger to the indefinite third persons with whom he may deal on his principal's behalf; he has no right of exoneration against them; he may buy the principal's right at a low figure and enforce it in full; he is an insurer and not a surety.[31]

A del credere agent is one who guarantees to his own principal the performance due him from third persons. The case of an agent who guarantees to the third person that his principal will perform in accordance with the contract must be distinguished; it is within the statute of frauds in the absence of any showing that his relation to his principal is other than that of a surety for him.[32]

This conclusion is not affected by the fact that the agent's promise is to pay the sum due from the third parties if they do not pay. It is quite unnecessary, therefore, as well as inaccurate in the great majority of cases, to assert that the agent's promise is merely a warranty that he will contract with only solvent persons or that the agent is a purchaser of the principal's

---

**30.**  U.S.—Bradley v. Richardson, 2 Blatchf. 343, Fed.Cas.No. 1,786, 23 Vt. 720 (C.C.Vt.1851).

Mass.—Swan v. Nesmith, 24 Mass. (7 Pick.) 220, 19 Am.Dec. 282 (1828), "the form of action is immaterial".

goods and not a mere agent to sell them.  Of course, a factor may be a purchaser instead of an agent,[33] and an agent may warrant solvency instead of guaranteeing payment;  if so, his promise is not within the statute.  But a del credere agent's promise is usually a guaranty of payment, and yet he is not an accommodation surety and his promise is not within the statute.[34]

## § 390.  Guaranty by an Assignor of a Debt

If as a part of an assignment transaction the assignor guarantees that the debt will be paid, the guaranty promise is not within the statute.[35]  This looks like a promise to answer for the debt of another;  but, even so, the promisor is an insurer and not a true surety, just as in the case of a del credere agent.  The assignor's promise is made solely to induce the payment of a larger purchase price to him and not in the least for the benefit of the debtor.  In fact, it does not benefit the debtor in the least.  If the assignor later on settles with the assignee he can by a reassignment regain his original position as creditor for the full amount, and it is only by buying a reassignment that he can get any reimbursement whatever from the debtor.

## § 395.  General Summary of Rules for Applying the Guaranty Clause

Without asserting that all the cases can be reconciled, it is believed that the following is an accurate general statement of the results of the decisions.

A promise is not one to answer for the debt or default of another and the promisor is not a surety in any of the following five instances:

(1) If there is no other obligor contemporaneously bound for the same performance.

    (a) No other one was ever bound at all.

    (b) Another was previously bound but has been discharged by novation of which the new promise is a part.

    (c) Another is still bound, but for a different performance.

(2) If it was not made to a creditor (an obligee) of another person.

(3) If the promisor is not entitled to exoneration by the third person, but instead owes him a duty of indemnity.

(4) If the promise is solely (or at least primarily) in return for a compensating benefit received by the promisor and constituting his object of desire and not at all for the benefit of the third person who is also indebted.

415

The promisor is here a primary debtor; and his performance will not ordinarily discharge the obligation of the third person at all. On performance, the promisor becomes an assignee. The "leading object" rule is included herein.

(5) If the promise is to pay out of funds of the third person.

On the other hand, a promise is within this clause of the statute if it complies with the four following requirements:

(1) It must be made to a creditor (an obligee).

(2) Its performance must be one that will discharge a present or future duty owed by a third person to the promisee.

(3) It must be aleatory in effect, performance being conditional upon nonperformance by a third person.

(4) It must have been made, in part at least, for the benefit of a third person, who is under a duty to exonerate and indemnify the promisor but whose duty is not in excess of exact indemnity.

# CHAPTER 17

## STATUTE OF FRAUDS—INTERESTS IN LAND

---

## § 396. Application of the Land Clause—in General

The fourth provision of section 4 is that "no action shall be brought . . . upon any contract or sale of lands, tenements, or hereditaments, or any interest in or concerning them." The phrase "contract or sale" is a little puzzling, for the statute was clearly not intended to include executed conveyances. The mode of making a conveyance is determined by the law of property quite independently of this clause of the statute. It has come to be applied as if the phrase read "contract for the sale." The terms "tenements and hereditaments" were added to "lands" perhaps in excess of caution to make sure that all real property should be within the protection of the statute and perhaps because tenements and hereditaments played a more important part in property law two hundred and fifty years ago than they do now. We need spend little time on these terms. A "tenement," in its modern sense, is within section 4 of the statute only if it is attached to land in some permanent fashion. A severed house is personalty. A "hereditament" is any form of property that descends to the heir; aside from lands and tenements it includes what are known as "heirlooms," certain movable articles that by custom descend to the heir. Probably there is little left of the custom in this country. Many of the statutory re-enactments of section 4 say nothing of tenements and hereditaments.

A conveyance of land must be distinguished from a contract to make such a conveyance. The acts that are necessary and sufficient to be operative as a conveyance are determined by the law of property, not by the law of contracts or by section 4 of the statute of frauds. These acts have varied with the history of property, chief among them being livery of seisin and delivery of a deed. An operative conveyance is a transfer of property, extinguishing the legal relations of the transferor with third persons and creating similar ones between the transferee and third persons. A contract for the sale of land, on the other hand, is meant primarily to affect only the legal relations of the two contracting parties. The conveyance creates "rights in rem"; the contract, "rights in personam."

In order that a contract may be within this clause of the statute, it must be one the performance of which involves a transfer of property in land; but it is not material when that transfer is to take place or what consideration is promised in exchange for it. A contract for a mutual exchange of lands is within the statute; [1] and so also is a contract whereby one promises to buy land and to convey it later on to the promisee,[2] or to buy back land that is then being transferred to the promisee,[3] or to receive land as part of a fee for services as an attorney.[4]

### § 397.  Promises by the Purchaser are within the Statute

A bilateral contract for the sale of land includes a promise to buy and pay the price as well as a return promise to sell and make conveyance. Part performance by either of the two parties may have an effect upon enforceability and will be given consideration hereafter; but as long as such a contract is wholly executory it is unenforceable against either party.[5] The promise to buy is as much within the statute as is the promise to sell. The words of the statute are "contract or sale of lands," not "promise to convey lands"; the phrase equally applies to the promises of both parties. Therefore, as long as conveyance has not yet been made and there is no sufficient memorandum, the seller can not enforce a promissory note or a check given for the price.[6] A promise to pay money is not, in itself and standing alone, within the statute; but it does not stand alone.

There are some statutes that expressly require that a memorandum of a contract for the sale of land shall be signed by the vendor, the grantor, or the lessor.[7] In a few other states, even though the statutory words are that the writing must be "signed by the party to be charged," these words are interpreted as requiring the signature of the vendor only.[8] This interpretation should not be followed, and generally is not. It must be based upon the notion that the statute was intended to protect landowners and not land buyers. In all of these states, the vendor can enforce the purchaser's promise without having the purchaser's signature; [9] but the purchaser cannot enforce the vendor's promise without the latter's signature. It has also been held that the vendor cannot enforce the contract against the purchaser unless he introduces a sufficient memorandum signed by himself, the vendor.[10] It would seem to be easy enough for the vendor to prepare such a memorandum and sign it at any time prior to bringing suit for enforcement, so that in the case of an oral contract for the sale of land the vendor would have the purchaser at his mercy. But the courts have tried to prevent this result by requiring some sort of "mutuality." They have held that a memorandum signed by himself does not enable the vendor to enforce the contract unless the memorandum so signed has been delivered to the purchaser or otherwise accepted by him as a correct memorandum of agreement.[11] The assent of the purchaser so required is more than his assent to the terms of the contract; it is an assent to the written memorandum as a correct expression of the terms of that contract. A requirement that the purchaser shall have signed, when he is the party to be charged, would be more effective to protect him against perjury and fraud than is a requirement that he shall have assented to the memorandum that is signed only by the vendor. The vendor can prepare a memorandum, sign it, and prove the purchaser's assent by oral testimony.

## § 400. Interests in Land—Estates, Property

The statute says "land or any interest in or concerning" land. The most difficult problem involved is to determine what is an interest in land within the intent of the statute. Until recent years, it was generally supposed that the interests in land recognized by law were comparatively few and could be enumerated in full by giving a list of technical names. A more improved legal analysis shows that this is not the case; but it remains true that all of the traditionally recognized interests for which the law provided a name are within the meaning of the statute. Thus, the statute includes all contracts that call for a conveyance of any of the so-called "estates" in land, with such exceptions only as the statute itself may expressly create. Among these "estates" are fee simple and fee tail, estates for life and for years, freehold and leasehold, reversions and remainders. In addition, the statute includes such interests in the land of another as are called easements and profits, although not dignified by the sounding title of "estate."

The definitions of the foregoing terms were never as exact and detailed as is desirable; and with the growing complexity of modern life new interests are being created that do not fall easily within any of the traditional classes. Whatever is regarded by the courts as an interest in real property is within the purview of the statute. The exact limits cannot be determined with absolute certainty, because here as elsewhere they must vary as the courts develop the concept of "interest"; but by collecting a number of illustrative cases an approximate and reasonably safe generalization can be made. No more than this can properly be claimed for any of the general rules of law.

The term "property" has two very general usages. The first and more general is to make it denote the tangible or intangible subject matter of manifold rights, powers, privileges, and immunities. These last are the legal relations with other persons that have been defined elsewhere. "Manifold" relations, as the term is here used, are those relations with numerous other but not specifically identified persons, each of these relations with one person being precisely similar to those with each other person. Thus, a landowner has a right that X shall not enter on the land and an exactly similar right that N shall not so enter. These many exactly similar rights may well be described as above by the word "manifold," to distinguish them from rights against one other person or against a few other specific persons, usually contractual or quasi-contractual in character.

The other and somewhat less general usage of the term "property" is to make it denote the above described manifold rights, powers, privileges, and immunities themselves rather than the subject matter. Whichever denotation we choose to adopt, the term connotes both the tangible or intangible subject matter and the manifold relations with other people that make the subject matter useful and enjoyable for men. It is the first and more generally accepted denotation that is adopted here.

The term "interest" on the other hand is practically always limited in its use to denote some combination of legal relations with reference to a subject matter. An interest in land, therefore, is some combination of rights, powers, privileges, and immunities that affect the use and enjoyment of specified land, the person having these rights, etc., being called the "owner." "Ownership" varies greatly, because "interests" consist of very numerous combinations of relations. Thus, a "fee simple" is perhaps the largest possible combination; but deprive the owner of his power to cut off his heir and the combination may become a "fee tail" or an estate for life. Again an owner of land may have manifold rights that others shall not enter thereon, except as against his adjacent neighbor and his assigns. In such case the owner is only a part owner of the land with a somewhat lessened interest; while the neighbor also has an interest in the land and is a part owner of it, his interest being perhaps called an "easement" or a "right of way."  In like manner every recognized interest can be analyzed and differentiated from others.[31]

It is only such property as is included within the term "lands, tenements, and hereditaments" that falls within section 4 of the statute.  Property that is described as "goods, wares and merchandise" falls within section 17, to be discussed later on.[32]

### § 401.  Interests in Land—Trusts

When land is held in trust by one person for the use and benefit of another, the former is called a trustee and the latter a *cestui que trust* or beneficiary.  Both the trustee and the beneficiary have an interest in the land, as that term is used in the statute of frauds; and a contract for the sale of his interest by either the trustee or the beneficiary is within section 4 of the statute.[33]

The creation of a trust in land is different from the transfer of one previously created.  It may be created by the voluntary declaration of an owner that he holds in trust, by a conveyance to a grantee with an express provision that he shall hold in trust for the grantor or for a third person, or by a contract that the owner shall hold as trustee.  It may also be created by operation of law, entirely without the assent of the party who is required to hold as a trustee for another.

The creation of an express trust by a voluntary declaration or conveyance might not be held to be within section 4 of the statute, even though an interest in land is being transferred.  When the owner of land turns himself into a trustee by a voluntary declaration, he is transferring an interest in the land to the beneficiary. When an owner transfers land to another in trust for a third, an interest in land is being transferred to the trustee and another interest to the third person.  When an owner transfers land to another in trust for the grantor himself, an interest is being transferred to the trustee and a remaining interest retained by the grantor.  Nevertheless, a transaction like these may not be re-

---

31.  This is the analysis that is recognized and followed by the American Law Institute, in its Restatement both of the law of Property and of the law of Contract.  Restatement, Contracts, § 195, reads as follows: "An interest in land within the meaning of the Statute is any right, privilege, power or immunity, or combination thereof, relating to realty which under the rules of law governing that subject, (a) is property in realty, and (b) does not fall within the definition of goods in Sec. 200."

32.  By the doctrine of equitable conversion, land was for certain purposes treated in equity as personalty.  This was true of partnership realty.  But this doctrine does not take a contract for the sale of such realty out of section 4 and put it within section 17. Brown v. Gray, 70 S.E. 276, 68 W. Va. 555 (1911).

garded as a "contract or sale" of an interest in land. It is not so easy to reach this conclusion, however, if the creation of either the interest of the trustee or that of the beneficiary is by a contract.

Under the original statute of 29 Chas. II, it was not necessary to answer these questions, because sections 7 and 8 of that statute applied to them in express words and forbade the recognition of express trusts in land unless properly evidenced in writing. These sections have been re-enacted in about three-fourths of the United States; [34] and the courts have frequently felt bound to carry out the statutory provisions by refusing to give effect to an oral express trust.[35]

Even where there is no statute requiring an express trust to be in writing, there are cases holding that such a trust cannot be established by evidence of an oral agreement or declaration made antecedently to or contemporaneously with an absolute documentary conveyance.[36] This is by virtue of the parol evidence rule, with the purpose of sustaining the stability of documentary titles. This has some reason if the document contains express words in conflict with the oral trust; otherwise it should not be approved.[37]

The English statute, however, expressly excepted from its provisions requiring a writing all those trusts that are created by implication or construction of law; and American statutes do the same. This has led to much litigation and to a good deal of conflict as to when a constructive trust can be established by oral evidence and enforced by the courts. That such an exception is necessary for the administration of justice can not be doubted. Without such an exception by statute, the courts must themselves have invented one, or the statute would not long have survived. It could not be endured that a promisor should be permitted to hide behind a statute and reap the benefits of his chicane and fraud, or, even in the absence of any fraud, to hide behind the statute and enjoy the benefits of the other party's performance while repudiating his own duty. His repudiation may be a part of an antecedently laid plan to defraud the other party, or it may be merely an afterthought by which he may retain something for nothing. In either case, no system purporting to be a system of justice can fail to require restitution, either specific or in a money equivalent, unless it goes farther and enforces the defendant's express promise itself. Courts of equity used the device of a constructive trust, generally to compel such restitution, but sometimes to enforce the express promise of the defendant. When consciously used for the latter purpose, it may seem to involve a judicial disregard of the express words of the statute; [38] but when used to compel restitution only it is within the express words of the statutory exception, and refusal of relief would be in disregard of the statute.[39]

## § 402. Oral Leases and Oral Contracts to Lease

Of course, the execution of a lease of land operates as a transfer of an interest in that land, whether the specified term is long or short. But the statute of frauds, in all of its adopted forms, expressly provides that oral leases for not more than a period specified in the statute shall be valid. The maximum period so specified is sometimes one year and sometimes as much as three years. As to this the particular statute must be consulted. If the lease agreed upon is for more than this maximum period, an oral contract for its creation is unenforceable, whether it purports to be an immediate transfer of the leasehold interest or to be a contract requiring the future execution of a documentary lease.[62] Such an oral contract can become enforceable by reason of part performance as in the case of contracts for other kinds of interests.[63]

## § 403. Interests in Land—Mortgages and Liens

It is clear that a mortgagee has an interest in the land. An agreement to create such an interest by executing a mortgage on land is within section 4; [75] so also is an agreement that a lender shall have a lien on land as security.[76] The oral promise of the lender to advance the money or credit is unenforceable, as well as the promise of the borrower to make conveyance, so long as the conveyance by the borrower has not been executed.[77] The oral agreement for a lien or a mortgage is not made enforceable by the fact that the promisor delivers possession of his own title deeds.[78]

It is the universally prevailing rule that an absolute conveyance can be shown by oral testimony to have been agreed upon as only security for a loan. The oral agreement that it shall be operative only as a mortgage is enforced.[95] This oral agreement seriously affects the interest that the deed purports to transfer. But the oral agreement itself purports to transfer nothing; it is merely a limitation on a transfer that appears to be made by the written deed. It is not itself a conveyance to the mortgagee; nor is it a conveyance from the mortgagee back to the mortgagor. It is not a conveyance back, because it prevents the grantee from ever being more than a mortgagee, and it retains *ab initio* in the grantor the equity of redemption.[96]

39. For a more complete discussion of trusts, express and constructive, the student is referred to the general treatise; also to works on

Trusts and Restitution. Some applicable rules will be found in Restatement, Trusts, § 44, and Restatement, Restitution, §§ 182, 183.

It remains true, however, that the only recognition of this equity is oral, and there is certainly no written promise to reconvey on payment of the loan.  The statute does not prevent equity from enforcing an express or implied promise of reconveyance, not because it is not a promise to transfer an interest in land, but because it would be a horrid injustice in hundreds of cases to allow the statute to have such an effect.

### § 404.  Interests in Land—Licenses

The legal relations of a person affecting the enjoyment of certain land may be very few and of comparatively slight value.  Such a slight combination of relations constitutes an interest in the land, as that term has been herein defined.  It may not, however, be regarded by the courts as such an interest as should be affected by the statute of frauds.  Thus an owner may give his neighbor's child the privilege of playing on his lawn.  This privilege has some value to the child measured in enjoyment, but not a market value, because he has no power to assign it to others and no immunity from revocation of the privilege by the owner.  It would be ridiculous to make the statute apply to the creation of such a limited interest or to require a formal deed of conveyance in order to create it.  It is the universal custom to create it by a friendly word; and the courts give this word a legally operative effect.  It terminates the child's legal duty to forbear from entering on the lawn and thus prevents his entry from being a trespass.  This is expressed by saying that he has the privilege of entering.

The friendly word by which the above privilege is created has been described in the law of property as a "mere license"; and the interest created thereby has been denied the dignity of any name at all, not being included among "easements" or "profits," and not even being called an "interest" within the statute of frauds.  But the friendly word that constitutes a "license" may create more than a single privilege in the grantee, and still be denied the dignity of the name "interest in the land."  Thus, in a Massachusetts case,[97] one Bryant by a friendly word gave to Taft the "privilege" of cutting ice on that part of a certain pond that was on Bryant's land.  It will be observed that Bryant's friendly word not only prevented Taft from being a trespasser in cutting the ice; it also gave Taft the power of making the ice his own by severing it.  Here, Bryant's friendly word created something of great value to Taft, even though it would have no market value for lack of the power to assign and the immunity from revocation.  The court therefore held, perhaps erroneously as matter of policy, that Taft had no interest that would be protected against injury

97.    Taft v. Bridgton Worsted Co.,
141 N.E. 119, 246 Mass. 444 (1923).

by a third party and no right to damages against one who lowered the water in the pond without just reason, and who totally destroyed the value of Taft's privilege and power of making the ice his own by causing it to settle into the mud.[98]  The court refused to recognize that Taft had an interest in property or to create in him any manifold rights against others.  There is no doubt, however, that had Taft actually severed the ice the court would have declared it to be his property and would have given him the usual manifold rights of an owner of chattels.  Such an interest as Taft had, therefore—the privilege and power of acquiring property by severance—could be created by a friendly word without any compliance with the statute of frauds and without any formal deed.[99]  Bryant, the grantor of this very limited interest, had manifold rights against third persons, including a right that the defendant should not reduce the water level without just cause; to convey these manifold rights to Taft would require a deed of conveyance, and a promise to convey such an interest is within section 4 of the statute.  Taft's interest would then be a "profit à prendre."

## § 405.  Interests in Land—Easements

An easement is a combination of legal relations of such importance affecting the use and enjoyment of land that any contract providing for the creation of an easement is within the statute.[4]  This is true whether the easement is appurtenant to a specific tract of land, and hence assignable only along with the tract itself, or is an easement in gross, not appurtenant to any land.  In either case it represents an important limitation on the ownership of the servient land.

A contract by a landowner to lay out and construct a street on his land for the use of the plaintiff is held to be within the statute.[5]  The legal relations contracted for would constitute an easement of way over the promisor's land.  But if the plaintiff is already the owner of such an easement, a contract whereby the owner of the servient land (or any third person) promises to build a road thereon for the plaintiff's use is not within the statute.[6]  Such a contract would be merely a contract for work and labor and would create no new privilege of use of the land, no new immunity from revocation, and no new manifold relations with third persons with respect to the use of the land.

## § 406.  Interests in Land—Restrictive Covenants

There is much difference of opinion as to whether a restrictive covenant creates an interest in land within the meaning of the statute of frauds.  In probably a majority of the cases it is held that it does, so that an oral agreement restricting the use to which specified land may be put is unenforceable as long as there has been no such part performance as to prevent the statute from being applied.[11]  In most of these cases the court merely assumes its conclusion, without discussing or analyzing the "interest" that is supposed to be created.  There is very respectable authority for the contrary rule, holding that a restrictive agreement is merely a limitation on the use of land and creates no "interest" in the covenantee.[12]

### § 407.  Interests in Land—Profits

One of the long recognized interests in land was called a profit à prendre.  When one is legally privileged for a considerable period of time to take some valuable thing that constitutes part of the land that chiefly belongs to another, such as turf, stone, firewood, hay, young trees, ice, minerals, and game, and has also manifold rights against third persons against interference with the enjoyment of his privilege, he has a profit.[17]  A contract is within the statute if its purpose is the buying or selling of such an interest.[18]  If, on the other hand, an owner of land promises to sever turf, stone, ore, trees, grass, and the like and to transfer the same after severance, the contract is not within the land clause of section 4.  The promisee acquires no profit à prendre or other recognized interest in the land.[19]

The term "profit à prendre" is no longer in very active use; and the question whether a contract for the severance and transfer of a portion of the earth or of its natural product is within the statute of frauds should not be made to depend upon the history and definition of such a term.  Nor is the question determined conclusively by the fact that the subject matter of such a contract, while unsevered, is clearly included within such words as "lands, tenements, and hereditaments."  The proper basis of determination is suggested in the succeeding sections dealing with buildings and growing trees.

### § 408.  Interests in Land—Growing Trees

A contract for the sale of trees not yet severed from the land may be such as to create a profit à prendre.  But ordinarily a profit includes the privilege of a perennial taking of the valuable thing.  In the case of a contract for the sale of specific standing trees, the buyer is not commonly said to acquire a "profit."  Nevertheless, the trees are a part of the land and will remain so until severance;  and if the parties agree that the ownership of the trees is to pass to the buyer before severance, it looks like a contract for the sale of part of the land.  On the other hand, it is also clear that the trees are to be severed and carried away, and that they will no longer be land after severance.  The courts have struggled with this problem and there is conflict in decision.

426

The question that arises in these timber transactions may be either a property question or a contract question. Property questions are: Who owns the trees, before severance or after severance? Who can maintain trespass for cutting the trees, or trover for exercising dominion over the logs? Does a subsequent transferee by deed from the vendor of the trees get the trees and buildings?[20] The contract question is: Can the oral promise of the vendor to sell, or of the vendee to pay, be enforced by the promisee either at law or in equity? It will appear from the cases that the answer to a property question does not depend upon the answer to the contract question; nor does the answer to the latter depend upon the answer to the former. The court may hold that no property in the trees has passed, even though the oral contract for their sale is held to be enforceable and even though there is a writing sufficient to satisfy the statute of frauds.[21] The vendor may be held to have the power to revoke the license to enter and cut the timber, even though it is the breach of an enforceable contract to exercise the power. Also, even though the oral contract is held to be unenforceable, the vendee may be held to have the power to make the trees his own by actual severance, so that he can maintain trespass or trover against third parties or even the vendor himself.

It is primarily the contract question that is considered herein. Is an oral contract for the sale of standing trees within the statute of frauds because it is for the sale of an interest in land? Sometimes the answer is said to depend on whether the parties contracted to pass "title" before severance or after severance. If the former, the contract is for the sale of land, because unsevered trees are land and descend to the heir. If the latter, the contract is for the sale of goods, because logs are chattels only.[22] This is a test that is frequently not capable of effective application. What it meant by the word "title" is itself highly uncertain, to be discussed rather in a work on property than in a work on contracts. But, in addition, in the majority of the cases the expressions used by the parties give no clear indication as to when they intend "title" to pass, even if they suppose that they know what "title" is.

It is quite possible for the parties to use the word "title" (or some similar term) and to say expressly that the vendee is to get none prior to severance. In such a case the court is almost certain to hold that no interest in land is involved.[23] The same is true if the expressions indicate that there is to be no sale of any kind of property, but that the owner is merely employing the other party to fell the trees and market them as logs.[24]

If by the contract it is the vendor who is to do the severing, it appears that no use of the land by the vendee is contemplated other than that necessary for the removal of the severed chattels.

In such cases, it is certain that the contract should be treated as one for the sale of chattels and not of land.[25] If, on the other hand, the severing is to be done by the vendee, some user of the land, for a longer or a shorter time, is involved. If this time is comparatively short, immediate severance being in contemplation, such user should be disregarded and the transaction held to be one for the sale of goods only. In some jurisdictions this result has been reached; [26] but a few cases reach it with no apparent regard for the length of time allowed for severance and removal.

If no time is specified for the removal, or if the period fixed is one of considerable length, the great majority of the decisions hold the contract to be within the statute as a contract for the sale of an interest in land.[27] In some of these cases, the court contents itself with merely saying that a contract for the sale of standing trees is within the statute.

Even if the contract is held to be within the statute and unenforceable, it is far from void. It is operative as a license, creating in the vendee the privilege of entry and the power to make the logs his own by actual severance.[28] The vendor has power of revocation; and an entry by the vendee after notice of such revocation, made before he has severed the trees, is a trespass. A notice of revocation, after severance, does not deprive the vendee of his already acquired property in the logs.[29]

What has been said in this section with respect to standing trees is equally applicable to contracts for the severance and transfer of any other subject matter that is properly included, so long as unsevered, within the phrase "lands, tenements, and hereditaments." Standing trees are certainly so included; so also are the agricultural soil itself, sand, water, ice, stone, coal, ore, and all other kinds of mineral in place.[30] If the severance, even though it is to be by action of the purchaser, is to be immediate and will not involve the use and occupation of the premises for a substantial period, the contract should be held to be one for the sale of chattels and not for the sale of land.[31]

---

31. The American Law Institute has approved of rules not greatly different from the text above. Restatement, Contracts, sec. 200: "Goods within the meaning of the statute" are held to include "things attached to or forming part of the realty which are agreed to be severed therefrom before sale or promptly after the formation of the contract." In the Comment, this is declared to include "minerals or ice or even buildings."

But the Illustrations seem not wholly consistent.

Restatement, Contracts, § 195, declares that "an interest in land within the meaning of the statute" is any group of legal relations "relating to the realty which . . . is property in realty, and does not fall within the definition of goods in Section 200." Here too, the illustrations appear to be lacking in consistency.

## § 409.   Interests in Land—Buildings and Fixtures

The word "tenements," as used in the statute, was no doubt meant in a general way to include buildings on land; but the application of the statute to contracts for the sale of buildings has not been made to turn upon the interpretation of the word "tenements." Instead, these contracts have been treated as substantially parallel with contracts for the sale of growing trees.

In the first place, section 4 does not apply to buildings that have not been so attached to the land as to be regarded as real property.[32] Whether or not a building has been so attached depends upon the character of the structure, the mode of physical attachment, and the apparent intent of the builder or owner. If after applying these tests the building is held not to be real property, a contract for its sale would not be within section 4, but may be within section 17.

As in the case of standing trees, however, the troublesome question is as to the application of the statute to contracts for the sale of buildings that have certainly theretofore been regarded as real property. The same distinctions have been drawn as in the case of trees, with a similar conflict in results. There is good authority for the rule that a contract for the sale of a building to be presently severed and removed is not within section 4,[33] even though the severance is to be made by the vendee. The holding is otherwise if the vendee is given control of the premises for some time before severance.[34]

## § 410.   Interests in Land—Growing Crops

Products of the soil that are dependent upon planting and cultivation by the hand of man are now not regarded as within the intent of section 4. A contract for their sale is therefore not within that section, even though at the time of making the contract the crops are attached to the soil and not yet matured.[37] This is true of biennial plants like winter wheat as well as of annual crops like Indian corn.[38] It has also been held to be true of crops that are gathered annually even though borne on perennial trunks or stems, such as apples, small fruits, and hardy shrubs and bulbs.[39]

The distinction between cultivated crops and uncultivated growths of the soil has been indicated by use of the terms *fructus industriales* and *fructus naturales*.[40] These terms are of no help in making the distinction, but have some convenience as descriptive catchalls.

## §§ 411–418.   Summary Statement as to Special Contracts

Only a brief statement can here be made concerning certain important classes of contracts.

Partnership agreements for dealing in land and for the sharing of profits and losses in the business are ordinarily held not to be within the statute; no transfer of land between the parties is contemplated.

An agreement between adjoining landowners settling a doubtful or disputed boundary line is held enforceable, without any writing, if the parties are not intentionally transferring a strip of land and if they make the agreement effective by marking the boundary or otherwise taking actual possession.

In like manner, oral partition agreements between tenants in common are effective if the boundaries are marked and separate possession taken.

One who has a right to a conveyance of land by virtue of a written contract can enforce specific performance and has an "interest;" his agreement to assign or transfer that interest is within the statute.

Contracts for the transfer of dower, curtesy, or "community" interests in land are within the statute; antenuptial agreements for the retention of existing separate property interests are not.

Agreements with a land broker to pay him a commission for procuring a sale of land are not within the original statute; but many States have enacted special statutes making such agreements unenforceable unless in writing.

Option contracts have been discussed in an earlier chapter. A contract whereby a party is given a binding option either to buy or to sell land is within the statute. It creates a conditional right in the option holder and is not revocable by the option giver.

## § 419.  Effect of Conveyance of the Land on Enforceability of Purchaser's Oral Promise

As is seen elsewhere, an oral contract that is plainly within the statute becomes enforceable specifically in case of certain kinds of "part performance" by one party. In such cases, equity compels the other party to perform his oral promise, even though the general effect of the statute is to prevent such compulsion. It seems obvious, therefore, that the oral promise of the vendee should be enforceable after conveyance by the vendor. The courts uniformly hold that the oral promise to pay the price is enforceable after its bargained-for equivalent, the transfer of the land, has been executed.[5]

The courts do not like to let a buyer get and keep the land without paying the agreed price; and it has not generally occurred to them that reasonable compensation to the extent of the value received by the defendant would be enough to avoid great injustice. The quasi-contractual remedy certainly would not be adequate where the land has been conveyed to a stranger to the contract, and the defendant, who was the only one promising to pay, has not himself benefited.[6]  This is clearly the reasoning of the courts when dealing with contracts within the one-year clause;  full performance by the plaintiff ordinarily enables him to enforce the defendant's oral promise to pay the price or to perform some other equivalent.

This rule differs from the "part performance" rule in important respects.  The "part performance" rule was exclusively an equity rule, the available remedy being a decree for specific performance and not money damages.  The rule here being considered made available to the vendor an action at law against the vendee;  if the latter had promised to pay a specific sum in money, an action of debt would be maintainable against him after conveyance by the vendor.  Such an action of debt was, however, substantially the specific enforcement of the vendee's promise, using common law execution in place of the chancellor's threat of imprisonment.

No doubt one reason for this action of the courts of common law is that the vendee's promise to pay money is not in itself within the statute at all;  and the part of the transaction that brought it within the statute—the promise to convey—has been performed.[7] The court did not feel that it was in any respect disregarding the statute;  whereas in applying the "part performance" doctrine, the court of equity is doing exactly that, even though it is doing so for reasons that make it equitable and just.

The foregoing reasoning is not available in case the oral contract is one for the mutual exchange of lands.  Here the defendant's promise to convey is as much within the statute because of its own content as is the promise of the plaintiff.  The performance of the plaintiff's promise by making his conveyance, therefore, does not completely perform everything that brought the transaction within the statute.  There are a few cases holding that the defendant's oral promise is not enforceable, even though the plaintiff has performed his part.[8]  It is no doubt consistent with prevailing doctrine to hold that a common law action for damages is not maintainable.  There is no money debt for land transferred;  and the "part performance" doctrine does not sustain an action for money damages.  It is clear, however, that the plaintiff has a good case for equitable relief.  Sometimes it may be desirable and sufficient to decree specific restitution of his own land to the plaintiff.[9]  There is ample authority, however, for a decree for specific performance compelling the defendant to convey the land promised by him.[10]  This is the only remedy that is fully adequate, and particularly so if specific restitution has become impossible.

The innumerable cases holding that an absolute deed can be shown to be a mere mortgage security lend support to the forego-

ing doctrine.[11]  In these cases the court compels a reconveyance
on payment of the loan.  This is the enforcement of an unwritten
promise, express or implied, to reconvey the land on payment.
The fact that it is a promise to reconvey the same land conveyed
by the promisee, instead of to convey other land, seems insufficient
to justify a refusal of enforcement in the latter case while granting it in the former.

## CHAPTER 18

## INTERESTS IN LAND—EFFECT OF PART PERFORMANCE OF ORAL CONTRACT

## § 420. Part Performance as a Ground for Enforcement of a Contract to Transfer Land

The statute of frauds says that no action shall lie for the enforcement of a contract for the sale of land; and it makes no exception in favor of a plaintiff who has rendered his own performance either in part or in full.[1] But a vendor who has made the agreed transfer is allowed to get judgment for the contract price; and there are innumerable cases in which a vendee has been given specific performance on the ground that he has rendered part performance prior to any notice of a repudiation by the vendor.[2]

The rules are the same whether the equitable relief asked is a direct decree for specific performance or for the enforcement of

---

1. In several states there is a special provision in the statute recognizing the doctrine of part performance but not defining its limits. See Svanburg v. Fosseen, 78 N.W. 4, 75 Minn. 350, 43 L.R.A. 427, 74 Am.St.Rep. 490 (1899), for one example. Other cases are collected in 101 A.L.R. 933 (1936).

Such statutes are merely declaratory of previously existing judicial law, inasmuch as nearly all the states recognize the doctrine though the statute says nothing about it. Probably such a statute encourages the courts to extend the application of the doctrine.

a contract by means of the reformation of a deed or the declaration of a constructive trust.[3]

It is sometimes said that part performance takes a case out of the statute. There is reason for this in the case of a sale of goods, because the statute applicable thereto is expressly limited to cases in which there has been no part payment, nothing given in earnest, and no acceptance and receipt of part of the goods.[4] But the usual statutory provision as to land contains no such limitation; and therefore part performance does not take a case out of that provision. Nevertheless, it is established law that, after certain kinds of part performance by a purchaser, the court will specifically enforce the vendor's promise to convey land, and there are numerous cases giving the same remedy to a vendor on similar grounds. By a course of judicial development, the statute has become inapplicable in these cases, in spite of the fact that they are clearly included within its words.[5] Part performance of a contract for the transfer of land does not take the case out of the statute; but it may be of such a character that it will take the statute out of the case.

In these cases, the plaintiff is permitted to prove the terms of the agreement by oral testimony; and he has the burden of proof as to what those terms were. It is equally permissible for the defendant to show that the agreement was not as alleged by the plaintiff, that his promise was conditional upon an event that has never occurred, that he promised to convey without warranty, or that he reserved a right of way or other easement.[6]

Part performance has been held sufficient to compel recognition of an easement in land as well as to compel a conveyance or a payment.[7] Being sufficient to enable the plaintiff to prove all the terms of an oral contract, it is necessarily sufficient to allow the use of oral testimony to supplement an existing memorandum that is deficient in some material respect.[8]

5. Dean Pound argues, in "Progress of the Law," 33 Harv.L.Rev. 933 ff. (1920), that the part performance doctrine is an anomaly, which ought to be held within narrow limits, and he cites various judges as being in agreement with him. But in most jurisdictions it has not been held within very narrow limits. And while it may be surprising that the courts will yield to the force of circumstances and act in the teeth of a statute, when they have done so in hundreds of cases the result is that the statutory rule has been varied by their judicial action. In time their action ceases to be an anomaly; the question merely is, What are the judicial limits?

The annotator in 101 A.L.R. 933 (1936) correctly says: "Their criticisms are merely protests against the inevitable. At all events, the doctrine of part performance is vital and thriving at the present day, and is so thoroughly established that its wisdom or unwisdom is, so far as the courts are concerned, a purely academic question." That this is the fact should also give pause to the *a priori* reasoners in "academic" circles.

The part performance doctrine applies to a contract for the sale of standing trees [9] or of any of the lesser interests in land; and cases are numerous in which it has been applied to oral leases of land, even though they are for so long a period as to be clearly within the one-year clause of the statute as well as within the land clause.[10]

If the vendor has made specific performance impossible, by a transfer to an innocent purchaser for value, the court may follow the equity precedent of awarding damages in lieu of specific performance.[11]

## § 422.  Part Performance Doctrine not Applicable in Actions at Common Law

The rule that part performance may make a contract for the sale of land specifically enforceable was the creation of the courts of equity and was not recognized at common law.  The result of this is, even in jurisdictions where law and equity are combined, that a suit solely for damages, or other purely common law remedy, for breach of the express contract is generally not maintainable, however greatly the plaintiff may have changed his position in reliance on the contract and however unjust it may be for the defendant to make use of the statute in defense.[18]  Part performance may make specific enforcement available;  it does not make a judgment for damages available.  This does not prevent an award of damages in a proper suit for specific performance where the latter remedy is too difficult of enforcement or is refused because of the intervention of an innocent purchaser.[19]  Nor does it prevent a court of equity from awarding compensation for defects and deficiencies, either by way of an abatement in price or otherwise, in conjunction with a decree for specific performance of the oral contract so far as that performance is possible.  Under the part performance doctrine, a court can decree specific performance in part with compensation for the rest.[20]  Most courts now have the powers of a court of equity and must apply equitable rules of law;  any such court should now be ready to award damages either as supplementary to specific performance or in lieu of it.[21]

21.   In White v. McKnight, 143 S. E. 552, 146 S.C. 59, 59 A.L.R. 1297 (1928), the remedy in damages was denied even though the transfer of land to an innocent purchaser for value made specific performance unavailable. The court regarded the action as a purely common-law suit for damages and not as a suit in equity for such specific or other equitable reparation as the facts justified. This seems to be true, also, of Wolfe v. Wallingford Bank & T. Co., 191 A. 88, 122 Conn. 507 (1937), the court expressing regret that the law was so well settled against the plaintiff. This case was sent back from a new trial; and on a second appeal, reported in 1 A.2d 146, 124 Conn. 507, 117 A.L.R. 932 (1938), the plaintiff's action for damages was sustained. No equitable relief was asked; and the

Two additional statements should accompany the foregoing common law rule in order that it may not mislead: (1) the rule has nothing to do with restitution of value received by the defendant; and (2) it does not prevent an action of debt for the purchase price in money for land that has actually been transferred by the plaintiff. The remedy of restitution is available to any one who has rendered to the repudiating defendant a part of the agreed performance; and this is true whether the part performance is such as to make specific enforcement available or not. So, one who has paid $1000 as part of the purchase price of land is not thereby enabled to compel conveyance by the vendor; but he can maintain suit for the restitution of the $1000 with interest, if the vendor refuses to convey.[22] Also, an action of debt, or its equivalent civil action, can be maintained for the agreed price in money of land already conveyed by the plaintiff in accordance with the oral contract.[23] This has sometimes been put on the ground that the only part of the contract that is within the statute has been fully performed. The recovery in these cases is for full performance by the plaintiff, not for a part performance; and it is for specific performance of the defendant's full duty.

## § 424. Part Performance Doctrine Applicable in Favor of Vendor

The doctrine that part performance may make an oral contract specifically enforceable is oftener applied in favor of a purchaser who seeks to compel a conveyance of the vendor than in favor of a vendor against the purchaser. This is because it is more often the vendor who refuses to perform and the purchaser who so changes his position as to make such enforcement necessary to avoid injustice. But a similar doctrine is applicable in favor of the vendor.

court describes the case as "one at law for damages." The trial court was one having full equity powers; and the decision might well be sustained as a proper exercise of those powers. The fact that the plaintiff's complaint does not refer to "equity" does not deprive him of the rights to which the existing law of the state entitles him. It is immaterial whether those rights derive from early common law, equity, law merchant, or more recent judicial development. The judgment for damages is sustained, not because of the transfer to an innocent purchaser, but because the plaintiff's action in reliance on the oral promise created an "estoppel" to plead the statute of frauds. The action in reliance was forbearance by a mortgagor to protect her interest in a foreclosure proceeding and the making of improvements on the premises. The decision nullifies the former decision in this case reported in 191 A. 88, 122 Conn. 507 (1937), and is a substantial extension of the part performance doctrine through the use of that flexible doctrine called "estoppel." The extension is a just one, if the court is careful to apply it only after weighing all equitable considerations.

## § 425.   Requisites of a Sufficient Part Performance

In order that acts of the plaintiff in reliance on the oral contract may make it specifically enforceable, there are several requisites, each being somewhat variable in character and enforced with varying degrees of strictness by the courts.   (1) The performance must be in pursuance of the contract and in reasonable reliance thereon, without notice that the defendant has already repudiated the contract.   (2) The performance must be such that the remedy of restitution is not reasonably adequate, making it very unjust for the defendant to hide behind the statute.   (3) The performance must be one that is in some degree evidential of the existence of a contract and not readily explainable on any other ground.

The various factors that constitute what is called "part performance" of the contract are numerous.   They occur in varying combinations, with varying degrees of importance to be attached to each one.   In each case, the court must weigh the sum total of factors, as they are found to exist;  and the weakness or absence of some one factor on which emphasis is often placed may be compensated by the unusual strength and character of the other existing factors.   Most courts are fully conscious that the "part performance" doctrine is a judicial device to prevent the terms of a formal statute from doing grave injustice.   It is a flexible device that has been, and may still properly be, molded to suit varying combinations of circumstances.

## § 426.   The Part Performance must be in Reasonable Reliance

It has been suggested a few times that the performance must be a part of the duty undertaken by the plaintiff, a part of his exchange performance; [34] but this is clearly shown to be incorrect by the multitude of cases giving decisive weight to the taking of possession and the making of improvements by a vendee.[35]   These constitute no part of his agreed exchange;  nor are they done in pursuance of the contract in any sense other than that they are done in reliance upon it.   The term part performance, therefore, is a misleading form of expression;  but it does not seriously mislead, because its frequent application has made its artifical connotation very generally understood.

There is no question, however, of the necessity that the performance on which the plaintiff relies must have been made by him in reasonable reliance on the contract.[36]   This means either that he rendered the performance without knowledge that the other party had repudiated the contract or that he rendered it under some kind of compulsion that justifies a disregard of the other's repudiation.   No doubt the fact that a contract was made by word of mouth only is never a reason that justifies its wilful repudiation in the eyes of honorable men.   With them a word

437

is as good as a bond. But in the cases now under discussion the legislature has said that an oral word is not quite as good as a signed writing; and in order to attain the purposes for which the statute was passed, it is necessary to permit repudiation without the usual legal penalty—at least where the result is not too shocking to honorable men. Therefore, if the repudiator informs the plaintiff of his refusal to abide by his oral contract, the latter is not reasonable in proceeding in reliance on the contract. Indeed, this is usually true, even though the contract is one not rendered unenforceable by the statute. It is not reasonable to enhance damages when they can fairly be avoided; nor can such unreasonable enhancement be accepted as a reason for specific enforcement.[37]

### § 429. Inadequacy of Other Remedies to Prevent a "Virtual Fraud"

The prevention of fraud and its successful consummation has for centuries been a favorite ground of equity jurisdiction. The courts of common law recognized certain kinds of fraudulent conduct as a tort and gave a remedy therefor; but they were slow to give fraud any effect in the law of contracts and conveyances. Therefore, for the noble purpose of thwarting defrauders, the chancellors became accustomed to direct interference with the operation of various rules of common law; and their so doing received general approval. Their interference with the strict application of the statute of frauds was made doubly easy, therefore, by explaining their action on the basis of the long-established and well-approved reason—the prevention of fraud. In addition, the statute itself was passed for the prevention of fraud and it would be shocking to allow the statute to defeat its own purpose.[43]

Without doubt, this explains why there are so many cases in which specific enforcement of an oral contract is justified by the court on the ground that there has been such part performance as would make it a "virtual fraud" to permit the defendant to repudiate his contract and to plead the statute of frauds in defense. A great majority of the cases make use of this language, either granting the relief asked on the ground that refusal of enforcement would result in the consummation of a "virtual fraud," or denying relief because no such fraud would exist.[44]

### § 430. Requirement that the Part Performance shall be Referable to the Oral Contract

The third generally stated requirement is that part performance will not make an oral contract enforceable unless it is such as to be directly "referable" to that contract. There is so much variation in the ordinary wordings of this requirement that it cannot be reduced to any very definite form; it must be explained rather

438

than stated. The phrase "referable to the contract" frequently appears; but nobody gives any exact meaning to "referable." It does not mean that in the process of performance, the plaintiff or the promisor makes oral references to their contract and says that such a contract is being performed. Some such statements may be admissible in evidence on various grounds; but the part performance must itself be shown to have the requisite characteristics before such statements are admissible to prove the fact that such a contract was made. They are not admissible to prove that the part performance has the requisite characteristics.

It is believed that the principal idea that is struggling for expression is that the part performance must be clearly evidential of the existence of a contract [48]—it must be such as would not ordinarily have taken place in the absence of a contract and therefore is not reasonably explicable on some other ground.[49]

If the performance rendered by the promisee consists wholly of forbearance to act, the fact is less likely to be evidential in character than when it consists of affirmative action. Where the alleged promise was to leave part of an estate by will in consideration of the promisee's forbearance to contest another will, the forbearance to contest until too late has been held not to make the oral promise enforceable.[50] It is clear that forbearance to file a contest is not of such a character as to lead directly to the inference that some contract for a reward had been made.

48. "The present case, resting entirely upon the parol evidence of one of the parties to the transaction, after the death of the other, forcibly illustrates the wisdom of the rule, which requires some evidentia rei to connect the alleged part performance with the alleged agreement." Maddison v. Alderson, 8 App.Cas. 467 (1883).

49. "Her mere continuance in Thomas Alderson's service, though without any actual payment of wages, was not such an act as to be in itself evidence of a new contract, much less of a contract concerning her master's land. It was explicable, without supposing any such new contract, as easily as the continuance of a tenant in possession after the expiration of a lease." Maddison v. Alderson, 8 App.Cas. 467 (1883).

In Burns v. McCormick, 135 N.E. 273, 233 N.Y. 230 (1922), the court said: "There must be performance un-

equivocally referable to the agreement—performance which alone and without the aid of words of promise is unintelligible or at least extraordinary unless as an incident of ownership, assured, if not existing. . . . What is done must itself supply the key to what is promised. It is not enough that what is promised may give significance to what is done." In this case the plaintiffs had abandoned their business and had removed to the home of the promisor, boarding and caring for him until he died. It was held that these facts were not sufficiently evidential of an oral contract to devise land as compensation and a decree for specific performance was denied. The court further said: "The plaintiffs did, indeed, while occupants of the dwelling, pay the food bills for the owner as well as for themselves, and do the work of housekeepers. One who heard of such service might infer that it would be re-

The statute of frauds is so worded as to seem to prevent proof of a contract to transfer land except by a signed memorandum. It would appear to be a direct and inexcusable nullification for the court to allow such a contract to be proved solely by oral testimony. We avoid this appearance by refusing to admit such testimony unless there has been action that speaks to the contract. The part performance must itself play a part in the proof.

How important a part must this be? How strongly evidential of a contract is the performance required to be? How clearly evidential of a contract to convey land? How much evidence must it supply as to the exact terms of that contract, showing how much land was promised and when it was to be transferred?

These questions are answered differently in different jurisdictions, and also differently in cases within a single jurisdiction. The first two questions can be answered with much less definiteness than the last two. Seldom, if ever, does the part performance afford much evidence of the exact terms of the contract; and no court requires that it should.[54] It may lead to the inference that a specific parcel of land has been promised; this is especially true where the plaintiff has taken possession of that parcel or has made valuable improvements upon it.[55] Even so, the time for conveyance and the conditions on which it is to be made are not indicated. The circumstances under which services have been rendered may lead to the inference that an aged person has promised to leave property by will; but it may not indicate the particular property or what proportionate part of the entire estate.

## § 431. Payment of the Price in Money Not Sufficient

An oral promise for the conveyance of an interest in land is not made specifically enforceable by the mere fact that the plaintiff has paid the price, or a part thereof, in money to the defendant.[58] Such a payment is, indeed, part performance; but the plaintiff can usually be put in statu quo by a judgment for the restitution of the money. The statute of frauds will not be disregarded if the injured party can be put in as good a position as

warded in some way. There could be no reasonable inference that it would be rewarded at some indefinite time thereafter by a conveyance of the land."

54. The Connecticut court asserts that there are "two rules; the stricter requiring the acts of part performance to be referable to the contract set up, and to no other one, and the more liberal holding the acts sufficient if they are such as clearly refer to some contract in relation to the subject matter in dispute, the terms of which may then be established by parol. We have adopted the latter and more liberal rule." Grant v. Grant, 29 A. 15, 63 Conn. 530 (1893). In Andrews v. New Britain N. B., 113 Conn. 467, 155 A. 838 (1931), the court was more hidebound.

he was in when the contract was made. Frequently restitution is far from the equivalent of the promised performance; but it prevents the defendant from making ill-gotten gains at the plaintiff's expense and it leaves the plaintiff in substantially the same position that would have existed had there been no performance at all.[59] The statute of frauds is an almost complete legal justification for the refusal of performance, even though it is no justification of profiting at the cost of the plaintiff.

### § 432. Part Performance in Reliance on Oral Promise to Devise Land

The service cases most commonly arising are those in which the plaintiff alleges that he has given support, nursing, attendance, and other personal service in reliance upon a promise to devise land by will. In such cases, even when the contract is evidenced by a writing that satisfies the statute, the court does not attempt to enforce the promise with literal exactness, this being an impossibility after the promisor's death. It does not order the execution of a will, with an injunction against its revocation or alteration, even though the promisor is still alive. The court can attain its ends by other means. It can compel heirs and devisees and purchasers with notice to hold the property in trust and to convey to the promisee.[64] It has also granted an injunction forbidding the promisor to convey away the land prior to his death.[65]

Generally, the suit to enforce an oral promise to devise land for services rendered is not brought until after the death of the promisor, because usually there has been no breach until such death. The courts have rightly looked with suspicion on such alleged contracts [66] and legislatures have often passed statutes affecting the evidence that is admissible to prove them. In refusing specific enforcement, while commenting on the quality of the evidence, the court may base its refusal upon generalizations as to the necessity of sustaining the statute of frauds or upon some stiff requirement as to the character of the performance rendered. These generalizations are certain to make difficulty when another case arises in which there is no doubt whatever about the contract.

In some cases the land that is to be devised is a specific parcel: an old father promises his son to leave him the homestead if the son will reside on it and cultivate it and care for the father.[67] In these cases it is possible for the promisee to take possession and make improvements. If he does so, the possession and improvements are themselves a sufficient part performance; and the services rendered merely afford added but unnecessary support. It is merely the payment of the price. If possession is not taken, or if it is not exclusive possession, the refusal of specific enforcement has been placed on that ground; [68] but the quality of the proof offered and the character of the services rendered must always be taken into consideration in weighing the decision.

### § 434.  Possession and Making Permanent Improvements

In nearly all jurisdictions [87] an oral contract for the sale or lease of land will be made specifically enforceable if possession is taken under the contract and valuable and permanent improvements are made upon the land.[88]  Doubtless in such cases varying degrees of weight are given to the possession and to the improvements; and if there has also been a part payment or other performance, that fact too will play a part.[89]  But it is clear that in many cases the making of the improvements has been the decisive element.  Of course, this means improvements made by the promisee in reliance on the oral contract.[90]

It is now pretty well established that when permanent improvements are made on the land of another, whether by mistake of fact or in reliance upon a contract that is unenforceable by reason of the statute of frauds, an action for their reasonable value or for some other remedy is maintainable; but this has not always been understood as existing law.  There are sufficient uncertainties about this restitutionary remedy, both as to its availability and as to the measure of value of the improvements, that it is not regarded as adequate to do complete justice and that it does not prevent specific enforcement.[91]

### § 435.  Oral Contracts to Transfer Land in Return for Services

Many courts are less willing to decree specific enforcement of an oral contract to transfer land where the part performance consists of services rendered than where it consists of possession and improvements.[11]  The reasons for this are, first, that the proof that the alleged oral contract was made is frequently less convincing in character; secondly, that the rendition of services is less likely to be evidential of such a contract and to be regarded as "referable" solely thereto; and thirdly, that certain kinds of services, at least, are capable of accurate valuation in money.

These reasons against enforcement are found to exist in varying combinations and in different degrees, with the result that there is conflict in decision and an appearance of conflict that is greater than the actual conflict.  However strongly the courts of some jurisdictions seem to be prejudiced against services as satisfying their part performance doctrine, it is believed that very few will be found that will never under any circumstances recognize services as sufficient.  Even the tough-minded courts that are most insistent upon logic and consistency are human enough to be affected by a showing of severe hardship and injustice.  Where the making of the oral contract is proved beyond

442

any reasonable doubt, and where the services have been long continued, onerous, and of a kind incapable of just estimation in money, the chancellor's conscience will be so moved as to lead to the conclusion that it is a "virtual fraud" for the defendant to hide behind the statute. If the principal terms of the contract and the rendition of the services are admitted by the defendant, even though he disputes other alleged terms and insists on the statute as a defense, there is no need that the performance rendered shall be such as to be "referable to" the contract and there is less necessity that performance rendered shall be difficult of valuation in money.[12] Rules may properly be relaxed when the facts are such as to demonstrate that the plaintiff is not attempting the consummation of fraud and that the defendant is refusing performance of a contract that has induced extensive action in justifiable reliance.

## § 441. Parol Gifts of Land

It has been previously explained that the part performance required by the courts as a prerequisite of specific enforcement is not necessarily any part of the agreed exchange for the defendant's performance that is compelled. It may be merely action in reliance on the defendant's promise. This is particularly evident in the case of a promise to make a gift of land; there is no agreed exchange of any kind, otherwise the transaction would not be a gift. These promises become specifically enforceable as soon as the promisee has so far acted in reliance on the promise as to make it very unjust (perhaps again called a "virtual fraud") not to compel execution of the gift.[51]

The kind of performance that is requisite in these cases is substantially the same as in the case of an oral contract, but not for exactly the same reasons. Usually it consists of taking possession of the promised land and the making of permanent improvements thereon, with the promisor's assent.[52] If the promise to make the gift is not evidenced by a signed memorandum, it is within the land clause of the statute and is therefore unenforceable while nothing has been done under it; but it is also made unenforceable by the lack of consideration.

If the promise to make the gift is evidenced by a memorandum sufficient to satisfy the statute, the lack of consideration still makes it unenforceable. But it is now understood that a promise without consideration may become enforceable if the promisee reasonably changes his position in reliance on the promise, in a way that is substantial and that the promisor had reason to foresee. Such a change of position is not a consideration for the promise, because it was not bargained for; but the courts often say that it is a sufficient consideration, doubtless meaning not that it is a subject of exchange by the parties but that it is a weighty consideration leading to enforcement by the court.[53]  In some cases it is difficult to determine whether or not the plaintiff's action was bargained for by the promisor as the object of exchange.  This is especially true in case he promises to make what he calls a gift, but makes it expressly conditional upon the performance by the plaintiff.[54]

### § 442.  Quality of Proof Required for Enforcement of Oral Contract

Part performance or other material change of position in reliance upon a promise affects in many important respects the legal relations of the parties and the remedies that are available to them.  In the case of an oral contract that is clearly within the statute of frauds, the words of the statute will be given their full effect as long as the contract remains wholly executory on both sides.  Mere disappointment in not getting something that was promised does not appeal to the chancellor's conscience sufficiently to cause him to decree specific performance of a contract for the breach of which the statute declares no action shall be brought.  After certain types of part performance, however, his conscience is more deeply stirred, and he is likely to talk about "virtual fraud" and to indulge the beneficial fiction that the case is taken "out of the statute."

Even in such cases, the chancellor wishes to be sure of his ground.  The statute exists for the prevention of fraud and perjury; and the means that it adopts is to refuse enforcement unless the contract is evidenced by a signed document.  When a plaintiff is asking enforcement without having such a document, there is always the possibility that he is attempting to effectuate the very kind of fraud that the statute was passed to frustrate.  Therefore, before decreeing enforcement, in disregard of the statutory prohibition, the court must be thoroughly convinced that the oral contract was in fact made as alleged.  This explains the various protecting limitations of the part performance doctrine.  One of these, and the most important and effective of all of them, is that specific enforcement will not be decreed unless the oral contract is proved to the entire satisfaction of the court.[57]

### § 443.  The Part Performance Doctrine in Kentucky, Mississippi, North Carolina, and Tennessee

In numerous cases, the courts of these four States have declared that they do not recognize the part performance doctrine and have refused specific enforcement.[a]  Yet there is much evidence

---

a. **Ky.**—Grant's Heirs v. Craigmiles, 4 Ky. (1 Bibb) 203 (1808).

**N.C.**—Ellis v. Ellis, 16 N.C. (1 Dev. Eq.) 341, 398 (1829).

**Miss.**—Box v. Stanford, 21 Miss. (13 Sm. & M. 93) 207 (1849).

of dissatisfaction with the resulting injustice; in addition to a restitutionary remedy, the courts have given damages measured by the value of the land that was promised, a remedy less consistent with the statute than is a decree for specific performance.[b]

b. See:

U.S.—Interstate Co. v. Bry-Block Merc. Co., 30 F.2d 172 (D.C.Tenn. 1928), specific enforcement granted.

Ky.—Waters v. Cline, 85 S.W. 209, 121 Ky. 611 (1905).

N.C.—Hager v. Whitener, 169 S.E. 645, 204 N.C. 747 (1933).

Tenn.—Robertson v. Heirs of Brooks, 158 Tenn. (Appendix) 43 (1814), a case unreported for 100 years.

# CHAPTER 19

## STATUTE OF FRAUDS—CONTRACTS NOT TO BE PERFORMED WITHIN ONE YEAR

## § 444. Statutory Words Very Narrowly Interpreted

The fifth provision of section 4 is: "No action shall be brought . . . upon any agreement that is not to be performed within the space of one year from the making thereof." Where actions on contracts are long delayed, injustice is likely to be done because of bad memory and because witnesses have died or moved away, so that mistakes will be made and perjury is more likely to be successful. And in the case of a contract whose performance is to cover a long period of time, actions are likely to be long delayed. These may be supposed to have been the reasons that underlay the enactment of this fifth provision.[1] In its actual application, however, the courts have been perhaps even less friendly to this provision than to the other provisions of the statute.[2] They have observed the exact words of this provision and have interpreted them literally and very narrowly. The words are "agreement that is not to be performed." They are not "agreement that is not in fact performed" or "agreement that may not be performed" or "agreement that is not at all likely to be performed." To fall within the words of the provision, therefore, the agreement must be one of which it can truly be said at the very moment that it is made, "This agreement is not to be performed within one year"; in general, the cases indicate that there must not be the slightest possibility that it can be fully performed within one year.

It makes no difference how long the agreed performance may be delayed or over how long a period it may in fact be continued.[3] It makes no difference how long the parties expect performance to take or how reasonable and accurate those expectations are, if the agreed performance can possibly be completed within a year. Facts like these do not bring a contract within this provision of section 4.[4] A provision in the contract fixing a maximum period within which performance is to be completed, even though that period is much in excess of one year, does not make the statute applicable.[5] A building contract is frequently such that it can be fully performed within one year, even though the fixed time limit is in excess of one year. If so, it is not within the one-year clause, however long the parties may expect to take or actually do take.[6]

## § 445. Promises Conditional upon an Uncertain Event

A certain performance that would not in itself take a year to complete may be promised at a definite future date more than one year from the time of making the contract. Such a contract is within the statute. But if such a performance is promised at an uncertain time, to be determined by the happening of a condition that may possibly occur within one year, the promise cannot be said to be one that is not to be performed within one year, and it is not within the one-year clause of the statute.[19] It makes no difference how improbable it is that the condition will occur within a year; if there is any possibility that it may so happen, the statutory provision is not applicable. Nor does it make any difference that the condition is one that may never happen at all. The following are promises conditional in such a way as to keep the promise outside the one-year clause, the condition being an event that may possibly happen within one year and the required performance being one that may possibly be completed within one year, even though it is also true that the event may not happen for many years or may never happen at all: a promise to pay money when X is married;[20] to charter a ship to the promisee if the promisor shall thereafter buy it;[21] to pay money when specified work is begun or is completed;[22] to render performance on the return of a ship;[23] to perform on the termination of pending litigation;[24] to account for proceeds after a sale is effected;[25] to render a performance on a date to be fixed by one of the parties or a third party;[26] to make a bequest by will or to pay money at the death of X.[27] In the case of a promise to pay money upon the death of X, it may be observed that the specified condition is one that is certain to happen at some time; and it may possibly occur

2. "These decisions are almost equivalent to a repeal of this clause of the statute." Blanding v. Sargent, 33 N.H. 239 (1856). Without question, however, this is too strong a statement.

3. U.S.—Warner v. Texas & P. R. Co., 17 S.Ct. 147, 164 U.S. 418, 41 L.Ed. 495 (1896), contract enforced after performance for 13 years.

within one year, although it may possibly be deferred for many years.

## § 446. Performance to Continue for an Uncertain Time

In the foregoing cases the specific performance that was promised was one that might take only a few minutes in the performing, or was at most a performance for no longer than one year. The statutory problem arose out of the fact that this performance was or might be deferred till some future time. There is another type of case, having superficial differences, to which the same principles are applicable. This is the promise of a long-extended performance, not a deferred brief performance, but one that the agreement provides shall come to an end upon the happening of some condition. If the condition is one that may happen within one year, the promise is not within the statutory one-year clause.[30]

Common illustrations are promises to support X as long as he shall live,[31] or to render some other continuing performance during the life of X.[32] Even though the promise is to render a performance throughout a specified period of years, it is generally held not to be within the statute if the continued life of some person is necessary to enable performance to be made and if upon that person's death the essential purpose of the parties is completely attained.[33] For these reasons, it has been held that a contract to maintain a child until he becomes of age, or for a specified number of years, is not within the one-year clause.[34] The death of the child would attain the object of the contract in so far as it is possible of attainment.

A contract for "permanent" employment is not within the one-year clause for the reason that such a contract will be fully performed, according to its terms, upon the death of the employee.[35] The word "permanent" has, in this connection, no more extended meaning than "for life." On the other hand, a promise to maintain a structure or an institution permanently is not conditional upon the continued life of a definite person or persons and is within the statute.[36]

---

30.　**U.S.**—Warner v. Texas & P. R. Co., 17 S.Ct. 147, 164 U.S. 418, 41 L.Ed. 495 (1896), oral promise to install and maintain a railway switch for use of plaintiff as long as he needed it, breach by the Railway Company occurring 13 years later; Mason-Walsh-Atkinson-Kier Co. v. Stubblefield, 99 F.2d 735 (C.C.A.9th, 1938), to buy and sell scrap accumulating in the course of performing a construction contract; Nester v. Diamond Match Co., 143 F. 72, 74 C.C.A. 266 (C.C.A.6th, 1906), to run, sort, and deliver plaintiff's logs continuously, as long as defendant controlled the river.

34.　**U.S.**—Wooldridge v. Stern, 42 F. 311, 9 L.R.A. 129 (C.C.Mo.1890), promise by the father of an illegitimate child, then 15 years of age, to support it until its majority. **Mass.**—Peters v. Westborough, 19 Pick. 364 (1837), to support a child of 11 until she became 18 years old.

## § 447. Contracts of Personal Service for a Definite Time

If A promises to work for B or B promises to employ A for more than one year, the promise is held to be within the statute.[47] This is in spite of the fact that A or B may die within a year and that death wholly extinguishes the duty of the promisor in contracts for personal service.[48] There seems to be as much reason for holding that A's promise to serve B is by implication conditional upon the continued life of one or both of the parties as for holding that a promise to support a child for a definite term of years is conditional upon its life. But in service cases it is generally recognized that termination of duty by operation of law is not identical with performance of a promise. The death of a party may terminate duty; but the contemplated work has not been done. It is otherwise if the parties have themselves agreed upon the limitation as one of the terms of the agreement that created the duty.

If A contracts to serve B for exactly one year, work to begin at a future time more than one day after the making of the contract, it is held that the contract cannot be performed within one year from its making and is within the statute.[49] If, however, the time set for beginning work is the next day after the making of the contract, the weight of authority is that the contract is not within the statute.[50] In such a case the agreed performance will be wholly completed on the anniversary of the day the contract was made and so is said to be within 365 days. If the contract was made at 10 o'clock in the morning on December 31, the one year's work would not be completed until the end of the working day on the following December 31, say, 6 o'clock in the evening. In such case the contract would not be fully performed until the lapse of 365 days and 8 hours. Here the rule is applied that the law disregards fractions of a day—a rule that ought to be applied in cases where the fraction of a day is of no practical importance. While legal fictions are often to be deprecated, there is no harm done in the instant case by slightly narrowing the operation of the statute in a class of cases where its more technical application would almost always do injustice.

Of course, if work is to begin on the very day the contract is made, a contract for exactly one year's work is not within the statute.[51] If no day is set for beginning the year's work, so that there is a possibility of its beginning on the same day or the next day, the statute does not apply, irrespective of when the work in fact begins.[52]

## § 449. Contracts with a Defeasance Clause or Option to Terminate

There are some contracts providing for a performance that certainly cannot take place within one year, but providing further that one of the parties shall have the privilege and power of terminating the contract by giving notice and ending the required performance within one year from the making. Such a contract as this should be held not within the one-year clause,[55] but a good many cases take the contrary view.[56] It appears to fall within the rules applicable to conditional promises and to contracts for alternative performances. Thus, where a contract of service provides that A shall work for B for ten years but that the contract shall be terminable at the will of either party at any time on giving thirty days' notice, it appears that the duty of A can be fully performed within a year on condition that either party shall give notice at least thirty days before the end of one year from the date of making the contract. The duty to work for ten years is expressly conditional upon the absence of any notice of termination. These are not cases where the duty of the promisor may possibly be terminated by operation of law independently of the terms of agreement; they are merely cases where the extent of the promised performance is to be determined in the future at the will of one of the parties, within the maximum limit named in the agreement. A contract by A to work for B as long as A or B desires would clearly not be within the one-year clause; [57] and it is not made so by the fact that the power is limited by express words setting a maximum period. The same is true of contracts to deliver goods within a set period at buyer's option.[58]

## §§ 451, 452. Rescission; Impossibility

A contract the terms of which require a performance beyond the expiration of one year is not taken out of the statute by the fact that it may be rescinded by mutual agreement or may become impossible of performance within the year. If the statute were thus made inapplicable, the one year clause would be entirely without effect, since mutual rescission is possible in all cases and events may render any performance impossible.

## § 453. Contracts in the Negative, Requiring Forbearance

In a leading case the defendant promised not to carry on a grocery business for five years in a certain town, and it was held that the promise was not within the statute. A distinction was drawn between affirmative contracts for personal service and negative contracts for personal forbearance. The court said: "An agreement to do a thing for a certain time may perhaps bind the promisor's representatives, and at any rate is not performed if he dies within that time. But a mere agreement that he will refrain from doing a certain thing is fully performed if he keeps it so long as he is capable of doing or refraining. The agreement of the defendant not to go into business again at Chicopee for five years was therefore not within the statute of frauds." [66]

There are some other cases in accord with this decision, even though the contract required a forbearance for a definite period in excess of one year.[67] Cases to the contrary appear to be more numerous.[68] Of course, if the promised forbearance is to be for life, or for an indefinite period of time that might be less than a year, the statute is not applicable.[69] There are many cases, however, in which no time limit was specified and the promised forbearance was to be forever.[70] Such cases should be regarded as supporting the leading case quoted above, the death of the promisor being regarded as completing the promised performance.

### § 456. Bilateral Contracts Performable within One Year by One Party but Not by the Other

A bilateral contract is one that includes promises by both parties and therefore requires a performance in the future by each of them. If either of these performances is one that cannot be completed within one year, the whole contract is within the one-year clause of the statute as long as the contract remains bilateral—that is, as long as neither party has fully performed his part. The fact that the performance promised by the other party is one that can be completed within one year does not take the case out of the one-year clause; and the contract is unenforceable by either party unless he has a sufficient memorandum signed by the other.[74]

As is seen in the following section, however, the rule is different with respect to a contract that from the beginning is unilateral, and also with respect to a contract that since its formation has become unilateral by reason of full performance by one of the parties. From this it appears that there is a "part performance" doctrine affecting the operation of the one-year clause, just as there is in the case of the land clause; but the two doctrines are not identical.

### § 457. Unilateral Contracts—Effect of Full Performance by One Party

A unilateral contract is one where only one of the parties thereto has made a promise. The statute of frauds is applicable only to executory promises; but to these it is ordinarily applicable whether the contract consists of a promise made by only one person or of mutual promises made in exchange by the two contracting parties. Thus, if S should guarantee payment of a debt, owed

66.    Mass.—Doyle v. Dixon, 97 Mass. 208 (1867). See contra Restate-       ment, Contracts, § 198, Illustration 4.

by P to C, in consideration of C's surrender of a lien on P's boat,[75] there is only one promise and the contract is commonly described as unilateral. That fact does not prevent the promise of S from being held to be within the guaranty clause of the statute. So, also, if A marries B as the consideration for B's promise to make a marriage settlement, the contract is unilateral and is also within the marriage clause of the statute. If A pays B $1,000 in cash for B's promise to convey Blackacre, the unilateral contract thus made is within the land clause of the statute.

Logical consistency may seem to require a like holding in applying the one-year clause; so that if A should pay $1,000 in cash for B's promise to build a fence after the expiration of two years, the unilateral contract, being one that could not be fully performed within one year, might be held to be within the statute. Likewise, in the case of a bilateral contract, where A exchanges a promise to pay $1,000 when his ship comes in for B's promise to serve as a seaman for two years thereafter, the bilateral contract is an entirety and might be held to be within the statute, because B's promise cannot be performed within one year, although the return promise of A is so performed. It has in fact been so held in some cases.[76]

The weight of authority, however, is very decidedly to the contrary. The rule to be applied has been stated in several different forms and the reasons upon which it has been based are not any too clearly stated in the opinions.[a]

a. Restatement, Contracts, § 198, Comment *a*, therein, reads: "Promises in unilateral contracts are not within [the one-year clause], however long the time performance of them may require, and promises in bilateral contracts as soon as they have been fully performed on one side are withdrawn [from its operation]."

# CHAPTER 20

## STATUTE OF FRAUDS—CONTRACTS IN CONSIDERATION OF MARRIAGE

### § 460. Form and Purpose of the Marriage Clause—Engagements to Marry

The third provision of section 4 is that "no action shall be brought . . . to charge any person upon any agreement made upon consideration of marriage." This is obviously aimed at the fortune hunter; but only at the fortune hunter who is also a perjurer. Marriage is recognized as a valuable and sufficient consideration for a promise. It has been held in New Jersey that a wife who innocently marries a man in consideration of an antenuptial transfer of property by him is a purchaser for value and may keep the property even though the transfer was an intentional fraud on creditors by the husband. But one who gives himself in marriage in return for a pecuniary promise needs the signed writing of the promisor in order to enforce it.

This clause of the statute has in one respect received an interpretation that may seem remarkable to those unacquainted with the history of the statute and its times. An "agreement made upon consideration of marriage" has been held to include promises of a pecuniary nature made in consideration of a promise to marry as well as such promises in consideration of an executed marriage—to include bilateral as well as unilateral contracts;[1] but it does not include the promises that constitute merely a mutual engagement to marry.[2] It was at first held that such engagements were within the statute;[3] but this was soon overruled[4] and the decisions are now uniform. In many States the statute expressly excepts mutual promises to marry.[5]

It is not certain what the draftsmen of the statute may have intended. Actions for breach of promise of marriage had been sustained shortly prior to the passing of the statute;[6] but it is unlikely that such actions were in mind when the words "contracts in consideration of marriage" were written.[7]

1. Mass.—Chase v. Fitz, 132 Mass. 359 (1882).

453

## § 461. Application of the One-Year Clause to Promises to Marry

Mutual promises of engagement to marry are held not to be within the marriage clause of the statute, if they involve no marriage settlement agreement. This rule may be some evidence of the tenderness of the courts for contracts of engagement, based on some underlying but unexpressed notion as to policy, or it may be based upon some purely historical ground. A few cases even went so far as to hold that an engagement promise to marry was not within the one-year clause of the statute, even though it was not to be performed within one year;[8] but the weight of authority is to the contrary.[9]

## § 462. Marriage Settlement Contracts

The contracts that are within the marriage clause of the statute are those making provision for a marriage settlement or for the regulation of the property rights of husband and wife. It includes all executory antenuptial settlement contracts, the consideration of which is in part or in whole either marriage or a promise of marriage. This is true whether the contracting parties are the two who are about to marry each other, or are one of such persons and a third person, or are two persons not themselves about to marry.

A contract is not within this clause of the statute merely because it is antenuptial; where two persons are contemplating marriage, they may contract in such a way that the consideration includes neither the marriage nor a promise to marry. Some courts have been rather more astute than others to find that this is the case.[10]

The following promises are within the statute: In consideration of a woman's promise to marry him, a man promises to make a settlement of money or other property in trust for her.[14] In consideration of Mary's promising to marry or actually marrying John, John promises to pay her an allowance[15] or to execute a will leaving Mary some or all of John's property at death.[16] In consideration of Mary's marrying John, Peter promises to convey property or to pay an annuity.[17] John and Mary mutually agree that their marriage shall not affect the existing property rights of each.[18] Mary marries John in return for John's promise to give Sarah a share in his estate,[19] or to adopt and care for Sarah.[20] Mary promises to release a money judgment against John in consideration of his marrying her.[21]

## § 463. Executed Marriage as Part Performance

The fact that the marriage ceremony has actually taken place, so that the consideration for the promise of a settlement is executed, is generally held not to take the promise out of the statute or make the promise enforceable.[22]   This is true whether the contract is unilateral, being a promise of a settlement offered in return for marriage, or is a bilateral contract consisting of mutual promises, the promise to marry being performed later.   It has been argued that the reason for this rule is that marriage cannot take the case out of the statute since it is marriage that brings the case within the statute.[23]   This argument is not sound, inasmuch as the statute applies to the bilateral as well as the unilateral contract; a promise to marry as well as actual marriage brings a promise to make a settlement within the statute.[24]   It is not merely the execution of the promise to marry that makes the statute applicable.   This flaw in the reasoning, the fact that several earnest arguments have been made to the contrary,[25] and the opinion of a few courts apparently to the contrary,[26] go far to show that the rule is hardly necessary to attain the purposes that may have lain behind this portion of the statute.   If there has been a part performance other than the marriage itself, as by change of possession and making improvements on land, the case may fall within the equity rules relating thereto and the unperformed part of the contract may become specifically enforceable.[27]   Also, specific enforcement has been granted where the oral contract and its consummation were induced by fraud or artifice.[28]

# CHAPTER 21

## STATUTE OF FRAUDS—CONTRACTS FOR THE SALE OF GOODS

---

### § 467. Section 17 of the Original Statute of Frauds

The provisions of the original statute of frauds, relating to contracts for the sale of goods, are as follows:

"Sec. 17. And be it further enacted by the authority aforesaid, that from and after the said 24th day of June [1677] no contract for the sale of any goods, wares, or merchandises, for the price of ten pounds sterling or upwards, shall be allowed to be good, except the buyer shall accept part of the goods so sold, and actually receive the same, or give something in earnest to bind the bargain, or in part payment, or that some note or memorandum in writing of the said bargain be made and signed by the parties to be charged by such contract, or their agents thereunto lawfully authorized."

The foregoing section was re-enacted, with very few changes, in the great majority of the States. In all of them, however, it has now been replaced by the corresponding sections in the Uniform Sales Act. The provisions of this Act, as adopted in New

456

York (Laws 1911, c. 571 [Consol.Laws, c. 41] § 85), are as follows:

"1.  A contract to sell or a sale of any goods or choses in action of the value of fifty dollars or upwards shall not be enforceable by action unless the buyer shall accept part of the goods or choses in action so contracted to be sold or sold, and actually receive the same, or give something in earnest to bind the contract, or in part payment, or unless some note or memorandum in writing of the contract or sale be signed by the party to be charged or his agent in that behalf.

"2.  The provisions of this section apply to every such contract or sale, notwithstanding that the goods may be intended to be delivered at some future time or may not at the time of such contract or sale be actually made, procured, or provided, or fit or ready for delivery, or some act may be requisite for the making or completing thereof, or rendering the same fit for delivery; but if the goods are to be manufactured by the seller especially for the buyer and are not suitable for sale to others in the ordinary course of the seller's business, the provisions of this section shall not apply.

"3.  There is an acceptance of goods within the meaning of this section when the buyer, either before or after delivery of the goods, expresses by words or conduct his assent to becoming the owner of those specific goods." [1]

### § 468.  Sale and Contract to Sell

In the early history of the statute, there was some doubt as to whether section 17 was intended to be applicable to executory contracts for the transfer of the property in goods at some future time.  The express words of the statute are "no contract for the sale of any goods"; and it was supposed by some that they were properly applicable only to contracts whereby the parties intended an immediate transfer of the property in the goods so that the contract could be properly described as an executed sale or a bargain and sale.  The decisions in the United States have uniformly held that both kinds of contracts for the sale of goods, whether called executory or executed, are equally within the statute. This rule is expressly adopted in the Uniform Sales Act.[2]

### § 469.  More than One Clause of the Statute may be Applicable

A contract for the sale of goods may also be a contract in consideration of marriage or for the sale of land or one that is not to be performed within one year.  In such case, it falls within section 4 as well as section 17 of the statute; and the fact that there has been part payment or an acceptance and receipt sufficient to satisfy the requirements of section 17 will not make the contract enforceable.[3]  There must also be a memorandum sufficient to satisfy the requirements of section 4.

## § 470. Definition of "Goods"

The American statutes, prior to the Sales Act, have frequently used the original words "goods, wares, and merchandise"; sometimes they have expressly included "choses in action" and sometimes they have substituted the words "personal property." The Uniform Sales Act used the words "goods or choses in action." In that Act, the term "goods" is defined as follows: " 'Goods' include all chattels personal other than things in action and money. The term includes emblements, industrial growing crops, and things attached to or forming part of the land which are agreed to be severed before sale or under the contract of sale." [4]

Separate sections are devoted herein to "choses in action" and "money," as well as to the distinctions made with respect to contracts for "work and labor." Contracts for the sale of standing trees, buildings, minerals, crops, and fixtures are sometimes held to be contracts for the sale of an interest in land, in which case the provisions of section 4 of the original statute of frauds are applicable, and not the provisions of section 17 or of the Sales Act. These topics are therefore considered as a whole in special sections among those devoted to contracts for the sale of land.[5] All of these, with the sole exception of tenants' fixtures, are included under the term "goods" except when they are regarded as a part of the land or an interest in land. If regarded as goods rather than land, of course the provisions of section 17 and of the Sales Act are applicable, observing particularly, however, that these provisions may be satisfied by the giving of earnest, by part payment of the price, or by acceptance and receipt of any part of the goods, as well as by a written memorandum.[6]

In the case of contracts for the sale of land, there is a "part performance" doctrine that often makes an oral contract enforceable. It would without doubt have been necessary for the

---

4. The Uniform Commercial Code —Sales, § 2—105 (1950 draft) thus defines the term: " 'Goods' includes all things which are movable at the time of identification to the contract for sale other than the money in which the price is to be paid, investment securities (defined in Article 8) and things in action. "Goods" also includes the unborn young of animals, growing crops and other things attached to, realty and capable of severance without material harm thereto as described in the section on goods to be severed from realty (Section 2—107)." Restatement, Contracts, § 200, is as follows: "Goods, within the mean-

ing of the statute, are:
"(a) Chattels personal, except current money bargained for as a medium of exchange;
"(b) Crops unsevered from the land, whether matured or not at the time when by the terms of the bargain they are to be sold, if they are of a kind subject to yearly cultivation;
"(c) Things attached to or forming part of the realty which are agreed to be severed therefrom before sale or promptly after the formation of the contract."
Presumably, this is intended to state, in other words, the effect given to the Sales Act by the courts.

courts to create a similar doctrine with respect to goods, but for the fact that by the express words of the statute itself any part performance is sufficient to satisfy the statutory requirements.

## § 471.　Contracts to Deal in Goods and Share Profits

A contract to form a partnership for dealing in goods, or to purchase goods jointly and divide them in a specified proportion, or to purchase goods and resell them, sharing the profits or losses, is not within section 17 of the statute.[7]　It is not a contract for the sale of goods from one of the contractors to the other; but it binds both of them to make purchases from and sales to third persons. There is no sufficient reason for holding the statute to be applicable to such a case.　The rule here stated is similar to the one that is applied to agreements to deal in land as a partnership, or to buy and sell land jointly, sharing profits and losses.

Just as in the case of land, also, an agreement that one party shall buy goods of a third and later transfer part or all of them to the other contracting party, is within the statute and unenforceable unless one of the several alternative requirements is satisfied.[8]

## § 474.　Differences Between "Price" and "Value"

Section 17 of the original statute contained the words "for the price of ten pounds sterling or upwards."　The Uniform Sales Act, however, following the example of Lord Tenterden's Act,[22] substitutes the words "of the value of five hundred dollars or upwards."　This raises the question as to whether "price" differs from "value."　In the case of ordinary sales of goods, a price in money is commonly named by the seller.　This is often varied in negotiation; and eventually an offer stating a price in money is accepted by the other party, so that the price is fixed by agreement of the two parties just as are the amount and quality of the goods and the other terms of the contract.　In every such exchange of goods for money, the goods are as much the price of the money as the money is the price of the goods.　In ordinary times, this fact is not often in mind; but it is otherwise in times of inflation, devaluation, and other governmental action affecting the currency.

Under the words of section 17 of the old statute, it might reasonably have been held that a contract for the transfer of goods was not within the statute unless it was a contract for the sale of those goods for a price "in money" fixed by the agreement itself. But it has been held in some cases, without any good discussion of the point, that a contract for the exchange of goods for other goods, or of goods for services, is within the statute.[23]　On this interpretation, a barter may be a sale of "goods for the price of ten pounds sterling or upwards."[24]　It follows from this that, under statutes containing the words "for the price of," if the agreed price named by the parties is not itself a sum of money, it must be valued in money before it can be known whether or not the contract is within the statute. This is because the words of the statute are "goods for the price of ten pounds." If the price is not already in pounds (or dollars), but is in some other commodity, that commodity must be translated into the terms used in the statute.

On the other hand, under a statute like the Uniform Sales Act, saying "goods of the value of $500 or upwards," it appears to be the "goods" themselves, rather than the price thereof, that must be valued before it can be known whether or not the contract is within the statute.

It seems highly probable that this distinction was not in the minds of the legislators who drafted or voted for the statute in either form. As a practical matter, in any case where the parties have themselves fixed the price in terms of money, or have themselves by the very terms of the bargain valued in money the goods sold, their valuation should be held conclusive for the purpose of applying the statute of frauds. The court still has before it, however, the problem of valuation in money, either of the price of the goods or of the goods themselves, in all cases where this valuation has not been made in the terms of the agreement.[25]

### § 475.  Amount and Character of the Price or Value

No contract for the sale of goods was within the terms of section 17 of the original statute of frauds unless it was "for the price of ten pounds sterling or upwards." In the re-enactments of this section in the United States, the price as specified in dollars has varied considerably, although most commonly it was stated at fifty dollars. The original draft of the Sales Act, as submitted by the Commissioners, made this sum five hundred dollars; so also does the Uniform Commercial Code (1950 draft). This is undoubtedly a wise substitution, since ten pounds at the time of the original statute had a much greater commodity value than has the sum of fifty dollars in the present century. There is no good reason for letting the continual depreciation of money in terms of commodities cause the statute to apply to myriads of small sale transactions of increasingly less significance. As the States adopted the Uniform Sales Act, however, they have not uniformly followed the recommendation of the draftsmen. The amounts inserted in substitution for the original "ten pounds sterling" have varied between $30 and $2,500. It would be wise not to create such a variation in the Uniform Commercial Code.

Frequently, two parties bargain for the sale of several articles, each having a separate price that is less than the statutory amount. But the bargain may be one bargain and the contract may be one contract for the sale of all the articles together, even though each article had a separate price. If such is the case, and the sum of the several prices equals the statutory amount, the contract is within the statute.[27] But if the several articles were bargained for separately and a separate contract was made for the sale of each, then none of the contracts is within the statute and each is enforceable even though wholly executory and not in writing. It is a matter of factual interpretation of the expressions of the parties whether they made a number of separate binding contracts for the sale of the various articles, or, after some preliminary inoperative negotiation, made one operative offer and a single operative acceptance. Frequently, indeed, the parties may not themselves know which they did.

## § 476. Sale of Goods Distinguished from Contract for Work and Labor

The contracts of mankind are of almost infinite variety, so that it is not easy to classify them into a few statutory categories. Further, a contract may be so complex and inclusive in its provisions as to fall within both section 4 and section 17, or within several of the classes of contracts that are separately enumerated within section 4. The subject matter of a contract of sale may be both land and goods. A contract may be one for the transfer of both land and goods in consideration of a marriage, the whole performance to be rendered after the expiration of one year. In such cases, it is generally but not always required that the requirements of both sections of the statute shall be satisfied.

It is obvious that an ordinary contract of employment is not a contract for the sale of goods. Illustrations are: A hires B to shovel sand at fifty cents an hour; a farmer hires a cowboy to round up the former's cattle; a school district hires a teacher for a year at a salary of $2,000. These are contracts for "work and labor," skilled or unskilled. The contract is not turned into one for the sale of goods by the fact that the shoveler agrees to bring his own shovel or that the cowboy rides his own horse; the shovel and the horse are goods, but the agreement does not provide that they are to become the property of the employer.

But suppose a contract by which A hires B to dig a well and B promises to supply the stone with which the walls are lined; or one by which a subcontractor contracts to do the plumbing work as required by a building contract, including the supplying of all fixtures involved therein;[32] or one in which a printer contracts to electrotype and print a book for an author and to deliver to him 1,000 finished copies, the necessary paper, ink, and covers to be supplied by the printer. In these cases, the stone, the plumbing fixtures, the paper and the ink, are goods, wares, and merchandise; as such they are on sale in every community, contracts for

461

their sale undoubtedly being within the statute if of the price or value named in the statute.

A contract may be one that requires both the transfer of property in goods and the doing of work and labor. The former is within the terms of section 17, but the latter is not. Such a contract might well be characterized for what it actually is—a contract that is partly within the statute and partly without it; [33] but the dual nature of the contract makes it possible to avoid the operation of the statute by calling the contract one for work and labor, disregarding the element in the promised performance that makes the contract also one of sale. In certain types of these dual-natured contracts, the courts seized this opportunity; but they did not agree with each other as to when it should be done.

If it is necessary or desirable to force such a contract having a dual aspect into a single category, calling it a contract for the sale of goods and therefore within the statute without regard to the element of work involved, or calling it a contract for work and labor and therefore not within section 17 without regard to the incidental transfer of title to chattels that is required, on what principle shall the forcing be now in the one direction and then in the other? When is an actually mixed contract to be treated as an unmixed sale of goods and when as a simon pure hiring of labor? One conceivable line of distinction might have been the comparative money value of the two constituent elements in the subject matter, putting the contract into the category of sales when the chattels that are to pass from one to the other are of greater value than the work and labor that full performance requires, and putting it into the category of work and labor when the converse is true. This basis of distinction has in fact been adopted nowhere, even though it may have played a material part in the actual determination of many cases.[34]

The English courts were less ready than the American to disregard the sale element and to take the contract out of the statute; but even the English courts might do so if this element is so small as to be practically negligible. In the leading English

---

34. Why, for example, did Blackburn, J., in Lee v. Griffin, 1 Best & S. 272 (1861), while holding that a contract of a dentist to fit a patient with a set of false teeth was a contract for the sale of goods, at the same time say that where an attorney is employed to prepare a deed "it cannot be said that the paper and ink he uses . . . are goods sold and delivered" and that "the case of a printer printing a book would most probably fall within the same category"? Are not the paper and the ink "goods"? And although no separate price is named, is not their value an element included in the price, and are they not in fact "delivered" so as to become the paper and ink of the other party? However, Blackburn expressly repudiated the comparative value test.

case on the subject,[35] the contract of a dentist to make and install a set of teeth to fit the mouth of a patient was held to be a contract for the sale of goods and within section 17, despite the fact that the skill and labor of the dentist added far more to the value of the completed article than did the materials out of which it was fashioned. In this case Blackburn, J., said: "On the other point, the question is whether the contract was one for the sale of goods or for work and labor. I think that in all cases, in order to ascertain whether the action ought to be brought for goods sold and delivered, or for work and labor done and materials provided, we must look at the particular contract entered into between the parties. If the contract be such that, when carried out, it would result in the sale of a chattel, the party cannot sue for work and labor; but, if the result of the contract is that the party has done work and labor which ends in nothing that can become the subject of a sale, the party cannot sue for goods sold and delivered. The case of an attorney employed to prepare a deed is an illustration of this latter proposition. It cannot be said that the paper and ink he uses in the preparation of the deed are goods sold and delivered.[36] The case of a printer printing a book would most probably fall within the same category. . . . In the present case the contract was to deliver a thing which, when completed, would have resulted in the sale of a chattel;[37]

35. **Eng.**—Lee v. Griffin, 1 Best & S. 272 (1861).

36. It both can and must be said that paper and ink are goods, wares, and merchandise, and also that upon the delivery of the document by the attorney to his client the property in the paper and ink passes to the client as in the case of any other sale of goods. The supposedly exact logical distinction of the learned judge requires us to shut our eyes to facts.

It may be true that the deed prepared by the attorney is not the subject of sale as a completed chattel, after it has been signed and delivered by the grantor; but is it not such a completed chattel after it has been drawn up by the attorney and before it has been delivered by him to the client for the latter's use? The printed books, expressing the author's ideas, are no doubt not chattels that the printer is at liberty to sell to third persons; but he is at liberty to sell them to the author himself and he is also at liberty to destroy them before delivery to the author, such destruction being the destruction of his own chattel and not the author's chattel.

The result reached by the learned English judge may be one that gives reasonable satisfaction in England and in other communities adopting his rule. The result reached by other and quite different rules may give an equal or greater degree of satisfaction. The supposition that either rule is determined by some compelling logic is illfounded. This is a practical, not a logical, world; and being so there is nothing to prevent a court from adopting a rule other than that declared by Blackburn, J. If it works as well or better, it is immaterial that it further narrows the operation of the statute.

37. As indicated in a preceding note, it is believed that this is no more true in case of false teeth than

in other words, the substance of the contract was for goods sold and delivered. I do not think that the test to apply to these cases is whether the value of the work exceeds that of the materials used in its execution; for, if a sculptor were employed to execute a work of art, greatly as his skill and labor, supposing it to be of the highest description, might exceed the value of the marble on which he worked, the contract would, in my opinion, nevertheless be a contract for the sale of a chattel."

The rule of this case was followed in a very few American cases.[38] It lays down an apparently simple rule, one that in most cases can be applied without great difficulty; but it has the defect of leaving within the statute a great many cases that our courts have desired to take out of it. This led to the general adoption of a contrary rule—first by the courts in interpreting and applying the individual statutes based upon section 17, and finally in express terms by the Uniform Sales Act.

### § 477. Goods to be Manufactured Especially for the Buyer

The courts of New York formerly held that a contract for the manufacture and delivery of goods not yet in existence in the form required for such delivery was not within the statute.[39] It was said to be a contract for work and labor. This made it necessary for the court to make fine distinctions in determining whether an article was in existence and ready for delivery at the time of contracting, and just how small an amount of labor required to fit the article for final delivery would be sufficient to make the statute inapplicable. It is no longer necessary to review these cases for the reason that the adoption of the Uniform Sales Act prescribed a different test and that the Uniform Commercial Code, if adopted, will do likewise.

The relevant words of that statute, as adopted in New York, are as follows: "The provisions of this section apply to every such contract or sale, notwithstanding that the goods may be intended to be delivered at some future time or may not at the time of such contract or sale be actually made, procured, or provided, or fit or ready for delivery, or some act may be requisite

---

in the case of a document to be drafted by an attorney or a book to be printed by a printer. False teeth are a chattel, and until delivery are owned by the dentist and salable by him to anybody. So, also, is a documentary deed; the attorney making it could sell it to anybody for use as a pipe light. The words used in the Sales Act exclude all such cases from the statute, not because they do not result

in the transfer of ownership in a chattel, for in fact they do, but because the teeth, the document, and the book are made especially for the buyer and are not suitable for sale in the usual course of the seller's ordinary business.

39. See:

N.Y.—Cooke v. Millard, 65 N.Y. 352 (1875); Parsons v. Loucks, 48 N.Y. 17 (1871).

for the making or completing thereof, or rendering the same fit for delivery; but if the goods are to be manufactured by the seller especially for the buyer and are not suitable for sale to others in the ordinary course of the seller's business, the provisions of this section shall not apply."

The rule thus adopted was derived very largely from the decisions in Massachusetts, decisions with which those rendered in a majority of other States agreed. In a leading case,[40] this rule was stated as follows: "The effect of these decisions we understand to be this, namely, that a contract for the sale of articles then existing or such as the vendor in the ordinary course of his business manufactures or procures for the general market, whether on hand at the time or not, is a contract for the sale of goods, to which the statute applies. But on the other hand, if the goods are to be manufactured especially for the purchaser, and upon his special order, and not for the general market, the case is not within the statute."

The adoption of this interpretation of section 17 of the original statute, or of a new statute worded like the Sales Act, affects somewhat the question to be determined, without altogether changing it. To fall within the statute, the contract must still be one for the sale of goods and not for work and labor; but, under the present rule, the fact that the goods are not in existence and ready for delivery when the contract is made is not itself sufficient to make the statute inapplicable. It is expressly provided, however, that if the contract requires the transfer of goods that are to be manufactured, in whole or in some material part, by the seller, on the special order of the buyer, and are in some material respect different from all goods that the seller makes in the usual course of his business and "are not suitable for sale to others in the ordinary course" of that business, the statute shall not be applicable. The issue, often a doubtful and difficult one, that this language raises is as to whether the goods that are to be made and transferred by the seller are of the sort that he makes in the usual course of his business for sale to the general

**40.**   **Mass.**—Goddard v. Binney, 115 Mass. 450 (1874), following Mixer v. Howarth, 38 Mass. (21 Pick.) 205 (1838).

The statute that is assumed for its discussion by the Restatement, Contracts, § 178, Class VI, is similar to section 17 of the old statute of frauds, not the Sales Act. It then follows the former Massachusetts rule in interpreting and applying its assumed statute. See § 199, limiting the statutory requirement thus: "except that where goods are to be manufactured by the seller especially for the buyer, and are not suitable for sale to others in the ordinary course of the seller's business, there is no such requirement." This shows that the Institute follows the interpretation that was given to the original statute by the Massachusetts court, rather than that given in New York or in England.

market. If the answer is yes, the contract is within the statute; if the answer is no, it is not within the statute.[41]

## §§ 478–481.    Choses in Action—Money and Credit

Many questions have arisen as to the coverage of the phrase "goods, wares and merchandise," questions that have received varying answers; many things have been included besides dry-goods, groceries, farm produce and livestock. Some of these things will be mentioned, without attempting definite conclusions or giving reasons. According to the English courts, choses in action are not included, the American courts usually deciding otherwise. Among "choses in action" are promissory notes and other commercial paper, certificates of corporate stock, and insurance policies. Patent rights, franchises, and contract rights not represented by any formal document are also included. The Uniform Commercial Code (1950 draft) treats choses in action in an Article entirely distinct from that dealing with contracts for the sale of goods.

Various forms of money, both foreign and domestic, are the subjects of bargaining transactions. In such cases they are treated as commodities. Nevertheless, in both the Uniform Sales Act and the Uniform Commercial Code they are expressly declared not to be included within the term "goods." Previously, some decisions were otherwise. Restatement, Contracts, § 200, excludes "current money bargained for as a medium of exchange"; its statement could stand much clarification.

An existing bank credit, foreign or domestic, is merely a chose in action; a contract for its transfer is to be treated accordingly. But a contract for the establishment of a new bank credit is not a sale or a contract to sell an existing chose in action; ordinary "letters of credit" are in writing but are not within the sale of goods section of the statute of frauds.

## § 482.    Acceptance and Receipt as a Method of Satisfying the Statute

Section 17 of the statute of frauds provides certain methods of satisfying its requirements for making a contract enforceable that are not effective when the contract is one that falls within the provisions of section 4. One of these methods is the acceptance and receipt of a part or all of the goods. The exact words of the statute are "except the buyer shall accept part of the goods so sold and actually receive the same." With respect to this provision, it must first be noted that it makes two requirements for enforceability of the contract, and not merely one. Acceptance and receipt are two separate acts or transactions.

Acceptance is the unilateral act of the buyer alone, or of his representative; it requires no action or expression on the part of the seller. Acceptance within the meaning of the statute is an expression of assent by the buyer to become the owner of specific goods as the subject matter of the contract made by him with the seller.[71] Receipt, on the other hand, involves a change in possession of the goods; it will be discussed in a subsequent section.

In order to be effective, acceptance and receipt need not be simultaneous, they need not occur at the time the contract is made, and there is no requirement that either one of them should be antecedent to the other.[72] They may make the contract enforceable even though they take place subsequently to the time that was agreed upon for performance.[73]

The requirements of the statute are satisfied by the acceptance and receipt of any part of the subject matter of the agreement to sell, and it may be a very small part indeed.[74] It must clearly appear, however, that the part so accepted and received was in fact a part of this subject matter, and not something collateral thereto, and that the acts that have taken place constitute a part performance of the contract.[75] When several articles or instalments are included in the terms of a single contract, the acceptance and receipt of any part of any one of them satisfies the statute as to the whole subject matter;[76] but if the articles are subjects of separate and distinct contracts, acceptance and receipt of part of the subject matter of one does not satisfy the statute as to the other.[77]

## § 486. Receipt Distinguished from Acceptance

Acceptance of part or all of the goods by the buyer is the expression by him of his state of mind, his manifestation of assent to "becoming the owner" of specific goods tendered or set forth by the seller as the performance of his part of the agreement. Receipt, on the other hand, is a change in the physical relations of those specific goods to the seller and to the buyer; at least, such appears to be the meaning of that term as understood by men under ordinary circumstances.[96] A creditor "receives" payment when money leaves the debtor's hand and rests in the creditor's; one "receives" a letter when the postman hands it to him in person; a housewife "receives" a package of coffee ordered by telephone when the delivery boy hands it to her at the back door. These are simple and obvious cases; but many purchase and sale transactions are not simple. In many such transactions there is no such change in physical relations. A threshing machine cannot be lifted in the seller's hand and placed in the buyer's; neither can a horse, although his halter strap can be so handled.

## § 487.  Operative Receipt Requires Assent of Party to be Charged

In order that the statutory requirement of receipt shall be satisfied, it is not enough for the buyer to make a forcible or other wrongful seizure of the goods.[97]  The contract is not made enforceable against the seller unless he in some way [98] participates in or expresses his assent to the change in possession and control.  Nor can possession be forced on the buyer so as to cause a sufficient receipt.[99]  If when delivery of the goods is tendered the buyer refuses them, there is no receipt even though the seller deserts the goods on the buyer's doorstep.[1]

## § 492.  Acceptance and Receipt by Delivery of Documents of Title or Other "Tangible Evidence"

If the ownership of goods is evidenced by some negotiable document of title, the acceptance and receipt of this document are sufficient to satisfy the requirements of the statute, if the document is so worded or indorsed as to require the delivery of the goods to the buyer; in such case, they stand in place of the acceptance and receipt of the goods themselves.[21]  The ownership of such a document carries with it the ownership and control of the goods.  It has been held that the statute is not satisfied by the acceptance of a document that is not negotiable or is not so worded or indorsed as to give to the buyer the ownership and control of the goods.[22]

## § 495.  What Constitutes a Part Payment—Money, Check, Goods, Services

Of course, the simplest and most obvious case is an actual handing over of money as part or all of the price.[39]  Even this, however, requires the assenting conduct of both parties.[40]  If the buyer sends money by mail and it comes into the seller's possession, it is not a part payment unless the seller accepts it as such.[41]  Whatever is paid must be assented to as part of the agreed price, although this may be at first called a "deposit" that is to be operative as a first instalment.[42]  Where several items are included in a single contract of sale, a payment on account makes the oral contract enforceable as to every item.[43]  The statute is not the less satisfied if the payment takes place subsequently to the making of the contract;[44] it must, of course, be made and received in part performance of the contract.[45]

When payment is made by check, note, or draft, instead of in cash, it has been held that the statute is satisfied if the instrument is accepted as absolute payment without regard to its ultimate cash results;[46] but otherwise, if it is accepted only as conditional payment and is in fact never cashed.[47]  In spite of the authority that supports the preceding rule, it is believed that a check ought to be held sufficient to satisfy the statute, whether it is received as absolute payment or as conditional payment. In either case, even though it is not technically a part payment operating as a complete discharge, it is a step in the process of payment and suspends immediate action; also it furnishes as definite evidence that there has been a sale transaction as would the payment of a few dollars in cash. For this purpose, it is immaterial that it was received as conditional payment.[48] The requirements of the statute are satisfied even though the drawer of the check causes its dishonor by stopping payment; the oral contract is still enforceable and the holder can maintain suit against the drawer for the amount of the check.[49]

The price for which goods are sold may take many forms other than money; whatever the parties agree upon as the price constitutes that which is to operate as payment so far as concerns the statute. The rendition by the buyer of that which they have agreed upon constitutes payment and satisfies the statute. So, the payment may be in the form of goods; and the transfer thereof, in full or in part, constitutes a payment.[50] The transfer requires mutual assent and the goods transferred must not be a performance that is part of a separate transaction.[51]

# CHAPTER 22

## STATUTE OF FRAUDS—NATURE AND CONTENTS OF THE WRITTEN MEMORANDUM

### § 498. Character of the Note or Memorandum Required by the Statute

Section 4 of the English statute of frauds made the specified classes of contracts unenforceable "unless the agreement . . . or some memorandum or note thereof shall be in writing, and signed by the party to be charged therewith, or some other person thereunto by him lawfully authorized." Section 17, affecting contracts for the sale of goods, wares, and merchandise, might be satisfied in several ways, one of these being "that some note or memorandum of the said bargain be made and signed by the parties to be charged by such contract or their agents thereunto lawfully authorized."

Certain differences may be noted in the wording of these two sections, with respect to the writing that is sufficient to make a contract enforceable. Under Section 4, the writing may be either "the agreement . . . or some memorandum or note"; while Section 17 specifies only "some note or memorandum of the said bargain." Section 4 requires only the signature of "the party to be charged"; Section 17 says "signed by the parties to be charged." The latter difference will be referred to in a later section dealing with "signature"; the former will be considered here.

Similar differences are to be found in the wording of the statutes of the various States, and in every case the exact words of the special statute must be considered.[1] Nevertheless, the variations are not so great as to prevent a general discussion.

It is obvious that the writing required by Section 4 is no different from that which will satisfy Section 17. Under either section, "some note or memorandum" is sufficient; and nothing is added or subtracted by stating as an alternative that "the agreement" may be in writing. Even though this alternative is not mentioned in Section 17, it is certain that a formal and complete integration of the terms of the agreement will satisfy its requirements; such an integration is certainly a "note or memorandum." If such an integration exists, the parol evidence rule comes into operation, preventing, in some uncertain and limited degree, the introduction of parol evidence to "vary or contradict" the integration. In so far as such evidence is thus prevented, it makes all the more certain the sufficiency of the writing to satisfy the statute of frauds; for it would seem that all such evidence would be excluded, even though its purpose is to show that the existing writing does not satisfy the requirements of the statute. The result is the enforcement of the contract as written; and if this happens to be the enforcement of a contract that is somewhat different from that in fact agreed upon, the responsibility for the injustice must be borne by the parol evidence rule and not by the statute of frauds.[2] The latter never operates to exclude oral evidence to show that a written memorandum is not a true and complete representation of the agreement made.[3]

Our problem, therefore, so far as concerns the operation of any statute that uses language similar to that of the original English statute, is to determine what is meant by "some note or memorandum." Without doubt, this meaning is to be discovered by a study of the thousands of cases in which the words of the statute have been interpreted and applied; but this study shows a considerable variation and some inconsistency, so that throughout the process we must consider court opinions critically in the light of the purpose for which the statute was adopted and for the attainment of which similar statutes are permitted to exist in the United States.

What is that purpose? It is the prevention of successful fraud by inducing the enforcement of contracts that were never in fact made. It is not to prevent the performance or the enforcement of oral contracts that have in fact been made; it is not to create a loophole of escape for dishonest repudiators.[4] Therefore, we should always be satisfied with "some note or memorandum" that is adequate, when considered with the admitted facts, the surrounding circumstances, and all explanatory and corroborative and rebutting evidence, to convince the court that there is no serious possibility of consummating a fraud by enforcement. When the mind of the court has reached such a conviction as that, it neither promotes justice nor lends respect to the statute to refuse enforcement because of informality in the memorandum or its incompleteness in detail.

Let us proceed, therefore, with a general consideration of what constitutes a sufficient note or memorandum. We may well start with this one general doctrine: There are few, if any, specific and uniform requirements. The statute itself prescribes none; and a study of the existing thousands of cases does not justify us in asserting their existence.[7] Some note or memorandum having substantial probative value in establishing the contract must exist; but its sufficiency in attaining the purpose of the statute depends in each case upon the setting in which it is found. A memorandum that is sufficient in one case may well be held insufficient in another. A complete admission in court by the party to be charged should dispense with the necessity of any writing whatever. With ample explanation and corroboration to be found in undoubted surrounding circumstances or even in the accompanying oral testimony, a writing may be sufficient even though it is cryptic, abbreviated, and incomplete. We are quite safe in trusting the courts to determine and administer justice, if it is made clear to them that this is their exact function and that there is no rule of thumb or detailed doctrine which they are appointed to apply literally and mechanically though the heavens fall. This does not mean that the courts are free to do as they please in spite of the statute; it means only that they need not construct straitjackets for themselves when the statute itself created none. The statute directs them that certain contracts, agreements, promises, or bargains shall not be enforced unless there is some written and signed note or memorandum thereof. That is the rule of law, to be applied with intelligence and discrimination and not like a pedant playing a game of logomachy.

§ 499.  **Informal Memorandum—Degree of Completeness in Detail**

Judicial dicta abound to the effect that the writing must contain all of the "essential terms and conditions" of the contract, and it is sometimes said that these must be so clear as to be understood "without any aid from parol testimony";[8] but the long course of judicial decision, which will be indicated throughout the discussion of the remainder of this topic, shows that "essential terms and conditions" is itself a term of considerable flexibility[9] and that the courts do not in fact blind themselves by exclud-

---

7.  In Packard **v.** Richardson, 17 Mass. 122 (1821), the court held that the consideration for a promise of guaranty need not be stated in the writing; it said: "It would seem, further, that the legislature chose to prevent an inference that the whole contract or agreement must be in writing; for it is provided that some memorandum or note thereof in writing shall be sufficient."

9.  "It must contain the essentials of the contract, so that they may be ascertained from the writing without a resort to oral evidence." But the court using this language found it immediately necessary to add that "the foregoing rule is sufficiently complied with if all the material elements of the contract or agreement are stated in general terms in the note or memorandum; all the details or particulars need

ing parol testimony when it is a necessary aid to understanding.[10] For certain purposes, parol testimony is invariably necessary; not otherwise can it be shown that even a formal document was in fact delivered or that an alleged signature is genuine. It is necessary for the purpose of showing that John Smith named in the memorandum is the very Smith who is now alleged to be a party to the contract, that "J.H.F." stands for John H. Flagler, that the agent who negotiated the contract and made the memorandum was in fact authorized, and that the words of description apply in fact to the tract of land as asserted in the action.

For purposes of applying the statute of frauds, as for other purposes, what terms are so "essential" that they cannot be supplied by parol evidence is a question of degree to be answered in the light of the circumstances of the particular case.[11] A rule stated in such words as these does not go far in helping a court to decide a case; but it should serve to warn the court that the application of the statute is not a mere matter of textual interpretation, that there is no easy hard-metaled road to justice, and that it must bear the responsibility for determining how best to attain the substantial purpose of the statute under the circumstances of the particular case before it.

There is some conflict in the decisions, due in part to a failure to keep clearly in mind the purpose of the statute and the informal character of the evidence that the actual words of the statute require, and in part to differences in the attitude of the judges as to the beneficence of the statute and the wisdom of its existence. Further, there are differences in the strictness of judicial requirements as to the contents of the memorandum. It is believed that sometimes these apparent differences can be explained by the degree of doubt existing in the court's mind as to the actual making and performance of the alleged contract. The better and the more disinterested is the oral testimony offered by the plaintiff, the more convincing the corroboration that is found in the surrounding circumstances, and the more limited the disputed issue because of admissions made by the defendant, the less that should be and is required of the written memorandum.[12]

## § 500.  Memorandum Must Identify the Contracting Parties

One of the "essential" elements of any contract is the existence of two competent parties who agree. No contract can be said to

not be stated therein." Lewis v. Aronow, 251 P. 146, 77 Mont. 348 (1926).

One of the best opinions on this subject fully sustaining the text above, is in Schafer v. Faylor, 60 N.E.2d 339, 74 Ohio App. 533 (1944). A written memorandum was held sufficient even though it did not state the time for possession, the kind of deed, who was to pay taxes, whether balance was to be secured by mortgage, or a complete description of the land.

be fully and formally integrated unless the document names or otherwise identifies the contracting parties. So, also, there is something missing from a note or memorandum of a contract that does not say who made it. There are many cases holding that a note or memorandum of an informal contract is insufficient to satisfy the requirements of the statute of frauds, even though it is signed by one party, unless the other contracting party is named, described, or otherwise so indicated in the memorandum as to make certain identification possible.[14] Some of these cases have without doubt shown too great a desire to magnify the requirements of the statute, when, so far as appears from the court's opinion, the result was to permit the unjust repudiation of an agreement, by a party known to have made it, in a case where there was no danger of successful fraud and perjury.[15] The courts have properly shown a willingness to admit parol testimony to supplement an informal memorandum that is itself evidential on the issue, to identify the contracting parties and show their agreed relation to each other, as well as for other purposes.[16] All agree that the party need not be formally named in the memorandum; it is sufficient that he is so described therein as to corroborate oral testimony identifying him.[17] His description in the writing need be no more complete and accurate than is the case with descriptions of subject matter or with statements of terms and conditions. If there is nothing in the memorandum to indicate that a specific person was a party to the contract, and the plaintiff's connection therewith is actually denied, the court must prevent such connection from being fraudulently established, either against him or in his favor. This would justify the exclusion of oral testimony.

### § 501. Must the Memorandum State the Consideration for Every Promise?

Must the note or memorandum contain a statement of "the consideration"? On this question there has been a long dispute and much litigation. It has gone so far that a few legislatures have intervened and passed supplementary statutes, some requiring that "the consideration" shall be stated,[29] others providing that it need not be stated.[30] The dispute and litigation were concerned with contracts of guaranty more often than with any of the other classes of contracts within the statute. A discussion of many of the reported cases is no longer profitable, either because of

14.   U.S.—Grafton v. Cummings, 99 U.S. 100, 25 L.Ed. 366 (1878); Storrow v. Concord Club of Wash. D. C., 70 F.2d 852, 63 App.D.C. 190 (1934); Peoria Grape Sugar Co. v. Babcock Co., 67 F. 892 (C.C.7th, 1895).

See also:

Mass.—Sanborn v. Flagler, 91 Mass. (9 Allen) 474 (1864).

N.Y.—Irvmor Corp. v. Rodewald, 171 N.E. 747, 253 N.Y. 472, 70 A.L.R. 192 (1930).

changes made in the words of the statute or because of the general confusion, both as to terms and as to policies.

In order to show why confusion exists, as well as to eliminate it, it may be helpful to discuss some preliminary questions: Is consideration a part of the contract or agreement? What is consideration? and consideration for what?

The definition of the term contract is a matter of choice; it is not an absolute. The American Law Institute has chosen to define it as "a promise or set of promises for the breach of which the law gives a remedy"; [31] while it says that an agreement is "a manifestation of mutual assent." [32] As thus defined, consideration is not a part of either a contract or an agreement. Indeed, it is expressly stated in comment that consideration "is not a part of the promise, and hence is not part of the contract as contract is here defined." From this, it would appear that a statute requiring a contract or agreement, or some memorandum or note thereof, to be in writing does not require the consideration to be stated. But the definition adopted by the Institute, for its use in stating the law of contracts, is not necessarily in accord with the meaning intended by the legislature. Even though we adopt this limited definition, however, for use in determining the application of the statute, "the promise or set of promises," or some memorandum or note thereof, must be in writing. The terms of the promise may show that the promisor's duty is conditional upon the giving of part or all of the consideration at some time or place. In such cases, if the statute requires all the terms of the promise to be stated in writing, then the agreed conditions must be so stated; and this might have the effect of showing what part or all of the consideration for the promise was. It would not necessarily have this effect, however; for the conditions of a promisor's duty are not the same as the consideration for the promise.[33] After knowing all of these conditions, we may still be quite ignorant of the agreed consideration or of any part of it.

The question, What is consideration? is discussed at length in another chapter; and the conclusions can only be summarized here. The term consideration has been used by the courts in so broad and so variable a sense that no statute can be clear and easy of application, if it merely requires a memorandum stating the consideration. Promises may be under seal, or made with other formality, and held to be binding without any consideration whatever. If in such cases there is no consideration, surely the writing is not insufficient for failing to state one. Informal promises, on the other hand, may also be binding without any consideration, if that term is given a comparatively narrow definition. Such promises may be enforceable by reason of something bargained for and given in exchange; [34] or because of certain transactions in the past, generally described as a past consideration; [35] or because of some subsequent action or forbearance by the promisee in reliance upon the promise.[36] If a statute requires "the consideration" to be stated in writing, does it mean to include all of these: the bargained-for exchange, the past transaction, and the subsequent reliance? When there is a bargained-for exchange, it is usually not difficult to state in writing what it is; and yet in certain kinds of cases, particularly guaranties, the parties very generally fail to do so. When a new promise is made to pay a past debt, especially one barred by statute of limitations, discharged in bankruptcy, or voidable for fraud or infancy, it is quite possible to state in writing what the past transaction was in which the debt arose; but this is seldom done in the new acknowledgment. In the third type of case, where a promise is made enforceable by reason of subsequent action in reliance upon it, it is not possible at the time the promise is itself made to state the action that may subsequently occur to make it binding.

In those cases where the consideration is a bargained-for equivalent, it may be either a performance already rendered or a promise of some future performance. It has been thought in numerous cases that the memorandum is required to state the consideration only if it is a promise of future performance and has not yet been rendered.[37] Yet the fact that some consideration has already been paid does not prevent the consummation of a fraud. Indeed, it is possible to establish by perjured testimony the fact that some payment has been made as well as the whole price for which the defendant agreed to exchange his land, goods, or services.

The foregoing is here inserted, merely to show that a requirement that the "consideration" must be stated in writing encounters serious difficulties in application and may operate as a trap for reasonably careful contractors and as an unexpected aid to repudiators. A further difficulty may be found in answering the second question: Consideration for what? The agreement of the parties may be a complex one, containing several promises. There may be mutual promises made by both parties; and the party to be charged may himself make several promises, that are all based upon a single consideration, or each of which has its separate consideration. Must the memorandum state all the promises and all the considerations?

The draftsmen of the original statute were indeed wise in making no detailed list of requirements and in contenting themselves with requiring no more than "some note or memorandum"; and, in applying it, the courts should require no more detail than is reasonably necessary to prevent the successful consummation of

---

35.　See chapter on Informal Contracts Without Assent or Consideration; also Restatement, Contracts, §§ 85-89.

36.　See preceding note; also Restatement, Contracts, § 90.

fraud. With respect to "consideration," how much is necessary in order to attain this purpose?

It must be admitted that fraud may be consummated not only by lying about the performance that a man is alleged to have promised to render, but also by lying about what he was to get in exchange for it and about the conditions under which it was to be rendered. A party is defrauded if, on the basis of perjured testimony, he is compelled to pay the debt of another that he never promised to pay; or if, having promised to transfer 10 acres of land, he is compelled to transfer 20 acres. It is as great a fraud if, by perjured testimony, he is forced to sell his automobile for $100 when he promised to sell it for $200; or if, having promised to transfer his farm on certain definite conditions, he is compelled to transfer it when those conditions have not in truth occurred.[38] Therefore, in some cases, it may be quite reasonable to refuse to enforce an alleged contract, if the note or memorandum fails to corroborate the plaintiff's assertions, not only as to what performance the defendant promised to render, but also as to what he was to get in return and the conditions under which his performance was to be rendered. In other cases, there may be so little doubt on these matters, and so slight a possibility of successful fraud, that a refusal to enforce the contract merely because of the incompleteness of the writing would clearly be giving aid and comfort to a dishonest repudiator and a denial of justice.[38a]

The foregoing is especially applicable in those cases in which it is customary to put a promise in writing without thinking much about the consideration for it or the conditions of its performance. Among these are the promises of sureties.[39] The consideration for the indorsement of a note may be the lending of money to the principal debtor or the forbearance to sue him on an existing debt; but it is seldom stated on the note itself.[40] Often a written promise of guaranty is given in order to induce the giving of

---

38a.    Such a case is Hanlon v. Hayes, 89 N.E.2d 51, 404 Ill. 362 (1949), where the only thing lacking in the signed writing was a statement of the price per acre, and both parties testified in court that the agreed price was $155 per acre. Had the agreed price not been established by the admission in open court, the decision could be approved, since the price per acre was an essential term and payment of that price was a condition of the vendor's duty to convey. This decision was rendered in spite of an express statutory provision that "the consideration of any such promise or agreement need not be set forth or expressed in the writing but may be proved or disproved by parol or other legal evidence." On using the word "consideration," the legislature probably made no distinction between consideration for a promise and the price of the land. Such a distinction should be made if it is regarded as necessary to attain the purposes of the statute. But in view of the testimony of both parties under oath, fully supplying the gap in the writing, the decision in this case should be emphatically disapproved.

credit from time to time in the future, without stating that fact or the form in which the credit is to be given. The consideration for such a guaranty may even be the payment of some premium direct to the guarantor, and yet not stated in writing along with the guarantor's promise. In such cases, the incomplete writing should not be held insufficient. Indeed, the courts have agreed with this in the great majority of the decisions.[41] Even though the State statute expressly requires the consideration to be expressed in writing, courts have held that it is enough to say "for value received," [42] and have been very astute in finding that the consideration is expressed in the writing by inference and implication.[43]

Even if the writing states definitely what the consideration for a promise is, it still remains to be proved by oral testimony that this consideration has been in fact performed. The statute of frauds, however it is interpreted, does not attempt to prevent fraud by requiring written proof that the agreed consideration has in fact been given or that the prescribed conditions of a promisor's duty have in fact occurred. These are usually overt performances capable of proof, and of disproof, by evidence other than the oral assertion of an interested party.

In contracts for the sale of land or goods, or for the rendition of services, the price to be paid in exchange is as much the subject matter of the contract as is the land, the goods, or the services, and is of equal importance in the transaction. The necessity that the memorandum should state the price is the same as that it should describe the land or goods.[44] But the price is not identical with "consideration" for the vendor's promise to transfer.[45]

Suppose, first, the case of a unilateral contract. The seller offers his promise to transfer land or goods in return for a cash payment. The actual payment of the money is the consideration; and there is no contract until the payment is made. Actual payment is the consideration and is also a condition of the promisor's duty to transfer. But we know that there is a price and what is its amount before it can be known whether there will ever be any consideration or any contract. The consideration is the paid price; while the price is the amount to be paid.

Suppose, secondly, a bilateral contract. The seller offers his promise to transfer land or goods in return for a promise of payment by the buyer. It is the buyer's promise to pay that is the consideration for the seller's promise to transfer. But the buyer's promise to pay is not the price of the land or goods; the price is the amount to be paid. In this case there is a contract as soon as the buyer accepts by making his requested promise; the consideration has been given, though the price has not been paid.[46]

478

In such bilateral contracts, the two promised performances, in the absence of some expression to the contrary, are to be rendered simultaneously; so that, as in the case of the unilateral contract, the actual payment of the price is a condition of the seller's duty to transfer, although it is not the consideration for the seller's promise. The transaction may, however, be a credit transaction; if so, the actual payment is neither the consideration for the seller's promise nor a condition of his duty to transfer.

The difference between price and consideration is perhaps even more obvious in the case of an option contract. In return for $50 in hand paid, the seller promises to transfer land or goods on payment of $1,000 by the buyer within 30 days. This is a unilateral contract, the buyer having the "option" between paying and not paying, and having made no promise. Here, the consideration for the seller's promise is the actual payment of $50. But that is not the price of his land or goods; the price is $1,000. And the payment of that price is a condition of the seller's duty to transfer, although it is not the consideration for his conditional promise to transfer.[47]

It will be observed that in the case of the option contract, it is far more important that the price of the land should be stated in the memorandum than that the consideration for the seller's promise should be so stated. If he gets the agreed price for his property, it is comparatively immaterial how much he got for his promise.

There is no doubt that, in the dispute as to whether the "consideration" must be expressed in the memorandum, part of the difficulty has been due to a confusion between consideration and price. It has been in part due, also, to confusion between consideration for a promise and condition of a promisor's duty, a subject that is discussed in the chapters dealing with those topics. For our present purposes, the conclusion to be drawn is that a statutory requirement of a "note or memorandum" in writing is not a requirement of any special detail. It does not purport to require a written statement of either the price or the consideration, or of the names of the parties or the description of the land or goods. So far as any or all of these are required specifically, the requirement is of judicial construction, and should be indulged in any particular case only so far as is necessary for the prevention of successful fraud in that case. The attention of the court should be devoted to attainment of the great purpose of the statute in the case before it, at the same time enforcing contractual promises as the rules of common law and equity require. There must be "some note or memorandum" of sufficient probative force, when taken with the surrounding circumstances and all other evidence, to make sure that these purposes are not being defeated.

In discussing the question "Consideration for what?" it should be made quite clear that what is meant is the consideration for the promise that is sued on, not the amount that is so promised for which the suit is brought. In a suit for a real estate commission, the broker introduced a memorandum in which the defendant promised "to compensate his agents to the amount that has been and is now understood." [48] This is insufficient because the terms of the defendant's promise are not in writing, not because the consideration for the defendant's promise is not in writing. The writing does not state what performance was promised. Even if, as in the case of guaranty promises, it is not necessary to state in writing the consideration for the promise, there must be a written memorandum of the terms of the promise itself, showing the performance promised and the conditions on which that performance is due.[49]

### § 503. Time of Making the Note or Memorandum—Written Offers

Any writing, signed by the party to be charged, and actually authenticating the existence and terms of a contract that he has made, is sufficient to satisfy the statute without regard to the time when it was made and signed. It may be made as a part of the process of agreement or subsequently to the final acceptance and closing of the contract.[56] The test is that the writing shall be an actual authentication; and the time of its preparation may have an important bearing as to whether it passes the test.

The note or memorandum may be made in the very process of contracting and as the operative expression of agreement by the party to be charged. Thus, if A prepares a written draft, signs it, and submits it to B as an offer to be accepted by B's signature, B's act of signing is the operative expression of acceptance. Such a document, signed by both parties, is usually referred to as "the contract"; and as a matter of course it is sufficient to satisfy the statute, irrespective of which one of them is afterwards the party to be charged.

Sometimes, however, A prepares and signs such a document and sends it to B as an offer, without requiring that B shall accept by signing it. In such a case, B has power to accept and to close the deal by an oral communication, or by a separate writing, signed or unsigned. The written and signed offer of A is a suffi-

56. Restatement, Contracts, § 214: "A signed memorandum that correctly states the terms of a contract satisfies the Statute, whether the memorandum is made before or at the time of the formation of the contract, or at any subsequent time during its existence." Quoted and approved in Kludt v. Connett, 168 S.W.2d 1068, 350 Mo. 793, 145 A.L.R. 1014 (1943).

cient memorandum of the contract making it enforceable against A, when he is the party to be charged in an action subsequently brought.[57] This is the law, even though the writing was signed before any contract came into existence, and even though it has no probative value in proving that B ever accepted. In a suit against A, B's acceptance can be proved by parol evidence. The document is indeed a written expression of the "offer"; it is not a memorial of a "contract." But it clearly authenticates the terms on which A was willing to make a contract; and it goes so far toward eliminating the danger of successful fraud against A that the courts were fully justified in holding it to be a sufficient memorandum. Of course, it is possible for B to lie about having accepted. He may possibly have at first rejected, and then attempted to accept after his power was ended. Or, he may have made a counter offer on different terms, that has been accepted by A. But the danger of successful fraud of this sort is very slight. A has sufficient protection in his own testimony and in the fact that B has the burden of proof that he accepted effectively. And at the very worst, A will be held to the very terms that he himself proposed. Perhaps the most common illustration of this sort of case is an offer made by letter or telegram and later accepted orally by the offeree.

### § 505.  Sufficiency of Description in Contracts for Sale of Land

A note or memorandum of a contract for the sale of land is insufficient to satisfy the statute unless it contains a description of the land constituting the subject matter of the sale. The cases that have passed upon the sufficiency of a description are almost innumerable; and a study of them will make it apparent that a description that is regarded as sufficient by one court has often been regarded as insufficient by another. No attempt will here be made to reconcile these cases, although a considerable number will be reviewed in the footnotes. They make it quite clear that it is possible to make a fetish of the memorandum, on the erroneous supposition that its contents have been fixed by statute. "Some note or memorandum" is indeed required, in the absence of which the oral contract is unenforceable, making oral testimony to identify the land quite immaterial. But it is going far beyond the express provisions of the statute to require a memorandum containing an exact and complete description or containing a description that needs no supplementary oral testimony to identify the property. Some contents a memorandum must have; and it is not unreasonable to require that it shall state that the contract is one for the sale of land. Further, it is agreed by all that there must be some descriptive identification of the particular tract of land. But if the court is convinced that no fraudulent substitution of property is being attempted and that the land actually agreed upon has been clearly established by all the evidence, including the written memorandum, the surrounding circumstances, and the oral testimony, little time should be wasted in listening to argument that the written description is inadequate.

Such description as the memorandum in fact contains, when reasonably interpreted and explained, must be accurately applicable to the land that is claimed to be the subject matter; but it need not be such that it cannot be accurately applied to any other tract. It need not be a full and complete identification in itself, excluding all possibility that any tract, other than the one asserted, was intended as the subject matter. The final identification and the exclusion of all other tracts may be made by admissions of the party to be charged and by proof of ownership, occupancy, and other surrounding facts.[71] Illustrative cases to this effect are collected below.[72] In a second footnote are collected other cases holding a description to be insufficient.[73] Without doubt it is not possible to reconcile some of the cases in these two groups; where such conflict exists, the case holding the memorandum to be sufficient should almost always be preferred as a precedent to be followed. This does not always mean that the opposing case was in fact wrongly decided. It is always possible that there was substantial doubt in the court's mind as to the making of the alleged contract or as to its terms, even though the decision appears to rest solely upon the insufficiency of the written memorandum. The mere existence of such a possibility, however, should not prevent us from criticizing the reasoning or from refusing to follow it as a precedent.

A description of the land by metes and bounds, mentioning monuments, general courses, and distances, is nearly always held sufficient.[74] The fact that the monuments can be identified only by the aid of oral evidence does not require a different result. Such a description as "my house," [75] an "estate on Congress street owned by H," [76] "my right in my father's estate," [77] has been held to be sufficient in the absence of proof that it is equally applicable to two or more separate tracts.[78] A tract of land can be sufficiently described by street and number or by a special name conferred upon the place by its owner or by the community.[79] Oral evidence is admissible to prove ownership of the tract and also to show its location in a particular city or county.[80]

### § 506. Memorandum of Contract for Sale of Goods—Statutes Prior to Uniform Commercial Code

An oral contract for the sale of goods, wares, and merchandise that is within the statute may be enforceable even if there is no memorandum of any kind. Old Section 17 and the Uniform Sales Act expressly provided that such a contract shall be enforceable if there is a part payment of the price, something given as "earnest," or an acceptance and receipt of any part of the goods sold. The actual occurrence of any one of these operative events may be proved by oral testimony as well as by documents; having been so proved, all the terms of the contract may likewise be proved by oral testimony. But in the absence of sufficient proof of some one of these operative events, specified in the statute, the oral contract is not enforceable unless it is evidenced by "some note or memorandum in writing of the said bargain."

The requirements of a sufficient note or memorandum for this purpose have been substantially the same as in the case of a contract that is within section 4. Since by the terms of the statute oral testimony is permitted to play so large a part in the enforcement of contracts for the sale of goods, it is obvious that the note or memorandum is merely an additional safeguard, specified as one of several alternatives. It should follow from this that informality, abbreviation, and even incompleteness in detail, are not fatal. Identity of the parties may be shown by a letterhead or a printed billhead.[81] The price of the goods, if some particular amount of money or any other kind of equivalent was agreed upon, has been required to be stated in the memorandum;[82] but if no price was determined by agreement, and it is proved that the parties meant to bargain for a "reasonable price," as that is commonly determined in lawsuits, the memorandum need say nothing whatever about it.[83] A contract to buy and sell goods, without mentioning price, is a contract to exchange the goods for a "reasonable price" in money. In like manner, if no time for delivery of the goods or for payment was agreed on, the law will imply a reasonable time, and the memorandum need say nothing as to time of performance.[84]

# CHAPTER 23

## THE MEMORANDUM—KINDS OF WRITINGS—SIGNATURE —ORAL EVIDENCE

---

### §§ 508–519.  Varieties of Written Memoranda

A deed of conveyance or a will may also constitute a sufficient memorandum of an antecedent contract if it states the terms of the contract; usually such documents do not do this. In order that the deed or will shall constitute the written evidence of a contract that the statute requires, it is not necessary that the deed shall have been delivered or that the will shall have been executed and witnessed. Even though the deed is not operative as a conveyance, it may be sufficiently evidential. The same is true of a will, even though it has been revoked and never is legally operative. Of course, a delivered deed may be operative as a conveyance even though it does not state the terms of the oral contract of which it is the consummation.

If a signed writing sufficiently acknowledges the making and the terms of a contract, it is not made insufficient by the fact that the party proceeds in the very same writing to repudiate the contract and refuse to perform it. The same thing should be true of an oral acknowledgement in court, even though at the very same time the statute of frauds is asserted as a defense; and there are cases so holding. On the other hand, no writing that denies the making of the asserted contract can operate as a sufficient memorandum.

A sufficient memorandum may consist of several separate writings no one of which would be alone sufficient. However, at least one of them must be signed and it must in some manner be so related to the others as to authenticate them also. An internal identifying reference to them is very desirable; but according to many decisions their authenticity and connection with the signed writing may be otherwise established. They may be physically attached or enclosed in a container; they may be in duplicate form or be so worded as to refer to the same transaction. If the court is convinced that there is in fact no fraud or perjury, parol evidence should be held admissible to identify documents and to explain their relation to each other. Some such evidence is almost always necessary; but some courts have stated strict requirements as to the internal reference in the signed writing to identify and connect the unsigned writings.

When the memorandum consists of letters and telegrams between the parties, it is seldom that any one of them is signed by both. Nevertheless, the contents may make it obvious that they are a continuous series sent in the course of a single transaction, so that the letters that are signed by the party to be charged fully authenticate the contents of the letters that are signed only by the other party. The several writings constituting the memorandum may include letters written to or by agents or other third persons and also recorded instruments and the minutes of boards of directors or other officials.

The cases are now so many and so variable, in their facts and in the stated rules and doctrines, that a court is now free to follow the ones that seem best suited to the case before it. It is proper to start anew with the words of the statute and to apply it with common sense, so as not to favor a dishonest repudiator while at the same time making sure that no fraud or perjury is being perpetrated. Any signed memorandum that is sufficient to attain this great object, when weighed along with all the other corroborating and explanatory testimony, should be held sufficient to satisfy the statutory requirements. Pleadings and depositions that are filed in court for other purposes may also be amply sufficient.

## §§ 520–526.  Signature of the Party to be Charged

The statute requires a note or memorandum that is "signed by the party to be charged or by his agent thereunto lawfully authorized." This does not require the signatures of both parties; the signature of the one against whom the court is asked to enforce it is enough. Except in the case of a unilateral contract, it can not be known in advance who will be the party to be charged; therefore each should be careful to obtain the signature of the other. As long as a contract that is within the statute is wholly executory it can not be enforced against one who has not signed; he can enforce it against the party who has signed, but in order to do so he must perform his own agreed equivalent and fulfil every condition precedent to the other's duty.

A signature may consist of part or all of the signer's name, even though misspelled or abbreviated to initials only. It may be inscribed by an agent or any third party who is authorized to do so, an oral authority being sufficient except in States where a special provision requires it to be in writing. Neither party can be empowered to sign for the other. In the case of signature by an agent, it is enough for him to sign either his own name or the name of his principal.

A signature is less likely to be questioned if it is subscribed at the end of the writing; but it is sufficient if it is inscribed at any place on the document and in any form, printed or typewritten. It is necessary, however, that it was inscribed or specifically adopted as a signature with intent to authenticate the writing as a note or memorandum of the contract. Oral testimony is admissible to show that the signature was so inscribed or adopted; and in some cases it may be absolutely necessary, as when it is part of a printed form or was stamped or inscribed before the agreement was made.

### §§ 527–531. Explanatory Testimony—Usage and Custom—Lost or Erroneous Writings

Courts have varied considerably in the extent to which they have permitted the use of oral testimony to explain, amplify, or apply written memoranda. Its admission should be very liberal indeed, so long as the writing is such that the purpose of preventing fraud and perjury is attained. However formal and complete a writing may be, oral testimony is admissible to aid in its interpretation and application. It should be equally so with respect to the cryptic and abbreviated memoranda that often are held to satisfy the requirements of the statute. An informal memorandum may be supplemented by oral evidence of the situation and relation of the parties and the surrounding circumstances, and also of relevant usages and customs not referred to in writing but which the parties had in actual contemplation. Enforcement of a contract is not prevented by the fact that the written document has been lost or destroyed; its contents may then be proved by oral testimony.

Without doubt, it is sound business policy to reduce important contracts to written form. However, in many situations it is not customary to do so; and in innumerable cases very important terms are left to mere usage and mutual understanding. The fact that the court believes that a contract should, as a matter of business policy, have been reduced to writing in great detail does not justify it in requiring more than the statute itself requires.

# PART III

# INTERPRETATION—PAROL EVIDENCE— MISTAKE

## CHAPTER 24

### INTERPRETATION—PURPOSES AND METHODS

## § 532. Rules of Interpretation Distinguished From Other Rules, with Respect to Wills and Contracts

Interpretation is the process whereby one person gives a meaning to the symbols of expression used by another person. The symbols that are most commonly in use are words, singly or in groups, oral or written; but acts and forbearances are also symbols of expression requiring interpretation.[1]

It is not only the words of a contract that require interpretation. Words and conduct used in the process of making a contract, offers, acceptances, preliminary communications not themselves operative in any way—all these need interpretation, before we can say that the parties have reached agreement, before we can determine whether or not agreement has resulted in contract, and before we can determine the operative effect that should be given to the contract. Such rules of interpretation as are stated in a work on contracts are applicable alike to all the communications just enumerated.

Much time and effort have been spent on the interpretation of wills and in the drafting of rules for determining their legal operation. From these one can gain some enlightenment respecting the interpretation of a contract. But he will gain only confusion unless he remains acutely aware of the fact that most of the rules given are rules respecting legal operation and not rules of interpretation at all.

First, we must distinguish all statutory and other rules prescribing the factors requisite for the execution of a valid will. There are analogous rules of law respecting the formation of a valid contract. In neither case are these rules of interpretation.

Next to be distinguished are those substantive rules limiting a testator's power to produce certain legal effects by will. There

1. Are rules of interpretation applicable to the communications in process of making a contract, the purpose being to determine whether or not a contract was made as well as what are its terms? In the case In re Kaufmann's Estate, 8 A. 2d 472, 137 Pa.Super. 88 (1939), the court said: "The general rule governing the interpretation of contracts applies not only where there is an admitted contract under consideration, but also where the controversy is whether there is a contract. Restatement, Contracts § 226 (Comment *a*). Whether the parties are merely negotiating a contract, or entering into a present contract, is purely a question of intention." Here the problem was to determine whether or not a depositary made an implied promise to pay interest. Undoubtedly its conduct as well as its words must be interpreted in the light of all surrounding circumstances. But some of the rules applicable to the interpretation of written language would not be applicable to the interpretation of actions and unworded expressions.

See Townsend v. Stick, 158 F.2d 142 (C.C.A.4th, 1946), interpreting the defendant's letter so that it was an operative offer to sell and not a mere statement of price, and interpreting the plaintiff's letter in reply so that it was an operative acceptance and not a conditional one or a counter offer.

Restatement, Contracts, § 226: "Interpretation of words and of other manifestations of intention forming an agreement, or having reference to the formation of an agreement, is the ascertainment of the meaning to be given to such words and manifestations."

488

are analogous rules limiting a contractor's power. These are certainly not rules of interpretation, although their existence has led to a rule that a writing, whether a will or a contract, should be interpreted *ut res magis valeat quam pereat*. Translated freely, this is a rule that a writing should be given a meaning that will make it legally operative rather than one that will not. This is not a rule that the court must give such a meaning to the writing, but only that it is sounder policy to give it such a meaning when other factors do not induce a conviction to the contrary.

Thirdly, we must distinguish those rules that determine whose meaning it is to which legal operation shall be given. Lawyers and judges are asked to advise and to adjudicate as to the juristic effect of wills and contracts. Interpretation is a preliminary to such advice and adjudication; and these will be found to depend upon the person toward whose meaning the process of interpretation is directed. Having determined who that person is, as required by some substantive rule of law, the process of interpretation begins.

As between wills and most contracts, there is a marked difference in the rules that determine whose meaning it is for which the court searches and to which legal operation will be given. In the case of a will it is the meaning of the testator and of nobody else. A will is made for the purpose of affecting the disposition of property by stating the desire of the testator. There is only one person whose symbols of expression are to be interpreted and whose meaning is to be given legal operation. The words of a will may convey very different meanings to an heir, to a stranger, and to the court, either before or after a careful process of interpretation. It is the court's meaning that must eventually prevail; but that meaning is the one that the court believes was given to the words of the will by the testator himself and the process of interpretation followed by the court is directed toward the discovery of that meaning. Thus is determined the issue that is before the court; and the field of relevant evidence is correspondingly limited.

In the case of most contract transactions there are at least two participants, each playing some part in the formation and the performance of the contract, each choosing some of the symbols of expression and each giving them a meaning that may differ materially from the meaning that is given to them by the other. In the making of a will the testator requires no other person's understanding or assent. He asks no one to make a return promise, to render an executed consideration, or to do any other act in reliance. These factors enter largely into the making and performance of a contract. The result is that the court must determine, in accordance with applicable law, whose meaning is to prevail, a determination far less simple than in the

489

case of a will. Once determined, however, the issue before the court is known and the field of relevant evidence again correspondingly limited.

Once having determined whose meaning is to be given legal operation, the process of interpretation by which that meaning is found is the same, whether the case involves a will or a contract. The rules as to the admissibility of evidence to aid interpretation are somewhat affected by the fact that the testator is always dead, while the contractors usually are not. The application of these rules undoubtedly affects the meaning that is found by the court; but their purpose—one that may be far from actually attained—is to insure the accuracy of the finding as to the meaning that was given by the person in question.

## § 533.   Can Interpretation be Either "Strict" or "Liberal"?

A distinction is often attempted between "strict" interpretation and "liberal" interpretation;[2] and since "liberal" is a word that is likely to excite pleasurable emotions, one making such a distinction usually prefers the "liberal" kind. Every one who uses a word or phrase is just as free as was Humpty Dumpty to give it any meaning that he desires; but it may take much circumlocution and play-acting to make others aware of that meaning. The hearer and interpreter of words used by another person is also as free as was Humpty Dumpty to give those words any meaning that he desires; but he would better be careful before he acts upon that interpretation. If "liberal" interpretation means the Humpty Dumpty kind, the pleasurable emotions are likely to be of short duration.

One who distinguishes between "strict" and "liberal" interpretation, at least in the field of contracts, may be one who thinks that there is one "correct" meaning, one "true" meaning, one "plain" meaning to words and phrases; that a strict interpreter is one who finds that meaning and declares it irrespective of results; and that a liberal interpreter is one who, although he knows that true and plain meaning, is willing to disregard it in order to produce what he thinks is a socially or morally desirable

2.   The terms used may also be "strict construction" and "liberal construction." And the choice that the court is making may be a choice, not between interpretations, but a choice between legal effects. Why one possible legal effect should be described as "strict" and another one as "liberal," the present writer can not see. He thinks that he understands, however, the difference between the exact adherence to an existing rule and a liberal departure from it.

"Liberal construction" as opposed to "strict construction" means merely that the words should receive a fair and reasonable interpretation so as to attain the purposes for which the instrument is designed. Mutual Life Ins. Co. v. Bryant, 177 S.W.2d 588, 296 Ky. 815, 153 A.L. R. 422 (1944).

result.[3]  At other times, the words may be used in precisely the
contrary manner;  in order to serve what is believed to be the
public interest a tax exemption statute may be "strictly" interpreted, restricting and narrowing its legal operation so as to
prevent it from creating a "contract" that is protected against
impairment by the Federal Constitution.[4]

Interpretation will not be described in this treatise as either
strict or liberal.  The effort will be made to look at language and
its limitations realistically and to state tentative working rules
of interpretation and construction, drawn from the decisions of
courts, that will measurably attain the purposes for which contract law exists.[4]  Usually the meaning that will be given to expressions used in a contract transaction is the meaning that one of the
parties in good faith gave to them, if the other party knew or
had reason to know that he gave it.  The meaning so adopted
by the court should be reasonably "plain and clear" after all the
relevant evidence is in.  It serves no useful purpose, after adopting this meaning, to describe it as either "strict" or "liberal."

## § 534.  Interpretation of Language Distinguished From Construction of Contract

Before attempting to lay down any rules of interpretation,
however tentative and variable they may be, we must first give
some thought to the word "interpretation" itself, as also to the
word "construction."  Without doubt, these two words are often
used in the same sense;  but they are also used in different senses,
the differences between them being variable.  The party who
writes or speaks these two words may have little or no awareness of the fact that there are such differences, or even of the
fact that he is himself using them variably—now as if exactly
interchangeable, and again as expressing very different ideas.
The most important matter is to identify the ideas that they are
used to express;  but the choice of the word to express the par-

---

**3.**  A friend of the Merchant of
Venice pleaded with Portia to be
more "liberal" in interpreting the
law of Venice as to penal bonds—
"to do a great right, do a little
wrong."  Portia's answer of refusal
is a classic;  but her refusal was
merely artistic camouflage, the
while she produced the same effect
in a more subtle fashion.

**4.**  Kales, "Art of Interpreting
Writings," 28 Yale L.J. 32, 49
(1918), says: "*Strict* and *liberal* as
applied to persons interpreting
written instruments are not much

more than epithets provoked in the
heat of controversy.  In the practice of the art of interpretation,
there must, in many cases, be a
fair ground of difference of opinion
by two experts, both adhering
strictly to all the rules and principles imposed upon them by the substantive law of interpretation and
the substantive law of evidence.
.  .  .  Both might be equally
*liberal* or equally *strict*.  The fact
is they merely differ in their judgment of the weight to be given opposing considerations on each
side."

ticular idea is of almost equal importance. The expressions of one whose ideas are themselves confused and uncertain will of necessity be equally confusing to others; but the effort to choose a word that will clearly convey an idea to others is of great assistance in clarifying to oneself the idea that should be conveyed. A clear and definite mind is a rarity; an artist in the use of words is as great a rarity.

It may be helpful to note that the word interpretation is commonly used with respect to *language* itself—to the symbols (the words and acts) of expression. In about the same degree, we speak of the construction of a *contract*. It is true that we also speak of construing language and of interpreting a contract; but by the latter phrase is certainly meant interpreting the *words* of a contract.[5] The word "contract" has been variously defined; but it is seldom identified with mere symbols of expression. By "interpretation of language" we determine what ideas that language induces in other persons. By "construction of the contract," as that term will be used here, we determine its legal operation—its effect upon the action of courts and administrative officials.[6] If we make this distinction, then the construction of a contract starts with the interpretation of its language but does not end with it; while the process of interpretation stops wholly short of a determination of the legal relations of the parties.[7]

---

**5.** The verbs "construe" and "construct" are now materially different in their signification, although they have the same Latin derivation. The words "constructive" and "construction" may be related to either of the two verbs, with corresponding variations in meaning. The usage of "construe" is almost identical with that of "interpret;" but a court does not discover a "constructive trust" or a "constructive condition" by a process that it would describe as "construing" or "interpreting." When a legal relation is declared to exist "by construction of law," its existence does not depend on the interpretation of a contractor's words.

**6.** In Brown v. Bedell, 188 N.E. 641, 263 N.Y. 177 (1934), the primary question was one of construction, whereby to determine whether a particular document created a "business trust," a partnership, or a "mere pooling agree-

ment or agency." The court held that it created the last of these three, without explaining how it reached that conclusion except to say "The court should be solicitous to gather the object and purposes of the parties from the language of their contract rather than from formulas applied to other cases."

**7.** This may be illustrated by taking a case from the field of joint contracts. Suppose that A and B employ X to build a ship, the agreement reading "We promise to pay therefor the sum of $40,000," the signatures being thus, "A three fifths; B two fifths." Did A promise to pay $40,000, or only $24,000? Did B promise to pay $40,000, or only $16,000? These questions are answered by process of interpretation alone. Suppose next that we hold X to have been reasonable in understanding that A and B both promised $40,000 to him and that the additions to the signatures were made merely to indicate the

When a court gives a construction to the contract as that is affected by events subsequent to its making and not foreseen by the parties, it is departing very far from mere interpretation of their symbols of expression, although even then it may claim somewhat erroneously to be giving effect to the "intention" of the parties.

The difference between interpretation and construction, as those terms are used herein, is often clearly indicated when we apply them in a case in which it is held that no contract has actually been consummated. The expressions used by the parties in the process of negotiation must be interpreted in order to determine whether or not an operative offer has been made and whether or not there has been an operative acceptance of an offer. Thus, to determine whether a letter constitutes an operative offer or is a mere quotation of prices requires the interpretation of the words used in the letter. A "meaning" must be given to the words before determining their legal operation. We must know the meaning that the recipient of the letter gave to the words, if the sender had reason to know that he would give them that meaning. We must know the meaning that the sender of the letter gave to the words, if the recipient had reason to know that such meaning was in fact given. So, if the court holds, after this process of interpretation, that the letter expresses a mere quotation of prices and should have been so understood by the recipient, it has no legal operation and the recipient got no power of acceptance. If, even assuming that an offer has been made, the reply is so expressed that the offeror has reason to know that the meaning given to his reply by the other party is not an expression of acceptance, again no contract has been made.[8] In neither case does the

---

shares of **A** and **B** as between themselves. Such questions as these may then arise: Can X get a joint judgment for $40,000? Can he get two separate judgments for that amount? If B pays $16,000 can X release him and still hold A bound to pay the balance? If A dies, can X get judgment against his executor, either jointly with B or separately? If B pays the whole sum can he get judgment against A's executor for contribution? These questions are not answered by "interpretation." They all involve the "legal operation" of the contract after its meaning has been found by interpretation, a legal operation to be determined by long study of the common law, equity and statutes.

See Ripley v. Crooker, 47 Me. 370 (1860); also Chapter 52, Joint and Several Contracts.

8. A good illustration of this is found in Williams v. Favret, 161 F. 2d 822 (C.C.A.5th, 1947). The defendant wished to make a bid for certain government construction. As a basis for such a bid, he asked the plaintiff to "submit quotations on the electrical work." The plaintiff submitted such an estimate and added: "If our estimate used wire us collect prior to June 6 or else same is withdrawn." The defendant sent the following telegram: "June 6. We used your bid for wiring on barracks and dispensary Gulfport." The court held, one judge dissenting, that the defend-

problem of "construction" of a contract arise. The interpretation of communications is necessary as a preliminary to the determination of their legal operation or total lack of legal operation.[9]

When a court is filling gaps in the terms of an agreement, with respect to matters that the parties did not have in contemplation and as to which they had no intention to be expressed, the judicial process should not be called interpretation. To call it so is merely convenient camouflage, the purpose of which is to reach a just result without seeming to disregard old and moribund doctrines. The time eventually comes when the doctrine should carefully be restated as the process of actual decision has required, and the camouflage thrown aside. The most common sort of "gap" that must be filled is found when, long after the parties have made their agreement, an event occurs that they did not foresee. In determining its legal effect, as the court must, the process may be called "construction"; it should not be called "interpretation."

The subject of the present Chapter is interpretation of language and other symbols of expression, not the construction of contract as that has been distinguished above. This is not to say that they are wholly independent of each other. Just as construction must begin with interpretation, we shall find that our interpretation will vary with the construction that must follow. Finding that one interpretation of the words will be followed by the enforcement of certain legal effects, we may back hastily away from that interpretation and substitute another that will lead to a more desirable result.[10] Nevertheless, our present topic is merely the

---

ant had made no contract with the plaintiff. Was the plaintiff's "estimate" an offer? Answering this question requires interpretation. Assuming that the defendant had reason to understand it so, was his reply an acceptance. The court held that the defendant merely said that he had "used" the estimate, that he was reasonable in thinking that the plaintiff would understand this as no more than preventing its withdrawal, and that the plaintiff had reason to know this. There was no contract for construction.

**9.** Restatement, Contracts, § 226, Comment c: "Interpretation is not a determination of the legal effect of language. When properly interpreted it may have no legal effect, as in the case of an agree-

ment for a penalty; or may have a legal effect differing from that in terms agreed upon, as in the case of a common-law mortgage."

**10.** Thus, the rule of interpretation *contra proferentem* makes a choice between meanings because of their legal effects. See § 559.

Where a lease was "on condition that in the event of an assignment . . . this lease shall immediately terminate," the lessor asserted that an assignment would merely create in him a power of termination by entry at his option, and the lessee asserted that it would at once discharge him from his duties as lessee. Here, the choice is between two inconsistent legal effects. See Judd v. Mutual Bank

interpretation of language.

The distinction here made between the terms "interpretation" and "construction" is by no means a necessary one; indeed, as is specifically indicated above, it is very often not made. But the fact that confused usage is the prevailing usage is not a good reason for adhering to it, even though any departure is sure to cause a temporary resentment in those whose complacency of mind is disturbed. Two good reasons can be given in justification of the distinction here made. First, there is no identity nor much similarity between the process of giving a meaning to words, and the determination by the court of their legal operation. Secondly, the distinction here made is consistent with that made in other chapters of this treatise and with the usage of the American Law Institute in its Contracts Restatement.[11]

### § 535. Do Words Used in a Contract have Only One True Meaning?

There is no single rule of interpretation of language, and there are no rules of interpretation taken all together, that will infallibly lead to the one correct understanding and meaning.[13] In understanding the variable expressions of others, men must do the best they can and results must be determined even though the understanding may be faulty. There is in fact no "one correct" meaning of an expression; and the party choosing the expression may have no clear and conscious meaning of his own. In reading each other's words, men certainly see through a glass darkly; and yet it is necessary for men to act upon their understanding, and it is necessary to hold men responsible for inducing others thus to act.

The statement that no word or phrase has one true and unalterable meaning is as true of proper names as it is of common

& T. Co., 159 A. 487, 114 Conn. 553, (1932).

Also, when a court says that as between two meanings the one that favors the public interest should be adopted it is making a choice between legal effects. A tax exemption statute will usually be "construed" not to be operative as an offer to contract; and even though a railroad is built in reliance on it the exemption can be withdrawn. When the court held that such a statute was a mere declaration of policy and not an offer, it was making a choice between legal effects, that is, between

no legal effect and the effect of creating a power of acceptance. Probably the exact question did not occur to the mind of any member of the legislature or even to that of one who built a railroad in reliance. Wisconsin & M. R. Co. v. Powers, 24 S.Ct. 107, 191 U.S. 379, 48 L.Ed. 229 (1903).

13. See Ogden and Richards, "The Meaning of Meaning; also the instructive articles by Chafee, "The Disorderly Conduct of Words," 41 Col.L.R. 381 (1941), and by Williams, "Language and the Law," 61 Law.Q.Rev. 71, 179, 293, 384 (1945), 62 id. 387 (1946).

nouns and verbs.　No name, whether "Peerless" or "John Smith" has any meaning in the absence of a user of it and of surrounding circumstances.[14]　One who speaks or writes such a name usually has a meaning for it.　The hearer or reader also gives it a meaning, perhaps a different one, one that is just as "correct," and one that may be just as reasonable to hold.　A "normal speaker of English" (or of Sanskrit) could give it no meaning without knowing surrounding circumstances;　and if he knew all the circumstances that were known to both the speaker and the hearer, he could still give it no "correct" meaning of his own.[15]

Sometimes it is said that "the courts will not disregard the plain language of a contract or interpolate something not contained in it";　also "the courts will not write contracts for the parties to them nor construe them other than in accordance with the plain and literal meaning of the language used." [16]　It is true

14.　Thus the term "Grand Coulee Dam" is a proper name and always has been;　yet it could be used at one period and by certain persons to mean a proposed low dam across the Columbia river, not yet built;　it could continue to be used with that meaning even after the government had determined upon the erection of a much higher dam, after the higher dam was under construction, and even after it had been completed.　The court was quite right in holding that, at the time of making the contract, the meaning of the parties had shifted to the higher dam.　Northern Pac. R. Co. v. U. S., 70 F.Supp. 836 (D. C.Minn.1946).

15.　Holmes, "Theory of Legal Interpretation," 12 Harv.L.R. 417 (1899) says this of proper names: "By the theory of our language, while other words may mean different things, a proper name means one person or thing and no other. If language perfectly performed its function, as Bentham wanted to make it, it would point out the person or thing in every case. But under our random system it sometimes happens that your name is *idem sonans* with mine, and it may be the same even in spelling. But it never means you or me indifferently.　In theory of speech your name means you and my name

means me, and the two names are different.　They are different words." As seen above, the present writer does not agree. They are not "different words." Just as in the case of common nouns, "meaning" can not exist without a speaker or a hearer.　The two persons give different "meanings," both equally true, to the one proper name.

16.　The quoted words are from Henrietta Mills v. Commissioner of Internal Revenue, 52 F.2d 931 (C. C.A.4th, 1931).　Such language can be found in many other cases.　See the many printed pages, almost wholly wasted by the printing of hundreds of such statements, in any Digest of cases dealing with "Interpretation and Construction."

In making such statements, judges are subject to the criticism made by Thayer, Prelim. Treatise on Evid., 428: "The Chief Justice [Holt] here retires into that lawyer's Paradise where all words have a fixed, precisely ascertained meaning; where men may express their purposes, not only with accuracy, but with fulness;　and where, if the writer has been careful, a lawyer, having a document referred to him, may sit in his chair, inspect the text, and answer all questions without raising his eyes. . . . But the fatal necessity of

that when a judge reads the words of a contract he may jump to the instant and confident opinion that they have but one reasonable meaning and that he knows what it is. A greater familiarity with dictionaries and the usages of words, a better understanding of the uncertainties of language, and a comparative study of more cases in the field of interpretation, will make one beware of holding such an opinion so recklessly arrived at.[17]

For statements such as those quoted above, the present writer might substitute something like the following: If, after a careful consideration of the words of a contract, in the light of all the relevant circumstances, and of all the tentative rules of interpretation based upon the experience of courts and linguists, a plain and definite meaning is achieved by the court, a meaning actually given by one party as the other party had reason to know, it will not disregard this plain and definite meaning and substitute another that is less convincing. Such a statement may be a mere truism; but it is not likely to lead to cocksure erroneous judgments.

Since the enforcement of a contract always necessitates the determination of its legal effect, and since this can not be de-

looking outside the text in order to identify persons and things, tends steadily to destroy such illusions and to reveal the essential imperfection of language, whether spoken or written."

17. Consider the following language of the court in Hurst v. Lake & Co., 16 P.2d 627, 141 Or. 306, 89 A.L.R. 1222 (1932): "The flexibility of or multiplicity in the meaning of words is the principal source of difficulty in the interpretation of language. Words are the conduits by which thoughts are communicated, yet scarcely any of them have such a fixed and single meaning that they are incapable of denoting more than one thought. In addition to the multiplicity in meaning of words set forth in the dictionaries, there are the meanings imparted to them by trade customs, local uses, dialects, telegraphic codes, etc. One meaning crowds a word full of significance, while another almost empties the utterance of any import. The various groups above indicated are constantly amplifying our language; in fact, they are developing what may be called languages of their own. Thus one is justified in saying that the language of the dictionaries is not the only language spoken in America. For instance, the word 'thousand' as commonly used has a very specific meaning; it denotes ten hundreds or fifty scores, but the language of the various trades and localities has assigned to it meanings quite different from that just mentioned. Thus in the bricklaying trade a contract which fixes the bricklayer's compensation at '$5.25 a thousand' does not contemplate that he need lay actually 1,000 bricks in order to earn $5.25, but that he should build a wall of a certain size. In the lumber industry a contract requiring the delivery of 4,000 shingles will be fulfilled by the delivery of only 2,500 when it appears that by trade custom two packs of a certain size are regarded as 1,000 shingles, and that hence the delivery of eight packs fulfils the contract, even though they contain only 2,500 shingles by actual count. Soutier v. Kellerman, 18 Mo. 509."

termined without first giving an interpretation to the words and acts of the parties, the report of almost every contract case shows that an interpretation has been made and contains a statement of some rule of interpretation. No treatise, however large, can cite all of these cases or attempt to state and criticise all of the stated rules. We shall here consider a considerable number of cases and discuss critically the rules constructed by the American Law Institute.

All rules of interpretation that are stated herein are to be taken as suggestive working rules only. They will be useful if they call attention to some of the possible aspects of a case and lead to the consideration of the various meanings of language that are worthy of comparison. They will be harmful if they are taken as dogmatic directions that must be followed, or if they mislead us into thinking that language has only one meaning, the one absolutely correct.[18] In every case, the first question is one of substantive law: Whose meaning and understanding is it to which it is the purpose of the law to give legal effect?

---

18. "The early English theory that words in a contract have a fixed and unalterable meaning . . . was not adopted here." Pettee **v.** Omega Chapter of Alpha Gamma Rho, 170 A. 1, 86 N.H. 419 (1934). The opinion contains a good discussion.

"It is not true that in practice (and I know no reason why theory should disagree with the facts) a given word or even a given collocation of words has one meaning and no other." Holmes, "Theory of Legal Interpretation," 12 Harv.L.R. 417 (1899).

It might be supposed that the word "wife" has a "plain and definite" meaning, or even one and only one true and correct meaning. Yet a court rightly admitted evidence to show that, in providing for a payment to his "wife," a contractor meant the woman with whom he was then living and not the lawful wife whom he had deserted. In re Soper's Estate, 264 N.W. 427, 196 Minn. 60 (1935).

Is not the meaning of the word "dollar" plain and definite when used in a promissory note? The answer must be No, until many factors have been weighed. The time and place of making and of payment must be known and many other circumstances as well. There have been Spanish dollars, Mexican dollars, gold dollars, paper dollars, and many others. In Thorington v. Smith, 75 U.S. (8 Wall.) 1, 19 L.Ed. 361 (1868), parol evidence was admitted to show that a note payable in "dollars" was payable in Confederate currency.

"There are instances where the Courts fall far short of the ideal interpretation as the ascertainment of meaning. A striking case of this sort is Re Gale, [1941] Ch. 209, where the testator, who had lived with an unmarried woman and had had four children by her, died leaving her certain property 'during her widowhood.' Farwell, J., held that the gift failed, because a woman who had not been married could not be anyone's 'widow.' This astonishing refusal to exercise intelligence in the construction of language cannot fairly be said to represent the customary attitude of judges; yet, though not the rule, it may be said, without disrespect, to be too frequent an exception." Glanville L. Williams, "Language and the Law," 61 Law Q.Rev. 393 (1945).

## § 536. Proof of Surrounding Circumstances—Application of the Words to Objects and Events

All through the history of the common law, and of other systems of law also, there is found a very common assumption of the existence of antecedent rules and principles, beginning no man knows when, coming from no man knows where, seemingly universal and unchangeable. And yet, at almost all periods, there have been a few jurists who took thought to the matter and who knew better. Nowhere is the truth of this more obvious than in the immense quantity of juristic writing about the rules of interpretation and the admissibility of evidence to aid in interpretation. Specific rules have been dogmatically laid down by judges of great repute. These have been repeated innumerable times, sometimes to apply them though justice weeps at her own blindness, sometimes to avoid them by making fine and specious distinctions, sometimes merely to state them with respect while disregarding them, and sometimes to voice criticism and disapproval. Among such rules are those indicating that words must have one, and only one, true and correct meaning, that this meaning must be sought only by poring over the words within the four corners of the paper, that extrinsic evidence of intention will not be heard, or that evidence of surrounding circumstances will be admissible only in cases of latent ambiguity.[19]

In view of all this, it can hardly be insisted on too often or too vigorously that language at its best is always a defective and uncertain instrument, that words do not define themselves, that terms and sentences in a contract, a deed, or a will do not apply themselves to external objects and performances, that the meaning of such terms and sentences consists of the ideas that they induce in the mind of some individual person who uses or hears or reads them, and that seldom in a litigated case do the words of a contract convey one identical meaning to the two contracting parties or to third persons. Therefore, it is invariably necessary, before a court can give any meaning to the words of a contract and can select one meaning rather than other possible ones as the basis for the determination of rights and other legal effects, that extrinsic evidence shall be heard to make the court aware of the "surrounding circumstances," including the persons, ob-

---

19. An extreme illustration is American Sumatra Tobacco Corp. v. Willis, 170 F.2d 215 (C.A.5th, 1948), where the appellate court reversed the trial court and jury, and held that a written promise to sell "my entire crop of 1946 Shade Grown Tobacco, to be grown by me on about 30 acres" legally bound him to sell all tobacco raised by him on two farms with twice such acreage, in spite of proof that he was already bound to sell the tobacco on one of the farms to another company holding legal title to that farm and that this was known to the plaintiff. The report should be read; for this seems almost unbelievable.

jects, and events to which the words can be applied and which caused the words to be used.[20] This is true, whether the court is trying to discover the meaning that the user of the words gave them, or the meaning that some hearer or reader gave them in the past, or the meaning that "a normal speaker of English" would have given them, or the meaning that a reasonable and prudent and intelligent man would have given them.

The first problem before the court is to determine whose meaning and intention it is to which the law will give legal operation; the next problem is to determine what that meaning and intention were. In interpreting a will, it is the meaning and intention of the testator that is sought; it is only the circumstances that surrounded and affected him that are relevant.[21] In interpreting the words of a contract, it is generally said that we seek for the meaning and intention of the parties; but inasmuch as two parties may have had different meanings and intentions, the court must determine to which one of them, if to either, is legal effect to be given. This choice depends upon a rule of substantive contract law, one that does not itself prescribe a method of interpretation of language. Having made this choice, it is only the circumstances that surrounded and affected the person or persons whose meaning and intention are sought that are relevant.[22]

The rules of substantive law applicable to a contract may, conceivably, be such that legal effect will be given to neither party's meaning and intention unless they are identical with those of the other party. It is often said that there must be a "meeting of the minds." If this is true, then the circumstances that surrounded and affected each of the parties are relevant, even though some of these circumstances may have affected one party and not the other. In the process of determining lack of identity in meaning, the meaning given by each party is a separate issue, to be determined in the light of the circumstances surrounding him.

It is conceivable also that, having identified the person or persons whose meaning and intention are in issue, the best that

---

20.    Even the statute of frauds does not exclude oral testimony to identify persons and things and to explain abbreviations in a written contract or memorandum.

Wigmore, Evidence, § 2470, has this title: "General Principle: All Extrinsic Circumstances may be Considered." After an enlightening review of ancient notions as to language and interpretation, he says:

"The truth had finally to be recognized that words *always* need interpretation; that the process of interpretation inherently and invariably means the ascertainment of the association between words and external objects; and that this makes inevitable a free resort to extrinsic matters for applying and enforcing the document."

a judge can do is to put himself so far as possible in the position of that person or persons, knowing their history and experience and their relations with other men and things, and then to determine what his own meaning and intention would have been. To do this requires a lively imagination, full and complete information obtained from the document and extrinsic testimony, and what we shall describe as sound judgment and common sense.[23]

If the foregoing suggests that it is not the meaning or intention of the party to the contract that is in fact given legal operation, but may be instead the meaning and intention that some imaginary reasonable, prudent, and intelligent man would have had (or, more realistically, the judge on the bench), we are not disposed to deny it.[24] Nevertheless, it is the circumstances that surrounded and could have affected the party to the contract that are relevant to the issue,[25] and not the circumstances that now surround the judge or the circumstances that might have surrounded some imaginary reasonable and prudent ghost.

### § 537. The Admissibility of Proof of Surrounding Circumstances Depends Upon the Person Whose Meaning is in Issue

In every case of interpretation, even though the contract is "integrated," the first question is: Whose meaning and understanding is it to which it is the purpose of the law to give legal effect? Before the relevancy and admissibility of evidence can be determined, we must know the issue with respect to which it is offered. In determining the existence and validity of a will, the first issue is the compliance by the testator with various statutory requirements. Those requirements are fixed by the substantive law of wills. The next question for determination is the meaning to be given to the words of the will, whereby can be determined the distribution of the estate. Here the purpose is to give effect to the will and intention of the testator. This rests upon the substantive law of wills, not upon rules of evidence or rules for determining the testator's intention by interpretation of his words. The words are the words of the testator; and it is the testator's meaning that the court is required to discover by process of interpretation. It is not the meaning that the heirs, or the next of kin, or the friends and neighbors, or the normal users of English, or the court itself, would have given or would like to give to the words. If by the substantive law it is the testator's meaning that is in issue, this fact definitely lim-

---

23.　Once, when counsel was citing case after case to establish the meaning of a will made by an old woman, Lord Mansfield is reported to have interrupted: "Sir, do you think that this old lady ever read those cases or would understand them if she had?" Holliday, History of Eng.Law, 127.

its the surrounding circumstances that may be proved. It is only those circumstances that are relevant to that issue—those that might have affected the meaning that the testator gave to his words—that will be admitted to aid in interpretation.

In the present treatise, however, we are concerned with the interpretation and effect of contracts and communications between contractors, not of wills. We must know what a contract is; we must know the requirements of a valid contract. As in the case of a will, these requirements are fixed by substantive law, although in major part it is not statutory law. Among these requirements is a promissory expression by one party, or by each of two or more parties. A promissory expression, however, must have "meaning," something that can be arrived at only by interpretation of the symbols of expression. Does the law of contract tell us *whose* meaning it is to which the law will give effect? The answer is that it does tell us; but it can not, as in the case of a will, tell us in a single sentence. The common statement that there must be a "meeting of the minds" in order to form a contract, with which we are all familiar, seems to require that at least two parties shall give to the words of the contract a common and identical meaning. If this is ever true, then in such a case the purpose of the law is to give effect to the meaning and intention of these two parties. But a study of decisions quickly shows us that the validity of a contract does not depend upon a "meeting of the minds" in this sense. Let us consider a few cases in trying to state whose meaning it is that must prevail.

Suppose, first, a unilateral contract of donation under seal, for which no one has given anything in exchange and in reliance on which no one has changed his position. To be specific, suppose that A signs and seals a document reading thus: "I promise to convey my Richland farm to my son John within a reasonable time." This document he delivers to C to hold for John's sole benefit. Here, just as in the case of a will, it is A's meaning and intention that must be found and given legal effect. The meaning and intention of John are immaterial; indeed he may have none at all, for he may not even know of the instrument. If this is correct, it is because of a rule of substantive law that is applicable before interpretation begins. It tells us whose meaning is to be found and made effective; but it gives us no rule or "standard" by which that meaning shall be found.

This sealed document, one that may be assumed to be fully "integrated," requires interpretation before a court can enforce the promise that it contains. What is "Richland farm"? Who is John? What is a "reasonable time"? What estate and by what form of deed must A "convey"? It is A's own meaning of these symbols that is the issue. Surrounding circumstances that are not relevant to this issue are not admissible. But every circumstance that might have affected the meaning that A gave to those symbols ought to be known by the court before it attempts enforcement. It should know that A called the 160 acre tract on which he lived "Richland farm"; [29] but that a contiguous 80 acre tract that he had bought from his sister he called "Emma's land." It should know that A lived with an illegitimate son named John Secundus, whom he dearly loved; and that much earlier his lawful wife from whom he had been estranged for forty years had borne him a son named John Primus. It should know that "Richland farm" was mortgaged for $5,000; that A had no resources out of which he could pay the debt; that A had no other home in which to live. It should know that A had frequently said to third persons that his little son John Secundus should have the home place.[30]

Suppose, next, that in consideration of $5,000 paid by B, the following promise is made by A: "I promise to convey to B my Richland farm within a reasonable time." Here, the words of A's promise are given a meaning by each of the parties; and it is in reliance on his own meaning that he assents to the exchange of land for money. Yet the two meanings so given to the written words may not be the same; and there may be no "meeting of the minds" in a subjective sense. By the substantive law, however, there may be an enforceable contract anyway. If A and B gave different meanings to the quoted words, we must proceed

---

29.   This could be proved by the contents of the donor's private diary, even though no other person ever used the name or knew that the donor used it.

30.   In Cheyney's Case, 5 Co. 68 (1592), a testator left property to his son "John." He had two sons so named. Evidence was admitted to show that the testator believed the first one to be dead.

In re Soper's Estate, 264 N.W. 427, 196 Minn. 60 (1935), is a case that is relevant here. An integrated escrow contract between two partners and a trust company provided for the control of the business after the death of either, and also that certain insurance money should be paid by the trust company to the "wife" of the partner who died. The court permitted proof that the *promisee* Soper intended the woman with whom he was then living, although he had a lawful wife abroad from whom he had been separated for many years. Here the contract was bilateral; but the "wife" was a donee beneficiary of the insurance provision. It was quite immaterial to the other partner, or to the trust company, to which woman the money should be paid. Therefore, it was the meaning of the promisee who was making a gift of the money that should be ascertained and made effective.

This reasoning is applied by Doe, C. J. in interpreting a will. Tilton v. American Bible Soc., 60 N.H. 377 (1880). "The question is not by what name any Bible society was known to others, but which of several Bible societies was intended by the testator. . . . A person known to a testator as A. B. and to all others as C. D. may take a legacy given to A. B."

to determine whether either one of them knew, or had reason to know, that the other gave a particular meaning to the quoted words and assented in reliance thereon. Consider the term "Richland farm." A meant the 160 acre tract that he had inherited from his mother, who had taught him to call it by that name. On the other hand, B understood the term to include the contiguous 80 acre tract that A had bought from his sister and that he was accustomed to call "Emma's land." The two tracts were separated by no fence or other boundary markings; and a continuous field of wheat crossed the line, partly covering both tracts. A had paid $1,000 for "Emma's land" some ten years earlier. No sales of land nearby had been made since then; and market values are doubtful. During negotiations, A had pointed out to B the fine field of wheat described above. All of these circumstances, and more, are relevant in determining the interpretation of "Richland farm." If the trial court finds as a fact that A knew or had reason to know that B understood the term to mean the 240 acre tract, there is a contract binding A to convey that tract. If A said nothing about a mortgage, then A is bound to convey a merchantable title in fee.[31]

The foregoing result is reached because, as our system of contract law has grown, one of its chief purposes is to secure the realization of expectations reasonably induced by the expressions of agreement, when that can be done without running counter to other expectations and understandings that were also reasonably induced. If, in the case above, A knew or had reason to know the meaning that B in fact gave to A's promissory words, then the substantive law declares that B's understanding shall be given legal effect.[32] This rule we can lay down before we know just what B's understanding was; but before determining legal effects the court must discover what his meaning was and whether A knew or had reason to know that he gave it. All surrounding circumstances that might have affected B's meaning should be admitted in evidence.

But there are now two separate issues before the court: (1) What was the meaning that B in fact gave to the quoted promissory words? (2) Did A know or have reason to know that B gave the words that meaning? On each of these issues, the court should admit all relevant evidence; it should know all surrounding circumstances that may have influenced B's interpretation of the words, and also all that tend to prove or to disprove knowl-

---

32. **U.S.**—Bowers Hydraulic Dredging Co. v. U. S., 29 S.Ct. 77, 211 U.S. 176, 53 L.Ed. 136 (1908), a contractor signed a second contract containing a provision identical with one in a previous contract, knowing the interpretation thereof asserted by the other party; United States Nav. Co. v. Black Diamond Lines, 147 F.2d 958 (C.C.A.2d, 1945); Ryan v. Ohmer, 244 F. 31 (C.C.A.2d, 1917).

edge, or reason to know, on A's part. All other circumstances are immaterial and should be excluded.

If the second of these issues is found affirmatively by the court, this determines *whose* meaning must be given effect; it is B's meaning. And the process of interpretation has been and still is the process of determining what B's understanding was. It is not the meaning that A gave; or the meaning that a normal user of English would have given; or the meaning that the court may hastily think is "plain and clear." All of these should be considered in the process of determining whether or not B in fact held any of them, and also in the process of determining whether or not A had "reason to know" the understanding that B had. But they are merely steps in the evidential search for B's meaning and A's reason to know it; no one of them is the one that must itself prevail. All of them together, even though they happen to be identical, may be wholly overpowered by other more compelling testimony.

The fact that B understood the term "Richland farm" to include 240 acres might be shown by the fact that he said so at the time to a third party, or by B's own testimony at the trial. The fact that such statements are self-serving, however, makes them suspect and clearly affects their persuasive effect. But if such a statement was made by B directly to A, at the time of agreement, that fact might be decisive, both that B understood 240 acres and that A knew that he did.[33] Such a statement made by B to a third person, and not in any way communicated to A, would not tend to prove that A either knew or had reason to know B's understanding. This shows that proof of B's statements as to his understanding or intention, not communicated to A, must be considered in relation to the issue before the court, as well as with respect to their weight and character. The same is true of similar statements by A uncommunicated to B.[34]

If it can not be shown that A in fact knew that B understood 240 acres, the fact that he had "reason to know" it must be shown by proof of circumstances. On this issue, it becomes very material what a reasonable man in A's position would have

---

**34.** If the issue is the meaning that B gave to the words of agreement, his own statements and conduct both antecedent and subsequent are admissible against him, even though they were wholly unknown to A. Suppose that B has said to C: "I knew that A did not intend to sell 'Emma's land;' but his description 'Richland farm' would be understood by any reasonably intelligent man to include that land and the law entitles me to get it." This would be admissible in A's behalf; no decree for reformation would be necessary. But A would not be permitted to prove a statement made by himself to C: "I have just sold Richland Farm to B; hereafter I shall make my home on Emma's land." See Allen v. Wolf River Lbr. Co., 172 N.W. 158, 169 Wis. 253, 9 A.L.R. 271 (1919).

known. But observe that it is such a man "in A's position" whose hypothetical meaning is given weight, not a reasonable man in vacuo, or a reasonable college professor, or a normal user of English in a different environment.

Of course, what has been said above, with respect to B's meaning and A's knowledge or reason to know, is equally applicable to A's meaning and B's knowledge or reason to know. It may be that neither one had actual knowledge of the other's understanding. It may be, also, that neither one can be shown to have had "reason to know" the other's understanding. If this last be true, then there is no valid contract; and B can get judgment for the restitution of the $5,000 paid by him to A, if A refuses to adopt B's meaning and to convey 240 acres. Neither one can enforce specific performance or get a judgment for damages for breach on the basis of his own meaning. This would equally be true had the agreement been bilateral in form, the price being promised but not yet paid.[35] And it is true whether the agreement was "integrated" or was not "integrated."

If the court finds that the meaning given by B to the phrase "Richland farm" was 240 acres and that A knew or had reason to know this, or if the court finds that the meaning given by A was 160 acres and that B knew or had reason to know it, a contract has been made even though there may not be a "meeting of the minds." In neither case is it an "objective" meaning (one that is or would be given by third persons) that prevails. It is either A's meaning or B's meaning.

### § 538. The Expressed Intention of the Parties

It is generally said that the purpose of interpretation is to become aware of the "intention of the parties." [40] In interpreting a will, it is the intention of one party—the testator. In contracts, other than purely unilateral contracts of donation that have never been acted upon by the donee,[41] there are always at least two parties whose intention and understanding must be considered. A contractor whose expressions induce another to understand and to act in reliance on that understanding may be held responsible therefor. In most cases, the officers who represent government are more interested in the understanding that is induced than in the meaning that the contractor himself had and intended to convey to the other. This has led very thoughtful and learned judges to say that the intention of the contractor is immaterial and that evidence of his intention—even his own testimony under oath

---

**35.** The case would then be illustrated by Raffles v. Wichelhaus, 2 H. & C. 906 (1864), discussed in a preceding section and also in the chapter on Mistake. The decision would be the same, whether the agreement was made orally, or by the exchange of letters, or by the execution of an "integrated" written instrument.

as to what his intention was—will not be received. The other party can not know what his intention was except so far as he expressed it in a manner understandable by others.[42] Therefore, he can not hold the other party bound in accordance with a meaning unless (1) the other party so understood his expressions, or (2) had reason so to understand them under the existing circumstances (meaning by this that any other understanding would be unreasonable).

Two parties may give the same meaning to the words of their contract, even though neither one had reason (in the light of the usage of other men) to suppose that the other would so understand, and even though no reasonable person put in the shoes of either one would so have understood. When such is the case, conflict is unlikely and litigation will probably not occur. In case this improbable litigation does occur, there is no good reason for refusing to enforce the contract. If the defendant admits that he gave the same meaning to the words as did the plaintiff, he should not escape liability by convincing the court that no reasonable man in his place would have given the words that meaning and that no reasonable man in the other party's place would have expected him to do so.[43]

If the foregoing is correct, a party should be permitted to determine the operative meaning of the words of agreement by proving that both parties so understood them, or that he so understood them and the other party knew that he did, or that he so understood them and the other party had reason to know that he did.[44] Once upon a time a party to the litigation was incompetent as a witness in his own behalf because of the fear that he might be a perjurer. For adequate reasons this ceased to be the law a good many years ago. Self-serving testimony does not have to be believed, however; and in most cases it can readily be rebutted when it is not true. Furthermore, the testimony of a party as to his own meaning becomes immaterial as soon as it is established that

**42.** As Brian, C. J., far back in 1478 (Y.B. 17 Edw. IV, 2), said: "the devil himself does not know the thought of man."

**43.** The writer therefore disagrees with Baron Bramwell when he said: "If a man intends to buy, and says so to the intended seller, and he intends to sell, and says so to the intended buyer, there is a contract of sale; *and so there would be if neither had the intention.*" Brown v. Hare, 3 H. & N. *484, *495. Would he exclude their antecedent declarations showing that the transaction was only frolic and banter, or their present admissions on the stand that such was the case?

When litigation actually arises, it may be very unlikely that the defendant will admit in court that he understood the words of the contract in the same unreasonable way as did the plaintiff. Even so, it may not be impossible to prove that he did so understand. His antecedent admissions, statements, and conduct may be convincing.

he knew or had reason to know that the other party had a different meaning and has materially changed his position in reliance thereon. Before this position is reached, the court must be convinced that the other party actually had and relied on this "different meaning;" so far from being immaterial, this meaning now determines the legal relations of the parties.

It must be remembered that the words in which a written or an oral contract is put are not the sole expression of either party's meaning. They may, indeed, agree that the contract now expressed in words shall be their only and entire contract, displacing and rendering inoperative all previous agreements and understandings, so that learned scholars may say that their contract has been "integrated" in the specific words used. This is not an agreement that the "integrated" language shall be the sole source to which either they or the court may go in order to determine their meaning and intention. No language, however fully and carefully "integrated," applies itself to the persons and objects and performances involved. Therefore, the meaning and understanding of one party may, and usually must, be drawn from his other expressions and surrounding circumstances as well as from the chosen contract words; but the other party can not be said to have reason to know this meaning and understanding unless the other expressions are communicated to him and the circumstances are known by him.[53]

It may be true to say that a mental state, totally unexpressed by either words or other acts, does not affect the interpretation of a contract; but the statement is almost certain to be misleading. In every case involving interpretation, the parties have used expressions, both words and other acts. The court is not searching for an unexpressed mental state; instead, it is searching for the meanings that each party intended to convey by his words and acts, and for the meanings that those words and acts conveyed to the other party. The meanings were in fact "expressed" in words and acts; but they may not have been successfully "conveyed." Even when a contract has been fully "integrated"

---

53. Learned Hand, J., said in Eustis Mining Co. v. Beer, Sondheimer & Co., 239 F. 976, 984 (D.C.N.Y.1917): "It makes not the least difference whether a promisor actually intends that meaning which the law will impose upon his words. The whole House of Bishops might satisfy us that he had intended something else, and it would not make a particle of difference in his obligation." This is quite true, if, as may be the case, he knew or had reason to know that the other party assented and acted in the belief that the words had a meaning different from the one held by himself.

The present writer believes that after thirty more years of experience on the bench the judge would be willing to modify his statement that in the process of imposing a meaning upon a party's words it makes not the least difference what the party intends.

in the form of written words, those words never have a single, necessary, legally imposed meaning, unaffected by the other words and acts of the parties whether antecedent or subsequent. Those other acts and words are admissible in evidence, to discover both the meaning that one party intended and the meaning that the other party received. If these meanings, so found, are identical, well and good; if they are substantially different, the court's problem is to determine which one of them, if either, should for reasons of policy be made legally effective.[54]

### § 539.  The Interpretation of "Integrated" Contracts

The contents of the preceding section are believed to be in substantial harmony with the rule stated in section 233 of the contracts Restatement by the American Law Institute.[56]  The rule of that section, however, is headed "Standard of Interpretation Applicable to Unintegrated Agreements."  The statements in this and the preceding sections are intended to apply to integrated as well as to unintegrated agreements; and most of them purport to state the substantive law of contracts as to whose meaning shall be operative.  The rule of the Restatement, Sec. 233, quoted in full below, is itself a rule of substantive contract law for determining the party whose meaning shall be made legally operative; it is not a rule of interpretation by which that meaning is to be discovered.

---

**56.**  This section reads: "Where there is no integration, words or other manifestations of intention forming an agreement, or having reference to the formation of an agreement, are given the meaning which the party making the manifestations should reasonably expect that the other party would give to them, except that

"(a) where a party manifests his intention ambiguously and neither party knows or has reason to know that the other party may give a different meaning to the manifestation, it is given the meaning in favor of each party that he intended it should bear; the same rule is applicable where both parties know or have reason to know of such uncertainty or ambiguity; and

"(b) where a party manifests his intention ambiguously, knowing or having reason to know that the manifestation may reasonably bear more than one meaning, and the other party believes it to bear one of those meanings, having no reason to know that it may bear another, that meaning is given to it; and

"(c) where the rule stated in sec. 234 requires a different result."

Section 234 is as follows: "Where the law gives to certain words an established meaning, this meaning is less readily controlled by the standard of interpretation otherwise applicable than is the meaning of other words."  Observe that here the Institute refrains from saying that the law ever establishes a meaning so that the parties cannot give those words a different meaning with legal effect if they make their intention to do so sufficiently clear. Of course, the law may forbid the production of a specified legal effect, whatever may be the words used and whatever may be the intention of the parties. This is not a rule of interpretation.

When an agreement has been reduced to writing, one that is assented to as the full and operative statement of terms, the writing has been described as an "integration".[57] This term may have some advantages; but there is danger that the adoption of so imposing and so unfamiliar a term may mislead us into giving effects to such a document that ought not to be given. It has been asserted that the interpretation of such a document is governed by special principles, that an "integration" may bind both parties in accordance with a meaning that was given to it by neither one of them. It is believed that this assertion is not correct. It is true that in such a case the parties are found to have assented to the written words as the definite operative expression of their minds. This is an assent to those words, not to any particular meaning of those words. When the court determines that the document is an "integration," it has determined only that the parties assented to it as the final verbal expression of their agreement. As yet there is no determination of the meaning of the words; and there is no determination that the parties have assented to be bound in accordance with a particular meaning. Such an integration may make antecedent expressions inoperative; but it does not deprive them of evidential value in the process of interpreting the language of the integration.[58]

A study of many cases shows that however "plain and clear" may be our chosen definition of the term "integrated," its application to the facts of any particular case may be very far from

---

57. The following is the definition given in Restatement, Contracts, § 228: "An agreement is integrated where the parties thereto adopt a writing or writings as the final and complete expression of the agreement. An integration is the writing or writings so adopted." It is wholly a question of fact whether there has been such an "adoption." The appearance of the written instrument is an evidential factor.

There is a discussion of the term "written contract" in § 31, herein.

58. Restatement, Contracts, § 231, limits the application of section 230 and is so worded as to reach very nearly the same results as those supported herein. This section reads: "Where application to an integration of the standard of interpretation stated in sec. 230 produces an uncertain or ambiguous result, the rules governing the interpretation of agreements which have not been integrated are applicable." Uncertainty and ambiguity are characteristic of all forms of human expression, the variation being only in degree. This is shown in the three Illustrations given under section 231. With the decision in the second Illustration, this writer does not agree; the injustice that it clearly perpetrates is not made necessary either by authority or by sound social policy. No court should hold that the parties by "private agreement cannot make buy mean sell." If, as is admitted in the Illustration, "reformation" would be decreed, the parties have succeeded in making *their* word "buy" mean "sell." This is discussed in the next succeeding section.

Olson v. Rossetter, 77 N.E.2d 652, 399 Ill. 232 (1948), is an excellent illustration at this point.

"plain and clear." A court exists for the purpose of doing justice to the parties before it, and should not be misled into doing something else by some third person's definition of a word even though the contracting parties both assented to a writing containing it.[59]

There is no sound reason for holding that parties are bound by any contract, integrated or not, in accordance with a meaning which the court now finds as a fact that neither of them gave to it. This is true even though the court thinks that this meaning is the only reasonable one, or is the one that accords with "good English" and the leading dictionaries, or is one that would be given to the words by a "normal" speaker or writer, or is the one that accords with ordinary and common usage in the local community or in the local trade or profession.

The fact that this meaning fits any one of these descriptions is some evidence that it was in truth held by either or both of the parties; and it is some evidence that either party had "reason to know" that the other party held it. If a court says that parties are bound by this meaning even though neither one of them held it, it is very probable that the court believes, either that both of them did in fact hold it, or that one of them did and the other had reason to know that he did. But to hold that, although A intends to sell Blackacre and B intends to buy Whiteacre, A must convey and B must accept Greenacre because their "integration" would so be understood by C or by a large community of third persons, is to hold justice up to ridicule.[60]

---

59. The better and more complete the Dictionary the more numerous and varied are the usages that it records and the less dogmatic are its assertions as to their relative merits. Compare the modern Oxford Dictionary with that of Dr. Samuel Johnson in the seventeenth century. Johnson is said to have defined "patriotism" as "the last refuge of a scoundrel," and "gratitude" as "a lively anticipation of favors yet to come." Other dictionary makers may have Dr. Johnson's weaknesses without having many of his merits.

60. In the comment to Restatement, Contracts, § 230, there is a statement that an integrated contract "may have a meaning different from that which either party supposed it to have." This comment is quoted in Koplin v. Franklin Fire Ins. Co., 50 A.2d 746, 160 Pa.Super. 182 (1947). The court actually interpreted and enforced an insurance policy in accordance with the meaning given to it by the insured, the insurer having chosen the words and having reason to know how they would be understood. It is believed that the courts would not now be willing to assent to the decision made in Illustration 1, under section 230, or that made in Illustration 2, under section 231. Illustration 1 seems to be drawn from the case of Preston v. Luck, 27 Ch.D. 497 (1884); but the facts of that case are not such as to justify the decision given in the Illustration. There it was clear that the seller intended to sell only his English patent and that the buyer had reason to know it. It is not clear that the agreement should be regarded as an "integrated" one, having been arrived at by a series of letters not very well expressed. See the next succeeding section herein dealing with Reformation.

The courts do not love an "objective" theory of contract or apply it in the process of interpretation merely because it is "objective." They apply it only when they find in fact that one of the parties understood the words of agreement in harmony with such an interpretation and that the other party had reason to know that he did. Indeed, the court may be convinced that both parties so understood the words, and that subsequently discovered self-interest has caused one of them to assert a different meaning.[61] But the reason for adopting the meaning of a reasonable person fails, after it has been found as a fact that neither party assented to the words with that meaning.

### § 540. Reformation of Contract Distinguished From Interpretation

One who files a bill for reformation of a written contract usually asserts that the written words do not express to others the meaning that he was trying to express; that he fully expressed that meaning outside the four corners of the document; and that the other party understood him, knew that meaning, and assented. He asks the court to interpret those extrinsic expressions and to make them legally effective. This is what the court does when it decrees reformation.[62] It is the extrinsic expressions, as well as the words of the writing, that are the subject of interpretation. The latter, in so far as their reformation by replacement is asked, are being either consciously abandoned or translated into a better and more complete form of expression. In any case of interpretation by a court, whether reformation is asked or not, the court will always be found to be translating the express words of the parties into a much more detailed and lengthy phraseology of its own.

One who asks the enforcement of a written contract without reformation does not seek replacement of any of the words written therein. Instead, he asserts that they properly express the meaning that he had and the meaning to which the other assented. He asks that these words be interpreted, by listening to evidence

See the discussion of the "objective" theory of contract by Frank, J., in Ricketts v. Pennsylvania R. Co., 153 F.2d 757, 164 A.L.R. 387 (C.C.A. 2d, 1946).

62.    In Sardo v. Fidelity & D. Co., 134 A. 774, 100 N.J.Eq. 332 (1926), the court refused reformation of a policy of insurance, although the insured had requested his agent to procure insurance against theft of "jewelry" and the company issued a policy against theft of "securities." The word "securities" was clearly defined in the policy, although the insured did not read it; and there was no evidence to indicate that the company's agents had any reason to know that the insured had asked for "jewelry" insurance. There was no contract to insure "jewelry," and the mistake was not chargeable to the insurer. Neither party used the word "securities" to mean "jewelry;" and no ground was seen for holding the insurer by estoppel.

of the surrounding circumstances, including other expressions of the parties extrinsic to the document. By this process, just as when "reformation" is granted, the meaning to which the court gives legal effect is derived in large measure, but not wholly, from the extrinsic expressions.*

## § 541. The Courts do Not Make Contracts for the Parties

In judicial opinions it is often stated that "the courts do not make a contract for the parties" and that the parties must be content to perform and to receive performance in accordance with their own agreement.[68] Such statements are usually made in a case in which the court refuses to make an implication that one party is asserting and the other is denying. It is true that a court never makes a contract for litigating parties; but court and jury may find that the parties made a contract when in fact they did not; and the court may decree the existence and enforcement of a quasi contract not created by mutual assent. Also, when the parties have themselves so far satisfied legal requirements that the court is willing to hold that a contract has been made, it will compel performance in accordance with what it believes to be required by good faith and fair dealing. To this end, the court makes use of processes called interpretation, implication, and construction, without making any fine distinctions between them or observing closely any juristic definitions.[69] Having made this interpretation and construction, with the resulting legal operation, it certainly is not proper to reform the contract or to put in new provisions merely because one of the parties is disappointed in the pecuniary outcome.[70]

As long as it is reasonably clear that the parties are still in the process of preliminary negotiation, some contemplated term of importance still to be agreed upon, no contract has been made, and the court will not supply the missing term. Such is the case when the court finds that the parties have merely made an "agreement to agree" on terms not yet made definite either expressly or by reasonable implication. An "option" to purchase creates no legal power, even though it is expressed as a part of a lease or other larger transaction, unless the terms on which the purchase is to be made are made clear.[71] But if the holder of such an "option"

---

* Full discussion of the subject of Reformation must be looked for at this point in the general Treatise.

69. Lord Wright, in Legal Essays and Addresses, 259, says of a court's compelling payment of a reasonable price: "The truth is that the court, or jury, as judge of fact, decides this question in accordance with what seems to be just and reasonable in its eyes. The judge finds in himself the criterion of what is reasonable. The court is in this sense making a contract for the parties—though it is almost blasphemy to say so. But the power of the court to do this is most beneficial, and indeed even essential."

has materially changed his position in reliance on it, the court may be more ready to find that the terms of purchase were to be in accord with some customary and well-known form.[72]

In order to prevent the disappointment of expectations that the transaction aroused in one party, as the other had reason to know, the courts find and enforce promises that were not put into words, by interpretation when they can and by implication and construction when they must. When unforeseen contingencies occur, not provided for in the contract, the courts require performance as men who deal fairly and in good faith with each other would perform without a law suit. It is thus that unanticipated risks are fairly distributed and a party is prevented from making unreasonable gains at the expense of the other. This is not making a contract for the parties; it is declaring what the legal operation of their own contract shall be, in view of the actual course of events, in accordance with those business mores known as good faith and fair dealing. By interpretation, implication, or construction, a promise will be held to have been made and its enforcement decreed. By interpretation, implication, or construction, an express promise will be held to be conditional and its enforcement denied unless the condition is performed. If these processes are too narrowly limited by judicial precedent to attain the ends of justice, such remedies as rescission and restitution are available.

## § 542. Are Words ever so "Plain and Clear" as to Exclude Proof of Surrounding Circumstances and Other Extrinsic Aids to Interpretation?

It is sometimes said that if the words of a contract are plain and clear, evidence of surrounding circumstances to aid interpretation is not admissible.[78] But some of the surrounding circumstances always must be known before the meaning of the words can be plain and clear;[79] and proof of the circumstances may make a meaning plain and clear when in the absence of such proof some other meaning may also have seemed plain and clear. Sometimes the circumstances proof of which is offered do not have any probative value and do not affect a meaning that is arrived at without them. When such is the case, such circumstances are immaterial.[80] In other cases, the testimony of additional factors may not be believed by the trial court after it has been admitted, in which case the meaning of words that is otherwise "plain and clear" will be adopted.[81]

**78.** Such cases are extremely numerous. Wigmore, Evidence, § 2461, quotes (disapprovingly) from the following:

U.S.—Bradley v. Washington, Alex-andria & Georgetown Steam Packet Co., 13 Pet. (U.S.) 89, 105, 10 L.Ed. 72 (1839), Catron, J.

Mass.—Goode v. Riley, 28 N.E. 228, 153 Mass. 585 (1891), Holmes, J.

Cases in which this is said should be carefully examined to determine whether or not the circumstances proof of which is offered would in fact have any probative value. Of course, an otherwise "plain" meaning should not be disturbed by the proof of irrelevant circumstances or of those having only a remote bearing or inconsequential weight. But until a court knows the circumstances it can not properly say that they have no probative value.[82] It seems highly probable that when a court says that it will enforce a contract in accordance with the "plain and clear" meaning of its words, the relevant surrounding circumstances have in fact been proved and have been carefully weighed; the losing party has merely urged the drawing of inferences therefrom that the court is unwilling to draw.[83] It is a very commonly reported statement that words are to be given "their plain, ordinary, and popular meaning;" but this is always limited by adding some such clause as the following: "in the absence of relevant evidence indicating that the words were used with a different meaning." If there is in fact a "plain, ordinary, and popular" meaning of words used by the parties, that fact is evidential that the parties used them with that meaning. It is fully overcome, however, as soon as the court is convinced that one of the parties used and understood the words in a different sense and that the other party had reason to know it.

There are, indeed, a good many cases holding that the words of a writing are too "plain and clear" to justify the admission of parol evidence as to their interpretation.[84] In other cases, it is said that such testimony is admissible only when the words of the writing are themselves "ambiguous." Such statements assume a uniformity and certainty in the meaning of language that do not in fact exist; they should be subjected to constant attack and disapproval. In many cases it is said that such testimony is offered in order to "contradict" the writing; but the existence of such "contradiction" can be determined only after the writing has been interpreted. It is easy to jump to a conclusion; and it is easy to dispose of testimony that is not believed by saying that it is "not admissible." [85]

In advising clients and in predicting court decisions, it must always be borne in mind that the assumption of uniformity and certainty in the meaning of language, however erroneous, has

---

82. Bowen, L. J., said in Re Jodrell, 44 Ch.D. 590 (1890), with respect to statements directed against admitting evidence to disturb the plain meaning of an instrument: "It seems to me that the only weight one can give to such language is to treat it not so much as a canon of construction as a counsel of caution, to warn you in dealing with such cases not to give way to guesses or mere speculation as to the probabilities of an intention, but to act only on such evidence as can lead a reasonable man to a distinct conclusion."

been made so often and so long that it will be repeated many times in the future. Also, that the decision in which such a statement is made may be thoroughly sustainable because of the relative weakness and the lack of credibility of the testimony that is said to be inadmissible.

Without a doubt, in supporting the interests of their clients, counsel often urge upon the court interpretations of the language of a contract that are far removed from common and ordinary usage, without producing any substantial evidence that the other party to the transaction gave the unusual meaning to the language or had any reason to suppose that the first party did so. In such cases the harassed judge is justified in saying that the words are too plain and clear to justify such an interpretation.

### § 543. Preliminary Negotiation and Statements of the Parties

Among the surrounding circumstances that are admissible for purposes of interpretation are included many acts and statements of the parties antecedent to and contemporaneous with the making of the contract. But, it may be asked, does not the "parol evidence rule" exclude evidence of such antecedent statements and understandings? The answer to this question is No. That supposed rule of evidence purports to exclude testimony only when it is offered for the purpose of "varying or contradicting" the terms of an "integrated" contract; it does not purport to exclude evidence offered for the purpose of interpreting and giving a meaning to those terms.[86] The terms of any contract must be given a meaning by interpretation before it can be determined whether an attempt is being made to "vary or contradict" them. The question in any particular case, therefore, may become this: When does interpretation cease and when does variance begin? So far as this question is concerned, any and all surrounding circumstances may be proved so long as they are material and relevant on the issue of what the contract is and what meaning should be given to its words.

Writers on the law of evidence say that, in the process of interpreting the words of an integrated written document, the extrinsic statements of the writer as to his intention in the writing are not admissible.[87] The case illustrations of this are almost wholly from the law of wills, where the writer who made those "extrinsic statements" is dead, thus making it possible to put false words into his mouth;[88] but the Contracts Restatement of the American Law Institute makes a similar statement with respect to the interpretation of a contract.[89]

89.    Section 230, that has been quoted heretofore in full, says that it is the meaning that a reasonably intelligent person would give to the words that must prevail, assuming that he is "acquainted with all operative usages and knowing all the circumstances prior to and con

This supposed rule of exclusion has certainly been disregarded, especially when the plaintiff asks for "reformation" as a mere verbal preliminary to final judgment. There are times when the actual understanding of one of the parties to a contract is directly in issue; when such is the case that party's antecedent statements should be admitted, and so also should his subsequent statements, especially when he is on the stand and under oath. There are other times when the actual understanding of one of the parties is immaterial; this is the case when the question is what was the understanding of the other party and did the first party have reason to know it. On this issue, evidence of the first party's uncommunicated state of mind is immaterial.[90] This has been more fully discussed in an earlier section.

It has been made apparent in preceding sections that the author of this volume does not believe that it is the meaning of a "reasonably intelligent man" or of a "normal user of English" that the court is trying to discover and make effective. Instead, it is the meaning of either one or both of the parties to the contract. The discovery of that meaning may indeed be difficult; and much evidence of surrounding factors may be necessary in the process. A better form of statement is believed to be this: The court will give legal effect to the words of a contract in accordance with

temporaneous with the making of the integration, other than oral statements by the parties of what they intended it to mean." Here, the exception is limited to "oral statements"; and we are given no explanatory comment or illustrative case regarding it. In the Comment, it is said with respect to "operative usages" that "Such usages may be confined to the parties themselves." This would seem to make admissible any definitions or statements of meaning and intention that were communicated to the other party. Very likely the words of section 230 were meant to exclude only oral expressions of intention that were not communicated to the other party.

Why are "oral statements by the parties of what they intended it to mean" excluded? In Restatement, Contracts, Comment *a* to § 230, it is stated that they are excluded, even "though these statements might show that the parties gave their words a meaning that would not otherwise be apparent. Such a common understanding may justify reformation, but cannot be the basis of interpretation of an integration."

In this treatise this Comment is not accepted. Statements by one party to the other as to the meaning of words or as to the terms of agreement, made in the course of their preliminary negotiation, are relevant and admissible to show what each of them had reason to understand by the words eventually embalmed in the "integration." And if they show a meaning that both gave to the words, or a meaning that one gave and that the other knew or had ample reason to know, no "reformation" is necessary for enforcement. If they show that no common meaning was given to the words and that neither party either knew or had reason to know the meaning given by the other, the only remedy to be granted is refusal of enforcement and rescission, with restitution of values that may have been received.

the meaning actually given to them by one of the parties, if the other knew or had reason to know that he did so. In determining the meaning so given by the one and the fact of knowledge or reason to know by the other, the court will hear all relevant evidence of the surrounding circumstances, including the admissions of the parties, the negotiations and antecedent communications between them, and all current usages that might have affected their choice of the words. In the process of interpretation, it is the court and not the parties who should be reasonably, or even remarkably intelligent.[91]

Extrinsic statements of meaning or intention made prior to or simultaneously with the making of a contract should be contrasted with such statements made subsequently. Statements made at either stage of the transaction may be wholly irrelevant. A party will not be permitted to build up his case by self-serving statements; they should be admissible against him, however, as admissions against his interest. They are admissible to aid in showing that he knew or had reason to know the meaning that the other party gave to the words of the contract. It is not correct to say that such statements are never admissible in evidence. They are excluded if they are irrelevant on the issue to be decided; but the issue that is before the court must be defined before we can say that they are irrelevant.

In determining whether the two parties gave the same meaning to their express words and what that meaning was, or in determining whether one party gave a particular meaning to the words and the other knew or had reason to know that he did, the court will need to know the preliminary negotiations and communications between the parties to the contract. These are among the relevant surrounding circumstances; and evidence of what they were is admissible.[92] This is true, even though the words of the contract seem to the judge to have a "plain and clear" meaning for him. A reasonably intelligent judge will not try to force *his* meaning upon the parties, when relevant and trustworthy evidence may convince him that one or both of them had

91. Read the very intelligent opinion of Lowrie, C. J., in Miller v. Fichthorn, 31 Pa. 252 (1858), in which the court held that parol evidence was admissible to show that a purchaser had assumed payment of a previously existing mortgage. Of judicial officers he spoke thus: "they have to deal with and manage the ever changing matters of a whole community, consisting of all degrees of intelligence, and of all classes of occupations, doing their business in all sorts of ways. It is the right of a free people so to deal; and those who participate in judging their acts are to find out and apply the pattern by which they act, and not to furnish it. Thorough training can best accommodate itself to the practical affairs of society by respecting the fact that others, of less or different training, must have liberty to act according to the training that they have, within the recognized limits of social morality, and must be judged accordingly."

another meaning.[93]  It is often said that the evidence is admitted to eliminate "ambiguity"; but the "ambiguity" seldom appears until the attempt is made to apply the words to existing facts by the use of parol evidence.[94]

Any existing usage of the specific written words is relevant and admissible to prove the meaning that either party actually gave to the words, if there is a reasonable degree of probability that the usage was known to him.  This is true however limited that usage may be; the extent of the usage affects merely the degree of probability of his knowledge.  The more general the usage and the more closely related to A's life and experience, the greater the probability that he knew of it and used the words in accordance with it.  On like conditions, the greater would be the probability that B knew the meaning that A in fact gave to the words.  The less general the usage and the less closely related to the life and experience of either A or B, the less its weight as evidence that he used the words in accordance with it or that he knew that the other party so used them.

It may be true that in most cases the proved usage is of such weight as to be decisive of the issues as to the meaning actually given by A and as to the knowledge of B.  It is not outweighed by the present assertion of A that he meant something else or by B that he didn't know.  This may sustain most of the actual decisions.  It does not justify the exclusion of other testimony leading to a different result.  Nor does it justify an appellate court in reversing the trial court's decision of these issues without knowing what relevant testimony was heard by that court or by declaring that such testimony was not admissible.

In interpreting written words, a party may always prove that they were to him a foreign tongue, that they are the words of a professor of philosophy and he is only a peasant, that they are the language of a lawyer and he is only a professor of philosophy.  Also he may prove the antecedent negotiations and communications between the parties for the purpose of determinating the meaning justly to be adopted and made effective by the court.

### § 544.  Parties may Adopt Special Codes and Choose Their Own Usage and Definitions

Many codes of communication exist, some of which are available to all alike.  Other codes are secret, or are supposed to be.  In addition, anybody can make his own code.  There is no limit as to the type of symbols that can be used as code symbols.  Ordinary English words can be deprived of their ordinary meanings and supplied with others—even with meanings that are the exact opposite of their ordinary ones.[95]  White can be made to mean

---

95.  **Conn.**—Norman P. S. Co. **v.** Ford, 59 A. 499, 77 Conn. 461 (1904).     **Ga.**—Penn Tobacco Co. **v.** Leman, 34 S.E. 679, 109 Ga. 428 (1899).

black, five can be made to mean ten, 500 feet can be made to mean 100 inches, and Bunker Hill Monument can be made to signify Old South Church.[96]

Proof of the use of such a code should determine interpretation even though it was invented on the spur of the moment for pur-

---

Ky.—Powers v. Commonwealth, 70 S. W. 644, 1050, 114 Ky. 237, 71 S.W. 627 (1902).

**96.** In a short article entitled "Theory of Legal Interpretation," 12 Harv.L.R. 417 (1899), Holmes said several things that the present writer can not accept and that the decisions do not support. One of these is the following: "I do not suppose that you could prove, for purposes of construction as distinguished from avoidance, an oral declaration or even an agreement that words in a dispositive instrument making sense as they stand should have a different meaning from the common one; for instance, that the parties to a contract orally agreed that when they wrote 500 feet it should mean 100 inches, or that Bunker Hill Monument should signify Old South Church."

He does not here deny that the parties could introduce their own private written "glossary" to interpret a contract written in their own private cipher-code; nor is he justified in laying down a dogmatic rule that would prevent a plaintiff or a defendant from proving by convincing testimony that the two of them had made a written glossary that has been lost or that they had orally agreed upon a special private usage for certain common words or numbers. The requirement is merely that the evidence shall be convincing. The fear that some consummate perjurer may work a successful fraud by his own unsupported testimony of a bizarre and improbable oral linguistic agreement is not a sufficient basis for a legislative addition to the statute of frauds, much less for a judge-made addition.

The illustration from Holmes, quoted above, is in part a repetition of his words used eight years earlier in Goode v. Riley, 28 N.E. 228, 153 Mass. 585 (1891); but his words in that court opinion were not limited to an "oral declaration or agreement." Hence, Wigmore, Evidence, sec. 2462, is justified when he writes: "Now the interesting feature of this illustration is that in important instances the very opposite fact is daily and hourly illustrated,—in the private cipher-codes of commercial houses. By these agreements words *are* employed in a sense totally alien, and sometimes exactly opposite, to the ordinary meaning. . . . No doubt some brokers . . . are accustomed to agree that 'buy' shall mean 'do *not* buy.' There are abundant instances in which not only there is no 'great risk' [as Holmes said], but there is an absolute necessity, of accepting proof of these private conventions; and these instances shatter the whole argument for the rule as a rule."

"A thousand" may be interpreted to mean twelve hundred, even though the parties have not said so, when such is the local usage in the rabbit business. Smith v. Wilson, 3 B. & Ad. 728 (1832, K.B.). Also "white" may be interpreted as black, where by trade usage "white selvage" meant a selvage that was relatively dark. Mitchell v. Henry, 15 Ch.D. 181 (1880), reversing Sir George Jessel who declared that 'nobody could convince *him* that black was white.' It is not uncommon for two business men to have their own limited cipher code, making use of words, numbers, and names that are commonly used with other meanings. See Bibb v. Allen, 13 S.Ct. 950, 149 U.S. 481, 37 L.Ed. 819 (1892).

poses of one contract.[97]  It may be invented by one of the parties only, but can not affect the other party unless communicated to him.  If so communicated, and the code words are then used in the contract, they mean what their inventor said they should mean.  The other party may expressly refuse to make such use of them; he in turn can force the words back into more normal meanings, under pain of refusal to make any contract.

### §§ 545–554.  Some Frequently Stated "Rules of Interpretation"

If the evidence is such that the court is aware of the principal purpose for which the parties entered into the contract, this should operate as a guide in the detailed interpretation of specific provisions.  Observe, however, that the parties to a contract do not ever have exactly the same purposes and ends in view; also, that before the court can know what these purposes are it is necessary to interpret the words used in the documents of agreement and the relevant words and acts of the parties extrinsic to such documents.[a]

As between two otherwise reasonable interpretations, preference may be given to the one that will make the agreement lawful and valid.  It may be true that parties usually intend to act lawfully and to produce a legal effect by their agreement; but at times they may consciously intend otherwise, and at other times they be wholly ignorant of the law and of the legal effects that an agreement will produce.  Observe further that interpretation and the determination of legal effect are quite different processes.[b]

Provisions in a contract that appear to be conflicting or repugnant can frequently be harmonized by reasonable interpretation.  In this process, words of general description should generally yield to words that are more specific.[c]  Likewise, printed provisions in a standardized "form" contract should generally yield to those that are specially typed or handwritten for the particular contract.[d]

In determining both the meaning and the legal effect of an agreement, the transaction should be considered as a whole.  This is true not only of a written document but also of oral agreements and agreements evidenced by a series of documents.  The meaning to be given to a single word, or phrase, or sentence,

a.  See Restatement, Contracts, § 236(b).

N.Y.—Outlet Embroidery Co. v. Derwent Mills, 172 N.E. 462, 254 N.Y. 179, 70 A.L.R. 1440 (1930).

b.  Some language, when properly interpreted, may have no legal effect, or a legal effect other than the parties in fact intended.  See Restatement, Contracts, § 226, Comment c.

c.  Restatement, Contracts, § 236(c).

d.  Illustrations are insurance policies, building contracts, railroad tickets.

or paragraph can never be determined without its context. Consideration of the rule reduces it almost to a truism; but its statement is useful as a warning.[e]

It is often said that a "construction" of a contract is to be favored that is in accord with the "public interest;" also that existing statutes are incorporated in a contract by "implication." These are rules for determining the legal effect to be given to a contract rather than rules of interpretation. It is certainly true that the court must consider and apply all relevant statutes in determining the validity and effect of a contract, even though the statutes may have been totally unknown to the parties or though well known may have been intentionally disregarded. Interpretations will be favored when they produce reasonable rather than unreasonable effects.

Certain rules have come to be known by and commonly expressed in Latin phrases: The meaning of a word or phrase used in a series is affected by that of the others in that series—*noscitur a sociis*. A general term that is accompanied by a more specific one may be held to include only matters that are similar in some degree to the one specifically named—*ejusdem generis*. If one or more matters are specifically listed, without accompanying them by any more general and inclusive term, other matters even though similar in kind are excluded—*expressio unius exclusio alterius*.

As the terms are used in this treatise, interpretation is always a matter of fact not a matter of law, and construction is always a matter of law not a matter of fact. Interpretation is always the determination of the meaning of symbols of expression—written, spoken, or otherwise acted, the thoughts that were actually intended to be conveyed by the party using the symbols or the thoughts that were actually conveyed to some other party or parties. Construction is the determination of the legal operation of the transaction after meanings have been found in fact and interpretation is complete. This usage, although not identical with that of many courts and writers, is adopted for the sake of greater clarity of analysis and expression. It is almost invariably stated that interpretation is a matter of law for the court. This is not to be disapproved even though it is merely one instance of the many in which the judges have, on grounds of policy, withdrawn questions of fact from the jury. It is a rule that is made necessary if the processes of interpretation and construction, as above defined, are not differentiated but are carried on together. The determination of legal operation—the application of the law to the facts—is always for the judge and not for the jury. On the other hand, if the symbols

**e.**   Restatement, Contracts, § 235(c).

of expression actually used or the circumstances under which they were used are doubtful or disputed, no one doubts that the issues involved therein are issues of fact.

## § 555.   Proof of Local or Limited Usage to Establish the Meaning of Words and Other Symbols

There is nothing surprising in the statement that evidence of usage is admissible in the process of interpretation of the words of any contract, or of any other symbols of expression. How else is interpretation possible? It is usage alone that gives meaning to any word or symbol. An appeal to a dictionary for aid in interpretation is an appeal to recorded usage—or rather, to recorded usages. The better the dictionary, the more varied and numerous are the usages that it records. The dictionary makers may incline to disapprove some of the usages that it records, characterizing them as "obsolete" or "dialect" or "slang" or "vulgar." Their judgments vary with the standards that they choose to adopt. But no large dictionary fails to record the many various usages of immense numbers of important words. Many of these they know that they must record, even while they indicate disapproval in accordance with some preferred standard, because they know that these usages exist and that the value and success of the book they are making depend upon the extent to which it gives aid in interpreting the expressions of men, in helping each one to convey his own meaning to others and to determine the meaning of the expressions of others. If "usage" were not admissible in evidence, then no dictionary would be admissible to aid a court or jury.[66]

There is no dictionary on earth, however, that can record all the usages of words or other symbols. We must appeal not merely to one dictionary, but to many of them together; and even then, our interpretation must be defective in some degree. This is obvious to the translators of works written in a foreign tongue, such for example as Greek drama and philosophy, Roman history, and the Holy Bible. It is just as true of our efforts to interpret the oral or written expressions of our mother tongue. The present volume is written in English. Is its meaning always clear? Will two readers give it the same meaning? The contracts with which we are dealing are usually in the English language; but they may be in any of the many kinds of English. They may be in slang or dialect, in vulgar or in obsolete words, in the finest literary style or in the carefully selected and specially defined words of a modern chemist, in the vernacular of the stock exchange or in a secret code prepared by the contracting parties themselves. There is no law requiring the contractors to express themselves in "good English;" and there is no law requiring interpretation to be in accordance with the standards of "good English." On the contrary, the law requires the court to put itself as nearly as possible in the position of the parties, with their knowledge and their ignorance, with their language and their usage. It is the meaning of one or both of the parties, thus determined, that must be given legal effect.[67]

In the interpretation of one particular contract, it is not all the usages of all the men on earth that are relevant; and yet any one of these innumerable usages may be relevant. No one of them should be definitely and finally excluded unless there is no reasonable probability that the parties were affected by it in expressing the terms of their agreement. Any litigant who asks that those terms shall be given the meaning that he asserts must give the court some basis for adopting that meaning. He must prove some usage among men by which the party or parties in question were probably affected; that is, he must prove it unless the usage is such that the court will take judicial notice of it. There are, indeed, common and ordinary usages of words which the court already knows, usages so common and ordinary that the court will be convinced, in the absence of evidence to the contrary, that the party or parties in question expressed themselves in accordance with them. Practical convenience does, indeed, require the court to assume that such a common and ordinary usage was the usage of the party whose meaning will control, unless some respectable evidence is introduced to show that

---

67. "There is no class of society that so much needs to keep itself free, within the bounds of a technical training, as those who are concerned with the administration of judicial affairs; for they have to deal with and manage the ever changing matters of a whole community, consisting of all degrees of intelligence, and of all classes of occupations, doing their business in all sorts of ways. It is the right of a free people so to deal; and those who participate in judging their acts are to find out and apply the pattern by which they act, and not to furnish it. Thorough training can best accommodate itself to the practical affairs of society by respecting the fact that others, of less or different training, must have liberty to act according to the training that they have, within the recognized limits of social morality, and must be judged accordingly." Miller v. Fichthorn, 31 Pa. 252 (1858).

"Technical treatises dealing with aeronautics, the radio, engineering, etc., generally contain glossaries defining the meaning of many of the words employed by the craft. A glance at these glossaries readily shows that the different sciences and trades, in addition to coining words of their own, appropriate common words and assign to them new meanings. Thus it must be evident that one can not understand accurately the languages of such sciences and trades without knowing the peculiar meanings attached to the words which they use. It is said that a court in construing the language of the parties must put itself into the shoes of the parties. That alone would not suffice; it must also adopt their vernacular." Hurst v. Lake & Co., 16 P.2d 627, 141 Or. 306, 89 A.L.R. 1222 (1932).

See Restatement, Contracts, §§ 245, 246.

it was not.  No respectable evidence of this sort should be excluded; but of course it may be outweighed by other factors and it does not have to be believed.

### § 556.  Proof of Usage and Custom to Add Provisions to a Contract

Usages and customs may be proved, not only to aid in interpretation of the words of the parties, but also to affect the contractual relations of the parties by adding a provision to the contract that the words of the parties can scarcely be said to have expressed.[81]  The purpose of such proof, however, is generally to ascertain and to give effect to the intention of the parties—or the intention and meaning of the party whose intention and meaning should be held to prevail.  Such proof is not for the purpose of compelling the parties to contract in accordance with usage.  The law makes no requirement that parties shall use words in accordance with common and ordinary usage.  Neither does it make any requirement that the terms and provisions of their contracts shall be the same as, or even similar to, those that their neighbors or trade associates are accustomed to agree upon.[82]  If proof of usage and custom is permitted to add a provision that is not expressed in words, it is because one of the parties asserts that they intended that it should be so included; intended it, at least, as much as they intend to include the provisions that they try to express in words.  In either case, it is enough if one of them intended it, and the other knew or had reason to know that he did so.

### § 557.  Pleading and Proof of Usage or Custom—When Operative against One without Knowledge of It

If a usage or custom is admissible to explain or interpret the meaning of words used in a contract, it should seldom or never be held necessary that the party offering to prove the usage or custom should have specially pleaded its existence.  In a number of cases, this has been expressly so held.[87]  Of course, a party must allege the contract on which he bases his action or defense; but he does not have to plead the evidence on which his allegation is based.  He may if he pleases set out verbatim the terms of a contract in writing; but he does not have to plead the evidence by which those terms must be interpreted.  Sometimes it has been held that the court will take judicial notice of a well-known general custom.[88]

Before the court will interpret words or add a provision in accordance with some special or local or trade usage different from that which is usual and general and ordinary, not only must the special usage be affirmatively proved to exist,[89] it must be further shown that the party against whom it is asserted knew of the usage and had reason to know that the other party assented to the words of the contract in accordance with it, or else that if he did not in fact know of the usage an ordinary person in his position would have known of it.[90] A party to a contract may not know the usual and general and ordinary meaning of a word; but he is bound in accordance with that meaning if the other party reasonably believes that he does. For the same reasons and to the same extent, a party may be bound in accordance with special usages.

### § 558. Practical Interpretation and Application of the Contract by the Parties Thereto

In the process of interpretation of the terms of a contract, the court can frequently get great assistance from the interpreting statements made by the parties themselves or from their conduct in rendering or in receiving performance under it. Parties can, by mutual agreement, make their own contracts; they can also, by mutual agreement, remake them. The process of practical interpretation and application, however, is not regarded by the parties as a remaking of the contract; nor do the courts so regard it. Instead, it is merely a further expression by the parties of the meaning that they give and have given to the terms of their contract previously made. There is no good reason why the courts should not give great weight to these further expressions by the parties, in view of the fact that they still have the same freedom of contract that they had originally. In cases so numerous as to be impossible of full citation here, the courts have held that evidence of practical interpretation and construction by the parties is admissible to aid in choosing the meaning to which legal effect will be given.[95]

It has been said that the practical interpretation of the parties will not be considered unless it is concurred in by both parties.[97] It is true that one party can not build up his case by making an interpretation in his own favor.[98] It is the concurrence therein that such a party can use against the other party. This concurrence may be evidenced by the other party's express assent thereto, by his acting in accordance with it, by his receipt without objection of performances that indicate it, or by saying nothing when he knows that the first party is acting in reliance upon the interpretation.[99]

### § 559. When Interpretation should be Contra Proferentem, against the Party Choosing the Contract Words

When the terms of a written contract have been chosen by one of the parties and merely assented to by the other, this fact will in some cases affect the interpretation that will be given to these terms by the court. After applying all of the ordinary processes of interpretation, including all existing usages, general, local, technical, trade, and the custom and agreement of the two parties with each other, having admitted in evidence and duly weighed all the relevant circumstances and communications between the parties, there may still be doubt as to the meaning that should be given and made effective by the court. This doubt may be so great that the court should hold that no contract exists. If, however, it is clear that the parties tried to make a valid contract, and the remaining doubt as to the proper interpretation is merely as to which of two possible and reasonable meanings should be adopted, the court will adopt that one which is the less favorable in its legal effect to the party who chose the words.[9]

Without doubt, there are great numbers of cases in which it can not be determined that one party rather than the other chose the specific language of the contract. In such cases the rule "contra proferentem" has no application. There are large classes of cases, however, in which one of the parties or his agent or attorney does substantially all of the drafting.[10] One who applies for an insurance policy, in any of its many varieties, has little or nothing to do with the provisions thereof. He may not even read the policy, the number of its terms and the fineness of its print being such as to discourage him. The insurance company executes thousands of such policies, using a printed form prepared and approved by its actuaries, officers, and attorneys. Perhaps nearly as much can be said of surety bonds, executed by any of the large surety companies that are in the business for profit. It is far less likely to be true of the contract of an individual accommodation surety, with whom the courts had so much sympathy that the contract was interpreted strictly in his favor.

In some lines of business, there are standard contract forms, prepared by business associations or attorneys, that may be used voluntarily by parties making such a contract. Thus, there is a standard form of building contract prepared on behalf of the American Institute of Architects. The use of such a form as this may be so definitely at the choice of either the owner or the builder that the rule contra proferentem is applicable against him. This is all the more likely to be so if the association or attorneys preparing the form are customarily associated with or employed by owners rather than by building contractors (or vice versa). The use of a standardized form does not in itself make the rule inapplicable.

## § 560. "Standards" of Interpretation

What has been heretofore said concerning the purposes of "interpretation," with respect to "whose meaning" it is that should be made legally operative, and with respect to the proof of various kinds of "usage" in the process of interpretation, now justifies a statement as to so-called "standards of interpretation." [21]

Any list of such "standards," by whomever constructed, must take into account the fact that human usage of words and other symbols of expression may be the usage of one person only, or that of two persons or of several, or that of many or of very great numbers. In considering any such supposed "standard," it should always be borne in mind that not one word or symbol in any language is ever used by all the people in any specified territory, large or small, with a single and uniform meaning; that no word or symbol is ever used by all the people of a sect or trade or profession with such a uniform meaning; and that the meanings that any word or symbol is used to express by any one individual vary with the time, the place, and the context in which he uses it.

There is, however, some approach toward uniformity in the usage of a word or symbol by one individual; there is such an

---

21. In his great work on Evidence, Wigmore constructed several such "standards"; and Restatement, Contracts, § 227, Comment a, enumerates six such standards: "1. The standard of general usage; 2. A standard of limited usage, which would attach the meaning given to language in a particular locality, or by a sect or those engaged in a particular occupation, or by an alien population or those using a local dialect (the distinction between 1 and 2 is a difference in degree, since generality of usage does not necessarily imply universality); 3. A mutual standard, which would allow only such meanings as conform to an intention common to both or all the parties, and would attach this meaning although it violates the usage of all other persons; 4. An individual standard, which would attach to words or other manifestations of intention whatever meaning the person receiving the communication understood from it; 5. A standard of reasonable expectation, which would attach to words or other manifestations of intention the meaning which the party employing them should reasonably have apprehended that they would convey to the other party; 6. A standard of reasonable understanding, which would attach to words or other manifestations of intention the meaning which the person to whom the manifestations are addressed might reasonably give to them." Comment on these standards continues as follows: "b. Standards, 1, 2, 5, 6 are objective; standards 3, 4, since they are based on the actual intention of one or both parties, are subjective. It is only in exceptional cases that the application of these several standards leads to different results; but as the results are different in some cases, the standards must be differentiated. c. These possible standards are enumerated merely to illustrate the meaning of the phrase 'standard of interpretation.' Other possible standards of interpretation could be suggested. The standards which the law adopts are stated in §§ 230, 233."

approach in a lesser degree by the members of a family, a sect, a trade, or a small community; in still lesser degree is the approach toward uniformity in the usage of all the inhabitants of New York, of the United States, of Great Britain and Ireland, or of the English speaking world. The degree of approach toward uniformity is such, however, that language is a useful instrument of communication; and dictionaries can record many of the usages to aid us in conveying to others the thoughts we wish to convey. The variation in the degrees of approach to uniformity and the utter absence of perfect uniformity in any instance should warn us that justice can not be attained by a mechanical application of any "standard," and that standards are useful only as evidential aids in determining the meanings that parties actually give to their words and other symbols and whether, under all the circumstances of a particular case, justice requires that a party should be held responsible to others in accordance with a meaning that he did not himself give.

Any one who tries to express his thoughts to others or to understand what another is trying to express to him should make the best use that he can of all the standards or means of interpretation that there are; but it is not possible to compel any one to observe any particular standard, to keep a large dictionary in his hand, or to be a skilled user or interpreter of language. When one party in fact makes his meaning clear to another, it makes no difference what mode of expression he uses or what standard he follows, except for the purpose of convincing a court that the other party is mistaken or dishonest in asserting the contrary.

In determining whether a party used or understood certain words or symbols with a particular meaning, his own admissions and conduct and communications made to him with respect thereto are relevant and admissible evidence. So also is evidence of the meaning that other reasonable persons would have given to the words or symbols under similar circumstances; such evidence as this, however, is never conclusive against the party whose usage or understanding is in issue. In making this determination, the issue is one of fact: What was the meaning that a particular person gave to the words and symbols involved?

If the court can not determine that two parties gave the same meaning to the words and other symbols that were employed by them, the issue then becomes this: Does justice require that either one of them shall be held responsible in accordance with a meaning given by the other and not given by himself? There is no easy and simple answer to the question What does justice require. It can not be answered by mere application of any stated "standard of interpretation." It can not be answered without considering all of the special circumstances of the particular case. The knowledge and conduct of each party must be considered. It is commonly said that they must be judged by the standard of a hypothetical "reasonable man," a standard that is also commonly said to be external and "objective." But it must be observed that this "reasonable man" has no existence, either subjective or objective, that before using this hypothetical character as a "standard" he must be put in the same setting of relevant circumstances as that of the party whose usage and understanding are in issue, and that to require the application of such a standard is to ask the court to apply its own intellect, emotions, and instructed judgment in that setting of relevant circumstances.

In applying this standard and in adjudging that a party shall be held responsible in accordance with an interpretation of words and other symbols that he did not give to them, the court is making effective the other party's actual interpretation because of a general belief that human transactions are thereby made an efficient instrument for the general welfare. To describe this as an "objective" method of interpretation does not seem to be perfectly descriptive. But, just as in the case of all other human conduct, the usage and understanding of contracting parties are critically considered in a frame of reference consisting of the usages and understandings of other men. Other things being equal, the weight given to these usages and understandings will be roughly proportionate to their generality—that is, to the degree of approach to uniformity; but other things are never equal and the degree of approach to uniformity is most difficult to measure. It should never be held that any usage or understanding is controlling if it is reasonably clear that it is not in accord with that of either of the two parties who are involved. The extent of its existence among men is no more than a weighty evidential factor. There is no "standard" that the law requires any contractor to observe in his choice of words or other modes of expression; but in attempting to convey his own meaning to another person or to understand the expressions of that other he must be alert to the customs and usages of other men and must conform to them sufficiently that a court will adjudge him to have been prudent and reasonable.[22]

22. Restatement, Contracts, § 227, says that "A standard of interpretation is the test applied by the law to words and to other manifestations of intention in order to determine the meaning to be given to them." If we are to use the word "standard" at all, the present writer prefers to say that "standards are the evidential tests by which to determine whether a man's modes of expression and understanding have been prudent and reasonable." But by what "standard" is the word "standard" itself to be interpreted?

# CHAPTER 25

## INTERPRETATION—THE PROCESS CALLED IMPLICATION

---

§§ 561–572.

These sections, dealing in detail with the process called Implication and Implied Promises, must be omitted from this volume. A skeleton outline of their contents follows.

Implication is itself a process of interpretation, by which meanings other than those that could be derived from words alone are discovered and made effective. Implied promises are also express promises, symbols of expression always including acts and other conduct of the parties in addition to written or spoken words. Language may consist of signs that are not commonly described as "words"; and meanings are expressed and conveyed by human conduct that is not commonly described as "language". Even when a court is interpreting an "express" contract, one that has been "integrated" in the form of written words, other acts and conduct of the parties play an important and necessary part in the process of interpretation.

The phrase "implied in law" must be clearly distinguished from the phrase "implied in fact." When a promise is "implied in law," as that phrase is used today, what is meant is that a legal duty has been imposed by operation of law. There is no promise that has been expressed in any manner; and none has been found by a process of interpretation. The legal obligation so created is now commonly described as a "quasi contract." [a]

The process of implication is used for the purpose of limiting contractual duties as well for creating them. Promises not otherwise expressed are found by "implication"; and promises that are expressed in words or conduct are found by "implication" to be conditional and limited. In both cases alike the process may be either one of true interpretation or one that is purely constructive to attain the supposed ends of justice.

The term "contract express or implied" is often found in statutes and formal documents. The meaning intended to be conveyed thereby can be found only by consideration of the context. The term renders no service at all except when it is intended to include quasi-contractual obligations—those that have frequently been described as "implied in law".

---

a. This distinction is brought out in the discussion of Upton-on-Severn R.D.C. v. Powell [1942] 1 All Eng. 220, in Section 561, Treatise.

The statement is often found that where the parties have made an express contract the law will not imply one. But the process described as implication in fact can not be avoided in the interpretation of "express" contracts; and it is always possible for parties who have executed the most formal of documents to vary it by their subsequent conduct from which a tacit agreement may be inferred. Furthermore, circumstances may make it quite improper to enforce an express contract and at the same time may be such that justice requires the enforcement of a different quasi-contractual obligation. It is a mere truism to say that after the proper interpretation of an express contract has been made, a different one should not be discovered by mere factual implications from the conduct of the parties in the process of making it; these implications were already involved in the interpretation process.

The field of impossibility of performance and frustration of purpose is full of striking illustrations of cases in which the phraseology of "implication" is used to justify holdings that are not based upon actual intention of the parties. Unforeseen circumstances require the construction of legal duties never in the contemplation of the parties and also the destruction or limitation of legal duties that they expressly intended to create. Thus, "implied" warranties are enforced; and enforcement of express promises is denied because they are held to be "impliedly" conditional.[b]

Sometimes performances that have been promised in unconditional terms are rendered impossible or "impracticable" or grossly expensive and difficult by some subsequent event not foreseen or contemplated by the parties. In other cases the known purpose for which one of the parties assented to the contract is wholly frustrated by an uncontemplated event. Cases are increasingly numerous in which the court has refused to enforce the unconditional promise, generally supporting the decision by saying that the promise was "impliedly" conditional. Full discussion must be reserved for the chapter dealing with impossibility and frustration.

In the expression of intentions and the making of contracts, it is the habit of all mankind to be cryptic, abbreviated, and incomplete. And yet the circumstances may be such that the expressions so used by one party are sufficient to convey fully and accurately to the other party the ideas and meanings of the first. Agreements for performances by agents and servants are frequently made and the services actually rendered without putting into words any promise of payment therefor. A doctor

---

b. A leading case is Taylor v. Caldwell, 3 Best & S. 826 (1863).

is called by telephone and he renders service; the subsequent rendition of his bill occasions no surprise, although the amount demanded may be surprising. On the other hand, the rendition of a bill for services rendered by a child to his parent or by a parent to his child may appear only as insulting effrontery. Whether a promise to pay is to be "implied" because it was understood in fact depends upon the surrounding circumstances. Even when these are established beyond doubt, decision may be difficult. The problem for the court is simplified in those cases in which it is convinced that "justice" requires payment even though the party receiving benefits may not have understood that they were to be paid for. Sometimes the law requires payment by one who was quite unaware that the beneficial services were being rendered. The term quasi-contract is then used rather than implied contract; but there is an intermediate zone including numberless cases which may be classified in either fashion.

In almost all kinds of commercial transactions the problem of implication of a promise, or of a condition of a promise, may arise. Does one who expressly promises to buy his "total requirements" of another also impliedly promise that he will have any "requirements"? Does one who promises to sell the "total output" of his factory also impliedly promise that his factory will run? If a performance expressly promised by one party is impossible or very difficult without the active cooperation of the promisee, does the latter impliedly promise to cooperate? The answers to these questions depend upon many factors other than the exact words used. Courts have been very willing to find by "implication" a promise by one party that he will do nothing that will hinder or delay performance by the other, even though the first party has used no promissory words whatever.

# CHAPTER 26

## THE "PAROL EVIDENCE RULE"

### §§ 573–596. General Statements as to this Supposed Rule

The cases that consider and purport to apply the so-called "parol evidence rule" are so variable and inconsistent as to be the despair of the teacher, the lawyer, and the judge. And yet the court opinions almost invariably refer to it as a definite and established rule; and when parol evidence is admitted in a case that would seem to require its exclusion, the decision is justified by listing it within one of the supposed "exceptions" to the rule or by making an artificial analysis of the facts. No student or lawyer can afford to disregard this supposed "rule" or to fail to submit to critical analysis many of the relevant cases. Otherwise, in cases in which a contract appears to have been reduced in whole or in part to written form, he may give erroneous advice to his client and may submit a very faulty argument to the court.

In the space that is available in this one-volume edition it is impossible to present an adequate discussion or to defend a theory by a critical analysis of a sufficient number of cases. The student is therefore referred to Chapter 26, in Vol. 3, of the author's general treatise. In the law schools, the subject has generally been dealt with in courses on Evidence; and an excellent and detailed discussion will be found in Wigmore on Evidence, §§ 2400, 2425–2453. See also Restatement, Contracts, §§ 237–244.

No more will be done here than to make a series of brief dogmatic statements to serve as points of attack and as direction guides in further study. No student who has been made aware of the evolutionary character of our law, with its continual breaking down of accepted rules and doctrines and the "restatement" of new ones, can accept any author's "dogmatic statements" as anything more than guides and points of attack, even when they are supported by critical analysis of cases and by citations of numberless "authorities."

When the terms of a contract have been embodied in a writing to which both parties have assented as the definite and complete statement thereof, parol evidence of antecedent agreements, negotiations, and understandings is not admissible for the purpose of varying or contradicting the contract so embodied. This is an attempted statement of the "parol evidence rule." The writing herein referred to has been described by Wigmore as an "integration", a term that has come into common use; but it is still unfamiliar enough to act as a "stop-light," diverting the attention to the phrase itself and away from the subject matter.

Although always referred to as the Parol Evidence Rule, it is not a rule as to the admissibility of testimony; instead, it is a rule of substantive law determining the legal operation of the written "integration" above described.

Whether any specific written document has been assented to by the parties as the complete and accurate "integration" of the terms of their contract is an ordinary question of fact. In determining this question, no relevant evidence is excluded on the mere ground that it is offered in the form of oral testimony.

No written document, however formal or lengthy, and however signed and sealed, can prove its own execution or the fact that either party assented to it as the accurate and complete embodiment of their agreement. Nevertheless, when one party asserts such execution and mutual assent and the other party denies it, the form of the document may have corroborative weight in favor of one and against the other.

If the court has found as a fact, after receiving all the evidence both parol and written, that the specific written document was assented to by both parties as the accurate and complete "integration" asserted, it operates as a nullification and discharge of all inconsistent agreements, statements, and understandings that were antecedent thereto. The contract of today controls that of yesterday. This is true and applicable even though the antecedent agreements were themselves in writing. It is equally true that any contract, even though wholly oral, discharges and nullifies a prior inconsistent contract even though that contract is embodied in a written "integration."

Prior agreements and understandings, oral or written, are not affected by a subsequent contract if they are not inconsistent in their meaning and operation. This is true even though they deal in some way with the same subject matter.

Appellate court opinions are often written so as to make it appear that the court is making an *assumption,* from the mere appearance of a document, that it was assented to by the parties as a complete and accurate "integration" and must be given effect as such. Of course, such an "assumption" is not necessarily false; but if it is made in the teeth of a finding by the trial court that the document was not such an "integration", the appellate court's action is erroneous. If the finding was not

535

supported by sufficient evidence, the case may be sent down for a retrial of the issue.

Before the legal operation of any agreement can be determined, however definitely it may be embodied in a written "integration", it must be interpreted by the court. For this process of interpretation, the "parol evidence rule" does not exclude evidence of prior communications and understandings (although there may be some other limitations on the extent to which such evidence may be used). Until a contract has been interpreted the court can not know whether there is an inconsistency between it and other agreements, oral or written, prior or subsequent. Before interpretation, a court cannot know what it is that cannot be "varied or contradicted." In addition, the "rule" does not purport to exclude any testimony to prove fraud, illegality, accident, or mistake; it does not prevent rescission or a decree for reformation and enforcement.

In innumerable cases, only a part of the terms of an agreement are reduced to writing; and the writing is not assented to as accurate and complete. This is often a difficult question of fact; in other cases there is no substantial dispute. It is upon the determination of this issue that the correctness of decisions giving or refusing effect to additional promises, warranties, and conditions must depend. Many documents, executed in the course of performance of an agreement, are not intended by either party as complete expressions of the terms of that agreement. Among such documents are deeds of conveyance, bonds, bills of exchange, and promissory notes. Formal leases are more likely to be regarded as "the contract."

In the leading case of Pym v. Campbell, 6 El. & Bl. 370 (1856) the parties, in order to avoid the necessity of another meeting, executed a written document containing the terms of a purchase and sale of an invention, accompanying it however by an oral statement that the obligation should be conditional on the approval of the invention by the purchaser's adviser Abernethie. In a suit on the written document to compel payment of the agreed price, the court held that the refusal of his approval by Abernethie was a good defense. It said that proof of the oral statement was not prevented by the "parol evidence rule" for the reason that no contract had been made. This reason is erroneous. Neither party had any power of revocation; and no further expression of assent by either one was necessary. The purchaser's obligation was merely conditional on Abernethie's approval. The legal relations of the parties were exactly what they would have been if the oral statement had been embodied in the document itself.

The foregoing decision has been followed in numerous cases, the same reason being generally given. Even though the reasoning is not applicable to the facts, the decision was sound and will continue to be followed. The court was convinced by the testimony that, in spite of its form, the written document was not assented to as a complete "integration." Of course, if the transaction was merely in the process of preliminary negotiation, no contract being yet made, the "parol evidence rule" does not purport to prevent oral testimony; but neither does it apply if a contract has been made and a writing has been signed but has not been assented to as the complete and accurate "integration."

Men often execute written instruments leaving many gaps and many contingencies unprovided for in the writing. Fundamental assumptions, wholly unexpressed in writing, are often said to be "implicit" in the circumstances. No reference may be made to usage and customs that materially affect performance. Oral testimony of these is not excluded. In a written bilateral contract, neither promise may be stated to be conditional on the performance of the return promise; nevertheless, its conditional character may be proved by oral testimony. Frequently, in the absence of any express written provision, the courts will draw inferences and make presumptions as to price, time, place, and other matters. The law does not exclude parol evidence either to establish or to rebut such inferences and presumptions.

With respect to issues involving third persons the courts make no assumptions as to the accuracy and completeness of written instruments; parol evidence to prove the facts for or against such third persons is not excluded. However, when it is found as a fact that a writing was assented to as a complete and accurate "integration" of the terms of a contract, its operation as a discharge of prior agreements and understandings is not affected by the fact that some third party is now involved.

# CHAPTER 27

## MISTAKE—KINDS OF SUBJECT MATTER AS TO WHICH MISTAKES ARE MADE

### § 597. What is Meant by Mistake and What Material Factors must be Considered

What is a mistake? Is it an act, or is it a thought? In the first sense, Cain seems to have made a mistake when he slew Abel. We are not dealing here with that kind of mistake; this is not a work on ethics or criminal law. In the present chapter we shall discuss mistaken thoughts and their juristic effects—thoughts that, when judged by the generally held thoughts of others, do not correspond with them or with what we call the facts, the truth, or reality.[1] In any human society we can not avoid being judged by the thoughts and opinions of other men, however variable and inconsistent they too may be.

It is perhaps true that a mere state of mind never has any juristic effect; but thoughts induce action that does have such effect. And the juristic effect that is caused by such action varies with the character of the thought that we believe to have produced the action. The juristic effect of homicide "with malice afore-

---

1. Restatement, Contracts, § 500, defines as follows: "In the Restatement of this Subject, mistake means a state of mind that is not in accord with the facts." This definition was adopted also in Restatement, Restitution, § 6.

At this point it would be easy to get lost in the verbiage of "metaphysics." In human society, "truth" and "justice" are merely conceptions of men, variables that are related to and determined by the experience and opinion of the specific period. We are indeed easily convinced that *others* have held mistaken opinions and have done "injustice" because of limited experience or evil will.

thought" is very different from that of homicide in the honest belief that it must be done in self defense. And likewise it will be found that the juristic effect differs with respect to a promise made in jest, the same promise made to A believing that he is B, the same promise induced by a mistaken computation as to costs, and the same promise induced by the belief that B has offered a fine consideration for it. We shall here be dealing with the juristic effects of action that has been induced by a mistaken thought.

This chapter is not a treatise on the law of Mistake in all of its aspects. Many mistakes, followed by injurious action, occur when the parties involved make no promises, whether valid, void, or voidable, and are not engaged in a bargaining process. Mistake as an operative factor in the law of torts and crimes is not dealt with in a treatise on Contracts, however closely related it may be. In the present chapter, there is another important limitation. Pecuniary benefits are often received because of another man's mistake; and a legal duty to make restitution is created even though the one on whom it is imposed made no promise and has not so acted as to lead anyone to believe that he made a promise. Money is paid to one to whom it was not due, and yet not paid as a gift; services are rendered to the wrong person; repairs are made at the wrong address; taxes are paid on property that one does not own: in these cases there may or may not be a duty of reimbursement or compensation. The law with respect to rights and duties in these cases may be found in works on Quasi Contracts and Restitution.[2]

We are now about to consider the effect of mistake in the process of bargaining and promising, the effect upon the legal relations of persons so engaged by reason of a mistake made by one or both of them. In that process, there may be mistakes in the forms of expression, oral or written; mistakes in execution or performance; mistakes as to identity of persons or as to the value or extent of property; mistakes in arithmetic or as to any one of the many factors on which a contractor's judgment is based.

It is not here denied—instead, it is affirmatively asserted, that there are many cases in which the facts are such that the case can not readily be classified as Contract or Quasi Contract, even if we

---

2. See Restatement, Restitution, Chapters 1, 2, and 4; Woodward, Quasi Contracts; Keener, Quasi Contracts.

If A pays to B the amount of a money debt, neither one then knowing that A's agent has previously paid it, A can compel restitution by B. The duty of B is in no sense contractual. B used no promissory words and intended to make none; A knew that B used no such words and had no such intention. No promise can be found by any kind of interpretation, whether we call it "subjective" or "objective." B's obligation is purely construction of law, on non-consensual grounds.

should make mutually exclusive definitions of those terms.[3]  At many points in this treatise it is necessary to deal with cases in which the interpretation of words and acts is doubtful and classification is impossible because of uncertainties in the process called "implication." [4]  Also, it is necessary to deal at great length with remedies that are commonly called quasi-contractual or restitutionary, in respect of transactions that are clearly promissory in character.

Before we consider how it is that we can discover the inducing thought, perhaps mistaken, of a man who has acted,[5] it may be helpful to suggest that his thought and action may be accom-

**3.**  "Quasi ex contractu" and "quasi ex delicto" were terms in use by Roman lawyers more than two thousand years ago.  They were confessions of the poverty of language and of the insufficiency of old classifications to contain the constantly multiplying transactions of men.  The use of such terms as "implied assumpsit" and "implied contract" in our own legal system is a similar confession.

**4.**  The following is a case that illustrates the problem of analysis and classification.  In Upton-on-Severn R. D. Council v. Powell, [1942] 1 All Eng. 220, a fire occurred on the defendant's land.  In the mistaken belief that his land was in the Upton Fire District (in which case he would have had a right to the Upton Fire service free of charge) he called the Upton Fire Department.  That Department rendered the requested service, also believing that the land was in the Upton District.  In fact the land was in Pershore.  The court held that the Upton Fire Department had a right against Powell to reasonable compensation, since benefits had been conferred at his request.  In this case there was no bargain in fact; and neither party supposed that there was one.  Powell made no promise to pay; and the Upton Fire Department did not suppose that he made one.  Both parties made a mistake of fact as to the location of the land with respect to fire boundaries.  This mistake caused the rendition of services in the belief that they were already due without charge not in the belief that Powell was promising to pay for them.  The legal duty of Powell to pay is not based upon any promise, express or implied; instead, it is based upon the common belief that benefits should be paid for when they are rendered and received in the mistaken belief that they were already legally due.  It is not based upon an interpretation, either subjective or objective, of Powell's request for the service.  There is no promise found by "implication", in the sense of "interpretation," because by his words of request Powell neither intended nor led anyone else to think that he intended to make a promise.

This interpretation and classification are by the present writer, not by the court.  The court was content to say that a promise to pay would be "implied" from the fact that the defendant requested and received the valuable service.

**5.**  In an ancient case, Y.B. 17 Edw. IV, 2, Brian, C.J., remarked, perhaps erroneously, that "the devil himself knoweth not the thought of man."  Every day experience shows that man himself believes that he can discover the thoughts of another man.  This he does by inferences from the other's external expressions, in words, in features, and in acts.  Such evidence may indeed lead to woeful error; but it is the best we have and we act upon it daily.

panied by a great variety of factors, and that juristic effects will be found to vary with these factors. Some of these many factors, to be discussed in the following sections, will be listed by putting the following questions:

1.   Did both parties, or only one, have a mistaken thought?

2.   Did the mistake induce mutual expressions of agreement; or did it merely induce action by one person toward another? E. g. a payment of money.

3.   If mutual expressions were induced, were they expressions that agreed in meaning, as interpreted by the parties themselves or by third parties?

4.   What was the fact as to which a mistaken thought existed? The possibilities are myriad.

5.   Was the fact of substantial importance?

6.   Did one party know of the other's mistake, or have reason to know it?

7.   Did one party cause the other's mistake, purposely or innocently?

8.   Was the mistaken party negligent?

9.   How soon was the mistake discovered and notice given?

10.   Has either party, or a third party, changed his position, so that restoration of his former position is impossible?

11.   Was the risk of such error assumed by one of the parties, by agreement or by custom?

12.   What remedies are available? Among these are Damages, Restitution, Specific Performance, Rescission, Cancellation, Reformation.

13.   Were there differences between Common Law and Equity, and do they still exist?

Cases involving mistake are difficult of classification because of the number and variety of factors to be considered. These factors are found in many combinations. The citation of authorities for a rule stated in general terms is made perilous by this fact. It is equally perilous, and it may be positively harmful, to construct a rule of law, unless it is so limited as to be applicable to a particular combination of many factors. If this exact combination does not recur, what we really have is merely one precedent, and not a rule.[6]

6.   Brown v. Lamphear, 35 Vt. 252 (1862), is a case with some comic aspects in which there was a serious mistake. The plaintiff conveyed to B a pasture from which spring water was piped to plaintiff's houses. B knew and agreed that an easement should be reserved; but by error of the scrivener no such reservation was made in the deed. B did not record the deed; and plaintiff executed it without

### § 598. Equitable Distribution of Risks According to Custom or Agreement

When a contractual promise is aleatory in character, the performance being expressly made conditional upon an uncertain and hazardous event, the promisee bets that it will happen and the promisor that it will not. The consideration exchanged for such a promise varies in proportion to their opinions as to probability. They consciously assume the risk. If the event occurs, or occurs sooner than the promisor expects, he is a loser; if it fails to occur, or occurs later than the promisee expects, it is he who is loser. The opinion of one of them as to probability is thus shown to have been erroneous; but his mistake is not ground for rescission, because he consciously assumed the risk.[7] An insurer can not escape payment of the amount promised because the insured was most unexpectedly struck by lightning two days after execution of the policy. An insured can not get restitution of his insurance premiums because he has paid them for forty years and has never had a fire. There will be no rescission of a contract to pay an annuity for life because the annuitant received only one annuity before dying in an accident or by reason of a hidden disease, or because the annuitant lives twice his life expectancy and the promisor is a heavy loser.[8]

The same result obtains in any case where the risk of the existence of some factor or of the occurrence of an event is con-

reading it. Later, B sold the pasture to defendant; and the plaintiff executed a second deed direct to the defendant, again leaving out the reservation. The unrecorded deed to B was cancelled. Defendant testified that he knew nothing of the spring, the pipe, or the reservation until two weeks after conveyance to him. There was testimony to the contrary; but accepting the defendant's statement as true, the court held the conveyance voidable. The defendant had been in possession for several years; and the plaintiff made use of the spring until finally the defendant destroyed the pipes. The court decreed that the defendant should either reconvey the pasture on restitution of the price that he paid, or convey an easement in the spring in accordance with the intended reservation. The court's solution of this complex case seems to be just and equitable and illustrates the extent of judicial power and the flexibility of equitable remedies. No rule of law or equity forbids such a solution.

**7.** Restatement, Restitution, § 11 (1): "A Person is not entitled to rescind a transaction with another if, by way of compromise or otherwise, he agreed with the other to assume, or intended to assume, the risk of a mistake for which otherwise he would be entitled to rescission and consequent restitution."

In U. S. v. Jones, 176 F.2d 278 (C. A.9th, 1949), agents of the government sold for $75 some "universal gear joints" that had cost $62,533, not knowing that they were "marine equipment" and made of bronze, these facts being known to the buyer. The court refused to set aside the sale, solely on the ground that by Act of Congress the government had made the documents of sale "conclusive." The effect of this holding (erroneous, it is believed) is that the government assumed the risk of such mistakes.

sciously considered in agreeing upon terms. There is no mistake; instead, there is awareness of the uncertainty, a conscious ignorance of the future. This is why an ordinary compromise of a doubtful or disputed claim is not subject to rescission when one of the parties turns out to have been correct in his assertions and the other incorrect. They were aware of the uncertainty, estimated their chances, and fixed the compensation accordingly.[9]

Releases of claims for personal injury have frequently been held voidable for mistake, on the ground that the claimant was unaware of the nature and extent of his injury when he assented to a settlement. Sometimes advantage has been taken of his weakness and ignorance; and the possibility of this, even though not definitely proved, has made courts readier to hold that the release was executed on a mistaken basic assumption as to the nature of the injury. The case for avoidance is stronger if the mistake was induced by untrue representations, either fraudulent or innocent, by the defendant, his doctors, or his claim agents; but mistake may be sufficient even though not so induced.[10]

In the absence of misrepresentations, the claimant must show that an injury existed that was outside of his contemplation when he executed the release. In settling any such claim, the claimant knows that there is some degree of uncertainty. In so far as he is aware of uncertainty respecting his future harm and loss, he is consciously exchanging this uncertainty for the liquidated amount received in settlement. To this extent the release is not voidable for mistake.[11]

A formal decree for cancellation of the release is not necessary. In nearly all jurisdictions the claimant merely brings his action for damages; and to a plea setting out the general release he makes replication of the facts showing the mistake that makes it voidable. Thus, in a single action, the claimant establishes his mistake, gets avoidance pro tanto of his general release, and gets judgment on the unreleased balance of his claim.

## § 599. Mistake in the Expression of Assent

Two parties may believe that an agreement has been reached, and act upon it, even though they said different things and meant different things, and neither one misled the other in any way. An agent, in order to get a commission fraudulently, by a substitution of typewritten sheets caused a builder to promise to erect a building for $33,500, and the owner to promise to pay $23,000 for the work. The difference was discovered after the work was completed. The solution had to be non-contractual, the owner being required to pay reasonable value. There was no meeting of the minds in any sense, no agreement in either intention or expression; and neither party was at fault.[19]

One party who has made an offer may be mistaken as to the expression of assent by the other. He may believe erroneously that the other heard his offer and accepted it. The mistake is not "mutual"; but there is no contract, for the reason that one party did not express assent and did not negligently cause the other to believe that he did.[20] A case that occurs more frequently is one in which each party misunderstands the expressions of the other. An offer is made in terms that the offeree misunderstands; and the latter accepts in terms that the former understands as an assent to the offer that he meant to make. In a case like this, each party is mistaken as to the meaning of the other; and sometimes this is not discovered until after important changes of position have taken place. It is very clear that no contract should be held to exist unless one of the parties so negligently expressed himself that the other was caused reasonably to believe that agreement existed.[21] For performance rendered in such a case, recovery must be quasi-contractual in character, generally based upon the value of benefits actually received by the other party.[22]

This is illustrated by an English case that has long played a leading part in discussions of the subject of Mistake. A buyer and a seller made what appeared to be an agreement for the purchase and sale of a stated amount of Surat cotton to arrive by the ship Peerless from Bombay. It happened that there were two ships then at Bombay, both named the Peerless. The buyer knew of only one of these ships; and he believed that there was a breach of contract by the seller when no cotton arrived by that ship. The seller knew only of the other ship, the one on which he shipped the cotton; and he asserted a breach by the buyer when he refused to receive and pay for the cotton. The court held that no contract existed and that the plaintiff had no right to damages.[23] The same result would obtain, had the parties to the action been reversed.

Some efforts have been made to reconcile this decision with the so-called "objective" theory of contract. Perhaps it can be done, if it is worth doing. It seems enough to say, however, that there was no convincing reason for charging one of these parties with the loss rather than the other or for penalizing one of them for the benefit of the other. The court was convinced that they meant different things and that each expressed his thoughts according to the usage of men and with reasonable prudence.[24]

19.  Mass.—Vickery v. Ritchie, 88 N.E. 835, 202 Mass. 247 (1909).

20.  Pa.—Royal Ins. Co. v. Beatty, 12 A. 607, 119 Pa. 6 (1888). The court held that there was no contract, since there was no sufficient proof that the offeree heard the offer. In such a case, it would be very difficult to make out an acceptance by estoppel.

23.  Eng.—Raffles v. Wichelhaus, 2 Hurl. & C. 906 (1864).

One who accepts an offer may do so because he is mistaken as to its terms, either by inaccurately hearing or reading the words in which it is expressed, or by giving them a meaning different from that intended by the offeror. In such a case, there is no "meeting of the minds" although there may be agreement in expression, as where the offeree merely says "I accept your offer." If the meaning asserted by the offeror is the only reasonable one under the circumstances and the offeree was negligent in not knowing that meaning, it is usually said that there is a valid contract; the offeree is bound in spite of his mistaken understanding.[26]

There are numerous cases in which the court has decreed rescission or refused enforcement of a transaction giving as a reason that there was no "meeting of the minds," when this reason is not truly applicable. Thus, where a bidder for a contract makes a mistake in computation, the result of which is that his bid is lower than he would otherwise have made it, the courts have very often refused enforcement against him if the mistake is discovered in time to prevent an irretrievable change of position.[29] Indeed, courts are in substantial agreement that if the other party knows, or has reason to know, that such a mistake has been made, he can not hold the bidder to the contract.[30] In these cases, however, there is actual agreement on terms, both in objective expression and in subjective intention. The mistake in computation is the bidder's alone and is antecedent to his offer. The offer that he then makes is definite and exact; there is no ambiguity and no misunderstanding. The bidder means exactly what the other party understands him to mean; he says what he means, and he means what he says.

Nevertheless, these decisions are not to be disapproved. They were made because justice so requires, as the court was convinced. Being confronted with an often stated doctrine that a contract is not made voidable by a "unilateral" mistake, the court avoided the necessity of expressly disapproving it by an appeal to the even more generally stated doctrine that there must be a "meeting of the minds." The fact is that this does not bear close analysis; but the decisions stand anyway and will generally be followed.

---

26. In Embry v. Hargadine-McKittrick D. G. Co., 105 S.W. 777, 127 Mo.App. 383 (1907), an employee said to his employer that he must have a year's contract or he would quit. After some discussion, the employer said: "Go ahead, you're all right. Don't let that worry you." The court held that it was a question for the jury whether the employee understood this to be an assent to a year's contract and whether the employer had reason to know that he did.

30. Illustrative cases are:

Conn.—Geremia v. Boyarsky, 140 A. 749, 107 Conn. 387 (1928).

Minn.—Tyra v. Cheney, 152 N.W. 835, 129 Minn. 428 (1915).

## § 600.　Mistake as to Existence of Subject Matter Necessary to Performance

If a contract for the purchase and sale of some specific thing is made after the thing has ceased to exist, the contract will ordinarily be rescinded and restitution in favor of the purchaser decreed.[33]　Also the non-existence of the thing is a defense in a suit by the seller for the purchase price or for damages.[34]　Of course, it is otherwise if by custom or agreement the purchaser or promisor has assumed the risk of previous destruction.　A ship at sea may be sold "lost or not lost"; and a marine or other insurance policy may expressly assume the risk of loss as of a date already past.　In such cases, there is no mistake; instead, there is conscious ignorance.

The same results obtain where there is a mistake as to the existence of some person or thing that is necessary to the performance that is promised.[35]　The duty of the promisor whose performance is thus prevented is constructively conditional, unless by custom or agreement he has assumed the risk, a question of fact and interpretation.　The other party is relieved of his duty by the fact that he will not receive the promised consideration.　But it is the fact that the parties were mistaken as to the existence of the necessary factor that caused them to make the contract and justifies the inference that neither one assumed the risk.

## § 601.　Mistake as to Identity of a Party to a Bargain

It is to be observed, first, that in some of the cases classified along with mistakes of identity no such mistake was made by either party.　Thus, if A makes an offer to B, and his offer falls into the hands of C, who attempts to accept, there is no contract.　A knows that C is not B; and C also knows that he is not B.　Neither party makes any mistake.[44]　In a case of this sort, however, C may cause A to make such a mistake.　He may ship to A goods of the kind that A ordered of B, at the same time inducing A reasonably to believe that the shipment was made by B.　Such action consummates no contract, either between A and B or between A and C; the solution must be worked out on a non-contract basis.

Next, the identity of a party may be wholly immaterial and known to be so, in which case the bargain is not invalidated by the fact that one is mistaken as to the "identity" of the other—as to his name, weight, age, features, parentage, family life, position in business, reputation in the community, or reported financial responsibility.

44.　Eng.—Boulton v. Jones, 2 H. & N. 564 (1857), is such a case.

Thirdly, "identity" is a variable concept, requiring analysis and definition, as is suggested in the preceding paragraph. One party may be mistaken as to the name of the other, but not as to his physical appearance.[45] He may know his true name, but be mistaken as to his physical appearance.[46] He may know both his name and appearance, but be mistaken as to his home or parentage or relations with third persons and position in the community.[47]

Fourthly, if such a mistake is made, it is always unilateral. The second party is aware of his own identity. He may know or have reason to know that the first party is mistaken, or he may not.[48]

Fifthly, the first party may have been negligent in making the mistake, and the other may have materially changed his position.

Sixthly, the mistake of the first party may or may not have been caused by the fraud of the second.

And lastly, the rights of an innocent third party may be involved, by reason of a resale of goods, transfer of money or negotiable paper, or otherwise.

These are factors not to be disregarded in determining the legal effect of a mistake as to identity.

In any case, if a party makes it clear that he intends to contract with X and with nobody else, no third person can consummate a contract by assenting or performing in X's place.[49] This is because he knows or has reason to know the intention of the first party and that the latter is mistaken if he believes him to be X.[50] This is true whether the mistake is caused by fraud or otherwise.[51]

45. As where a defrauder Richard Roe tells a merchant that he is the well-known John Doe, and induces a sale of goods on credit. Edmunds v. Merchants' Despatch T. Co., 135 Mass. 283 (1883).

46. John Doe number one makes an offer which the other party accepts in the belief that it is John Doe number two.

47. John Doe appears in person and induces a sale on credit, the merchant believing him to be the John Doe who married Mary Smith and is president of a bank.

See Phillips v. Brooks, [1919] 2 K.B. 243; also, an amusing article by Glanville Williams, "A Lawyer's Alice", 9 Cambridge L.J. 171 (1946), the value of which as a discussion of the problem of identity, respecting name and attributes, is not reduced by the fact that it is amusing.

51. In Cundy v. Lindsay, 3 App. Cas. 459 (1878), one Blenkarn ordered goods of Lindsay, fraudulently using the name Blenkiron and Co., giving a street number directly across from that of Blenkiron and Son, a firm with good credit. Lindsay shipped the goods as requested, thinking that they were ordered by Blenkiron and Son. The carrier delivered them to Blenkarn. It was held that Blenkarn got no title and could give none to Cundy, an innocent purchaser for value. In accord, Mayhew v. Mather, 52 N.W. 436, 82 Wis. 355 (1892).

If Y ships goods to A, knowing that they were ordered of X, and A accepts them in the reasonable belief that they were shipped by X, A's acceptance of the goods is made under a mistake as to identity of the shipper. It has been held that his consumption of the goods under a mistake thus induced does not create any duty, contractual or quasi-contractual to pay for them.[55] In cases of this sort, it is to be observed that X could accept A's offer, delegate performance of it to Y, and assign to Y his right to payment.[56]

### § 603. Cases in Which Identity is Immaterial

When the identity of a party to a bargain is in fact immaterial to the other party, the latter will seldom attack its validity on the ground of mistake. There are a few cases, however, expressly holding that the identity of the party was immaterial and enforcing the contract.[64] Thousands of contracts are made in which one party neither knows nor cares to know who the other party is. This is true of practically all cash sales of goods over the counter. Even if the buyer of the goods thinks that the clerk is the owner of the store, and the clerk mistakenly thinks that the buyer is the Prince of Wales, the contract will be valid as soon as mutual assent is expressed. Also, one who makes an offer to the world at large by publication, promising a reward for information or other performance, will be bound to the person who performs as requested. The offeror may not know or think that he knows who the acceptor is, and so makes no mistake; but he is bound to pay even if he mistakenly thinks the acceptor is A instead of B. Likewise the acceptor will be entitled to the reward, even though he accepts believing that the offeror is X instead of Y; of course, it is Y and not X who is bound, X having made no offer.[65]

### § 604. Mistake in Sales of Land, as to Title, Area, Quality, or Price

There is an obvious difference between mistake as to the existence of a physical res and a mistake as to ownership of a property interest in such a res; but the results reached are the same. If one pays for a release or assignment of a leasehold interest that the parties mistakenly believe to exist, rescission and restitution

---

56.   In Boston Ice Co. v. Potter, 123 Mass. 28 (1877), there probably was a bilateral contract between the defendant and the Citizens Ice Co.; and the Boston Ice Co. should probably have been regarded as the assignee of the rights of the Citizens Ice Co. and as its delegate in performing its duty to deliver ice. The court, however, regarded the delivery of ice by the Boston Ice Co. to Potter as constituting a new offer to sell ice from day to day. Potter supposed that the deliveries were being made by the Citizens Ice Co., and, on this theory, was mistaken as to the identity of the offeror. The Boston Ice Co. had reason to know of this mistake. The decision may be defended on the ground that Potter had expressly ordered the Boston Ice Co. not to supply him with ice.

will be decreed.[68]  The same should be true of other interests in land, large or small; but this requires explanatory discussion.[a]

In contracts for the purchase and sale of land, a mistake is not infrequently made as to the identity or area or quality or value of the land.  If in the making of the contract the parties agree upon the sale of tract A, but by mistake the deed of conveyance describes tract B, of course the courts will decree reformation of the deed and enforce the true contract, unless the rights of an innocent purchaser have intervened.[80]  Here the mistake is in the performance of the contract.  The same result obtains if the parties orally agree upon the sale of tract A, but by mistake in reducing it to writing the written contract describes tract B.[81]

In the process of making the contract, a mistake may be made as to the identity of the tract of land that is the subject of sale. In most such cases, the vendor knows the tract that he intends to sell, but he does not know that the purchaser intends to buy a different tract.  The purchaser usually knows the tract that he intends to buy, but he does not know that the vendor intends to sell a different tract.  As long as they do not reduce their agreement to writing, their overt expressions may differ, so that no contract exists.  But when reduced to writing, the written description usually (but not always) applies accurately to the tract that the vendor meant to sell.  The vendor then makes no mistake as to the tract described by the instrument; as to this fact the mistake is by the purchaser alone—this mistake is unilateral.[82]  If the written description is clear and accurate, the purchaser's mistake may have been negligent in failing to read it at all or in failing to observe that it does not describe the tract he means to buy.  Often, however, the discrepancy between the written description and the land he has in mind cannot be determined by merely reading the description.  It may require the examination of other documents or records and an inspection of the ground itself.  Even by these methods, identification may not be easy.  Generally, the purchaser's error is due to the fact that he looked at the wrong tract.  The wrong tract or the wrong boundary lines, may have been pointed out by the vendor or his representative.  Whether this last is the case or not, the purchaser usually is held entitled to rescission,[83] with mutual resti-

---

**a.** For this discussion the student must be referred to works on Real Property and Conveyancing; or for a briefer treatment, to the corresponding section in the author's general treatise on Contracts.

**80.**  In Cole v. Fickett, 49 A. 1066, 95 Me. 265 (1901), the same error was made in a series of convey-ances.  In a deed from A to B, the description erroneously *omitted* a certain lot.  The same error was made in a deed from B to C.  Later A conveyed his adjoining land to X, erroneously *including* the certain lot.  It was held that C could compel a conveyance of the lot by X, who is not an innocent purchaser for value.

tution if performance has occurred. Mistake as to identity of the land is a material and vital mistake.

There are cases in which the purchaser was held bound by the contract, his mistake having been due to his own carelessness, the vendor having neither knowledge nor reason to know, with sometimes a material change of position.[84]

A mistake as to the area of land that is the subject of a contract of sale may be such as to require remedy. If the contract was for the sale at a specified price per acre, justice may require an abatement in the price in proportion to the deficiency [85] or an additional payment for the excess.[86] Even though the agreed price was by the tract, and not by the acre, its amount may have been determined with reference to a basic assumption of a specific area. Whether or not such was the case is a question of fact, and may be a difficult one.[87] When such was the assumption, and the error is material, the court should award an appropriate remedy. If the difference in area is so great as to cause a substantial degree of frustration of the purpose for which the land was bought, the buyer should be awarded a rescission if he seeks it.[88] For less important differences the remedy is proportionate abatement in price, this taking the form of restitution if the price has been paid. Sometimes, the remedy may well be a decree giving to the defendant a choice between rescission and his repairing the deficiency by an abatement or a payment or even an additional conveyance.[89]

If the sale was strictly by the tract, in gross, and the price was not determined at so much per unit of area, the fact that a mistake was made as to area will probably be held to be immaterial.[90] If the mistake did not affect the price, and did not otherwise cause the making of the sale, the contract stands as made.

### § 605. Mistake or Ignorance of Value or as to Factors that Affect Value

Market value is a material factor in transactions for the purchase and sale of any commodity. This is true whatever may be the nature of the commodity, whether it be land or goods or corporate shares or bonds or dollars or marks or rubles. But market value is a variable quantity. It varies with time and place and circumstance. It varies with the appetite of him who buys and with the needs of him who sells. This fact is generally known to buyers and sellers of such commodities.[91] When they contract for an exchange, of goods for dollars, of dollars for rubles, of land for goods, they are themselves agreeing upon value and are helping to determine market value. Each party is in the market when he contracts.

In making this contract of exchange, either party may be mistaken in his estimate of market value, mistaken as to the appetite of others for the commodity. He finds that he can not sell for as much as he paid. Practically never is this such a mistake as will justify rescission.[92] The parties are conscious of the uncertainty of value. Value is one of the principal subjects of agreement. Each party is consciously assuming the risk of error of judgment. As to this, by business custom, by prevailing mores, by social policy, and by existing law, the rule is caveat emptor. It is also, and in equal degree, caveat vendor.[93]

But although the value of a commodity is a variable that is determined by the opinions and desires and ability of those who deal in that commodity, and although a buyer and a seller ordinarily assume the risk of error of judgment as to such value, it must be borne in mind that the opinions and desires that determine value are themselves dependent upon many subsidiary factors, such as quality and capacity and scarcity. One or more of these subsidiary factors may be believed by one or both of the parties to be definitely established. In most cases, the risk as to the factors on which value depends is assumed along with the risk of value itself, their resultant. There are many cases in which it has been so held, mistake as to such a factor not justifying rescission.[94] In the older cases of this sort, it is often said that the mistake is as to a collateral matter, in others that there was "no implied warranty." A factor that so directly and vitally affects the purposes for which a contract is made should not be described as "collateral"; and it is possible that, even though nobody is "warranting" anything, justice as that is commonly seen and practiced may require rescission.

There are many cases in which one or both of the parties did not consciously assume the risk as to one or more of the subsidiary factors. One or both may assent to the contract on the assumption that this factor is definitely established and that there is no risk. If this assumption is mistaken, the fact that it is material only because it affects market value does not prevent the contract from being voidable by the party who is harmed by the mistake. Cases allowing rescission because of a mistake such as this are cited below.[95]

The market value of a stone depends on whether it is a diamond or a topaz. But if the parties assume without question that the

**95.  Cal.**—Wedge v. Security-First Nat. Bank, 25 P.2d 411, 219 Cal. 113 (1933), a power transmission way made the land nearly valueless for residence use; Hannah v. Steinman, 112 P. 1094, 159 Cal. 142 (1911), lease of a lot, both supposing that the law permitted erection of a wooden building.

**Ky.**—Neale v. Wright, 112 S.W. 1115, 130 Ky. 146 (1908), sale of corporate shares, the corporate books misrepresenting the merchandise owned.

**Mass.**—Jeselsohn v. Park Trust Co., 135 N.E. 315, 241 Mass. 388 (1922), mortgage on a vacant lot believed to have a building on it.

stone is a diamond and agree upon a price on that basis, the buyer assumes the risk as to the market value of such a diamond, but he does not assume the risk that the stone may turn out to be a topaz.[96] If the agreed price is fixed with consciousness of the fact that the stone may be either a diamond or a topaz, the second risk is being assumed as well as the first.[97]

When a contract is made for the sale of a cow, it may be true that the buyer generally assumes the risk of her barrenness. But if parties assume that the cow is barren and of no use except for butchering, the risk that they consciously assume is only as to the market value of a barren cow for use in steaks and roasts. A mistake as to her fecundity has been held to make the contract voidable by the seller.[98]

In these cases, the decision involves a judgment as to the materiality of the alleged factor, and as to whether the parties made a definite assumption that it existed and made their agreement in the belief that there was no risk with respect to it. Opinions are almost sure to differ on both of these matters, so that decisions must be, or appear to be, conflicting. The court's judgment on each of them is a judgment on a matter of fact, not a judgment as to law. No rule of thumb should be constructed for cases of this kind.

After a conveyance of land has been made, the grantor is not entitled to a reconveyance or to a rescission or to an additional payment, on the ground that the land has since become more valuable in the market by reason of the discovery of oil or gold on or near the property or because of unexpected changes in the prices of commodities or in the surrounding circumstances of transportation or population. In such cases, the grantor was ignorant of underground conditions or of the waves of the future; but he must have been conscious of this ignorance and made no operative mistake. As to these matters the correct maxim is caveat grantor.[2]

---

96. **Mass.**—Chapman v. Cole, 12 Gray (Mass.) 141 (1858), goods exchanged for a piece of money, believed to be a 50 cent piece, in fact, a gold piece.

97. Such was the case in Wood v. Boynton, 25 N.W. 42, 64 Wis. 265 (1885). See also U. S. v. Jones, 176 F.2d 278, 285 (C.A.9th, 1949), where agents of the government sold some "universal gear joints," as war surplus, for the price of $75, although their cost to the government had been $62,533 and their value even as scrap was $2,260. The selling agents did not know that the gear joints were "marine equipment" and made of bronze; the buyer did know these facts. The court would have set aside the sale except for the fact that it believed (erroneously, it is submitted) that Congress had intentionally made the documents of sale conclusive.

98. **Mich.**—Sherwood v. Walker, 33 N.W. 919, 66 Mich. 568 (1887).

# CHAPTER 28

## MISTAKE—EFFECT OF NEGLIGENCE—MUTUAL AND UNILATERAL MISTAKES

### § 606. Negligence and Delay of Mistaken Party and Change of Position by Others

Relief for mistake depends, not only upon the materiality of the mistake, but also upon the stage in the transaction at which the mistake is discovered and notice given. How far has performance already gone? To what extent and at what cost can the status quo ante be restored? What changes of position in reliance on the contract, by a party to it or by third parties, have occurred? Before making a decision, these questions should be considered and answered. The fact that they are questions of degree, that answers must be relative to many factors, and that decision may be difficult, should come as no surprise to court or lawyer. It is true that in many cases the court opinion does not show that they have been considered; but it is probable that in most cases there has been an awareness of them and that the proved facts afforded ground for answers.

It is often stated as a reason for denying relief that the mistaken party was negligent in making the mistake.[1] A century ago it was often thought that in refusing relief it was sufficient to say that a man must bear the consequences of his own "folly." Court decisions now indicate that prevailing opinion is less harsh in its judgment of those who fail to act in accordance with some standard of care and prudence. We must still bear "the conse-

---

[1] Cases saying that equity will not relieve against unilateral mistake if due to want of ordinary care:

U.S.—Grymes v. Sanders, 93 U.S. 55, 23 L.Ed. 798 (1876), here the mistake was not very material; Bailey v. Lisle Mfg. Co., 238 F. 257 (C.C. A.8th, 1916).

Iowa —Reid M. & Co. v. Bradley, 74 N.W. 896, 105 Iowa 220 (1898), further credit advanced on a mistaken guaranty.

553

quences" of our own folly; but the court decisions have moderated some of those "consequences." They seem to justify the statement that one is held responsible for harm to others if it is caused by his "folly" or his negligent mistake, but his responsibility need not be carried so far as to permit others to profit by reason of his mistake.[2]

It is frequently said, also, that rescission will be denied to one who has negligently made a mistake, if the other party was innocent and has materially changed his position. It is better to say, however, that such relief will be denied unless the other party is put in statu quo.[3] In some cases, at least, in spite of a material change that has occurred, the original position of the other party can be substantially restored by money payments and other equitable adjustments. Like the former Chancellors, the courts of today have ample power to mold their decrees as justice may require in the particular case.[4] They are no longer to follow old decisions that were rendered under the inflexible procedure of the ancient common law.

A bidder who enters into a contract for construction work at too low a price, because of his antecedent mistake in computation or in interpreting plans and specifications or in estimating difficulties and costs of excavation, may be given relief if he can and does put the other party in statu quo. But after performance has been rendered, he certainly can not get a decree rescinding the contract and compelling the other party to pay the reasonable value of the work.[5] If the other party did not cause the mistake and did not know of it, it is not just to force him to pay an amount that he did not promise to pay. To the facts that the contractor was negligent and the other party innocent, we must add a change of position that calls for enforcement of the contract.

Likewise, after goods have been delivered and consumed, the contract stands, in spite of a mistake by the seller in computing the price that he asked or a mistake of the buyer in estimating costs or market values.[6]

2. In the following cases negligence did not prevent relief, the other party being in statu quo or being put so by the decree:

U.S.—Moffett, H. & C. Co. v. Rochester, 20 S.Ct. 957, 178 U.S. 373, 44 L. Ed. 1108 (1909); Hearne v. New Eng. Mut. Marine Ins. Co., 20 Wall. 488, 22 L.Ed. 395 (1874), clerical error by bidder's employee; Columbian Nat. Life Ins. Co. v. Black, 35 F.2d 571, 71 A.L.R. 128 (C.C.A.10th, 1929); Skelton v. Federal Surety Co., 15 F.2d 756 (C.C.A.10th, 1926);

Connecticut v. McGraw, 41 F.Supp. 369 (D.C.Conn.1941).

Eng.—Kelly v. Solari, 9 M. & W. 54 (1841).

3. Relief denied unless other party can be and is put substantially in statu quo:

U.S.—Grymes v. Sanders, 93 U.S. 55, 23 L.Ed. 798 (1876); Star-Chronicle Pub. Co. v. Evening Post, 256 F. 435 (C.C.A.2d, 1919).

Conn.—Milford Yacht Realty Co. v. Milford Yacht Club, 72 A.2d 482, 136 Conn. 544 (1950).

One who by a negligent mistake executes a mortgage or a suretyship undertaking can not have it set aside after an innocent party has made a loan in reliance upon it.[7]  To put that party in statu quo requires the repayment of the loan with interest; and that is just what the instrument was given to secure. One who makes such a negligent mistake will not be given relief at the expense of an innocent purchaser of value, whether of lands, goods, or choses in action.[8]  Such mistakes as these are often caused by fraud, making the transaction voidable against the defrauder; but unfortunately for the one induced to make the error, the rights of an innocent third party have become involved.

Deeds of conveyance and other documents, even including negotiable instruments, have been set aside at the expense of innocent purchasers, if the mistake was as to the character of the instrument executed and was caused under such circumstances that the mistaken party was not guilty of negligence.[9] It is best not to pass judgment on the merits of these decisions; but usually, as between two equally deserving persons the defendant will prevail.

## § 607.  Mistake Caused by Failure to Read a Document before Signing

One who signs or accepts a written instrument without reading it with care is likely to be surprised and grieved at its contents later on.  In most cases he has been held bound in accordance with its written terms.[15]  Broad general statements are frequently to be found to the effect that he is estopped by his "negligence," or that he must suffer the consequences of his "folly," even though he trusted to the other party or his agent as to the contents of the writing.  In these cases, however, the other party had no reason to know that the one signing or accepting the document was unaware of its contents and usually was able to show that he materially changed his position in reliance on the written provisions.

It is quite possible for a party to assent to be bound in accordance with terms of which he is then ignorant, just as he may promise to pay a sum yet to be determined by the future market or by an arbitrator.  He may sign a document that has been drawn by his lawyer, saying: "I have no time to read this; but I trust my lawyer's judgment and assent to what he has written." In these cases he may be bound by promises that he did not consciously know he was making but by which he leads the other party reasonably to believe that he intends to be bound.[16]

9.  Eng.—Lewis v. Clay, 2 L.J.Q.B. 224, 77 L.T. 653 (1898); Foster v. Mackinnon, L.R. 4 C.P. 711 (1869); Thoroughgood's Case, 2 Coke 9a (1584).

The fact that a written instrument was signed or accepted without reading it is not sufficient ground for refusing a decree of reformation if its contents are at variance with the antecedent agreement and understanding of the parties. That the failure to read the instrument was negligent is not enough to prevent correction of the mistake by a decree of reformation.[23] Such a mistake can be proved in an action for the enforcement of the written instrument, without first getting a decree of reformation.[24]

If the mistake of the party who signs or accepts an instrument without reading it is induced by the artifice or misrepresentation of the other party, of course the contract is voidable by the mistaken signer.[25] This is most often illustrated by cases in which the signer is illiterate or is unfamiliar with the language in which the contract is written; [26] but it is equally applicable in any case in which one party causes the mistake that the other is making when he signs.[27] Indeed, the same result obtains in any case in which one party is mistaken as to the contents of the document and the other party has actual knowledge of that fact at the time the instrument is executed.[28]

### § 608. Must Mistake be "Mutual"? Unilateral Mistake Compared

Statements are exceedingly common, both in texts and in court opinions, that relief will not be given on the ground of mistake unless the mistake is "mutual." Such a broad generalization is misleading and untrue. Seldom is it accompanied by either definition or analysis. A study of thousands of cases is not necessary to convince us that to err is human, both in the sense of having mistaken ideas and in the sense of performing acts that are evil or unwise. But such a study will show that human mistakes are of great variety in kind with a great variety of causes, that they have a great variety of results, and that the juristic effects vary as the combinations of factors vary.

Cases do not always submit readily to be classified with either "mutual mistake" or "unilateral mistake." And even when they do submit, the solution does not mechanically follow in accordance with a separate set of rules for each class. Very often relief has

24. Mass.—Martin v. Jablonski, 149 N.E. 156, 253 Mass. 451 (1925).
The contrary was held in Northern Assur. Co. v. Grand View Bldg. Ass'n, 22 S.Ct. 133, 183 U.S. 308, 46 L.Ed. 213 (1902), in a 55 page opinion, three justices dissenting, reversing two lower federal courts. Thereupon, suit for "reformation" and enforcement was brought and sustained in the courts of the State where the contract was made and to be performed. Grand View Bldg. Ass'n v. Northern Assur. Co., 102 N.W. 246, 73 Neb. 149 (1905). This action was held not to have been barred either by election of remedy or by res judicata in Northern Assur. Co. v. Grand View Bldg. Ass'n, 27 S.Ct. 27, 203 U.S. 106, 51 L.Ed. 109 (1906), opinion of only 2 pages by Holmes, without dissent.

been and will be, granted where the mistake is unilateral. And relief is not necessarily granted, even though the mistake is mutual. It depends very materially upon the form of relief sought. Reformation is often refused on the ground that the mistake was not "mutual," when the correct reason is that the parties never agreed upon any terms other than those in the erroneous writing. In such cases the appropriate remedy is rescission or cancellation, unless there is sufficient basis for an estoppel.[31]

As we have seen in other connections, the term "mutuality" has an appeal that must not be overlooked, even though it has blinded us at times to facts and reality.[32] The idea behind the term is of importance; but it is not one that lends itself easily to the statement of broad principles and just working rules. Statements are very numerous to the effect that the mistake of only one of the parties to a contract is not a ground for relief either at law or in equity.[33] Such a statement can be accepted only in case the party seeking relief proves no more than that his action was induced by his erroneous thought. The statement will seldom be found in cases in which relief is granted; in the cases refusing relief and making the statement as a reason for so doing, the court has always considered and weighed the additional factors that accompanied the mistake.

Let us consider, first, mistakes made in the process of making a contract. Sometimes one party is mistaken as to the identity of the other, clearly a case in which the other party would not be laboring under the same mistake; but if that other party knows or has reason to know of the mistake, seldom if ever can he hold the first party to the agreement. The rights of innocent purchasers and other third parties will depend upon a variety of factors.[34]

In the famous case of the ships named Peerless, neither party made a mistake in expression; each one correctly described the ship that he meant to describe. The mistake that each one made

---

31. See § 614, Reformation.

32. Consider, for example, "mutuality of assent," "mutuality of obligation," "mutuality of remedy."

33. Restatement, Restitution, § 12: "A person who confers a benefit upon another, manifesting that he does so as an offer of a bargain which the other accepts or as the acceptance of an offer which the other has made, is not entitled to restitution because of a mistake which the other does not share and the existence of which the other does not know or suspect." Observe that this rule deals only with cases in which a performance has already been rendered and received. In the Reporter's Notes to Restitution, § 12, p. 6, the Reporter states that "where the contract is wholly unexecuted but where a deposit has been made by one of the parties who, however, made a unilateral mistake, the cases are more in doubt. Cases on both sides are cited.

34. See § 601, Identity.

was in believing that the other party intended to describe the same ship that he himself described. Here they were "mutually" mistaken, which means that both were mistaken. Were these "mutual" mistakes identical? Not quite, although they had common elements. Both parties believed that there was only one ship named Peerless sailing from Bombay, when in fact there were two; both believed that there was agreement in meaning, when in fact there was not. But in believing that the other party meant the same ship as himself, they were making closely similar but not identical mistakes. Here, it is not the fact of mutuality that is decisive; rather it is the fact that neither one made a negligent mistake and caused harm thereby.

When one party, in expressing his assent, so negligently chooses his words that the other reasonably gives them a meaning different from the one intended, a valid contract is often held to have been made, in spite of the fact that, as in the Peerless case, both parties are making a mistake. Just as in that case, both parties believe that there is agreement in meaning, that the other party means the same as himself. Just as in that case, the parties are "mutually" mistaken, though their mental errors are not quite identical. In spite of this "mutuality," there is a contract, due to the negligence of the one and the reasonableness of the other.

If the mistake of one party to a written instrument is in thinking that it contains a larger promise by the other party than in fact it does, and the other party has no reason to know of this mistake, of course the mistaken party can not hold the other to the large promise that he did not make, by getting reformation or otherwise. In such a case, the court may say that there can be no relief unless the mistake was "mutual," or that a party is "conclusively presumed to know its contents." But when a mistaken party asks for rescission and restoration of the status quo, he is asking for a remedy that is very different from enforcement against the other party of a contract that the mistaken party thought was made but was not.[36]

36.    Such a case is Metzger v. Aetna Ins. Co., 125 N.E. 814, 227 N.Y. 411 (1920), where an insurance policy was expressly limited to the period during process of construction of a building. The plaintiff can not hold the insurer bound to pay a loss that occurred later merely because he thought erroneously that the policy read for a calendar year.

In Page v. Higgins, 22 N.E. 63, 150 Mass. 27 (1889), a deed was so worded as to convey lot C as well as another lot. The grantor knew that he did not own lot C, but supposed that the deed did not include it; he was illiterate and the deed was not read to him. The grantee knew that the deed included lot C, for he drafted it; but he supposed that the grantor owned and intended to include lot C. Here each made a material mistake, but as to different facts. They were both mistaken in think-

Frequently, the existence of a factor as to which a mistake is made, is of material importance to only one of the contracting parties; and he is the only one who is likely to seek relief or who will be given it if he does. In such a case, it is practically immaterial whether the mistake was made by both parties or by one only. What the court needs to know before giving a remedy is whether the mistake substantially affects the party seeking relief, whether the other party can be put in statu quo, how the granting of relief will affect third parties, and whether the petitioner's conduct has created an estoppel. The fact that the defendant also made the same mistake may add nothing to the determination of the issue.

In these cases the fact that the defendant did not make the same mistake may aid the plaintiff's case, the defendant's conduct being regarded as fraudulent or in bad faith.

In the case of a unilateral contract of donation, its words are to be interpreted for the purpose of giving effect to the actual intention of the single promisor. If in the drafting or execution of such a contract the promisor labored under a mistake that causes the legal effect produced to be materially different from that intended by him, he has a right to correction of the instrument. The fact that the mistake is unilateral does not prevent relief. The same is true of other donative acts, such as the change of beneficiary of an insurance policy by the insured. If such a change was made under a mistake that leads to a result different from that intended by the insured, the change will be modified in equity at the suit of the original beneficiary or other party in interest so as to carry out the actual intention of the insured.[37]

The distinction between "mutual" mistake and "unilateral" mistake has some importance. In the matter of the remedy to be granted, it may be a decisive factor. But we must not begin with any broad generalizations based upon this distinction. We must not say that relief will be denied unless the mistake is "mutual"; or that a "unilateral" mistake does not affect the validity

ing that they were agreed on the land to be conveyed. This is clearly a case for rescission and restitution; but the court decided only matters of procedure.

One who buys property from the defendant, through the latter's agent, the contract being in some substantial respect beyond the agent's authority, can rescind the transaction, return the property and compel restitution of his money. He paid it by mistake as to a factor whereby his purpose is substantially frustrated. Observe that the plaintiff's mistake is as to the agent's authority. The defendant's mistake is as to the agent's making the unauthorized part of the contract. Rackemann v. Riverbank Imp. Co., 44 N.E. 990, 167 Mass. 1 (1896); Seifert v. Union Brass & M. Mfg. Co., 254 N.W. 273, 191 Minn. 362 (1934).

37. N.Y.—Rosenblum v. Manufacturers Trust Co., 200 N.E. 587, 270 N.Y. 79, 105 A.L.R. 947 (1936).

of a contract. Every attempt at a generalization or stated rule must take into account a variety of factors and must be limited to some particular combination of them.[38]

The American Law Institute states the law to be that a contract is not made voidable by a unilateral mistake, however material it may be to the interests of the mistaken party.[39] Without doubt, this has been the prevailing form of statement, along with the even more common form that mistake is not operative unless it is mutual. It is supported by some decisions and by many dicta; but the decisions that are inconsistent with it are too numerous and too appealing to the sense of justice to be disregarded.[40]

It must be borne in mind, however, that the circumstances accompanying the mistake must always be considered, just as they were considered by the former courts of Chancery. It has never been asserted, and it is not being asserted here, that a party ever makes out a sufficient case for relief, either affirmative or defensive, by merely proving that he was caused to execute a deed or to make a promise by the fact that he had a mistaken thought. Many of the pertinent factors have been listed in the first section of this chapter. No one of them can be said to be absolutely necessary for the granting of relief; the combination of factors existing in the specific case must be considered. Here are two of the more important factors: Did the other party participate either intentionally or innocently in causing the mistake? Is it still possible to restore the other party to his original position? [42]

### § 609.  Unilateral Errors of Computation in Preparing Bids and Offers

There are many cases in which one party has assented to a definite bargain because of some antecedent error of computation that he has made. Their number is due to the fact that men are poor accountants and inaccurate in doing simple mathematical problems. If the mistake is discovered and corrected by notice before an acceptance of the mistaken offer, no harm results and no relief is necessary. But if an acceptance has taken place, trouble may arise. If the error was made by the offeror, then the offer is one that would not have been made but for the mistake. This is the frequently occurring case. It is quite possible, however, for the error in computation to be made by the offeree, his error leading him to believe that the offer is an advantageous one, or the best one, or one that he can afford to accept.

In this type of case, it is very often said that there has been no real meeting of the minds, no true assent to identical terms. This statement is not correct. By making it, a decision that the court feels that justice requires is made to appear consistent with accepted doctrine. If no mutual assent, then no contract was made, and the mistaken party escapes disagreeable consequences. In these cases, however, the mistake of the offeror is made before he makes his offer. When he makes his offer, he says exactly what he then intends to say and he conveys to the other party exactly the meaning that he intends to convey. The thought expressed by his words and understood by the other party is exactly the thought that is in the offeror's own mind. We have exact agreement in intention as well as in expression. His mistake was one of computation, wholly antecedent to his expressed and communicated offer. In adding together two and two, he made the sum three—an important mistake, to be sure, and one that caused him to make the offer that he in fact made; but it was the result of the addition and not the erroneous addition itself that was offered for acceptance by the other.[43]

The truth of the foregoing statements is seen by many courts; and they are led thereby to hold that there is a valid contract enforceable against the mistake maker.[44] Nevertheless, it is believed that their decision is frequently unjust and should not be followed. There are several important factors to be considered. Cases of such unilateral mistakes are not such that they can all be put into one basket and dumped into the ash can.

Suppose, first, a case in which a bidding contractor makes an offer to supply specified goods or to do specified work for a definitely named price, and that he was caused to name this price by an antecedent error of computation. If, before acceptance, the offeree knows, or has reason to know, that a material error has been made, he is seldom mean enough to accept; and if he does accept, the courts have no difficulty in throwing him out. He is not permitted "to snap up" such an offer and profit thereby.[45] If, without knowledge of the mistake and before any revocation, he has accepted the offer, it is natural for him to feel a sense of disappointment at not getting a good bargain, when the offeror insists on withdrawal; but a just and reasonable man will not insist upon profiting by the other's mistake.[46] There are now many decisions to the effect that if the error was a substantial one and notice is given before the other party has made such a change of position that he can not be put substantially in statu quo, the bargain is voidable and rescission will be decreed.[47]

**44.** Rescission and restitution denied:

U.S.—Sanitary Dist. v. Ricker, 91 F. 833 (C.C.A.7th, 1899).

Md.—Mayor of Baltimore v. Robinson Const. Co., 91 A. 682, 123 Md. 660 (1914).

**45.** U.S.—Moffett, H. & C. Co. v. Rochester, 20 S.Ct. 957, 178 U.S. 373, 44 L.Ed. 1108 (1900).

**47.** U.S.—Moffett, H. & C. Co. v. Rochester, 20 S.Ct. 957, 178 U.S. 373, 44 L.Ed. 1108 (1900); State of Conn. v. McGraw, 41 F.Supp. 369 (D.C.Conn. 1941); Nason Coal Co. v. U. S., 64 Ct.Cl. 526 (1928).

Conn.—Geremia v. Boyarsky, 140 A. 749, 107 Conn. 387 (1928).

Sometimes it is also said that the mistake must not have been grossly negligent; but this is generally a mere make-weight, one that is not easy to apply with accuracy or justice. The law does not penalize for negligence beyond requiring compensation for the loss it has caused. Most errors of computation are careless in some degree, though no doubt differences in degree may be perceptible.

It has often been asserted to be the weight of authority that rescission will not be permitted or decreed for a unilateral mistake of the sort here under discussion; and numerous cases have so held.[48] Where authorities are apparently so divided, it is not desirable to generalize dogmatically; and courts are free to do justice as they see it after weighing all the factors of the specific case. Much depends upon the time factor and upon change of position and inability to restore the status quo ante. Some of the cases, at least, can be reconciled.[49]

In some of the cases cited above, the bid or offer that was based upon an erroneous computation was accompanied by a deposit or certified check to secure execution of the contract if it should be awarded. This either made the bid irrevocable, even before acceptance, or it was a contract to forfeit the deposit in case of a withdrawal of the bid. The mistake was discovered in time to prevent execution of a written contract, and perhaps even before notice that the bid would be accepted. The question, therefore, was whether the mistake made the deposit contract voidable so that return of the deposit could be compelled.[50]

Courts refusing to decree rescission for unilateral mistake often say that to do otherwise would tend greatly to destroy stability and certainty in the making of contracts.[51] In some degree, this may be true; but certainty in the law is largely an illusion at best, and altogether too high a price may be paid in the effort to attain it. Inflexible and mechanical rules lead to their own avoidance by fiction and camouflage. A sufficient degree of stability and certainty will be maintained if the court carefully weighs the combination of factors in each case, is convinced that the substantial mistake asserted was in fact made, and gives due weight

---

48.   **U.S.**—U. S. v. Conti, 119 F.2d 652 (C.C.A.1st, 1941), Mass. law.

**Md.**—Baltimore v. Robinson Const. Co., 91 A. 682, 123 Md. 660 (1914), the deposit small and "equitable" relief not asked.

**Mass.**—John J. Bowes Co. v. Milton, 151 N.E. 116, 255 Mass. 228 (1926), the extent or circumstances of the error are not stated; Wheaton Bldg. & Lbr. Co. v. Boston, 90 N.E. 598, 204 Mass. 218 (1910), underbid caused by misinterpretation of specifications, erroneously treated as error of law.

**Ill.**—Steinmeyer v. Schroeppel, 80 N. E. 564, 226 Ill. 9 (1907), mistake of addition, seller said to be negligent and error not to affect the "subject matter".

to material changes of position. Proof of the mistake should be required to be strong and convincing; but in many of the cases it is evident that such proof existed.

## § 611.  Contract may be Voidable by One Party and Not by the Other

A unilateral mistake may make a bargain voidable but it does not make it void. It is not voidable in favor of the party who made no mistake; [60] nor is it voidable by the mistaken party unless the mistake operates in some substantial manner to his disadvantage. Where a vendor is mistaken in believing that he has perfect title and in fact conveys less than be supposed, he has no right to rescission if the purchaser is content with the bargain as it was performed. Of course, he has no right of rescission, if the risk of defective title was on him and he bound himself by the contract to transfer good title.[61]

# CHAPTER 29

# MISTAKE—LEGAL AND EQUITABLE REMEDIES

## § 613. Remedies for Mistake—Effect of Amalgamation of Law and Equity as Legal Systems

It is unfortunate that courts still have to spend time and effort in trying to determine whether a particular court proceeding is "at law" or "in equity." Once there was a reasonably distinct but never perfect boundary line, because there were two sets of courts, with judicial officers having the separate titles of Judge and Chancellor, sitting on different sides of Westminster hall, each making its own system of rules and jural relations and remedies, sometimes glaring across at each other with jealousy or malevolence. Since the two systems varied in important respects, the learned jurists who knew most about them and realized the importance of these differences came to believe that law and equity are different "in the nature of things" and that a dual system of doctrines and jural relations is inevitable and eternal.

There is in fact just as much reason, both logical and practical, for believing that our juristic system must be quadruple or quintuple or worse. The Lord High Admiral also had his bench and his doctrines; admiralty must not be forgotten, in the debate as to the nature of Common Law and Equity.[1] Even now, we have an "Admiralty bar"; while the "Chancery barrister" seems to have disappeared. There were, also, special courts for the Merchants, with a system of doctrines and jural relations called the "Law Merchant"—a name of mystery to the modern law student, so thoroughly has it been absorbed and amalgamated. Once there were Ecclesiastical courts, with officers who fought and died for their "jurisdiction." Their system still exists within a limited field, separate from Equity since the Chancellor ceased to be an Archbishop.

---

1. See the discussion as to reformation for mistake in Admiralty in Rice v. Dreifus Co., 96 F.2d 80 (C. C.A.2d, 1938).

Each of these systems of law was in constant evolutionary change. Each could, and did, borrow from the others. The "Law Merchant" was once almost unknown to the Court of King's Bench; but, long since, the law of bills and notes became part of the ordinary judge's domain. The jural relations created by a negotiable instrument differ in some respects from those created by an ordinary contract; but so do those created by any contract from those created by another. They merely exist in varying groups and combinations. So also, the courts of Common Law borrowed from the Chancellors. Equitable defenses became legal defenses; equitable causes of action became legal causes of action. Somewhat to the dissatisfaction of stand-pat judges, Lord Mansfield not only learned and applied the Law Merchant, he also made his court a Court of Conscience by expanding the use of the action of assumpsit. Fraud and mistake may once have been solely the domain of the Chancellors; but the King's Bench and the Common Pleas took them within their jurisdiction. By such processes, that which was equity became common law as well, or even exclusively.[2]

Some of our States still have Chancellors as well as Judges, with their more or less separate jurisdiction, special remedies, different procedure. They may well have a "dual" system of law as well as of courts, with sets of variant and even conflicting rules and doctrines. In other States, there are no Chancellors, but there are two kinds of procedure and the same two sets of doctrine as in the States where Chancellors still flourish. Such was the situation in the Federal courts, when there was an "equity side" and a "law side", and the lawyer had to know his "bill in equity" and the "federal equity rules." Since the adoption, by authority of Congress, of the new Federal Rules of Procedure, the court no longer has two "sides". Having only one judge and a uniform procedure, the federal courts should no longer imagine two sets of substantive laws and jural relations, jangling against each other in disharmony and conflict. This is the same situation as that existing in the States having a uniform Code Procedure.

The problem is complicated by the fact that constitutions and statutes have been drawn using the English language of the past. They give their courts jurisdiction "in equity and at common law." Federal courts also have "admiralty" jurisdiction, something that State courts too must consider. Probably they no longer mention the law merchant or canon law. Each State must work out its own problem with respect to the powers and jurisdiction and procedure of its particular courts. But a strong effort should be made to hold that they have but one system of law to apply, but one set of jural relations consequent upon a specific set of facts; that they no longer have common law as distinct from equity, anymore than they have a distinct law Merchant.[3]

It is not to be supposed that, in applying this advice, any State or any court can wholly escape from history. Instead, its law and its judicial system are the product of that history. It is a complicated product, in spite of more or less effective efforts at reform and simplification. But it is one net product, one system of law. Under it, any specific set of facts creates a single set of jural relations among the participating parties. We no longer have actions "at law" and suits "in equity"; no longer the common law in the "strict sense", as was once set opposite to equity or law merchant. We now have *common* law, in its only sense, whether "strict" or otherwise.[4] We still have "trusts", express or constructive. We still know what is an "equity of redemption". They are a part of our juristic heritage, a part of our common law. Injunctions, and decrees of reformation or rescission, are still granted. They are granted by our courts of common law; and they are to be sought in a civil action, not by a "bill in equity." The remedies that were created by the Court of Chancery differ from those created by the old courts of common law; and the terms and conditions on which such equitable remedies were granted differed from those justifying common law remedies. Like differences existed between any two equitable remedies, and also between any two common law remedies. These differences still must be known in order to determine whether or not they still exist and are to be respected.

If one has been induced by fraud or mistake to sign a contract or to pay money or to convey land, where does he go for relief? To the courts of the present common law. If he asks for reformation of a writing, or for the repayment of his money, or for the surrender and cancellation of a note, or for something called rescission, or for a declaratory judgment stating his rights and powers, to what courts does he go? To the courts of the present common law. The particular court in which he must file his com-

---

3. What is said above does not deny that the business or occupation in which one is engaged may not be an operative fact in determining the rule of law or usage that is applicable to his case. Brokers have special usages, and special rules of law may be applicable; but we should not speak of "broker's law" as a separate system. No doubt, there are special usages in transactions between merchants, or between clothing merchants, or between merchant Smith and merchant Jones; but we should not, for that reason, say that there is now a "law merchant" or a "law clothing-merchant" or a "law Smith-Jones."

4. Of course, this does not mean that the 48 States and the United States have identical laws, although some rules and doctrines may be commonly applied in all of them. There are many "Uniform" statutes, interpreted and applied with varying degrees of uniformity.

plaint or make his petition may depend upon county lines, or upon where process must be served, or upon the place where an act occurred, or upon the size of the judgment that he asks. The distinction is not between "law" and "equity"; it is between the county of Calaveras and the county of Los Angeles, or between the Superior Court and the Municipal Court. One who has been induced by fraud to pay $625 for some worthless stock has a right to damages for the tort (or perhaps for breach of a promise) and, in the alternative, a right to the restitution of $625. Such is the existing common law. It may be that many years ago the courts of King's Bench and Common Pleas would have given the plaintiff neither of these remedies, and that the plaintiff would have had to petition the Chancellor.[5] At the time of Lord Mansfield, he could maintain an action of indebitatus assumpsit. His right of restitution was not thereby changed in the nature of things, from "equitable" to "legal".[6] A new court was open to him, with a different jurist, different formalities, different modes of proof,[7] and different process of enforcement. These are indeed important matters. Statutes may have eliminated the varieties of "jurist", the difference in "formalities", and possibly may have established uniformity in modes of proof. It is still advantageous for our common jurist to be able to choose among a variety of remedies, enforceable by a variety of processes.[8]

A number of remedies will be listed as being available to cure the effects of various kinds of mistake, and some of these will be discussed more at length in later sections. But it should be remembered that in each case the exact form of the judgment or decree is still in the hands of the courts. The remedies here listed and discussed were themselves invented by the courts because justice made them necessary. The power of the courts to make the remedy fit the special case is not extinct. Under modern statutory reorganizations and codes of procedure, that power is not diminished. Instead, under a very flexible procedure, a single court may now have all the powers of all the earlier complex systems of courts and may have available all the remedies of common law and equity, to be used separately or in combination. The decree of the court, therefore, should be moulded to suit the facts of each case as justice may require.

5.  His petition might have read thus, possibly in Latin: "To the most reverend Fader in God, John, Archbishop of Caunterbury and Chauncellor of England: Mekely besechith your good and gracious lordshyp your continuell orator, Sebastian Giglis, merchaunt of Venyce, that Whereas . . . [stating the facts and the remedy sought] . . . this at the reverence of God and in the wey of charitie." See Giglis v. Welby, 1 Calendars of Proceedings in Chancery, cxx; Ames' Cases on Suretyship, 583.

A judgment or decree for the restitution of money paid by mistake was available, both at common law and in equity under certain circumstances and on certain conditions. Such a judgment or decree is now generally available in a single court. Mistake became an effective defense, in the common law courts as well as in equity, in actions for the enforcement of contracts.[9] It can still be made so. Deeds and written contracts, incorrectly drawn, can be reformed or set aside. Specific performance or damages can be awarded for the enforcement of a true agreement not correctly reduced to writing. Conveyance can be compelled in case of a mistaken omission. Decrees may be made conditional on the making of compensation, or on other terms. Defendants may be required to elect between specified alternatives.[10]

The court must be acutely aware of the wide extent of its powers and of the variety and flexibility of its remedies. Mould the decree so as to fit the mistake and to correct its unjust results, giving due consideration to the situation as it now exists, to changes of position, to the character of each party's conduct, and to the rights and interests of third parties. In some states, there may still be courts whose jurisdiction and remedies are severely limited as at earlier common law.[11] In those states, as of old in England, a supplementary court with a different procedure stands ready to give relief with all the powers and remedies of the Chancellors.

### § 614. Reformation of Mistaken Instruments

Reformation of a written instrument will be decreed when the words that it contains do not correctly express the meaning that the parties agreed upon, as the court finds to be convincingly proved. The writing may omit a provision that they agreed should be put in; or it may contain a provision that they agreed to leave out or that was not in fact assented to.[12] A very common mistake is the insertion of an incorrect description of the subject matter; street numbers, survey numbers, boundary lines, area, may be erroneous by reason of a typist's error, bad memory, copying from an earlier document that was itself erroneous.[13] A person may be incorrectly named or his relation to the transaction may be incorrectly stated.[14] If by reason of a mistake of law,

10. Ill.—Hoops v. Fitzgerald, 68 N. E. 430, 204 Ill. 325 (1903), an excellent opinion.

Mass.—Keene v. Demelman, 52 N.E. 188, 172 Mass. 17 (1898), rescission unless purchaser accepts deed without warranty as to area.

Mo.—New York Life Ins. Co. v. Gil-bert, 256 S.W. 148, 215 Mo.App. 201 (1923).

N.Y.—Haviland v. Willets, 35 N.E. 958, 141 N.Y. 35 (1894).

R.I.—Lawrence v. Staigg, 8 R.I. 256 (1866), election between rescission and making an additional payment for excess area.

the legal effect of the words in which a contract or conveyance is expressed is different from that on which the parties were agreed, reformation is a proper remedy.[15]

Reformation is not a proper remedy for the enforcement of terms to which the defendant never assented; it is a remedy the purpose of which is to make a mistaken writing conform to antecedent expressions on which the parties agreed. These antecedent expressions of agreement may have been such as to constitute a valid informal contract, in which case reformation is merely a step in the enforcement of that contract. The written document was intended to be no more than the integration in writing of the terms already agreed upon. In so far as it differs from those terms it is mistaken and will be corrected.

## § 616.   Mistake of Law—Its Effect upon a Contract

We must first make an effort to explain what is meant by a mistake of law. It is commonly believed, not incorrectly, that law consists of rules by which men's legal relations with each other can be determined, rules that can be, and are, stated in words, rules that any one can read and know and understand. It is conceivable that this statement itself is mistaken, in which case there would indeed be a huge mistake of law; not a mistake as to a particular rule, but as to the existence and nature of all rules.

If we assume the correctness of the statement, it is easy to see how mistakes of law occur. Law books are almost innumerable; the words in which they are expressed are tricky things; the printed books of rules may leave some rules out and misstate others, else why so many Restatements; a man may not read some or all of these books, or be able to read them; one who reads a rule, even assuming it to be correct, may fail to know and understand; a rule that is read and understood may later be forgotten.

Rules of law are made and are read and understood, not merely for their own sake, but in order to determine our relations with other men—our rights (or, to be somewhat more analytical, our rights, powers, privileges, and immunities). One will certainly be mistaken as to these "rights" if he is mistaken as to the "rules of law"; but it is possible for one to be mistaken as to his "rights," even though he knows all the rules.[41] To say that a legal "right" exists means only that the facts and events necessary to the judicial recognition of the right, under our prevailing system of rules, exist or have occurred. Therefore, in order to know whether or not a legal right exists, it is necessary to know both the specific facts and events and also the applicable rules of law. Mistakes are possible as to either of these prerequisites—mistakes of fact and mistakes of law.

To know and apply the rules of law, it is necessary to know the sources from which the applicable rule will be drawn if litigation shall occur. These sources are numerous and are not easily known. Often, they are conflicting and difficult of interpretation. They include statutes and constitutions, both of the state of the forum and elsewhere; judicial decisions of many courts, unreported as well as reported; judicial dicta; administrative pronouncements, interpretations, and decisions; the treatises, articles, commentaries, and restatements of scholars; the mores and customs of men in analogous situations. The law is not written in shining letters against the sky. Its rules are not such that he who runs may read. It may seem strange that common men are required to know the law when savants and jurists do not. The truth is that they can not be, and are not, expected or required to know all the law upon which their rights depend. They are merely required to know enough law to avoid harming others by crime or tort or breach of contract. Even an ignorant man has reason to know that harm to others may lead to resentment and punishment by others; and the public welfare requires that thus far he must be held responsible even though ignorant. Hence, the maxim, *ignorantia juris non excusat.*

The public welfare does not require that men must know all the law upon which their rights depend. That is indeed to require an impossibility. They are not required to suffer for their ignorance or mistake when harm to others is avoided. Nor is it justice to permit others to make a profit out of such ignorance or mistake.

A man may be mistaken as to his "rights," whether property or contract, for either of two reasons: First, he may be mistaken as to the specific operative facts to which the rules of law, from whatever source drawn, are to be applied. He may not know that he is the son of John Doe, who died leaving lands to his heir. He may not know the fact that his uncle Richard left a will devising Blackacre to him. He may not know that X contracted with Y to pay money to him as a third party beneficiary; or knowing that X so promised, he may not know that the promisee Y gave a consideration for the promise. In all such cases, his mistake is a mistake of fact, a mistake not only of his rights, but of the specific facts upon which his rights depend. In such a case he may be the wisest jurist in the world, knowing all the law and all its sources; he would still be mistaken as to his rights. If such a man, thus mistaken, should, for a small consideration, promise to transfer his property and contract rights to another, shall that other be permitted to profit by keeping the property or the money that the transferor truly owned but mistakenly supposed that he did not? Our system of justice permits no such result; and this is so whether the other party was likewise mistaken or knew the facts and seeks to profit thereby.

Secondly, a man may be mistaken as to his "rights" because, although he knows the specific facts upon which they depend, he does not know the rules of law that the courts will apply to these facts. The wisest jurist may be mistaken in this manner, although he is less likely to be than is the ordinary layman. He may know that his father John left a will devising land to a stranger; but he may not know that the applicable statute requires three attesting witnesses. He may know that X orally contracted with Y to transfer land to him; but he may not know that the statute of frauds requires such a promise to be in writing and that the common law requires a consideration. If, for a small consideration, he contracts to transfer all his lands to another, shall that other be permitted to keep the land that he mistakenly believed to belong to the stranger, when in fact it belonged to him as the heir of his father because of the invalidity of his father's will? Surely, our system of justice permits no such result as this, even though his mistake as to his rights, the ownership of the land, was due solely and directly to his ignorance or mistake as to the statute of wills.[42]

There are cases in which the court has denied relief, giving as a reason that the mistake was a mistake of law, and that such a mistake is not a sufficient reason for enforcing restitution or rescission or reformation or other remedy, legal or equitable.[43] Without doubt, some of these decisions must be flatly disapproved; but in many instances, while disapproving the broad generalization stated by the court, an examination of the facts will show that another and better reason existed and that injustice was not done.[44] Unfortunately, there are cases in which the facts are not reported with sufficient fullness to enable us to say whether another and better reason existed. It can only be hoped that there was one, while counting the case and its ratio decidendi on the wrong side.

It must be remembered that mistake of fact does not always justify granting the relief sought. In the mistake of law cases, the facts may be such that the mistaken party would not have been entitled to relief even if his mistake had been a mistake of fact. That his mistake was a mistake of law should put him in no better case.[45]

The American Law Institute, in its chapter on Mistake, Contracts Restatement, chapter 17, makes no distinction between mistake of law and mistake of fact. This is to be commended, although the reader might well have been expressly warned that the applicable rules of law are not affected by the distinction and that judicial dicta to the contrary are disapproved. Without mentioning mistake of law as such, one illustration is given in which a lease is declared to be voidable, although the mistake made by the parties is clearly one of law.[46]

In the Restatement of the law of Restitution, the Institute distinguishes between mistake of law and mistake of fact.[47] It is severely critical of the cases in which the distinction was first drawn and in which restitution of money paid by mistake of law was refused.[48] Nevertheless, because those cases have not been overruled and because there are so many cases in the United States in which they have apparently been followed and approved, the Institute forbears to state as a general rule that money paid by mistake of law can be recovered back. Instead, it goes to great length to state the many exceptions to that rule, in which restitution may be had, and to indicate when it is that the distinction between mistake of fact and mistake of law is immaterial in awarding restitution or creating a constructive trust. In spite of the many decisions and dicta pro and con—indeed, because of them, it is believed that the time has come to say that the exceptions now make the rule, that social policy requires that mistake of law and mistake of fact be treated alike, and that in granting relief for mistake the attention of the court should be directed to the other factors in the case. There will still be left enough difficulty in the court's determining what justice requires.

In this and several succeeding sections, we are dealing with mistake of law as it affects the validity and enforcement of contracts. A treatise on Restitution deals with the recovery back of money paid or property transferred; it deals with executed transactions, cases in which a court may believe that "possession is nine points in the law," including cases in which no contract may ever have been made. Here, we are dealing with cases in

---

48.   **Eng.**—Brisbane v. Dacres, 5 Taunt. 143 (1813, C.P.); Bilbie v. Lumley, 2 East 469 (1802).

In Restatement, Restitution, Topic 3, Introductory Note, it is correctly stated that, prior to Bilbie v. Lumley, the English courts had made no such distinction. "Until the nineteenth century no distinction was made between mistake of fact and mistake of law and restitution was freely granted both in law and in equity to persons who had paid money to another because of a mistake of law." In this same note, the Institute further says: "Before long, the injustice which would result from the universal application of such a broad rule led to many

limitations upon it and by a process of attrition it has been limited to cases similar to that of Bilbie v. Lumley, that is, to cases where a benefit has been conferred upon another because of a supposed duty to him in response to an honest demand by him." The Institute does not itself purport to correct Lord Ellenborough's mistake of law, but carries on the "process of attrition" by stating various rules under which restitution has been granted. The volume quoted here deals only with "restitution"; but the courts have gone even further in decreeing rescission and reformation of contracts and other instruments for mistake of law.

which a contract was made, in the making or performance of which one or both parties acted under some mistake of law. The mistake may have been discovered before any performance has been rendered, so that there is as yet no question of "unjust enrichment" or of "recovery back." The question may take one of these forms: Does the mistaken party have a power of avoidance of the contract? Does he have a good defense when he is sued for breach of the contract? Is he legally privileged to refuse to perform? Will a court recognize or create such a privilege by decreeing rescission or cancellation? Will a court correct the mistake by a decree of reformation and enforce the contract as reformed?

On the other hand, we can not and should not exclude cases in which the contract has been partly or fully performed, by either or both of the parties. We can not avoid questions of restitution of money paid or property transferred in the course of such performance, or questions of compensation for services rendered and benefits conferred. This treatise and one dealing exclusively with Restitution have a considerable amount of overlapping; and the rules laid down should be identical or consistent with each other.

It should be constantly borne in mind that we are not dealing with cases in which a wrongdoer is seeking to be excused from the consequences of an unlawful act, whether crime or tort. Nor is anyone asking to be excused for a wrongful breach of contract, although he is asking the court to hold that the contract as made does not bind him.[49] It is not in itself wrongful to be mistaken as to the law. In the light of the complexity of our law, of the evolutionary nature of its growth and judicial application, and of the continuing necessity of its statement and restatement, no contractor should be penalized, or even characterized as "negligent," for not being able to predict correctly the effect that a court will give to a transaction, so long as he has done no harm to others and asks nothing but correction of his error and the restoration of the status quo.[50]

## § 617.  Restitution of Money Paid by Mistake of Law

According to commonly stated doctrine, one who pays money under a mistake of law has no right to restitution thereof, even though it was not legally due, if the payee claimed it as of right honestly and in good faith.[51] How the payee can, in the absence of additional factors, be regarded as "honestly" keeping the money so paid, after he learns of the mistake of law and that his claim was unfounded, has never been made clear. It is certain that in several jurisdictions this rule has never been recognized.[52] In all jurisdictions, there are large classes of exceptions.[53] In most jurisdictions, cases may be found in which the decision rendered was inconsistent with the rule, though nothing was said of it and the court may have given no thought to the distinction between law and fact. And it is believed that the cases to be considered herein, dealing with rescission and reformation for mistake of law, or of legal "rights," strongly indicate the injustice and incorrectness of the stated rule.[54]

It must always be borne in mind, in cases denying restitution of money paid on the stated ground that it was paid by mistake of law and not of fact, that the circumstances may be such that restitution would have been denied even though the money had been paid by mistake of fact instead of mistake of law. When a court is convinced that restitution should not be decreed, in the pressure of work it is likely to seize upon the first plausible rule that comes handy;[55] and the reader surely well knows how handy the "mistake of law" rule has become. This would be nearly conclusive in its favor, if there were not so many actual decisions in conflict with it, such definite disapproval by writers on grounds of policy and justice, such obvious error on the part of Lord Ellenborough in the case that started it, and such weight of opinion to the contrary in the Roman law and the many legal systems based upon the Roman law. In view of these facts, we may properly disregard the stated rule—the ratio decidendi—in the very large numbers of cases that should have been decided as they were, but for a very different reason.[56]

A list of other reasons for refusing restitution, that may also be reasons for refusing other forms of equitable relief, will here be given. It may not include every such reason.

Restitution for mistake of law may properly be refused because (1) the mistake may not have been material or followed by much harm;[57] (2) the money may have been due in equity and good conscience, though not in law;[58] (3) the interests of some innocent third party must be protected;[59] (4) the mistake may have been wholly unilateral and the other party can not be restored to his former position;[60] (5) the payment may have been made in settlement of a disputed claim, with consciousness that the legal right was doubtful;[61] (6) there may have been negligence in making the mistake and delay in seeking relief, with subsequent change of position;[62] (7) the evidence to prove the mistake may not have been clear and convincing;[63] (8) the plaintiff may have sought the wrong remedy, such as rescission when he could have got reformation, or reformation when no agreement different from the written one has been proved.[64]

In the following classes of cases, the restitution of money paid under a mistake of law is very generally required, by both common law and equity, these classes being described as "exceptions" to the general rule. When considered as a group, with the reasons given for enforcing restitution, it is practically impossible to justify a contrary decision in the cases not falling within one of these supposedly exceptional classes.

Money paid or other benefit conferred in the belief that it is legally due, this belief being caused by mistake of law, is recoverable just as if the mistake were one of fact if (a) the payment or benefit is given by a municipal or other governmental corporation, [65] or (b) the recipient is a court or court official and the benefit is within the control of the court, [66] or (c) the mistake is one of foreign law, [67] or (d) the benefit was given in accordance with a judgment since reversed.[68]

Money paid by one under compulsion of a contract believed, by mistake of law, to be valid, can be recovered, provided that the bargained-for equivalent has not been received.[69]

### § 618.   Mistake of Law Caused by Misrepresentation

If the mistake of law that induced the making or the performance of a contract by one party was caused by a fraudulent misrepresentation of the law by the other, or by his innocent misrepresentation if the relations of the parties are such as to make it reasonable for the one to rely upon the representations of the other, the appropriate relief by rescission, restitution, or reformation will be given to the injured party.   Doubtless, this statement represents a variation from older views and earlier decisions; but it is believed to be in harmony with modern notions of justice and with the trend of recent decisions.[72]

### § 619.   Mistake as to the Legal Effect of Words Used in a Contract or Deed

If two parties are in clear agreement as to the factual and legal result that they wish to accomplish, and a deed or other document is drawn by a scrivener using words that do not produce that result, the case is a proper one for reformation of the instrument.[74] The scrivener has made a mistake, either as to the result that he was instructed to produce, or as to the legal effect of the words that he used.   It makes no difference whether this is called a mistake of fact or a mistake of law or a mistake of both together. With respect to the legal effect of the words, the two parties no doubt make the same mistake that the scrivener made; and they make it because they relied on him.   They are not denied reformation by calling this mistake a mistake of law.   If the parties thought that the instrument contained words that it did not contain, their mistake is one of fact.   If they knew the words that were used and assented to them, their assent being induced by the belief that the legal effect of those words was an effect that they do not have, their mistake is a mistake of law.[75]

# PART IV

# CONSTRUCTION AND LEGAL OPERATION OF CONTRACT—CONDITIONS OF LEGAL DUTY

## CHAPTER 30

### DEFINITIONS AND TERMINOLOGY—CONDITIONS CLASSIFIED

## § 622. The Legal Operation of Contract

After having considered the formation of a contract and the requirements for its validity, it is necessary to consider its legal operation and to discover, if possible, the rules applicable to its performance. This is a more difficult and complex undertaking than that of stating the law of contract formation. It requires a more detailed knowledge of the performances for which people make agreements, of the practices and mores of contractors. This means a more detailed knowledge of the manifold relations between buyers and sellers of goods and of land, between em-

576

ployers and workmen, between builders and owners, between landlords and tenants. It means a detailed knowledge of the manifold relations and performances of all kinds of people with each other.

The "legal operation" of a contract, after it is made, can not be determined by reading the contract (assuming it to be in writing), or by interpreting the language used by the contractors, or by what is often referred to as "construction." It can not be determined by finding, in some occult manner, the supposed "intention of the parties." Such terms as these may serve a useful purpose; but they also cause obfuscation and always involve a supposition of clarity and certainty that is very largely false.

In order to determine the "legal operation" of a contract, it is necessary to know what the courts will do in all the possible contingencies of performance or non-performance. Sometimes these contingencies are foreseen and provided for by the parties in making their agreement. In more instances, however, the contingencies that actually later occur are not foreseen by the parties, or at least are not provided for in any way by them. Yet, in such cases the courts have to determine the rights and wrongs of the matter, the remedies to be awarded, what the parties ought to have done and ought not to have done. This is what is meant by the "legal operation" of the contract. These are the "legal relations" that are created by the contract and the subsequent events.

### § 623.   The Life History of a Contract—a Series of Facts and Events

When a contract bargain is made, we have a transaction between two or more specific parties. This transaction is a series of facts and events: the tentative approaches, the preliminary negotiation, the offers and counter-offers, the acceptance, the integration in writing, the performance or non-performance, partial or total. All this is a chronological series of events, including acts of the contracting parties and of third parties and also events that are acts of nobody. Any of these acts or events may affect the action of the courts in a given case. If they do affect it, they are legally operative facts and help to create new legal relations. Therefore, one who advises a contractor on the "legal operation" of his contract must know these subsequently occurring acts and events, must have experience with the conduct of the courts as affected by them, and must be able to predict that conduct for the benefit of his client. The "construction" of a contract has often been said to be hard. It is hard because it is necessary to know all of these facts as well as to know what is called "the law." It is necessary to know the business that is involved. Such knowledge can be gained from books as well as from living experience.  Indeed, most of it must of necessity come from books, especially the records of cases;  for no one can live many lives at once or become immediately experienced in the business of all of his clients in time to advise them.  Many a case will be such that advice must be tentative and provisional and that a large element of uncertainty will exist.  This work on contracts can not eliminate that uncertainty;  but the attempt is made to supply an analytical method and to indicate how the degree of uncertainty can be reduced.

Each contractual transaction has the chronological history indicated above;  there is a sequence of events.  In any case, these events should be considered in their chronological order.  They constitute the life history of a contract.[1]

### § 624.  What is a Legal Relation

By the process of contracting, parties create legal relations.  A conveyance of land creates new legal relations and extinguishes old ones.  "Property" in land or chattels consists of manifold legal relations with the other people of the world.  Certain kinds of facts are called "operative" facts because they create legal relations.  We have reason to know what is meant by these innumerable "relations" that play such an important part in life.

The truth is that legal relations are nothing other than groups of facts that enable us to predict with some degree of accuracy the future action of the judicial and administrative officials of an

---

1.   Thus:  *Fact one:*  A says to B, "If you will agree to pay me $100 for this horse you may have him and you may indicate your agreement by taking him."  This is a physical fact, called an offer, consisting of certain muscular acts of A (his spoken words) producing certain physical effects in B.  The legal relations immediately following are (in part) as follows: B now has the privilege of taking the horse;  B has the power of making the horse his own by taking him, with the correlative liability in A to the loss of his ownership;  no new rights or duties are created and no new immunities or disabilities;  by giving B a privilege and a power, A has lost a previous right and a previous immunity.

*Fact two:*  B says to A, "How old is the horse?"  This fact operates to create no new legal relations

whatever.  The operative legal effect of fact one is still intact.

*Fact three:*  A, knowing the horse to be 12 years old, replies, "6 years." This false representation changes the character of B's power by adding to it;  he still has the power to make the horse his own by accepting the offer, but now his acceptance will create in addition the power to "rescind" on discovery of the fraud.

*Fact four:*  B takes possession of the horse.  This is the fact called acceptance.  It operates at once to create in B all those multitudinous legal relations that are called "ownership" or "title" and to extinguish the ownership of A;  also to create a right in A as against B and the correlative duty in B to pay $100. Because of fact three, B also has the power to restore the legal *status quo* by tendering the horse back

organized society of men.   These facts are chiefly the events of the past, including acts of men and other physical changes around us.   Suppose that A delivers goods to B in exchange for B's promise to pay money in thirty days: we say that this creates a legal relation between A and B; it is a "right" in A against B and a duty in B to A.   We say this because we know, from past history, that if B does not pay, A can get assistance from societal officers—that is, he can get judicial and administrative remedies.   The "legal relation of right and duty," thus existing between A and B, is nothing more than a shorthand description of the group of facts: the delivery of goods, the promise, the long and consistent practice of courts and sheriffs.

We can classify the facts of life into various kinds of groups, including various kinds of societal action, and give them a series of separate names.   Thus, we get rights, powers, privileges, immunities, conditional rights, and as many varieties as we choose. There is no limit to the possibility of classification and the giving of names.   But we quickly meet a limit of practical usefulness in this process, due to the mental habits and capacity of men.   Many have been content to classify very little and to be satisfied with the one term "rights."   All desirable relations are included under "my rights"; and if such words as "power," "privilege," and "immunity" slip into use, it is almost inadvertent and is without any clear consciousness that a difference in meaning exists and that a new classification has been made.

### § 625.   Right to Future Performance Compared with Right to Immediate Performance

A contract is usually made for the purpose of getting some bargained-for performance.   It may also be made for the conscious purpose of getting a legally enforceable right to such a performance.   The creation of this legal relation of right and duty need not be within the contemplation of the parties; it may be the result of their expressions of agreement, without regard to their conscious intention.   Of course, each party may promise something, in which case there are mutual rights and duties and the contract is described as "bilateral."   When we say that one party has a "right" to a performance that it is the "duty" of the other to render, we mean that our organized society of people commands the performance by one for the benefit of the other, and provides some remedy in accordance with a stated procedure in case of non-performance.   This is what is meant by the "legal relation" of right and duty.

But performance may not be promised immediately; in which case society does not command that it be rendered immediately. The distinction between a right to a performance in the future and a right to immediate performance seems perfectly obvious; and yet attention must be called to it as a preliminary to explaining conditional rights and duties.[2] It is our custom, both juristic and popular, to say that a contract creates rights and duties, even though the performance is not yet due and even though some event must still occur before it becomes due.[3] An executory promise to repay money lent creates a right in the creditor and a duty in the borrower. There is an existing debt, even though the due date is still to arrive.

## § 626.  Conditional Rights and Duties

The group of operative facts that cause us to say that A has a right against B do not occur at one moment of time. When we say that a right is "conditional," we mean that some of these operative facts exist, but that one or more other facts necessary to perfect the legal relation that we have in mind do not yet exist. Any one of these other necessary facts is a "condition" of the existence of the contemplated legal relation. This indicates the difference between a conditional right and an unconditional one. If it is unconditional, all of the necessary creative facts exist; if it is conditional, at least one of these facts has still to occur.

How many of the group of necessary operative facts must exist before we begin to say that a legal relation exists and give it a name? The answer is that most of them must exist, but not all of them. There must be an organized society of men with a system of law—an established habit of consistent judicial and administrative action that enables confident prediction of like action in the future. Assuming that this actually exists, and that A and B are living persons, still A has no right against B. Other facts are necessary. It would be possible to say that A already has a right that B shall pay him $100, conditional on their subsequently making a sale of goods on credit; but we have not found such language to be practically convenient.[4] If A offers his goods

2. Restatement, Contracts, § 250, Comment *c:* "A duty of immediate performance exists when all things have happened and the necessary time has elapsed to make present performance by a promisor obligatory. A duty to make compensation and a right of action arise when performance has become immediately due and has not been rendered (see § 385, Comment). In some cases a right of action may arise before the time fixed for the stipulated performance (see §§ 315, 318)."

3. In Corson v. Mulvany, 49 Pa. 88 (1865), the court said: "If one contracts to purchase a vessel at sea upon her safe arrival in port, no one will dispute that the obligation to deliver on one side, and to pay on the other, arises upon her safe arrival. The vessel may never arrive, and the contract is not absolute to performance on either side till the contemplated contingency occurs; but the contract is binding and only awaits the event, to become binding also to performance."

4. In Kelly v. Grimshaw, 167 P.2d 627, 161 Kan. 253 (1946), a government contract provided that the contractors should pay a specified minimum wage to unskilled labor-

to B for $100, on thirty days credit, one more step has been taken; but we still do not say that A has a right to $100, conditional on B's acceptance and the delivery of the goods. As soon as the offer is accepted and there is mutual assent to the terms proposed, we use the term "contract" and we begin to talk about A's "right" to payment. This is true even though the money is not yet due and even though it may never become due.

If A has delivered the goods in exchange for B's promise to pay $100 in thirty days, we say that A has a "right" and that B is indebted, even though no societal remedy will be available until after the passage of thirty days time. This is a right to future performance, not a right to immediate performance. It is not usually called a "conditional" right, for the reason that the passage of time is regarded as a matter of such certainty that it is disregarded in description.[5]

Suppose that A delivered the goods in exchange for B's promise to pay $100 *if and when his ship comes in.* We still say that A has a right, even though there is one additional fact necessary

---

ers. It is not convenient usage to say that X, who is competent to do unskilled labor, has a conditional right to the minimum wage, even before he has been employed by the contractor. Too many operative facts are still lacking, including mutual expressions of assent to employment as unskilled laborer. After such employment, he would have the right of a third party beneficiary to payment of the minimum wage, conditional on his rendition of the service as agreed. If X is employed by the contractor as a watchman, he still has no right to the minimum wage, conditional or otherwise, if the work of "watchman" has been classified as not "unskilled labor."

**5.** The difference between "future" and "conditional" was recognized in Roman Law: "*Condicio* is a more important matter . . . a conditional obligation is one subject to an event both future and uncertain. . . . The first point to be considered in relation to conditions is the question of the attitude of the law to a conditional *obligatio* while the *condicio* was outstanding. There were many rules which resulted from the

proposition that pending satisfaction there was as yet no complete *obligatio.* . . . But the transaction was not a mere nullity, in the meantime. It could not be renounced (except in cases where a right of renunciation was a tacit or express term in the contract). The capacity to contract must have existed when the agreement was made. There was a *spes debitum iri* which passed to and against representatives. A conditional creditor could claim *bonorum separatio.* . . ." Buckland, Roman Law, 419 (1921).

Restatement, Contracts, § 250, Comment *c:* "The nature of the promisor's duties involves a further distinction. A duty arises whenever a contract is made. This duty is called absolute if nothing but lapse of time is necessary to make immediate performance by a promisor obligatory, since though time must elapse before performance need be rendered, lapse of time is not usually called a condition and is not so designated in the Restatement of this Subject. The duty is conditional when an event other than lapse of time must happen in order to make the duty one of immediate performance."

to a societal remedy, and even though that fact may never occur. The coming in of B's ship is this necessary fact; it is a condition precedent to A's right to immediate payment of $100. Now, we say that A has a conditional right. Such usage is convenient. Most of the facts necessary to judicial enforcement exist; and a shorthand descriptive term serves a useful purpose.

Fire insurance policies are valid contracts. They create rights in the insured, even though there may be several conditions precedent (such as loss by fire, proofs, inventories, appraisals, and the like) to a right that the insurer shall make an immediate payment.

An indorsement of a note is a valid contract, even though the holder's right is conditional on default, demand, and notice.[6]

The difference between a conditional right and an unconditional one is merely that in the latter case there are no necessary operative facts still to occur, while in the former case most of those facts exist but one of them (or a few of them) is missing.

In a similar way, any other legal relation may be conditional. The explanation is the same in character. There may be conditional powers, conditional privileges, and conditional immunities, although these terms are not so commonly used as are the terms conditional right and conditional duty.[7]

The terms "vested right" and "expectancy" are troublesome terms that have often been used to explain a decision without explaining it. The ideas behind them are so variable and uncertain as to make their use both deceptive and confusing. It is clear that the fact that rights are future and conditional does not prevent their recognition and protection; they are within the protection of the Constitutional provision against impairment of obligation by a State. A contract creating such rights is legally effective according to its terms; if the payment of money is promised therein, to either the promisee or a third party beneficiary, the existence of a "contract right" is not denied merely because

6. An employers liability statute provided that no action should be maintained unless notice of injury be given to employer within 30 days after the injury. Of this, the court says: "This notice . . . is a condition precedent to the right of action. It is not simply one of the steps in enforcing a right of action already existing, but is the last circumstance necessary to the creation of such right . . . it must precede the writ. . . . If it be said that the notice is given for the purpose of enforcing a right which, although not yet complete, is so far inchoate as to be beyond the power of the person against whom it may be enforced when made complete, it may be answered that such is the liability of an indorser upon a note, or any other contingent liability which depends upon an option to be exercised and made known by notice, as in the case of an agreement to renew a lease." Healey v. Blake Mfg. Co., 62 N.E. 270, 180 Mass. 270, (1902).

the money is payable in the future and only on the happening of an uncertain event or because some one has a power of termination or modification. If a right has to be "vested" in order to be recognized and protected, these rights are vested. It is immaterial whether the parties "expect" or "hope" that payment will take place. The holder of a fire insurance policy very seldom gets the money promised him, and yet he is not disappointed in his "expectations." He both hopes and expects that his house will *not* burn down; yet no one doubts that he has "rights" created by the policy contract.

## § 627. Condition Defined

Like all other words, the term "condition" is used in a variety of senses. There is no law against this; and there is no single "correct" definition. People can not be compelled to use a legal term in the sense preferred by the present writer or by the makers of a dictionary. A good dictionary attempts to report all usages that are common and respectable. The only basis for choice among definitions is the extent and the convenience of the usage. Without doubt, this results in ease and variety of expression; but in many instances, in which exactitude and clarity are especially needed, it results also in inexact thinking and in misunderstanding by others. It is to avoid such inexactness and misunderstanding that the term "condition," for use in the present work, is defined as an operative fact, one on which the existence of some particular legal relation depends.[8] In contract writing, it is often used as synonymous with "term," "provision," or "clause," a list of such provisions often being headed as "conditions of the contract." This will be strictly avoided in the present work.[9] The three words in quotation marks adequately supply the need of expression and accord with the most common usage; while there is no other word than "condition" to express the meaning herein adopted. This will appear more fully when we differentiate among conditions precedent, concurrent, and subsequent.

As the term condition is defined here, it is an "operative" fact or event. This means that it is a fact or event that affects legal

---

8.  Restatement, Contracts, § 250, states that a "condition is . . . either a fact (other than mere lapse of time) which (a) must exist or occur before a duty of immediate performance of a promise arises, in which case the condition is a 'condition precedent,' or (b) will extinguish a duty to make compensation for breach of contract after the breach has occurred, in which case the condition is a 'condition subsequent,' or a term in a promise providing that a fact shall have such an effect."

The last fifteen words of this definition were added to satisfy the demand of some critics who liked the alternative usage of the term; but in the Restatement itself the term "condition" is never used in this alternative sense. It is never used to mean a "term" of the contract— a mere group of words.

relations; it is a cause of some change in those legal relations. To say that the fact or event is a cause (or condition) of the change does not mean that it is the *sole* cause (or condition). It is merely one of the group of factors that are necessary to produce the change.[10]

The terms of a contract are all of its words, taken individually and also in groups known as phrases, clauses, sentences, and paragraphs. Anyone can, if he likes, use the word "conditions" to mean exactly this and nothing more; he will find common usage of the sort. Also, anyone can, if he likes, use the word to mean both this and other entirely different things, without stopping to consider or explain whether in any particular instance he means one or the other; again, he will find plenty of common usage as his warrant. But the test of success in the expression of an idea so as to induce that same idea in the minds of others is not solely common usage as to the words chosen for the purpose. So far as mere usage is concerned, it is common enough to be as opaque as mud, even though each word chosen has justifying usage.

Now, however beautiful and exact may be the usage and terminology of this book, comparatively few people will read it; and it is impossible to compel millions of contractors to conform to it. It will not even be possible to induce lawyers, and other supposedly skilled draftsmen of contracts and statutes and constitutions, to conform to it. The courts, and the lawyers and law writers, must take the raw material that is prepared for them by contractors and draftsmen and determine its meaning and operation. The problem is one of interpretation and construction and the problem now before this writer is to give aid in this process of interpretation and construction. Most assuredly, it is not to force meanings upon contractors that they did not intend, or to penalize them for not choosing their words according to a system that is more beautiful and exact.

The limited definition of the term "condition" that is adopted herein, in accordance with which the term will be used throughout, is supported by plenty of judicial usage.[11] The author is not

---

11.   Note the difference in usage in the two following instances. In Boone v. Eyre, 1 H.Bl. 273 (1777), the reporter of a decision by Lord Mansfield, feeling his way in the expression of a new rule of law, said: "Where mutual covenants go to the whole of the consideration on both sides, they are mutual conditions, the one precedent to the other." This sentence is sufficiently obscure in numerous respects, quite apart from its identifying "condition" with "covenant" and

indicating that each of them is "precedent" to the other. Seventy-five years later, Pollock, C. B. repeated the rule and attempted to apply it in Ellen v. Topp, 6 Exch. 424 (1851). He found it necessary to limit the application of the rule and also to reword it. He said that after a part performance, if the partial breach can be compensated in damages, "the covenant is independent and *the performance of it* is not a condition precedent." Thus, the "condition" of the duty

snatching the word out of its native tropical habitat and lifting it into the cold and unfamiliar region of the aurora borealis. Every sentence in which it is used will have a familiar ring to the reader; and the fact that it is used with a single and limited significance will make the text less difficult of interpretation by anyone accustomed to read law books.[12]

### § 628.  Condition Precedent and Condition Subsequent

Analysis and definition are of no importance unless they render us a service in solving problems, advising clients, and determining what courts should and will do.  We do not care what a "condition" is, or how a condition precedent differs from a condition subsequent, unless such knowledge renders the desired service.  It is clear, however, that we need to know whether A has a right against B, whether that right is a right to immediate performance by B, whether non-performance by B is a breach of duty making available a judicial remedy.  In order to satisfy this need, we must know what facts will create these rights and will induce the giving of the judicial remedy.  It is merely a mode of stating this question when we ask What are the conditions precedent to A's right to immediate performance by B and to the obtaining of a judicial remedy for B's non-performance.  It is a matter of utter indifference to anyone what is a "condition precedent" in the abstract or in vacuo.  Indeed, no such thing exists.  The term "condition precedent" is an expression of a relation between two facts, a relation between facts and the action of a court.  In general, therefore, we wish to know what are the facts necessary to justify putting court machinery in motion in favor of A against B.  These are the "conditions precedent" to A's right to immediate performance, to B's instant duty to perform, to any breach of duty by B, and to remedial action by the court.

So, therefore, this abstruse and unattractive process of analysis and definition turns out to be only a mode of describing the very practical and interesting things that we need to know in order to gain our ends in life.

Before A has a *contract* right to an immediate performance by B, a contract must have been made.  We have already considered the mode of making it.  Various facts must exist and events

of one promisor was the *performance* that was promised by the other, not his *promise* to render the performance.

12.  This is not to say that the reader may not find the author's text obscure for other reasons, or that the reader may not himself add to its obscurity by giving to the author's words meanings other than those that he intended to convey.  But the probability of misunderstanding is at least doubled when the author uses an important term in two or more senses, often without making clear in his own mind the thought that he is trying to express.

must take place. These facts and events, such as legal capacity, offer, acceptance, consideration, delivery, etc., are conditions precedent to A's right and remedy. Nevertheless, it is not customary to refer to them as conditions precedent, and we shall adhere to custom in this treatise.[13] Assuming the occurrence and existence of these particular conditions precedent, assuming that a valid contract has been made, we focus our attention on those additional facts and events necessary to A's case against B, facts and events subsequent to the making of the contract but precedent to A's right to immediate performance. It is these facts and events that by custom are called conditions precedent.[14]

The words precedent and subsequent express relationship in time. Any fact or event is precedent to what comes after and is subsequent to what has gone before. Therefore, before speaking of a conditioning fact or event as a condition precedent or a condition subsequent we must know what it is to which we are relating it. Precedent to *what*? Subsequent to *what*? Until we have answered this question, it is meaningless to describe a fact or event as a condition precedent or a condition subsequent. And by relating it both to something in the future and to some other thing in the past it may properly be described as both a condition precedent and a condition subsequent. The use of these two terms is often very puzzling; and the reason is that they are used with respect to a fact or event, without indicating in any definite way what it is to which it is being related.[15]

Sometimes an equitable remedy is available even though there has been no breach of duty; but generally the remedy must follow breach. This is true of the most common remedy of all—a judgment for money damages. In general, therefore, it is the right to immediate performance of a promise to which it is convenient to relate our conditioning facts.[16]

14. Restatement, Contracts, § 250, Comment *d:* "The 'fact' which according to the definition constitutes a condition most commonly is the occurrence of an event after the formation of a contract, as where an insurance policy is conditional on a specified kind of future loss, but the fact sometimes relates to the past, as where a marine policy insures against a loss that may already have occurred, and sometimes to the present, as where present soundness is a condition under a contract to buy a horse. The fact also may be either a fortuitous event or a voluntary act by one party or the other."

15. That the confusion between conditions precedent and conditions subsequent is both ancient and respectable, in property law as well as in contract law, witness 2 Coke's Inst. ch. 27, 11: "Many are of opinion against Littleton in this case . . . and that here Littleton of a condition precedent doth make it subsequent." Coke states the arguments *pro* and *con,* and then adds: "*Benigne lector, utere tuo judicio, nihil enim impedio.*"

16. Observe clearly that this whole matter of analysis and definition is merely one of convenience. **Any**

Conditions precedent, for our present purposes, are those facts and events, occurring subsequently to the making of a valid contract, that must exist or occur before there is a right to immediate performance, before there is a breach of contract duty, before the usual judicial remedies are available.[17]

Conditions subsequent, for our present purposes, are those facts and events that occur after breach of contract duty and that terminate the right to immediate performance and also the right to a judicial remedy.[18]  The term could be used to denote those facts

other mode of analysis and definition could be adopted without violating any rule or canon except that of practical convenience. Indeed, it may well be that in some cases another sort of analysis and other definitions and usages of words would be more convenient and serviceable. When such is the case, we should shift our method and be conscious of the fact that we are shifting and of the reasons for doing so.

In the law of property, conditions precedent and subsequent are generally related to the group of property relations called "title" or "ownership." A will or deed is executed providing for the creation of an estate in land on the happening of some condition—a condition precedent to the "estate," or providing for the immediate creation of an estate subject to be divested on the happening of some condition—a condition subsequent to the "estate." See Carpender v. City of New Brunswick, 39 A.2d 40, 135 N.J.Eq. 397 (1944), for a discussion of these terms with respect to the vesting and divesting of an estate, the court finding its definitions in Coke or Littleton.

17.    The following are illustrations:

I promise to pay such an amount as X may determine:

Mass.—Old Colony Ry. v. Brockton Ry., 218 Mass. 84, 105 N.E. 866 (1914).

Eng.—Thurnell v. Balbirnie, 2 M. & W. 786 (1837, Ex.); Scott v. Avery, 5 H.L.Cas. 811 (1856).

I promise to pay as soon as I am able:

N.Y.—Work v. Beach, 13 N.Y.S. 678, 59 Hun 625 (1891).

See also Ulpian, Dig. 2, 14, 49.

I promise to pay after architect X has certified that the work is properly done:

N.Y.—Granger Co. v. Brown-Ketcham Iron Works, 97 N.E. 523, 204 N.Y. 218 (1912).

Eng.—Clarke v. Watson, 18 C.B.N.S. 278 (1865).

Cf. Nolan v. Whitney, 88 N.Y. 648 (1882).

We promise to buy and to sell (specified goods) if the Government issues a permit: Atlas Trading Corp. v. Grossman, 169 F.2d 240 (C.A.3d, 1948).

In these cases the determination by X, the financial ability, the architect's certificate and the issuance of a permit are facts that operate as conditions precedent to the legal duty to pay, although all of these facts are subsequent in time to the creation of a valid contract.

18.    Examples of conditions subsequent to the secondary obligation and terminating it are to be found in:

U.S.—Semmes v. Hartford Ins. Co., 13 Wall. 158, 20 L.Ed. 490 (1871).

Conn.—Chambers v. Atlas Ins. Co., 51 Conn. 17 (1883).

Iowa—Read v. Insurance Co., 72 N. W. 665, 103 Iowa 307 (1897).

Or.—Ward v. Warren, 74 P. 482, 44 Or. 102 (1903).

Eng.—Smart v. Hyde, 8 M. & W. 723 (1841, Ex.).

and events that occur after a contract has been made and operate as its discharge and termination, without regard to whether there has been a breach or not. By this usage, the facts and events would be related to the primary contractual rights and duties, rather than to the right and duty of immediate performance and the breach thereof. Since the issue that is involved in nearly every litigated case is whether or not a contract *has been breached*, not merely whether or not it *has been made*, it is more convenient and more consistent with judicial usage to relate conditioning facts and events to the *right and duty of immediate performance* and the breach thereof. As used herein, conditions will be either precedent to the duty of immediate performance (and its breach) or subsequent to that duty (and its breach). [19]

## § 629.  Concurrent Conditions

The mutual duties of the parties to a bilateral contract may be concurrently conditional, in which case the conditions are sometimes described as conditions concurrent. This situation does not exist unless the agreement requires the simultaneous performance of the mutual promises. Such is the case when A and B mutually agree upon the simultaneous exchange of some chattel for a price in money.[20] The promise of each is conditional upon a tender of performance by the other; the duty to deliver the chattel is conditional upon tender of the price, and the duty to pay is conditional upon tender of the chattel. Observe that in each case the duty to render immediate performance is subject to a condition precedent. No condition is ever "concurrent" with the legal relation that it helps to create.[21]

Either or both of the promises in a bilateral contract may be independent of the other and not conditional at all; but usually the promises of a simultaneous exchange of performances are not thus independent. When they are mutually dependent and con-

For instances of a condition subsequent to the primary obligation, its non-occurrence being a condition precedent to the secondary obligation, see:

Mass.—Gray v. Gardner, 17 Mass. 188 (1821).

Ohio—Moody v. Amazon Ins. Co., 38 N.E. 1011, 52 Ohio St. 12 (1894).

19.    See Restatement, Contracts, § 250, quoted previously.

21.    This is why the Contracts Restatement, in § 251, says that "a concurrent condition is a condition precedent which exists only when parties to a contract are bound to render performances at the same time," with a following comment saying, "Concurrent condition is an elliptical expression for a condition precedent where performances are due at the same time." The section proceeds: "and the fact constituting the condition is, in the alternative, either (a) performance by one party before performance by the other, or (b) an offer, accompanied with manifested present ability to make it good, to perform if the other party simultaneously performs.

ditional, either party can put the other in default only by rendering actual performance himself or by tendering such performance so as to assure the other party that the exchange will be simultaneous.[22]

## § 630. Contractual Duty Not Discharged Merely because it is Not Yet Enforceable

A contractual promise may not yet be enforceable, while at the same time the legal duty that it created may not yet be discharged. A party to a transaction may ask his lawyer the following questions: (1) Was a valid contract made? (2) Can I now maintain action against the other party for breach of contract? (3) Has his contractual duty or my own been discharged and terminated?

With the first of these questions we have dealt in the previous chapters. We are at present dealing with the second question. The third question will be given detailed consideration in subsequent chapters. Nevertheless, the second question is closely related to the third; and in discussing the "conditions" of legal duty we may at times also use terms of "discharge." But the fact that a condition of a party's promissory duty has not yet occurred or been performed does not show that that duty has been terminted and discharged; it merely shows that the party has not yet committed a "breach" of his duty and that an action may not yet be maintainable against him. If it appears that the "condition" of his duty has become impossible of performance, it is proper to say that his duty has been discharged; but as long as it is still possible of performance he can assert no more than that he is not guilty of a breach, not that he has been discharged from duty.

At present, therefore, we shall be dealing primarily with the facts and events that must exist or occur after a contract has been made but before a "breach" can be asserted and before there is a "right of action" for breach.[23]

Certain judicial remedies may be available and an action for them maintainable even before any "breach" of contractual duty has occurred and while the duty in question is still future and conditional. There may be sufficient reason for determining the validity of a contract before it has been broken and for preventing a breach before it has occurred. Justiciable disputes arise as to the legal operation of an agreement, promise, or transaction before anyone is charged with committing a "breach;" and the harm to be caused by an imminent breach may be such that it ought to be prevented rather than to be compensated after it oc-

22. Where a payment and the conveyance are to be concurrent, if neither party makes tender neither is in default, even though the day fixed for the exchange of performances has passed. Weiser v. Rowe, 170 N.W. 753, 185 Iowa 501 (1919).

curs.  For these purposes, declaratory judgments and equitable remedies are available.

## § 631.  Express Conditions and Implied Conditions

What is it that causes a fact or event to be a condition precedent to a duty of immediate performance of a promise, or a condition subsequent that will discharge such a duty?  First and foremost, it may be made such a condition by agreement of the parties, expressed in definite language when the contract is made.  The condition is then called an "express" condition.  But contractors can "express" their intentions otherwise than by the use of specific words.  Just as parties can make promises without using words to do so, they can also express an intention that a fact or event shall be a condition of legal duty without putting it into words.[24]  Just as we have promises implied in fact, so also there are conditions that are implied in fact.  Such promises and conditions are really express promises and express conditions, using the word "express" in a broad but quite reasonable sense.  However, the distinction between expression by words and expression by conduct other than words is of importance, justifying the use of the two words "express" and "implied."  It serves a purpose; and it causes no misunderstanding except when the word "implied" is used to include cases in which the parties had and expressed no intention whatever.  "Implied" promises of this latter kind are now usually referred to as "quasi contracts," and such "implied" conditions are now usually called "constructive" conditions.[25]

## § 632.  Constructive Conditions

A fact or event may be a condition of a contractual right or duty, even though the parties had no intention that it should so operate, said nothing about it in words, and did nothing from which an inference of intention can be drawn.  When such is the case, the condition is one that can be described as neither an express condition nor an implied condition.  Such a fact or event will be called herein a constructive condition.[26]  It is operative as

24.  See discussion of the process of Implication in Chapter 25.

25.  Restatement, Contracts, § 252, defines thus: "An express condition is a condition that is such because a promise or agreement so provides."  This wording is such as to include implications of fact as well as definite words.  The term "implied condition" is not used and is not defined.

26.  Restatement, Contracts, § 253, reads: "A constructive condition is a condition that is such because of a rule of law, and is not based on interpretation of a promise or agreement."  The present writer believes that many constructive conditions are held to be such by a court even though there is no antecedent "rule of law" that is applicable to it. Out of such hold-

a condition for the reason that courts have held or will hold it so on grounds of justice that are independent of expressed intention. Frequently, however, the holding of the court will be so stated as to make it appear that it is based upon a "presumed" intention or even upon actual intention that is discovered by some mysterious kind of interpretation or inference.[27] In many cases, indeed, it may be difficult to determine whether the parties intended such a condition or not; and this need not be determined at all if the court is willing to hold that justice requires the condition whether the parties intended it or not.

Suppose that A contracts to render personal service for B for a period of one year. Neither party thinks of the possibility that A will be stricken with an incapacitating illness; and A's promise to serve is absolute and unconditional in form. A's duty to serve will be held to be conditional upon the existence of a reasonable degree of physical health. By construction of law, it is a condition of A's duty to serve. This has been held to be so in so many cases that a "rule of law" has been constructed and is regularly applied. Had it occurred to their minds, it may well be that the parties would have intended that A's duty should be conditional on his physical health; but this fact does not make the condition one that is implied in fact, or one that is such by reason of interpretation of their words and conduct.[28]

ings, however, a "rule of law" soon grows, one that will govern in like cases. The principal "rule of law" is merely this, that a promisor should not be penalized for non-performance if, because of some fact or event for which the parties did not provide, that mores and practices of men make it "unjust" to require performance.

27. "Supposing a contract to have been duly formed, what is its result? An obligation has been created between the contracting parties, by which rights are conferred upon the one and duties are imposed upon the other, partly stipulated for in the agreement, but partly also implied by law, which, as Bentham observes (Works, III, 190), 'has thus in every country supplied the shortsightedness of individuals, by doing for them what they would have done for themselves, if their imagination had anticipated the march of nature.'"

Holland, Jurisp. (10th ed.) 278. In Leonard v. Dyer, 26 Conn. 172, 178 (1857) the court said: "And if we were to add stipulations to the contract which the parties themselves did not make, it appears to us that such only should be inferred as the parties themselves would have made, had they foreseen the circumstances that rendered such stipulations important." See also Bankes, L. J., in Groves v. Webb, 114 L. T. Rep. 1082, 1089 (1916, C.A.).

"You can always imply a condition in a contract. But why do you imply it? It is because of some belief as to the practice of the community or of a class, or because of some opinion as to policy, or, in short, because of some attitude of yours upon a matter not capable of exact quantitative measurement, and therefore not capable of founding exact logical conclusions." Justice O. W. Holmes, The Path of the Law, 10 Harv.L.Rev. 466 (1897).

In the modern cases dealing with Impossibility of performance, especially those using the phrase "Frustration of Contract," there has been much discussion of the use and meaning of the words "implied term" and "implied condition." Frequently the court has said that the "implication" is nothing other than an honest interpretation of the expressions of the contracting parties, by which their actual meaning is discovered, that the court can not "make contracts for the parties," and that "no court has an absolving power."[29] In other cases it is declared that the court is merely drawing an "inference" as to what the parties themselves would have provided if they had foreseen subsequent events.[30] In the more recent cases the courts are beginning to see and to admit that the finding of an "implied term" or an "implied condition" is frequently a pure construction by the court itself for the purpose of attaining a "just" result under circumstances that the parties did not foresee and as to which they had no ideas and made no provision.[31]

## § 633.  Promise and Condition Distinguished

From the definitions already given, it is obvious that promise and condition are very clearly different in character. One who makes a promise thereby expresses an intention that some future performance will be rendered and gives assurance of its rendition to the promisee. Whether the promise is express or implied, there must be either words or conduct by the promisor by the interpretation of which the court can discover promissory intention; a condition is a fact or an event and is not an expression of intention or an assurance. A promise in a contract creates a legal duty in the promisor and a right in the promisee; the fact or event con-

28.    This is recognized by the House of Lords in Fibrosa Spolka Ackyjna v. Fairbairn L. C. B. Ltd. [1943] A.C. 32, [1942] 2 All Eng. 122, a case in which a seller's duty to deliver machines in Poland was discharged by outbreak of the second World War; it was held that he must make restitution of the part of the price paid in advance.

29.    See Lord Loreburn, in Tamplin S. S. Co. v. Anglo-American Petr. Prod., [1916] 2 A.C. 397.

30.    See supra, quotations from Bentham and from the court's opinion in Leonard v. Dyer, 26 Conn. 172 (1857). Numerous English opinions have contained similar expressions.

They were effectively criticised by Lord Sumner in Hirji Mulji v. Cheong Yue S. S. Co., [1926] A.C. 497.

31.    See especially, Lord Wright in Denny, Mott, & Dickson v. Fraser, [1944] A.C. 265, 1 All Eng. 678; the full review of the cases and the various theories in Webber, "The Effect of War on Contracts, ed. 2 (1946), Parts III and IV; and the keen analysis by Dr. Glanville Williams in his article on "Language and the Law—IV," 61 Law Q.Rev. 400–406.

This is considered more fully in chapters 74 and 77 dealing with Impossibility of Performance and "Frustration of Contract."

stituting a condition creates no right or duty and is merely a limiting or modifying factor.

This may be illustrated by the early case of Constable v. Cloberie.[32] In this case, there was a bilateral contract in which the plaintiff expressly promised to sail with the next favoring wind with a cargo supplied by the defendant. The latter promised to pay a specified sum as freight if the ship went the intended voyage and returned to the Downs. The plaintiff succeeded in making the voyage and returning; but he had not kept his promise to sail with the next wind. The court held, nevertheless, that the freight was due and payable. The plaintiff had promised to sail with the next wind, and committed a breach of that promise; but sailing with the next wind was not a condition of the defendant's duty to pay freight. Making the voyage and returning to the Downs was expressly made a condition precedent to the defendant's duty to pay freight; but the plaintiff made no promise that the voyage and return would be successfully accomplished.

To put a contract in this form would be entirely reasonable to-day; but there were special reasons for doing so in 1626. Long voyages then were perilous and uncertain, so that the shipowner did not wish to be liable in damages if his ship should be lost. He was quite willing, however, to make the lesser promise that his ship would sail promptly with the next favorable wind. On the other hand, although starting promptly was desirable it was not of vital importance and did not go to the "essence" of the shipper's trading venture. In 1626 all voyages were by sail and were long and slow; the goods shipped were not perishables. Also, markets were steady and not quickly variable as in the present days of radio, railway refrigeration, and transport planes. So, therefore, a contract was made whereby the shipowner risked his ship and his freight against the non-completion of the voyage back to the Downs and the shipper risked his goods and his profits against the perils of the sea as well as against the absence of a market at destination. The promise to sail promptly was thrown in by the shipowner for good measure, but was not regarded as of essential importance by either party. It might be quite otherwise as to this, under modern conditions of transport.

A promise is always made by the act or acts of one of the parties, such acts being words or other conduct expressing intention; a fact can be made to operate as a condition only by the agreement of both parties or by the construction of the law. The purpose of a promise is the creation of a duty in the promisor; the purpose of constituting some fact as a condition is always the postponement

32. Palmer 397 (1626), also reported in Latch, 12, 49, and in Popham, 161.

or discharge of an instant duty (or other specified legal relation). The non-fulfilment of a promise is called a breach of contract, and creates in the other party a secondary right to damages; it is the failure to perform that which was required by a legal duty. The non-occurrence of a condition will prevent the existence of a duty in the other party; but it may not create any remedial rights and duties at all, and it will not unless someone has promised that it shall occur.[33]

Of course a contract can be so made as to create a duty that the fact operative as a condition shall come into existence. If in Constable v. Cloberie the plaintiff had promised to make the voyage and return, we should have a case where the future existence of the fact (voyage and return) was expressly promised by the plaintiff and was also a condition precedent to any instant duty of the defendant to pay. The non-performance would then have double operation, on the one hand preventing any instant duty in the defendant to pay freight and on the other creating a secondary duty in the plaintiff to pay damages. Such a condition might be described as a promissory condition.[34]

---

33.    Restatement, Contracts, § 260: "If in an agreement words that state that an act is to be performed purport to be the words of the person who is to do the act, the words are interpreted, unless a contrary intention has been manifested, as a promise by that person to perform the act. If the words purport to be those of a party who is not to do the act they are interpreted, unless a contrary intention has been manifested, as limiting the promise of that party by making performance of the act a condition."

34.    See Home Ins. Co. v. Union Trust Co., 100 A. 1010, 40 R.I. 367 L.R.A.1917F, 375 (1917), holding that a certain proviso created a condition but was not a promise and created no duty.

Also Coykendall v. Blackmer, 146 N. Y.S. 631, 161 App.Div. 11 (1914).

For cases holding that the particular proviso was promissory and created a duty and did not merely create a condition of the other party's duty, see:

Kan.—Boston S. D. Co. v. Thomas, 53 P. 472, 59 Kan. 470 (1898).

N.D.—St. Paul F. & M. I. Co. v. Upton, 50 N.W. 702, 2 N.D. 229, (1891).

Restatement, Contracts, § 257, reads: "Failure of a condition to exist or to occur, even though the condition is some performance by a party to the contract, is not a breach of contractual duty by him unless he has made an enforceable promise that the condition exists or shall occur. Whether he has done so is a question of interpretation."

In Constable v. Cloberie, supra, failure to sail with the next wind was a breach of duty because it was promised, yet it was not the non-performance of a condition of the defendant's duty to pay freight; failure to go the voyage and return would not have been a breach of duty because it was not promised, but it would have been the non-performance of a condition of the defendant's duty to pay.

There are numerous cases in which the parties to a contract expressly promised to submit disputes to arbitration, yet in which the plaintiff was held able to maintain suit in spite of his refusal to arbitrate. The "express promise" did not

The word "covenant" has come to be not much more than a synonym of "promise," although once its only proper meaning may have been a formal promise under seal. Whether a covenant is a formal promise, or an informal promise, or both, it is not itself a "condition" of the duty of the covenantee to keep his return promise or "covenant." But the *performance* of a covenant, or other promise, may be such a condition, either express or constructive. A landlord who promised in the lease to grant a renewal, "upon the lessee's paying rent and performing his covenants," made such performance a condition.[35]

It may be observed that both a promise and a condition are means that are used to bring about certain desired action by another person. For example, an insurance company desires the payment of premiums. One means of securing this desired object would be to obtain a promise by the insured to pay premiums; on failure to pay them an action would lie. In fact, however, insurance policies seldom contain such a promise; the payment of the premiums is secured in a more effective way than that. The insurance company makes its own duty to pay the amount of the policy expressly conditional upon the payment of premiums. Here is no express promise of the insured creating a duty to pay premiums, but there is an express condition precedent to his right to recover on the policy. Payment by the insured is obtained not by holding a lawsuit over him in terrorem, but by hanging before him a purse of money to be reached only by climbing the ladder of premiums.

The first step, therefore, in interpreting an expression in a contract, with respect to condition as opposed to promise, is to ask oneself the question: Was this expression intended to be an assurance by one party to the other that some performance by the first would be rendered in the future and that the other could rely upon it? If the answer is yes, we have found the expression to be a promise that the specified performance will take place. The alternative question to be asked is: "Was this expression intended to make the duty of one party conditional and dependent upon some performance by the other (or on some other fact or event)? If the answer to this question is yes, we have found that the specified performance is a condition of duty, but we have not found that anyone has promised that the performance will take place. It is not difficult to draw the logical distinction be-

make arbitration an "express condition." See:

U.S.—Hamilton v. Home Ins. Co., 11 S.Ct. 133, 137 U.S. 370, 34 L.Ed. 708 (1890); Oregon Short Line R. Co. v. Teton Coal Co., 35 F.2d 919 (C.C.A.9th, 1929); Aktieselskabet, etc., Co. v. Rederiaktiebolaget Atlanten, 232 F. 403 (D.C.N.Y.1916).

Mass.—Brocklehurst & P. Co. v. Marsch, 113 N.E. 646, 225 Mass. 3 (1916).

tween a promise that a specified performance will be rendered, and a provision that makes a specified performance a condition of the legal duty of a party who promises to render another performance. The first creates a legal duty in the promisor; the second limits and postpones a promisor's duty. Often the contracting parties do not make this logical distinction and therefore so word their agreements as to make interpretation difficult. When such is the case, the court is free to give the contract the "construction" that appears to be the most reasonable and just.[36]

### § 634.  Can a Condition be "Broken"?

Not infrequently courts may speak of a "right of action for condition broken." Such usage makes "condition" the equivalent of promise. Breach of contract is always the non-performance of some duty created by a promise. In the sense adopted herein, a condition should not be described as "broken." The condition merely does not exist or does not occur. If the condition consists of action by some person, it may properly be said not to be performed; but such non-performance is not a breach of contract unless he promised to render the performance—to perform the condition. If A promises to deliver goods, and in return B promises to pay $100 ten days after delivery, non-delivery by A is both a breach of his promise and the non-performance of a condition precedent to B's duty to pay. If an insurance company issues a unilateral policy contract to pay loss sixty days after a fire and proof made, a fire and making proof are conditions of the company's duty; but nobody has promised to perform them. The non-occurrence of a fire is not a "breach of condition" or a breach of contract; nor is the non-performance by the insured of the act of making proof.[37]

In view of the uncertainties and inconsistencies of language, especially the variation in the usages of terms, it must not be asserted here that there is no such thing as a "breach of condition." Too much depends upon the meaning given to "condition" and to

36. Southern Surety Co. v. MacMillan Co., 58 F.2d 541 (C.C.A.10th, 1932), is a case in which the distinction is well understood and clearly discussed. The words of a contract were "Provided that notice of default shall be given"; but failure to give the notice was held to be a mere breach of promise and not the non-performance of a condition of the duty of the Surety to pay a loss. It is not so certain, however, that the majority judges made the right choice between the two alternatives; and if they did not the decision was unjustly expensive to the Surety.

37. Restatement, Contracts, § 257: "Failure of a condition to exist or to occur even though the condition is some performance by a party to the contract, is not a breach of contractual duty by him unless he has made an enforceable promise that the condition exists or shall occur. Whether he has done so is a question of interpretation."

"breach." It is explicitly asserted, however, that as the terms are used in this treatise there is never a "breach of condition;" because "breach" is used to mean nonperformance of something promised, and "condition" means a "fact of event" on which some legal duty is dependent. In interpreting contracts drawn by others, it is necessary for this author, as for the courts, to determine the usage of the contracting parties, however different it may be from his own, and to give full legal effect to their meaning and intention.

Moreover, it must always be borne in mind that a performance that one party promises may also be a condition of the other party's legal duty; so that failure by A to perform would be a breach of contract by A and would prevent B's failure to pay from being a breach of contract by B. Interpretation and construction are made more difficult by the fact that both a promise and a condition of a promissory duty may be either "implied" or "express" and may be either actually agreed upon by the parties or an outright construction by the court in its quest for justice. But the fact that it is necessary for us to seek the meaning of the parties as expressed in their obscure, elliptical, and variable language, does not justify an author or a court in adopting and using a similar obscurity, ellipsis, and inconsistency.[38]

Striking illustrations of the existing variable usage may be found in that common but also variable contract called a "bond." Where an obligor gave bond to assure certain performances on condition that the obligee would build a railroad, it was found that by accepting such a bond the obligee (not the bond obligor) impliedly promised to build the railroad.[39] Here the obligee promised and the obligor's duty was conditional. This is quite dif-

---

38. A case in which the obscurity of its terminology is very obvious and caused great trouble to the court and cost to the litigants is McNeal-Edwards Co. v. Frank L. Young Co., 51 F.2d 699 (C.C.A.1st, 1931). Space will not be taken here to make a re-analysis of the case, although many of the court's statements (partly taken from Massachusetts opinions) will not bear such analysis. In the first place the District Court had made a correct decision. This was reversed, as reported in 35 F.2d 829, with an opinion wholly erroneous. Thereafter, the District Court again rendered a correct decision. This was again erroneously reversed, as reported in 42 F.2d 362.

This reversal was itself reversed by the U. S. Supreme Court, on a jurisdictional point. 51 S.Ct. 538, 283 U.S. 398, 75 L.Ed. 1140. Now considering the District Court's judgment on the merits, the Circuit Court of Appeals correctly reverses its original opinion and affirms that judgment. A seller's duty to pay $10,730 damages for breach of a warranty of quality of oil sold was not discharged by the buyer's subsequent wilful failure to return promptly the empty oil drums, to the seller's damage found to be $100. Of course, the return of the drums was not a condition of the seller's duty to ship oil as warranted.

ferent from the ordinary "penal" bond, where the obligor binds himself to pay a sum of money, this obligation on "condition" to be void if he builds a house properly. This has long since been interpreted to be a promise by the obligor to build the house.[40]

In the case of an ordinary bilateral contract for the exchange of property for money, the duty of immediate performance by either party is generally conditional on a tender of the exchange performance by the other. If neither one makes such a tender neither one is guilty of a breach of legal duty (in the absence of a repudiation). If time of performance was expressly made "of the essence," failure to make tender within that time operates as a discharge of the other party; but the failure is not itself a breach of contract. In Louisiana, where the usage as to "conditions" is derived from Roman and French law, such a failure has been described as a "passive breach." [41]

## § 635. Presumption That Words are Promissory Rather Than That They Create a Condition of Duty

In discussing the difference between a unilateral contract and a bilateral contract, it is sometimes said that where the expressions used by the parties are doubtful the presumption is in favor of a contract bilateral in character.[42] The reason for such a presumption is that, where some performance is still to be rendered, the party to be benefited thereby usually desires an assurance that such performance will take place. This means that he desires a "promise"; and, as the other party has reason to know, it means that he understands that a promise is being given. He thereby obtains, under our legal and social system, an assurance that is backed by our societal organization.

The expressions of the parties may, indeed, be so clear that a promise of the particular performance is not being made that they negative the presumption above stated. If it is clear that they intend a unilateral contract, then the specified performance is a condition. One promise is being made; but the promisor will not be bound by any legal duty until the specified performance is rendered, or at least is begun or tendered.

Of course, it is quite possible that a valid unilateral contract may exist even though the specified performance has not yet been begun. A single promise may be a binding unilateral contract because it is under seal or because there is some other fully executed consideration. Thus, most insurance policies are valid unilateral contracts, either because they are under seal, or because the first premium has been paid by the insured, or for both reasons. Nevertheless, certain performances may be specified that are still to be rendered by the insured. If the reasonable in-

---

39. **Colo.**—Pueblo & A. V. R. Co. v. Taylor, 6 Colo. 1 (1881).

42. See Restatement, Contracts, § 31.

terpretation is that these performances are promised by the insured, the insurance contract is not a unilateral contract.  Both parties have made promises and both parties have assumed legal duties.  The reasonable interpretation, based on clear expressions or on common usage and understanding, may be quite otherwise, so that the insured has made no promise.  It is in cases in which this process of interpretation reaches no such definite conclusion that the presumption is indulged that the specified performances are merely being promised and are not conditions of the existence or continuance of legal duty.[43]

From the foregoing, it appears that the supposed presumption of promise rather than condition will not often be the decisive matter in a case.  Such a presumption does not relieve the court of the necessity of interpretation; and the process of interpretation will usually be decisive without making use of this presumption.  The most that can be said for it is that it is more usual to promise a performance than to make that performance merely a condition of another's duty, and that this fact is one of those that play a part in the process of interpretation.[44]

The fireproof safe provision that was contained in numberless fire insurance policies has afforded unusual opportunities for interpretation.  As reported in one case, it reads thus: "The assured will keep such books and last inventory  .  .  .  in a fireproof safe at night  .  .  .; or, failing in this, the assured will keep such books  .  .  .  in some place not exposed to a fire which would ignite or destroy the building; and in case of loss, the assured specifically warrants, agrees, and covenants to produce such books for the inspection of the company.  In the event of failure on the part of the assured to keep and produce such books, this entire policy shall become null and void, and such failure shall constitute a perpetual bar to any recovery thereon."  Without question, this language makes some fact a condition precedent to the duty of the insurer to pay the amount of a loss.  It is not so clear, just what that fact is.  In one case, the assured kept his books at night in a trunk above the store that was insured, so that they were burned along with the store; and the court properly held that the company was not bound to pay.[45]

43.  In a contract where the parties promised to settle disputes amicably and also to arbitrate disputes if any should arise, it was held that an attempt at amicable settlement, though promised, was not a condition precedent to the duty to arbitrate.  Britex Waste Co. v. Schwab, 12 A.2d 473, 139 Pa. Super. 474 (1940).

Restatement, Contracts, § 261: "Where it is doubtful whether words create a promise or an express condition, they are interpreted as creating a promise; but the same words may sometimes mean that one party promises a performance and that the other party's promise is conditional on that performance."

45.  Kan.—Hammond  v.  Niagara Fire Ins. Co., 142 P. 936, 92 Kan. 851 (1914).

In another case, the assured took his books home with him at night, so that they were not burned in the fire; the court held that this fulfilled the required condition precedent and that the insurer must pay, even though the books disappeared in some other fashion and were never produced.[46]

If both of these decisions can be justified, as it is believed they can, the provision above quoted was not meant to make actual production of the books after the fire a condition precedent, in spite of the words in the last quoted sentence in the provision. If such actual production was intended as a condition precedent, why should the insurer also include careful provisions for keeping the books in a safe or in a place not exposed to fire? It would be to the direct interest of the company to have the books kept in a bale of hay and burned up. The requirement of a fireproof safe indicates that the intended condition of duty to pay was no more than the keeping of the books in the fashion that was so carefully described. This is a matter of interpretation; and the whole provision must be interpreted together. If the policy had merely stated that it should be void in case of failure to produce the books after the fire, the decision ought to be otherwise.

A further question that might arise as to this fireproof safe provision, but probably never has arisen is this: Did the assured promise the insurer that he would keep the books in the manner specified, so that the insurer could maintain an action for breach of duty in case of his failure to do so? The answer to this question is believed to be No, even though the words are "the assured specifically warrants, agrees, and covenants to produce such books." It is true that, in general, these words are words of promise. But if the keeping the books as strictly specified is a condition of the insurer's duty to pay, the failure to keep them so does no harm to the insurer. The insurer is much better secured and protected by having a condition precedent to its duty to pay than by having a promise by the assured to keep the books in a safe. Such a promise would render no service to the insurer and, so far as it is concerned, would better be broken than kept. Therefore, it is reasonable to believe that the whole provision, including the words "warrants, agrees, and covenants," was drafted for the single purpose of creating the protective condition precedent and not for the purpose of creating a right to damages in case of non-performance. This does, indeed, require us to suppose that the insurer's draftsman did not mean what the three quoted words, standing alone, seem to mean, and that he had never clearly distinguished between a promise and a condition in his own mind. This is not a violent supposition, since he has had much distinguished company.

46.   **U.S.**—Liverpool & London & Globe Ins. Co. v. Kearney, 21 S.Ct. 326, 180 U.S. 132, 45 L.Ed. 460 (1901).

In leases and other conveyances, the question often arises whether a provision is operative as no more than a promissory covenant that certain things shall be done, or as one that makes nonperformance a condition subsequent on the happening of which the property interest is extinguished. The latter interpretation will be avoided, if possible, because the courts dislike an interpretation the effect of which will be what they regard as a "forfeiture." [47]

## § 636. Promises to Pay Money Out of Funds yet to be Acquired

If one promises to pay money out of funds yet to be acquired, the problem arises whether the acquisition of the fund is a condition of the promisor's duty to pay or whether the provision should be interpreted as a promise that the fund will be acquired. If the promise is to pay an already existing debt out of a fund to be raised in some specified manner, it is very likely to be interpreted as a promise to pay the debt within the time reasonably required for the raising of the money. If so interpreted, an action will lie for a non-performance of the promise after the expiration of such reasonable time, even though the fund has not actually come into existence.[48] Of course, if the debt has an independent existence and its collection has not been barred in any way, an action will lie for its collection without making use of a new conditional promise at all. In such a case the new promise may be given as a mere pledge of the funds to be collected, or as a mere collateral promise to assure the creditor that payment will be made.

If the promise is to pay a debt that has been barred by statute of limitations or has been discharged in bankruptcy and is to pay the debt as soon as financially able or out of some fund to be acquired, the acquisition of the money is usually held to be a condition precedent to an enforceable duty to pay.[49]

Promises to pay wages for services received by the promisor, payment to be made out of some fund yet to be acquired, will frequently be interpreted to be promises to pay within a reasonable time, and not to be absolutely conditional upon the acquisition of the fund.[50] If it appears from the circumstances that the wages

---

47.    **U.S.**—In re Pennewell, 119 F. 139 (C.C.A.6th, 1902), covenant not to sublet.

**Ill.**—Rubens v. Hill, 72 N.E. 1127, 213 Ill. 523 (1905), covenant to repair.

**Tex.**—Johnson v. Gurley, 52 Tex. 222 (1879), tenant was not to cut or sell growing timber.

In Hague v. Ahrens, 53 F. 58 (C.C.A. 3d, 1892), the court said: "A clause

in a lease will not be treated as a condition if it can be construed to be a covenant without doing violence to its terms; and if the purpose to create a condition or conditional limitation is not expressed in clear, unequivocal language, the clause will be treated as a covenant simply."

to be paid were not intended to represent the mere market value of the services received, but that the promisee as well as the promisor intended to carry a part of the risk involved in the business, the acquisition of the fund will be held to be a condition precedent to the defendant's duty to pay.[51]

A seller of goods is not infrequently willing to assume part or all of the risk of the buyer's being unable to make a resale of the goods. If the buyer promises to pay the agreed price only out of the proceeds of the resale of the goods, such resale is a condition precedent to the buyer's duty to pay.[52] In such cases the buyer will usually be held to have made a promise by implication, either to use reasonable effort to make a resale of the goods,[53] or, at least, that he will not do any act making the happening of the condition impossible.[54]

Where a debtor assigns a claim against a third person to one of his creditors, the latter promising to collect it and to pay other creditors after his own claim is satisfied, the other creditors have no action for damages against this creditor if he makes a reasonable compromise with the third person because of some bona fide dispute and not enough is realized from the claim to pay all the accounts due.[55]

## § 637. Dependent and Independent Promises

For several centuries a distinction has been recognized between dependent and independent promises, although attempts at definition have been meager and unsatisfactory. The two terms are used only with respect to the mutually exchanged promises in a bilateral contract. If the duty of rendering performance of one promise is conditional upon the antecedent performance of the other, or of a tender of such performance, the first mentioned promise is said to be a "dependent" promise. The two promises may both be concurrently conditional in this manner; they are then both "dependent" promises. An illustration of this is the ordinary case of a bilateral contract for the sale of goods for cash. Each promisor's duty is conditional upon performance, or tender thereof, by the other party. If the agreement is for a sale of goods with a period of credit, the buyer's promise to pay is dependent on delivery of the goods, and the seller's promise to deliver is not conditional on payment.

The terms dependent and independent are now rendering no necessary service. There is much greater clarity in saying that a promise (or the duty that it creates) is conditional, indicating definitely the fact or event that is the operative condition.

## § 638. Other Classifications of Conditions

In the previous sections, we have classified conditions in two ways, (1) according to the mode of their creation; (2) according to the mode of their operation. The first classification is into Express, Implied, and Constructive. The second is into Precedent, Concurrent, and Subsequent. There are other methods of classification that may at times be useful and convenient.

Thus, (3) conditions may be

    (a) facts or events not in themselves the consideration for the promise sued on; these are usually express—e. g., architect's certificate;

    (b) facts constituting the expected equivalent, being generally acts of the promisee (he sometimes having promised to perform them and sometimes not)—these are more often not express.

Or, (4) they may be

    (a) acts or events that are certain to occur at a definite time —e. g., the arrival of a future date;

    (b) those certain to occur, but at an uncertain time—e. g., the death of X;

    (c) those not certain to occur at all—e. g., the arrival of a ship, or the construction of a building.

Or, (5) they may be

    (a) conditions not within the volitional control of any person—e. g., a fair wind, as in Constable v. Cloberie;

    (b) those within the volitional control of a third person— e. g., architect's certificate, or the king's return to London;

    (c) those within the volitional control of the promisor; [56]

    (d) those within the volitional control of the promisee—e. g., ordinary option contracts.[57]

(6) By the Louisiana Code, conditions precedent and subsequent are called suspensive and resolutory, each of these being again subdivided into casual and potestative.[58]

No doubt still other classifications are useful, and no classification is indispensable. The cases present facts in many combinations and they are not easily classified.

56.   In Scott v. Moragues Lbr. Co., 80 So. 394, 202 Ala. 312 (1918), the defendant contracted to charter a certain ship to the plaintiff at specified rates if the defendant should buy the ship. The defendant in fact bought the ship, thus voluntarily performing the condition precedent to his own duty; and his refusal to charter to the plaintiff was held actionable. He had the free choice, or option, between buying and not buying the ship; but if he chose to buy he was bound to charter to the plaintiff.

# CHAPTER 31

## EXPRESS CONDITIONS—TYPES AND ILLUSTRATIONS

## § 639. Forms of Expression That Will Make a Duty Conditional

A fact or event may be made a condition of a contract right and duty by any form of words capable of interpretation. There is no one required form; but there are several common modes of expression that are familiar. Every common school pupil who studies grammar is taught to recognize a conditional clause in a sentence. A promisor's duty is expressly conditional if his promise to render the specified performance is limited and modified by such a conditional clause. I promise to pay "if my ship comes in"; [1] or "on condition that the goods are delivered by June first"; or "provided that there shall be no liability unless father wills me the farm"; [2] or "this promise is to be null and void if the assured does not keep the books in a fireproof safe" [3]— all these are recognized modes of making the promise conditional. A promise can be made conditional by using language fixing the *time* of performance. [4] Thus, I promise to pay "sixty days after proof of loss"; or "on receipt of the goods"; [5] or "when Smith returns to New York." In all of the foregoing cases, the fact or event is a condition for the reason that interpretation of the

---

1. In Guerrette v. Cheetham, 193 N. E. 836, 289 Mass. 240 (1935), defendant promised to pay the plaintiff's claim against a third person "if he (defendant) took over the premises."

604

words indicates that such was the intention of the contracting parties.

A very common method of making some fact or event a condition of a promisor's duty is to provide that no action shall be brought against the promisor unless the fact or event exists or has occurred. This indicates in express words that the fact or event is a necessary part of the cause of action and that the promisor can not be regarded as in default of duty if it has not occurred.[6]

Sometimes parties use language that makes interpretation very doubtful.[7] Such poor draftsmanship does not relieve the court of the necessity of deciding the issue, but it will justify the court in giving greater weight to what now seems fair and reasonable. No doubt, the court will hesitate to interpret any contract so as to make the promisee's right to performance subject to an unfair and unreasonable condition; but the parties are free to make such a contract and the language may clearly require such an interpretation.[8] In determining what fact or event, if any, the parties intend shall be a condition of contractual duty or of some legal power or privilege, the court will consider the surrounding circumstances, the negotiations and communications of the parties, just as in the interpretation of promissory words and other parts of a contract.[9]

In order that the promise of one party may be expressly conditional upon some performance by the other party, it certainly is not sufficient that the latter makes an express promise to render the performance. An express promise by one party is an entirely different thing from an express condition of the other party's duty. In an ordinary bilateral contract, each party promises something, as where A promises to deliver goods by June first, and in exchange B promises to pay $100. The fact that A promises delivery does not in itself make such delivery an express condition of B's duty to pay the price. For at least two centuries after the common law recognized the validity of such a bilateral agreement, the courts held that each of the two promises was independent and unconditional. They hold differently now where the two promised performances are the agreed equivalents of each other; but this is because we now believe that justice requires that B should not have to pay the price unless he receives the goods, it is not because we understand that B expressly made his promise to pay conditional on delivery of goods. This will be discussed under the heading "Constructive Conditions."[10]

10.  For an excellent discussion of the differences between express and constructive conditions, see Patterson, "Constructive Conditions in Contracts," 42 Col.L.R. 903 (1942).

In a case that has previously been used as an illustration, the plaintiff had taken the defendant's goods on board his ship, and he expressly promised to sail with the next favoring wind for Cadiz. In return, the defendant expressly promised to pay specified freight "if the ship should go the intended voyage to Cadiz and return to the Downs." The court held that the plaintiff had a right to payment of the freight even though he did not sail with the next wind. The delay in sailing was a breach of the plaintiff's promise, entitling the defendant to such money damages as he could prove; but it was not the non-performance of a condition of the defendant's duty to pay freight. Going the voyage and return was expressly made a condition of the defendant's duty; but prompt sailing was not.[11]

Any fact or event can be made a condition of a contractor's duty to perform, by the use of language that expresses such a meaning and intention when interpreted by the usual processes of judicial interpretation. The difference between express conditions and those that are herein described as "constructive" conditions is reasonably clear and definite; but in specific cases it is not always possible to classify the condition involved in the case as being an express condition or a constructive one. The reason for this is that the factors of fairness and reasonableness, which are the principal basis of constructive conditions, are also given great weight in the interpretation of language used by the parties. Express language may, indeed, be such as to overcome these factors and make something a condition however unfair it may seem to others; seldom, if ever, is such language found in a contract. If a condition is found by the processes of interpretation of language, it is called an express condition; if otherwise, the condition is not express. We have an express condition whenever the parties have used language that makes some fact or event necessary to the creation of the right and duty of immediate performance of a promise, or makes it operative to extinguish such a right and duty. The same is true with respect to the creation and extinguishment of any other legal relation, however it may be named; but it is the above-described right and duty that constitute the chief subject of contract litigation.

As long as the English courts of common law thought that there could be no condition unless it was express, there were many cases in which the courts carried the process of interpretation to an extreme that made it seem a fiction, in order that their sense of justice should not be outraged. It was thus that it came to be recognized that the law might make a contract right conditional, even if the parties had not themselves done so. If in a bilateral

11.   Eng.—Constable   v.   Cloberie, Palmer, 397 (1626); Latch, **12, 49;** Popham, 161.

contract one of the parties promised to render his performance "for" the performance that was promised by the other party, this little word "for" was held to make the first promise expressly conditional and dependent.[12]   Fine distinctions were made in many cases [13] that the later growth of the law has rendered unnecessary.

## § 640.   Performance by Plaintiff a Condition When Defendant's Performance is Impossible without It

One kind of case in which it is said that a performance by the plaintiff is a condition precedent to the defendant's duty, by plain implication of fact, is that in which the defendant's promise is impossible of performance until after the plaintiff has performed his part.   A defendant, who promises to deliver any motor car that the plaintiff may select out of the defendant's stock of one hundred used cars, can not be held liable for a failure to deliver unless the plaintiff has made his selection.[14]

Other illustrations are these:  promise to make repairs with timber to be furnished by the plaintiff; [15]  to pay for machinery by delivering paper made by a secret process which the plaintiff is to disclose to the defendant; [16]  to do construction work according to the directions of an engineer to be appointed by the plaintiff; [17]  to deliver coal on a ship to be named by the plaintiff; [18]  to make and deliver goods, times and sizes to be specified by the buyer.[19]   In cases like these, not only will the contractor's duty be held to be conditional on the co-operation of the other party, but that other may be held liable in damages for breach of an "implied" promise to render the necessary co-operation.[20]

It would indeed be gross injustice to make the defendant pay damages for failing to do that which can not be done for the reason that the plaintiff has not made it possible.   It is quite reasonable to hold that the parties agreed upon such a condition precedent, by plain implication of fact; but, also, it is equally reasonable to hold that the plaintiff's performance is a condition, without stopping to consider whether or not the parties agreed that it should be.

Such an implication and decision may also reasonably be made where the plaintiff's failure to render a promised performance makes it materially more difficult or expensive for the defendant to perform on his part.   Thus, where the defendant promises to construct a building on a specified lot, now occupied by an old building that the plaintiff promises to remove, removal by the plaintiff is a condition precedent, even though it may be both possible and lawful for the defendant to remove the old building himself.[21]

## § 641.  Promise to Perform When Able, or out of Earnings

The promisor's own financial ability to pay is sometimes made a condition of his promise, in which case the court must give a reasonable meaning to the word "ability" having reference to all the other calls upon the promisor's resources.[22]  A contract to pay a salary "as the financial condition permitted out of profits of the defendant's business" was held to make the existence of this financial condition an express condition precedent and one that must be proved by the plaintiff.[23]  A promise by a Port Authority to repay money advanced by a county has been held to be a promise to repay when able out of receipts in excess of those necessary for other operations, such necessity to be determined in accordance with the honest and reasonable judgment of the Port Authority itself.[24]

In all cases the express words of the contract must be interpreted in the actual context of those words and in the light of all the surrounding circumstances.  Such an interpretation may show that "ability" to pay, was not intended to be a condition of the promise, but that the promise was that payment would be made at a reasonable time.[25]  The problem then becomes one of weighing the factors upon which "reasonable time" depends.  A promise to pay a debt when the promisor shall be "able to effect a sale" of certain property has been interpreted as a promise to pay within the time in which a sale could be consummated by reasonable effort and with reasonable price concessions.[26]

A contract to ship goods may be made expressly conditional on the promisor's ability to get railway cars for the purpose, in which case "ability" requires reasonable effort and does not mean financial ability to pay for the cars.[27]

## § 642.  Express Provisions as to Strikes, Fires, and Causes Beyond Promisor's Control

In contracts for the manufacture and delivery of goods, and in other kinds of contracts also, there is often included a so-called "strike clause" in some form like this: this contract is "contingent on strikes, fires, breakage of machinery, and other causes beyond our control."[28]  Such words require amplification by the

---

22.  **N.Y.**—Work v. Beach, 13 N.Y.S. 678, 59 Hun 625 (1891).

27.  **U.S.**—Edwardsville Coal Co. v. Crown Coal & Coke Co., 20 F.2d 890 (C.C.A.8th, 1927).

28.  See New Eng. Concrete Const. Co. v. Shepard & Morse Lbr. Co., 107 N.E. 917, 220 Mass. 207 (1915).

In Baetjer v. New Eng. Alcohol Co., 66 N.E.2d 798, 319 Mass. 592 (1946) and Cleveland & W. Coal Co. v. Cyclops Steel Co., 123 A. 320, 278 Pa. 346 (1924), the contract contained two separate sentences as to strikes and other causes beyond control, one of them being expressly applicable to the buyer.

court. They are generally intended to make the seller's duty conditional, but not the buyer's; and that duty is conditional only upon the non-occurrence of a strike or fire that is serious enough to be a material interference with performance or to frustrate the purpose for which the contract was made.[29] The provision may be so drawn as to affect merely the time for performance and not the duty of performance altogether, thus: "contract is subject to delay from strikes, fires, and other causes beyond our control." [30]

When a promisor's duty is made "contingent on strikes, fires . . . . . and causes beyond our control," the fact constituting the actual condition of his duty is not the absence of a strike or fire itself. What the parties really mean, and what they actually say, is that the promisor's duty is conditional on the absence of some factor material to performance that is "caused" by a strike, a fire, or other "cause" beyond control. A strike, a fire, or an earthquake that has no material effect on the cost or difficulty of performance is wholly immaterial. When such a material increase in cost or difficulty of performance occurs, it operates as an excusing factor if its "cause" is a strike, a fire, or other event that is beyond the promisor's control.[33] The extent of the increase in cost or difficulty necessary to be an excusing factor is a matter of degree, and is in no respect determined by mere interpretation of the "strike clause" itself. If it makes performance "commercially impracticable," it is clearly an excuse; this might be true, under modern law, even if there were no "strike clause."[34] It may be correct to say that when a promisor has taken care to put in a "strike clause," he will be excused from performing if some "cause" not in reasonable contemplation and beyond his control renders performance as agreed impossible except at a net loss, although no case so holding has been found. If this is true, a "strike clause" has a material effect in reducing the promisor's risk.[35]

### § 643.    Promises to Render Performance "on Demand"

Where a contractor promises to render his performance "on demand" or at a specified time after demand, the reasonable interpretation would seem to be that an actual demand for performance is an express condition precedent to the duty of immediate performance. With the exceptions mentioned hereafter, this appears to be the rule; action does not lie unless demand has been made and the statute of limitations begins to run from the date of demand.[46] It is often held that, by proper interpretation of the contract, demand must be made within a reasonable time, as a condition precedent to the promisor's duty of immediate performance; [47] and in the absence of special circumstances the statutory period of limitation is often taken to be the reasonable time.[48]  But if the demand is made within this reasonable time, it is generally held (and should be) that the statutory period for barring action begins to run from date of the demand.  There seems to be slight reason for measuring a reasonable time for demand by the period of limitation for bringing suit.  It may be that some courts have felt that a promisee should not have power by merely delaying demand, to let a claim go stale and yet keep it enforceable.  Yet it has not been held that a contract clearly so providing is against public policy and invalid.[49]

It is held that when a negotiable instrument, is made payable "on demand," with nothing more to indicate that an actual demand is intended, the money is payable at once and that an action can be maintained without first making a demand.[50]  In such case the statutory period of limitation begins to run from the date of the contract.[51]  Such a holding has been justified on the ground that the phrase "on demand" is used not to make an actual demand a condition precedent but to show that a money debt already due and payable exists.[52]

## § 644.  Promises Conditional on Personal Satisfaction

In spite of depressions, political changes, and group pressures backed by force, we still have freedom of contract in a high degree;  and the contract that we have chosen to make will usually be enforced by the courts as we have made it.  So, a contractor can, by the use of clear and appropriate words, make his own duty expressly conditional upon his own personal satisfaction with the quality of the performance for which he has bargained and in return for which his promise is given.  Such a limitation on his own duty does not invalidate the contract as long as the limitation is not so great as to make his own promise illusory.  Let us consider some hypothetical cases.

Suppose that A sends a book (or other goods) to B by mail, saying: "I send this at the price of $5 subject to your approval. If you do not like it, please send it back at my expense."  There is no contract; A has only made an offer of one.  Here, B's satisfaction with the goods and the price is not a condition precedent to his duty to pay.  The only condition is his expression of acceptance of the offer.  It is true that in most cases he will not accept unless he is satisfied with the book (or goods);  but he can accept and bind himself to pay from any collateral motive, even though he believes the book to be worthless and the price a hold-up.  Furthermore, there is no contract in this case, and B is not bound to pay the price, however well satisfied he may be with the quality and the price.  Many excellent bargains are offered to us, with which we express entire satisfaction but which we do not accept for lack of the money or for other reasons unconnected with the satisfactoriness of the bargain as a bargain. Of course, B's acceptance is a condition precedent to his duty to pay; but this is not a case of conditional promise, for he has made no promise at all. We do not talk of the conditional rights and duties of contractors until they have gone far enough to be said to have made a valid contract.[58]

Secondly, suppose that A writes thus to B: "I offer my motor car to you for $500; but you need not pay anything unless you wish to do so when you see the car. Please wire acceptance." B telegraphs: "I accept your offer." Here, again, no contract has been made; and B's satisfaction with the car or with the price is not a condition of his duty to pay. There is no contract because B's telegraphic acceptance makes no promise of any kind, either to be enforced against him or to constitute a consideration for A's promise to transfer the car.[59]

If A's offer in the preceding case had contained these additional words, "The car is yours for nothing if you do not wish to pay," the analysis above would not be changed; but the actual delivery of the car to B on such terms would be the execution of a gift, so that B could keep it and pay nothing. In the case as first stated, there was no offer of a gift; and delivery of the car would not pass title without payment. Payment of the $500, however, would execute the sale, without regard to B's motives or his satisfaction with the car.

Thirdly, suppose that A offers to sell his car to B for $500, making representations as to the mileage it has run and the condition of its engine. B replies: "I accept your offer on condition that I am satisfied personally that your representations are correct." This conditional promise made by B is a counter-offer. If, in his turn, A assents to it, there is a valid contract. B's promise is not an illusion, even though it makes his duty to pay conditional upon his personal satisfaction that the mileage and condition of the engine are as represented. This condition of personal satisfaction is a "state of mind"; but it is a fact that is capable of proof like other facts. A jury may find that it exists, even though B denies it under oath and violently asserts that the mileage was misrepresented. In order to enforce B's promise to pay, A must prove affirmatively that B does in fact believe the representations to be correct. Such belief by B is an express condition precedent to his duty to pay the price. It is not enough for A to prove that the representations were in fact correct, that any reasonable man would believe them, and that in disbelieving them B is an honest but crotchety old curmudgeon.

In order that B's personal satisfaction shall be held to be a condition of his duty, irrespective of reasonableness, the intention to make it so must be clearly expressed. It is not enough for B to say that he will pay "if your representations are satisfactorily established," or "if the condition of the engine is satisfactory." Somebody's satisfied state of mind is, indeed, made a condition of B's duty to pay; but it is not B's state of mind. The condition is here the satisfaction of reasonable men, to be tested in case of dispute by court and jury.[60] The disinclination of the courts to interpret the contract as making B's personal state of mind a condition of his duty is especially marked in cases where performance by A has been rendered to some considerable extent and where the result is either that B gets something for nothing or that there is economic waste and A suffers an inevitable loss.[61]

If a principal employs an agent and promises to pay a commission on all orders sent in by the agent and "accepted" by the principal, the latter's personal satisfaction with the terms of the orders and the credit of the purchasers, as evidenced by his "acceptance," is a condition of his duty to pay a commission. But if orders that are obtained are rejected "in bad faith" by the principal, he is bound to pay the commission. In one case it was said that the burden of proving that he had a reasonable ground for rejecting an order is on the principal.[62]

### § 645. Promise of Satisfaction Compared with Condition of Satisfaction

Just as in other cases, the difference between an express promise and an express condition must be observed. A may promise to repair B's house to B's entire satisfaction, in return for B's promise to pay $500 after completion. A has expressly promised to satisfy B; but B has not made his promise to pay expressly conditional on his own mental state of satisfaction, although he has made it expressly conditional upon completion of the work.

Here, as elsewhere, we must not put undue weight on form of expression or upon grammatical rules. If B thinks that, to make his duty to pay conditional upon his own state of mind, it

---

60. Restatement, Contracts, § 265, reads thus: "A promise in terms conditional on the promisor's satisfaction with an agreed exchange gives rise to no duty of immediate performance until such satisfaction; but where it is doubtful whether words mean that a promise is conditional on the promisor's personal satisfaction with an agreed exchange, or on the sufficiency of that exchange to satisfy a reasonable man in the promisor's position, the latter interpretation is adopted."

61. Justice Holmes said in Hawkins v. Graham, 21 N.E. 312, 149 Mass. 284: "When the consideration furnished is of such a nature that its value will be lost to the plaintiff either wholly or in great part unless paid for, a just hesitation must be felt, and clear language required before deciding that payment is left to the will, or even to the idiosyncrasies of the interested party." The court in that case seized upon the words, "or the work demonstrated," as offering an alternative to the owner's acknowledgment.

is enough to get a promise by A to do the work to his satisfaction, and A, with reason to know that B thinks this, makes such a promise, they have expressly made B's personal satisfaction a condition of B's duty to pay.[65]  In order to prove that A had reason to know this, B must prove something more than the mere promissory words of A and B.  He must prove that he expressed his intention to A in some additional way, or that A had reason to know that common usage in the community was to understand A's promise to give satisfaction as the equivalent of making B's promise conditional on satisfaction.[66]  In certain kinds of cases, involving matters of artistic taste or personal fancy, this usage can readily be shown.  These cases are discussed in another section.

Consider and compare the following bilateral contracts:

I { A promises to do certain work.
{ B promises to pay $100.

In this case there are mutual promises that are mutually dependent, but nothing is said about anybody's satisfaction.  If A does the work in accordance with specifications, he has fully discharged his duty and B has no claim for damages even though he is not satisfied.  Also, B is under a duty to pay the full amount promised even though he is not satisfied.  B's personal satisfaction has not been promised by A, nor is it a condition precedent to B's duty to pay.

II { A promises to do specified work to the personal satisfaction of B.
{ B promises to pay $100.

In this case also we have mutual promises that are mutually dependent.  The only difference between this and the first case supposed above is that now A has not only promised to do the work according to specifications; he has also promised to do it to the satisfaction of B.  If he does not do the work to B's satisfaction, he has broken his promise; and B could maintain an action for damages, although these damages would be only nominal, in case the work is proved to be in accordance with specifications.  In this case B's duty to pay the contract price is not expressly made conditional upon his own satisfaction.  The fact that A has expressly promised to satisfy B is not at all the same thing as to make B's duty to pay expressly conditional upon his satisfaction.  Nevertheless, if the character of the work that is promised by A is of such a kind that its excellence or accuracy is largely a matter of personal taste and feelings and cannot readily be determined by objective standards, performance of A's promise to the satisfaction of B will probably be held to be of the essence of the contract.  If such is the case, B's personal satisfaction will be held by construction of law to be a condition precedent to B's duty to pay, even though the terms of the contract did not make it such a condition in express words.[67]

III
{
A promises to do specified work.

B promises to pay $100 if the work as done is satisfactory to him personally.
}

Here we have another valid bilateral contract. A has promised to do the work in accordance with specifications, but he has not promised to produce satisfaction in B. If the work is done according to specifications, A has completely performed his contractual duty, even though B is not satisfied with the result; and B can maintain no action for damages against A.[68] On the other hand, B has expressly made his duty to pay $100 conditional upon his own personal satisfaction; and if he is in good faith not satisfied he is not bound to pay the $100 even though, in the opinion of other competent critics, A's work is exactly in accordance with specifications. A has not fulfilled a condition precedent to B's duty, although he has fully performed his own duty as required by his express promise. This is applicable to building contracts and other kinds, as well as to those more definitely involving matters of personal taste and feeling; but in such cases we may find the court failing to observe the express condition, or else refusing to give it effect, in order to avoid an unjust result.[69] Courts prefer to interpret even such words as these as requiring only the satisfaction of a reasonable man.[70]

### § 646. Performances Involving Artistic Taste and Personal Fancy Compared with Those Measurable by Objective Tests

When A promises to do certain work involving artistic taste or personal fancy "to B's personal satisfaction," it may be this state of mind that is B's chief object of desire, a fact that A has reason to know because it would be the chief object of desire on the part of men in general. "Substantial performance" of his promise by A may be impossible without producing this state of mind in B; and in most cases "substantial performance" by A is a constructive condition of B's reciprocal duty even though not an express condition. When such is the case, it is unnecessary for us to determine whether the condition should be classified as "express," or "implied," or "constructive." It is enough for us to be sure that according to standards of men in general B ought not to be compelled to pay without being personally satisfied.

Where the performance contracted for is one that involves operative fitness and mechanical utility rather than personal taste and fancy, the personal satisfaction of the promisor is much less likely to be regarded by the average man as his chief object of desire.  There can be substantial performance in accordance with generally held opinion even though the promisor thinks otherwise.  The extent and quality of the performance rendered can be measured by objective tests, scientific and mechanical in character, that have uniform application for all persons alike.  In these cases, the fact that A promises expressly to complete the performance entirely to B's satisfaction is not enough to make B's personal satisfaction a condition of his duty to pay.  A renders substantial performance, and B will be compelled to pay, if application of the objective tests shows that reasonable men would be satisfied and that B has received substantially what he bargained for.  Even in these cases, however, B can, by apt and convincing language, make his personal satisfaction a condition of his duty.[77]

## § 648.  Judicial Disregard of Express Words of Condition

Where two parties have made a bilateral contract in which A promises to render a specified performance and B promises to pay therefor on the express condition of his personal satisfaction with the performance rendered, should the courts ever enforce B's promise to pay in spite of his honest but unreasonable dissatisfaction?  When A has convinced court and jury that he has performed his promise according to specifications, it often seems harsh and unjust to deny judgment for the promised compensation.  In the absence of fraud or mistake, courts generally deny that they can or will ever set aside an express condition, even though it is the personal state of mind of an interested party.  But they often can and do produce the same result by indulging in a process of pseudo-interpretation, finding that the language used means the "satisfaction of a reasonable man."  When this is in fact what is done, it is a substitution by the court of a reasonable condition precedent in place of what seems to the court an unreasonable condition precedent.  Such pseudo-interpretation as this constitutes a judicial limitation upon the freedom of contract of the parties. It may perhaps be justifiable at times, because of inequality in the economic bargaining power of the parties at the time they make the contract.  Such inequality, however, has not yet consciously and openly been recognized by the courts as a reason for limiting freedom of contract and for depriving the party in the superior economic position of some of the advantages that would be his by the express terms of the agreement.  Moreover, in a particular case there may have been no inequality in economic bargaining power; or, if there was, it may have had

---

77.  Illustrative cases are analyzed and discussed in the remainder of this section in the general treatise.

Also § 647 deals with Personal Dissatisfaction as a Condition of a Power to Terminate.

nothing at all to do with the inclusion of the condition of personal satisfaction in the contract.

It should be remembered that there are effective methods of preventing injustice other than by making false interpretations or by limiting freedom of contract. Thus, if B has received and is actually profiting by a performance of value that A has rendered, a restitutionary remedy is available to A, even though he has not fulfilled a condition precedent to B's promissory duty to pay. Although A cannot enforce B's express promise, he can get a judgment for the reasonable value of the performance that B has received from him and retained. As has been stated above, A's failure to fulfil a condition precedent to B's contractual duty is not necessarily a breach of his own promise. Even if A has committed such a breach, all that justice requires against him and in B's favor is that A shall pay to B compensatory damages measured by the extent of B's actual injury; it does not require that B should go scot-free and enjoy large benefits from A's performance without paying anything in return. A can get judgment, therefore, for the reasonable value of the performance that he has rendered under the contract, less such damages as B may be entitled to by reason of A's breach, in so far as B has actually received A's performance and enjoys the benefits thereof. If A's failure to fulfil the condition precedent to B's contractual duty is not also a breach of A's promise, B has no right to damages and there is no deduction to be made.

The only limitation on the foregoing restitutionary remedy in favor of A seems to be that he has no such remedy if he is guilty of a wilful and deliberate breach of his own contractual duty. A full discussion of this will be reserved for the Chapter dealing with Remedies.

### § 649. Appraisal, Approval, or Certification by a Third Person as an Express Condition of Duty

In many contracts it is expressly provided that some act of a third person shall be a condition of a promisor's duty to pay money or to render some other specified performance. A promise to pay for property or service such a sum of money as X may determine makes the determination of X a condition precedent.[5] Similar cases are a promise to pay specified sums on certificate of an architect or engineer that work has been completed,[6] or to buy and pay for land "subject to" approval of title by X,[7] or to perform as agreed subject to the approval of the deal by X,[8] or to buy property contingent on the approval by a zoning board of its use for a dental office.[9]

In making a contract the parties may use language indicating that the "contract" itself is conditional on some collateral event, such as the approval of a third person or court or commission, or the award of some collateral construction contract.[10]   In such cases, it is quite incorrect to say that until the event occurs there is no contract; neither party has the privilege of revocation and no further expression of assent by the two parties is necessary. The binding character of such a conditional contract has been recognized by sustaining a bill for specific performance or an injunction.[11]   Courts have often held that the "parol evidence rule" does not prevent proof of an oral agreement making the contract thus conditional, even though the contract is otherwise embodied in a writing that is apparently complete, giving as a reason that the oral testimony shows that no contract was ever consummated.[12]   This reasoning is unsound, although the decision holding the evidence admissible should be supported.   In some of these cases, the parties may intend that the promises of both shall be conditional on the event, in others that only one of the promises shall be so.

In insurance contracts, the duty of the insurer to pay has often been made conditional upon the presentation of the sworn statement or certificate of a physician, near-by magistrate, or other person that in his opinion the claim made by the insured is honest and correct.[13]   This has sometimes made a hard case for the court where the third person refuses his oath or certificate on what are alleged to be unreasonable grounds.   A court must determine when justice requires dispensing with a condition as well as when to find one, either express or constructive.[14]

### § 650.   Certificate of Architect or Engineer as a Condition Precedent

In contracts for building and construction, there are plans and specifications with which the contractor promises to make his work conform.   Failure of such conformance is a breach of contractual duty, except when there are justifying reasons for such failure.   Failure of conformance is a breach of duty even though the failure is slight in character.

If the failure of conformance is slight, relatively to the whole and to the purposes for which the contract was made, it does not in itself justify the other party in refusing to perform his re-

10.   Illustrative cases are:

U.S.—Watson Bros. Transp. Co. v. Jaffa, 143 F.2d 340 (C.C.A.8th, 1944).

Ky.—D. L. Walker & Co. v. Lewis, 101 S.W.2d 685, 267 Ky. 107 (1937),

sale of stone conditional on buyer's being awarded a highway contract.

Mass.—Nigro v. Conti, 66 N.E.2d 353. 319 Mass. 480, 165 A.L.R. 752 (1946).

Eng.—Pym v. Campbell, 2 El. & B. 370 (1856).

turn promises. It is a breach of contract; but it is not the non-fulfilment of a condition of the other party's duty to pay or perform his part of the agreed exchange.

By express terms of the agreement, however, the parties can make small and otherwise immaterial performances "conditions" of a promisor's duty. Often, in construction contracts, the party for whom the work is being done, makes his promise to pay expressly conditional upon the presentation of a certificate by a supervising architect or engineer. This may be a certificate that the work has been completed in accordance with the plans and specifications, or that it has been performed to the satisfaction of the engineer, or that a stated portion of the work has been so completed. The certificate may be made a condition precedent to the promisor's duty to pay the entire contract price; but it is more likely to be a condition precedent to the duty to pay a final balance of the price, or to the duty to pay an intermediate instalment of the price.[15] The so-called "progress payments" of building contracts are such intermediate instalments; the owner's duty to make such payments is usually conditional upon a certificate of the architect or engineer that a specified amount of progress has been made toward completion. The finding of the engineer determines the amount of the progress, and so also determines the amount that is due from the owner.

### § 651. Refusal of Certificate Fraudulently or Unreasonably

Under some circumstances, all courts will refuse to give effect to an express provision making the expert's certificate a condition precedent to the duty to pay compensation. If the expert's refusal of his certificate is not "in good faith," his certificate will be eliminated as a condition, and the promise of compensation becomes enforceable without it.[18] All agree that it is eliminated if its refusal is the result of the fraudulent collusion of the expert and the employing owner. Fraud and bad faith will be found to exist if the expert fails and refuses to make an examination of the performance by the contractor.[19] Refusal of the certificate because of conscious and neglectful ignorance of the facts may not be as bad as an intentional misrepresentation of facts known to exist; but it is bad enough to induce the courts to compel payment in the absence of the certificate. The owner must pay even though he did not act in collusion with the expert and had no part in causing the refusal of the certificate; it is enough that the expert himself acted in bad faith. The expert must express an honest judgment after a fair consideration of the facts in issue.[20]

20. Restatement, Contracts, § 303: "Where a certificate of an architect, surveyor or engineer is a condition precedent to a duty of immediate payment for work, the condition is excused if the architect, surveyor or engineer

    (a) dies or becomes incapacitated, or

    (b) refuses to give a certificate because of collusion with the promisor, or

    (c) refuses to give a certificate after making examination of the work and finding it adequate, or

    (d) fails to make proper examination of the work, or

    (e) fails to exercise an honest judgment, or

    (f) makes a gross mistake with reference to facts on which a refusal to give a certificate is based."

# CHAPTER 32

## CONSTRUCTIVE CONDITIONS—FAILURE TO PERFORM THE AGREED EXCHANGE

### § 653. Constructive Conditions Distinguished from Implied Conditions

It has already been stated that a condition that is truly "implied" is substantially an express condition. It is a condition for the reason that the parties have so agreed; but their intention to make it so has not been expressed in definite language. Their intention must have been expressed in some manner, however; otherwise it could not be found by implication or inference. A constructive condition has been defined as a fact or event that is operative as such on grounds of fairness and justice, even though the parties expressed no intention whatever, either in definite language or by methods from which an inference or implication is possible. We are now to deal with these constructive conditions, at least to the extent of discussing a good many illustrations in various kinds of contracts.

In this process, we shall frequently be on the borderline of express and implied conditions; for, although these are discovered by the processes of interpretation of the words and conduct of the parties, the fairness and justice of the result is one of the prime factors in making the interpretation. In few cases will it be necessary to spend much effort in classifying the condition in a particular case. The problem for the court and the lawyer is to determine whether the fact or event should operate as a condition. If the words used in the agreement give us a clear and prompt answer to this question, we shall easily call the condition "express." If we find that the parties in no manner expressed an intention concerning it, we shall easily describe the condition as "constructive." In an immense number of cases, the question admits of neither answer to the exclusion of the other; and in these cases the fairness and justice of the result must be the really determinative factor.[1] This is the factor on which the attention ought to be focussed. Such is the reason for using the topical heading "constructive conditions." When justice seems to require that a contractor's duty to perform his promise should be conditional on some fact or event, the court should hold it to be a condition of the duty unless the parties clearly expressed an intention to the contrary. To be sure if they did express such an intention, justice generally is best served by carrying out that intention.

As the law of contract assumed increasing importance in human affairs, there was for some centuries an increasing tendency to regard the intention of the parties as the sole operative factor in determining the legal relations consequent upon agreement. No contract without an actual mutual assent; and no rights and duties based upon that assent unless the parties willed that they should exist. The word was the "sovereign talisman." A promise was held to be independent and unconditional unless words were used to indicate otherwise. But the strict application of this doctrine failed to be in harmony with the mores and beliefs and acknowledged interests of men; it shocked the conscience of the judges, leading to the use of fiction and pretense to avoid it. The actual decisions of the courts have long been out of harmony with it; and the opinions of our leading jurists now often speak a different doctrine.[2] By this, we do not mean to

---

1. Restatement, Contracts, § 267, Comment a, says: "How far such conditions are constructive rather than based on an interpretation of the manifested intention of the parties may be subject to dispute, and the answer may differ in different kinds of contracts. In some kinds long usage of treating promises falling within the rules of the Section [sec. 267] as concurrently conditional has now resulted in making the inference natural and perhaps necessary that the parties intended simultaneous performance, and that neither performance should be rendered unless the other is also. It is immaterial, however, whether such an intention is manifested. Justice requires the result unless a contrary intention is clearly manifested."

For excellent discussions of the distinction between express and constructive conditions, see Patterson, 42 Col.L.Rev. 903 (1942), and Williams, "Language and the Law," 61 Law Q.Rev. 400–406.

2. It is far from universal even now. In Comptoir Commercial Anversois v. Power & Sons, [1920] 1 K.B. 868, Scrutton, L. J., said: "The court . . . ought not to imply a term merely because it would be a reasonable term to include if the parties had thought about the matter or because one party, if he had thought about the matter, would not have made the contract unless the term was included; it must be such a necessary term that both parties must have intended that it should be a term of the contract and have only

deny the importance and operative effect of the expressed intention of the parties; it is merely to assert that it is not the sole operative factor and that justice must and will be done in cases where no intention was expressed. Seldom should a court hold that a promise is "constructively" conditional if it would be clearly in conflict with some other provision of the contract reasonably interpreted.[3]

## § 654.  History of Implied and Constructive Conditions

The law of a country is not a system of eternal principles or doctrines, controlling all future human transactions and from which the decisions in all future cases can be deduced.  Go back only a thousand years in English history — a mere watch in the night of the evolution of man — and one can observe how clearly

not expressed it because the necessity was so obvious that it was taken for granted." Scrutton, L. J., used similar language in Reigate v. Union Mfg. Co., [1918] 1 K.B. 592. To the present writer, this seems quite sound in so far as it deals with implications of intention in fact and on the assumption that the legal relations resulting from a contract depend solely upon expressed intention. If we make a contrary assumption, the statement is much too narrow. The quoted language is more nearly correct when applied to the 'implication' of promises than when applied to the 'implication' of a condition; and it is more nearly correct with respect to a condition that does not constitute any part of a bargained-for equivalent than with respect to one that does.

Compare the following statement of Mr. Justice Holmes, in his essay on "The Path of the Law," 10 Harv.L. Rev. 466, and reprinted in his collected essays:

"The language of judicial decision is mainly the language of logic. And the logical method and form flatter that longing for certainty and for repose which is in every human mind. But certainty is generally an illusion, and repose is not the destiny of man. Behind the logical form lies a judgment as to the relative worth and importance of competing legislative grounds, often an inarticulate and unconscious judgment, it is true, and yet the very root and nerve of the whole proceeding. You can give any conclusion a logical form. *You always can imply a condition in a contract.* But why do you imply it? It is because of some belief as to the practice of the community or of a class, or because of some opinion as to policy, or, in short, because of some attitude of yours upon a matter not capable of exact quantitative measurements, and therefore not capable of founding exact logical conclusions."

See, also, Leonard v. Dyer, 26 Conn. 172, 178 (1857); Bankes, L. J., in Grove v. Webb, 114 L.T. 1082, 1089 (1916); Evans & Co. v. U. S., 169 F.2d 500 (C.A.2d, 1948).

3.    In Evans & Co. v. U. S., supra, the court said: "Like the court below, we agree with plaintiff that a 'constructive condition of cooperation' may appropriately be implied in construction contracts, where consistent with the terms of such contracts. If, however, a contract on its face discloses a legal provision which specifically contemplates the situation which did arise; and if the provision sets out the responsibility of each of the contracting parties in that eventuality, there can be no inference to the contrary."

impossible such a system is and how clearly contrary to truth and fact. Before the victory of William the Norman at the battle of Hastings, we have the traditional laws of Alfred the Great; and after that battle we have the nostalgic yearnings of the Saxons for the "good laws of Edward the Confessor." They tell us how many shillings must be paid for an eye; but they say next to nothing about the law of "contract." There were folkmoots and a witenagemot, but no King's Bench or English Common Law. The transactions of men were simple and few, as the common individual lived and died within sight of his own rooftree.

In the first few centuries after the Norman conquest, the kings made England a united country and established much law as "common" law. Forms of action were developed, most of them limited in use and soon obsolete and forgotten. The great jurist Bracton and a few others knew something of the Roman system that had developed during a previous period of more than another thousand years. But the growth of what we now call the law of contract was very slow. Seals came into use. Recognizances before magistrates and promises that were in writing and under seal were enforced by the courts. A debt was an enforceable unilateral obligation based upon the receipt of an executed quid pro quo. An amorphous and undefined concept called "consideration" began to be talked about; and informal promises given in exchange for an executed consideration became enforceable in assumpsit. It was not until the fifteenth century that an exchange of a promise for another promise — the modern "bilateral" contract — obtained judicial recognition as creating obligation.

Prior to this recognition of the bilateral contract, nothing could be said about the mutual dependency of promises; and failure by a promisor to perform his promise did not affect the other party's duty, for the reason that he had made no return promise and wasn't under any duty.

The recognition of the bilateral contract, however, created a new situation with many new problems. In the previously recognized informal contract, whether enforced in debt or in assumpsit, the single promise created no obligation until the quid pro quo was received or the "consideration" actually performed. The performance of this consideration by the promisee was a condition of the promisor's duty, because it rather than the promise was conceived of as the source of obligation. Expressed in our present legal language, we would say that until performance by the promisee no contract had been made. In the newly recognized bilateral contract, this was not so; there was obligation, and a "contract" existed, as soon as the promises were exchanged and before any performance. It was a return promise that took the place of the quid pro quo or the executed consideration.

623

It should not surprise us, therefore, to find that for a few more centuries either party to a bilateral contract could get judicial enforcement of the other fellow's promise without first performing his own, and even though he had expressly repudiated it. He had already done that which made the other party's promise enforceable; he had given his own promise. The two promisors were in like case; each could enforce the promise of the other. This was equal justice. It was recognized that either party could limit his own promise as he saw fit by the use of appropriate words of condition; express conditions must be performed. But in the absence of an expressly stated condition, mutual promises were held to be independent of each other and unconditional. If one promisor was compelled to pay damages for breach of his promise, when he had not received and was not likely to receive performance of the return promise, the courts seemed not to care. For he could have done exactly the same to the other promisor; and he now had exactly the same remedy. He had bargained for a promise instead of a performance; and he must have relied upon his remedy for non-performance.[4]

As time went on, this newly-discovered learning as to bilateral contracts did not give satisfaction to the contracting parties.[5] They had contracted; but they did not know the difference between bilateral and unilateral. No doubt they realized that they had exchanged promises; but they also knew that they were bar-

---

4. In Thorpe v. Thorpe, 12 Mod. 455 (1701), Holt, C. J., said: "What is the reason that mutual promises shall bear an action without performance? One's bargain is to be performed according as he makes it. If he make a bargain, and rely on the other's covenant or promise to have what he would have done to him, it is his own fault. If the agreement be, that A shall have the horse of B and A agree that B shall have his money, they may make it so; and then there needs no averment of performance to maintain an action on either side."

This shows how completely ill-founded is the commonly repeated doctrine that at common law "time is of the essence," although in equity it is not. To say that "time is of the essence" means that if A does not perform his promise exactly on time he can not maintain suit for a subsequent refusal of B to perform the return promise—that is, that performance exactly on time is a condition of B's duty. That this was not true for several centuries at common law is shown by the fact that no performance at all, whether on time or otherwise, was a condition. This is fully discussed later in Chapter 37.

5. Where the defendant had bound himself by a covenant to pay a sum of money as the price of land or goods, there being no enforceable return promise by the plaintiff to transfer title, the courts were very astute to find that the defendant's covenant was in words that made his duty conditional. They had no liking for requiring the defendant to do something for nothing.

See Pordage v. Cole, 1 Wms. Saund. 319 (1669); Lock v. Wright, 1 Strange 569 (1723); Collins v. Gibbs, 2 Burr. 899 (1759); Austin v. Jervoyse, Hob. 69 (1615).

gaining for the performance that was promised as well as for the promise to render the performance. When one was sued for breach of his promise, he argued that the other had not performed or tendered performance and that he had never himself received the promised equivalent. Defendants continued to make these arguments and to fight these cases; and the constant dropping finally wore through the judicial stone of doctrine.[6]

The memory of the unilateral contract — the only contract that had once been enforceable — must have affected the judges; and they came to realize that in most bilateral contracts each promisor bargains for performance as well as for promise, that the agreement is for an exchange of performances as well as for an exchange of promises.[7]

The first step in breaking down the doctrine that mutual promises in a bilateral contract are independent was taken by discovering express words of condition in language that very poorly expresses such an intention.[8] The defendant's defense that the plaintiff had himself failed of performance was sustained by holding that the defendant's promise was expressly conditional on such performance. The next step was to find such a condition by implication even though not in express words; the facts are such that the parties must have so intended. The final step is to hold the defendant's promise to be a dependent promise — to be conditional on performance or tender thereof by the plaintiff — for

6.   "Although many nice distinctions are to be found in the books, upon the question, whether the covenants or promises of the respective parties to the contract are to be considered independent or dependent; yet it is evident, the inclination of Courts has strongly favored the latter construction, as being obviously the most just. The seller ought not to be compelled to part with his property without receiving the consideration: nor the purchaser to part with his money without an equivalent in return. Hence, in such cases, if either a vendor or a vendee wish to compel the other to fulfill his contract, he must make his part of the agreement precedent, and cannot proceed against the other without an actual performance of the agreement on his part, or a tender and refusal. And an averment to that effect is always made in the declaration upon contracts containing dependent undertakings, and that averment must be supported by proof." Bank of Columbia v. Hagner, 1 Pet. 455, 7 L.Ed. 219 (U.S. 1828).

7.   Restatement, Contracts, § 266(1): " 'Promises for an agreed exchange' in the Restatement of this Subject means mutual promises in a bilateral contract where the performance promised by one party is the agreed exchange for the performance promised by the other party."

Such a transaction differs from a "barter" in that the parties first make an exchange of reciprocal promises on which they rely to bring about performance in the future; but as in the case of "barter" they are agreeing upon an exchange of the two performances as equivalents. Whence the phrase of the Restatement "agreed exchange."

the reason that justice, as determined by the practices and mores of men, requires it to be so conditional. In taking this last step, the courts have created what is herein described as "constructive conditions." In taking the first two steps, also, they had often done substantially the same thing; for their interpretations and inferences of intention were often so far-fetched that they should be recognized and described as fiction. This is not to say that these interpretations and inferences may not in most cases have been correct; at least they may have been in harmony with what the parties thought but did not say, or in harmony with what they would have thought and said if they had foreseen the future.[9] It is thus that the express fades into the implied, and the implied fades into the constructive. The dividing lines disappear; and in a specific case we may not know which description of the condition is correct. Indeed, it is not necessary for a court to determine which is correct, if the same result is going to be reached in any event. But a restatement of the law must make and express the distinctions in order to make clear what the courts have in fact done and to instruct lawyers and judges as to how and why new cases should be decided.

We shall now proceed to discuss and analyze specific cases, of various classes, illustrating the development and application of the doctrine of dependency of promises and of the concepts of implied and constructive conditions. The problem is a complex one because bilateral contracts often contain many promises instead of only two, and many performances are promised to be rendered at various times and in various instalments. One such contract may create many duties instead of only two, each of which may have one or more "conditions" peculiar to itself. Although all the promises on the one side are exchanged for all the promises on the other, any one of the various performances promised may have its own separate bargained-for exchange or it may not.[10]

The complexity is increased because the kinds of performances promised are of infinite variety. Contracts for the sale of goods differ from contracts for the sale of land; building contracts differ from service contracts; charter parties differ from leases. Each such class develops its own special business practices and understandings and language; and at the same time the con-

9.  Holland, Jurisprudence (ed. 10), p. 278, writes thus: "Supposing a contract to have been duly formed, what is its result? An obligation has been created between the contracting parties, by which rights are conferred upon the one and duties have been imposed upon the other, partly stipulated for in the agreement, but partly also implied by law, which as Bentham observes (Works, III, 190) 'has thus in every country supplied the short-sightedness of individuals, by doing for them what they would have done for themselves if their imagination had anticipated the march of nature.'"

tracts within any one class present important differences. Samples from each class will here be considered; but no one class can be exhaustively dealt with.

## § 656.   Bilateral Contracts for Simultaneous Performances

When the two full performances reciprocally promised in a bilateral contract are the agreed exchange each for the other, and the contract provides that they are to be rendered and the exchange effected at the same moment of time, it has now long been held that the two promises are mutually dependent.[11]   The two performances are said to be "concurrent conditions" of the reciprocal duties of the parties.   Each promisor's duty of immediate performance is conditional on a tender by the other party of his return performance in execution of a simultaneous exchange. There must be an offer of the return performance and the ability to make it good.

A transfer of ownership of goods or land and the payment of the agreed price in money or in other goods or land are performances that can be completely rendered simultaneously.   A bilateral contract requiring such an exchange is a cash transaction, not a "credit" transaction.   Neither party can require the other to give "credit."

By exchanging promises in advance, each party acquires a conditional right to future performance at the agreed time, a right that he has power to turn into a right to immediate performance by making the proper tender.   There is some degree of risk involved; for each carries the risk that the other party may be unable or unwilling to perform his part.   But this is merely the risk of not getting the expected profit of the bargain; it is not the risk of giving something for nothing.   Each party risks disappointment; but neither one risks the loss of his money or his property.   In a "credit" transaction, the party giving credit risks the loss of his money or his goods, as well as the expected profit (the benefits of the bargain).   In either case, however, if the

---

11.   As has been previously stated, the rule was otherwise in the early history of bilateral contracts in England; the promises were mutually independent unless they were made conditional in express terms.   The rule had changed, however, when the famous note to Pordage v. Cole was written by Serj't Williams in his edition of Saunders' reports in the 18th Century.

Serjeant Williams's rule 5 is as follows: "Where two acts are to be done at the same time, as where A covenants to convey an estate to B on such a day, and in consideration thereof B covenants to pay A a sum of money on the same day, neither can maintain an action without showing performance of, or an offer to perform his part, though it is not certain which of them is obliged to do the first act: and this particularly applies to all cases of sale."

necessary conditions precedent are fulfilled, he may be able to get reparation by a law suit.

In many cases, the parties make a bilateral agreement for the exchange of two such performances as above without specifying any time for the rendition of either one. Custom supplies the missing specification; the parties are now bound to perform at and within "a reasonable time." The contract is a valid one; and each has a conditional right to performance by the other and a conditional duty to render his own performance. The "condition" to be fulfilled in this case, however, is not a tender at a specified moment of time. An operative tender can be made at any time after making the contract; but it must be kept good for such a length of time as by custom in such cases is regarded as a reasonable time for the other party to prepare and execute the return performance. Neither party having agreed to give "credit," the two performances are again required to be simultaneous; the two promises are mutually "dependent" and concurrently "conditional."

In still other cases, the bilateral agreement for such an exchange specifies a definite time for the rendition of one of the performances without specifying a time for the return performance. In a contract for the sale of land or goods at an agreed price, the seller may promise to execute his transfer on a specific day, with no time stated for the return transfer.[12] Again, custom supplies the missing specification; but now the return performance must be rendered on the day that is specified for the other performance, the two to be rendered simultaneously. The lack of one of the time specifications does not indicate that

---

12.   Ziehen v. Smith, 42 N.E. 1080, 148 N.Y. 558 (1896), is such a case. It was a contract for the sale of land, no time being specified for conveyance by the vendor. The purchaser made a down payment of $500, and promised to pay $300 more on September 15, to assume an existing mortgage, and to give bond and mortgage for a balance of $1,700. The court held that the closing day was September 15, the reciprocal duties being concurrently conditional.

The decision in Pordage v. Cole, 1 Wms. Saund. 319 (1669), was directly contra to the text above. A time was set for payment, but none for conveyance of the land. Judgment was rendered for the price without requiring a tender of conveyance. Serjt. Williams was not able to deny that such was still the law, and therefore so limited his rule (1) as to be consistent with it. This is quoted and discussed in the next section.

Mattock v. Kinglake, 10 Ad. & E. 50 (1839), is another good illustration of the older law. In a sealed contract, a buyer promised to pay on or before Feb. 19, 1825; and the seller promised to convey but specified no date. In a suit for the price, the buyer pleaded that no deed had been tendered. A demurrer to this plea was sustained. Pordage v. Cole was followed and Serjt. William's rule (1) was applied. Littledale, J., said that the buyer might have sued for non-conveyance *before* the day set for payment.

a "credit" transaction is intended. If the parties intend that one of them shall give "credit" and run the larger risk, that intention must be expressed in words or otherwise. Absent such an expression, the contract is the same as if it had specified an identical time for both performances; tender at that time is a condition of each party's duty of immediate performance.

A fourth kind of provision is found in bilateral agreements such as these. It may be agreed that one or both of the performances shall be rendered within a stated period of time, or "on or before" a specified day. Here, too, there is no "credit" period and performances are to be concurrent. Each party has the entire period within which to perform; the effect of the contract is the same as if it had provided for performance on the last day of the stated period. Each party's duty of immediate performance is conditional on a tender by the other, a tender that may be made at any time during the specified period but that is insufficient to put the other party in default unless it is kept good until the termination of that period or is repeated at that time. Because of the express time provision, each one has the full period within which to render his performance. Non-performance is not a breach until the period is ended, and even then is not a breach in the absence of a tender of the agreed exchange. If neither one makes a tender, neither one is under a duty of immediate performance.

So, when a vendor promised to convey land "on or before 2d of September" in consideration whereof the purchaser promised to pay £210 "on or before 2d of September," it was held that tender of conveyance was a condition precedent to the purchaser's duty to pay.[13] Lord Kenyon, who is not suspected of being a radical judge, recognized that his decision was contra to many decisions of the past, decisions which he said "outrage common sense." At the same time, he appeared not to believe that the

---

13. **Eng.**—Goodisson v. Nunn, 4 T. R. 761 (1792, K.B.). Lord Kenyon, C. J., said: "Suppose the purchase-money of an estate was £40,000 it would be absurd to say that the purchaser might enforce a conveyance without payment, and compel the seller to have recourse to him, who perhaps might be an insolvent person. The old cases, cited by the plaintiff's counsel, have been accurately stated; but the determinations in them outrage common sense. I admit the principle on which they profess to go: but I think that the Judges misapplied that principle. It is admitted in them all that where they are dependent covenants, no action will lie by one party unless he has performed, or offered to perform his covenant. Then the question is, Whether these are, or are not, dependent covenants? I think they are; the one is to depend on the other; when the one party conveyed his estate he was to receive the purchase-money; and when the other parted with his money he was to have the estate. They were reciprocal acts, to be performed by each other at the same time."

law itself had changed. He said, "I admit the principle on which they profess to go; but I think that the judges misapplied that principle." This "principle" he stated thus: "Where they are dependent covenants, no action will lie by one party unless he have performed, or offered to perform his covenant." To state a principle thus, in order to make the law appear to be static, is a mere unconscious juggling with words. It is no better than to say "when covenants are dependent they are dependent." The old judges did not misapply that principle, because it is not a principle and can not be applied. The old rule was that the mutual promises in a bilateral contract are independent and unconditional unless the parties, by some expression of intention, make them otherwise. The new rule, one which Lord Kenyon was applying but did not state, is that when the two performances, mutually promised in a bilateral contract, are the agreed equivalents of each other, and by custom or agreement are to be performed simultaneously, the promises are concurrently conditional and dependent.[14]

In the contract that Lord Kenyon was considering, each party expressly promised to perform "on or before 2d of September." If the vendor executed and delivered a conveyance on August 15, this would be a full discharge of his duty and exact performance of his promise. Yet, he could not require the purchaser to pay the price on that day. Payment of £210 on September 2 would

---

14. The statements in this section are supported by Restatement, Contracts, § 267, as follows: "Promises for an agreed exchange are concurrently conditional, unless a contrary intention is clearly manifested, if the promises can be simultaneously performed and the parties can be assured that they are being so performed, where by the terms of the promises

    (a) the same time is fixed for the performance of each promise; or

    (b) a fixed time is stated for the performance of one of the promises and no time is fixed for the other; or

    (c) no time is fixed for the performance of either promise; or

    (d) the same period of time is fixed within which each promise shall be performed."

The insertion in this section of the words "and the parties can be assured that they are being so performed" seems to indicate that the two promises are independent as of olden time in case the two performances are to be rendered at different places with no means of instantaneous communication. The writer now sees no reason for this and would therefore eliminate the quoted words. A tender by each party at the appointed place is a condition of the other party's duty, even though the party making tender can not at once know whether the other party is also tendering performance; his tender is not sufficient if he makes it conditional on such knowledge. Such lack of knowledge makes a tender somewhat more risky than it would otherwise be; but neither party can maintain suit for breach by the other without making it. If neither party makes a good tender, both insisting on knowledge, neither one can maintain suit; there has been no breach.

be exact performance of his promise by the purchaser. Each party was privileged to choose the day for his own performance, so long as it was not later than September 2. In this case, the parties do not say that the performances are to be rendered simultaneously. Nor do they say that either promise is dependent on performance of the other, or that either duty of rendering immediate performance is conditional on tender of performance by the other. Each has a limited option as to the time of performing his own promise; neither one has the power to shorten the time within which the other party must perform.

Why, then, were these promises mutually dependent, concurrently conditional? It must be because "justice" requires that the purchaser shall not have to hand over the price unless he gets the land and that the vendor shall not have to convey the land unless he gets the money. This is "justice," not because the parties have expressed such an intention, but because of the customs and beliefs of men, the business mores of the time. Something in exchange for nothing is not justice, by these mores, even though the one getting nothing has a good law suit. If the parties had clearly expressed the intention that one or both of the promises should be independent and unconditional, the same "justice," having the same basis, generally requires the court to give effect to that expressed intention.

In this case each party had the legal privilege of performing his part before September 2 if he so desired; but, by the decision of the court, neither one had a legal right that the other should so perform. The right to each (and the correlative duty of each) was that the other should render his promised performance on September 2, on condition that he himself should tender his own performance in simultaneous exchange, unless he had exercised his privilege of rendering it earlier.

In cases within this section, it is always possible for one party to make his promise expressly conditional on concurrent performance by the other, while the other party is not so foresighted and omits to do the like. It is believed that this does not change the legal result. Such a provision does not make the transaction a "credit" transaction. One of the promises is expressly conditional and the other is not; but the law does for the other party what he failed to do for himself because fairness and justice still so require. A provision that clearly requires one performance to be rendered in advance of the other is a different matter.

### § 657.  Dependency of Promises When One is to be Performed before the Other

If the parties have in express terms provided that one of the promised performances shall be rendered before the return performance is begun, or if, in the absence of any express words, such is required by the custom of men, it is possible for the one who promises the earlier performance to commit a breach even though the other party has not performed or tendered the equivalent. The promises are not concurrently dependent and conditional. The first promise is said to be independent while the second one may be dependent and conditional.[15] The duty to render the earlier performance can not be made conditional on tender of the return performance without changing the terms on which the parties have agreed.

Serjeant Williams, in his much-used footnote to Pordage v. Cole,[16] constructed the following rules:

" 1. If a day be appointed for the payment of money, or part of it, or for doing any other act, and the day is to happen, or may happen, before the thing which is the consideration of the money, or other act, is to be performed, an action may be brought for the money, or for not doing such other act, before performance; for it appears that the party relied upon his remedy, and did not intend to make the performance a condition precedent; and so it is where no time is fixed for performance of that which is the consideration of the money or other act.[17]

"But, 2, When a day is appointed for the payment of money, etc., and the day is to happen after the thing which is the consideration of the money, etc., is to be performed, no action can be maintained for the money, etc., before performance."

One of the performances may be such that it cannot be rendered in a single instant of time, although the other can be so performed. It is obvious that such a contract does not require simultaneous performance. If A promises to render personal service for B, and the latter promises to pay therefor the sum of

---

15.    See Loud v. Pomona Land & Water Co., 14 S.Ct. 928, 153 U.S. 564, 38 L.Ed. 822 (1893).

U.S.—Phillips & Colby Const. Co. v. Seymour, 91 U.S. 646, 650, 23 L. Ed. 341.

Md.—Speed v. Bailey, 139 A. 534, 153 Md. 655.

16.    1 Wms. Saund. 319 (1669).

17.    In support of this rule Serjt. Williams cites a number of antecedent cases, and then adds: "This seems to be the ground of the judgment in this case of Pordage v. Cole, the money being appointed to be paid on a fixed day, which

might happen before the lands were, or could be, conveyed."

This Rule 1 has often been repeated in modern cases. See:

Ill.—Powers Reg. Co. v. Hoffmann, 169 Ill.App. 657 (1912).

Me.—Allard v. Belfast, 40 Me. 369 (1855).

Md.—Speed v. Bailey, 139 A. 534, 153 Md. 655.

Mass.—Massachusetts Biog. Soc. v. Russell, 118 N.E. 662, 229 Mass. 524 (1918).

N.M.—Glaser v. Dannelley, 170 P. 63, 23 N.M. 593 (1918).

$100 per month, payment and service are not to be simultaneous; and the two promises are not concurrently conditional and mutually dependent. If the time of payment is not otherwise expressly agreed upon, the custom of contractors in such cases is that $100 shall be payable at the conclusion of a month's service.

The inclusion of the words "or may happen" in Serjeant Williams Rule 1 is subject to criticism, even though he may have justly felt that the decision in Pordage v. Cole forced him to include them. The duty to render a promised performance should not be held to be independent of the return performance, merely because the time set for rendering it was indefinite at first and might turn out to be either before or after the time set for the return performance. If the time, at first indefinite, turns out to be simultaneous with the time set for the return performance, or subsequent thereto, the dependency of promises should be determined in the light of the facts as they have eventually turned out to be. The question is not exclusively one of expressed intention; it is even more one of what justice requires. Thus, if A promises to convey land on June 1, in return for B's promise to pay the price when his ship comes in, A's duty should be held to be conditional on tender of the price in case B's ship comes in on or before June 1.

The mere order of performances in time is a matter of importance. The one promising the earlier performance may reasonably be supposed to calculate the risks involved, including the risk that, having himself performed, he will not receive the promised exchange therefor. As the courts have said, he has put his trust in the business honor of the other party and in the efficacy of the legal remedies that are available in case of breach. Standing alone, however, the mere order of performances in time is not always decisive of the case. The promise to render the earlier performance is not conditional on tender of an agreed equivalent by the other party; but it may be conditional on other factors even though it is not expressly so provided.

For example, the promisor's duty to render the earlier performance is constructively conditional on the absence of a material increase in his risk of not getting the agreed exchange. He is privileged to withhold his performance if the other party repudiates in advance or if for any reason he becomes prospectively unable to render the agreed exchange, whether because of objective impossibility or of insolvency or other personal inability.[18]

18.    If a seller promises to ship goods on a certain day, in return for the buyer's promise to pay for them after delivery, the seller's duty to ship is constructively conditional on the buyer's prospective ability to pay. If the seller can show that the buyer will not in fact be able to pay, he is privileged not to ship; this is true in spite of the fact that shipment was to be first in time. McCormick v.

This will be dealt with hereafter.

Furthermore, if the other party has promised to give a surety bond or other security for his own ultimate performance, the duty to render the earlier performance will be held to be conditional on the execution of the bond or security.[19] This is true even though the bond or security is not the agreed exchange. The requirement of security shows that the promisor did indeed calculate the risks and did not trust to the other party's business honor or to the efficacy of the legal remedies against him.

The duty of the party who has promised the later performance is conditional on the actual rendition (at least "substantially") of the earlier performance if that earlier performance is the agreed exchange for the later one. However, it may be very much less than that "agreed exchange;" and delay in rendering it may be of comparatively little importance and no more than a

---

Tappendorf, 99 P. 2, 51 Wash. 312 (1909). Indeed, the seller is privileged to stop the goods after transit has begun, if the buyer becomes insolvent.

The Uniform Commercial Code— Sales, § 2—609 (1950 draft) provides: "(1) A contract for sale imposes an obligation on each party that the other's expectation of receiving due performance will not be impaired. When reasonable grounds for insecurity arise with respect to the performance of either party the other may in writing demand adequate assurance of due performance and until he receives such assurance may if commercially reasonable suspend any performance for which he has not already received the agreed return."

The Code further provides in § 2— 702: "(1) Where the seller discovers the buyer to be insolvent he may (a) refuse delivery except for cash including payment for all goods theretofore delivered under the contract, and stop delivery under the provisions of this Article."

19. In the leading case of Kingston v. Preston, decided by Lord Mansfield in 1773, reported in 2 Doug. 689, the defendant promised that he would transfer his business and stock in trade to the plaintiff and the plaintiff promised that "at and before" the transfer he would give sufficient security for the payment of £250 monthly. In an action for refusing to execute the transfer, the defendant pleaded that the plaintiff had not tendered sufficient security. As against an argument that the promises were "mutual and independent," counsel for the defendant replied that "it would be highly unreasonable . . . to oblige the defendant to give up a beneficial business and valuable stock in trade and trust to the plaintiff's personal security (who might and indeed was admitted to be worth nothing)." This argument of the defendant was sustained and the plaintiff's demurrer of the plea was overruled. Tender of the security "was clearly a condition precedent." Observe, first, that the promise to transfer was not expressly conditional; and, secondly, that the giving of security was not the agreed exchange for the property, although it was to be given when the transfer was executed. But the security would greatly reduce the defendant's risk of getting nothing for his goods.

minor breach.[20]　　Again, there is no agreed exchange of the two performances if the contract is "aleatory," a matter to be dealt with in full hereafter.

## § 658.　When is Nonperformance of a Condition also a "Failure of Consideration"?

When there is no consideration for an informal promise, it is generally not binding on the promisor.[21]　When the courts speak of "failure of consideration," they do not mean absence of consideration or that the promise whose consideration has failed never was binding.　They mean that a promisor has not received something for which he bargained; and they give that as a reason why his promise ought not to be enforced.　Ordinarily, the contract with respect to which the phrase is used is a bilateral contract, one in which the parties not only exchange promises but one in which they also are bargaining for an exchange of the promised performances.　If A promises to deliver a cow in return for B's promise to pay fifty shillings, we have such a bilateral contract.　The consideration for B's promise to pay is A's promise to deliver the cow, not the cow herself.　Yet, if without sufficient excuse A fails to deliver as agreed, the courts now hold that B is justified in not paying the fifty shillings; and they often say that he is so justified by "failure of the consideration." [22]　It is the non-performance of A's return promise and the consequent failure of B to receive that for which he bargained — that for which he agreed to exchange his fifty shillings.　For B is regarded as bargaining for the cow, as well as for A's promise to deliver a cow.　The promise is merely a preliminary step toward the ultimate object.　He exchanges his promise for A's promise; but also he agrees to exchange his money for a cow.　As the word is used in the phrase "failure of consideration," the cow is the "consideration" for the money; and that consideration has failed to be rendered.[23]

---

20.　The rights and remedies of the parties are not dependent, as is sometimes supposed, upon which one committed "the first breach." Order in time is of importance but there are other factors having much greater importance.

21.　In some cases it will later become binding by reason of action taken by the promisee in reliance on the promise. See Restatement, Contracts, § 90, and chapter 8, herein.

22.　This was the old case of Nichols v. Raynbred, Hob. 88 (1615), in which the court held that the two promises were "independent" and that the seller could get judgment for the price without averring either delivery or tender of the cow.

23.　This usage of the word is broader than that of the American Law Institute, Contracts Restatement, or that of this treatise in the chapter on Consideration. In determining the validity of a contract, we need to know what, if anything, was exchanged for the promise. In determining the remedy for an asserted breach of the

This is another way of saying that B's promise is dependent and conditional—the delivery or tender of the cow is a condition precedent to B's duty of paying over the price. To say that B's promise is dependent and conditional does not necessarily mean that B expressly made it so, or even that he gave the matter a thought. If he said, "I promise to pay fifty shillings if and when the cow is delivered to me," he has made his promise expressly conditional; but his promissory duty is conditional even though he used no express words of condition, and even though he did not think of the matter at all. In either case, by the present usages of mankind and the modern court decisions, the delivery or tender of the cow is an event that must occur before it is B's duty to make payment. It is a condition precedent to the duty to pay.

Failure to deliver or to tender the cow is non-performance of a condition precedent to B's duty to pay; but this does not show that A has committed a breach of his contractual duty or that B has been discharged from his. Assuming that the parties contemplated concurrent performances, the duty of A to deliver was just as conditional in character as was the duty of B to pay. If B has made no tender of the price, A's failure to tender delivery is not a breach. Neither party can justly complain or maintain an action for damages as long as he has not tendered his own performance;[24] but neither one is discharged from duty by "failure of consideration" as long as it is still possible for the other to

---

promise, we often need to know what was the agreed equivalent of the performance that was promised. In an executed barter, two executed performances are exchanged as a "consideration" for each other.

See a discussion by Patterson, "Constructive Conditions in Contracts," 42 Col.L.Rev. 903, 920 (1942).

In Fibrosa Spolka Ack. v. Fairbairn L.C.B., [1942] 2 All Eng. 122, [1943] A.C. 32, Lord Simon said: "In English law, an enforceable contract may be formed by the exchange of a promise for a promise . . . and thus, in the law relating to the formation of contract, the promise to do a thing may often be the consideration; but, when one is considering the law of failure of consideration and of the quasi-contractual right to recover money on that ground, it is, generally speaking, not the promise which is referred to as

the consideration, but the performance of the promise. The money was paid to secure performance and, if performance fails, the inducement which brought about the payment is not fulfilled. If this were not so, there could never be any recovery of money for failure of consideration, by the payer of the money in return for a promise of future performance. Yet there are endless examples which show that money can be recovered, as for a complete failure of consideration, in cases where the promise was given but could not be fulfilled."

See a similar analysis in Bliss v. California Co-op. Producers, 181 P.2d 369, 30 Cal.2d 240, 170 A.L.R. 1009 (1947).

24. There are cases in which equity would have sustained a bill for specific performance even though the plaintiff had made no tender prior to suit; the decree would be

make a proper tender in compliance with the contract. There is such a discharge, however, just as soon as it has become impossible for substantial performance to be rendered, either because the time limit (specified or "reasonable") has expired or for other reasons. If the contract requires concurrent performances, the expiration of the time limit operates as a discharge of both parties alike.

"Failure of consideration" is almost wholly restricted in its use to a case where the non-performance has gone so far as to discharge the promisor from any further duty. If A has not yet tendered delivery of the cow, an action against B for refusing to pay is premature; tender is a condition precedent to B's duty to pay. Yet, the time for delivery may not have fully expired, and B can not be said to be wholly discharged. There has not as yet been a "failure of consideration," although it has not yet been performed. As soon as it has become impossible for A to render substantial performance, there is failure of consideration and B may properly be said to be discharged.[25]

### § 659.   Partial Failure of Consideration as the Nonperformance of a Condition

After the courts had abandoned the theory that the mutual promises in a bilateral contract are always independent unless they are made conditional in express terms, they were soon confronted with the problem as to what justice requires when there has been a partial, but not a total, failure of performance by the plaintiff. The first attempt at a solution was to lay down the rule that the defendant is not justified in refusing to perform his promise if the plaintiff's failure is only partial and is such that full and just compensation can be made by the payment of money damages. This was a reasonable beginning toward a solution of the new problem, although the forms in which the rule was stated were often very unclear and the analysis of the facts of cases left much to be desired.

Lord Mansfield, in 1777, expressed the rule thus: "The distinction is very clear, where mutual covenants go to the whole of the consideration on both sides, they are mutual conditions, the one precedent to the other. But where they go only to a part, where a breach may be paid for in damages, there the defendant has a remedy on his covenant and shall not plead it as a condition

conditional on actual performance and the costs would be equitably adjusted. In any such cases, similar relief is available in the courts of today; indeed, it may be granted even more liberally than formerly. Since the plaintiff offers performance in court, the defendant's repudiation or refusal in his answer becomes itself a breach justifying a judgment for damages.

**25.**   See §§ 1255–1263, Failure of Consideration as a Discharge, in Chapter 68.

precedent." [26]   Although this was an intelligent groping toward
the felt justice of the time, by a great judge whose contribution
to the growth of law and to justice is not exceeded by that of
any other judge, the words that he chose made the rule unclear
in meaning and application, and have compelled many an attempted "restatement." [27]

Like other attempted "rules," this one of Lord Mansfield can
be given meaning only by stating facts to which it is applied.  The
plaintiff was the grantor in a deed of conveyance in which the defendant grantee had covenanted to pay an annuity of £160 for
life to the plaintiff.  The defendant pleaded in defense to an action for this money that in return for his promise of the annuity
the plaintiff had conveyed a plantation in the West Indies with
a stock of slaves thereon and had covenanted that he had good
title to both land and slaves and that the defendant should have
quiet enjoyment;  also that the plaintiff's title to the slaves was
bad.  On demurrer this plea was held insufficient;  and the above
quoted rule was stated as the reason.

Observe that here was a bilateral contract under seal, with mutual covenants.  The consideration for the defendant's promise to
pay an annuity to the plaintiff for life was the plaintiff's deed of
conveyance with its warranty of title to both the land and the
slaves.  The defendant pleaded only that title to the slaves was
bad, a partial failure of the consideration.  It does not appear that
title to the land failed, nor what was the ratio in value of the

---

26.   **Eng.**—Boone v. Eyre, 1 H.Bl.
273 note (1777).  The words quoted
above are probably the words of
the reporter or commentator and
not the words of Lord Mansfield.
To say that "mutual covenants go
to the whole of the consideration
on both sides" is to be very obscure; and to say that "they are
mutual conditions, the one precedent to the other" is worse.  It is
the promised performance, and not
the promise, that may be a condition precedent to the duty of the
other promisor; and in no case
will performance by each party be
a condition precedent to the other's
duty, although tender of such performance may be.

27.   When Serjt. Williams prepared
his edition of Saunders' reports,
he appended to the earlier case of
Pordage v. Cole, 1 Wms. Saund.
319 (1669) his famous analytical
note on dependent and independ-

ent promises.  His third and fourth
"rules," undoubtedly based in part
upon Lord Mansfield's words above
quoted, are as follows:  "3. Where
a covenant goes only to part of
the consideration on both sides
and a breach of such covenant may
be paid for in damages, it is an
independent covenant, and an action may be maintained for a
breach of the covenant on the part
of the defendant, without averring
performance in the declaration.
.  .  .

"4.  But where the mutual covenants
go to the whole consideration on
both sides, they are mutual conditions, and performance must be
averred."

In thus stating his "rules" Serjt.
Williams made no improvement
in clarity of either analysis or
expression, although he did give
some assistance in his accompanying discussion.

slaves to the land. The court was not willing to hold that the defendant need not pay the annuity without being informed as to the amount of his injury in not getting the slaves, inasmuch as he got the land and still kept it. A more just remedy for the grantor's partial breach was an action for money damages. Under modern procedure this would be maintainable as a cross action in the same suit.

This was a case in which the performances promised by the two parties were not to be simultaneously exchanged. The plaintiff's performance was the conveyance of land and chattels by warranty deed. The defendant paid £500 in cash and promised to pay an "annuity" of £160 per annum during the plaintiff's life. Because of the aleatory character of the defendant's promise, the performances promised were not regarded by them as agreed equivalents; the performance promised by the plaintiff was definite and certain, while the payments promised by the defendant were wholly uncertain in number and amount. In the report of the case nothing is said of these facts, but the court must have been conscious of them. In the light of subsequent decisions as to aleatory contracts, this decision was clearly just and reasonable. The plaintiff's duty to give good title to the slaves was not conditional on the making of the annuity payments (although doubtless conditional on tender of the cash payment of £500), since they were to be subsequent in time and a credit risk was contemplated; his failure of performance as to the slaves was a breach of his duty, but it was only a partial breach. The defendant had received and continued to enjoy the benefits of the plantation. No court has ever held that the duty of a contractor who has received and retains large benefits is at once completely discharged by any breach however small by the other party. It is believed that, in spite of the aleatory character of the defendant's promise, if the plaintiff had in the beginning tendered a conveyance of the plantation without the slaves, the defendant would have been justified in refusing to pay anything. Before any part performance, the defendant's duty to make the cash payment of £500 would be held to be constructively conditional on tender of complete and perfect title to all the property as warranted. After the mutual part performances had taken place, a minor breach by one does not operate as a discharge of the other.[28] As we shall see, however, a major breach with substantial failure of consideration may operate as such a discharge if the contract is not aleatory in character.

28. In Graves v. Legg, 9 Exch. 709 (1854), it was said that, after the consideration has been performed in part, "it is no longer competent for the defendant to insist upon the nonperformance of that which was originally a condition precedent; and this is more correctly expressed than to say it was not a condition precedent at all."

## § 660. Analysis of Another Illustrative Case: Ellen v. Topp

From the form of the "rule" stated in Boone v. Eyre above, a form that has often been repeated in other cases, the inference might be drawn that if one promisor in a bilateral contract has performed in part, the other promisor is always bound to perform in full, in spite of a partial failure of the performance for which he bargained—that while the duty of one promisor may be conditional on the absence of a total repudiation or total failure of performance by the other party, it can never be conditional (in the absence of express words to the contrary) on the rendition of any portion of the return performance after some of it has been rendered as agreed. It became apparent that such an inference is erroneous. The part that has failed to be performed may be of vital importance to the other party, so as to make it quite unjust to require him to proceed with his own promised performance.

Even as stated in its early form, the "rule" took this into account somewhat obscurely, saying that the partial non-performance shall not be pleaded "as a condition precedent" if it goes "only to a part, where the breach may be paid for in damages." Whatever this was intended to express, it is perfectly clear that a party should not in all cases be allowed to go free and clear of all performance on his own part if he has received and retains something of value rendered by the other; and it is equally clear that he should not have to pay the whole price or otherwise render his full performance when he is not going to receive the full agreed equivalent thereof. If the partial nonperformance is such that the harm to the injured party can be fully compensated by a money payment as "damages," it may be proper to require him to perform his own part in full, making due allowance of compensatory damages for his harm (by deduction when that is feasible). Ancient procedure at law might not have permitted this in a single action; but in modern practice there is generally no difficulty other than that of measuring the damages. Another possible solution would be to privilege the injured party to refuse to render any performance if he can and does return to the wrongdoer the part performance received or its value in money. A third possible solution is to give to the injured party the privilege of rendering no further performance even though he can not or does not return what he has received, giving to the other party a right to reasonable compensation for the part performance that he has rendered, insofar as he can show that its value exceeds what he has already received on account and the harm that his breach has caused.[29] It is obvious that in cases in which a breach has occurred in the course of performance a just solution can not be reached by sole dependence on the methodology of "conditions," whether they are described as express, implied, or constructive.

Let us consider at this point another case, one that arose some 75 years after Boone v. Eyre. An indenture of apprenticeship was entered into between George Topp, father of Richard, and Frederick Ellen, whereby the latter acknowledged payment of £70 and covenanted to instruct Richard in the business of auctioneer, appraiser, and corn-factor, and George Topp covenanted that his son would serve faithfully as an apprentice for five years. After serving for three years, Richard departed from service; and the master Ellen sued George Topp for damages in an action of covenant. The defendant Topp pleaded that before Richard quit service Ellen had abandoned the business of corn-factor and so had ceased to teach Richard therein. The court sustained this plea, although it is obvious that it alleged only a partial failure of consideration.[30] Richard had received the full instruction for three years; and the plaintiff was ready and willing to continue to instruct him in the business of auctioneer and appraiser.

The court repeated the "rule" in Boone v. Eyre,[31] and thus commented on it: "It cannot be intended to apply to every case in which a covenant by the plaintiff forms only a part of the consideration, and the residue of the consideration has been had by the defendant. The residue must be the substantial part of the contract; and if, in the case of Boone v. Eyre, two or three negroes had been accepted and the equity of redemption [the land] not conveyed, we do not apprehend that the plaintiff could have recovered the whole stipulated price, and left the defendant to recover damages for the non-conveyance of it." [32]

This decision and the reasoning of both court and lawyer, show that there had been born the doctrine that we have learned to describe as the doctrine of "substantial performance". One prom-

29.  This method is sometimes necessary to avoid an unjust penalty or forfeiture. It is dealt with in Chapter 62, dealing with the Remedy of Restitution in Favor of a Plaintiff in Default.

30.  Eng.—Ellen v. Topp, 6 Exch. 424 (1851).

31.  Pollock C. B., made one logical improvement in it. He does not say that "the covenants . . . are mutual conditions." Instead he says that after part performance, if the partial breach can be paid for in damages, "the covenant is independent, and *the perform-*

*ance of it* is not a condition precedent." He thus recognizes that a covenant or promise is not a condition of the return promise; it is *the performance* of one promise on which the other may be conditional.

32.  The court had been well instructed by the defendant's lawyer, Macnamara, who thus argued: "The exercise of the trades, or rather the non-abandonment of any one of them by the master, is a condition precedent to the service of the apprentice. . . . The non-exercise of the trade for a few days merely would not

isor in a bilateral contract can not enforce the return promise if he fails to perform the substantial part of his own; that is, the duty of one promisor is conditional on substantial performance of the consideration for which he bargained. This doctrine is most often seen referred to in the discussion of building contracts; but it is applicable to all bilateral bargains for an exchange of equivalents.[33]

The justice of the decision in this case is not demonstrated by merely saying that continuing to teach corn-factoring was a constructive condition of Richard's duty to remain in service, or even by saying that continuing to teach the boy to be auctioneer and appraiser would not be "substantial performance" of the agreed exchange. The court must have some evidential basis for "constructing" the condition and for believing the curtailed performance to be less than the "substantial" equivalent. However, there are no obvious reasons for criticising the decision made. Richard's quitting service deprived Ellen of his services as an apprentice for the two years in which their value would be the greatest; but Ellen was relieved of the necessity of further teaching and support. Ellen's prospective failure to teach was only partial; but the harm caused by it to Richard's career is not easily measurable with money. Further, Ellen had already received £70 in cash in addition to Richard's immature services for the first three years. Justice must often be arrived at by a process of rough approximation.

justify the apprentice in leaving; but the relinquishment of any one of them would." Then after quoting the "rule" of Boone v. Eyre, he continues: "The question seems to be, whether, notwithstanding the breach, the contract can be substantially carried out, and whether adequate compensation can be obtained for such breach. The reason of the rule is that the damages would be unequal if a breach of a comparatively unimportant part of the contract afforded ground for rescinding it altogether. The chief tests to be applied appear to be the materiality and importance of the covenants broken and the difficulty of assessing damages thereupon. . . . The rule adopted for the construction of covenants as dependent or independent is this: That the good sense of the case, the nature of the instrument, and the intention of the parties, are to decide the question."

See, also, Chanter v. Leese, 4 M. & W. 296, 5 M. & W. 698 (1838), plaintiff agreed that defendant might make and sell under several patents; one patent was void; the defendant was held privileged to repudiate the whole, nothing having as yet been done under the contract; Jansen v. Schneider, 78 Misc. 48, 138 N.Y.S. 144 (1912), where one agreed to instruct another to become an aviator for $250, but did not complete the instruction as to the construction of the machine within a reasonable time, the breach went to the essence; Vigers v. Cook, [1919] 2 K.B. 475, an undertaker is entitled to nothing if he performs the service in all except that he fails to preserve the body so that it can be taken into the church.

33. The doctrine of "substantial performance" is considered in detail in Chapter 36.

# CHAPTER 33

## CONSTRUCTIVE CONDITIONS IN SALES OF LAND OR GOODS

---

This Chapter (§§ 661–673), omitted as a whole herein, deals briefly with problems in the construction and operation of contracts for the sale of land and sale of goods. Full treatment must be looked for in treatises on Vendor and Purchaser and Sales.

# CHAPTER 34

## CONSTRUCTIVE CONDITIONS IN SERVICE CONTRACTS, CHARTERPARTIES, LEASES

This Chapter (§§ 674–686) is also omitted as a whole. Consult treatises on the law of Master and Servant, Charter parties, and Leases.

# CHAPTER 35

## CONDITIONS IN INSTALMENT CONTRACTS— DIVISIBILITY

### § 687. Instalment Contracts—Effect of a Nonpayment

An instalment contract is one in which the agreed performance of at least one of the parties is to be rendered, not as a whole at one time and place, but piecemeal at different times or different places.

1. A seller delivers a bill of goods to a buyer who pays one third cash and promises to pay the balance in two equal amounts at thirty and sixty days. The price of the goods is divided into three instalments.

2. A seller promises to deliver enough brick for the erection of a building, at the rate of at least 5000 brick per day (or in amounts to be specified later by the buyer), the price to be paid on completion of all deliveries. Here the whole price is to be paid at one time and place; but the goods sold must be delivered in instalments.[1]

3. A workman is employed by contract for one year at a salary of one hundred dollars per month. It is obvious that both the work and the wages are to be given in instalments, the wages in twelve instalments and the work in as many as we care to say.

4. A builder contracts to erect a building by a specified date, for a total price of twenty thousand dollars, payable as work proceeds in amounts to be certified by the architect. The price of the labor and materials is here payable in instalments of an undetermined number and amount; it is obvious that the labor and materials will also be given in instalments. Here the instal-

---

[1] Such a case, as decided, is Kelly Const. Co. v. Hackensack Brick Co., 103 A. 417, 91 N.J.L. 585, 2 A.L.R. 685 (1918). No time for payment was expressly determined. The price was stated to be "$7 per thousand;" and deliveries were to be as needed for construction of a large building. It was not enough to say, as the court did, that this was an "entire" contract. A consideration of trade custom in such cases might well lead to a different interpretation and result. Cf. Uniform Commercial Code— Sales, § 2—307 (1950 draft).

ments of the price are usually not the agreed equivalents of the instalments of labor and materials previously rendered; building contracts generally provide that the payments shall bear an estimated ratio to the work previously done, as where the owner promises to pay seventy per cent of the value of completed work as certified by the architect.

In each of the foregoing cases, the transaction is a credit transaction, not only in the sense that each party puts faith and credit in the word of the other, but also in the sense that one of the parties evidences that faith and credit by rendering in advance part or all of his own performance. He risks an actual performance on the mere word of the other party that he will later give the equivalent. In case 1, it is the seller who gives the credit, with respect to two thirds of the price. In case 2, the seller gives credit for the whole price. In cases 3 and 4, it is the workman and the builder who give partial credit.

A transaction may be an instalment contract without being a credit transaction at all. Both parties may agree to perform in instalments without promising to render any performance in advance of full payment of the price of each instalment so rendered. Thus, a seller contracts to deliver wheat straw at the rate of three specified loads per fortnight, for the price of thirty three shillings per load, payable on delivery; simultaneously with each delivery, the full price of each load is to be paid.[2] Both parties promise to perform in instalments; but neither one promises any performance in advance of its exact agreed equivalent. Neither one risks an actual performance upon the mere word of the other.

It is always a matter of interpretation to determine whether a party has promised to deliver, or to pay, or otherwise to perform, in instalments, an interpretation that at times is difficult. It is a matter of interpretation whether one party has promised a part or all of his performance in advance of the payment of its price, a credit transaction. Upon the result of this interpretation depends the existence of a breach and the determination of whether an action can be maintained against a promisor. In making the interpretation due weight should be given to the surrounding circumstances and the custom of men in like cases.[3]

The principal question now to be considered, however, is not primarily one of interpretation, in the majority of cases. We

---

**2.** See Withers v. Reynolds, 2 Barn. & Adol. 882 (1831).

**3.** The Uniform Commercial Code —Sales, § 2—307 (1950 draft) provides: "Unless otherwise agreed all goods called for by a contract for sale must be tendered in a single delivery and payment is due only on such tender, but where the circumstances give either party the right to make or demand delivery in lots the price, if it can be apportioned, may be demanded for each lot."

now assume that performance by one of the parties is to be in instalments; and we assume that the failure to render an instalment as promised is a breach of contract for which an appropriate action can be maintained.[4] Our question now, however, is as to the effect of such an instalment breach by one party upon the reciprocal duty of the other. When does an instalment breach go to the essence of the contract, discharging the other party from further duty and giving him an immediate action for damages as for a total breach? Also, when is the performance of a promised instalment a condition of the duty of the other party to proceed with his agreed performance?

These two questions are not identical in either form or substance. For example, the failure of an owner to make a specified progress payment under a building contract may justify the suspension of work by the builder, without immediately discharging the builder from further contractual obligation; it may enable him to maintain an action for the overdue instalment, without at once enabling him to maintain an action for damages for a total breach.

As a matter of course, the parties may provide in clear language that performance of an instalment by one of them shall be a condition of the other's duty to proceed, or that it shall not be such a condition; they may provide that failure to perform an instalment as agreed shall go to the essence and shall operate as a total breach and as a total discharge of the other party or that it shall not so operate. The question whether they have so provided is, indeed, one of interpretation. In litigated cases, however, the contract generally contains no such express provision. It merely contains an express promise to perform in specified instalments. The effect of a failure must be determined by the court, on the basis of what the court thinks that justice requires. This is not mere interpretation.

Our present job is to suggest tentative rules to aid in determining what "justice" requires in these cases. Like other rules of law, these rules are, in the main, to be drawn, by an inductive process, from the court decisions. Though they can not be absolute, and should not be stated in dogmatic form, they can nevertheless render useful service in aiding a court to a decision and in enabling us to predict the decision that a court will make.

## § 688. When is an Instalment Contract "Divisible"?

It is obvious that a failure by one party to render one instalment of his promised performance is not a failure of the whole performance. It is not a total failure of the agreed exchange. As the courts use the term, it is not a total "failure of consideration" for the other party's promise.

If the other party also has promised to render his performance in instalments, and if the promised instalments have been apportioned into pairs of separate agreed equivalents, then the failure to render one of these instalments is a total failure of the consideration for the reciprocal instalment with which it was paired by the parties. Such a contract is often said to be "divisible," as if the transaction consisted of a number of separate contracts, one for each of the apportioned pairs of instalments. The term "divisible," however, is used in other senses, so that it renders a very precarious service in the analysis of a problem or in the statement of a rule.[a]

Sometimes it has been thought that since the failure to render an instalment is not a total "failure of consideration," its performance can not be a condition of the other party's duty, and its failure can not operate as a discharge of the other party from further duty.[5] That this is not correct will be shown later on. The relative importance of the failure of one instalment varies with the circumstances that surround it.[6] The question

a. "Divisibility" and "Apportionment" are dealt with in detail in the general treatise §§ 694–699.

5. Mersey Steel & Iron Co. v. Naylor, Benzon & Co., L.R. 9 App.Cas. 434 (1884, H.L.) was a case in which a seller promised to deliver 5000 tons of steel blooms in instalments of 1000 tons monthly. Payment also was to be in instalments, cash within three days after receipt of shipping documents. One of the instalment payments was withheld without legal justification; and the seller at once refused to make any further deliveries. For reasons to be considered later on, it was rightly held that the seller's refusal was wrongful; but the court's idea that the failure to pay a part by the buyer could not be a condition of the seller's duty, in a contract that the court called an "entire contract," is not to be approved. Lord Selborne said that the fact that payments and deliveries were to be in instalments "does not split up the contract into as many contracts as there shall be deliveries." He then proceeded: "It is perfectly clear that no particular payment can be a condition precedent of the entire contract,

because delivery under the contract was most certainly to precede payment; and that being so, I do not see how, without express words, it can possibly be made a condition precedent to the subsequent fulfilment of the unfulfilled part of the contract, by the delivery of the undelivered steel." If other factors, such for example as insolvency, had accompanied the nonpayment, the court would have easily seen the possibility.

6. See Los Angeles Gas & E. Co. v. Amalgamated Oil Co., 106 P. 55, 156 Cal. 776 (1909), where the failure of the buyer to keep its promise to buy oil of no one other than the defendant was held to justify the defendant in refusing further deliveries, even though the oil was to be delivered in instalments each of which had its apportioned price. In spite of this apportionment of goods and price, the contract was said to be "entire." Without doubt, if an instalment of the price of oil delivered was not paid, a separate action could be maintained therefor. For purposes of such a suit, the contract was "divisible." At the same time the seller's duty to deliver was con-

whether the performance of a particular instalment is of such importance that its failure makes it fair and just either to discharge the other party entirely, or to privilege him to suspend his own performance, is not one that can be answered by any stated rule of law. We can, however, collect and compare the specific cases of the past, thereby acquiring knowledge of what has seemed fair and just to the courts in those cases. Here, as elsewhere, we can construct helpful working rules.

### § 689.  Nonpayment of an Instalment of the Price of Land

Where the purchase price of land is payable in instalments, and the contract provides that conveyance is to be made, or possession given, at a date that precedes some of the instalments, it is clear that the purchaser's duty to pay these later instalments is constructively conditional on the execution of the conveyance or the giving of possession.[7] This does not mean that failure to convey on the exact date will operate as a total discharge of the purchaser from further duty. In such contracts, performance by either party at the exact time specified is ordinarily not of the essence except when expressly so provided. But the law will not treat the contract as an unsecured credit transaction any further than the agreement itself clearly indicates.

So it is that if the due date for conveyance and the date for the payment of one instalment of the price are identical, the duty to pay that instalment is conditional on tender of conveyance, and the duty to convey is conditional on tender of that instalment. This is true even though it is plain that the conveyance and the one instalment are not agreed equivalents. If an instalment is made payable at a date that precedes the date set for conveyance or for possession, the vendor's duty to convey or to give possession is conditional on actual payment of the earlier instalment.

**§§ 690–692.**  At this point in the general treatise, contracts for the Sale of Goods and contracts of Employment are dealt with. Such contracts are very often Instalment contracts. Courts have to determine the effect of failure to pay an instalment of the price, or of wages, as agreed; also to determine the effect of failure to deliver an instalment of the goods or to perform one or more days' service. Works on the law of Sales and of Master and Servant give fuller treatment.

ditional on performance of the buyer's promise to take its whole supply of oil; for this purpose the contract was said to be "entire."

7.  **N.Y.**—Grant v. Johnson, 5 N.Y. 247 (1851). Some of the reasoning in this case should not be approved; and the explanation given of the earlier English case Boone v. Eyre, 1 H.Bl. 273, is not sound.

### § 693. Remedies Available to Building Contractor in Case of Nonpayment of an Instalment

Nonpayment of an instalment when due is a breach of contract duty. The remedies that are available to the contractor are considered more fully in the chapter dealing with remedies for breach. They may be stated briefly here also.

One remedy that is always available is an action for the specific sum due, with interest as damages for the delay. If the nonpayment is held to be a partial breach only, not going to the essence, this remedy is the builder's only remedy.[41] As long as the nonpayment continues, the builder will generally be privileged to suspend performance;[42] but this is not a judicial remedy, although the legal privilege to suspend performance is itself a legal relation created for the benefit of the injured party. This legal privilege is the automatic result of the nonpayment, requiring for its existence no declaration by a court or other judicial action.

If the nonpayment is held to be a vital breach, going to the essence, either because it is expressly so provided in the agreement, or because it is relatively so important and its results so injurious to the builder, the builder is at once legally privileged not only to suspend performance but to renounce the contract forever. This privilege is likewise the automatic result of the vital breach. It is not a judicial remedy, although it is a legal relation of benefit to the injured party. When the breach is such as to create this legal relation, the builder has three alternative courses to pursue:

1. He may stop performance and forget it, bringing no suit and asking no remedy.

2. He may continue performance, treating the breach as if it were partial, and either giving further indulgence, or bringing a suit for the instalment with interest as stated above.

3. He may renounce the contract entirely, and bring suit for reasonable compensation for his labor and material already performed and transferred.[43] This is often referred to as "rescission"; but it is very different from a mutual agreement to rescind. The remedy asked is a judicial remedy, often described as "quasi-contractual."

4. He may renounce the contract entirely, and bring suit for damages for a total breach, these damages being measured by the full contract price, after deducting all payments received on account and also the cost of completion that is saved by the refusal to complete. If the breach causes other losses that the owner had reason to foresee, they may be added in the judgment that is awarded.[44]

5. Under some circumstances he may proceed with his own performance and get a decree for specific performance by the owner. This is an "equitable" remedy, that is considered elsewhere under its appropriate title.

There is no serious doubt as to the foregoing remedies available to the injured party. The hard problem is to determine whether the breach is total or partial, whether or not it goes to the essence. This is the problem that has been discussed in preceding sections.

# CHAPTER 36

## SUBSTANTIAL PERFORMANCE, ITS CHARACTER AND EFFECT

## § 700. The Problem of "Substantial Performance"—Cases in Which It is Involved

The phrase "substantial performance" is one that has played a part in the enforcement of contracts and in the statement of contract law. Sometimes courts and writers refer to "the substantial performance doctrine"; and they may assert that it is, or that it is not, a part of the law of the particular state. It is necessary for us to devote some time to a consideration of the concept, or concepts, behind this phrase.

When one party has failed to render a part of the performance as and when promised by him, the following questions may arise:

1. Is the other party privileged to refuse to render a reciprocally promised performance?

2. Is the other party wholly discharged from his contractual duty?

3. Can the other party maintain suit for damages, regarding the breach as "total"?

4. Can the other party maintain suit for damages for a partial breach, while still maintaining an enforceable right to further performance, one for breach of which he can maintain a second action later on?

652

In the present chapter we are considering only the first of these four questions; but a brief discussion of them all may be useful in showing that they are closely related. All four are questions as to the legal effect of a partial failure of performance by one party; but the particular legal effect that is questioned in each one is separate and distinct. In each case the answer will depend in large measure upon the character and extent of the partial failure—upon its relative importance to the party affected by it. In all alike we need to know whether the failure is "substantial" or minor and whether the part that has not failed is "substantial" or unsubstantial. This ratio between the part that is not performed and the full performance promised varies with the case. It can not be said that any stated ratio will determine the answer to any one of the questions, much less that the answers to all four will depend on a uniform ratio. In the first two questions the party who has failed in performance is the plaintiff; in the last two it is the defendant.

When a contract has been made for an agreed exchange of two performances, one of which is to be rendered first, the rendition of this one substantially in full is a constructive condition precedent to the duty of the other party to render his part of the exchange. The first of the above four questions can not be answered in a specific case until it is determined as a fact whether the performance actually rendered is "substantially in full."

The second one of the above questions can not be answered until it is determined as a fact that substantial performance, not only has not yet been rendered by the plaintiff, but also that the defendant is justified in believing that it will not be rendered. If it is now too late for such performance, or if for any other reason the defects can not be cured, the defendant is not only privileged not to perform his part of the exchange now, he is so privileged forever and he is discharged from his contractual duty.[1] If the defective performance, though less than "substantial" has conferred benefits on the defendant in excess of his injury, he may be under a quasi-contractual duty to pay that excess.[2]

In the third question the parties are reversed; it is the defendant who is in default by partial failure of performance.[3] The

1. See Restatement, Contracts, §§ 397–401, Discharge of One Party by Breach or Non-Performance of the Other or by Failure of Consideration. See Chapter 68, herein.

2. See Restatement, Contracts, § 357, Restitution in Favor of a Plaintiff Who Is Himself in Default.

3. Questions 3 and 4 are not involved in those cases in which the defendant has a good excuse for his failure to perform. If such an excuse exists, he is not guilty of a "breach" of contract. And yet, if he has rendered a part performance, the question whether it may properly be described as "substantial" is involved; and questions numbered 1 and 2 above may be in issue before a court.

answer to this question also requires the determination of a fact whether the partial failure is such as to prevent the performance that has been (or still may be) rendered from being "substantial". Does the breach already committed by the defendant go to the "essence"? In making this determination the same factors must be weighed as in the case of questions 1 and 2. Even for a minor breach the law gives a remedy, but it is a minor remedy. The plaintiff is not privileged to refuse his own performance; and he has no right to damages for a large or "total" breach that the defendant has not yet committed.[4]

In answering question 4, as in the other three, we must determine as a fact whether the defendant's breach is such as to prevent the performance that is rendered by him from being "substantial" performance. The question is often put thus: Does his breach go to the essence? If the breach is relatively minor and not "of the essence", the plaintiff is himself still bound by the contract; he can not abandon performance and get damages for a "total" breach by the defendant. He can, however, maintain suit for damages for the minor breach at any time until his action is barred by a statute of limitations. But even if the breach is a major one, one that causes the rendered performance to be less than "substantial," there are cases in which the plaintiff can "waive" the condition of his own duty and require continued performance by the other party. The cases in which this is possible are often "instalment" contracts; and they are never cases in which the defendant has definitely repudiated the contract. Difficulty and conflict are encountered on this question.[5]

In the sections that follow, we are considering only the first of the four questions. To what extent is performance by one party a condition of the other party's duty to render a return performance? How great, relatively, must a plaintiff's nonperformance be in order to justify the defendant in refusing to proceed with his return performance. If the plaintiff renders "substantial," but less than full, performance, is the defendant bound to pay the agreed price (render the agreed exchange)? How do we determine what constitutes "substantial" performance?

### § 701. The Problem is Not Restricted to Building Contracts, Although Commonly Appearing Therein

Before trying to determine the difference between a performance that is substantial and one that is not substantial, our attention should be directed to identifying the performance in question. What is this "performance" that is to be weighed and valued,

---

4. See Restatement, Contracts, Chapter 11, Breach of Contract, §§ 312–317; also Chapter 53, Breach of Contract, herein.

5. See Restatement, Contracts, Chapter 11, and Chapter 53 herein.

whose performance is it, and what is the relation that it bears to the other elements of the particular transaction? The performance in which we are now interested is the performance of a promissory contractual duty by one of the parties to the contract. In order to determine whether a building contractor is entitled to payment of an instalment of the price, we do not need to know whether or not he has rendered substantial performance of his duty to his wife and children; what we seek to know is whether he has built the house as he promised and whether he is asking that the defendant be compelled to pay for something that he has never received.

This problem of "substantial performance" is involved in contracts of all kinds, contracts for the sale of land or of goods, contracts for the rendering of personal service,[6] and contracts for manufacture and transportation,[7] as well as contracts for the building of buildings or for other creative construction. For the present, it will be convenient to restrict our discussion chiefly to building contracts. Such tentative rules and suggestions as may be made will generally be applicable to other kinds of contracts; but the language will mostly be the language of a building transaction.

The ordinary contract between a builder and an owner is a bilateral contract, consisting of a promise by the builder to construct in accordance with plans and specifications and a promise by the owner to pay a price therefor in one or more instalments. The owner's promise to make these payments may be expressly conditional on the performance or happening of anything in nature, on which the parties care to agree; it may be expressly conditional on an architect's certificate, on the mathematically exact performance of every detail of the specifications, on the driving of the last nail prior to May 1. Theoretically, at least, people are free to contract as they choose, limiting their rights and duties in ways that are unusual or absurd or unprofitable. Their language is subject to judicial interpretation; and in this process of

---

6. In Poussard v. Spiers & Pond, 1 Q.B.D. 410 (1876), a singer who was hired for the leading part in an opera was too ill to appear for rehearsals or the opening performance, but she became able a few days later. The employer was held justified in hiring a substitute for the entire period. The singer was not guilty of a breach of contract; but the performance she tendered was not "substantial."

There was a similar holding in Hong v. Independent School Dist., 232 N.W. 329, 181 Minn. 309, 72 A.L.R. 280 (1930), where a teacher was ill for the first five weeks of school.

On the other hand, in Bettini v. Gye, 1 Q.B.D. 187 (1876), a singer hired for concert work was unable to appear for rehearsals until four days later than agreed, there being no serious interference with an advertised program. The performance that he tendered was close to "full" performance and was "substantial."

In the above cases the term "substantial" was not used.

interpretation the tendency away from the absurd and the unreasonable is so strong as to amount to a practical limitation upon our freedom of contract. But it is not with express conditions or interpretation that we are now primarily concerned. We are now dealing with a contract that consists of two exchanged promises requiring the rendition of two promised performances, without making either promise expressly conditional on anything. The builder promises to build and the owner promises to pay.

In such a contract as this, the parties exchange their promises; but also they are providing for an exchange of performances. By agreement, their promises are equivalent; but equally by agreement the promised building is the equivalent of the promised price. The consideration for the owner's promise to pay is the builder's promise to build; and yet it is customary to say that the failure of the builder to keep his promise and to build the house is a "failure of consideration" for the owner's promise. Even though the agreement was a perfectly valid contract, each promise being supported by sufficient consideration, the customs and beliefs of men are such that substantial non-performance by one party is held to justify non-performance by the other. Though both parties are bound, neither one of them is bound to do something for nothing. This means that, even though they have not said so in terms, the duty of each party may be conditional on performance by the other. Such "conditions" as these are herein described as "constructive conditions." And we may now say at once that "substantial performance" by the builder is a constructive condition of the owner's duty to pay.

It is substantial performance of what the builder promised to do, of the construction work, of the equivalent for which the owner has promised to pay, that is the "condition" of the owner's duty to pay. It is not substantial performance of "a condition" that must be rendered; "substantial performance" *is* the condition— the fact that must exist before payment is due. It is now the general rule in the American courts that a contractor who has rendered "substantial performance" of the promised equivalent of the contract price can get judgment for that price, with a deduction for minor defects and nonperformance.[8]

## § 702. Substantial Performance is Not a Complete Discharge of Duty

When we use the term "substantial performance of a promissory duty," we always mean something less than full and exact performance of that duty. As so used, therefore, substantial performance is not a complete discharge of duty. It is not a defense in a suit against the building contractor for damages. Judgment will not be prevented from going against him in such a suit by his averring and proving that he performed almost in full, that his deviations have been small, that the owner can live comfortably in the house, or that the value to the owner is very nearly as great as it would have been had exact performance been rendered.[9]

If the difference in value is slight, the damages allowed for the contractor's breach will approach that minimum limit called "nominal damages." But the award of even "nominal" damages requires a finding of fact that the performance rendered is less than full and exact. There has been a breach of duty; but the breach is relatively small and unimportant.

One who has rendered substantial performance, but less than full performance, and has already received the agreed price, has a defense in a suit by the owner for the restitution of that price.[10] There has been no such "failure of consideration" as to create a quasi contractual duty of restitution. The reason is not merely the fact that the contractor is in possession or that "possession is nine points" in the law. It is because the contractor had a right to the payment when it was made and could have maintained suit for it. This is not to say that "possession" does not still have weight in the courts—it still has its "points." This is especially true in those cases in which the court says that it does not recognize the "substantial performance doctrine", or in which the performance rendered is held to be less than "substantial."

### § 703. Substantial Performance Does Not Mean Any Performance Having Substantial Value

Almost any part performance of a building contract has some value in the market. Thus, if the contractor excavates the hole for the cellar and stops work forever at that point, the excavation

---

**9.** One who contracts, (1) to put in gas pipes for both natural and artificial gas is not excused by the fact that natural gas is not in use in the town; or (2) to put in flue linings in the chimneys, by the fact that he uses another equally good method; or (3) to use Acme paint, by the fact that Princess paint is as good. See Morgan v. Gamble, 79 A. 410, 230 Pa. 165 (1911).

"The courts never say that one who makes a contract fills the measure of his duty by less than full performance. They do say, however, that an omission, both trivial and innocent, will sometimes be atoned for by allowance of the resulting damage, and will not always be the breach [nonperformance] of a condition to be followed by a forfeiture. The distinction is akin to that between dependent and independent promises and conditions." Cardozo, J., in Jacob & Youngs v. Kent, 129 N.E. 889, 230 N.Y. 239 (1921). The distinction that this refers to is not merely "akin," it is identical. The question is, upon what performance by the plaintiff is the defendant's legal duty to pay conditional. So far as the construction of the law is concerned, in its effort to do justice, the condition of the defendant's duty is "substantial performance" by the plaintiff of the agreed equivalent.

See also Karlinski v. P. R. & H. Lumber & Const. Co., 281 N.W. 898, 68 N.D. 522 (1938).

has value; indeed that value may be a very substantial amount. The existence of the hole may now save $500, or even $50,000, in the cost of erecting the complete building. These are "substantial" amounts of money. But when we speak of "substantial performance," we mean something different from this. The hole has substantial value; but it is far from substantial performance of the builder's promissory duty, and it is far from enough to enable the builder to maintain suit for the contract price of the building.

Of course, the contract may be what is often called a "divisible" contract, meaning by this that the parties have clearly apportioned the mutual performances into pairs of smaller agreed equivalents. The work of the builder may have been expressly divided into parts, for each of which the owner has promised to pay a specified portion of the entire contract price. For the excavation work as a separate performance, the contract may provide that the owner shall pay the sum of $5,000 as soon as it is completed. If such is the agreement, the excavation of the hole is not merely "substantial performance," it is full and complete performance of the agreed equivalent to be exchanged for the $5,000—the apportioned part of the total price.

### § 704.  How Great may be the Deviation Without Preventing "Substantial Performance"?

It is not easy to lay down rules for determining what amounts to "substantial performance," sufficient to justify a judgment for the contract price (subject to a counterclaim for injury, if asserted) in any particular case. It is always a question of fact, a matter of degree, a question that must be determined relatively to all the other complex factors that exist in every instance.[11] The variation in these factors is such that generalization is difficult and the use of cases as precedents is dangerous.

This is not to say that rules are impossible or that precedents are useless. Here, as elsewhere, guiding suggestions are of value; but they must not be taken as rules of thumb, or used as implacable major premises. Here, as elsewhere, case experience can not be dispensed with; and justice is not to be expected from one who scorns the light of such experience. In the cases are found illustrations of the factors that judges have considered, and sometimes an indication of the weight given to them. Without doubt, in every case there have been factors of importance that are not listed in the opinion of the appellate court; sometimes the appellate court may not be aware of some of the important

11.  In Jacob & Youngs v. Kent, 129 N.E. 889, 230 N.Y. 230 (1921), Judge Cardozo said: "The decisions in this state commit us to the liberal view, which is making its way, nowadays, in jurisdictions slow to welcome it. Dakin & Co. v. Lee, 1916, 1 K.B. 566, 579. Where the

factors that influenced the trial court; sometimes the trial court itself was not advised of such a factor or was not aware that it should be considered. In spite of all this, it is a study of such cases as we have that informs us of the factors to look for and gives us advice as to their weight. If at times it seems that the blind are leading the blind, that is no justification for our going it blind, cock-sure that there is nothing for us to learn.

The problem with which we are dealing here, under the title "substantial performance" is not limited to building contracts or to plumbing contractors. What is essentially the same problem recurs in many guises and is discussed herein under other headings. What is the effect of non-payment of an instalment of the price, or of the non-delivery of some tons of iron rails? When is "time of the essence"? How shall we determine the difference between a partial breach and a total breach? When is a contractor's failure of performance of such importance as to entitle the other party to the restitution of money paid in advance? When does a breach go "to the essence"? Is there any matter that is "material," or any essence that is "essential," or any substance that is "substantial?"

It is not necessary to go astray into a feckless logomachy. Without knowing how to define a "fact," or a "rule of law," it is possible to work out a practical system of justice by which men can live, keeping our stumbling feet in the ploughed fields and not blinding our eyes by metaphysical clouds. What, then, are some of these earthy factors that influence the action of contractors and should affect the court in reaching its final judgment? The reader must not expect a complete list of these factors; the writer is not sufficiently experienced to make such a list. Perhaps no

line is to be drawn between the important and the trivial cannot be settled by a formula. In the nature of the case precise boundaries are impossible. The same omission may take on one aspect or another according to its setting. Substitution of equivalents may not have the same significance in fields of art on the one side and in those of mere utility on the other. Nowhere will change be tolerated, however, if it is so dominant or pervasive as in any real or substantial measure to frustrate the purpose of the contract. There is no general license to install whatever, in the builder's judgment, may be regarded as 'just as good.' The question is one of degree, to be answered, if there is doubt, by the triers of the facts, and, if the inferences are certain, by the judges of the law. We must weigh the purpose to be served, the desire to be gratified, the excuse for deviation from the letter, the cruelty of enforced adherence. Then only can we tell whether literal fulfilment is to be implied by law as a condition."

Where a grain elevator had a capacity of only 3,300 bu. per hour, instead of 4,000 as specified, the court held that the jury ought to have been instructed that substantial performance had not been rendered. Steel Storage & Elevator Const. Co. v. Stock, 121 N.E. 786, 225 N.Y. 173 (1919).

more can be done than to lay out a few samples for study and to indicate a method of investigation and analysis.

## § 705.  Relative Extent, Degree, and Value of the Nonperformance

One obvious factor for consideration is the extent of the nonperformance by the plaintiff.  This is a matter that can be considered and weighed only in relation to the full performance that was promised.  The ratio between that left unperformed and the total performance promised will frequently be decisive.  This may be a ratio that is stated in terms of acres, of pounds avoirdupois, of bushels, or of pounds sterling.  If one has promised to ship about 1000 tons of old iron T rails for each of the next six months, has he rendered "substantial" performance by shipping 400 tons in February, 885 tons in March, and 1571 tons in April? [12]  The court held that this was not substantial performance, although it did not put it in those terms.  Instead, it said that "In contracts of merchants time is of the essence."

In the case of a building contract, it is not as easy to find the arithmetical ratio between the unperformed part and the full promised performance.  The difference may be in quality of materials and workmanship, rather than in board feet or bags of cement.  It is obvious that any rule stated in terms of extent of the nonperformance can not be a rule of thumb.

The extent of the nonperformance can also be stated in terms of value in money, its ratio to full performance being the ratio of the two respective money values.  This ratio is an influential factor in almost all cases, even though it is often a difficult matter to make a valuation.  However, the parties have themselves valued the full performance promised by the contractor, very often in dollars and cents;  and generally the court is willing to make a finding as to the cost of completion and of curing the defects in performance.  The higher the ratio of this cost of curing defects to the total contract price, the less likely it is that the performance rendered will be held to be "substantial performance."  If defects are such that they cannot be cured without unreasonable economic waste, it is not the cost of curing them that will be awarded as damages.  In such cases, the ratio factor is that between the market value of the defective performance rendered and the market value of the full performance promised.[13]  In ei-

---

12.  **U.S.**—Norrington v. Wright, 6 S. Ct. 12, 115 U.S. 188, 29 L.Ed. 366 (1885).

13.  Structural variations by the contractor that are not material and that are not wilful and deliberate will not prevent the contractor from getting judgment on the contract.  In these cases, if the owner is given any damages at all for the non-performance, they will be measured by the difference between the value of the building as con-

ther form, this ratio is far from being a conclusive factor;[14] and no attempt will be made here to name an arithmetical ratio that separates the substantial from the less than substantial. It will only be said that the higher this ratio the more likely it is that the performance will be held to be less than "substantial performance;" and this is not because the "value" itself is so important, but rather because of the other factors that underlie "value" and determine what that value is in terms of money and of other commodities.[15]

## § 706.  Degree of Frustration of Purpose

Extremely important factors in solving the present problem are the character of the performance that the plaintiff promised to render, the purposes and ends that it was expected to serve in behalf of the defendant, and the extent to which the nonperformance by the plaintiff has defeated those purposes and ends, or would defeat them if the errors and omissions are not corrected.[16] One who contracts to erect a dwelling house has not rendered substantial performance by erecting a garage, or an automobile trailer, or by excavating a cellar. The writer may be over-confident in making this statement; for the fact is that a person can dwell in a garage or in a trailer, and that a cellar hole in times of modern war might be a better dwelling place than the king's mansion. But the fact that the statement can plausibly be made shows that a high degree of difference in form and usefulness may be decisive on the question of substantial performance, and that even a law writer or a judge might decide a case on the sole basis of his own past experience.

A glue factory, getting its power from an 80 horse power boiler, contracted with the plaintiff for the installation of a new one having 120 horse power. When the new one was installed on a brick foundation it was found to have less horse power than the old boiler had. The defendant requested its removal, but used it to keep his factory running. The trial court thought that, in view of this user, there was substantial performance, and gave judgment for the contract price. The appellate court thought this to be error and that it had sufficient knowledge of the facts to

tracted for and the value of the building as actually constructed. If this difference is great, no doubt the variations by the contractor would be held to be material, and would prevent him from getting any judgment other than for a possible quantum meruit. The cost of reconstructing and correcting the defects will not be allowed as damages in this kind of a case, for the reason that it would involve too much tearing down of the completed structure and an unnecessary and disproportionate economic waste. See Jacob & Youngs v. Kent, 129 N.E. 889, 230 N.Y. 239 (1921).

14.   Ill.—Errant v. Columbia Western Mills, 195 Ill.App. 14 (1915).

justify a reversal of the trial court. If the defendant should refuse to permit the removal or reconstruction of the boiler, the plaintiff might yet have a right to quantum meruit.[17]

If the errors and omissions are such that they can not be corrected without tearing down and starting anew, or can not be corrected at all, it would seem that performance has not been "substantial;" but this is frequently not true. It would be true if the errors and omissions are such as to defeat the main purposes for which the contract was made by the defendant, in the absence of correction. In a case in which Judge Cardozo wrote one of his most enlightening opinions, the contractor put in "Cohoes" drainage piping instead of "Reading," as the specifications required. It was set in the walls, floors, and foundation; its replacement meant the practical destruction of the completed $77,000 building; the house was as valuable in the market and as satisfactory a dwelling as it would have been with "Reading" pipe. It was held that the performance was "substantial" and that the contractor had a right to the full contract price without any deduction for nonexistent injury.[18] Such questions as these are best answered by architects, engineers, and other witnesses expert in the specific subject matter.

The errors and omissions may be such as to defeat the purposes of the injured party as long as not corrected; but if they can be corrected without great difficulty, the performance rendered may be held "substantial" in spite of them. A money allowance, out of the balance of the unpaid price for which the plaintiff is suing, will be sufficient compensation. If the defendant already has the money in his hands, he is not required to pay it all over to the defaulting plaintiff, provided that he asserts and establishes the amount of his injury.[19]

17.  Wis.—Manitowoc Steam Boiler Works v. Manitowoc Glue Co., 97 N.W. 515, 120 Wis. 1 (1903).

A contract to build a house, with garage and driveway, is not substantially performed by building in such a way that the driveway is too narrow for use by automobiles. Younger v. Caroselli, 232 N.W. 378, 251 Mich. 533 (1930).

A heating boiler of only two thirds the specified heating capacity is not substantial performance. McElraevy & Hauck Co. v. St. Joseph's Home, 143 N.Y.S. 235 (1913).

18.  N.Y.—Jacob & Youngs v. Kent, 129 N.E. 889, 230 N.Y. 239 (1921).

"There may be omissions of that which could not afterwards be supplied exactly as called for by the contract without taking down the building to its foundations, and at the same time the omission may not affect the value of the building for use or otherwise, except so slight as to be hardly appreciable. Notwithstanding such omission, there might be a substantial performance of the contract." Handy v. Bliss, 90 N.E. 864, 204 Mass. 513, 134 Am.St.Rep. 673 (1910).

19.  A plumbing contract may be "substantially" performed so as to entitle the plumber to the contract price, less damages for his minor breach, even though the defects are such as to make the plumbing unusable with safety until remedied. Jones & Hotchkiss Co. v. Davenport, 50 A. 1028, 74 Conn. 418 (1901).

### § 707.  Is Substantial Performance Affected by the Cause of the Defects—"Wilful" Breach

The cause of a contractor's breach of his contract is seldom, if ever, material in determining whether or not his incomplete performance deserves to be described as "substantial"; but it is of importance in determining whether or not he has any remedy against the owner, either contractual or quasi contractual. It is very commonly stated that if the contractor has been guilty of a "wilful" breach, he can maintain no action for compensation, either for the contract price or for reasonable value.[20] Sometimes this statement is said to be true, even though the contractor's nonperformance is of a very minor character, so long as it is not so small as to fall within the doctrine "de minimis non curat lex." [21]

In most cases making the statement, however, it is a mere dictum, the contractor being actually given a judgment for compensation, either on the basis of the contract price or for reasonable value of the part performance. In many cases in which the plaintiff's action is sustained on the ground that he has rendered substantial performance, nothing whatever is said on the question of wilfulness; [22] it may well be, however, that we are meant to presume that the evil quality was absent. In other cases denying a recovery to the plaintiff on the ground that his breach was wilful, it is probable that his breach was actually such as to prevent his performance from being "substantial." Often the case is one in which the plaintiff has "abandoned" performance; [23] but even here there are cases giving quantum meruit less damages for breach.[24]

Seldom, if ever, have the courts attempted to define wilfulness in any detail. They have sometimes used other accompanying terms, saying that there can be no recovery if the breach was "wilful and deliberate" or "wilful and intentional" or if the per-

---

20.  In Gillespie Tool Co. v. Wilson, 16 A. 36, 123 Pa. 19 (1888), the plaintiff contracted to drive an exploratory gas well 2000 feet deep and 8 inches in diameter. Instead, he drilled most of the hole with the diameter of 5⅝ inches, with still further reduction near the bottom. Of course, the plaintiff did this knowingly. The court held that he could maintain no action for the price, and that it was not material whether the smaller bore was equally good for exploratory purposes. It clearly would not have been equally good for production if gas had been struck. The court said: "The equitable doctrine of substantial performance is intended for the protection and relief of those who have faithfully and honestly endeavored to perform their contract in all material and substantial particulars, so that their right to compensation may not be forfeited by reason of mere technical, inadvertent, or unimportant omissions or defects. It is incumbent on him who invokes its protection to present a case in which there has been no wilful omission or departure from the terms of his contract. If he fails to do so, the question of substantial performance should not be submitted to the jury."

formance rendered did not evidence an attempt to comply "in good faith" with the contract requirements. This matter has been discussed at some length in the Chapter on Restitution,[25] and the discussion will not be repeated here.

A variation from specifications does not necessarily prevent recovery of the contract price even though it was conscious and intentional.[26] The purpose of the departure must be considered, as well as its effect upon the value and usefulness of the result. A contractor who finds, and can prove, that a specified quality of cement is unsuitable for successful construction, in view of weather and other conditions, is not denied a right to full payment merely because he uses an improved mixture that is in all respects advantageous to the owner.[27]

The Massachusetts court, in particular, has appeared to be exceptionally strict in denying a contractor, whose breach is described as "wilful," any remedy even for quantum meruit.[28] He is supposed to have no merit. It should be observed that this operates to enforce a penalty and forfeiture, the extent of the penalty being in inverse proportion to the size of the breach. Probably, as actually applied, the penalties have not been very great; and there are recent cases indicating some modification of the doctrine.[29]

## § 708. Performance Less Than "Substantial" May Justify Nonpayment Without Justifying Repudiation of the Contract

The failure of a contractor's performance to constitute "substantial" performance may justify the owner in refusing to make a progress payment, without at the same time giving him the privilege of discharging the contractor. Substantial performance of some portion of the work may be a condition precedent to the owner's duty to pay a promised instalment, so that no suit will lie for its collection or for damages; but the time for curing defects may not have expired. The owner's refusal to pay is not a breach by him; but the defects or unfinished character of the contractor's performance may not yet constitute a breach of his duty, or if such a breach it may not yet go to the essence of the whole contract.[30]

---

25. Chapter 62, Restitution in Favor of a Plaintiff in Default.

Breach is not "wilful" if it is due to financial difficulties. Commercial Discount Co. v. Plainfield, 180 A. 311, 120 Conn. 274 (1935).

30. Also, the buyer's failure to pay an instalment may not justify repudiation by the seller. As Judge Cardozo said in Helgar Corp. v. Warner's Features, 119 N.E. 113, 222 N.Y. 449 (1918), a buyer's failure to pay an instalment on time may be a breach and justify an action to collect: "But it does not follow that he may be equally precipitate in his election to declare the contract at an end. That depends upon the question whether

If the refusal to pay an instalment is justified on the owner's part, the contractor is not justified in abandoning work by reason of that refusal. His abandonment of the work will itself be a wrongful repudiation that goes to the essence, even if the defects in performance did not.

In very many cases in which the question of substantial performance has been raised, both parties have already partly performed; the building is apparently completed, and the owner has paid some instalments of the price. It is only the final instalment of the price that is in dispute; and if the court finds that performance is less than "substantial," it is only the final instalment that the contractor loses.[31] It is believed that very seldom would the courts compel the contractor to repay all the instalments previously received.[32] If the owner seeks such a heroic remedy as this, the court would give renewed consideration to the question whether a substantial performance had been rendered. In such a suit for restitution, the courts would certainly allow for the value actually received by the owner; and this whether the performance was substantial or not.[33]

### § 709.  Measure of Recovery by One Who Has Rendered "Substantial Performance"

There seems to be some variation and doubt as to the burden and method of proving the amount to which the plaintiff is entitled in the case of merely "substantial performance." This is a case in which both parties are in the wrong; but the defendant is in the greater wrong.[34] Both are guilty of a breach; but one is a little breach and the other is a large breach. The plaintiff has failed to perform in minor details and must make compensation therefor. Yet, the defendant is not justified in refusing payment; and he must make compensation for this greater wrong. Having completed substantial performance on his own part, the plaintiff is entitled to its agreed equivalent or price, according to the contract, with incidental damages for the defendant's delay in paying. The defendant, however, is not asking for payment for a performance rendered; he asks damages for a nonperformance. The plaintiff's position is such that at common law he could maintain an action of debt, or indebitatus assumpsit, for the agreed price. The defendant, on the other hand, would be restricted to an action of express assumpsit for unliquidated damages.

the default is so substantial and important as in truth and in fairness to defeat the essential purpose of the parties." Here, the purchaser's failure to pay on time the price of an instalment of goods delivered, although a breach justifying suit for that instalment, did not justify the seller's repudiation of the rest of the contract. The seller had no right to damages as for a total breach, beyond the unpaid instalment. Without doubt the purchaser did have such an action for total breach.

Because of the existence of this claim and counterclaim, it is generally stated as the rule of recovery that the contractor has a right to the contract price, less compensatory damages for the injury caused by his breach.[35]  In stating and applying this rule, the court frequently says nothing about the mode of pleading or the burden of proof.  One who asserts a breach by another and a right to compensation in himself is ordinarily required to allege and prove facts establishing such a breach and such a right.  In the present case, according to the theory stated above, each party has committed a breach and each has a right to compensation. It would seem that each one must state his own claim, and must allege and prove the facts that constitute the other's breach and that create his own right.  There is no very strong reason for requiring the plaintiff to prove that the defendant has any counterclaim or its amount.  Generally the plaintiff alleges full performance by himself, at least until prevented or discharged by the defendant;  and his testimony tends to prove such full performance. The defendant denies the plaintiff's allegations, asserts a substantial breach, and counterclaims for damages.  Thus are raised the issues, full performance or not, substantial performance or not, and the amount of injury suffered.  If it is found that each party has a right against the other and that each has committed a wrong, the court must liquidate the claims in money, deduct the smaller and give judgment for the balance.  If the damages payable for the plaintiff's breach exceed the unpaid balance of the price, the plaintiff gets judgment for nothing.[36]

Critics of the "substantial performance" doctrine are likely to make a fundamental error.  They appear to assume, if not to state positively, that at common law the contractor has no right to the agreed compensation unless he has performed his part in full, without defect or omission.  No such rule has ever been a part of the common law, much less has it been a rule in equity. At the early common law, bilateral agreements were not enforced at all.  Assumpsit was not yet invented as a form of action.  No promises were enforced, except those under seal and those that were identical with a debt that was created by the receipt of a quid pro quo.  In the fifteenth or the sixteenth century mutual promises came to be regarded as enforceable;  each promise came to be regarded as a consideration sufficient to sustain an assumpsit for the breach of the return promise.  But the plaintiff did not have to allege or prove performance of his own promise except when the defendant's promise was expressly conditional on such performance.[37]  The two promises were thought to be indepen-

35.  See Kauffman v. Raeder, 108 F. 171 (C.C.A.8th, 190₁).

36.  Cal.—Herdal v. Sheehy, 159 P. 422, 173 Cal. 163 (1916).

37.  Eng.—Nichols  v.  Raynbred, Hob. 88 (1615);  Pordage v. Cole, 1 Wms. Saund. 319 (1669).

dent and unconditional. It took two or three centuries, with innumerable decisions, before the mutual dependency of promises was discovered and enforced.[38] Even then, a mere partial breach by the plaintiff was no defense to the defendant; the plaintiff's non-performance must go to the whole of the consideration and not be compensable in damages.[39] By this, however, was meant that the plaintiff would not be deprived of his agreed compensation by reason of minor breaches for which an allowance in damages would be an adequate remedy. This is exactly the "substantial performance" doctrine; and it is the common law.

Just how, during the latter half of the nineteenth century, some of the courts came to believe that the plaintiff could be given no remedy unless he had performed his part in full, has not been made clear. Some of them have assumed, however, that it is not possible for both parties to commit a breach of contract, that any breach by one party discharges the other, and that the defendant establishes a good defense if he shows that the plaintiff committed a breach first. By this theory all "breaches" are alike, and any breach is a vital breach. The theory has always been erroneous. There have always been little breaches and big breaches, partial breaches and total breaches. A plaintiff who has rendered substantial performance may have committed a small breach, and it may have been "first"; but this does not justify nonperformance by the defendant.

In many cases, the contract provides for compensation of the contractor in some other form than in money. For example, as compensation for the contractor's work, labor, and materials, the owner may promise to convey a tract of land, or to deliver a motor car, or to sink an oil well to the depth of two thousand feet. In such cases, if the contractor has rendered "substantial performance," with minor defects or omissions, the owner's claim for damages for those minor defects can not be used as an arithmetical deduction from his own performance. Substantial performance having been rendered by the contractor, it is the owner's immediate duty to convey the land, or deliver the car, or sink the well. He is not privileged to deduct two acres from the tract of land, or to substitute a less expensive car, or to drive the well ten feet less in depth. His refusal to convey the land, because of the

---

See, also, discussion and cases cited in § 653 (Implied and Constructive Conditions).

The Massachusetts court purported to follow these cases, unaware that it was applying a rule much more liberal to the plaintiff than the substantial performance rule. See Prest v. Cole, 67 N.E. 246, 183 Mass. 283 (1903).

38. See Kingston v. Preston, 2 Doug. 689 (1773), quoted in Jones v. Barkley, 2 Doug. 684.

39. Eng.—Boone v. Eyre, 1 H. Bl. 273 (1777).

See Serjt. Williams's notes to Pordage v. Cole, 1 Wms. Saund. 319 (1669).

plaintiff's minor breaches, is itself a total and unjustifiable breach; and his failure to perform in full, in an attempt to get even for the plaintiff's breach, is likewise wrongful and might also be a breach going to the essence.

It is true that when the contractor sues for damages in these cases, the owner can recoup and counterclaim; and when the two claims are liquidated in money, by a finding by the court or jury, an arithmetical subtraction will be made, the judgment being entered for the balance of the larger amount.

The foregoing statements are substantially true, also, in a case where the agreed price promised by the owner is expressed in money. Substantial performance by the contractor makes it the owner's duty to pay; he certainly is not justified in refusing the entire price. It is dangerous for him to withhold any part of the price, as compensation for the plaintiff's minor non-performance; this compensation is not a liquidated sum, and the owner can not render it certain by his own action or accounting. Nevertheless, under the statutes and practice of many states, the owner will escape payment of costs and interest if he withholds no more than the damages eventually allowed him, making continuous tender of the balance to the contractor.[a]

a. Sections 710–712 of the general treatise deal with Burden of Proving the Deduction to be made from the Full Contract Price; Benefit to the Defendant—Necessity of Acceptance or Use of the Result; and Method of Pleading Substantial Performance.

## CHAPTER 37

## CONDITION OF PERFORMANCE ON TIME—CONDITION OF NOTICE

### § 713. When is Time of the Essence—Common Law and Equity Compared

A statement very commonly made by both judges and text writers is that "at common law" time is of the essence of a contract, but that it is otherwise "in equity." [1] As thus made, it is applicable to all contracts alike, for the sale of land or of goods, for services, for manufacture and delivery, for transportation. It seems to make no difference what performance it is that is delayed, what ratio it bears to the amount that is rendered on time, how great or how slight the delay, how little is the injury that is caused. By the blind eye of the common law, it would seem, "time" is read as a master word in the contract jungle, absolute and uncompromising in its significance and power.

It can be asserted with confidence that never were the common law judges so blind as this. They did not need to be advised of the relativity of time and space to be aware that the importance of the time element is relative to all the surrounding factors, that the question is always one of degree, and that there is no absolute and universal rule. They stated no such dogmatic and almost meaningless rule of thumb as that "time is always of the essence of a contract at common law."

---

1. Thus, in Colbath v. Stebbins Lumber Co., 144 A. 1, 127 Me. 406 (1929), it is said: "In general, it may be said that at law time is always of the essence of the contract, although in equity a different rule prevails. Time in equity is held to be of the essence or not, according to the circumstances of the case." This statement the court partly nullifies by adding: "And under some circumstances, in law time may or may not be of the essence according to the intent of the parties." This case is one of special interest and is analyzed in the next succeeding section herein. See also Snowman v. Harford, 55 Me. 197 (1867).

Here, as in other connections, much confusion is due to the very common failure to distinguish (1) between a promise and a condition, and (2) between an express condition and a constructive condition. A party may promise to render his performance by a specified time; this gives the other party a right that it shall be then rendered. The other party may make his reciprocal promise conditional on performance by the first party by a specified time; this makes the duty of the other party conditional, but does not in itself give him a right that the condition shall be performed. Again the agreement may be in such terms that the first party promises performance by a stated time and the second party expressly makes his return promise conditional on the exact performance; in such a case, failure by the first to perform on time gives to the second a right to damages and also the legal privilege of not performing his own promise. And still further, although the second party's return promise may not be in terms conditional, it may be made so by construction of law because the first party's failure to perform on time will deprive the second of the substantial benefit for which he bargained.

No doubt, it is true that one who contracts to pay $500 on May 1, or to complete a building by June 15, or to render any other performance by a specified time, is guilty of a breach of legal duty if his performance is not exactly on time. Even as to this, however, custom may allow days of grace for certain purposes; and we must always be on the lookout for good legal excuses that prevent nonperformance from being a breach of duty.[2] Observe as to this, that if the nonperformance exactly on time was the breach of a duty at common law, it was nearly always the breach of an equitable duty as well. Equity recognized some excuses that the common law did not recognize; but it laid down no such rule as that one who promises to perform by a stated time is not bound "in equity" to perform by that time.

The foregoing, however, is not what is meant by saying that time is of the essence of a contract. What is meant is that one who does not perform in full his own promised performance, within the exact time specified in the contract, can not maintain any action at law for the enforcement of a return promise.[3] It

**2.** For example, by admiralty law applicable to time charters, the failure of the charterer to return the vessel within the expressly stated time may not even be a breach of duty. The exigencies and emergencies of voyages by sea brought about a custom to this effect. This is an addition to the rules to the effect that a promisor's duty may be discharged by impossibility. See Straits of Dover S. S. Co. v. Munson, 100 F. 1005 (C.C.A. 2d), affirming 95 F. 690 (D.C.); Anderson v. Munson, 104 F. 913 (D.C.N.Y.). Compare Munson v. Elswick S. S. Co., 214 F. 84 (C.C. A.2d), affirming 207 F. 984 (D.C.), where the excess time claimed by the charterer was too long.

**3.** Tex.—Dayvault & Newsome v. Townsend, 244 S.W. 1108 (Civ.App. 1922).

is a rule that purports to be applicable to all bilateral contracts. Performance in full within the exact time, by one promisor, is a condition of the duty of the other promisor to render his return performance, even in the absence of any express provision indicating that the counter promise is thus conditional. Any failure to perform *on time* goes to the essence, is a vital breach, discharges the other party, and gives him a right to damages for total breach of contract. A statement in this form is not, and never has been, a correct statement either "at law" or "in equity."

In some sense, it can be said that time is always of the essence of every bilateral contract. Some performance at some time is always necessary for the enforcement of the return promise of an agreed equivalent. This is true except when the court is willing to hold that the mutual promises are totally independent. But this is very different from saying that performance in full at exactly the agreed time is of the essence.

This matter has already been discussed in dealing with the meaning and effect of "substantial performance." Time of performance is merely one element in determining whether a defective or incomplete or belated performance is "substantial." It has already been stated that when the common law came to recognize and enforce bilateral contracts, it made no such requirement that a plaintiff could maintain no action unless he had performed in full as promised. This includes the lesser statement that it made no requirement that the plaintiff must have performed exactly on time. Performance on time by the plaintiff was not held to be a condition of the defendant's duty unless the terms of agreement expressly made it so. Instead, for more than two centuries, the common law rule was that in a bilateral contract the exchanged promises are mutually independent and unconditional, in the absence of a clear expression to the contrary. Instead of having to perform in full, and *on time,* in order to maintain suit, he was not required to perform at all.

This was, indeed, a bad rule that gave dissatisfaction. Later on it was displaced by a rule that a promisor who has substantially failed to perform his agreed exchange can not maintain suit for failure of the other party to perform his promise. It was not displaced by a rule that a promisor who has failed in the least degree, or for the least time to perform his promise can not maintain suit. Instead, it was laid down that the defendant is not discharged unless the plaintiff's failure goes to the whole consideration and is not compensable in damages.

It is true that, in the nineteenth century, cases began to appear in which it was stated that "at law time is of the essence," or that "in contracts of merchants time is of the essence." Sometimes, the statement has been used to justify a decision against the plaintiff.[4]  But it is believed that in almost every such case, the plaintiff's failure to perform was a substantial failure.  These cases do not justify the statement that at common law time is always of the essence of a contract.  They are sufficient to indicate an inadequate terminology and analysis;  and probably they demonstrate, also, continuing doubt as to what rule and what actual decisions are required by good social policy.

The idea that time is of the essence at common law, and that at law a contractor cannot maintain suit for the price or for damages unless he has rendered full performance of his own part in every detail, may have originated in erroneous statements by the chancellors, who felt strongly the injustice of denying recovery to a contractor who has rendered substantial performance and who assumed that the more tough-minded common law judges would fail to see the injustice.  The tough mindedness of the judges, however, had long been evidenced by the holding that mutual promises were wholly independent unless so worded as to be expressly conditional.[5]  The notion has been further disseminated by judges whose jurisdiction covers both common law and equity, and who rightly assert that equity permits them to do justice even though the common law might be otherwise.

Gradually, the two systems known as equity and common law have been amalgamated.  Our present law of contracts is a compound of these two major elements and of many lesser ones, including the "law merchant" and many a rule or custom that was once very limited and local.  The compounding process has been largely judicial;  but great statutes such as Procedure Acts and Judicature Acts have also been necessary.  For our present purposes, we do not need to distinguish between law and equity, or to recognize the existence of two conflicting rules as to the necessity of performance on time.  Our present rule, the product of both systems, can not be said to be so definite in form or sub-

---

4.  **U.S.**—Norrington v. Wright, 6 S. Ct. 12, 115 U.S. 188, 29 L.Ed. 366 (1885);  Meier Dental Mfg. Co. v. Smith, 237 F. 563 (C.C.A.8th, 1916).

In the case of The Bank of Columbia v. Hagner, 1 Pet. 455, 7 L.Ed. 219 (U.S.1828), there was a contract for the sale of land, conveyance and payment to be made on January 1, 1820.  On May 8, 1821 the buyer gave notice repudiating the contract.  Prior thereto, the vendor had made no tender of a deed of conveyance.  The court held that the vendor could maintain no action for damages and argued at great length that a tender of conveyance by the vendor on the exact day fixed by the contract was of the essence thereof.  Could the vendor have got a decree "in equity" for specific performance in spite of his delay of a year and four months?  And would the judgment for damages have been refused if the vendor had tendered conveyance on Jan. 2, 1820?

5.  Such a statement was made by the Master of the Rolls in Parkin v. Thorold, 16 Beav. 59, quoted at length in Secombe v. Steele, 20 How. (U.S.) 94, 15 L.Ed. 833 (1857).

stance that it can be mechanically applied. Instead, it requires the court to weigh the importance of many factors in each particular case.[6]

Sometimes, failure of the plaintiff to perform on time will be a good reason for denying him a judgment for damages, or a decree for specific performance. In either case, allowance must be made for the injury he has caused by his delay. In either case, the judgment or decree may be entered on such conditions as seem just. Sometimes one remedy rather than the other may be the more satisfactory; a court should cut the coat according to the cloth.

In holding that time is not of the essence in any particular case, the court is not "making a new contract for the parties." A bilateral contract whereby V promises to convey land on May 1 and P promises to pay a price on March 1, is nothing more than two promises to convey and to pay. Neither one is in terms conditional on performance of the other, either on time or otherwise. The parties have not thought about making their promises conditional; indeed, when they do think about it, they use additional words of condition. If the courts hold, as they now do, that one promise is conditional upon substantial performance of the other, it might be said with reason that something is being added to the agreement of the parties. But nothing is being added by refusing to hold that either promise is conditional upon performance of the other exactly on time, by refusing to hold that time is of the essence. Nor is anything being subtracted or altered. Each party has promised to perform at a specified date. If P fails to pay on March 1, he has committed a breach of duty for which V has a remedy. This is not affected by the further holding that V must still convey, even though P fails to pay exactly on time.

It is true that by interpretation and construction, courts often add much to the work of the parties, in determining the legal operation of their agreement. This is true of both law and equity. Some contracts are wholly refused enforcement, express penalty provisions are disregarded, and many excuses for nonperformance are recognized.

## § 714. Avoidance of Forfeiture by Eliminating an Express Condition of Performance on Time

If a contract expressly provides that performance by one party by a stated time shall be a condition of the other party's duty,

---

**6.** Restatement, Contracts, § 276: "(a) Unless the nature of a contract is such as to make performance on the exact day agreed upon of vital importance, or the contract in terms provides that it shall be so, failure by a promisor to perform his promise on the day stated in the promise does not discharge the duty of the other party." Nothing is said here of any difference between "law" and "equity."

"time" is as much of the essence in "equity" as it was at "law." One difference, however, is that equity would sometimes give relief against the provision in order to avoid a forfeiture. It may be that this was the cause of statements that time is not "of the essence" in equity. In these cases equity prevented the enforcement of a contract in accordance with its express terms, or it decreed equitable enforcement in spite of an express provision to the contrary. No such relief as this was given by the courts of common law.[7] This does not mean that the two courts gave different interpretations to the terms of the contract or that one regarded performance on time as of more importance than the other. It indicates that the two systems of remedial justice were so different that equity could and did give an effect to events subsequent to the making of the contract that the courts of common law never did.

If a promise is expressly conditional on the rendition of a performance by the other party, or on the happening of any other event, by a specified time, no court of law or equity should set aside the limitation and enforce the promise in spite of nonperformance of the condition, unless the condition has been excused by action of the promisor himself or there has been such performance or change of position by the promisee that an unjust forfeiture will result unless the condition is disregarded. Consider the case of an aleatory contract, made in the course of the settlement of an uncompleted transaction. It was provided as follows: "If by December 31, 1921, it proves that Colbath now has cut and in Squa Pan Lake . . . logs in excess of 4,590,666, we will pay you an amount equal to $10. a thousand on such excess . . . If it should prove by December 31, 1921, that the amount of logs now cut is less than 4,590,666, Colbath agrees to pay an amount equal to $10. a thousand on such shortage." It did not appear that either party promised either to bear or to share the cost of count-

7.    Thus, where a vendor had given a bond for conveyance of land on the express condition that payments should be made on specified dates, it was held that the purchaser who had failed to make two payments for 4 and 16 months could not maintain Debt on the obligation for the vendor's refusal to convey. The remedy, if any, was said to be in equity. Hill v. Fisher, 34 Me. 143 (1852). If the purchaser had taken possession and made valuable improvements, he might have been able to make a case that would induce a Chancellor to set aside the express condition.

"It is said, that it is not the province of the court of chancery, any more than of a court of law, to make contracts for parties, but to enforce them. This is true, as a general proposition. But it is also true, that the court of chancery looks to the substance of a contract; and when the substance of a contract is fulfilled, and the general intention of the parties carried into effect, the court relieves against any forfeiture or penalty, inserted for the purpose of enforcing the contract." Edgerton v. Peckham, 11 Paige 352 (N.Y.1844).

ing the logs. Nor was it made to appear that the plaintiff would suffer an unjust forfeiture if payment by the defendant should not be compelled. The court held that time was of the essence.[8]

In this case the contract was aleatory, both of the promises having the same aleatory character. It was like a bet on a horse-race, except that it was not unlawful; in no event would both parties have to make a payment. Unless the settlement can be attacked on some other ground, it would be inequitable for the court to increase the risk of either party by eliminating or varying the condition on which either promise was expressly conditional. One who has promised to pay if Alpha beats Omega should not be compelled to pay if the race is a dead heat. Observe that the condition in this case was not a performance that was promised by the other party; it was a determination of the number of logs by December 31.

### § 715. Express Provisions Declaring That "Time is of the Essence"

Time may be made of the essence by an express provision to that effect; there is no limit in this respect upon our freedom of contract, as long as no part performance has taken place.[9] If the enforcement of such an express provision will have the effect of enforcing an excessive penalty or an unjust forfeiture, equity will prevent such enforcement; this is one limit upon our power to determine our own contractual rights and duties.[10] But the vendor can make his duty to convey expressly conditional upon a payment on or before a specific day or hour;[11] and the purchaser can make his duty to pay expressly conditional upon conveyance, by a specified time. Such a result is not achieved by merely promising to pay or to convey on a stated day;[12] either party can achieve it by making his own promise expressly conditional upon such an exact performance by the other.

It is not desirable to try to achieve this result by merely putting into the contract the words "time is of the essence of this contract." Such a provision may be effective for the purpose, because the context may make clear what the intention is and what the expression means. What the court must know, in order to give effect to such a cryptic provision, is: What performance at what time is a condition of which party's duty to do what? In some cases, the answer to this question is simple and obvious. Often, however, it is not clear whether the provision is meant to limit the duties of both parties alike, or to limit the duty of one and not the other. Was it meant to make the vendor's duty to convey conditional upon payment at the exact time, without mak-

---

8.    Colbath  v.  Stebbins  Lumber Co., 144 A. 1, 127 Me. 406 (1929).

ing the purchaser's duty to pay similarly conditional? The context may, indeed, show that this was the intention.[13] Courts must interpret as best they can; but a contract draughtsman ought to be so specific as to leave no doubt and to avoid unnecessary litigation.

In some states there is a statute declaring that time shall not be considered of the essence unless expressly so provided. Such a statute leaves many questions unanswered, although it weights the scales against a finding that performance by the exact date promised is a condition of the other party's duty.[14] One who promises to ship goods by August 15, knowing that they are for the buyer's fall trade, can not hold the buyer if shipment is delayed until Sept. 28.[15] The facts may make performance on time, or within some time, clearly of the essence, even though the express words of the parties do not. The statute makes it clear that merely promising to ship by a named date is not per se sufficient to make that time of the essence; this should be clear without the statute, but the contrary is often stated as being the rule "at law." [16]

A contract may have in it many promises for sundry performances, varying in amount and importance. A general provision that "time is of the essence" should not be held to be applicable to all of them alike, especially in the case of instalment payments for which interest is provided in case of non-payment.[17] Such an often repeated provision as this may be inserted in a contract without any realization of its significance; and other terms contained in the agreement, interpreted in the light of the conduct of the parties, may show that it should be given no legal effect.[18]

In contracts for the sale of goods to be manufactured or to be shipped from a distance, the buyer is not bound to accept them if they are materially defective, and he has a reasonable time for inspection. A general provision that "time is of the essence" would not affect the length of a reasonable time. It would affect only those performances for which a definite time is specified, as is usually the case with respect to delivery of the goods and payment of the price. But the parties may also specify a time limit for inspection and for giving notice of rejection for defects. If the parties intend that failure to give this notice within the stated time shall operate as an acceptance of the goods and a waiver of defects, they should say so expressly. Such a statement clearly shows that the power and privilege of rejection terminate at the end of the stated time.[19] A particular performance is thereby related to a particular legal effect; a mere general statement that "time is of the essence of this contract" does not do this.

## § 716.  When Time is of the Essence in Contracts for Sale of Land

In an ordinary bilateral contract for the purchase and sale of land, the fact that a specific time is fixed for payment or for conveyance does not make "time of the essence"—at least, it does not make performance at the *specified* time of the essence. Failure to  pay at that time is not per se sufficient to terminate the seller's duty to convey;  and failure to convey on the exact date does not per se discharge the buyer.[20]

This is not to say that tender of payment or conveyance can be delayed forever.  Performance within some time, limited by what is reasonable under the circumstances, will always be of the essence.[21]  Indeed, the promisee has power to fix an exact time by giving notice, if he is careful to name a time beyond the "reasonable" limit that the law would allow.[22]

Nor, in saying that time is not of the essence, have we said that tender of payment or tender of conveyance may not be a constructive condition precedent to the other party's duty.  If the time fixed for a payment is prior to, or concurrent with, that fixed for conveyance, tender of the money is a condition precedent to the duty to convey, even though tender on the exact day is not.  If the time fixed for conveyance is prior to, or concurrent with, the time fixed for a payment, tender of the agreed conveyance is a condition precedent to the duty to make that payment, even though tender on the exact day is not.[23]

The reason that payment or conveyance at the exact time is not "of the essence," even though delay will be a breach of contract and a cause of action, is that the injury caused by delay is little or nothing.  Delays are frequent in these transactions; and it is the custom of men to overlook them, even though they may have stated in advance that they would not.  The reason can also be stated in this form: performance at a time later than that specified in the contract is "substantial performance." [24]

Conveyance with good title, promptly on the time agreed or within a very short time later, may be held to be of the essence for the reason, known to the vendor, that the buyer expected to make immediate use of the premises either as a home, or for continuing a business that was already a going concern on the place, or for making improvements and starting a new business.[25] In a contract whereby one party promises to start drilling for oil or gas by a certain date, performance on time is likely to be

---

20.  See Restatement, Contracts, §
276.

24.  See the rules in Restatement, Contracts, § 276, for determining the "materiality" of delay in performance.

of the essence because values are fluctuating and because of the "vagrant and fugitive nature of oil and gas." [26]

A purchaser's failure to make payment on time may be held to go to the essence and justify the seller in refusing to convey, if values are rapidly fluctuating and the delay has already shown that the purchaser is a gainer by the deal.[27]  There are various other factors that may make it seem inequitable to enforce a contract in favor of a vendor or a purchaser who has not performed at the time fixed in the agreement.[28]

## § 718.  Mercantile Contracts for the Sale or Transportation of Goods

It can not truthfully be said that, in contracts for the sale of goods, or in "contracts of merchants," time is always of the essence.  Here, as elsewhere, the parties can make it so by the use of express words; but, if they do not, then it depends on circumstances.  "Merchants" make all sorts of contracts for all sorts of purposes.  "Goods" of many kinds are bought and sold for many purposes.  If delivery or payment is promised at a specified date, a later delivery or payment is a breach of duty; but whether the lateness is such as to justify the other party in not paying or delivering depends on circumstances.

It is true that delay is likely to be of more importance in transactions for the sale of goods than in those for the sale of land; a short delay is more likely to be fatal.  Without doubt performance is customarily more prompt; and delay is less likely to be overlooked by the parties themselves.  In this treatise, the author will not attempt to review the innumerable cases or to classify the factors that have been held to make delivery, or payment exactly on time a condition of the other party's duty to pay or to deliver.  Sometimes a brief delay in shipment or in delivery has been held to go to the essence and to discharge the buyer.[34] It must always depend, however, upon the quantity that is delayed, the length of the delay, the character of the subject matter, the purposes for which the goods are bought, the degree of injury caused by the delay, and other matters.[35]

A contract for the sale of a restaurant and retail liquor business, including an assignment of a lease, partakes somewhat of both a sale of goods and a sale of land; the facts may be such that the buyer can get a decree for specific performance even though he has not himself rendered full performance by the agreed closing day.[36]

After a part performance has already been rendered, a subsequent delay is less likely to be fatal.[37]  This is in part because

37.  See Restatement, Contracts, §
276(b) and (c).

the one party has already received benefits and partly because to the party in default the consequences of non-enforcement are more serious.  A seller who has as yet made no delivery has the goods at his own disposal.  If they are not received and paid for, he can sell them in the market.  If the market has fallen, and he suffers loss, that is about the same loss that his delay in delivery might have caused the buyer.

If no time for shipment or delivery is specified, there is a duty to perform within a "reasonable time" ;  and performance within a "reasonable time" is a condition of the buyer's duty to pay.[38] Presumably this "reasonable time" is the same for both purposes.

Contracts for the transportation of goods, or for a ship or vehicle in which to transport them, have much in common with sales of the goods.  Time is more likely to be held of the essence.[39] Delays are likely to be of more importance and to be customarily so treated by the parties.  Charter parties, and bills of lading have their special rules and special customs.

## § 719.  Goods to be Manufactured

In a contract for the manufacture and sale of as yet non-existent goods, the time specified for delivery is somewhat less likely to be held to be of the essence than in a contract for the sale of goods already in completed form.  The chief reason for this lies in the fact that the work and labor of manufacturing is involved;  in this process the probability of delays is somewhat greater, and also the loss to the manufacturer is likely to be greater in case the buyer is permitted to refuse to accept and pay. This last is especially true if the goods are made to special order and are of a kind not readily salable in the general market.[40]

The truth of the foregoing is not surprising to one who realizes that rules of law are never absolute and that their application is never purely logical or mechanical.  The legal operation of expressions of agreement never depends solely upon literal interpretation;  and, in the present instance, literal interpretation tells us only that performance was promised by a stated time, it does not tell us whether the return promise is conditional upon such exact performance.  A court of justice, therefore, whether it is called Kings Bench or Chancery or District Court will take into consideration all those factors that appeal to ordinary men in the performance of their business transactions.  One of these factors is the comparative amount of loss to the parties.  Even one who has broken his promise in the matter of time will not be forced to scrap the entire performance when some small payment will be ample compensation to the other party.[41]

40.  U.S.—Beck & Pauli Lithographing Co. v. Colorado Milling & Elevator Co., 52 F. 700, 3 C.C.A. 248 (C.C. A.10th, 1892).

## § 720. Building Contracts—Time Commonly Not of the Essence

In contracts for the erection of buildings or other permanent structures on land, it is customary to fix a time at which it is the builder's duty to begin work and another time by which the work is to be completed. It is not often, however, that either beginning or completing on time is expressly made a condition of the owner's duty to pay the agreed compensation. In the absence of such an express provision, courts will rarely hold that either beginning or completing on time is of the essence—that is, a constructive condition of the owner's duty.[42] Construction contracts are subject to many delays, for innumerable reasons, the blame for which may be difficult to assess. The structure, as fast as it rises, becomes part of the land and adds to the wealth of its owner. Delays are generally foreseen as probable; and the risks thereof are discounted. Payment by the owner is seldom refused because of short periods of delay, or even for long ones causing no exceptional harm. The complexities of the work, the difficulties commonly encountered, the custom of men in such cases, all these lead to the result that performance at the agreed time by the contractor is not of the essence.

By this it is not meant that a contractor who promises to begin or to complete by a definite time is not bound by his promise. Of course, he is so bound; his unexcused failure is a breach of duty, for which the owner has a right to damages. Often, indeed, the contract expressly provides for the payment of a stated sum of money for each day's delay as liquidated damages. A provision like this will be enforced, as long as the amount so fixed is not found to be a penalty and not a measure of the injury actually suffered. Such a provision as this leads strongly to the conclusion that performance on time, although a plain and enforceable duty, is not a condition of the owner's duty to accept and pay for the structure.[43]

As matter of course, time can be made of the essence of a building contract by the use of clear language to that effect, although excuses and waivers will very frequently be found to exist. If the owner promises to pay a bonus, beyond the stated contract price, in return for completion by a stated time, such completion on time is an express condition precedent to a right to the bonus.[44] It is possible, also, for such special circumstances to exist as will make time of the essence, even though not expressly so provided; but the case will be a rare one. Sometimes the court will say that "time is of the essence," but at the same time enforce payment of the contract price less damages for the delay.[45] Here, either the statement is quite erroneous, or the court has found some waiver or other excuse for non-performance of the condition.[a]

---

**a.** The titles of §§ 721–723 in the general treatise are as follows: § 721.      Failure of Performance on Time May Create a Power to Terminate,

## § 724. Notice as an Implied or Constructive Condition Precedent

There are many contracts in which there is a promise the performance of which is impossible, unless the promisor obtains knowledge of certain facts. In other cases the promise is to render a performance after the happening of a certain event. Of course it is possible and, no doubt, it is frequently desirable for the promisor to make his promise expressly conditional upon the giving to him of notice of these facts or events by the other party to the contract or by some third party.[61] With respect to such notices, questions often arise as to whether the requirement of notice has been waived by the party whose duty is conditional thereon or whether the fulfilment of the condition by giving notice has been excused by the law by reason of impossibility or otherwise. These questions will be discussed in subsequent sections.[62]

When a promisor has not expressly made notice a condition precedent to his duty of performance,[63] in what kinds of cases will the giving of notice to him be a condition precedent to his duty to perform, either by implication or by construction of law? It is believed that the most general rule that can safely be laid down in this matter is as follows. Notice need not be given to a promisor who has the same or substantially equivalent sources of information with respect to the facts or events, knowledge of which is necessary for performance, as those that are available to the promisee.[64] If the promisor can find out the facts for himself as easily as the promisee can find them out and give notice of them, the giving of notice will not be a condition precedent to the promisor's duty of performance, unless he has clearly so specified in the contract. If, on the other hand, the sources of information available to the two parties are not equivalent and

without Itself Terminating Contract Duty; § 722. Waiver of Time Limit—Effect of Extension—Effect of a New Notice; § 723. Power of One Party to make Time of the Essence by a Notice.

**61.** Where a seller promises to ship goods as directed by the buyer, the giving of "shipping directions" is an express condition of the seller's duty. This requires notice by the buyer. The seller has no other means of determining his wishes in the matter. Weil v. American Metal Co., 54 N.E. 1050, 182 Ill. 128 (1899).

The failure to give such shipping directions within a reasonable time may also be a breach of contract duty. Kingman & Co. v. Hanna Wagon Co., 52 N.E. 328, 176 Ill. 545 (1898).

**62.** In Chapter 78, dealing with Impossibility, will be found a discussion of cases in which the giving of notice became impossible or difficult by reason of supervening events. In some of these cases, the condition of giving notice was held to be excused. Contracts of insurance and option contracts are types in which express provisions requiring the giving of some sort of notice are to be found. Such problems as what constitutes "immediate" notice frequently arise. See American Cas. Co. v. Purcella, 163 A. 870, 163 Md. 434 (1933).

it is much more difficult for the promisor to find out the facts for himself than it is for the promisee to find out and give notice, it should usually be held that the giving of notice to the promisor is, by construction of law, a condition precedent to his duty to perform. It is obvious that this latter rule involves questions of degree. No exact limits in the application of this rule can be established; but a careful comparative study of cases will afford a guide to its application capable of being followed with a reasonable degree of confidence.[65]

65. See:

Eng.—Holmes v. Twist, Hob. 51 (1615).

Mass.—Hayden v. Bradley, 72 Mass. (6 Gray) 425 (1856).

Eng.—Vyse v. Wakefield, 6 M. & W. 442 (1840).

The titles of §§ 725–727 in the general treatise are as follows: § 725. Notice of Defects as Condition Precedent to Duty to Make Repairs; § 726. Notice as a Condition in Suretyship Contracts; § 727. Notice as a Condition Precedent to a Right of Action.

# CHAPTER 38

## ALEATORY CONTRACTS—NO AGREED EXCHANGE OF PERFORMANCES

## § 728. Aleatory Contracts are Not Agreements to Exchange Equivalent Performances

The term "aleatory contract" has not been in very general use in Anglo-American law. The American Law Institute has adopted it; and it supplies a lack that previously existed. What are the contracts that are properly described as "aleatory"; and how do the rules of law that are applicable to them differ from those in other cases?

When two parties make a bilateral contract, they are making an exchange of promises. Each party accepts the promise of the other party as the agreed equivalent of his own. Both parties, however, are looking forward to the performances that are being promised. Each party is induced to make his promise not merely by his desire for the return promise of the other party, but also because of his desire for the performance that is promised by the other party. In most such cases the parties contemplate not merely an exchange of their mutual promises, but also an exchange of the two performances that are being promised. The promised performances are the subjects of an agreed exchange. This does not mean that either of the contracting parties regards the two promised performances as of exactly the same market value or as equally advantageous to himself. The principal inducement for making the contract is the fact that each party has a stronger desire for the performance that is being promised him than for that which he is agreeing to give up in exchange. Nevertheless, the mutual willingness to make the exchange is some evidence that the market values are not far apart.

It is upon the facts stated in the foregoing paragraph that the rules of law respecting implied and constructive conditions, the rules of mutual dependency of exchanged promises, are based. It is not regarded as a square deal for one of the promisors to be required to render the performance promised by him when he has not received and is not going to receive the performance that was promised to him in return. Having reasonably anticipated an agreed performance in exchange for his own, it is not in accordance with prevailing notions of justice that he should be forced to give something for nothing.

The rules with respect to implied and constructive conditions, with respect to mutual dependency of promises, and with respect to failure of consideration, are not altogether applicable to what are now being described as aleatory promises. An aleatory promise is one the performance of which is by its own terms subject to the happening of an uncertain and fortuitous event or upon some fact the existence or past occurrence of which is also uncertain and undetermined.[1] The performance that is promised may never actually be rendered, and yet the failure to render it may not be a breach of the promise. Both parties to such a promise— the promisor and the promisee—are incurring a hazard or taking a chance; and the hazard is so far consciously incurred that neither party can justly complain if the chance goes against him. The promisee may be disappointed because the fortuitous condition does not occur and the promised performance is not rendered.[2] The promisor may be disappointed because the fortuitous condition does occur and he is obliged to render the promised per-

1.  "Aleatory" is thus defined in the Oxford Dictionary: "Dependent on the throw of a die; hence, dependent on uncertain contingencies." In derivation it is related to alea (meaning a die) and to aleator (meaning a dice player).

The La.Civ.Code, art. 1776, says: "A contract is aleatory or hazardous when the performance of that which is one of its objects depends on an uncertain event." Art. 2982 says: "The aleatory contract is a mutual agreement, of which the effects, with respect both to the advantages and losses, whether to all the parties or to one or more of them, depend on an uncertain event."

Restatement, Contracts, § 291: "An 'aleatory promise' in the Restatement means a promise conditional on the happening of a fortuitous event, or an event supposed by the parties to be fortuitous."

"Comment: *a.* . . . It may be beyond the power of any human being to bring the event to pass; it may be within the control of third persons; it may even be a past event, as the loss of a vessel, provided that the fact is unknown to the parties. But the fact that the time or amount of performance is dependent on a fortuitous event does not make a promise aleatory." In the last sentence here quoted there is error.

2.  If one conveys land for a small sum in cash and a note for another sum payable only if the seller is living on the day of its maturity, nothing is due from the buyer if the seller is not living on that day. Village of Clyde v. Mohn, 4 Ohio C.C. 537 (1890), affirmed 52 Ohio St. 635 (1894).

formance when he hoped that he would not be so obliged. When such aleatory promises are exchanged, it is not necessarily contrary to the prevailing notions of justice that one of the two parties should get something for nothing. This is because he himself took a similar chance and might have been compelled to give something for nothing.[3]

The typical and most common form of an aleatory contract is a betting contract. There are numberless wagers laid on horse races, elections, and games, as well as on the future price of wheat and other uncertain events. Originally these were not illegal, although most of them have become so. But there are great numbers of aleatory contracts that are not illegal wagers, especially in the fields of insurance and suretyship, where the carrying of other people's risks for compensation is an established business.[4]

In an English case nearly two centuries ago,[5] a bilateral contract was made between Martindale and Fisher whereby Martindale promised to deliver to Fisher 3 yards of cloth and Fisher promised in return to pay to the plaintiff £5 12s., in case Sir Marmaduke Wyvill's horse should beat a horse belonging to Martindale in a race about to be held; but if Martindale's horse should beat Sir Marmaduke's horse, then Fisher was to pay nothing for the cloth. This was very evidently a bet on a horse race, the plaintiff Martindale making a hedging bet against his own horse. It differs from most racing bets in that one of the promises— the one made by Martindale—was an unconditional promise; the 3 yards of cloth were to be delivered in any event. The return promise of Fisher, however, was performable only upon a fortuitous condition and was an aleatory promise.[6]

---

3. See, for example, Rishel v. Pacific Mut. Life Ins. Co., 78 F.2d 881 (C.C.A.10th, 1935), holding that the amount paid for an annuity contract is not recoverable even though the annuitant died soon before receiving any payment.

If A promises to pay a specified amount of money to B in exchange for B's promise to support A (or a third person) for life, the promise of A is enforceable in B's favor, without regard to the length of time that A (or the third person) lived.

Cal.—Roy v. Pos, 191 P. 542, 183 Cal. 359 (1920).

4. See the full discussion of Wagering Contracts in Chapter 88.

5. Eng.—Martindale v. Fisher, 1 Wils. 88 (1745).

6. At the date of the above case, wagering contracts were not illegal at common law. Such a contract would not be enforced today. See Bates v. Clifford, 22 Minn. 52, (1875), where the plaintiff delivered a horse to the defendant who promised in return that he would pay $500 if Grant should be elected President, and would pay only $150 if Horace Greeley should be elected. Grant being elected, the court refused to enforce the defendant's promise or even to make the defendant pay the reasonable value of the horse. The contract was rightly regarded as a bet on the election.

Similar cases are Givens v. Rogers, 11 Ala. 543 (1847), promise to pay double price for a wagon if Polk should defeat Henry Clay; and

It should be observed that, although Martindale's promise to deliver the cloth was not, standing alone, an aleatory promise, he was nevertheless incurring a hazard of loss and obtaining a chance of gain to the same extent as was the defendant Fisher. Martindale consciously incurred the hazard of selling his cloth for nothing, for he was to get nothing if Sir Marmaduke's horse lost the race. He also obtained the chance of selling his cloth at an unusually high price, £5 12s., for he was to receive that amount if Sir Marmaduke's horse won the race. Martindale was willing to incur the hazard of selling his cloth for nothing at all because he also got the compensating chance that he would get more for it than it was worth in the market. Fisher was willing to incur the hazard of having to pay more than the cloth was worth because he got the compensating chance that he would get the cloth for nothing at all. The contract in this case differs from the most common form of "betting" agreements in that one of the promises was to be performed in any event. In an ordinary "bet," one of the promises is conditional on the happening of the specified event and the other promise is conditional on its not happening.

Sir Marmaduke's horse won the race; and Martindale sued Fisher for payment of the £5 12s. Martindale did not aver in his declaration that he had delivered the cloth to the defendant in accordance with his promise. The court held that such an averment was not necessary. The only reason given by the court is that the contract was a promise for a promise; and the defendant's promise was not expressly made conditional upon performance or tender thereof by the plaintiff. The £5 12s. were not promised "for the cloth." This reasoning was characteristic of the English courts during the 18th century. The mutual promises in a bilateral contract were commonly held to be independent of each other, unless there were such express words as would make one or both of the promises conditional. There was a strong and often a successful effort to find such words by liberal interpretation. It was thought to make a promise conditional if the performance was promised expressly "for" the return performance. In Martindale v. Fisher, however, the defendant did not promise £5 12s. for 3 yards of cloth. They were not supposed by the parties to be exchanged for each other as agreed equivalents. The cloth was clearly considered by both parties as being of less value than the £5 12s. Justice did not require, therefore, that Fisher should be entirely freed from his duty by reason of the plaintiff's non-performance of his promise. The two performances not having been valued by the contracting parties themselves as equal subjects of exchange, the value of the cloth should now be determined by a jury and the defendant should be required to pay such part of the

Smithson v. Love, 270 P. 23, 132 Okl. 214 (1928), promise to pay     $1326 extra for a Ford car, if a test oil well should strike no oil.

£5 12s. as is in excess of the value of the cloth. The hazard having gone against him and having lost his bet, Fisher should not be allowed to go scot-free and pay nothing, as would be the case if the court should hold that his promise was subject to the condition precedent of delivery of the cloth by Martindale. It is sufficient to reduce the amount of Fisher's payment by the amount of his own injury caused by Martindale's breach, to be determined by making a counter-claim therefor. This would be complete justice today, just as it was in 1745, even though the courts have developed new law with respect to bilateral contracts that are not aleatory in character. Today, it would be quite proper to give judgment for the full £5 12s., making execution conditional on delivery of the cloth into court, or to give judgment for that amount diminished by the value of the cloth as found in fact.

Perhaps the case that has been most discussed in connection with aleatory promises is Christie v. Borelly.[7] In this case the defendant held two bills of exchange for £100 and £62 respectively, both drawn by Owen & Co. The plaintiff was about to sell certain Scotch whiskey for the price of £300 to one B. Fisse on credit. The parties thereupon made the following bilateral agreement. The plaintiff guaranteed the payment by Owen & Co. of the two bills of exchange amounting to £162. In return the defendant guaranteed the payment of the price of the whiskey amounting to £300. The plaintiff sued the defendant for breach of this latter promise of guaranty, and the defendant pleaded that Owen & Co. had become in default on the two bills of exchange and that the plaintiff had committed a breach of his guaranty of payment of said bills before the £300 had become due for the whiskey. The court held that the plea was bad, the two promises being mutually independent promises. The court said: "It appears that the damages in respect of the breach on one side must be very different from the damages arising from the breach on the other side; on the one side they would be £300 and on the other only £162; it is consequently apparent on the face of the contract itself that it was not intended by the parties that performance of the one stipulation should be a condition precedent to performance of the other."

In this case both promises were aleatory promises, although the court does not refer to that fact or so describe them. Each promise was conditional upon an uncertain event, while at the same time they were not conditional upon the same uncertain event. It is this fact that causes the two promises to be sufficient consideration each for the other; otherwise the agreement would have been a promise by one to pay £162 in return for a promise by the other to pay £300. As the agreement was, however, the plain-

---

7.　Eng.—Christie v. Borelly, 29 L. J.Com.Pl. 153 (1860).

tiff undertook the hazard of having to pay £162 to the defendant, although the defendant might not have to pay anything in return because Fisse, the purchaser of the whiskey, might pay the price himself. On the other hand, the defendant undertook the hazard of having to pay £300 to the plaintiff without getting anything whatever from the plaintiff in return, inasmuch as Owen & Co. might pay their own bills. There was also the hazard that the defendant might have to pay £300 to the plaintiff, while at the same time the plaintiff might nave to pay £162 to the defendant, the result of this being to the defendant's disadvantage in the sum of £138. This shows the difference between this case and an ordinary "bet;" both conditions precedent might occur and both parties might have to pay. In an ordinary "bet" this is not so.

Of course it is obvious that the parties to this agreement did not contemplate a mere exchange of £300 for £162. They knew in advance that the promised performances were not in any sense the equivalents of each other and they knew exactly the extent to which they were unequivalent. They were merely exchanging hazardous aleatory promises.[8]

It is obvious further, as the court clearly stated, that total non-performance by the plaintiff does not cause as much injury as does total non-performance by the defendant. Furthermore it is not in accord with prevailing notions of justice that the defendant should go scot-free from his duty to pay £300 merely because the plaintiff has failed to perform his promise to pay £162. Instead, justice requires merely the setting off of one amount against the other, with the result that the plaintiff gets judgment for the balance due him.

A contract may be similar to a betting agreement without falling within a prohibition against betting, because the purpose for which it is made is a different and approved purpose. A lawful but hazardous investment may be made, one party promising to share profits in exchange for the other party's promise to pay losses.[9] Here it is certain from the beginning that there will not be both a profit and a loss. Honest disputes over the quantity of land or goods transferred are sometimes settled by mutual promises, by one to pay in case of a deficit, by the other to pay in case of an excess.[10]

---

9. **N.Y.**—Coleman v. Eyre, 45 N.Y. 38 (1871), profits or losses on a shipment of coffee.

**Eng.**—Guy-Pell v. Foster, [1930] 2 ch. 169, defendant induced plaintiff to invest in bonds, promising to indemnify the plaintiff against loss and the latter promising to pay one fourth of the profits to defendant.

10. **Me.**—Colbath v. Stebbins Lbr. Co., 144 A. 1, 127 Me. 406 (1929), difference or doubt as to number of logs cut.

**Tenn.**—Seward & Scales v. Mitchell, 1 Cold. 87 (1860), dispute as to acreage of land.

**Eng.**—Cook v. Songat, 1 Leon. 103, 4 Leon. 31 (1588), dispute as to title, each promising to abide by the decision of J. S.

The two promises in a bilateral contract may both be conditional upon exactly the same uncertain event; in such a case the contract is not aleatory.  On the other hand, the two promises may be conditional upon two separate and entirely unrelated uncertain events, as in the case of Christie v. Borelly; or one of the promises may be conditional on such an event, and the other promise entirely unconditional, as in the case of Martindale v. Fisher,[11] or the two promises may be conditional—the one upon the happening of an uncertain event, and the other upon the event's not happening.  In the last described case, the parties know in advance that it is impossible for both of the conditions to occur, and that one of the promises will certainly not have to be performed; but they cannot tell in advance which one of the promises this will be.

### § 729.  Aleatory Promises Distinguished From Other Conditional Promises

In the great majority of bilateral contracts, the legal duty of each promisor is either expressly or constructively conditional upon substantial performance by the other contractor or at least upon his willingness and ability to render such performance.  Thus, in a contract of employment, if the servant does not work, the master is not required to pay.  In a contract for the sale of goods, if the buyer becomes insolvent, the seller can withhold delivery unless payment is sufficiently secured.  In the case of a building contract, if the builder does not substantially perform, the owner is not required to pay the price.  The fact that these promises are thus conditional in their legal operation does not make them aleatory, however.  The performance of the condition in these cases may be uncertain; and a promisor may, therefore, never come under a duty of rendering the promised performance.  In these cases, however, the condition precedent to a promisor's duty is concerned with the very return performance for which he has promised to give his own performance in exchange.  In these cases the parties contemplate and actually promise their performances with an equal degree of certainty.  A contract is aleatory only when the parties contemplate that one of them may have to perform even though the other does not have to, only when the promises are so expressed that one party promises to perform under certain circumstances even though the other party does not perform at all.  The legal result of this is that in case of an aleatory contract one of the parties may come under a legal duty of rendering immediate performance even though the other party does not and never will come under such a duty.  In ordinary bilateral contracts the performances are promised and the legal duties of the two parties will accrue with an equal degree of certainty; in aleatory contracts this is not the case.  Since the promises in the ordinary bilateral contract for an agreed exchange are held to be conditional and dependent for the very reason that they are not aleatory, they can scarcely be called aleatory because they are held to be conditional.

A contract is not made aleatory in character by the fact that one of the performances is to be rendered upon the happening of an uncertain event, if reasonable interpretation shows that the parties regarded the two performances as agreed equivalents. If the contract is still bilateral, it may be understood that the two performances are to be simultaneous when the event occurs. Thus, if A promises to convey his land to B in exchange for B's promise to pay $5,000 when his ship arrives from Spain, the reasonable interpretation (in the absence of evidence to the contrary) is that conveyance is promised to take place when the money is paid.

## § 730.    Effect of Repudiation or Other Breach by a Party to an Aleatory Contract

If in a bilateral contract one of the promises is aleatory and the other looked at separately is not, it may reasonably be assumed that the performance that is promised conditionally is more valuable than the one that is promised with certainty. Therefore, if the aleatory promise is repudiated or becomes impossible of enforcement before the determination of the event that constitutes the condition, the duty of the other party may properly be held to be discharged.[17] Even though there was a chance that the other party might have to render his less valuable performance for nothing, he should not be required to continue to carry that risk after it has been materially increased by the other party's wrongful act or by events the risk of which he did not assume. The consideration for his own promise was the conditional assurance of the aleatory promise. The value of that assurance is destroyed by a repudiation or by the other unforeseen events and his purpose is wholly "frustrated." A repudiation substitutes a costly lawsuit for his assurance; unenforceability for other reasons substitutes nothing.[a]

17.    A repudiation by an insurer of its obligation on a life policy justifies the refusal of the insured to pay a note given for the first premium. Sydnor v. Boyd, 26 S.E. 92, 119 N.C. 481 (1896). In such a case the only aleatory promise is that of the insurer; its repudiation greatly increases the risk of the insured that his premium payment will never be compensated, even though his premium note was not in itself an aleatory promise. This is applicable in the case of fire insurance also; but the contrary was held in New Eng. Mut. Fire Ins Co. v. Butler, 34 Me. 451 (1852), on the stated ground that the promises were wholly "independent." The court thought it was enough that the insured could still maintain action on the policy in spite of an anticipatory repudiation.

a.    In the general treatise there is further discussion of the effect of repudiation by one party and of the rule expressed in Restatement, Contracts, § 293.

## § 731.   Insurance as an Aleatory Contract

One of the most common forms of an aleatory promise is to be found in contracts of insurance. These are customarily unilateral, so that the problem of mutual dependency does not arise, and the rules with respect to implied or constructive conditions are not applicable. The promise of the insurance company is a promise to pay money on the happening of some uncertain and fortuitous event, and it is, therefore, an aleatory promise; it is usually made expressly conditional upon the payment of stated premiums by the insured, although the insured makes no return promise to pay these premiums. There are a good many instances, however, in which an insurance contract assumes a bilateral form. Instead of an actual payment of the premium in cash by the insured, the insurance company may accept the promissory note of the insured or even a mere non-negotiable promise on his part to pay the premium at some stated period. In such a case, if the insurance company makes its promise to pay the amount of the policy expressly conditional upon exact performance by the insured of his return promise to pay premiums, there is again no problem with respect to implied or constructive conditions.[28] In such a case the court merely has the problem of determining whether or not it will enforce the insurance contract exactly in accordance with its express terms and not otherwise. There are many cases, however, in which the insurance company has not made its promise to pay the amount of a policy expressly conditional upon the exact performance by the insured of his return promise to pay the premium. Such cases are exactly like the case of Martindale v. Fisher, previously discussed. The promises of the two contracting parties are exchanged for each other and are both binding according to their terms. The insured has made an absolute and unconditional promise to pay the amount of the premium. The insurance company, on the other hand, has made a conditional and aleatory promise to pay a much larger sum upon the happening of an uncertain event. The two promised performances are not agreed to be given in exchange for each other as agreed equivalents. In an action on the policy by the insured against the insurance company, it is no defense that the premium note was not paid when due.[29] There is merely a counter-claim for the amount of the premium, with interest during the period of delay.

On the other hand, a repudiation of its policy contract by the insurer justifies the refusal of the insured to pay his premium note.[30] The transaction is bilateral in form, the premium promise being exchanged for the insurance promise. A repudiation by either party before the risk undertaken has changed materially causes a total failure of the consideration for the return promise.

Repudiation by the insurer causes the insured to lose substantially the benefit of his "protection", as insurers describe it. A "lawsuit" has been substituted for "assurance"; and even a good lawsuit is not a good substitute. Although there is no agreed exchange of the performances promised, there is such an exchange of the promises themselves and of the promissory obligations.

### § 732.  Suretyship as an Aleatory Contract

While the fact that a promise is aleatory in character tends strongly to the conclusion that the duty of the promisor is not impliedly or constructively conditional upon the performance of a return promise by the other party, it cannot be said that this is universally true. Thus, the promise of one who is a surety for the debt of another is always aleatory in character. This is because, even though it may not be expressly so provided, the surety's duty is conditional upon non-performance by the principal debtor.[32] Even though it may be perfectly clear that the performance thus conditionally promised by the surety is not being exchanged as the agreed equivalent of any return performance by the promisee, the surety's duty of performance may, nevertheless, be constructively conditional upon the performance of a return promise by the creditor. The surety's duty may be conditional on other factors than the performance of an "agreed equivalent" and he may be discharged for other reasons than "failure of consideration."

In an early California case[33] Smith had a judgment against Richardson for $3,900. A bilateral agreement was thereafter made whereby Compton guaranteed payment of Richardson's debt, and, in return, Smith promised to suspend proceedings on the judgment against Richardson for a period of four months. Smith sued Compton on his promise of guaranty, and the latter moved for a nonsuit, because the plaintiff had not proved that he in fact suspended proceedings on the judgment. It was held that the nonsuit ought to have been granted because performance by the plaintiff was a condition precedent to the duty of the guarantor. It appeared later, however, that the defendant had acquiesced in the proceedings on the judgment by the plaintiff, thus waiving the condition.

The holding in this case is quite correct, in spite of the fact that Compton did not agree to exchange $3,900 for Smith's forbearance of proceedings on the judgment against Richardson. These performances were not to be exchanged as agreed equivalants. One who has, by making an aleatory promise, incurred

---

33.  Cal.—Smith v. Compton, 6 Cal.
24 (1856).

some degree of hazard or risk certainly has a right that the other party to the contract shall not do anything that will increase materially the degree of this hazard or risk except such things as it was clearly contemplated by the parties that he might properly do; and, further, the duty of the promisor is, by operation of law, constructively conditional upon the other party's so conducting himself as not materially to increase the risk.[34]

In a case like the one just stated above, the action of the creditor Smith in pressing his judgment against the debtor Richardson might seriously affect the risk that Compton would have to pay, inasmuch as the agreed extension of time to Richardson was probably for the very purpose of enabling him to get on his feet financially and to pay the debt himself. In such a case as this, therefore, the duty of the surety, by reason of his aleatory promise, is constructively conditional upon performance by the creditor of his return promise. It should be observed that the same result would be reached in many cases, even though the creditor's conduct was not a breach of any promise by him to the surety. Thus, a surety is discharged from his duty to the creditor, if, without the surety's consent, the creditor either releases the principal debtor or gives him a binding extension of time.[35] The result is not necessarily based upon the non-performance of a return promise; but whenever the non-performance of such a return promise by the creditor will materially increase the promisor's risk of having to perform, the surety will be discharged by reason of the non-performance of a constructive condition precedent. There seems to be no doubt that this would be true not merely in cases of suretyship and guaranty, but also in all other cases of aleatory promises.[36]

In the case of a construction bond, the obligation of the surety is conditional on default by the building contractor, the principal obligor. If the obligee promised to supply the money with which to finance construction the principal obligor's duty is constructively conditional on substantial performance of the obligee's promise; so also is the promise of the surety.[37]

In these cases the plaintiff's breach of his promise may have been the cause of the defendant's being called upon to pay in accordance with his promise. If the defendant would not otherwise have been called upon to pay, it is clear that the injury caused by the plaintiff's breach of his promise is identical with the amount due from the defendant. Therefore, in spite of the aleatory nature of the contract, it falls within the reason underlying the rules as to implied and constructive conditions.

693

The extent to which the risk of the defendant has been increased by the plaintiff's breach of promise cannot be determined with certainty. It cannot be established with certainty that the principal debtor would have paid his own debt if the creditor had forborne in accordance with his promise to the surety. Neither can the contrary now be established. Inasmuch as it is the plaintiff's own wrongful conduct that has caused this situation to arise, all doubts as to the matter should be resolved against him.

# CHAPTER 39

## CONDITIONS SUBSEQUENT—ANALYSIS—PLEADING AND BURDEN OF PROOF

## § 739. Condition Subsequent Distinguished From Condition Precedent

In distinguishing a condition subsequent from a condition precedent, not only must a specific definition of the word "condition" be adopted, but also the character of the modifying adjectives must be considered. A condition has been defined as a fact or event, the occurrence of which changes in some way one or more of the legal relations of two persons. Proceeding from this, a moment's thought must make it apparent that the adjectives "subsequent" and "precedent" add nothing whatever in and of themselves with respect to the character of the fact or event. A condition subsequent is not a condition of some peculiar character that enables us to distinguish it from a condition precedent. The terms are frequently used, however, so as to lead one to suppose that a condition precedent is one kind of fact or event, and that a condition subsequent is a different kind of fact or event. The truth is that the terms are meaningless until the fact constituting the condition is related to something else. If it is precedent, it must be precedent to something; and if it is subsequent, it must be subsequent to something. Therefore, the first question must always be: Precedent to what? and subsequent to what?

If a condition is a fact that changes a legal relation, it is believed that it is convenient to relate the condition to the legal relation in question, and that this is in fact what the courts and legal writers are doing, even though it is frequently done confusedly. A fact is a condition precedent to the legal relation for the creation of which it is necessary. A fact is a condition subsequent to the legal relation that it extinguishes. It is evident that the same fact is a condition precedent to one legal relation,

695

the while it is a condition subsequent to another. Therefore, before it can be described as either precedent or subsequent, it is necessary to know the particular legal relation with respect to which it is being considered.

### § 740.  Illustration—Time Limit for Suit as a Condition Subsequent

The analysis and discussion of a number of cases are necessary, in order to make clear the usage that is here adopted and to demonstrate the existing confusion that must be eliminated. An insurance policy contained the following provision: "Payment of losses shall be due in 60 days after the proof required by this company shall have been received at this office and the loss shall have been satisfactorily ascertained and proved as required by the foregoing provisions of this policy. It is furthermore hereby expressly provided that no suit or action of any kind against this company for the recovery of any claim by virtue of this policy shall be sustainable in any court, unless such suit or action shall be commenced within the term of 12 months next after any loss or damage shall occur; and in case any such suit or action shall be commenced against this company after the expiration of 12 months next after such loss or damage shall have occurred, the lapse of time shall be taken and deemed as conclusive evidence against the validity of the claim thereby so attempted to be enforced." Proof of loss was made on September 14, 1881. From the provision in the policy quoted above, it appears that payment by the company thereafter became due on November 14, 1881. Prior to that date non-payment by the company would not be a breach of its duty, and no action could be maintained against it. After November 14, however, non-payment by the company would be a breach of duty, and an action could be maintained. Therefore, it was on November 14 that there first came into existence a duty of immediate performance on the part of the insurance company, as distinguished from its duty of future performance that existed from the time of the execution of the insurance policy.

A suit for breach of contract was brought by the insured on November 11, 1882. This was more than 12 months from the date when the loss occurred, the fire injuring the insured property having occurred on September 1, 1881. The court, therefore, held that the action could not be maintained, because the lapse of more than 12 months from the date of the loss had terminated the plaintiff's right and had discharged the duty of the defendant.[1]

The operative facts in this case should be considered in relation to the insurer's duty of immediate performance (the duty to pay

1.  Conn.—Chambers v. Atlas Ins. Co., 51 Conn. 17 (1883).

over the counter), the breach of which at once constituted a cause of action for damages. There were a number of different events that had to occur before this duty of immediate performance by the insurer could exist. These events were conditions precedent to the existence of such a duty. Among these events, conditions precedent to the duty, were the following: The fire itself, which occurred on September 1; proof by the insured of the amount of loss caused by this fire, such proof being actually made on September 14; the lapse of 60 days' time after the making of this proof of loss; the payment of the premium, no doubt expressly required by the policy as a condition precedent.

These conditions precedent all having occurred, the defendant's duty of making immediate payment was born. By express provision in the policy, however, the failure of the insured to bring any suit within the period of twelve months next after the occurrence of the loss would wholly extinguish and discharge the company's duty to make payment. This is what the court actually decided. Certain events, already named above, were conditions precedent to the existence of the company's duty to make immediate payment; we now have a fact, however, which is likewise a condition of the existence of that duty on the part of the company, but which terminates it, instead of initiating it. This fact is the failure of the insured to bring any suit during the twelve-month period after the loss. From November 14, 1881, when the defendant's duty of making immediate payment first accrued and when its breach first existed, a right of action existed in the insured; and a duty of paying the amount of the loss, and also a duty of paying compensatory damages by reason of its delay, existed in the insurance company. This right and this duty terminated on September 14, 1882, by the occurrence of the specified condition subsequent—the failure to bring suit.[2]

## § 741. Illustration—Note Conditioned to be Void on a Specified Event

In the days when the whaling industry was active, the plaintiff sold to the defendant a quantity of oil. The two agreed that the price to be paid therefor should be dependent upon the extent of the season's supply; therefore, the defendant paid 60¢ per gallon and gave his promissory note for 25¢ more per gallon, on condition, however, that the note should be void if a larger amount of oil should arrive at certain ports before October 2 than had arrived the previous season. In an action on the note, it was held that the condition was a condition subsequent, and that the plaintiff had a right to judgment for the amount of the note, unless the defendant affirmatively proved that a larger amount of oil had arrived.[3] This holding was decisive in the case for the reason that evidence was lacking as to the relative amounts of oil. The ship "Lady Adams" had arrived with a cargo of oil on the night of October 1. If she came to anchor before midnight, a larger amount of oil had arrived and the note was not payable. If she cast anchor after midnight, a larger amount had not arrived and the note was payable. Apparently proof was lacking as to whether she arrived before midnight or after.

This raises two questions for analysis and discussion: First, as to the character of the condition; secondly, as to the burden of proof. The reasoning on which the court held that the condition was subsequent, rather than precedent, seems to have been this: The note was a valid and operative note from the time it was delivered, but it was to be made void and invalid by a subsequent event—the arrival of a larger quantity of oil. There is no error in this reasoning; but it does not lead to the result reached by the court. The fact that the note was valid and operative from delivery does not show that it created a duty of immediate performance; it does not show that non-payment by the maker was a breach of contractual duty. In actions for enforcement of a contract, the crucial issue is not merely whether a valid contract was made; it is also whether it has been broken. The plaintiff's cause of action is not merely that money was lent or goods sold and a good note given in return; it also requires that the time should have come for payment, and that the defendant failed to make payment. It is not enough to show that a primary contractual obligation was created by the making of a valid contract; it is necessary also to show that it became the defendant's duty of making immediate performance in accordance with that primary obligation, and that he committed a breach of such duty.

A bargaining transaction consists of a series of operative facts. First, there is an offer, stating the terms, the conditions, and the promises that are to be agreed upon. Next comes the acceptance by the offeree. It is useful to say that the offer created a power in the offeree. The acceptance is the exercise of this power. After acceptance, the new situation of the parties is that neither can withdraw. It is useful to say that they are under obligation, that rights and duties have been created; but usually still other facts and events must occur before actual performance is due. These facts and events, although occurring subsequently to the acceptance of the offer and to the primary obligation created thereby, are conditions precedent to the duty of immediate performance and to any right of action for breach.

In the case of the sale of oil, stated above, the note was a valid note but it was not due and payable prior to October 2; nor was

3. Mass.—Gray v. Gardner, 17 Mass. 188 (1821).

it due and payable even then, unless the casting of the anchor of the "Lady Adams" occurred after midnight, instead of before. Upon the arrival of the larger amount of oil, the note was to become void; but the note never became due at all, unless the amount of oil that had arrived was a smaller amount. Specifically, therefore, the fact that the amount of oil arriving before October 2 was not greater than that of the year previous was a condition precedent to the duty of payment; and it was the duty of making payment that the plaintiff had to establish, not merely the existence of a valid primary contractual obligation.[4] To establish this fact, it was necessary to prove that the anchor of the Lady Adams was not dropped before midnight.

The second question to be discussed relative to this case is the question of the burden of proof. The court threw this on the defendant with respect to the arrival of the "Lady Adams," thinking that her arrival before October 2 was a condition subsequent, and that this fact determined the incidence of the burden of proof. As to both matters, it is believed that the court was in error. Proof of the time of her arrival was necessary only because the duty to pay the note depended on the amount of oil that had arrived by midnight. It never became due if she cast her anchor before midnight; and, inasmuch as no evidence was available as to whether she cast anchor before or after midnight, it appears that the court made the defendant pay the note because it could not tell whether the note was due or not.

Some courts have thought that the burden of proving a "negative" ought not to be put upon the plaintiff. There is seldom any good reason for such a rule. But in the oil case discussed above it was not a "negative" that had to be established. The plaintiff, asserting breach of the duty to pay the note, merely had to prove the amount of oil that had arrived before October 2 and its relation to the amount of oil that had arrived the year before. In making this proof, the plaintiff would not have had to mention the Lady Adams at all, or any other whaler that he believed had brought no oil. But if the defendant introduced testimony that the Ladybird had unloaded 10,000 gallons of oil in August, it would have been necessary for the plaintiff to convince the jury that the testimony was untrue.

It does not appear to be any more difficult for the plaintiff to prove the amounts of oil that arrived during each of the two seasons than for the defendant to prove them. The evidence to be produced for that purpose would be identical. The mere form of the words used in the note appears to be an insufficient reason for shifting the burden of proof.

The question who has the burden of proof is not necessarily dependent on whether the condition is a condition precedent or a condition subsequent. Even though it is the former, as in the instant case, it may be sound policy to throw the burden of going forward with the evidence on the defendant, on the ground that he is in better position to know the truth as to the happening, or non-happening of the event. Less often it may even be proper to throw on him the final burden of persuasion—the "burden of proof." This is a matter of policy, not to be determined solely by the logical character of a particular condition as being "precedent" or "subsequent." In general, however, the plaintiff has the burden of proving the facts necessary to his right of action.[a]

### § 747. Duty of Immediate Performance Distinguished From Remedial Duty to Make Compensation

In some cases it may be necessary to distinguish between the promisor's duty of immediate performance and his duty to make compensation for a breach. It is possible for parties to control not only the primary contractual obligation and the duty of immediate performance, but also to control to some extent the remedy that is available for breach—the legal sanction. Parties cannot create remedies unknown to the existing legal system; but they can discharge remedial rights and duties, either by agreement in advance creating a condition subsequent or by an agreement made subsequent to breach. It appears also that they can postpone the remedy for an already existing breach, making some fact a condition precedent to the duty of making compensation, without at the same time making it a condition precedent to the duty of immediate performance of the promise.

Thus, it is frequently provided that, in case of a dispute arising out of performance of the contract, no action shall be maintainable except after an arbitration and award. This makes the award a condition precedent to a right of action and to the defendant's duty to make compensation for an already existing breach. It is not, however, a condition precedent to the defendant's duty of performing in accordance with his promise. Long before the award of the arbitrator and probably before the dispute arose, it was the defendant's duty to render immediate performance. The absence of an award is not a postponement of that

a. Further illustrations are given in the general treatise and specific cases analyzed. § 742. Illustration from Insurance—Condition of Survivorship—"Vested" Interest. McGowin v. Menken, 119 N.E. 877, 223 N.Y. 509, 5 A.L.R. 794 (1918). § 743. Sale with Privilege of Return—Condition Subsequent to "Title". Ray v. Thompson, 66 Mass. (12 Cush.) 281 (1853). § 744. Exercise of a Reserved Power of Withdrawal or Termination. Wilmington & R. R. Co. v. Robeson, 27 N.C. 391 (1845). § 745. Time Limit on Warranty of Quality—Form of Pleading. Smart v. Hyde, 8 M. & W. 723 (1841). § 746. "Conditional Delivery" of an Instrument and the "Parol Evidence Rule." Pym v. Campbell, 6 El. & Bl. 370 (1856).

duty. His failure to perform at that time is a breach of duty; but the contract partly controlled the remedy and postponed the remedial right and duty until after an award.[18]

The failure to arbitrate the dispute in cases like this does not necessarily operate as a discharge and, therefore, is not necessarily a condition subsequent to the duty of immediate performance. It may, however, be provided in the contract that the failure to arbitrate within a specified time or the failure to make a claim for defects within a specified time shall operate as a discharge after breach. Thus, where a seller warranted an engine and promised to accept the return of it if defective, the court stated that the contract provided "that seller should not be liable to claims for damages or failure of consideration, unless such claims were made by registered letter to the seller within ten days after starting engine." The buyer gave no notice by registered letter within the ten days; and, therefore, the plaintiff got judgment for the contract price, in spite of alleged defects in the engine.[19]

This seems to be a case where notice is a condition precedent to any right of action for damages, but not a condition precedent to the duty of immediate performance. It was the seller's contractual duty to deliver a perfect engine. That duty was either performed or broken at the time of delivery. Nevertheless, no action for a breach would be maintainable until after giving notice by registered letter. Furthermore, since the time for giving this notice was limited to a period of ten days, failure to give the notice would be a condition subsequent, operating as a complete discharge. Of course, in this case the giving of notice within the ten days was a condition precedent to the seller's duty to accept return of the engine and to repay the contract price.

## § 748. Forfeitures are Regarded with Disfavor

When it is said that courts do not favor forfeitures, the meaning is that they do not like to see a party to a contract getting something for nothing. It is for the same reason that they refuse to enforce an express provision for the payment of a penalty. Therefore, the courts do not greatly favor express conditions precedent where the condition is itself no part of the subject-matter of exchange by the parties and where giving effect to the condition will result in one of the parties enjoying benefits under the contract without giving the agreed equivalent in exchange therefor. The courts do not hold such express conditions to be contrary to public policy, however; they are not yet ready to limit our much prized freedom of contract so greatly. Nevertheless, they are very ready to put an interpretation on a contract so as

19. Ga.—Walker v. Malsby Co., 67 S.E. 1039, 134 Ga. 399 (1910).

to avoid such a harsh condition; and they are very ready to dispense with the necessity of such a condition by holding that it can be waived without consideration, and that it can be excused and made entirely unnecessary by supervening facts making its performance impracticable.[20]

Likewise, express conditions subsequent will be regarded with disfavor if they are such as to cause a forfeiture, that is, if they permit a party to keep benefits received under the contract without giving their agreed equivalent. Supervening occurrences beyond the control of the parties which make the occurrence of such a condition subsequent inevitable are very likely to lead to the entire nullification of the condition by the court.[21]

If the dislike of forfeitures has caused the courts to treat express conditions with some degree of severity, it is certain that the courts will not of their own motion create by implication or by construction a condition, either precedent or subsequent, that will result in a forfeiture. If a contract contains a provision providing for some performance that does not constitute any substantial part of the subject-matter of exchange by the parties, the courts much prefer the interpretation that this provision is a promise to render the performance, rather than that it makes the performance a condition precedent to the defendant's duty. By the former interpretation, the failure to render the performance merely creates a right to damages for such injury as may be caused thereby; while by the latter interpretation, the failure to render the performance would privilege the defendant to refuse to render his part of the agreed exchange. Express provisions in a contract, therefore, providing for an arbitration and award under certain circumstances, or for the certificate of an architect or engineer, or for the giving of a notice, or for the making of proof of loss, will be held to be merely promissory in nature, and not to create a condition precedent to the defendant's duty of performing unless the express words of the contract very clearly show a different intention. Thus, where a contract of fidelity insurance provided that proof of the amount of the loss should be made within a certain ninety-day period, it was held that, in the absence of express words, the time element was not of the essence, and that, while the making of the proof was itself

---

**20.** See Elberton Cotton Mills v. Indemnity Ins. Co., 145 A. 33, 108 Conn. 707, 62 A.L.R. 926 (1929). Also, Chapter 78, Impossibility of Performance of a Condition.

**21.** Thus, in Semmes v. Hartford Ins. Co., 13 Wall. 158, 20 L.Ed. 490 (U.S.1871), where an insurance policy provided that no action should be maintainable upon it unless commenced within the period of twelve months next after the occurrence of the loss, the court held that this provision became entirely inoperative when the occurrence of the Civil War made the bringing of such a suit either impossible or extremely difficult.

a condition precedent to the insurance company's duty to pay, the making of such proof within the ninety-day period was not a condition precedent.[22]

## § 749. Burden of Proof, as Affected by the Form of Stating a Condition—Statutory Rule of Pleading

The problem of burden of proof is not wholly solved by determining whether a fact is a condition precedent or a condition subsequent; there are other elements to be considered. If a fact is a condition precedent to the defendant's duty of immediate performance, it is a necessary part of the plaintiff's cause of action; but there are cases in which its existence will be assumed, unless the defendant disproves it. Thus, the plaintiff often has no right to performance by the defendant if the plaintiff was guilty of fraud or had an illegal purpose; but the burden of proving the existence of either is thrown on the defendant. This is so for reasons of general public policy, not because fraud and illegality are conditions subsequent. There are cases also in which a fact that is plainly a condition precedent to the defendant's duty is one that is peculiarly within the knowledge of the defendant himself; in such cases, it may be sound policy for the court to assume that the condition has occurred, unless the defendant affirmatively proves that it has not.[23] Except for such reasons of social policy, however, if a fact is a condition precedent to the defendant's duty of immediate performance, the burden of proving it should be on the plaintiff.[24] If that duty accrued and the defendant committed an actual breach, the burden should usually be on him to prove the occurrence of a subsequent fact operating as a discharge.

The performance of all conditions precedent must ordinarily be affirmatively alleged by the plaintiff and affirmatively proved by him. It has frequently been held, however, and there are some statutes that expressly so provide, that it is sufficient for the plaintiff, in his declaration, to make a general and blanket allegation of performance of all conditions precedent.[25] Such a rule as this does not change the burden of proof; it merely relieves the plaintiff of the necessity of listing all possible conditions precedent and alleging their occurrence. The defendant may, of course, raise an issue as to the occurrence of any or all of them; but if he wishes to do so, he is required to specify the particular condition precedent, the performance or occurrence of which he wishes to deny. Having thus raised such an issue, the burden of proof is generally put upon the plaintiff.[26]

22. Elberton Cotton Mills v. Indemnity Ins. Co., 145 A. 33, 108 Conn. 707, 62 A.L.R. 926 (1929).

Where a plaintiff had sold machinery to the defendant, promising to instruct the defendant in a secret process of making paper, and the defendant promised to pay the price in paper to be manufactured by the process, it was held that the teaching of the process and the privilege of manufacturing by it were conditions precedent to the defendant's duty to pay, that the declaration was demurrable for not specifically alleging their performance, and that the burden of proving them was on the plaintiff. A mere blanket allegation of performance of all conditions precedent was not sufficient.[27] Under most modern codes of procedure, the demurrer would not be sustained, although the burden of proof would be on the plaintiff if an issue were raised as to the instruction and use of the process.

Even before the passage of statutes regulating common law procedure, it was held that if a defendant pleaded the nonfulfilment of one express condition, not mentioning another, and permitted the case to proceed to trial and verdict on that one issue, it was too late after verdict for him to move in arrest of judgment on the ground that the plaintiff had not alleged or proved the fulfilment of the second condition.[28] This decision is in accord with sound policy in the matter of procedure, whether the second condition was precedent or subsequent to the plaintiff's "right of action."

27.  Mass.—Cadwell v. Blake, 6 Gray, 402 (Mass.1856).

# CHAPTER 40

## ELIMINATION OF CONDITIONS BY WAIVER
## OR PREVENTION

## § 752. Waiver and Estoppel Compared

The term "waiver" has been given various definitions; the fact is that it is used under many varying circumstances. There is no one "correct" definition; it can not be defined without reference to the kind of circumstances to which it is being related. Nor can we determine the legal operation of a "waiver" without knowing the facts that the term is being used to describe. In particular, if the question is asked whether a "waiver" can be legally effective if it is not accompanied by a "consideration," it can not be answered without knowing what it is that is being "waived" and what is the mode in which the "waiver" is being attempted. Let us analyze and classify a few hypothetical cases.

Suppose that A has given his note to B for money lent. B has a legally enforceable right to repayment of the money. Can B effectively discharge this right by merely saying to A "I waive my right to repayment"? The answer to this appears to be No. The question is one of Discharge of a contract right created by a promissory note given for an executed consideration. There are various ways in which such a right can be discharged; and in the case of some of these, there is no necessity that B should receive any consideration for the discharge. There are ways of effecting a gift discharge. But these should not be sought for or discussed under such a heading as "waiver."

Suppose that A and B have exchanged promises (a bilateral contract), A promising to pay for services that B promises to render. Can B effectively discharge his right to payment by merely saying to A "I waive the right to payment for my services"? The answer to this also is No. Again, the search for an answer should be made in some chapter dealing with Discharge of contractual duties.

Suppose further, in the immediately foregoing case, that A has repudiated the contract, refusing either to receive B's services or to pay for them. B has a remedial right to damages for A's breach. Can B effectively discharge his right to damages by merely saying to A "I waive my right to damages"? Here again the answer is No; and the methods of discharge that are effective must be considered in chapters dealing with Discharge instead of one dealing with waiver.

And yet we can find court opinions in which it is said that rights like these have been "waived," this term being used to denote the particular set of facts by which the right in question has been discharged.

In the present chapter, we are not dealing with "waiver" as a method of terminating rights and discharging duties. We are dealing with the operation of a contract after it has been made, with promissory duties that are expressly or constructively conditional, with the "conditions" on which a duty of immediate performance depends and which must be proved to exist in order to show that there has been a breach of duty. In the present and succeeding sections we are dealing with the subject of "waiver of conditions."

If a promise is conditional, if the promisor's duty of immediate performance is dependent on the existence or occurrence of some fact or event, is it possible that such promise or duty may become unconditional and not dependent on that fact or event? Of course, as soon as the fact or event occurs or comes into existence, the duty becomes thus unconditional and independent. It may still be conditional on the happening of other events; but it is no longer conditional on the one that has happened.

But there are methods by which a promisor's duty of rendering immediate performance may cease to be conditional on some fact or event, even though that fact or event has not occurred or come into existence. The condition may be eliminated—it may cease to be a condition of the duty's existence—by processes that are known as "waiver" and "estoppel." This is what is meant when we say that a condition has been "waived"—the duty once conditional has become unconditional; a duty of immediate performance accrues and nonperformance is a breach, even though the fact or event constituting the condition never occurs or exists.

In many cases, a vendor has promised to make conveyance of land on the express condition of payment of some instalment of the price by a specified date. Here, payment on time is the stated condition of the vendor's duty. It is quite possible, however, for him to disregard this limitation on his duty. He can make actual conveyance, even though he has not been paid on time, and even though he has never been paid at all. By such action, he not only waives the condition of his duty; he performs when he was under no legal duty to render the performance.[1] But waiver of the condition is possible without making actual conveyance; if he merely states to the purchaser that he does not insist on payment on time, he thereby eliminates it as a condition. Thereafter, his duty to convey is not conditional, as it had been by the contract as made. He may be able to restore the conditional character of his duty; but as long as he does not retract his statement, he is bound to convey even though payment on time is not made. His statement to the purchaser is called a "waiver"; and by it he has enlarged his duty by removing the limitation on it and eliminating the condition.

The vendor's "waiver" in the foregoing case is his own voluntary action; and in order to be legally effective, it is not necessary that the purchaser shall have given any consideration for it or shall have changed his position in reliance upon it. If the vendor offers to eliminate the condition in exchange for a requested consideration, and the purchaser gives that consideration, the case can still be described as a "waiver"; but it is also a modification by mutual agreement—by a substituted contract—a modification that is not subject to retraction by the vendor.

If the vendor requests and receives no consideration for his waiver, but, as he had reason to foresee, it causes the purchaser to change his position materially in reliance upon it, this too deprives the vendor of his power of retraction for, at the least, a reasonable time. The vendor is then said to be estopped; his own action can still be described as a "waiver", while the resulting action of the purchaser justifies the added description of estoppel.[2]

By the usage thus explained, it appears that "waiver" consists of the voluntary action of the obligor alone. A contractual modification by substituted agreement, requires the assent of both parties;[3] and it produces the usual effects of other valid contracts.

1. Observe, however, that the waiver of the condition is not a dis- charge of the purchaser's duty to pay.

To create an "estoppel," also, action by both parties is required, but not mutual expressions of agreement or an exchange of agreed equivalents.[4]

### § 753.  Waiver of a Condition may be Effective Without a Consideration

In the chapter on Consideration, we have seen that a promise can become enforceable by reason of other factors than a bargained-for exchange.  Substantial action by the promisee in reliance on the promise may be such a factor; and so also may certain kinds of antecedent events called "past consideration."  We need not be surprised, therefore, to find that a promisor can sometimes turn his conditional duty into an unconditional one by a "waiver" of the condition, without any consideration therefor.  It depends, however, upon the kind of condition that is being waived.

Generally, the waiver of a condition by a promisor is followed by a substantial change of position by the promisee.  At the very least, he will be induced by the waiver not to perform the condition, if it was one that consisted of some act or forbearance of his own.  Thus, where a promisor's duty to convey is conditional on payment by a stated day, the promisor's waiver of the condition may induce the promisee to cease his efforts to raise the money and to forbear to pay on the day.  Here we have ample reason for an estoppel, or for the enforcement of a promise because of subsequent reliance.

In many cases, however, the waiver takes place after the failure to perform the condition has already occurred, and there is no subsequent change of position by the promisee on which to base an estoppel.  Suppose that an insurance company, after the failure of the insured to pay a premium on the last day allowed, promises him to "waive the forfeiture" and to reinstate the policy on "satisfactory evidence of insurability."  This new promise is binding in accordance with its terms.[5]  The past transaction, including the execution of the policy and the payment of premiums by the insured, is a sufficient basis on which to rest the new promise, without any new consideration for it or any new action in reliance on it by the promisee.  Of course, he must show performance of the conditions of the new promise, whatever they may be.

In a New York case, there was a contract between a publisher and a writer, wherein the latter promised to write a law book and to refrain from drinking intoxicants while so occupied.  The publisher promised to pay two dollars per page, if the manuscript should be accepted and published; and to pay an additional four dollars per page, if the writer actually forbore to drink.  The writer did not forbear to drink, as the publisher knew; but, when the manuscript was done, he accepted and published it. In a suit by the writer to collect the extra four dollars per page, he alleged a waiver of the condition by the publisher—that is, the forbearance to drink. As constituting such waiver, he asserted, first, that the publisher permitted him to continue writing, with knowledge of his drinking, and accepted the manuscript; secondly, that, with full knowledge of his having consumed liquor, the publisher expressly promised to pay the additional four dollars per page. The court sustained the second contention, held that there was a waiver of the condition, and that the defendant must pay the additional four dollars per page.[6]

It should be observed that the plaintiff's first contention was certainly unsound. By the express terms of the contract, the publisher had a right to the delivery of the manuscript, whether the plaintiff drank or not; if the plaintiff drank, the price was to be only two dollars per page. No estoppel would arise from the fact that the publisher "permitted" the writer to continue to do what he was bound to do, or from the fact that the publisher received and used the manuscript to which he had a contract right.

The plaintiff's second contention, that the defendant expressly waived the condition of his duty to pay the extra four dollars per page, can be sustained only in case a voluntary waiver should be held operative without either a consideration given in exchange or any subsequent action by the plaintiff sufficient to support an estoppel. In supporting this voluntary waiver, the court said that the forbearance to drink was no part of the consideration for the publisher's promises to pay two and four dollars per page. This statement is inconsistent with the express terms of the contract. However, it may well be that, as things turned out, it was not a material, or essential, part of the consideration. It can not be proved with certainty whether or not the plaintiff's drinking materially decreased the value and quality of his manuscript. The fact that the defendant published it establishes no more than the fact that he thought it was good enough to publish. Expert legal opinion, however, may be convincing on this question of value, and the answer might properly be left to the jury.

In a land sale, the making of a payment, or of the conveyance itself, exactly at the agreed time, is a part of the consideration for the promise to convey, or the promise to pay. Nevertheless, it may be of comparatively little importance. Therefore, payment, or conveyance, exactly on time, even though it is expressly made a condition of legal duty, can be waived by a mere voluntary expression of such intention.

6. N.Y.—Clark v. West, 86 N.E. 1,
193 N.Y. 349 (1908).

On such a basis as the foregoing, therefore, we can construct the following tentative working rule of law: A condition of a promisor's duty can be eliminated by a mere voluntary expression of his willingness to waive it, if its performance does not constitute a material part of the agreed equivalent of the promise and its nonperformance does not materially affect the value received by the promisor.[7] If the condition that is waived constitutes no part of the agreed equivalent, this suggested rule is not difficult to apply. If it does constitute a part of that equivalent, the question whether it is so material as to invalidate a waiver will not always be easy to answer.

In order to illustrate the kind of condition that can not thus be voluntarily waived, let us suppose the following case: A contracts to erect a building for B, and the latter promises to pay $10,000 therefor after completion. In such a contract, the completion of the building, substantially according to plans and specifications, is by construction of law a condition of B's duty to pay the price. Suppose that B should, without consideration, agree to waive this condition and to pay $10,000 to A without getting any building whatever. It is believed that no court would enforce this promise of B to pay $10,000 for nothing. A promise to make a gift of $10,000 would not be enforced, if no antecedent building contract had been made. One can not "waive" himself into a duty to make a gift of the money. And the fact that a building contract had formerly been made is not a good reason for reaching a different result, when the waiver eliminates the building and causes the new promise to be, in a substantial part at least, the promise of a gift.

Many conditions of a promisor's duty, however, do not constitute any substantial part of the agreed equivalent to which the contract entitles him. The waiving of such a condition, al-

7. Such a rule is adopted by the American Law Institute. Section 88(1), Contracts Restatement, reads as follows: "a promise to perform all or part of an antecedent conditional duty in spite of the nonoccurrence of the condition is binding, whether the promise is made before or after the time for the condition to occur, if performance of the condition is not a substantial part of what was to have been given in exchange for the performance of the antecedent duty, and if the uncertainty of the happening of the condition was not a substantial element in inducing the formation of the contract."

§ 297. "Excuse of Condition by Waiver.

A promisor whose duty is dependent upon performance by the other party of a condition or return promise that is not a material part of the agreed exchange can make that duty independent of such performance, in advance of the time fixed for it, by a manifestation of willingness that the duty shall be thus independent. Such a waiver, unless it is a binding promise within the rules for the formation of contracts, can be retracted at any time before the other party has materially changed his position in reliance thereon, but not afterwards."

though it does effect a change in the contract, does not require the promisor to give something for nothing. So, if an accident insurance company promises to make a payment, on the express condition that notice of accident be given within ten days, the waiver of the condition does not affect its receipts or the size of the fund out of which losses must be paid. The insurer's promise to pay, even though notice has not been given, will be enforced, in the absence of other defenses.

In an aleatory contract, it is the degree of uncertainty of the happening of the condition that determines the extent of the risk of having to perform the promise, and determines "the odds" that are given—that is, the ratio between the promised performances. The total elimination of such a condition would greatly affect "the odds" and this ratio. Therefore a mere voluntary waiver of it should be held ineffective. In the case of a wager on a horse race, one promises to pay on condition that a specified horse wins. Suppose that he "waives" this condition, promising to pay even though the horse does not win. Must he pay, even though the wager has been turned into a case of "heads I win, tails you lose"? A life insurer promises to pay at death of the insured; will he be bound to pay if he waives the condition and promises to pay even though the insured does not die? A voluntary waiver of a condition in an aleatory contract like insurance will not be effective if the extent of the risk assumed is thereby materially increased.[7a]

## § 754. Waiver of Condition of Payment or Other Performance on Time

Where a contract expressly provides that "time shall be of the essence," or that in case of nonpayment of an instalment on time the rights of the obligor shall be forfeited, or that in such case the obligee may declare a forfeiture, performance on time is thereby made a condition of the obligor's reciprocal rights under the contract. But the courts do not favor forfeitures, either of a property interest in land or goods or of money payments already made for which no equivalent will be received in case the "condition" is insisted on and a "forfeiture" enforced.

To avoid such a forfeiture, the courts have been very astute to find and declare the existence of a waiver or an estoppel. Even though the contract expressly declares that nonpayment on time shall automatically terminate all rights of the obligor and that all

---

**7a.** So an insurer who has promised to pay double indemnity in case of death outside of military service does not become bound, by a mere voluntary waiver, to pay such an indemnity in case of death while in military service also. A general inclusion of such an additional risk in its policies would make necessary the material enlargement of the company's reserves to pay the losses. See Laurendeau v. Metropolitan Life Ins. Co., 71 A.2d 588, 116 Vt. 183 (1950).

overdue payments shall remain due and collectible, such a provision will not be enforced if the creditor has in any way contributed to the default or has in any way indicated that he will not insist upon the forfeiture.[8] If the delay is induced by an expression of waiver or assent, there is an estoppel to take advantage of it as a reason for refusing to render a return performance or as a basis for claiming damages or a forfeiture.[9]

The anxiety of the court to find a waiver or an estoppel increases in proportion to the extent and inequity of the forfeiture. In case the payments already made have been small, the property interest to be forfeited is slight, and the value to be kept by the obligee is no more than reasonable compensation for the obligor's existing breach, the terms of the contract may be enforced with no shock to the conscience of the court. The obligee is then not enforcing a penalty and is not getting something for nothing. Even in these cases, however, the condition of the contract may be eliminated by voluntary waiver.

In any case, the continued recognition of the contract as mutually valid and operative will prevent the obligee from asserting the obligor's existing default as a complete discharge of his own obligation.[10] The acceptance of a delayed payment, whether of part or all of the amount then due, without any notice of intention to claim a forfeiture or a discharge, is operative as a waiver with respect to the default that then exists.[11] This is true in spite of the fact that the payment that is then made is no more than is owed by the obligor and is not a sufficient consideration for a return promise. A waiver of performance on time as a condition of contract rights and duties is effective without any consideration. This is true, of any condition that is not a material part of the consideration,—that is, a material part of the agreed equivalent of the obligee's reciprocal performance under the contract.[12]

The mere receipt of a delayed payment without objection is not operative as a waiver as to defaults that occur subsequently.[13] For such a result, there must be such conduct on the creditor's part as causes the obligor reasonably to believe that payment on time will not be insisted on in the future. The receipt of one payment, of money to which the obligee is then entitled, is not enough standing alone to induce such a reasonable belief.

Any expressions or conduct of the obligee that leads the obligor reasonably to believe that performance on time will not be insisted on will operate as a waiver of the time condition, as to

12. See Restatement, Contracts, §§ 88, and 297.
Restatement, Contracts, § 302, states: "A condition may be excused without other reason if its requirement

(a) will involve extreme forfeiture or penalty, and
(b) its existence or occurrence forms no essential part of the exchange for the promisor's performance."

subsequent defaults as well as to antecedent ones.[14]   Such a belief by the obligor may be reasonable where it is induced by the obligee's receipt of a series of delayed payments without objection.[15] Such an effect can be avoided by the obligee by a definite statement to the obligor that he means no such waiver and will insist thereafter on payment as agreed.

There are a good many cases in which it is said that forfeiture for delay in payment will be regarded as waived by a vendor unless he asserts the forfeiture "promptly."[16]   From this it might reasonably be inferred that mere silence and inaction for some length of time, in the face of one or more failures to make payment, will operate as a waiver of the condition of payment on time.   Usually, if not always, in such cases there has been more than silence;  there have been circumstances accompanying such silence that are evidence of the vendor's intention to waive the condition or that now raise an estoppel against him.   If the vendor has reason to know that the obligor is making improvements, or otherwise changing his position, in the belief that the vendor does not intend to enforce forfeiture, an estoppel quickly arises.[17] In many cases, the vendor has received delayed payments without objection.   This is more than mere silence and inaction by the vendor;  and it involves material changes of position by the obligor.[18]

As matter of course, the fact that a buyer in default is permitted to occupy the property and to make improvements, in reliance on statements or conduct by the creditor that a provision for forfeiture will not be enforced, greatly strengthens his position.   Courts will then speak in terms of "estoppel" as well as of waiver.[19]

### § 755.  Waiver by Continuing to Perform or to Receive Performance

The primary contractual obligation of one whose duty is subject to a condition precedent is terminated just as soon as that condition can no longer be performed.   So, if one promises to deliver goods (or to render other performance) on condition that the promisee shall pay a sum of money by a specified date, after that date has gone by without payment, the promisor is no longer bound by the contract.   His duty to make immediate delivery was subject to a condition precedent, a condition that now can never be performed;  though his contract was valid and binding, his duty of immediate performance will now never arise, and the previously existing conditional duty of future performance is terminated.

Nevertheless, such a contractor has power to recreate his former duty—sometimes by a mere voluntary expression of waiver, and nearly always by continuing to render his own performance

713

or by receiving further performance from the other party, with knowledge that the condition has not been performed.[20]

A contractor's continuing to receive deliveries of goods, in disregard of antecedent material delays, is a waiver of the condition of delivery on time. He is still bound to perform his own promises. Timely insistence upon his privilege to discontinue performance would have been a good defense. In the language of the courts, he had a "right to rescind," meaning by this that he was under no further duty to render performance of his own part. By his subsequent receipt of further deliveries, he waives the condition of his duty and thus re-establishes it.[21] Likewise, a seller waives the condition of his duty if he continues to fill belated orders by the buyer,[22] or to make shipments knowing that the required banker's credit has not been "confirmed." [23] A seller who has expressly reserved power to terminate the contract in case of delay in payment cannot exercise that power on the basis of delayed payments with knowledge of which he continued to make deliveries.[24]

A buyer may not be bound to receive a short, or otherwise defective, first instalment; but if he does receive it with knowledge of the facts, he has waived the condition of his duty and he is again bound to receive subsequent instalments if they are tendered as the contract requires.[25]

The performance of one party may be a condition precedent to the return duty of the other to render a series of performances in instalments. Thus, the conveyance of land by a vendor may be a condition precedent to the duty of the purchaser to make payment of any of a series of instalments of the price that fall due at or after the time set for the conveyance. If the purchaser pays one of these instalments without first receiving the conveyance, he is voluntarily doing that which he is then not bound to do; but he is not waiving or eliminating the condition of his contractual duty. The mere voluntary payment of one or more of these instalments does not make it his duty to pay subsequent instalments without getting the conveyance.[26]

### § 756. Waiver of Conditions in Building Contracts

Delays in the performance of a building contract by the builder are frequent and are to be expected. Under ordinary circumstances, time of completion will not be held to be of the essence

25. **Mass.**—Service v. Goodnow-Pearson Co., 136 N.E. 623, 242 Mass. 594, 29 A.L.R. 1513 (1922), applying Uniform Sales Act, G.L.Mass.Ch. 106, § 58(3); Craig v. Lane, 98 N.E. 685, 212 Mass. 195 (1912), shortage in the first carload of potatoes.

**N.J.**—Blackburn v. Reilly, 1 A. 27, 47 N.J.L. 290 (1885).

**N.Y.**—Cahen v. Platt, 69 N.Y. 348 (1877).

unless the contract expressly so prescribes. Even if it does so pre-scribe, the condition of prompt completion can be waived by the mere expression of assent thereto by the owner or by making a payment in disregard of the condition.[31]

Often, it is a condition of the owner's duty to permit the be-ginning of work, or to make a payment, that the builder should procure and deliver a surety bond; such a condition is eliminated by a voluntary statement or by merely permitting work to pro-ceed.[32]

Even though an architect's certificate is made an express con-dition precedent to the owner's duty to make certain payments on a building contract, it is not itself a part of the agreed equivalent for which those payments are to be made. The condition of such a certificate, therefore, can be waived by a mere voluntary ex-pression of such intention by the owner, or by the architect if he is an authorized agent.[33] It has even been held that the owner's making payment of several instalments without any certificate may operate as a waiver of the condition of such a certificate with respect to the final instalment.[34] This may be regarded as doubtful, in the absence of a change of position by the builder in the reasonable belief that the certificate will not be required.[35]

In building contracts it is frequently provided that there shall be no claim for extra work done unless the written order of the architect is first obtained and claim therefor made in writing by the builder within a specified period. Such a provision makes the written order of the architect a condition precedent to an en-forceable right to payment for extra work. This condition can be dispensed with, however, in various ways. If, before certain extra work is done by the builder, the owner promises to make a payment therefor, this is a new and valid contract, wholly sep-arate from and independent of the original building contract. The owner receives a new and sufficient consideration for his promise, and it is enforceable according to its own terms, just as in the case of any other contract. In such a case, the written order of the architect is not a condition precedent to the duty of the owner to pay the agreed extra amount. The provisions of the original building contract do not limit the owner's power to make a new contract on different terms. Very frequently the making of a new contract such as this is said by the courts to be a "waiver" of the condition precedent. It is merely an illustration, however, of a new and valid contract, making no requirement of such a con-dition.[36]

In cases like the foregoing, the owner has power to dispense with the condition of a written order by the architect, by a mere expression of waiver, without any consideration and without mak-ing a new contract. A promise of extra pay made after the extra work is all completed, clearly indicating an intention to dispense with the requirement of the architect's written order, would be enforceable.

The making of a progress payment on time may be a condition of the builder's duty to continue performance of a construction contract; his continuing to perform or to require performance under the contract is a waiver of this condition.[37] This does not mean that he must now continue to wait forever; he can reestablish the condition with respect to future duty by giving a reasonable notice. By proceeding with the work when not bound to do so, the contractor does not "waive" his right to damages for the delay caused by the nonpayment.[38]

A construction contract may require completion of the work by a fixed date and at the same time reserve power to the owner or his engineer to terminate the contract by notice in case of unreasonable delay or failure to make progress with the work. Whether completion on time is expressly made of the essence or not, it is certain that the owner remains bound by the contract if he permits performance to continue after the fixed date has gone by; but performance within a reasonable time thereafter is still required and the owner's power of termination in case of failure to make reasonable progress with the work still persists.[39]

Construction contracts frequently contain a provision that the contractor shall have no right to an extension of time or to damages for delay because of any prevention or interference by the other party or his representatives unless he gives prompt notice (usually in writing) of the act or event constituting such prevention or interference. The giving of notice is thereby made a condition of the contractor's privilege not to complete within the agreed time, of his privilege not to pay damages (liquidated or otherwise) for the delay, and of his right to damages for the prevention or interference. Such a provision as this is frequently disregarded by the parties in the course of performance. The requirement of notice can be eliminated by waiver or by estoppel. An express waiver is so operative, even though it is oral and without consideration, either before or after the time when the notice should have been given. A like effect is produced by conduct that causes the contractor to omit the notice in the reasonable belief that it is not necessary.[40]

### § 757. Condition Subsequent made Inoperative by Waiver, Estoppel, or Subsequent Events

Conditions precedent may cease to be such by reason of waiver, estoppel, or subsequent agreement, and occasionally by reason of impossibility of fulfilment. The same is true with respect to facts that are operative as a condition subsequent, terminating an already existing right of immediate performance and duty of making compensation for breach. Thus, where an insurance policy provided that no suit for breach should be maintainable, unless brought within a specified period of twelve months, the bringing of a suit by the insured within that period was made very difficult and almost impossible by the breaking out of the Civil War. It was held that this fact nullified the condition subsequent and prevented it from operating as a discharge of the insurance company.[41] Observe that the condition subsequent in this case was the failure of the insured to bring suit within twelve months. The occurrence of this condition was not prevented by the war; instead, it was rendered almost inevitable. For this reason, the court thought that it was inequitable to permit the occurrence of the condition to have the legal effect that was expressly provided in the written contract.[42]

In the case of another insurance policy containing a similar provision, the reason that the insured did not bring a suit within the required twelve-month period was that throughout the period negotiations for the settlement of the claim were actively proceeding, and the claimant was lulled into a sense of security in the matter, thus causing the occurrence of the condition subsequent. It was held that the insurance company was estopped from taking advantage of this condition, and its occurrence no longer had the legal effect that the policy stated that it should have.[43]

### § 758.  Waiver of "Legal Tender" as a Condition

There are many contracts in which the tender of a money payment is a condition of a promisor's duty to render some return performance. Unless the contract clearly specifies some other kind of money, the money that exact performance requires is the kind of money that has come to be called "legal tender". What kinds of money constitute this "legal tender" money, and in what amounts, must be determined by the study of federal statutes. A personal check on a bank is certainly not such "legal tender." It is not difficult, however, for the party, to whom such

---

**41.**   **U.S.**—Semmes v. Hartford Ins. Co., 13 Wall. 158, 20 L.Ed. 490 (1871). The same was held in Scovill v. McMahon, 26 A. 479, 62 Conn. 378 (1892), where land was conveyed on condition to revert to the grantor when no longer used as a cemetery, and later the Legislature forbade its use for that purpose.

**42.**   Restatement, Contracts, § 307: "The happening of a condition subsequent that by the specific terms of a contract is to terminate a prom-

isor's duty does not operate as a termination if the happening of the condition is caused or rendered inevitable by

  (a) the promisor's unjustified conduct, or

  (b) events that occur without the promisee's fault, and that cannot have been within the contemplation of the parties when the contract was made, unless continuance of the duty subjects the promisor to a materially increased burden."

payment is required, to waive the condition.  If tender is made in the form of a bank check, drawn on a solvent bank and against an ample deposit, the party to whom the tender is made waives the requirement of "legal tender" money if he fails to object to the tender because not "legal tender."  Of course, an estoppel to insist on such a tender may quickly arise, since the time for making payment may soon expire and the party making the tender may reasonably change his position, by failing to make "legal tender" or otherwise, because of the failure to make objection.[46]  A waiver will be held to exist if the payee states that the actual production of the money is unnecessary or that it will be refused if produced.[47]

## § 759.  Waiver of Condition of Notice

There are many cases in which the giving of a notice of some kind is a condition precedent to a promisor's duty of rendering his promised performance.  It may be either an express or a constructive condition.  Thus, an accident insurance policy may be expressly conditional on prompt notice of the accident.  Notice of disrepair may be a constructive condition of a landlord's duty to his tenant to repair defects.  The requirement of a notice is usually for the convenience or protection of the promisor; but, whether the condition is express or constructive, it is practically never a substantial part of the consideration constituting the agreed equivalent of the promised performance of the other party.  Therefore, the condition of notice can be eliminated by a voluntary waiver of the promisor, either before or after the time when the notice is due.[50]  As a matter of course, the promisor may by his conduct easily become estopped to insist upon the condition of notice.

## § 760.  Waiver of Defects in Title to Land

In the absence of expressions to the contrary, the purchaser of land has a right to a marketable title; and his duty to pay the price is conditional on his getting it.  Nevertheless, he can waive this condition and enforce the contract.  Of course, if the vendor has not promised a title that is free from the defect that in fact exists, the purchaser has no claim for damages by reason of the defect.  Even so, he may have limited his own promise, so that his duty to pay is conditional on the absence of defects.  This condition he can waive; and he can compel the vendor to transfer such title as he has.  By such a waiver, the purchaser is now bound to pay the agreed price in full.  He has no counterclaim for damages, or any right to a deduction from the price, for the reason that the vendor is guilty of no breach of duty.[51]

The situation is different if the vendor has promised a title that is free from the defects that actually exist.  Here, not only is the purchaser's duty to pay conditional, but also he has a right to damages for breach by the vendor. This right to damages is not discharged by a mere expression of "waiver" by the purchaser, without consideration or change of position in reliance.[52] Here too, however, the purchaser can waive the condition of his own duty. Usually, he can insist upon the transfer of such title as the vendor has, and can get a decree for specific performance. If he does so insist, he must pay either a proportionate part, or all, of the price. In either case, he has eliminated the condition of his duty. In most such cases, he can get a decree for specific performance, with a deduction for defects from the agreed price. There may be a few cases in which this equitable remedy will work undue hardship on the vendor; if it so appears to the court, it may leave the purchaser to his remedy in damages or by restitution. Even here, the purchaser can get a decree that the vendor shall transfer such title as he has, if he is himself willing to pay the full price into court. Such action by him is often called "waiver" of the defects. At no time prior to entry of the decree, however, is the purchaser legally bound to accept defective title or to pay the price. By no mere expression of "waiver" can he put himself in such a legal position. Even the decree of the court may not put him in such a position. The decree that is entered may be no more than an order that the vendor shall execute the conveyance, on condition that the purchaser shall pay the full price into court within a specified period.[53]

It should be observed that a defect in title materially affects the extent and value of the equivalent received by the purchaser in return for his money. Mere failure to convey on time, or to pay one or more instalments of the price on time, generally does not do this. That performance on time can be effectively waived, in so far as it is a condition of a promisor's duty in a contract for the sale of land, is considered in a previous section.[54]

## § 764. Power to Re-establish a Condition That has been Eliminated by Waiver

A vendor who has deprived himself, by a mere waiver, of the advantages of a provision for a forfeiture in case of failure to pay on time, has power to terminate the effect of such a waiver by giving a notice to the obligor of such intention.[78] Such a notice does not nullify the effect of a waiver with respect to defaults occurring prior to the notice; it will not now make possible a forfeiture by reason of such past defaults. The notice

54. §§ 761–763 in the general treatise are thus entitled: § 761. Waiver of Provision that Contract shall be Void on Specified Conditions. § 762. Waiver and Estoppel by Failure to State an Existing Ground of Defense. § 763. Effect of Express Provisions against Waiver or Variation.

merely prevents past conduct from operating as a waiver with respect to new defaults occurring after the notice. Even after giving notice, the obligor must be given a reasonable time within which to make payment of instalments that are overdue or are then falling due.[79] Until the expiration of this reasonable time after receipt of notice, the previously existing waiver is still operative.[80]

### § 766.  Waiver of a Condition of One's Own Duty is Not a Discharge of his Right to Damages for the Other's Breach

The voluntary waiver, by one promisor in a contract, of some condition of his duty to render performance, often has the effect, as has heretofore been shown, of eliminating the condition, so that failure to perform is a breach of contract. If, however, the condition that is thus eliminated happens to be a performance that was promised by the other party to the contract, its nonperformance by that party may have been a breach of contract on his part. If it was such a breach, it created a liability in damages that is not discharged by a mere voluntary waiver. The various ways by which a claim for damages for a breach of contract can be discharged must be looked for in the chapter on Discharge; a mere voluntary expression of "waiver" is not among them. There are, indeed, several methods that may be described as a "gift discharge"; these methods require more than an expression of "waiver."

A waiver of a condition removes a limitation on the duty of the party who does the waiving. It does not discharge an already existing duty of the other party to make compensation for a breach that he has committed.[88] When a party has failed to deliver goods, or to render other performance, on time, he has committed a breach of contract; and a waiver by the other party of the condition of prompt performance, even though it now makes him bound to pay, or to proceed with his own further performance, does not discharge his right to damages for the first breach.[89] When sued for payment, or for damages for his own failure of performance, he has a basis for recoupment or counterclaim.

Although there has been some conflict in the law of sales, it has been held, and should be, that the buyer's receipt and user of defective goods does not discharge his right to compensation for the defects, even though it may make it his duty to pay the price and to proceed with further performance under the contract.[90] His acceptance and use of the goods, accompanying express words of waiver or discharge, may operate as a discharge; this is discussed in Chapter 67 on Discharge.

It must be here remembered that the term "waiver" is often used to describe an agreement based on a sufficient consideration;

also that an expression of waiver may be followed by such a change of position in reliance upon it as to create an estoppel. Claims to compensatory damages for a breach can be discharged by agreement or estoppel, at the same time that the party so agreeing or so estopped, eliminates a condition of his own duty.[91] It should be remembered also that a waiver may prevent a subsequent nonperformance from being a breach of duty. One party may prevent the other from performing within the prescribed time by merely assenting to the delay. Having thus caused the delay, he can not take advantage of it, either as a reason for refusing his own performance or as a reason for claiming damages or a forfeiture.

## § 767. Elimination of a Condition by Unjustified Prevention of its Fulfilment

One who unjustly prevents the performance or the happening of a condition of his own promissory duty thereby eliminates it as such a condition. He will not be permitted to take advantage of his own wrong, and to escape from liability for not rendering his promised performance by preventing the happening of the condition on which it was promised.[92] One who himself induces the failure of the other to perform within the time agreed upon can not take advantage of such failure, either by enforcing a prescribed penalty or forfeiture, or by claiming damages for breach.[93] This is closely related to the rule that in such case he can not use the failure to perform on time as an excuse for his own failure to perform.

It is to be observed that since the defendant's duty to pay was originally conditional on a performance by the plaintiff, the defendant's refusal to pay would not have been wrongful except for the fact that the nonperformance of the condition was unjustly caused by himself. It is his prevention of performance of the condition that makes his refusal to pay a breach of contract. Prevention eliminates the condition, for purposes of remedy. But the extent of that remedy is governed by the usual remedial rules. If the defendant's prevention has saved some expenditure on the plaintiff's part, the amount of that saving must be deducted from the full contract price. It is only the balance to which judgment will be given as damages for defendant's breach.[94]

## § 769. Hindrance of a Condition—Making Its Fulfilment more Difficult or Expensive

Restatement, Contracts, section 295, states that the performance of a condition may be excused by the promisor's hindrance

---

92. **U.S.**—Dupont DeNemours Powder Co. v. Schlottman, 218 F. 363 (C.C.A.2d, 1914); Camden v. Jarrett, 154 F. 788 (C.C.A.4th, 1907).

as well as by his prevention, its opening clause being, "If a promisor prevents or hinders the occurrence of a condition or the performance of a return promise." No statement is made as to how great must be the degree of "hindrance" in order that it shall operate as an excuse. Perhaps it must be so great as to justify a jury in describing it as "prevention." The stated rule further provides, however, that prevention or hindrance is no excuse if it "is caused or justified by the conduct or pecuniary circumstances of the other party" or if "the terms of the contract are such that the risk of such prevention or hindrance as occurs is assumed by the other party."

# PART V

# RIGHTS OF THIRD PARTIES — ASSIGN-MENT — JOINT AND SEVERAL CONTRACTS

---

## TOPIC A

## THIRD PARTY BENEFICIARIES

---

### CHAPTER 41

### PRELIMINARY ANALYSIS—INTENT TO BENEFIT—INCIDENTAL BENEFICIARIES

---

## § 772. Introductory Statement

For some years before work was begun on the present treatise, the author published a series of articles on the subject of the present chapter. That subject has been a puzzling one to many jurists in many countries. It has been thought, and very learned writers have said, that two parties can not by contract create rights in a third person; others, while recognizing the possibility

723

that rights may be so created, doubted that it was sound legislative or juristic policy to give recognition to such rights. Fears were expressed that the enforcement of such rights might result in serious injustice to the contracting parties, and that in any case it would greatly complicate judicial procedure and lead to a flood of litigation.

In spite of such doubts and opinions, in all jurisdictions there has been a constant pressure for the recognition and enforcement of such rights. By the tens of thousands, third parties have brought suits in all existing courts, however described (such as common law, equity, admiralty, merchant), and have asked and have often obtained all the sorts of remedies that have been available to persons who are parties to a contract and are said to be in "privity."

A study of thousands of these cases in which an enforcing remedy has been given to the third party shows no injustice to the defendants; instead it demonstrates that refusal of remedy would have been out of harmony with generally prevailing ideas of justice and convenience and that cases in which a remedy was refused have often come to be regarded later as in shocking conflict with existing mores. At the same time, it also appears that there has been an immense amount of litigation, and that the defendants have continually asserted their immunity and have fought hard to maintain it. In some instances this litigation has been woefully repetitious, substantially the same issues having been fought over and over again, even up to the highest available appellate court. In some States the complex cases were so poorly analyzed and there has been so much direct conflict in decision that no litigant could be safely advised by his attorney without first taking his case to the court of last resort. The existence of such a morass as this, with its great economic waste and its resulting mental and moral dissatisfaction, indicates both the difficulty of analysis and the uncertainty as to policy.

Eventually it became clear that there was a decided "trend" in the decisions, less obvious in some States than in others,[1] and vigorously resisted by the courts of Massachusetts and Michigan. Even in the minority states, however, statutes were enacted in favor of certain classes of beneficiaries, such as the beneficiaries of insurance policies and mortgagees; and their courts in "hard

---

1. Pennsylvania maintained two continuous lines of decisions, wholly inconsistent and each maintaining its existence without reference to the other. Since the publication of Restatement, Contracts, the Pennsylvania courts have followed it.

"Many of the early cases and the distinctions therein set up are not pertinent since Pennsylvania has placed itself in line with the prevailing view in other jurisdictions as to the rights of persons not party to the contract." Williams v. Paxson Coal Co., 31 A.2d 69, 346 Pa. 468 (1943).

cases" gave judgment to a third party by finding a fictitious "privity" or a "trust" relationship. Some judges thought that the claim of a third party might properly be recognized "in equity" though not "at law." The amalgamation of law and equity into a single system and the adoption of reformed and simplified procedure[2] have caused this last distinction to be almost lost in the historical obscurity of forgotten lore.

In the series of articles mentioned above, the present author developed the "trend" and reasons for it, reviewing with an approach to completeness the many cases in a number of particular jurisdictions.[3] These articles have been embedded, with various amendments and additions in the general treatise. And the American Law Institute, in its Restatement of the Law of Contracts, has constructed a series of working rules based upon the judicial "trend" and in harmony with the present author's conclusions. Of course, it can not be said that these rules represent the old "common law," or that they are in exact harmony with the existing law of any jurisdiction (whether common law, equity, or other law). Furthermore, like any other series of legal generalizations, they are subject to amendment and variation, as life and litigation proceed. But these rules offer a roadway out of the morass and make an analysis that many courts have found useful.

## § 773.  Preliminary Questions of Interpretation

It is perfectly obvious that third parties have no enforceable contractual rights if there is no contract. Like other plaintiffs, they have the burden of proving that a contract has been made. It is equally obvious that if such a contract has been proved and if they assert that under it they have a right to the rendition of some performance by the defendant, they must show that the defendant made a promise to render that performance. When the contract is in writing, this is largely a question of interpretation.

**2.**   The New Federal Rules of Procedure make the flexibility of equity procedure available in all cases, and have abolished the complexity and inconvenience of maintaining two "sides" in a single court. A few states have not gone so far; but they can not be expected to lag behind much longer. Observe the court reorganization in New Jersey in 1948.

**3.**   "Contracts for the Benefit of Third Persons," 27 Yale L.J. 1008 (1918).

"Contracts for the Benefit of Third Persons In Connecticut," 31 id. 489 (1922).

"Third Parties as Beneficiaries of Contractors' Surety Bonds," 38 id. 1 (1928).

"The Law of Third Party Beneficiaries in Pennsylvania," 77 U. of Pa.L.Rev. (1928).

"Contracts for the Benefit of Third Persons" in England, 46 Law Q. Rev. 12 (1930).

"Contracts for the Benefit of Third Persons in the Federal Courts," 39 Yale L.J. 601 (1930).

Some of the cases that are cited as refusing to recognize any right in a third party beneficiary and as adhering to the supposed requirement of "privity," are really cases in which the court finds that the defendant made no promise to anybody to render the performance claimed by the plaintiff.[4] Such cases turn on interpretation, not on the rules that will be discussed in this chapter. Moreover, some of the cases that deny relief because of a lack of intention to benefit are also cases in which such lack of intention is evidenced by the absence of any promise to render the beneficial performance that the plaintiff desires. In these cases the defendant's failure to render this performance is no breach of duty to anybody, neither to the other contracting party nor to third persons.

The manufacturer or seller of goods (examples are automobiles and canned foods) is generally bound by a warranty to the buyer to whom the goods are sold. In innumerable cases an action has been brought by a sub-buyer or user of the goods for breach of the warranty. In some of these the question arises as to whether the injured party can maintain suit as a beneficiary of the contract made by the seller with the first buyer or intermediate dealer. The "warranty" for breach of which action is brought may be one not put into words but is said to be "implied by law". Most such actions by a sub-buyer are tort actions, not within the scope of this treatise. The law, on grounds of policy, may impose a duty upon manufacturers and sellers to many remote sub-buyers and users of the goods who can not fairly be regarded as beneficiaries of a contract. The manufacturer or seller may also authorize an intermediate dealer to make a warranty on his behalf to a sub-buyer, in which case the latter sues as a direct promisee.[5] If the manufacturer or seller makes an express warranty to the first buyer or intermediate dealer, it may be in such terms as to make it clear that it is intended for the benefit of sub-buyers and users or that its performance is one that directly benefits them. In such a case they fall readily within the rules of the present chapter.[6] Cases denying a remedy to sub-buyers or users seldom deal with the question whether a warranty "implied by law" extends to others than those with whom the manufacturer or seller directly dealt. An express warranty against defects in the goods

4. The following cases are illustrative:

U.S.—Baltzer v. Raleigh, etc., R. Co., 6 S.Ct. 216, 115 U.S. 634, 29 L.Ed. 505 (1885); Twin Falls Canal Co. v. American Falls Reservoir Dist. No. 2, 59 F.2d 19 (C.C.A.9th, 1932); Kentucky Rock Asphalt Co. v. Fidelity and Casualty Co., 37 F.2d 279 (C.C.A.6th, 1930), promise to indemnify A against claims is not a promise to pay the claimants.

Conn.—Shea v. United States Fid. & G. Co., 120 A. 286, 98 Conn. 447 (1923), liability insurance policy.

5. See Timberland Lbr. Co. v. Climax Mfg. Co., 61 F.2d 391 (C.C.A. 3d, 1932).

may at times justify the implication of a promise to indemnify against loss from such defects; but such a promise may be only to indemnify the immediate promisee, not a more remote sub-buyer or user.

## § 774. Third Party Beneficiaries are Donees or Creditors

In the United States there are various persons who are recognized as having enforceable rights created in them by a contract to which they are not parties and for which they give no consideration. They are called herein "third party beneficiaries." These persons can be loosely grouped into two classes; (1) donee beneficiaries, and (2) creditor (or obligee) beneficiaries. The third person is a donee beneficiary if the promisee who buys the promise expresses an intention and purpose to confer a benefit upon him as a gift in the shape of the promised performance.[7] He is a creditor beneficiary if the promisee, or some other person,[8] is under an obligation (a duty or a liability) to him and the contract is so made that the promised performance [9] or the making of the executory contract itself [10] will discharge that obligation.

7.  A conveys land to B who promises A to pay to A's daughter C $1000. C is a donee beneficiary, as to the promised payment.

A insures his life in the B insurance company for $1000 to be paid to C on A's death. C is a donee beneficiary, as to the promised payment.

8.  See McClare v. Massachusetts Bonding & Ins. Co., 195 N.E. 15, 266 N.Y. 371 (1935), where A promised B to pay C's debt to D, and D was held to have an enforceable right against A.

9.  A gives a consideration to B for B's promise to pay to C a debt of $1,000 owed to C by A (or by X). C is a creditor beneficiary.

C has a power to file a lien on A's house, for money due from X, a building contractor. A gives a consideration to B for B's promise to pay C and discharge or prevent the lien. C is a creditor beneficiary.

See Caldwell v. Ryan, 190 S.W. 1078, 173 Ky. 233 (1916), contract by bank directors, made with shareholders, to pay all debts of the bank to its creditors. Here the creditors were not creditors of the promisee but of a third party, the bank, who was not itself a party to the contract.

This definition, also, includes some cases that are not clearly included within the definition of creditor beneficiary given by the Restatement, Contracts, § 133(1b). It may be, however, that the words there chosen are intended to include such cases as the second illustration in this note. Subsequent sections herein will show that they should be included.

10.  A sells a lot to C, covenanting that all other lots sold by A shall be subject to a building restriction. Later A sells a lot to B, who covenants in return to abide by such a restriction. The making of this second contract fully performs A's duty to C; A owes no further duty to C even if B does not perform his covenant. C is a creditor beneficiary of B's contract with A.

A appoints a selling agent C with exclusive territory, promising C that he will require all other agents to pay C a commission on sales they may make within C's territory. Later A gives B a similar

There may well be included within this definition cases in which the promisee is not actually under obligation to the third party, but the existence of such obligation is asserted or believed to exist, and the promised performance will operate to discharge the claim.

The consideration for the promise practically always is given by the promisee and practically never by the third party. In nearly all cases, therefore, if the third party is given an enforceable right against the promisor, this right comes to him at no cost to himself. This is true even though he is a creditor beneficiary and the promised performance comes to him in satisfaction of his claim and not as a gift. The classification of third parties into donees and creditors is not perfect; but it has become familiar to the legal profession and has seemed to have some legal significance. It is adhered to in this treatise for these reasons. Something will also be said of sole beneficiaries and mixed beneficiaries; but the existing law has not been much affected by these concepts.

It might be supposed that the one essential classification of beneficiaries should be into "intended" beneficiaries and "unintended" ones. Such, however, is not the case. The decided cases have established that many "unintended" beneficiaries have rights and that some "intended" beneficiaries have no rights; it would be foolish to say that they are erroneous merely because they can not be forced into a simple classification. The conception underlying the term "intention to benefit" requires consideration at some length.

## § 775.  Various Forms of Benefit to the Third Party

One who is not a party to a contract may be benefited by it in various ways. He may be materially benefited, even before performance by the promisor, by the fact that the contract has been made. If the law recognizes a right in the third party, this right itself may be of value to him. As a matter of course, we must not predicate the existence of a right in him upon the fact that it will be beneficial to him if he has it. The kind of benefit now to be considered in determining whether or not he has a right against the promisor is the benefit that he will receive from the promised performance.

agency and B makes the promise as to commission. C is a creditor beneficiary of B's contract with A. Of course, in these cases, A may promise C not only that he will cause B to make the desired covenant or promise, but also that he will be surety for B's performance of it. See Vogeler v. Alwyn Improvement Corp., 159 N.E. 886, 247 N.Y. 131 (1928), the beneficiary of a restrictive covenant was held to have an enforceable right.

These cases are not clearly included within Restatement, Contracts, § 133(1b); but they should be governed by the same rules.

While the existence of a right in the third party cannot be said to depend entirely upon the form of benefit that may come to him by reason of performance of the contract, it may be helpful to consider some of the different forms that this benefit may take. The right of a third party beneficiary rests chiefly upon the fact that the contract will create reasonable expectations on his part and will induce him to change his position in reliance. But it rests also upon the fact that permitting enforcement by the beneficiary will carry out the intentions and satisfy the expectations of the promisee with the least amount of litigation. The character of the benefit that will result to the beneficiary from the contract is of some value in determining whether his expectations and his action in reliance are reasonable and also whether enforcement by him will produce at least cost to society the result intended by the promisee.

The promised performance may be beneficial to the third party in two respects: First, it may be a performance that will in itself create new and beneficial legal relations between him and other persons; and secondly, without affecting his legal relations at all, it may beneficially affect his physical, social, and economic relations with the surrounding world. In either case the promisee may have expressed an intention to produce the result for the purpose of benefiting the third person; and in either case the third party may have an enforceable right against the promisor. But the fact that the promised performance is one that would beneficially affect the legal relations of the third party has a very considerable evidential weight in determining what the intentions of the promisee were; it also aids the court in determining whether judgment and execution in favor of the third party will attain the result for which the promisee contracted. If the promised performance will not affect the legal relations of the third party, this evidence and this aid to the court are lacking; and the third party will have no right against the promisor unless other sufficient evidence is produced. Inasmuch as usually no evidence of the promisee's intentions and purposes is produced outside of the terms of the contract itself, this difference has importance; the third party is more likely to win in the first class of cases than in the second.

The following are illustrations of cases in which the promised performance, whether it comes as a gift or in satisfaction of a debt, will affect the third party's legal relations: (1) B promises A to convey to C land or money or other chattel; here the promised conveyance will create in C a property interest, and this is contemplated by A as the effect of performance. (2) B promises A to deposit $100 in the City Bank to C's credit; the deposit will create a right in C against the bank.[11] (3) B promises A to deliver to C a sealed promise to pay him $100; such delivery will

create a right in C against B.    (4) B promises A to make C his
agent or to make an offer of Blackacre to C at $1000; the agency
or the offer will create a legal power in C.[12]    (5) B promises A
to execute a release to C of his debt to B; the release will extinguish C's debt and create in him a privilege not to pay.  Observe that in these cases the promised performance would create
beneficial legal relations in C quite irrespective of whether the
promise of B is enforceable by C.  In cases of this sort A must
almost invariably have contemplated a resulting benefit to C
from the promised performance by B.[13]  This does not mean,
however, that A's chief motive or desire was to benefit C; it
means only that he contemplated the performance as one that
would itself create beneficial relations in C.

The following are illustrations of the second class, where the
performance is one that will not in itself create new legal relations
in C, but is nevertheless beneficial to him by affecting his physical, social, or economic relations with the surrounding world:
(1) B promises A to build a handsome building or a subway or
a railway on land adjacent to the land of C; this will increase
the value of C's land but will not necessarily affect his legal relations.[14]    (2) B promises A to forbear to sell goods in York, where
C happens to be a dealer in such goods; this will merely avoid
disadvantageous competition.[15]    (3) B promises A to maintain a
water pressure of 80 pounds in a fire hydrant near C's house;
such pressure will not affect C's legal relations, but it will protect his house.[16]    (4) B promises A to keep a street pavement in
repair,[17] or to exhibit beautiful fireworks, or to carry the mail

14.    In Klingler v. Wick, 109 A. 542,
266 Pa. 1 (1920), the defendant
promised to maintain a switch for
the use of a neighbor; it would
also have incidentally been useful
to a railroad company, but the latter was held to have no right.

15.    A promise by a lessee to his
lessor not to sell any beer on the
place except beer made by the
plaintiff brewing company was held
enforceable by injunction for the
plaintiff.  Here performance is a
forbearance that merely decreases
competition, leading to greater profits.  The court believed that the
promisee contracted for the plaintiff's benefit.  Ferris v. American
Brewing Co., 58 N.E. 701, 155 Ind.
539, 52 A.L.R. 305 (1900).

16.    A promise to repair a weak
spot in a levee, made to a drainage

district for the benefit of all the
inhabitants thereof was held not to
be sufficiently for the benefit of one
landowner to give him a right to
damages caused by an overflow
through the unrepaired spot.  Rod-
house v. Chicago & A. Ry. Co., 76
N.E. 836, 219 Ill. 596 (1906).  This
is like some of the Water Company
Cases.  See § 806.

17.    Where the defendant contracted
with a county to keep a bridge in
repair, the performance thereof
would be of physical benefit to
travellers.  It would not affect
their legal relations.  They were
held not to be intended as beneficiaries of the contract and to have
no action for its breach even though
they suffered special injury.  Styles
v. F. R. Long Co., 57 A. 448, 70 N.J.
Law 301 (1903), "It is not enough
that the plaintiff may be benefited

from York to Troy; these performances will merely protect C's legs or please his eye or make communication easy.   (5) B promises A to give A enough money to pay his debts or to supply him with materials necessary to enable A to perform his contract with C;  the promised performance by B will not affect the legal relations of A's creditor C, and yet it might lead to C's receiving what is due him.[18]   In the foregoing five cases the promised performance does not necessarily involve C's person and does not affect his legal relations with others;  and it seems clear that to bring him within the range of beneficiaries with a right there must be evidence that A had C's benefit in actual contemplation as one (at least) of his objects of desire.   (6) A sixth case may be supposed in which C's legal relations will not be affected but where performance will necessarily involve his person, as where B promises A to render personal service to C, such as instruction, advice, or personal care.   There are a few cases in which such a beneficiary has got judgment;[19]   the personal contact necessarily involved no doubt makes it easier to show an intention on the part of the promisee to make C the beneficiary.

## § 776.   Intention to Benefit the Third Party

The recognition of a right in a third person is often thought to depend upon the intention of the contracting parties, particularly that of the promisee who pays for the promise in question,

by the performance of the contract; he can only maintain the action when the contract is made for him." It would have been held otherwise if the defendant had also promised to pay damages to any person injured. See Pennsylvania Cement Co. v. Bradley Contracting Co., 7 F.2d 822 (C.C.A.2d, 1925).

18.   See Ferguson v. Marsh, 174 P. 678, 37 Cal.App. 482 (1918), where the defendant promised a contractor to pay for all gasoline and oil used by him in performing the contract, this appearing to be merely a means of determining the total compensation of the contractor; also First Nat. Bank v. Perkins, 87 So. 912, 81 Fla. 341 (1921), holding that a contract whereby a city withholds 15 per cent of the contract price as security for performance by a contractor does not amount to a promise by the city to use the money in payment of

claims against the contractor for labor and materials.

The case would be very different if B promised A to pay money to A in trust for C. Here the promised performance, the delivery of the money to A, would have created a right in C against A. It would have made A a trustee and C a cestui que trust. Yet, in Percival v. Luce, 114 F.2d 774 (C.C.A.9th, 1940), the court held that C could maintain no action against B in case B broke his promise to A. As the dissenting judge argued, C should have been held able to maintain a suit against B and A jointly, to compel the performance of the promise by B and the performance of the trust by A (or by a new trustee to be appointed).

19.   Gooch v. Buford, 262 F. 894 (C. C.A.6th, 1920), wife sued on a contract of defendant with her husband to furnish her with special hospital attendance.

to confer a benefit upon him. This has been variously expressed in scores of cases.[21] But the ideas that lie behind such terms as "purpose," "motive," and "intention" are obscure and elusive, as has been found in the criminal law as well as the civil. When a contract is made, the two or more contracting parties have separate purposes; each is stimulated by various motives, of some of which he may not be acutely conscious. The contract itself has no purpose, motive, or intent. The two parties have purposes, motives, and intentions; but they never have quite the same ones.

In third party cases, the right of such party does not depend upon the purpose, motive, or intent of the promisor. The motivating cause of his making the promise is usually his desire for the consideration given by the promisee. In few cases will he be moved by a desire to benefit a third person. If A buys Blackacre of B and promises B to pay the price to C, he makes this promise in order to get Blackacre, not to benefit C; and this is true whether C is a creditor of B's or is B's dearly beloved daughter or is a home for imbeciles. In the present chapter we can disregard the purposes and motives of the promisor after we once determine that he has made a legally operative contract with his promisee.

How is it with the purposes and motives of the promisee? If B conveys Blackacre to A in return for A's promise to pay $1000 to B's dearly beloved daughter C, it will usually be a desire to make C happy and comfortable that motivates B and causes him to convey his land to A. There is a purpose and intent to "benefit" C by making her a gift of money. This "intent to benefit" C is given weight by the courts and the prevailing law is that C has a right against A.[22] Suppose, however, that C is Shylock to whom B owes $1000 in life blood with compound interest. No love is lost on C in this case; and yet B makes the identical contract that he made above. B conveys Blackacre to A in return for A's promise to pay $1000 to B's dearly hated creditor C. Here, too, the prevailing law is that C has a right against A. It is certain that "intention to benefit" cannot be identified with love and affection. It is now a desire to escape from C's clutches that motivates B and causes him to convey his land to A. Of course, a difference in legal result could be made between these two cases, giving C a right against A in the one case and not in the other; but such is not the prevailing law.[23] Some courts have indeed made such a difference; but they did not agree in the difference that they made. Some courts held that creditor C has no right, because B had no desire to "benefit" him, or because it would be

21. Simson v. Brown, 68 N.Y. 355 (1877); Austin v. Seligman, 18 F. 519 (C.C.N.Y.1883); Garnsey v. Rogers, 47 N.Y. 233, 7 Am.Rep. 440 (1872); Sayward v. Dexter, 72 F. 758, 19 C.C.A. 176 (1896).

unjust to make A liable to two suits.[24]　Others denied a remedy to daughter C because B owed her no legal duty that would be discharged by the promised payment.[25]

Since the prevailing law now is that C has a right against A in each of the above cases, they should be separately explained and not be alike based upon the indefinite phrase "intent to benefit." In both contracts alike, A promised a specified performance. In both alike B desired that performance and paid for it, although the antecedent motivating causes of his action were very different. In both alike, the performance would result in the direct pecuniary benefit of C, his benefit in the second case being a bird in the hand in place of one in the bush. In the one case it would come as a gift accompanied by love and affection and in the other case it would not. In both cases, B contemplated the specific result that affected the interest of C and "intended" that exact result. In both cases enforcement at the suit of C would produce the "intended" result with the least amount of litigation and expense. The following is an attempt at a consistent statement of the generally prevailing law: A third party who is not a promisee and who gave no consideration has an enforceable right by reason of a contract made by two others (1) if he is a creditor of the promisee or of some other person and the contract calls for a performance by the promisor in satisfaction of the obligation; [26] or (2) if the promised performance will be of pecuniary benefit to him and the contract is so expressed as to give the promisor reason to know that such benefit is contemplated by the promisee as one of the motivating causes of his making the contract.[27] A third party may be included within both of these provisions at once,[28] but need not be.[29] One who is included within neither of them has no right, even though performance will incidentally benefit him.

It is clear that if the "primary" and "paramount" purpose seems to be to benefit the third person, as in the case of all sole and donee beneficiaries, he should have an enforceable right as the court says. But rights have not been limited so narrowly as this. In the case of most creditor beneficiaries, it is the purpose and intent of the promisee to procure the discharge of his obligation. The attainment of this end involves benefit both to himself and to his creditor. This "benefit" he intends to bring about as an entirety, having no idea in his own mind as to its division between the persons receiving it or as to "primary" or "paramount" purpose. Neither should the court make such a division. It should content

24. Second Nat. Bank v. Grand Lodge F. & A. M., 98 U.S. 123, 25 L.Ed. 75 (1878). The same reasoning was used in Blymire v. Boistle, 6 Watts 182 (1837, Pa.).

25. The case most often cited is Vrooman v. Turner, 69 N.Y. 280, 25 Am.Rep. 195 (1877).

itself with bringing about the entire result that the promised performance would attain.   That result was the "paramount" object of desire and that result was the "primarily" intended result, including not only the ultimate end in view but also the means used to bring it about.   The great majority of the courts attain this desired result in full by giving a remedy to the creditor against the promisor.   The question is not "whose interest and benefit are primarily subserved," but what was the performance contracted for and what is the best way to bring it about.[31]   Of course, the defendant should not be compelled to render a performance that he did not promise to render—to pay a bill that he did not promise to pay.[32]   This is a question of interpretation of the defendant's promise, not one of probing into the intentions and motives of the promisee.   The question of interpretation is the same, whether the promisee or the third party is the plaintiff.[33]

## § 777.   Intent to Create a Right in the Third Party

It is sometimes given as a reason for denying a right in a third party that the contracting parties did not intend that he should have a right.   A distinction should be drawn between an intent to create a "right" in a third party and an intent that a performance beneficial to him shall be rendered.   In the making of contracts parties do not often consciously advert to the legal relations that will be created by their expressions.   They attempt to make no analysis of those relations, even if they are competent to do so.   The existence of legal relations is not dependent upon an intent to create them.   If one party makes a promise to another who gives a sufficient consideration in return, these facts will create a right and a duty even though the parties are quite unaware of the law or of what a "consideration" is.   There is no more reason for requiring an intent to create a "right" in a third party than for requiring an intent to create one in a direct promisee.   If any particular intent is required at all, the only intent that is necessary is an intent on the part of the promisee that the performance beneficial to the third party shall be rendered by the promisor.[37]

On the other hand, the contracting parties have power to control their legal relations with each other in great measure if they care to do so and consciously advert to them.   If two parties go through the forms of agreement but at the same time express an intention that their agreement shall not be legally operative there is no contract between them.[38]   To some extent, also, parties have power to determine their legal relations with each other by specifying exactly what they shall be, the power being limited to methods recognized by the courts.   There is no reason why this should not also be true in third party cases in about the same degree as in other cases.   Therefore, **if two contracting** parties expressly provide that some third party who will be benefited by performance shall have no legally enforceable right, the courts should effectuate the expressed intent by denying the third party any direct remedy.[39]  It is well established that if the parties to a life insurance contract expressly provide that the named beneficiary shall have no immunity from a change of beneficiary or from a rescission of the contract, the provision is effective.[40]  The form of words adopted often is, "power is reserved in the insured to change the beneficiary."  Likewise, if two contracting parties expressly provide that some third party shall have an enforceable right against the promisor, the intent expressed should be effectuated unless the creation of such a right would be contrary to statute or public policy.[41]  It is no longer thought that public policy requires a denial of a right merely because the party in question is not "in privity of contract."

### § 779.  Consideration Moving from One Not the Promisee

A third party beneficiary is usually neither a promisee nor the one who gave a consideration for the promise.  The question of his rights has often been put in either of the two following forms: (1) Can a contract be enforced by one who is not "in privity" with the promisor;  (2) Can a contract be enforced by a "stranger to the consideration."  These two questions are not identical. The consideration for a promise may be given either by the promisee or by some third person;  and the benefit involved in performance of a promise may be received by the promisee or by some third person.  It is possible therefore that a party may be the promisee and the one who will be benefited by performance and yet not the one who gave the consideration.  Such a promisee is not a "third party" beneficiary;  but he is a beneficiary of the party who gave the consideration.  The fact that the words of the promise are directed to him brings him "in privity" and prevents him from being third party or stranger to the contract.[51] In his case the only problem is as to whether consideration can move from a third person and create a right in a promisee who gave none.  This has been discussed previously.  It has been said to be the law of England that a promisee has no right unless consideration moves from him; [52] but the strong current of authority in the United States is to the contrary.[53]

### § 779A.  Trust Beneficiaries Compared with Contract Beneficiaries

Where a property res, real or personal, is conveyed to B to hold in trust for or to the use of C, the court of equity has had

---

52.  .Eng.—Dunlop Tyre Co. v. Selfridge, [1915] A.C. 846.  But see Chapter 46, Law of England.  Contra: Rookwood's Case, Cro. Eliz. 164 (1590, C.P.); Body v. A——, Gouldsb. 49 (1587).

no difficulty in recognizing and enforcing a right in C against B, even though C gave no consideration and knew nothing of the conveyance when it was made. This recognition of a right in C was established, however, as a part of the law of property rather than contract and as a part of the system of law called equity rather than the system called the common law. It is quite possible that as a result of the conveyance in trust C has rights against third persons as well as against B. But if this is possible, there seems all the less reason for a court's laying down the rule that two persons cannot create a contract right in a third. The operative facts are very similar indeed; and in neither case has C, the beneficiary, had any part in them. If the defendant has received a sum of money or other specific res from one whom he promised to deliver it to the plaintiff, the latter can maintain an action on the express promise.[54]

### § 779C.   Incidental Beneficiaries

The term "incidental beneficiary" has been frequently used to denote a person who will be benefited by the performance of a contract in which he is not a promisee, but whose relation to the contracting parties is such that the courts will not recognize any legal right in him.[69] This is not a particularly helpful definition, however; for the problem of the courts is to determine what kinds of claimants asserting themselves to be beneficiaries have rights and what kinds have not.

In other sections it appears that donee beneficiaries and creditor beneficiaries have enforceable rights against the promisor; and an attempt is made to define these two classes of beneficiaries. It is also suggested that the distinction between them may turn out to be unnecessary; but since it is certain that not every sort of beneficiary has a legal right, it is necessary to find some basis for distinguishing those who have from those who have not. The concepts of "gift" and "debt" are useful for this purpose. As the law has been developed in the decisions up to date, it is possible to say that the only third parties who have legal rights are the donees and the creditors of the promisee. If in buying the promise the promisee expresses an intent that some third party shall receive either the security of the executory promise or the benefit of performance as a gift, that party is a donee of either the contract right or of the promised performance or both. If, on the other hand, the promisee's expressed intent is that some third party shall receive the performance in satisfaction and discharge of some actual or supposed duty or liability of the promisee, the third party is a creditor beneficiary. All others who may in some way be benefited by performance have no rights and are called incidental beneficiaries. This term is a sort of omnium gatherum and is not very clearly descriptive; but it is used in default of a better. It can be defined only by a statement that negatives the existence of gift and debt: Incidental beneficiaries are all those who are not donees or creditors of the promisee.[70] It will not always be easy to draw the line between incidental beneficiaries and the others; questions of intent and motive are involved, and the application of the definition of "donee" and "creditor" as here used is not without difficulty.[71]

Sometimes a suit is brought by a third party on the theory that he is a beneficiary when in fact the promised performance would not benefit him at all. Thus, a surety bond may be so worded that the surety promises to protect the promisee against liens of laborers and materialmen; such a promise is not a promise to pay the debt for which such liens may possibly be filed. An attempt by a third party to become a beneficiary by strained and unusual interpretation, expanding the terms of the promise and increasing the extent of the promised performance, should always fail. Such third persons are not even "incidental" beneficiaries; they are merely "would-be" beneficiaries.[72]

The same can be said of liability insurance policies in which the insurer undertakes to indemnify the insured against loss by reason of injury to third persons and to defend suits by such persons, expressly providing that no action shall lie against the insurer except by the insured after he has paid a judgment against him. Under this insurance contract, the injured party is not a beneficiary, because the promised performance will not actually benefit him; and he can maintain no action against the insurer.[73]

### § 779D.  Beneficiaries of Contracts to Supply Money or Materials to the Promisee

Where A owes money to a creditor C, or to several creditors, and B promises A to supply him with the money necessary to pay such debts, no creditor can maintain suit against B on this promise.[74] The same is true in any case where A is under a contractual duty to C the performance of which requires labor or materials, and B promises A to supply to him such labor or material; C has no action against B on this promise.[75] In such cases the performance promised by B does not in itself discharge A's duty to C or in any other way affect the legal relations of C. It may, indeed, tend toward C's getting what A owes him, since it supplies A with the money or material that will enable A to perform, but such a result requires the intervening voluntary action of A. B's performance may take place in full without C's ever getting any performance by A or receiving any benefit whatever. In such cases, therefore, C is called an "incidental" beneficiary and is held to have no right. It would be possible for A to make his contract with B in such terms as to show that A was making it for C's benefit and intended C to have an enforceable right.   C would be a donee of the right though not of the promised performance.   But in fact such contracts are never so worded.[76]

The foregoing is applicable to most cases of contracts between a principal building contractor and subcontractors.   Such contracts are made to enable the principal contractor to perform; and their performance by the subcontractor does not in itself discharge the principal contractor's duty to the owner with whom he has contracted.   The installation of plumbing fixtures or the construction of cement floors by a subcontractor is not a discharge of the principal contractor's duty to the owner to deliver a finished building containing those items;  and if after their installation the undelivered building is destroyed by fire, the principal contractor must replace them for the owner, even though he must pay the subcontractor in full and has no right that the latter shall replace them.   It seems, therefore, that the owner has no right against the subcontractor, in the absence of clear words to the contrary.[77]   The owner is neither a creditor beneficiary nor a donee beneficiary;  the benefit that he receives from performance must be regarded as merely incidental.

A contractor entered into a contract with the Government, the latter promising to pay the cost plus a fixed fee and assenting to the letting of subcontracts.   In such a case it is clear, in the absence of evidence of a different intention, that the subcontractor is not a beneficiary of the Government's promise to the contractor to pay the cost, even though the amount payable to the subcontractor is reckoned as a part of the cost.   The Government made no promise to pay anything to the subcontractors.[77a]   For similar reasons, the Government is not a beneficiary of a subcontractor's promise to the contractor, even though the performance promised may enable the contractor to perform his contractual duty to the Government.

One who undertakes to pay certain classes of creditors of the promisee is under no obligation to other classes of his creditors. The promised performance puts no money in their pockets.   The specified creditors have rights as beneficiaries;  but the unspecified creditors have not.   This is true even though payment of the specified creditors brings an incidental benefit to the unspecified ones.   It reduces the sum-total of debts, thereby increasing the possible dividends payable to other creditors out of the debtor's assets.   It is conceivable that they could maintain a creditors' bill to compel the promisor to keep his promise to pay the specified creditors;  but they can compel no payment direct to themselves.[78]

## § 779E.   Beneficiaries of Contracts between Principal and Agent

The contract between a principal and his agent is seldom to be regarded as for the benefit of a third person and will seldom create a right in such person. If A puts B in possession of certain goods as A's servant and custodian, the fact that B has assented to A's instructions to deliver them to C will not make C a beneficiary with an enforceable right. In such case the facts stated do not operate to make B a trustee of the goods for C's benefit or to confer any property interest upon C. Instead, B is custodian solely for A's benefit; and A has the whole property interest. Also, the promise made by B to A is solely for A's benefit; the performance that B promises will not necessarily confer any benefit upon C. The performance promised is to hold and protect the goods for A and to deliver them to A's order. A has the power to revoke the agency at any time and to extinguish B's powers and privileges with respect to the goods. Although A's instructions may have been to deliver to C, it is B's duty to obey A's later instructions if he cares to give any. C can maintain no action against the agent, whether A has changed his instructions or not.[87]

### § 779F.  Payees of Checks and Drafts as Beneficiaries of Drawer's Contract with Drawee

The rule above stated with reference to property deposited with an agent is applicable in the case of money deposited in bank, although the relation is that of debtor and creditor and the bank holds no property in trust. The bank contracts with the depositor to honor his checks and drafts—to pay out to his order. This contract is not made for the benefit of the holders of such checks and drafts, and does not give them a right against the bank.[91] The legal position of the bank is sufficiently like that of an agent to give to the depositor the power of stopping payment, the power to revoke and extinguish the bank's power to honor a check and charge to the depositor.

### § 779J.  The Third Party's Right is a "Contract Right"

The right of a third party beneficiary is properly described as a "contract right" whether he is a creditor or a donee. The right is created by a "contract" between promisor and promisee, the validity and operation of which are determined by the law of "contracts." This is not affected by the fact that the beneficiary is not himself a promisee or one of the constituting parties. It has been held that the beneficiary's right is within the protection of the provision of the Constitution against impairment by a State.[7]

At a time when "privity" was a talismanic word, many of the courts that recognized an enforceable right in a third party beneficiary contented themselves with saying that "privity" was created by the law.[8] This has no reasonable meaning other than that the courts will hold that a contract made by two persons for the benefit of a third creates an enforceable right in the third. That is to say, the "contract" creates rights in the third party just as it does in the first and second parties.

## § 779K.  The Beneficiary's Right is both Legal and Equitable

This involves a discussion of the difference between legal and equitable rights.  It is believed that the distinction, regarded as a fundamental and necessary distinction between kinds of rights, is an illusion and that it should no longer be used in classifying legal relations.  In certain fields, such as trusts, it may still be a useful term of classification.  The distinction is based upon the fact that the Court of Chancery and the courts of Kings Bench and Common Pleas administered different and to some extent conflicting sets of rules and enforced their decrees by different remedies.  The conflict in the rules has now been largely abolished by statute, and few jurisdictions any longer maintain separate courts of equity.

If rights are to be classified in accordance with the courts in which as a matter of history they originated, we should not only have equitable rights and king's bench rights, but also exchequer rights, admiralty rights,[11] ecclesiastical rights, merchant rights, and many others.  That is, indeed, a possible classification; and once it may have been a convenient one.  It is so no longer.  The right of a third party beneficiary cannot be said to have originated in any one of these courts and is not enforced in some particular one of them.  Instead, it is being enforced and developed in the system of courts that now exists.

If rights are to be classified in accordance with the remedies that have been or are now available for enforcement, this will not lead to classifying the right of a third party beneficiary as either legal or equitable, using each term so as to exclude the other.  According to the actual administration of the law, the remedies available to a third party beneficiary are substantially identical with those available to promisees.  Remedies are exceedingly important and various in character, and a reasonable and useful classification of rights could be based on them; but, again, this would not lead to classifying the third party's right as either legal or equitable.

## § 780.  The Beneficiary may Acquire Privileges and Immunities (Defenses) as Well as Rights

It is now well-established law everywhere that a debtor will be discharged from his obligation by a payment made by a stranger and accepted as a discharge by the creditor.[22]  This is true even

---

**22.**    See § 1251, Chapter 67, Discharge of Contract.

though the payment accepted in full satisfaction is less than the amount due from the debtor.   Likewise, the legal duty of any other obligor can be discharged by a substituted performance rendered by a stranger and accepted by the obligee as accord and satisfaction.   It had once been held that lack of "privity" would prevent this result.[23]   While this early decision has long been abandoned, it is not generally appreciated that the present rule recognizes that the obligor in such a case is a third party beneficiary of a contract made by others for his benefit.[24]   This is because the beneficial relation created in him is a privilege and not a right, a privilege of not performing what he was previously bound to do.

In a Connecticut case a note and mortgage executed by the defendant were assigned by the mortgagee to the plaintiff who promised the mortgagee that he would forbear to demand payment of the defendant for one year.   The plaintiff sued in breach of this promise within the year, and the court held that the contract was an operative defense in the suit.[25]   While the court spoke only in terms of "rights," it is clear that what the court in fact held was that the defendant was legally privileged to forbear to pay the debt for a year with immunity from foreclosure.   He had a defense.   Doubtless the contract also gave him a right that the plaintiff should not sue, for breach of which he could maintain an independent suit for damages or a counterclaim;  he had ground for *attack*—a cause of action.   But this was not necessary to the decision of the case.

## § 781.   When Must the Beneficiary be Identified

Of course the beneficiary must be identified before he has an enforceable right;  but it is not necessary that he should be identified or identifiable at the time the contract is made.[29]   It is enough that he be identified at the time performance is due.   Thus, if B contracts with A to pay money to A's child, as yet unborn, the child when born can enforce B's promise.[30]   Again, if B contracts with A to pay the debts of a certain class that A may owe in the future, A's creditors of that class can enforce B's promise even though it was not until after the contract was made that they became creditors.[31]   Surety bonds for the payment of laborers and materialmen can be enforced by the individual beneficiaries separately when they become such.[32]   If a class of per-

23.   Eng.—Grymes v. Blofield, Cro. Eliz. 541 (1594).

25.   Conn.—Baurer v. Devenis, 121 A. 566, 99 Conn. 203 (1923).

30.   Kan.—French v. French, 167 P. 2d 305, 161 Kan. 327 (1946).

Mass.—Gardner v. Denison, 105 N.E. 359, 217 Mass. 492, 51 L.R.A.,N.S., 1108 (1914), in this case the court regarded the unborn child as a promisee.

sons is clearly designated as beneficiaries, an individual of that class can maintain suit though not specifically named.[33]   A contract to pay all the debts of another person, living or deceased, sufficiently identifies the beneficiaries, even though it is still necessary for them to present and to prove their claims.[34]   Under the Labor Relations Act the employees of one who has made a collective bargain with their union bargaining representative are beneficiaries of that bargain.[35]   A contract to furnish heat for the tenants of a building during a specified period is enforceable by one who became such a tenant subsequently.[36]

An insurance policy taken out "for whom it may concern," or for a changing group of employees, may be enforced by a person who later fulfils the description.[37]   Some of these cases are rested on the theory of an unauthorized agency ratified by the plaintiff. Industrial insurance policies often contain a "facility of payment" clause, whereby the insurance company has the option of making payment either to the estate of the insured or to a needy and deserving relative.   Until the company exercises its power, no beneficiary is identified or has an enforceable claim to payment; it is otherwise after the power has been properly exercised.[38] Also, where liability insurance is taken out for the benefit of third parties who may be injured in the future, of course they cannot be identified until long after the making of the contract.[39]   And a contract to subscribe for shares of stock in a corporation yet to be formed can be enforced by the corporation after it is created.[40]

## CHAPTER 42

## BENEFICIARIES CLASSIFIED—DONEES, CREDITORS, MORTGAGEES

### § 782. Donee Beneficiaries

A donee beneficiary of a contract is a third party to whom the promised beneficial performance comes without cost to himself as a donation from the promisee.[1] If B should make a donative promise under seal direct to C, the promisee would be the sole beneficiary thereof and also a donee beneficiary; but the case would not fall within the subject matter of this chapter since that is *third party* beneficiaries.

The promisor as well as the promisee may have the purpose of benefiting the third party. He may consciously promise something of much greater value than the consideration that he receives; as where, in return for $5 received from A, B promises to convey Blackacre to C. In such a case, Blackacre is the gift of A to C only to the extent of $5 and is the gift of B to C as to the rest of its value. In fact, this seldom takes place; if B wishes to make a donation to C, he makes it direct to C and not by making a promise to A that he will later make a donation to C. It is reasonably accurate and complete therefore to base the definition of donee beneficiary upon the donative intent of the promisee and the absence of cost to the beneficiary.[2] If the performance promised by B can be accepted by C only as the discharge of an obligation owed to him by A, or at some other cost, C is not a donee—at least not as to the entire performance.[3] In such a case, also, C is hardly ever the "sole" beneficiary.

1. See definition in Restatement, Contracts, § 133 (1a).

743

It is now established law in the United States that a donee beneficiary has an enforceable right, if the contract is one that he could enforce if he were the promisee therein.[4] It may be doubted, indeed, whether there is a single jurisdiction consistently holding the contrary.[5] The Supreme Court of the United States has expressly recognized the "sole" beneficiary;[6] and a donee beneficiary is almost always a sole beneficiary. Many early cases, both English and American, expressly stated the rule that one for whose benefit a contract is made can enforce it;[7] and while there was a tendency away from it in the middle of the last century, as new and complicated cases began to press upon the courts, the recent decisions are all in favor of the intended beneficiary and the opinions express no doubt.[8] A few types of donee beneficiaries may be specially mentioned.

The beneficiary of a life insurance policy, when he is other than the insured himself in an endowment policy, is usually a donee beneficiary. It is believed that no American jurisdiction would now refuse to allow him to maintain action on the policy, although in England and a few states the recognition of his right was brought about by statute.[9] Nothing is ever said about "privity" ; and there is no requirement that he shall give any "consideration." The beneficiary's right is enforceable in an ordinary contract action. The English statute is a part of the Married Women's Property Act of 1882,[10] and applies only to widows and children. Prior to the statute there was one case, at least, that recognized a daughter's right to the insurance money on the theory of a gift advancement.[11]

It has been held in many cases that where parents give a child up to one who promises that he will support it and that it shall share in his estate, the child can enforce the promise, often by getting a decree for specific performance or other similar relief.[12] The same result is reached where two persons agree to make mutual wills in favor of specified beneficiaries.[13] There are numerous cases, also, in which judgment is rendered in favor of an illegitimate child enforcing a promise made by its father to its mother.[14]

Contracts made by municipalities for the benefit of their inhabitants have been held enforceable at the suit of one or more of such inhabitants in a good many cases. These are cases of a promise to render some specific service to the beneficiaries, to

4.   **U.S.**—Second Nat. Bank **v.** Grand Lodge, F. & A. M., 98 U.S. 123, 25 L.Ed. 75 (1878), semble (see § 832, Federal Courts).

**Conn.**—Baurer v. Devenis, 121 A. 566, 99 Conn. 203 (1923), assignee of a

debt promised the assignor to forbear to collect for one year, the performance to be donated was *forbearance* and the legal relation created was *privilege* not to pay; Schneider v. Ferrigno, 147 A. 303, 110 Conn. 86 (1929), semble.

charge no more than specified rates, to pay damages caused to individuals by the construction of a public improvement.[15] In these the right against the defendant comes as a gift, but the performance promised is usually paid for in some form. In some such cases, especially those involving water companies, the individual was denied a remedy for various reasons expressed and unexpressed.[16] Similar to the public contract cases are a few in which a member of a trade union has been held to have an enforceable right by virtue of a contract made by the union with his employer.

In making a "collective bargain" the contract is usually regarded as being between the employer and the union as an organization. Even so, the bargain is made for the benefit of individual workmen; and if it is so worded as to require the employer to pay them at a specified rate or for a specified time a workman can base on it an action for unpaid wages or for a wrongful discharge, even though his own personal hiring agreement was less advantageous.[17] Such a workman is a donee beneficiary, just as he is of a bargain in which a contractor promises an owner that he will pay wages at a stated rate.[18] On the other hand, a "collective bargain" may deal solely with general working conditions and require no performance by the employer for the direct benefit of an individual workman.

United States Savings Bonds are frequently made payable, in accordance with Treasury regulations, to the purchaser or in case of his death to a named third party. The latter is a donee beneficiary, with a conditional contract right. Questions arose as to whether the money belonged to the executor of the promisee or to the beneficiary, if not paid prior to the promisee's death. A few courts erroneously held that such a bond was an attempt to make a testamentary gift without complying with the law of wills.[19] It is well established that the law of contract applies, not the law of property. The money is payable to the named beneficiary; and the promisee has no power to extinguish the beneficiary's right except by cashing the bond during his life as the bond itself provides.[20] Neither an assignment nor a provision in the promisee's will can have any such effect.

The New York Court of Appeals held in a number of cases that a third party could have an enforceable right against the promisor only in case the promised performance would satisfy a legal or equitable obligation owed to him by the promisee;[21] but there are now so many recent New York cases to the contrary that their former rule would probably not be applied.[22] Some

22.  See § 827, infra, for a statement of New York law; and especially McClare v. Massachusetts Bonding & Ins. Co., 195 N.E. 15, 266 N.Y. 371 (1935), and Fata v. Healy Co., 46 N.E.2d 339, 289 N.Y. 401, 144 A.L.R. 1031 (1943).

of the earlier cases will no doubt continue to be quoted enough to keep the law in a somewhat unsettled state; but the rule they lay down should be totally abandoned. Cases may be found in other states in which the court was satisfied with a tenuous "moral obligation" in lieu of a "legal or equitable" one.[23] No obligation of any kind, on the part of the promisee to the third person, need be looked for if there is a sufficient expression of intent to make a gift to the third party of either the performance or the executory promise.

There is here an illustration of a curiously conflicting tendency that is not uncommon in the great field of the law. Some courts have said that a creditor of the promisee cannot have been intended as a beneficiary because the promisee is seeking a discharge from his own onerous obligation and is buying the promise for his own benefit. They therefore deny the creditor beneficiary a remedy, while granting one to a donee beneficiary. Other courts have said that if the third party is not in some kind of "privity" with the promisee, as by being one to whom the promisee is indebted, he cannot be supposed to have been intended as a beneficiary and is therefore denied a remedy.[24] Both lines of reasoning are out of harmony with prevailing law, often with the law of the very jurisdiction in which the reasoning is used. But the second is the worse of the two, because it would deny a remedy to all sole and donee beneficiaries, the ones who are most definitely "intended" as beneficiaries by the contracting parties, a result that no state would endure. Such erroneous reasoning is not infrequently the expedient chosen for explaining a decision that might well rest on other grounds. The plaintiff may have been one whose benefit was too remote and incidental or the justice of the case as a whole may have been doubtful. This may explain the use of the false expedient and the failure to observe its falsity, but it does not justify it or save it from operating to the confusion of the law.

The right of the donee beneficiary against the promisor has the following basis: First, the promisor has made a valid contract; and, as in the case of other contracts, the social interest is subserved by its efficient enforcement. Secondly, it was the expressed intent of the promisee that the third party should receive the beneficial performance as his gift, and it is generally felt that the intent of one who has paid for the promise should be effectuated.[25] Thirdly, beneficiaries in fact rely upon such promises and are disappointed by failure of performance; and one of the chief purposes of the law of contracts is to avoid this kind of disappointment. Fourthly, the purposes of the law are best served by making legal remedies available to the one who has a direct pecuniary interest in their use; in this case that person is the beneficiary and not the promisee.

It may here be observed that all third party beneficiaries are donees in one respect; even if he is a creditor of the promisee, and the promised performance is to operate in satisfaction of the promisee's debt, the creditor is still getting something for nothing. The promised performance does not come to him for nothing and as a gift, because his receipt of it will discharge his right against the promisee; but his contract right against the new promisor is an added security that he gets for nothing.[26]　However, since the promised performance satisfies his claim as a creditor, he is described as a creditor beneficiary, and not as a donee.

Sometimes one party contracts with another to pay a debt due from a third party to a fourth, as where A promises B to pay C's debt to D.　In this case D is a creditor beneficiary and can sue A;[27] but the facts may also clearly show that B bought A's promise for the purpose of making a gift to C, in which case C is a donee beneficiary and also has a right enforceable against A.[28]

## § 783.　Bank Deposits to the Credit of Another as a Donee

Problems have arisen in a number of cases as to bank deposits. Suppose, first, that A deposits money with the B bank to the credit of C, but not as a separate fund to be held in trust.　This is generally held to be an executed gift; and doubtless much would be said about title to the money being in C.　But such "money" as A may deposit is mingled with the funds of the bank and becomes the property of the bank.　C is the beneficiary of a contract of deposit on loan between A and B.　B has merely promised A to honor C's checks for the amount deposited; and A has retained no power of revocation.　On the facts stated above, C is a donee beneficiary of B's contract with A.　Of course it is possible for B to make its promise direct to C, and it is also possible that C may be a creditor of A.

Suppose, secondly, that A already has a deposit in the bank and wishes to give it to C.　There are two ways in which this can be done without withdrawing the money from the bank.　A can assign to C his right against the bank.　This is a transaction between A and C, the assent of the bank not being necessary, although C's full protection requires notice to the bank.　If there is a true assignment, third party beneficiary law is not involved. Or, A can have the bank transfer the account on its books to C. This is a transaction between A and the bank, C's knowledge and assent being unnecessary.　Here, as in the first case supposed, C is the beneficiary of a contract between A and the bank.　As such, C can enforce the bank's promise to A.

Suppose, thirdly, that A deposits money, or transfers an existing deposit, to the joint credit of A and C, each to have the power to draw against the account, and the whole to go to the survivor on the death of either.　As in the second case above, this result can be attained by assignment by A of a joint right to C. But if there is no assignment, and the transaction is wholly between A and the bank, C is a mere beneficiary of the bank's promise to A to pay to the order of C as well as to the order of A. The fact that in these cases A as well as C has power to draw should make no difference except so far as A may exercise this power before his death. C's right as beneficiary that the bank shall honor his drafts is merely conditional on A's not having drawn ahead of him. Nearly all the cases dealing with this problem have reached the result that C gets all the money remaining after A's death; [29] but the analysis is of various inconsistent sorts. Nearly always the discussion is in terms of gifts of property. Sometimes a trust theory is invoked. Sometimes the beneficiary is regarded as a promisee. Rarely has the third party been regarded as the beneficiary of a contract between A and the bank.[30] This is due either to insufficient analysis or to the uncertainty and conflict that until recently existed in third party beneficiary law. In all such cases, so long as there is no fraud on A's creditors, C should get the money that A has not drawn out, either as an assignee, a promisee, the beneficiary of a trust, or the beneficiary of the banking debtor's promise to the depositor. The fact that the promisee may have retained a power to revoke should be held to be immaterial,[31] inasmuch as any joint depositor has power to terminate the other party's right against the bank by withdrawing the whole deposit. Of course, the beneficiary has power to do the same thing with respect to the donor.

### § 784.  Devises, Bequests, and Conveyances on Condition of a Payment to a Third Party

There have been many cases in which a testator has made a specific devise or bequest on condition that the devisee or legatee make a certain payment to some third party. The latter party is usually some member of the family of the testator; although this should have little bearing upon the third party's right. It is universally held that acceptance of the conditional devise or bequest creates an enforceable right in the third party to the payment specified by the testator.[32] The acceptance of the devise or bequest has the effect of a binding promise, although it is hardly a promise to the third party and is certainly not a promise to the testator. The third party need know nothing about it and no communication to him is requisite. It may perhaps be regarded as a promise to the executor for the benefit of the third party. The same result is reached where the conveyance is by deed directly from the grantor instead of by will, if the deed is so worded that its acceptance is interpreted as a promise to pay.[33] The acceptance of a transfer of land, expressed as "subject to" a mortgage or other lien then existing, is not so interpreted.[34]

748

## § 785. Effect of Blood Relationship between Promisee and Beneficiary

A number of English and American cases based the right of the donee beneficiary upon relationship by blood or marriage between the promisee and the beneficiary.[35]  It is believed that no effect other than evidential should be given to such relationship.  It is the expression of donative intent by the promisee and the fact that the promisor has contracted to perform to the benefit of the third party that create a right in him.  Close relationship may indeed be evidence of donative intent, showing the reason or motive that induced the promisee to buy the promise.  But such intent can be shown by other kinds of evidence, and proof of relationship can be and often has been dispensed with.

## § 787. Creditor Beneficiaries—Promises to Discharge Obligations Owed by the Promisee to a Third Party

If the promisee in a contract contemplates the present or future existence of a duty or liability to a third party and enters into the contract with the expressed intent that the performance contracted for is to satisfy and discharge that duty or liability, the third party is a creditor beneficiary.[41]  With respect to this definition the following observations may be made:

(1) The obligation or liability need not have a present existence when the contract is made.[42]  If B contracts with A to pay A's future debts, and A later borrows money of C, C is a creditor beneficiary.

---

35.  The leading case is Dutton v. Poole, 2 Lev. 210 (1677, K.B.), where, in consideration that the plaintiff's father would forbear to cut certain timber, the defendant (the plaintiff's brother) promised the father to pay £1,000 as a marriage portion to the plaintiff. Judgment was given for the plaintiff on this promise, the court saying: "There was such apparent consideration of affection from the father to his children, for whom nature obliges him to provide, that the consideration and promise to the father may well extend to the children." Tweddle v. Atkinson, 1 Best & S. 393 (1861, Q.B.), is directly contra; but Dutton v. Poole was decided by the higher court.

41.  This definition is not identical with that in Restatement, Contracts, § 133(1b); but it is believed that the definition of the Restatement should be interpreted and applied to the same effect.  The material part of that definition is: "No purpose to make a gift appears . . . and performance of the promise will satisfy an actual or supposed or asserted duty of the promisee to the beneficiary." There are many cases, discussed herein at various points, in which "no purpose to make a gift appears" and yet where the promisee is under no legal duty, actual or asserted, to the beneficiary.  This is particularly true in the case of construction bonds in which the surety promises an owner to pay laborers and materialmen.

See the preceding section for a recognition of the fact that even a creditor beneficiary is also a donee—a donee of the contract right, given him by the law as a new and additional security.

(2) The contemplated obligation need not be a valid and enforceable one. If C asserts incorrectly that A owes him money, and A, though doubting and disbelieving, contracts with B for a performance that is to operate to satisfy and bar C's asserted claim, C is a creditor beneficiary. A's duty to C may be equitable as well as legal; but if there is no more than a moral duty, C should be classified as a donee.[43]

(3) The obligation may be either primary or secondary and may arise out of either contract, quasi-contract, or tort.[44] If C asserts that A owes him damages for some tort, and A contracts with B for a performance in satisfaction of C's claim, C is a creditor beneficiary.

(4) The promises on which a creditor beneficiary has been given judgment are nearly all cases where the consideration was executed and the promisor is a money debtor. The term "creditor," however, may properly be used broadly to include any obligee to whom the promisee owes a duty. There seems to be no good reason for restricting the rule to cases where the third party is a creditor in the narrow sense of one to whom the promisee owes a liquidated debt. Thus, if the promise is to perform labor or deliver goods instead of to pay money, or is to pay claims for unliquidated damages,[45] the obligee should be able to maintain suit against a promisor who has assumed the duty. Further, the promisee's obligation need not be unilateral, for an executed consideration.[46] The promisor's duty arises out of his contract with the promisee and is limited solely by its own terms and conditions. His promise may itself be given for an executory consideration and may be enforceable as an independent promise; but the beneficiary's right is subject to any conditions, express or constructive, that it would have been subject to had he been the direct promisee. The third party's claim against the promisee may itself be ill-founded; and it may itself be a claim based upon executory consideration. If the defendant has promised to perform a duty of the promisee that was not itself a liquidated debt, on breach of the promise the third party can maintain assumpsit for unliquidated damages but not an action of debt.[47] Even if he sues in the code "civil action," the very same distinction must be made as to his recovery.

(5) The expression "obligation or liability" is here used in order to include both a legal duty (the correlative of a "right") and a legal liability (the correlative of a "power"). If C is a laborer who has done work for D on a building owned by A, he may have power under a mechanic's lien law to put a "lien" upon A's building or to foreclose one already existing. A thereupon contracts with B for a performance by B that will satisfy C's claim against D and destroy C's power of creating or foreclosing a lien on A's house. A is under no "obligation" (owes no legal duty) to C, but

has a "liability" that C will affect his property by a lien.[48] C is a creditor beneficiary, because the promised performance by B will discharge both D's legal duty to C and A's legal liability to a lien.[49]

Another case that may properly be regarded as an illustration of this kind of "creditor" is to be found in the law of mortgages. If a mortgagor sells his equity to B, who does not promise to pay the mortgage debt, the mortgagee can get no personal judgment against B; but B is under the liability that his property interest (called "equity of redemption") will be terminated by foreclosure and sale. Hence, if B sells to D, who expressly promises to pay the debt, the promisee B is not indebted to the mortgagee; but he had a liability prior to his conveyance to D and the mortgagee had a power of foreclosure. Where the mortgagee can enforce D's promise, as in many states he can, he should be classified as a creditor beneficiary. Payment by the promisor will discharge the mortgagee's right against the mortgagor and his power of foreclosure as to the land.[50]

A legatee under a will is not exactly a creditor of the executor, having merely a right that the executor shall distribute the trust estate as the law requires; but the legatee can maintain suit against one who contracts with the executor to pay the legacy and is rated as a creditor beneficiary.[51]

(6) The obligation or liability must be contemplated by the promisee; and he must express an intent that it shall be discharged by the promised performance.[52] A, not knowing that C has a claim against him for $100, contracts with B for the latter to deliver a horse to C. Performance by B will not discharge A's debt to C, and C is a donee, not a creditor beneficiary.

(7) The performance contracted for need not be identical with the one owed by the promisee to the third party, although in the case of money debts it usually is. A owes C $100 and contracts with B for the latter to deliver a horse to C in satisfaction of the debt. C is a creditor beneficiary. Delivery of the horse, assented to by C with knowledge of the facts, will operate as an accord and satisfaction. C's right to such delivery is a conditional right—conditional on his assenting to receive it as satisfaction of his claim. This is a case in which the contract between A and B creates a conditional right in the third party and also operates as an offer to him. In its latter aspect an expression of assent by the third party is necessary before his right is enforceable. In many cases not of this sort the courts have said that assent by C is necessary to deprive A and B of the power to rescind, but in those cases the assent was not the acceptance of an offer.

(8) The third party is a beneficiary; but he is not the sole or a donee beneficiary. Performance benefits him, but at the cost

of discharging his right, or his power as a lienor, against the promisee. Performance also benefits the promisee, for the reason that his debt to the third party will be discharged.[53]

(9) The performance promised must be one that will in fact discharge the promisee's (or another party's) obligation to a third person; if it will not do this, the third person may be a creditor of the promisee but he is not a creditor beneficiary of the contract.[54] Such is the case where the defendant has promised an obligor (or debtor) to indemnify him and save him harmless with respect to the obligation or debt.[55] A promise to indemnify a debtor is not in form a promise to pay the creditor. The mere form of the words should not be conclusive, however; surrounding facts may indicate that payment direct to the creditor was the kind of indemnification that the parties intended.

A promise to pay money to a debtor for him to use in paying his debts is not a promise to pay the debt; and the creditor has no enforceable right.[56] So, also, if a principal contractor contracts with a subcontractor for the supply of materials to be used by the former in erecting a structure, the owner is not a beneficiary of the subcontract. The same will ordinarily be true even though the subcontractor undertakes the incorporation of the materials into the structure, for the reason that this incorporation will not discharge the contractual duty of the principal contractor and the parties do not contemplate that it should.[57] It is the principal contractor's duty to erect and deliver the complete structure according to plans and specifications; and the subcontractor's work does not discharge that duty to any extent. His work is merely a preliminary step that will enable the principal contractor to perform. If the structure is destroyed after the subcontractor's work is done but before completion and delivery of the whole, the principal contractor is still under his contractual duty as a whole; the subcontractor's performance discharged it in no respect. This is of great importance to subcontractors, because it is possible that the principal contractor's breach may cause large consequential injury to the owner. In so far as this consequential injury was the foreseeable result of the subcontractor's breach of his contract with the principal, no doubt the latter can charge the former with the amount that he is compelled to pay to the owner. But the question whether it was a foreseeable result of the principal contractor's breach of the main contract is far from identical with the question whether it was a foreseeable result of the subcontractor's breach of his subcontract. Each question should be separately litigated between the two parties who are directly concerned.

If the subcontract is not so made that its correct performance will discharge the duty of the principal contractor to the owner, the latter is not a creditor beneficiary of the subcontract. He

752

is merely a creditor of the principal contractor; and he can make use of the principal contractor's claim against the subcontractor only as can any other creditor.

If the parties to the subcontract contemplate the existence of the principal contractor's duty to the owner and the subcontract is so made that its correct performance will discharge that duty, the owner is a creditor beneficiary within the meaning of the term as used in this chapter.[58]

(10) If the rendition of the promised performance will discharge the obligation of the promisee (or of another party) to the third person, it is immaterial whether or not the right of that third person will now be transferred, by subrogation, assignment, or otherwise, to the new promisor who renders the performance.

Thus, if A promises B to pay B's debt to C, the last named is a creditor beneficiary, whether A is paying with the understanding that B shall subsequently reimburse him, or that he shall be subrogated to C's right against B, or that B shall be totally discharged from duty to anybody. If B transfers property to A as the full and complete consideration for A's promise to pay B's debt, the payment to C will discharge B's duty to C, without resulting in A's having any right against B, by subrogation, assignment, or otherwise. But C's right, as a creditor beneficiary of A's promise to B, is not dependent upon this fact.

Again, if A contracts with B to pay C's debt to D, the right of D against A is not dependent upon whether or not, after such payment, A is to have some claim to reimbursement by B or is to be subrogated to D's right against C. In a recent New York case,[59] a surety company executed a bond to the State Athletic Commission assuring the payment of certain debts of an Athletic Club, including one for printing done by the plaintiff. It was held that the plaintiff could maintain suit against the surety company on the bond. As matter of course, the surety company would be subrogated to the plaintiff's rights against the Athletic Club. Many similar illustrations may be found in the field of building and construction bonds.[60]

Where A promises B to pay C's debt to D, it is quite possible that it is B's intention to make a gift to C and that it is understood that A shall have no claim against C. This does not prevent D from having a right as creditor beneficiary. In such a case, C also may be a beneficiary; but if so he must establish his claim against A as that of a donee beneficiary.[61]

(11) The performance that the defendant promises to render may be one required by the duty or liability of a third party who is not a promisee in the contract. If A promises B to pay C's debt to D, the last named party D is a creditor beneficiary and can maintain suit against A in case of breach.[62] In this case, the

promisee B is under no obligation; it is the third party C who owes the debt. D is a beneficiary of the contract; and he is a creditor (but a creditor of a third party, not a creditor of the promisee). In these cases, it may be that C also has a right against A, as a donee beneficiary of the contract.[63]

(12) The decisions of the future may require an expansion of the definition; or else the recognition of new classes of beneficiaries under other names.[64]

## § 788. Lawrence v. Fox, the Leading Case Now Generally Followed

The leading case dealing with creditor beneficiaries is Lawrence v. Fox.[65] In this case one Holly owed Lawrence $300 and was about to pay the debt. Fox induced Holly to lend him that sum of money, promising Holly that he would pay Lawrence and thereby discharge Holly's debt the next day. Lawrence sued Fox on this promise and was given judgment. Lawrence was not a promisee and gave no consideration for Fox's promise to Holly.[66] The contract between Holly and Fox was a perfectly valid one; and the performance promised by Fox would discharge Holly's debt to Lawrence. Fox was a borrower of the money for his own use and did not receive it as a trust fund for Lawrence. Further, in spite of some expressions of certain of the judges, Holly was not acting as agent for Fox and made no pretense of contracting in Fox's name.

The decision was subjected to much criticism for a considerable period, even in the New York courts; the theories on which it has been explained are not in harmony. Nevertheless, it has been followed in an immense number of cases; and creditor beneficiaries now have rights enforceable by common law remedies in all but a small number of states.[67] The cases sustaining this statement are distributed under various headings throughout this chapter. Only a few are cited at this point.

Where one sells his business, stock in trade, choses in action, or other property and the buyer undertakes to pay the seller's debts, an action by a creditor lies against the buyer on his promise.[68] And this is true even though the creditor who sues may not have been specifically pointed out.[69] In fact he often is not. Massachusetts allows such suit, but appears to regard the right as being of an equitable nature.[70]

65.    20 N.Y. 268 (1859).

66.    "The doctrine of Lawrence v. Fox is progressive, not retrograde. The course of the late decisions is to enlarge, not to limit, the effect of that case." Pound, J., in Seaver v. Ransom, 120 N.E. 639, 224 N.Y. 233, 2 A.L.R. 1187 (1918); Merchants' Mut. Cas. Co. v. U. S. Fid. & G. Co., 2 N.Y.S.2d 370, 253 App. Div. 151 (1938).

If one who has contracted to buy property assigns the contract rights to one who expressly assumes payment of the price, the vendor is a creditor beneficiary and can maintain action for the full price against the assuming assignee.[71]  If a leasehold is assigned and the assignee (or sublessee) promises the assignor to pay the rent or to perform other obligations of the assignor to the landlord, the landlord can enforce this promise.[72]

The New York Court held at one time that a promise to a debtor to pay one quarter of his indebtedness created no right in any particular creditor either pro rata or otherwise.[73]  Even though such a promise may be too indefinite to create a money debt in any one creditor, it should create rights in all the creditors enforceable by a creditors bill.

Bonds given by principal contractors with sureties promising that laborers and materialmen shall be paid are enforceable by these third parties even though they are not capable of being specifically named when the contract is made.[74]  Where a new partner enters a firm and promises the old members to pay a share of the previous debts, his promise can be enforced at law by the creditors.[75]  Where a mortgagor insures premises and the policy is made payable to the mortgagee as his interest may appear, the mortgagee can sue the insurer.[76]  An agent or broker who has negotiated a sale, lease, or charter for his principal can maintain suit on a promise of the other party to his principal to pay a commission for the service.[77]  The agent is not a promisee in such a case; but the fiction has been indulged that the principal was receiving the promise as a "trustee" for the agent.[78]

A few states once held, and possibly one still does, that a creditor beneficiary can not sue in a common law action.[79]  These will always give him some form of equitable relief.[80]  There is no longer any good reason for maintaining such a distinction, especially where only a single system of courts is maintained and there is uniform procedure.

If the mortgagee, or other creditor beneficiary obtains an assignment from the mortgagor (the promisee), of the latter's right against one who has assumed the debt, he can maintain suit on the contract.[81]  By the assignment he gets all of the common law rights of the promisee, without derogating in any way from such rights as he may have had in his own person as beneficiary.  By recognizing a right in the beneficiary as an assignee when no such right would have been recognized had the assignment been to an entire stranger, the court is enforcing a right possessed by the third party beneficiary before any assignment to him.  He may thus be able to get a money judgment that neither the assignor himself nor any other assignee could have obtained.[82]

The right of a creditor beneficiary has in some respects a different basis from that of the donee beneficiary. There is no expressed intent of the promisee to make him a gift of the promised performance, inasmuch as that performance is to discharge an obligation of the promisee to his creditor. The right of the creditor beneficiary may be based on the following grounds: First, the promisor has made a valid contract to render the beneficial performance and the social interest is subserved by its enforcement. This is the same as in the case of the donee beneficiary, or indeed in the case of any contract. Secondly, it was the expressed intent of the promisee that the third party should receive the benefit of performance at a price (the discharge of the promisee), although it was not the desire to benefit the third party that was the ultimate and decisive motive of the promisee in buying the promise.[83] Thirdly, the beneficiaries of this class will in fact rely upon the promise as much as do donee beneficiaries and will be equally disappointed by failure of performance (unless the promisee should pay his own debt). Fourthly, the beneficiary has a direct pecuniary interest in performance and he is therefore a proper party to make use of legal remedies, although the promisee also has such a pecuniary interest. Fifthly, direct enforcement by the beneficiary will tend to reduce litigation, inasmuch as it attains a result that might otherwise require a suit by the creditor against the promisee and another suit by the promisee against the promisor.[84] While this reduction of litigation is not a necessary result of the rule, it is believed that in fact the suit by the beneficiary is nearly always the only suit brought. Sixthly, direct enforcement by the beneficiary is beneficial to the promisee's other creditors also, since it reduces the amount of the promisee's debts, leaving his assets available to the other creditors. They cannot justly say that the beneficiary is being given an improper preference, since the promised performance was in no case to go to them. If the promisee was insolvent when the contract was made, it may be voidable as in fraud of other creditors;[85] but if it was not then so voidable, the subsequent enforcement of the valid contract does nothing but good to other creditors. The decisions holding that a creditor of the promisee can maintain action on the contract of which he is a beneficiary have been based upon no one well-defined theory. Where the promised performance will come as a gift to the third party, his legal right is clearly based upon the expressed intention of the promisee to make such a donation to the specific third person. In the creditor cases, also, an intention to benefit the third person is very generally asserted to be the reason for giving him an enforceable right. It is very clear that the stated reason is not the correct one, if by "intention to benefit" is meant an intention to make a gift or a desire to enrich. Some of the conflict and con-

756

fusion has been caused by this error. Courts have not infrequently denied the creditor a remedy because they saw clearly that the promisee did not make the contract with the conscious purpose of conferring a benefit upon him. Other courts, with a better instinct for justice and social convenience, in an exactly similar case give the creditor a remedy, perhaps justifying the decision by asserting that he was the intended beneficiary. It is clearly evident that when a debtor buys the defendant's promise to pay his creditor, he is not doing this with a donative intention or motivated by a desire to confer a benefit upon his creditor. His mind is intent upon his own interests; and his purpose is to secure relief from his own onerous burden. That he need have no specific third person's interest in mind is shown by the fact that the creditors who will be paid by the promisor may be entirely unidentified and unknown when the contract is made; indeed, they may not even yet exist and the obligations to be discharged may not yet have been assumed.[86]

In cases where the debtor is not himself insolvent the promised performance may be of very slight benefit to the creditor. His right to payment by the debtor has a value in the market that may be equal to the performance itself; and the performance always comes to him from the promisor at the cost of the discharge of his right.

## §§ 789-794. Various Theories Held in the Past

In the process of breaking down the supposed requirement of "privity" and in order to maintain an appearance of consistency, various theories have been advanced in the past as a basis for recognition of rights in third parties. In this volume these theories will be merely mentioned, without any full explanation and analysis. Such explanation and analysis require much space; and the result reached is merely to abolish the theories. In decisions of the present time, the courts seldom mention them; and in Restatement, Contracts, the rights of third party beneficiaries are stated without reference to them.

Some courts held that the third party could maintain suit against a promisor if the latter had in his possession "assets" which in equity and good conscience belonged to the beneficiary. However they did not require these "assets" to be held *in trust,* and they did not limit recovery to the amount of the "assets" so held.

Some jurists argued that a creditor beneficiary could maintain suit against the promisor because his promise to the debtor was an "asset" of the debtor, of which the creditor beneficiary could make use just as he could levy on other assets of the debtor. This promissory "asset", however, was unlike the debtor's other assets in this—no creditor other than one whom the promisor had undertaken to pay could make use of it. This "asset" theory could not be used by a donee beneficiary for the reason that he was not a creditor. Observe that this "asset theory" is very different from the "assets" theory just previously mentioned. Those "assets" had to be in the possession of the promisor whose promise to pay formed no part of them whatever. In the present "asset theory", the promise to pay is itself the only "asset" in view; and it is an "asset" belonging to the promisee.

A third theory was the theory of Subrogation. Borrowing the term from Equity as applied in the law of Principal and Surety, it was strenuously argued that after a party has promised a debtor to pay the latter's debt to his creditor, the promisor has made himself the principal debtor, putting the original debtor (the promisee) in the position of a surety with a right that the promisor shall pay off the creditor and thus exonerate the surety. With this as a basis, the creditor beneficiary was said to be "subrogated" to the surety's right to exoneration by the promisor. This right of the creditor's "by subrogation" was described as "derivative"; he had no "direct right" of his own, but could merely step into the promisee's shoes and enforce the latter's right (of course keeping the money himself when collected). This theory, like the "asset theory" was not available to a donee beneficiary.

In a few cases a "Novation theory" was used. The promise made to the promisee to pay the latter's debt to the creditor was said to be an offer to the creditor that the promisor should be substituted for the original debtor. If thereupon the creditor assented by bringing suit against the promisor, he thereby wholly discharged the original debtor and completed a novation. This theory received very little approval, the supposed offer and acceptance being seen to be, what in nearly every case they plainly are, pure fiction. The creditor reasonably regards the promise as an additional security and has no reason to suppose that a novation has been proposed. The creditor can bring suit without any prior expression of assent; his bringing suit is not the acceptance of any offer, and he is not required to give any consideration.

Finally, a theory that has been made much use of in England is that the promise is made to the promisee as an "agent" of the third party or as his "trustee". The *promise* is held by the promisee "in trust" for the beneficiary, thus making available to the beneficiary the rules found in the law of trusts. The chief weakness of this theory is that the promisor and promisee have no such idea or intention. They use no such words as "agent" or "trustee", or any other words that can be so interpreted.

These theories were merely complex rationalizations, used for the purpose of attaining a desired result, a result that is now very generally attained without them and a result that is desirable in many cases to which none of them can readily be applied.

### § 796. Mortgagee Beneficiaries—Assumption of Debt by Purchaser of Property

One of the most common among creditor beneficiaries is the mortgagee. Suppose that C has lent money to A, taking A's note and a mortgage on land or chattels as security. Later A sells the mortgaged property to B, who as part of the consideration therefor promises A to pay the debt due to C. Almost all of the American states now permit C to enforce the promise made by B.[43] In some courts, the subrogation theory has been used to reach this result, the grantee who has assumed payment being regarded as principal debtor and the promisee as a surety, to whose right against the promisor the mortgagee is subrogated.[44] The promise to pay the debt is a valid contract and is enforceable independently of the mortgage security; there is no necessity of foreclosure before action on the promise.[45]

The mortgagee can get judgment not only against the grantee of the mortgagor but against all subsequent grantees of the equity of redemption, provided every grantee in the series has himself assumed payment of the mortgage debt.[46]

Of course the contract made by A and B does not operate to discharge A from his obligation to C; there can be no novation without C's assent. C can foreclose the mortgage and apply the property in payment of the debt; and he can also get a judgment against A for any deficiency. Also, C can get judgment against A on his note without first foreclosing the mortgage.[47] But the new promise made by B to A now operates to give C an additional security. Indeed, as between B and A, B is now the principal debtor and A is a surety.[48] C can get judgment against B for breach of his promise to A, either without foreclosure of the mortgage or for the deficiency after foreclosure if one exists.

The assumption of the mortgage debt may be oral, or in a separate writing, and the conveyance itself may be to a different party.[49] The promise of the grantee need not be in express words other than those contained in the deed of conveyance to him. The acceptance of such a deed, with knowledge of all of its terms, is an assent thereto and a promise to pay the debt.[50] The creditor's right against the grantee exists in spite of the fact that the

---

44.  U.S.—Keller v. Ashford, 10 S.     N.Y.—King v. Whitely, 10 Paige 465
Ct. 494, 133 U.S. 610, 33 L.Ed. 667     (1843).
(1890).

deed was a deed poll and was neither signed nor sealed by the grantee. The assumption by the grantee is to be regarded as his sealed promise, provided that he did enough to be regarded as his adoption of the grantor's seal as his own and as a "delivery" to the grantor. It seems true, however, that the grantee ought seldom to be held to have sealed or delivered the instrument; his acceptance with knowledge is rather to be regarded as a tacit informal promise to pay the debt.[51] The fact that the assumption promise is in a sealed instrument has given the courts no difficulty in sustaining an action against the grantee.[52]

An irreconcilable conflict still exists in the following case. Suppose that C, as above, holds the personal note of A secured by mortgage. A sells the mortgaged property to B, who takes it subject to the mortgage but does not promise to pay the debt to C. Later, B sells the mortgaged property to D, who not only takes it subject to the mortgage but also promises B expressly to pay the mortgage debt. A majority of the decisions hold that C can get judgment against D on his promise to B.[53]

## § 797. Assumption Clause in Purchaser's Deed Not Conclusive

The production by the mortgagee of a recorded deed containing an assumption clause, with evidence showing acceptance of delivery by the grantee, is no doubt sufficient to make a prima facie case against the grantee.[66] Indeed, some courts have felt a hesitation in permitting the grantee to introduce oral testimony in contradiction to the terms of the recorded document.[67] All courts, however, will admit evidence that the assumption clause was inserted by fraud or mistake either in a suit for reformation or by way of defense in an action on the assumption promise.[68] There are some cases in which the defendant won by showing that he made no antecedent agreement to assume payment of the mortgage debt and to show that the delivery and acceptance of the deed were under such circumstances as did not charge him with actual knowledge that the deed contained an assumption clause.[69] But the acceptance of a deed,

---

53.  **U.S.**—Calder v. Richardson, 11 F.Supp. 948 (D.C.Fla.1935), semble; Duvall-Percival Trust Co. v. Jenkins, 16 F.2d 223 (C.C.A.10th, 1926), Missouri law.

**Conn.**—Schneider v. Ferrigno, 147 A. 303, 110 Conn. 86 (1929).

**Contra:**

**Cal.**—Ward v. De Oca, 52 P. 130, 120 Cal. 102 (1898).

**S.D.**—Fry v. Ausman, 135 N.W. 708, 29 S.D. 30, 39 L.R.A.,N.S., 150, Ann. Cas.1914C, 842 (1912).

The American Law Institute, Restatement, Contracts, takes no position on this disputed question; but it is not clear that the mortgagee in these cases falls within the definition of either a donee or a creditor beneficiary. It is believed, however, that no inference should be drawn that the Institute definitely intended to deny the mortgagee a remedy in such cases. No illustration of this sort is given in the Restatement.

with full knowledge of the assumption clause contained therein, is sufficient to bind the grantee, even though there had been no antecedent agreement to assume the mortgage debt.[70]   These rules are equally applicable whether the grantor (and promisee) was himself bound to pay the debt or not.

The assumption by a grantee of a debt previously owed by his grantor does not have to be put into the deed of conveyance itself.   An oral contract by the grantee to pay such a debt is just as enforceable as is a written contract.   Whether the grantee has made such a contract, either by oral words or by reasonable implication, is merely a question as to the weight of the evidence offered.[71]   There is no assumption of the debt by one who does no more than accept delivery of a deed that states that it is "subject to" an existing mortgage.[72]   Such a deed transfers merely the grantor's equity;  and there is no implied promise by the grantee to relieve the grantor by paying the debt.

# CHAPTER 43

## BENEFICIARIES OF SPECIFIC TYPES OF CONTRACTS: SURETY BONDS—MUNICIPAL—INSURANCE— SEALED CONTRACTS

## § 798.  Contractors' Surety Bonds—Rights of Workmen and Materialmen

The giving of surety bonds to secure the performance of building and construction contracts, both public and private, is now a large part of the commercial surety's business.  Such bonds create legal relations among at least four kinds of parties: (1) the owner for whom the construction work is being done—the direct obligee in the bond; (2) the principal contractor or obligor who is responsible for the construction work and who hires labor and buys material; (3) the laborers, materialmen, and subcontractors, whose work and material go into the construction; (4) the surety, who promises to answer for the defaults of the principal contractor.  Still other parties than these sometimes attempt to secure advantages under the bond, but they will not be considered at this point.  With the legal relations between the owner and the principal contractor, between the owner and the surety, and between the principal and the surety, we have at present nothing to do.  They are the parties who make the contract and execute the bond.  Our problem in this chapter is to determine the relations between the surety on the bond and the laborers, materialmen, and subcontractors.  Does the bond create rights in these last named parties against the surety?  Are they third party beneficiaries of the surety bond so that they can compel payment for their labor and materials by the surety?

These questions have already caused an immense amount of costly and unnecessary litigation.  There is much apparent and some actual conflict among the court decisions, a fact that is bound to continue to breed more costly and unnecessary litigation.  It is typical of our continuing struggle for law, a struggle for uniformity that can be used as a basis for future advice and prediction, in a huge community with some fifty nearly independent jurisdictions.  Simplicity and a greater degree of certainty can be achieved; but it will require the active efforts and coöperation of many jurists possessed of a high degree of political and judicial intelligence. The result can be achieved by clearly stating and regularly applying what is already the generally prevailing law, totally abandoning minority views not supported by the social interest, and frankly repudiating outworn dogmas.[1]

We should now start with the general proposition that two contracting parties have power to create rights in a third party. This has long been a general rule; it is not an "exception." "Privity" is not necessary: the third party need not be a "promisee" nor need he give consideration.[2] Secondly, it is not necessary to the creation of rights in the third party against the promisor that the promisee should owe any legal, equitable, or moral duty to the third party. This, also, has long been the prevailing rule; but there is a line of cases stating the contrary, though very often keeping the actual decision in harmony with it. And thirdly, the third party has an enforceable right if the surety promises in the bond, either in express words or by reasonable implication, to pay money to him. If there is such a promissory expression as this, there need be no discussion of "intention to benefit." We need not speculate for whose benefit the contract was made, or wonder whether the promisee was buying the promise for his own selfish interest or for philanthropic purposes.[3] It is a much simpler question: Did the surety promise to pay money to the plaintiff?

A "simpler" question, but not always a simple one. There will continue to be badly drawn bonds, although clarifying the law would tend toward improvement in draftsmanship. A fair share of the past litigation has been due to doubtful interpretation; such litigation cannot altogether be avoided. Nor is it meant that "intention to benefit" can be wholly eliminated from

---

1.   Since this was published in Article form, 38 Yale L.J. 1 (1928), a reasonably clear statement of the prevailing law has been presented by the American Law Institute, Restatement, Contracts, Chapter 6. That this is having a considerable degree of success in achieving the purpose expressed above is now evident. As an example, see Wilmington Housing Authority v. Fidelity and Deposit Co., 47 A.2d 524, 4 Terry 381, 170 A.L.R. 1288 (Del. 1946), citing the Restatement and the above Article.

2.   Quoted with approval in Commonwealth of Pennsylvania v. Great Amer. Indemnity Co., 167 A. 793, 312 Pa. 183 (1933); Concrete Products Co. v. United States Fidelity & Guaranty Co., 165 A. 492, 310 Pa. 158 (1933); Pennsylvania Supply Co. v. National Casualty Co., 152 Pa.Super. 217, 31 A.2d 453 (1943); and Harris v. American Surety Co., 24 N.E.2d 42, 376 Ill. 361 (1939).

3.   In Pennsylvania Supply Co. v. National Casualty Co., 31 A.2d 453, 152 Pa.Super. 217 (1943), the court said: "What may have prompted the obligee to require protection for third parties is unimportant. She was protected by the stipulation against liens and her motives may have been altruistic or even sentimental without affecting the obligation of the surety."

third party beneficiary law. It is merely asserted that in the case of a surety bond for the payment of money, if there is a promise to pay money to an ascertainable person, the fact that he is a third person who gave no consideration for the promise does not prevent him from enforcing it. The fact that he was not identified at the time of making the contract does not prevent him from being "ascertainable" at the time of performance.[4]

The first important classification is that dividing statutory bonds from non-statutory bonds.[5] The second is to divide the non-statutory bonds into those that promise to pay the third persons and those that do not. Less important classifications to which some attention must be given are those separating public construction contracts from private ones, and cases in which the third person has a power to create a lien on the obligee's property from those where he has not.

### § 799. Common Law Surety Bonds

The cases grouped in the note below are cases of non-statutory bonds where laborers, materialmen or other subcontractors were held to have a right to payment by the surety.[6] The court believed that there was a promise to pay the third party, although in some cases it was expressed in the form of a "condition" and in others it was found only by a liberal interpretation of the bond

6.   **U.S.**—Maryland Casualty Co. v. Portland Const. Co., 71 F.2d 658 (C.C.A.2d, 1934), applying Vermont law; Maryland Casualty Co. v. Board of Water Com'rs of Dunkirk, 66 F.2d 730 (C.C.A.2d, 1933), citing 38 Yale L.J. 1, the article on which this section is based.

**Ala.**—Fidelity & Deposit Co. of Baltimore, Md., v. Rainer, 125 So. 55, 220 Ala. 262, 77 A.L.R. 13 (1929).

**Conn.**—Byram Lumber Co. v. Page, 146 A. 293, 109 Conn. 256 (1929), bond in the form adopted by the American Institute of Architects.

**Del.**—Wilmington Housing Authority v. Fidelity & Dep. Co., 47 A.2d 524, 4 Terry 381, 170 A.L. 1288 (1946).

**N.Y.**—McClare v. Massachusetts Bonding & Ins. Co., 195 N.E. 15, 266 N.Y. 371 (1935).

It is believed that the laborers and materialmen are creditor beneficiaries within the definition given in Restatement, Contracts, § 133 (1b), by a liberal but reasonable interpretation of that definition.

But no illustration of this sort of case is given and no decision is made. It is possible, also, to regard these third parties as donee beneficiaries under the Restatement definition, since there may be sufficient evidence of an intention on the part of the promisee to confer upon them a security right as a gift, even though the payment when received will not come as a gift but as satisfaction of money due.

This view is supported in Restatement, Security, § 165: "Where a surety for a contractor on a construction contract agrees in terms with the owner that the contractor will pay for labor and materials, or guarantees to the owner the promise of the contractor to pay for labor and materials those furnishing labor or materials have a right against the surety as third party beneficiaries of the surety's contract, unless the surety's contract in terms disclaims liability to such persons."

along with the construction contract.[7]   The cases cited include both public construction contracts and private ones.

A surety bond that is conditioned on full performance of his contract by the principal, will operate in favor of such third parties as the principal, by his contract with the promisee, undertakes to pay; the bond need be no more specific.[8]   The surety bond may be broader in its terms than was required by the principal construction contract, but it is an independent contract and is enforceable according to its own terms.[9]   Of course both contracts should be considered together if there is any doubt or ambiguity as to the interpretation of the bond.   There are cases holding that third parties can enforce provisions in a bond, given to comply with a statutory requirement, that are in excess of those required by the statute.   As to the excess, the effect of the bond is determined by the common law rules.[10]

There are numerous cases holding that laborers, materialmen, and other subcontractors have no enforceable right against the surety, even though the terms of the principal contract make it the duty of the contractor to pay the third parties, and even though the surety bond is expressly conditioned on full performance of all of his promises by the contractor.[14]   Indeed, in some of the cases the bond is specifically conditioned on payment of the debts for labor and material.   These cases at times evince a fondness for the supposed common law rule requiring "privity"; some cases rest upon the false but still lingering idea that the third party's right depends upon there being some pre-existing duty owed to him by the promisee, thus explaining why the promisee came to make a contract requiring payment to the third party; and in other cases the court interprets the contract as solely for the indemnity of the promisee.   On the last of these three grounds, a few of the cases may possibly be reconciled with the majority cases; but in most of them the facts and the terms of the contract afford no reasonable basis for distinguishing.   Cases where such a distinction by interpretation of the contract was reasonable are collected in the succeeding section.

### § 800.   Does the Surety in Fact Promise to Pay the Third Parties?

In the case of a surety bond given to an owner to assure performance of a building contract, the legal duties of the surety ought not to be expanded beyond the terms of the surety's promise.[15]   He is paid for his undertaking; but he is not paid for more than his undertaking.   The extent of this undertaking is to be determined not only by the surety's words of express promise, but also by the "condition" of the bond.   Words of "condition" are not words of "promise" in form; but in the case of a penal bond they must be construed to be words of promise, inasmuch as the only express words of promise are those in which payment of the penal sum is promised.[16]  The alternative seems to be between enforcing the penalty and construing the words of condition as a promise and enforcing that.  The courts have adopted the latter alternative, penalties no longer being collectible.  A bond conditioned to be void on fulfillment by the principal contractor of all of his duties is operative as a promise either that all those duties will be performed or that the promisee will be indemnified within the limit of the penalty in case of non-performance.  The cases denying a remedy to third persons on a private surety bond nearly always interpret it as exclusively the latter promise and rest the decision on that ground.

A promise to indemnify the promisee against loss is one that could be fully performed, in many instances, without paying anything to the third persons.[17]  Even if they have power to put a lien on the promisee's property, they may not do so in fact, or the lien that is put on may be disposed of otherwise than by paying the debt.  Such a promise therefore cannot surely be said to have been "intended" for the benefit of the third persons, since the promised performance will not necessarily benefit them.  And to give the third party a judgment for his debt would often compel the surety to do more than he promised to do.[18]

If on reasonable interpretation the surety bond contains no promise to pay laborers and materialmen, of course they have no right against the surety.  There are numerous cases, even in states where the rights of third party beneficiaries are fully recognized, holding that the particular bond in suit contained no promise to pay the third parties who were suing.[19]  These cases show the usual variation in the process of interpretation; but the current of authority now is that the contract of a compensated surety is to be interpreted liberally in the interest of the promisee and beneficiaries, rather than strictly in favor of the surety.[20]  Some of the older cases, interpreting the bond narrowly and strictly in favor of the surety, are explainable on the ground that the surety was not compensated and the growth of the commercial suretyship business had not then taken place.[21]

The words used in building contracts and in accompanying surety bonds are now usually such that they are and should be

16.　In Byram Lbr. & Supply Co. v. Page, 146 A. 293, 109 Conn. 256 (1929), the court says: "We attach little significance to the fact that the provision here in question is stated in the 'condition' of a bond. 'An enforceable provision may be contained in that part of a bond called the condition.' New Britain v. New Britain Tel. Co., 50 A. 881, 1015, 74 Conn. 326, 329." See also Tomlinson v. Ousatonic Water Co., 44 Conn. 99, 104 (1876); and 28 Yale L.J. 9, 13.

21.　See:

N.M.—Southwestern Portland Cement Co. v. Williams, 251 P. 380, 32 N.M. 68, 49 A.L.R. 525 and note (1926).

Ohio.—Royal Indemnity Co. v. Northern Ohio Granite & Stone Co., 126 N.E. 405, 100 Ohio St. 373, 12 A.L.R. 378 (1919).

interpreted as a promise by the surety to pay laborers and materialmen in case of default by the contractor. Often the construction contract contains an express promise by the contractor; and the bond is either conditioned expressly on such payment or on full performance by the contractor of all his promises.[22] The third parties are often definitely indicated in that part of the bond specifying the conditions. Words of "condition" are not words of "promise" in form; but in this class of cases it is sound policy to interpret the words liberally in favor of the third parties.[23] In a majority of states, it is already done; and without question the surety's rate of compensation for carrying the risk is sufficiently adjusted to the law. The compensated surety has become an institution that is well suited to carry the risk of the principal contractor's default, whereas individual laborers and materialmen are frequently very ill prepared to carry the risk. The legislatures have recognized this fact, and in the case of public contracts have required surety bonds to protect the third parties. While this has not been done in the case of private construction, and while the courts should not on their own motion put such a provision into a private surety bond, they may well interpret a bond that is expressly conditioned on the payment of laborers and materialmen as being a promise to pay them and made for their benefit. The words reasonably permit it, and social policy approves it.[24] The court need not strain the words of the bond, as has sometimes been done, to hold that the third persons were not intended as beneficiaries thereof, even though the promisee may have been thinking chiefly of himself when he paid for the bond.[25]

## § 804. Official Bonds and Public Service Bonds

Public officials and persons or companies rendering some kind of public service are often required to give bond to secure individuals affected by the public service against loss caused by default therein. The named obligee is usually the state or municipality or a public trustee. In many such cases it is clear that the individuals are the beneficiaries intended to be protected, in which case they should experience no difficulty in maintaining suit.[61] If the official bond is solely for the protection of the state or municipality, as it is in the case of an official treasurer's bond to secure public funds deposited with him, third persons are not beneficiaries thereof and can maintain no action on the bond.[62] Some official bonds may be for both purposes, in which case what has been said herein concerning contractors' surety bonds would be applicable.

25. In §§ 801–803, at this point in the general treatise will be found discussions under the following titles: § 801. For Whose Benefit is the Surety Bond Executed? § 802. Is the Beneficiary a Creditor or a Donee? § 803. Statutory Surety Bonds.

Even though an official bond is primarily for the benefit of the state or municipality employing the officer, it may also be for the benefit of third persons having transactions with the officer in his official capacity. It is frequently so provided by the statute under which the official bond is required. In accordance with such a statute the beneficiaries can maintain suit on the bond, being careful to comply with the statutory requirements.[63]

## § 807. Beneficiaries of Insurance Contracts

Life insurance policies are very frequently contracts between the insured and the insurance company whereby the latter promises upon certain conditions to pay money to a third party beneficiary. Usually this third party is a sole and donee beneficiary. In all jurisdictions alike, such beneficiary can now maintain suit on the policy, and the proceeds belong to the beneficiary and not to the estate of the insured.[88] It should be obvious in these cases that the third party is not a promisee and does not ordinarily give any consideration for the promise. It is sometimes said that the insured has made an executed gift to the beneficiary, but this merely means that the beneficiary can enforce the executory contract and has the beneficial right. There is no executed gift of the money as property until after such money has been actually paid. Of course, the law of third party beneficiaries is not involved where a party with an insurable interest insures the life of another. In such case, the beneficiary is the promisee himself.

Fire insurance policies are often taken out by a mortgagor and made payable to a mortgagee "as his interest may appear." Here the mortgagee is not the promisee; he is a creditor beneficiary, because the payment by the insurance company to him will operate to discharge pro tanto the mortgage debt due to him. The mortgagee is allowed to maintain action against the insurance company on these policies.[89] In many instances fire and marine insurance policies have been taken out by one party "for the benefit of whom it may concern," the intended beneficiary frequently being an as yet unidentified party who may become a purchaser of some interest in the property insured. The right of the beneficiary when he becomes identified is everywhere recognized, sometimes by permitting suit on his behalf in the name of the promisee as a "trustee of an express trust," [90] and sometimes by maintaining a suit brought by the beneficiary himself.[91] A large automobile manufacturing company has recently contracted with an insurance company whereby the latter insures all purchasers of automobiles from the promisee against loss by fire and theft. There is no doubt in this case that the purchaser

63. Sections 805 and 806, omitted here, are entitled thus: § 805. Contracts with a Municipality for the Benefit of the Inhabitants; § 806. Municipal Contracts with Water Companies.

could maintain suit against the insurer, whether the latter issues a special policy to the purchaser or not.[92]  There are cases in which an employer of labor has contracted with an insurance company for the insurance of all his employees.  An employee fulfilling the conditions of the policy can maintain action against the insurance company. [93]

Liability and indemnity insurance is a form of insurance that has had rapid growth in recent years, particularly in connection with the use of automobiles.  These policies may be so worded as to make it clear that they are intended solely for the protection and indemnity of the insured.  Indeed, the promise may be merely to reimburse the insured in case he is compelled to pay damages to some third party.[94]  If the contract is clearly for the sole benefit of the promisee, being merely for his indemnification or reimbursement, no third party has an enforceable right by virtue of the policy.[95]  There is a tendency, however, for the states to require by legislation the carrying of liability insurance for the protection of third parties.  Policies that are issued by virtue of such legislation should be interpreted as being for the benefit of the injured third party and should be held to give him an enforceable right against the insurer.[96]  Even in the absence of such legislation the injured third party should have an enforceable right against the insurance company if the policy is so worded as to indicate that it was executed for the protection of third persons,[97] or as to amount to a promise to pay the debt of the insured to the injured party; [98] and there are cases in which the terms of the insurance policy have been given a strained interpretation in favor of the injured party, particularly where the insurer undertook to "defend" suits against the insured.[99]  There are cases in which the insurer has contracted and has fixed his premiums on the basis of indemnifying against liability rather than on that of indemnifying by reimbursement after payment; if so, the fact that the insured is insolvent and never pays does not relieve the insurer.[1]  After the claim against the insured has been reduced to definiteness by a judgment in favor of the injured party, the insured can get judgment for that amount against the insurer.[2]  On collection of this amount, the insured should be compelled to hold it in trust for the benefit of the injured party; but an English case has held that the amount so collected must be distributed pro rata among the general creditors of the insured, the injured party getting only his pro rata share.[3]  A promise by the insurer to pay a judgment, after it shall be rendered, should be held to make the injured party obtaining the judgment a creditor beneficiary of the insurer's promise to the insured.[4]

4.  After some further discussion of Insurance Contracts, the general treatise contains two sections entitled thus: § 808. Covenants Running with the Land. § 809. Beneficiaries of Contracts under Seal.

# CHAPTER 44

## REMEDIES OF BENEFICIARIES AND DEFENSES AGAINST THEM—RIGHTS AND POWERS OF THE PROMISEE

---

## § 810. Remedies of a Beneficiary

Inasmuch as the term "legal right" is merely an expression of the fact that organized society will employ its force for the benefit of one person against another, it is merely a truism to say that in all cases where a third party is recognized as having a right he has also some legal remedy. But there are a good many remedies known to the law, and not all of them are available in the case of every legal right. There is no difference in this respect between the contract right of a third party beneficiary and the contract right of any promisee. The remedies available to a beneficiary are exactly the same as would be available to him if he were a contractual promisee of the performance in question. This might not have been true under the old common law system of remedies. For example, he might not have been able to maintain an action of covenant on a promise under seal. But this was not tested out in the courts after it became settled that beneficiaries had rights. Those rights have been developed and enforced mainly since the forms of action at common law have been much altered by statute. Cases holding that a third party has no enforceable right under a sealed contract hold that no form of action is available and not merely that *covenant* is not; they hold (erroneously, as is stated in another section) that neither assumpsit nor the civil action of the codes will lie.

Whatever forms of action are now available to a promisee should be available in like case to a beneficiary. Where a promisee might maintain an action of debt for a specific sum of money, such an action is available to a beneficiary. In like manner he should have an assumpsit (or a civil action) for damages, measured by the value of the promised performance.[1] In like manner, also, equitable remedies should be given him when in like circumstances they would be given to a promisee of the identical performance. Injunction and decree for specific performance are obtainable in proper cases.[2] Thus where B has contracted with A to convey specified land to C, both C and A should be able to get a decree for specific performance. In case a pledge, mortgage, or other security has been given by B, the usual remedies by way of foreclosure and sale should be available to C. So, also, where the father of an illegitimate child promises the mother to support and educate it, the child can get a decree for specific performance of the promise.[3] In a good many cases the parent or guardian of a child has surrendered it to another on the latter's oral contract to care for it and devise property to it by will. Such a contract contemplates filial service and obedience by the child; and after this has been rendered it is a "part performance" that makes the oral contract specifically enforceable by the child.[4] Specific enforcement of the promise to support and educate the child has been decreed, as well as of promises to transfer property.[5]

In suits brought by a contract beneficiary, it is seldom if ever thought necessary that the promisee should be joined as a party.[6] Certainly, the promisor when sued must make prompt objection for the nonjoinder; and it seems clear that in most cases the

---

1. Numerous cases hold that an illegitimate child can maintain an action for damages for breach of its father's promise to its mother, such damages being measured by the value of the support or of the property promised.

Ky.—Bowling v. Bowling, 300 S.W. 876, 222 Ky. 396 (1927); Doty v. Doty, 80 S.W. 803, 118 Ky. 204 (1904); Stowers v. Hollis, 83 Ky. 544 (1886).

N.C.—Redmon v. Roberts, 150 S.E. 881, 198 N.C. 161 (1920).

Unliquidated damages, determined by a jury to be $2500, were given to a donee beneficiary in Pierce v. Northern Pac. R. Co., 271 P. 976, 127 Or. 461, 62 A.L.R. 644 (1928), without discussion of the point. The defendant had failed to provide a pullman berth for the plaintiff, in breach of a contract made with the plaintiff's son.

In Waterhouse v. Waterhouse, 72 A. 642, 29 R.I. 485 (1909), assumpsit was maintained by a donee beneficiary.

2. U.S.—Maumee Valley Elec. Co. v. City of Toledo, 13 F.2d 98 (C.C.A. 6th, 1926), injunction.

Mich.—Smith v. Thompson, 230 N.W. 156, 250 Mich. 302 (1930), specific performance; Jones v. Ireland, 196 N.W. 369, 225 Mich. 467 (1923), to adopt and leave property to child.

Restatement, Contracts, § 138, is as follows: "If specific enforcement of a duty owed to a donee beneficiary or to a creditor beneficiary is possible and in accordance with the rules of equity, a suit for such enforcement can be maintained. The suit may be brought either by the promisee or by the beneficiary."

promisor may and must take his own steps to have the promisee joined as a party. In practically all cases the promisee is a proper party to be joined; for not only has he a formal right as the promisee, but frequently he has some substantial interest, and in all cases the promisor has an interest in avoiding a possible second litigation brought by the promisee.[7]

### § 811. Power of Beneficiary to Discharge or to Assign

There is no question that the beneficiary has the same power over his rights derived from contracts between other persons that he has over his rights created by contracts made with him in person. So, a release sealed and delivered by him, a substituted contract or novation, an accord and satisfaction, may all be operative to discharge his right against the promisor.[8]

It has been said that any contract beneficiary has power to extinguish his right by a mere expression of disclaimer, at any time prior to expressing his assent to the contract.[11] There appear to be no decisions on the point. If it be correct, the beneficiary has a power that he would not possess if he were the promisee in the contract.[12] It is supported, however, by analogy with cases where specific property has been delivered by A to B for the benefit of C; when such delivery comes to C's knowledge he has power by disclaimer to nullify the delivery to B for his benefit.

### § 812. The Right of the Promisee

In a jurisdiction denying an enforceable right to a third party beneficiary there ought to be no doubt that the promisee has such a right. He is "in privity" and ordinarily the consideration moves from him. If the third party was the sole beneficiary and the contract was made as a donation to him, breach of the promise seems to cause no pecuniary damage to the promisee. For this reason, it was doubted in an early case [15] whether the promisee had an enforceable right; and a few American cases have denied such a promisee any right to damages on the ground of lack of pecuniary interest.[16] Two early English common law cases held that such a promisee could maintain action; [17] and it seems difficult to deny him a right on a promise that he bought and paid for.[18] If the only damages that he can collect are pure-

---

11. Restatement, Contracts, § 137.

12. See Chapter 67, Discharge, §§ 1238–1247. There are statutes that create a power to discharge by a signed writing without the necessity of consideration.
See Neg.Inst.Law § 122.
N.Y.Pers.Prop.L. § 33(2).

18. In O'Neill v. Supreme Council, 57 A. 463, 70 N.J.Law 410 (1904), where a benefit insurance society repudiated its policy, the insured (promisee) was held to have a right to damages for such repudiation. If he has such a right because of an *anticipatory* repudiation, it would seem that he would certainly have one for actual nonperformance.

ly nominal his remedy is not an adequate one, and he should no doubt often be able to obtain a decree for specific performance.[19] The alternative remedy of restitution of the consideration paid by him would often operate with unfairness to the promisor, who would still be held bound by his duty to the beneficiary in most jurisdictions.[20] The promisor could, however, prevent a double recovery against him, in this case as in cases where he is sued by two persons for damages, by making use of equity or code procedure and joining all parties in the suit.[21] Cases of this sort are not numerous, for the reason that the beneficiary is the one having the pecuniary interest in performance and is the one who in fact sues.[22]

In creditor beneficiary cases, where the performance promised was to be the satisfaction of some debt or obligation of the promisee to the third party or was to be otherwise beneficial to him in a pecuniary way, the promisee has a pecuniary interest and has a right to substantial damages for breach of contract.[23] The remedy of specific enforcement is also available to the promisee if the case is one in which that remedy would ordinarily be available; the fact that the performance to be compelled is one going to a third person does not in itself make the remedy unavailable to the promisee, although it may have some weight in determining whether or not his remedy in damages would be fully adequate.[24] If the defendant's promise was to pay the debt and not merely to indemnify the promisee, the promisee can maintain suit for breach without first himself paying the debt, the measure of recovery being the full amount of the debt.[25] It is immaterial that the promisor is liable to two suits, as he has ample means to prevent a double payment.

If sued by the creditor, the promisee can join the promisor to compel performance.[26] And if he has been compelled to pay the beneficiary he can of course get judgment for damages against the promisor.[27] The promisee can always maintain suit in those states purporting to deny a remedy to the beneficiary.[28] Where the third party is not given a right against the promisor, the latter can nevertheless compel the promisee to hold the payments collected by the promisee as a trust fund for the third party, in case the third party has a mortgage on land of the promisor or other such security for performance of the obligation that the promisor undertook to satisfy.[29]

There are a good many English cases and also a few in the United States that allow the promisee to sue as a "trustee" for the beneficiary, and to recover not merely his own damages but also the damages suffered by the beneficiary by reason of the promisor's breach of contract.[30] This is a clear recognition and enforcement of the third party's right rather than the right of the promisee. Many states have provided by statute that one who makes a contract for the benefit of another is a "trustee of an express trust" and can maintain suit without joining the beneficiary even though the latter is regarded as the real party in interest.[31] Such a statute does not prevent the beneficiary, as the real party in interest, from suing alone and in his own behalf.[32]

## § 813. Power of the Promisee to Discharge—Revocation Distinguished

A distinction must first be drawn between the power of the promisee to discharge his own right against the promisor and a power to discharge the right of the third party beneficiary against the promisor. Although there may be only one operative transaction, it may create, and in this case it does create, separate rights in two different parties. The power of the promisee to discharge his own right against the promisor presents no unusual features. It is dealt with in the chapter on Discharge of Contract. The question that we must deal with in this place is that of the power of the promisee to extinguish the right of the third party beneficiary without the latter's consent.

In a good many suits brought by a beneficiary against the promisor, the latter has set up in defense a rescission or other discharge by the promisee. The question of the power of the promisee has not been very well analyzed or thoroughly considered and in certain aspects it remains still unsettled. Two possible powers on the part of the promisee should first be distinguished—(1) the power of revocation, and (2) the power of discharge.

The power of discharge differs from the power of revocation in this: revocation is a term that is used with respect to an existing power in some other person; the power to revoke is to extinguish the existing power in the other person, whether that power is a power to accept an offer, or the power of an agent, or some other kind. The term "discharge," on the other hand, applies with respect to existing rights and not merely with respect to powers. In the case of a bilateral contract creating mutual rights and duties, neither party acting alone can discharge the entire contract. A discharge of such a contract terminating the rights and duties of both parties ordinarily requires the assent of both of the contracting parties, their mutual expressions of assent then being described as a rescission. In the case of a unilateral contract, only one of the parties has a right and only the other party is under a contractual duty. In this case, the party having the right has a power to discharge the other party without the latter's assent.[40] For an operative dis-

40.　Of course, the two contracting parties can expressly reserve the power to rescind the contract by their mutual agreement without the

charge, however, it is usually required that there should be a consideration for the discharge or that it should be a release under seal.

The contract whereby a third party beneficiary is given a right may be either bilateral or unilateral; and its entire discharge would be governed by the rules just suggested. The right of the third party against the promisor, however, assumes the aspect of a unilateral contract as between the third party and the promisor. The third party has a right but no duty. It is clear, therefore, that the third party has a power to discharge his right and the promisor's duty to him just as any contractor can do in the case of unilateral contracts. The question here, however, is as to whether the promisee has a power not only to discharge the promisor, with or without the promisor's assent, but also to discharge the promisor from his duty to the third party without the third party's assent.

## § 814.　Promisee Has no Power to Discharge the Right of a Donee Beneficiary

In determining whether the promisee has the power to discharge the right of the third party beneficiary, it is necessary to distinguish between donee beneficiary cases and creditor beneficiary cases. The line of distinction between these two classes is not well marked in some respects; and it is not altogether certain that there should be any difference in the legal relations created by the two types of transaction. The existing cases indicate, however, that there is such a difference in the matter of the promisee's power to discharge. It seems that he has no such power whatever where the third party is the sole and donee beneficiary of the contract that has been made.[41] In such a case the promisee has no pecuniary interest in the performance. This fact led some courts in a few early cases to hold that he has no enforceable right; and it has led most courts to hold that he has no power of discharge as against the third party. Most of the illustrations of this sort are found in life insurance, where the promised payment is to go to the beneficiary and not to the insured. In the case of ordinary life insurance policies, it is held that the insured has no power to discharge the right of the bene-

consent of the beneficiary. In re Connecticut Co., 95 F.2d 311 (C.C. A.2d, 1938).

41. In accordance with this, it is said in Restatement, Contracts, § 142: "Unless the power to do so is reserved, the duty of the promisor to the donee beneficiary cannot be released by the promisee or affect-ed by any agreement between the promisee and the promisor, but if the promisee receives consideration for an attempted release or discharge of the promisor's duty, the donee beneficiary can assert a right to the consideration so received, and on doing so loses his right against the promisor."

ficiary, even though the latter is not aware that the contract has been made for his benefit.[42] The insured can create such a power by an express reservation in the policy. This provision usually takes the form of a power to change the beneficiary.[43] If there are restrictions as to the mode of exercising this power they must be complied with, although the courts have generally been favorable to the insured in determining what is substantial compliance.[44] For reasons that are not obvious, there is a different rule in the case of certain types of mutual benefit insurance. Members of mutual benefit associations which contract to pay benefits to specified persons, have been held to have the power to change the beneficiary without an express reservation to that effect.[45] It may follow from this that the member will also be held to have a power to discharge the association altogether.

As a matter of course, when a contract for the benefit of a third person is made, the promisee can reserve the power to discharge the promisor from his promissory duty. A very common case, one that is usually digested under other headings, is this: Suppose that A deposits money in the bank to the joint credit of A and B, payable to either A or B or to the survivor. When such a deposit is accepted by the bank, it is making a binding promise to A of which B is in part a donee beneficiary. By the very form of the promise, A has reserved the power to discharge the bank's duty to B by drawing out the money. Likewise, B has the power to discharge the bank's duty to A in the same manner. After A's death, with money still in the account, A's personal representative has no right to the money and no power to discharge the bank.[46]

There should be no doubt whatever that if A makes a deposit in a bank in the name and for the benefit of B, reserving no power in himself, he has no power to discharge the bank's duty to B, by a notice of revocation, the drawing of a check, or otherwise. It is commonly said that the "gift is executed," but the truth is that no money is deposited as a "bailment" and generally not as a fund to be held "in trust". The transaction is merely a unilateral contract; for money received and added to its general assets, the bank promises the depositor to pay it over to B, the donee beneficiary, or to his order. In some cases, B may himself be one of the promisees; but generally he is not.

## § 815. Promisee's Power to Discharge the Right of a Creditor Beneficiary

In cases where the third party is a creditor beneficiary, the promised performance coming to him in satisfaction of a debt

45.    U.S.—Supreme Council of Royal Arcanum v. Behrend, 38 S.Ct. 522,          247 U.S. 394, 62 L.Ed. 1182, 1 A.L. R. 966 (1917).

owed to him by the promisee and not as a mere donation, the general rule seems to be that the promisee and the promisor have some power of rescission. In a few cases involving donee beneficiaries and not creditors, the courts have laid down a general rule denying all power in the promisee to extinguish the right of the third party by a rescission, the rule being stated in such a general form as to apply to all third party beneficiaries alike.[60] In addition to these, there are a few cases where the third party involved was a creditor of the promisee in which the court held that from the very making of the contract the promisee had no power to discharge.[61] In a much greater number of cases, however, it has been definitely held that the promisor and the promisee can rescind their contract at any time before the creditor beneficiary has "assented" or "accepted" or acted in reliance upon the contract.[62]

No general statement has been agreed upon by the courts as to the exact moment when the promisee first loses his power to discharge. There seems to be no doubt that such power is lost as soon as the beneficiary has begun to act in reliance upon the contract; and the rule is generally stated to the effect that the power of discharge is gone as soon as the third party has expressed his assent.[63] The basis of this rule seems to be in part the ideas underlying the doctrine of estoppel, and in part the ideas involved in the acceptance of an offer. As has been explained, the transaction between the promisor and the promisee should not be regarded as an offer to be accepted by the third party. It seems better to construct a rule on the basis of estoppel unless the transaction ought to be regarded as an irrevocable gift to the third party from the beginning. In creditor beneficiary cases the promised performance does not come to the creditor as a gift, because it comes to him in satisfaction of a claim he has against the promisee; but the new right against the promisor conferred upon him by the contract does come to him as a gift. Such a new right cannot possibly be detrimental to him and, as in the case of other gifts, it is quite possible here to indulge the presumption of assent to such a donation without any knowledge or expression of assent on the part of the creditor.

---

**62.** Ala.—Copeland v. Beard, 115 So. 389, 217 Ala. 216 (1928), mortgagee beneficiary.

**63.** Ark.—McCown v. Nicks, 284 S.W. 739, 171 Ark. 260 (1926).
N.Y.—New York Life Ins. Co. v. Aitken, 26 N.E. 732, 125 N.Y. 660 (1891); Gifford v. Corrigan, 22 N.E. 756, 117 N.Y. 257, 6 L.R.A. 610, 15 Am.St.Rep. 508 (1889).

The rule constructed by the American Law Institute is believed to be a useful rule that is not out of harmony with the existing decisions. It has not been found in any judicial opinion in the exact terms, however. Restatement, Contracts, § 143, reads as follows: "A discharge of the promisor by the promisee in a contract or a variation thereof by them is effective against

Inasmuch as a creditor beneficiary is now generally regarded as having a legal right against the promisor, it is desirable to accompany this right with such an immunity from revocation or rescission as will make the right of some value to the creditor. He should certainly be safe in acting in reliance upon the promise without running the risk of a discharge by the promisee. This safety in acting in reliance upon the promise could be created by depriving the promisee of all power to discharge. It is not necessary, however, to go quite so far as this. It would be sufficient to hold that the promisee has no power of discharge after the creditor has received knowledge of the transaction. The courts have already said so much about assent and acceptance by the creditor that they may not adopt this rule. Another possible rule would be to deprive the promisee of power to discharge from the moment that the beneficiary changes his position in reliance upon the contract. This rule would not give the beneficiary the full protection desired, because the promisee might discharge the promisor and the beneficiary might thereafter act in reliance upon the contract without knowledge of the discharge. It seems best, therefore, that the discharge by the promisee should be operative as against the beneficiary only in case he learns of the discharge before he has assented to the contract or has acted in reliance upon it. This rule is not inconsistent with the decisions heretofore rendered.

### § 817. The Beneficiary's Right may be Conditional

As is stated in the following sections, the right of the beneficiary is subject to defenses of various kinds and to such conditions precedent as may be provided in the contract or determined by the court on grounds of justice. The point to be made here is that the third party should not be denied a right merely because there is some condition precedent. The rights of any contractor are frequently conditional rights; and there is no reason why the third party's right may not be the same.[70]

Thus, if B should contract with A to pay C $100 if B's ship comes in, C has a conditional right to the payment, a right that

a creditor beneficiary if, (a) the creditor beneficiary does not bring suit upon the promise or otherwise materially change his position in reliance thereon before he knows of the discharge or variation, and (b) the promisee's action is not a fraud on creditors." This section is approved in Morstain v. Kircher, 250 N.W. 727, 190 Minn. 78 (1933).

**70.** A donee beneficiary has rights even though the contract was made primarily for the promisee's own benefit and only contingently for that of the beneficiary. Thus, an endowment insurance policy is primarily for the benefit of the promisee and the benefit goes to him if he survives to maturity of the policy. But if he dies before such maturity, the beneficiary collects. The insured has no power to discharge or vary the policy as against such a beneficiary except as reserved therein. Union Central R. Ins. Co. v. Buxer, 57 N.E. 66, 62 Ohio St. 385 (1900).

becomes unconditional and enforceable after B's ship arrives. The fact that there is an express condition precedent to C's enforceable right does not show that the contracting parties intended that C should have no right at all or that it was not their purpose to benefit C. It merely shows that their intent was that the payment should be made only on the specified condition. The fact that insurance policies are payable only on various burdensome conditions has never been held to deprive the beneficiary of a right; his right is merely subject to the specified conditions.

## § 818. Defenses and Conditions as Against a Beneficiary

The claim of a beneficiary is dependent upon the validity of the contract that creates it. If that contract is void, voidable, or unenforceable, his claim is likewise affected.[79] Thus an informal promise without consideration cannot be enforced by a beneficiary;[80] nor can he enforce a promise void for illegality.[81] If the promisor is lacking in legal capacity, or if the promise is void or voidable (as for fraud, mistake, infancy, insanity, or coverture) the claim of the beneficiary as well as that of the promisee is subject to the defect.[82] If the promise as made is within the statute of frauds, the beneficiary cannot enforce it unless the provisions of the statute are complied with.[83] It should be observed here, however, that a promise by B to A to pay A's debt to C is not within the statute of frauds, although a promise by B to C to pay A's debt to C would be within the statute.[84]

If the promise is expressly, impliedly, or constructively conditional, the right of the beneficiary is a conditional right.[85] So, if B promises A to pay money to C if C shall marry D, or if C survives A, or if war is declared by Spain, C's right against B is subject to the specified condition. If B promises A to pay money to C in exchange for A's promise to deliver a chattel to B concurrently with B's payment, C's right to the money is conditional upon delivery of the chattel. The defense in such a case is often called failure of consideration.[86] A breach of contract by the promisee A will thus often operate as a defense to B as against the beneficiary C; but the fact that B's promised performance is

---

79. It is provided in Restatement, Contracts, § 140, as follows: "There can be no donee beneficiary or creditor beneficiary unless a contract has been formed between a promisor and promisee; and if a contract is conditional, voidable, or unenforceable at the time of its formation, or subsequently ceases to be binding in whole or in part because of impossibility, illegality or the present or prospective failure of the promisee to perform a return promise which was the consideration for the promisor's promise, the right of a donee beneficiary or creditor beneficiary under the contract is subject to the same limitation."

to go to C may sometimes be of influence to cause the promise of B to be an independent promise. A holding that it is independent is a holding that C's right is not conditional upon performance of a return promise by A.

The facts discussed above, operating against the beneficiary as well as against the promisee, are facts that affect the contract in its formation, operating to determine the primary legal relations of the parties and modes of proof.[91] After the contract is made, however, and the primary legal relations of promisor, promisee, and beneficiary have been created, it is not at all correct to say that supervening defenses that would be good against the promisee are good also against the beneficiary. The right of the promisee and the right of the beneficiary, although born of the same creative factors and with the same inherited defects, now have separate lives of their own; and the vicissitudes that are met by the one do not necessarily affect the other. Thus, the promisee has power to discharge the promisor's duty to himself; but his power to discharge the promisor's duty to the third party is almost wholly lacking.[92] Wrongful acts of the promisee, subsequent to the making of the contract, that would greatly affect his own right, may not affect the beneficiary's right at all. Thus the surrender of securities by a promisee to a principal contractor will often discharge his right against a surety bondsman; but it will not discharge the beneficiary's right against that same surety.[93] The statute of limitations or a provision in the contract itself may bar the promisee's right and yet not bar the beneficiary's;[94] frequently they would be barred together.

Observe further that the promisee may have many good defenses in a suit brought against him by the third party that would not be operative in a suit against the promisor by the third party. The contract may have been made by the promisee for the purpose of settling some ill-founded claim of the third party; this is discussed in a succeeding section. The duty owed by the promisee to the third party may have become barred by statute of limitations or in bankruptcy; such a bar will not avail the promisor.[95] If the right of the third party were based on "subrogation," it would be dependent upon the validity of both the third party's claim against the promisee and the promisee's claim against the promisor. Of course, a donee beneficiary's claim cannot be so based; and in general the claim of a creditor beneficiary has not been so based either.

## § 821. Promises to Discharge an Ill-founded Claim

There is nothing to prevent a promisor from undertaking a larger duty than the duty owed by the promisee to the beneficiary. He can make his own promise unconditional, although the duty of the promisee to the beneficiary is conditional upon an uncertain event.[10] If he promises to pay a third party a sum claimed by him against the promisee, irrespective of defenses that the promisee may have, he is bound by his promise in the teeth of those defenses, so long as the contract does not run afoul of some principle of public policy.[11] Promises of this sort are often made; a grantee from a mortgagor who assumes the debt usually cannot question the validity of the mortgage or the debt that he promises to pay.[12] Where such a defence is not available to the promisor, in whole or in part, the question arises whether the beneficiary should be regarded as a donee or as a creditor.

One who makes an ill-founded claim against another is not in fact a creditor; but he asserts that he is one. In such a case if the asserted debtor contracts with a promisor for a performance that will satisfy the asserted claim, the claimant should be classified as a creditor beneficiary.[13] This is because the performance does not come to him as a gift, but in return for his agreement to accept it in discharge of his claim. Such an agreement on his part, assuming that his claim was asserted in good faith, is a sufficient consideration for a return promise. Even if his claim was not asserted in good faith, his receipt of the promised performance will operate as a bar to his further prosecution of his claim, even though the promisee may have had some other good defense. The promisee intends it to operate in this way and does not have an intent to make a gift. Therefore, such a third party should not be in as favorable a position as is a donee beneficiary; but he should have the right of a creditor beneficiary unless the promise was made conditional on the validity of his claim.

## § 823. Effect of Performance by the Promisor

In the case of a donee beneficiary, performance by the promisor in accordance with his promise has exactly the same effect as would such performance if the beneficiary were himself also the promisee. It discharges the beneficiary's right against the promisor and also the promisee's right against the promisor.[20] It does not discharge any right of the beneficiary against the promisee, because he had none. Also a tender of performance by the promisor has the same effect as it would have if the beneficiary were himself also the promisee.

After a breach of duty by the promisor, or after a judgment for such a breach has been entered in favor of the beneficiary, a discharge can be obtained by the promisor in the very same ways as would be the case were the beneficiary also the promisee. The commonest ways are release and accord and satisfaction.

In the case of a creditor beneficiary the matter cannot be stated quite so simply. A creditor beneficiary has been herein defined as one whose right against the promisee will be discharged by the promisor's performance. The promisee's purpose in making the contract is to obtain the discharge of his own duty to the third party by means of the performance by the promisor. Whether he and the promisor can effectuate such a discharge without the assent of the third party depends upon whether the performance that the promisee owed to the third party was a personal performance by the promisee or was a performance that was delegable by him to others. If it was the latter, the performance due from the promisee can be rendered by the promisor; and such performance by the promisor will discharge the duty of the promisee to the third party, the duty of the promisor to the promisee, and the duty of the promisor to the third party. If, on the other hand, the performance tendered by the promisor in satisfaction of the promisee's obligation is not substantially identical with that due from the promisee, the third party's right against the promisee will not be discharged or affected in any way unless the third party accepts it on the terms offered. In most creditor beneficiary cases the duty owed by the promisee is a duty to pay money, and the performance tendered by the promisor would be identical with that due from the promisee.

After a breach of contract by the promisor, the legal relations have so changed that no longer will a performance by him discharge all three duties as above unless the other two parties who are involved assent thereto. The third party may have obtained two separate judgments, against the promisee (his own original debtor) and against the promisor (the additional security). Since the third party had a right to only a single performance, the satisfaction of either judgment should operate pro tanto as a satisfaction of the other, except as to court costs.[21] If he collects from his original debtor (the promisee), such debtor has his right over against the promisor and will be subrogated to the third party's judgment against the promisor provided the third party has been fully satisfied.[a]

a. Chapters 45 and 46 of the general treatise are omitted here. They deal in detail with Third Party Beneficiary law and its development in Massachusetts, New York, Pennsylvania, Michigan, the Federal Courts, and England. In the chapter on English law, the theory that the promisee contracts as a "trustee" for the benefit of the third party is critically considered.

# TOPIC B

# ASSIGNMENT

---

## CHAPTER 47

### ASSIGNMENT IN THE LAW OF CONTRACT—HISTORY AND ANALYSIS

---

## § 856. Historical Development of the Law of Assignment

The problem of assignment of "choses in action" has had a long history, the tracing of which in detail will not here be attempted. When business transactions were few and when many of the kinds of contracts in common use today were not enforceable, it cannot be supposed that men felt a very compelling need for a simple and flexible law of assignment. In early English history, the bilateral contract seems not to have been enforceable at law, enforceable contracts being restricted to promises under seal, various kinds of recognizances and specialties, and promissory debts for a *quid pro quo* received. Thinking as much as they did in terms of formal documents and physical objects, it is not surprising that the idea of transfer of an incorporeal contract right had very slow development. It was a personal relation that was incapable of delivery.

Very likely the first step was the use of the power of attorney, the owner of the "chose in action" thereby authorizing another to enforce it in the name of the owner and to keep the pro-

783

ceeds so obtained.[1] The courts of common law recognized the power of attorney and gave it full effect, while all the time declaring that a "chose in action" was not assignable. Later, words of assignment were held to authorize the use of the assignor's name, without any express power of attorney;[2] but a tradition was established that "choses in action" were not assignable at common law, and this was solemnly declared by judges and law teachers even as late as the beginning of the present century.

In an early case,[3] the defendant had certain claims against third parties and sold and assigned them to the plaintiffs, the latter giving their obligation for the price. The plaintiffs later came into Chancery, alleging that the assignment was ineffective "to give them any action for the recovery of the debts," and asking that their obligation should be delivered up to be cancelled for lack of any *quid pro quo*. The chancellor granted the relief asked and committed the defendant to jail for refusal to obey. This shows that the court recognized difficulties in enforcement by an assignee; but it does not in itself show that at that date an assignee had no remedies at all. If the plaintiffs had held a formal power of attorney from the defendant, it seems certain that they could have collected the debts assigned to them; and it could not have been long afterwards when the courts became willing to regard the assignment as itself an implied power of attorney.

The law against champerty and maintenance was once thought to make the assignment of a "chose in action" illegal. A distinction was made between an assignment of a "chose in action" as security for an existing debt, owed by the assignor to the assignee, and an assignment for a consideration and not as security, the former being lawful and the latter unlawful.[4] This distinction has long since faded out; and "choses in action," contractual in character, as well as many non-contractual ones, have been recognized by the courts as a form of property that is law-

---

1. Holdsworth, "History of the Treatment of Choses in Action by the Common Law," in Selected Readings on the Law of Contracts, p. 710, taken from Holdsworth, History of English Law, vol. 7.

The common law courts acknowledged a power in the king to assign his "choses in action"; and the king's assignee could sue in his own name. Winfield, Assignment of Choses in Action, 35 L.Q. Rev. 143, citing Mich. 39 Hen. 6, f. 26; Breverton's Case, 1 Dyer 30 b (28 Hen. 8); R. v. Wendman, Cro.Jac. 82 (3 Jac. 1); Lambert v. Taylor, 4 B. & C. 138 (1825). Holdsworth, op. cit. supra, at 714.

2. Ames, Lect. on Leg. Hist., p. 214.

3. **Eng.**—M. P. & J. B. v. J. R., 37 Hen. 6, f. 13, pl. 3 (1458).

4. Y.B. 34 Hen. 6, Mich. pl. 15; 15 Hen. 7, Hil. pl. 3.

**Eng.**—Barrow v. Gray, Cro.Eliz. 551 (1597); Harvey v. Bateman, Noy 52 (about 1600); Anon., 2 Freeman Ch.Cas. 145 (about 1670). See Winfield, "Assignment of Choses in Action in Relation to Maintenance and Champerty," 35 L.Q. Rev. 143.

fully assignable.[5]  Modern statutes often make it illegal for an attorney at law to buy property in litigation or to buy a "chose in action" for the purpose of recovery by suit; [6] but these are meant to prevent the abuse of their position by officers of the court, who may be tempted to foment litigation for their own profit.

There are some modern cases in which it was held that an assignment was invalid because it was champertous.  This is not because assignments in general are invalid as involving maintenance, but because the court found that the assignment to the plaintiff was itself merely a champertous agreement whereby he undertook to prosecute the claim at his own expense and to share the net proceeds with the assignor.[7]  Such a transaction is not an ordinary assignment for a consideration;  it is a bargain to maintain a suit for a share of the thing to be recovered.

At some stage in the process, the court of chancery took a hand in the game and enforced the assignee's claim.  A power of attorney could be revoked;  and there were cases in which the assignor would thus prevent his assignee and "attorney" from maintaining suit against the obligor and obtaining his due.  The chancellor might grant an injunction against the assignor;  but this was not always effective, and the chancellor would also allow the assignee to maintain suit in his own name against the obligor.[8]  Thus, the legal tradition was expanded to say that "choses in action" were assignable in equity, though not at common law.

The chancellor developed his law of assignment in reasonable fashion, holding that the assignee's claim was subject to defenses that the obligor could have used against the assignor, and protecting the obligor in case he paid the assignor without notice

---

**5.**  In Fitzroy v. Cave, [1905] 2 K.B. 364, the plaintiff wished to get the defendant off a board of directors by getting him into bankruptcy; so he got an assignment from some of defendant's creditors, giving to them as sole consideration his promise to pay over to them all he could collect over and above costs. This was held to be valid and not maintenance.  The plaintiff's motive was immaterial.

**6.**  See §§ 1420 et seq., Champerty and Maintenance.

**7.**  Pa.—Ames v. Hillside Coal & Iron Co., 171 A. 610, 314 Pa. 267 (1934), relying chiefly upon Restatement, Contracts, § 542 [§ 547].

See also:

Mass.—Sherwin Williams Co. v. J. Mannos & Sons, 191 N.E. 438, 287 Mass. 304 (1934).

Conn.—Slade v. Zeitfuss, 59 A. 406, 77 Conn. 457 (1904).

**8.**  Eng.—Row v. Dawson, 1 Ves. 331 (1749, Ch.);  Lord Carteret v. Paschal, 3 P. Wms. 199 (1733, Ch.); Peters v. Soame, 2 Vern. 428 (1701, Ch.);  Fashion v. Atwood, 2 Ch. Cas. 36 (1680).

Barbour, "History of Contract in Early English Equity," in 4 Oxford Studies in Social and Legal History, p. 108.

of the assignment. It thus came to be said than an assignee obtained only an "equitable interest" and not "legal title," supposing that if his "legal title" should be admitted the protection of the obligor would be impaired. These terms, however, were not used with a clear and exact signification.

Meantime, the common law also was developing; and it was being affected, more than its judges openly admitted, by the competing legal systems of equity and law merchant. Those judges, too, were able to give protection to the obligor and could prevent the assignor from rooking the assignee by a revocation.[9] Before 1800, they declared that the assignor could not control the action brought by the assignee in his name and could not discharge the obligor by release or otherwise, after notice of the assignment.[10] An action brought by the assignor for his own use would be dismissed.[11] So far did they go, that the court of chancery appeared to retire from the field almost altogether,[12] not following its usual custom of retaining jurisdiction that had once been assumed. Notwithstanding all this, it was still taught that "choses in action" were not assignable "at law" and that the assignee had only an "equitable interest," not "legal title."

This led to discussions of the relations of law and equity and of the supposed differences between equitable rights and legal rights.[13] Partial assignments involved further complications and differences of opinion.

9. The King's Bench disregarded a revocation by the assignor in Carrington v. Harway, 1 Keble 803 (1676). The same was done by the Pennsylvania court in M'Cullum v. Coxe, 1 Dall. 139 (1785).

Again, the King's Bench recognized that after an assignment the assignor had no right that would pass to his later assignee in bankruptcy. Winch v. Keeley, 1 Term R. 619, 99 Eng.Rep. 1284 (1787).

10. U.S.—Welch v. Mandeville, 14 U.S. (1 Wheat.) 233, 4 L.Ed. 79 (1816).

Vt.—Newell Bros. v. Hanson, 123 A. 208, 97 Vt. 297 (1924).

Eng.—Legh v. Legh, 1 Bos. & P. 447 (1799, C.P.).

In Tripp v. Brownell, 66 Mass. (12 Cush.) 376, 380 (1853), Shaw, C.J., said: "It is called an 'equitable'

assignment, and it is so far an equitable transfer only of the debt, that if the assignee have occasion to go into a court of law, he must sue in the name of the assignor, that the debtor may have the benefit of any payment, or set-off, or other defense he may have against the assignor. But it is so far a transfer of the right to the debt, or the balance due, that, after notice of it, the debtor cannot discharge himself by paying the original creditor, the assignor; and it is so far recognized as a right in a court of law, that, in a suit brought in fact by the assignee, but in the name of the assignor, the court will take notice of the right of the assignee, and protect it, and will not permit the assignor to discontinue or release the action, or in any way to control it."

Meantime, the commercial world had gone its own gait, puzzled, it may be, by the curiosities of legal theory, and obstructed now and then by court decisions that were judicial anachronisms.[14] The needs of modern commercial business caused the "chose in action" to become a subject of daily transfer; and the assignee assumed that the right was his with as much confidence as if the subject matter had been the property in a horse. This commercial custom was of necessity paralleled by the course of judicial decision. The American courts, from the beginning of our national existence, exercised their powers in favor of the assignee and in giving due protection to the obligor.[15] This was made easier by legislation, liberalizing court procedure, welding common law and equity into a uniform legal system, and declaring that assignments should be legally operative and enforceable at the suit of the assignee as the real party in interest. Nearly everywhere, statutes have formally declared contract rights and other "choses in action" to be assignable, so that in an ordinary civil action the assignee can (and generally must) maintain suit in his own name.[16]

The present law of assignment can now be stated as a single system of rules, without distinguishing between law and equity or between an "equitable interest" and a "legal title." This has been done by the American Law Institute;[17] and it will be done in this treatise. The assignee has a legal right if the assignor had one. Prior to notice to the obligor, the assignor still has the power to discharge; and none after such notice. The relations of the parties can be fully stated in this fashion, in accordance with business custom and with the results actually reached by the courts. Outworn juristic theory and antiquated terminology that is no longer accurately descriptive can be abandoned. It can also be stated with conviction that in no field of the law more than in assignment is greater profit to be obtained from a clear and detailed analysis of the operative facts and the legal relations resulting therefrom.

## § 857.  Non-assignability of Tort Claims and of Claims Against Government

There are certain kinds of claims, mostly not arising out of contract, that are still declared to be non-assignable, either ex-

14.  For a recent case in which long obsolete reasoning caused the court to render a decision that would, if supported, invalidate an infinite number of security transactions, amounting to billions of dollars in government war-production contracts alone, see Rockmore v. Lehman, 128 F.2d 564 (C.C.A.2d, 1942),

frankly reversed and corrected by the court on rehearing, 129 F.2d 892 (C.C.A.2d, 1942).

17.  Restatement, Contracts, §§ 148–177 (1933). See also Corbin, "Assignment of Contract Rights," 74 U. of Pa.L.Rev. 207 (1926), reprinted in Selected Readings on the Law of Contracts, 718 (1931).

pressly so declared by statute or so held for some special reason of supposed public policy. Various statutes have declared that claims against the government or some branch thereof shall not be assignable. These may be directed primarily against attempts by contractors to delegate to others the performances that they have promised to render. In so far as they apply to claims against the government to compensation for work actually performed, there has been much relaxation either by judicial interpretation or by more recent legislation.[18]

A right to a federal pension has been made nonassignable; and the right of a public officer or employee to future salary or wages not yet due for performance rendered has been held not to be assignable.[19] Perhaps the purpose is to protect pensioners from loan-sharks. A public employee who has enjoyed and expended his wages by anticipation is perhaps expected to scamp his job thereafter—one does not like "to pay for a dead horse"; but the law no longer protects a private employer against such anticipatory assignments.

In this treatise on the law of contract, we are dealing with the assignment of contract rights, including money debts, primary rights to some specific performance promised, and secondary rights to damages or restitution for breaches of contract. We are not dealing with the assignment of claims to unliquidated damages for tortious injuries. It is only in comparatively recent times that claims of this latter kind have been regarded as assignable, and then only with respect to claims for injuries to property rather than to person. A claim to unliquidated damages for tortious injury to person or reputation is still nonassignable, although the distinguishing line may sometimes be hard to recognize. When any claim, of whatever kind, is reduced to judgment, it becomes a money debt and is assignable.[20]

Some rights are so closely connected with the use of specific land that a conveyance of the land carries the right with it even though not specifically mentioned; it "runs with the land." Some such rights may not be assignable at all, separately from the land, a problem dealt with in works on real property. After a breach has occurred, however, the secondary right to compensation is assignable. A similar problem may arise in the case

20. Restatement, Contracts, § 547: "(1) An assignment of a claim against a third person or a bargain to assign such a claim is illegal and ineffective if the claim is for

(a) the salary or pay, not yet due, of a public officer or employee, or

(b) a pension granted at least in part for continuing future services, or

(c) alimony, judicially awarded, and either not yet due or still subject to modification by the court, or

(d) damages for an injury the gist of which is to the person rather than to property, unless the claim has been reduced to judgment."

of personal property. The seller of specific goods may make an accompanying promise to the buyer, such as a warranty of quantity or quality. A sub-purchaser of the goods does not, by virtue solely of the transfer of ownership, become an assignee of the seller's contract right against the warrantor; there must be some expression of an intention to assign the contract right. If such an expression accompanies the sale, there should be no doubt in any ordinary case that it is legally operative, whether at the time of sale there has already been a breach of the warranty or not. If a breach has occurred, the right to compensation therefor is assignable to anyone. Even before breach the primary contract right created by the warranty can certainly be assigned to a sub-purchaser of the goods. Although it would not "run with the goods," the seller has power to realize full value by transferring it along with the property.[21]

### § 858.   Are the Rights of an Assignee "Equitable" as Opposed to "Legal" ?

Even before the amalgamation of law and equity that has taken place in most jurisdictions, the assignee of a contract right had an adequate remedy in the common law courts. In addition, those courts gave substantially the same protection to the obligor as the court of chancery had done. The various jural relations existing among the assignor, the assignee, the obligor, and other creditors and assignees, came to be substantially identical as recognized by the two systems of courts.[22] In so far as these jural relations had been developed in equity, they were taken over by the courts of common law. Except for purposes of historical explanation, therefore, it became unnecessary to describe the assignee's right as a solely "equitable" right.[23] Not only unnecessary, it became misleading and injurious, causing false distinctions and unjust decisions in cases of partial assignments, perpetuating the survival of the notion that there is some universal and eternal distinction between an "equitable" right and a "legal" one, and tending to prevent the full realization by the courts that they are empowered and in duty bound to act as chancellors as well as judges and to apply the rules of equity in cases of conflict between the two systems.

It must, indeed, not be overlooked that in various states there still exists a dual system of courts, and that in other jurisdictions there are separate systems of procedure to be followed in a single set of courts. The amalgamation of the two courts and the two systems of law is not complete, and is not everywhere at the same stage of development. This means that the degree of amalgamation must always be considered and the rules of the local system of procedure complied with. Even where a separate court of chancery still exists, however, it is misleading to describe the right of an assignee as solely "equitable." This is supported by the opinion of a Vice Chancellor of such a court in the note below.[24]

## § 859.  What is a Chose in Action?

We think in terms of the objects of sensation. In the history of our law, "chose in action" is opposed to "chose in possession." The word chose is from the French and expresses the same concept as does the Latin word res and the English word thing. My book, my hat, and my horse are choses in possession. If I lend my book to B, the book is still a chose in possession; but it is not in my possession. It might well be called a "chose in action" with respect to me; for it is certainly a "chose" in the material sense, and it may take an action in order for me to recover its possession. But the book is not called a "chose in action," in whosesoever possession it may in fact be.

Again, if I lend $100 to B to be repaid in the future, the specific money is a chose that goes from my possession to that of B. The money is a chose in B's possession; as against B it is said that I have a "chose in action." But observe: B spends this money and it scatters into unknown hands; B no longer has this chose in his possession, but as against B it is still said that I have a "chose in action." Doubtless, the origin of such usage is the fact that a material thing once went out of my possession into that of B.

Again, suppose that I work for B, and he promises me wages of $100. No material thing has come into B's possession from me, and yet I am said to have a "chose in action" as against him. Evidently there can be a "chose in action" without any material thing, or specific res, being in anybody's possession or having passed from one's possession to another's.

It may be that the use of "chose in action" in the case of the loan of money or the promise to pay wages is to be explained on the ground that the performance of his duty by B will ordinarily result in the delivery of some material thing by B to his creditor. Yet performance does not always have such a result. The parties may have agreed that B can discharge his debt to me by merely instructing his bank to credit my account.

It appears from all this that the term "chose in action" has come to be used to denote a right against another person, not including those manifold rights that are called property rights. Whether this is true or not, the term "chose in action" will not be used in this chapter wherever clear analysis is necessary.

24. The case is Farrell v. Passaic Water Co., 88 A. 627, 82 N.J.Eq. 97 (1913). The opinion by Vice Chancellor Stevens is too long to be quoted in this volume.

We shall not discuss the alienability or inalienability of "choses in action"; instead we shall discuss the assignment of rights, and in a lesser degree the assignment of powers and privileges.[28]

### § 860.　Is a Contract Right "Property"?

The term "property" is an abused term, seldom defined or subjected to careful analysis, and nearly always used to attain some desired end with variable underlying assumptions that are not expressed.　Only the briefest possible analysis will be given here;[29] but something is necessary in order to deal intelligently with contract rights and their assignment.　The term "property" is used to denote some subject matter, usually physical in character, such as a tract of land, a cow, or an automobile;　but, also, it is used to denote the complex group of jural relations between the individual owner of such subject matter and all other individuals.　In the first of these two senses, an automobile *is* property;　in the second sense, it is the subject matter of property relations.　In the first sense, I may say that the land is my property;　in the second, I have property in the land.　In either usage, it is clear that "property rights" are manifold rights against innumerable unidentified persons, operating as a constraint upon their action for the benefit of the "property owner."

It is quite clear that by nobody's usage is a contract right one of these manifold property rights just specified.　A contract right is a right against a particular and identifiable person, operating as a constraint upon his action only.　We may start, therefore, with the assumption that a contract right is not a "property" right.　When a court says that a contract right is property, it is using the word in the first of the two senses, as a subject matter of property relations.　It is indeed different from a tract of land, a cow, or an automobile;　but like them, it can be the subject of transfer by sale or gift, and its ownership involves not only the right against the specific identifiable person but also manifold jural relations with innumerable unidentified others.　Thus, while the contract right is not a property right, it may be and is regarded as the subject matter of property rights.　The owner of land or chattels has manifold rights against others that they

---

28.　The American Law Institute, Restatement, Contracts, Ch. 7, does not use the term "chose in action." Instead, it deals with the assignment of "rights" and the delegation of performance of "duties."

29.　The American Law Institute has presented the best jural analysis of "property." See its Restatement, Property, Tentative Draft No. 1, Chapter 1. It is based

directly upon Hohfeld, "Fundamental Legal Conceptions," first printed in 23 Yale L.J. 16 (1913), and 26 id. 710 (1917), later published in book form by the Yale Press. That the application of this type of analysis is necessary to the development of sound theories of economics and political science, see Commons, "Institutional Economics" (1934).

shall not trespass; the owner of a contract right has manifold rights that others shall not interfere to prevent performance by the obligor. The owner of land or chattels has a power of transfer; so also has the owner of a contract right. After the transfer of a chattel, the transferor no longer has the manifold rights against others; after the assignment of a contract right, the assignor no longer has either his manifold rights against others or his particular contract right against the identified obligor.

Certain income tax cases have considered the effect of an assignment, by gift or for value, of contract rights, for the purpose of determining whether money payable after such an assignment is to be taxed as income of the assignor or income of the assignee. With the question whether Congress, by its income tax legislation, has intended to prevent a man from reducing his tax by reducing his income, a work on contracts has nothing to do. But that question should not be permitted to confuse our understanding as to the nature and effect of an assignment of a contract right.

### § 861. Meaning of Assignment

If we abandon the term "chose in action" and also disapprove of the expression "assignment of contract," it is nevertheless necessary to explain what it is that we "assign" and what we do when we assign it. The term "assignment" is used in the law of property as well as in the law of contract; indeed, it may be said to have application only in cases involving property, for contract rights are "property" as that term is used by the courts. The term has much the same usage as have the terms "alienation," "conveyance," and "transfer." In this book, however, next to nothing will be said of the assignment of lands or of physical chattels; primarily, the subject matter of this chapter is the assignment of contract rights and of other purely contractual relations between two parties.

The distinction should first be pointed out between the tradition from hand to hand of a physical thing and an assignment of rights. It is far easier for the human mind to grasp the idea of a physical object or a physical change than the idea of a right or other legal relation, even though the latter is merely a foresight of future physical changes. The earlier processes of commerce involve bartering rather than promising, physical possession is almost ten points in the law, and conveyance of land lies in "livery of seisin." Later on, assignment and alienation take place more often without any physical tradition of a thing (except a token or document of title), and we begin to talk of the assignment of rights rather than of the transfer of a thing.

792

Alienation, conveyance, and transfer of land or chattels may take place without physically touching the res in question. It is often said that "title" is transferred or conveyed. "Title" means legal relations—"rights" in the broadest usage of that term. A more exact and specific analysis would indicate that "title" consists of rights, powers, privileges, and immunities,[32] defining these terms so that they are mutually exclusive. It is these legal relations that are transferred or conveyed or aliened. An alienation or transfer or conveyance of "title" is the substitution of a new party to some or to all of the legal relations of which "title" consists. The grantor extinguishes his relations with others respecting the subject matter and creates similar relations between the grantee and others. If the grantor had rights (in rem) that other persons shall not trespass, the grantee now has such rights. If the grantor was legally privileged as against others to use or abuse, the grantee now has such privileges. If the grantor had power of alienation, the grantee now has such power. The conveyance, alienation, or transfer may have been of only a part of the legal relations of the grantor, as in the case of a mortgage or of an option; in such case both parties now have "title," or a part of the "title."

Alienation, conveyance, and transfer, therefore, consist of some operative action that extinguishes and creates, that substitutes a new party as the focus of legal relations with respect to the subject matter. Such also is an "assignment" in the law of contracts.[33]

The term "assignment" may be used to denote the *act* of the party assigning [34] or it may be used to denote the change in legal relations created by that act. In the case of an assignment in writing, the written document is sometimes referred to as the "assignment." Such variation in usage is also to be observed in the case of "contract," and of "alienation," "conveyance," and "transfer." They may all mean either acts, documents, or legal relations, or some combination of the three.

---

32. See American Law Institute, Restatement, Property, Ch. 1.

33. The Institute defines an "Effective Assignment," in Restatement, Contracts, § 150, as follows: "An effective assignment is one by which the assignor's right to performance by the obligor is extinguished and the assignee acquires a right to such performance."

34. Restatement, Contracts, § 149, defines assignment in this way: "An assignment of a right is a manifestation to another person by the owner of the right indicating his intention to transfer, without further action or manifestation of intention, the right to such other person or to a third person." The terms "assignor," "assignee," "subassignee," and "assignment for value" are also there defined.

## § 862. Assignment Distinguished from Power of Attorney, or Agency

Even in the days when the transfer of a contract right was regarded as impossible, and an attempted assignment was therefore regarded as a "power of attorney," the assignee was not in any proper sense an "agent" of the assignor. In attempting to enforce the claim, he was not acting for the benefit of the assignor but for his own benefit; he had not undertaken to follow, nor was he bound to follow, the directions of the assignor. The "power of attorney" theory was used only in order to surmount the difficulties created by the erroneous notion of impossibility of transfer; and having served this purpose, it receded into the background and was not allowed to carry the assignee into the field of agency.[35]

An assignee is not an agent; and the converse is equally true that an agent is not an assignee. One to whom a power of attorney is given, its terms and the accompanying expressions showing an intention that the power is to be used under the direction and control of the grantor of the power, is not an assignee.[36] The holder of such a power as this is governed by the rules of agency; with the well-known exceptions created by those rules, the power is revocable by notice and is terminated by the grantor's death. The grantor still owns the right against the obligor and retains the power to discharge. Whether the acts and expressions of an alleged assignor are to be regarded as an assignment, or as a mere power of attorney, is a question of interpretation that is sometimes difficult to answer. It is more likely to arise in the field of gift assignments than in that of assignments for value.

Where one has a right to funds in the possession of another, a communication to that other requesting and authorizing him to transfer a portion of them to a third person is not necessarily an assignment. The owner of the right undoubtedly has power to make an assignment at once transferring his right to a third party; but he also has power to create in the holder of the fund a power to effectuate such a transfer by a subsequent act. One who has power to assign also has power to do something less than a present assignment. Whether he has done the former or the latter is a matter of reasonable interpretation of his communication to the holder of the fund.

35. An assignment is not a mere power of attorney even though the assignee undertakes to collect and pay over the proceeds to the assignor, and even though the assignee is expressly given a power of attorney to maintain suit. Titus v. Wallick, 59 S.Ct. 557, 306 U.S. 282, 83 L.Ed. 653 (1939).

Restatement, Contracts, Ch. 7, retains no vestige of the "power of attorney" theory of assignment.

There is no question that an effective assignment of a right can be made without any communication to or assent by the assignee; [37] but the usual method of assignment includes a communication to the assignee. Therefore, a communication to the holder of the fund (the obligor) is somewhat less likely to be intended as a present assignment. An expression of intention to assign, communicated to the assignee, should hardly ever be interpreted as being a mere power of attorney to the assignee. But a mere communication to the holder of the fund (the obligor), containing no words of present assignment and merely authorizing and directing him to pay to a third party, may properly bear the interpretation that it is a mere power of attorney to the obligor himself, empowering him to effectuate a transfer by his own subsequent act. [38] With this interpretation, the communication to the obligor is not an assignment; and, like most other powers of attorney, it is revocable by its creator and it is terminated by its creator's death.

### § 863.  Negotiable Instruments Distinguished.

No attempt will be made in this work to state the law of negotiable instruments, or even to reprint the uniform act known as the Negotiable Instruments Law. It is desirable to point out, however, a few of the differences and a few of the similarities between that law and the law of assignment here stated. A negotiable instrument is a special kind of formal contract, including bills of exchange and promissory notes drawn in a required form. The rules applicable to this form and to the legal effects of transfer are the result of centuries of commercial usage. The evolution of these rules was long quite independent of the English common law and equity, being referred to as "law merchant" to indicate that independence. It fell to the lot of Lord Mansfield to incorporate most of that law into the common law of England, by his judicial action; but the usage of merchants was becoming the usage of Englishmen, so as to make the judicial incorporation inevitable.

In so far as the rules applicable to negotiable instruments differ from those applicable to the assignment of other contract rights, they are due to the commercial advantages accruing from the use of a readily transferable credit instrument. The same influences that created the negotiable instrument, and the rules applicable thereto, have also created the rules of assignment applicable to other contracts; and there is an observable tendency to give to other formal documents some of the attributes of negotiability. In earlier times, bills of exchange were said to be assignable and ordinary contract rights were not; in this respect, the ordinary contract eventually caught up with the bill of exchange. But under certain circumstances, the transferee of a negotiable instrument obtains an enforceable right against the maker and indorsers, even though his transferor and the original promisee had none. The rules determining when this is so are part of the negotiable instruments law. In the case of ordinary contract rights, the assignee is said to take subject to defenses, to get no better right than the assignor had. If the holder of a negotiable instrument fails for some reason to come within the rules applicable to such instruments, he may nevertheless fall back upon the law of assignment and obtain such advantage as that law will give him.

A negotiable instrument is a written promise, or order, to pay to the order of a named payee, or to bearer, a specified sum of money. It is on its face unilateral and unconditional. This fact shows that the law of assignment must deal with many problems and situations unknown to the law of negotiable instruments. The latter law does not need to deal with the problems involved in complex, bilateral transactions, with the matter of delegation of performance of reciprocal duties, with the performance of conditions precedent. But negotiable instruments may be drawn for accommodation, may pass through many hands and have many indorsements. Also such an instrument may be given as a part of a large and complex transaction, creating many legal relations not peculiar to negotiable instruments; and in such cases it is necessary to know and apply both the law of negotiable instruments and the law of ordinary contracts.

The law of negotiable instruments is so specialized and so definitely crystallized into a statutory system that it must be studied apart. The law of assignment can also be stated independently, for those innumerable transactions in which no negotiable instrument is involved. If the transaction involves such an instrument, reference must then be made to the special law applicable to it; in many instances that law will be found not to vary the effect that is produced by the law of assignment, and in other instances it will vary it in only a few respects, often minor in character.

### § 864. Can a "Contract" be Assigned?

It is very general usage to speak of the assignment of "the contract." Such usage, however, is based upon lack of analysis and definition. By no acceptable definition of the term "contract" can the usage be justified; and it is not possible to construct clear and accurate rules by making use of the term "assignment of contract." [39]

39.   Restatement, Contracts, Ch. 7, speaks solely of the assignment of "rights," not of the assignment of contracts.

If a contract is defined as consisting of the facts operating to create a binding obligation—offer, acceptance, consideration, etc. —these facts are merely a part of recorded history and surely cannot be assigned. It is meaningless to speak of assigning a past event.

If a contract is defined as a promise enforceable at law, we are merely placing emphasis upon one of the operative facts and indicating that it is in fact operative. A promise is merely a past event and cannot properly be said to be assignable by the promisee; much less can a promise be assigned by the promisor who made it, and it would be equally erroneous to say that either party to a bilateral contract can assign *both* promises.

If contract is defined as denoting the legal relations of the parties created by agreement or promise, it is again erroneous to say that the "contract" can or cannot be assigned. Some of the legal relations can be assigned and some cannot. The legal relations created by any particular contract must be analyzed and the assignability of each one must be considered separately. The legal relations created by some complex contracts are very numerous; and it would usually be absurd to try to determine whether they could all be assigned in a group. The issues that arise in actual cases never require such a determination; instead they always raise the question whether one of the parties (and not the other) has power to assign certain specific legal relations created by the contract (and not the others).

It may be helpful to consider some specific cases, either hypothetical or actually taken from the reports. Case (1): In consideration of $100 lent by A to B, the latter promises to repay in thirty days. Here A has a right to payment at a definite date— a right that is not conditional on any performance to be rendered by A or by any third person; and B has no right whatever against A. Nobody doubts that A has the power of assignment of his right or that the assignee can maintain an action against B for breach of his promise to pay the money.

Case (2): In consideration of services actually rendered by A to B, the latter promises to pay $100 to A. This is exactly like (1) except that the consideration is service rendered, instead of money paid. A has power of assignment exactly as in Case (1).

Case (3): A promises to sink an oil well for B; and B promises to pay $1,000 at the completion. Here the contract is bilateral; and A's right to payment is conditional on substantial performance of his own part. If A sinks the well as agreed, the contract becomes unilateral and the condition precedent to his right to payment of the $1,000 is performed. Again A has power of assignment exactly as in Case (1). Even before the sinking of the well, however, A has power to assign his right to payment. The right so assigned is a conditional right to payment in the future; but A's act of assignment is a present act and is operative to put the assignee in A's present legal position and to make him the holder of a conditional right to a future payment.

In this Case (3), A has no power to get rid of his duty to B to sink the well by assigning it to C. The performance required by this duty is not any performance by A in person; he has not promised to sink the well with his own hands or even to have others sink the well under his direct supervision. He can delegate the performance to others; but this does not mean that, by such a delegation, he escapes from the legal duty. It merely means that his legal duty requires him to cause the sinking of the well. If he produces this result, he has performed his promise, whether he causes it by sinking the well himself or by employing servants to do so or by inducing an assignee who is an independent contractor to do so. If the well is sunk in accordance with the contract, the assignee C has a right to the promised payment. If the well is not sunk substantially in accordance with the contract, the assignee has no right to the payment; and B can get a judgment for damages against A for breach of his contract. A did not escape his duty to B by the assignment. If C promised A to sink the well, B can also get judgment for damages against C for breach of his contract with A to sink the well and to satisfy A's legal duty to B. With respect to this contract, B is a creditor beneficiary, since the performance that C promised A to render was a performance that A owed by virtue of a legal duty to B.

In this case, B also has a power of assignment; he can assign his right that A shall sink the oil well. This right is indeed a conditional one; it is conditional on B's remaining able and willing to pay the price on completion of the well. Of course, B can perform this condition vicariously; there is nothing personal about the act of payment. But financial credit is personal; an attempt by B to substitute an assignee's credit for his own would be a breach of contract and would discharge A from further duty. But no harm is done by getting the assignee of B's right to undertake the payment of the $1,000. A must sink the well; and he would then have a right to payment of the $1,000 against both B and his assignee.[40]

Case (4): In consideration of the promise of A, who is a great portrait painter, to paint a portrait of B's wife, B promises to pay A $1,000. Just as in Case (3), A has an immediate power of assignment of his right to payment. The right so obtained by the assignee, however, would be a right to future payment, conditional upon substantial performance of his contract by A. This case differs from Case (3) in that such substantial performance requires A's own personal performance. By the custom of portrait painters, it may perhaps be proper for A to have the canvas prepared, the background laid, outlines drawn, and some other of the easier matters done by assistants; but the more vital matters it is clear that the master has himself promised to do, and his personal performance is a condition precedent to his right to payment and also to his assignee's right to payment. It is a breach of his contract to delegate these to another person. Of course in this case, no more than in Case (3), can the painter escape from his duty to produce the portrait by delegating any part of the work to another, either a part requiring the highest artistic skill or a part requiring no skill at all.

Case (5): A more complex situation can be found in the facts of a case in North Carolina.[41] The plaintiff, the Atlantic & N. C. R. Co., contracted with one Ives to buy from him a large quantity of wood for wood-burning locomotives. Later, the railroad company leased its road to the Howland Improvement Company, this lease being interpreted by the court as containing a promise by the lessee to perform the existing contracts of the lessor, including the contract with Ives. This lease was then assigned by the Howland Improvement Company to the Atlantic & N. C. Co., the defendant, who also is treated as having assumed and promised to perform the Ives contract. It did not keep this promise, the result being that Ives sued the plaintiff and got judgment for damages. The plaintiff now sues the defendant, the assignee of the lease, for breach of its contract with the Howland Improvement Company.

The relations of the four parties are graphically represented in the accompanying diagram below, each solid arrow representing a promise to the party to whom it points.[42] The promise of the plaintiff to Ives is numbered "1." The promise of the lessee to the plaintiff lessor is numbered "2." Ives is a creditor beneficiary of this promise No. 2; and the broken arrow numbered

41.   N.C.—Atlantic & N. C. R. Co.
v. Atlantic & N. C. Co., 61 S.E. 185,
147 N.C. 368 (1908).

42.    Atl. & N. C. R. Co. (Pff.)

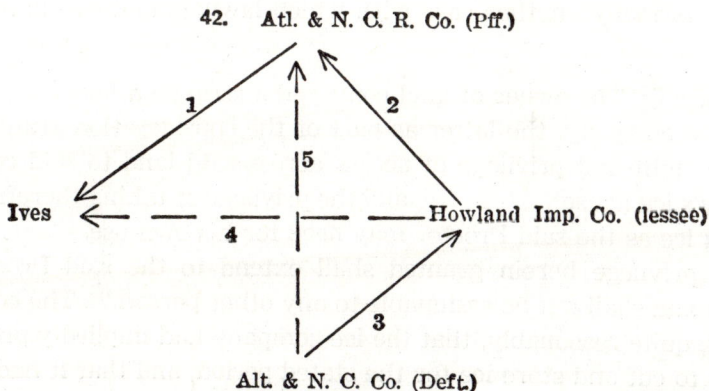

Ives     Howland Imp. Co. (lessee)

Alt. & N. C. Co. (Deft.)

"4" represents the legal duty that the lessee owed to Ives as such beneficiary. Ives preferred, however, to enforce his own contract with the plaintiff. The assignment and lease by the plaintiff to the Howland Improvement Company did not discharge the plaintiff from its duty to Ives; but the plaintiff's right to delivery of the wood by Ives was assignable and it was not conditional on any *personal* performance by the plaintiff, inasmuch as the performance due in return for the wood was the payment of money, and the money of one person is as good as the money of another.

The Howland Improvement Company, lessee, assigned its lease to the defendant; and the latter promised to perform the lessee's contract with the plaintiff. This promise is numbered "3." The plaintiff is a creditor beneficiary of promise No. 3; and the broken arrow numbered "5" represents the legal duty of the defendant to the plaintiff as such beneficiary. It is this duty that the court enforces by a judgment for damages. By the assignment contract of the Howland Improvement Company and the defendant, the latter obtained the right to the delivery of wood by Ives; and the former delegated performance of a duty to pay the agreed price. If Ives had refused to deliver the wood to the defendant, the latter, as second successive assignee, could have got judgment for damages against Ives. The fact that the original contract with Ives was bilateral and that payment of the price was delegated to the defendant would not relieve Ives from his duty to deliver the wood; but Ives committed no default. Instead, the defendant failed to perform its promise to take and pay for the wood—promise number "3." That promise was made to the Howland Improvement Company; but it created a duty to the plaintiff and doubtless also to Ives. The plaintiff does not sue as an assignee; instead, the defendant is the assignee and is sued by the plaintiff as the beneficiary of the defendant's promise to perform the duty delegated to it by the assignor.

This analysis may seem complex and hard to follow; but its complexity lies in the actually existing facts and is no greater than in many another case with which lawyers and courts have to deal.

Case 6: The owner of land conveyed a strip on a lake shore to an ice company, the latter as part of the consideration granting "the right and privilege of access across said land to said company's ice house . . . and the privilege of taking therefrom such ice as the said Proctor may need for his own use. . . . The privilege herein granted shall extend to the said Proctor only and shall not be assignable to any other person." The court held, quite reasonably, that the ice company had impliedly promised to cut and store ice for the stated period, and that it had no power to terminate its duty by selling its land and business.[43] Without doubt, it had power to perform vicariously, by delegating the cutting and storing of ice to other individuals. The legal privilege of crossing the land and taking ice for his own use was created in Proctor; this privilege was not assignable by him and would not have been even in the absence of the express prohibition. This means that he could not by assignment create in another person the privilege of taking ice for the latter's use; it does not mean that Proctor could not legally privilege his servant to cross the land and bring away ice for Proctor's use. The "contract" was a unilateral one.

43.   Mass.—Proctor v. Union Coal Co., 137 N.E. 659, 243 Mass. 428 (1923).

# CHAPTER 48

## ASSIGNMENT OF RIGHTS AND DELEGATION OF PERFORMANCE—ASSENT OF OBLIGOR

## § 865. When is a Contract "Personal"—Delegation of Performance

In the matter of assignability as affected by the supposed "personal" nature of the contract, or by the existence of "liabilities" as well as rights, or by the existence of a relation of "trust and confidence," it will be helpful to consider the following questions:

(1) What was the performance required of the defendant obligor?

(2) What were the conditions on which it was the defendant's duty to render that performance?

(3) What performance, if any, was the assignor under a duty to render?

In the case of a simple contract debt for money lent, all three questions are easy to answer. (1) The performance required of the defendant was the payment of money. (2) There are no conditions precedent to his duty to pay other than the arrival of the date of maturity, except where his promise to pay was expressly made conditional. He may have made a promise to pay "on demand," or "after I sell Blackacre," or "if X is elected president." (3) The creditor is under no duty to render any performance. In all these, nothing appears to make the creditor's right non-assignable. Of course, the creditor has put "trust and confidence" in the debtor; but this does not affect the power of the creditor to assign his right to payment. It does not even affect the power of the debtor to delegate performance, because payment of money by one person is not substantially different from payment by another person. Of course, the debtor cannot discharge his duty by assigning it to another—no promisor can do this without the creditor's assent; but he can discharge it by an actual vicarious performance.

Suppose a second case: The X Electric Co. pays Caruso $5000 in advance and Caruso promises in return to sing three songs over the radio. (1) The performance required of Caruso is his personal singing. (2) There are no express conditions precedent to Caruso's duty; but the existence of proper facilities would be such a constructive condition. (3) Again, the Electric Company is under no duty.[1] Just as before, there is in all these nothing that makes the Electric Company's right non-assignable. And if there are any conditions precedent on its part, they can readily be performed by an assignee or other delegated person. This second case differs from the case of the money debt in this, that the performance promised by Caruso is strictly personal. It is impossible for Caruso, not only to discharge his duty by assigning it to another, but to discharge it by an actual vicarious performance. This fact has no bearing on the power of the Electric Company to assign its right. It has put "trust and confidence" in Caruso; but Caruso has put no trust and confidence in it.

A third case follows: A bilateral contract is made whereby Hackley promises to keep certain city streets clean and the city promises to pay specified sums in instalments as the work proceeds. Before work begins, Hackley assigns his rights to Devlin, who undertakes to perform Hackley's duties. (1) The performance required by the defendant city was the payment of money, as in the first case put. Of course, Hackley put "trust and confidence" in the city. (2) It was a condition precedent to the city's duty to pay that the streets should be kept clean as agreed. It was not such a condition that Hackley should clean them with his own broom. Cleaning by Devlin or by men employed and directed by Devlin, would do as well. (3) This case differs from the two preceding cases in that the assignor Hackley promised a return performance; it was his duty to see that the streets were cleaned. His rights against the city were connected with "liabilities"—that is to say, reciprocal duties to the city. But this fact does not deprive Hackley of his power to assign his right to payment. Nor does it deprive him of his power to perform vicariously. He cannot discharge his duty to the city by assigning it (or by delegating performance of it) to Devlin, any more than the city can discharge its duty to pay by assigning it

---

1. It is quite possible that all the circumstances would justify a court in finding by implication a promise by the Electric Company to furnish appropriate facilities to enable Caruso to enhance his artistic reputation by the wide distribution of his voice. If so, the bargain is to that extent bilateral.

to another. But Hackley can discharge his duty by causing Devlin, or Devlin's workmen, to clean the streets, just as the city can discharge its duty by causing some one else to pay the agreed sum. Hackley's assignment of his right to payment and his delegation of performance to Devlin involved no breach of duty by him. If Devlin does not perform, Hackley is still bound to do so and is liable to a judgment for damages. His duty has not been repudiated by him, nor has he escaped his liability to judgment.[2]

In a bilateral contract for the hire of railway cars, the lessor promised to keep them in repair. The lessor went into liquidation and assigned the rentals to a new company, the plaintiff. It was held that the lessee was not justified in refusing to perform further, personal performance by the lessor corporation or its particular officers and servants not being a condition of the lessee's duty.[3] The plaintiff was ready and willing to perform in place of the lessor, and its ability was not questioned. Of course, the right to the rentals was assignable; the question is whether the lessor could delegate performance of its own duty. Being a corporation, such delegation to individuals must have been contemplated from the beginning.[4]

If, in the foregoing case, the lessor should be totally dissolved, so that an action could not be maintained against it in case of default in performance by its delegate and assignee, it would be reasonable to hold that the defendant lessee is discharged from further duty. Even though he did not contract for personal performance by the lessor, he did rely upon its financial responsibility. Even as to this, however, the lessee should not be discharged by the lessor's insolvency or dissolution, if the assignee can and does tender full performance at once (in this specific case it could not), or if no serious question is raised as to the sufficiency of his financial responsibility and the security that he will perform in full.[5]

In the case of a contract to render personal service, the employee can assign his right to salary or wages; but he cannot delegate performance of the service. Unless the employee himself performs as agreed, the assignee of the wages cannot collect them, just as the assignor himself could not. In like manner, the employer can assign his right to the services and he can delegate performance of his duty to pay wages; but the employee's duty to render the service remains conditional upon the original employer's readiness and willingness to pay the wages or upon a tender of ample security by the assignee.

2.   This third case is Devlin v. Mayor, etc., of City of New York, 63 N. Y. 8 (1875). In full accord are Ernst v. Kunkle, 5 Ohio St. 520 (1856); and British Wagon Co. v. Lea & Co., 5 Q.B.D. 149 (1880).

3.   Eng.—British Wagon Co. v. Lea & Co., 5 Q.B.D. 149 (1880).

The statement that the employer can assign his right to the promised service does not mean that he can by assignment change in any material way the service to be rendered.[6] If it was service as a valet, to be rendered to himself in person, he cannot by assignment make it the servant's duty to act as a valet for a different person; but the right that the servant should serve him as a valet can be assigned, so that the enforcement thereafter, by damages or otherwise, would be in favor of the assignee and at his suit. If the service is to be rendered under the personal supervision and direction of the employer, he can assign his right to such service; but his own readiness and willingness to supervise and direct is still a condition precedent to the servant's duty to proceed with the service, just as it was prior to the assignment.[7] In such a case, the death of the employer, or his refusal to perform the condition of supervision, will operate to discharge the employee from further duty.[8]

In almost all cases where a "contract" is said to be non-assignable because it is "personal," what is meant is not that the contractor's right is not assignable, but that the performance required by his duty is a personal performance and that an attempt to perform by a substituted person would not discharge the contractor's duty.[9] In this sense the statement is correct if a proper interpretation of the agreement shows that the performance by a particular person is required.

A second possible correct meaning is that personal performance by the contractor is a condition precedent to his right to performance by the other party, and an assignee of that right will fail in case of non-fulfilment of this condition. In this case, as in the preceding one, performance cannot be delegated.[10] If it should be meant that the assignee of the right would fail even

---

**6.** Restatement, Contracts, § 152, is as follows:

"(1) If the performance which an obligor is under a duty to render involves co-operative action by the obligee of such a nature that the obligee has power to delegate the action to an agent, an effective assignment of the obligee's right subjects the obligor to a duty to perform with the co-operation of the assignee instead of that of the obligee.

"(2) The performance that an obligor is under a duty to render can be changed by assignment of the obligee's right, except in slight and unimportant details, only as stated in Subsection (1)."

**8.** N.C.—Woodley v. Bond, 66 N.C. 396 (1872).

In such cases, the death of either the employer or the employee operates as a discharge of the duties of both parties. See Spalding v. Rosa, 71 N.Y. 40 (1877); Yerrington v. Greene, 7 R.I. 589 (1863); and Chapter 75, Discharge by Impossibility.

**9.** See, for example, Paige v. Faure, 127 N.E. 898, 229 N.Y. 114, 10 A. L.R. 649 (1920), where the court says that "rights arising out of a contract cannot be transferred if they are coupled with liabilities, or if they involve a relationship of personal credit and confidence."

though the contracting assignor himself performs as originally agreed, thus fulfilling the condition precedent, the statement is entirely erroneous.[11]

A third possible correct meaning is that in a bilateral contract the contractor has no power to assign both his right and his duty. Thus it has been said: "When rights arising out of a contract are coupled with obligations to be performed by the contractor and involve such a relation of personal confidence that it must have been intended that the rights should be exercised [12] and the obligations performed by him alone, the contract, including both his rights and his obligations, cannot be assigned." [13] As has been seen previously, a legal duty cannot be escaped by assignment; and, as has just been said, a truly personal performance cannot be delegated.

It is sometimes said that where the contract makes it the duty of one party thereto to render a personal service, special trust and confidence being reposed in him, a valid assignment is impossible "as long as such contract is executory on the part of the party in whom such trust and confidence is reposed." While this is correct if the assignment is meant to include both duties and rights, it is not correct if it is meant to say that a right cannot be assigned as long as a duty of the assignor, requiring his personal performance remains executory. The assignor's right is assignable in spite of the personal character of the performance he is still under a duty to render; but if it is a right that was conditional upon some personal performance by the assignor, it remains so conditional after the assignee gets the right by assignment.[14] Thus a school teacher can assign his wages to be-

---

11. In Restatement, Contracts, § 160 (3), there is the following general statement as to when performance can be delegated: "Performance or offer of performance by a person delegated has the same legal effect as performance or offer of performance by the person named in the contract, unless, (a) performance by the person delegated varies or would vary materially from performance by the person named in the contract as the one to perform, and there has been no such assent to the delegation as is stated in § 162; or (b) the delegation is forbidden by statute or by the policy of the common law; or (c) the delegation is prohibited by contract." This statement applies when the ques-

tion is whether the performance by the delegate has discharged the assignor's duty, and also when it is whether that performance has fulfilled the conditions of the other party's duty so that the assignor (or his assignee) can maintain suit.

14. American Lith. Co. v. Ziegler, 103 N.E. 909, 216 Mass. 287 (1914).

It has been supposed that the right was too personal to be assigned in Arkansas Valley Smelting Co. v. Belden Min. Co., 8 S.Ct. 1308, 127 U. S. 379, 32 L.Ed. 246 (1888). The trouble was, however, that the assignor not only assigned his right to delivery of ore, but also became unready to perform his purely personal duty of crushing, sampling,

come due under an existing contract even though his services are still to be rendered; but the assignee's right will be exactly the same as the assignor's, conditional upon proper performance of the work by the teacher in person.

In a contract for a sales agency, the personal performance of the agent is practically always a condition precedent to the duty of the principal and employer. The performance of the agent's duty cannot be delegated to a substitute. The assignee of the agent's right must fail, therefore, in his attempt to enforce it, if he merely tenders a substituted performance.[15] The same is true in the case of one who has contracted to render personal care and support for another.[16] Indeed, no one who has contracted to render any kind of service in person, even though it is shoveling dirt, can discharge his duty or make his wages payable by furnishing a substitute; but if he performs in person, his assignee can collect the wages.

Even in cases where the required performance is not "personal," the non-personal performance that is required may be a condition precedent to the right to payment contracted for in return. In such cases the right is assignable before fulfilment of the condition precedent; and the fact that fulfilment of this condition is delegated to the assignee of the right to payment does not in any way affect the validity of the assignment.[22] Thus, where the duty to pay for coal is conditional on certain instalment deliveries being made, the making of these deliveries is a condition precedent to the seller's right to payment by the buyer; but the making of these deliveries is in no sense a personal performance. A tender of delivery by an assignee of the seller's right would fulfil the condition precedent and the assignee could then enforce the right against the buyer.

In case of a bilateral contract to sell goods ordinarily obtainable in the market, the seller can assign his right to the price and can delegate performance of the duty to deliver the goods. The assignee can maintain suit for the full price after making actual delivery; and he can maintain suit for damages, just as the assignor could, if the buyer repudiates before tender or refuses to accept and pay for goods tendered according to contract.[23]

In the much criticized case of Boston Ice Co. v. Potter,[24] the defendant had become dissatisfied with the Boston Ice Company,

and assaying the ore so as to determine the amount to be paid, and it was not alleged that he remained ready and willing to pay for ore subsequently delivered. His right to delivery (and therefore the right of the assignee also) was conditional upon his continued readiness to perform in person and to pay if the assignee did not. Had he fulfilled this condition, the assignee should have won the suit. The right to delivery was not non-assignable.

24.    123 Mass. 28 (1877). With the plaintiff's quasi-contractual right to payment on the ground of unjust enrichment, we are not here concerned.

terminated his relations with it, and "made a contract with the Citizens Ice Company to furnish him with ice." Thereafter, the Citizens Ice Company "sold its business to the plaintiff, with the privilege of supplying ice to its customers"; and the Boston Ice Company delivered ice to the defendant for a year before he knew of the change. The court held that the plaintiff had no right to compensation for ice delivered and used. It did not discuss the law of assignment. There is no doubt that the Citizens Ice Company could assign its right to payment for ice delivered by it, without Potter's assent, in the absence of an express or implied prohibition; and the fact that Potter had ceased buying of the plaintiff was not sufficient evidence of such prohibition. Assuming that the Citizens Company had assigned its right to payment, the real question was whether the performance of its duty to deliver ice could be delegated to an efficient substitute. As the law has since developed, it is clear that it could be so delegated; again, however, in the absence of a prohibition in the contract. Of course, if the substitute tenders ice of a different quality, the tender is bad; but Potter's long use of the ice shows that the performance was satisfactory. If the transaction between the two ice companies was actually an assignment of right and delegation of duty, the case would now be decided otherwise.

In building and construction contracts, it is seldom that the general contractor undertakes the duty of personal performance. There are special reasons for this when the contractor is a corporation. In the absence of expressions to the contrary, the contractor can perform vicariously; it is no breach of duty for him to delegate his promised performance, in part or in whole, to others and to make subcontracts with them to render such performance.[25] As a matter of course, the subcontract, or delegating transaction, may properly include an assignment by the general contractor of his right to payment, in part or in whole. A subcontract may be made in such a way that the party for whom the work is being done is a creditor beneficiary and can enforce the promise of the subcontractor. Generally, this is not the case, the subcontract being merely a step in the performance of the general contractor, the performance by the subcontractor not in itself discharging any part of the general contractor's duty to the owner.[26]

A building contract may be made in such a way as to require personal performance or supervision by a particular person. This is a matter of interpretation, in the light of the expressions used and the circumstances of the case. The work of an architect or designer nearly always involves such a degree of artistic skill or knowledge as to deprive him of the power of delegation.[27] Portions of his work he may delegate to subordinates; but this is not to say that he may desert the job entirely on the appointment of a good substitute.

Where the contractor whose duty it is to erect a building is a corporation, that fact may in itself be sufficient to show that the other party did not contract for anyone's "personal" service. A corporation can perform only through individual persons acting as its agents and employees; and generally it can enforce its contracts even though it changes all of its officers, all of its shareholders, and all of its employees. However, this is not necessarily true. Under many circumstances the courts will "pierce the corporate veil" and see the human beings that are operating behind it. One who makes a bilateral contract with a corporation may not even see the "veil"; he is dealing with the officers who wear it, and it may be reasonable for him to require them to continue to do so and to perform in person some substantial part of the performance promised by the "corporation" acting through them. In such a case the corporation can not delegate this performance to others.[28]

The question of delegation of performance has no necessary connection with assignment of contract rights. It arises in exactly the same form and is answered in exactly the same way where the plaintiff is the original contractor and not an assignee at all. Thus, if A sues B on the latter's promise to pay for the service of A as a teacher, A must lose if, without B's assent, he has tendered the performance of X as his substitute teacher. A's promised performance was "personal"; his own work as a teacher was a condition of his right to salary. Again, if B sues A for the latter's failure to perform his promise to teach, it is no defense for A to show that he tendered performance by X, a superior substitute. Whichever party is plaintiff, the question is merely what was the performance that was required on A's part. The assignment by A of his right to salary does not affect this question.

Where a performance is personal and not possible of delegation, the condition of personal performance is waived if the obligor assents to the substituted performance; and failure to object, with knowledge that the work is being performed by a substitute, may operate as assent.[29]

The parties can make personal performance by one of them a condition of the other's duty to pay by expressly prohibiting delegation of performance. In such case, the delegated assignee can recover nothing for services rendered by him without the defendant's assent.[30]

## § 866.  Assignment of Legal Duties

Before proceeding to determine what rights are assignable and what are not assignable, the easier problem of the assignment of duties will be disposed of. This disposal consists of the flat statement that no duty can ever be effectively assigned, if we adhere to our description of an assignment as a unilateral expression of the assignor. Applying that definition to duties instead of rights, we have: An assignment is an expression of intention by the assignor that his duty shall immediately pass to the assignee. Many a debtor wishes that by such an expression he could get rid of his debts. Any debtor can express such an intention, but it is not operative to produce such a hoped-for result. It does not cause society to relax its compulsion against him and direct it toward the assignee as his substitute. In spite of such an "assignment," the debtor's duty remains absolutely unchanged. The performance required by a duty can often be delegated; but by such a delegation the duty itself is not escaped.[31]

Suppose the following cases: 1. A is under contract with B to deliver for compensation a ton of coal to B's house. A employs C to deliver it for him. By so doing A is not a repudiator of his contract; but he is still bound by the contractual duty. If C delivers the coal, A has a right to payment of the compensation by B.[32] If C does not deliver the coal, B has a right to damages against A for breach of duty.[33] C's failure to deliver the coal may also give to both A and B a right to damages against C. This depends on whether C made a valid contract with A; if he did, A can sue for its breach,[34] and nearly everywhere B can sue C as an obligee-beneficiary of his contract with A. The assumption of the assignor's duty by the assignee merely gives to the other party a new and added security.

2. A is under contract with B to play the part of Hamlet in B's theater. In B's absence, A employs C to play Hamlet and C actually does so. In this case A has no right to the agreed compensation;[35] and instead B has a right to damages from A for breach of contract. No more than in the first case could A escape his duty by such an arrangement with C; but in addition, A could not perform vicariously as he could and did do in the first case.

3. In the case of a contract for the sale of goods, the assignment and delegation may be by the buyer as well as by the seller.

---

31.  Restatement, Contracts, § 160 (4), states this as follows: "Neither the delegation of performance by an obligor, nor a contract with the obligor by the person to whom performance is delegated to assume the obligor's duty, extinguishes it or prevents recovery of damages from him if the duty is not performed."

35.  Of course, if A has no right to the compensation, an assignment to C is ineffective; and C, having rendered some performance in attempted substitution for A, without B's assent, cannot get judgment against B. Zetterlund v. Texas Land & Cattle Co., 75 N.W. 860, 55 Neb. 355 (1898).

The buyer's assignment of his right to the goods and his delegation of the duty to pay the price are both effective; but he himself remains bound to pay the price just as before.[36]  If the assignee contracts with the assignor to pay the price, the seller can maintain suit for the price against the assignee also, as a creditor beneficiary of the assumption contract; [37] the seller has merely obtained a new and additional security.

A duty can never be escaped by assignment or delegation; but any duty can be extinguished by performance.  Some duties require a performance by a specific person; others do not.  In the coal case, the performance required was the delivery of coal at B's house, and it made no difference whether by team or by truck or by whom driven.  In the Hamlet case, the performance required was the physical acting of A, involving the co-ordination of A's trained body and brain.  Whether or not a contractual duty requires personal performance by a specific individual can be determined only by interpreting the words used in the light of experience.  In many cases there will be ample room for a difference of opinion.  But whether the performance required is a personal performance or not, the legal duty is not escaped by an assignment or delegation of performance.[38]

It is easy to put striking cases where the performance required is not solely the personal action of the contractor.  A contracts with B that C will not expose a trade secret or that D will play Hamlet.  Here A can neither escape his duty by assignment, delegate performance to a new person, nor satisfy his duty by performing himself.  The contract puts neither C nor D under any duty whatever; but the duty of A can be satisfied only by the silence of C and the acting of D.

If it is impossible for A to assign his duty, how can he get rid of it?  Only by some one of the recognized methods by which a contractual duty is discharged.  Most of these require the assent of the obligee, the party having the right correlative to the duty to be discharged.  One of these methods is called "novation," by which, with the obligee's assent, a substitution of debtors is effected.[39]  This is not assignment.

If it clearly appears from the terms of the assignment transaction that the assignee intends to undertake the duty to perform for the assignor, and that the latter intends to be himself no longer bound, there is a discharge of the assignor by novation if the third party accepts performance by the assignee with knowledge of the terms of the assignment or otherwise assents to those terms.[40]

If the assignor, on making the assignment, manifests an intention to repudiate his own contractual duty, he thereby discharges the other party's duty to render the agreed exchange;

and the assignee gets no right to the performance of that exchange. This is true even though the assignor's duty was one that did not require his personal performance, and even though the assignee expressly promised to perform it.[41] The other party may assent to the substitution and complete a novation; but he need not do so. The only exception to this rule would seem to be a case where the assignee, immediately after the assignment and repudiation by the assignor, can and does tender immediate and full performance in the assignor's place. He can do this if the assignor's only duty was the payment of money or the transfer of title to property by a single act of conveyance without personal warranty.

The assignor cannot by assignment materially change the performance to be rendered by the obligor or the conditions of the obligor's duty to render it. Nor can the assignor escape from his own duty by assignment of it or by delegating its performance. In spite of these limitations on his power, however, he may take comfort in the fact that there are like limitations upon the power of the obligor and the assignee. He remains bound by his original duty, as before the assignment; but the obligor and the assignee cannot without his consent change the performance that he is bound to render or the conditions on which he is bound to render it. This is obviously sound doctrine, although the question has not often arisen and there is little case authority.

This may be illustrated by the case of a bilateral contract for the future sale of goods or land. The buyer can assign his right to the goods or land and can delegate performance of his duty to pay the price.[42] He himself remains bound as before by his duty to pay that price. But observe that he remains bound "as before"; the assignee and the seller cannot, by agreement or by waiver, make it the assignor's duty to pay a different price or on different conditions. If the seller is willing to make such a change, he must trust to the assignee alone. It has been held that, if a tender of delivery by a certain time is a condition precedent to the buyer's duty to pay, the assignee of the buyer has no power to waive this condition, and substantial delay by the seller will prevent his getting judgment against the assignor for the price.[43] If the assignee has contracted to pay the price, his waiver of the condition will be effective in a suit against him, but it will not be allowed to prejudice the position of the assignor, who now occupies substantially the position of surety.

§ 867.  Assignment of Rights under a Bilateral Contract

If the analysis and discussion given in the preceding sections are sound, it is obvious that a contract right is never made non-assignable by the mere fact that it was created by a bilateral contract. It is true that under such a contract, the assignor has duties as well as rights; but the fact that he cannot escape from his duties by assignment or delegation does not cause his rights to be nonassignable.[44] It is true that in many cases the performance required by his duty is a purely personal performance, one that cannot be delegated to any substitute, however competent; this too does not deprive him of the power to assign his rights.

Faulty analysis and inadequate consideration of underlying policy have united to produce some confusion and have resulted in a few unjust decisions and in some often repeated doctrines that ought to be abandoned. One of these doctrines is as follows: "When rights arising out of a contract are coupled with obligations to be performed by the contractor and involve such a relation of personal confidence that it must have been intended that the rights should be exercised and the obligations performed by him alone, the contract, including both his rights and his obligations, cannot be assigned."[45] This statement can be supported if it means that the contractor cannot assign "both his rights and his obligations." It has been taken to mean, however, that he cannot assign *either* his rights or his obligations; when so understood, it must be disapproved.[46]

In a Massachusetts case[47] that repeated the above quotation, the facts were that the owner of a patent granted to the defendant a license to use, make, and sell the patented machines, the licensee promising to use diligence in extending the business and to pay a royalty, and the owner promising to aid and instruct in the manufacture and use, to patent new improvements and license the defendant to use them, and to aid in conducting infringement suits by or against the defendant. Later the owner assigned his patent to the plaintiff company, subject to the license and contract of the defendant, and specifically assigned also his

---

45. **U.S.**—Delaware County Com'rs v. Diebold Safe & Lock Co., 10 S.Ct. 399, 133 U.S. 473, 33 L.Ed. 674 (1890); quoted also in Burck v. Taylor, 14 S.Ct. 696, 152 U.S. 634, 38 L.Ed. 578 (1894).

In Arkansas Valley Smelting Co. v. Belden Min. Co., 8 S.Ct. 1308, 127 U.S. 379, 32 L.Ed. 246 (1888), the court quoted from Pollock on Contracts (see ed. 9, p. 512) as follows: "Rights arising out of contract cannot be transferred if they are coupled with liabilities, or if they involve a relation of personal confidence such that the party whose agreement conferred those rights must have intended them to be exercised only by him in whom he actually confided." See to the same effect Paige v. Faure, 127 N.E. 898, 229 N.Y. 114, 10 A.L.R. 649 (1920).

47. **Mass.**—Paper Products Machine Co. v. Safepack Mills, 131 N.E. 288, 239 Mass. 114 (1921). This case should be considered in connection with the preceding and the following sections. See also Fenn v. Pickwick Corp., 4 P.2d 215, 117 Cal.App. 236 (1931), distinguishing the Safepack Mills case; Sloan v. Williams, 27 N.E. 531, 138 Ill. 43 (1891).

right to all money to become due from the defendant under the license agreement, and all rights and remedies thereunder. The assignee sued for the defendant's breach of contract in failing to use diligence and to pay money due. The court held the declaration to be demurrable. It used the quotation above, and finally said: "It is plain that the right to maintain an action for the breach assigned in the first count is a right which is not separable from the contract; that contract was not assignable, and the plaintiff has no right to an action for the defendant's nonperformance in its own right and name or in the name and right of the licensors. Nor do we think the plaintiff has a standing to maintain its action under the allegations of the second count. The license agreement is still executory, the licensors remaining bound by its terms to personal services during the terms of the existing patents and of the pending applications for patents. We are also of opinion that a contract which involves personal services, and is one of trust and confidence, cannot be assigned in part and abide in the original parties to it in part."

These statements, particularly that in the last sentence, must be disapproved. It amounts to a statement that a contractor cannot assign his rights if he is still under executory duties, at least if those duties require a performance by him that is personal and incapable of delegation. For purposes of assignment, or of delegation of performance, a contractor can separate his rights from his duties. (1) He can assign his rights to another and perform his duties himself; as where a teacher assigns his right to future salary and goes on teaching, or where a builder assigns his right to progress payments and proceeds with the work. (2) He can assign his rights to an assignee, and delegate performance of his duties to the assignee or to a third party if the performance is not of a personal character.[48] (3) He can

---

**48.** The seller of goods can delegate performance to another and assign to him the right to payment. Petroleum Products Co. v. Alton Tank Line, 146 N.W. 52, 165 Iowa 398 (1914).

The buyer of land or goods can assign his right to a conveyance to another and at the same time delegate the payment of the price in cash to the assignee. See Carluccio v. 607 Hudson St. H. Co., 57 A.2d 452, 141 N.J.Eq. 449 (1948), Gulf States Creosoting Co. v. Loving, 120 F.2d 195 (C.C.A.4th, 1941).

**U.S.**—Rockmore v. Lehman, 128 F.2d 564, reversed 129 F.2d 892 (C.C.A.

2d 1942), appears to be an illustration of the text above. In this case, the Circuit Court of Appeals first decided that the assignment of rights to future instalments, for services yet to be rendered was not valid as against the assignor's subsequent trustee in bankruptcy On rehearing, the court correctly reversed its own decision. The services to be rendered seem not to have been "personal"; for they had in part been performed by the assignee. See also Canister Co. v. National Can Corp., 71 F.Supp. 45 (D.C.Del.1947).

retain his rights, and at the same time employ a substitute to render the performance of his duties and conditions precedent.

The case before the court belongs under class (1). It is true that the duties of the defendant, and the assignor's correlative rights, were conditional on the personal performance of the assignor and upon his continued readiness and willingness to perform. But the court did not sustain the demurrer on the ground that such readiness and willingness were not alleged. The assignee's rights were conditional upon the assignor's continued readiness and willingness to perform in person. This is all that is necessary for the obligor's protection. The rule of the American Law Institute is clearly correct: "Rights under a bilateral contract can be assigned as effectively as rights under a unilateral contract, but if rights are conditional on the performance of a return promise, no assignment can extinguish or vary materially the condition." [49]

An attempt by the assignor to assign both his right and his duty under a bilateral contract will sometimes be interpreted as a repudiation of his duty, particularly where the performance required by the duty is personal to the assignor and not possible of delegation. This will prevent any enforcement of the right by the assignee thereof,[50] unless the right is wholly independent of the duty and not conditional upon performance or readiness to perform.

If a promisor in a contract delegates to another the performance of his duty, at the same time clearly indicating that he is himself no longer to be bound, his expressions seem to be a repudiation of the contract. It may appear further, however, that this transaction with the delegated party is intended to be communicated to the promisee in the contract only as an offer of novation, in which case it is no repudiation. If such an offer is assented to by the promisee, either in words or by accepting performance by the delegate with knowledge of the terms on which his performance is offered, there is a novation and the promisor is discharged.[51] In such case, also, there is a new contract between the delegate and the acceptor.

The fact that a party to a bilateral contract makes an assignment of the "contract," purporting thereby not only to transfer his rights to the assignee, but also to appoint the latter as a substitute for the performance of the assignor's duties, is not regarded as a repudiation of the contract. In spite of such an assignment, the assignor remains bound by his duties just as before; and his assignment of the "contract" is no assertion to the contrary.[52]

---

49.    Restatement, Contracts, § 161,
   "Assignment of Rights under a Bilateral Contract."

If the assignor's duty requires a performance of so personal a character as not to permit of a vicarious performance by a substitute, the appointment of such a substitute is ineffective except as an offer of a novation or of an accord executory. It should not be regarded as in itself a repudiation, however; there must be a clear expression that amounts to a refusal to render the promised performance.

## § 868. Assignment does not Affect Performance

The performance, whether action or forbearance, that an obligor is under a duty to render cannot be changed in any material way by assignment of the right by the obligee. It must be admitted that it is some disadvantage to a debtor that his creditor has power to substitute a new creditor without the debtor's consent. It would be a much greater disadvantage, without any particular gain to the community, to give the creditor power to change the performance due from the debtor. If B has a right that A shall serve as his valet, he cannot by assignment make it A's duty to serve C as valet; also, if B has a right that A shall supply his needs for coal he cannot make it A's duty to supply the needs of C.[53]  In like manner, if A owes B a debt of $100 payable at the First National Bank on May 1, B can assign his right to the Second National Bank; but he cannot make it A's duty to pay at the Second Bank or on any other day than May 1. If A sells his stock of hardware, business, and good will to B and promises to forbear from competition for five years, B can assign his right along with the business to C; but he cannot by such assignment make it A's duty to forbear to solicit hardware business in any greater territory than the business covered previously, even though C's business may be more widely extended.

Where a teacher, agent, or other employee has agreed to render personal service under the direction of a particular master or employer, the latter cannot require performance under the direction of a different person, and an attempt to reach that result by an assignment of the right to service must fail.[54]  Likewise, a school that has contracted to give instruction to student A cannot be required to instruct student B.[55]  A can assign his right that he shall be given instruction; but he cannot change the instruction that is to be given the person to be instructed, or the conditions under which it is to be given.

53.  Ga.—Tifton, etc., R. Co. v. Bedgood, 43 S.E. 257, 116 Ga. 945 (1903), R. R. contracted to haul all lumber cut by H. & S.

Ky.—Frankfort & C. R. Co. v. Jackson, 156 S.W. 103, 153 Ky. 534 (1913).

Md.—Crane Ice Cream Co. v. Terminal Freezing Co., 128 A. 280, 147 Md. 588, 39 A.L.R. 1184 (1925), one having a right to all the ice he may use in his business for three years cannot create in an assignee a right to all the ice such assignee may use in its business.

From what has preceded, it has been made to appear that a party to a contract cannot by any process called assignment change in any material way the performance to be rendered by the other party. He has power to substitute a new party as holder of the right; he has no power to change the performance that the right requires. In other sections, also, it has been made to appear that one cannot by assignment change the conditions on which the other party has promised to perform—the limiting facts the non-occurrence of which prevents duty of immediate performance. This is true whether the limiting conditions are prescribed in words or by implication or by construction of law. Special attention is here directed to the application of this rule to aleatory contracts.

If the obligor's duty is aleatory in character—that is, if he has promised to perform only upon the happening of some event that is not certain to occur and that is not within the control of either party—the element that may be described as hazard, chance, or risk, is of special importance. And in such cases an assignment is defeated if the risk of the obligor is materially increased—that is, if the happening of the uncertain event is made more likely. The promisee cannot change the performance to be rendered; and also he must not, in the aleatory case, increase the risk that the performance will have to be rendered. An unjustified act increasing this risk discharges the obligor's duty altogether.

### § 869.  Risk of Nonperformance of the Agreed Exchange must not be Materially Increased

Impossibility of performance of an agreed exchange, or a repudiation of the duty to render it, operates as a discharge of the contractual duty of the other party. Even though not wholly impossible, a material increase in the risk that the agreed exchange will not be performed may justify the other party in requiring further security. Such is the case where a buyer of goods on credit becomes insolvent before delivery. These rules operate against an assignee the same as against the assignor. Therefore, if the assignor, by the act of assignment itself or otherwise, has materially increased the risk that the obligor will not receive his promised exchange, the assignee cannot enforce his claim against the obligor without giving sufficient security.[64]

### § 870.  Effect of Obligor's Assent to an Assignment

The effectiveness of an assignment does not depend upon the assent of the obligor. If in other respects the assignment is good, his duty is now a duty to the assignee; to this extent the obligor has no delectus personae, however unwilling he may have been to contract with the particular assignee. When notice of assignment is given to the obligor, it is not necessary that he should promise the assignee that he will perform. If the assignment is in the form of an order, the obligor is bound without giving his "acceptance" of the order.[72]

Even in the case of a partial assignment, assent of the obligor is not necessary, except for the purpose of maintaining a separate suit against him.[73] And, to attain that purpose, his assent must clearly include the severance of the part from the rest of the claim. A mere acknowledgment of receipt of notice of a partial assignment works no such severance.

The case is quite different if the so-called "assignment" purports to be more than the mere transfer of the assignor's right. If by its terms it purports to make a material change in the performance to be rendered by the obligor, his assent is necessary. If the original transaction between the assignor and the obligor is still bilateral in character, with reciprocal rights and duties, either party has power to assign his rights without the assent of the other; but he has no such power to substitute a new duty-bearer in his place. An assignment proposing such a substitution is an offer of a novation, and assent is necessary.

When notice of an assignment of a contract right is given to the obligor, he may or may not express assent thereto. If the case is one in which the obligee had a power of assignment, the assent of the obligor is entirely unnecessary. In many of the older cases in which it is said that the assignee cannot maintain suit unless the obligor assents to the assignment, the court is merely carrying out the old fiction of non-assignability;[74] what is meant is no more than that the assignee must sue in the assignor's name unless the obligor has assented to the substitution. The assent is no longer necessary even for that purpose.

Likewise, when there is a delegation of performance by the assignor, either in discharge of his own reciprocal duty or in performance of some condition precedent, the obligor may or may not express his assent to such delegation. If the performance in question is not of such a character as to be personal to the assignor, the assent of the obligor is again entirely unnecessary. So, if A has a contract to sell 100 tons of coal to B, A can assign to C his right to the price and can delegate to C (or to D) the delivery of the coal, the assent of B being entirely unnecessary with respect to both the assignment and the delegation.

But there are rights that are not assignable because of a prohibition in the terms of the contract. Such a prohibition is for the benefit of the obligor; and he has power to annul it. His assent to an assignment operates as an annulment; after the assignment has been made or other material change of position in reliance upon the assent has been made by the assignor or assignee, there can be no retraction of the expression of assent.

Also, there are cases in which the assignor has no power to delegate the performance of his own duty or of some condition precedent to the obligor's duty; in these cases the assent of the obligor to the proposed delegation is necessary in order to make the substituted performance effective.[75]

It is to be observed, therefore, that an expression of assent by the obligor may have any of the following effects: (1) it may be nothing more than an assent to be himself bound to the assignee, the new holder of the right to his performance; (2) it may be an assent to receive a substituted return performance, in accordance with a proposed delegation by the assignor; (3) it may be an assent to a novation, immediately discharging the assignor. In any particular case, whether the assent is one or another of these is a question of interpretation of the expressions of the two parties.

## § 871.  Effect of Contracting With a Party "and His Assigns"

Many contracts are to be found in which a party purports in express words to contract with the other party "and his assigns," or with the other party and "his executors, administrators, and assigns." The meaning and legal operation of such an expression cannot be determined or stated without knowing the context and the surrounding circumstances. It is highly probable that in many cases the words are inserted without any definite idea as to their meaning or operation, the parties having a vague idea that they are thereby making themselves more secure, on the analogy of a deed of conveyance to a man "and his heirs." In other cases, however, the context and surrounding facts may indicate a definite meaning, and may determine the legal operation.

If A promises to render a specified performance to B and his assigns, the form of the promise indicates an intention that B shall have power to assign his right.[79] If such is the sole purpose, the addition of the phrase is of no effect in the great majority of cases, for B's right has become assignable without A's assent by statute and judicial action. If in a building contract it is provided that the builder may "sublet and assign" portions of the work, the words indicate that he may delegate performance of those portions, so that performance by the delegate will discharge pro tanto the builder's duty and will also fulfil a condition of his right to the compensation. The inclusion of the phrase "and his assigns," without specifying its application to promisor or to promisee, to rights or to duties, should generally tend in the direction that performance is delegable and not personal.[80] It should seldom, if ever, be held to mean that a party is intended to have power to substitute another party as obligor in place of himself, that is, to assign his duty.[81]

## § 872. Contract Provisions Forbidding Assignment

It is frequently expressly agreed by the contracting parties that the "contract" shall not be assignable at all, or shall not be assignable by one party without the assent of the other. Such a provision must first be interpreted to determine how the parties intended it to apply to the facts of the case; after such interpretation there remains a question of validity and legal effect.

The parties themselves seldom analyze their concept of "contract"; so that a provision against assignment is of varying inclusion, in accordance with the nature of the transaction and the number and kind of the legal relations created. Ordinarily, the provision is made applicable against only one of the parties and in favor of the other; but even so, it may not be intended to deprive that one party of his power to assign all of his legal relations. Even though the parties may not have been conscious of the distinction between the assignment of a right and the delegation of performance of a duty, it may be perfectly clear that the limitation of power referred to one of these and not to the other. Thus if a building contract provides that the builder shall not assign the contract, it is almost certain that the parties intend that he shall not delegate supervision of the work wholly to another, and leave the job himself. In the absence of very apt words to the contrary, they do not intend that the builder shall not assign his right to instalments of the price as they fall due.[85] It may be of great importance to have the personal supervision of the builder; but it is of much less importance to whose hands the money is to be paid. If the owner desired to deprive the builder of the power to assign his right to the money, he would have said that the builder's right to the money shall not be assigned,[86] not that the builder shall not assign the "contract." Had the personality of the receiver of the money been deemed important to the owner, that fact would have caused him to use words that would clearly differentiate the right to the money from the duty of supervision.[87]

When a contract contains express words forbidding one party to assign the contract, usually more is intended than that he shall not repudiate his duty by assigning it to another and escaping; it indicates that his duty is one that he cannot perform vicariously by delegating the performance to another.[89] Such a provision makes the party's reciprocal right to compensation dependent and conditional on his own personal performance of the agreed ex-

---

87.     But in City of Omaha v. Standard Oil Co., 75 N.W. 859, 55 Neb. 337 (1898), the court gave old-fashioned weight to the importance of the identity of the party to receive payment of money. It said that where "assignment of the contract" is prohibited it would be a "perversion of terms" to restrict its application to the delegation of performance of duties.

change;  but it does not make his right to compensation non-assignable, either before or after he has performed the condition.[90]

## § 873.    Validity and Effect of a Provision Forbidding Assignment

A shift, from the doctrine that a "chose in action" is of such a nature that it cannot be assigned and that an attempt to assign it as a subject of sale is illegal because involving maintenance, to the doctrine that a provision in a contract forbidding the assignment of rights is invalid because it involves an improper restraint on the alienation of property, marks a great change in the climate of judicial opinion.   Such a shift, however, has to some extent occurred.   It cannot be said that the new doctrine is yet established; nor should it be predicted as yet that it will be established.

In one case, however, the United States Supreme Court has said that a prohibition against assignment, contained in a written contract for building construction, was ineffective, likening the contract right to personal chattels.[94]   Limitations on the alienability of goods and chattels are certainly not to be favored;  but a contract right is in many respects not analogous.   According to expressions used by the court, not only are existing contract rights not inalienable;  they cannot be made inalienable *ab initio* by the party who is their original creator.   It should be observed, however, that in this case the obligor did not insist upon his immunity, and paid the money into court.   The prohibition was solely for his protection, not that of third parties.

It has been held that a provision in a contract of employment that the employee should not assign his right to wages, and that an attempt to assign should be null and void, is itself contrary to law and is ineffective even against an assignee who had notice.[95]   The decision is not well sustained in the opinion, either by the court's analysis of jural relations, or by its citation of authorities; and its assertion that public policy need not be considered cannot be accepted.

The fact that the courts have long recognized that the holder of a right to wages has the power of assignment is not in itself proof that the creators of the right cannot by agreement prevent its being accompanied by such a power.   The fact that the law ordinarily gives to a creditor the "privilege" or "liberty" to assign his

---

94.    **U.S.** — Portuguese - American Bank v. Welles, 37 S.Ct. 3, 242 U. S. 7, 61 L.Ed. 116, Ann.Cas.1918D, 643 (1916).   See criticism of this case in 26 Yale L.J. 304.

See also Martin v. Nat'l Surety Co., 57 S.Ct. 531, 300 U.S. 588, 81 L.

Ed. 822 (1937), holding that a statutory prohibition of assignment was for the benefit of the State only, and that, as between an assignee and a subsequent assignee with notice, money paid by the State to the latter is held in trust for the former.

right, does not prove that he cannot by contract deny himself that "privilege" or "liberty." No proof lies in the fact that the court calls the power or the privilege of assignment a "property right." The right to wages is a contract right. For various purposes the courts have described contract rights as "property"; this commonly, but not necessarily, includes the power to transfer.

There is no sufficient analogy between chattels and "choses in action" on which to rest the conclusion that contract rights, once inalienable at common law, must now of necessity be alienable even though the contract by which they are created says that they are not. In all cases, assignees are held to take the assigned right with all its native weaknesses and subject to many defenses. Alienability is desirable, and it has been accomplished; but care has been taken to protect the obligor, in ways that are not applicable in the law of chattels. The sale of a chattel habitually involves only two specific persons; the assignment of a right always involves three.

There is nothing wrong, however, in the court's making new law, if it is good law in accord with existing mores and the public interest. This is true even though the court is unaware that its law is new. In the present case, however, the court gives no facts that evidence the public interest. The weight of previous judicial decision has been to the contrary; and an investigation of the conditions in Chicago, that led the employer to insert the provision against assignment, tends strongly to indicate that it would operate to the advantage of both the employer and the employee.[96]

There are statutes in most of the states limiting or regulating the power of assignment of wages and the mode of exercising it.[97]

Provisions forbidding assignment of his right to payment by a building contractor,[3] and by a contractor to supply street lighting,[4] have been held effective; and the assignee of a non-assignable bill of lading has been denied a remedy.[5] A salesman's right to payment of commissions has been made non-assignable.[6] No one doubts that railway passenger tickets can be made non-assignable;[7] but they may be regarded as exceptional in that assignment by the holder involves a different performance by the carrier—that is, it must carry a different person. A rule made by a savings bank that payments would be made only to the depositor in person was held not to prevent an assignee of the entire deposit, presenting the pass book also, from maintaining suit;[8] the rule might have been held effective as to partial withdrawals. Where a contract provided that no assignment of the right to payment should be valid without the assent of the contractor's surety, the right of an assignee without such assent was held inferior to that of the surety.[9]

---

96.    See Fortas, "Wage Assignments in Chicago," 42 Yale L. J. 526 (1933).

As has been stated in a previous section, the question of validity of a provision against assignment is quite apart from the question of interpretation of such a provision.  General words against assigning the "contract" should not readily be interpreted to mean that rights created by the contract shall not be assignable.  More frequently they are meant to require the personal performance of duty—to prevent delegation of performance.  Such a provision makes a contract right conditional on personal performance of the exchanged consideration, and it remains thus conditional after an assignment; but it does not invalidate the assignment.[12]  If, however, reasonable interpretation shows an intent to make the right itself non-assignable, there should be no hesitation in giving the intended effect.[13]

A provision forbidding one party to make an assignment of his right is solely for the advantage of the other party who is under the correlative duty.  That other party can waive the benefit of the provision, either before or after an assignment has been made.  A mere expression of willingness, made to either the assignor or the assignee, acted on by them, makes the assignment effective.  And such an expression made to the assignee when he presents his claim, or brings suit on it, is likewise effective.[20]  Third parties cannot, in such case, maintain the invalidity of the assignment.

So, too, the assignor is in no position to assert the invalidity of the assignment, even though the debtor might do so.[21]  If he collects the money and then refuses to pay it over to the assignee, he is certainly guilty of breach of contract, if not of breach of trust and conversion.[22]  Even though the prohibited assignment is held inoperative to create any enforceable right in the assignee that the obligor shall pay the assignee, the assignment transaction may be operative as between the assignor and the assignee, making it the duty of the former to hold in trust any amount that he receives from the obligor.[23]  Likewise, an assignee is entitled to money paid by the obligor to a subsequent assignee with notice.[24]

20.   U.S. — Portuguese - American Bank v. Welles, 37 S.Ct. 3, 242 U.S. 7, 61 L.Ed. 116, Ann.Cas.1918D, 643 (1916), can be rested on this ground.

# CHAPTER 49

## ASSIGNMENT OF VARIOUS KINDS OF RIGHTS—MODES OF ASSIGNMENT

## § 874. Assignment of Future and Conditional Rights

Many courts have seemed to think that the effectiveness of an assignment of future contract rights depends upon whether or not they have a "potential existence" at the time of the assignment. Supposed analogies are drawn with the wool to be grown on the backs of sheep already alive and with the fruit of an existing orchard to be harvested over a period of years.[1] Such physical analogies as these are of little service; instead, they divert the attention from the real issue. In the assignment cases, the real problem is one of public policy, not one of potential existence. The real questions are: (1) to what extent should an assignee of future rights be preferred over other later assignees and creditors; and (2) to what extent should an individual have power to anticipate his own future income. These questions can not safely be answered dogmatically; they have not been subjected to enough conscious scrutiny in the light of collected experience. As to the second, it may be suggested that, while a blanket assignment of all future earnings would seem to reduce the assignor to a state of near-slavery or peonage,[2] there seems to be no limit upon his

2. See Porte v. Chicago & N. W. R. Co., 156 N.W. 469, 162 Wis. 446 (1916).
Such an alleged danger as this may be merely fanciful in case the assignment is given for ample new consideration. It may be that by means of the assignment the assignor obtains new credit and resources that will enable him to create new

power to incur unlimited contractual obligations. The latter, however, are rendered ineffective in some degree by exemption laws; and the bankruptcy laws afford means of escape. Certain assignments of non-existent future rights, even though ineffective as against later assignees and creditors, have been held to be effective against the assignor himself as creating a contractual obligation to make an effective assignment after the rights are born.[3] No doubt there are limits beyond which the courts would refuse to go, and beyond which the assignment of future rights would be held utterly ineffective.[4]

The first of the two questions has already been given a reasonably definite answer by the courts, in spite of the fact that it has been envisioned rather as a question of "potential existence" than as one of public policy. The policy aspect is always in the background and given decisive weight even though not given expression. After a contract has been made, rights created by it are assignable, even though the promised performance is deferred to some definite or indefinite future date, or the duty to render it is subject to some condition precedent.[5]

Thus, no one doubts that the right to payment of a unilateral money debt is assignable, even though its maturity is long deferred.[6] If a man gives consideration for a promise that a sum of money shall be paid if A survives B, or shall be paid if cotton rises to twenty cents a pound by Christmas, the right is assignable; it is not made non-assignable by the fact that the promise is aleatory, the promisee having no control over the happening of the condition.[7] Again, if a building contractor makes a contract whereby he has a right to payment of various sums in instalments as the work progresses, his right to these payments is assignable although the work has not yet been done and the money is not yet due.[8] His right is not made non-assignable by the fact that the owner's duty to pay is conditional upon substantial performance by the builder or upon the certificate of an architect that the work has been properly done. In these cases, the assignee's right is subject to the same conditions as was that of the assignor; but he is not defeated by the mere fact that the assignor makes a second assignment after the money has become due or that other creditors have made advances to the builder in ignorance of

income and new economic power. Matters like this should certainly be considered and weighed before holding that an assignment is void for reasons of public policy. It would not be unreasonable to distinguish between the assignment of future wages by an employee and

the assignment of future accounts by a merchant.

3.    See:

Me.—Edwards v. Peterson, 14 A. 936, 80 Me. 367 (1888).

N.Y.—Field v. Mayor, etc., of City of New York, 6 N.Y. 179, 57 Am.Dec. 435 (1852).

the assignment and in the belief that they could attach the money to be earned.[9]

An assignment of an existing debt is not invalidated by the fact that the debt is not yet due; but the contract or other transaction creating the debt must have taken place. So a blanket assignment by a merchant of all his book accounts present and future, whether given as security for a loan or as an outright sale of the accounts, is not effective, as against other creditors of the assignor, with respect to money due by reason of transactions that are wholly subsequent to the assignment.[10] Such blanket assignments may no doubt be a very useful means of financing a business and preserving the value of a going concern in times of difficulty; but they may also be used in fraud of other creditors.[11] Very likely they can be made serviceable and safe by statutory regulation similar to that with respect to conditional sales and chattel mortgages.

Assignments of existing and future book accounts may also be invalidated as a fraud on creditors by reason of leaving entire control over them in the assignor. It was so held in a case where the assignor was given the privilege of collecting the accounts and of reinvesting the proceeds as he desired, without substituting any other security in their place.[12] It was so held where a company made an assignment of its accounts receivable to a bank as security for a loan, the agreement being that the company should collect the amounts due and deposit them to its own credit in the bank, where they would still be subject to its own check. The bank had the power to apply the deposit at any time in reduction of the loan; but this did not validate the assignment as against creditors of the assignor after its insolvency.[13]

It has long been established, also, that an employee has power to assign his right to future wages, to become due only after performance of services not yet rendered; and this is true even though there is no enforceable contract binding him to render the service or binding the employer to keep him employed.[14] It is sufficient that at the date of the assignment there is an existing

---

9.    **U.S.**—Rockmore v. Lehman, 129 F.2d 892 (C.C.A.2d, 1942), reversing on rehearing the court's own former decision in 128 F.2d 564; In re Talbot Canning Corp., 35 F.Supp. 680 (D.C.Md.1940).

12.    **U.S.**—Benedict v. Ratner, 45 S. Ct. 566, 268 U.S. 353, 69 L.Ed. 991 (1925), reviewing New York cases and applying the applicable New York statutes as to fraudulent transfers. This case is discussed

again in a subsequent section. It seems directly contra to Union Trust Co. v. Bulkeley, 150 F. 510 (C.C.A.6th, 1907). It is very intelligently distinguished by Hincks, J., in In re New York, N. H. & H. R. Co., 25 F.Supp. 874 (D.C.Conn. 1938). From the early drafts of the Uniform Commercial Code it appears likely that the doctrine of Benedict v. Ratner will be abandoned.

employment, an existing relation of master and servant, under which the wages assigned may reasonably be expected to be earned, and which is notice to other assignees and creditors that an assignment of such future wages may have been made.[15] But if the assignment purports to include a right to compensation for services yet to be rendered under a contract not yet made and in an employment not yet formed, it will be held ineffective as against subsequent assignees for value and subsequent attaching creditors.[16]

It is thus that the hazards of giving credit to an individual are restricted so as not to include those of antecedent blanket assignments or of assignments looking far into the future and anticipating the earnings and receipts of transactions both distant and uncertain.

A present assignment of rights under a contract or employment that does not yet exist, may, as between the assignor and the assignee, be regarded as a binding contract to assign in the future when the operative facts creating the right shall have occurred.[17] When those facts have occurred, there being no intervening creditors or assignees, the premature assignment becomes an effective assignment. There are some cases holding that the premature assignment is effective, even as against subsequent creditors and assignees, if it has been recorded as provided by statute, so that there is constructive notice to all concerned.[18] It has also been held that an assignment by a building contractor to his surety of all deferred payments and retained percentages is valid, as against a subsequent attaching creditor of the contractor, even though the assignment transaction was antecedent to the execution of the building contract.[19] A reason for this holding was that the assignment, the building contract, and the surety bond were all parts of one large transaction. Another reason for the decision might have been that the surety should have had preference, without any assignment, because of subrogation to the rights of laborers and materialmen, whose rights were superior to that of the attaching creditor by the terms of the building contract itself, and whose claims the surety had paid.

## § 875. Conditional Assignments

Conditional rights and duties have not been well understood, with resulting confusion in decisions.[20] Full explanation of them

17.    **U.S.**—Union Trust Co. v. Bulkeley, 150 F. 510 (C.C.A.6th, 1907) [but see Benedict v. Ratner, 45 S.Ct. 566, 268 U.S. 353, 69 L.Ed. 991 (1925)].

**Mich.**—Preston N. Bank v. Geo. T. Smith M. P. Co., 47 N.W. 502, 84 Mich. 364 (1890).

**N.Y.**—Field v. Mayor, etc., of New York, 6 N.Y. 179, 57 Am.Dec. 435 (1852).

20.    See §§ 247–251, Conditional delivery in escrow; and § 589. Conditional contracts and the parol evidence rule.

must be sought in another chapter.[21] At this point, attention is called to the fact that the right of the assignee may be a conditional right because the assignor's right is itself conditional, or because the assignment is itself a conditional assignment although the assignor's right is wholly unconditional. Thus, firstly, a building contractor's right to a future payment is conditional upon his substantial performance and, it may be, upon an architect's certificate of approval. This fact does not prevent an effective present assignment; it merely causes the assignee's right to be conditional exactly as is that of the contractor before the assignment. Also, it does not affect the date of the assignee's priority in relation to other assignees and attaching creditors.[22] Secondly, the building contractor may assign his right to payment to a bank as security for a loan, conditional upon the non-payment of the loan by a certain day. This assignment makes the right of the bank subject to an additional condition, the condition of non-payment of the loan, a condition to which the builder's own right was not conditional.[23] Again, this assignment is an effective present assignment, its priority being determined by its date, not by the happening of the condition.[24]

In a recent case, a builder gave to his surety an assignment of all "deferred payments and retained percentages and all moneys that may be due and payable at the time of any breach." He later borrowed money of a bank, and gave it another assignment of all moneys to become payable under the contract. The court gave preference to the bank on the ground that its assignment was "unconditional," whereas that of the surety was conditional on a future breach by the contractor. "The assignment to the bank, being absolute, had attached and was operative against said funds before the assignment to the bonding company became effective." [25] This reasoning is not to be sustained, even though the decision may be.

---

21. See Chapter 30, Conditions.

22. **U.S.**—Rockmore v. Lehman, 129 F.2d 892 (C.C.A.2d, 1942), reversing on rehearing the court's own former decision in 128 F.2d 564 (C.C.A. 2d).

Tex.—O'Neil Engineering Co. v. First N. Bank of Paris, 222 S.W. 1091 (Tex.Com.App.1920).

23. An assignment as security is of this kind, the assignee's right being conditional upon non-performance of the obligation that it is given to secure. If the right that is assigned is itself a right to immediate performance, while the obligation secured is not yet one requiring immediate performance, the assignee may enforce the assigned right and hold the proceeds in trust for the specified purpose, unless the assignor has limited the assignment otherwise.

24. **U.S.**—In re Allied Products Co., 134 F.2d 725 (C.C.A.6th, 1943).

25. **Iowa**—Coon River Co-op. Sand Ass'n v. McDougall Const. Co., 244 N.W. 847, 215 Iowa 861 (1932).

What does the court mean by "had attached" and "became effective"? In one respect the claims of the two assignees were alike conditional; both were conditional upon such performance of the contract as to create in the builder a right to a payment. His right being conditional, it is a certainty that neither assignee had an unconditional one. In addition, the surety's right to moneys to become due was conditional upon some breach by the builder. This was so provided because the surety's own duty to the employing owner was itself conditional on the builder's breach. But it no more prevented the assignment from being a present and effective assignment, than did the fact that the bank's right was conditional on the builder's performance of his contract. Both assignments were given as security.[26] Both were conditional on substantial performance of the contract, because without that no money would ever be payable. Both, likewise, were conditional upon a non-performance by the builder, although not the same one; the surety's right was conditional upon breach of the builder's contractual duty to the owner, and the bank's right was conditional upon the builder's non-payment of the loans for which the assignment was a security. The fact that this condition of the surety's right was in express terms and that the condition of the bank's right was merely necessarily implied is not material for the present purpose. The priority of the two assignees, with respect to each other or to third parties, is not dependent upon the date of the happening of a condition.

It must be observed, however, that no conditional right becomes immediately enforceable unless the condition occurs. This may be found to justify the decision in favor of the bank, even though its assignment was the later one in time. If the conditions precedent to the bank's right occurred, and some condition precedent to the surety's right did not and can not occur, then the money belongs to the bank. It is evident that the surety did not wish to prevent the builder from getting the instalment payments upon which a builder normally depends to enable him to carry on. As long as no breach by him should occur, no instalment falling due would belong to the surety; and having then been collected by the builder, the surety would never have any right thereto.

In the instant case, the money in dispute was such an instalment. It had become payable before any breach by the builder; and the owner had issued a warrant for the amount to the assignee bank. This was proper procedure by the owner, even though he was aware of the surety's earlier assignment. The owner would have been justified in paying the builder, so far as the surety was concerned; and he was equally justified in paying the assignee whose loan had enabled the builder to use the payment by anticipation. The money was then due to the assignee and not to the builder. The surety's assignment meant to include

829

all moneys that should be due and payable *to the builder* at the time of breach; and this instalment was not so payable. A condition precedent to the surety's right to it did not and never could occur. On this ground the decision of the court can be approved. But all "deferred payments and retained percentages" belong to the surety and not to the bank, in spite of the conditional character of the surety's assignment, unless there are other and independent reasons to the contrary.

## § 876.  Conditional Assignments of Rights to a Series of Future Payments

Assignments are often made of a series of claims to future payments, such claims to become mature and payable on a series of dates in the future. There is nothing illegal or improper in such an assignment. An illustration of this is an assignment by a lessor of his right to future rents to become due monthly. Such assignments have been made as security for a loan or in other credit transactions. Furthermore, the fact that the assignment is itself expressly made conditional on the assignor's default as to principal or interest on the loan does not invalidate the assignment.[28]

Where, as in the case of monthly rents, sums of money are to become due periodically, it is quite possible for the claimant to assign his rights separately, the right to the May rent to one assignee and the right to the June rent to another. It is possible also to assign these successively accruing rights to a single assignee, making each assignment conditional on the assignor's default on the loan that the assignment is given to secure. If, when the May rent falls due, there has been no default on the loan, the May rent is not payable to the assignee, because the condition (the default) precedent to his right has not occurred. The May rent is due to the assignor just as if there had been no assignment at all. After a default has occurred, however, all subsequently accruing rentals under the leasehold that are included within the assignment are now payable to the assignee.[29]

It should be observed that the above discussion is not dealing with a general assignment of book accounts not yet in existence or of other claims to arise in the future out of employment that does not yet exist. Such assignments have been thought to be in fraud of the assignor's other creditors.[30] There is no such fraud in the present instance. The rentals that fall due before the default (or other condition precedent) occurs belong to the assignor

28.   **U.S.**—In re New York, N. H. & H. R. Co., 25 F.Supp. 874 (D.C. Conn.1938).

30.   **U.S.**—Benedict v. Ratner, 45

S.Ct. 566, 268 U.S. 353, 69 L.Ed. 991 (1924).

**Mass.**—Taylor v. Barton-Child Co., 117 N.E. 43, 228 Mass. 126 (1917).

Restatement, Contracts, § 154(2).

and are subject to attachment by his other creditors. The rentals that fall due after the default belong to the assignee and are not subject to attachment by the assignor's creditors. In this respect they are no different from other effective assignments.[31]

It should be obvious from what has just been said that an assignment of future instalments of rent (or of moneys due in other kinds of transaction) that may fall due after a default by the assignor in his duty to the assignee is not an attempt to assign his rights and at the same time to retain "dominion" over them or the "jus disponendi." No inherent contradiction or inconsistency is involved; the assignor is making no attempt to have his cake and eat it too. His rights to payments to be made prior to a specified future event he does not assign at all; his rights to payments accruing thereafter he assigns without any reservation whatever.

As much cannot be said, however, of the following transaction: Suppose that one doing a continuing business should make what purports to be a present and unconditional assignment of his book accounts, at the same time being expressly authorized by the assignee to collect the accounts himself and to use the proceeds in the business until notice to the contrary from the assignee. This certainly involves the retention by the assignor of something that may be called "dominion" or "jus disponendi." At the same time the assignee has the power, merely by giving notice to the assignor, to terminate that "dominion." Such a transaction as this, unknown to the public or to the assignor's other creditors, or even to the customers whose debts to the assignor are involved, may well seem to be unfair to the assignor's other creditors and

---

31. An excellent example of a conditional assignment of a conditional right is found in In re New York, N. H. & H. R. Co., 25 F. Supp. 874 (D.C.Conn.1938). The Railroad had a right to the payment of certain sums by a realty company, conditional on the accrual of a new income from certain property. As security for a loan made by the R. F. C., the Railroad assigned its right against the realty company, it being "expressly understood and agreed by the corporation (the R. F. C.) by the acceptance of this assignment, that so long as the New Haven R. Company shall not be in default in respect of said loan, the New Haven Company may collect, receive and retain all moneys due and to become due under said agreements [with the realty company]." Thus, the right of the assignee against the realty company, the obligor, was conditional on default by the assignor on the loan for which the assignment was security. Indeed, all moneys that became due from the obligor, and were collected by the assignor before any default by it on the loan, escaped wholly from the coverage of the assignment. Only such sums as were not collected by the assignor prior to its default on the loan were effectively assigned. Of course, it could not be told in advance what sums these would be. In an excellently reasoned opinion, Judge Hincks held that the assignment was valid in exact accordance with its terms.

contrary to general welfare.  Even though others are well aware
of the possibility that rights have been assigned, they have little
reason to suspect such an assignment as this.  The assignor still
has his business as a going concern, giving to him an appearance
of having assets that justify giving him credit, among these assets
being the very book accounts that have been secretly made subject to the will of the assignee.  The weight of this argument is
the greater as the proportion of the assets covered by the assignment increases; it is especially weighty if the assignment covers
all future book accounts as well as those now on the books.  It
is for these reasons that a number of the existing decisions can
be supported.[32]

### § 877.  Promises to Make an Assignment, or to Pay Over a Fund When Collected

If the holder of a contract right makes a promise for a sufficient
consideration to assign it to another, what is the legal operation
of the transaction?  Beyond question such a promise is a valid
contract if there is no legal impediment to the assignment of such
a right as that involved.  There would be a legally enforceable
duty to the promisee to perform in accordance with the promise as
in the case of any other contract.[38]  But how does such a promise
to assign affect the legal relations of the obligor (the debtor) to
the assignor and the assignee?  It is quite impossible to answer
this question in one general statement, because the term "promise
to assign" has several distinct meanings.

In some cases the "promise to assign" has been held to be itself a completed assignment, extinguishing the right of the assignor against the debtor and creating a similar right in the
promisee.  In such cases the "promise to assign" is self-executing
and makes the "promisee" in fact an assignee.  Such a holding
is quite correct if the words and conduct accompanying the "promise to assign" express an intention to convey the right immediately.  That the assignor's words are in promissory form is not
conclusive to the contrary.  It is clear that such an intention may
exist and may be expressed, even though the parties contemplate
the subsequent execution of a documentary assignment.  In such
case the document is to be a mere memorial of an already operative transaction and is not itself to be the operative assignment.[39]

Even though a promise to assign in the future is held not to be a
present assignment or to create any right in the promisee against
the obligor, it is possible to hold that as against the promisor himself it is a promise to treat the contract right and the fund when
collected as a trust fund, and to give to the promisee a preference
with respect to it over the promisor's personal representative [40]
and his general creditors.[41]  It is not easy to see why this is not
a preference of one promisee whose claim is based on a mere contract no better than that of general creditors, unless the promise

to assign is so far a self-executing assignment as to create in the assignee a right against the obligor. It seems clear that the claim of a subsequent assignee for value and without notice should be preferred to that of such a promisee.[42]

On the other hand a promise that the promisor will on his own behalf collect the money due him and thereafter pay that specific money over to the promisee is not an assignment.[43] The promisor's right against the debtor is not thereby extinguished and payment by the debtor to the promisee would not operate as a discharge;[44] nor is a right against the debtor created in the promisee. Such a promise is a promise to collect and to pay out of the proceeds. Words of present assignment, however, are not made inoperative as a present assignment by the fact that the assignor at the same time promises to collect the money due as an agent of the assignee and to pay it over to him.[45]

For an effective assignment it is necessary that the right assigned shall be clearly identified.[48] A promise to assign book accounts as security is not operative as a present assignment if the accounts are not clearly indicated and the terms of the assignment are left to future agreement or if the parties understand that the promisor is to be privileged to collect the accounts and use the money in his own affairs.[49] In such a case there is great probability that the agreement is too uncertain in subject matter or terms to be regarded even as a valid contract between the promisor and the promisee.

A promise to pay to the promisee a sum of money to be received from a third person is not an assignment to the promisee. So, also, a promise to apply money received from the promisee (or due to him) in payment of a debt due to a third party is not an assignment to the third party;[50] it is merely a contract of which he is the creditor beneficiary.

A direction by a principal to his agent that the latter shall pay money then in his hands, or to be collected by him, to some specified third person is not an assignment;[51] but it is quite consistent with an order on the agent delivered to the third person and operative as an assignment, and it may be accompanied by other expressions that taken as a whole are so operative.[52]

---

42. Restatement, Contracts, § 166 (1), reads as follows: "A contract to assign a right in the future is not an assignment. But a contract to assign as security a right which is specified and capable of effective present assignment under §§ 151, 154, gives the promisee a right against the obligor inferior to that of an assignee only in that the right will be extinguished if, before satisfaction is obtained by the promisee, an assignment of the obligee's right is made to a bona fide purchaser for value without notice of the prior contract."

52. § 878. Assignment of Powers and Privileges, is here omitted.

## § 879. What Constitutes an Effective Assignment—Oral Assignments and Orders

There is no required form in which an assignment for value must be made; all that is necessary is for the assignor so to express himself as to indicate an intention then and there to transfer his right to the assignee.[57] This he may do, by any communication to the assignee or to some one as his representative, either orally, or by a writing sealed or unsealed, or by some combination of expressions.[58] The most obvious form of assignment is a writing signed by the assignor and delivered to the assignee, stating that the assignor assigns to the assignee his right against a third person. This right must be described so as to be identifiable and the third person who is under the correlative duty must be identifiable. Assignment is the transfer of an already existing subject matter; and that subject matter must be specific and must be identified. This does not mean, however, that any greater degree of definiteness is required than in the conveyances of other kinds of property.

Gift assignments are discussed in another section. The existence of the element of consideration, or of an obligation to be secured, is a strongly evidential factor in proving intention to assign. This factor is missing in gift assignments; and therefore other evidential factors must exist in its place.

An assignment may be fully effective as between the assignor and assignee without any notice to the obligor; and it is effective as to the obligor too so long as there is no change of position on his part due to his lack of such notice.[59] An insurance policy has been assigned by a written statement to that effect filed with the insurance company and nothing but a later oral notice to the assignee;[60] also by a signed statement delivered to the assignee, even though not a compliance with provisions in the policy.[61]

A contract right that is evidenced by some written document executed by the obligor can be assigned by indorsement and delivery of the document,[68] or by delivery, without indorsement, accompanied by words expressing intention to assign.[69]

The sale of specific goods, by one who had previously bought them with a warranty or other promise by the seller, is not in itself operative as an assignment to the buyer of the seller's rights against the previous seller on his warranty or other promise. There must be some expression of an intention to assign the contract right along with the goods.[73] Parol testimony of such an expression should always be admissible. If the owner of a business, to whom a previous party had made a promise not to compete, sells it with no mention of such restraining promise, the buyer is not an assignee of the contract right.

## § 880. When an Order on the Debtor is an Assignment

It is now the established rule that an ordinary draft or check, whether negotiable or non-negotiable, is not an assignment of rights against the drawee, in part or in whole.[74]  This is because it is regarded as an order on the drawee to charge the amount against the general credit of the drawer.  It is not the custom of either the drawer or the payee of the draft to regard it as a transfer of a right; in most cases they do not consider the legal effects of their transaction.  The drawer of the draft has power to control those legal effects, however, by modifying the form of the transaction.  He can put the draft in the form of a non-negotiable assignment if he desires.  Moreover, he can draw a negotiable draft or check and at the same time accompany it by an oral statement or a written memorandum that will make the whole transaction operate as an assignment.[75]

The owner of a right can make an effective assignment of it by delivering to the assignee or to the obligor a written order that the latter shall pay the assignee;[76] but it must be an order that directs the obligor to extinguish the specific debt, or other duty owed by him, by rendering performance to the party named in the order.  It must not be an order to pay and to charge against the general credit of the drawer.[77]  Just as in the case of a negotiable draft, a non-negotiable order may not purport to be the transfer of a specific right; it, too, may be drawn against general credit.  If so, it is not itself operative as an assignment; but, here, too, other expressions by the drawer of the order may show that a present assignment of a specific right is intended, making the whole transaction an effective assignment.[78]

An agreement made between a debtor and his creditor that instead of paying the creditor the debtor shall pay a third person to whom the creditor himself is indebted, is not operative as an assignment.  The third person may have an enforceable right by virtue of this agreement, but if so, it is a right as a creditor beneficiary, and not as an assignee.  An assignment is a transaction between a creditor and the assignee.  In the case just stated, the transaction is an agreement between the debtor and creditor.  The former requires no assent by the debtor; the latter, in order to be operative, requires his assent and promise.[80]

## § 881. Assignments as Security

Assignments are frequently given as a collateral security only.[82]  In such case, the assignee's right against the obligor is conditional

---

**82.**   See:

**U.S.**—Rockmore v. Lehman, 129 F.2d 892 (C.C.A.2d, 1942), superseding s. c. 128 F.2d 564; Brierley v. Commercial Credit Co., 43 F.2d 724 (D.C.Pa.), affirmed 43 F.2d 730 (C. C.A.1930); In re New York, N. H. & H. R. Co., 25 F.Supp. 874 (D.C. Conn.1938).

on nonperformance of the duty to which the assignment is collateral. When that duty has been fully performed, the claim assigned as security reverts to the assignor, so that payment to him is a good discharge of the obligor's debt and the money received by him is his to keep.[83] As long as the debt has not been paid in full, the assignee for security may collect the assigned claim and apply the proceeds in satisfaction of the debt secured;[84] the balance, if any, belongs to the assignor.[85]

## § 882.   Assignments for Collection

An assignment of a claim may be for purposes of collection only, the money when collected to belong to the assignor. There seems to be no very good reason for refusing full recognition to such an assignment in a suit against the obligor. It cannot be doubted that suits by such assignees are very numerous, the debtor not knowing the limited character of the assignment, or making no objection if he does know it. A suit brought by such an assignee in his own name should be sustained, in the absence of a statutory requirement to the contrary. It may be thought that a statute providing that a suit must be brought in the name of the real party in interest should be held to prevent action in the name of an assignee for collection only.[89] If so, such an assignment is nothing more than a power of attorney, authorizing collection by suit, or otherwise, in the name of the assignor himself. An assignment may once have been regarded as merely a power of attorney; but such a power of attorney should not now be called an assignment.[90] There are cases sustaining an action, brought in the name of an assignee for collection, in spite of statutes providing for suit in the name of the real party in interest.[91] The fact is that there may be more than one "real" party in interest; and such a statute should, if possible, be prevented from creating a new procedural pitfall. Property interests in land and chattels are complex quantities, capable of division into parts; "title" is not an indivisible entity. A contract right or other claim is likewise capable of subdivision and distribution.

An assignment absolute in form can be shown to have been for collection only; and the assignee on collection will hold the proceeds in trust for the assignor.[92]

90.   See Spencer v. Standard Chemicals & Metals Corp., 143 N.E. 651, 237 N.Y. 479 (1924), so applying N. Y. Code of Procedure, § 111. The power of attorney here authorized suit in the attorney's own name without purporting in terms to be an assignment; the suit so brought was thrown out.

See also Heiskell v. Mozie, 82 F.2d 861 (App.D.C.1936).

Suit by the assignee was sustained in Titus v. Wallick, 59 S.Ct. 557, 306 U.S. 282, 83 L.Ed. 653 (1939), where the document was in express terms an assignment of the right as well as a power of attorney, distinguishing the Spencer case above.

## § 883.   Power of Assignment in Option Contracts

The holder of an "option" is in one major respect similar to the offeree in an ordinary offer: he has a power to create new contractual relations by an expression of assent. Indeed, any ordinary offeree has an "option" between accepting and not accepting. But it is not customary to use the word "option" unless there is more than a mere power of acceptance; it usually means what is a little more fully expressed by the phrase "binding option." This means that the transaction is to be described as a contract, rather than as an offer. The option holder has a power of acceptance, but it is an irrevocable power. Since the option giver has made a binding promise, to sell or to buy, on specified conditions, it is quite accurate to say that he has made a contract and that the option holder has a conditional contract right.[95]

In the case of an ordinary revocable offer, the power of the offeree is not assignable, meaning by this that the offeree cannot substitute a third party in his own place as the party who is to make the contract with the offeror.[96] In the making of such a rule as this, the phrase *delectus personae* and the idea behind it have played a part. But it seems, now that contract rights have become freely assignable and that in very many cases performance of a duty can be delegated, that there remains no very good reason for maintaining this rule of non-assignability. Of course, if the proposed contract is one that involves a promise by the offeree, it is the personal credit of the offeree that the offeror is willing to trust, and he can not be required to accept the promise of a substitute. Even after acceptance by the offeree, he can not substitute a new obligor in his place, there being no difference either before or after acceptance. But there are many offers that do not request any promise of the offeree; and the performance that is requested of him may not be his personal performance.

Thus, if A offers to employ B as a salesman, B can not assign his power of acceptance to C, meaning thereby to substitute C's promise to serve and C's salesmanship for his own. Even after acceptance by B, he can not substitute C by assignment or delegation, although he can assign his right to wages.[a]

## § 889.   Partial Assignment

Even after assignments were given operation at common law, there were special difficulties in the case of an attempt to assign a part only of a larger claim. It is unjust to subject the debtor to a possible horde of claimants, or even to make it necessary for

---

a.   The following Sections are omitted at this point: § 884. Output and Requirement Contracts; § 885. Assignability of Rights against Competition; § 886. Assignability of Rights of Action for Damages; § 887. Assignment of Rights under a Life Insurance Policy; § 888. Assignment of Rights in Fire Insurance.

him to defend several suits in case he disputes the validity or the amount of the claim. The earlier procedure at common law included no effective method of preventing such injustice; and it was therefore many times held that the partial assignee's remedy, if any, must be in equity, where there was greater flexibility in the joinder of parties. The fusion of law and equity has proceeded so far, however, and the procedure of modern courts has been made so flexible, that it is now possible for the American Law Institute to lay down the general rule that a partial assignment "is operative as to that part or amount as if the part had been a separate right, subject to the limitation that if the obligor has not contracted to make such a partial performance no legal proceeding can be maintained by such an assignee against the obligor over his objection, unless all persons having collectively a right to the entire performance are joined in the proceeding." [51] This is supported by all decisions that are in favor of the partial assignee whether they purport to be "in equity" or are clearly understood to be in a "civil action" under modern codes in a jurisdiction where law and equity are fused; [52] but the court in which his action should be brought and the procedure by which his claim is enforced will vary in accordance with the local system.[53]

Even where law and equity are still administered by separate courts, or as separate systems of law, the partial assignee's right should be enforced in any court whose procedure has been made flexible enough to permit joinder of all parties in interest.[54] The assignee may himself join all other partial claimants in the suit, either as co-plaintiffs or as defendants. If he fails to do this, the obligor may either make no objection and let judgment go against him, without affecting the rights of other partial claimants; or he may ask the dismissal of the suit for non-joinder of necessary parties; [55] or he may himself bring these parties into the proceeding.

Some of the cases holding that a partial assignee gets no right unless the obligor assents to the assignment may be justified on the ground that the partial assignee is suing in a separate action for the amount assigned to him.[56] Even so, the court should consider its equity powers, and also should give full effect to its rules of procedure permitting joinder of parties. If the plaintiff will not join the other parties necessary to the final adjudication of the entire claim, or if they cannot be joined, the refusal to give judgment for the sum assigned may be justified.

There are cases holding that a partial assignment is not effective as against the assignor's subsequent assignee of the whole,[57]

---

**51.** Restatement, Contracts, § 156; quoted with approval and applied in New York Trust Co. v. Island Oil & T. Corp., 34 F.2d 649 (C.C.A. 2d, 1929); Commercial Discount Co. v. Town of Plainfield, 180 A. 311, 120 Conn. 274 (1935).

his attaching creditors,[58] or his trustee in bankruptcy.[59]  The fact that the assignment is a partial one only should have no bearing upon this subject.  The partial assignee should be preferred, except where the assignment can be avoided as an improper preference or in fraud of creditors.  This means that the assignment should be held effective in exactly the same cases in which it would have been held so had it been an assignment of the entire claim.[60]

After notice of a partial assignment, a payment in full to the assignor or to a second assignee does not operate as a discharge to the debtor; [63] nor does a compromise agreement or an accord and satisfaction.[64]  This is now true even in a court that persists in saying that a partial assignee has only an "equitable interest" and not "legal title."  Cases to the contrary should now be disapproved and the Law Institute rule followed, giving full effect to its limiting provision against subjecting the obligor to more than one action.[65]

## § 890.   Power of Assignor to Release the Obligor

Before the obligor has been notified of the assignment he is justified in believing that his duty is still owed to his original obligee, the assignor.  It follows that payment to the assignor, or the rendition of other required performance to him, operates as a discharge; [70] and the assignee must look to the assignor for his remedy.  Likewise, an accord and satisfaction, by agreement with the assignor, operates as a discharge; and so does a substituted executory contract or novation, and any other mode of discharge that involves a material change of position by the obligor.[71]  The assignee could have prevented such change of position, and thereby protected his own rights, by giving notice of the assignment.

After notice of the assignment has been given to the obligor, or knowledge thereof received by him in any manner, the assignor has no remaining power of release.[72]  The obligor must pay the assignee.  Even though a suit is brought in the name of the assignor, he cannot control that suit; even at strict common law, the assignee could bring a new action in the assignor's name after a wrongful dismissal.[73]

To deprive the assignor of his power to discharge, it is not necessary that the obligor shall be given a formal notice in writing or otherwise.  It is enough that he has actual knowledge of the assignment, however it was obtained.  It is enough, also, that he has knowledge of facts that would have caused a prudent business man to withhold payment from the assignor until obtaining further in-

---

60.  This is fully supported in Schwartz v. Horowitz, 131 F.2d 506 (C.C.A.2d 1942), an excellent decision supporting a partial assignment as against a trustee in bankruptcy, with clear analysis of the problem.

71.  See in general, Restatement, Contracts, § 170.

formation as to the claim of the assignee.[74]  The obligor must have such knowledge of facts as would "put him on inquiry," an inquiry that would have given him definite knowledge of the assignment.

### § 891.  Assignment Extinguishes the Assignor's Right

After an absolute and unconditional assignment of a contract right, the assignor has no further right to the performance.[76]  In some jurisdictions, his name can still be used as the nominal plaintiff;[77] but there are cases holding that such a suit will be dismissed in the absence of a showing that the suit is brought in behalf of the assignee—the real party in interest.[78]  It has also been held that the assignor cannot maintain a bill for specific performance, to compel the obligor to render performance to the assignee.[79]  The assignor is not a necessary party to a suit to enforce the assigned right, although it is proper to join him as a party of record so as to protect the obligor against future liability.[80]

The statements in the foregoing paragraph are not applicable in case the assignment is for collection only or is given as a mere collateral security.  The assignor in these cases is certainly a party in interest, although not the sole one;  he has an existing right against the obligor, as well as against the assignee, and he should be given an appropriate remedy consistent with the rights of the other interested parties.[81]

Since under ordinary circumstances a debt carries with it the securities that are given for its payment, after a debt is assigned the assignor has no further right as to the security as well as to the debt.  After the transfer of a note that was given as conditional payment of a previous debt, the transferor is generally held to be unable to maintain suit on the original account or against one who guaranteed payment of it.[82]  A few cases have reached a different result, because they regarded the note itself as a mere security for the primary debt.[83]  Such cases should not be followed.

For two centuries after the courts of common law recognized the rights of an assignee and enforced a judgment in his behalf, they required the suit to be brought in the name of the assignor.  This requirement was in most jurisdictions done away by statute, either permitting suit by the assignee in express terms or by requiring the suit to be brought in the name of the real party in interest.  Equity always permitted the assignee to sue in his own name; and no court with equity jurisdiction needs the aid of statute to follow this procedure.  Nevertheless, courts often say that in the absence of statute the assignee must sue in the name of the assignor.[84]  This is merely adherence to the old common law formality.

# CHAPTER 50

## LEGAL EFFECTS OF ASSIGNMENT—DEFENSES AND PRIORITIES

## § 892. Defenses to Which the Assignee is Subject

The recognition of the power to assign has led to some complexity of relations and to new conflicts of interest and desire. Suppose the following series of transactions: X employs A for a month's service at a salary of $500. During the first week, A purchases goods of Y, promising to hold his salary in trust to pay the bill. Later, by fraud, B induces A to assign his claim for salary to B and induces X to advance him $100. Without good excuse, A renders no service during the last two weeks. B makes a further assignment of the claim to C, who purchases for value and without knowing any of the facts that might injure his claim.

Observe that in a suit by A against X, the wilful breach of A would give to X a defense and a counterclaim for damages. In a suit by B against X, the advancement of $100 operates in reduction of B's claim, and also to give X a right of restitution. In a suit by C against X, can X make use of his defense and counterclaim against A and his reduction and counterclaim against B? In more general terms, does an assignee take the claim subject (1) to defenses and counterclaims of the obligor against the original obligee, and (2) to defenses and counterclaims of the obligor against an intermediate assignee?

Observe, further, that in a suit by A against X, Y could intervene for the enforcement of his right against A; also that in a suit by B against X, A could intervene and avoid the fraudulently induced assignment to B. In a suit by C against X, can A and Y likewise intervene and deprive C of the money? In more general terms, does an assignee take the claim subject to the prior equitable claims of third parties, arising out of transactions with the obligee or with an intermediate assignee?

It is generally stated that the assignee, even though he is a purchaser for value and without notice, takes subject to defenses and counterclaims that were available to the obligor against the assignor.[1] Like other generalizations, this requires some elaboration and limitation. With respect to counterclaims and set-offs, it makes some difference whether they arose out of the same contract or transaction as did the assigned claim itself or arose out of some collateral contract or transaction.

The purpose of the rules with respect to defenses against an assignee is the protection of the obligor against being put in a substantially worse position by reason of an assignment to which he has not assented. In any case, the assignment obligates him to a person with whom he has never consented to deal; such disadvantage as this involves he must bear, because of the public advantage derived from assignability, but no additional disadvantages need be thrust upon him.

The obligor has been protected against procedural disadvantages, affecting the forum of enforcement rather than the right. Thus, if the obligor could have caused the abatement of the action against the assignor, because the nature of the claim or the place of the original transaction is such as to make the forum an inconvenient and undesirable one, he can cause its abatement against the assignee as well.[2] This would not be true if the change in the personality of the claimant makes inapplicable the obligor's reason for the abatement.

If the obligor's contract with the assignor provides for arbitration of disputes arising out of the contract, this provision is applicable for and against the assignee just as it was against the assignor. The assignee can obtain specific enforcement just as could

---

1. **U.S.**—Wagner v. Central Bkg. & Security Co., 249 F. 145 (C.C.A. 4th, 1918).

Restatement, Contracts, § 167(1), reads as follows: "An assignee's right against the obligor is subject to all limitations of the obligee's right, to all absolute and temporary defenses thereto, and to all set-offs and counterclaims of the obligor which would have been available against the obligee had there been no assignment, provided that such defenses and set-offs are based on facts existing at the time of the assignment, or are based on facts arising thereafter prior to knowledge of the assignment by the obligor."

the assignor, if an arbitration statute provides for such a remedy.[3] No doubt, if the arbitration term provides for the personal appointment of an arbitrator by the assignor, an appointment by the assignee would not be effective; but the arbitration term should seldom be interpreted as making such a requirement.

### § 893.  Original Transaction Void or Voidable

The claim transferred to the assignee depends for its existence and character upon the original transaction between the defendant (the alleged obligor) and the assignor.  The assignee has no right if that transaction was void of legal operation.  It may have been void for lack of mutual assent or of consideration or for noncompliance with other requirements.[4]  If the original transaction was voidable, and not wholly void, as may be true in cases of fraud, duress, mistake, lack of capacity, and some forms of illegality, the obligor's power of avoidance is not affected by the assignment.  No doubt the obligee can, by an assignment, put the assignee in as good a position as his own; but the assignee has no right if the obligor properly exercises his power to avoid.[5]  If an effective avoidance preceded the assignment, the assignee got no right thereby; and even if no avoidance had as yet occurred, if the time for exercising the power of avoidance has not expired, it can be exercised against the assignee.  The contract may be unenforceable by reason of the statute of frauds, a defense equally available to the defendant against the assignee.

A power to terminate the obligor's contractual duties may be reserved by express agreement, the power to be exercised by notice; or the power may be reserved to discharge the obligation by payment to a third party or in some other specified manner.[6] The right of the assignee is subject to such a power.

In these cases, the assignment puts the assignee in as good a position as that occupied by the assignor, but in no better.  The assignee holds and can enforce the voidable claim, as long as it has not been avoided.  As against him, as well as against the assignor, the power of avoidance must be exercised within the time and in the manner required in case there had been no assignment.

For the obligor to be able to make use of the assignor's fraud as a defense in a suit by the assignee, it has been held in England that it is necessary for the obligor to disaffirm the contract entirely; if he does not disaffirm, and retains the consideration received, his only remedy is an action for damages against the de-

---

6.  The assignee of a contractor's right to payment takes subject to the power of the obligor, reserved in the contract, to apply the unpaid price in settlement of the claims of laborers and materialmen for work and materials furnished by them to the contractor. Yancey v. Stark, 129 S.E. 81, 132 S.C. 171 (1925); Twentieth St. Bank v. Summers, 110 S.E. 478, 90 W.Va. 90 (1922).

frauder.[7] This is a separate action for the fraud, and cannot be maintained against an innocent assignee for value. It is believed, however, that since the fraud induced the very transaction creating the assigned right, it should have been held available as a recoupment in reduction of the assignee's claim.

## § 894.   Discharge by Release, Payment, Accord and Satisfaction

A third class of defenses consists of those that arise out of facts occurring subsequently to the making of the contract, or even subsequently to breach by the obligor, and that are commonly described as affirmative defenses. This classification is of some convenience; but it must not be supposed that the line of separation between this class and the second is clear and distinct or that the question of burden of proof can safely be determined by means of it. There are many ways in which a contract right and duty can be discharged by a new and independent transaction between the parties. Among these methods of discharge are release, rescission, payment, accord and satisfaction, novation and substituted contract. If any one of these methods of discharge has occurred, prior to the assignment, or even thereafter but prior to notice of the assignment by the obligor, the discharge is effective against the assignee.[8] After the obligor knows or has reason to know of the assignment, none of these methods of discharge is effective against the assignee. As to such discharges prior to notice, the rule applicable to the assignee is caveat emptor; after he has received notice, the obligor must get his discharge from the assignee only.[9]

The defenses included in the first two classes are effective against the assignee even though they occur after notice to the obligor. They thus differ from the defenses now being considered.

A payment made by the obligor to his original creditor is fully operative in defense against an assignee if it was made in good faith without notice, actual or constructive, of the assignment. It is otherwise of payments made with such notice or with knowledge of facts sufficient to put the obligor on inquiry.[10]

The rules just stated as to the effect of a discharge by the assignor upon the right of the assignee apply equally to the effect of a discharge by an assignee upon the right of a sub-assignee.[11] As long as the obligor has no notice of the sub-assignment, he is justified in settling with the assignee, just as he would have been justified in settling with the original obligee before notice of the first assignment. This section is not dealing with set-offs and counterclaims; nor is it dealing with the rights of two successive assignments by the same assignor.

11.   Restatement, Contracts, § 170 (2a).

## § 895.  Nonperformance of a Condition and Failure of Consideration

Even assuming that the original transaction was perfectly valid and in no respect voidable, the duty of the obligor thereby created may be expressly or constructively conditional.  The right of the assignee is subject to the same conditions as was that of the assignor.  In many instances, a condition precedent to the obligor's duty to perform his part is the substantial performance of the agreed exchange;  his not receiving this performance is often called failure of consideration.  Such defenses as these, although arising by reason of facts subsequent to the original contractual transaction, are operative defenses because of the character and terms of that transaction upon which the assigned right depends for its existence.  The assignee must know at his peril the conditional character of the right that is assigned to him.  As in the case of the purchase of a horse, the rule is caveat emptor, except that here the rule is used in favor of the obligor, instead of the seller, and is applied in full vigor.  The reasons for its obsolescence that exist in the field of sales of goods, where it once gave an injurious license to the seller, are not applicable as against the obligor, who is not even a party to the assignment transaction.  To the assignee, the nature of the transaction on which his right depends is sufficient warning to him of what he may demand of the obligor in accordance with the mores of reason and justice.  He is, therefore, subject to the doctrines of express and constructive conditions, precedent and subsequent, and of actual and prospective failure of consideration.

This is applicable whether the event that would be a good defense against the assignor occurs before or after the assignment or notice thereof, and before or after a breach by the obligor.[13]  Even after the obligor has committed a breach of his duty, both his primary duty and the duty to make compensation for breach may be discharged by the happening of an express condition subsequent [14] or by an event that shows that there would have been a total failure of consideration if the obligor had performed his promise.[15]  In cases of this sort, if the obligor has performed before the failure of the agreed exchange has become apparent, he has a right of restitution;  and if the performance was made to the assignee rather than to the assignor, this right of restitution is a right against the assignee himself.[16]

If the assigned claim arose out of a contract the terms of which are such as to make the claim either expressly, impliedly, or con-

13.  Cal.—Bliss  v.  Calif.  Co-op. Producers, 181 P.2d 369, 30 Cal.2d 240, 170 A.L.R. 1009 (1947).

14.  Restatement, Contracts, § 396.

15.  Restatement, Contracts, §§ 274, 277.

16.  Conn.—Munson v. De Tamble Motors Co., 91 A. 531, 88 Conn. 415 (1914).

structively conditional upon some performance by the assignor or upon any other fact or event, the non-occurrence of the condition is a good defense against the assignor and also against the assignee.[17]  This is a case where a defense exists because the plaintiff's right never became a right to immediate performance and no breach of the obligor's duty has occurred;  it is not a case of counterclaim or set-off.  Within this rule would fall those cases of mutually dependent promises, in which the court holds that the obligor's contractual duty is dependent and conditional upon performance or tender thereof by the other party.  If it is so dependent as against the assignor, it is equally so as against the assignee, except that the obligor may by his own representations to the assignee estop himself from using the defense.

§ 896.  Counterclaims Arising out of the Original Transaction

What is the difference between a "defense," on the one hand, and recoupment, set-off, and counterclaim, on the other?  And what difference, if any, does this difference make in the law of assignment?  In its broadest sense, no doubt the word "defense" includes the others;  and no attempt will be made here to combat that broad usage.  But the facts that have been dealt with in the preceding sections are facts that differ in their effects from the facts to be dealt with in this one;  and it is the difference in the effects upon which emphasis will be placed.

We say that a promise is void for lack of consideration, or has been avoided for infancy, or is conditional upon some event that has not occurred, or has been discharged by payment.  By such a statement we mean that the court will deny a remedy to the promisee and will declare the promisor to be under no duty.  But in these cases the court will not declare that the promisee has himself committed a breach of duty.  When we say that a defendant has a counterclaim, we mean that the plaintiff has committed a breach of duty to the defendant.  Each party has done wrong;  each is entitled to a remedy, although there must be an adjustment of remedies.  Set-off is a term commonly used to denote a particular limited form of counterclaim, in case of which the adjustment of remedies takes place by the mere process of subtraction.  Recoupment likewise refers to an adjustment of remedy, but without necessarily indicating that the plaintiff has done wrong so that the defendant can establish a separate and independent claim to a remedy against the plaintiff.  Sometimes, when a defendant pleads "in recoupment," he may have an affirmative claim for damages against a third person, but not against the plaintiff;  at other times, he may have such a claim against the plaintiff himself, but cares to use it only by subtraction as a reduction of the claim of the plaintiff.

Whether the defendant asserts a counterclaim, a set-off, or a recoupment, he is not thereby denying his own wrongful breach; but he is asking an adjustment in the remedy, affecting the judgment or decree and the execution thereof.

The availability, as against an assignee, of counterclaims, set-offs, and recoupments that would have been available against the assignor, has been very generally dealt with by statute, such provisions being commonly included in codes of procedure.[18] The question with which we are dealing, however, is not merely a question of pleading and procedure. Just as in other cases, procedure and substantive law cannot be wholly separated. What the assignee wishes to know is how much he has a right to collect from the obligor; what the obligor wishes to know is what deductions he may make from the face of the assigned claim and how much he must pay. This is as much a matter of right and duty, of substantive law, as is any other question of right and duty; and it can be determined only by finding out what remedies, either direct or indirect, are available.

In a suit by an assignee, the counterclaim, set-off, or recoupment of which the defendant wishes to make use may arise either (1) out of a transaction between the defendant and the assignee, (2) out of some contract by the assignee of which the defendant is beneficiary, or (3) out of some transaction between the defendant and the assignor. Questions arising in the first two classes are not peculiar to the law of assignment; counterclaims in such cases are available against the plaintiff on the same terms that they would be available if he were not an assignee at all.[19] Such questions need not here be considered; it is the third class of cases with which we must deal.

To what extent are counterclaims, set-offs, and recoupments, arising out of transactions by the assignor that did not involve the assignee, available against the assignee? No broad generalization in answer to this question is entirely safe, partly because such generalizations have been attempted by statute and the statutes vary, and partly because of variation in court decision. With this warning as to their possible inapplicability in some jurisdictions, a few limited generalizations will be constructed.

A counterclaim, set-off, or recoupment, arising out of the same transaction as that by which the claim of the assignee was itself created, is usable against the assignee in precisely the same cases that it would be so usable if it were operative as a complete defense. Its operation against the assignee is not affected by the fact that some of the events creating it occurred after the assignment or even after notice of the assignment. The transaction on which the assignee depends is itself a sufficient warning to him that counterclaims may grow out of that transaction requiring an adjustment of remedies. It is therefore thought just to require him to bear the risk that such counterclaims will be used in reduction or total extinction of his own claim. This does not mean that the counterclaim against the assignor is enforceable also as a counterclaim against the assignee; it is not so enforceable unless the assignee himself undertook the duty of performance and has been guilty of a breach.[20] But the counterclaim, set-off, or recoupment is as effective in reducing the assignee's remedy as it would have been in reducing the assignor's remedy if he were the plaintiff.

It may be difficult at times to define the limits of a single "transaction," and to determine whether or not the counterclaim arises out of the same transaction as did the assigned claim. Thus claims and counterclaims between partners may all be regarded as arising out of their "partnership" business, all of their doings as partners being regarded as part of a single, long-continued, partnership transaction. There seems to be no objection to this, so long as the claim and counterclaim arise out of matters that are within the contemplation of the partnership contract.[21] Liberality in this direction makes for the reduction of litigation and should not be regarded as unjust to an assignee.[22]

There are breaches of contract that do not "go to the essence" and that are not operative as defenses to the other party. Such breaches give rise to counterclaims for damages against the assignor and may be used in reduction of the assignor's claim. They arise out of the same contractual transaction as did the assigned claim. Such counterclaims as these are available against the assignee, even though he had no knowledge of them and even though they had as yet no existence either at the time of the assignment or at the time of notice thereof to the obligor.[23] The assignor's breach of contract which is the basis of the counterclaim may occur subsequently to notice of the assignment; and yet it would have been available to reduce the claim of the assignor and it is likewise available as a recoupment against the assignee.[24] On such counterclaims as these, the defendant cannot get an affirmative judgment against the assignee, unless the assignee has contracted with the assignor (or with the defendant) to render the omitted performance.[25] If the assignee has so contracted with the assignor, the defendant is a creditor beneficiary of the contract.

23.  **Ala.**—Jefferson Co. Sav. Bank v. Carland & Co., 77 So. 704, 201 Ala. 178 (1918).

**Cal.**—Suhr v. Metcalfe, 164 P. 407, 33 Cal.App. 59 (1917), assignee of balance due on a building contract is subject to counterclaims of the owner based on the builder's failure to keep off liens.

## § 897.　Counterclaims Arising out of Collateral Transactions

The availability of a set-off or counterclaim depends in large part upon the existing statutory provisions. In general, these ought to be liberally construed in favor of the obligor who is defendant. If the obligor has a counterclaim or set-off against the assignor that arises, not out of the transaction that created the assigned claim, but out of some collateral transaction, it is available against the assignee also in case it existed as a matured claim at the time of the assignment.[26] But it is held in some jurisdictions that it is not available against the assignee if it became a matured and enforceable claim after the date of the assignment.[27] In no jurisdiction is the counterclaim or set-off effective against the assignee if it was acquired by the obligor after notice of the assignment.[28]

It has been held also that a matured counterclaim of the defendant against the assignor, arising out of a different transaction, is not available against an assignee whose claim was not yet matured at the date of the assignment and was dependent upon further substantial performance by the assignee himself.[29] To allow this antecedent counterclaim, the existence of which was not known to the assignee, would enable the defendant to lie by and receive the performance of the assignee without paying him anything therefor. It would not be just to do that, even though the assignee should be subrogated to the defendant's collateral counterclaim against the assignor.

## § 898.　Defenses and Counterclaims of the Obligor against Intermediate Assignees

A set-off or cross-claim, that arises out of the same transaction by which the assigned claim was itself created, almost necessarily is one that would be available against the original obligee if he were now the plaintiff. But set-offs and counterclaims that arise out of collateral transactions would not be so available if the collateral transaction was not one to which the original obligee was a party or of which he was a beneficiary. The question therefore arises as to set-offs and cross-claims arising out of a transaction between the obligor and some holder of the claim after it has been assigned by the original owner. As against that holder himself, they are, of course, available; but are they available also against a subsequent purchaser for value without notice? In other words, is a defense, set-off, or cross-claim that would have been available against an assignee (but not against the original obligee), available also against a sub-assignee?

The American Law Institute answers this question in the negative. It says: "A sub-assignee's right against the obligor is not subject to the set-off or counterclaim of a right of the obligor against a prior assignee unless the obligor's right was acquired prior to any sub-assignment by the prior assignee, nor even in that case if a sub-assignee claiming under such prior assignee is a bona fide purchaser for value of the assigned right, without notice of the existence of the obligor's right." [32]

Here, again, some favor is shown to the sub-assignee, putting him in a better position than that occupied by his immediate assignor. But the rule of the Institute is not universally followed.

### § 899.  Defenses and Counterclaims may become Ineffective by Estoppel

The doctrine of equitable estoppel may prevent an obligor from setting up defenses and counterclaims as against an assignee. To create such an estoppel, the obligor must have so conducted himself as to induce the assignee to believe that the defense or counterclaim that is later asserted did not exist and to change his position materially in reasonable reliance thereon. Also, the obligor must have had reason to foresee some such change of position in reliance. A few illustrations of conduct creating an estoppel will be given; but whether the facts of a case justify an estoppel must always be largely a question for the court that hears the evidence.

If a document, that on its face evidences the existence of an obligation that is normally assignable, is executed and delivered by the obligor for the purpose of enabling the obligee to assign it for value, the obligor will be estopped to defend on such a ground as lack of consideration.[35] The same may be true where the executed document expressly states that there are no defenses and counterclaims.[36] The obligor may estop himself by oral representations made to the assignee [37] or by standing silent when he hears the assignor make them.[38] Estoppels often arise by entrusting to the assignor documents of such a sort that the obligor ought to foresee their successful use to induce a purchase for value.[39]

### § 900.  Latent Equities of Third Persons against an Assignor

An assignee takes subject to many defenses and counterclaims which were available to the obligor against the assignor, even though the assignee is a purchaser for value and without notice. The more generally prevailing rule is, however, that such an assignee takes the claim free from the equities of all others than the obligor.[40] Thus, where A, the owner of a claim against X, is induced to assign it to B by fraud, and B then assigns it to C

---

39.   **Md.**—Eversole v. Maull, 50 Md. 95 (1878), obligor held estopped because he entrusted the possession of the note and mortgage to his attorney for collection, and the latter sold them to an innocent purchaser.

**N.Y.**—McNeil v. Tenth Nat. Bank of N. Y., 46 N.Y. 325 (1871), owner of stock certificate entrusted it to a broker, having on it his own executed assignment in blank.

Restatement, Contracts, § 170(3) and (4).

for value and without notice, C is preferred over the original assignor A, who was defrauded by B.  C's claim would be subject to such defenses as the obligor X might have against the original assignor A, but not to the claim of the defrauded assignor A against B.[41]  So, also, if one holds a claim against another in trust for a third and fraudulently assigns it to a purchaser for value without notice of the trust, such an assignee can enforce the claim against the obligor free from the claim of the cestui que trust.  It may be that this rule comports with the public interest; the equities of the two claimants appear to be equal, and the opposite rule would clog the honest transfer of such claims by the ever existing fear of a latent equity not discoverable by reasonable inquiry.  There are decisions, however, laying down the opposite rule and preferring the prior equity.[42]

If the assignee is not a purchaser for value without notice of the latent equity, his claim is subject to that equity; [43] and he is not regarded as such a purchaser if he received the assignment as a gift or as a new security for a pre-existing debt.[44]

There are many cases in which the "equity" of the third party can not be properly described as "latent" ; and, indeed, where his claim should not be described as an "equity."  Such is the case where the third party's right is created by the terms of the very contract creating the right that has been assigned.  In such cases the right of the third person is superior to that of the assignor himself; and the assignor has no power to assign more than he has or to put the assignee in a better position than his own.[a]

## § 902.  Successive Assignments of the Same Right

An assignment of a contract right is operative to extinguish the right of the assignor and to create a like right in the assignee.  To produce this effect, it is not necessary that notice shall be given to the obligor, although until such a notice is given, the assignor or his subsequent assignee has power to discharge the obligor by receiving payment and otherwise.[58]  The more generally prevailing American rule now is that, as between two successive assignees of the same right whose claims are otherwise equal, the earlier in time is preferred.[59]  By the first assignment, the right became his, so that at the time of the second assignment, the assignor had no right and could therefore transfer none.  There are certain exceptions to this rule, as will be discussed below.  This result, preferring the first assignee, is now

**a.**  Section 901, Equities of Third Persons that are Not Latent—Subrogation of a Surety, is omitted.

**59.    U.S.**—Salem Trust Co. v. Manufacturers' Finance Co., 44 S.Ct. 266, 264 U.S. 182, 68 L.Ed. 628, 31 A.L.R. 867 (1924), noted in 33 Yale L.J. 767;  Wilson v. Duncan, 61 F.2d 515 (C.C.A.5th, 1932) ; In re Ideal Upholstering Co., 28 F.2d 791 (D. C.Mass.1928).

reached without regard to whether an assignee's right is called legal or equitable; and it is reached even though the first assignment is a partial assignment or is an assignment as security only.[60]

In England and in some of the states, a different rule is applied, the second assignee being preferred over the first if he is a purchaser for value without notice and if he is first to give notice to the obligor.[61] By this rule, the assignees, if otherwise equally deserving, are ranked in the order of giving notice to the debtor. This rule has very considerable merit, from the standpoint of convenience; but the opposite rule has been adopted by the United States Supreme Court, and the decision has been followed by the American Law Institute.[62]

Whatever rule is adopted as to preference between successive assignees, care must be taken to protect the obligor. If without notice of any assignment he pays the assignor, he is discharged; the assignor is a wrongdoer in granting this discharge, but the obligor is innocent and will not be made to pay twice. If the obligor pays a second assignee, without notice of the first assignment, again the payment operates as a discharge, and for the same reasons.[63] Such is the result, even though the second assignee knew of the first assignment and intends to perpetrate a fraud. In such a case, the second assignee will hold the money as a constructive trustee for the rightful claimant; [64] but the latter's claim against the obligor is discharged.

The first exception to the general rule stated above is that, if the second assignee collects the money in good faith and is not a mere donee, he will be allowed to keep the money so received.[65] This would once have been explained by saying that he has got "legal title" to the money and his "equities" are equal to those of the first assignee. We may wholly avoid the problem of what may be the meaning of "legal title" by saying that mere priority in time of assignment does not seem to be a sufficient reason for taking away from the second assignee money that he has innocently collected by the exercise of diligence and effort.[66]

65. **U.S.**—Judson v. Corcoran, 58 U.S. (17 How.) 612, 15 L.Ed. 231 (1854).

Mass.—Rabinowitz v. People's Nat. Bank, 126 N.E. 289, 235 Mass. 102 (1920).

66. "There are various ways in which this can be described in terms of legal doctrine. One can say that the rights of an assignee are equitable (as they no doubt once were) and that the man who has changed his equitable right into legal title prevails, equities being equal. Or one can draw the analogy of reduction to possession, like sinking the harpoon into the still active whale. Or one may speak of estoppel, though this simply labels a result, for the elements of an estoppel in pais are not present. However explained, the favored position acquired by the subsequent assignee in the situations noted in Restatement, Contracts, § 173, comes not from his status as bona fide purchaser, but from his activities following his belated assignment." In re Rosen, 157 F.2d 997 (C.C.A.3d, 1946).

It is held, also, that if a second assignee for value, still acting in good faith, gets judgment against the obligor, he may enforce the judgment and keep the money so obtained, even though after judgment rendered both he and the obligor are notified of the first assignment.[67] This is the general rule where the judgment-getter is merely an attaching creditor of the assignor; and it would apply with even more reason in favor of a purchaser for value. It should be observed that the judgment is collectible against the obligor, even though notice of the first assignment had been given to him previously. His failure to make use of his defense would not invalidate the judgment; but he would still be bound to pay the first assignee. If the obligor had no notice of the first assignment, the judgment should operate as a discharge of duty to the first assignee.

A third case in which the second assignee for value has advantage over the first is where he has innocently entered into a contract of novation with the obligor. As in the case of the judgment, this contract is enforceable against the obligor, even though he had notice of the earlier assignment; but he would be bound to pay a second time. If the obligor had no such notice, he is bound by the novation and his duty to the first assignee is discharged. If the second assignee makes the novation contract without notice of the earlier assignment, he may keep what he gets even though the first assignee gets nothing. Otherwise, he holds as a constructive trustee.

Fourthly, the second assignee is preferred over the first in any case in which the first assignment was voidable by the assignor. The second assignment will in such case operate as an avoidance. Whether or not an assignment is voidable because given without consideration will be discussed later. Observe that in this class of cases, too, a payment by the obligor to the first assignee, without notice of the second assignment, will discharge the obligor; but the first assignee will hold as a constructive trustee if he collects knowing that there has been a valid revocation.

Finally, the second assignee is preferred over the first if he is a purchaser for value [68] without notice and the facts are such as to create an estoppel against the first assignee.[69] If the assignor's claim is evidenced by some formal document that is customarily identified with the claim itself, and that under ordinary circumstances must be produced and surrendered on collection or enforcement, it is negligent for the first assignee to leave that document in the possession of the assignor, with nothing on its face to warn a second purchaser that the assignor is not the complete owner. It is reasonable for the second assignee to advance his money on the faith of such a document. There may be an estoppel against the first assignee because of other conduct on his part. In such cases as these the second assignee is preferred over the first.[70] This preference is without regard to priority of notice to the obligor, although there are cases in which payment by him to the first assignee without notice of the second assignment will operate as a complete discharge. Illustrations of the documents of title above referred to are savings bank books, insurance policies, indorsed certificates of stock, promissory notes, and certificates of deposit.

It should here be observed that we have been discussing successive assignments of the identical right. In the case of a building contract, or a leasing contract, the assignor may have a series of rights to a series of instalment payments. If the first assignment covers only sums to fall due after a certain date, or after a default in performance of the building contract under which the assigned rights were created, the later assignment will have priority as to sums payable before that date or default. Here the rights assigned are not the same rights.[71]

### § 903.  Assignees and Subsequent Attaching Creditors

There are numerous cases in which, after a claim has been assigned for value, a creditor of the assignor makes an attachment or brings a garnishment proceeding against the obligor. Even if the obligor then has no notice of the previous assignment, the assignee is preferred over the creditor if he gives notice to the obligor in time to enable him to use it as a defense in the attachment proceeding.[72] In a very few states the attaching creditor is preferred if the assignee had not given notice prior to the attachment.[73]

### § 904.  Assignor's Duty to Assignee—Implied Warranties

In the law of assignment the difficult questions have been those that involve the relations between the assignee and the obligor. No such difficulties exist in determining the relations of the assignor and the assignee. Between them there is direct privity; and the assignment transaction can be found to contain contractual promises, express and implied, in accordance with the rules and customs of ordinary contract law.

Until notice of the assignment has been given to the obligor, it is necessary to his protection that the assignor shall still retain the power to discharge. Prior to such notice, payment to the assignor is an operative discharge of the debt. So also is an accord and satisfaction, or a voluntary release by the assignor followed by a change of position by the obligor.

70.  Mass.—Herman v. Connecticut Mut. L. Ins. Co., 105 N.E. 450, 218 Mass. 181 (1914), insurance policy; Bridge v. Connecticut Mut. L. Ins. Co., 25 N.E. 612, 152 Mass. 343 (1890).

However effective as to the obligor, his discharge by the assignor by any of these processes, or by any other, without the assignee's assent, is a wrong to the assignee. Usually it has been held that the assignor, at the time of the assignment, impliedly promises that he will do nothing to prevent or to impede collection by the assignee. In case of breach of this implied promise, the assignee can maintain action for an appropriate remedy. He can sue for money damages in a contract action.[78] An action for wrongfully discharging the debtor could be just as well explained on a tort theory, the assignor's action being a wrongful destruction of the assignee's right, but the measure of recovery would be the same. If the assignor has enriched himself by wrongful collection from the obligor, the assignee can maintain suit for the amount so received; [79] this is a restitutionary or quasi contractual remedy. It, too, can be regarded as a remedy for a tortious wrong—as a suit in assumpsit on the old theory of waiver of tort.[80] This remedy is equally available to the assignee against any other person who wrongfully induces payment by the obligor.[81] In addition, the usual equitable remedies are available; the assignee can prevent the wrongful destruction of his right by obtaining an injunction or can hold him as a constructive trustee of the amount collected.[82]

Even if the assignment is of only a part of the entire claim, the assignor may properly be regarded as impliedly promising not to collect from the debtor the part so assigned by him.[83]

Not only does the assignor promise not to impede collection; it is also held that by implication he warrants the genuineness and validity of the claim that he purports to assign, unless at the time he manifests a contrary intention.[84] In like manner, he warrants the existence and validity of accessory securities transferred by him along with the assigned right.[85] He may expressly guarantee collection as well; but there is no implied warranty of this sort.[86] If the assignor delegates to the assignee the performance of his duties and of conditions precedent, he may or may not represent that such performance is delegable and that performance by the substitute will be accepted by the obligor. For breach of such a warranty, the assignee can maintain action for damages.[87]

The character and extent of warranties that are implied in fact on the part of the assignor must depend upon the transaction of assignment itself and the facts that form its setting. Little, if any, basis for such an implication exists in case of a gratuitous assignment. There is more reason for an implication in case of

78.     U.S.—Cavalliotis v. Gray & Co.,
293 F. 1018 (C.C.A.2d, 1923), affirming 276 F. 565 (D.C.N.Y.1921).

an assignment given to secure an antecedent debt, and still more in case of a purchase for value then paid. In any case, much turns upon the knowledge of existing facts possessed by the assignee or that the assignor reasonably supposes him to possess.

### § 905. Remedies Available to an Assignee

The right of the assignee is the same as was that of his assignor, subject to the same conditions and in general to the same defenses. Likewise, under generally prevailing modern law, he can enforce it by the same remedies. If he sues for a money judgment, he can maintain the proper modern form of action— the modern equivalent of the common law actions of covenant, debt, and assumpsit. This action he can now maintain in his own name; but in some jurisdictions his suit will not be dismissed because it is brought in the name of the assignor. The mere fact that he is an assignee is not a sufficient reason for asking for a remedy that was formerly obtainable in a court of equity only; but if the claim is one that would have been enforceable in equity at suit of the assignor, it is likewise so enforceable by the assignee in the absence of new reasons that were not applicable to the assignor.[88] The assignee of a right under a contract for the conveyance of land can get a decree for specific enforcement; [89] he has the usual remedies for the foreclosure of liens and mortgages and for the discovery and application of assets.

### § 906. Does the Assignee Undertake to Perform for the Assignor

The transaction between an assignor and an assignee may take many forms and affect their legal relations in many ways. The determination of its legal operation requires a careful analysis of the facts of that transaction; this includes the interpretation of their expressions in the light of all the circumstances.

The simplest assignment transaction is one in which the assignor purports to transfer to the assignee his contract right to some performance to be rendered by a third party (the obligor). If this right is enforceable only after the performance of certain conditions precedent, the assignee's right is conditional accordingly. These conditions precedent may be the performance of certain nondelegable acts by the assignor (or some third party) in person; and, if so, a tender of performance by the assignee is not sufficient. But if their performance is not personal, and is delegable, a tender of their performance by the assignee is a sufficient tender.

In his transaction with the assignor, the assignee may or may not promise the assignor to perform the conditions precedent to an enforceable right against the obligor. This is true irrespective of whether the assignor had undertaken to perform them. Also the assignee may or may not promise the assignor to perform and discharge the duties owed by the assignor to the third party. Again, this is quite irrespective of whether such performance was or was not a condition precedent to an enforceable right against the third party.

If the assignee contracts with his assignor to discharge the duties of the assignor to the third party, the latter is a creditor beneficiary of that contract. If the duties of the assignor were such as to require his own personal performance, of course the third party may properly refuse to accept the substituted performance tendered by the assignee; and if the assignor refuses to perform, the third party can maintain suit against him for breach. Even in such a case, however, the third party can accept the substituted performance tendered by the assignee, thus completing an accord and satisfaction. Also, if the assignee fails to perform his contract with the assignor, the third party can maintain suit against the assignee, as a creditor beneficiary of the assignee's contract.[90]

It is not always easy to determine whether or not the assignee actually contracts to perform the duties of the assignor. If he has not so contracted, no action can be maintained against him, either by the assignor, or by the third party as a beneficiary.[91] If he has so contracted, an action for his breach can be maintained by both of them.[92] In order for the third party to maintain such an action, it is not necessary for him to discharge the assignor from his duty; the promise of the assignee to the assignor is an additional security to the third party—excepting only those cases where it is offered to him as a discharge of the assignor by novation.

If the words of the assignment transaction clearly purport to do nothing but transfer to the assignee the assignor's right against the third party, interpretation is simple. The same is true if the assignee's words are clearly promissory.[93] The difficulty exists in those cases in which the parties make no clear analysis and do not differentiate in terms between rights and duties; and the assignor purports to assign the "contract" or all of his "right and title to the contract." [94] If the contract is still bilateral in character, so that the assignor has a duty to perform as well as a right to a performance by the third party, interpretation must depend chiefly upon the context and the surrounding circumstances. In such a case, the American Law Institute has laid down a rule of presumptive interpretation, to the effect that the assignor is presumed to have delegated performance of his duties to the assignee, and that the assignee is presumed to have promised to perform them.[95]  This seems reasonable;  and it is supported by a number of decisions.[96]  The New York Court of Appeals, however, has preferred to follow its former decisions that there is no such presumption, rather than the Institute doctrine.[97]

The factual basis for the inference of a promise varies with each case; generalizations are perilous, and are to be used merely as guides to assist in the making of a reasonable inference.  Sometimes, the matter may properly be determined by the subsequent conduct of the parties themselves.  Presumably there is no assumption of duties when the assignment is as security only.[98]

Whenever a party to a bilateral contract assigns his rights thereunder, it should always be made perfectly clear in words whether the assignee contracts to perform in the assignor's place. Generally, the surrounding circumstances will make this clear, but they should not be expected to bear the entire burden.

## § 907.  Assignment of a Right Carries Securities with it

In the absence of expressions to the contrary,[2] the assignment of a claim transfers not only the claim itself, but also all securities therefor then held by the assignor.[3]  This is the general rule, not because of any necessary and inherent connection between debt and security, but because such is usually the intention of the assignor and assignee and there is ordinarily no reason for letting the assignor keep the security or for giving it back to the obligor or other party who charged it with the security burden.[a]

---

95.   Restatement, Contracts, § 164.

Uniform Commercial Code—Sales, § 2—210 (1950 draft), provides: "(4) An assignment of 'the contract' or of 'all my rights under the contract' or an assignment in similar general terms is an assignment of rights and unless the circumstances indicate the contrary (as in an assignment for security) it is a delegation of performance of the duties of the assignor and its acceptance by the assignee constitutes a promise by him to perform those duties.  This promise is enforceable by either the assignor or the other party to the original contract."

97.   N.Y.—Langel v. Betz, 164 N.E. 890, 250 N.Y. 159 (1928).

a.   Section 908, Effect of Assignor's Bankruptcy upon an Assignment of Rights to Future Payment is omitted.

# CHAPTER 51

## GIFT ASSIGNMENTS

## § 909.   Gift Assignments of Contract Rights

The force of human convenience and business practice was too strong for the common-law doctrine that choses in action are not assignable. They have proved too strong, also, for the doctrine that a gratuitous assignment is not effective because equity will not aid a volunteer. As long as an assignment was regarded as nothing but a power of attorney, the assignee's claim against the obligor was declared to be equitable only; and it was thought that, in case of a revocation by the assignor or of repudiation by the obligor, the affirmative aid of equity was necessary in order for the assignee to enforce his claim and obtain possession and enjoyment. This affirmative aid would be refused unless it appeared that the merit of the applicant was reinforced by his having given valuable consideration, the result being that an assignee would be remediless unless he was an assignee for value.

At the present time, it is not necessary to review the learned arguments that were made for and against the theory that an assignment was ineffective unless it was for value. It is sufficient to say that time has decided the controversy; the cases holding a gift assignment to be effective are legion—it is no defense to an obligor that the assignee gave no consideration.[1] The American

---

1. The cases supporting this statement are distributed throughout the sections dealing with gift assignments. Among the cases in accord are:

U.S.—Sunnen v. Com'r of Int. Revenue, 161 F.2d 171 (C.C.A.8th, 1947); Cook v. Commercial Cas. Co., 160 F.2d 490 (C.C.A.S.C.1947). See articles by Jenks, Anson, and Costigan in 16 L.Q.Rev. 241, 17 L.Q.Rev. 90, 27 L.Q.Rev. 326; by Rundell, "Gifts of Choses in Action," 27 Yale L.J. 643; and by Dickinson, "Gratuitous Partial Assignments," 31 Yale L.J. 1.

Law Institute therefore correctly states that "an assignment is not ineffective because it is conditional, revocable or voidable by the assignor for lack of consideration or for other reason, or because it is within the provisions of the statute of frauds." [2]   This means that the lack of consideration does not prevent the assignment from being effective as a transfer to the assignee of the assignor's right against the obligor.

This we may regard as wholly settled.   The present litigation, of which there is a vast amount, is concerned with the question whether the gift assignment can be revoked by the assignor and whether the assignor's death before enforcement terminates the gift-assignee's right.

By "effective" the Institute means that the assignment terminates whatever right against the obligor that the assignor had and creates a like right in the assignee; and by the section just quoted it means that this result can be attained by a gift assignment.   The right assigned may itself be conditional, or voidable by the obligor; if so, it remains thus conditional or voidable as against the assignee.   But, also, the assignment may be conditional, or revocable or voidable by the assignor.   If it is conditional, enforcement by the transferee will depend upon the performance of the condition.   If it is revocable or voidable by the assignor, the assigned right is nevertheless the right of the assignee until the assignor exercises his power.[3]

By the quoted section the Institute does not indicate whether or not the lack of consideration given for the assignment makes it revocable or voidable.   That question is dealt with in a different section; and it is dealt with farther on in the present volume.   The fact is, however, that there are numerous gift assignments that are not revocable or voidable; and the question later to be discussed is as to what methods are effective in attaining such a result.

A transaction that does not purport to be a present assignment cannot be operative as a contract to assign in the future unless the facts satisfy the usual requirements of an executory contract.   In such cases, there must be a sealed writing, or a consideration, or some sufficient basis for an estoppel.

### § 910. General Requirements of an Irrevocable Gift Assignment—Delivery

The ordinary method of making a gift of a chattel is by delivering it to the donee or to his representative.   There are some other methods, however; and these vary to some extent, partly by statute, in different states.   It is believed that any of these other methods that would be legally operative to make an irrevocable gift of

2.   Restatement, Contracts, § 150.

a chattel is equally effective to make an irrevocable gift assignment.[4]

With respect to delivery, as a method of gift, it is clear that a contract right cannot be delivered, unless we construct some unusual meaning for that term. It is no more difficult to make a physical delivery of a contract right than to make such delivery of a property right; but in the case of a chattel, it is the chattel that is delivered, not the rights and other manifold relations that constitute property therein. The chattel is a physical subject matter capable of user and of being moved from place to place; and it is held that a gift transfer of the manifold legal relations that constitute "ownership" or "property" can be effected by the physical delivery of this subject matter, with appropriate expressions of donative intention.

In the case of a contract right, on the other hand, there is no physical subject matter, about which are clustered those manifold legal relations called "ownership" or "property." There may be some testimonial document, evidencing the right; and such a document is indeed a subject of property. But a chattel is the very subject the use and enjoyment of which are desired and are protected. In the case of the contract right, it is never the mere testimonial document that is regarded as the subject of ultimate use and enjoyment. Whether such a document exists or not, the contract right contemplates and requires a performance by another particular person, frequently involving the creation or the delivery by him of money or chattels. This is why our ancestors described a contract right as a "chose in action"; they were thinking not of the right-duty relation itself, but of the thing (the "chose") that the required performance would eventually create or deliver.

Thinking in terms of this future "chose," therefore, it seemed obvious to our ancestors that a "chose in action" was quite incapable of transfer by assignment. So it is, if we mean the "chose" that does not yet exist. Thinking, as we now do, of the right-duty relation itself as the subject of transfer, it is equally obvious that it is incapable of a physical delivery. Nevertheless it can be transferred, in the sense of legal recognition of a new holder of the right. Our question therefore is, What acts by a donor will effectuate such an irrevocable gift transfer?

In view of the foregoing, it is obvious that if a gift assignment is to be effected by an act of delivery, it must be some testimonial document, token, or other physical symbol or representative of the right that is delivered. Just what documents or symbols are

---

**4.** It is so stated in Restatement, Contracts, § 158. Included among these methods is an assignment in writing, formal or informal. This is dealt with in a later section.

sufficient to serve this purpose is considered in the sections that follow. If such a document or symbol exists, an irrevocable gift assignment can be effected by its delivery, with appropriate expressions of donative intention. Thus it is that in the case of contract rights, just as in the case of chattels, a physical delivery is one of the most important operative facts in the process of giving. The requirements as to this delivery and as to the accompanying expressions are the same as in the case of a chattel.

There are numerous cases holding that a gift assignment was not effectively made, because of absence of delivery of an evidential document, the retention of control by the assignor, or absence of proof of expressions of intention to make an executed gift.[5] Many claims are asserted, especially after the death of the alleged donor, that a gift was made, either inter vivos or causa mortis. Convincing proof should, of course, be required. Mere possession of the document, however formal, is not conclusive evidence of a delivery for any purpose; and delivery alone, even if proved, does not establish donative intention.[6]

There is no complete gift assignment if the documents evidencing the right are retained in the alleged donor's control and his expressions indicate an intention to retain the power of disposition. This is true even though he expressly indicates that the donee is to have the ownership after the donor's death, or directs the depositary of a fund to pay it over to the donee at the donor's death.[7] But the reservation of the income to the donor for life does not in itself prevent the gift of the principal from being valid and irrevocable.[8] If the donor clearly reserves no power of disposition or control of the principal, there is a valid gift assignment of the right to that principal, even though the donee's possession and enjoyment are postponed until some definite or indefinite future time.

6. "Mere possession of a chattel does not carry with it the slightest presumption as to the mode in which possession was acquired. Such possession may have resulted from the voluntary delivery of the chattel as a gift by some one who formerly had possession of it, but it may have been the result of any one of a large number of contracts of bailment, or it may have been the result of a trespass or a theft." Dunn v. Houghton, 51 A. 71 (N.J.Ch.1902).

7. U.S.—Ratterman v. Lodge, 13 F. 2d 805 (C.C.A.8th, 1926).

Where the donor handed to the donee a sealed envelope containing a certificate of deposit, with words of gift, and the donee without knowing what was in the envelope handed it back to the donor for safe keeping, the gift was held effective. In re Westerton, [1919] 2 Ch. 104.

An effective gift of an undivided half of certain bonds was made in Collins v. McCanless, 169 S.W.2d 850, 179 Tenn. 656, 145 A.L.R. 1380 (1943), even though the bonds were left in the donor's safe-deposit box. The donee later went with the donor to the box and received her half of the interest coupons.

If the document or symbol is delivered to a third person as the agent or bailee of the donor, with instructions to make a final delivery to the donee later on, the gift is held not to be effective and irrevocable until the final delivery. This is because the agent or bailee is still understood to be subject to the direction of the donor whom he serves; and the instructions are revocable.[9] It is otherwise if the third person is directed by the donor to take and hold possession as the bailee or trustee for the donee.[10] It is often difficult to interpret the meaning of the donor's acts and words, and to determine whether the third party is the donor's agent or is a bailee or trustee for the donee; the question of revocability turns on this interpretation.[11]

Not infrequently it is said that no more is required by way of delivery than the nature of the subject matter makes possible. If there is no testimonial document, or other symbol or token, that is representative of the right that is the subject of gift, the effectiveness of a gift assignment must depend upon the existence of factors other than delivery. These other factors are considered in accompanying sections. It is frequently held, also that when the document or symbol is already in the physical possession of the donee, an irrevocable gift can be consummated without any physical transfer of possession. This has been held in the case of the gift of chattels; and whatever is effective in such cases should likewise be effective in the case of incorporeal rights.[12]

### § 911.  Meaning of "Dominion and Control"

It has often been said that for the gift to be irrevocable and complete, the donor must do acts sufficient to strip him of all "dominion" or deprive him of all "control" over the property. With respect to a chattel or a particular piece of paper, these statements render service, provided that by dominion and control is meant the physical possession of the chattel or paper. In most cases involving gifts of choses in action, however, this is not what is meant by those terms. Instead, there is a subtle begging of the question by an unconscious shift from the idea of physical relations to that of the legal relations of the parties. In the case of many contract rights, the holder thereof has in his possession no "document of title," no voucher or other evidential document or token. In such cases, to say that the donor must deprive himself of dominion and control can mean nothing except that he must successfully extinguish his right against the obligor. The relinquishment of dominion and control of the chose in action is not the test of an irrevocable assignment by gift; it is identical with it. There is no more reason for saying that the gift is effective because dominion and control are gone than for saying that they are gone because the gift is effective.

The problem is to determine what acts by the donor ought now to be regarded as sufficient to execute his gift, to deprive him of further dominion and control, to have the legal effect that other unquestioned assignments produce. It is clear that in all cases the donor's overt expressions must have been such as to indicate his intention to make an irrevocable gift. This is not to say that he must consciously advert to the specific legal relations that are to be effected; he does not need to be an analytical jurist, or even to know the definition of "irrevocable." But ordinary persons are aware of the difference between gift and loan and give overt expression of that awareness; and it is the function of the courts and of legal analysis to give effect to that overt expression and to invent a juristic terminology that will aid in serving this purpose.

It is clear that the donation may be irrevocable even though it is conditional. Gifts causa mortis are conditional upon the donor's death in the impending crisis; meantime, while awaiting the occurrence of the condition, they are generally said to be revocable. Gifts inter vivos may be conditional upon some uncertain event other than the donor's death and yet be irrevocable meantime. Such a conditional but also irrevocable gift may be made either by delivery to a third person with final instructions to hold for the donee,[13] or by delivering a sealed assignment, on specified conditions. If a donor delivers a book or a bond or a written assignment of an orally created debt to A with definite instructions to hold it and deliver it to B in case X is elected governor and to return it to the donor only if X is not elected, the conditional donation is effective and irrevocable from the delivery to A.

In an often cited case,[14] the New Jersey court said: "The reason is that the donor parted with nothing that was essential to dominion over the moneys in question. After she had transferred the slip of paper in question [containing only a column of figures and no written words] her dominion over her deposits remained plainly intact. The paper was in no sense a voucher of the receipt of the moneys; they could have been collected without its production; nor was it necessary to a suit for their recovery. It is impossible to believe that the parties intended this slip of paper, which contained nothing but a line of figures and an addition of them, as a testimonial showing the transaction to which it immediately appertained . . . it carries on its face no indication whatever that it was drawn or given as a voucher of the indebtedness of the person making it. The delivery of so insignificant a paper as this cannot, in our opinion, operate to legalize the transaction." The inference from this is that, if the document had been a "voucher of the receipt of moneys" and a "testimonial" of indebtedness, the gift assignment would have been fully effective. And yet the possession of such a "voucher" or "testimonial" does

14.     N.J.—Cook v. Lum, 26 A. 803,
55 N.J.L. 373 (1893).

not create "dominion and control." Such a voucher or testimonial is evidential of the validity of the claim made; but it is far from conclusive, and also it is far from "necessary" to the winning of a suit. The trouble with the slip of paper was that it was "so insignificant a paper." For the delivery of a document to effect an assignment, the document that is delivered must have "significance," it must have meaning to a reader and serve an evidential purpose.

In the same opinion, the court also said a valid gift of a non-negotiable note or bond can be effected by delivery, "although the title of the donee is not ceremoniously perfect, as it wants the finishing touch of a written assignment; but the transaction is validated on the ground that it is possessed of the all-important quality of depriving the donor of all control over the property. After the delivery of such a bond or note, the donor can exercise not a single act of ownership with respect to it; he cannot sue upon it, nor collect it, nor regain its possession." But, with respect, it must be asserted that the mere lack of physical possession of such a note or bond does not prevent its owner from suing or collecting or regaining possession. If he has delivered it with accompanying expressions of gift, it is true that he cannot do these things; but, if there are no such accompanying expressions, he can do all of them, although he may have difficulties of evidence and he may have to explain the absence of the document. If it has been delivered with gift expressions, it is an effective gift assignment; but his physical relation to the document is not a conclusive factor. The gift assignment of the right is not irrevocable because he has lost dominion and control of the document; and it is begging the question to say that it is irrevocable because he has lost dominion and control of the right that is assigned. Instead, the gift is irrevocable because the acts and other expressions of the donor manifest an intention that it should be so, one of the most important of these being the delivery of a significant voucher or testimonial of great service in the process of collection.

An effective gift assignment of a depositor's right against a savings bank can be made by delivery of the bank book. The loss of that book deprives the depositor of "dominion and control" of the book; but it does not deprive him of the power of assignment. The mode of assignment that he uses need not comply with the savings bank rules, so long as the bank itself is protected.[15] Of course, he must use a method that will deprive him of "dominion and control" of his right against the bank; that is, for an effective assignment, his method must be effective.

"Dominion and control" are not lost, and a gift assignment is not effective, as long as the acts and expressions of the donor indicate an intention to retain control. He writes an assignment, and even seals it, but retains it in his own possession; there has been no effective assignment. Even if he had received a consideration, the writing and sealing of the undelivered document would not in themselves be operative acts. So, also, where the alleged donor encloses his written assignment or his testimonial documents of title within a sealed envelope, to be opened only by the donor or after his death, his intention not to cross the Rubicon is apparent; for that reason he has not lost "dominion and control" of his right and he has as yet made no effective and irrevocable assignment.[16]

Even though an assignment is in writing and is supported by a sufficient consideration, the assignor can retain a power of revocation and control by the use of express words. Of course, the same is true of an assignment by gift. The reservation of such a power does not make the assignment inoperative, so long as the reserved power is not exercised; but it may cause the income derived from the assigned right to remain taxable under federal or other income tax statutes as income of the donor rather than that of the donee.[17]

### § 912.   Gifts Causa Mortis and Gifts Inter Vivos

It has been suggested, no doubt correctly, that the development of gifts causa mortis was greatly stimulated by the statute of frauds. The habits of a people cannot be changed overnight by a statute; and those who would previously have profited by the enforcement of oral wills now had a lively interest in the enforcement of oral gifts causa mortis. But the art and practice of giving is not restricted to testamentary donation; and the development of the law of giving involves gifts inter vivos as well as gifts causa mortis. People wish to have the power of gift and they attempt to exercise it in many informal ways. Even more intensely, people wish to be able to profit by the gifts of others, even though the gift is manifested in an informal way. As contract rights, and other choses in action, came to be regarded as assignable property, it is natural that they should be assigned by way of gift as well as for a price; and the law has become increasingly liberal in recognizing and making effective the methods by which a gift may be made.

Inasmuch as gifts causa mortis are not fully consummated until the donor's death, and, further, such gifts may be used as a substitute for a will, it would not be surprising to find that the requirements for such a donation are stricter than in the case of a gift inter vivos.[18] In the earlier growth of this law, there were cases in which the court indicated some differences. But it is believed that at the present time and in the United States there is substantial uniformity in the requirements, with respect to what constitutes delivery and what kind of document must be delivered.[19]  Whether a gift is causa mortis or inter vivos, the donative intention must be proved by expressions of the donor in addition to mere delivery; and in either case the evidence of such expressions and delivery must be clear and convincing if the trial in which the proof is offered is after the donor's death.[20]

The gift of a chattel is consummated by delivery; this, in general, means the physical tradition of the object itself.  The purpose and effect of this delivery is the creation in the donee of that complex body of legal relations that were previously in the donor, called property.  In the case of a contract right, or other chose in action, there is no chattel.  The purpose of its assignment is the same as in the case of a chattel, the creation of a right in the donee like that previously had by the donor; but the method of evidencing this purpose and of producing the intended effect is of necessity different.  A right cannot be grasped out of thin air and handed to the assignee.  If the right is evidenced by and traditionally identified with some document or other physical token, the method of transfer may follow the example of the chattel; the delivery of the document or token may be regarded as a delivery of the right—a delivery of the "chose in action."  If the right is evidenced by a document that has not been traditionally identified with the right, and has not itself been called the "chose in action," still its delivery may be regarded as sufficient, and as the law has grown has frequently been so held.  But if there is no evidential document of any kind, neither the right nor a representative of it can be delivered; and the effect of assignment must be otherwise produced.

## § 913.  Gift by Novation Distinguished from Gift Assignment

A gift can be executed, not only by an assignment of an existing claim against an obligor, but also by bargaining with an obligor and causing him to make his note or other promise direct to the donee.[21]  A donor who pays money for such a promise does not execute a gift of the money, for it goes to the obligor, not to the donee.  Instead, he causes the note or other promise of the obligor to go to the donee as a binding obligation to him, without any consideration moving from such donee.  The donee gets the con-

20.  See Knight v. Mears, 159 S.E. 119, 156 Va. 676 (1931).

In the case of a gift inter vivos, the donor's acquiescence in the continued possession by the donee constitutes corroborative evidence of the gift.  Drew v. Hagerty, 17 A. 63, 81 Me. 231 (1889).

21.    U.S.—Garrett v. Keister, 56 F. 2d 909, 61 App.D.C. 25 (1932), donor sold land to A, causing A to exe-

cute a purchase money note payable to B; Ratterman v. Lodge, 13 F.2d 805 (C.C.A.8th, 1926), donor paid money for notes and mortgages of A, causing A to execute an assignment of them direct to B.

Md.—Curley v. Wolf, 196 A. 285, 173 Md. 393 (1938), mortgage certificates surrendered to obligor who issued new certificates payable to donee.

tract right as a gift. This right he does not get by assignment from the donor; but the net result attained is substantially the same.

The contract that the donor makes can take either of two forms: (1) he may cause the obligor to make a promise to the donee as the promisee; or (2) he may cause the obligor to promise the donor that he will render a performance to the donee. The donee gets a right against the obligor in either case, as a gift from the donor who paid the price; but in the second case he is not a party to the contract (in "privity"), but is a third-party beneficiary. Had the donor wished to effectuate the same result by a gift assignment, he would have caused the obligor to make a promise to the donor to render performance to the donor himself; and afterwards, by making a gift assignment, the donee would be substituted as holder of the right.

Thus if A desires to make a gift of a bank account of $1000 to B, he may use the following methods: (1) deposit $1000 with a bank in return for the bank's issuance of a certificate of deposit or promissory deposit book direct to B; (2) deposit the money in bank, taking the bank's promise to himself that it will honor B's checks for the amount or will hold it in trust for B; (3) make the deposit as usual in his own name and later make an effective assignment thereof to B.[22]

## § 914.  Gift of Bank Account by Means of a Novation

There is no question that an irrevocable gift of a bank account can be effected by the process of novation, involving the extinguishment of the depositor's right against the bank and the substitution of such a right in the donee. It is often a difficult question, however, whether the transaction between the depositor and the bank was intended to operate as such a substitution.

If the depositor has given a written assignment to the assignee, or an order on the bank authorizing it to make such a substitution, and this writing is presented to the bank by the holder, the bank is thereby given power to effectuate a novation by assenting and making a new promise to the assignee.[23] In the case of a written assignment, the gift is generally held to be effective and irrevocable even without any notice to or acceptance by the bank. It is much less likely to be so in the case of a mere signed order, the gift assignment becoming certainly irrevocable only on acceptance or certification by the bank.

Even an oral authorization by the depositor to the bank, followed by its recognition of the assignee as a new depositor with

22. There is an excellent statement in Dunn v. Houghton, 51 A. 71 (N.J. Ch.1902).

promise to pay on his order, will also operate as a novation and a transfer of the depositor's right. In these cases, after the assent by the bank, the old depositor's check or order on the bank will rightly be dishonored and that of the new depositor respected.

There is also no doubt that, by this novation process, the depositor can determine exactly what the rights of the substitute depositor are to be. He can make his proposal to the bank on such terms as he desires. The bank may promise to hold in trust for the new party for a period of time, or to pay to his order only after the death of the depositor or on some other specified condition. The new party's rights in such a case are determined by the terms of the bank's new promise. The gift has been effected by novation, and not by mere assignment; and the character of the new rights and duties is governed thereby.[24]

In order to effect such a substitution by novation as stated above, it is not necessary that the new party be brought into the transaction or even informed of it. On being so informed, he may indeed refuse the benefit of the transaction; his assent to a beneficial donation will be presumed, but in case of actual refusal to assent, his disclaimer is effective to defeat the gift. But prior to such a disclaimer by him, the novation contract has created in him enforceable rights. If the depositor has offered to discharge the bank from further duty to him, and in return the bank has promised him to pay to the order of the new party, that new party has rights as a donee beneficiary of the transaction, the character and conditions of these rights being determined by the terms of the new contract between the bank and the depositor.[25]

Just as a depositor can effectuate a gift by assignment and novation with respect to a deposit already made, so also can he effectuate such a gift by making a new and original deposit in the name of the donee; notice to the donee is not necessary in order that the gift shall be effective and irrevocable.[26] If the bank accepts the delivered money as a trust for the donee, the law of trusts is perfectly clear. If the bank accepts it with a promise to pay it to the order of the donee, the law of contract beneficiaries is also now perfectly clear. Cases holding the contrary are either wrong because of bad analysis or sustainable by reason of facts indicating that the depositor reserved a power of revocation.[27] Parol evidence is admissible to prove the facts that accompany the deposit.

The difficult cases are those in which a depositor makes a new agreement with the bank, attempting to create rights and powers

25.　See the discussion of this problem in Dunn v. Houghton, 51 A. 71 (N.J.Ch., 1902). Also, Chandler v. Hardgrove, 2 A.2d 661, 124 N.J. Eq. 516 (1938); Mutual B. L. Ins. Co. v. Ellis, 125 F.2d 127, 138 A. L.R. 1478 (C.C.A.2d, 1942); Kittredge v. Manning, 59 N.E.2d 261, 317 Mass. 689 (1945).

in a new party and at the same time to retain rights and powers in himself. Among the commonly repeated transactions of this sort are the following: (1) the depositor has his account altered so that the promise of the bank is to pay to him "as trustee" for a named third person; (2) he has it altered so that the promise of the bank is to pay to the order of either the depositor or a named third person and to the survivor in case of the death of either.

As to the first of these, the novation is just as complete and effective as it would be if the bank's promise were to the third person himself, provided only that the intention is made clear that the depositor is given power to draw thereafter only as a trustee for the sole benefit of the new party. This intention is often far from clear; and many cases have held that an irrevocable gift is not effected by a depositor's merely altering the form of his account so that it stands in his name "as trustee for X," in the absence of any other evidence of a gift intention.[28] In such a case the depositor still has rights against the bank and the power to discharge it from all further duty to anybody by withdrawing the total sum due; and a court may say that he still retains "dominion and control." But if there are additional expressions of intention to create a real trust relation, the gift is effective—not the less so because the trustee still has such "dominion and control." [29] The transaction is then one that has transferred to the third party certain rights against the bank, at the expense of the rights of the depositor himself. In this respect, at least, it operates as a kind of partial novation. A court should look carefully to the facts of such a transaction, and not jump to the conclusion that the words "as trustee for X" were intended to have no meaning.[30]

As to the second of the two cases, that of the joint account payable to either party or to the survivor, it is clear that, if the depositor intends to execute a gift by assignment or novation, the extent of the gift to be made is subject to some serious limitations. The law does not deny to a depositor the power to make such a limited gift, nor does it prescribe one sole and exclusive mode of executing it. By a novation contract with the bank, making the third party either a direct promisee or a donee beneficiary, the depositor can create rights in such third party against the bank and the power to discharge the bank by withdrawal of the deposit. He can at the same time preserve in himself similar rights and powers.[31] It is reasonably clear, also, that he can

29.   **Me.**—Rose v. Osborne, 180 **A.** 515, 133 Me. 497 (1935).
**Mass.**—Harrington v. Donlin, 45 N. E.2d 953, 312 Mass. 577 (1942).

31.   See:
**U.S.**—Cashman v. Mason, 166 F.2d 693 (C.C.A.8th, 1948); Mutual B. L. Ins. Co. v. Ellis, 125 F.2d 127, 138 A.L.R. 1478 (C.C.A.2d, 1942).

create in the donee a right to any balance that remains at the depositor's own death. If the new contract of the bank is to pay such balance to the third party named and to no other party, there is no sufficient reason for denying validity to such a contract. There are a good many cases giving effect to transactions of this kind, where the expressions of the depositor are clear;[32] and there are statutes intended to give them full legal operation.[33]

On the other hand, there are many cases refusing to find that the gift was executed, and decreeing that the balance on deposit at death of the depositor shall go to his executor and not to the party claiming as donee.[34] These cases generally fail to see that the transaction is one of assignment or novation, the gift of an existing contract right against the bank or the creation of such a right by a novation contract. They regard it as an effort to give away *money*,[35] while at the same time retaining "dominion

**Mass.**—Kittredge v. Manning, 59 N.E. 2d 261, 317 Mass. 689 (1945).

**N.J.**—Hickey v. Kahl, 19 A.2d 33, 129 N.J.Eq. 233 (1941).

By exercising his power of withdrawal, each of the co-depositors can totally extinguish the rights of both against the bank. Neither one, however, can extinguish the rights of the other by making an assignment of his rights, even though it purports to cover the entire deposit. Upon the death of the assignor, the amount then in the bank belongs wholly to the survivor, the assignee taking none of it. Hopkins Place Sav. Bank v. Holzer, 2 A.2d 639, 175 Md. 481 (1938).

**32. Cal.**—Kennedy v. McMurray, 146 P. 647, 169 Cal. 287 (1915).
**Or.**—Beach v. Holland, 142 P.2d 990, 172 Or. 396, 149 A.L.R. 866 (1943).
Many other cases are in the note in 149 A.L.R. 879, and in earlier notes there cited.

**33.** The Banking Law of New York (Laws 1914, ch. 369, § 249) provides, "When a deposit shall be made by any person in the names of such depositor and another person and in form to be paid to either or to the survivor of them, such deposit thereupon and any additions thereto made, by either of such persons, shall become the property of such persons as joint

tenants . . . and may be paid to either during the lifetime of both or to the survivor after the death of one of them." In Moskowitz v. Marrow, 167 N.E. 506, 251 N.Y. 380, 66 A.L.R. 870 (1929), it was held that the transfer of a deposit by M into the joint names of M and H was so operative as a gift to H that H was entitled to the whole deposit remaining at the death of M. Neither the death of M, nor a notice of revocation given to the bank by M, was operative to make the gift ineffective, even though M might have had such power by an actual withdrawal of the money. The effect of this New York statute is further considered in Re Porianda, 176 N.E. 826, 256 N.Y. 423 (1931), and in other cases collected in 103 A.L.R. 1133.

**35.** "A great deal of our language in relation to bank accounts and contracts is figurative. Of course, in fact there is no 'money' of the depositor 'in the bank,' and the depositor has no title to any fund in the bank. The so-called depositor has absolutely parted with his money in every instance, and instead thereof has accepted a contract of the bank to pay him either an equal amount of money from time to time to that which he has paid to the bank, or a

and control," and perhaps also as an evasion of the statutes regulating wills. It is true that such transactions, if held operative, have an effect similar to that to be attained by a will; but gifts causa mortis and contracts for the payment of money after death of promisor or promisee have thus far not been held to be invalidated by the law of wills. Some of the cases refusing a remedy to the donee claimant can be defended on the ground that the depositor's expressions do not as a whole indicate an intention to execute a gift, either as a gift assignment or as a novation contract. Sometimes, the deposit is made a joint account solely for the convenience of the depositor himself.[36] In general, however, and in the absence of evidence to the contrary, it would seem that there is sufficient evidence of donative intention when a depositor causes his bank to change an account into a joint account of himself and another, giving to that other the power to withdraw money, and providing that any balance at death shall belong to the survivor. Retaining possession of the deposit book is not at all inconsistent with such intention.[37]

## § 915. Gifts of Notes and Bills, Bonds, Insurance Policies

The holder of a negotiable instrument can make a valid and irrevocable gift assignment of his right by delivering it, with an expression of donative intention, to the donee or some one as his representative.[38] This has been applied in many cases involving bills of exchange, promissory notes, and bank checks certified [39] and uncertified. An indorsement, in blank or in full, aids the proof of intention, but is not absolutely necessary.[40] Delivery to the custody of a third person, without instructions to hold it as representative of the claimant or to deliver it to the claimant, is not sufficient evidence of gift.[41] The evidence of such intention must be stronger in cases where the making of a gift would be a fraud on creditors.

An effective and irrevocable gift assignment can be made by the delivery with expressions of donative intention, of other more or less formal documents. Among these are bonds [42] and life insurance policies.[43] Both of these are testimonial documents, evidencing the existence and terms of a contract right; they are generally under seal; and they are expected to be presented for cancellation on payment, although this is not absolutely necessary under all circumstances. The rights of a corporate shareholder can also be transferred as a gift by the delivery of the certificate of stock,[44] although the transferee will not have the full powers of a shareholder until the transfer is entered on the books of the corporation. The holder of a life

greater amount, according to the terms of the contract and the existing usury laws." Dunn v. Houghton, 51 A. 71 (N.J.Ch.1902).

42.   U.S.—Muir v. Gregory, 168 F. 641 (C.C.A.2d, 1909).

insurance policy payable to himself or to his estate can effect an irrevocable substitution by a novation as well as by assignment, as where he surrenders the policy and procures the issuance of a new one payable to a named beneficiary.[45]  One who was insured under a group insurance policy, not held by himself, effected a valid gift assignment by delivering to the assignee a written and sworn statement "I want my insurance paid to H." [46]

## § 916.  Delivery of Savings Deposit Book

One of the most common of testimonial documents is the savings bank deposit book, containing entries of all deposits and withdrawals and definitely evidencing the extent of the depositor's claim against the bank.  It is not conclusive evidence, since mistakes can be corrected and interest or dividends may not have been entered.  All courts hold that the depositor can make an irrevocable gift assignment of his claim against the bank by the delivery of the deposit book with expressions of donative intention.[47]  These accompanying expressions may be in writing, but need not be; it is by them that it is to be determined whether the gift assignment is meant to be conditional or unconditional, a gift causa mortis or a gift inter vivos.[48]  It cannot be said that the deposit book is the "debt itself"; it is merely the generally accepted evidence of ownership, under normal conditions required by the bank to be presented before permitting a withdrawal.  In this important, but limited, sense it complies with the Law Institute requirement of a "tangible token or writing the surrender of which is required by the obligor's contract for its enforcement." [49]

## § 917.  Commercial Bank Pass Book

It has been held in a great many cases that one who has made deposits of money in a commercial bank cannot make an executed and irrevocable gift of his right against the bank by merely delivering to another person the ordinary bank book or "passbook" in which the bank has entered the various amounts that have been deposited.[50]  These cases can be distinguished from those holding that an assignment by executed gift can be made by the delivery of a savings bank book, a certificate of deposit, or a written receipt acknowledging an indebtedness and stating the terms of the obligation.  The ordinary bank book is nothing more than a memorandum showing that certain deposits have been made at definite times, but not stating in any way the terms of the contract between the depositor and the bank.  The bank book does not indicate the amounts that may have been withdrawn by the depositor by check or otherwise and does not indicate what balance, if any, is due from the bank to the depositor.  Such a bank book is not required to be presented when withdrawals are made, and, therefore, it seldom indicates the extent of the right that the depositor may have against the bank. Such a bank book is evidence of the receipt of money by the bank, but it is not evidence as to withdrawals that may have been made, or of the terms of the contract between the parties, or as to the amount that is actually due from the bank.[51]

## § 920. Delivery of a Token or Symbol

A gift assignment has in various cases been held to be effected by the delivery of a token or symbol. Such a token or symbol is certainly not to be regarded as "the debt itself"; its possession is seldom, if ever, absolutely necessary to the enforcement of the right and the realization of performance; and its delivery cannot be said to be in itself a surrender of "dominion and control" of anything other than the token or symbol itself. Gifts causa mortis and inter vivos have been effected by the delivery, with expressions of donative intention, of a key to a safe deposit box or other locked receptacle not itself near to the donor and easily deliverable itself. The contents of such a deposit box may include testimonial documents such as notes, bonds, savings bank books. If these documents are such that a gift assignment could be effected by their delivery, such an assignment can also be effected by a delivery of the key that gives access to the box.[67] This is not because the surrender of the key is "required by the obligor's contract" for the enforcement of his contract, or because anybody has appointed the key to be a token or symbol of the contract right; it is because possession of the key gives a degree of access to the box and is rightly treasured by the owner for that reason, so that its delivery is strong confirmatory evidence of the donative intention.

Again, the warning should be given that the key to the box has no mystic quality; but it has a practical serviceability. Its mere possession is conclusive evidence of nothing; and the fact that it was actually delivered is nothing more than corroborative evidence, insufficient when standing alone to establish a donative intention. In every case, therefore, dealing with the delivery of a key or other "symbol or token," care must be taken to weigh the accompanying evidential factors; by such a process the appearance of conflict in decision frequently disappears.[68]

51. Section 918 deals with Gifts of Certificates of Deposit and Written Receipts. The case of Cronin v. Chelsea Savings Bank, 87 N.E. 484, 201 Mass. 146 (1909) is discussed at length.

Section 919 deals with Gift Assignment by Delivery of the Obligor's Informal Written Contract. There is some authority that an irrevocable gift of a contract right can thus be made.

## § 921.    Gift by the Assignor's Written Assignment, Sealed or Unsealed

In spite of some conflict in the past, based chiefly on the abandoned view that an assignment is a mere power of attorney, it seems now to be well settled that an irrevocable gift can be made by the delivery of a written assignment under seal.[69]  The modern statutes that abolish or limit the effect of a seal should not prevent the delivery of such a writing from operating as an irrevocable gift.[70]

In some states where common law seals have been abolished, the effect has been to give to unsealed documents substantially the same effect that they would formerly have had if sealed.  In such a state, a written unsealed assignment should be held to be effective and irrevocable.  More often, however, the abolition of seals is intended to have no such effect; and if a written, unsealed assignment is fully effective, it is because the delivery of such a document properly evidences donative intention.  If this reason is accepted, it is equally operative in a state where seals retain their common law effect.

## § 922.    Gift Assignment by Mere Oral Communication

As has been seen above, there has been a progressive liberality in the direction of sustaining gift assignments made in various informal ways.  This liberality has even been extended so far as to hold that an irrevocable gift of a chose in action can be made by a mere oral communication to the donee or to the obligor.  Delivery is impossible if the donor's right is not evidenced by any testimonial document; and in such a case a mere oral statement to the donee has been held effective.[80]  Of course, it was quite possible for the donor to execute a written assignment.  There are also cases holding that where the testimonial document is already in the possession of the donee,[81] or in the possession of a third person who refuses to give it up,[82] a gift assignment can be made by an oral statement.

In some cases a gift assignment has been effected by the donor's oral direction to the obligor to pay the donee and the obligor's assent thereto, the obligor sometimes expressly promising the donee.[83]  Such a decision can be rested on the theory of novation, if the evidence shows that the donor discharged the obligor from further duty to him, but the court has attained its end without

69.    Chase Nat. Bank v. Sayles, 11 F.2d 948, 48 A.L.R. 207 (C.C.A.1st, 1926), is a striking recent case, although the right assigned was not a contract right.  A woman, who was the beneficiary of a bequest of $4,000,000 in trust, delivered a sealed assignment of a part thereof amounting to $1,500,-000 to her attorney, as a gift.  Later she tried to revoke it, and was held to have no power.  The court talks in terms of "equitable title."

reference to such evidence.  Also, such a decision can be rested
on the theory that the donee is not an assignee, but is instead a
donee beneficiary of a contract between the obligor and the
donor.[84]  To support this theory, the donor must be shown to have
given a consideration for the obligor's promise.

There are cases definitely holding that an irrevocable gift assignment cannot be made by a mere oral communication; [85] and
there can be no doubt that this accords with the great weight of
judicial dicta.  Nevertheless, the door has been opened; and courts
are not unlikely to give effect to an oral gift when the evidence
is convincing and the circumstances are such that the making
of the gift was justifiable and reasonable.  Evidence of an oral
gift will very frequently be unconvincing in cases where the
donor is now dead, where actual delivery of documents could have
been made and was not made, and where the donor during his
life continued to treat the subject matter as his own.[86]

85.   **Cal.**—Adams **v.** Merced Stone
Co., 178 P. 498, 176 Cal. 415, 3 A.
L.R. 928 (1917), holding that a
mere oral expression of gift was
not enough even though the donee
was the president of the obligor corporation, with access to its books
and full power to make entries
therein indicating changes in its
obligations.

# TOPIC C

## JOINT AND SEVERAL CONTRACTS

### CHAPTER 52

### JOINT AND SEVERAL CONTRACTS

### § 923.  Parties to a Contract—Complexity of Relations

In a transaction by which a contract is made, the individuals taking part may be few or many. It takes only one to make a promise, although the act of promising must be directed at someone else; it takes two to make a bargain and there must be at least two in order that there may be an agreement. In a bargain or agreement, there may be no promise made by either party, there may be a promise by one party only, or promises may be made by both parties. As the number of persons in a transaction increases it grows in complexity; and the legal relations of the participants with each other increase in geometrical progression. In such a transaction two or more persons may act together, with interests and desires more or less in common. Two or more may thus contract with one, together making a promise to him, or together receiving a promise made by him. Two or more persons may thus as a group all promise that a single performance shall be rendered; or they may each promise a separate performance. Thus, when A, B, and C sign a note saying "We promise to pay to the order of D $1,000", there is only one payment to be made; D has a right to only $1,000 not to $3,000. On the other hand, in return for services or a transfer of property by D, separate amounts of money may be promised, by A $500, by B $300, and by C $200.

Instead of money, A, B, and C may promise to render service, or to transfer Blackacre owned by them in common, or to cause a building to be erected; and in return D may promise them $1,000 in a single undivided payment or in three payments (equal or unequal) to be made separately to each one. In such a transaction D also may have associates. The promise or promises of A, B, and C may be made to D, E, and F; and they in turn may promise the single payment of $1,000, or the three payments. In such cases we have co-promisors and co-promisees. We may also call them "joint" promisors and "joint" promisees; but this term "joint" has had a long history, with varying legal significance at common law, in equity, and by many statutes. This variation is so great that it is misleading to classify contracts as "joint" or "several" or "joint and several" as though these terms had a constant significance.

The complexity may increase further. On either side the parties may all promise as "principals", or one may be a "principal" and the others his "sureties"; or each may be a principal as to one part of the performance, with one or more of the others his surety therefor. The promises may be made expressly in this form, the other parties assenting thereto; or they may be made with no indication of suretyship, and yet with a clear agreement among the promisors determining their relations with each other, an agreement that may be either known or unknown to other parties to the transaction.

The end is not yet. Promisors and promisees may not aline themselves in two groups only. It is possible for them to make their promises in a circus, each promising something to the next; or they may divide into three or more groups. Three neighbors may agree to exchange farms, A to B, B to C, and C to A, with additional provisions as to crops, livestock, money payments, mortgages and suretyship.

As the final indication of growing complexity, we may suggest the "collective bargain," affecting a million workers in a hundred mills owned by numerous individuals and corporations, the workers organized but not incorporated, and represented by a few union leaders. Alongside, or it may be within, this collective bargain is the individual bargain of each workman with his separate employer, determining his special place in the collective whole. Great bargaining transactions such as these, of great variety among themselves, have not yet received clear analysis. Who is legally bound and to what extent? This remains for the future, to be determined perhaps by legislation, perhaps by conflict. They do not fit into such categories as "joint" or "joint and several".

### § 924. Displacement of Common Law by Equity and by Statute—the Law of Suretyship

In a general treatise on contract law, we can not hope to analyze or to solve all of the complex problems suggested in the preceding section. In this treatise the problems of individual "capacity" to make a contract will not be considered: the powers of an infant, a married woman, an agent or trustee, a person suffering from abnormality in some degree, a group of persons acting as an "incorporated" company. Some of the simpler and more frequently recurring transactions involving more than two parties will be dealt with, recounting to a limited extent the history of "joint" and "joint and several" contracts. Doctrines that are dead should not continue "to rule us from their graves" because of ignorance of their demise. The common law has itself never been uniform and static. The law of the present must be sought in the history of equity as well as in the decisions at common law. The general character of statutory changes must be indicated, even though no attempt is made to present the statutory law of any jurisdiction. In so far as ancient rule and doctrine were based on the narrow and inflexible character of primitive procedure, they have been or must still be abandoned under the compulsion of modern systems of procedure, the state codes and the federal rules. In so far as those rules and doctrines were caused by an inadequate analysis of jural relationships, by conceptual obsessions as to "jointness," or by notions of "justice" that have become obsolete with the changing mores and practices of men, their abandonment by progressive courts must be made to appear, whether those courts purported to administer "equity" or the "common law" or a modern system of law that is the product of both, along with statute and other sources, in a continuing judicial evolution.

Let us first consider briefly the extent to which the law of suretyship, so largely the construction of courts of equity, is necessarily involved in a transaction in which two or more persons make promises for the rendition of a single performance. If between two or more promisors the relation of principal and surety exists, their present legal relations with each other and with their promisee are determined by the equitable law of suretyship, not by the contrary rules and decisions of the earlier common law. It is everywhere provided by statute that in case of conflict between the two systems, equity shall prevail; and even without such a statute the same result should obtain, by reason of judicial history alone, in any court that is the successor of the court of Chancery as well as of the Common Bench. By reason of unawareness of this, injustice has sometimes been done, with frequent repetition of displaced doctrines.

Let us first suppose the simple case in which A and B borrow $1,000 of C and execute their note to him thus: "We, A and B, promise to pay to C or order $1,000, thirty days after date, for value received." A and B use the money together, either for business or pleasure, either as a business partnership or in a single common transaction. This note is called a "joint" note; and it is clear that A and B are both borrowers and users of the money, that they are both principal debtors. And yet they are also both sureties. In the absence of a contrary agreement between them, it is the duty of each to the other to pay his just proportion, in this case $500. If A pays the full debt to C, whether by compulsion of a judgment or merely in performance of his contract, he has a right of contribution by B in the sum of $500. Even before making payment, A could get a decree in equity against B that he shall exonerate A by paying his share of the debt. After paying more than his own share, A could get a decree for reimbursement of the excess by B. This right of reimbursement was at length recognized at common law also and was enforced in the action of assumpsit. In equity, as between themselves, each was a principal debtor as to his own share and a mere surety as to the balance. This did not deprive C of his right against both A and B to full payment, the amount being collectible against either; but he was required nevertheless to recognize the existence of the suretyship relation and to do nothing that would increase the risk of non-reimbursement in case one should pay more than his share.

If in the foregoing transaction the fact had been that the full amount borrowed had been solely for B's use and benefit, A signing the note only for the purpose of lending his credit to B, the latter is the sole principal debtor and A is a surety with a right to full exoneration and reimbursement by B.

Hereafter, when we are considering the effect of payment by one obligor, or of the death of one obligor, or of a discharge of one obligor, or of a judgment against one obligor, as to all of which the common law laid down some early and now unreasonable rules, we must not fail to remember the equitable law of suretyship and that this law may nullify the common law rules in many respects.[1]

### § 925. Promises of One Performance made by Two or More Persons

Suppose that two persons, John Doe and Richard Roe, sign a document which reads: "We, J. Doe and R. Roe, promise to pay Styles $1,000." This is a single promissory sentence, although it has a plural subject and two distinct persons are named as promising. Each of these persons signs his name by a separate and distinct act; and it is clear that each one is promising that Styles shall receive payment. But it is also clear that the two men are promising only one payment. It does not appear in what proportion Doe and Roe may have agreed between themselves to raise and tender the money. They may be co-principals, having either equal or unequal shares of the burden; or they may be principal and surety, the latter having a right to full exoneration by the former.

The early common law judges did not regard the relations of Doe and Roe inter se, the document saying nothing on the subject. These judges saw only a single indivisible promise creating a single indivisible obligation—a *vinculum juris* with Doe and Roe handcuffed together at one end. The one promise was a "joint" promise; and Doe and Roe were "jointly" bound by a "joint obligation." Enforcement could only be by a single judgment requiring a single payment.[2] If Roe died and vanished,

---

1. Restatement, Contracts, Chapter 5, purports to state the "common law" with respect to "joint" "joint and several" and "several" contracts, disregarding the part played by equity and the various statutes. In two sections the stated rule is limited thus: "except in the cases and to the extent required by the law of suretyship." There is no statement as to what the law of suretyship requires. There seems to be no other warning that the stated rules may not now be in effect in many jurisdictions or in any jurisdiction.

2. In Fuller & Co. v. Morrison, 169 A. 9, 106 Vt. 22 (1933), the court held that it could not render judgment against several defendants for separate amounts.

In U. S. Printing & Lith. Co. v. Powers, 135 N.E. 225, 233 N.Y. 143 (1922), it was held that a judgment against joint guarantors could not be reversed as to one and affirmed as to another. This would be affected by later New York statutes.

Cornish & Co. v. West, 84 N.W. 750, 82 Minn. 107 (1901), excellently illustrates the flexibility of modern

Doe alone was bound to Styles. If in order to free Roe, Styles let loose the chain, Doe likewise was set free.

It was always possible, of course, for Doe and Roe to make their promises separately by signing separate documents, even though they promised a single payment of $1,000. Principals and guarantors often have done this. Here the judges could readily see two separate promises, each with its own *vinculum juris,* each enforceable by a separate judgment, each easily loosened without affecting the other. These promises were "several". Doe and Roe were "severally" bound, the obligation of each being a "several obligation." [3]

At some time or other, it became possible for Doe and Roe to produce this second juristic result even though they signed but a single document. It could be done by the use of mystic words. The word "several" had become the "sovereign talisman". Needs only to have Doe and Roe sign thus: "We, J. Doe and R. Roe, promise severally only to pay Styles $1,000."

Creditor Styles further found that he might as well have the advantages of both forms at once; and he had his debtors sign thus: "We, J. Doe and R. Roe jointly and severally promise to pay Styles $1,000." There was still but one document and but one promissory sentence; there was but one performance to be rendered. But the mystic words enabled the judges to see three promises, one "joint" and two "several", each surrounded by its appurtenant doctrines and enforceable by its appropriate judgment.[4]

It would have been of no importance whatever to the obligee Styles, or to the obligors Doe and Roe, whether they promised "jointly", or "severally" or "jointly and severally", except for

---

procedure. Twenty-one men signed a subscription contract promising to pay $3,000 for the erection of a creamery. Ten of them put specific amounts by their signatures, these amounts having been paid. Eleven others signed, naming no specific amounts. The court interpreted the document as binding these eleven men to pay each one-eleventh of the balance. It held that they were properly joined in a single action, and that the ten who had paid were also properly joined because of the plaintiff's claiming a lien on the property. Where 20 men (including A) contracted to buy land of A and B, the 20 promising severally, and not jointly, to pay their stated portions of the price, it was held that A and B could get a decree for specific performance against the 19 buyers other than A, the fact that their promises were several not preventing. Welling v. Crosland, 123 S.E. 776, 129 S.C. 127 (1923).

3. One who by agreement with a debtor assumes payment of the latter's debt to a third person can be sued in a separate action by the creditor beneficiary. He is not jointly bound with the original debtor. As between themselves, the debtor is now a surety and the new promisor the principal obligor. Under modern procedure the original debtor and the new promisor can be joined in one action.

certain collateral doctrines that became attached to the "joint" contract by reason of inadequate analysis and inflexible procedure. In all three forms alike, Doe and Roe were promising one identical performance, not two distinct and separate performances to be rendered by each separately. This is a fundamental distinction, to be observed long after the analytical and procedural excrescences have disappeared. In a modern court, administering a system of law based on equity as well as common law,[5] by a flexible procedure created by statute and by rules of court, the main issue with respect to co-promisors is as to whether they promised only one performance or separate and distinct performances, and with respect to co-promisees is as to whether they were all promised one identical performance or a separate and distinct performance for each of them. This is the issue of which it is correct to say that it is determined by "interpretation."

The issue just stated is the one most likely to be in the court's mind when it asks whether two parties promised jointly or promised severally. Did they promise one and the same performance or did they promise two different performances? But it is seldom what the courts meant in earlier days when they asked whether two parties promised jointly, or severally, or jointly and severally. They assumed that only one performance was promised; and they asked whether that performance was promised in the "joint" manner or not, whether the words were words of "jointness". And their purpose in asking was to determine the applicability of the ancient collateral doctrines as to survivorship, discharge, and joinder of parties, doctrines that if not wholly extinct are certainly moribund.

It is unfortunate that we still have to use the same language, the same terminology, now that the law to be applied has changed. Its use produces intellectual confusion. A joint contract is no longer the "joint contract" of old; but how does it differ? Once its connotation included those doctrines just described as "procedural excrescences"; it no longer includes them all, if any, but it may take fifty pages to explain why and to what extent.

If two or more persons promise one and the same performance, there is necessarily a relation of suretyship between them, gov-

---

5. One who speaks of the "common law" of the present time seldom means to contrast it with "equity". He means to include within the term all those rules that are not obviously the result of formal legislative enactment, from whatever source they may have been drawn. Our law is "common law", whether it comes from the old law of the King's courts, from the equity of the Chancellors, from the law merchant of international traders, from the civil and the canon law known to the Chancellors while they were also ecclesiastics, or by conscious and unconscious borrowings from other systems.

erned by the rules of law that originated in the court of Chancery but now fully incorporated into our existing legal system. There are two alternatives: (1) one of the promisors is sole principal debtor and another his surety only, or (2) each of them is a principal debtor as to his just proportion and a surety as to the just proportions of the others. This is true whether their promises are in form "joint", or "several", or "joint and several;" it is true whether their promises are made orally, or in a single written instrument, or in separate writings executed at different times and places.

If, however, the two or more persons promise separate performances, a different one for each, each one is necessarily a sole principal as to the performance that nobody else has promised; and there is no suretyship involved. Also, the problems of "jointness" that perplexed the courts of early law are non-existent. Questions may arise as to the joinder of parties plaintiff or defendant, but these will be answered as required by the modern and flexible rules of procedure.

In innumerable cases it is said that if the words of a promise that is signed by two or more persons are in the "conjunctive" form, the presumption is that they mean to be bound "jointly." [6] In a modern case this may mean no more than that they are promising one and the same performance and not separate performances; formerly it meant that they are promising "jointly," but not "severally" or "jointly and severally." To indulge such a "presumption" when we do not clearly know what is the result of indulging it has its dangers; but these dangers must be dealt with, they can not be ignored. The forms of language that raise this presumption include such as the following: We, Doe and Roe, promise to pay (a plural subject with a single predicate); Doe and Roe are held and firmly bound to pay; we jointly promise (the word "jointly" being a strong though not a necessary word); obligamus nos.

The "presumption" that the promisors mean to be bound "jointly" can easily be overcome by adding words of "severance". If Doe and Roe mean to promise separate performances, one for each, they can easily do so by using two sentences and avoiding the "conjunctive" form: Doe promises to pay $60; Roe promises to pay $40. They can produce the same result while using the "conjunctive" form in a single sentence: We, Doe and Roe, promise to pay the amounts set opposite our signatures. Cases involving separate performances are considered in the section that follows.

Even if Doe and Roe intend to promise only one identical performance, they can prevent their promise from being a "joint promise" with its old common law connotations. The traditional word of severance was "severally": We, Doe and Roe, promise severally (or jointly and severally). The words might also be such as these: We, and each of us, promise; we bind ourselves as individuals; obligamus nos et singulos. These, too, will be considered in a subsequent section.

### § 926.   Promises of Separate Performances by Two or More Persons—Factors in Interpretation

The question whether two or more promisors have promised a single undivided performance, or have each promised a limited and separate performance, is wholly a problem of interpretation. The question is merely what was the performance promised and who promised it. This question is quite distinct from the question whether the two or more promisors are bound jointly, or jointly and severally, with the significance given to those terms by the old common law.

For example, let us suppose that a dealer receives an order for goods, part to be delivered to A and part to B, with direction that the prices of the goods so delivered shall be charged to them separately. In such a case, the dealer can not get judgment against A for the price of the goods shipped to B; nor can he get judgment against A and B jointly for the price of the goods shipped to both of them. A and B have made separate purchases of goods and separate promises to pay separate amounts of money.[7]

Let us suppose however that the dealer replies to the order saying that he will ship no goods to B unless A assures payment for them, and that A replies that he will do so. With respect to the goods shipped to A the dealer can get judgment against A alone; B has made no promise to pay for them, either jointly or severally. With respect to the goods shipped to B, the dealer can get judgment against B; and he can also get judgment against A. For the goods shipped to B, both A and B have promised to pay. Their promises were made in separate letters, B's in the first order, A's in the succeeding letter; but these two promises are for one single performance, the payment of the price of B's goods. Under modern procedure there should be no difficulty in joining A and B as co-defendants in an action for the price of B's goods, even though they would not be described by the old common law as "jointly" bound, and even though B is principal debtor and A his surety.

One who guarantees payment of the debt of another is always promising the same performance as is the principal debtor. This is true even though he limits the amount of his liability. Up to that limit, the performance promised is one and the same. As between themselves, two or more co-sureties or guarantors may bind themselves for separate portions of a principal debt;[8] but merely fixing a maximum limit to the liability of each does not have this effect.  Up to the amount of the lowest of these limits they are all promising one and the same performance.  Their words may, of course, be such that they can be separately sued.[9]

An employer may make wholly separate contracts with each of his employees; but he can produce the same legal effect by a single contract with several employees.  Each employee may therein promise to render separate service, for which the employer promises each of them a separate compensation.  The performances promised are separate performances; and there is no "joint" promise under either modern or ancient law.  Whether or not this is what the parties mean is a matter of interpretation on which reasonable minds may at times differ; but when so interpreted each one can sue or be sued separately for breach, and the common law doctrines affecting joint contracts were never applicable.[10]

### § 927.  Subscription Contracts—Promises in One Instrument to Make Individual Payments

It is not at all uncommon for a good many persons to sign a common "subscription" paper.  It may read: We the undersigned .  .  .  (for a stated purpose and consideration) subscribe and promise to pay the amounts set opposite our names.  This purports to be a single promise, with a plural subject in conjunctive form.  And yet, because the amounts of money to be paid are separate and different, the inference that each signer means to bind himself for his own specified amount and for not a cent more, either as principal or surety, is irresistible.  Each is separately bound for a separate payment, just as clearly so as in the cases in which he signs a separate subscription card reading "I subscribe and promise to pay."  In the case of charitable subscriptions a different intention is hardly conceivable.

To these promises, the law of "joint" and "joint and several" contracts has no application.  The promises of the subscribers may indeed be described as "several"; but they are very different from the cases in which two or more persons "severally" promise one and the same performance.[24]  When two or more persons promise

---

10.    Kan.—Curry v. Kansas & C. P. R. Co., 48 P. 579, 58 Kan. 6 (1897).
In Beckwith v. Talbot, 95 U.S. 289, 24 L.Ed. 496 (1877), A, B, and C made a contract with D to care for his herd of cattle for two years, to be paid one half of the excess over $36,000 for which the herd would then sell.  On breach by D, A was allowed to maintain a separate action for one third of the promised money.  Presumably, but not necessarily, for a breach by A of his duty to serve, D could have sued him separately.

24.    Restatement, Contracts, § 113: "Where two or more parties to a contract promise separate performances, to be rendered respectively by each of them, or where each of them makes only a separate prom-

one and the same performance, a suretyship relation is necessarily created between them, however separately they may make their promises. A full payment by one of them necessarily discharges the obligee's rights against the others; and so does any other substituted performance that is received as the agreed equivalent of the performance that was promised. Although the obligee can get separate judgments against the promisors, he is entitled to only one satisfaction, except as to the costs. If the performances promised are separate and distinct, the foregoing statements can not be made. In neither case was the doctrine of survivorship applicable; but that doctrine is practically extinct even as to joint promises.

Even though the "subscription" promises are for a business purpose, with a single consideration for which all the subscribers are bargaining, the legal duty of each subscriber is just as separate as in the case of a charitable subscription, if such an intention is expressed with sufficient clearness. This has often been held to be sufficiently clear, even though the signatures are on a single document that starts out with the words "We subscribe and promise", if they are followed not by a gross and total sum of money, but by such words as "the amounts set opposite our names".[25] Other factors may have evidential significance in interpretation, such as the manner in which the subscriptions are solicited and the lack of acquaintance or business relationship among the subscribers. The practical construction given to the document by the obligee himself may be conclusive; and occasionally there has been a usage in the community that is relevant.[26]

The setting of a separate amount against each signature should practically always be sufficient to justify a separate action against him for that amount, even though other factors may show that each signer intended also to be a surety for the others. In some

ise that the same performance shall be rendered, each is severally bound for the performance which he promises and is not bound jointly with any of the others."
See also the Comment and Illustrations thereto.

This statement deals with two different kinds of transactions, the legal effects of which are very different.

It leads to what appears to be erroneous statements in other sections. For example, the statements made in Section 120 are true only of persons severally bound for *the same performance*, not of those severally bound for *different performances*.

25. Groups of farmers have often formed co-operative associations for erection of a creamery, subscribing wholly separate amounts.

U.S.—Davis & Rankin B. & M. Co. v. Barber, 51 F. 148 (C.C.Ind.1892), "each shall be liable only for amount subscribed by him".

Subscriptions for corporate stock are ordinarily wholly separate from each other, and an unpaid balance is separately collectible by the corporation or its creditors.

of the cases, the court merely sustains such an action, overruling the defendant's objection that others are not joined in the action.

Some of these business subscription contracts for a co-operative undertaking are very complex; they may provide for forming a corporation, for joint management by a committee, for procurement and transfer of a tract of land by all the subscribers. Even though some joint duties and powers may thus be created, the promise of money payments may be wholly separate.[27]

In some cases, a promisee who supplied goods or erected a building in reliance on the promises of several subscribers was held to have been reasonable in his understanding that each subscriber bound himself for the whole amount, even though as among themselves the subscribers divided the total into parts and limited the ultimate responsibility of each to one of those parts.[28] On the facts as reported it can not be said that the interpretation by the court was unreasonable.

### § 928.  Each Joint Promisor is Bound for the Whole Performance Promised

If two or more persons promise the payment of a stated sum of money, one identical amount promised by all, the promisee can get judgment against all the promisors; and execution may be levied on the goods of any one of them as may be most convenient.[29] Each one is bound to pay the full amount, although one full payment will discharge them all. This is true whether they all sign a single promise in conjunctive terms ("jointly"), or sign separate promises in separate documents (indicating that they refer to one payment only), or all sign one promise in terms both conjunctive and disjunctive ("jointly and severally," all and each of us).

At common law great differences in procedure were dependent on which form was used; and the legal effect of one obligor's death, or of his discharge, or of a judgment against one only, varied greatly with the words. But in all alike, and by modern law as well, the extent of the duty of each and every one was the same and was enforceable against him in full. The differences just mentioned have been mostly wiped out by equity or by statute; but they will be developed in some detail in succeeding sections in order to show the extent to which they have been wiped out and to help make sure that the process continues.

---

27.   See:

Idaho —Buster **v.** Fletcher, 125 P. 226, 22 Idaho 172 (1912).

Iowa —McArthur v. Board, 93 N.W. 580, 119 Iowa 562 (1897).

Minn.—Gibbons v. Bente, 53 N.W. 756, 51 Minn. 499 (1892).

29.   **Ala.**—Leinkauff **v.** Munter, 76 Ala. 194 (1884).

Me.—Ripley v. Crooker, 47 Me. 370 (1860).

If the single performance that is promised by two or more persons is the building of a house, or the transfer of land or goods, or the rendition of specified objective service not allocated to the promisors separately, the promisee can get judgment for damages for breach against all the promisors; and, as in the case of the money promise, collection may be made out of the goods of each or any of them, one full satisfaction operating as a discharge of all.[30]  At common law the same differences existed as stated above with reference to money promises; and they have likewise been largely wiped out.

There being but a single performance due from all the promisors, the rendition of that full performance, or of its full agreed equivalent, by anyone, operates as a discharge of all; and the rendition of a part of that performance, or of the agreed equivalent of such a part, operates as a discharge of each and all in equal proportion.[31]

If two or more make separate promises of different performances, the case is very different; and what has been said above is not applicable.  Even if they all promise one and the same performance, each can make his own legal duty to the promisee subject to one or more conditions precedent that are special to himself.  He thereby distinguishes his promise from the others, not in the performance to be rendered but in the conditions of his legal duty to render it.[32]

The legal relations among themselves, of the two or more promisors of one and the same performance, are determined by agreement express or implied among themselves; or, if there is no such agreement, by equitable considerations in accordance with the facts.  If all of them bargained alike for the same consideration, each for his own beneficial use, they are co-principals, each being a principal as to his pro rata share of the performance promised and a surety as to the shares of the others.  If the consideration exchanged for their promises was bargained for and received to the beneficial use of only one of the promisors, he is the sole principal debtor and the others are his sureties.

30.   In Alpaugh v. Wood, 23 A. 261, 53 N.J.L. 638 (1891), the two defendants agreed "to take entire charge of the manufacturing department of said pottery and to give their whole time, labor and skill towards the proper management of said business."  The court held that for any breach they could be sued for damages jointly, irrespective of whether the neglect was by one or by both of them, and even though one of them had specially promised his skilled service in modeling.  "The promisors have undertaken to accomplish together a single result; for in such cases the promisee evidently relies upon a joint performance.  The inference of a joint obligation is not defeated by the fact that it appears, either in the terms of the contract or from the circumstances of the transaction, that each promisor is to contribute separately to the entire result for which they bargain."

## § 929. Effect of Non-joinder of a Joint Promisor, and of a Judgment against One Only

As we consider the common law procedure for enforcement, we must constantly remember that we are not stating present day law. Today's law, varying in some respects with the jurisdiction, is determined more by equity and by statutes, both substantive and procedural, than by the common law. Note, too, that this instant discussion deals with the common law procedure for enforcement of a promise or promises made by two or more persons for the rendition of a single performance. Whether these persons promise this performance jointly, or severally, or jointly and severally, each promisor is under a legally enforceable duty to cause this performance and the whole of it to be rendered.

If these two or more persons have promised in the "joint" form, thus: "We Doe and Roe, promise to pay Styles $1,000," although each bound himself for the full amount, the promisee could not get judgment at common law against one alone, or against less than all, if objection was properly made.[33] So obsessed with the supposed unitary character of the promise made by Doe and Roe was the judicial mind in very early times, that if Styles brought action against Doe alone, alleging that Doe had promised to pay $1,000 and making no mention of Roe, Doe could plead the general issue. It was believed that he had made no such promise. Also, if Styles declared on the promise as one made by Doe and Roe, without joining Roe as defendant, a demurrer to the declaration would be sustained.[34]

This led to futile delay and injustice, since Roe might be dead, insolvent, or beyond the jurisdiction; and finally a judge appeared with sufficient intellectual vigor and judicial prestige to effect a change. Lord Mansfield held that Doe could object to the non-joinder of Roe only by a plea in abatement.[35] Such a plea was sustainable only by "giving the plaintiff a better writ," that is by naming the man not joined and showing that he is alive and subject to process. If Doe could not do this, or omitted to do it, the action proceeded to judgment against him for the full amount unpaid.[36]

This change in the procedure by Lord Mansfield in no way affected the terms or the character of a joint promisor's contract. It was a change of procedure of importance to such a promisor, making it measurably less likely that he would escape perform-

33. **U.S.**—First N. Bank of Clarion v. Hamor, 49 F. 45 (C.C.A.9th, 1892).
Restatement, Contracts, § 117: "Each person bound by a joint promise is bound for the whole performance thereof, but by making appropriate objection can prevent recovery of judgment against him unless there are joined as defendants all promisors who were originally jointly bound with him, except such of them as are at the time of suit dead or beyond the jurisdiction of the court."

ance; it did not change that performance or affect the interpretation by which such performance and the conditions of his duty to render it are determined. By the old common law itself, Doe is in duty bound to render the full performance and to render it without any suit, with or without joinder of Roe. Even under the former procedure, a judgment against Doe and Roe jointly being rendered, execution could be levied against Doe alone. Nor did the change in procedure affect in any way Doe's equitable right to contribution against Roe.[37]

If Doe, when sued alone, did not plead in abatement, Roe being alive and within the jurisdiction, the judgment so obtained against Doe alone, even though uncollectible, was held to bar any subsequent action against Roe by the obligee.[38] Various reasons were given for this, one being that the original obligation is merged in the judgment and so discharged. This is really no explanation; it is merely a statement of the result in other terms. A more plausible reason is that Roe has the same right not to be sued alone as had Doe; and he ought not to be deprived of it by the fact that the obligee sued Doe alone and the latter made no objection. Yet Doe can not now be sued again on the same cause of action. Therefore, Roe is allowed to plead that he has been discharged by reason of the suit and judgment against Doe.[39] Justice does not really require this, since even the technical common law recognized the fact that Roe owes the full amount, just as much as Doe; and modern statutes generally permit separate actions just as if Doe and Roe had promised jointly and severally.

In the course of time the common law judges further recognized that Doe and Roe are two separate individuals, each making a promise to pay the money, even though they used the word "jointly" and signed a single document. They held that if Roe can not be joined in the action against Doe because he is out of the jurisdiction, judgment will be rendered against Doe alone, and that judgment is not a bar to a later action against Roe alone wherever process can reach him, whether in a different jurisdiction or in the same one after he returns to it.[40] This was a marked recognition of the individual obligation of joint obligors and of the fact that separate actions are not unjust.

There are many statutes expressly authorizing judgment against one joint obligor, or against all such obligors as are made parties defendant, and providing for enforcement against others by a subsequent proceeding.[41] Some of these have been rather

41. The Uniform Joint Obligations Act as adopted in New York, Consol.Laws 1930, Ch. 12, § 232: "A judgment against one or more of several obligors, or against one or more of joint, or of joint and several obligors shall not discharge a co-obligor who was not a party to the proceeding wherein the judgment was rendered."

narrowly interpreted.   In addition, almost all the states provide that a contract joint in form shall be in effect joint and several.

Under such a statute, a judgment against one obligor alone is no bar to action against another;  but it is conclusive against him on the issues actually determined therein, now said to be res judicata. If in the action against the first obligor judgment is given in his favor and against the obligee, those issues are certainly now res judicata against the obligee in a subsequent suit against a second obligor.   If such issues go to the merits of the plaintiff's case, the judgment bars action against the second obligor.[42]   The judgment does not bar such action if the issues determined in the first action were merely as to defenses purely personal to the first defendant. Such defenses are infancy, insanity, or other contractual incapacity, discharge in bankruptcy, and statute of limitations.[43]

Such statutes eliminate the old doctrine of survivorship to be discussed later;  and they enable the obligee to get separate judgments against the obligors, except as the court may apply the modern procedural rules as to joinder of parties in interest for reasons other than mere "jointness" in the form of a contract.[44] Of course they do not prevent each promisor from being bound to pay the whole, if such was the meaning of his promise;  and they have no application to promises of wholly different and separate performances made by two or more persons, whether in one or in several documents.

### § 930.   Survivorship—Effect of Death of a Joint Obligor

Perhaps the most unreasonable of the common law doctrines applicable to joint contracts was that as to survivorship.   Assume once more this contract: "We, J. Doe and R. Roe promise Styles to pay him $1,000."   According to the common law, there was here but a single promise;  and the obligee Styles had a single right enforceable by a single action.   Upon the death of Doe the right of Styles did, indeed, survive; but it survived against Roe alone.   It made no difference that Doe may have been principal debtor and Roe a mere surety, or that Doe was the only financially responsible promisor and Roe a mere straw man.   Styles could not maintain action against Doe's executor, either separately or as a co-defendant with Roe.[45]   Doe had made no separate promise and his executor had made none;  and there were what seemed insuperable objections to the joinder of Roe and Doe's executor.

45.   **U.S.**—Pickersgill v. Lahens, 82 U.S. (15 Wall.) 140, 21 L.Ed. 119 (1873).

**N.Y.**—Davis v. Van Buren, 72 N.Y. 587 (1878).

The cases, before abrogation of the rule by statute, are very numerous. See 67 A.L.R. 609 (1930).

After the death of all the joint obligors, the obligee's only remedy was against the estate of the last one to survive.

This last has been said to have been due to the fact that in creating common law procedure the judges were not inventive enough to enter a judgment requiring two kinds of execution: a judgment against Roe, the survivor, with writ of execution for the full amount against his goods (de bonis propriis), and a judgment against Doe's executor, also for the full amount but with writ to be executed only against the goods held by him as executor (de bonis testatoris).[46] If this is the true explanation of the doctrine of survivorship, or if the reason lies in the supposed "oneness" of the promise and the indivisibility of the "vinculum juris,"[47] there is no longer any good reason for the continued survival of the doctrine. In most if not all the states it has been abolished by statute, or rendered practically impotent by a statute declaring that an obligation of two or more shall be construed to be "joint and several," even though expressed in strictly "joint" form.[48]

This doctrine of survivorship, as between obligors "jointly" bound as principals for one and the same performance, was not applied in the court of Chancery. That court and American courts conscious of their "equity" powers took steps to nullify the doctrine substantially, at least in favor of those fortunate enough to employ a Chancery barrister or a lawyer with a fair knowledge of equity as a system. On the death of one of two joint obligors, the obligee could get judgment at common law against the survivor only, even though he was in fact only a surety for the deceased obligor in part or in whole. The estate of the deceased was immune from execution. Not so in equity. By proper application to the Chancellor, either before or after judgment was rendered against him, the surviving obligor could get a decree against the executor of the deceased for exoneration and contribution out of the goods of his estate. If as between themselves the deceased had been principal and the survivor only a surety, the decree was for full indemnification; if in some measure they had been co-principals, and sureties for each other as to the remainder, the decree was for pro tanto indemnification.

It is obvious, however, that the survivor's right of indemnification, in part or in whole, against the estate of the deceased, did not in itself give a remedy to the obligee. But the obligee was not in serious need of a remedy if the survivor was solvent and full collection could be made from him. Some inconvenience and expense were indeed caused to the survivor, who had to make an expensive application to the Chancellor while the sheriff was on his trail with a writ of execution from the court of common law. But for a long time this was not regarded as serious injustice, the dual system of courts of law and equity being generally regarded as not only beautiful and wise but even as unavoidable "in the nature of things."

If the surviving joint obligor was insolvent or for some reason not subject to process or execution, the survivorship doctrine did grave injustice to the obligee. In such case the Chancellor gave him a remedy also. He could be "subrogated" to the survivor's right of indemnification against the estate of the deceased obligor; and this meant full payment if the deceased was principal debtor as to the whole debt. But the chancellor did not limit the obligee to this remedy by "subrogation;" if he could not collect in full from the survivor he was given a decree for payment in full against the estate of the deceased.[52] This was in truth and substance a holding that death does not end all, that the two joint obligors are two and not one, that a *vinculum juris* may be an indivisible chain "in the eye of the law" but has two distinguishable strands in the keener sight of the Chancellor, and that the "doctrine of survivorship" is itself an unjust and unnecessary procedural excrescence.

In many American cases the court has given the obligee a remedy against the estate of a deceased joint obligor whenever necessary for full collection, either by expressly applying "equity" or by merely following precedents without drawing a line, between equity and law.[53] This should itself be sufficient, under any modern rules of procedure, to justify an action against the surviving obligor and the executor of the deceased obligor with a single judgment against them both.

The doctrine of survivorship was not given its mortal wound by equity alone. Nearly every state has a statute declaring that obligations in form "joint" shall be in effect "joint and several"; and the doctrine was never applicable, even at common law, in favor of obligors who bound themselves for one performance using the mystic password "severally." Some statutes expressly provide that the personal representative of a deceased joint obligor may be joined as defendant with the survivor or survivors.[54] Rules of court and codes of procedure have liberal provisions as to joinder of parties. Courts of today do not need to rest upon these statutes; but there is no reason for failing to give them the fullest effect.

The Uniform Negotiable Instruments Law, in force throughout the United States, provides that when the joint payees, or the joint indorsees, of a negotiable instrument themselves sign as indorsers thereon, the indorsement without more shall bind them severally as well as jointly.[62]   Indorsers can limit this obligation as they see fit by the use of express words above the indorsed signature.

In view of the prevailing statutory law, the decisions in equity independently of statute, and the near-certainty that its sole reason for existence lay in the inadequacies of early common law procedure, the doctrine of survivorship which prevented an obligee from enforcing the contract against the estate of a joint obligor should be treated as extinct.[63]   It appears that the cases applying it have receded into history.

### § 931.   Release of One Co-obligor Without Receiving Full Payment or its Equivalent

When two or more persons are bound for the rendition of separate and distinct performances, the release or other discharge of the obligation of one has no effect whatever upon the obligation of the other.   Even full performance by one has no such effect. It is otherwise when they are under obligation to render one and the same performance.   This is true whether the obligation arises out of tort or out of contract.   The legal relations of the parties are not identical in the two kinds of cases;  and the reasons for applying the same rule of discharge are not in all cases the same. In contract, the primary right of the obligee, created by the contract, is a right against the two or more obligors to a single performance;  in case of breach by the obligors, the secondary, remedial right of the obligee is a right to compensation measured by the harm suffered, one full compensation whether rendered by one of the obligors or by all of them together.   Whether or not more than one action is maintainable against the obligors, the injury is single and the law denies double compensation.

In tort, the primary right of the injured party is merely the right not to be harmed, a right that may be specifically enforceable at times by injunction or by direct police action but is not enforceable by a pecuniary judgment or decree.   When the tort is committed and the injury suffered, the compensatory right to money damages arises, a secondary and remedial right as in the case of a breach of contract.   For one and the same injury, even though it is caused by the tortious conduct of two or more persons,

---

62.   N. I. L. § 68;  Restatement, Contracts, § 116.

63.   Nevertheless the old common law rule is given in Restatement, Contracts, § 125: "On the death of a joint promisor in a contract when one or more of the joint promisors are still surviving, the estate of the deceased promisor is not bound by the joint promise unless all the surviving joint promisors are insolvent;  nor in that event if the deceased promisor was a surety. In the many volumes of State annotations of this Restatement, it is uniformly said that section 125 does not represent the existing law.

the right of the injured party is a right to one full pecuniary compensation. The extent of the harm suffered is the measure of this compensation; but frequently the harm suffered is not itself pecuniary in character, and in measuring the compensation court and jury must be given a large degree of discretion. Even so, however, court and jury must be directed to avoid double compensation.[64] In general, it is more difficult in tort than in contract to determine whether or not the injured party has received more than the one full compensation to which the law entitles him, although in a good many contract actions the measurement of the unliquidated damages for breach is not easy.

In a contract case, the early common law made procedural distinctions in respect of joint, several, and joint and several contracts, distinctions that came to be regarded as "substantive," some of which worked such injustice that they have been largely eliminated by equity, by statute, and by common law judges themselves, with a vast deal of complexity and confusion. In the law of torts, most of these procedural distinctions did not exist and the resulting "substantive" law is less complex and difficult. Two or more persons responsible for the same tortious injury are both jointly and severally liable.[65]

Another important distinction between tort and contract is that when two or more are bound by contract for the rendition of one and the same performance, there is always a relation of suretyship between themselves, a relation that caused equity to create rights of contribution and indemnity, rights that the courts of common law eventually recognized and enforced. This has had important effects upon the existing law of discharge. As between two joint tort-feasors there has generally been no right of contribution or indemnity, so that the law of suretyship has not affected the law as to discharge. This probably still remains true, even though in some cases a party liable for a tort may now have a right of contribution or indemnity against another liable for the same injury.[66]

65. The fact that liability for a tort is joint and several did not prevent a vast amount of litigation over releases, with much confusion and some conflict. Some of the discussion herein and the cases cited will show this, because they are largely applicable to releases of joint and several contracts. An absolute release of one tortfeasor operates to discharge others who are liable for the same tort. See annotation in 104 A.L.R. 846 (1936).

But courts have gone through the same struggle as in contract cases to find a "reservation" of rights or to interpret the document as a "covenant not to sue."

66. The best discussion of this, in a tort case, is by Rutledge, J., in McKenna v. Austin, 77 U.S.App.D. C. 228, 134 F.2d 659, 148 A.L.R. 1253 (1943). See also Manthei v. Heimerdinger, 75 N.E.2d 132, 332 Ill.App. 335 (1947).

At early common law, two or more parties who made a "joint promise" could not be sued separately for breach, if objection was properly made. It followed that if the obligee released or otherwise discharged one joint promisor, he likewise released or discharged the other joint promisors. Such discharge made it impossible to maintain action against the particular one discharged; and the others could prevent action against them without joining the one. Therefore, the rule was that a discharge of one was a discharge of all.

This reasoning was not applicable with respect to two or more persons who made a joint and several promise or who made separate promises of one and the same performance. Such promisors could be sued separately, with separate judgments rendered against them. It might be supposed therefore that one such promisor could be discharged without affecting the obligation of another. In the case of the joint and several promise, however, the common law courts generally held that a release or other complete discharge of one discharged them all. Sometimes this may have been due to simple confusion of mind, because of the complexity of the situations involving more than two parties and the barren technicality that arose out of this complexity.

Another and somewhat better reason may be suggested, however, in the fact that however separately the parties may have promised, their promises are for the rendition of one performance only. The rendition of that performance would certainly discharge the obligation of all; and so would a substituted performance received in full satisfaction. When the obligee voluntarily released one of the persons under obligation to him, the court might assume (or "presume") that the release would not have been given except for full performance or satisfaction. To give judgment against the other obligors, severally liable though they are, would or at least might result in double compensation, more than justice to the obligee and unjust to the obligors.[67] The trouble is that this assumption (or "presumption") may be quite false; and collection of the unpaid balance would cause no double compensation.

Finally, a still more plausible reason was suggested, one that could never have been given until the equitable right of contribution and indemnity came to be recognized as between obligors of the same performance. It was thought that a release of one such obligor is unfair to the others because it deprives them of their right of contribution or indemnity; or if they are not so deprived, as is manifestly the case,[68] then it is unfair to the one released to compel him to make contribution or indemnity after being released.[69] Co-obligors have such a right of contribution whether they are co-principals or are co-sureties for a third party.

The rule that the voluntary release of any one of a number of persons obligated for a single performance discharges all the others operated as a trap into which many an obligee has fallen.[70] In many states it may still so operate. Suppose that one obligor pays or otherwise performs his pro rata share of the promised performance and receives from the obligee a sealed release from obligation, the latter expecting to receive from the other obligors their pro rata shares. This is a natural and not unreasonable proceeding; but the unexpected and unjust result is that the obligee can compel no further performance by anybody. The release of one is the release of all, without regard to the amount received.[71] If the release of one is granted to him as a mere favor, with intent to compel performance of the whole by the other obligors, they might reasonably complain; but not so if they are asked for only their pro rata shares. It may indeed be human nature to be sore and envious at a gift bestowed on another in which one does not himself share; but no one can justify the discharge rule on such a ground.

There are hundreds of cases in the field of torts holding that the release or other unqualified discharge of a tortfeasor at once discharges all others who are liable for the same tort.[72] The fact that they are jointly and severally liable does not prevent this result. In the tort field, also, the rule has operated as a trap to injured parties not well advised by counsel. In some states the rule has been changed by statute.

The American Law Institute has refused to accept the rule that a release of one joint and several obligor releases the others also from their several obligations.[73] The grounds for this are, first, that the reasons anciently given at common law in the case of a joint contract were never applicable to joint and several contracts; secondly, a judgment against one such obligor does not bar action against another, and the analogy is so close that there should not be a different rule in the case of a release. Of course, the Institute's rule is limited to the field of contract. Its rule has not been applied in joint tort cases, except by statute, although it ought to have been.

For many years, courts have not liked the rule that a discharge of one joint or joint and several obligor operates as a discharge

---

**70.** "Many, not knowing this, accept less [than full satisfaction] only to find later they have walked into a trap." Rutledge, J., in McKenna v. Austin, 77 U.S.App.D.C. 228, 134 F.2d 659, 148 A.L.R. 1253 (1943).

**73.** Restatement, Contracts § 123: "Where the obligee of joint and several contractual promises discharges a promisor by release, rescission, or accord and satisfaction, the other promisors are thereby discharged from their joint duty, but not from their several duties, except in the cases and to the extent required by the law of suretyship."

of all even though full payment or satisfaction had not been received. In order to avoid applying it they have recognized exceptions and have indulged in fiction, as will be developed in the next succeeding section. But the rule became so firmly fixed in the declared common law that they have not felt able to abolish it outright without the aid of statute. In order to restrict its operation within the narrowest limits, the courts have often definitely stated that the rule is applicable only when the discharge of one obligor is effected by a formal release under seal, making no distinction between a joint obligation and one that is joint and several.[74] In some of these cases, however, the one obligor had merely made a part payment, doing nothing that he was not already bound to do, so that the one obligor himself would not at common law be discharged as to the balance in the absence of a sealed release.[75] In others the transaction asserted as a discharge was interpreted to be only a "covenant not to sue" the one obligor and hence not a discharge even as to him. If the rule stated in these cases were wholly accurate, in the many states that have abolished seals the discharge of one obligor would never in itself discharge the others; but such is not the case.

When two or more persons are bound by contract for the rendition of one and the same performance, whether jointly, or severally, or jointly and severally, the courts of equity recognized the existence of a suretyship relation and constructed rules of discharge that ought now to be held applicable in all cases. Even if the obligors are co-principals, each one is bound to exonerate and indemnify the others to the extent of his just proportion, this being a pro rata share unless otherwise agreed.[76] The same rule applies as between co-sureties. As between a sole principal and his surety, the latter's right to exoneration and indemnity is applicable to the whole debt.[77]

If an obligee does any act that materially increases the risk that one who is in the position of surety for another will not be exonerated or indemnified, the latter is discharged from his duty to the obligee. If an obligee releases one obligor with reason to know that in his relation with the other obligors he is in part or all a principal debtor and they his sureties, he is thereby increasing their risk.[78] This is made perfectly obvious when he proceeds to sue them without joining their principal or levies execution against their property and not against that of the principal. This equitable rule is applicable only in favor of a surety and only to the extent that he is a surety. Therefore the release of a co-obligor should release the others only to the extent that they are his sureties, only to the extent that they have a right that he shall exonerate and indemnify them.

If A and B are indebted to C in the sum of $100, each is bound to exonerate and indemnify the other up to $50. The release of A by C should therefore discharge B to the extent of $50, leaving him bound to pay his own share. As to that share he is himself a principal debtor with no rights against A. This should be the result whether A pays C his own full share of $50 or a lesser sum or nothing at all; and it should be the result whether C discharges A by a sealed release or by any other effective method. Any payment by A to C on account, however small or large, necessarily discharges B up to the amount so paid, because the debt is to that extent satisfied.

If C lends $100 to A as principal, with B as surety (whether signing as co-maker of a note, or as accommodation indorser, or as a guarantor by a separate instrument), the discharge of A by C operates as a complete discharge of B; but a discharge of B by C does not affect A's legal duty in the least, C has merely dispensed with his secondary security. If A is principal debtor, with B and S as his sureties, the discharge of B by C leaves S bound as A's surety to the extent of $50 only.[79]

But prior to the Judicature Act, 1873, unifying the court system, and the Common Law Procedure Acts, making equitable defenses available in a common law action, the English courts of law were unable to escape from their old and technical rules as to discharge. Nor were the Chancellors themselves quite sure how far they should go in nullifying those common law rules.[80] In the United States, the courts generally failed to see the existence of the suretyship relation, or failed to realize their own equity powers except when the procedure and terminology of equity were used by the plaintiff in bringing his suit, and in general followed the common law rules of discharge in the case of both joint torts and joint contracts, ameliorating their operation by fictions and exceptions.[81] In a good many states there are statutes providing that the discharge of a co-obligor shall not operate to discharge the others if the intention of the parties is that they shall not be discharged.[82]

The statute that obligations in form joint shall be in legal effect joint and several renders no service, in respect of the law of discharge, in any jurisdiction following the English decisions that a discharge of one joint and several obligor discharges the others also from their several as well as from their joint obligation.

81.   Some of the cases holding that a discharge of a joint or joint and several obligor is a discharge of all can be justified on the ground that the performance rendered by one of the obligors was received by the obligee as full satisfaction of his claim against all. Full payment as agreed necessarily so operates; and so does an accord and satisfaction received as a complete substitution.

There was no sound reason for starting or following such a line of decisions. If a judgment against one such obligor does not bar an action against another, neither should a release or other discharge except so far as required by the equitable principles of suretyship. On this ground the American Law Institute states as the rule that a discharge of one does not discharge the others. The Uniform Joint Obligations Act also states the law of discharge in accordance with the law of suretyship.[83] This Uniform Act is rightly made applicable to obligations for the rendering of one performance, whether joint or several or both.

### § 932. The Legal Operation of an Obligee's Covenant not to Sue an Obligor

Something remains to be said with respect to the effect of an obligee's covenant not to sue one of his joint or joint and several obligors. The fictitious covenant discovered by the courts, in what is in express terms a release with reservation of rights, is always merely a covenant not to sue the one obligor who is said to be released or discharged. It certainly never includes a covenant not to sue the other obligors; for they are the very ones against whom rights are reserved. There are many settlement agreements, however, that are drawn by lawyers who know the history of joint obligations, and that are put in express terms in the form of a covenant not to sue. These express covenants may be so worded as to protect third parties as well as the one covenantee. Generally they are not so worded, being in express terms only a covenant not to sue the obligor who is making the settlement. In such case, the effect is the same as that given to a release with reservation. What is this effect?

---

**83.** Uniform Joint Obligations Act as adopted in New York, Consol. Laws 1930, § 234: "Subject to the provisions of § 233, the obligee's release or discharge of one or more of several obligors, or of one or more of joint, or of joint and several obligors shall not discharge co-obligors, against whom the obligee in writing and as part of the same transaction as the release or discharge, expressly reserves his rights; and in the absence of such a reservation of rights shall discharge co-obligors only to the extent provided in § 235."

§ 235: "(a) If an obligee releasing or discharging an obligor without express reservation of rights against a co-obligor, then knows or has reason to know that the obligor released or discharged did not pay so much of the claim as he was bound by his contract or relation with that co-obligor to pay, the obligee's claim against that co-obligor shall be satisfied to the amount which the obligee knew or had reason to know that the released or discharged obligor was bound to such co-obligor to pay.

(b) If an obligee so releasing or discharging an obligor has not then such knowledge or reason to know, the obligee's claim against the co-obligor shall be satisfied to the extent of the lesser of two amounts, namely (1) the amount of the fractional share of the obligor released or discharged, or (2) the amount that such obligor was bound by his contract or relation with the co-obligor to pay."

In the first place, as we have already seen, it does not discharge the other obligors or prevent action against them for any unpaid balance, except insofar as they are sureties and are protected by the law of suretyship. The question now is, what is its effect with respect to the obligor making the settlement, the one whom the obligee releases with reservation, or whom the obligee expressly covenants not to sue. The word "covenant" as here used means no more than "valid contract." The facts must be such as are sufficient to make a promise binding. In the absence of statute, sealing and delivery are sufficient; otherwise there must be a sufficient consideration (including so-called "past consideration") or sufficient action in reliance under the modern rule. In the absence of all of these factors, the "covenant" is inoperative and protects no one.[84]

At early common law, a covenant never to sue for enforcement of a claim was not pleadable in bar if such a suit were brought. The bringing of such a suit was merely a breach of covenant, for which an action for damages would lie. In that action, the damages recoverable would include the full amount recovered in the wrongful suit. Therefore equity would specifically enforce the covenant and prevent the wrongful suit by an injunction. The common law courts also saw the point and changed their law, holding that the covenant never to sue could be pleaded in bar to prevent "circuity of action." Though not a "release," it was a good defense.[85]

The fact that the covenant not to sue was not called a "release" enabled the courts to maintain an appearance of consistency when they held that a release of one releases all but a covenant not to sue one does not discharge the others. If necessary, they blandly ignored the magic word "release" actually used, and also the entire absence of the word "covenant." They did not wholly overlook the fact that a covenant never to sue could be pleaded as a bar to suit; they merely said that in joint obligation cases it

84. Thus, if all that the one obligor has done is to pay a part of a larger liquidated sum of money then due from him, most courts still hold that he has given no sufficient consideration; a mere informal promise by the obligee not to sue him would not be made binding thereby. In some of the contract cases, this is all that the obligor has done, a fact that may explain some of the statements that other obligors are not discharged unless the obligee has executed a formal release to one obligor. When one tortfeasor makes a payment in settlement, it is usually received on account of a claim previously unliquidated, leaving a balance that is also unliquidated. The claimant's promise not to sue is thereby made valid; and the same is true when the payment made is on account of a wholly unliquidated claim to damages for breach of contract. The obligee's promise not to sue one obligor may be made binding by that obligor's subsequent change of position, as where in foreseen reliance he forbears to take necessary steps to compel exoneration by co-obligors.

should not be so pleadable, conceding to it only its earlier common law effects. Hence, a covenant not to sue one joint obligor is merely a valid contract for breach of which an action for damages will lie.

Any such case is certainly one that is proper for equity jurisdiction, for several reasons: several parties are involved with issues so complex that full justice could not be done in a single action at common law; principles of suretyship are involved, principles that originated in equity and some of which were not recognized by common law; and thirdly, money damages might not be an adequate remedy to the covenantee himself, if in breach of the covenant the obligee joined him as a defendant and threatened to levy execution against his property. And yet equity would not specifically enforce the obligee's promise by enjoining him from joining the one obligor as a co-defendant with the other obligors, if such joinder is necessary or useful in compelling them to pay their just proportion of a debt.[86] Equity would protect the covenantee from irreparable injury by a wrongful levy on his property; but it would not protect the other obligors from having to pay what they justly owe.

At the present day, practically all courts are both empowered and in duty bound to apply those rules of law that derive from the old courts of equity. Their procedure is flexible enough to deal with many parties at once, to protect their various rights, and to render a decree properly enforcing the duties of all. If an obligee, having covenanted not to sue one obligor, nevertheless joins him as a co-defendant with the other obligors, the court can dismiss the suit as to him if his presence is not necessary, or it can compel the obligee to indemnify him against loss. At the same time it can enforce payment by the others of any balance that is due in those equitable proportions required by the law of suretyship or of quasi-contract.

In the light of the statutes declaring joint obligations to be joint and several, of the power of the court to apply the law of suretyship, and of the flexibility of modern procedure in the joinder of parties and the issuance of decrees, none of the difficulties that beset the old courts of common law should exist. The obligee can avoid committing a breach by not joining the released obligor, and yet have a complete remedy against the others. If the joinder is necessary, the obligee can avoid any substantial breach by preventing any execution against the released obligor.[87]

As between the obligee and the one obligor, the covenant not to sue should be treated as a complete discharge. As between the

86.  Restatement, Contracts, § 124, states that it is not a breach of a covenant not to sue one obligor for the obligee merely to make him a formal defendant along with the remaining obligors, so long as no levy is made on assets of the covenantee.

obligee and the other obligors, they should be held to be discharged to the full extent that they are sureties for the first obligor, to the extent of the full amount for which they have a right to exoneration and indemnity by him.[88]  As between the first obligor and the others, if in making his settlement the former has paid more than his just share he can join voluntarily in the suit or bring a separate one to compel contribution; and the other obligors can bring the former in as a party if they wish a declaration that they owe him no contribution.

Such should now be the solution in any case where two or more are bound for one and the same performance and one of them has made a separate settlement that is in fact only a partial satisfaction. This should be so whether the obligee executed an unqualified release, a release with reservation, or a covenant not to sue the obligor making the partial settlement.

### § 933.  Release with Reservation of Rights—Covenants Not to Sue One Obligor

The rule that a release of one joint obligor is operative as a release of all was based on remedial difficulties caused by ancient common law procedure, and perhaps also on the inability of judges to imagine that one "joint" obligation could consist of multiple relations. Such difficulties could be and were avoided, in making a settlement with one joint obligor, by the obligee's executing a covenant not to sue the one obligor instead of a sealed release. By such a covenant not even the one obligor was discharged at common law; the obligee could still join all the obligors in one action and get a joint judgment against them as common law procedure required. Execution could then be levied on the goods of the obligors who were not parties to the covenant.[93]  By such action the favored obligor would not be harmed; if by any chance he was so harmed, his only remedy was an action against the obligee on his covenant. Thus was one technical rule of law frustrated by the use of another. The fact that a covenant never to sue came to be a perfect defense at both law and equity in an action against a single obligor was not allowed to be such a defense when it would discharge other obligors as well.[94]

The complexities of the common law as to joint obligations were such that no ordinary contractor could be expected to understand them, or to know and intend the legal effects that his agreements,

---

93. Restatement, Contracts, § 121: "(1) Where the obligee of a joint contractual promise discharges a promisor by release, rescission or accord and satisfaction, the other joint promisors are thereby discharged.

"(2) Where such an obligee contracts not to sue a joint promisor, the other joint promisors are not discharged except in the cases and to the extent required by the law of suretyship."

by way of either promise or discharge, would be given by the judges. In his efforts to obtain payment or other performance promised him by two or more obligors the obligee has often found it advantageous to settle with them separately. The obligors find it to their advantage also, each one being glad to be discharged on paying some amount less than the whole, whether his own proportionate share or not. How natural, therefore, for an obligor to demand his own release as a condition of making the part payment. The obligee did not know the great historic differences between a release and a covenant not to sue; but he did know that he intended to discharge one obligor without discharging the others.

The exact form in which the obligee expressed this intention was largely accidental, except when he was advised by an astute lawyer. If he executed a general release under seal, on receiving the part payment, he would be shocked to learn that it was his "folly" not to have hired a lawyer. If, in executing his release of A, he added the words "reserving all my rights against B," he would have been told for some centuries that his "reservation" was quite inoperative, that he had tried to do that which was impossible "in the nature of things." There was only one obligation, only one *vinculum juris;* in releasing one obligor he had dropped his end of this legal "chain" so that all attached to the other end were free. He had only *one right,* even though it was against many; he had released that, and there were no other rights to be reserved.

It is because of this antiquated view of a "joint" obligation that it is even now often said that the release of one with reservation of rights against others is a "contradiction in terms." There is no such contradiction in the minds of the contracting parties themselves, or in the mind of a court that looks at words in the light of the usages of the time instead of through a thick legal veil that has often blinded "the eye of the law." [95]

Finally the common law judges themselves saw what justice required and gave a partial remedy. Without abandoning the "unitary" conception of a joint obligation, and still insisting that a release with reservation was a legal impossibility, they declared that such a document must be held to operate as a "covenant not to sue"—such must have been "the intention of the parties." [96] Previously they had declared the release effective and the reserva-

---

95. This does not mean that the common law judges had a vision inferior to that of the common man on the street. In general it was much superior. The vision of the Chancellors was often superior to that of the judges; but the Chancellors enjoyed the great advantage of having second sight. With time and experience the vision clears, so that jurists of today have less excuse than their predecessors for not lifting the veil.

tion void; they now attacked the release and supported the reservation. The magnifying glass through which they discovered the creditor's intention to execute a mere "covenant not to sue" has not been handed down to us.

With the aid of this artificial interpretation, the courts held that a release of one obligor with reservation of rights against the others is not pleadable as a defense in an action on either a joint or a joint and several obligation, whether the action is against them all jointly including the one released, or against the unreleased obligors separately. This is generally followed today.[97] In so holding the courts removed one veil from before their eyes and substituted another. A "covenant not to sue" a debtor had already become pleadable as a bar to an action against him. They would not let it be so pleaded in this case, because to do so would again defeat the "reservation," a result that the obligee did not intend. It does indeed seem reasonable to hold that the obligee did not intend that such an effect should be given to a "covenant not to sue" that he did not know he had made.

A retrospective survey of the many long opinions, in cases of both contract and tort, in which a release with reservation has been held to be a covenant not to sue, and in which also this imaginary "covenant" has been refused its normal effect as a discharge because otherwise the "reservation" would be made ineffective contrary to the obligee's intention, creates the impression of legalistic verbiage gone mad.[98] How much simpler to hold directly that a release effective as to one obligor does not release the others if the intention not to release them is clear and full satisfaction has not been received![99] What a vast amount of litigation, some of it still going on, would have been avoided! What price justice!

The device of a reservation of rights was held to be effective against sureties as well as against co-principal debtors.[4] Frequently such a holding must do grave injustice to a surety, by greatly increasing the risk of being compelled to pay money that he has a right that others shall pay. This increase of risk is not prevented by holding that a release with reservation is merely a covenant not to sue. Nor is this increase of risk prevented by the fact that the surety can get judgment for exoneration against his principal or a co-surety. But for this unfair "covenant not to sue" them, they might have performed as their equitable duty to him required; a judgment for exoneration or indemnity may be too late.

The law of discharge with respect to two or more who are bound for one and the same performance should be brought into harmony with the rules of suretyship as created and applied in equity, displacing the old common law rules of joint obligations as the general provisions of modern statutes require. This should be done by judicial decision as an application of those statutes, and even without such statutes since our courts are themselves courts of equity. To compel such a result, the Uniform Joint Obligations Act should be enacted. Under these rules, the fiction of the "covenant not to sue" would disappear, rights against others would be reserved by the law until full satisfaction is rendered, and an express "reservation of rights" would not prevent the discharge of a surety who has in fact been injured.

What then are these equitable rules? Their applicability depends on the fact that the obligors are bound for one and the same performance, not on the use of the words "joint" and "several," and not on their signing one document or separate documents.[5]

Rendition of the agreed performance in full, or of any substituted performance assented to as the full equivalent of the one originally due, discharges all alike from further duty to the obligee. Adjustments among the obligors themselves depend upon their own understanding or agreement.

The effect of a discharge of one obligor should not depend upon its particular form, whether by sealed release, accord and satisfaction, substituted contract, executed gift, or otherwise.[6] Any voluntary discharge by the obligee that is effective as to one obligor should discharge all the others to the extent that they have a right to exoneration and indemnity by the one discharged and to no greater extent, provided that the obligee at the time of the discharge, knows or has reason to know that they have such right.[7]

If the obligor discharged is thus known to be the sole principal obligor and the others his sureties, these others are all discharged in full, for they have a right to complete exoneration and indemnity by the principal.[8]

As between two obligors who are equally principal debtors, the discharge of one discharges the other as to half the debt, leaving him bound still to pay his own share. If by agreement among obligors their shares are not equal, and the obligee has reason to know this, the discharge of one leaves the others bound to pay their separate shares as agreed. This is true whether the one discharged paid his full share or a lesser amount or nothing at all; as to that full share the others were his sureties and had a right to be exonerated and indemnified by him.[9] Of course, if he paid or otherwise satisfied more than his agreed share, the others owe merely their shares of the balance to the obligee and owe to the discharged obligor their shares of the excess paid by him.[10]

If the obligor who is discharged is in fact only a surety for all the others, their obligation to the creditor is not affected at all, except as to the part that their surety may have paid or otherwise satisfied; as to that part the others must indemnify the surety.   This rule should be applied even though the obligee did not know that the one he discharged is a surety only.

If the obligor who is discharged is, as the obligee then has reason to know, one of several co-sureties for a principal debtor, the other sureties are discharged to the extent that they had a right to contribution by the one discharged, each of them remaining bound for his own agreed share of the balance.[11]

### § 934.   Effect of Release with an Oral Reservation of Rights

If, without intending to discharge other obligors, the obligee discharges one joint obligor by a written release or accord and satisfaction, and in this writing there is no express reservation of rights against others, it has been stated that parol evidence is not admissible to prove that it was clearly understood that the other obligors were not to be released or discharged.[12]   The so-called "parol evidence rule" is supposed to require this result. There appears to be no sufficient reason for such a holding.   Such an oral understanding neither contradicts nor varies the writing; and even if it did so, the parol evidence rule is inapplicable for the reason that the writing does not purport to be a complete "integration" of a contract.   It expressly purports to be nothing but a release or discharge of the one obligor.   The oral understanding is quite consistent with the writing, interpreting it just as the rules of interpretation require.   It is indeed repugnant to the "legal effect" that the common law would otherwise give to such a writing; but it is not at "legal effect" that the parol evidence rule is directed.   Moreover, it is not repugnant to the "equitable effect" required by the law of suretyship as developed in equity.

The parol evidence rule did not prevent the common law courts themselves from "interpreting" an express release with "reservation of rights" as a covenant not to sue, thus changing the legal effect that the writing with its specific words of release of one obligor would otherwise have had.   The parol evidence rule should not be perverted to preserve a "legal effect" that the parties to it do not intend, for the benefit of third parties who ought still to be bound, a "legal effect" so inequitable in operation that the courts have themselves made many successful efforts to avoid it, and that in many states has been expressly abolished by statute. If it is preserved in such a way, its operation will chiefly be against the small obligee who drafts his own release according to common

12.   Restatement, Contracts, § 122, states that "a written discharge cannot be varied by an accompanying oral statement or agreement that rights against other promisors are reserved."

sense and the normal usage of words, without paying a fee to an accomplished lawyer. If, contrary to intention, the other obligors are held to be discharged, they are receiving without merit and without cost a benefaction from the confusion of the present and the procedural technicality of the distant past.[13]

There are also cases holding that the parol evidence rule is not applicable to exclude testimony to the effect that a release absolute in form was intended as a covenant not to sue or was understood not to apply to other obligors, for the reason that these other obligors are not parties to the instrument.[14] It is generally said that the rule is not applicable either in favor of or against third parties. This is considered in the chapter dealing with the parol evidence rule. The refusal to let such third parties hide behind the parol evidence rule, when the documentary "release" was not in fact intended to discharge claims against them and does not on its face purport to express such an intention, is a thoroughly justified refusal. Testimony that is offered for this purpose should never be excluded whoever may be the parties to the suit in which it is offered.

## § 935. Discharge of the Joint or Several Duties of Co-obligors by Payment or Other Agreed Satisfaction

Where two or more persons have either jointly or severally undertaken to render a single performance, the legal duty or duties so created can be discharged in exactly the same ways as can any contractual duty of any one person. They may be discharged by performance, accord and satisfaction, release, failure of consideration, nonperformance of a condition, or impossibility. These need no special discussion here, except in the troublesome cases in which the obligee releases or otherwise discharges one without

13. In accord with the text above see:

Pa.—Schock v. Miller, 10 Pa. 401 (1849).

S.C.—Massey v. Brown, 4 S.C. 85 (1872); and Conn. G.S.1930, § 5557.

In McKenna v. Austin, 77 U.S. App. D.C. 228, 134 F.2d 659, 148 A.L.R. 1253 (1943); the reservation of rights was in the writing and the parol evidence rule was not discussed; but no one can read the full discussion in the opinion of Rutledge, J., without seeing the correctness of the argument in the text above.

The correct reasoning is well given in Massey v. Brown, supra, the court saying: "The declarations of Brown at the time of the execution of the release were not offered to explain, vary, or contradict the language of the instrument discharging him. It was not to add conditions or restrictions which would impose on the immediate parties to it, as between themselves, any other obligations than those which it plainly expressed, or in any way to contravene or disturb the contract between them; but they were offered to show that . . . . the rights of Massey as to the other surety Barnes were not to be prejudiced by reason of his [Brown's] release. They were to show something extrinsic to, and outside of, the discharge."

meaning to discharge another. Since the obligee, in the case now assumed, has a right to only a single performance, the full rendition of that performance extinguishes his right, whether the performance is rendered by one obligor alone, by all of them together, or by a third party.[15] This is true whether the performance contracted for is the payment of money, the transfer of property, or the rendering of services. Likewise, the problem of whether a mere part performance can operate as a discharge of the whole is the same as in other cases.

If the obligee executes a proper release of his rights against all his obligors or assents to a full discharge by novation, substituted contract or accord and satisfaction, the legal duties of the obligors are all discharged. The fact that there are more than one obligor does not affect the obligee's power of discharge so long as he treats all the obligors alike.

If the claim to be settled is unliquidated in amount, as it is in the case of a tort or of most claims for damages for breach of contract, the receipt of a sum of money from one of the obligors as the full and agreed equivalent of the injury suffered operates as an accord and satisfaction, not only of the legal duty of the obligor paying it but of all the other obligors. If the claim to be settled is for a liquidated sum of money, the receipt of something other than money from one of the obligors as the full and agreed equivalent of the whole money debt operates as an accord and satisfaction in favor of all the obligors who owe that debt. Where such full satisfaction has been received, just as in the case where full payment is received or other full performance rendered as agreed, an express reservation by the obligee of rights against any of the obligors is of no effect. There are no rights to be reserved because he has been paid in full or otherwise satisfied in full, and the law does not permit double recovery.[16] It is a question of fact for the jury whether a performance rendered by one obligor was received as the full equivalent and satisfaction of his claim by the obligee.[17] The mere fact that a formal and absolute release of one obligor has been executed has been held to require the inference that full satisfaction has been received. To hold that this "inference" is conclusive is merely to hold that it is quite immaterial, and that the release of one releases all even though nothing at all was given or received. This has been considered in a previous section.

### § 936. A Payment or Other Performance Received from One Obligor must be Credited in Favor of All

The rendition of any part of the exact performance promised by two or more operates as a discharge pro tanto of everyone of them; all of them still owe the balance and no more than that balance. The rendition of a part of that which is already legally due is not, according to the great weight of authority, a sufficient consideration for the obligee's promise or assent that it shall operate as a discharge in full, even as to the one obligor who renders such part performance. Any different performance, substituted for part or all of that which the obligation requires, and accepted by the obligee in satisfaction of part or all of that obligation, is a sufficient consideration and operates as a discharge by accord and satisfaction to the extent agreed. This too operates to discharge all the obligors alike and in the very same proportion.[26] If the obligee accepts the substituted performance in satisfaction of one tenth of the debt, all the obligors now owe nine tenths.

Suppose, however, that one obligor makes a separate settlement wholly for his own benefit, either by paying one tenth of the debt and receiving a release under seal applicable to himself alone, or by rendering a substituted performance that is accepted as satisfaction of his proportionate share. It is perfectly clear that the other obligors are discharged also to the extent of the performance or satisfaction received; one tenth being paid, they owe no more than nine tenths; or, an agreed satisfaction having been received as to one share, they now owe no more than the remaining shares. This is true, even though in making the special settlement with one obligor it was expressly agreed that it should not reduce the obligation of the other obligors. Such an agreement is ineffective, for the reason that the obligee is entitled to only one full performance or satisfaction, not to double satisfaction even as to any small part.

## § 937. Joint and Several Promises of a Single Performance

As has already been stated, it is possible for two or more persons to enter into an obligation by which they are bound separately as individuals and also jointly bound as a group for the rendition of one and the same performance. Such an obligation is said to be "joint and several" and a contract creating it is called a "joint and several contract." These are the technical words of the common law.

The typical form of promise is as follows: "We, J. Doe and R. Roe, jointly and severally promise to pay John Styles $1,000." Exactly the same legal effect is produced by any other language indicating that the promisors mean to bind themselves for the same performance as a group and also as individuals. Whether or not their language has this meaning is a matter of interpretation according to the usual process. It would do just as well for them to say "we promise both as a group and as individuals"; or "we bind ourselves and each of us." [31] In several cases the promissory words were in the singular number, as where they read "I promise to pay" followed by two or more signatures. The obligation created by such a document is held to be "joint and several." [32]

The use of the first person singular is a factor in interpretation; but such words may be overpowered by other words in the instrument, or by extrinsic factors commonly used in the process of interpretation.[33]

It must be borne in mind that two or more persons may, by a single instrument containing only one promissory expression, bind themselves to pay wholly separate sums of money or to render any other entirely distinct performances. In the present section we are dealing only with the obligation of two or more persons who promise one and the same performance. Many persons have often signed what is called a "subscription" paper, in which they "subscribe" separate amounts of money. The paper may read "we subscribe the amounts set opposite our names," or "I promise to pay the amount set opposite my name." The use of the singular or the plural form of pronoun is not the matter of chief importance. An informal subscription paper should in many cases be found not to be a complete "integration" of the terms of agreement. Usually the signers intend to bind themselves separately for their separate amounts, just as if they had signed separate instruments; but it is possible that each signer intends to be a surety for each of the others.[34] When a modern court is discussing whether or not two or more promisors are jointly bound, the problem is very likely to be merely this: did they all promise one and the same performance or did each one promise only a separate part of the total.

It is by "interpretation" that we determine the amount of money or other performance for which each signer intends to bind himself or for which he leads the promisee reasonably to believe that he so intends. The mere words of the document can seldom if ever be regarded as wholly decisive of the question; they certainly are not decisive as to the extent to which one obligor is principal and another his surety.

After completing the process of interpretation, in the light of the written words and of all the admissible extrinsic factors, and having thus determined that all the obligors intend to be bound for one and the same performance, both as a group and as individuals, the legal effect of what they have said and done remains to be determined. This is not a matter of mere interpretation. What are the legal relations of the obligors between themselves and of each one of them with the obligee? What is the effect of the death or insolvency of one obligor, or of a release or other form of discharge? What is the procedure for enforcement?

At common law the differences in legal effect between promising "jointly" and promising "jointly and severally" were very great. Those who promised in the latter form were regarded as having made two kinds of promises at once, even though each and every one of the promisors bound himself for only one performance. Having promised "jointly", the parties were bound in some respects in accordance with the law of "joint" contracts; but having promised "severally" also, they were bound in some respects in accordance with the law of "several" contracts. Since the law applicable to these two kinds of contracts was in some respects quite inconsistent, the legal relations resulting from promising "jointly and severally" could not be determined by merely adding the two sets of legal relations together. In legal effect, therefore, instead of the promisor's binding himself both jointly and severally, the truth is that he binds himself neither jointly nor severally. This must be demonstrated by briefly stating the differences in the legal relations that are created in these cases. This is necessary even in those states that have enacted statutes declaring that contracts in form joint shall be in effect joint and several.

If one joint obligor were sued alone, he could successfully plead in abatement if another one bound jointly with him was living and within the jurisdiction. This is not true of a joint and several obligor; having promised "severally", he can be sued alone. A judgment obtained against one joint obligor, who failed to plead in abatement when he might have done so, operated as a bar to an action against others jointly bound with him. Again, this is not true of joint and several obligors; against them separate actions are maintainable and separate judgments obtained.[35] Thus by adding the word "severally," or its equivalent, is cancelled out one of the important effects of a "joint" contract.

Of course, joint and several obligors can not be sued both jointly and severally. There is but one cause of action and no one of the parties may be twice vexed by litigation thereon.[36] It was held further, at common law, that if there are three or more such obligors they may all be sued together or each may be sued separately; but in a suit brought against more than one but less than all the defendants could plead in abatement as in the case of a joint contract.[37] Modern rules of procedure very generally wipe out this peculiarity, making very liberal and flexible provision for the joinder of parties and for the granting of judgments and decrees.[38]

Although a judgment against one joint and several obligor does not bar an action against another one, it has been held to limit the amount of possible recovery in the later action.[39] This seems to be sound, because the issue in the two cases is identical and because of the law of suretyship that is applicable when two or more are bound for the same performance. For similar reasons, the satisfaction of the judgment against one such obligor operates as a satisfaction of the obligee's claim against another.[40]

If in an action by the obligee against one of two or more joint and several obligors judgment is rendered against the obligee and in favor of the defendant, this bars a later action against the other obligors if the defense that was sustained is one that would be equally good if made in the later action.[41]   It does not bar the later action if the defense is one that is personal to the obligor who made it.[42]   The issues determined in the first action are res judicata against the obligee in an action by him against the other obligors.[43]   This is quite consistent with the law of suretyship.

The common law doctrine of survivorship that was applicable to joint obligors was never applied to obligors bound jointly and severally, with respect to the separate obligation.   Upon death of one obligor, his executor succeeded to his separate obligation and could be sued separately by the obligee.[44]   At common law it was said that such executor could not be joined as defendant with the surviving obligors; [45] but there is not the slightest reason for maintaining such a rule where equity or modern code procedure prevails.[46]

The statement has often been made that a voluntary release of one joint and several obligor is a release of all, just as if the obligation were joint only.   There were English cases so holding. Some decisions and many dicta in the United States asserted the same rule.[47]   It is even now generally applied, except where statutes provide otherwise, in the case of tortfeasors who are jointly and severally liable.[48]   In some cases in which the rule is stated the court does not make clear whether the obligation was joint only or was joint and several and gave no thought to the fact that each obligor was separately bound.   Nor is it always clear whether the discharge of one obligor was not by reason of some substituted performance received by the obligee as satisfaction of his entire claim.   The rule never should have been applied with respect to obligors who are separately as well as jointly bound.   Both statutes and suretyship decisions to the contrary effect are numerous.[49]

---

41.   **Neb.**—Galt v. Hildreth, 158 N. W. 366, 100 Neb. 15, 3 A.L.R. 114 (1916).

Restatement, Contracts § 119 (2): "A judgment by a court in favor of one or more of such promisors, unless based on

(a) lack of jurisdiction, or

(b) contractual incapacity, or

(c) a discharge in bankruptcy, or

(d) a discharge or barring of the remedy by the Statute of Limitations,

discharges the joint duty of the other joint promisors."

42.   **Cal.**—Arocena v. Sawyer, 213 P. 523, 60 Cal.App. 581 (1923), statute of limitations.

**Conn.**—Belden v. Curtis, 48 Conn. 32 (1880), bankruptcy.

**Ind.**—Davis v. Statts, 43 Ind. 103 (1873), coverture; McKee v. Harwood Auto Co., 162 N.E. 62 (App. 1928), infancy.

49.   If one surety pays his "just proportion" of the debt for which he and other sureties are bound, or is otherwise discharged, his co-sureties remain bound to pay their

Just as in the case of "joint" obligations, with even more convincing reason, the rules as to release or other discharge of a joint and several obligor should be those that were developed in equity with respect to co-obligors, whether principal or surety. By those rules, without regard to the form of the original obligation, the discharge of one co-obligor discharges another only to the extent that he may be injured thereby. The discharge of a principal obligor discharges his surety because it increases the latter's risk of having to pay, when, as the obligee has reason to know, the surety has a right that the principal shall exonerate him. The discharge of a surety has no effect upon the obligation of his principal. The discharge of a surety discharges his co-surety to the extent that the latter has a right to be exonerated by the discharged surety. Whether two co-obligors are to be regarded as principal and surety or as co-sureties is determined in accordance with the facts that the obligee had reason to know at the time he assented to the release or discharge.

Just as in the case of joint obligors, a mere covenant not to sue one joint and several obligor was never held to discharge the others insofar as those others are themselves principal debtors.[50] But a covenant not to sue, or any binding extension of time given to the principal debtor operates to discharge one who is a surety and is known to be such, unless the covenant is expressly limited by a reservation of rights against the surety. The decisions holding that an express reservation like this prevents a surety from being discharged by a release or a covenant not to sue his principal were based on confusion of mind. Such a reservation does not prevent his risk of having to pay the debt from being much increased by the release or covenant; and it in no respect protects his rights against the principal since those rights would not be affected by a release or covenant however absolute.

It is a matter of course that if one obligor makes payment in full or otherwise satisfies the entire obligation by a substituted performance, the obligee's right against all others who are bound for the same performance is extinguished.[51] This is true whether

remaining just proportions, but no more.

Pa.—Klingensmith v. Klingensmith, 31 Pa. 460 (1858); Shock v. Miller, 10 Pa. 401 (1849), "equity is part of our law."

S.C.—Massey v. Brown, 4 S.C. 85 (1872).

Any two co-obligors, bound for the same debt or other obligation, are principal obligors only as to the just proportion determined by their own agreement or understanding; beyond that, each is a surety for the other.

Restatement, Contracts, § 123: "Where the obligee of joint and several contractual promises discharges a promisor by release, rescission or accord and satisfaction, the other promisors are discharged from their joint duty, but not from their several duties, except in the cases and to the extent required by the law of suretyship."

they were jointly bound or severally bound. Any part payment or part satisfaction reduces the obligation of the others in like measure.

### § 939.    Joint Promisees—Promises may be made to More than One Person Jointly or Severally

A single promise can be made to two or more persons. Styles may sign a promissory note: "I promise John Doe and Richard Roe to pay to them or order $1,000". He may execute a bond saying that "Styles is held and firmly bound to Doe and Roe in the penal sum of $1,000." A promise may be made to Doe and Roe, partners in business. Such promises may also provide for performances other than money payments, to erect buildings, to perform services, to deliver goods, to forbear from competition. In such cases, there are joint promisees. Styles makes but one promise to render only one performance; but the promise is made to two persons. These two are said to have a "joint right," a phrase that is used to connote the group of jural relations created by such a contract. But, Doe and Roe are not one person, not even a "quasi-person." The contract creates rights and powers in each of them, against Styles and against each other; but these rights are limited and the procedure for their enforcement may vary with circumstances and with the court.

Since Styles has made one promise to render but one performance, in most cases it has seemed just that he should be harassed by but one action in case of alleged breach. Doe and Roe must join as co-plaintiffs; and if one should sue alone, alleging a promise to him alone, at common law a plea of the general issue by Styles would be sustained.[57] At common law, just as in the case of joint promisors, there was a doctrine of survivorship; if Roe dies, his executor could not join with Doe in suing Styles. Doe alone, the survivor, was recognized as the only holder of a right against Styles; he had to sue alone, alleging the promise to Doe and Roe as it was made and that Roe was dead.[58]

Such was the "tontine" character of the rights of joint promisees at common law, not because the judges knew or admired the

---

58.    **Ark.**—Trammell v. Harrell, 4 Ark. 602 (1842).

Mass.—Donnell v. Manson, 109 Mass. 576 (1872); Draper v. Jackson, 16 Mass. 480 (1820).

Restatement, Contracts, § 132: "On the death of a joint obligee, the surviving obligees, if more than one, become the only joint obligees. If but one obligee survives he becomes the sole obligee; and on the death of the last surviving obligee, his estate becomes solely entitled to performance by the obligor." This was the old common law rule, although it was mitigated somewhat by a readiness to find that separate interests made the obligation several but the rule should be wholly disregarded by any court willing and able to apply the principles of equity under modern procedure.

quality of "tontine" insurance or because they thought that a contract right could not survive its owner's death. It was because they were strait-jacketed by their own rules of procedure, aided by confusion in the analysis of an "obligation" when there were more than two persons involved. Such was the common law of old, if the words of promise were directed to Doe and Roe conjunctively, even though the performance promised by Styles was a payment to be made to Doe alone,[59] or to a fourth person.[60]

The court of Chancery, having a very different procedure and tradition, reached a very different result. Roe's executor was recognized as having the same rights as Roe had had in person, with ample remedy to compel Doe to pay over Roe's share of the recovery.[61] Today, the rights of promisees of a single performance are determined in accordance with the rules of equity, either by statute abolishing the common law doctrine or by the general amalgamation of law and equity in a single court system with a flexible procedure. There should be no difficulty in joining Doe and Roe's executor as co-plaintiffs. Under modern rules, if a joint promisee refuses to join as a co-plaintiff the others can make him a party against his will, if not as a formal plaintiff then as an additional defendant.[62] In one judgment or decree the rights of all are determined and the proper distribution compelled. The defendant Styles can not object if one joint promisee sues in a representative capacity for the rest, where parties are numerous. And modern codes frequently provide that the non-joinder of a co-obligee is waived if not objected to as the code specially requires, usually by a demurrer or by answer.[63] The rules of procedure are now flexible enough to eliminate mere technicality; but they do not empower a court to adjudicate the rights of a co-obligee who is not properly before the court and they afford ample opportunity to the defendant to avoid multiple litigation and to insist on the joinder of all parties necessary to the complete disposition of the case.[64]

In many cases in which a promise is made to two or more persons, the performance promised is not divisible into separate parts, each one to be rendered to a definite person and for his benefit. Suppose that A and B make a contract with C, in which they promise to make a specified excavation or construction or to render any other service, and in return C promises to pay them $5,000. A and B are joint promisees as to this sum of money. It

---

64. Neither a court of common law nor a court of equity should attempt to determine the rights of one not made a party to the suit. See Gregory v. Stetson, 10 S.Ct. 422, 133 U.S. 579, 33 L.Ed. 792 (1890). This is true whether such party was a joint promisee or otherwise.

66. Compare Beckwith v. Talbot, 95 U.S. 289, 24 L.Ed. 496 (1877), discussed in the section that follows.

does not appear what may be their individual shares by their agreement with each other. If A sues alone, whether for all or for a part, C may justly object for the non-joinder of B.[65] It would be otherwise if A and B join in a contract with C by which they promise to render their individual service for two months at the rate of $8 per day each. C's promise may be to A and B; but that promise is to pay them separate wages for separate service.[66]

If in return for the service of A and B the promise of C is to build a house for them on land jointly owned, or to sink an oil well, or to deliver a carload of coal at a particular place, or to forbear to enter into the employ of any competitor of theirs for a limited time, the probability that a separate action by A would be sustained in spite of objection duly made by C is very much less.[67] Parol evidence of the surrounding facts is always admissible to aid in interpretation; indeed, such evidence of the actual understanding of A, B, and C should seldom be excluded, since it will be provable in actions between A and B in any case, and the modern law of procedure sufficiently protects C's interest against unnecessary litigation.[68]

In determining whether the interests of two or more obligees are sufficiently separate to justify the maintenance of separate actions, the courts have not been consistent.[69] This is not surprising. It should be clearly realized that the problem is largely one of "interpretation"; also that it can not be solved by the deductive application of some definition of "joint contract" or some simple contract rule. It should be solved as a problem of procedure, in accordance with the convenience and protection of the parties concerned and the public interest in the avoidance of unnecessary litigation.

### § 940. Joint Promisees of Separate Performances—Severance of Interest

In the American courts the boundary lines between law and equity became more and more blurred, even while jurists were in terms insisting that there was a difference "in the nature of things" between a "legal" and an "equitable" right, and while they were maintaining two kinds of procedure.[73] The English common law judges had not themselves been unaffected by the equitable system operating alongside of them. Progressive and understanding men like Lord Mansfield had applied equitable principles, expanded the use of the common law action of assumpsit, and incorporated rules and practices of the "Law Merchant." American courts were able in many cases to ameliorate the operation of ancient doctrine as to joint contracts, without openly repudiating the doctrine or consciously appealing to their powers as courts of "equity". Thus, they observed that, although the promissory words in a contract might be "joint", the practical and economic interests of the promisees might not be so. They were able to enforce separate rights by interpreting "joint" language in the light of the separateness of "interest".

A "contract" may be a complex transaction. The parties to it may be many; and these parties may not be divided into two separate "groups", the members of each group having common "interests" and acting as a "unit." And yet they may execute a single document, with two or more making certain promises together and in conjunctive form, and with promises being made to two or more others. The performances promised may be separate instead of single and undivided, one payment or transfer to go to A and another to go to B. In such a case the "interests" of these promisees, A and B, are separate; A and B are separate persons and they want their separate payments for their separate use and benefit. In many cases the American courts recognized the separateness of these "interests," and held that A and B had separately enforceable rights in spite of their being "joint" promisees in form of words.[74]

The English courts of common law were much less ready to sustain a separate action by one promisee on the ground of separateness of interest. Proof of such separateness could be made only as an aid in the interpretation of language that would otherwise be ambiguous. If one covenanted with A and B to pay a sum of money to B, it was held that B could not maintain a separate action.[75]

It is seldom that two or more promisees are in express words declared to be either "several" or "joint and several," the latter form being excluded by the fact that the English judges declared that an obligation could not be owed to two or more persons "jointly and severally." When obligees are declared to be entitled "severally," the meaning seems invariably to be that each

74. **U.S.**—Jewett v. Cunard, 13 F. Cas.No.7,310, 3 Woodb. & M. 277 (C.C.Me.1847).

**Md.**—Rent-A-Car Co. v. Globe etc. Ins. Co., 148 A. 252, 158 Md. 169 (1930), insurance policy payable to mortgagee and mortgagor; Jacobs v. Davis, 34 Md. 204 (1870), promise to two adjoining landowners.

Where three owners of undivided interests in property were insured against fire by a single contract, it was held that two of them could recover the amount of their loss according to their interests, even though the third set the fire himself and could recover nothing.

Even though the insurer intended to insure them "jointly", the owners were justified in understanding that each was insured. Also, although their interests were several, it was proper to join in one action and to be given separate recoveries. Hoyt v. New Hampshire Fire Ins. Co., 29 A.2d 121, 92 N.H. 242, 148 A.L.R. 484 (1942).

75.    **Eng.**—Anderson v. Martindale, 1 East 497 (1801).

The rule in Anderson v. Martindale, supra, is repeated in Internat'l Hotel Co. v. Flynn, 87 N.E. 855, 238 Ill. 636 (1909).

of them is entitled to a separate and distinct payment or other performance. This is often what courts mean when they hold that their "interests" are separate. There is a practical and working distinction between a case where A promises B and C to pay to them $100 and one in which A promises B and C to pay $60 to B and $40 to C. These two cases are mutually inconsistent. It may be that the common law judges who said that the rights of two or more promisees might be either "joint" or "several," but could not be both "joint and several" had in mind the foregoing case.

The following case came to the Supreme Court of the United States. A, B, and C promised to care for D's herd of cattle for two years; and D promised them in return to sell the herd with its increase and to pay to them one half of the selling price in excess of $36,000. It was held that A could maintain a separate action against D for breach of his promise.[76] The court assumed that the amount to be paid was payable in thirds, an equal sum to each of the three promisees, as the agreed equivalent of the services rendered by each. Other cases are stated below.[77]

It has even been held that when the "interests" are thus severed, the two or more promisees can not maintain a single action jointly.[78] This surely would not be followed in any court permitted to enter a judgment for a division of the amount collected according to the terms of agreement, as any court of equity could do.[79] It was the old common law court that made itself helpless to render a judgment for payment to two persons separately, a fact that may account in part for the old rule that promisees could not be both joint and several but must be either joint or several.[80] The American Law Institute has abandoned this old doctrine in its Re-

---

76. **U.S.**—Beckwith **v.** Talbot, 95 U. S. 289, 24 L.Ed. 496 (1877). Doubtless it was of some importance in this case that B and C were both sons of D and that A was unrelated. The fact seems to be that A, B, and C were not mere "hired hands", selling their separate labor to D. If the cattle had not been cared for by them as agreed, it seems clear that D could have maintained an action for damages against all three, as was held in Alpaugh v. Wood, 23 A. 261, 53 N.J.L. 638 (1891). But the three might be separate promisees even though they were joint promisors.

77. Each beneficiary can sue separately on a policy in which the in-

surer promises to pay them $5000 "share and share alike." Emmeluth v. Home Ben. Ass'n, 25 N.E. 234, 122 N.Y. 130 (1890).

A promise by one partner to two retiring partners to indemnify them against antecedent debts of the firm is one on which each promisee can sue separately. Morgan v. Wordell, 59 N.E. 1037, 178 Mass. 350, 55 L.R.A. 33 (1901).

Where two contract to render joint service, each to be paid separate salary or wages, they are joint obligors but are several obligees; each can sue separately for his pay. Curry v. Kansas & C. P. R. Co., 48 P. 579, 58 Kan. 6 (1897); Alpaugh v. Wood, 23 A. 261, 53 N.J.L. 638 (1891).

statement.[81]  This does not abolish the distinction between promising to pay one entire sum to two persons and promising to pay a portion of that entire sum to each of two persons.

If the contract and the relations of the promisees are such that clearly separate interests are created by the contract, the maintenance of a separate action should not be prevented by the use of the word "joint;" and yet the joinder of the other promisees should be permitted and encouraged since the claims arise out of a single transaction.[82]  Such joinder should be permitted even though the word used is "several".  Also, even though the right and the interest are both clearly "joint", the executor of a deceased joint promisee should always be allowed to join and to participate in the distribution.  Statutes declaring that a contract in form "joint", shall be in effect "joint and several" should be given at least this much effect as to joint promisees.

### § 941.    Power of One Joint Promisee to Discharge the Obligor

At common law any one of two or more joint obligees had power to terminate the joint right of all and to discharge their obligor from further legal duty.  To produce this result all that he had to do was to discharge the obligor from further duty to himself.  The other obligees had no enforceable right remaining, because they could not maintain action without joining all surviving obligees, and the one who had granted the discharge could not be joined.  Indeed, it is still generally stated as the existing law that each joint obligee has power to discharge without any participation therein by the other obligees.[86]

This rule is, of course, not applicable to a contract in which two or more obligees have rights to wholly separate performances.  If

---

81.  Restatement, Contracts, § 128, says: "(1) If a promise in a contract is made to several persons, the intention of the promisor as expressed in the contract determines whether the right thereby created is joint or whether rights are created which are several or are joint and several.  (2) If no intention is expressed in such a promise, the rights are several if the interests of the obligees in the performance of the promise are distinct; but if their interests in its performance are joint, or if any one of the obligees has neither a separate nor a joint interest in the performance, the right is joint."
The text above is worded differently from this Restatement and would lead to somewhat different results.

86.  Restatement, Contracts, § 130: "Except as the rules of this Section are qualified by § 131 [effect of fraud],

(a) any joint obligee may sue for the enforcement of the promise in the name of all the joint obligees; he also has the power to discharge the promisor by collection and receipt of the performance promised or by release or otherwise;

(b) a discharge by a joint obligee of his individual right operates as a discharge of the joint right of all;

(c) a tender to one of several persons jointly entitled is equivalent to a tender to all of them."

in one contract and for one undivided consideration, A has promised to pay $60 to B and $40 to C, B has power to discharge A's duty to pay him $60 and has no power to discharge A's duty to pay $40 to C. On pure common law theory, if two or more are promisees of one and the same performance, in a contract that is "several" and not "joint," a discharge by one obligee of his own right against the obligor would not discharge the obligation of the latter to the other obligees, each of them having been able to maintain action alone. Full performance as required by the contract would, indeed, discharge the obligor; and part performance would operate pro tanto as against all the obligees alike. Thus, if A promised B and C severally to pay $100 to either one of them, payment of $100 to B would end A's duty to C; and payment of $60 to B would reduce C's claim as well as B's to $40. If in return for $60 paid by A, he was given a sealed release by B, A would still be bound to C to pay $40 more.

No cases illustrating the statements in the preceding paragraph have been found. Where the obligees have been held to have separate rights, the performances to which those rights applied were held to be separate also. Even the ancient common law judges, however technical, did not press their theories of joint and several contracts to their logical conclusion. When they said that obligees could be joint or several but could not be both joint and several, it may well be that the idea that was pressing for expression was that obligees can be promised one performance jointly or separate performances severally, and that one performance and separate performances are inconsistent.

Even when two or more obligees are jointly entitled to a single performance by the obligor, there have been limitations on the power of one obligee to discharge the duty of the obligor to the others. These limitations may have originated in equity; but in considerable degree they have been made effective in ordinary actions for common law remedies. Thus, if the discharge by one obligee is made with intent to defraud a joint obligee, and this fact is known to the obligor, the discharge is no defense in an action brought against him.[87] Without question, the discharge is good except as to the equitable share of the defrauded obligee.

# PART VI

# BREACH OF CONTRACT

---

## TOPIC A

## BREACH OF CONTRACT

---

### CHAPTER 53

### VARIETIES OF BREACH—PARTIAL, TOTAL

---

## § 943. Breach of Contract—When Nonperformance Constitutes a Breach

A breach of contract is always a non-performance of duty; but it is not every non-performance of duty that is a breach of contract. Every executory contract creates legal duty; but in most cases it is not a duty that requires immediate performance. There is a difference between a duty to perform in the future and a duty to perform immediately.[1] One who has contracted to pay

---

1. Restatement, Contracts, § 312, says: "A breach of contract is a non-performance of any contractual duty of immediate performance. A breach may be total or partial, and may take place by failure to perform acts promised, by prevention or hindrance, or by repudiation."

$1000 on the first of next June has undertaken a duty and owes a debt. Nevertheless, non-payment of the money prior to the first day of June is not a breach of contract.

The legal duty created by a contract may not only be a duty to render a performance at some time in the future; it may be a duty to perform contingently upon the happening of some uncertain event. This is a future conditional duty. In such a case failure to render the performance promised will not be a breach of contract unless the time fixed for such performance has expired and all conditions precedent have occurred. If an owner has contracted to pay a builder $1000 as soon as the roof of the building is completed, non-payment of the money will not be a breach of contract unless it occurs after the completion of the roof.

There are various ways in which a contractual duty can be discharged before any breach of it has been committed. Such a discharge renders any breach of that duty impossible. Of course a discharge may occur after a breach of contract has already been committed. Such a discharge may bar further judicial remedy; but the breach of contract has already occurred as an operative fact and some of the changes effected by its occurrence may still exist. Whenever there is legal justification for the non-performance of a promise there is no breach of contractual duty.[2]

### § 944. Breach of Duty Assumed Impliedly or Unintentionally

When a contract is made, legal duties may be created that the parties themselves did not intend. They expressly promise certain definite performances. Neither one may expressly promise that he will forbear to put hindrances in the way of performance by the other or that he will not prevent the fulfilment of some condition precedent to his own duty or that he will not repudiate the contract before the date set for the promised performance. Nevertheless, a contract creates duties of this sort; and a breach of contract may be committed by prevention, hindrance or repudiation.[3]

2. Restatement, Contracts, § 312, Comment a: "Justification may be due to the fact that the duty arising when the contract was formed has been discharged, or if that is not the case, to the fact that a duty of immediate performance has not arisen because some condition precedent has not occurred."

3. In Kirke LaShelle Co. v. Paul Armstrong Co., 188 N.E. 163, 263 N.Y. 79 (1933), the court found an implied promise not to do acts that would impair the value of contract rights that had been granted. The defendant had granted production rights in a drama, at a time before the "talkies" were commercially known; and the court held that there was an implied promise not to grant "talkie" rights to a third party. Another case involving a similar implication is Palmer Elec. & Mfg. Co. v. Underwriters Laboratories, 188 N E. 257, 284 Mass. 550 (1933).

## § 945.   Breach may Vary in Extent and Importance

A breach of contract may be large or small, total or partial.  A debtor may pay nine-tenths of his debt, but fail to pay the other tenth.  He has committed a breach of contract.  A building contractor may fail even to start excavation for the foundation, or he may erect the building as a whole substantially in accordance with specifications and fail merely to use the brand of sewer pipe that his contract required.[4]  In either case the builder has committed a breach of contract, but his two breaches are not of the same size or importance.  An employer may discharge his servant at the very beginning of the employment, paying him nothing;  or he may employ the servant to the end, paying him his full salary, omitting only to pay a small bonus promised at the end.  In either case he has committed a breach of his contract with the servant, but the breaches are not alike.

## § 946.   The Terms "Total Breach" and "Partial Breach"

For every breach of contract, irrespective of its size or kind, the law will give an immediate remedy.  What this remedy may be, is discussed in the chapter dealing with Remedies for Breach of Contract.  The terms total breach and partial breach are frequently used by the courts in determining the remedies that are available to the injured party.  It might reasonably be supposed, from the form of these expressions, that a total breach is the non-performance of everything undertaken in the contract, and that a partial breach is the non-performance of something less than the whole.  Actual usage by the courts, however, is somewhat different.  A total breach of contract is a non-performance of duty that is so material and important as to justify the injured party in regarding the whole transaction as at an end.  Whether or not a breach is thus material and important is a question of degree;  and it must be answered by weighing the consequences in the light of the actual custom of men in the performance of contracts similar to the one that is involved in the specific case.  A total breach by A will usually terminate B's duty to perform any further on his part, but it does not always do so.  The promises of the two parties may have been independent promises, or the breach by A may occur after he has already performed all conditions precedent to B's duty to proceed.  Nor does a total breach by A always effectually terminate A's own duty to render the promised performance.  B can sometimes get a decree for

---

4.   See Jacob & Youngs v. Kent, 129 N.E. 889, 230 N.Y. 239 (1921), breach too small for any substantial compensation;  Helgar Corp. v. Warner's Features, 119 N.E. 113, 222 N.Y. 449 (1918), breach by 48 hours delay in payment of a large instalment.
See Chapters 30, 35, 36, dealing in detail with Conditions, Substantial Performance, Instalment Contracts, etc.

specific performance; and even in cases where this is not possible, the subsequent rendering by A of the promised performance has often been held not to be a sufficient consideration for a new promise by B, for the reason that A is doing nothing more than his contractual duty still requires of him. Nor does a total breach by A always terminate the power of B to earn the full compensation promised to him by continuing to render his own performance. In spite of his breach, A may still assure B that he will perform or he may request B to go ahead.

Circumstances may be such as to make it unreasonable to require B to stop performance, as where he is bound by a duty to others to proceed or where greater injury will result from stopping than from continuing. Therefore, it is not correct to say that a total breach terminates all the primary contractual relations and substitutes secondary and remedial ones; but it is clear that, wherever the court will hold that A's breach is a total breach, B can regard A's performance as at an end and at once maintain action for damages for all of his injury, past, present, and future.[5] If A's breach is not sufficiently material and important for this, the breach is called a partial breach.

For a partial breach the injured party can maintain action at once; but he is not permitted to stop further performance by the wrongdoer and get damages for the anticipated future nonperformance, as well as for the past non-performance constituting the partial breach. The non-payment of an instalment of money when due will always create a right of action for that money, but it will not always be a total breach.[6] A partial breach by one party, as here defined, does not justify the other party's subsequent failure to perform; both parties may be guilty of breaches, each having a right to damages.[7]

While in the case of a total breach the injured party can at once get judgment for his entire injury, it is not always necessary for him to elect this remedy. In some cases he may elect to regard the breach as partial, proceed with his own performance, sue for the partial injury, and maintain a second suit in case a further

6.   In Helgar Corp. v. Warner's Features, 119 N.E. 113, 222 N.Y. 449 (1918), the purchaser of a large amount of film to be delivered and paid for in instalments was guilty of a delay of 48 hours in making a payment of $10,000. The court held that although this was a breach of contract it was a minor one and did not justify repudiation by the seller. The seller could get judgment for the instalment due with interest, but not for damages as for total breach including prospective profits.

Restatement, Contracts, § 313, Comment c: "Though a breach to any extent of a contractual duty of immediate performance gives rise to a right of action, a slight breach does not terminate the duty of the injured person or the right of the party committing the breach (§ 274), unless non-performance of an express condition requires this result."

breach occurs.[8]  He generally has no such election, however, in case the wrongdoer has repudiated the contract, expressing his intention to perform no further.  In such a case the injured party has one entire cause of action.  The breach must be treated as total, and no such second action will be maintainable.  Thus, if on a building contract the owner fails to make payment of a large instalment in the course of performance, the building contractor will usually be privileged to stop work and can maintain suit for damages as for a total breach.  But if the owner does not also repudiate the contract, the builder can get judgment for the instalment due, proceed with construction, and get a second judgment in case of a later breach.

If the seller of goods delivers an instalment of nonconforming goods, in breach of some warranty, even though the breach may be such as to operate as a total breach the buyer is not required to treat it so.  He may keep the defective instalment, retaining his right to damages or recoupment, and demand delivery of the remaining instalments required by the contract.  When sued for the price of the instalments received by him, he may recoup for breach of warranty and claim damages for the seller's failure to deliver the subsequent instalments.[9]  The seller has committed one breach, treated by the buyer as partial, and a second breach that is total.

The terms "total breach" and "partial breach" can render useful service, even though actual usage is not altogether consistent, if it is recognized that such a variation exists and that they do not in themselves determine the result that a court should reach.  They may be properly used in stating a result that the court has reached by a careful weighing of the importance of the facts and events before it, a reasonable interpretation of the expressions of the parties, a consideration of existing doctrines and antecedent cases, and a determination of what public welfare and sound policy require.  In this they differ in no respect from other legal terms and phrases.[10]

8.  Restatement, Contracts, § 317: "(2) Where there has been such a total breach of contract as is stated in subsection (1) the injured party may by continuance or assenting to the continuance of performance, or by otherwise manifesting an intention to do so, treat the breach as partial, except that where there has been one of the acts of repudiation enumerated in Section 318, whether anticipatory or not, subsequent assent of the wrongdoer to the continuance of the contract is requisite in order to permit this result."

See § 1039, Avoidable consequences.

10.  Restatement, Contracts, § 313: "(1) A total breach of contract is a breach where remedial rights provided by law are substituted for the existing contractual rights, or can be so substituted by the injured party.

(2) A partial breach of contract is a breach where remedial rights provided by law can be substituted by the injured party for only a part of the existing contractual rights."

In one sense of the word, there is never such a thing as an immaterial breach. For any breach of contract, an action lies; any breach is material enough for that, although if no substantial injury is shown the damages recoverable are only nominal. But not infrequently the term material breach is used to mean one that the injured party can elect to treat as a total breach.[11] If a contractor's failure of performance causes such slight harm that the courts will give no remedy therefor, adopting and applying the maxim *de minimis non curat lex,* it is proper to say that there has been no breach of duty.

## § 947.   Prevention or Hindrance of Performance as a Breach

Elsewhere in this work will be found a discussion of implied promises.[12] Among such promises there discussed is the implied promise not to prevent or hinder performance. Such prevention or hindrance is a breach of contract in any case where the facts justify the implication of a promise.[13] There are a few cases in which the implication is not justified, cases in which the prevention or hindrance was reasonably necessary in carrying on a party's other business or supplying his wants and in which both parties contemplated the possibility of such prevention or hindrance when the contract was made.[14] Generally however, the parties contemplate no such possibility and neither say nor think anything about it; and prevention or hindrance should clearly be regarded as wrongful. It is practically immaterial whether the implied promise is a fiction of the court to attain a desirable result or is a justifiable inference of fact. In some cases the wrongful conduct could have been treated as a tort; and it can still be so treated if the courts find it of advantage in the course of justice. Even so, it can be made use of both for defense and for attack, in contract actions.

To one who is sued for nonperformance of his promise it is a defense if he can prove that his performance was prevented or substantially hindered by the plaintiff.[15] This is a case of discharge by wrongful action of the plaintiff and is considered in the chapter on Discharge. It is another aspect of prevention with which we are dealing at this point—that in which it appears as a basis for attack against the wrongdoer. In the majority of cases the duty of a contractor is a conditional duty—his duty of immediate performance is dependent on some condition or conditions precedent. But suppose that he steps in to prevent or to interfere seriously with the performance of those conditions? What is the effect? For example, in a building contract the duty of the owner to pay is usually conditional on performance of the work; it may also be expressly conditional on

11.   See Restatement, Contracts, §§ 270, 271, 311.

15.   U.S.—U. S. v. Peck, 102 U.S. 64, 26 L.Ed. 46 (1880).

completion by a fixed time and on a certificate of the architect. Has the owner committed a breach of the building contract if he excludes the contractor from the premises, if he delays completion by changing the plans, or if he induces the architect to refuse a certificate?

Exclusion from the premises is a breach of contract by the owner; and this is so whether the action is accompanied by an express repudiation or not. Its legal effect is the same as that of repudiation.[16] It is a total breach; and the contractor can get judgment for the contract price, less what he saves by not having to do the rest of the work (the cost of completion). He is prevented from performing the full equivalent and therefore he is not entitled to the full contract price.

If the owner wrongfully prevents the architect from giving his certificate as a prerequisite to a final payment, this too is a breach of contract; but the condition that it prevents is an act of a third party and it does not prevent the contractor from performing the agreed equivalent of his money or from getting judgment for the contract price in full. Prevention by one party of the fulfilment of any condition precedent to the other party's right to the agreed compensation is a breach of contract unless such prevention was regarded as permissible when the contract was made.[18]

One who has promised to pay an attorney compensation for negotiating settlement of a claim or for prosecuting a case to judgment is guilty of a breach if he prevents performance of the condition of the attorney's right to payment by unjustifiably settling the claim himself or dismissing the case without the attorney's consent.[19]

One who sues for damages, alleging as a breach the prevention or hindrance by the other party must prove that the condition on which his rights depended would have occurred or been performed but for the prevention or hindrance.[20] Those terms presuppose a relation of cause and effect. If his performance would not have been rendered anyway, he has not been harmed by the alleged prevention or hindrance. The existence of this causal relation is a question of fact, one that may at times be difficult of determination.

## § 948.  Remedy Available at Once for any Breach

It has often been said that "there can be but one action for damages for a total breach of an entire contract".[21] This statement renders nothing but disservice so long as the terms "total breach" and "entire contract" are incapable of exact definition.

21.  N.Y.—Pakas v. Hollingshead, 77 N.E. 40, 184 N.Y. 211 (1906).

But it is true that the remedies that are available and the procedure necessary to obtain them depend in large measure upon the character and importance of the breach that has occurred.

The first rule to be stated is that for any breach that has occurred, be it large or small, "partial" or "total", an action can be maintained and the law will give an appropriate remedy. This remedy may be a judgment for a sum of money (compensatory damages or money debt), or in some cases a decree for specific performance.[22] If a contract provides for the payment of money in instalments, an action will lie for each instalment as it falls due.[23] A judgment rendered in any one of these actions will not operate as a bar to the maintenance of the others. So also if a contract requires the rendition at separate times of performances other than the payment of money, when the duty of immediate performance of any one of these accrues and a breach is committed, an action therefor is at once maintainable.[24] Such a contract, even though it is one contract and not many, and even though it may properly be described for many purposes as "entire" and "indivisible", it is certainly capable of several separate breaches for each of which a separate action will lie.[25]

Care must, of course, be taken not to bring suit prematurely. If a minor breach has occurred, but there is sufficient assurance that defects will be cured and losses compensated, the bringing of suit at once may properly be regarded as vexatious and an unreasonable enhancement of damages. Furthermore, if the breach is minor it does not justify the injured party in refusing further performance of his own and suing for damages as for a total breach. Such action by him constitutes a total breach on his own part and puts him in the position of a defendant rather than a plaintiff.

## § 949.  Contracts to Pay Money or Deliver Goods in Instalments

Instalment contracts formerly caused great difficulty with respect to the character of the duty or duties that they create and with respect to the number of actions that may be maintained for their non-performance. In earlier times it was held that only one action could be maintained on one contract, whether it was performable in instalments or not. Where a sum of money was payable in instalments at separate dates, the creditor could not maintain an action of debt until all the instalments fell due.[26] As is well understood, the action of assumpsit was used to expand and to change the common law, the substantive

---

**24.** "If one contracts to do several things, at several times, an action of assumpsit will lie on each default; for, although the agreement is entire, the performance is several, and the contract divisible in its nature. Knight v. New England Worsted Co. 2 Cush. (Mass.) 271." Goodwin v. Cabot Amusement Co., 149 A. 574, 129 Me. 36 (1930).

changes involved being concealed by making the determinations deal solely with procedure and forms of action. Such a change was made in the case of instalment contracts. Assumpsit was held to lie just as soon as there had been a non-performance in the case of any instalment. It was still maintained, however, that only one action would lie and that, therefore, if assumpsit was brought after the failure to pay one instalment, but before the others were due, the plaintiff might get judgment for the whole amount promised as damages, prospective as well as past. Still further on in the process of development such an instalment contract came to be regarded as divisible into parts, creating separate duties enforceable in successive actions.[27] Indebitatus assumpsit, which was the equivalent of the action of debt, was maintainable for each definite instalment as it fell due.[28] It was not necessary thereafter to ask damages for the prospective defaults as well as for the overdue instalment. This amounted to a total abandonment of the rule that only one action would lie for breach of such a contract; and, indeed, of the rule that the action of debt could not be maintained until after all the instalments came due. The failure to perform any one of the instalments when it is due is now regarded as a breach of contract for which an action will lie; and if there are several definite and independent performances which are to take place at different times, the contractor is regarded as under duties to render these performances that are separately enforceable.[29] Action lies for each instalment even though it is not the agreed and apportioned equivalent of any specified part of the service or property in return for which the payments are promised.

The rule applicable to instalments of money is equally applicable to contracts for the delivery of goods in instalments. Failure to deliver a definite instalment as promised is a breach for which an action will at once lie. The same should be true of all other types of performance in instalments so long as the rule is not abused by bringing actions for very small breaches.

## § 950. Only One Action Maintainable for all Previous Breaches

Although an action lies at once for failure to render an instalment performance as promised and a second action for similar failure thereafter, if no action is brought until after there have been two such failures only one action can thereafter be maintained for the two. One judgment bars any further action for breaches that existed at the time suit was brought and that might then have been included in a single action. This rule is to reduce the cost of litigation and to prevent unnecessary and vexatious actions.

So only one action is maintainable for all instalments of money under a single contract that are overdue when suit is commenced,[30] or for all instalments of rent that are due under a single lease.[31] The same is true of all other kinds of breaches as well, failure to make repairs or to insure as well as failure to pay a money instalment or to deliver goods or to perform services.[32]

The same rule applies to all other kinds of contracts requiring a series of performances such that a series of breaches can occur by failure to render the performances as required.[33]

No doubt an acceleration clause can be so drawn as to cause an entire debt to become due upon failure to pay an instalment as agreed and to cause a judgment for the instalment to bar action for the balance of the debt. Probably such clauses are not generally so drawn, but instead merely give to the creditor the option of declaring the balance due and enforcing payment of the whole. If he forbears to exercise the power so retained and sues for the overdue instalment, judgment should not bar a suit for the balance.[34]

In any case where the plaintiff brings an action for less than the whole of the amount of one entire claim, he has no power to prevent the judgment from merging the entire claim or of preserving his right as to the part not sued for, by expressly excluding a part of the claim in his declaration or expressly reserving a right of action.[35]

## § 951.  Effect of a Statute of Limitations on Actions for a Partial Breach

The period fixed by a statute of limitations begins to run from the "accrual of the cause of action." Since "cause of action" is so uncertain and variable a concept, serious injustice may be done unless the court uses judicial discretion in applying such a statute in the case of "partial" breaches of a single contract. No doubt there is much authority for the statement that where separate actions would lie for a series of such breaches, the statute operates against each one separately as of the time when each one could have been brought, and that this rule is not affected by the fact that after two or more such breaches have occurred the plaintiff must join them all in one action.[36] Of course, if an action for a first instalment is barred by the statute, it can not properly be included in an action for later instalments that are not yet barred.

There are many cases, however, in which an injured party has reason to be uncertain whether such a "partial" breach has occurred as to justify immediate action; and in other cases it may be unreasonable to apply the statute against him with technical strictness. For example, an anticipatory repudiation is a breach for which an action will at once lie, and yet it is reasonable for

31.  Conn.—Burritt v. Belfy, 47 Conn. 323 (1879).

the injured party to continue to demand performance and to hold open an opportunity for retraction of the repudiation. In such a case the statutory period is held not to begin to run until the day set for the actual performance promised or until the injured party has definitely expressed his intention to regard the repudiation as a breach.[37] Also, where a building contract provides for payments as the work progresses, on certificates by the architect, an action will lie for each payment as due; and yet if the promisee forbears to sue until completion of the work his action for the whole price is maintainable for the period beginning when that whole price was due.[38] The bar of the statute is not raised piecemeal.

Where a contract contains an acceleration clause making all instalments payable in case of failure to pay any one instalment when due, the creditor is not required to join subsequent instalments in his action for the first instalment, if the acceleration clause is regarded as giving him an option. In such case, the statute does not begin to run against later instalments until each falls due in regular course.[39] In some cases the contrary has been held because of the positive wording of the acceleration clause, with nothing to indicate an option.[40] Such a holding may be unduly harsh on the plaintiff who has delayed in good faith without harm to the debtor.

It is perfectly clear, also, that where a non-performance is so material that the injured party may treat it as a "total" breach if he wishes but is not accompanied by a repudiation of the contract, he may sue as for a "partial" breach only and the statute will not begin to run against an action for a subsequent failure of performance until it in fact occurs.

## § 952.  Breaches of Separate Contracts—Negotiable Notes

The rule stated in the previous section is not applicable where the breaches involved are breaches of separate and independent contracts.[41] The court may in a proper case order the consolidation of actions brought on such contracts; but in the absence of such an order separate actions are maintainable even though the parties are identical. Cases frequently arise in which it is difficult to determine whether the parties made two separate contracts or only one contract; in such cases a plaintiff should not be penalized unnecessarily. The applicable rule of law is not so absolute and inflexible as that. In matters of remedial procedure the modern courts have wide discretionary powers. At times it may be sufficient to charge costs against a plaintiff instead of barring his action.[42] The result should often depend on determinations as to "good faith" and the actual inconvenience caused.

37.  **U.S.**—Foss-Schneider Brewing Co. v. Bullock, 59 F. 83 (C.C.A.6th, 1893).

**N.Y.**—Ga Nun v. Palmer, 96 N.E. 99, 202 N.Y. 383 (1911).

See §§ 788, 789. Anticipatory breach.

Negotiable bills and notes have long been regarded as separate contracts; and courts have held that separate actions can be maintained for non-payment even though they have been given for instalments of the price on a single sale or in accordance with any other bargain in a single transaction, and even though they are all overdue and held by a single plaintiff.[43]  Such bills and notes have always been transferable by the law merchant; and when they are held by different persons each holder may properly bring his own action.  Some holders may be innocent purchasers for value and others not; so that the issues involved, as well as the parties plaintiff, may not be identical.  But as between the original payee and the maker of several notes in a single transaction the duty to pay them is not to be determined independently of the consideration and the other terms of agreement; and the bringing of several actions by the payee on the notes may be vexatious and unnecessary.[44]

### § 953.  A. Series of Transactions may Merge into One Running Account

Where there has been a series of purchases and sales between two parties, constituting a running account, payable as bills may be rendered, there is but one right of action for a balance due at any one time.[45]  This is true even though each purchase was by a separate order and a period of credit was agreed upon.  By custom and implied agreement the separate transactions are merged into one.[46]  Of course, when a suit is brought no item can properly be included the price of which is not yet due.  It is just like a case of a contract to pay a definite sum of money in separate instalments.  An action lies at any time for an instalment that is due; but only one action can be maintained for instalments then due that have not already been sued for.  A judgment with respect to such instalments is not a bar to an action for instalments that fell due after the bringing of the suit in which the judgment was rendered.[47]

It is possible for two persons to make a series of purchases and sales, each price payable at a distinct time, without treating them as a single running account with total balances payable on bill rendered.[48]  Even in such a case, if the parties have reviewed the series of transactions and struck a balance due, the account so stated constitutes a single cause of action.[49]

### § 954.  Breach by Repudiation of Obligation

The unexcused failure of a contractor to render a promised performance when it is due is always a breach of contract for which an action for an appropriate remedy can be maintained.  Such failure may be of such great importance as to constitute what has been called herein a "total" breach.[50]  This is true even though there may be a large part of his promised performance that is not yet due; and it is true also even though the failure to perform is not accompanied by any expression of repudiation of the contractual obligation. For a failure of performance constituting such a "total" breach, an action for remedies that are appropriate thereto is at once maintainable. Yet the injured party is not required to bring such an action. He has the option of treating the non-performance as a "partial" breach only and getting a judgment therefor without barring a later action for some subsequently occurring breach. It is reasonable for him to expect performance of the remainder of the contract as agreed and to ask a judicial remedy in case of disappointment.

Thus a contractor can get judgment for an unpaid progress payment, while proceeding with the work. By so proceeding he does not waive his right to damages for delay in completion caused by the non-payment [51] or for subsequently occurring breaches.

Likewise a seller who delivers a non-conforming instalment of goods commits a breach of contract, one that may be treated as "total" dependent on the relative materiality of the defect; but if there has been no repudiation the buyer may continue to insist on further deliveries. If sued for the price of the instalment delivered the buyer may recoup for the breach of warranty involved in the defective delivery. By obtaining such recoupment he bars any claim for further damages for such breach of warranty, a claim that he might have enforced by bringing his own action against the seller; but he does not bar his right to damages for the seller's failure to make further deliveries or for any other subsequent breach.[52]

An employee who has not been paid his wages or salary as it falls due, but has not been discharged or prevented from continuing to perform the service, has an immediate right of action for the amount so unpaid; he does not by getting such a payment bar his action for any subsequent breach, either an action for subsequently overdue wages or for damages for a subsequent discharge or repudiation of contract.[53] The failure to pay wages or salary may be under such circumstances as to justify the employee in stopping work and suing for damages for "total" breach; but if he does not choose to do this he is not, in the absence of a discharge or other repudiation, "splitting" his cause faction or vexatiously multiplying suits.

How are the rights of the parties affected and what is the character of the breach when a failure to render some performance when due is accompanied by a repudiation of the contractual obligation? In the first place, such a repudiation is called an "anticipatory breach" when it occurs before any performance by the repudiator is actually due.[54] The injured party is not required to bring action before the due date for performance; but if he can avoid losses without unreasonable effort or expense his damages will be limited accordingly.[55] If a contract requires a performance at one time only and it is not then rendered, the breach is not "total" if time is not of the essence; but it will certainly be "total" if then accompanied by a repudiation, and thereafter only one action is maintainable.[56] If time is of the essence, the non-performance is a "total" breach without any accompanying repudiation; and in any case time becomes of the essence when the delay continues so unreasonably long a time that patience ceases to be a virtue.[57]

Suppose next that the contract requires performance in instalments or continuously for some period and that there has been such a partial failure of performance as justifies immediate action for a partial breach. If this partial breach is accompanied by repudiation of the contractual obligation such repudiation is anticipatory with respect to the performances that are not yet due. In most cases the repudiator is now regarded as having committed a "total" breach, justifying immediate action for the remedies appropriate thereto. In determining the damages recoverable in such an action, it is necessary for the court to look into the future. In spite of the uncertainty involved in this, the trier of fact is permitted to make an estimate to be added to the damages awarded for the actual non-performance that has already occurred.[58] In most cases this remedy is regarded as adequate and the injured party is allowed only one action for his wrong. The non-performance plus the repudiation constitute one and only one cause of action.[59]

If the buyer of goods in instalments fails to pay for one of them and also refuses to take and pay for any more, there is a "total" breach; and the seller can get but one judgment for damages.[60] If the seller fails to deliver one instalment of goods, or delivers a defective instalment, and also repudiates his obligation to deliver any more, the buyer can get only one judgment for damages.[61]

In any case of repudiation by one party, the injured party is expected to avoid losses if he can do so without unreasonable effort and expense, and his damages are limited accordingly. Where such avoidance is possible we have a sound reason for not permitting the injured party to proceed with his performance and compel payment of the agreed price. He must stop performance, avoid loss, and be content with compensatory damages obtained in one action.[a]

## § 958. Breach of Contract of Employment by the Employer

Breaches of an employment contract by the employer may be either total or partial; and the courts have not, in some matters,

a. The following sections are here omitted: § 955. Rule against "Splitting a Cause of Action", with analysis and illustrations; § 956. Successive Breaches of "Continuing" Contracts; § 957. Severability for Purpose of Different Remedies.

followed a uniform course as to remedies. A contract of employment to begin at a future time is totally broken by the employer's refusal to begin such employment at that time.[89] On such refusal, the employee has a single action for his injury, measured by the full amount of salary or wages promised, less what he can earn by reasonable effort in other similar employment.[90] The fact that the amount of such possible earnings may be uncertain and hard to prove is not a sufficient reason for allowing a series of actions. The burden of proving the amount of such possible earnings is on the employer who is in default, a disadvantage that is counterbalanced by the fact that he escapes the vexation of a series of suits by the employee. If the employer has promised to give the opportunity to do the work as well as to pay for it, the loss of opportunity as well as the loss of pay is to be measured. A total breach by the employer can take place without an absolute discharge; a demotion from a position of honor and power to one with different duties and inferior advantages may be a total breach even though there is no breach with respect to salary.[91]

If an employee is wrongfully discharged by his employer, this is a total breach for which only a single action lies, judgment being obtainable for all wages past due and for all future promised wages less what can be earned by reasonable effort in similar employment.[92] If all the agreed services have been fully rendered and all that remains is a series of payments by the employer, as a pension or other deferred compensation, the transaction has be-

---

91.　Demotion as a breach:

N.Y.—Marks v. Cowdin, 123 N.E. 139, 226 N.Y. 138 (1919); Sigmon v. Goldstone, 101 N.Y.S. 984 (1906).

The loss of opportunity is material in those cases in which performance will enhance the skill or the reputation of the employee as in the case of actors, musicians, and apprentices. See Collier v. Sunday Referee Pub. Co., [1940] 4 All Eng. 234; Marbe v. Edwardes, [1928] K. B. 269.

If the employer has not promised actual work and remains ready and willing to pay the promised salary or wages, there is no breach. Turner v. Sawdon & Co., [1901] 2 K. B. 653; Lagerwall v. Wilkinson, Henderson & Clarke Ltd., 80 L.T. 55 (1899).

92.　U.S.—Pierce v. Tennessee Coal, Iron, & R. Co., 19 S.Ct. 335, 173 U. S. 1, 43 L.Ed. 591 (1899); Russell v. Barnes Foundation, 52 F.Supp. 827 (D.C.Pa.1943), affirmed 143 F.2d 871 (C.C.A., 1944).

W.Va.—Jameson v. Board of Ed., 89 S.E. 255, 78 W.Va. 612 (1915), a judgment for past wages bars a later action for damages.

Eng.—Emmens v. Elderton, 4 H.L. Cas. 625 (1853).

Instead of suing for damages measured as above stated, the employee has the alternative remedy of quantum meruit for services actually rendered. A judgment in either form bars a second action. It was an unnecessary hardship for the court to bar the second action in Goodman v. Pocock, 15 Q.B. 576 (1850), where it was the court and not the plaintiff that prevented a total recovery in the first action. See also James v. Parsons, R. & Co., 78 P. 438, 70 Kan. 156 (1904), where the court might have been less severe on the plaintiff.

come a unilateral instalment contract and an action lies for each instalment as it falls due.[93]　This seems to be true in spite of a flat repudiation by the employer.

It has been held in some cases that the right of action for wages or salary due before a wrongful discharge is separate and distinct from the right of action for damages for the repudiation and that judgment for one does not bar an action for the other.[94]　At common law the action for wages due was debt, or its equivalent indebitatus assumpsit, while the action for damages was special assumpsit.　Even so, the two claims could have been adjudicated in one assumpsit action.　In a modern civil action there is no reason for maintaining two separate actions, but a court can hardly be blamed, in view of the conflicting decisions, for refusing to deprive an employee of damages for a total discharge on the ground that he "split" his cause of action by first suing for unpaid wages actually due.

If the employer has not discharged the employee or otherwise repudiated, and service continues, an action lies at once for nonpayment of an instalment of salary or wages when it is due.　For two or more such wage instalments overdue, only a single action lies.[95]　Each non-payment is a partial breach, although it may be accompanied by circumstances that justify the employee in treating it as total;　but he is not required to do this as long as there has been no discharge or repudiation.

## CHAPTER 54

## BREACH OF CONTRACT BY ANTICIPATORY REPUDIATION

## § 959. Anticipatory Breach of Contract

The law of contract is the law of promises; it consists of the rules that have been empirically developed for determining the legal effect of promises and of facts closely connected with them. By the term "promise" we mean an expression of intention by the promisor to conduct himself in a certain way or to bring about a certain result, made so as to justify and induce reliance thereon by another person. From these facts, one is easily led to suppose that a "breach" of contract is necessarily the failure to perform as promised, and that such failure can occur only at the time that the terms of the promise prescribed and under the conditions therein specified. If, in 1950, A promises to take B to Europe as his courier in 1952 and to pay him $500 on return from the trip, since the only performance that A expressly promises to render is to take place in 1952 it may seem that no breach can occur in 1950 or 1951.

The existing law, however, is otherwise. Such a promise creates duties of immediate performance long before the time set for starting to Europe. A is required by the law not only to perform in 1952, but also to forbear from repudiating his promise in 1951.[1] It is now the generally prevailing rule in both England and the United States that a definite and unconditional repudiation of the contract by a party thereto, communicated to the other, is a breach of the contract, creating an immediate right of action and other legal effects, even though it takes place long before the time prescribed for the promised performance and

---

1. This has seemed strange and illogical to some scholars, born in a community whose political and legal ideas were first developed under pioneer conditions by a people looking for unlimited personal liberty (at least for themselves) and were first written into statute and decision on a large scale in the time of revolution (American and French). The preferred theory was that, in the field of contract law, a person could be bound only by the expression of his own will, and that there could be no legal duty to be enforced against him beyond the terms of his own consensual promise. This may account for the many statements that "logically" or "in the nature of things" there can be no breach of contract except by failure to perform something that was prom-

ised. But as social conditions change, the prevailing notions of what is desirable change with them. Personal liberty, always necessarily limited in any society of men or beasts, becomes more narrowly limited. The legal rights and duties growing out of and regarded as a part of "contract" are determined more and more by the needs of the all, and less and less by the mere will of the contractor. Contract law approaches tort law, though still far from being identified with it. The pendulum, once swinging "from status to contract" now swings in the opposite direction; and the line where personal privilege ceases and legal duty begins is now more greatly determined not by the will of the individual for himself, but by the desires and wills of the many.

before conditions specified in the promise have ever occurred.[2] In a very few jurisdictions there have been decisions contra;[3] but it should not now be regarded as assured that any of these minority jurisdictions will continue to adhere to their formerly expressed rule. The pressure for uniformity, respect for the opinions of others, observation that the majority rule has produced no dire effects in operation—these have already led some courts to change their position and may be expected to have a similar effect on others.[4] The American Law Institute has adopted the general rule, with some limitations that have judicial support and that may possibly be retained hereafter. The history of the doctrine of anticipatory breach, the full exposition of its legal effect, and the statement of its exact limitations, require a comparative study of the leading cases and a discussion of considerable length. In this discussion there will be stated the effect of a repudiation, whether it is wholly anticipatory or is accompanied by a breach by an actual failure of performance as and when promised.[5]

An anticipatory breach of contract by a promisor is a repudiation of his contractual duty before the time fixed in the contract for his performance has arrived. Such a repudiation may be made either by word or by act. If the promisor makes a definite statement to the promisee that he either will not or can not perform his contract, this is a repudiation and will operate as an anticipatory breach unless the promisor had some justifying cause for his statement. Likewise, if a promisor does any voluntary act rendering performance of the contract impossible by him, this, too, is operative as an anticipatory breach. If one who has contracted to sell specific land, goods, or other subject matter, to another, either sells or contracts to sell to a third person the same

---

**2.  U.S.**—New York Life Ins. Co. v. Viglas, 56 S.Ct. 615, 297 U.S. 672, 80 L.Ed. 971 (1936); Central Trust Co. of Ill. v. Chicago Auditorium Ass'n, 36 S.Ct. 412, 240 U.S. 581, 60 L.Ed. 811, L.R.A.1917B, 580 (1916); Roehm v. Horst, 20 S.Ct. 780, 178 U.S. 1, 44 L.Ed. 953 (1900); Hawkinson v. Johnston, 122 F.2d 724, 137 A.L.R. 420 (C.C.A.8th, 1941), Missouri Law; Barnebey v. Barron G. Collier, 65 F.2d 864 (C. C.A.8th, 1933); Colorado Yule Marble Co. v. Collins, 230 F. 78 (C.C. A.8th, 1915); Weber v. Grand Lodge of Kentucky, F. & A. M., 169 F. 522 (C.C.A.6th, 1909).

**Ill.**—Lake Shore & M. S. Ry. Co. v. Richards, 38 N.E. 773, 152 Ill. 59,

30 L.R.A. 33 (1894); Roebling's Sons Co. v. Lock Stitch Fence Co., 22 N.E. 518, 130 Ill. 660 (1889); Kadish v. Young, 43 Am.Rep. 548, 108 Ill. 170, 177 (1883); Follansbee v. Adams, 86 Ill. 13 (1877); Fox v. Kitton, 19 Ill. 519 (1858).

**Eng.**—Synge v. Synge, [1894] 1 Q.B. 466; Johnstone v. Milling, 16 Q.B. D. 460 (1886); Frost v. Knight, L. R. 7 Ex. 111 (1872); Danube, etc., Ry. Co. v. Xenos, 11 C.B.(N.S.) 152 (1861), affirmed on appeal in Exchequer Chamber, 13 C.B. (N.S.) 825; Avery v. Bowden, 5 El. & Bl. 714, 6 El. & Bl. 953 (1855); Hochster v. De la Tour, 2 El. & Bl. 678, 22 L.J.Q.B. 455 (1853).

subject matter, this act is a repudiation of his contract. Neither a sale nor a contract to sell specific subject matter makes performance of the prior contract absolutely impossible. They make performance more difficult, however, and they amount to a positive manifestation of intention not to perform the first contract.

## § 960.   The Leading Case is Hochster v. De la Tour

The leading case in the long line of cases that have established the doctrine that an action for damages can at once be maintained for an anticipatory breach is Hochster v. De la Tour.[6] The facts and the reasoning of this case deserve some special consideration here. In April, 1852, the parties had made a bilateral contract for the employment of the plaintiff by the defendant in the capacity of a courier, service to begin on the following June 1 and to continue for a period of three months, at a specified salary. On May 11 the defendant sent a communication to the plaintiff totally repudiating the contract. The plaintiff asserted that this repudiation was a breach of contract by the defendant and on May 22 brought his action for damages, this action being ten days before actual performance under the contract was to begin. The defendant objected to the action, on the ground that it was premature, and that there could be no breach of contract before June 1.

It was argued for the defendant "that an announcement of an intention to break the contract when the time comes is no more than an offer to rescind. It is evidence till retracted of a dispensation with the necessity of readiness and willingness on the other side; and, if not retracted, it is, when the time for performance comes, evidence of a continued refusal; but till then it may be retracted." Thereupon, Crompton, J., asked: "May not the plaintiff, on notice that the defendant will not employ him, look out for other employment so as to diminish the loss?" The defendant's barrister replied: "If he adopts the defendant's notice, which is in legal effect an offer to rescind, he must adopt it altogether." Lord Campbell, C. J., then added: "So that you say the plaintiff, to preserve any remedy at all, was bound to remain idle."

It is believed that it was by this argument that the defendant's barrister lost his case. He claimed too much for his client in asserting that the repudiation was an offer to rescind the contract. No doubt the defendant would have been glad to have the plaintiff assent to a mutual rescission of the contract; but the repudiation was a manifestation of his intention to commit a breach of the contract, even though the plaintiff would not assent to a rescis-

6.    2 El. & Bl. 678 (1853).

sion.[7]  In answer to the question of Justice Crompton, he should have replied that, upon repudiation by the defendant, the plaintiff was at once legally privileged to look for another job and was discharged from his duty of remaining ready and willing to render the agreed service under the repudiated contract.  This is certainly in accordance with existing law; and without doubt it was the existing law of England at the time the argument was being made.  The answer actually given to Justice Crompton's question was that the plaintiff had a choice between only two alternatives: The plaintiff must either accept the defendant's offer to rescind, thereby apparently giving up all claim to damages for breach; or he must refrain from looking for other employment and remain ready and willing to begin service on June 1, if the defendant should change his mind and withdraw the repudiation. The court saw that both of these alternatives were unreasonable and unsound in policy.  It, therefore, disapproved of the defendant's whole contention and gave judgment for the plaintiff.  Apparently, it did not occur, either to the defendant's barrister or to the court, that the legal effect of the defendant's repudiation might be to make it unnecessary for the plaintiff to remain ready and willing to perform under the contract and to privilege him to look for another job without at the same time sacrificing his right to damages for breach, while at the same time the plaintiff's right of action for such damages might be postponed until the date set for actual performance under the contract and a breach by non-performance existed.

That the defective argument for the defendant played an important part in leading to the decision recognizing the possibility of a breach by anticipation is indicated by the following excerpts from the opinion of Lord Chief Justice Campbell: "The defendant's counsel very powerfully contended that, if the plaintiff was not contented to dissolve the contract and to abandon all remedy upon it, he was bound to remain ready and willing to perform it till the day when the actual employment as courier in the service of the defendant was to begin; and that there could be no breach of the agreement before that day to give a right of action. . . . . If the plaintiff has no remedy for breach of the contract unless he treats the contract as in force and acts upon it

---

7.    In the course of argument it was said by Crompton, J.: "When a party announces his intention not to fulfill the contract, the other side may take him at his word and rescind the contract. That word "rescind" implies that both parties have agreed that the contract shall be at an end as if it had never been. But I am inclined to think that the party may also say: "Since you have announced that you will not go on with the contract, I will consent that it shall be at an end from this time; but I will hold you liable for the damage I have sustained; and I will proceed to make that damage as little as possible by making the best use I can of my liberty."

down to the first of June, 1852, it follows that till then he must enter into no employment which will interfere with his promise to start with the defendant on such travels on the day and year, and that he must then be properly equipped in all respects as a courier for a three months' tour on the continent of Europe. But it is surely much more rational and more for the benefit of both parties that, after the renunciation of the agreement by the defendant, the plaintiff should be at liberty to consider himself absolved from any future performance of it, retaining his right to sue for any damage he has suffered from the breach of it. Thus, instead of remaining idle and laying out money in preparations which would be useless, he is at liberty to seek service under another employer, which would go in mitigation of the damages to which he would otherwise be entitled for a breach of the contract."

The court failed to see that it was perfectly easy for it to declare that the plaintiff was at liberty to seek service under another employer, without at the same time holding that it was proper for him to bring an action for damages on May 22—ten days before the time set for the beginning of performance under the contract. Lord Campbell further said: "If it should be held that, upon a contract to do an act on a future day, a renunciation of the contract by one party dispenses with a condition to be performed in the meantime by the other, there seems no reason for requiring that other to wait till the day arrives before seeking his remedy by action. And the only ground on which the condition can be dispensed with seems to be that the renunciation may be treated as a breach of the contract." But if it is a ground at all, it is certainly not the only ground. The efficient reason is that by dispensing with the condition and requiring the plaintiff to get another job, the injury that he will suffer is reduced and unnecessary economic waste is eliminated.

### § 961. Objections to the Rule of Hochster v. De la Tour

Objections of several kinds have been made to the rule laid down in Hochster v. De la Tour allowing an action to be maintained at once for an anticipatory repudiation. First, it is objected in the name of logic that the breach of a promise is impossible except by non-performance in accordance with its terms, and that a mere statement of intention to commit a breach in the future made before a specific time fixed for the performance of the promise cannot be a breach. Even assuming that this argument is sound in its asserted logic, this is a case in which logic has not controlled the development of law; but there is nothing illogical in making a rule of law to the effect that an anticipatory repudiation is a breach of contractual duty, even though such a repudiation is not a failure to perform any express or implied promise in that contract. Contractual duties are not restricted merely to those that are consciously foreseen and assented to by the parties; the legal duties arising out of a contract and in the course of its performance or breach are created in the furtherance of social policy. These duties may well be and have actually been made to include a duty not to repudiate in advance, as well as a duty to render performance in accordance with a promise. Whether such a duty has been created is a question that has been determined by the historical course of judicial decision. Whether such a duty should be created is a question of social and judical policy and is not a question of logic at all.[8]

Secondly, it has been thought to do injustice to the defendant in making him pay damages for the breach of a promise that he never made. But what justice is and what justice requires, cannot be determined on *a priori* grounds. The action taken by the courts in a long line of decisions, over a considerable period of time, is the best test that we have as to the requirements of justice. Moreover, the action is neither brought nor maintained against the defendant because of his failure to perform in accordance with his promise; it is brought and maintained because of his unjustified and injurious repudiation of his contractual duty—a repudiation that in many cases is without any moral justification.

The third and most serious objection is that the bringing of a suit before the time fixed for performance increases the difficulty of ascertaining the extent of the injury suffered by the plaintiff, causing him in some cases to get much less than his due and in other cases to get judgment for a large amount that subsequent events demonstrate is greatly in excess of his injury. This objection cannot be passed over as being one without any practical importance. It is possible that in some of the cases in which the rule has already been applied, the damages awarded were more inaccurately estimated than they would have been, had the bringing of the suit been postponed until the time set for performance of the contract. In most of these cases, however, although the action may have been brought before the time set for performance, its trial is seldom reached until after that time has arrived. Our system of administering justice is much more subject to criticism on the ground of its delay than on the ground of its too hasty action. In general, it would seem to be fortunate that the plaintiff can avoid some of the delay by bringing his suit at an early date. Moreover, it is not doubted that justice frequently requires the awarding of damages for injury that is yet to be suffered in the future in both tort and contract cases. There are many cases in which trial is reached before the time fixed for com-

---

8.  In Daniels v. Newton, 114 Mass. 530 (1874), a case that has not yet    been overruled, the court refused to follow Hochster v. De la Tour.

pletion of performance, even though the breach is not anticipatory and in which values must be determined by prediction.[9] It is believed that the difficulties involved in the award of damages for future injuries are not greatly increased by the anticipatory breach doctrine. In the rare cases where there is danger of substantial injustice, it would seem that the trial court has an adequate preventive remedy in its power to postpone trial until a later date, when the uncertainties have been, to a sufficient degree, removed.[10]

A partial justification for allowing an immediate action in case of an anticipatory repudiation is that such a repudiation causes injury to the other party at once, an injury that is different from that caused by actual non-performance. In the Chapter on Remedies for Breach of Contract, it is said: "A contract right, as contrasted with a promised performance, frequently has its own market value. The amount of this value is determined by the advance opinions of possible buyers as to what the value of the promised performance is going to be, making due allowance for the degree of probability that the performance may never in fact take place. The repudiation of a contract duty in advance is almost certain to destroy part or all of the market value of the other party's correlative contract right. Repudiated contract rights are assignable; but purchasers will be lacking, because no one wishes to buy a lawsuit." It is true that the courts generally refuse to award damages for this kind of injury; but the fact that it exists is one justification for the bringing of an early action.

The repudiation by the defendant is generally morally indefensible. It disturbs the confidence and security of the promisee; it causes him immediate pecuniary injury; and the allowance of an immediate action makes for an early settlement of the dispute and a timely payment of damages.[11]

Equitable remedies, as well as damages and restitution, are available in cases of anticipatory repudiation. Just as in cases where the breach is not anticipatory, the decree will be moulded to suit the requirements of justice. If specific performance is ordered, it will ordinarily be performance at the time agreed upon; [12] and the decree will be made conditional on performance by the

---

9.   This was considered by the judges in Hochster v. De la Tour, 2 El. & Bl. 678 (1873); Coleridge, J. "No doubt it was possible, in this case, that, before the 1st of June, the plaintiff might die, in which case the plaintiff would have gained nothing had the contract gone on." Lord Campbell, C.J., "All contingencies should be taken into account by the jury in assessing the damages." Crompton, J., "That objection would equally apply to the action by a servant for dismissing him before the end of his term, and so disabling him from earning his wages; yet that action may be brought immediately on the dismissal."

plaintiff of the agreed equivalent and of other conditions precedent to the duty of the defendant. Today practically all courts have power, even in suits for damages only, to grant relief only in accordance with justice and equity.

## § 962. Repudiation of Unilateral Contracts

It has been frequently stated that repudiation before the time fixed for performance of a contract can never operate as an anticipatory breach thereof if the contract was unilateral at the time of the repudiation.[13] Such statements are based upon the erroneous idea that the reason for holding an anticipatory repudiation to be a breach of contract is that otherwise the injured party must himself continue to be ready to perform on his own part. It would follow from this that, if the injured party never had any performance to render on his part, or, having such a performance, has already fully performed it, it would not be necessary for his protection to give him an immediate action for damages for the anticipatory breach. It has been shown elsewhere herein that the rule allowing an action for an anticipatory breach cannot properly be rested upon this reason. The reasons upon which it can actually be sustained are equally applicable to unilateral contracts. The harm caused to the plaintiff is equally great in either case; and it seems strange to deny to a plaintiff a remedy of this kind merely on the ground that he has already fully performed as his contract has required.[14]

## § 963. Repudiation of Unilateral Contracts for the Payment of Money

One of the most common kinds of unilateral contracts consists of promises to pay a sum of money in return for a consideration already fully executed. The following are examples of such contracts: promissory notes for money lent; bills of exchange and letters of credit already paid for in advance; insurance policies payable at a future day, the insured having paid the premium in advance. There has been some hesitation on the part of the courts in these cases to recognize a repudiation before the time fixed for payment as a breach of contract permitting an immediate action at law. To permit such an action appears to be allowing an action for the collection of a money debt before the debt is due.

There are a good many cases refusing to give judgment for instalments not yet due at the time of suit, if the consideration was fully executed and there were no conditions precedent yet to be performed by the plaintiff.[15] Although the author of this

15.   **Ark.**—Manufacturers' Furniture Co. v. Read, 290 S.W. 353, 172 Ark. 642 (1927). The plaintiff had fully performed services in negotiating a lease, and the defendant had repudiated his obligation to

volume believes that the distinction should make no difference in the result reached, attention must be called to the fact that some courts have distinguished unconditional money debts from those in which the debtor's duty to pay is conditional on some performance yet to be rendered by his creditor, recognizing anticipatory breach in the latter cases and not in the former.

There are plenty of cases holding that the fact that it is a duty to pay money that is repudiated is not in itself enough to prevent the recognition of the repudiation as an anticipatory breach. If the contract is bilateral and not yet fully performed by the plaintiff, he can at once maintain suit against the repudiator, even though the latter's duty was merely to pay money for land, goods, or service.[16] Also, even though the contract is wholly unilateral, the plaintiff having made no promise at all or no promise that remains unperformed, he can maintain suit if his right to payment by the repudiator is conditional on some performance still to be rendered by the plaintiff. The repudiation excuses the plaintiff from performance of the condition and also enables him to get judgment for damages at once. There are some cases in which the distinction has been disregarded, and judgment given for the plaintiff, even though the repudiated debt was unilateral, unconditional, and not yet due; [17] but no such decision has been

---

pay, this repudiation being partly anticipatory. The court held that the repudiation did not accelerate the maturity of instalments which were not yet due and refused to allow damages to include such instalments. The court overruled the earlier case of Aetna Life Ins. Co. v. Phifer, 254 S.W. 335, 160 Ark. 98 (1923), a case in which the court had allowed damages, including future instalments reduced to their present value. Cases in accord with the Read case are Leon v. The Barnsdall Zinc Co., 274 S.W. 699, 309 Mo. 276 (1925); Huffman v. Martin, 10 S.W.2d 636, 226 Ky. 137 (1928); Operators' Oil Co. v. Barbre, 65 F.2d 857 (C.C.A.10th, 1933); and Sheketoff v. Prevedine, 51 A.2d 922, 133 Conn. 389, 171 A. L.R. 1009 (1947).

In Dudzik v. Degrenia, 138 A. 57, 48 R.I. 430, 57 A.L.R. 823 (1927), the plaintiff sold a motor bus to the defendant, payment to be made in installments. After some payments had been made, the defendant failed to pay one installment; and the plaintiff alleged that the defendant repudiated his duty to pay the balance. The court held that this repudiation would not accelerate the time for making the subsequent payments. The plaintiff was given judgment only for the installment that had fallen due at the date of the writ.

16. A life insurance and trust company promised to pay $32,500 to the plaintiff when the latter had completed a building, to be repaid only in the form of annual premiums on a life insurance policy. The defendant repudiated before the building was built. It was held that the plaintiff could recover damages, including expenses involved in his preparation of the land. Holt v. United S. L. Ins. Co., 72 A. 301, 76 N.J.L. 585 (1909).

17. It was definitely so held in Universal Life & Acc. Ins. Co. v. Sanders, 102 S.W.2d 405, 129 Tex. 344 (1937); and Pollack v. Pollack, 46 S.W.2d 292 (Com.App.1932).

found where the debt was evidenced by a formal bond, a promissory note, a bill of exchange, or other formal commercial paper.[18]

## § 964.   Repudiation of Unilateral Money Contracts and of Bilateral Contracts Compared

In the case of a bilateral contract for the sale of goods or land, or for the rendition of service, an anticipatory repudiation by the buyer or employer not only makes tender of performance by the seller or employee unnecessary, but also enables him to maintain action at once.   The fact that it is a duty to pay money in the future that the defendant has repudiated does not prevent his repudiation from being an anticipatory breach, for which an action lies at once.[19]   The measure of damages in such a case is the amount promised, less the saving to the plaintiff in not having to perform his part.   If the money is being collected in advance of the due date, it should be properly discounted; this has been given due consideration in a number of cases.[20]

If a judgment for future instalments of money will be given in favor of a plaintiff who has not himself performed, deducting only the saving involved in his own non-performance, it would seem that a similar judgment should be given in favor of a plaintiff who has himself fully performed.   The fact that in the latter case no deduction is to be made merely indicates that the plaintiff's injury is greater; it is not a reason for postponing a remedy.[21]   If repudiation does not accelerate the date of pay-

---

19.  In the leading case on anticipatory breach, Hochster v. De la Tour, the defendant's duty was to employ the plaintiff and to pay him money therefor.  Nothing was said in the case about the possible educational value to the plaintiff of being employed as a courier; and, therefore, the defendant's repudiation of his duty to employ the plaintiff is of importance only in that it involves also the non-payment of the promised wages.  The fact that it was a duty to pay money in the future that was repudiated in advance by the defendant was not referred to by either court or counsel as a possible reason for denying the plaintiff an immediate remedy.

In Roehm v. Horst, 20 S.Ct. 780, 178 U.S. 1, 44 L.Ed. 953 (1900), there was a bilateral contract for the sale and purchase of hops.  It was repudiated in advance by the buyer,

and the seller brought action for damages before the time for payment had arrived.  The court followed Hochster v. De la Tour and held that the action was maintainable, even though the duty repudiated by the defendant was a duty to pay a definite sum of money at a specified future time.

21.  Dale F. Stansbury, in a student's manuscript on repudiation of unilateral contracts, wrote: "It requires no doctrine of anticipatory breach to put it out of the mouth of the repudiator to say that the injured party has not performed, and even if we admit that estoppel has anything to do with the case, the only difference in this respect between a bilateral and a unilateral contract is that in the case of the former the defendant cannot assert the plaintiff's failure to perform because he is estopped,

ment in the case of a contract to pay instalments of money for a fully executed consideration, neither does it do so in case of a contract to pay instalments of money for a mere promissory consideration. If judgment will be given for an anticipatory repudiation in the latter case, it should likewise be given in the former. In either case, if, by reason of the anticipatory repudiation, payment is compelled in advance of maturity, there should be a discount for cash in advance.[22]

### § 965. Recognition of Anticipatory Breach of Money Contracts does not Involve "Acceleration of Date of Maturity"

It is believed that the refusal to recognize an anticipatory repudiation of a unilateral money debt as an immediate breach is mainly to be found in the notion expressed by the unfortunate phrase "accelerate the date of maturity." Money due next year cannot be made due now by the debtor's saying that he is not going to pay it. But neither can services that by the contract are to be performed next year be rendered immediately performable by the employee's saying that he is not going to render the service. The same is true with respect to contracts for the sale of goods or the conveyance of land. It is probable that the court should never decree the specific performance of these duties ahead of the time fixed for performance by the contract. What the plaintiff asks for and what he is given is a judgment for money damages. It is merely an accidental circumstance that where the contractual duty is a duty to pay money, the performance that is expressly promised is identical in character with the performance that is required by a judgment for money damages. Obviously, a judgment for money damages is not a judgment for the specific performance of a promise to deliver goods, to convey land, or to render service. In the case of an express contract for the payment of money, however, a judgment for money damages may appear to one who looks at the matter only superficially to be a judgment for specific performance. This, it certainly is not if the judgment is not for the full sum promised, but is merely for its present value after making proper discount for advance collection.[23] Furthermore, in an action for damages for breach of a promise to make a money payment, the plaintiff can get judgment for much more than the amount promised him if he can prove with reasonable certainty the amount of additional losses that the defendant had

and in the latter he cannot so assert because the assertion would be false. Truth ought to be even a better weapon than estoppel."

23. The discount should be determined as of the date of the judg-

ment not of the repudiation. Even though the suit is brought before the date of maturity, the judgment may not be rendered until after that date has arrived.

reason to foresee.   Therefore, a plaintiff should not be deprived of his remedy in damages for an anticipatory repudiation merely because the promised performance is similar in character to the performance that is required by the judicial remedy that is commonly given for all kinds of breaches of contract.

## § 966.   Repudiation of Money Contracts that is only Partly Anticipatory

In many of the cases refusing to give judgment for the amount of money instalments that have not yet matured, there has been an actual non-payment of an instalment already due.   In such cases there is a present breach of contract; and a judgment can certainly be obtained for the amount already due, with interest as damages.   It should be observed in these cases that, if the contract has become wholly unilateral, there being no further performance to be rendered by the plaintiff, the defendant's mere failure to pay one or more of the instalments when due would not in itself be a repudiation of the balance and would not be a breach going to the essence of the contract.   In such cases there is only a partial breach; and, of course, judgment cannot be obtained for the later instalments that are not due and have not been repudiated.[24]   In other cases, however, accompanying the non-payment of one instalment there has been a definite repudiation of the balance.   Here, the cases that give judgment for damages for a partly anticipatory breach might well be followed.[25]   In an

25.   In New York Life Ins. Co. v. Viglas, 56 S.Ct. 615, 297 U.S. 672, 80 L.Ed. 971 (1936), the court held that the insurer's assertion in good faith that the disability of the insured had not continued and that the policy had lapsed for non-payment of premiums was not a repudiation of the contract, because it did not deny its obligation under the terms of the policy and was ready and willing to perform in accordance with the facts. If it was mistaken on the facts, its failure to pay benefits was a present partial breach for which action would lie; but there was not total breach because this non-payment was not accompanied by a complete repudiation. In this case the Circuit Court of Appeals had regarded the insurer's action as a total repudiation [see 78 F.2d 829 (C.C.A.1935)] and said: "Nor does the fact that the defendant's obligation was only to pay money prevent the assessment of damages for the entire value of the contract including future payments." The Supreme Court does not deny the accuracy of this statement, but does deny the repudiation and says that the "law will be able to offer appropriate relief where compensation is wilfully and contumaciously withheld." It may be here observed, however, that in the instant case the action of the insurer left the insured without his promised means of support in time of total disability (as he alleged); and the decision of the Supreme Court leaves him dependent on charity (or other resources, if he has any) while his series of expensive actions for payments as they fall due drags wearily through the courts. This would be "frustration of the ends it was expected to subserve." Of course, such a result can and would be avoided by an equitable decree.

excellent case the repudiation of a unilateral leasehold contract, accompanied by non-payment of an instalment of rent already due, was held to be a total breach justifying a judgment for future damages.[26] It was not necessary to wait until subsequent instalments of rent fell due. The action is not for those instalments as an accelerated debt, but for the full agreed rental less the reasonable rental value of the premises for the remainder of the term.

In cases where there is some minor breach by actual non-performance at the due date, accompanied by a repudiation of the remaining duty, the fact that the contract was unilateral at the date of repudiation is not regarded as an objection to recovery of damages as for a total breach, if the remaining duty is not solely for the payment of money. Thus, damages will be given for the total future injury in case of a repudiation of a contract to give a free pass for life over a railroad.[27] The same judgment was given in a case where the defendant promised that the plaintiff might take ice from the defendant's ice house for life, in consideration of land conveyed by the plaintiff, and the defendant later sold the land and put up no ice whatever.[28] The plaintiff's damages were reckoned on the basis of life insurance tables.

### § 967. Repudiation of Unilateral Money Contract that is Conditional on Some Performance by the Plaintiff

It is well established that the fact that a contract is entirely unilateral at the time of repudiation by the defendant is not in itself sufficient to deprive the injured party of an immediate right of action; this is true, even though the contract is a unilateral contract for the mere payment of money instalments in the future. The contract, even though unilateral, may be conditional upon some performance to be rendered by the plaintiff. If it is thus conditional, the cases hold that the plaintiff can maintain an action at once for the anticipatory repudiation, without performing the condition. It has been so held, even where the condi-

26. **Conn.**—Sagamore Corp. **v.** Willcutt, 180 A. 464, 120 Conn. 315 (1935). The more recent case of Hawkinson **v.** Johnston, 122 F.2d 724, 137 A.L.R. 420 (C.C.A.8th, 1941), is similar except that the repudiated lease still had nearly 70 years to run and was bilateral, in that it contained a covenant of quiet enjoyment binding upon the lessor. Judgment for damages was given covering a period of ten years, the amount being the promised rent and taxes for ten years, diminished by the estimated rental value of the surrendered premises for ten years, commuted to present value on a four per cent interest basis. Evidently, the court thought that no convincing opinion evidence was presented as to future rental value and taxes beyond the ten year period.

27. **Pa.**—Erie & P. R. Co. **v.** Douthet, 88 Pa. 243 (1878).

28. **Mass.**—Proctor v. Union Coal Co., 137 N.E. 659, 243 Mass. 428 (1923).

tion to be performed by the plaintiff is not any part of the agreed exchange for the performance promised by the defendant.[29]

In one case, an insurance company, for a consideration fully executed, promised to pay $25 a week during the plaintiff's total disability. It later failed to make payment when due and also wholly repudiated the contract. The court held that the plaintiff could maintain action as for an entire breach and had a right to a judgment for all future damages. The contract was entirely unilateral, since the plaintiff was under no duty whatever to the insurance company; but the company's duty to make payment was expressly conditional on the plaintiff's submitting himself to a monthly medical examination. The court said: "It is not merely a technical requirement, but a substantial and continuing burden, involving the expenditure of time and money on the part of the assured. It is said, however, that this is merely a condition precedent to the payment of these instalments, and not a condition that could be enforced by the company. The latter may be true so far as enforcement by action is concerned; nevertheless, it is a provision binding on the plaintiff, the non-performance of which may be enforced by refusal to pay. In this respect it does not differ from a tender of property under a sales contract or the tender of service under an employment contract." [30]

**29.** **U.S.**—Roehm v. Horst, 20 S.Ct. 780, 178 U.S. 1, 44 L.Ed. 953 (1900); Lovell v. St. Louis Mutual Life Ins. Co., 4 S.Ct. 390, 111 U.S. 264, 28 L.Ed. 423 (1884); Federal Life Ins. Co. v. Rascoe, 12 F.2d 693 (C.C.A. 6th, 1926); Equitable Trust Co. of New York v. Western Pac. R. Co., 244 F. 485 (D.C.N.Y.1917); Northwestern Nat. Life Ins. Co. v. Gray, 161 F. 488 (C.C.A.8th, 1908), semble.

**N.J.**—O'Neill v. Supreme Council, American Legion of Honor, 57 A. 463, 70 N.J.L. 410 (1904).

**Wis.**—Merrick v. Northwestern Nat. Life Ins. Co., 102 N.W. 593, 124 Wis. 221 (1905).

This is discussed with great clarity and understanding by Judge Learned Hand in Equitable Trust Co. of N. Y. v. Western Pacific R. Co., 244 F. 485 (D.C.N.Y.1917).

**30.** **U.S.**—Federal Life Ins. Co. v. Rascoe, 12 F.2d 693 (C.C.A.6th, 1926). One judge dissented in this case. He thought that a repudiation by the defendant is a breach of contract only when it amounts to a prevention of performance by the plaintiff, and not even then, unless it was a performance that the plaintiff had promised to render. He said: "I do not understand that a contract sued upon is executory as against a plaintiff, unless it binds him to do something, so that an action may lie against him for specific performance or for non-performance. By that definition, the contract here sued upon is not executory on the plaintiff's part. . . . It is a condition, not an obligation." It seems certain that the learned judge is in error in this. The prevention by one party of the performance of a condition by the other is a breach of contract. Indeed, the prevention of a performance that was promised by the other party is not a breach, unless that performance was also a condition. Prevention of performance is an injury only in case it prevents the other party from earning the promised compensation.

The foregoing decision has been twice disapproved by the United States Supreme Court;[31] but this is expressly on the ground that the partial breach committed by the insurer in failing to pay several instalments was not enlarged into a total breach by a declaration that the policy had lapsed, this declaration being made in good faith in the honest belief that the plaintiff's disability had ceased. The insurer did not repudiate the policy as such, and professed to stand strictly by it and to be ready to pay the cash surrender value and to perform other alternatives. Had the insurer's repudiation been "wilful and contumacious," a different decision might have been rendered. These cases are discussed at length in a following section, dealing with disability insurance requiring the payment of an uncertain number of future instalments.

The United States Supreme Court has held that a unilateral money debt, not yet matured, is provable in bankruptcy against the debtor, expressly on the ground that an adjudicated bankruptcy constitutes a breach by anticipation.[32] While it is true, as shown in a later section, that the legal effect of bankruptcy differs in several respects from that of an anticipatory repudiation, the reasoning of the court makes it clear that the fact that the contract before it was a unilateral money debt did not make impossible its breach by anticipation prior to maturity.[a]

## § 970. Repudiation of a Contract Specifying no Definite Time for Performance

If the time for the defendant's promised performance was not definitely fixed in the contract but the defendant promised to perform whenever requested by the plaintiff or as soon as the plaintiff should have performed certain conditions precedent, a repudiation by the defendant is regarded by all courts without exception, as a breach of the contract, creating an immediate right of action.[62] Inasmuch as the conditions precedent to the defend-

---

31.   U.S.—New York Life Ins. Co. v. Viglas, 56 S.Ct. 615, 297 U.S. 672, 80 L.Ed. 971 (1936); Mobley v. New York Life Ins. Co., 55 S.Ct. 876, 295 U.S. 632, 79 L.Ed. 1621, 99 A.L.R. 1166 (1935).

32.   U.S.—Central Trust Co. of Ill. v. Chicago Auditorium, 240 U.S. 581, 36 S.Ct. 412, 60 L.Ed. 811, L.R.A. 1917B, 580 (1916).

a.   Two sections are here omitted: § 968. Repudiation of Unilateral Insurance Contracts; § 969. Repudiation of Insurance Contracts Re-

quiring Payment in Instalments during Disability.

62.   Lovelock v. Franklyn, 8 Q.B. 371 (1846), and Short v. Stone, 8 Q.B. 358 (1846), were cases of this sort, the first being a promise to assign a lease at any time within seven years at the option of the promisee, and the second being a promise to marry within a reasonable time after request. In Daniels v. Newton, 114 Mass. 530 (1874), the court discussed these cases with apparent approval, saying: "It was held that request was not necessary, and need not

ant's duty of immediate performance had not been performed at the time of the repudiation, it seems clear that the repudiation was an anticipatory one, and that it no more constituted a non-performance of the defendant's promise than does a repudiation antecedent to a definitely specified date for performance. All agree, however, that the defendant's repudiation excuses the plaintiff from performing conditions precedent; and, therefore, it is said that the defendant's performance becomes instantly due, and that there is a breach by non-performance in addition to the defendant's repudiation. While this reasoning reaches a just result, it is believed that the reasons why this is so are substantially the same as those justifying the decision in cases like Hochster v. De la Tour.

## § 971.   Repudiation as Breach of an Implied Promise—Status of Betrothment

One of the reasons commonly given for recognizing an anticipatory repudiation as a present breach and sustaining an immediate action for damages is that the repudiation is the breach of an implied promise. Thus, Lord Chief Justice Campbell said: "There is a relation constituted between the parties in the meantime by the contract, and they impliedly promise that in the meantime neither will do anything to the prejudice of the other inconsistent with that relation." [63] Of course, it is possible for the parties to promise expressly that they will not repudiate the contract before the time fixed for performance. In some cases, also, such a promise may be made tacitly, to be discovered by implication from the conduct and words of the parties interpreted in the light of surrounding circumstances. If such a promise has been made as a part of the contract, a repudiation is a breach of contract by actual non-performance; such a breach is not anticipatory. It is not necessary to sustain the decisions upon this theory of an implied promise; and frequently the theory would be wholly inconsistent with the facts. If the finding of such an implied promise is a mere fiction and subterfuge for the purpose of attaining justice, it is better to explain and justify the result by giving the reasons that have induced the fiction and the subterfuge.[64]

The doctrine has also been sustained by merely asserting the existence of a right that the contract shall not be repudiated with-

---

be alleged. It was rendered unavailing, and therefore unnecessary, by the act of the defendant, which was of itself a breach of the contract by rendering performance impossible. No question arose, or could arise, whether the action was premature, because there was no future time certain for performance. The defendant had made the only limit of time impossible."

63.   Eng.—Hochster v. De la Tour, 2 El. & Bl. 678 (1853).

out attempting to base it upon the fiction of an implied promise. Thus, Lord Chief Justice Cockburn said: "The promisee has an inchoate right to the performance of the bargain, which becomes complete when the time for performance has arrived. In the meantime, he has a right to have the contract kept open as a subsisting and effective contract. Its unimpaired and unimpeached efficacy may be essential to his interest. His rights acquired under it may be dealt with by him in various ways for his benefit and advantage." [65]   There is no resort to fiction or subterfuge in this; it is merely the creation of a right against repudiation by asserting its existence and giving a judicial remedy for its non-performance. This is the way in which most of our rights against others have been established. It may not be the most desirable language to say that the contractor "has a right to have the contract kept open as a subsisting and effective contract"; but the court is declaring with sufficient clearness that an anticipatory repudiation is wrongful and a breach of legal duty.

It has been thought that the foregoing argument and assertion are especially applicable in the case of contracts of engagement to marry. In these cases it has been said that there is a "status of betrothment," and that a repudiation is the actual non-performance of a duty involved in that status.[66]   Nothing is really explained or justified, however, by the use of such an expression as "status of betrothment." It is not at all difficult to find a "status of agreement," that exists in the case of all contracts alike. It may well be that the anticipatory repudiation of an engagement to marry causes a kind and extent of injury that is different from the injury that is caused by the repudiation of a commercial contract. Human feelings and opinions might be so affected by this difference as to induce the courts to give a remedy in one case, and not in the other. In fact, however, the courts have not drawn such a distinction, except perhaps in the case of money debts.[67] A right against repudiation inheres not only in the status of betrothment, but also in the broader relation—the status of agreement.[68]

## § 972.   Repudiation of Part of a Contract only

As has already been shown in an earlier part of this chapter, a breach of contract may be either total or partial; and an action for damages can at once be maintained for a partial breach, just as it can for a total breach. The so-called partial breach may be the non-performance of a comparatively immaterial part of the contract, not going to the essence; in such case, it does not justify the other party in refusing to render his agreed performance in

65. Eng.—Frost **v.** Knight, L.R. **7** Exch. 111 (1872).

exchange, and he cannot in a single action get judgment for damages as for a total non-performance of the contract, unless he awaits the occurrence of an additional breach by the other party that is so material in character that, when added to the partial breach, the two taken together go to the essence and make the breaches so substantial as to be total.[71] Or, secondly, a partial breach may be of so material a part of the contract as to go to the "essence" and justify the other party in refusing further performance, and yet be unaccompanied by an indication that the one committing the breach does not intend to perform the rest of the contract. In such a case, the injured party is not required to treat the breach as total, but may proceed with performance and claim damages for the partial breach only.

The repudiation of a contract is almost always total in character. It is either a refusal to render any further performance whatever under the contract, or it is a refusal to render such a material part of the promised performance that it goes to the essence of the contract and can properly be regarded as total by the injured party.[72] It is quite possible, however, for a contractor to repudiate a minor part of his contract, while remaining ready and willing to perform the balance when the time comes. This partial repudiation may be anticipatory in character. At present, however, there seems to be no authority for saying that, for such a partial anticipatory repudiation, an action for damages can be at once maintained. There is one English case in which the question was given some slight consideration, although the decision rested mainly on other points. This case is deserving of analysis and discussion here.

In a long-term lease of land, it was provided that, at any time after the expiration of the first four years of the term, the landlord would forthwith proceed to rebuild, provided that the tenant had given him six months' notice that such rebuilding was desired. By another provision in the lease, the tenant was also given power, by giving a six months' notice, to terminate the lease at his option at the end of four, seven, or fourteen years. During the first

---

**71.** Such was held to be the case in New York Life Ins. Co. v. Viglas, 56 S.Ct. 615, 297 U.S. 672, 80 L.Ed. 971 (1936), where the insurer asserted that the total disability of the insured had not continued and therefore refused to continue to waive premiums and to pay benefits. It also declared the policy to be "lapsed;" but it did not deny the validity of the policy or its duty to pay the cash surrender value as provided therein. Its actual breach was not anticipatory; it committed the present breach of not paying benefits that were already due in case the facts were as asserted by the insured, but denied in good faith by the insurer.

**72.** It is believed that in New York Life Ins. Co. v. Viglas, supra, the insurer's repudiation of duty might well have been held to be a total breach.

four years, the landlord repeatedly told the tenant that he was unable to rebuild for lack of money. Because of these statements of inability on the part of the landlord, the tenant never gave the six months' notice to rebuild; but, instead, he gave the six months' notice of termination of the lease under the power reserved. After vacating the premises, the tenant made claim for damages for the landlord's anticipatory repudiation of his duty to rebuild. The court held that the tenant had no cause of action.[73]

The breach by the landlord, if any existed, was an anticipatory breach. There was no breach by actual non-performance, because the contract did not require the landlord to rebuild until after the expiration of four years; and when that time arrived, the lease had been terminated by the tenant. The court held that there had been no anticipatory breach, for three reasons: First, the landlord's declarations of inability did not amount to a repudiation. Secondly, even if they were such a repudiation, they affected only a part of the leasehold contract and did not go to the essence. Thirdly, even if there had been a repudiation of the entire contract by the landlord, it was not an anticipatory breach, because it was not assented to as such and acted upon as final by the tenant.

The court reasoned as follows: "The first question is whether the plaintiff intended to repudiate the contract when he made the statements relied upon with regard to his inability to find the money for rebuilding. Did he mean to say that, whatever happened, whether he came into money or not, his intention was not to rebuild the premises? It does not seem to me that what he said naturally leads to the inference that such was his intention. . . . If we ought not to draw that inference from what the plaintiff said, it seems to me to follow as a matter of course that the defendant was not entitled to draw it; and the result is that the defendant fails in the very first point which it is necessary for him to establish. . . . But, assuming the contrary, then comes the question whether the defendant elected to treat the plaintiff's statement as a wrongful repudiation of the contract. That involves, first of all, the question whether he could so treat it. The contract made between the plaintiff and the defendant was the whole lease. The covenant in question is a particular covenant in the lease, not going to the whole consideration. If there were an actual breach of such a covenant at the time fixed for performance, such breach would not, according to the authorities, entitle the tenant to throw up his lease. That being so, I do not hesitate to say, though it is not necessary in this case to decide the point, that an anticipatory breach could not entitle him to do so, and that it does not appear to me that he could elect to rescind part of the contract."

73. Eng.—Johnstone v. Milling, L.R.
16 Q.B.D. 460 (1886).

The court's first reason for holding that there was no anticipatory breach was that the landlord's expressions of inability did not amount to a repudiation. There is, of course, a clear logical difference between the statement, "I cannot perform," and the statement, "I will not perform." From the standpoint of a practical man of affairs, however, it would seem that this logical difference is not a sufficient basis for giving to the two statements substantially different legal effects. Statements of inability to perform, especially when repeatedly made, as in the instant case, would be regarded by the ordinary man as justifying a refusal to render a return performance, in failing to perform conditions and in taking other steps to avoid anticipated losses. Also, the reasons that in the case of Hochster v. De la Tour were thought to be sufficient to justify the maintenance of an immediate action for damages would seem to be almost equally applicable in a case of definite and repeated declarations of inability to perform. It has already been indicated, however, that the courts have shown a tendency to limit the anticipatory breach doctrine and to make it applicable only to definite, unconditional, and morally unjustifiable declarations of intention not to perform the contract. The first reason given by the court in the present case is a strong illustration of this tendency.

The court's second ground of decision is that the landlord's declarations of inability to rebuild affected only a part of the entire leasehold contract. The covenant to rebuild did not go to the essence of the contract; and an actual failure to rebuild at the time fixed for performance would not be such a breach of the leasehold contract as would empower the tenant to terminate the lease. This is in harmony with the weight of authority respecting contracts for the leasing of land; the tenant is not privileged to quit by reason of some breach on the part of the landlord, unless the breach amounts to an actual or constructive eviction of the tenant from the premises, or unless the lease contains such an express provision for the tenant's benefit.

But although an actual failure to rebuild might not be a total breach of the contract, it would nevertheless be a partial breach, for which an action for damages could at once be maintained by the tenant. So, an anticipatory repudiation of the covenant to rebuild might also be held to be an anticipatory partial breach, for which the tenant could at once maintain action. There is no clear discussion of this matter in the court's opinion; but whatever is said with respect to it bears directly against the recognition of an anticipatory partial repudiation as creating an immediate right of action. Such other decisions on the point as have been found seem not to recognize an anticipatory repudiation of a part of the contract as a breach unless the part is so substantial as to go to the essence.[74]

The court's third ground of decision is that, even if the landlord's declarations had amounted to a total repudiation, they did not constitute an anticipatory breach of the contract, because the tenant did not assent to them as such and at once terminate the lease because of the repudiation. The tenant, in fact, occupied the premises until the end of the four-year period, and at that time terminated the lease by exercising his power of termination that was expressly reserved to him. It is believed that this third reason is surely bad. As recent American cases have decided, the tenant ought not to be penalized for urging performance and giving the repudiator an opportunity to repent. Although the tenant waited and urged performance, the landlord never retracted; and finally, without having caused any injury to the landlord or any substantial change of position on his part, the tenant acted and terminated the lease by reason of the landlord's statements. It is true that the tenant had the power and the privilege of termination of the lease, even though the landlord had made no repudiation; but in the actual case, the exercise of the tenant's power was itself caused by the landlord's declarations of inability. But for those declarations, he would not have terminated the lease. By terminating it, he assented to them as final and proceeded to claim damages.

## § 973.  No Breach unless Repudiation is Definite and Unequivocal

In order to constitute an anticipatory breach of contract, there must be a definite and unequivocal manifestation of intention on the part of the repudiator that he will not render the promised performance when the time fixed for it in the contract arrives.[75] Doubtful and indefinite statements that the performance may or may not take place and statements that, under certain circumstances that in fact do not yet exist, the performance will not take place, will not be held to create an immediate right of action.[76] A mere request for a change in the terms or a request for cancellation of the contract is not in itself enough to constitute a repudiation.[77]

A case in the United States Supreme Court [78] shows how definite and positive an anticipatory repudiation must be before it will be held to be a breach for which action will lie at once. The defendant had promised to deliver a quantity of ice to the plaintiff

75.  U.S.—Dingley v. Oler, 6 S.Ct. 850, 117 U.S. 490, 29 L.Ed. 984 (1886); Kimel v. Missouri State L. Ins. Co., 71 F.2d 921 (C.C.A.10th, 1934); Suburban Improvement Co. v. Scott Lbr. Co., 67 F.2d 335, 90 A.L.R. 330 (C.C.A.4th, 1933); Higgins v. California Prune & Apricot Growers, 16 F.2d 190 (C.C.A.2d, 1926).

78.  U.S.—Dingley v. Oler, 6 S.Ct. 850, 117 U.S. 490, 29 L.Ed. 984 (1886).

during the season of 1880, in return for a like quantity that the plaintiff had delivered to the defendant in 1879. This arrangement had been made in 1879, at the plaintiff's request, because he then had an excessive supply, ice then selling at 50 cents per ton. When the plaintiff requested delivery the following season, ice was selling at $5 per ton. A correspondence ensued, each party thinking that the other was unreasonable. Finally the plaintiff brought suit, before the end of the season and before the expiration of the time within which the defendant could have performed according to his promise, the breach alleged being a repudiation by the defendant. The court held that there had been no such repudiation as would operate as an immediate breach. It stated its reasons as follows:

"We differ, however, from the opinion of the circuit court that the defendants are to be considered, from the language of their letters above set out, as having renounced the contract by a refusal to perform, within the meaning of the rule which, it is assumed, in such a case, confers upon the plaintiffs a right of action before the expiration of the contract period for performance. We do not so construe the correspondence between the parties. In the letter of July 7th the defendants say: 'We must therefore decline to ship the ice for you this season, and claim, as our right, to pay you for the ice, in cash, at the price you offered it to other parties here, or give you ice when the market reaches that point.' Although in this extract they decline to ship the ice that season, it is accompanied with the expression of alternative intention, and that is, to ship it, as must be understood, during that season, if and when the market price should reach the point which, in their opinion, the plaintiffs ought to be willing to accept as its fair price between them. This, we think, is very far from being a positive, unconditional, and unequivocal declaration of fixed purpose not to perform the contract in any event or at any time. In view of the consequences sought to be deduced and claimed as a matter of law to follow, the defendants have a right to claim that their expressions, sought to be converted into a renunciation of the contract, shall not be enlarged by construction beyond their strict meaning." [79]

If one party to a contract, either wilfully or by mistake, demands of the other a performance to which he has no right under the contract and states definitely that, unless his demand is complied with, he will not render his promised performance, an anticipatory breach has been committed. Such a repudiation is conditional in character, it is true; but the condition is a performance to which the repudiator has no right.[83] Thus, where a

83.    U.S.—Michigan Yacht & P. Co. v. Busch, 143 F. 929 (C.C.A.6th, 1906).

contract for the sale of a cargo of tea was rescinded by the parties and a new contract substituted therefor, the buyer's refusal to accept the tea under the new contract was a repudiation and an anticipatory breach, even though it was coupled with a demand for the delivery of the tea under the original contract.[84]

Where the two contracting parties differ as to the interpretation of the contract or as to its legal effects, an offer to perform in accordance with his own interpretation made by one of the parties is not in itself an anticipatory breach. In order to constitute such a breach, the offer must be accompanied by a clear manifestation of intention not to perform in accordance with any other interpretation.[85] So, also, the making of a demand upon the other party to a contract that he shall perform in accordance with an interpretation that is not justified by the law is not in itself a repudiation; such a demand, however, does not require much by way of accompanying expressions in order to justify the other party in understanding that no performance other than that demanded will be accepted.[86]

A defective tender of a performance that is substantially different from that required by the contract will frequently not be operative as an anticipatory breach. Of course, if there is no time remaining in which substantial performance of the contract can be rendered according to its terms, there is a breach by actual non-performance. If time still remains for substantial performance in accordance with the terms of the contract, a subsequent tender in accordance with the provisions of the contract will be operative and sufficient.[87] If the first and defective tender was made in such a way as to be a manifestation of intention not to perform the contract in any other manner, there is an anticipatory breach, even though there is still sufficient time remaining in which a proper performance could be rendered. As in the case of other anticipatory breaches, however, such a breach may be nullified by retraction so long as there has been no material change of position by the injured party. A subsequent tender of proper performance as required by the contract would operate as such a retraction.

In order that a mere expression of intention not to perform in the future may be an anticipatory breach, it is necessary that the expression shall be communicated to the other party. A letter of repudiation that is written but never mailed, a statement to a third person without in any way authorizing him to repeat it to the other party to the contract, will not be operative as an anticipatory breach.[88]

The manifestation of intention to repudiate may, of course, be made and communicated by conduct other than words.[89] Such is the case when a promisor acts so as to make performance impossible; and a breach by actual failure of performance when due frequently manifests an intention to perform no longer without putting such intention into words.

## § 974.   Expressions of Doubt as to Ability to Perform

It has been thought that a mere expression of inability to perform in the future is not a repudiation of duty and cannot be operative as an anticipatory breach.[91]  Of course, the expression of a doubt as to whether the ability to perform in accordance with the contract will exist when the time comes, is not a repudiation.  A statement of inability to perform, however, may be so made as to justify the other party in understanding it as a definite repudiation.[92]  There may be cases in which expressions of inability by one party or an existing appearance of inability on his part to perform will justify the other party in non-performance of his part of the contract or in materially changing his position so as to make performance impossible, without at the same time operating as an anticipatory breach, for which an action for damages could be maintained.[93]  It would seem, however, that, if the other party has such justification and actually so changes his position, it would be well to allow the parties to adjudicate their differences in an immediate action.  If the situation is such that there can be no retraction or subsequent performance, and a breach of the contract is now certain to occur, there seems to be little reason for not including the case in the anticipatory breach doctrine.

## § 975.   When Repudiation Discharges the Duty of the Other Party

In the case of a bilateral contract for an agreed exchange of performances, a repudiation of his duty by one of the parties terminates the duty of the other.  It gives to the latter the legal privilege of refusing to render the return performance; if sued for such refusal, the plaintiff's repudiation is a good defense.[94]  This is true even though the plaintiff's repudiation was long in advance of the time when his performance would have been due and also in advance of the time set for performance by the defendant.  In such a case, the defendant's duty was not conditional upon performance or a tender thereof by the plaintiff; but it was nevertheless conditional upon the plaintiff's continued willingness and ability to perform as he agreed.  A promisor is discharged not only by actual failure of consideration, but also by a prospective failure of consideration; and this is true whether the exchange was to be effected by simultaneous performances or otherwise.[95]

94.  That a repudiation suspends the other party's duty of further performance, see:

Conn.—Wetkopsky v. New Haven Gas Light Co., 96 A. 950, 90 Conn. 286 (1916).

## § 977. Repudiation or Other Total Breach Makes Further Tender of Performance Unnecessary

A repudiation or other total breach by one party enables the other to get a judgment for damages or for restitution without performing acts that would otherwise have been conditions precedent. It is no longer necessary for the plaintiff to perform or to tender performance.[1] This is true whether the repudiation is in express words or is by an act that makes performance by the repudiator apparently impossible or very improbable.[2] If a vendor of land makes conveyance of it to a third party, it is not necessary for the buyer to tender the price before bringing suit.[3] The cancellation of an order for goods to be shipped or manufactured makes it unnecessary for the seller to make or tender the goods.[4] Where arbitration as to amount of loss or as to any other disputed issue is expressly made a condition precedent, of course the defendant's repudiation and refusal to arbitrate will excuse performance of the condition and enable the plaintiff to maintain suit.[5]

Sometimes a written notice of termination is made a condition of one party's privilege of treating delay in performance as a total breach and of his right to damages measured by increased cost; a repudiation or other statement of intention by the contractor not to perform eliminates the necessity of giving this notice.[6]

Where a valid option contract for the purchase of land has been made and the option giver serves notice of his repudiation on the option holder, the latter can maintain a suit for specific performance without giving any formal notice of acceptance or making a tender of the price.[7]

## § 978. Ability to Perform Remains a Condition even Though Actual Tender of Performance is Eliminated

In an action for breach by an unconditional repudiation it is still a condition precedent to the plaintiff's right to a judgment for damages that he should have the ability to perform all such conditions. If he could not or would not have performed the substantial equivalent for which the defendant's performance was agreed to be exchanged, he is given no remedy in damages for the defendant's non-performance or repudiation.[8] Of course, the willingness and ability that remains a condition precedent in spite of the defendant's repudiation, is willingness and ability to perform if there had been no repudiation. The defendant's

8.   U.S.—U. S. v. Penn Foundry & Mfg. Co., 69 S.Ct. 1009, 337 U.S. 198, 93 L.Ed. 1308 (1949); Western Grocer Co. v. New York Oversea Co., 28 F.2d 518 (D.C.Cal.1928); Petersen v. Wellsville, 14 F.2d 38 (C.C.A. 8th, 1926).

Wash.—McCormick v. Tappendorf, 99 P. 2, 51 Wash. 312 (1909).

wrongful repudiation justifies the plaintiff in taking him at his word and at once taking steps that may make subsequent performance impossible. The willingness and ability to perform need not continue after the repudiation; it is merely required that they should have existed before the repudiation and that the plaintiff would have rendered the agreed performance if the defendant had not repudiated.

### § 979.   Restitution as a Remedy for Anticipatory Repudiation

If a repudiation is recognized as a breach of contract, the injured party is given the alternative remedy of restitution on the same conditions as in other cases of total breach. It makes no difference whether the repudiation was anticipatory or accompanied by a breach by non-performance of a promise. Indeed, it appears that even courts that do not like to recognize an anticipatory repudiation as a breach for which an action for damages will lie are willing to maintain an immediate action for restitution of the consideration paid.[16]

This may be supposed to be upon the theory that, although there has been no breach of contract, there has been a "rescission"; but there is no more reason for sustaining this theory in an action for money back than in an action for damages. The repudiation is a mere expression of unwillingness to perform. The repudiator does not make an offer to rescind; and his repudiation certainly does not include any promise to make restitution. Such a remedy, therefore, is a remedy for the defendant's wrongful and injurious act, just as is the alternative remedy in damages. Because of the nature of this remedy, however, it is not open to one of the objections that is made to an immediate award of damages. The remedy in damages looks to the future; and the earlier the remedy is granted, the more difficult it is to determine the correct amount to be awarded. The amount to which the plaintiff is entitled by way of restitution, however, is as easily and certainly established from the beginning as it ever can be in the future. This is merely an additional reason for sustaining an immediate action for restitution; it is not a reason for supposing that restitution can be granted without recognizing that the anticipatory repudiation is a breach of contractual duty.

### § 980.   Power of Retracting a Repudiation—Effect of Retraction

One who has committed an anticipatory breach by a manifestation of an intention not to perform his contract has power to nullify its effect as a breach by notifying the promisee that he has changed his wrongful intention and will perform the contract.[17] This power of retraction will cease to exist as soon as the promisee has materially changed his position in reliance on the repudiation.[18] The bringing of a suit by the promisee for the anticipatory breach is one sort of reliance making retraction impossible.[19] If the repudiation consisted of a voluntary act rendering further performance of the contract impossible, of course there is no power to retract. If the repudiation consisted of selling or contracting to sell specific subject matter to a third person, it would seem that the repudiator may have power to retract by repurchasing the subject matter or by obtaining a rescission of his contract to sell. In order to operate as such a retraction, the repudiator must now be in a position such that he can perform in all material respects as he contracted to do; and, further, he must notify the promisee of this change of position by him before the promisee has materially changed his position in reliance on the repudiation and without knowledge of the retraction.[20]

There are some cases in which it seems clear that the repudiator would have no power of retraction from the very moment of repudiation. If the substantial performance of the contract requires the maintenance of a relation of trust and confidence between the parties and the repudiation is of such a character as to shatter this relation beyond repair, the repudiation in itself creates such a change of position as to prevent retraction.[21] One who repudiates his contract to marry can seldom restore either the social or legal relations of the parties by a subsequent offer to perform. The same would be true in cases of personal employment involving close personal contact and association.

A retraction not only restores the duty of the other party, so that it again becomes enforceable; it also reinstates conditions precedent to the duty of the repudiator, so that performance of such conditions is now again necessary before the repudiator can be charged with a breach and suit maintained against him. Thus, in the case of an option contract whereby the defendant had promised to convey land for $1,300 on or before April 10, the defendant wrongfully revoked and afterwards retracted the revocation in ample time for the option holder to procure and tender the money. It was held that no action could be maintained without first tendering the $1,300.[22] Time being of the essence of an option contract, it again became so after the retraction. If the time left after the retraction had been unreasonably short, no doubt a reasonable time thereafter would have been allowed.

18.　**Mich.**—Rayburn v. Comstock, 45
N.W. 378, 80 Mich. 448 (1890).
**Eng.**—Ripley v. McClure, 4 Exch. 345
(1849).

22.　**Mass.**—Smith & Rice Co. v. Canady, 99 N.E. 968, 213 Mass. 122
(1912).

## § 981.  Theory that Repudiation is No Breach until Accepted by the Other Party

In a number of cases it has been said that a repudiation before the time fixed for performance of a contract, does not become an anticipatory breach thereof unless the promisee accepts it as such a breach.  Thus, Lord Chief Justice Cockburn said: "The promisee, if he pleases, may treat the notice of intention as inoperative and await the time when the contract is to be executed and then hold the other party responsible for all the consequences of non-performance; but in that case he keeps the contract alive for the benefit of the other party as well as his own; he remains subject to all his own obligations and liabilities under it and enables the other party not only to complete the contract, if so advised, notwithstanding his previous repudiation of it, but also to take advantage of any supervening circumstance which would justify him in declining to complete it." This statement was a mere dictum, inasmuch as the plaintiff, in the case under consideration, brought suit for the repudiation and was given judgment; but since the statement was made in a leading case in the early history of the doctrine, it is still being repeated by the courts and it has affected some actual decisions.[24]

In a number of well-considered recent cases, this doctrine that an anticipatory repudiation is not a breach until it is accepted as such by the injured party has been repudiated.[25]  Their reasoning is convincing and they should now be accepted as having established the law.[26]  In repeating the older forms of statement, the courts did not sufficiently analyze a complex situation and give due consideration to its separate aspects.  In the first place, the repudiator has a power of retraction as long as there has been no substantial change of position by the injured party; and the latter's continuing to urge performance may be properly held

24.  See:
U.S.—Hettrick Mfg. Co. v. Waxahachie Cotton Mills, 1 F.2d 913 (C.C.A.6th, 1924); Roller v. Leonard & Co., 229 F. 607 (C.C.A.4th, 1915).

Conn.—Belisle v. Berkshire Ice Co., 120 A. 599, 98 Conn. 689 (1923); Home Pattern Co. v. Mertz Co., 85 A. 19, 86 Conn. 494 (1913).

Pa.—Zuck & Henry v. McClure, 98 Pa. 541 (1881).

25.  U.S.—Bu-Vi-Bar Petroleum Co. v. Krow, 40 F.2d 488, 69 A.L.R. 1295 (C.C.A.10th, 1930), annotated in 69 A.L.R. 1295; Lagerloef Trad-

ing Co. v. American Paper Products Co., 291 F. 947 (C.C.A.7th, 1923); United Press Ass'n v. National Newspaper Ass'n, 237 F. 547 (C.C.A.8th, 1916), later appeal in 254 F. 284 (C.C.A.1918); Tri-Bullion Smelting & D. Co. v. Jacobsen, 233 F. 646 (C.C.A.2d, 1916).

N.Y.—De Forest Radio T. & T. Co. v. Triangle Radio S. Co., 153 N.E. 75, 243 N.Y. 283 (1926); Blumenthal v. Gallert, 148 N.E. 215, 240 N.Y. 217 (1925); Henderson Tire & R. Co. v. Wilson, 139 N.E. 583, 235 N.Y. 489 (1923); Canda v. Wick, 2 N.E. 381, 100 N.Y. 127 (1885).

to keep this power of retraction alive. A notice of retraction, seasonably given, nullifies the effect of the anticipatory repudiation; and an offer to perform, before any change of position by the injured party, is operative as a retraction.[27] Some of the cases in which the older language is repeated can be supported on this ground.

Not even the older cases held that a notice of acceptance must be given to the repudiator before bringing suit.[28] Further, mere delay in bringing a suit does not disentitle the injured party to relief.[29] And the newer cases, cited above, rightly hold that one who has received a definite repudiation is not to be penalized for his efforts to bring about its retraction and to get that which is his due without a law suit.[30] His failure or refusal to assent to the repudiation does not make it his duty to proceed with his own performance in the teeth of an unretracted repudiation. It is enough that he thereby continues to hold out the opportunity for repentance. Moreover, in the absence of a retraction he can at any time cease urging performance and maintain suit without performing acts that in the absence of the repudiation would have been conditions precedent. The repudiation terminates his own duty to perform his promises and it excuses performance of conditions precedent.[31]

### § 983. Anticipatory Repudiation Makes Rule as to Avoidable Consequences Applicable at Once

Not only are the injured party's duties terminated and his conditions precedent excused; it is now the general rule that when a definite repudiation is communicated to him the rule as to avoidable consequences is at once applicable. He must not proceed with his own performance if his so doing will increase the extent of his injury. He will not be given damages for any part of his loss that he could have avoided by refraining from continued performance or by making reasonable effort.[37] Such decisions as these are clearly in conflict with the notion that by refusing to assent to a repudiation the injured party remains bound as before. Not only is he not bound to perform; he cannot get damages for the additional injury suffered by him if he does perform.

31.    **Mass.**—Daniels v. Newton, 114 Mass. 530 (1874), semble.

**N.Y.**—Strasbourger v. Leerburger, 134 N.E. 834, 233 N.Y. 55 (1922).

In Lagerloef Trading Co. v. American Paper Products Co., 291 F. 947 (C. C.A.7th, 1923), where the buyer repudiated, the seller refused to consent to cancellation and proceeded to make an insufficient tender. The buyer did not retract his repudiation. It was held that the seller could maintain suit for the buyer's breach without making any further attempt at a valid tender of performance.

In § 982, here omitted, is discussed The Relation between Repudiation and Rescission.

Because of the rule as to avoidance of losses, one effect of a repudiation in advance of some performance by the other party is to deprive that party of his contract right to the full price or compensation promised him. But for the repudiation he would have had the power of earning the full contract price by completing what he was to do as the agreed exchange. If the price was to be in money, he could have completed his work and thus created a liquidated debt for the full price. If the price was to be paid otherwise than in money, he could have created a right to the full performance promised in return and to its full value in money in case of nonperformance. After a repudiation, the injured party is deprived of this power, provided that his resulting injury will in fact be less if he stops work than it will be if he continues.

A repudiation by one party after the other has already fully performed his part does not affect that other's right to the full price promised or the full value of the promised equivalent. Having already performed in full, he can not reduce his claim by avoiding some part of his own performance. One who has borrowed money or bought goods on credit owes a money debt; and he can not reduce it by repudiation. One who has received the full consideration for his promise to render services or to transfer property can not by repudiation reduce the other's claim for the full value of the services or property. There may, however, be harms and losses other than the value of the performance that the repudiator refuses to render. There may be what the courts have called "consequential injuries." If they are such that the repudiator had reason to foresee them as a result of his breach, they will be included in the other's claim for damages. The fact that the other has already performed his own part in full does not necessarily prevent him from being able to avoid part or all of these consequential harms and losses; and as to them the rule as to avoidance applies. He can not get damages for such harms occurring after notice of repudiation, if by reasonable effort they could have been avoided.

## § 984.  Repudiation by Making Performance Impossible

Repudiation is a manifestation of intention not to perform a contractual duty. Such manifestations are usually communicated by words; but they may be evidenced in other ways. It has become a proverb that actions speak louder than words. Therefore, if a promisor so conducts himself as to make the substantial performance of his promise impossible, this is a repudiation of his promise and has the same legal effect as would a repudiation in words.[42] If the time for the performance of the promise has not yet arrived, there is an anticipatory breach for which an action lies.[43]  Also, the performance of conditions precedent by the other party is rendered unnecessary to his right of action.[44]

The word "impossible" is a strong word; but its use in the law of contracts is shifting and uncertain.  In the present instance it is so used as to mean much less than "physical impossibility." If the promisor so acts as to make subsequent performance by him so difficult or expensive that it is reasonable for the other party to believe that the promisor intends not to perform, there is a repudiation and an actionable breach.[45]  So, where one who has contracted to convey specific land in the future, and then makes a conveyance of it, or of some material interest in it, to a third person, there has been a repudiation even though such conveyance does not make performance of the contract wholly impossible.[46]  The promisor could repurchase the land in most cases and perform his promise as agreed; but there is a clear manifestation of intention not to do this, and the promisee is justified by the long history of such cases in believing that it will not be done. If one who has contracted to sell a specific chattel destroys it or sells it to another, he has repudiated his contract.[47]  If one who has promised to marry the plaintiff then marries another person, there is a repudiation for which action lies at once;[48] and this is true even though no date was set for the promised marriage or though the date depended upon an uncertain contingency.[49]

## § 985.  Bankruptcy as an Anticipatory Breach of Contract

Mere insolvency on the part of one who is under a contractual duty has never been held to be operative as a breach of the contract.  Insolvency will often have a very material effect upon the legal relations of the parties, but it is not in itself a breach, for which an action can be maintained.  The United States Supreme Court has said, however, that adjudged bankruptcy is operative as a breach of contract, apparently as soon as the petition in bankruptcy has been filed and apparently, also, whether the petition is a voluntary one or an involuntary one.  In so holding, the court used the following language: "It must be deemed an implied term of every contract that the promisor will not permit himself, through insolvency or acts of bankruptcy, to be disabled from making performance.  And in this view, bankruptcy proceedings are but the natural and legal consequence of something done or omitted to be done by the bankrupt in viola-

43.  **U.S.**—Cavalliotis v. Gray & Co., 293 F. 1018 (C.C.A.2d, 1923), affirming 276 F. 565 (D.C., 1922);  In re Swift, 112 F. 315 (C.C.A.1st, 1901); Wm. Cramp & Sons Ship & Engine Building Co. v. U. S., 50 Ct.Cl. 179 (1915).

44.  **Pa.**—Weinglass v. Gibson, 155 A. 439, 304 Pa. 203 (1931), manager of theatrical troupe need not tender performance when the theater has been rented to another by the owner.

tion of his engagement.   .   .   .   We conclude that proceedings, whether voluntary or involuntary, resulting in an adjudication of bankruptcy are the equivalent of an anticipatory breach of an executory agreement within the doctrine of Roehm v. Horst." [50]

The purpose of the court, in laying down this rule, was to make certain unmatured and unliquidated claims provable in the bankruptcy proceedings. It may not be regarded as settled that, under our present bankruptcy law, such claims are provable for the purpose of sharing in the bankrupt's estate; but it is not within the scope of the present volume to determine the exact limits of the doctrine.[51]

It was not necessary for the court to find justification for its decision in the field of anticipatory breach of contract. Moreover, in spite of the court's language, there are certain differences between the effect of bankruptcy and the effect of an anticipatory repudiation that cannot fail of recognition. The repudiation of almost any kind of a contract will be recognized as a breach, creating a right of action for damages. Bankruptcy, however, will not affect certain kinds of contracts at all. If the contract has created a money debt, or is one the performance of which requires the expenditure of money, bankruptcy often makes it very nearly certain that the obligation will not be performed.[52] Bankruptcy has no such effect, however, in the case of a contract that requires only the rendition of personal service. A second distinction between bankruptcy and repudiation is to be found in the fact that bankruptcy does not always justify the other party in assuming that performance will not be rendered and in changing his position in reliance thereon. The trustee for the creditors may have power to elect to perform the contract in spite of the bankruptcy; and where he has such power, he must have a reasonable time within which to determine whether or not to exercise it.[53] Upon an anticipatory repudiation, the injured party may assent to it as final and change his position in reliance thereon at once, thus depriving the repudiator of any further power of retracting his repudiation.

No doubt, the theory that bankruptcy operates as an anticipatory breach has played an important part in establishing the provability of unmatured and contingent claims; but in such cases, the right of the claimant to share in the estate of the bankrupt should not be made to depend upon such a theory. His right to share in the estate should depend upon the fact that his own assets have gone to make up that estate, just as much as in the case of those holding claims already matured. By dividing

**50.** U.S.—Central Trust Co. of Ill.
v. Chicago Auditorium, 36 S.Ct. 412,
240 U.S. 581, 60 L.Ed. 811 (1916).

up the estate among the others, his own collection is made more highly improbable.[a]

## § 987.  Repudiation that is Partly Anticipatory—Damages for Future Injury

In most of the cases dealing with repudiation and discussing the law of anticipatory breach, the repudiation was only in part anticipatory. There was a breach, either great or small, by actual non-performance at a time when performance was required by the terms of the contract, accompanied by a repudiation of the duty to render any further performance under the contract. That such a repudiation is operative to make a total breach out of what otherwise would be merely a partial breach, has already been stated. All courts agree that in these cases the plaintiff's damages are not restricted to the injury suffered by him prior to the repudiation or prior to the bringing of the action or even prior to judgment; they include also all future injury that the repudiator ought to have foreseen and that the plaintiff can establish with a reasonable degree of certainty.[62] Indeed, most of the courts hold that, if a partial breach by non-performance is accompanied by a repudiation of the contract, the injured party has only one right of action. If, in the first action that he presses to judgment, he fails to make proof of any part of his injury, whether past or future, his right to compensation therefor will be forever barred.[63]

## § 988.  Place and Time that a Repudiation Becomes Operative as a Breach

Questions have arisen as to both the place and the time that a repudiation becomes operative as a breach. If a repudiation is sent by mail, does the breach occur at the place of mailing, or at the place of receipt, or at the place where the injured party first expresses his intention to treat the repudiation as a breach, or at the place where he mails a letter expressing such intention? The legal operation of the repudiation may vary with the place selected, thus raising a question in the conflict of laws. Again, it may be necessary to determine whether or not an action is barred by Statute of Limitations. Did the repudiation operate as a breach when it was mailed, or when it was received, or when the injured party elected to regard it as final? Is non-performance on the due date also a breach, starting the statutory period to run, even though an action might have been brought at the time of repudiation?

a.  § 986, omitted here, deals with Repudiation of Lease by the Tenant as an Anticipatory Breach. Special problems are involved.

The answers to these questions have not yet been clearly settled, but there are several cases in point. It should be borne in mind that an answer may depend upon the purpose for which it is given. A repudiation may not become operative at a single point of time for all purposes alike.

When two parties are in the same jurisdiction and the repudiation is made by an expression directly communicated, no question as to place will ordinarily arise; but repudiations have been by correspondence and questions have arisen. In one case the repudiation was cabled from New York, addressed to and later received by the other party in South America; and it was held that the breach occurred in New York.[69]  The purpose of this holding was to bring the case within a statute giving the court jurisdiction of a case brought by a non-resident against a foreign corporation "where the cause of action arose within the state." *Boni judicis est ampliare jurisdictionem.* The court likened the cable message of repudiation to the acceptance of an offer, finding them both to be operative at the time and place of transmission; but there is slight parallel between them. The acceptance is an invited communication of benefit to the offeror; the repudiation is uninvited, undesired, probably unexpected, and injurious.

Nevertheless, the decision can be sustained on the ground that the term "cause of action" as used by the Legislature is a term of uncertain meaning, and the case may well be held to fall within the terms of the statute. When the question is whether or not a plaintiff has stated or has proved enough operative facts to justify the rendition of a judgment in his favor, the term "cause of action" must frequently include a great many facts and events. In an action for breach of contract, the term will include the acts of both parties in making the contract, the existence of a consideration, the performance of all conditions precedent, and conduct constituting a breach of duty by the defendant. In interpreting a jurisdictional statute like that of New York, however, it would be very unreasonable to interpret the term "cause of action" as including so much. It is believed that the result reached by the court was quite reasonable in including within the term "cause of action" nothing more than the defendant's wrongful act in transmitting his cable message of repudiation.

It seems certain that much more than the mere transmission of this message was necessary to constitute a cause of action sufficient to justify a court in giving judgment for damages against the defendant. The making of the contract would certainly have to be alleged and proved by the plaintiff. If there

69.   **N.Y.**—Wester v. Casein Co., 100 N.E. 488, 206 N.Y. 506, Ann.Cas. 1914B, 377 (1912).

were conditions precedent that would not be excused by the defendant's repudiation, such as the plaintiff's own willingness and ability to perform his part of the contract, the performance of these conditions constitutes a necessary part of the cause of action. Indeed, it is believed that, if the defendant's cable message of repudiation had been lost on the way and never delivered, or had been withdrawn by the defendant before delivery to the plaintiff so that the plaintiff never became aware that it was sent, there would have been no actionable breach of contract and no cause of action justifying a judgment for damages. But in the case before the court, the cable message of repudiation had not been lost or withdrawn; it had been received by the plaintiff, and the intended injury consummating a cause of action justifying a judgment for the plaintiff undoubtedly existed, unless the statute deprived the New York court of jurisdiction. There is no reason to interpret the statute so narrowly as to deny jurisdiction. No doubt the statute was passed under the supposition that a cause of action is an indivisible quantity; this supposition is incorrect, and the courts must mold the statute so that its application to the facts of life will do no injustice.

## § 989.  Time when Statute of Limitations Begins to Run

In a leading case in New York, the plaintiff made a contract with one Jane Sands to care for her the rest of her life; and in return, Jane promised to pay the plaintiff $70 a month for the running of the house and also to give the plaintiff $20,000 at Jane's death. In November, 1900, after living with the plaintiff a few months, Jane repudiated the contract and went to live with the defendant under a similar contract. In 1906 Jane died, leaving everything to the defendant as her sole beneficiary and executrix. In May, 1907, the plaintiff brought an action for breach of the express contract by Jane. The court held that, as to the monthly payments that fell due more than six years prior to the bringing of the suit, the plaintiff's action was barred by the Statute of Limitations. With respect to the $20,000 payable at Jane's death, the court held that the action was not barred. Even though the plaintiff could have brought suit at once upon Jane's repudiation of her promise to give the $20,000, the court said that the plaintiff might disregard the repudiation and postpone her action until after the day set for performance, when the breach by non-performance took place. In such case, the statutory period begins to run only from the day fixed for performance.[74]

74.  **N.Y.**—Ga Nun v. Palmer, 96 N.
E. 99, 202 N.Y. 483, 36 L.R.A., N.S.,
922 (1911).

If the defendant's repudiation had been wholly anticipatory, no objection should be made to the decision of the court. There is no necessity for making the statutory period of limitation begin to run against the plaintiff until the day fixed by the contract for the rendition of performance, at least unless the plaintiff definitely elects to regard the anticipatory repudiation as a final breach. It is generally said that he need not so elect and that he may properly wait until the time that performance was due, before regarding the contract as broken. He is not justified in forbearing to take steps that will mitigate his injury; but the defendant ought not to be allowed to complain at the delay in bringing action against him. For the purpose of determining when the period of limitation begins to run, the defendant's non-performance at the day specified may be regarded as a breach of duty as well as the anticipatory repudiation. The plaintiff should not be penalized for leaving to the defendant an opportunity to retract his wrongful repudiation; and he would be so penalized if the statutory period of limitation is held to begin to run against him immediately.

•

# PART VII

# DISCHARGE AND IMPOSSIBILITY

---

## TOPIC A

## DISCHARGE OF CONTRACT

---

### CHAPTER 67

### PERFORMANCE—TENDER—RESCISSION—RELEASE— GIFT—SURRENDER—CANCELLATION— CONTRACT NOT TO SUE

---

### § 1228. Introductory Analysis—Question Usually Involved is Merely Whether One Party's Contractual Duty has been Discharged

The term "discharge of contract" may be as confusing as is the term "assignment of contract" and for the same reason. The word "contract" is used to express a variety of very different ideas. It is often used to denote a written document. Such a document may be cancelled or surrendered or destroyed; but no one says that the document is discharged.[1] The word "contract" is used to denote the acts of the parties in expressing their mutual assent. Again, no one says that the "acts" of the parties are discharged. Thirdly, "contract" is used to denote the legal relations that are created between parties by their acts in executing a document or otherwise expressing their assent.

These legal relations are very often complex. Clear thinking and writing require that they be identified and considered separately. When it is said that a contract is discharged, it is always meant that one or more of the legal relations of the parties have been terminated. The meaning that is most commonly intended is that the legal duty of one of the parties has been terminated; it is in this sense that the term will be used in this treatise. A party who is asserted to be under a legal duty by virtue of his contract may reply that the duty has been "discharged" by some factor that has occurred since the making of the contract. This is very different from a reply that such a duty never existed, either because no contract ever was made or because the contract that was made created no such duty; these are matters that have been discussed in the chapters dealing with formation of contract and with interpretation and construction of contract.

No inconvenience or obscurity is involved when we say that a contract duty has been discharged or that a party has been discharged from his contractual duty. The point to be borne in mind is that very seldom are all the legal relations of the contracting parties terminated at one and the same time. A party may be discharged from further contractual duty, by some act of the other party or some other event, and continue to retain all the rights and powers and privileges that he himself possessed. It is indeed possible for the entire complex group of legal relations to be terminated at once, as where a power of "termination" is expressly reserved by agreement; in other cases, however, this seldom happens and it is usually necessary to consider them separately and one at a time.

In the case of a simple unilateral contract, such as a promissory note for money lent, only one party is under a duty. A discharge of the debtor's duty to pay may be described as a discharge of the "contract" for the reason that there are no other legal relations to be terminated.

Throughout this treatise the distinction has been continually insisted on between a future and conditional duty and a duty of immediate performance; also between a primary contractual duty, whether future or immediate, and a secondary duty to make reparation for breach of contract. Contract actions almost always involve a claim to pecuniary compensation or other reparation for a breach. It is practically always necessary, therefore, for the plaintiff to allege and prove both the making of a valid contract and its breach; he must show that the defendant came under a contractual duty, that it became immediately performable by the fulfilment of all conditions precedent, and that it was not performed. The burden is not thrown upon him, however, of alleging and proving that there has been no discharge.

The primary contractual duty of a party may be discharged either before, at, or after the time when it became immediately performable. Since the plaintiff must ordinarily establish the fact of breach of duty, it would seem that he must prove that nothing occurred to discharge the duty either before or at the time for its immediate performance. The burden of persuasion on such an issue varies with circumstances; but if the defendant relies upon the existence of some discharging factor, the burden of proceeding to establish it is on him—he must allege and offer respectable evidence of its existence.

If, after it is established that a duty of immediate performance arose and that a breach occurred, the defendant relies upon a subsequently occurring factor that discharged his secondary duty to make reparation he must assuredly allege and prove its occurrence. The risk of persuading the court that such a discharge occurred is on the defendant guilty of the breach.

The American Law Institute in its Restatement considers the matter of Discharge under twenty topical headings. Most of these will be given consideration herein.

## § 1229.  "Discharge," "Termination" and "Cancellation"

The terms "discharge," "termination," and "cancellation" are commonly used with variable meanings. Since the word "contract" is so widely used to include all the legal relations of the two parties thereto, it is a common supposition that when a "contract" is said to be discharged, or terminated, or cancelled, all of those legal relations cease to exist, the rights and duties of both parties alike being ended.  In litigated cases, it is far more common to use the word "discharge" with respect to the legal duty of one of the parties only.  When a defendant is sued for an alleged non-performance, he defends by asserting that his duty has been "discharged" by failure of consideration, by condition subsequent, by the plaintiff's own breach, or by some other operative event.  It is not meant by this that the contractual duty of the plaintiff has also been discharged;  indeed, the defendant may insist that the plaintiff is still bound to proceed with performance, may ask for specific enforcement, or may counterclaim for damages for either a partial or a total breach.

When, by express terms, a party reserves a power to "terminate" or to "cancel," it is more likely to be intended that the exercise of the power shall affect the rights and duties of both parties and that further performance according to the contract shall be no longer required of either one.  The inference of such an intention should never be drawn from the mere quoted words themselves.  Just as in all other cases, the result must be reached by process of interpretation, using all the aids thereto that may exist in the particular case;  the words must be interpreted and given legal effect in the light of all the surrounding circumstances, those extrinsic to the instrument as well as to those that are to be found within its four corners.

The exercise of a power to "terminate" or "cancel" the contract, by reason of a breach or other nonperformance by the other party, does not discharge a right to the agreed price of a performance already rendered by the party exercising the power or his right to damages for a breach that has been committed previously.  The same is true, even though the power was one that was reserved in express terms and was not dependent on a breach by the other party.[2]

In contracts of agency or other employment, it is often provided that one or both of the parties shall have the power to terminate the agency or employment at any time (or on specified conditions) by giving notice.  When the required notice is given, neither party is under a duty of further performance;  the contract may be said to be "discharged."  Yet the rights of the parties with respect to performances rendered or breaches committed before the notice became operative still depend upon the provisions of the "discharged" contract.

### § 1230.  Discharge of Duty by Performance

Any legal duty is discharged and terminated by full and exact performance.  This is true of a primary contractual duty and also of a duty to make compensation or restitution after breach of the contract.  Full and exact performance means not only performance of the character, quality, and amount as required, but also performance within the time agreed upon. The performance that is required by a duty to make compensation for a breach of contract is usually the payment of an unliquidated amount of money. As long as it is unliquidated, there is difficulty in determining just what the performance is that is required by the duty. Even in such cases, however, it is certain that, just as soon as it can be determined what the required performance is, the duty will be discharged by rendering that exact performance.

In an action for damages or other type of reparation for a breach of contract, the plaintiff must allege and prove the making of the contract and the fact of breach. In the case of unilateral money debt it is often said that payment is an affirmative defense.[3] Doubtless, this was true in the common law action of debt, which was not regarded as an action for breach of a promise. It was receipt of the quid pro quo that made the defendant a debtor; and in an action of debt, the creditor was regarded as merely suing for his own, not as asking for damages for breach of a promise to pay. But for reasons that are well known and that are stated herein the action of debt was largely displaced by assumpsit; and they have both been swallowed up by the civil action in code procedure. Burden of proof has long been confused with the burden of proceeding in the case. The decisions are such that the problem can not be treated as one of mere logic; but if a plaintiff asks damages for a breach he must allege and prove action or inaction by the defendant that constitutes a breach.[4] A discharge that takes place subsequent to breach must be alleged and proved by the defendant. Payment that is subsequent to breach or any other performance that is accepted as satisfaction must be shown by the defendant.

It may not be improper to plead "payment" as a defense, even though the settlement made was not exactly as required by contract, provided that the other party is not misled to his disadvantage.[5] Such a settlement is not exact "performance," however. It is clearly a kind of discharge by accord and satisfaction or new agreement and the burden of establishing the discharge is clearly on the defendant.

The primary contractual duty to render a promised performance may continue to exist even after a breach has been committed by the promisor. The duty to make compensation for

---

4. The plaintiff must aver breach by non-payment. Lent v. New York & M. R. Co., 29 N.E. 988, 130 N.Y. 504 (1892).

In a suit against a guarantor, the plaintiff must allege and prove non-payment by the principal debtor;

in the absence of such proof, the defendant is entitled to a directed verdict in his favor. Security Finance Co. to Use of Bernheim v. Linker, 176 A. 76, 115 Pa.Super. 523 (1935).

the breach is merely an additional secondary duty. A liquidated money debt is one illustration. The performance required is the payment of the money and this can be rendered by the debtor after the due date as well as at the exact time. Payment of the amount of the debt operates as a discharge thereof, whenever it is made; it does not discharge the duty to make compensation for delay in making the payment. Payment is a performance that requires co-operation by the creditor or someone representing him; this is as true on the exact day of maturity as it is thereafter. But the creditor's co-operative action is no more than the actual receipt of the money. A secondary duty to pay unliquidated damages for breach is not discharged by merely making a payment that is received. The creditor must assent to receive it as a liquidation and discharge; there is no "satisfaction" unless there is also an "accord."

### § 1231. Application of Payments when More than One Debt Exists

A debtor has power to determine the application of any money payment that he tenders to his creditor, except when he holds the money as a trustee or under a duty to apply it in a particular way and the creditor knows or has reason to know that he so holds it.[6] Aside from such a duty, a debtor can tender a payment on his own terms and the creditor must receive it on those terms or not at all. If the debtor owes more than one debt to his creditor, matured or unmatured, he can direct that any payment tendered by him shall be applied to any one of the debts, or to none of them, or to more than one of them in any specified proportion. To attain his end, all that is required is that he shall cause the creditor to be aware of his directions at the time the money is tendered.[7]

If a debtor makes a money payment to his creditor without any direction as to its application, the creditor has power to apply it in satisfaction of any matured and lawful debt, unless he has reason to know that the debtor is under a duty of applying the tendered money in a particular way. The creditor can apply the payment in discharge of a debt that is unsecured rather than one that is secured, or even in discharge of a debt that is barred by a statute of limitations or is not enforceable because of the statute of frauds.[8] The creditor's power to determine the application of a payment must be exercised within a reasonable time by giving notice to the debtor that such application has been made.[9] His application must not be made on a claim that is in dispute, or such as to cause the payment to be a breach of a legal duty by the debtor, the existence of which the creditor has reason to

7. See Restatement, Contracts, §§ 387–394.

know, or such as to cause the debtor to suffer an unreasonable loss or forfeiture that a different application would avoid.[10]

If a payment is made and the power of application is exercised by neither the debtor nor the creditor, its application will be determined by the court in the manner that is most just and equitable, having special regard to the interests of third parties.[11] The application will be in accordance with the debtor's duty to a third person if he is under such a duty; otherwise the payment will ordinarily be applied to overdue interest rather than to principal, to unsecured debts rather than to one that is secured, and to matured principal debts in the order of their maturity.

## § 1232. Tender of Performance

One who is under a contractual duty to render immediate performance will be guilty of a breach unless he takes some affirmative and independent action. All conditions precedent have occurred and the next move is his. Just what such action is, however, and just what its legal operation will be, depend upon the character of the performance that it is his duty to render. It may be a performance that requires the co-operation of the other contracting party or one that requires no such co-operation, either by the party or by any representative; it may be a performance that requires only a moment of time, or one requiring a period more or less extended.

Thus, a duty to pay money requires the co-operation of the receiver as well as of the payor; but the first step is to be taken by the latter and the consummation requires but a moment of time. The duty to make a conveyance of land requires the delivery of a document to the grantee or his representative, thus involving two parties but not requiring a long-continued performance. The performance of a service contract, on the other hand, may at times involve no co-operation of the employer, and may require a long period for completion. It is obvious that in such a variety of cases the phrase "tender of performance" will have a variety of meanings.[12] Money or a bank check can be tendered on a platter. The tender of three barge loads of hard coal would be made quite differently. And two years' service as a collector of specimens on the Amazon can not be tendered at all, although there can be an expression of willingness and readiness to start for South America.

The effect of the obligee's refusal to receive performance, his prevention of such performance by other means, and his repudiation of his own duty to render an agreed exchange are considered elsewhere.

## § 1233. Legal Operation of Tender

A tender or an offer to perform is not the equivalent of actual performance and never, standing alone, operates as a discharge of the duty. If the promised performance is one that requires no co-operation on the part of the promisee or of any one representing him, a tender or an offer by the promisor to perform would ordinarily have no operation whatever. It is the promisor's duty to render the performance, and not merely to tender it. If he wishes a discharge, all that is necessary is for him to proceed with the performance until completion. Thus, if A contracts to build a building on his own land or to set sail in his own ship for South America, an offer to build or to set sail would have no effect as a discharge.

If, however, the performance promised is one that requires the co-operation of the promisee or of some representative of the promisee, a tender or an offer of performance by the promisor at the proper time and place will make it incumbent on the promisee to render the necessary co-operation. Whether the promisee has himself promised to render the co-operation or not, the promisor's duty of performance is conditional upon the giving of the requisite co-operation. In such a case, the promisor's duty to perform may be discharged by the failure of the other to co-operate. It is not the promisor's offer of performance, however, that discharges him; instead, it is the refusal of the necessary co-operation by the other party.

Statements may be found that a proper tender of performance operates as a discharge of duty, in cases where the performance due is the rendition of service or the transfer of goods.[13] Such a tender, or offer to perform, undoubtedly has some legal operation; but standing alone it does not operate as a discharge. Its effect will be considered not under the head of tender, but under that of refusal to receive performance.[14]

An offer to perform or a tender of performance, made conditional upon some return performance by the other party that he is then under no duty to render is not an effective and operative tender, either as a discharge or otherwise.[15] Where in a bilateral contract the parties are required to render performances concurrently, each party's duty being conditional on such concurrent performance by the other, a tender by either one may properly be made conditional on such performance.[16]

---

13. If one who has a duty to sell and deliver goods has power to pass title to the goods by tender of delivery, such tender operates as a discharge because it is actual performance in full and the goods are now at the risk of the obligee. See Miles v. Roberts, 34 N. H. 245 (1856). Also, Uniform Commercial Code—Sales, §§ 2—703, 2—709 (1950 draft).

14. The Uniform Sales Act contains provisions as to what constitutes a proper tender of goods by a seller to the buyer. See Sections 11, 19, 20, 43, 46, 51. The Uniform Commercial Code—Sales, §§ 2—503 to 510 contains like provisions with amendments.

The question of the effect of a tender of performance arises most frequently in the case of a unilateral money debt. In such a case, tender of payment does not operate as a discharge of the debt, even though the exact amount due is tendered at the very time and place specified in the original contract.[17] Nor does the creditor's refusal to accept the money so tendered operate as a discharge of the debt. Such a refusal by the creditor is, indeed, a prevention of performance by the debtor; but it does little or no harm to the debtor. The latter is not being deprived of any return performance to which he has a right; and under ordinary circumstances the creditor's refusal to accept the risks of ownership and possession of the money is of no serious disadvantage to the debtor. Where his refusal to accept these risks is a serious matter to the debtor, and there is a subsequent loss to him because of these risks, it will very likely be held that he is discharged to the extent of the loss suffered.

The refusal by the creditor of a proper tender of the money due him is operative to prevent the debtor from being guilty of a breach of duty, although it is not a discharge of his duty. It is the creditor's own fault that he is deprived of the use of his money, and he has no right to interest or to other damages. Interest as damages for breach is not collectible, for there is no breach;[18] and any promise of interest that the debtor may have made in the contract of loan is discharged for the reason that the debtor is no longer in a position to make use of the principal. The debtor has withdrawn the money from his business and is justified in keeping it segregated and unproductive in order to make payment of his debt.

For the same reasons, the creditor no longer has a right of enforcement of securities held by him.[19] He cannot require a surety to pay the debt, because by his own act he has caused the failure of payment by the debtor and has thus increased the burden on the surety. And it is equally unjust for the creditor to enforce mortgages and other liens on property of the debtor, when the latter has made a proper tender and remains ready to pay the amount for which the liens were created.

### § 1234.　Purpose for Which Tender is Made

A tender of performance, or an expression of readiness and willingness to perform, may be for more than one purpose. The performance tendered, or the tender itself, may be a condition precedent to the duty of immediate performance by the other party, in which case the purpose of the tender is to produce an effect upon that other party's duty and to put him in default. The discussion of tender as a condition precedent is to be found in the chapters on conditions. Secondly, the performance tendered may be one that it is the immediate duty of the tenderer to render, in which case the purpose of the tender is to perform a duty and to be discharged therefrom. It is the latter aspect of the subject of tender that is being dealt with in the present chapter. Under what circumstances does a tender of performance operate as a discharge of duty, or what is its effect in that direction? It may be that usually there is no difference in what constitutes an operative tender, whatever may be its purpose; but it is only as a fact leading to a discharge of duty that we shall now consider it.

## § 1235.   Requisites of a Proper Tender of Money

In order that tender of payment shall have the foregoing operation, the tender must be a proper one and it must be kept good. To make a proper tender there are several requirements.[20] (1) The money must be of the kind required by the contract;[21] if the promise was to pay in gold coin, it is gold coin that must be tendered; [22] if in the notes of the Traders' Bank, then the notes of that very bank must be tendered. In case the contract provided only for the payment of "dollars," the tender may be in any kind of dollar currency provided by the law of the land as a medium of exchange, provided that it is also specified by law as "legal tender" money. Under the Federal constitution, the Congress has power to determine what shall constitute "legal tender" money; and it seems to have power to make changes therein, even with respect to pre-existing contract debts. The ordinary forms of "legal tender" money are gold coin and gold certificates, silver coin and other subsidiary metal in variously limited amounts, and United States notes (greenbacks) that are expressly declared to be "legal tender" by act of Congress.[23] The statutes must be consulted for an exact determination of what constitutes "legal tender" money at any particular time, as well as the effect of attempts by express contract provisions to require payment in some particular kind of money.[24]

The sufficiency of a tender of payment must be determined with reference to the customs of business as well as to the exact terms of the contract. Payment by check is a customary method among most businessmen; and a tender of payment by check is an operative tender, if the creditor does not expressly object to the form of payment and if the check is one that would be honored on proper presentation to the drawee bank.[25] The same is true of a tender in non-legal tender currency.[26]

(2) The money must be produced in such a way that the creditor can take possession of it without unreasonable exertion, un-

22.    The Act of Congress withdrawing gold coin from circulation made it legally impossible to tender it as required by many contracts. The condition of tender in gold is thus eliminated and is replaced by the condition of tender of the same number of dollars in any form of legal tender money.

less by words or other conduct the creditor makes it evident that the money will not be received even if it is produced.[27]  In the latter event, the money need not be physically produced; but the debtor must have it available.[28]

(3)  The money tendered must be either the exact amount due, or a larger amount without requiring the making of change.[29]

(4)  Tender must be at the time and place required by the contract.[30]  It must be made to the creditor in person, or to his authorized representative.[31]  A tender of payment in advance of the due date and the creditor's refusal to receive it then do not affect the debtor's duty to make payment as agreed.[32]  He must make a new tender on the date of maturity or be in default. Likewise a tender of money made after the debtor has already committed a default was not, at common law, a proper tender, for the reason that the amount then due is no longer a liquidated and definite sum.[33]  After default there is a right to damages as well as a right to the principal sum.  In most cases, however, these damages are the interest value of the use of the money at the agreed rate or at market rates, the amount of which can easily be calculated.  This has led to the passing of statutes providing that a tender of payment after default shall be fully operative if the amount tendered is large enough to include the principal of the debt, accrued interest, and any further amount to which the creditor may afterwards be found by a court to have been entitled.  Refusal of such a tender may therefore have all the effects that a tender on the due date would have had.  It may be, indeed, that such would now be held to be the case even in the absence of a statute.[34]

(5)  The tender must be kept good.[35]  This means that, if the creditor repents of his refusal to receive the tendered payment and takes such action that he can no longer be reasonably regarded as preventing payment by the debtor, the debtor must make actual delivery of the money.  If the creditor brings an action at law on the account, even though he demands more than the amount tendered, the tender is not regarded as being "kept good" unless the debtor actually pays the amount into court for the creditor's use.[36]  Where the suit is in equity, however, or in any modern court that has equity powers and a flexible procedure, the actual payment into court may not be required; such a court can do full justice by making its decree conditional and can thus give the creditor complete security.[37]  Unless the debtor complies with the conditions prescribed, the advantages of a tender will be denied him.

A payment of the money into court, in accordance with a previously made tender according to contract, operates as actual performance of duty and as a discharge.[38]  The only judgment to which the creditor is then entitled is a judgment that the amount held by the officer of the court shall be delivered to him.[39]  No judgment whatever will be entered against the debtor on which any writ of execution could be issued.  Instead, the debtor will be given judgment for his costs against the creditor.  To have this effect, the tender must be a proper one as heretofore described.  If not such a tender, the creditor may get the amount that was paid into court, but he will also get judgment for a proved balance and for interest and costs.

(6) For a tender of money in payment of a debt to be a proper one it must be unconditional.[40]  There is an exception to this in the case of a negotiable note or bill, a tender of payment not being rendered ineffective by the fact that the tender is expressly made conditional upon the production and surrender of the note.[41]  Of course, in the case of a bilateral contract the duty to pay may be conditional upon the concurrent rendition of the agreed exchange, in which case the defendant can be put in default by a tender that is conditional upon such concurrent performance.[42]  Also, the duty to pay may be conditional upon the concurrent surrender of securities held by the creditor, in which case the tender is not ineffective by being made conditional on such surrender.[43]  It has been held that tender is not good if it is conditional on the giving of a receipt in writing by the creditor;[44] but the contrary has also been held.[45]  Of course, it is not good if it is conditional on a receipt in full or upon an acknowledgment of full satisfaction;[46] and the same has been held if it is conditional upon the execution of a release of mortgage security.[47]

It should be observed that an offer to pay a sum of money in compromise or in full settlement of a larger claim is not a tender of performance of the sort here under consideration, even though the money may be produced.  This is a conditional offer that requires acceptance like any other offer.  Until such an acceptance, prior claims and securities are not affected.[48]  A tender of the amount due is not made ineffective by the fact that the amount tendered is less than the amount claimed; but it must not be made in such manner that the receipt of the money by the creditor prejudices his claim to a larger amount, either as a discharge or as an evidential admission.

(7) Non-compliance with any or all of the formal requisites of a proper tender will not prevent its being fully effective, if compliance is prevented by the creditor, intentionally waived by him, or if his expressed objections to the tender as made are wholly on other grounds.  That this applies especially to the form of the payment that is tendered has been shown above in the discussion of that part of this topic.  It applies to other requirements as well, such as that the tender is not kept good,[49] and the

actual production of the money.[50] For such a result to be reached, it must appear that the debtor would in fact have complied with all requisites but for the waiver or prevention of the creditor. The fact that the creditor claims too much is not itself a waiver or prevention.

## § 1236. Discharge by Rescission

As the term is used in this treatise, rescission means a mutual agreement by the parties to an existing contract to discharge and terminate their duties under it. Just as in the case of the formation of a contract, so also in the case of its rescission there are expressions of assent by both parties—usually in the form of an offer by one and an acceptance by the other. The legal effect of a rescission as thus defined is the discharge of all rights and duties on the part of both parties with respect to the contract that has been rescinded. If any contractual right to further performance under the contract or if any right to damages for a breach of the contract continues to exist, there has been no complete rescission.[51] If all such rights have been discharged there has been both "rescission" and "accord and satisfaction." [52]

As long as any primary contractual right and duty are recognized by the law as existing, they are subject to discharge by rescission, even though there has been a breach of the contract creating a secondary right to compensatory damages. In such a case an operative rescission in general terms has been interpreted as intended to discharge the primary contractual rights and duties and also the secondary right and duty of compensation for injury. The court should not jump to such a conclusion without a careful search for actual intention of the parties.

A mutual agreement of rescission after part performance has already been rendered or a breach has already occurred may raise a difficult question of interpretation. Is any compensation to be made for a part performance rendered?[53] Does the agreement discharge all right to compensatory damages for a breach that has already been committed?[54] If the antecedent contract contained a provision exempting the contractor from liability for negligence, and there has been harm negligently caused, does the rescission destroy this exemption?[55] Does the rescission operate only in futuro, making the contract inoperative as to matters as yet unperformed, but leaving it still operative as to performances fully or defectively rendered under it? The answers to such questions as these can be made only after interpretation of the terms of the agreement of rescission, in the light of the circumstances that surrounded its making. In this process the same common-sense rules should be applied as in the interpretation of the contract that is being "rescinded".

Some efforts have been made to distinguish "rescission" from the "termination" or "cancellation" of a contract, the latter two terms being applicable only to the rendition of further performance as provided in the contract, leaving intact all claims for performance rendered or breaches committed in the past.[56]  No doubt this distinction is supported by some usage; but this usage is not so uniform as to be decisive in interpretation.  All relevant factors must be considered;  and in rendering judgment and awarding the remedies the court should frequently be aware that it must fill a gap on a matter as to which the parties did not advert and that the result must depend on equitable considerations.

If the existing contract that is the subject of rescission is a unilateral contract, it cannot be discharged by a rescission that consists merely of mutual expressions of assent to rescind.  This is because only one of the parties to the contract has any contractual right under it, and only the other bears the burden of a contractual duty.  The one has everything to lose by a rescission and nothing to gain;  the other has everything to gain and nothing to lose.  In agreeing to a rescission, therefore, one of the parties is doing nothing that could be operative as a consideration sufficient for the formation of a contract.  It is true that an agreement that is purely and simply a rescission contains no promise by either party and is not an executory contract.  It is not necessary, therefore, that the requirement of a sufficient consideration for an executory promise should be satisfied in order to make a rescinding agreement operative as a discharge of an existing contractual obligation.  Indeed, this is made fully evident by the fact that there are a number of modes of discharge of contract by executed gift.  These modes of discharge will be discussed hereafter.  It remains true, nevertheless, that mutual assent to a rescission is not operative as a discharge when only one of the parties is under any contractual duty to the other.

If the existing agreement that is the subject of rescission is still a bilateral contract, each of the parties has one or more rights under the contract to be given up, as well as one or more duties under it from which to be discharged.  In such a case a mutual assent to a rescission is at once operative to discharge both parties.  This is true even though the original contract that is the subject of rescission has been partly performed by one or by both of the parties thereto.  Each of them still has certain advantages under the contract to give up; and by analogy with the doctrine of consideration in the formation of contracts, there is no requirement that each of the parties should have the same amount to give up or that the rescission should be equally advantageous to both parties.[57]

Even though the antecedent contract is in writing, rights and duties under it can be discharged by an oral agreement of rescission; and by modern law, the same is true even though the antecedent contract is under seal.[58] The "parol evidence rule" has no application to agreements made subsequently to the execution of a written contract. In almost all cases, an agreement of mere rescission is not required to be in writing by the statute of frauds, even though the contract to be rescinded was so required and was fully expressed in writing. The new agreement may be more than a mere rescission, however; if it makes a new or modified contract to be substituted for the antecedent one, this may be such as to be within the statute and unenforceable in any of its aspects unless there is a signed writing.[59] This may be true even though the antecedent contract was not itself within the statute and was not in writing.

Just as in the case of the formation of a contract, an operative agreement of rescission can be made tacitly as well as expressly.[60] Also, it is possible to make a valid rescission even though it is only one of the parties who has an active desire for it and even though he is threatening a breach of his contract. If an offer of rescission is made under such circumstances, an acceptance of the offer completes the discharge of the existing contract, even though the acceptance is accompanied by feelings of regret and dissatisfaction.

It should be observed, however, that a mere expression of repudiation by one party to a contract is not an offer of a rescission. Acquiescence in such a repudiation by the other party is not an acceptance of an offer of rescission and does not prevent the repudiation from being a breach of contract creating the usual remedial rights. Thus, suppose that A, who is under a contract for the construction of a building for B, should tell B that he is not going to perform the contract. B replies: "Very well, I shall at once get another builder." This conversation is not operative as a rescission of the contract. B's duty to A is indeed discharged by A's repudiation; but the repudiation is a breach of contract, for which B can maintain an action for damages. If there were a true and complete rescission, this would not be the case.[61]

When two parties make a new contract that is inconsistent with the terms of a previous one dealing with the same subject matter, it may be described as both a rescission and a discharge by substitution. If the new contract contains no statement as to the intended effect upon the old contract, the court may have a difficult problem of interpretation. At times it will be reasonable to hold that the rescission and substitution are only partial, part of the old contract being still enforceable.[62]

### § 1237. Rescission Distinguished from a Mere Attempt to Mitigate Damages

Without doubt a considerable amount of injustice has been done by reason of variation and confusion in the use of the term "rescission." When one party repudiates the contract or otherwise commits a very material breach, this fact may in itself discharge the other party from further duty under the contract.[63] This is not a "rescission" or even an offer of a rescission; yet is it often said that such a breach privileges the other party to "rescind" the contract. This usage has caused serious difficulty; it should not be hopeless to try to eliminate it.[64]

Again, it is often said that the injured party may "elect to rescind", but that by such an "election" he deprives himself of his right to compensatory damages for the breach. This is explained on the theory that "rescission" is inconsistent with "enforcement". It is true that an agreement to rescind is inconsistent with enforcement of that which is rescinded; but an agreement to rescind can be restricted by the parties in any way that they see fit; and it should never prevent the enforcement of any rights and duties that they did not intend to discharge.

A mere expression by the injured party of recognition of the fact that a vital breach has occurred and an assertion of his own discharge thereby is no part of an "agreement to rescind"; it is not an offer to rescind, nor is it the acceptance of such an offer.[65] Furthermore, it is not an "election" between remedies, the very existence and character of which he can not know until advised by a competent lawyer.

When the injured party asserts his own freedom from the duty to perform further, he is merely trying to avoid further loss from the other's wrong—something that the law often requires of him whether he is willing or not. There are other methods by which he may reasonably endeavor to avoid or reduce injury: he may contract for some substitute material or service; [66] he may ask the repudiator to repent and retract; he may demand replacement or the repair of defects; he may ask compensation for what he has done; he may demand his money back or the reconveyance of property; and he may demand compensatory damages. In doing these things, he is trying to avoid harms and losses; he is not offering a "rescission" or "waiving" his rights or "electing" a remedy. These also are things that the injured party can do; but they are clearly distinguishable.[67]

The original Uniform Sales Act, 1906, contributed to the confusion by providing that "rescission" by a buyer of goods deprived him of his right to damages for breach of warranty, at least

67. If the parties actually agree upon return of the goods and repayment of part or all of the price in settlement of a disputed claim as to defects and injury, there is a discharge by accord and satisfaction. See Stanley Drug Co. v. Smith, K. & F. Lab., 170 A. 274, 313 Pa. 368 (1934), where such may have been the agreement. Likewise a satisfaction can be agreed upon and effected by any other substituted performance.

"when the buyer has claimed and been granted" such a remedy.[68] Even if this may have been confusedly intended to prevent an aggrieved buyer from mitigating his injury by getting his money back and at the same time reserving his claim for compensation for other consequential harms, it should never have been so interpreted or applied.[69] The Uniform Commercial Code—Sales avoids the confusion and rejects the theory of "election" when only mitigation of loss is intended.[70]

If a substantial breach has been discovered by the buyer before he has paid the price, he can properly refuse payment and retain the money. His doing so is not a "rescission" and is no bar to a suit for damages measured according to the usual rules therefor; the retention of the money goes merely to a mitigation of damages, by avoidance of loss. Exactly the same is true, if unfortunately the price was paid before the breach was discovered; if the buyer then succeeds in getting his money back, he is merely mitigating his damages unless he gets the money by agreeing that it shall have some other effect as a mutual rescission or an accord and satisfaction.

### § 1238.　Discharge by Release

One who has a contractual right against another, or a right to compensation or to restitution by reason of another's breach of his contractual duty, has the power to discharge his right and the other's duty by the execution and delivery of a release.[71] Even though the right in question does not actually exist, but is merely asserted to exist, a release executed and delivered by the claimant will be a good additional defense in any action by him for its enforcement. A release is a writing manifesting an intention to discharge another from an existing or an asserted duty. In order to be effective as a discharge at common law, the writing was required either to be under seal or to be given in exchange for a sufficient consideration.[72] It seems not improbable, however, that, in states that have abolished the common law effect of a seal by legislative action, a formal written release would be effective, even though there was no consideration. The statute might well be interpreted as manifesting a legislative intention to deprive a promisor of the power of binding himself by merely adding a seal after his signature, without, at the same time, depriving a promisee of the power of discharging his claim against another person by an executed gift evidenced by a formal written statement.[73] Under the Negotiable Instruments Law, in effect everywhere, the holder of a negotiable instrument has power to discharge the duty of any party to it by a signed written renunciation.[74] There is no good reason for not giving like effect to a

---

74.　N.I.L. § 122. The same provision appears in the Uniform Commercial Code—Commercial Paper, § 3—605 (1950 draft).

similar written discharge of any contract right.[75]

Inasmuch as an executory promise will sometimes become legally binding by reason of subsequent action by the promisee in reasonable reliance upon the promise, no doubt it is equally true that a written release, given without any consideration for it, will become legally effective as a discharge, if the obligor takes the same kind of justified action in reliance upon it that would be held to be sufficient to make an executory promise binding. The same result should be reached, even if the words of release are entirely informal and unwritten; the circumstances that would make an oral promise binding should likewise be sufficient to make an oral discharge effective.[76]

If a documentary release is dependent for its validity entirely upon its form, and not upon consideration or some action in reliance, there must be a delivery of the document either to the one who is being released or to a third person for his benefit. It is by such a delivery that the party executing the release expresses his intention to make it immediately operative. There has been some variation in the holdings as to what acts will constitute an effective delivery. The problem is identical with that existing in the matter of delivery of a sealed executory promise.[77]

If, on the other hand, the validity of a release is supported by a consideration given or by subsequent action in reliance upon it, the transaction may be fully effective as a discharge even though there has been no delivery. A purely oral release would be effective in such cases; and no delivery is possible in such a case. The problem is not one of delivery, but one of bargaining agreement or of a communicated expression actually inducing action in reliance. Of course, delivery may be a part of a bargain or the mode of communication of intention; but in these cases the document is merely one factor in the larger transaction, and it is not an indispensable one. Such a transaction falls within the field of accord and satisfaction.

Statutes have been passed providing that in an action upon a sealed instrument the seal shall be only presumptive evidence of a consideration. It has been held that such a statute does not make a gratuitous sealed release inoperative, since the form of the statute is such as to be applicable only in actions for the enforcement of promises under seal.[78] A sealed release is not the basis of an action; it is merely set up as a defense to an action that is based on something else. The form in which the statute is worded is probably due to an erroneous belief that at common law the seal was "conclusive evidence" of a consideration. If a leg-

---

75.   In New York a special statute so provides. N.Y.Pers.Prop. Law, § 33.

78.   N.J.—Braden v. Ward, 42 N.J. L. 518 (1880).
N.Y.—Stiebel v. Grosberg, 95 N.E. 692, 202 N.Y. 266 (1911).

islature means to make seals ineffective, on promises and releases alike, it should use accurate and appropriate language.

Statutes sometimes purport to abolish all distinction between sealed and unsealed instruments. In adopting such a statute account should be taken of its effect upon conveyances, assignments, and releases as well as contracts. This fact has been discovered by the New York legislature and its Law Revision Commission.[79] In abolishing the seal as an operative factor, there is no doubt that provision should be made for the making of valid gift assignments, promises, and releases. Of course, the abolition of the seal does not in any way diminish the effect of those instruments that were previously legally operative without having anything purporting to be a seal.

There is no particular form of words that is required in order to make a written release effective. All that is necessary is that the words should manifest a present intention to discharge. This is to be determined by the process of interpretation, just as in the case of determining the meaning of an executory contract.

## § 1239. Conditional Release and Temporary Suspension

It is possible to execute a written release in such a form that it will not be operative until a future date or will not be operative until the happening of some condition precedent; just as in the case of executory promises, a release may be either conditional or unconditional.[82] If a creditor gives to his debtor a release to be effective only on condition that the debtor shall deliver a certain chattel to the creditor or shall render specified service for him, on the delivery of the chattel or on the rendition of the service, and not before, the release will become effective. In such a case as this, the written release is identical with an offer by the creditor of an accord and satisfaction; and the performance of the condition by the debtor is his acceptance of the offered accord, and operates as a satisfaction of his debt.

As shown in the preceding paragraph, a temporary suspension of a claim could be practically effected by executing a document that would be pleadable as a release if the claim should be sued on within a stated period; also, without any temporary suspension, a valid release could be executed so as to be operative in the future on the occurrence of a specified condition precedent. Another device that was sustained was a sealed release, by its terms immediately effective, but subject to defeasance on the happening of a specified condition subsequent.[83] This, too, is in effect a temporary suspension, but one that will be permanent if the condition never occurs.

A release, like a deed and other formal instruments, can be delivered "in escrow." This means delivery to a third party, for

---

82. Stiebel v. Grosberg, 95 N.E. 692, 202 N.Y. 266 (1911); Gibbons v. Vouillon, 8 C.B. 483 (1849); Restatement, Contracts, § 404.

further delivery by him to the obligor on the happening of some specified condition.[84]  Such a delivery in escrow is operative as a release subject to a condition precedent.[85]  After such a delivery, the party executing it has no power of revocation unless he has expressly reserved such a power.  On the happening of the condition, the release becomes fully operative as such without the making of any second delivery by the holder to the obligor.  The so-called "parol evidence rule" does not prevent parol proof of the conditional delivery, even though such proof makes the document operate just as if the condition had been incorporated in the writing.[86]

### § 1240.  Gift Discharge by Creditor's Oral Release or Renunciation

A mere oral statement by a creditor to his debtor that the debt is discharged and the debtor released is not legally operative as a discharge.[88]  The creditor can disregard his statement and get judgment for the amount of the debt.  This seems to be true, without regard to the particular form of words that the creditor uses, and in spite of the fact that the creditor is proved to have made the statement with donative intent.  He may say that he gives him the debt or the money;  or he may promise him (without consideration) that he will never insist on payment or will never sue for the money.[89]

Such a statement or such a promise, however, may become binding, and operative as a discharge, by reason of the debtor's subsequent action in reliance upon it before notice of its withdrawal by the creditor.[90]  The debtor's action must be substantial in character and of a kind that the creditor had reason to foresee.  There then exists a discharge by a sort of promissory estoppel.

In some cases in which an oral gift discharge was held inoperative, the debt was evidenced by a promissory note or other document that was capable of delivery, and by the delivery of which a discharge by gift could have been executed.[91]

A mere oral waiver of the right to damages, whether liquidated or unliquidated, for a breach of contract that has already been committed, is not operative as a discharge thereof; [92] but as appears in a succeeding section, if such a waiver is accompanied by

---

90.    In Millett v. Temple, 182 N.E. 921, 280 Mass. 543, 84 A.L.R. 378 (1932), a woman lent $2300 to her son-in-law to help him to build a home.  For two years he paid interest at 5 per cent, the mother living in the house so built.  She then said, in 1917, that she felt she had not been paying her full share of the living expenses, and told her son-in-law orally that he might "forget the $2300 loan." Thereafter she lived in the same house for five more years, nothing being said of the loan.  In 1929, the son-in-law having obtained a divorce, the woman attempted to collect the debt.  The court held that it had been discharged by gift in 1917.

continuing to render or to receive further performance under the contract, it is almost certain to be held that there has been a discharge by agreed modification or by executed gift.[93] A voluntary promise to extend the time for payment of a sum due is not enforceable.[94]

There is, indeed, no necessity, either logical or social, for extending the requirement of a consideration to the discharge of a contractual duty. Even though it may be thought that an executory informal promise should not be legally enforceable in the absence of a consideration, it might reasonably be held that a discharge requires none. In enforcing a promise, the promisee is seeking affirmative action by society; one who asserts a discharge is not. The first asserts the creation of duty; the other asserts its termination. It is true that a large part of the time we assume that justice requires an exchange of equivalents, a quid pro quo; but it is equally true that we make little effort to test the actual equality of values and that we are quite willing to give effect to executed gifts, both inter vivos and causa mortis.

In the matter of a discharge by an oral or an unsealed written exoneration, therefore, the question is merely whether or not we think it desirable to regard the transaction as an executed gift. If we refuse so to regard it, it seems clear that we must do so, in part at least, because the evidence of the donor's intention is not entirely satisfactory. We do not hesitate in the case of a sealed gratuitous release; or in the case of surrender or cancellation by gift; or in the case of a "horse, a hawk, or a robe" [95] (or, it may be, a peppercorn) given in satisfaction; or in the case of a written renunciation by the holder of a negotiable note.[96] Why, then, should we not give full effect to a written discharge of any other unilateral obligation, or to an oral exoneration, if it is expressed definitely, is not improperly induced, and is satisfactorily proved? [97]

## § 1241. Cases Giving Effect to an Oral Discharge

Cases can be found in which full effect seems to have been given to an oral gift discharge.[98] The rule contra is no doubt supported by greater authority; but it is obvious that the courts have not always known it or have not felt the necessity of applying it. It may be that in some cases denying the validity of an oral gift discharge, the evidence supporting it was not convincing. It is easy for an obligor to expand loose statements of intention not to press him for payment into definite expressions of im-

97. It has been adopted by statute in New York, on the recommendation of the State Law Revision Commission. N.Y.Pers.Prop.Laws, § 33(2) provides that an agreement to modify or discharge an existing contract shall not be invalid for lack of consideration if it is in a signed writing.

mediate discharge by gift. The evidence, especially where the donor is dead, should be subjected to careful scrutiny.

The owner of a chattel that is in the possession of another can make an executed gift of it to that possessor by merely saying to him that it is his.[99] It is unnecessary for the donor to take back his chattel and then make a new physical delivery of it to the donee. The same result has been reached where the subject of the gift was money instead of a chattel.[1] If the money was specific coins or bills, the rule as to chattels properly applies. If there was merely a money debt, then an oral gift discharge is being supported.

## § 1242. Differences between Gift Discharge of a Debt and the Gift Transfer of a Chattel

It is sometimes said that a gift can not be regarded as executed unless there has been such a "delivery" as is sufficient to convey "title" or "ownership" or "dominion" over the subject of the gift. Such language may be applicable to the gift of a physical chattel; but it is not applicable to gift discharges of a contract right, even though that right may be evidenced by some written instrument, formal or informal in nature. The purpose of a discharge is not a conveyance of any kind of property to the donee; it is not a transfer of the donor's contract right to his debtor. It is merely the extinguishment of the donor's right and the debtor's duty, the termination of their legal relation. After the discharge, the debt is not now "owned" by the debtor; it merely does not exist. There is no "title" to a debt; for debt means nothing more than a relation of creditor and debtor, a right-duty relation. After a discharge, there is nothing over which to have "dominion." Language that is suitable to express jural relations with respect to material chattels is not suitable in describing a contract right or in expressing the manner and effect of its termination.

It is to avoid the supposed necessity of "delivery" that courts have often said that it is enough if there has been such delivery as the nature of the subject matter makes possible, and that a contract right is not capable of delivery. The purpose thus attained is wholly commendable; but we might as well attain that purpose without any reference to "delivery." The attention of court and jury should be directed to the question of the donor's expression of intention to make a present and irrevocable gift discharge; satisfactory evidence of that must be required in order to prevent debtors from perpetrating a successful fraud. Our rules of gift discharges should be so constructed as to direct the court's attention to the weight and character of the evidence presented.[a]

a. § 1243 discusses the supposed Distinction Between Discharge "Before Breach" and Discharge "After Breach."

### § 1244.   Discharge of Right to Compensation for a Breach by Voluntary Waiver and Proceeding with Performance

Even if a liquidated money debt, due in return for a fully executed consideration, can not be discharged as a gift by mere informal words of renunciation, the rule seems to be otherwise of a right to unliquidated damages for the material breach of a bilateral contract that has not yet been fully performed by the injured party.[6] The material breach by the one party has operated to discharge the duty of the other to render the promised equivalent; and if, under such circumstances, he says to the wrongdoer that he now regards the contract as wholly discharged and at an end, the wrongdoer is discharged as well as the injured party himself. The latter's discharge is by material breach, often described as "failure of consideration"; but the wrongdoer's discharge is a gift discharge by the mere words of renunciation.

The explanation of this may well be that the courts regard the contract as still bilateral in its effect so that each party still has something to give up. If we assume that the breach by one is so material as to discharge the other, the wrongdoer no longer has rights to give up; but in any specific case the assumption is never an absolutely safe one until there has been an adjudication as to the materiality of the breach. Therefore, a mutual agreement of rescission by the parties would be a valid agreement, with sufficient consideration on each side; the resulting discharge by either party would not be a "gift" discharge.

Under ordinary circumstances, merely proceeding with performance in spite of the nonfulfilment of some condition precedent by the other party is not operative as a discharge of an existing right to damages for such nonfulfilment.[8] It does not manifest an intention to discharge the right; it is merely a waiver, for the time being at least, of the condition of one's own duty to proceed. In order to operate as a discharge by gift there must be an expression of intention by the injured party when he proceeds with his performance that it shall operate as a discharge. In proceeding with performance when one is not bound to do so it is good policy to protest against the breach by the other party and to assert a right to damages therefor.[9]

### § 1245.   Discharge by Voluntary Acceptance of a Defective Performance

It is frequently stated that a claim for compensatory damages for a breach of contract can be discharged by a voluntary "waiver," without consideration and with no basis for an estoppel. This is not true, however, if the injured party has performed the full agreed equivalent, creating in the defendant the duty to pay a liquidated sum of money (a money debt). A liquidated money debt can not be discharged by a mere oral "waiver," even though it is given in return for a part payment. If the plaintiff has not fully performed, however, the statement appears to be sustained by the courts.

Undoubtedly, the rule here stated, that a claim for damages for a breach can be discharged by a mere voluntary statement, is an important limitation on the supposed rule against voluntary informal exoneration. It is illustrated chiefly by the many cases in which a building is defectively constructed, or work is improperly done, or defective goods are delivered, and such building or work or goods are accepted as a sufficient performance.[10] The mere receipt of the defective performance is not in itself sufficient to discharge the claim to damages for the breach. There must be an expression of assent to accept it in satisfaction and as a complete discharge.[11] In such cases, the obligor may or may not acknowledge the defects in his performance, and the obligee may or may not call attention to the defects; but the latter must be aware of the performance that is being tendered or that has been rendered and he must express his assent to accept it as a complete discharge of the obligor's duty to him.

If the seller of goods tenders a defective delivery, defective in either quantity or quality or time, the buyer's receipt of the goods so tendered does not in itself operate as a discharge of his right to the balance of the goods or his right to damages for the seller's breach.[12] To operate as such a discharge there must be an assent to the discharge; the defective delivery must be accepted as a full performance or as a sufficient substituted performance, or there must be other sufficient basis for an estoppel.

The discharge here described is not a discharge by an accord and satisfaction. The performance of the obligor is not something new and different that is being offered in satisfaction as a substituted performance. It is merely a part performance or an otherwise defective performance that can not in itself operate as a discharge of duty. The obligor has committed a breach and the obligee is giving up his claim to compensation therefor. The discharge is effected solely by the expression of assent to discharge.

Nor is the case here considered a case of compromise and settlement of a doubtful or disputed claim. Even if there is neither doubt nor dispute, and nothing whatever is said about compromise, the discharge is operative.

Further, the discharge here described is not a discharge by mutual "rescission." The transaction may be one in which the wrongdoer has nothing from which to discharge the other party

10.   U.S.—Gregory v. Baer, 149 F. 2d 411 (C.C.A.4th, 1945), short delivery.
Restatement, Contracts, § 411.

12.   U.S.—Robberson Steel Co. v. Harrell, 177 F.2d 12 (C.A.10th, 1949), citing 14 recent cases.

who assents to discharge him.  That party may already have paid in advance or otherwise fully performed his part.  It is merely a case in which, by accepting a defective performance as a discharge, he is extinguishing the duty of the wrongdoer to correct the defects or to make compensation for them.

### § 1246.  Gift Discharge by Delivery of Receipt in Full or by Informal Written Renunciation

There are statutes, especially in states that have abolished seals or have made them only prima facie evidence of a consideration, providing that a signed release or renunciation in writing shall be operative as a discharge according to its terms.[15]  This makes possible a gift discharge by a writing less formal than the sealed release of the common law.  It shows a felt need for such a method of making a gift, a need the satisfaction of which appeared to have been made impossible by the abolition of seals.  It tends strongly to show, also, that the courts should, without the aid of statute, give full effect to a written renunciation.  Time and modern business practice have caused the "seal" to lose the superstitious solemnity that it once had; and it should now be recognized that an unsealed renunciation has the same value as evidence of intention as has a sealed release.[16]

The delivery of a receipt in full, without stating the amount received, is evidence that payment in full was actually made; but it is not conclusive evidence.  A signed statement is not conclusive even though it specifies the amount, the receipt of which is acknowledged.  But the intentional delivery of a receipt in full, making no mistake as to the sum due or as to the sum received in fact, is strong evidence of a gift if the sum actually paid is less than the sum due.  The Connecticut courts have held it to be operative as a discharge by gift in such a case, if there is no sufficient evidence in rebuttal.[17]

There are many cases in other states holding that a "receipt in full" is not itself sufficient evidence of a gift discharge.[18]  Nevertheless, it is always helpful in making out such a defense as payment or accord and satisfaction; it should be of great weight also in establishing a gift discharge when there is evidence of expressions of donative intention.

15.  In New York, Laws 1936, c. 281, amended Personal Property Law, § 33, and Real Property Law, § 279, by adding: "An agreement hereafter made to change or modify, or to discharge in whole or in part, any contract, obligation, or lease, or any mortgage or other security interest in personal or real property, shall not be invalid because of the absence of consideration, provided that the agreement changing, modifying, or discharging such contract, obligation, lease, mortgage or security interest, shall be in writing and signed by the party against whom it is sought to enforce the change, modification or discharge."

There are some very well-considered cases that give effect to a gift discharge by written renunciation not under seal. Thus, in a New York case, it was held that a money debt of $821 was discharged by the following facts: the creditor proposed to make a gift of the debt, and in order to make it certainly effective, he received a payment of $1, executed a receipt therefor "in full to balance all accounts," and entered in his own ledger the payment of the dollar, with the additional words "Gift to balance account $820."[19] Surely it would be a strange court that would refuse to give this the effect of a discharge.

The Negotiable Instruments Law, everywhere adopted, provides that the written renunciation of his right by the holder of the instrument, even though gratuitous, shall be effective.[20] No words should be required other than those expressing an intention to make a gift discharge. If it is sound policy to give effect to such a writing in the case of a negotiable instrument, there is at least equally good reason for giving it the same effect in the case of other contracts.

§ 1247. Part Payment of a Debt, and Gift Discharge of the Balance

As we have seen elsewhere, the part payment of a liquidated debt, then due, is not a sufficient consideration for a promise given in return therefor by the creditor. But this does not prevent the creditor from otherwise discharging his debtor, not even from executing a gift discharge. Such a gift discharge, to be operative, must not depend for its validity upon the part payment; the facts operating as a discharge must be such that they would be so operative if the creditor were executing a gift discharge of the entire debt instead of merely a part of the debt.

Inasmuch as by the present weight of authority the part payment of a larger sum then due is not operative in itself as a consideration for a promise or as a discharge of a duty to pay the larger sum, the question in these cases becomes, Was there an intention to make a gift of the balance due, and if so was the intention expressed in such a way as to make an executed gift and not merely an executory promise of one? A mere statement that the creditor will accept a part of the debt as a full discharge and satisfaction does not, standing alone, make an executed gift. It is believed that there is no good reason, however, for refusing to follow the New York court in Gray v. Barton [21] in holding that an entry of full satisfaction in the books of the creditor and a receipt in full delivered by him to the debtor are facts sufficient to make an executed gift and, therefore, to operate as a full discharge.

19.   Gray v. Barton, 55 N.Y. 68 (1873).

20.   Consol.Laws N.Y., c. 38, § 203; Mass.St.1898, c. 533, § 122.

21.   55 N.Y. 68 (1873).

The rule in Foakes v. Beer,[22] to the effect that part payment of a liquidated debt is not operative as a discharge of the whole, even though the creditor assents to receive it as such, was based upon a dictum of Lord Coke in Pinnel's Case.[23]　But that dictum was merely to the effect that £10 can not discharge a debt of £20. Lord Coke had, in other cases, held that the payment of £4, due on a judgment debt of £5, was a sufficient consideration for the creditor's promise to acknowledge full satisfaction of the judgment on the court records.[24]　Moreover, neither Pinnel's Case nor Foakes v. Beer held that the creditor can not make a gift discharge of a part of the debt by something less than a sealed release.

The facts in Foakes v. Beer show that the creditor had no actual intention of making a gift to her debtor.　Julia Beer promised that, if Foakes would pay the full amount of her judgment against him in stated instalments, she would accept such payments in full satisfaction.　This promise was broad enough in its terms to include her right to interest on the judgment as well as the principal of the debt; but it appears that at the time she made this promise she did not know that her judgment bore interest, or else did not have it in mind at all.　Her promise really amounted to no more than that she would give her debtor time within which to pay his debt and would not levy execution.　Most decisions indicate that such a promise is not binding; but since it appears that Mrs. Beer did not intend to make a gift of the interest, the decision is not an authority against the validity of a gift discharge.

Cases following the decision in Foakes v. Beer, holding that part payment of a liquidated debt is not a sufficient consideration for any promise by the creditor, and that it does not operate as a discharge of the entire debt, ought to be distinguished from cases in which the creditor clearly expresses his intention to execute a gift discharge of part or all of the debt due him.[25]　The former are cases in which the parties make an actual bargain. Even though the creditor is conscious, as Julia Beer was not, that the payment made is less than the sum due, he assents to the transaction and makes his promise of forbearance in order to get the offered consideration—the part payment.　The part payment is offered by the debtor on those terms.　In order to get what is so offered, the creditor gives the required assent and promise. This is a bargaining transaction, not a gift.　It may well be, as Lord Blackburn thought,[26] that the creditor gets a sufficient consideration of benefit to himself and detriment to the debtor; but

22.　L.R. 9 A.C. 605 (1884).

23.　5 Coke 117a (1602).

24.　See Reynolds v. Pinhowe, Cro. Eliz. (1595).

26.　See his opinion, nearly dissenting, in Foakes v. Beer, supra.

even if we adhere to the holdings to the contrary, we are not denying effect to a gift, for the creditor expresses no intention to make a gift. Even if the creditor signs a "receipt in full" in such a case, he does it in order to get the part payment offered to him as part of a bargain, not as an expression of an intent to execute a gift.[27]

The distinction here made between a bargaining transaction and a gift discharge has, in many cases, not been perceived by the court. Without doubt, in some of them in which there was held to be no effective discharge there was evidence of a gift intent; and the court consciously refused to make it effective. Indeed, there are cases in which there was no part payment made, and therefore no bargaining transaction, holding that a gift discharge was not effected. In such cases, however, the trouble is that the intent to execute the gift was not sufficiently expressed; it was thought not to be an "executed" gift.[28] Many of the cases that are cited as holding that a parol discharge is inoperative are cases in which the reported evidence is not sufficient to show that the creditor intended to make a gift discharge.[29]

### § 1248.    Discharge of Another's Duty by Gift of One's Own Performance

Suppose that A contracts to serve B for $90 a week. In spite of this contract, A still has power to render his service as a gift. All that A needs to do, in order to make such an executed gift, is to express his intention to B as he begins his work: This work is done as a gift to you, and not for the purpose of earning a reward. In such a case the doing of the work would discharge A's duty under the contract; in order not to have this effect, it would be necessary for the work to be understood to be work other than that contracted for. Further, B would be under no duty to pay the agreed wages; B's duty under the contract, as well as A's duty, would be discharged. He is under no duty to pay for the services received, for they were rendered as a gift; and he is under no duty to pay for other services, since no other services have been rendered.

Likewise, it is possible for A to render a part of the service as a gift. This is the effect if he says to B at the time of beginning a piece of work: I do this work as a gift to you. The same effect is produced if, on beginning work, A says to B: I will reduce my pay and will do the work for $80 a week. Thus, by executing a gift of a part of the work, he discharges B from his duty to pay a part of the wages. The employer's duty to pay at the former contract rate has been discharged by the employee's voluntary rendition of the full service with knowledge of the cut in pay.[30]

30.    U.S.—Hines v. Ward Baking Co., 155 F.2d 257 (C.C.A.7th, 1946).

In the same way B can make an executed gift of a sum of money, either by paying the full $90 a week for less work than that contracted to be done by A, or by paying a larger amount for the same work. All that is necessary is for B to say to A when he pays the money: I pay you this money for the work you have done. Of course either party can manifest his intention to execute a gift of the work or the money otherwise than by express words.

Observe, however, that, according to the majority rule still applied by the courts, neither the employer nor the employee can bind himself by a promise to make such a gift of either work or money. A promise of B to pay more money for the same work, or the same money for less work, would not be binding in the absence of other facts; and the same would be true of a promise by A to do the same work for less money. After such executory promises as these, either party could enforce the original contract exactly as it was made. The making of such a promise, however, is an expression of intention to make a gift; and if the other party, at the time the money is paid or the service rendered, is still reasonable in understanding that this intention continues, performance executes the gift. To prevent this result, the promisor should give notice of his change of intention.

In the case of a contract to sell goods at a specified price, the buyer's duty to pay will be effectively discharged by the seller's assent to forgo his right to all or part of the price at the time that he makes delivery of the goods to the buyer; the seller's duty to deliver the goods will be discharged by the buyer's assent to forgo his right to them at the time that he makes payment of the agreed price. There is a discharge by executed gift.[31]

In the case of a construction contract, where there is a bona fide dispute as to whether certain work is "extra," if the contractor goes ahead and performs this work knowing that the other party insists that there is to be no extra pay, his claim for such extra pay when made later will not be sustained.[32] Even if the work was in fact "extra" work, for which a charge could otherwise have been made, voluntary performance with knowledge of the other's refusal to pay extra, is the performance of a gift.[a]

---

31.    Restatement, Contracts, § 416, reads: "Where one party to a bilateral contract at the time when he renders performance manifests to the other party assent to forgo all or part of the performance promised as an agreed exchange by the other party, the latter's duty is to that extent discharged."

32.    **U.S.**—United Dredging Co. v. United States, 81 F.2d 118 (C.C.A. 6th, 1936), extra work done with knowledge that the owner believed it to be included in the contract price.

a.    § 1249, omitted here, discusses Gratuitous Reduction of Rent by a Landlord.

### § 1250.  Gift Discharge by Surrender or Cancellation of a Document Evidencing the Right [38]

The contract right of a creditor or obligee may be evidenced by various kinds of written instruments, more or less formal in character. Some of these, if properly executed and delivered, are given special kinds of legal operation that others do not have. Even in these cases, however, such legal operation is not established without evidence, extrinsic to the instrument itself, that it was in fact executed and delivered. Sealed bonds, insurance policies, and other sealed contracts are illustrations. So also are negotiable bills and notes. It has long been held that a gift discharge of the rights evidenced by such formal instruments can be made by the surrender of possession of the instrument with intent to discharge [39] or by its cancellation or destruction with like intent.[40]

In the chapter on Assignment, we have already dealt with the gift of contract rights to an assignee. There can be an assignment by executed gift; and such a gift, whether causa mortis or inter vivos, can be executed by the delivery of various kinds of instruments evidencing the right that is assigned. In such cases, the right is not destroyed or discharged; it is assigned and transferred to the assignee, who can thereafter enforce it against the obligor. It seems, however, that any method by which a gift assignment can be executed should be equally operative when used for the purpose of a gift discharge. If the delivery of a certain kind of instrument to an assignee would be an operative gift assignment, its delivery to the obligor with intent to discharge should be operative as a gift discharge.

The holder of a sealed bond or insurance policy can make a gift assignment of his rights by delivery of the formal document with intent to execute the gift. In like manner, he can make a gift discharge of his rights by surrender of the instrument, or by cancelling or destroying it, with intent to make such a discharge.[41] A discharge in this manner should be held to be effective, even in a state that has abolished seals.

Besides negotiable instruments and formal contracts under seal, a contract right may be evidenced by less formal papers. There are savings bank books, certificates of deposit, receipts, and acknowledgments of indebtedness such as an I. O. U. With respect to all of these, it has been held that a gift assignment to a third party can be made by delivery of the paper with a proper

38. Observe that such terms as "discharge," "termination," and "cancellation" are commonly used with variable meanings, as will appear in other sections. Here, the term "cancellation" is used to mean an act that alters the physical appearance of a document with intent to destroy its legal effect.

donative expression. In jurisdictions so holding, it is reasonable to suppose that the surrender of the paper to the obligor with a proper donative expression would be held to effect a gift discharge. There are some such decisions.[42]

## § 1251. Discharge or Suspension by Contract Not to Sue

A contract by a creditor never to bring action against his debtor for the enforcement of the debt is legally operative as a discharge of the debtor's duty.[43] This is true, whether the contract is with the debtor himself or is with a third person for his benefit. Such a contract as this is not in terms a release. Being in the form of a promise by the creditor, it might seem to be intended to create a duty in him, rather than to discharge an existing duty in another person. To refuse to give it effect as a discharge, however, would result in an unnecessary and highly undesirable circuity of action. If the creditor should sue the debtor for the enforcement of his original claim, the debtor could at once maintain a counteraction for damages for the breach of the creditor's promise never to sue. The damages to which the debtor would be entitled in this counter-action would be exactly the amount of the creditor's recovery in his action against the debtor. In spite of its promissory form, such a contract by the creditor clearly indicates an intention to discharge the obligor, in any case not involving a joint obligor; and the parties should be held to have consummated a discharge because they intended it to be one. In the case of joint obligors, the device of a contract not to sue was adopted in order to escape the technical rule, applicable to joint contracts, that the discharge of one joint obligor necessarily discharges all the others. Not wishing to give effect to their own unreasonable rule, the common law courts held that a release of one joint obligor, expressly reserving all rights against the other joint obligors, would be interpreted as a mere contract not to sue the one instead of a release.[44] Such a contract never to sue one of the obligors really evidences an intent not to discharge the others rather than an intent that the one shall remain bound.

---

42. In the following cases, the evidential document was a receipt for money due, stating the amount and the terms on which it was to be repaid:

N.Y.—Champney v. Blanchard, 39 N. Y. 111 (1868), "Received from J. H. $2,803.50, also $500 from A. S. F., both of which sums are on account of and belonging to Mrs. Mary Champney and are to be disposed of in any manner she may direct as paid to her individually, together with whatever interest I may obtain for their use. F. Blanchard".

Eng.—Moore v. Darton, 4 De G. & Sm. 517 (1851), "Received October 22, 1843, of Miss Darton £500, to bear interest at 4% per annum, but not to be withdrawn at less than six months notice. William Moore."

If a creditor makes a valid contract by which he undertakes not to bring action against his debtor for a limited time, the English courts held at an early period that the contract was not operative as a defense to the debtor even during the specified period.[45]  One reason for this is that it was thought that the existence of a right could not be temporarily suspended without necessarily discharging it forever, and that sustaining a "plea in bar" caused that action to be forever barred.  If there was ever a sound basis for such a thought it has been completely forgotten.  It was always possible for the court to dismiss a case as premature without prejudice to a new action after expiration of the agreed period of extension.  Nevertheless, the English decisions were followed by most of the American courts for many years.  A "doctrine" that once gets into printed words is tough to kill.

A covenant never to bring an action for enforcement could be pleaded in bar as a "release" in order "to avoid circuity of action", the action wrongfully brought being exactly counterbalanced by the action for damages that would lie for bringing it.  It was rightly seen that this argument did not apply to a contract not to bring suit for a limited time only.  The damages for breach of the latter promise would not equal the amount of the recovery in the action wrongfully brought on the original claim.  This, too, was believed to support the English decisions.

The insufficiency of the above reasoning and the injustice of the result must often have been suspected; but suspicion alone is not sufficient to break down a "doctrine".  An English Vice Chancellor had in one case extracted the sting from the doctrine by granting an injunction specifically enforcing the contract for a temporary suspension and preventing the enforcement of a judgment on the original claim;[46] but apparently few were aware of his action.  Although most of the American judges had the powers of a Chancellor, the procedure for getting equitable relief was a distinct procedure and few lawyers were accomplished chancery practitioners.  Moreover, the problem was practically identical with the problem that is involved in the contract known

46.  The leading English case entering judgment on the original claim in an action brought in breach of the new contract for a suspension is Ford v. Beech, 11 Q.B. 852 (1848).  Even then the defendant had a suit pending in Chancery asking an injunction.

In Beech v. Ford, 7 Hare 208 (1848), the Chancellor, after waiting to see what judgment the Court of Exchequer Chamber should render in the case of Ford v. Beech, supra, entered a decree specifically enforcing Ford's contract to suspend suit against William Beech.  After the Judicature Act of 1873, creating a unified system of courts, the effect of the Chancery rule is that the new agreement can be used as a defense in an action on the original debt.  The same is true under the American Codes of Procedure, including the new Federal Rules.

as an "accord executory". Here, too, there was a "doctrine". "Upon an accord no remedy lies." Blinded by the "doctrine", judges, lawyers, and professors were confused in their analysis and wrong in their results. It is only recently that the law has been "restated" and an opposing "doctrine" started on its way: an action lies for breach of an "accord"; and the "accord executory" suspends the right of action on the original claim as long as the obligor has committed no breach of the new contract.[47]

Those who constructed the new "Restatement" were not new discoverers, although they put the new doctrine into printed words and supported it by the prestige of a Law Institute. In actions "at law" as well as in suits for specific enforcement in equity, several courts had knocked the support from under the old doctrine. In 1826, the Maryland court refused to apply the rule that a covenant not to sue for a limited time would not operate as a temporary defense, holding in an action of assumpsit on a promissory note that a contract made by the holder and an endorser that suit on the note should not be brought for three years was a good defense for three years.[48]

In 1852, the Michigan court repudiated the old doctrine root and branch, explaining its origin and exploding its supposed reasons.[49] A surprised bar perhaps did not believe its eyes; a new case was taken to the court within three years. A convinced and able court boldly stood its ground in a second carefully prepared opinion, holding that the contract not to sue, whether for a limited time or forever, was a modification of the old contract, the plaintiff's legal rights now being determined by the new agreement and such terms of the old one as were not replaced.[50] The reason given is the correct one that such a result accords with the intention of the parties and reaches a just result by the shortest path. The court was aware that it was going against the "weight of authority;" it cites seventeen cases that it refused to follow. These two Michigan decisions did not get the publicity and influence that they deserved. They are now supported, however, by the American Law Institute and by the modern decisions enforcing an accord executory as a temporary suspension.[51]

48.   Md.—Clopper v. Union Bank, 7 Har. & J. 92 (1826).

In Baurer v. Devenis, 121 A. 566, 99 Conn. 203 (1923), the plaintiff sued to foreclose a mortgage. The defense was that the plaintiff was assignee of the note and mortgage and had promised the assignor (for a consideration) not to sue for one year. This was demurred to by the plaintiff on the ground that the defendant was not the promisee, and the demurrer was overruled.

It was assumed without discussion that if a beneficiary can enforce a promise not to sue him, the promise would operate as a defense also. This is on all fours with Clopper v. Union Bank, supra, decided nearly a century earlier. See § 780, Chapter 41, Third Party Beneficiaries.

49.   Mich.—Robinson v. Godfrey, 2 Mich. 408 (1852).

50.   Mich.—Morgan v. Butterfield, 3 Mich. 615 (1855).

## CHAPTER 68

## DISCHARGE BY NONPERFORMANCE OF CONDITION— BREACH — FAILURE OF CONSIDERATION — PRE- VENTION — POWER RESERVED — CONDITION SUB- SEQUENT

## § 1252. Discharge of Duty by Nonperformance of a Condition

When a contractual duty is subject to a condition precedent, whether that condition is express, implied, or constructive, there is no duty of immediate performance and there can be no breach of that contractual duty by mere nonperformance, unless the con- dition precedent is either performed or excused. If such a condi- tion precedent is neither performed nor excused within the time that is required, such failure now makes it impossible for a breach of contract to occur. Nonperformance of the primary contractual duty can now never operate as a breach of it; and no remedy for enforcement will ever be available. Therefore, the contractual duty must be regarded as discharged.[1]

---

1. Restatement, Contracts, § 395: "A contractual duty is discharged by the unexcused failure of a condi- tion to occur within the time neces- sary to create a right to the im- mediate performance of the duty." Restatement, Contracts, § 274: "(1) In promises for an agreed exchange, any material failure of perform- ance by one party not justified by conduct of the other discharges the latter's duty to give the agreed ex- change even though his promise is not in terms conditional. An im- material failure does not operate as such a discharge.

In applying this rule, care must be taken to determine that the time for performing the condition has in fact expired. The condition may be an express one; and its performance by a fixed date may be expressly made of the essence. Even if performance by a fixed date is not made of the essence of the contract in express terms, there must almost always come a time after which performance would be too late and the promisor would be discharged.[2]

Frequently, the condition precedent consists of the performance, in part or in full, of the agreed exchange by the other party. That party's failure to render such performance ordinarily constitutes a breach of contract on his part; and the discharge of the one party may be said to be a discharge by the breach of the other. But even though the other party has not promised to render the agreed exchange, and his failure to perform is no breach whatever, nevertheless if his performance is a condition precedent of the first party's duty, that duty is discharged as soon as the condition cannot be performed. In such case, the discharge is a discharge by nonperformance of a condition precedent, not a discharge by breach of the other's contractual duty.

If A has contracted to deliver goods to B on a specified day, for a price thereafter to be paid, time being made expressly of the essence, A's performance by that day is a condition precedent

---

"(2) The rule of Subsection (1) is applicable though the failure of performance is not a violation of legal duty."

This statement forces the word "material" to bear weight that it can not bear successfully without much explanation. That explanation is attempted in Restatement, §§ 275, 276, stating a number of important factors upon which the materiality of a failure of performance (including delay) depends.

If performance by one party of a condition of the other party's duty is rendered impossible by the enactment of a statute, the other party's duty is discharged. American Merc. Exch. v. Blunt, 66 A. 212, 102 Me. 128 (1906).

See the discussion of Ziehen v. Smith, 42 N.E. 1080, 148 N.Y. 558 (1896), at § 1258, Effect of Failure to Tender Either of Two Concurrent Performances.

contract for the sale of land, made on Nov. 17, 1931, provided for payment on delivery of abstract and deed, but that payment could not be made after Dec. 1, 1932. Here, the promises were concurrently conditional, payment within the stated time being expressly made essential. Tender of a deed within that time by the seller was not so made; and yet he could not put the buyer in default without making tender, one that the law would surely require to be made within a "reasonable time." Neither party made tender until 1940, when the buyer made tender and demand. Of course, it was too late. The seller's duty was discharged long before 1940. Neither party was in default, although both were discharged. By Louisiana usage the buyer's failure to make tender on time was described as a "passive breach."

2.   In Goudeau v. Daigle, 124 F.2d 656 (C.C.A.5th, 1942), a bilateral

See also Dewenter v. Mott, 27 So.2d 444 (La.App.1946).

to B's duty to pay, and failure of such performance is a total discharge of B. The latter is discharged, not merely because A has committed a breach of duty but because the performance that has failed was a condition of the continued existence of B's primary contractual duty and was a condition precedent to the very birth of his immediate duty to make payment of the price.

The condition precedent may consist merely of some act of co-operation by the other party. If his co-operation within a specified time is of the essence of the contract, his unexcused failure to co-operate within that time operates as a discharge. Even if no time is specified, a time will eventually come beyond which it is unreasonable to expect or require a contractor to be ready to perform his part. Sometimes the contract provides that he can aid his case by giving a notice fixing a definite time limit. In the absence of such a provision, the court must determine what is the time limit of his discharge, beyond which he is justified in refusing to perform. If without such a contract provision a party attempts to establish a time limit by giving a notice, the notice will have no such effect unless the court finds that the time stated is not less than a reasonable time.

In the case of an ordinary money debt, unilateral in character, the co-operation of the creditor or his agent is to some extent necessary to effectuate a payment. A mere tender of the money, refused by the creditor, is not payment. The casting of a sum of money on a table before the creditor may indeed be payment, if the creditor remains wholly silent and inactive;[3] but possession and ownership can scarcely be forced upon him in the teeth of his express refusal. In the case of such money debts, no time limit for the necessary co-operation by the creditor has ever been fixed by the courts. Refusal to accept a tender, or to receive payment if it should be tendered, prevents the debtor's non-payment from operating as a breach of contract, but it does not operate as a discharge. It seems that in this case there is never a discharge by the creditor's nonperformance of the condition.

Such is not the case, however, if the debtor's unilateral contract requires the performance of service or the delivery of goods within a specified and limited time. If the creditor's co-operation by receiving the service or the goods within that time is a condition of the debtor's duty, failure of such co-operation operates as a discharge. The problem is merely to determine what is the time limit. The same may be said of the place fixed for the rendition of performance. Thus, if one who is bound to deliver

---

3. See Flower's Case, reported in Noy, 67, about the year 1600, where the debtor was held to have paid his debt by casting a bag of money on the table before his creditor, even though the creditor at once returned it to the debtor *as a gift.*

goods to another on May 1 at the corner of Broadway and 42d Street is ready and willing to make such delivery, and that other is never at that corner on May 1, the duty to deliver is discharged by the nonperformance of a condition.

A contractor's duty may be expressly conditional upon some fact or event that does not constitute any part of the agreed exchange or any part of the other party's promised performance. If the fact or event does not and can not exist or occur, the contractor's duty to render the performance promised by him can never accrue and the conditional obligation of the contractor is discharged.[4]

## § 1253.   Discharge or Suspension of Duty by the Other Party's Breach of Contract

It is not always that a breach of contractual duty by one party to a bilateral contract discharges the duty of performance on the part of the other. As the term "breach" is used, a contractor who has committed a breach is guilty of a wrong for which some remedy is available, the remedy varying with the case.[5] Being guilty of a wrong does not make him an outlaw or deprive him of all rights, even the rights that were created by the very contract that he breaks. This is true, in spite of many a contrary dictum, even when his breach is "wilful." [6] Indeed, it seems best to say that breach by one party never discharges the other party, regarding breach merely as a wrong without regard to the extent and quality of its ill effects. When those "effects" are so material to the interests of the other party that a mere judicial remedy is not sufficient to satisfy the requirements of justice as felt by the community, the legal duty of that other party is either suspended or discharged.

The fact that it is not breach as a mere wrong that discharges the other party is indicated by the fact that the very same failure of performance may operate as a discharge, whether it is a wrongful failure or not. The failure of performance may not be wrongful because of some intervening factor that we describe as "impossibility"; there is no breach, and no judicial remedy may be available. Nevertheless, justice will not require the other party to pay something for nothing. There is substantial failure of the agreed equivalent, generally called "failure of consideration;" it is this that justifies withholding the promised return performance. It may be true that when this "failure of consideration" is wrongful, when it is a "breach", the court is more likely to make it operate as a discharge; but it must be remembered that in such a case the law gives a compensatory judicial remedy that is not available when the failure is not wrongful. Should one having such a compensatory remedy be more readily discharged than one who has none? If yes, then the discharge operates as an added judicial "penalty", one that seems inconsistent with prevailing ideas of justice.[7] Breach or no breach, it is better to say that the fact operating as a discharge is substantial failure of the agreed equivalent.

Mere delay in rendering a promised performance may be so material as to justify suspension of work by the other party without being sufficiently material to justify his total abandonment of the contract. In most cases performance on the exact time is not "of the essence," and yet an unexcused failure to perform exactly on time is a breach, a minor breach. Such a minor breach will in some cases suspend the other party's duty to proceed with immediate performance, even though it is far from discharging him from all contractual duty. A building contractor may be justified in stopping work when a "progress payment" is delayed, without being justified in abandoning the contract. When a buyer of goods by instalments fails to pay as agreed for one instalment, the seller may be justified in holding back the next instalment without being privileged to repudiate further obligation. The failure to pay on time is a breach; but it is not a "total" breach. The time element being of minor importance, the failure of consideration is slight, not substantial; it is material enough to justify suspension but not to justify discharge.[8]

**8.** Restatement, Contracts, § 397: "A breach or non-performance by one party to a bilateral contract, so material as to justify a refusal of the other party to perform a contractual duty, discharges that duty."

At first sight, this appears to be a mere truism, merely saying that a promisor's duty is discharged if he doesn't have to perform. But reference back to §§ 274–279 is made for the tests as to when a non-performance by one party is "so material" as to operate as a discharge. In particular, § 276 gives rules for determining whether a breach by delay in performance is so material as to discharge the other party.

Restatement, Contracts, § 276: "In determining the materiality of delay in performance, the following rules are applicable:

"(a) Unless the nature of a contract is such as to make performance on the exact day agreed upon of vital importance, or the contract in terms provides that it shall be so, failure by a promisor to perform his promise on the day stated in the promise does not discharge the duty of the other party.

"(b) In mercantile contracts performance at the time agreed upon is important, and if the delay of one party is considerable having reference to the nature of the transaction and the seriousness of the consequences, and is not justified by the conduct of the other party, the duty of the latter is discharged.

"(c) If delay of one party in rendering a promised performance occurs before any part of his promise [promised performance] has been rendered, less delay discharges the duty of the other party than where there has been part performance of that promise.

"(d) In contracts for the sale or purchase of land delay of one party must be greater in order to discharge the duty of the other than in mercantile contracts.

"(e) In a suit for specific performance of a contract for the sale or pur-

At what time it will become substantial, as the delay continues, depends on the variant circumstances and the express words of the contract.

If one party to a bilateral contract commits a partial breach of his duty, one that is not so material as to discharge the other party's duty of performance, the latter's only remedy is damages for the partial breach. His own subsequent nonperformance of his promise will, in turn, be a breach of the contract by him, for which the first party will, in his turn, have an appropriate remedy. The first party will certainly have a right to damages for this breach, whether it is regarded as partial or as total. If it is a total breach and a substantial failure of the agreed exchange, he will be privileged to render no further performance on his own part and can maintain action for full damages for the defendant's total breach. In such an action he will be subject to the defendant's counterclaim for the partial breach first committed by him.[9]

chase of land, considerable delay in tendering performance does not preclude enforcement of the contract where the delay can be compensated for by interest on the purchase money or otherwise, unless

(i) the contract expressly states that performance at or within a given time is essential, or

(ii) the nature of the contract, in view of the accompanying circumstances, is such that enforcement will work injustice".

In several of the illustrations given under this section it is made clear that non-payment of an instalment on time may justify the other party in refusing to proceed with performance without justifying his refusal to perform forever. The delay in payment, unaccompanied by other factors, is a minor breach for which an action will lie. His own duty to proceed with immediate performance is conditional on the actual payment, and he is privileged to suspend performance. He is not bound to give added credit, with its added risk of an increased bad debt; but for the avoidance of this risk a complete discharge is not necessary.

See Chapter 53, for a discussion of Partial and Total Breaches; and Chapter 37, Condition of Performance on Time.

In City of Farrell v. H. Platt Co., 15 A.2d 718, 142 Pa.Super. 242 (1940) the court made use of the Restatement sections.

The following are illustrative cases holding that one party was not discharged by the other's partial breach:

U.S.—Princess Amusement Co. v. Wells, 271 F. 226 (C.C.A.6th, 1921).

Ala.—Worthington & Co. v. Gwin, 24 So. 739, 119 Ala. 44 (1898).

Conn.—Frederick Raff Co. v. Murphy, 147 A. 709, 110 Conn. 234 (1929); M. J. Daly & Sons v. New Haven Hotel Co., 99 A. 853, 91 Conn. 280 (1917); Bridgeport v. Aetna Indemnity Co., 99 A. 566, 91 Conn. 197 (1916).

Ind.—Pickens v. Bozell, 11 Ind. 276 (1858).

N.J.—Kinney v. Fed. Laundry Co., 68 A. 111, 75 N.J.L. 497 (1909).

Vt.—Tichnor Bros. v. Evans, 102 A. 1031, 92 Vt. 278 (1917).

Eng.—Boone v. Eyre, 1 H.B.L. 273 (1777).

Where a contract has been divided by the parties into pairs of apportioned equivalents, a party who has rendered a part performance may be able to get judgment for the agreed price of that part, even though he has repudiated his duty to render the remaining part performances.[10] For his repudiation he is, of course, bound to pay compensatory damages. Whether the contract has in fact thus been divided is a matter of reasonable interpretation depending on the terms of agreement and the circumstances of the case. It is not so divided if the failure as to a part substantially affects the value of the remaining parts to the other party.

The material breach of contract by one party involving such a failure of consideration that it discharges the other may take any of the forms in which a breach can occur. It may be an actual nonperformance at the time when performance is due by the contract; or it may be a repudiation of the contractual duty, either anticipatory or otherwise; or it may be a prevention by one party of the performance of a condition precedent to the right of the other.[11]

### § 1254.  Discharge of One Party by the Other's "Wilful" Breach

There is an often repeated doctrine to the effect that any wilful breach by one contractor discharges the other from further duty, without regard to the extent or materiality of the performance that is wilfully refused or withheld. The harshness with which such a rule as this would often operate, grossly penalizing the one party for a comparatively slight harm to the other, has generally been avoided, either by making no reference to the doctrine at all or by strained interpretations of the word "wilful." It is generally true that, in cases where the doctrine is expressly relied on, the breach is not only wilful but is also material in character and extent;[12] frequently the breach that the court has in mind is a wilful and total abandonment.

But if the doctrine is strictly and honestly applied, in a case where one party wilfully commits a slight and immaterial breach, then there is a discharge by wilful breach, even though the non-performance is one that would not in itself have been of the essence and there is no discharge by failure of consideration or by nonperformance of a condition. This is not justice.

The law should be stated as follows: 1. If a promisor's duty is subject to a condition precedent (either express or constructive) and that condition has not been performed or its perform-

12. A case with a very interesting history is McNeal-Edwards Co. v. Frank L. Young Co., 35 F.2d 829 (C.A.1st 1929); 42 F.2d 362 (reversed 51 S.Ct. 538, 283 U.S. 398, 75 L.Ed. 1140); 51 F.2d 699 (1931).

ance excused, the promisor's nonperformance is not a breach; if that condition can not now be performed, the promisor is discharged from contractual duty.[15] This is true whether the nonperformance of the condition is wilful or is not wilful. 2. If in a bilateral contract one party commits a small breach, by failing (wilfully or otherwise) to render a performance that was not expressly made a condition of the other party's duty and did not constitute a substantial part of the agreed equivalent for which the other party bargained, such breach does not justify the other party in refusing to perform or discharge him from contractual duty—much less does it discharge him from his duty to pay damages for a breach of contract that he has already committed. 3. If after one party to a bilateral contract has committed a breach that does not itself justify nonperformance by the other, a subsequent breach by that other may or may not be so substantial as to justify refusal by the first party to proceed further; in any case it gives to the first party a counterclaim for damages, one that may or may not be large enough to counterbalance his duty to make compensation for his own previous breach.[16]

### § 1255.   Discharge by Failure of Consideration Either Existing or Prospective

In the case of a promise that is not entirely independent, the promisor may be discharged by his failure to receive the agreed equivalent for which his promised performance was to be exchanged. This is true, even though the other party has not promised in return to perform this agreed equivalent. The promisor's duty to render his performance may be either expressly or impliedly conditional upon the giving of something recognized by the parties as the agreed equivalent of that which he himself promises to do, even though there is no promise by anybody in return. In such a case, if the promisor has not received and is not going to receive the agreed equivalent of his own performance, he will not be required to perform at all. There is a failure of consideration, even though there is no breach of contract. In most cases, doubtless, when the parties have agreed upon an equivalent to be exchanged for a promised performance, the contract is put into a bilateral form, with a return promise to render the agreed equivalent. In such a case failure of consideration may also be a breach of contract; and the discharge could be called a discharge by breach, as well as a discharge by failure of consideration. The failure to render a promised performance may not be a breach of contract for the reason that performance has become impossible without fault; but it is nonetheless a failure of consideration discharging the other party from his duty to make the agreed return and giving him a right to the restitution of payments already made or other benefits already conferred.[17]

1017

A promisor may be discharged by a prospective failure of consideration, even though the time has not yet arrived for the giving of this consideration.  If the party who is to give it definitely expresses to the promisor his intention not to perform the agreed equivalent, the promisor will be discharged from his duty, unless the other party retracts his statement of intention before any substantial change of position on the part of the promisor in reliance upon his statement.  It may well be that the same result would be reached if, instead of manifesting an intention not to render the agreed equivalent, the other party merely gets into such a position, financial or otherwise, that a reasonable man in the promisor's place would be justified in believing that the equivalent is not going to be rendered.  In such a case as this, it would seem that he would be justified in changing his position, because of the anticipated failure of consideration, and that such a change of position by him would operate to discharge his duty altogether.[18]

### § 1257.  Nonperformance of a Condition Compared with "Failure of Consideration"

In general, a bilateral contract is an agreement for the exchange of mutual promises and also for the exchange of the performances that are promised.  Each promise is the "consideration" for the other promise in the sense that it is its agreed exchange;  and each performance can in the same sense be regarded as the "consideration" for the return performance.  At first, neither performance has yet been rendered;  and yet the contract is valid and binding.  If the agreement is for a concurrent exchange of performances, the duty of each of the parties is conditional on tender of the performance by the other;  and if the performances are not to be concurrent, the rendition of the earlier one may be a condition of the duty to render the later one.

Thus, if during April an owner promises to sell a parcel of land for $1,000, and the buyer promises to pay that price, conveyance and payment to be made on May 1, the enforceable duty of each is conditional on tender of performance by the other.  Yet nonperformance by either party during April would not be a breach of his duty;  nor would such nonperformance be called "failure of consideration."  The point is that the nonperformance of the agreed exchange by one party may prevent the other party's duty of rendering his performance from arising without being operative · as a discharge of the other party from the duty to render it.  The continuance of the nonperformance, however, will eventually operate as such a discharge;  and so also will the prospective certainty of its future continuance.  It is at the point of discharge that the nonperformance by one party is described as "failure of consideration," actual or prospective.  Just when that point is reached, in various sorts of cases, will vary with the circumstances, involving a question of fact that may be difficult to answer. All that we can lay down as a matter of law is that there is a discharge as soon as the delay has made what is described as "substantial performance" impossible. If the purpose for which a party entered into the contract, a purpose that the other party had reason to know, can no longer be attained, a tender of performance is too late and there is a discharge.

### § 1258.  Effect of Failure to Tender Either of Two Concurrent Performances

When two performances, agreed equivalents, are to be exchanged simultaneously, a tender of his performance by either one of the parties is a condition precedent to the duty of performance by the other. This is a case of so-called concurrent conditions. If time is of the essence in a case of this kind, the failure of both parties to make tender within the time limit operates as a discharge of the contract. Neither one can thereafter put the other in default. But the fact that a specific time for mutual performances is agreed upon does not necessarily make that time "of the essence." If the stated time is not of the essence, then each party has a "reasonable time" within which he can tender his performance and enforce the contract.

This "reasonable time" may be long or short, according to circumstances; but whatever it is, tender of performance within this reasonable time is of the essence. If both parties alike fail to make tender within this time, the contract obligation is discharged.[22] In some such cases, it has seemed to be the court's idea that there is no discharge until one of the parties has notified the other to that effect; but it is believed that this is incorrect.[23]

It is true that the failure of either party to make a tender and demand may tend to show that a reasonable time has not yet expired; but it is not conclusive on that point. We must not fail to realize that the absence of tender by one party does not put him in default; it is no breach of duty for which he deserves a penalty. The other party is in exactly the same position. Furthermore, the fact that one party gives notice to the other that the contract is discharged can not be conclusive that such is the case. If it is given before the "reasonable time" has expired it is ineffective;[24] and if given after that time has expired, it is unnecessary.

Suppose a bilateral contract for the sale of land, the buyer making a down payment of $1000, balance payable on delivery of deed on a specified later date. In this case, the conveyance and the final payment are concurrent conditions. As long as neither party makes a tender, of the deed or of the money, neither party is in default. If tender at the exact time is of the essence, and there is no waiver or estoppel, the contract obligation is discharged. If performance on time is not of the essence—as generally it is not in land sales—it is not easy to say how soon the parties will be discharged by mutual failure to tender performance. Very likely the time will be much longer, after payments have been made or possession given, than when there has been no part performance. But when the end has come, the purchaser should have a right to his money back and the vendor should be able to regain possession and enforce a claim for the value of use and occupation.[27] A tender of performance would be useful before bringing any suit; but this involves the risk that the other party will also then perform. If he does not perform when tender is made, either he is in default and is liable in damages, or the contract was previously ended by mutual nonperformance and restitution will be enforced for that reason.

## § 1259.  Prospective Failure of Consideration

When two parties have made a bilateral contract for an exchange of equivalent performances to be rendered simultaneously, the two promises are said to be concurrently conditional. The duty of each is conditional upon tender of performance by the other. If supervening events make it impossible for one of the parties to render substantial performance of his promise, two effects are at once produced: the other party is discharged from duty to render the return performance; and his right of action, if he has one, is no longer conditional upon his tendering this return performance.[28] The condition of making such tender is eliminated by inability of the defendant to perform the agreed equivalent.

If the two promised performances are to be performed at different times, the duty to render the later of the two performances is conditional upon the actual performance of the first. Thus, if A promises to pay B $100 for a week's service, the completion of the service is ordinarily a condition precedent to A's duty to pay. In such cases, it is sometimes said that A's duty is conditional and dependent, and that B's duty is unconditional and independent. This statement as to B's duty is not entirely correct. It is true that the contract requires B's performance first; and his duty to perform is not conditional upon performance or tender of performance by A. Nevertheless, it is not just to require B to perform the service if he can show that he is not going to be paid. B's duty is conditional upon the continuing ability of A to pay when the time comes; it is not wholly independent. A's inability to perform his part is a prospective failure of consideration; and as in the case of concurrent performances there are at

27. Compare Ziehen v. Smith, 42 N. E. 1080, 148 N.Y. 558 (1896), a case that is discussed and criticised in the general treatise at this point.

once two effects: B is discharged from duty to perform the service; and B's right of action against A is no longer conditional upon his either tendering or performing that service.[29]  Likewise, if substantial performance by one who has promised to do construction work becomes impossible, the other party is no longer bound to continue making instalment payments and can get judgment for restitution of instalments already paid.[30]

## § 1260. Proof of Prospective Failure of Performance

A promisor is not justified in failing to render his promised performance by the mere fact that he reasonably believes that there will be a failure of consideration in the future.[35]  A prospective failure is more difficult to prove than is an already existing failure.  It is determined by process of prediction, not by history.  Proof of the past is often difficult enough; foresight of the future, however vital it may be to our lives and fortunes, may be almost impossible.  Sometimes it is said that prospective inability is no defense unless it is established beyond a reasonable doubt.[36]  This introduces a concept that has played its part in our criminal law; it is not necessary to use it here.  It seems enough to say that the court must be thoroughly convinced that the agreed equivalent will not be rendered.  The plaintiff certainly should be given ample opportunity to show that present appearances are not final or conclusive, and even to give security in some reasonable form that he will perform when the time comes.[37]  It would be entirely proper for the court to postpone trial of the issues so that the uncertainties of prediction are reduced and that history may be substituted.

## § 1261. Insolvency is Not Impossibility

Proof of insolvency is not enough to establish the fact of prospective inability to perform.  This is true especially in cases where the promised performance is something other than the payment of money.[41]  The insolvency of one who has promised to render a personal service does not in itself disable him from rendering the service.  The same is true where the promise is to transfer land or to deliver specific existing goods; but in such cases one must consider the possibility that a transfer might be set aside at the suit of other creditors as an illegal preference.  The insolvency of a building contractor, with added proof of

35. **Conn.**—Wonalancet Co. v. Banfield, 165 A. 785, 116 Conn. 582 (1933).

**Mich.**—F. W. Kavanaugh Mfg. Co. v. Rosen, 92 N.W. 788, 132 Mich. 44 (1902), that the seller has received an unfavorable report from a financial agency does not justify withholding delivery.

**N.J.**—Keppelon v. Ritter Flooring Corp., 116 A. 491, 97 N.J.L. 200 (1922), "that the credit of a party . . . has become impaired, so that he is no longer a good credit risk."

his inability to get labor and materials on credit, may be a sufficient showing of prospective failure of performance.[42]

The insolvency of one who has promised to pay money is a relevant factor in proving prospective inability; but it is not a conclusive factor. If the contract is an advantageous one to the insolvent promisor, it is an asset upon which he may be able to realize by borrowing or by assignment. Lenders of money may be willing to advance the necessary money on the faith of an assignment of the insolvent party's contract right, thus making possible the promised payment when it is due. Therefore, the insolvency of one party does not in itself discharge the other party from further duty or eliminate the condition of the other party's performance in establishing his right of action.[43] Insolvency may create a seller's lien or a right of stoppage in transit;[44] but this is not discharge. If the insolvent buyer does not tender payment in cash, the seller may dispose of the goods in the market and enforce his claim for damages.[45]

### § 1264.  Prevention by Promisee as a Defense to the Promisor

There are many cases in which a defendant who is being sued for breach of his promise sets up in defense the fact that he was unjustly prevented from performing by the plaintiff. Prevention by the plaintiff may take many forms. Whatever its form, if the plaintiff's action is unjust and is such that it made performance by the defendant impossible or substantially more difficult or expensive, it is a good defense against the action.[57] The prevention terminated the defendant's legal duty.

It is clear that such preventive action by the promisee would in nearly all cases be unjust. In the case of a construction contract, if the owner prevents completion on time and according to specifications by failing to excavate as agreed, or by insisting on substantial changes in the work, or by refusing to supply promised materials, or by holding the contractor off with a shot gun,[58] his action will certainly prevent the contractor's failure to complete as agreed from being a breach of contract.[59] But there are cases in which the contrary would be true. Thus, suppose that the government is in the market for the immediate supply of millions of feet of lumber for army cantonments. First, a contract is made wherein A promises to supply a million feet at once. As A had reason to expect, the government proceeds to contract with B and C and many other lumber dealers for the supply of many millions more feet. This greatly increases the difficulty and the cost of performance by A; yet he would not be discharged thereby, since he had reason to expect such action by his promisee and it was not unjust.[60]

Prevention may result in a discharge even though it is in itself not at all unjust. If the promisee tells the promisor that he no longer desires performance and thereby leads the promisor to change his position materially, the latter is discharged. If one who has the "first right to buy" property—the right that the owner shall not sell to others without first making an offer to the promisee—tells the owner that he is no longer interested in buying and thereby causes the owner to contract to sell to another party, the owner's duty to submit an offer is terminated.[61] The prevention is not unjust; but it has caused performance to be more difficult and expensive, so that enforcement would be very unjust indeed.

The acts of prevention by one party may go no further than to cause or induce the other party not to render his performance within the time allotted therefor in the contract. Prevention such as this may not increase the cost or difficulty of performance; indeed, it may be desired and even requested by the other party. In such a case, the other party is not discharged from his contractual duty as a whole. But his failure to perform within the required time is not a breach for which damages must be paid; and the delay so caused does not justify the other party in refusing to render his own performance or enable him to enforce a penalty or forfeiture that would otherwise have been enforceable.[62] The act of prevention need be nothing more than an assent to the delay.

It is regarded as prevention of performance if the promisee acts in such a way as to increase materially the cost or difficulty of that performance.[63] The application of this rule involves questions of degree, as is so often the case with rules of law. Also, some acts that increase difficulty or expense may have been contemplated by the parties as within the privileges of the promisee.

If a buyer knows that the seller is negotiating with a third person for a supply of the goods required by the contract, and with intent to prevent performance induces the third person not to deal with the seller, these facts constitute a good defense against the buyer in a suit for nondelivery.[64]

### § 1266.  Termination of Contract by Exercise of a Power Reserved

When a contract is entered into, a power of termination may be expressly reserved to either party or to each of them. A bilateral contract of employment for a year may be made terminable by written notice to be given by one party to the other.[69] A contract for the sale of a chattel may expressly provide for a period of trial or examination with a "right of return." [70] A contract for the purchase and sale of goods in instalments over a long pe-

---

64.   **U.S.**—United States v. Peck, 102    **N.Y.**—Taylor v. Risley, 28 Hun (N.Y.)
U.S. 64, 26 L.Ed. 46 (1880).          141 (1882).

riod at specified prices may provide for termination by one or both parties on specified conditions.[71]  If there are such conditions specified, the power to terminate is a conditional power.[72] A contract for a selling agency may be made subject to the power of either party to terminate it by the giving of notice.[73] If a period of notice is required, the contract remains in force and must continue to be performed according to its terms during the specified period after receipt of the notice of termination.

A power to terminate in case performance is not satisfactory may be expressly reserved without invalidating the contract, whether the satisfactoriness is to be determined by a party to the contract, by his engineer, or by a stranger.[74]  Here the power is conditional and can not be exercised in the absence of a good faith determination.

# CHAPTER 69

# THE LEGAL OPERATION OF AN EXECUTORY ACCORD

## § 1268. Definition of Accord—Compromise Agreements

What is an accord executory? The term has a long history; and its signification is not doubtful. But the fact that an accord executory has so many times been said to be an unenforceable agreement has brought confusion into the law of the subject. An agreement is brought before a court for enforcement, one that the court sees to be fully in compliance with every rule for the formation of valid contracts. The court can conceive of no good reason for refusing to apply ordinary contract law; and when the argument is made that executory accords are not enforceable, the court thinks that the perfectly valid contract before it can not be an executory accord. Thus what is an accord becomes not an accord; and definitions become impossible to use and the law is in confusion.[1]

The term "accord executory" is and always has been used to mean an agreement for the future discharge of an existing claim by a substituted performance. In order for an agreement to fall within this definition, it is the promised performance that is to discharge the existing claim, and not the promise to render such performance. Conversely, all agreements for a future discharge by a substituted performance are accords executory. It makes no difference whether or not the existing claim is liquidated or unliquidated, undisputed or disputed, except as these facts bear upon the sufficiency of the consideration for some promise in the new agreement. It makes no difference whether or not a suit has already been brought to enforce the original claim; or whether that claim arises out of an alleged tort or contract or quasi-contract.[2]  Nor does it make any difference whether the former claim is not yet mature when the new contract is made, or that it had matured and an alleged breach committed, although an executory accord is seldom made until after an alleged breach.[3]  It makes no difference that the debtor gives collateral security that the new performance will be rendered, even though that security may consist of the promise of a third person, thus bringing in a new party to the transaction.  And finally, it makes no difference whether or not the original claim can now be shown to have been ill-founded, except so far as that fact affects the sufficiency of consideration;  and if the claim was made in good faith on any reasonable ground, it does not affect it at all.

If the foregoing statements are true, one does not get out of the field of executory accords by calling the new agreement a "compromise" or a "composition with creditors."  Of course, every one knows that executory compromises are enforceable, even though it was performance of the compromise that was to operate as a discharge of the claim compromised.  And composition agreements are every day enforced, even though not until they are performed are the prior claims of the creditors discharged.  All this shows that the law of compromises and compositions is also the law of executory accords.

Most compromise agreements are executory accords, although they too may be substituted contracts.[4]  Compromises are known to be favored by the law;  and if the court is asked to enforce a valid compromise it generally does so without question.  By thinking and speaking in terms of "compromise," the existing befuddlement in regard to "executory accords" is avoided.  Compromises are frequently made in the course of a pending action;  and such compromises, if one party refuses to perform, have frequently been specifically enforced by a summary order in the very proceeding that is compromised,[5] without any discussion of executory accords or any nice discrimination as to whether the compromise was a substituted contract.  In most such cases it seems reasonably clear that the parties intend that the plaintiff's claim and the pending action are to be discharged only when the compromise performance is rendered.  The compromise agreement may be made with respect to a disputed claim before any action has been brought;  and it may be specifically enforced in an independent suit brought for that purpose, whether an action has already been started or not.[6]

In some cases it has been thought that a "compromise" is always to be distinguished from an accord executory.  The law favors "compromises" and therefore they should be enforced.

2.   See  Restatement,  Contracts,  §
417, Comment b.

But there is no such valid distinction.[7]  It is true that an accord executory may be an agreement for the future discharge of an undisputed claim, in which case it should not be described as a compromise.  But most executory accords are agreements for the future discharge of unliquidated claims; and in many cases the amount actually due is in dispute.  If the "compromise" is an agreement for the discharge of the disputed claim by rendering some specified performance in the future, it is an accord executory; [8] and it is no more a favorite of the law than is any other executory contract based upon sufficient consideration.  The existence of the bona fide dispute is merely one ground for holding that the consideration is sufficient.  If an accord executory that happens to be the compromise of a disputed claim is enforce‐ able, so are other accords executory that have sufficient consideration.

Of course, a compromise agreement, like any other "accord," may be made as a substituted contract, immediately discharging the original claim.  But there are many compromise agreements that are not substituted contracts, in which it is the "performance" that is to operate as a future discharge and not the "promise" that is accepted in present discharge.  Such compromise agreements are not prevented from being enforceable contracts by the fact that they are also accords executory.

It has been said that "there is a distinction which is usually made between a compromise and settlement and accord and satisfaction.  An unexecuted accord and satisfaction does not offer a bar to an original cause of action, while a valid compromise agreement, although executory, operates as such bar." [9]  Aside from the confusion of terms in this statement, the case is clearly one in which the "compromise" was an accord executory, in which the debtor promised to pay $900, "upon receipt" of which the claimant agreed to release him from an unliquidated tort claim.  Judgment was given against the debtor on this promise.  But it is not true that every valid compromise operates as a final bar.  If it is not agreed upon as a substituted contract, and in many cases it is not, it should be held to operate only as a temporary suspension as in the case of other accords.  In such cases it is the "performance" of the compromise that is to operate as final satisfaction.  If the debtor breaks the compromise agreement, the suspension is lifted and the creditor can again enforce his former claim.

### § 1269.  Accord Executory Distinguished from Accord and Satisfaction

An accord executory is an agreement that an existing claim shall be discharged in the future by the rendition of a substituted

---

**9.  Ky.—Barr v. Gilmour, 265 S.W. 6, 204 Ky. 582 (1924).**

performance.  The reason that such an agreement is not in itself at once operative as a discharge of the claim is that the agreement itself does not so provide.  If it does so provide, it operates accordingly and is a substituted contract.  But a creditor who has agreed to accept a gold watch or a week's labor in satisfaction has not agreed to accept the promise of such watch or labor in satisfaction.[10]  And if he has not so agreed, it is grossly unjust to restrict his damages to the value of the watch or labor in lieu of the original claim in case the debtor does not keep his new promise and the creditor is forced to go to law.[11]  There is unlimited authority to the effect that an accord executory, providing for a future discharge of a claim, is not itself a present discharge.[12]

This is true even though the debtor has committed no breach of the accord, and has even tendered performance, thus putting the creditor in default.[13]  In most of the cases the possibility of using the accord as a temporary defense was not raised or in any way suggested.  The only alternatives considered by the court were (1) holding that the unexecuted accord was a discharge of the original claim and (2) holding that it was not a discharge.  The first of these is at variance with what the parties intended and would not be just;  but it is otherwise with a temporary suspension.[14]

Of course, a part performance of the accord by the debtor, accompanied by unjustified failure to perform the remainder, is not operative as satisfaction and does not bar action on the original claim.[15]  Credit is given on account for the part performance.  It has even been held that part performance is no bar even though the failure of the remainder is due to the creditor's own refusal to receive it.[16]  In such case, the part performance is not operative as a full discharge;  but it should operate to suspend the prior claim as is explained hereafter.

In correctly so holding, the courts have frequently fallen into the error of saying that it is not a discharge because it is not an enforceable contract.[17]  The real issue before the court in these cases is whether an action can be maintained on the original claim and not whether the accord is an enforceable contract.  If the accord is so enforceable, it should be held to operate as a temporary suspension as long as it is itself unbroken by the debtor;  but after he has committed a total breach the suspension is lifted.

Dissatisfaction with the former rule that the accord is not operative as a suspension caused the court in some cases to misinterpret the terms of the agreement and to hold that it is a substituted contract operating as a present discharge and not an accord at all.[18]  As a result of such an interpretation, the executory agreement for a future discharge, instead of being totally unenforceable in spite of the intention of the parties, became effective far beyond their intention. In such cases the court would say that it is true that an accord executory is wholly invalid and unenforceable, but the present contract is enforceable because it was intended as a substituted contract. The first half of this statement is now an error of law; and the second half is in these particular cases an error in fact.

Thus in a leading English case [19] the holder of a bill of exchange agreed with the debtor "to accept payment . . . by his covenanting to pay to a trustee of our nomination one third of his annual income and executing a warrant of attorney." The plaintiff never named a trustee; and so the covenant and warrant of attorney were never executed. In a suit on the bill it was held that the new agreement was sufficient to sustain a plea of the general issue. Of course, it should have been operative to suspend action on the bill; but it was the covenant and warrant of attorney that were to constitute satisfaction, and they were never executed. If the debtor had wrongfully refused to execute them, it is inconceivable that the creditor's action would have been restricted to the new agreement to the exclusion of the bill of exchange. It is clear that the agreement was a mere accord executory.[20]

There is, of course, no question that contract rights and duties, and asserted claims of any kind, whether disputed or undisputed, can be immediately discharged by a new executory contract substituted therefor. Whether the new contract is in fact such a substituted contract is a question of interpretation of its terms.[21] The process of interpretation may be a difficult one; for sometimes the parties had themselves no clear idea to express on the matter, or having such an idea failed to express it. Substituted contracts are dealt with herein under the title "substituted contracts," although courts frequently say that they operate as an accord and satisfaction.

## § 1270.  A Mere Offer is Not an Accord

By common usage the word "accord" connotes agreement between two parties; and it should never be applied to a case in

19.  Eng.—Good v. Cheesman, 2 Barn. & Adol. 328, 109 Eng.Rep. 1165 (1831).

20.  Lord Tenterden said: "It certainly appears that this was not an accord and satisfaction properly and strictly so called, but it was a consent by the parties signing the agreement to forbear enforcing their demands."  Parke, J., said:

"I think, therefore, that a mutual engagement like this, with an immediate remedy given for non-performance, although it did not amount to a satisfaction, was in the nature of it, and a sufficient answer to the action."  This is as much as to say that an accord is not satisfaction but can be held to be satisfaction if the court so desires.

which one party has made an offer of a settlement of a previous claim but the other party has not yet accepted the offer.[22]  In such a case there is no agreement, although there is an offer that may perhaps lead to one.

Such an offer may be made either by the obligor (debtor) or by the obligee (creditor); either by the party against whom the claim is made or by the claimant.  Thus if A asserts (B either denying or not denying) that B owes $100 to A, it is possible for B to make various offers of settlement.  He may tender his gold watch to A in satisfaction of A's claim.  This gives to A a power of acceptance; but it is a power that he can exercise only by doing an act that will entirely extinguish his right against B.  He may accept delivery of the watch, after which A's right is discharged and B's property in the watch has passed to A.  This is called accord and satisfaction; there is agreement, but it is fully performed on both sides and there is no executory contract.  As the facts are stated above, neither party has made any promise to the other.

It is quite possible, however, for the offer to include a promise, either by the offeror or by the offeree.  B may offer his watch, asking in return A's promise never to sue on the former claim. The acceptance of this offer by A is also operative as an accord and satisfaction; but it is clearly also the making of a promise for breach of which an action for damages would lie.  The accord resulting would be a unilateral contract, as well as a satisfaction. Similarly, B's offer might be as follows: I offer you my watch in immediate satisfaction of your claim and I promise in addition to pay you $20 on May 1, if you will promise in return never to sue on your claim.  A's acceptance of this offer would instantly discharge his claim and at the same time make a bilateral contract. In these cases, prior to A's acceptance there is neither an accord nor a satisfaction.  A could still maintain suit on his existing claim; but neither could maintain suit on the basis of B's unaccepted offer.

On the other hand, the offer of settlement may come from A, the claimant.  He may say to B: I will accept your gold watch in full satisfaction.  Of course, B is not bound to accept such an offer; and no action will lie against him for failure to deliver his watch.[23]  Again, there is neither an accord nor a satisfaction. Such a promise as this by the creditor, signed, sealed and delivered, is an enforceable unilateral contract, whether or not it be called an accord.  It empowers the debtor to discharge his debt by

22.   See Restatement, Contracts, § 417, Comment a: "An accord is a contract (not merely a revocable offer nor a bargain invalid for lack of a sufficient consideration or any other reason) between a creditor and debtor for the settlement of the claim by some performance other than that which is due."

rendering the specified performance. It does not itself operate as a satisfaction; but upon its breach the debtor can maintain an action.[24]

Some of the cases in which it is said that "upon an accord no remedy lies" are of the sort discussed above; they are mere unaccepted offers, and no action will lie because there is no contract. Thus, in an action to enforce an existing claim, the defendant pleaded that the plaintiff had promised to discharge the same if the defendant should on or before July 10 pay to the plaintiff a specified part of the debt, sign a release of a certain claim, and make a certain return to the probate court. He pleaded further that on July 10 and for two days preceding he had tried to find the plaintiff and his attorney so as to make the payment and execute the documents, but that they could not be found. After the bringing of the present action he had tendered full performance. Of course, this plea was bad.[25] There was no satisfaction, for lack of performance. The statement of the court that "it was not an accord with mutual promises" is correct as a statement of fact; its additional dictum that "unperformed it is a mere accord" is a poor use of the word "accord". There was a mere offer, the attempt to accept which had failed.

Such an offer of settlement by either the debtor or the creditor is revocable just as other offers are revocable; [26] and the applicable rules governing the mode of acceptance are the same. In a New York case [27] a creditor promised his debtor to accept a lesser sum in satisfaction of the mortgage debt if the debtor would pay it by a specified date in advance of maturity. The debtor then made no return promise; but on the date specified he came to the creditor's house with the money and knocked at the door. The creditor, without opening the door, asked who was there. The debtor replied, saying that he was there with the money to pay off the mortgage debt. The creditor then told him to go away, that the money would not be accepted. The court held that the debtor had no right to damages for breach of the creditor's offered promise. The correctness of this decision turns wholly upon the rules governing modes of acceptance. If the debtor's statement at the door was not an operative acceptance, the creditor still had power to revoke and exercised it. It may be suggested, however, that somewhat greater liberality is desirable in determining the operative modes of·acceptance. The mortgage debt most certainly was not discharged until the money in the debtor's pocket was paid to the creditor. But the court might properly have held that the creditor's offer could be accepted either by paying the money or by promising to pay it, and that

25. **Conn.**—Francis v. Deming, 21 A. 1006, 59 Conn. 108 (1890).

27. **N.Y.**—Petterson v. Pattberg, 161 N.E. 428, 248 N.Y. 86 (1928).

the debtor had made a promise to pay before receiving any notice of revocation. There would then have been an "accord with mutual promises," although not as yet a full discharge. To reach this result, the court must be willing to hold the debtor to the promise that he made outside the door. If he should change his mind and refuse to pay, an action by the creditor would lie against him.

### § 1271.  An Accord Executory is an Enforceable Contract

"Upon an accord no remedy lies." Such is the traditional form of statement that has come down to us from past centuries and that is still being gravely repeated. In most of the cases in which this statement is made, it is a mere dictum, the question before the court almost always being whether the executory accord can be set up in defense by the debtor when he is sued on his original obligation.[28] As is shown in a later Section, it has come about that even in this kind of an action, the accord executory can be successfully pleaded as a temporary suspension of the creditor's cause of action if the debtor himself has as yet committed no breach of the accord.

There are some cases, however, in which the plaintiff's action was one for breach of the executory accord itself, and in which the court gave judgment for the defendant, giving as a reason that upon an accord no remedy lies. The case of this type that is most often cited as authority is the case of Lynn v. Bruce.[29] In this case the defendant owed the plaintiff a debt of £105. There is nothing to show that this debt was in any way disputed or unliquidated. Nevertheless, the two parties made a bilateral agreement whereby the debtor promised to pay 14s. in the pound, in consideration of the creditor's promise to accept that sum in full satisfaction, the total amount so to be paid being somewhat less than £74. Of this amount the debtor had paid a little more than £70, leaving a balance of £3 and some shillings. For this balance the creditor brought suit, alleging the new bilateral agreement as the basis of his action. The court gave judgment for the defendant, the opinion of the Lord Chief Justice Eyre being reported as follows: "It was settled in the case of Allen v. Harris, 1 Ld. Raym. 122, upon consideration of all the cases, that upon an accord, which this is, no remedy lies; it was said that the books are so numerous that an accord ought to be executed, that it was impossible to overturn all the authorities; the expression is 'overthrow all the books.' It was added that, if it had been a new point, it might have been worthy of consideration. But we think it was rightly settled upon sound principles. *'Interest rei publicae*

29.    2 H.Bl. 317, 126 Eng.Rep. 571 (1794). See also Tassall v. Shane, Cro.Eliz. 193.

*ut sit finis litium'*; accord executed is satisfaction; accord executory is only substituting one cause of action in the room of another, which might go on to any extent."

Of this case, it should first be observed that the new bilateral agreement between the parties was not enforceable against the creditor for lack of a sufficient consideration, since the debtor promised in return only to pay a part of his already existing debt.[30] Of course, no more than any other contract is an accord executory enforceable unless there is a sufficient consideration for the promise to be enforced.[31] It might well be held, therefore, that, since the creditor's promise was not enforceable, it was in itself not a sufficient consideration for the debtor's promise to pay 14s. in the pound. It would better have been held, however, that the debtor's promise was enforceable without regard to whether or not the creditor's return promise was enforceable. A debtor's repeated promise to pay the debt that he then owes is amply supported by that debt and is an enforceable promise without any new consideration at all. So, therefore, the defendant's promise to pay 14/20ths of his existing debt was amply supported and was a binding promise.[32]

In rendering its decision, the court appealed to notions of public policy as well as to authority. The decision that is appealed to was in fact decided as the court represents; but the public policy ideas that the court expresses are quite erroneous as applied to executory accords. The enforcement of an accord executory does not in fact substitute one cause of action in the room of another; this is the result of a substituted contract, which all agree to be enforceable. Nor does it cause any unreasonable increase in litigation. If the debtor commits a breach of the contract of accord, the creditor is compelled to elect between the old obligation and the new. If it is the creditor who commits a breach of the contract of accord, there is no unreasonable increase in litigation if we permit the debtor to enforce the contract of accord, either specifically or by a counter-action for damages.

It seems quite probable that the notion that an accord executory is not an enforceable contract arose, not only out of the confusion over the use of the accord as a defense in an action on the original claim and its use as the basis of an action for damages for its breach, but also out of the history of bilateral contracts. In the early history of English law, the only contracts that were recognized as enforceable were unilateral transactions that had created a debt and formal covenants under seal. Parol bilateral agreements were not recognized at all. Most executory accords are parol bilateral agreements. In very early times, therefore, it was quite correct to say that upon an accord no remedy

30. See Restatement, Contracts, §
417, Comment *c.*

32. This is supported by Restatement, Contracts, § 86(1).

lies. [34] Even then, however, as the cases in the Year Books show, the question usually arose out of an attempt by a debtor to set up the accord executory as a defense when sued upon his original obligation. He tried to make it operative as an accord and satisfaction, and he failed.

There is now ample modern authority justifying us in saying that an accord executory is an enforceable contract, for the breach of which either party can maintain an action for damages if it complies with the usual requirements for the making of valid contracts.[35] In order to be so enforceable, it is not necessary that the new agreement shall be a substituted contract immediately discharging the previous obligation. A composition with creditors is hardly ever such a substituted contract. If it is not performed by the debtor, the creditors can maintain action for the enforcement of their entire original claim;[36] and yet no one doubts that the composition agreement is itself an enforceable contract. If a breach of the accord executory is committed by the creditor, it is now held that the debtor can maintain an action for damages.[37] If a breach of the accord is committed by the debtor, the creditor can at his election maintain an action for breach of the accord,[38] instead of falling back upon the original obligation.

In some cases the error has been made of supposing that, if the accord executory is not a "bar" to suit on the original claim, there is no consideration for the promise to render the substituted performance.[41] This may have had some foundation in the very early times when bilateral contracts were not enforceable; but since that ceased to be the law, the foundation for the notion ceased to exist. In practically every sort of case, a promise is a sufficient consideration if the promised performance would be.

35.    **U.S.**—Union Central Life Ins. Co. v. Imsland, 91 F.2d 365 (C.C.A. 8th, 1937), quoting Contracts, Restatement; Archibald McNeil & Sons Co. v. United States, 1 F.2d 39 (D.C.Pa.1924), affirmed 10 F.2d 1016 (C.C.A.3d, 1926); Kahn & Co. v. Clark, 178 F.2d 111 (C.A.5th, 1949), quoting Restatement, Contracts.

37.    Restatement, Contracts, § 417 (d), says: "If the creditor breaks such a contract, the debtor's original duty is not discharged. The debtor acquires a right of action for damages for the breach, and if specific enforcement of that contract is practicable, he acquires an alternative right to the specific enforcement thereof. If the contract

is enforced specifically, his original duty is discharged."

**Mass.**—Hunt v. Brown, 15 N.E. 587, 146 Mass. 253 (1888).

**Minn.**—Schweider v. Lang, 13 N.W. 33, 29 Minn. 254 (1882).

38.    Restatement, Contracts, § 417 (c), says: "If the debtor breaks such a contract the creditor has alternative rights. He can enforce either the original duty or the subsequent contract."

**Eng.**—Nash v. Armstrong, 10 C.B. (N.S.) 259 (1861), action on tenant's oral promise to pay £70 rent, the original lease, promising an amount to be fixed by appraisal, being under seal and not discharged.

Therefore, the claimant's promise to accept the substituted performance in satisfaction is ample consideration for the other party's promise to render it.[42]

The fact that this error has persisted over so long a period and appeared in so many cases cannot be permitted to cause its recognition as sound or existing law. It may be that *communis error facit jus*. But in this case the error is not universal; and, in addition, it conflicts with one of the most generally accepted doctrines of consideration, that a promise is a sufficient consideration for a return promise.

## § 1272.  An Accord Executory may be Either a Unilateral or a Bilateral Contract

Most accords are in bilateral form, consisting of a promise by a creditor to accept a substituted performance in the future, in satisfaction of a previously existing claim, and a promise by the debtor to render such substituted performance. If, however, a creditor should deliver to his debtor a sealed promise to accept a substituted performance in full satisfaction of his claim, the contract so made would be an executory accord and it would be unilateral, for the reason that the debtor makes no return promise to the creditor.[44] In like manner the debtor might execute such a valid unilateral sealed promise to render a substituted performance in satisfaction. In addition to this, either party can bind himself by promises similar to those just described, if the other party gives an executed consideration in return. Thus, in consideration of $10 paid by the debtor, the creditor can bind himself to accept a substituted performance in full satisfaction, even though the debtor makes no promise whatever to render that substituted performance. This would be a unilateral accord executory.[45]

## § 1273.  An Accord Executory is Specifically Enforceable

Since the early courts of common law did not enforce an accord executory, either as a temporary defense against a suit on the prior claim or as the basis of an action for damages, it was incumbent on equity, as in so many other cases, to supply the need. Application for specific enforcement seems not to have been made in many cases; but in a number of well considered cases it has been actually decreed.[46] In a leading English case at common

---

45.  See Restatement, Contracts, § 417, Comment *a*, and Illustration 2.

46.  This is accepted in Restatement, Contracts, § 417(d), where it is said: "If the creditor breaks such a contract, the debtor's original duty is not discharged. The debtor acquires a right of action for damages for the breach, and if specific enforcement of that contract is practicable, he acquires an alternative right to the specific enforcement thereof. If the contract is enforced specifically, his original duty is discharged."

law,[47] the court held that an accord executory was not a defense to a suit on the original obligation, even though the debtor had partly performed and had committed no breach. Application was at once made to the Chancellor, however, and an injunction against the enforcement of the judgment was granted, conditional on performance of the accord by the debtor.[48] This is specific enforcement of the accord; and under modern law, in which defenses that were formerly equitable only are recognized in all cases, it amounts to a temporary suspension of the former right of action.

In another case, in the United States Supreme Court,[49] the holder of a bond brought a bill in equity to foreclose a mortgage given to secure it. The defendant answered that before the bond became due there was a bilateral parol agreement by which the defendant agreed to deliver jewelry at reasonable prices within one year, and the plaintiff agreed to accept such goods at Little Rock in full settlement. The defendant delivered part of such goods, and was ready and willing to deliver the rest all the year; but the plaintiff was never there to receive them. The court specifically enforced the accord, and decreed the appointment of a receiver to take and value the goods sufficient to pay the debt and that the delivery of such goods should satisfy the debt and mortgage.

The agreement of accord was in this case made before breach of the sealed bond and mortgage obligation; but this fact would have no weight in the direction of making the parol accord enforceable. Before breach, a parol agreement could not discharge a specialty at common law, but it was not so in equity.

See also Comment *d*, and Illustrations 4 and 5.

The Restatement is quoted and followed in Union Central L. Ins. Co. of Cincinnati v. Imsland, 91 F.2d 365 (C.C.A.8th, 1937). Also, it is approved in Corrigan v. Payne, 45 N.E.2d 829, 312 Mass. 589 (1942), but specific performance had not been asked in the case.

47. Eng.—Ford v. Beech, 11 Q.B. 852 (1848).

48. Eng.—Beech v. Ford, 7 Hare 208 (1848). A third person was also a promisor in the new agreement; but this is not material except as supplying additional consideration for the creditor's promise. The facts of these two cases are stated in the succeeding Section.

49. U.S.—Very v. Levy, 13 How. (U.S.) 345, 14 L.Ed. 173 (1851).

This case was followed in Bufton v. Crane, 143 A. 382, 101 Vt. 276 (1928).

Very v. Levy was again followed in Chicora Fertilizer Co. v. Dunan, 46 A. 347, 91 Md. 144 (1900), contract by a creditor to discharge a debt upon payment of part in money and part in goods before maturity; and in Union Central Life Ins. Co. of Cincinnati v. Imsland, 91 F.2d 365 (C.C.A.8th, 1937), specifically enforcing an accord between mortgagor and mortgagee. In accord also is Boshart v. Gardner, 77 S.W. 2d 642, 190 Ark. 104, 96 A.L.R. 1130 (1935).

### § 1274. An Accord Executory Operates as a Temporary Suspension of the Right of Action

An accord executory does not in itself operate as a discharge of the previous claim, for the reason that it is not so intended or agreed. In nearly every case, however, the parties intend that the duty created by the previous transaction shall be suspended during the period fixed for performance of the accord. As long as the debtor has committed no breach of the accord, therefore, the creditor should be allowed to maintain no action for the enforcement of the prior claim. His right of action should be held to be suspended as the parties intended.[51]

The courts of common law at first prevented themselves from reaching this just result by laying down the technical rule that, if a right of action should be once suspended, it could not be revived.[52] This may have been due to a misleading figure of speech—the personification of a right. If a person dies, we assume that he cannot be recalled to life; but there is no analogy between this and a right of action for breach of contract. Erroneously believing that a judgment holding the accord executory to be a good temporary defense in an action on the previous claim would necessarily operate as a complete discharge, it was held that the accord was no defense at all and that the defendant's only remedy was a counterclaim for damages.[53]

The very case that established this rule was itself substantially nullified in equity. The plaintiff in the law case, Ford, held two promissory notes for £340 in all, signed by William Beech. It was then agreed by them with Alfred Beech that the latter would pay the sum of £200 and that Ford would accept that payment in full satisfaction. In breach of this accord, Ford sued William Beech on the notes and got judgment, the court holding that the provision in the agreement for a suspension of the notes was not a defense. Thereupon William and Alfred Beech brought a bill in equity for relief; and the Chancellor decreed that the agreement should be specifically performed, that Alfred Beech should pay £200 as agreed, and that on such payment satisfaction of the judgment should be entered. This decree though not affecting the power of the common law court, unquestionably operated to

---

51. A rule in harmony with this is laid down in Restatement, Contracts, § 417(a): "Such a contract does not discharge the duty, but suspends the right to enforce it as long as there has been neither a breach of the contract nor a justification for the creditor in changing his position because of its prospective non-performance." This is paraphrased with approval in Milici v. Di Francesco, 188 A. 884, 122 Conn. 267 (1936); it is quoted also in Union Central Life Ins. Co. of Cincinnati v. Imsland, 91 F.2d 365 (C.C.A.8th, 1937).

53. Eng.—Ford v. Beech, 11 Q.B. 852 (1848).

suspend collection of the judgment at law against William Beech until the date set for payment of the £200 by Alfred Beech.[54]

Even without the aid of equity, the common law courts made much progress in breaking down their own bad rule. Thus, in the case of a money debt, the giving of a negotiable note by the debtor, payable at a definite future time, operated to suspend the creditor's prior claim until maturity of the note.[57] Of course, if the note was received as an absolute discharge, the case is not one of accord executory. Secondly, it has been held that a composition with creditors operates to suspend their claims against the debtor as long as the composition agreement is not broken.[58] That the composition is a mere accord executory is shown by the fact that, if it is not performed as agreed, the creditors can get judgment on their original claims. Thirdly, an agreement under seal that no suit shall be brought for a specified time and that if such a suit is brought the agreement shall operate as a total release will be given effect in accordance with its terms.[59] Such a release, to be operative only in case of suit in breach of the agreement, is in fact a suspension. Fourthly, the courts recognized a release with a condition subsequent to the effect that if the accord is broken the release of the original claim shall be no longer operative.[60] This also is a repudiation of the doctrine, even though some courts may have been deceived by their own camouflage.

In any case where an accord has been agreed upon and there has been no material breach by the debtor, when sued by his creditor on the original claim he should plead the accord and his continued readiness to perform it as an equitable defense. Under modern code procedure he does not need to describe the defense as "equitable" or to file a cross-bill for specific performance of the accord. He should not assert in his plea that the original claim is already satisfied, unless the new agreement was itself a substituted contract. But if he pleads the accord and his own continued readiness to perform (sometimes including a tender of performance), any court now having the powers of the former courts of chancery should recognize the facts pleaded as operating as a temporary suspension, and should give judgment for the defendant conditional upon his rendering the performance agreed upon in the accord. This involves the repudiation and abandonment of those cases holding that an accord executory is no defense even though tender of performance has been properly made by the debtor and wrongfully refused by the creditor.[61] Such

54.   **Eng.**—Beech v. Ford, 7 Hare 208 (1848).

61.   The following are cases of this type:

**Mass.**—Corrigan v. Payne, 45 N.E.2d 829, 312 Mass. 589 (1942); Waitzkin v. Glazer, 185 N.E. 927, 283 Mass. 86 (1933).

cases have done enough injustice already. But attention should be called to the fact that in these cases the question of temporary suspension was not raised and the court was unaware that it could amply protect both parties by a conditional decree. In the more numerous cases in which it is the debtor who is in default on the accord, the facts do not justify even a temporary suspension and he has no good defense whether sued on the original claim or on the accord. In these cases it is only the reasoning of the court, or perhaps only the judicial dicta, that must be disapproved.

## § 1275. Material Breach of Accord by the Debtor Makes the Previous Claim Again Enforceable

Since an accord executory operates at best no more than as a suspension of the antecedent claim, a material breach of the accord by the debtor lifts the suspension and makes the creditor's prior claim again enforceable.[62] This is true whether the accord is a compromise agreement, a composition with creditors, or any other form of agreement providing for a future discharge by substituted performance. To have this effect, however, the debtor's breach must be a material breach, going to the essence, and discharging the creditor from his contractual duty.[63] Part performance of the accord is not itself operative as satisfaction.

If the new executory agreement is itself substituted by the parties for the original claim, it is an accord and satisfaction, operating as a final discharge; so that thereafter the rights of both

---

**N.Y.**—Larscy v. T. Hogan & Sons, 146 N.E. 430, 239 N.Y. 298 (1925); Reilly v. Barrett, 115 N.E. 453, 220 N.Y. 170 (1917).

The New York decisions, supra, have been nullified by statute in cases where the accord is in writing. Sess.Laws N.Y.1937, ch. 77, amending Pers.Prop.Law, § 33. If the accord is not in writing the Appellate Division has continued to apply the older and erroneous rule as to an accord executory. Di Roma v. Chambers Drug Store, 28 N.Y.S.2d 170, 262 App.D. 856 (1941); Atterbury v. Walsh Paper Corp., 26 N.Y.S.2d 43, 261 App.D. 529 (1941). Even though the legislature did not overrule these cases, the Court of Appeals should do so.

**62.**   **U.S.**—Brown v. Spofford, 95 U.S. 474, 24 L.Ed. 508 (1877); In

re Plaza Music Co., 10 F.Supp. 310 (D.C.N.Y.1934); The Joy, 290 F. 407 (D.C.N.Y.1923); Olympia Shipping Corp. v. Morse Dry Dock & Repair Corp., 275 F. 199 (C.C.A. 4th, 1921); Ransom v. Geer, 12 F. 607 (C.C.N.Y.1882).

**Eng.**—In re Hatton, L.R. 7 Ch.App. 726 (1872).

Restatement, Contracts, § 417(c), says: "If the debtor breaks such a contract the creditor has alternative rights. He can enforce either the original duty or the subsequent contract." See also Illustration 3, under § 417.

The accord may be expressly conditional on performance by a specified time, making time of the essence. See:

**Cal.**—Scheeline v. Moshier, 158 P. 222, 172 Cal. 565 (1916).

parties are determined solely by the substituted contract. Even though the debtor commits a breach of it, the creditor can not maintain suit on his old claim.[64] There are cases, however, in which damages for breach of the substituted contract may be an inadequate remedy. In such a case there is no reason why a present day court should not decree the restitution of rights under the antecedent contract for which the new one was "substituted." This is discussed in Sections 1121 and 1293.

64. There is no revival of the original right in case the debtor's check or promissory notes were given and accepted in instant satisfaction, even though these notes are never paid. But if the substituted contract is voidable for fraud or other reason, and the power of avoidance is exercised, the original claim is enforceable.

# CHAPTER 70

# ACCORD AND SATISFACTION

## § 1276. Accord and Satisfaction—Discharge by Substituted Performance

The preceding discussion of executory accords has laid the foundation for a somewhat briefer discussion of accord and satisfaction. This is a term that has been in use for centuries, denoting one of the recognized methods of discharging and terminating an existing right and constituting a perfect defense in an action for the enforcement of a previous claim, whether that claim was well founded or not. Discharge by accord and satisfaction means a discharge by the rendering of some performance different from that which was claimed as due and the acceptance of such substituted performance by the claimant as full satisfaction of his claim. The previously existing claim may be one arising out of contract, quasi-contract, tort, or otherwise; it may be one arising out of a breach of duty and including a claim for damages, or one of which no breach is asserted.[1] The settlement may be

---

1. Since most settlements by accord and satisfaction of contractual claims occur after an alleged breach of contract, it is worth while to call attention once more to the fact that an accord may be agreed upon before any breach has occurred. In such case, the claim to be discharged is one based on primary obligation. The rules that are applicable are the same in either case. Thus, there are many

either before breach or after breach.

The two parties may first make an accord executory, that is, a contract for the future discharge of the existing claim by a substituted performance still to be rendered. When this executory contract is fully performed as agreed, there is said to be an accord and satisfaction, and the previously existing claim is discharged.[2] It is quite possible, however, for the parties to make an accord and satisfaction without any preliminary accord executory or any other executory contract of any kind. A debtor may offer the substituted performance in satisfaction of his debt and the creditor may receive it, without any binding promise being made by either party. So, too, the creditor may ask for some specified performance in satisfaction of his claim and the debtor may comply with this request, again without either party's making any binding executory promise. In such cases, the new transaction is wholly executed at the very moment of acceptance. The substituted performance is fully rendered and the antecedent debt is discharged, leaving nothing more to be done by either party.[3]

If the parties have reciprocal claims against each other, an accord whereby they agree that one shall pay and the other receive a specified sum in full settlement, or shall give and receive any other substituted performance, there is a discharge of both claims just as soon as there is a discharge of either one. Thus, where a seller claims the price for goods sold, and the buyer claims damages for breach of warranty, an agreement to return the goods and to return the purchase money notes in full settlement is an agreement to discharge the buyer's claim as well as the seller's.[4] The law of accords is operative, not only against

cases holding that a part payment before maturity is operative as an accord and satisfaction. See Princeton Coal Co. v. Dorth, 133 N.E. 386, 191 Ind. 615 (1921), with note in 24 A.L.R. 1471, citing other cases in quantity. Also, Lonergan v. Highland Trust Co., 192 N.E. 34, 287 Mass. 550 (1934).

2. Full performance of a valid accord by the debtor operates as satisfaction and is ground of defense in an action previously brought on the claim so satisfied, even though the claimant has repudiated the settlement. There is therefore no need for an injunction against further prosecution of that suit. Savage v. Edgar, 98 A. 407, 86 N.J. Eq. 205, 3 A.L.R. 1021 (1916).

3. Many illustrations of this type of accord and satisfaction can be found in the cases holding that the cashing of a check, sent as payment in full of an unliquidated claim, is a full discharge. Deuches v. Grand Rapids Brass Co., 215 N.W. 392, 240 Mich. 266 (1927), is such a case, the court specifically holding that no antecedent accord is necessary, the acceptance of the tendered check being enough.

See Weld v. Weld, 81 P. 183, 71 Kan. 622 (1905), where a creditor agreed that marriage of the debtor to himself should discharge the debt. In an action on the debt, the consummation of the marriage was held to have operated as satisfaction, even though there was no writing sufficient to satisfy the statute of frauds.

creditors to whom money has been promised, but also against obligees of all sorts making other kinds of claims.

The principal questions to be asked in determining whether a discharge by accord and satisfaction has taken place are: (1) Did the parties in fact agree that the performance rendered should have this operation? and (2) Does that performance constitute a sufficient consideration for a return promise or for a discharge? The chief problem that has arisen concerns those cases in which the performance rendered is nothing more than the part payment of a liquidated money debt.

### § 1277.  No Accord and Satisfaction without Expression of Assent

The process of making an accord, of interpreting the words and acts of the parties, and of determining the legal effect thereof, is the same as in the case of other contracts.[5]  In order that a performance rendered by an obligor shall operate as a satisfaction of the claim against him, it must be offered as such to the creditor.  There must be accompanying expressions sufficient to make the creditor understand, or to make it unreasonable for him not to understand, that the performance is offered to him as full satisfaction of his claim and not otherwise.[6]  If it is not so rendered, there is no accord, either executory or executed, for the reason that there are no operative expressions of agreement—no sufficient offer and acceptance.[7]

Questions of this sort arise most frequently when the amount of a money obligation is in dispute, and the debtor tenders a sum less than the amount claimed.  Such a payment may be tendered either as a part payment on account or as full satisfaction.  The debtor when making the payment has power to direct its application;  but if he does not then express his will in the matter, the creditor may receive it as discharging that part of his claim equal to the amount paid, leaving the balance subject to litigation.

So, where there are two or more claims, the payment of the amount of one of them may reasonably be taken by the creditor as intended to settle that one claim alone;  it will not operate as a satisfaction of both claims unless the debtor, when paying, clearly expresses to the claimant an intention that it shall so operate.[8]  Also, the payment and acceptance of a sum of money in discharge of a claim for services rendered or goods sold does not operate as satisfaction of a counterclaim of the payor for damages for an alleged breach by the payee, unless the counterclaim was clearly included in the expressed terms on which the payment was made.[9]

5.  An offer by a creditor to receive something less in satisfaction can be revoked before acceptance, like any other offer.

9.  **Ark.**—Beeson-Moore Stave Co. v. Brewer & Storey, 250 S.W. 518, 158 Ark. 512 (1923).

It is not enough for the debtor merely to write on a voucher or on his check such words as "in full payment" or "to balance account," where there has been no such dispute or antecedent discussion as to give reasonable notice to the creditor that the check is being tendered as full satisfaction. Such an indorsement on the check is merely an evidential fact, to be weighed along with other facts. In case there is no other evidence of an offer of accord, the creditor may strike out the writing on the check;[10] or he may cash the check without doing so. There is some risk that there may be other evidence;[11] and in any case he would be well advised to inform the debtor at once that he receives the payment as on account only. If the debtor has given adequate expression to his intention that his check must be taken as full satisfaction or not at all, the creditor does not obviate its effect as such by merely crossing out words that may be written on the check, such as "in full settlement."[12]

The question whether a payment, in money or by check, or other performance rendered by the obligor and later asserted to be in satisfaction, was so tendered to the claimant that he knew or should have known that it was tendered as full satisfaction, is a question of fact; and frequently the evidence is so conflicting or doubtful that it is a question for the jury.[13] Statements that accompanied or preceded the tender may be disputed; or, if not disputed, the interpretation that the claimant should have given them under the circumstances may be far from clear.

## § 1278. The Relation of Compromise to Accord and Satisfaction

In our digests, cyclopedias, and treatises we find "compromise and settlement" and "accord and satisfaction" listed as two separate and apparently independent titles. In fact they are not separate and independent. As the term is actually defined and applied in cases and treatises, an accord is an agreement for the settlement of some previously existing claim by a substituted performance. It will be found that this definition of accord also includes all compromises; they are agreements for the settlement of a previously existing claim by a substituted performance. But the previous claim may be one that is in doubt or in dispute, or one that is certain, liquidated, and undisputed. It is only the former claims that are the subject of compromise. Any claim can be discharged and satisfied by some substituted performance that is agreed upon; but it is only doubts and disputes that are com-

Acceptance by a discharged workman of a check for his wages, due without dispute to the date of his discharge, is not a settlement of his claim for damages for wrongful discharge, even though the check was indorsed "in full to date." Those words may be reasonably understood as referring solely to the claim for wages for service rendered. Murphy v. Menke Groc. Co., 201 S.W. 650 (Mo.App. 1918).

promised. From this it appears that a compromise is always an accord, but that an accord is not necessarily a compromise.

No distinction is to be drawn with respect to the character of the substituted performance. The transaction is never called either an accord or a compromise unless the new performance agreed on is in some respect different from that previously claimed by the obligee. If the claim is for the payment of $100, whether disputed or not disputed by the obligor, the new agreement made by them is called neither an accord nor a compromise unless it calls for a performance that differs in some respect from the payment of $100. If the obligor merely promises to pay $100 and the obligee promises to receive that sum in satisfaction, the validity of the new agreement depends almost wholly upon the validity of the previous claim. If for any reason that claim was invalid ab initio, the new agreement is equally invalid. If the previous claim was a valid debt for $100, the obligor's new promise is mere repetition; it is sufficiently supported by the existing debt, but it is neither an accord nor a compromise. It is true that the new promise is itself called a contract [14] and that it may have the effect of recreating a legal duty the enforcement of which has been barred by the statute of limitations or by a discharge in bankruptcy. Also it may operate as a ratification of an obligation that was voidable for infancy or fraud. But even in these cases it is not called either an accord or a compromise, and no new consideration is required for its validity and enforcement.

If, on the other hand, the new agreement is for the settlement of the claim by rendering a performance in any respect different from that previously claimed, the agreement is an accord; and its validity and enforceability depend upon the existence of sufficient consideration. If the prior claim was a disputed one, then the new agreement is a compromise; and a consideration can usually be found in the obligor's promise to render the additional performance and in the obligee's promise to give up some part of what he previously claimed. But a sufficient consideration is lacking if the obligor promises nothing more than was admittedly due or if the obligee gives up nothing whatever. The most common sort of compromise is a case in which the claimant agrees to be satisfied with less than the whole of what he claims and the other party promises to render more than that which he admits that he owes.[15]

It is not a prerequisite to an accord that the creditor's claim shall be either doubtful or disputed, although the fact that the claim is liquidated and undisputed will have a bearing on the question of consideration and of validity.[16] If A owes B an undis-

14.   Restatement, Contracts, §§ 85-
87.

puted debt of $100, an agreement whereby A promises to give and B promises to accept a used car in full satisfaction is an accord executory and a valid contract; upon delivery of the car, the transaction becomes an accord and satisfaction. On the other hand, the term "compromise" is inapplicable to this transaction; it is only doubtful or disputed issues that are the subject of compromise.

## § 1279.  What Constitutes Assent by the Creditor—Cashing or Retention of a Check

There is no accord, either executory or executed, unless there is an offer either by the debtor to give or by the creditor to receive a substituted performance in full settlement, and an acceptance by the other party of the offer so made. Usually the offer is made by the debtor, and the problem of acceptance involves the action of the creditor. Where the amount due is in dispute, and the debtor sends cash or check for less than the amount claimed, clearly expressing his intention that it is sent as a settlement in full, and not on account or in part payment, the retention and use of the money or the cashing of the check is almost always held to be an acceptance of the offer operating as full satisfaction, even though the creditor may assert or send word to the debtor that the sum is received only in part payment.[17] The creditor's action in such case is quite inconsistent with his words. It may, indeed, be clear that he does not in fact assent to the offer made by the debtor, so that there is no actual "meeting of the minds." But this is merely another illustration of the fact that the making of a contract frequently does not require such an actual meeting. This has been discussed in the chapters on offer and acceptance and interpretation. The court is in these cases faced with the alternative between holding that the creditor is a wrongdoer in cashing the check or using the money, and holding that his conduct is operative as an acceptance and is therefore not wrongful. The latter holding is a short cut to complete justice, protects the debtor against injury, and prevents unnecessary litigation. It is true that the creditor may bring suit for the balance claimed; but he loses his case and is taxed with the costs. If the contrary rule were adopted, the creditor would get judgment for such balance as he can prove; and the debtor would have to support a counter action, or a counterclaim in the same action, for damages for the creditor's wrongful retention of the money or check. It has seemed to the courts more beneficial to hold that the creditor's action speaks louder than his words and is operative as an acceptance of the offer as made.[18]

18.   This has the approval of the American Law Institute. Restatement, Contracts, § 72 (2), is as follows: "Where the offeree exercises dominion over things which are offered to him, such exercise of dominion in the absence of other circumstances showing a contrary

The cashing, or the certification, of a check expressly sent in full settlement of a disputed claim, operates as an accord and satisfaction if, at the time, no word of dissent is sent to the party offering it in satisfaction.[19]

In these cases it is held that it makes no difference that the creditor did not know that the effect of his cashing the check or keeping the money would be the discharge of his entire claim.[20] This is supported by fundamental legal doctrine. The acceptance of an offer makes a contract even though the parties do not know the law or the legal consequences of their agreement.[21] It is the prevailing rule that ignorance of legal consequences does not prevent one's voluntary acts from having such consequences.

There are some cases in which the conduct of the creditor is less clearly wrongful, even though he may temporarily retain the money or cash the check. If he at once informs the debtor that he does not accept it in full settlement and requests the debtor to say at once whether he assents to the retention as a part payment only or requires its immediate return, his action is not so clearly wrongful. If the debtor then makes no objection to the retention, his silence may be regarded as assent, so that no full satisfaction has occurred.[22] The action by the creditor is not so unreasonable in this case and the notice of his non-acceptance of the offer may with nearer approach to justice be given its normal effect. But if the debtor replies that the part payment must be accepted as offered or at once returned, the continued retention by the creditor should be held to operate as full satisfaction.[23] If the court is unwilling to hold that the debtor's silence is an assent by him to the creditor's counter-proposal to hold the money or check as part payment only, its continued retention by the creditor will be held to be full satisfaction.[24] The retention of the check for an unreasonable time, even though not cashed, will have the same effect if no objection was made to the form of payment and if the check would have been honored on presentation at the bank.

If, before the payment is made or check sent by the debtor, the creditor informs him that it will not be accepted as full satisfaction, and in spite of such information the debtor sends the money or check without a new assertion that it must be accepted as

intention is an acceptance. If circumstances indicate that the exercise of dominion is tortious the offeror may at his option treat it as an acceptance, though the offeree manifests an intention not to accept."

The rule applies to goods tendered as full satisfaction, accepted and kept by the creditor while protest-ing that there was no satisfaction. Citizens & Southern Bank v. Union Warehouse & C. Co., 122 S.E. 327, 157 Ga. 434 (1924).

23.    Iowa —Sparks    v.    Spaulding Mfg. Co., 139 N.W. 1083, 158 Iowa 491 (1913).

N.Y.—Fuller v. Kemp, 33 N.E. 1034, 138 N.Y. 231 (1893), annotated in 20 L.R.A. 785.

full payment if at all, the creditor is justified in supposing the payment to be on account. In such case his cashing the check will not operate as satisfaction. The same result is reached if the creditor returns a check sent in full payment, rejecting the offer of the debtor, and the latter again sends the check without a new assertion that it is again offered only on the same terms.[25] If the debtor keeps sending the check, each time stating that it must be taken as full satisfaction, and the creditor at last cashes it, the claim is discharged.[26]

### § 1280. Burden of Proving an Accord and Satisfaction

Accord and satisfaction is properly called an affirmative defense; it must be specially pleaded and the burden of proof with respect to every necessary element of it is on the party alleging it as a defense.[27] Of course, the creditor as a plaintiff must allege and prove a breach of duty by the defendant; he must prove non-payment at maturity. But he need not allege or prove that there has been no mutual accord providing for a substituted performance, whether such accord has been executed or not.

### § 1281. Acceptance of Part Payment of a Liquidated Debt as a Discharge—Foakes v. Beer

When a debtor merely pays a part of his already overdue money debt, he is doing no more than to perform a part of his already existing legal duty to his creditor. The sufficiency of such a performance as a consideration for a return promise or as a satisfaction of the debt is a matter that has excited endless discussion. It has already been considered at length in the Chapter herein dealing with the subject of consideration. The matter was debated in the time of Lord Coke; and in Pinnel's Case[28] "it was resolved by the whole court that payment of a lesser sum on the day, in satisfaction of a greater, cannot be any satisfaction for the whole, because it appears to the judges that by no possibility a lesser sum can be a satisfaction to the plaintiff for a greater sum; but the gift of a horse, hawk, or robe, etc., in satisfaction is good. For it shall be intended that a horse, hawk, or robe, etc., might be more beneficial to the plaintiff than the money in respect of some circumstance, or otherwise the plaintiff would not have accepted it in satisfaction. But when the whole sum is due, by no intendment the acceptance of parcel can be a satisfaction to the plaintiff." This statement was a mere dictum and the case was decided on quite another ground; but without doubt it represented the prevailing judicial notion as to the law. The actual ground of decision was one that would not now be sustained.[29]

28. 5 Coke 117a (1602).

29. "Pinnel's plea was, that before the maturity of his bond for the

larger sum, plaintiff had accepted a lesser sum agreed upon between the parties, in full satisfaction of

Some 280 years later this dictum in Pinnel's Case was made the basis of a decision by the House of Lords in the case of Foakes v. Beer, a case that is now usually referred to as the leading case on this subject and a case that is followed in most of the United States. In this case it was held by the House of Lords that the payment by instalments of a liquidated debt, all of which was overdue, was not operative to discharge the debtor's obligation to pay an additional sum by way of interest, even though the creditor had expressly agreed that it should be operative as a total discharge.[30]

The American decisions in accord with Foakes v. Beer are innumerable, some of the more recent ones being collected in the footnote below.[31] In some states the contrary rule has been adopted by statute, either providing that the part payment of an overdue debt shall operate as full satisfaction if so accepted by the creditor, or that it shall so operate if the creditor gives a receipt in full or other written acknowledgment of full satisfaction.[32] Two states have rendered decisions contrary to Foakes v. Beer without the aid of statute.[33] The doctrine that part payment of a liquidated debt can not operate as satisfaction of the whole will be very acceptable to a court when the debtor is a large employer and the creditor a small workman, especially when the debt is a sum awarded by statute for breach of a "Fair Labor

the original debt. Now, all the authorities, American and English, including Coke himself, agree that this was a good defense, and that the plaintiff was bound by it, if defendant should properly plead it to a suit for the entire original debt. But the hapless Pinnel, in that remote period when courts were almost as jealous for the observance of technical rules of special pleading as for the execution of justice according to right, was adjudged to pay the whole debt, the plaintiff having judgment against him because of his 'insufficient pleading, for,' says Coke, 'he did not plead that he had paid the £5 2s. 2d. in full satisfaction (as by law he ought), but pleaded the payment of part generally, and that the plaintiff accepted it in full satisfaction.'

"However amusing and absurd this may appear to us, it was the point decided in Pinnel's case, and the question before us was not only

not decided, but it was impossible that it should have been. There Pinnel pleaded payment of the lesser sum before the date of the maturity of the greater sum named in the bond, and its acceptance by his creditor in full satisfaction, and he lost, unhappy wretch that he was—born two or three centuries too soon, and not knowing the difference betwixt legal tweedledum and legal tweedledee—because he pleaded that he paid a part of the greater original sum and that the plaintiff accepted it in full satisfaction, and did not plead that he paid it in full satisfaction." Clayton v. Clark, 22 So. 189, 74 Miss. 499 (1896).

30.    Eng.—Foakes v. Beer, 9 App. Cas. 605 (1884).

33.    Miss.—Clayton v. Clark, 21 So. 565, 22 So. 189, 74 Miss. 499 (1896).

N.H.—Frye v. Hubbell, 68 A. 325, 74 N.H. 358 (1907).

Standards Act." [34]    A more complete discussion will be found in the chapter on consideration for a promise.

New York now has a statute wholly abolishing the requirement of a consideration for any agreement in modification or discharge of a prior contractual obligation, provided that the agreement is in writing and signed by the party whose contract rights are being modified.[35]  Under this statute a gratuitous written promise to receive a lesser sum in full satisfaction is at once operative as a pro tanto discharge of the debtor's obligation to pay the balance,[36] and undoubtedly a signed receipt in full will operate as a discharge if so intended, whether it is given in exchange for a part payment or as a gift discharge without any payment.

There should no longer be any doubt that a promise by a creditor to accept a part payment in full satisfaction will be made fully operative by any substantial change of position by the obligor in reliance on the promise, other than the part payment itself, provided that the creditor knew or had reason to know when he made the promise that the obligor would thus change his position.  On this ground an English court has held that a landlord's promise to reduce the rent by one half became binding when, to his knowledge, the lessee continued to occupy the leased premises and to do business.[37]  The decision was based on modern cases since the fusion of law and equity, the court distinguishing Foakes v. Beer because the effect of action in reliance had not been considered in that case.

### § 1282.    Part Payment in Advance of Maturity or at a Different Place

Even in the case of a liquidated and undisputed money debt, a payment of anything by the debtor prior to the maturity of the debt is a performance that it was not his legal duty to render. The payment of any sum whatever prior to maturity of the debt is a sufficient consideration for a promise;  and it operates as satisfaction of the entire debt if the creditor accepts it as such.[38] Even if the amount paid is relatively small and is much less than the present value of the debt, discounting it at market rates of interest, it operates as satisfaction in full if the creditor accepts it as such.  Even the very early cases admitted this to be the law. In like manner, payment of a lesser sum at a different place than that required by existing duty operates as full satisfaction if so agreed.

---

34.    See Fleming v. Post, 146 F.2d 441, 158 A.L.R. 1384 (C.C.A.2d, 1944) ; Rigopoulos v. Kervan, 151 A.L.R. 1126, 140 F.2d 506 (C.C.A. 2d, 1943).

35.    N.Y.Pers.Prop.Laws, § 33(2).

37.    Eng.—Central London P. Trust v. High Trees House, [1947] 1 K.B. 130.

## § 1283.  Compositions with Creditors

A composition with creditors is an agreement between a debtor and two or more of his creditors,[39] or between such creditors for the benefit of the debtor,[40] or between such creditors and any outside person, whereby the creditors agree to accept in full satisfaction something different from or less than that which they originally claim.[41]

This agreement may take different forms.  (1) It is most commonly a bilateral contract whereby the debtor promises to render the substituted performance and the creditors promise to receive it in full satisfaction.  Such a composition agreement is an accord executory, resulting in a satisfaction and discharge of the original claims only when the new performance is rendered.[42]  After it is made, however, unless the contrary is clearly agreed on, it operates as a suspension of the original claims as long as the debtor has committed no material breach of it.[43]  It is an enforceable contract, so that either the debtor or the creditors can maintain action thereon in case of breach by the other party.  In case of breach by the debtor, the creditors have alternative rights:  they can maintain suit on their original claims [44] or on the accord itself.[45]

(2) The creditors may offer their promise to receive in full satisfaction a substituted performance by the debtor or by a third person, no promise of such performance being made by the latter. This is not an accord;  it is a mere offer, revocable by the offeror at any time before the requested performance is begun or tendered.  When this performance is completed, there is an accord and satisfaction, and the original claims are discharged.  After the requested performance is begun, the creditors are bound by their promise;  and after it is completed, they are bound to forbear further action against the debtor.  The contract, made thus, is unilateral.

(3) The debtor, or some third person, may offer an instant performance in satisfaction of the claims of the creditors.  Their receipt of such performance at once operates as accord and satisfaction.  If they make no return promise, express or implied, there is never any executory contract;  but there is agreement and an exchange has been made—an accord and satisfaction.  The re-

---

39.  The validity of a composition does not depend on assent by all the creditors, unless by its own terms it is made thus conditional.

41.  An assignment of property to a trustee for the benefit of named creditors is not a composition agreement and does not suspend

enforcement of their claims.  It is a mere security.  Reynolds v. Pennsylvania Oil Co., 89 P. 610, 150 Cal. 629 (1907).

43.  U.S.—In re Clarence A. Nachman Co., 6 F.2d 427 (C.C.A.2d, 1925).

ceipt of the offered performance, however, may involve the making of a promise to surrender notes or other evidential documents or to take no future action against the debtor, in which case there is here too a unilateral contract.

In the case of a composition agreement made by a debtor with two or more of his creditors, or made by such creditors between themselves for the debtor's benefit, the rule in Foakes v. Beer has never been applied.[46]  Even though the claims are liquidated, mutual promises to receive a percentage of the claims, however small it may be, as full satisfaction of the claims, are binding and enforceable while executory;  and the actual payment of the specified amount operates as accord and satisfaction.[47]

While this can be regarded as merely an exception, based on notions of policy, it can also be defended on the ground that there is a sufficient consideration for each creditor's promise.  Each one gets a benefit to which he was not entitled by virtue of his original claim;  and each creditor and the debtor also incur a detriment by virtue of the composition.  If the composition provides for a payment of merely 25 cents on the dollar, in receiving the 25 cents a creditor gets only one fourth of that to which he had a legal right;  but he also gets the advantage of equal treatment with the other creditors, something to which the common law did not entitle him, and to which even a bankruptcy act entitles him only conditionally.  The detriment incurred by each creditor is similar to that involved in any bilateral contract, each one promising to give up something to which he has a right.[48]  If the debtor is a party to the composition, as he nearly always is, the detriment incurred by him is that involved in his promise to pay his creditors pro rata.  The common law did not make it a debtor's duty to share his assets equally among his creditors or to pay them proportionate amounts.  In promising to do this he is giving up a privilege that has great value, the privilege of preferring one creditor over another.  Under our bankruptcy laws, the creditors have power to compel an equal division;  but as long as no bankruptcy proceeding has been started it is not wrongful for a debtor to pay any honest debt in full.[49]

### § 1284.  Some Performance Different from That Previously Required

The rendition of a performance in any way different from that required by his existing legal duty, in accordance with the mutual agreement of debtor and creditor that it shall operate as full satisfaction of the latter's claim, is a discharge of the claim.  As Coke said in an early case,[53] the delivery and acceptance of "a

49.  In accord with this, see Restatement, Contracts, § 84(d), and Comment d.

53.  Eng.—Pinnel's Case, 5 Coke 117a (1602).

horse, hawk, or robe in satisfaction is good." It has even been said that a liquidated debt, however large, is discharged by the delivery and acceptance in satisfaction of even so small an article as a "tomtit" or a "canary." [54] It is immaterial that the market value of the performance rendered is greatly less than that of the performance previously due. The law does not require adequacy of consideration for a promise; nor does it require adequacy of value in the case of an executed accord.[55] Whatever is sufficient as a consideration for an executory promise given in exchange for it is equally sufficient to operate as a satisfaction and discharge. The following are illustrations of substituted performances constituting sufficient consideration: goods and chattels of any kind; [56] the assignment of a chose in action; [57] a new chattel mortgage or other collateral security; [58] some action by the debtor that he is under no duty to perform, for the purpose of enabling himself to pay part of the debt; [59] a forbearance by the debtor to apply for a discharge in bankruptcy or to make an assignment for the benefit of creditors; [60] some personal service rendered at the creditor's request.[61]

In several cases it has been held that the acceptance of the debtor's own unsecured promissory note, for an amount less than the debt or for the same amount payable at a future day, is not operative as satisfaction even if the creditor accepts it as such.[62] It was at first so held in England also; but later cases held otherwise, carrying out with strict logic the doctrine that a money debt can be discharged by the acceptance of a substituted performance that differs in any respect, without regard to values.[63] A few American cases have held likewise.[64] The delivery of a note, bill, or check is certainly payment in a different form of performance from that required by a money debt; and, in view of the great number of expressions of dissatisfaction with the rule in Foakes v. Beer, it may be regarded as strange that the American courts have not uniformly followed the later English cases as to discharge by substituting the debtor's note. Of course, it is hard to suppose that his note for $50 is more valuable than is $50 in cash; and this is often stated in the cases. But this is out of harmony with the generally accepted doctrine that adequacy of consideration, in the sense of equivalence or reasonableness in market value, is not required.

The truth seems to be that courts are human and are subject to conflicting tendencies and varying emotions, now standing stiffly for logical consistency and again giving weight to practical

---

54.   A creditor "might take a horse or a canary or a tomtit, if he chose, and that was accord and satisfaction; but by a most extraordinary peculiarity of the English Common Law, he could not take 19s. 6d. in the pound; that was *nudum pactum*." Jessel, M. R., in Couldery v. Bartrum, 19 Ch.D. 394, 399.

or emotional considerations. This makes it seem sometimes that the creditor should keep his word when he accepts part payment as full satisfaction, and at other times that the debtor reaps an unfair advantage by settling with a peppercorn.

### § 1285. Payment or Other Performance by a Third Person as Satisfaction

An accord may be an agreement between a claimant and a third person who is not the obligor; and a performance rendered by such third person and received by the claimant in satisfaction of the claim operates as a discharge of the obligor.[69] It is not necessary that he should express his approval or ratification or that he should even have knowledge that the transaction has occurred.[70] He is a donee beneficiary of the transaction, except where he is himself a party to the transaction and has given a consideration to the third person. Of course, if he is sued later by the claimant, judgment will go against him unless he alleges and proves the accord and satisfaction; but his discharge has already occurred before he makes this defense. All that is necessary is that he shall get knowledge of his discharge by a third person in time to make use of it as a defense when sued by his creditor.[71] Failure to make use of it in the suit will of course result in the rendition of judgment against him, as in other cases where there is a good defense that is not pleaded or proved. Making use of it as a defense has been called a ratification; this maintains an appearance of consistency with the doctrine that there is no discharge without authorization or ratification. It may be true that the obligor after a discharge by a third person, has power to renew his obligation by a disclaimer of all benefit of the transaction.[72] Such a disclaimer might help to prevent the third party from having a restitutionary remedy against him; but it would not prevent the third party from being subrogated to the rights of the creditor or from enforcing the claim as the creditor's assignee.

The acceptance by a creditor, as full satisfaction of his claim against his debtor, of a lesser amount paid by a third person out of moneys not belonging to the debtor,[75] or of a third person's note or bill or check for such a lesser amount,[76] is operative as a discharge of the whole claim against the debtor. It has even been held that such a settlement is not rendered invalid by the fact that the money paid by the third person was supplied to him for the purpose by the debtor himself.[77] But this decision should be

70. "It is not necessary that the debtor should have formally adopted the satisfaction before pleading it; the plea itself is an adoption." Bennett v. Hill, 14 R.I. 322 (1884). If the plea is a good plea, the satisfaction was operative before pleading.

72. See Restatement, Contracts, § 137.

regarded as substantially in conflict with the decision in Foakes v. Beer.

The note or bill of the third person may be taken as only a conditional payment or discharge, in which case there is a temporary suspension of the creditor's former claim, action on that claim being again maintainable on dishonor of the note or bill. But in these cases, in the absence of manifested intention to the contrary, the presumption is that the note or bill is accepted as accord and satisfaction and in complete discharge.[78]

### § 1286.  Mutual Discharge of Reciprocal Obligations

The substituted performance accepted in satisfaction of a claim may itself be the discharge of some counterclaim; and nothing more is necessary to effectuate such mutual discharges other than the agreement that they shall be so discharged. Such a transaction is not an accord executory; it is accord and satisfaction. Thus, where A holds B's note for $100, and A is indebted to B and C in the sum of $125 for services rendered, if it is agreed by A with B and C that the debts shall be mutually cancelled, the agreement is instantly operative as satisfaction of both.[83] Had A's counter obligation involved no third party but had been owed to B alone, both debts being due and payable, there would have been no sufficient consideration for A's total discharge of B; but such a mutual agreement by A and B would instantly operate to discharge A's debt to B in full and to discharge B's debt to A to the extent of $100.

If the reciprocal claims of the two parties are disputed or otherwise unliquidated, their assent to reciprocal discharges operates at once as a mutual accord and satisfaction; this may be so even though the parties contemplate the execution of formal releases or the surrender of documents.[84] Mutual expressions of assent are enough, unless an intention to the contrary is expressed.

### § 1289.  Discharge of Unliquidated Claim by Performance of a Part That is Admittedly Due

There are numerous cases holding that where the debtor admits that a certain balance is due on an otherwise disputed claim, as where he admits the correctness of the creditor's claim in every respect except as to a deduction based upon a disputed recoupment, set-off, or counterclaim, a payment by the debtor of the amount admitted to be due is not legally operative as a full satisfaction of the claim, even though it is tendered as such by the debtor and is so accepted by the creditor.[89] Cases so holding are carrying out logically the generally stated rule that performance of a legal duty is not sufficient as a consideration for a return promise. The sum paid is one that is then legally due and payable, for which the creditor could have got judgment. The payment is not a compromise, as both parties are clearly aware. The creditor is being asked to surrender the whole of that part of his claim that is in dispute; and in return he gets nothing but the payment of that which is not in dispute.

A greater number of cases, however, hold the contrary; [90] and it is believed that they are supported by the better considerations of policy. The strict application of the doctrine of consideration in the field of discharge of contract has given much dissatisfaction, as appears from the opinions of the judges themselves. Performance of legal duty should, perhaps, be regarded as insufficient to support a promise to render some return performance, although even this may be regarded as doubtful. But by his acceptance of the rendition of such a performance of legal duty as full satisfaction of a larger claim, the creditor is not merely making a promise to render some return performance. Instead, he is assenting to a discharge of the debtor. Instead of undertaking a new duty to the other party, he is extinguishing a previous duty of that party to himself. Instead of creating a new enforceable right in the other party, he is extinguishing his own previous right against that party. The parties themselves do not regard the transaction as an executory contract but as a finished and executed transaction; and there is no good reason why the courts should not also so regard it. It is not ordinarily supposed that consideration is required for that which is executed. It is true that it is sometimes said that the creditor is making an implied "promise" never to sue for the balance of his claim; but even if this has any foundation in fact, there is no reason for overlooking his express assent to the immediate extinction and discharge of the claim. After such a discharge, a subsequent suit by him should be fruitless.

### § 1290.  Illustrations of Claims That are Unliquidated

As has been stated heretofore, the part payment of a liquidated and undisputed debt, already due, does not operate as a discharge by accord and satisfaction even though both parties mutually agree that it shall so operate. A different result is reached, however, if the debt is unliquidated or disputed. It is important, therefore, to determine what is meant by "unliquidated." It may be of assistance to group the cases within a number of separate classes, although they may not be exhaustive and are not mutually exclusive.

(1) The amount of the plaintiff's original claim may never have been determined either by agreement of the parties or otherwise. Thus, where A has rendered service for B without agreeing in advance upon the compensation to be paid, B is bound to pay a reasonable sum; what this sum may be is a question of

fact for court or jury. Prior to judicial determination, no man can say with certainty how much B owes for the service. Another illustration of this type of unliquidated claim is a claim for damages for an alleged breach of contract or for a tort. The breach or wrongful action may itself be denied; and in addition the extent of the harm done and the amount to be paid as damages are uncertain. After final adjudication of the amount, the debt becomes a liquidated debt. It may also be turned into a liquidated debt by mutual agreement of the parties. This agreement may itself be substituted for the prior unliquidated claim, operating as an immediate discharge and sometimes called an accord and satisfaction; or it may provide that the payment of a specified sum by B shall operate as satisfaction, in which case the agreement is an accord executory. In either case the agreement is itself an enforceable contract; it makes no difference whether the amount agreed upon is large or small. The payment of this amount as agreed operates as full satisfaction.[91]

(2) A rate of payment per unit of performance may have been agreed upon by the parties; but the number of units may be undetermined or disputed. It may have been agreed that A shall be paid $5 per day for his service, but the number of days that he has worked is undetermined or disputed.[92] It may even be true that no one knows whether or not A has worked at all, as where the work was to be the searching for a fugitive or some lost chattel and A has died before rendering any report. The amount due is unliquidated and doubtful; and a mutual agreement fixing the amount is an enforceable contract, whether it is a substituted contract or an accord executory.

(3) The exact amount to be paid may have been exactly determined in advance, but the duty to make the payment may have been conditional upon some fact or event, and it is unknown, uncertain, or in dispute whether that fact or event has or has not occurred.[93] Or, it may be in doubt or dispute whether the promise to make the agreed payment was or was not conditional on some event. Thus, the purchase and sale of a patent may be expressly conditional upon the approval of X; and X has died without expressing to others his approval or disapproval. Again the agreed price of goods sold may be fixed and certain; but the seller asserts that title passed and the price was due instanter, and the buyer asserts that title was to pass only on delivery, after which the price was to be paid, the goods meantime having burned before delivery. In these cases, a mutual agreement fixing the amount at any figure between zero and the maximum that is possible under the alleged original agreement will be valid, just as in the first two classes.

(4) The terms of the contract or the meaning to be given them may be doubtful and disputed.[94] The performance rendered may

be definite and certain, but the amount to be paid therefor is in dispute, whether that amount was a lump sum or a sum to be determined at a rate per unit. Thus, a broker employed to make a sale succeeded in his efforts, asserting that his commission was to be 5 per cent of the price obtained, while the employer asserted that it was to be 1 per cent only. Here the amount due is unliquidated, except that according to the assertions and evidence of both parties there is a maximum and a minimum. A mutual agreement fixing the amount to be paid at any sum between 5 per cent and 1 per cent is enforceable according to its terms, whether executory or executed. According to the weight of authority, if the debtor tenders payment of the exact amount that he has admitted to be due, making it clear that he offers it as satisfaction in full of the creditor's claim, the acceptance of the tendered payment operates as accord and satisfaction of the whole.[95] There are cases holding the contrary,[96] the reason being that the debtor performed no more than his admitted legal duty. It is certain that the majority courts reach their conclusion in part for the reason that they are not satisfied that the rule in Foakes v. Beer is just and convenient; but an argument, of some plausibility, has been made that in a case of this kind the debtor is not wholly bound by his admission that any sum was due, and that prior to the adjudication of the dispute, the amount payable was uncertain in its entirety.

(5) The amount claimed by the creditor may be definite and certain, except that the debtor asserts that a reduction should be made by way of set-off or recoupment arising out of the very same transaction. Thus, the claimant may have rendered service or delivered goods for a definite price to be paid, but the debtor alleges that the service or goods were defective and not according to contract. The defects asserted by the debtor may be such as to go to the essence of the contract, so that if his assertions are true the claimant may be entitled to nothing; or they may be such as do not go to the essence, so that the debtor merely has a counterclaim for his damages. In either case, however, it can not be told prior to adjudication how much, if anything, is legally due. It can not even be said that there is a definite minimum. In this kind of case, a mutual agreement fixing the amount to be paid in satisfaction is valid and enforceable; and most courts agree that the amount so paid and received operates as a satisfaction in full.[97] Some cases are contra if the debtor pays a balance no greater than he admits to be due.[98] Again, the amount due to the claimant may be definite and certain in all respects, except that the defendant alleges a discharge of part of the claim by a part payment on account or by some substituted performance accepted by the claimant. In a case of this sort, no doubt the same conflict will be found as in the cases in class (4) above, the

majority holding that the payment of the amount of the difference between the whole claim and the alleged part payment will operate as satisfaction in full if so agreed, even though the amount so paid was no more than the debtor admitted to be legally due.

(6) There may have been two transactions between the parties, the result of one of them being that the plaintiff has a just and undisputed claim for a definite amount, while the defendant has a counterclaim for damages arising out of the second transaction. If the amount due from the plaintiff to the defendant on this second transaction is fixed and certain, the rules of law as to set-off may operate so that there remains but one debt, measured by the difference between the two fixed sums. This would make the rule in Foakes v. Beer applicable; a payment of this difference would be a discharge by exact and complete performance, while the payment of a lesser amount could not be made a full satisfaction. If the amount due on the second transaction is uncertain and in dispute and may possibly be as large as the amount of the plaintiff's claim on the first transaction, an agreement fixing the net balance to be paid by either party to the other will be valid and the payment of such agreed balance will operate as full satisfaction of both claims.[99] If the amount due on the second transaction is in dispute, but there is a maximum beyond which the defendant makes no claim whatever, the case is similar to class (5) above. In such case, if the defendant tenders in full satisfaction no more than the difference between the sum claimed by the plaintiff and the maximum counterclaimed by himself, and this sum is accepted by the plaintiff, there is once more a conflict in the decisions as to whether the plaintiff's entire claim is discharged.[1] The fact that the counterclaim arises out of a separate and independent transaction has been given weight by some courts, leading to the result that there is no such discharge.[2] It may well be that weight should be given to circumstances of economic coercion by the debtor, enabling him to hold up the creditor by the threat that even the amount admittedly due will be litigated.

(7) Finally, the plaintiff may claim as his due a gross amount that consists of two or more separate items; these items may be parts of a larger complex transaction or may be independent transactions that occurred at different times and that were not connected in the minds of the parties. Thus, where two articles were sold as part of one complex transaction, separate prices of $50 and $30 being fixed for them, and the buyer wrongfully rejected one and tendered $30 (the price of the other) as a full satisfaction of the seller's entire claim, it was held that the seller could accept the $30 and yet maintain suit for $50, the separate price of the other article.[3] If the articles had been sold at times

so far apart as to make the transactions wholly independent and unrelated to each other in the minds of the parties, the number of courts holding that payment of the amount admittedly due for one article could not operate as satisfaction of the disputed claim for the other would be somewhat increased. A similar result has been reached where the creditor has two claims for services, one liquidated and certain, the other in dispute; [4] also where under a single insurance policy the insured made claims for one loss that was undisputed and a further one that was denied by the insurer as not being within the terms of the policy.[5]

### § 1292.   Effect of Mistake upon Accords and Compromises

There is no doubt that if no part of the claim is in dispute and the creditor sends by mistake a bill showing less than the amount actually due, the payment of that amount does not operate as a full satisfaction even though the debtor sends his check indorsed "to balance account to date." [9] Under such circumstances, a promise by the creditor to accept the check as full satisfaction would be without any sufficient consideration.

Just as in the case of other contracts, an accord can be set aside, or reformed and enforced, on the ground of fraud, accident, or mistake.[10] This is true whether it is an accord executory or an accord and satisfaction. It is true, also, even though it is an accord that is also a compromise of a disputed claim; but in these cases it should be borne in mind that where the parties are consciously disputing an issue and agree upon a compromise in order to settle it, they are making no mistake as to the matter in issue and thus settled.[11] There must be a mistake as to matters that were not in issue and were not compromised in order that the settlement may be voidable on the ground of mistake.[12]

If a claim is made for damages for an injury, a compromise settlement is ordinarily not made voidable for mistake because the injury was greater and lasted longer than was expected at the time of the settlement, if the parties knew or had reason to know that the extent of the injury was uncertain and that was the very reason for the compromise.[13] But if the settlement was made in

12.   A release executed by an insured on the supposition that the policy had lapsed for failure to pay premium on time, this supposition being due to a mistake as to the date when the policy became effective, can be set aside and the policy contract can be enforced. Penn Mut. Life Ins. Co. v. Forcier, 24 F.Supp. 851 (D.C.Mo.1937).

Where a mutual settlement of a claim the amount of which is doubtful is made by payment of more or less than was in fact due, the excess or deficiency is not recoverable. It is otherwise, however, if the excess or deficiency was due to a mistaken belief that a specific payment had been made on account, this payment not being in dispute at the time of settlement. Stuart v. Sears, 119 Mass. 143 (1875).

contemplation of one kind of injury, minor in character such as a flesh bruise, when in fact but unknown to the parties, there was a very different injury such as a broken back, the settlement or release may be voidable for mistake.[14] The difference in the one case is a difference in degree; in the next case it is a difference in kind. But a great difference in degree may well be more important than a difference in kind.[15]

Where a claimant executes a release of all claims thinking that the amount paid is solely to compensate for loss of wages, he has not compromised his claim for damages for injury to person. Nor is he bound by the release if his failure to read it was caused by a false statement as to its contents by an attorney whom he had not authorized to settle the latter claim.[16] In such a case there is seldom sufficient reason for an estoppel because of a change of position by the releasee.

# CHAPTER 71

## SUBSTITUTED CONTRACT—NOVATION

## § 1293. Discharge by a Substituted Executory Contract

An existing claim can be instantly discharged by the substitution of a new executory agreement in its place.[1] This is true whether the prior claim is not yet matured at the time of the substitution, or is a claim to reparation for some prior breach of duty. The substituted contract may be either unilateral or bilateral. Suppose that two parties to a contract are each asserting a breach by the other and making conflicting claims. They finally reach an amicable agreement whereby each agrees to the immediate extinguishment of his claim and that in total substitution therefor A gives to B his promise to pay $1000 in 30 days. This is a unilateral contract, the exchange given by B being the extinguishment of his claim and wholly executed; this is given for two things in return, the extinguishment of A's claim and A's new promise of $1000.[2] If their new agreement had been that B should transfer 10 shares of stock within 30 days and that A should pay $1000 to B, their previous claims being both immediately extinguished, we should have a bilateral substituted contract.[3] In either case the new agreement is executed and performed with respect to the discharge of the old claims. The legal effect of their agreement to substitute is an immediate discharge.

It happens very frequently that a party to a valid contract attempts, either as plaintiff or as defendant, to show that a new contract has been substituted, either as a total discharge or as a partial modification and discharge. The existence of such a new contract of substitution or modification must be established in the same way as is any other contract. No one will be held to have surrendered or modified any of his contract rights unless he is shown to have assented thereto in a manner that satisfies the requirements of a valid contract.[4]

It will be observed that the term "substituted contract" is closely related to such terms as novation, accord and satisfaction, and rescission. It is frequently described by the courts as one kind of accord and satisfaction; and rightly, because the agreement instantly operates as satisfaction and discharge.[5] But there are many instances of accord and satisfaction that are not substituted contracts. A mutual agreement to pay and to receive $1000 in the future as a satisfaction of a prior unliquidated claim is an accord executory; upon payment of the $1000 we have accord and satisfaction, but we do not have a substituted contract, because there is now no executory promise left to be enforced. The money is paid, the claim is discharged, and everything is executed. Accord and satisfaction can take place without any antecedent executory accord. The debtor may merely offer his cash in immediate settlement and the creditor may take it, in which there is an accord operating as satisfaction but with no promise whatever.[6]

All novations are substituted contracts; and the converse is also true that all substituted contracts are novations, unless we follow the more usual custom of using the term "novation" only in cases where the substituted contract involves a substituted debtor or creditor as a new party. The term "substituted contract" is more likely to be used where there are no new parties; and the term "novation" where a new party is involved.[7]

A substituted contract is also a rescission, if the former claim was itself of a contractual character; unless we choose to restrict rescission so as to denote a mutual agreement of total discharge without making any payments or new promises. When rescission is so restricted, it is never identical with either a substituted contract or an accord and satisfaction; it merely has the common element with them that it operates as a discharge.

It is frequently difficult to determine whether a new agreement is a substituted contract operating as an immediate discharge, or is an accord executory the performance of which it is agreed shall operate as a future discharge. It is wholly a question of intention, to be determined by the usual processes of interpretation, implication, and construction.[8] Where the new agreement is oral and the words used are in dispute, the ques-

8. The following language is very clear as showing an intention to substitute the new contract in immediate discharge of the former one and all claims arising thereunder: "Whereas, said parties desire to compromise and release said claim for damages and release all parties from any further obligations under said contract;" and further, "Except for the rights and obligations created hereby, all contracts, claims, demands, rights, duties, obligations and liabilities ex-

tion becomes one for a jury.[9]  When two persons are jointly indebted to a third, the creditor may accept the note of one of them either as a mere collateral security or as a substituted contract and satisfaction.  If the latter is found to be the fact, the co-obligor is at once discharged by novation.[10]

If the substituted contract has itself been broken by either party, the other party's rights are dependent on the substituted contract.  The breach has often been held not to revive the former discharged claim.[11]  In this respect it differs from an accord executory; the accord operates only to suspend the prior claim so that on breach that claim becomes again as enforceable as it ever was.  But if a creditor accepts, in lieu of his liquidated debt of $1000, the debtor's new promise to deliver a used automobile, on breach by the debtor the creditor's damages are measured by the value of the automobile and he can not get judgment for the $1000 debt.  Of course, the new contract may expressly provide that upon breach the old claim is to revive; in this case its operation is rather to suspend than to discharge.

If a promissory note is given and accepted as immediate discharge of a prior claim and in substitution for it, there is no revival of the original right even though the note is never paid.[12]  The presumption in such a case is usually said to be that the note was taken as only "conditional payment," in which case it is only an accord executory and a temporary suspension.  Likewise, if a promissory note is discharged by assenting to a substituted executory contract, the repudiation of that contract does not revive the note.[13]

On the other hand, the substituted contract may itself be voidable for fraud, infancy, or other reasons; and if the power of avoidance is exercised, the avoided contract is nullified both as an executory contract and as a discharge.  The prior claim then becomes again enforceable.[14]

In spite of the cases holding, or saying, that the antecedent rights are not revived by the breach of the substituted contract by which they were discharged, it is clear that courts of equity could and sometimes did declare the reinstatement of the former legal position as a remedy for the party injured by a total breach of the substituted contract.  For such a breach, restitution as an alternative to damages was a remedy available to the injured party under certain circumstances just as in the case of other con-

isting at any time up to the time of the execution hereof . . . are hereby mutually satisfied, discharged and released."  In re Kellett Aircraft Corp., 77 F.Supp. 959 (D.C.Pa.1948), affirmed 173 F.2d 689 (C.A.3d, 1949).  Of course, more words were used than necessary.

11.    U.S.—In re Kellett Aircraft Corp., 173 F.2d 689 (C.A.3d, 1949).

Iowa —Merry v. Allen, 39 Iowa 235 (1874), substituted contract, even though broken, barred foreclosure of a mortgage; Hall v. Smith, 15 Iowa 584 (1864).

tracts, at common law as well as in equity. The explanatory theory usually has been that the breach gives the injured party a power to "rescind"; this is considered in Chapter 61, dealing with Restitution as a remedy for breach. If for some reason money damages computed on the basis of the substituted contract are not an adequate remedy, one form that the restitutionary remedy may take is the reinstatement of former rights, contract rights as well as property rights, and their enforcement in spite of their intervening discharge.[16]

### § 1294.  Oral Discharge or Variation of a Written Contract

Excepting as otherwise provided by statute,[24] any simple contract can be varied or rescinded by the oral agreement of the parties. This is true even though the contract is embodied in a written instrument, not under seal.[25] The rules as to mutual assent and consideration must, of course, be complied with;[26] but the validity of the oral agreement as a discharge or variation is not dependent on whether it is before or after breach of the former contract. If there are mutual duties still existing under the old contract, the mutual discharges of these duties are sufficient consideration for each other or for new promises.[27] These rules are now very generally held to be applicable even though the written contract is also under seal.[28] Seals and their legal effect at common law have been abolished in about half of the states; other states have modifying statutes.

If the contract as orally modified is within the statute of frauds, it is not enforceable unless there has been such a "part performance" as prevents the statute from being applied. It is often stated that a written contract that is itself within the statute of frauds can not be modified by a parol agreement; but such a rule should not be applied if the contract as orally modified is one that the statute does not require to be in writing.[29]

### § 1295.  Effect of an Express Provision Forbidding Oral Variation or Discharge

Very frequently the parties to a written contract include an express provision therein that there shall be no discharge or variation of its terms except by a new agreement that is itself

---

26.  It must be remembered, of course, that there are many informal contracts that are valid without regard to mutual assent or consideration. See the chapter herein dealing with such informal contracts. Such contracts include agreements to modify or discharge antecedent contracts and claims. There are statutes expressly applicable to agreements to modify or discharge. See Neg.Inst.Law, § 122; and N.Y.Pers.Prop.Laws, § 33 (2).

28.  It is so stated in Restatement, Contracts, § 407.

29.  See Chapter 13, Agreements to vary or rescind.

embodied in a signed writing.  The purpose of such a provision as this is to give added protection against fraudulent or mistaken oral testimony as to transactions subsequent to the written contract and affecting the rights of the parties that are created by it.

The purpose of the statute of frauds is to give this protection with respect to alleged transactions never reduced to writing. The statute gives no such protection as to oral discharges or variations of a written contract unless this subsequent oral transaction is itself one that falls within one  of the classes of agreements that are enumerated in the statute.[30]  Frequently the subsequent oral agreement does not fall within the statute, even though the original agreement itself does fall within it.

The purpose of the so-called parol evidence rule is to give protection against fraudulent or mistaken oral testimony as to oral expressions antecedent in time to the final effective delivery of an integrated written memorial.  Even for this limited purpose, the parol evidence rule is a broken reed on which to depend.[31]  But it does not even purport to affect in any way subsequent oral discharges or variations of a writing.

It is not surprising, therefore, that careful and experienced men attempt by express terms to create protection of a sort that the common and the statute law do not otherwise afford.  This attempt, however, is in the main unsuccessful.  Any written contract, other than specialties not now being considered, can be rescinded or varied at will by the oral agreement of the parties; and this is held to be true, except as otherwise provided by statute,[32] even of a written agreement that the contract shall not be orally varied or rescinded.[33]  Two contractors cannot by mutual agreement limit their power to control their legal relations by future mutual agreement.  Nor can they in this manner prescribe new rules of evidence and procedure in the proof of facts and events. The power of an agent to make or to vary or to rescind a contract on behalf of his principal can be limited by the latter as he sees fit;  but a principal cannot limit his own power to make future contracts with those who will agree.

### § 1296.  Inconsistent Contracts

The new agreement may make no reference to the previous contract or claim;  and yet it may operate as a substituted contract.  If the new agreement contains terms that are clearly inconsistent with the previously existing contract or claim, the fact of inconsistency is itself a sufficient indication of intention to abrogate the old and substitute the new.[35]  The inconsistency may exist as to the whole of the former contract or claim or only as to

---

**30.**    See Chapter 13, Oral variation of contract within the statute.

a part. It operates as a discharge by substitution only so far as the inconsistency extends.

## § 1297. Discharge by Novation

The term "novation" is never used except to denote a substituted executory contract. There must always be a prior obligation, actual or asserted, that is discharged and a new obligation that takes its place.[36] If the parties to the new executory contract are identical with the parties to the former obligation that is being discharged, the term "novation" is less often used. It is generally used only when the substituted contract involves at least one new party; and according to the more general practice, this new party must be a substituted obligor in place of a former obligor or debtor who is discharged.[37]

A substitution of a new creditor can be brought about by an assignment.[38] This is seldom referred to as a novation.[39] It is discussed in full in the Chapter dealing with assignments. Thus, if we suppose that A owes B $100, B can assign his right to C, without A's assent. Thereafter, A owes the money to C and is no longer indebted to B. If A should thereafter express his assent to this assignment, and expressly promise to pay the money to C, he is merely promising to perform his already existing duty to C. A's new promise to C is wholly unnecessary, but, nevertheless, it is a binding promise. This new promise served a real purpose as long as the common law courts refused to recognize the full effectiveness of an assignment. It enabled C to bring an action in his own name against A; and, therefore, it was sometimes said to have effected a novation in place of a mere assignment.[40]

**37.** See Riverside Coal Co. v. American Coal Co., 139 A. 276, 107 Conn. 40 (1927).

Some of the statutory codes of contract law include within the term "novation" all substituted executory contracts, whether there is a substituted debtor, a substituted creditor, or no new party at all. See City Nat. Bank of Huron, S.D. v. Fuller, 52 F.2d 870 (C.C.A.8th, 1931), affirming 52 F.2d 865, applying South Dakota statutes.

The novation contract may include the old debtor along with a new obligor. See Bennett v. Hill, 14 R.I. 322 (1884), where the creditor accepted in substitution for the debt a new promise of the debtor and a third person to carry on the business and to pay the debt out of its profits.

Restatement, Contracts, § 424, defines novation as "a contract that (a) discharges immediately a previous contractual duty or a duty to make compensation, and (b) creates a new contractual duty, and (c) includes as a party one who neither owed the previous duty nor was entitled to its performance." This includes the case of a substituted creditor as well as that of a substituted debtor.

**38.** Restatement, Contracts, § 423, reads: "A contractual duty or a duty to make compensation can be discharged by the creditor's effective assignment of his right." This means that the obligor's duty *to the assignor* is thereby discharged and a new and similar duty *to the assignee* is substituted.

There is more reason for describing the transaction as a novation if A undertakes to render a new and different performance to C in place of the payment of $100. Such a result as this could not be brought about by a mere assignment on the part of B. Such a result is reached, however, if B discharges A from his duty to pay $100, and, in return, A promises C to deliver fifty bushels of wheat. After this transaction, A is still the obligor, but he owes a different duty. There is a substituted creditor and also a substituted performance. This new transaction cannot be described as an assignment, and it may well be called a novation.[41]

A novation that consists in the simple substitution of a new debtor is as follows: Suppose that A owes B a debt of $100. A transaction thereupon takes place between B and C, whereby B discharges A in return for C's promise to pay B $100. By this transaction, A is effectively discharged and C becomes bound in his place.[42] To bring about this result, A's knowledge or assent is not necessary. Illustrations of such discharge by a simple novation are very numerous. They frequently involve a serious question of fact as to whether the creditor really agreed to discharge his prior debtor before performance has actually been rendered by the new promisor; but the rule of law applicable is not doubtful.[43]

In any form of novation there may be a substituted performance as well as a substituted debtor. Such a case is as follows: A owes B a debt of $100. A transaction thereupon takes place between B and C, whereby B discharges A, and C promises to deliver to B fifty bushels of wheat. This is an effective novation. In this case, A's assent was not necessary. He was not a party to the novation, but he was a beneficiary of it. A was a donee beneficiary of the contract between B and C. By that contract, he did not acquire a new right against anybody; instead he ob-

41. A new creditor can be substituted by novation without procuring his assent. Suppose the following case: A creditor says to his debtor, "In consideration of your executing your promissory note to X for $100, I will discharge you from your debt to me." The debtor thereupon executes the note and delivers it to X, or to any other person for X. The promissory note is enforceable by X, and the debtor's original debt is discharged. See Restatement, Contracts, § 425.

Again, suppose that the creditor says to his debtor, "promise me that you will pay $100 to X and I will accept that as an immediate discharge of your debt to me." The debtor makes at once the requested promise. Here, the new promise being to the creditor, X is a third party beneficiary and the creditor is the promisee in the new contract. This too is a novation, enforceable by both the promisee and by X; it instantly discharges the debtor's previous duty. See Restatement, Contracts, § 426.

42. See:
Ala.—Perry & Walden v. Gallagher, 82 So. 562, 17 Ala.App. 114 (1919).

Mich.—Gleason v. Fitzgerald, 63 N.W. 512, 105 Mich. 516 (1895).

tained a discharge from an existing duty, that is, he acquired the legal privilege of not paying his previously existing debt.

The illustration of a novation that is most commonly given in legal treatises is not as simple in character as some of those just discussed. It starts with two existing debts, discharges both of them, and substitutes a third. Thus, suppose that A owes B a debt of $100 and B owes C a debt of $100. By the assent of all three parties, both of these debts can be discharged and a new debt substituted whereby A owes C $100.[46] This result can be reached by an agreement between B and C alone, without any assent on the part of A. All that is necessary is an agreement between B and C, whereby C discharges B from his pre-existing debt and B assigns to C his right against A to the payment of $100. After such a transaction, A's duty to B is certainly discharged; but it must be remembered that C's protection requires that a notice of the assignment should be given to A. Until such a notice, received by A, the assignor B has it in his power to defraud C by discharging A. The common law courts would not have held that a novation was consummated in this case as long as they refused to enforce an assignment of a "chose in action" and thought that a debtor could not be discharged without his own assent.

In order to effectuate such a novation as the foregoing one, it is not at all necessary that the two debts that are discharged by the novation should be identical in amount. It is not even necessary that they should be money debts at all. Thus, if A owes B a debt of $100, and B owes C fifty bushels of wheat, a complete novation will be effectuated if C gives B a discharge in return for B's assignment to C of his right to $100 against A.

Additional forms of still more complex novations can be suggested as follows: Suppose that A owes B a debt of $100 and B owes C fifty bushels of wheat. The three parties—A, B, and C— thereupon mutually agree that B will discharge A, that C will discharge B, and that A will deliver to C a horse. This transaction is a novation, whereby the two existing obligations are discharged and A undertakes a duty to a new creditor to render a new performance. Because of this change in the performance to be rendered by A, the assent of A is as necessary as is the assent of B and the assent of C.

### § 1298. Novation by Accepting a Third Person's Note

The note of a third person may be offered to and accepted by a creditor either as an additional security for the note he already holds or as an immediate substitution and discharge by novation. If the intention of the parties is not otherwise expressed, the presumption is that the new note was taken in immediate satisfaction,[49] although the comparative sums involved and the surrounding circumstances must not be disregarded. There may be a discharge by novation even though the former debtor's note is not cancelled or surrendered and there is no written renunciation;[50] but the fact that the original debtor's note is not surrendered or cancelled is of some weight to the effect that a substitution of debtors by novation was not intended.[51] If the debtor gives merely his own new note, the presumption is that there is merely a temporary suspension and not a discharge.

### § 1299.  Assent by the Debtor Not a Requisite of Novation

It is frequently said that there can be no novation without the assent of three parties, the creditor, the new party, and the debtor.[54] If this was ever the law, it is so no longer. The assent of the new party is necessary, because it is his promise that is being substituted for the obligation of the debtor. The assent of the creditor is necessary, because the proposed result is that he shall give up his existing claim against his debtor. But a debtor can be discharged without either his knowledge or assent. A sealed release delivered by the creditor to a third person for the debtor's benefit always had this effect. The acceptance of money paid by a third person, or of any other performance actually rendered by such a person, operates as a discharge of the debtor if it is tendered for that purpose. There is nothing to prevent the third person from tendering his promise as an immediate substitute for and a discharge of the debtor's obligation; and the acceptance of this offer by the creditor at once effectuates the substitution. In cases like this, the debtor is a donee beneficiary of the transaction. It is now well established law that two parties can create an enforceable right in a donee beneficiary, without his knowledge or assent; and in like manner they can discharge him from a pre-existing duty, creating in him the legal privilege not to pay.[55] Of course, the debtor does not have to assent to the benefit; if, when sued, he pleads it in defense he is then assenting. If he does not plead it in defense, judgment will go against him, just as in case he fails to plead some other good defense that may actually exist.

The assent of the debtor is necessary if the proposed novation involves not only the discharge of the debtor from his pre-existing obligation, but also his assumption of some new duty or the incurring of some new deprivation. Even in such a case, the creditor and the third party can make a valid contract between themselves, that is conditional on the debtor's subsequent assent to assume the new duty or incur the new detriment; in such case

55.   Ala.—Underwood v. Lovelace, 61 Ala. 155 (1878).
Conn.—Baurer v. Devenis, 121 A. 566, 99 Conn. 203 (1923).
Md.—Clopper v. Union Bank, 7 Har. & J. 92 (1826).

there is no novation until this condition has been performed by the debtor.

## § 1300. Novation Distinguished from Accord Executory

At this point it is necessary to repeat the distinction that exists between an accord executory and an accord and satisfaction. The latter operates as a discharge; the former does not. And yet the former may itself be a valid and enforceable contract. A novation is like accord and satisfaction; and unless the transaction operates as an immediate discharge, it is not called a novation. If the agreement between the creditor and a third person provides that on the rendition of some performance by the third person the creditor will accept that performance in full discharge of his debtor, the new agreement is not a novation; instead, it may properly be called an accord executory, and it has been so called herein. The fact that it does not instantly operate as a novation, or substituted contract, or accord and satisfaction, does not prevent it from being an enforceable executory contract.

## § 1301. Assumption of Obligation by Third Party is Not Necessarily an Offer of a Novation

Frequently an assignee of contract rights undertakes to perform the assignor's duties also. This is not operative as a novation, since the assignor remains bound by those duties so long as his creditor does not accept the assignee's new promise in lieu of the duty of the assignor.[57] The creditor's actually receiving a payment or other part performance from the assignee, knowing that he has undertaken to perform, is not an assent to a novation discharging the assignor unless the assignee's performance is tendered not merely as a satisfaction pro tanto of the assignor's duty but also on condition that the assignor shall be discharged from any further duty.[58] In like manner, the creditor's written expression of assent does not operate as a discharge of his debtor by novation where he has merely been notified that an assignment of contract rights has been made and that the assignee has assumed the performance of the assignor's duties.[59] Such an as-

**58.**　**Mass.**—Coral Gables v. Granara, 189 N.E. 604, 285 Mass. 565 (1934).

**59.**　**U.S.**—City N. Bank of Huron, S. D. v. Fuller, 52 F.2d 870, 79 A.L.R. 71 (C.C.A.8th, 1931).

In Klinkoosten v. Mundt, 156 N.W. 85, 36 S.D. 595 (1916), a note was given to the Unitype Co. by defendant for machines sold. Later the defendant sold his business and machinery to the Messenger Publishing Co., which wrote to the Unitype Co. that it assumed Mundt's rights and obligations on the machinery contract and agreed to pay the notes. On this letter, Mundt wrote authorizing the Unitype Co. to give bill of sale of machines to the Messenger Publishing Co. On this letter also was written, "Accepted. Unitype Co." It was held that this did not operate as a novation, and that Mundt was not discharged. The assent by the Unitype Co. was thought to be merely

sumption merely gives to the creditor an additional security.[60] His expression of assent does not go beyond this, unless the notice to which he assents is clearly a proposal for a substitution of debtors instead of a mere assumption of duty by the assignee. The question is one of reasonable interpretation.[61]

A frequent illustration of this type of case is found in cases where a new partnership or corporation takes over the assets of a previous one and assumes payment of the debts.[62] If the parties previously bound to pay those debts wish to be discharged from them by novation, they must make sure that there is a clear proposal that the successors shall become the sole debtors and that the creditors assent to this proposal.[63]

## § 1302.   Effect of Promisor's Erroneous Belief That He is Indebted to the Discharged Obligor

A novation is the promise by a new party to render some performance, the promise itself being both offered and accepted as an immediate discharge of the creditor's antecedent claim against a debtor. Normally, the consideration for this promise is the discharge so given by the creditor. Such a discharge is itself a sufficient consideration; it is not necessary that the debtor should give any consideration. If the debtor is thus discharged, he is a donee beneficiary of the transaction.

Sometimes the third party makes his promise to pay the debtor's debt to the creditor in the belief that he is himself indebted to that debtor and that his payment to the creditor will be in discharge of both debts. Thus, in the case of a building contract, the owner may think that he owes a balance to the building contractor, and this makes him willing to promise to pay a materialman the amount of the contractor's debt for materials. If he makes this promise in consideration of a discharge by the materialman of the latter's claim against the contractor, the transaction is not invalidated by the fact that the owner actually owes no balance to the contractor. The novation is nevertheless effective as a discharge and the owner's promise to the materialman is enforceable.[64] Of course, the owner can make his promise conditional, in express terms, on the existence of a balance due; or he can promise merely that he will apply such balance in payment of the materialman's claim.

an assent to the delivery of the machines to the Messenger Co. and to its becoming the primary obligor for the price but not the sole and substituted obligor.

64.   Idaho—McCallum v. McClarren, 98 P. 200, 15 Idaho, 374 (1908).
Ala.—Perry & Walden v. Gallagher, 82 So. 562, 17 Ala.App. 114 (1919).

# CHAPTER 72

## ACCOUNT STATED

## § 1303. What Constitutes an Account Stated—Striking the Balance Due on an Open Account

The term "account stated" has been used to denote a number of diverse transactions, the facts of which are so different that the legal relations created thereby must also be different. And yet in almost every instance in which this term is used in a court opinion or in a treatise it seems to be assumed that it invariably denotes a single type of transaction; general rules of law are laid down as if they were applicable to any transaction to which the term "account stated" has been applied. The truth is that the writers are dealing with diverse types of transactions and that the "general rule" laid down may be applicable to some "accounts stated" and not applicable to others.

In spite of the slippery terminology, the confused analysis, and the inconsistent legal doctrines, it seems probable that not a great many of the actual decisions need to be disapproved. In each case, the court is dealing with a specific set of facts, constituting the transaction between parties who are actually before the court. Facts are stubborn and impressive; and it is facts rather than legal doctrines that play the major role in judicial decision. Facts always precede rules; and it is only after a court has knowledge of the facts of a case that it finds or constructs the rules of law that it applies.

Persons who carry on business with each other often have a series of transactions constituting an open running account with various items of debit and credit. For long periods neither one may know which one is actually indebted to the other. Under such circumstances, they may get together and compare their books and their memories, cast up their mutual accounts, and strike a balance. In Latin phrase, they were formerly said to have accounted together—insimul computassent.[1] Assumpsit lay for the recovery of the balance so found due, before the development of many of the principles of present-day contract law.

At first, this custom of maintaining a continuing open account, with an occasional or a final mutual accounting and agreement on the balance due from one to the other, was probably restricted to merchant traders dealing with each other. As trading transactions multiplied and dealing on credit was extended to include many classes of people, the custom of mutual accounting and striking a balance was likewise extended. If this suggested history is accurate, it would follow that the effect of an "account stated" was originally determined by merchant custom and not by the common law of England that was then being created by the King's judges. The rules that developed out of this custom were a part of the "law merchant," then clearly demarked apart from the common law.

The custom of maintaining continuing open accounts has now prevailed for a very long time, between others as between merchants. Common illustrations of such accounts, with recurring debits and credits, are those between banker and depositor [2] between customer and grocer or department store,[3] between principal and agent,[4] and between partners in business.[5] In all such cases, if the items are liquidated in money, one of the parties is a debtor to the other in an amount that can be determined at any time by an accounting process. The amount of the debt is the

---

1. In Swaller v. Williamson Milling Co., 226 P. 1001, 116 Kan. 329 (1924), Burch, J., said: "In its origin account stated was a fact. Parties met, canvassed the items of their transactions, struck a balance, concurred in it, and then, putting the items behind them, agreed to stand on the balance. The adjustment and the agreement actually occurred. . . . With the advent of modern business methods the conception lost reality. The parties did not meet and canvass items, mutual concurrence in balance became an implication, and agreement to pay the balance became a legal fiction." See also

City of St. Petersburg v. Meyers, 55 F.2d 810 (C.C.A.5th, 1932).

In White v. Schrafft, 56 A.2d 62, 94 N.H. 467, 175 A.L.R. 242 (1948) there had been a long series of transactions. For certain years, bills had been rendered, assented to, and paid; these, even though settled by compromise or accord and satisfaction, could be reopened on proof of fraud. For the last two years, the account was open and continuing, with no bills rendered and no balance struck; there was neither a compromise and settlement nor an account stated, although an action was maintainable for unliquidated reasonable value of goods and services.

balance of debits over credits. The debt becomes due and payable only as the parties may have agreed; this may be in instalments or as a whole, at regular intervals or as demanded by the presentation of drafts or statements of account.

For the collection of any liquidated amount, whether a mere instalment or the full balance, the common law forms of action were Debt and Assumpsit. For complex accounts and undetermined balances a Bill in Equity for an accounting was available; and there was the common law action of Account, the functions of which were later performed by Assumpsit. The problem involved in a complex case was greatly simplified for the courts when the parties themselves accounted together and arrived at the result called an "account stated." Such an account stated might be reached by the parties before any balance became due or any breach committed; or it might be after a breach had already occurred, in which case the law applicable to "accords" became involved.

As between any two parties, whether they are maintaining a continuing open account or not, there may be debt items that are wholly independent of the open account; and there may be other separate and independent items consisting of unliquidated claims that cannot be entered as a debit or a credit in an account, uncertain in amount either because never agreed on or because they are in dispute.[6] Such claims as these may also be reduced to a sum certain by agreement; and the result is now often referred to as an "account stated." These will be considered separately; for the law applicable to them is in important respects a different law.

### § 1304. Liquidated Money Debts and Account Stated

Only a few words need be said about the relation of account stated to a simple debt consisting of one item, a sum certain that is due and payable. Usually it is assumed that there can be no account stated in the case of such a debt; and yet the creditor may, and frequently does, send his bill for the amount due and the debtor may expressly or tacitly assent thereto and promise to pay. As we have seen in other chapters herein, such a promise is itself an enforceable contract.[7] It is so, even though the antecedent debt has been barred by statute of limitations or has been discharged in bankruptcy; and it is so, even though the creditor presents no bill and makes no demand.[8] It is so where there have been several loans with payments on account and the parties agree upon the balance due, even though each of the loans had become barred.[9]

Such a new promise by the debtor is a contract without the necessity of either assent or consideration. Nothing is given in exchange for it. Its validity rests solely upon the preexisting debt, commonly called a "past consideration." The obligation of the new promise is limited in two ways: first, by its own terms; and secondly, by the amount of the pre-existing debt. If the new promise is merely a promise to pay five dollars, it is enforceable for that amount only; if it is a promise to pay in instalments, it is enforceable only as the instalments mature; if it is conditional on some stated event, its enforcement must await the happening of that event. And secondly, if the new promise is to pay an amount larger than the pre-existing debt it is not enforceable as to that excess.[10]

It is quite possible for two parties to owe liquidated debts to each other, created by wholly separate transactions and independently enforceable in separate actions. As procedure at common law grew more flexible and liberal, it became possible for the defendant to assert set-offs and counterclaims. Even before this occurred, however, it was possible for the parties to account together, make the correct additions and subtractions and strike a balance. Such a transaction as this may properly be described as creating an account stated. It is the equivalent of payment of the smaller debt in full and of an equal payment on account of the larger debt, leaving one of the parties wholly discharged and the other owing the balance as the only remaining liquidated debt.[14]

## § 1305. Agreements Reducing Unliquidated Claims to Certainty or Compromising Disputed Claims

Another type of transaction to be considered in its relation to an account stated is one that creates an unliquidated claim instead of a money debt. (1) Goods may be sold or services rendered for compensation, without any agreement as to the amount to be paid. In the absence of agreement on price or compensation, there is no sum certain or liquidated money debt; but there is a legal obligation to pay a "reasonable" price and "reasonable" value.[15] This amount must in some way be reduced to certainty before enforcement by judgment and execution. It can not be reduced to certainty by any mere arithmetical process. The determination of the amount to be paid requires the weighing of evidence and the exercise of discretionary judgment. It requires the work of an arbitrator or a jury, not that of an expert accountant or a bookkeeper. If the parties do not themselves agree upon the amount, within the time fixed by them or by the law for that purpose, the claimant may bring his action and have it determined

15. See White v. Schrafft, 56 A.2d 62, 94 N.H. 467, 175 A.L.R. 242 (1948), involving past accounts agreed upon and settled by payment, an open running account for goods sold for which bills had never been rendered prior to suit, and claims for the reasonable value of services rendered but never valued by the parties.

by court and jury.   This action could not have been an action of account or a bill for an accounting.

In most cases of the foregoing type, the parties do in fact agree upon the amount and thus turn the unliquidated claim into a money debt for a sum certain.   The claimant demands a named amount of money;  the obligor suggests a smaller amount that he is willing to pay;  after more or less haggling they either assent to one of these two amounts or to an intermediate amount. The promise that the obligor has thus made, expressly or tacitly, is enforceable as is any other liquidated debt;  in very numerous cases it has been described as an account stated.   It is to be observed, however, that the parties did not arrive at their result by mathematics or by bookkeeping;  it was by a process of haggling or compromise, a process of demanding and yielding, a process of discretionary give and take.   We shall demonstrate that the legal effects of this kind of an account stated are very different from those that are consequent upon one that is reached by a mere accounting or bookkeeping process.   Before doing so, let us consider certain other unliquidated claims that may be thought to differ from the foregoing ones.

(2)  When one party harms another by a breach of contract or a tort, that other usually has an enforceable claim for compensatory damages.   Like the claim for reasonable compensation for goods sold or services rendered, this too is an unliquidated claim, one that is enforceable by action at law unless the parties make settlement otherwise.   This, too, can be settled by amicable agreement;  but, as in the previous case, it can not be settled by mere accounting or bookkeeping.[16]   If the parties reach such a settlement, by a process of haggling, compromising, and yielding, it is sometimes expressly denied that they have created an account stated.[17]

If there is any difference between the two cases, it lies merely in the fact that in the latter ones it definitely appears that there is a cause of action for a wrong before the settlement agreement takes place, while in the former ones it does not so clearly appear.   And yet the obligation to pay a reasonable price for goods sold or services rendered is enforceable by action immediately after delivery of the goods or completion of the services, unless there was an agreement for a period of credit;  and, in any case, at the expiration of such a period an action will at once lie.   Action does not have to await liquidation by agreement;  and many such settlement agreements are made after a time when suit could have been maintained.   Yet enforcement is not denied for that reason and the agreement is generally said to create an account stated.

17.   See Murphy v. Oregon Engr. Co., 186 P. 12, 94 Or. 534 (1919), and Laycock v. Pickles, 4 B. & S. 497, 33 L.J.Q.B. 43 (1863).

Just as in the case of mutual debts that may be set off against each other by agreement, two parties may have separate and independent unliquidated claims against each other, arising out of entirely separate incidents and transactions. These too may all become the subject of a settlement agreement. The parties may agree to cancel them all out against each other without liquidating any one of them into a definite sum of money; no debt is created thereby and there is no account stated. Or they may by special agreement liquidate each one of them separately, and then set them off against each other as in the case of other mutual and independent money debts, thereby striking a balance due from one to the other which that one then promises to pay.[18]

### § 1307.  Account Stated That is a Mere Arithmetical Computation

It might be supposed that an account stated that is no more than a mere arithmetical computation would have no legal operation whatever, that it would merely confirm the truth when it is correct and would not in any way nullify the truth when it is incorrect. Such accounts, however, have important legal operation in addition to their evidential weight.

A mutual accounting and the striking of a balance due are always accompanied by the debtor's promise to pay that balance and by the creditor's promise to accept it as full satisfaction. These promises, if not express, are reasonably to be inferred. If the accounting is accurate and the balance found is arithmetically correct, each party is promising exactly that which he is already legally bound to perform. Such a promise is ordinarily said to be insufficient as a consideration for a return promise. Nevertheless, the debtor's new promise, express or implied, may properly be described as a contract, even though there is no sufficient consideration given for it by the promisee—no bargained-for equivalent given in exchange. It is a promise to pay a pre-existing debt. This pre-existing debt has been called by the courts a sufficient "past" consideration. The American Law Institute has preferred to say that such a promise is enforceable without consideration. At any rate, the existing debt forms a sufficient basis for an enforceable new promise; and this is true even though the past debt has been barred by the statute of limitations. The past debt, however, is a sufficient basis only so far as it in fact existed; the new promise is enforceable only so far as it is co-extensive with that debt. It appears, therefore, that the courts are quite correct in treating such an account stated as this as merely prima facie evidence of the pre-existing debt, the payment of which is promised, and in letting either party prove error if he can.[21]

21. **U.S.**—Standard Oil Co. v. Van Etten, 1 S.Ct. 178, 107 U.S. 325, 27 L. Ed. 319 (1882), is an illustration of this type of account stated. The plaintiff sold barrel headings to the defendant. The latter had a count

The new promise of the debtor is a contract, because it is enforceable by action on it; but it is a contract only so far as it is antecedently well supported.  The new promise of the creditor is not binding and not a contract in so far as it is a promise to accept less than is due; the debtor has given no sufficient consideration for such a promise.  This is true even though the mistake is that of the creditor himself in omitting an undisputed item from his rendered account.[22]

### § 1308.   An Account as an Evidential Admission

The rendition of a bill or statement of account is in itself an admission by the claimant that there is no claim in excess of the bill.   Such an admission is not conclusive against him.[23]   The bill or account, even though actually received, has no effect whatever, as an admission or otherwise, against the alleged debtor.[24] His continued silence for an unreasonable time may be held to be an admission that the bill is correct or even an expression of a promise to pay it.  But a tacit admission like this would be no more conclusive than an express admission; and a tacit promise like this would be enforceable only if it would be so if put into express words.

Statements by the courts are numerous to the effect that an account stated is merely prima facie evidence of the balance due.[25] Such a statement must not be taken to mean that the creditor cannot properly declare upon the debtor's promise, express or implied, that he makes when he assents to the account as correct.  But whether the creditor declares on the original debt or on the new promise, the account stated is prima facie evidence of the amount due.  It is no more than that, if the account is merely a numerical computation; it is much more than that if the agreement is a compromise or settlement of an unliquidated claim.

made by an inspector, rendered an account thereof, and paid the sum shown to be due.   The plaintiff assented by some months' silence; but he eventually sued for a balance due, alleging and proving a mistake in the count by the inspector.  Judgment was given for the plaintiff.  The mutual assent as to the number of headings and the amount due was an assent to a computation believed to be correct, not the compromise of a claim known to be doubtful.

A promise to pay a sum of money, when there was no antecedent debt or dealing whatever, cannot be made enforceable by calling it an account stated.

25.   U.S.—Perkins   v.   Hart,   11 Wheat. 237 (1826).

Cal.—Green v. Thornton, 30 P. 965, 96 Cal. 67 (1892).

Kan.—Swaller v. Williamson Milling Co., 226 P. 1001, 116 Kan. 329 (1924), quoted at length in a previous section.

"The general rule is that an account stated may always be impeached for mistake. An account stated is only prima facie evidence of its correctness." Wussow v. Badger State Bank of Milwaukee, 234 N.W. 720, 236 N.W. 687, 204 Wis. 467 (1931).

### § 1309. Account Stated as a New Cause of Action

If a claimant renders his account and this is assented to as correct by the other party, with an express or implied promise to pay, suit can be maintained on the promise.[26] This is true whether the parties have thus created an account stated as to antecedent liquidated claims or have thus turned an antecedent disputed or unliquidated claim into a liquidated debt. If it is the former, the debtor's promise is merely one to pay his already existing debt and is enforceable against him unless he shows errors or omissions in the accounting. If it is the latter, it is binding as a wholly new contract of accord or compromise, without regard to the accuracy or validity of the claim previously made, provided it was made honestly and in good faith. Although an agreement of this latter kind would once have been open to the objection that it is an accord executory (assuming that it was not itself accepted as an immediate discharge and satisfaction of the previous claim), this objection has at last been openly recognized as invalid. In numberless cases it was by-passed by the device of calling the transaction an account stated instead of an accord.

### § 1310. Effect of Mistake in an Account Stated—Burden of Proof and of Producing Evidence of Errors and Omissions

One who is sued upon an account stated may deny ever having assented thereto, or he may assert the total absence of any transactions out of which a debt could arise. The burden is on the plaintiff to establish the existence of the defendant's assent and promise to pay and also the existence of a basis for it if these are denied. But it is not necessary for the plaintiff to list or allege in his complaint the items on which the account stated was based.[32] If the defendant does not deny the existence or validity of the account stated, he must, in order to overcome the plaintiff's prima facie case, proceed with evidence to establish specific errors and omissions. In the absence of such evidence, it is unnecessary for the creditor to introduce any evidence as to the transactions on which the account is based.[33]

The courts often say that an account stated is conclusive unless the defendant proves "fraud, accident, or mistake"; but, in the present instance, this means that the defendant may attack the balance shown in the account, in spite of his having assented thereto, by evidence of errors of computation and errors in the inclusion or exclusion of items. His previous assent merely puts on him the burden of showing wherein the account is incorrect.[34]

### § 1311. Action by Creditor for an Amount in Excess of the Account Stated

If there is no new consideration for the creditor's promise to accept the amount of the stated account as full satisfaction, his promissory admission is only prima facie evidence against him. Such a promise is not binding, if the sum promised by the debtor in the stated account is actually less than is then legally due from him. Therefore, the creditor may prove the antecedent transactions to show that a larger amount was due.[39] As to this excess over the stated account, the burden of establishing it is on the claimant.[40] As to this excess, he has no admission by his debtor to make a prima facie case; and the account stated is a prima facie defense against the creditor's claim to the excess.[41]

## § 1312.  Account Stated Compared with Compromise or Accord

If the amount due from one party to the other is unliquidated and uncertain, whether because the claims or counterclaims are in dispute or because the sum to be paid has never been agreed upon, an offer by either one to settle for a specified sum, assented to by the other, consummates a contract of compromise and settlement. This is true whether the offer so made specifies that the act of acceptance shall constitute an immediate discharge of all prior claims, thus consummating an accord and satisfaction by the substitution of the new contract, or specifies instead that the acceptance must be followed by payment before discharge takes place. In the latter case, the acceptance of the offer constitutes what is called an "accord executory"; but it is a valid contract just the same.

There are many cases in which the court has described a transaction as an account stated, when it could more properly be described as an accord executory or as an accord and satisfaction.[44]

**39.  U.S.**—Standard Oil Co. v. Van Etten, 1 S.Ct. 178, 107 U.S. 325, 27 L.Ed. 319 (1882); Bowen Motor Coaches v. N. Y. Casualty Co., 139 F.2d 332 (C.C.A.5th, 1944); City of St. Petersburg v. Meyers, 55 F.2d 810 (C.C.A.5th, 1932).

**Kan.**—Swaller v. Williamson Milling Co., 226 P. 1001, 116 Kan. 329 (1924).

A common case of this kind is action by a bank depositor for an amount erroneously charged against him by the bank, often because of its cashing forged checks. The depositor's assent to bank statements of balances does not prevent recovery.

**N.Y.**—National Surety Co. v. Manhattan Co., 169 N.E. 372, 252 N.Y. 247, 67 A.L.R. 1113 (1929); Shipman v. Bank of the State of N. Y., 27 N.E. 371, 126 N.Y. 318 (1891).

**44.**  In the following cases, the stated account appears to have been either a compromise of a dispute or the settlement of an unliquidated claim with knowledge that its amount was uncertain.

**U.S.**—Kretni Development Co. v. Consolidated Oil Corp., 74 F.2d 497 (C.C.A.10th, 1934), accord and satisfaction; Vance v. Chicago Portrait Co., 19 F.2d 981 (C.C.A.7th, 1927), compromise with satisfaction; Bank of N. Y. v. U. S., 76 F.Supp. 549 (D.C.N.J.1947), same, but said by the court to be an "account stated and settled".

**Mass.**—Rizkalla v. Abusamra, 187 N. E. 602, 284 Mass. 303 (1933).

**Eng.**—Laycock v. Pickles, 4 B. & S. 497, 33 L.J.Q.B. 43 (1863); Homes v. Savill, Cro.Car. 116 (1628); Bard v. Bard, Cro.Jac. 602 (1620).

In such cases as these, the term "account stated" tends to confusion of thought, as leading to an incorrect inference that the legal relations created by every account stated are identical with those created by a contract of accord or compromise. Its use rendered some service in enabling courts to disregard the old rule that an accord executory is not an enforceable contract; but it is no longer necessary for that purpose.

The striking of an agreed balance between two parties by the arithmetical process of computing numerical debits and credits, is neither a compromise nor an accord; and the law applicable to it is not the law of compromise or the law of accord and satisfaction.[45] The monthly bank statement rendered to a depositor states the balance due and may properly be called an account stated as soon as it is tacitly assented to by the depositor. It is not a compromise; the items of the bank statement are numerical debits and credits. If A buys goods of B, at agreed prices, paying $100 on account, and a bill is rendered by B crediting the payment and stating the balance, there is an account stated as soon as A expressly or tacitly assents to the correctness of the bill.

On the other hand, if services are rendered by a lawyer or a doctor, for compensation not made definite, the rendition of a bill for a specific sum of money is an offer to liquidate the claim and to reduce it to certainty. The assent to such an account rendered is an assent to the offer and is frequently said to create an account stated.[46] But it is more than a mere accounting; it is an agreement to pay and to receive a specific sum of money in satisfaction of an unliquidated claim—it is an accord executory. The same is true in case of a bill rendered for goods sold at a price that was not determined, or for a sum as the damages claimed for a breach of contract or for a tort.[47]

---

**45.** The distinction here made is clearly stated by Selden, J., in Lockwood v. Thorne, 18 N.Y. 285 (1858), and in Handley v. Baretta, 181 So. 828 (La.App.1938).

**47.** In Gardner v. Watson, 150 P. 994, 170 Cal. 570 (1915), the claim settled was one for uncertain damages for alleged fraud. This case made trouble for the court in Walsh v. Parker, 74 P.2d 531, 24 Cal.App.2d 224 (1937), but it did not follow it. The court held that a promise to pay $2,000 per year for services of a minor character rendered over six past years was not an account stated and was not en-

forceable. There certainly had been no mutual accounting with balance struck. Nor was the promise made as a compromise of a doubtful claim. It was merely a promise by an aged woman that an amount far in excess of the value of services received would be paid out of her estate.

The American Law Institute's Illustration 2, under § 422, Contracts Restatement, is as follows: "A orders goods from B his grocer, no price being fixed. B employs A, an attorney at law, to render certain services for which no price is fixed. A and B agree that the value of the groceries is $125 and

If the transaction that is described by the court as an account stated is in fact a compromise of a doubtful or disputed claim or is an agreed liquidation of a claim theretofore uncertain in amount, the validity of the agreement does not depend on the validity of the antecedent claim. The new agreement is then either an accord executory or a substituted executory contract (an accord and satisfaction). For each party's promise in the new agreement there is an entirely new consideration—the return promise of the other party.[48]

The great expansion in the use and coverage of the term account stated is largely due to the fact that it enabled courts and counsel to by-pass the old doctrine that "upon an accord no remedy lies". Transactions that are in no way distinguishable from an executory accord were thus made enforceable without seeming to run afoul of that ancient doctrine.[49] Eventually, that doctrine has itself been more directly nullified under its own name.[50] Of course, if the new agreement, under whatever name,

the value of the legal services is $100, and that the balance due B is $25. There is an account stated." This is quite correct. They have struck a balance between two liquidated debts; and it is the correct balance. But their valuation of the groceries at $125 was not the mere striking of a balance; nor was their valuation of A's services at $100. Each of these was a valid contract, with no error or mistake of any kind, even though others might have made different valuations. The agreement effected the cancellation and set-off of $100 of each of the debts; but A's promise is merely a promise to pay $25 still due for groceries. If by an error in subtraction, they had stated the balance due as $35, the account would likewise have been "stated"; but it would have been erroneous and not binding on the debtor beyond $25. Yet the agreed valuation of the groceries at $125 and of the services at $100 would still be binding. There was no "mistake" in either of those agreements. The two valuations might have been so related as to make both of them constructively conditional on the accuracy of the subtraction made; that is, the grocer's assent to the valuation of his goods at $125

might have been conditional on the valuation of the legal services at $35 less. If this had been their agreement there would be a "compromise and settlement" of both claims at once without a separate liquidation of either one.

Illustration 1 immediately adjacent, seems to be in conflict with Illustration 2. It reads: "A owes to B a thousand dollars. A has a claim against B for B's failure to do certain work that B had contracted to do. Subsequently A and B agree that A's damages amount to $300, and that therefore the net amount due B is $700. This is not an account stated, but there is a valid compromise." The correct conclusion is as follows: There is a valid compromise of A's unliquidated claim against B, reducing that claim to the liquidated sum of $300. There are now two liquidated cross claims, just as in Illustration 2. The parties have also struck a balance of these two claims at $700. This is the correct balance, and the account is stated. There has been a mutual set-off of claims for $300, resulting in an account stated just as in the other illustration. B can sue for the balance of $700 on his original debt, or on A's new promise to pay it.

is assented to as in substitution for and in settlement of previous claims, the rule as to executory accords did not purport to be applicable and the new agreement is an enforceable contract as well as a discharge of the antecedent claims.

### § 1313.  Mutual Assent Necessary—Silence as an Assent

It is always said that there is no account stated unless both parties have expressed assent to it as correct.[54]  Here again it is necessary to analyze and classify the cases, and to differentiate between agreements liquidating or compromising doubtful or disputed claims and a mere arithmetical accounting of liquidated items.  In any case, the mere rendition of a bill or statement of account, by either party, is in the nature of an admission by him alone, that the amount stated therein is correct.[55]  This has evidential weight;  but it is not conclusive and does not prevent the party who rendered the statement from showing its incorrectness.  The same is true even though the party receiving the statement also assents to it, thereby making a similar admission.

If either the creditor or the debtor offers to liquidate a claim theretofore uncertain in amount or to compromise a doubtful or disputed claim by the payment of a specified amount, it is without question that an assent by the offeree is necessary.[56]  Such an offer is not even an admission as to an amount due.  In cases of this sort, it is not often that silence should be interpreted as an expression of assent;  in rare cases the surrounding circumstances may justify such an interpretation.[57]

Even if an account is rendered as a mere computation believed to be correct, and not as an offer of compromise and settlement, it is never called an account stated unless the party receiving the account assents to it, expressly or tacitly;  but as to the necessity of such assent there is a marked difference between an account rendered by the creditor and an account rendered by the debtor.  Most accounts are rendered by the creditor;  and it is obvious that, unless the debtor expresses assent, he has made neither a promise to pay nor an evidential admission.  Of course, no action will lie in favor of the creditor on a new promise by the debtor that has never been made.  If an account stated is regarded as a contract, the debtor has made no such contract;  if it is regarded as an evidential admission, he has made no such admission.  Until the debtor has assented, there is no account stated in any sense of that term.  There has been a statement of account by the creditor, but not an "account stated."

In the comparatively smaller number of cases, however, in which the account is rendered by the debtor to the creditor, the transaction is substantially different and the necessity of the creditor's assent may not exist.  Here, again, if the debtor's accounting is an offer to compromise and settle a claim then understood to be doubtful or disputed, the creditor's assent is necessary.[58] Without it there is only an unaccepted offer, one that is conditional on acceptance just as in the case of other offers. But if the debtor renders a statement of account that purports to be an accurate computation of items that are themselves neither doubtful nor disputed, his action in so doing is an evidential admission and also justifies the inference that he promises to pay the amount so admitted to be due.

If when the debtor renders his statement of account he promises, either expressly or impliedly, to pay the amount therein stated, his promise is binding from the time that it is made, insofar as the statement is correct. To make it thus binding on the debtor, no assent by the creditor is necessary.[59] And if the amount stated by the debtor is in excess of the amount actually due, his promise to pay that excess is not made binding by the fact that the creditor expresses his assent. The statute of limitations begins to run against enforcement of the new promise from the time it is made, not from the time of any expression of assent by the creditor.

When a statement of account is rendered by one of the parties, the retention of this statement by the other party, without objection made, for more than a reasonable time for its investigation, has very often been held to be an expression of assent to its correctness.[62] This is one of the cases in which silence, in the light of the preceding relations of the parties, may be operative as an expression of assent. The inference of such assent may readily be rebutted by other evidence as, for example, that the claim on which the account is based was a disputed claim.[63]

A common illustration of a case in which an account rendered by a debtor is held to become an account stated, by reason of the creditor's retention of it without objection, is the monthly bank statement rendered by a debtor bank to its depositor along with the latter's cancelled checks.[64] It should be remembered, however, that this does not prevent either party from proving errors and omissions, unless and until there has been such a change of position in reasonable reliance as to create an equitable estoppel.[65] Negligence by the depositor and change of position by the bank may lead to such an estoppel; [66] but errors and omissions in the bank statement and the charging of forged checks against a depositor are negligence on the part of the bank and must be weighed in determining what justice requires.[67] Seldom is either a debtor or a creditor justified in refusing to correct an erroneous accounting merely because of the lapse of time; but the lapse of time and the loss of records and other evidence may make it difficult to determine whether an alleged error was in fact made. It is for this reason that courts of equity often refused to sustain a bill for the reopening of closed accounts and the determination of stale claims.

## § 1314. Does an Account Stated Operate as a Discharge?

An account stated, in the sense of a mutual assent to a statement of the balance found by mere arithmetical computation of debits and credits in a running account between the parties, does not operate in any case as a discharge of the debt that was previously due; nor can it create a debt in excess of the one that was previously due. This statement is not in harmony with a rule adopted by the American Law Institute, at least in appearance.[77] The only debt previously enforceable was the correct balance, arithmetically determined; and that is the debt that is still payable, whether the account was correctly or incorrectly "stated."

If the balance struck by agreement is the correct one, we have no more than a promise by the debtor to pay his existing debt and a promise by the creditor to receive payment as a full discharge. Such a promise by the debtor, if not made in such a solemn form as to operate as a "merger",[78] does not discharge the previously existing debt. Instead, an action will lie on that debt.[79] As already stated an action will lie on the debtor's new promise, also.

Next, if the balance struck in the agreement is larger than the existing debt, by reason of the omission of a credit or of errors in computation, the promise of the debtor to pay the larger sum does not discharge the previous debt for the same reasons as before. Just as before, there is no sufficient consideration for the debtor's promise; and in so far as it is in excess of the existing debt, that debt furnishes no support for it. The creditor's promise to receive a larger sum than is due, in discharge of the debt, is not a sufficient consideration for any promise. In a suit on the debtor's

---

**77.** Restatement, Contracts, § 422, reads: "(1) Matured debts are discharged by a manifestation of assent in good faith by debtor and creditor to a stated sum as an accurate computation of the amount of the matured debt or debts due the creditor, or if there are cross demands as the amount of the difference between the total indebtedness due one party and the total indebtedness due the other party. A new duty arises to pay a sum so fixed. . . .
"(3) Where there is an omission of some item or an error in computation or in the amount of an item in a statement of account, the duty to pay the stated sum can be avoided by a party who has assented thereto in ignorance of the omission or error, unless in justifiable reliance on the statement of account the other party has materially changed his position."
In the accompanying "Comment," the Institute clearly distinguishes between "account stated" and "compromise."
In par. *f* of the Comment, it is said: "Obvious insufficiency of consideration also invalidates an account stated. Though an antecedent liquidated debt will support a promise to pay it, such a debt will not support a promise to pay a sum that the parties must have known was larger; nor will a promise to pay an obviously smaller sum discharge the antecedent debt."
This Comment is in harmony with the present text; and the four Illustrations under § 422 are believed to be likewise.

new promise, there is nothing to prevent the debtor from proving the mistake—the omission of a credit or the errors of computation.[80] If he has already paid too much by mistake, he has a right to the restitution of the excess.[81]

Finally, if the balance struck in the agreement is smaller than the existing debt, the debtor's promise to pay that sum in satisfaction is not a sufficient consideration for the creditor's promise to receive it in satisfaction.[82] The creditor may sue, if he likes, on the debtor's little promise; but if he sues instead on the old debt, there is again nothing to prevent him from proving its actual amount and the reason for the deficiency in the erroneous account.[83]

If the so-called statement of account is in fact a compromise of disputed claims or an agreed liquidation of an unliquidated claim, it is itself enforceable without regard to the validity of the claims previously made.[86] In such cases, however, the new agreement may be either an accord executory or a substituted executory contract. In the latter case it is a discharge of the previous claim;[87] but in the former it operates only to suspend action on the previous claim as long as there has been no substantial breach of the accord by the debtor.[88] The law applicable to these cases should be sought under these headings, not under "account stated."

It seems almost certain that statements to the effect that an account stated operates to discharge the pre-existing debt, are made with respect to cases in which the previous claim was disputed or otherwise unliquidated. At all events, the statement is true only as to them; and even as to them it is not wholly true if the new agreement was not understood to be a substituted contract, but was instead an executory accord.[a]

---

80.   **U.S.**—Perkins v. Hart, 11 Wheat. (24 U.S.) 237, 6 L.Ed. 463 (1826), dictum.

**N.Y.**—Lockwood v. Thorne, 18 N.Y. 285 (1858), per Selden, J.; Donald v. Gardner, 44 App.Div. 235, 60 N.Y.S. 668 (1899); Sedgwick v. Macy, 24 App.Div. 1, 49 N.Y.S. 154 (1897).

**Tex.**—Dodson v. Watson, 220 S.W. 771, 110 Tex. 355 (1920), the defendant, sued on an account stated, proved an item omitted by him from the account that he had himself rendered.

81.   **Kan.**—McCue v. Hope, 154 P. 216, 97 Kan. 85, 11 A.L.R. 581 (1916).

a.   Chapter 73, here omitted, deals with Discharge of Specialties, and of Discharge by Alteration, Judgment, Arbitration and Award, and Merger.

# TOPIC B

# IMPOSSIBILITY

## CHAPTER 74

## IMPOSSIBILITY OF PERFORMANCE—PERSONAL INABILITY

## § 1320. Impossibility as a Defense—Evolution of the Law

A study of the cases indicates that there has been an increasing liberality in determining what constitutes a justifying "impossibility" or frustration of purpose. A portion, at least, of the risk of disappointment by supervening events is being put upon the promisee. The earliest stated doctrines were that impossibility does not discharge; and when those statements first began to break down, the courts were very strict in refusing a discharge unless the impossibility was absolute.[1]

Before the recognition of bilateral contracts in the sixteenth century, the problems of impossibility and frustration were much less complex. One who promised to compensate for services or

1088

goods certainly did not have to pay if an unexpected event prevented the service or the transfer; and no action would lie against the promisee for his failure to serve or to transfer, whether his failure was caused by *force majeure* or was obstinately wilful. Having made no promise, he was guilty of no breach. If, after the service was rendered or the goods transferred, some event made the specific form of compensation impossible, the promisor's enrichment would have been grossly unjust if the impossibility had been held to discharge him from the duty to pay its value in money. This would be equally true in similar transactions today.

For two centuries after bilateral agreements became enforceable the mutual promises, in the absence of express words of condition, were thought to be mutually independent. Failure of performance by one promisor, whether wilful or caused by death or destruction, was no defense in a suit for nonperformance of the return promise; the defendant merely had a counter action, and in this counter action "impossibility" should, in justice, be no defense. As business agreements became increasingly bilateral in character, the law of mutual independency became in conflict with the practices and mores of men. It was, after much travail, changed by the judges, a change in which Lord Mansfield played an important part, but in the wake of earlier judicial action. The change was effected largely by the method of the "implied condition". Long before the decision in Taylor v. Caldwell,[2] Taylor's duty to pay rent was made conditional on his getting the use of the music hall that he had hired from Caldwell. After this rule became established, discharging Taylor in case of failure to get the hall, whether by its destruction or otherwise, it became imperative to change the rule that Caldwell would be liable in damages for non-delivery that was caused by fire or other *force majeure*.

The differences between impossibility of performance of a promise and frustration of the purpose for which a contract was made will be discussed in the succeeding sections. At this point it may be noted that when a promisor is sued for nonperformance he may set up, among various kinds of defenses, the three following that are very different in character: (1) he may assert that supervening events have made his own performance impossible; (2) he may assert that performance of the agreed equivalent has become impossible; (3) he may assert that the purpose for which he made the contract has been frustrated. These are alike in being asserted as a justifying reason for the defendant's not performing his promise; but the first is that he himself can not perform, and the second is that the plaintiff can not. The second of

2.    3 Best & S. 826 (1863), a leading
      case that is discussed in §§ 1331
      and 1337.

these defenses is often described as "failure of consideration"; but failure of consideration may be caused in many ways not involving impossibility. The third of these defenses is frequently not an assertion of impossibility of performance of either party's promise; it is an assertion that it has become impossible for him to attain the end and aim for which he had assented to the bargain. All three assert that something has been made impossible by supervening events. The existence of this common factor has caused the three types of cases to be discussed together. The last two will be found to overlap other topics discussed elsewhere in this work.

With respect to all three of the foregoing types of defenses, there has been a progressive development in the law, lessening the risks to be carried by a promisor. This has no doubt been based upon a similar development in the practices and understandings of contractors.

### § 1321. Supervening Impossibility of Rendering a Promised Performance—Distribution of Risks

If the specific performance promised by a contractor becomes impossible, either by the destruction of the specific subject matter, the death of a necessary person, or the non-existence of the specifically contemplated means of performance, his duty is discharged—unless the parties expressed a contrary intention. So, one who promises to give possession of a music hall is discharged by the destruction of the hall before the time for delivery.[3] A like result obtains where a seller promises to deliver specific goods,[4] or where one promises that he (or a specific third person) will render personal service.[5]

In cases like the foregoing, the custom of men has indicated by whom the risk should be carried, and the extent of the risk that is carried. The one promising the performance that has later become impossible bears the risk of loss of property value by reason of his ownership; and he also bears the risk of not getting the agreed exchange (the price) for the performance that he promises to render. The other party also bears a risk— the risk of not getting the profit that performance of the bargain would have brought him; he can maintain no action for the profits of his bargain, however certain it is that they would have been made. But, on the other hand, he does not bear the risk of having to pay the promised price for nothing. If he does not get the house, or the goods, or the service, he does not have to pay the

3. Eng.—Taylor v. Caldwell, 3 Best & S. 826 (1863).

horse became sick and was shot by order of the S.P.C.A.

4. N.J.—Gouled v. Holwitz, 113 A. 323, 95 N.J.L. 277 (1921), a hired

5. N.Y.—Spalding v. Rosa, 71 N.Y. 40 (1877), illness of artist.

price;  and if he has paid part or all of the price in advance, he
has a right of restitution.[6]  Thus are the risks of loss and disappointment divided between the parties;  and the subdivision does
not give dissatisfaction in the community.  Either it was in accord with common usage before the judicial decisions, the usage
being the basis of the decisions;  or else the decisions created a
workable rule that has been accepted and has resulted in common
usage.

The same result is reached, and for the same reasons, if one
party's specific promised performance is made illegal, or otherwise actually impossible, by a supervening law or by the act of
government domestic or foreign.

In the cases just discussed, the specific performance promised
by one has become impossible or illegal;  and there seems to be
no sufficient reason for compelling him to make compensation for
the other party's disappointment—for his loss of bargain profits.
The risk of this loss is therefore carried by the other party.  Observe, however, that the purpose for which this other party made
the contract and promised an agreed exchange has been "frustrated."  His purpose was to get the use of the hall, or the goods,
or the valuable services.  This frustration of his purpose, even
though the first party is without blame, discharges him, too, from
his duty to pay the price, and gives him a right to restitution if
he has already paid it.  In subsequent sections, we shall discuss
the allocation of risks, and the effect of frustration of one party's
purpose in entering into the contract, in cases where there is no
impossibility or illegality of rendering a specific promised performance.  Frustration of purpose may be no less complete, even
though not caused by supervening impossibility of rendering one
of the specific promised performances.

### § 1322.  Impossibility of Performance Compared with Frustra-
tion of Purpose

Before proceeding to discuss specific cases or to construct general rules, it will be helpful to compare briefly two closely related
concepts:  impossibility of performance, and frustration of purpose.  Generally, in a contract transaction, there are performances rendered, or promised to be rendered, by each of the contracting parties.  Either one or both of these performances may
become impossible, or illegal, or dangerous, or difficult, or expensive.  The effect of these supervening changes in the situation,
upon the rights and duties of the parties, must be considered.

---

6.    The English courts formerly refused to recognize this right to
restitution;  but the House of
Lords has recently changed their

law in this respect.  See Fibrosa
Spolka Akcyjna v. Fairbairn etc.
[1943] A.C. 32, [1942] 2 All Eng.
122, 167 L.T. 101, 111 L.J.K.B. 433.

They are usually discussed under the general heading, "impossibility of performance."

Secondly, each of the two parties to a contract has an object or purpose for which he joins in the transaction. These purposes are not identical; each party has his own separate purpose. There is no "purpose of the contract"; instead, there are the purposes of the parties to the contract. Supervening events may frustrate the purpose of either one of the parties. Very much less often, they may frustrate the purposes of both parties. If the frustration of one party's purpose is held to discharge his duty to perform, the law thereby frustrates the purpose of the other party also, making available to him the defense of failure of consideration.

Generally, the purpose that induces contractor A to express assent and to render a performance, or to promise to render it, is the attainment of an agreed equivalent that is given or promised by the other party B. If that agreed equivalent becomes impossible, or is not for any reason actually performed, the purpose of contractor A is frustrated. But the fact that the performance promised by contractor B becomes impossible does not, in itself, frustrate B's purpose at all. Two quite distinct questions, therefore, arise out of the supervening impossibility of B's promised performance: (1) Is B discharged from duty, or must he pay damages for breach? (2) Is the contracting purpose of A frustrated; and, if yes, is A still bound to perform his return promise—to pay the agreed price? These two questions do not answer themselves; and they are not necessarily answered alike. Observe that if we discharge B from further duty, it is because his promised performance has become impossible, not because his purpose is frustrated. If we discharge A from duty to pay the price, it is not because his performance is impossible, but because the attainment of his purpose has become impossible— his purpose is frustrated by the fact that B can not perform the bargained-for equivalent and is under no duty to pay damages for the non-performance.[7]

We must observe, further, that the purposes of contractor A may be complex; his purpose is to get the return performance promised by B, but he bargains for that performance for the further purpose of making use of it in some profitable way. Some-

---

7. So, if a government order fixing a maximum price invalidates a previously made contract fixing a higher price, the seller of the goods is not bound to deliver the goods. In re Kramer & Uchitelle, 43 N.E.2d 493, 288 N.Y. 467, 141 A.L.R. 1497 (1942). Such a government order does not require the seller to deliver at the lower rate; and his contractual duty to deliver was certainly conditional on payment at the contract rate. The government order frustrates the seller's purpose by making performance by the buyer illegal.

times it is this further use that becomes impossible; it is this further and ultimate purpose of A that is frustrated by supervening events. Such a frustration as this may come about, even though neither one of the actual performances promised by A and B has become impossible, or even difficult. The frustration of such an ultimate purpose as this should not be described as an "impossibility of performance," although it is true that something has become impossible.[8]

We can not lay down one simple and all-controlling rule for these various kinds of frustration and impossibility. Many varying factors must be considered in each case that arises. These factors are capable of classification, and a number of tentative working rules may be constructed—not the less rules of law by reason of their being tentative working rules. The problem is that of allocating, in the most generally satisfactory way, the risks of harm and disappointment that result from supervening events.[9]

The leading case in the field of impossibility is Paradine v. Jane, Aleyn, 26 (1647, K.B.), a case that has been cited innumerable times, apparently with uniform approval. It states a rule to the effect that one who contracts to render some performance is not discharged from legal duty by the fact that this performance subsequently becomes impossible without any fault in him. Both the facts of the case and the reported reasoning of the court deserve extended discussion here.

The plaintiff declared in an action of Debt, "upon a Lease for years rendering Rent," the tenant not having paid for three years. The tenant pleaded that a royalist army under Prince Rupert had invaded the kingdom, expelled him from possession, and kept him out for the three years during which rent was not paid, "whereby he could not take the profits." The plaintiff's demurrer to this plea was sustained.[10]

The court held that the tenant must pay the rent even though the army was composed wholly of alien enemies. "And this difference was taken, that where the Law creates a duty or charge, and the party is disabled to perform it without any default in

---

8. It has been held that such a "frustration" as this, the frustration of a lessee's purpose of operating a grain elevator at a profit, does not discharge him from his duty to pay the agreed rent. The Interstate Commerce Commission had made such a change in transportation rates that grain would no longer be shipped to this elevator. But "the elevator . . . still stands. The railroads . . . are still in opera-tion. The Omaha Grain Market still functions, and the elevator business continues as before. [Not the lessee's business.] The frustration complained of related to a more remote objective—the making of a profit out of the use of the leased premises." Megan v. Updike Grain Corp., 94 F.2d 551 (1938). Like enough, the risk of rate changes may as well be left on the lessee.

him, and hath no remedy over, there the Law will excuse him. As in the case of waste, if a house be destroyed by a tempest, or by enemies, the tenant is excused.[11] . . . but when the party by his own contract creates a duty or charge upon himself, he is bound to make it good, if he may, notwithstanding any accident by inevitable necessity, because he might have provided against it by his contract. And therefore if the lessee covenant to repair a house, though it be burnt by lightning, or thrown down by enemies, yet he ought to repair it." [12]

There was some question whether the tenant's duty to pay rent in this case was really contractual, since the lease was a conveyance with a "reservation" of rent, and there were no express words of covenant or promise by the lessee to pay rent. But the court held, very reasonably, that the reservation of rent (in a lease accepted by the lessee) amounted to a covenant to pay it.[13]

The report of the case goes on: "Another reason was added, that as the lessee is to have the advantage of casual profits, so he must run the hazard of casual losses, and not lay the whole burthen of them upon his lessor." Here the court was making a conscious allocation of risks. The leasehold estate is "property," just as is the landlord's "reversion." Indeed, some leases are for very long terms, so that the value of the tenant's interest may be very much greater than that of the landlord's interest.[14] If the parties have not otherwise agreed, as by an express covenant to repair, the risk of loss by fire or storm is borne by both parties as their several interests appear. The tenant loses the use of a destroyed building during the term; the landlord loses its use thereafter. Each bears his own loss; and rent is payable as usual. So, if an alien army occupies the land, the tenant loses the use

---

11. This means that if the duty of a tenant not to permit waste is a duty created by law, and not by his contract, he is excused therefrom in case of destruction by storm or by enemies. This means no more than that the law makes it the tenant's duty not to commit waste himself or to permit waste by other individuals, but does not make it his duty to repair the destruction by storm or by enemies. The tenant is not excused from performance of a duty in the latter cases; it is merely that the law puts no duty upon him.

12. A lessee who covenants to maintain buildings in repair, saying nothing as to cause of disrepair, is bound to repair injuries caused by the explosion of an enemy bomb.

Redmond v. Dainton, [1920] 2 K.B. 256. This is not a case of impossibility. The question is what risks were included in the lessee's express promise. The cause of a disrepair may be of importance in allocating risks; but the possibility of performing the promise to repair does not depend upon the cause of the harm.

14. See Cricklewood Prop. & Inv. Trust v. Leighton's Inv. Trust [1945] A.C. 221, 61 T.L.R. 202, [1945] 1 All Eng. 252, where the duty of a lessee to pay rent as provided in a lease for 99 years was held not discharged by the fact that the erection of buildings on the land, as contemplated by the parties, had been made temporarily impossible by the war.

during his term and the landlord loses the use during the occupancy after the term has expired. This distribution of risks is not a necessary one. That it is not always regarded as the just distribution will appear in the sections that follow. A different distribution of risks may be required by the terms of the contract, and also by reason of the varying circumstances of the particular case.

In Paradine v. Jane, there was no promised performance that was made impossible by Prince Rupert's army of invasion. The plaintiff had fully conveyed the leasehold interest in the land; and we are told of no covenant of quiet enjoyment. The defendant had covenanted to pay rent; and there is nothing in the report to show that Prince Rupert's seizure made this payment impossible, or even difficult. It was the tenant's use and occupation (his "enjoyment") that were made impossible. He was deprived of his expected profit and advantage. The purpose for which he made the contract of lease was "frustrated," without fault by either party. Nor does it appear that there was any failure of consideration; the agreed equivalent for the defendant's promise to pay rent was the conveyance of the leasehold property interest and delivery of possession. There was merely a frustration of the tenant's purpose of enjoying the profits of use and occupation.

The real question for decision, therefore, was not whether impossibility of rendering a promised performance operated as a discharge of either party; it was whether the frustration of the tenant's ultimate object in taking the lease, caused by the royalist army, operated as a discharge of his duty to pay rent. How should the risks of loss by such a frustration be distributed? Should the tenant's duty to pay rent, assumed by contract, be constructively conditional upon the absence of such a frustration? It would certainly be held to be conditional upon the absence of a wrongful eviction by the lessor himself. Should it be conditional also upon the absence of a wrongful eviction by Prince Rupert?

The court answered this last question in the negative. Its decision on this exact issue is probably in accord with the existing modern law, although there are other leasehold frustration decisions that remain to be compared.[15] Since this issue was what it was, the decision is not a precedent for cases in which a promised performance has become impossible by destruction of sub-

---

15. In Pollard v. Shaaffer, 1 Dall. (Pa.) 210 (1787), a tenant, ousted by the English army, was held bound to continue to pay rent. "As he was to have the advantage of casual profits, he ought to run the hazard of casual losses during the term, and not lay the whole burthen of them upon the lessors; as resolved in Aleyn, 27."

In Leonard v. Autocar S. S. Co., 64 N.E.2d 477, 392 Ill. 182, 163 A.L.R. 670 (1946), seizure of the leased property by the government

ject matter, death of a necessary party, or even by virtue of the invasion of a foreign army. When a later court held that a promise to deliver possession of a music hall was discharged by the destruction of the hall by fire, it was dealing with an issue not decided in Paradine v. Jane. Its decision was in direct conflict with the dictum reported in Paradine v. Jane; and that dictum must now be regarded as an inaccurate generalization. The court's effort to distinguish its case, by saying that the defendant's promise to deliver possession of the music hall was impliedly conditional on the continuing existence of the building, is (or at least, it may be) based upon a fiction derived from false interpretation. But the court knew how the risks of loss in case of such a fire ought to be allocated; and it found an "implied condition" as a means to serve its end, an end that was justice. Of course, if the promise to give possession of the hall was in fact conditional on its continued existence, performance as promised never became impossible at all. Performance as promised became impossible for the very reason that the promise as the parties made it was not conditional.

The American Law Institute, in its Restatement of the Law of Contracts, clearly differentiates between impossibility of performance and frustration of object. It devotes an entire chapter containing sixteen sections to the statement of the effect of impossibility of a promised performance upon the duty of the party who promised to render it.[16] The result there reached is, in most of its aspects, directly contra to the once much repeated rule that supervening impossibility is no defense.

The Institute likewise differentiates between impossibility of performance and failure of consideration. It devotes five sections in the chapter on Discharge of Contracts to the latter topic.[17]

for a limited period was held not to discharge the lessee's duty to pay rent. He had a right of compensation by the government. In accord is Swift v. Macbean [1942] 1 K.B. 375.

16. Restatement, Contracts, Chapter 14, §§ 454–469. Although "Impossibility" as a ground for discharge of duty is given the importance of a separate chapter, it is listed in Chapter 13, Discharge of Contracts, § 385, as one of the many "methods" by which contractual duties may be discharged.

17. Restatement, Contracts, Chapter 13, Topic 5, §§ 397–401, entitled:

"Discharge of One Party by Breach or Non-Performance of the Other or by Failure of Consideration." If the nonperformance of the other is caused by impossibility for which he is not at fault, his duty is discharged in accordance with the rules stated in Chapter 14; but the first party is discharged by failure of the bargained-for equivalent, whether such failure was wrongful or was due to an excusing form of impossibility. This rule had been stated previously in § 274, "Failure of Consideration as a Discharge of Duty." This is now incorporated in § 397 by reference back to § 274.

Although it is perfectly clear that failure of the consideration or equivalent for which one party bargained is a "frustration" of the purpose or object for which he entered into the contract, whether it is due to a wrongful breach or to an excusing impossibility, the Institute says nothing about "frustration" either in the sections dealing with Impossibility or in those dealing with Failure of Consideration.[18]

The only rule given by the Institute as to Frustration, as distinguished from Impossibility and Failure of Consideration, is that contained in Section 288, in Chapter 10, "Conditions." This section is entitled "Frustration of the Object or Effect of the Contract." This is quoted below in full, with some criticism of its form and substance. In the form there used, the rule is expressly stated solely as a rule of discharge of a promisor from his contractual duty. It would be more appropriately placed in the chapter on Discharge of Contract; and in that chapter there should have been a reference back to Section 288.[19]

18. In listing the various "methods" of discharging contractual duties in § 385, however, method numbered (c) is thus described: "breach by the other party or failure of consideration, or frustration." There seems to be no reference back to § 288, where a rule as to frustration is given.

19. Restatement, Contracts, § 288, says: "Where the assumed possibility of a desired object or effect to be attained by either party to a contract forms the basis on which both parties enter into it, and this object or effect is or surely will be frustrated, a promisor who is without fault in causing the frustration, and who is harmed thereby, is discharged from the duty of performing his promise unless a contrary intention appears."

"The possibility of a desired object" may be said to be "the basis on which" the party who desired it entered into the contract. If the other party does not know that the one assented on such a "basis," it certainly does not form his own "basis;" but even knowledge of the other party's "basis" does not make it his own. Further consideration of this section since its publication has led the present writer to disapprove the quoted wording. Two bargainers never have the same purpose or "desired object." The section is expressly worded so as to apply in cases where "a desired object or effect to be attained *by either party*" is frustrated; and it is only the party "who is harmed thereby" who is said to be "discharged from the duty of performing his promise." Seldom, indeed, can it be said with accuracy that the attainment of one party's purposes "forms the basis" on which the other party assents to the bargain. The "basis" on which each party assents is the possibility of attainment of his own purposes and "desired object"— the attainment of that for which he bargains. If it is argued that the "basis" on which each party assents is the possibility of attainment of the other party's purposes as well as his own, because his own can not be attained unless the other party's are also, we are merely begging the question. Moreover, if such is the reason for the rule, the section should say that both parties are alike discharged from duty. The court's attention should be directed, not to the discovery of a non-existent "basis" or intention of a party, but

## § 1323. Impossibility of Performing the Defendant's Promise That is Caused by the Plaintiff

With respect to the first of the three defenses, described in the first section of this topic, it may be stated with very little qualification that if the plaintiff has himself made it impossible for the defendant to perform his promise, the nonperformance is not an actionable breach of duty.[20]  No one doubts that it is unjust for the plaintiff to make performance impossible and then to complain of it.  Indeed, action by the plaintiff that causes much less than objective impossibility will deprive him of a remedy and discharge the defendant from duty.  If the plaintiff's action causes no more than a personal inability to perform on the part of the defendant, the latter is discharged.  Nor is total inability necessary to such a result.  If the plaintiff makes performance by the defendant materially more difficult or expensive, the latter will be discharged.[21]  It is merely stating this rule in another form to say that the duty of a contractor is constructively conditional on the absence of material interference by the other party.

There are a few cases in which the foregoing doctrine is not applicable.  These are cases in which the terms of the contract or other facts make it clear that the parties contemplated the possibility of interference by the promisee, and that the promisor undertook to render his performance despite such interference.  This means that the promisor consciously assumed the risk of interference by the promisee.  Probably no case can be found in which the promisor has bound himself to perform, or to pay indemnity, even though the promisee renders the performance utterly impossible objectively.  But there are cases in which the parties contemplated a type of interference by the promisee that might increase the difficulty or expense of performance, and making it reasonable to hold that the promisee is privileged so to

to the allocation of risks in accordance with the business practices and mores of men in similar cases.

**20.**  A builder who warrants that walls will be water-tight can not be held liable for breach or prevented from recovering compensation if the defects in the walls is caused solely by the defective specifications and supervision of the owner's engineer. See MacKnight Flintic Stone Co. v. Mayor, 54 N.E. 661, 160 N.Y. 72 (1899).

**21.**  See United States v. Peck, 102 U.S. 64, 26 L.Ed. 46 (1880).

Where the defendant contracted to buy land of the plaintiff, knowing that the latter did not then own it and expected to buy it at an approaching auction sale, the court held that the defendant's going to the auction and bidding against the plaintiff was wrongful.  Not only was the plaintiff promisor discharged from his duty to defendant, but also the latter was guilty of a breach of an implied promise not to interfere at the auction. Patterson v. Meyerhofer, 97 N.E. 472, 204 N.Y. 96 (1912).

See further Discharge of Contract, §§ 1264, 1265.

interfere and that the promisor is bound to perform in spite of the increased difficulty.

For example, suppose that the government needs a hundred million feet of lumber for immediate construction of cantonments. A and B are persons who have supplies of such lumber. Government agents go to both A and B, explain the facts in full, and solicit contracts for as much as each will promise to deliver. A contracts to deliver two million feet. He then has only one million feet; and he expects to procure an additional million from B. When he reaches B, he finds that B has already contracted to deliver his entire supply to the government. The result is that performance by A is made more difficult and expensive. This does not discharge A from duty to deliver two million feet. He knew all the facts; the government was privileged to buy of B and others; and A must bear the risk of such interference.[22] Here the promisee's action was in the direction of cornering the market; but under the circumstances it was not illegal. In cases where the promisee's purchases amount to an illegal corner of the market, no doubt the promisor would be discharged from duty.

## § 1324. Impossibility of Performance as a Discharge of Contractual Duty—"Act of God"

It was formerly supposed to be the law that impossibility of performance was not operative to discharge a contractual duty. A duty created by the law, and not voluntarily assumed by contract, would be discharged, it was supposed, by facts making performance impossible; otherwise, however, of duties voluntarily assumed by contract. The extent and conditions of the latter duties were supposed to be determined solely by the expressed will of the parties; limitations, conditions, and exceptions had to be provided for by the parties themselves in the express terms of the contract, or they would not exist. Such was the stated law of the courts; and it was the taught law of the schools. It may be doubted whether the actual decisions ever justified such statements. Even our primitive ancestors may have had ways of ameliorating the operation of the supposed "strict law" of their time. At any rate, if it was ever the applied law of the land, it is so no longer.

Supervening impossibility was formerly often said to discharge the contractual duty of a promisor, only in case it was caused by

---

22. In United States v. Peck, supra, the promisor had no reason to foresee that the government would buy up the supply on which he depended. Therefore, the usual rule was applicable, making the duty of the promisor conditional on non-interference.

In Iron Trade Products Co. v. Wilkoff, 116 A. 150, 272 Pa. 172 (1922), a seller was not discharged from duty by the fact that the buyer competed in the market for additional such goods.

"act of God." [23] The term has been extensively used in the law of carriers. It may be that in former times men supposed themselves to be able to see the hand of the Almighty in the occurrences about them; today, the phrase is out of fashion as a mode of determining when to throw the risk upon a promisee, rather than a promisor. Other phrases, particularly in a foreign language, have also been used. A promisor has been said to be discharged in case the promised performance was prevented by *vis major* or by *force majeure*, depending upon a preference for Latin or for French. These phrases, too, serve no useful purpose as a test of responsibility, although they are catchwords that may occasionally be convenient to describe the facts that lead a court to decide in favor of the promisor.

The kinds of impossibility that are held to discharge legal duty, or to eliminate a condition precedent, in very many instances are caused by human beings.[24] On the other hand, impossibility caused by act of God (assuming that we can determine this) is not always an operative discharge.[25] The question of a promisor's responsibility would better be approached (1) from the standpoint of interpretation of the contract, (2) from the custom of business men in like cases, and (3) from prevailing opinion of public welfare as evidenced by the judicial decisions.

### § 1325. What is Meant by the Term Impossibility

As the discussion of the modern law proceeds, it will be noted that there are several degrees and kinds of "impossibility," as that term has in fact been used. At one end of the category is the so-called absolute impossibility, sometimes called "physical" impossibility, based upon all human experience and applicable to all manner of men, whatever may be their wisdom, strength, or scientific training. "All the king's horses and all the king's men cannot put Humpty Dumpty together again." No one can go to the moon. Even the Creator was thought to be unable to

---

24. For example, destruction of the subject matter or the necessary means of performance will discharge the promisor even though the destruction was by human hands. So, also, will death of a necessary person, even though due to murder or suicide.

25. One who has contracted to erect a building is not discharged by the destruction of the almost completed building by a fire caused by lightning. School Dist. v. Dauchy, 25 Conn. 530 (1857). In such a case, however, it may be only performance *on time* that has become impossible. Time may not be of the essence; and substantial performance can be rendered. See § 1333, Unexpected difficulty.

The closing of the Panama Canal by a slide at Culebra Cut was held not to be an "Act of God", within the meaning of that phrase in the contract, in Gans S. S. Line v. Wilhelmsen, 275 F. 254 (C.C.A.2d, 1921). The slide was "the result of a deliberate widening of the canal."

make a two-year old colt in a minute.[26]  This kind of impossibility has sometimes been described as "objective" impossibility.[27]

The term is also used with respect to performances that are extraordinarily difficult for anybody to do and yet that experience has shown can be done by exceptionally wise and efficient men. Samson can lift a ton, the average man cannot;  and a paralytic cannot even stand erect.  Some men may be able to pay a million dollars, while others might as well promise to deliver the moon to Jupiter.  Such impossibility has been described as "subjective" impossibility.[28]

A performance may be so difficult and expensive that it is described as "impracticable," and enforcement may be denied on the ground of impossibility.  The subject must be considered, therefore, in relation to past human achievement of all time, in relation to degrees of difficulty and economic cost, and in relation to the capacities and economic power of particular persons.

There will be found in common use such terms as physical impossibility, legal impossibility, impracticability, subjective and objective impossibility, personal inability, increased difficulty, and frustration of object.  These express varying concepts;  and the applicable rules of law are not uniform.[29]

## § 1326.  Impossibility Existing at the Time the Bargain is Made

Antecedent impossibility, in the objective, absolute sense stated above, of rendering a performance that is promised, prevents the promise from being enforceable as a contract.[30]  It prevents the existence of contract;  no contractual duty arises. This may be explained on various grounds, as that the parties cannot be supposed to have meant what they said, in case the impossibility was known to them, or that they have entered into the transaction by mutual mistake.[31]  The same result may be reached when the antecedent impossibility is not absolute, but consists of such a degree of difficulty or economic unprofitableness as to make performance impracticable;  but it is much less likely, because there may have been no mistake at all, or the promisor may be held to have assumed the risk.  The law that is applicable in these cases may be postponed for consideration, along with like cases where the impossibility or impracticability supervenes after the contract has been made.

If two parties make an agreement that is not impossible of performance, but it is erroneously reduced to writing so that the

---

31.　The promise of a lessee to pay a specified rent, in the form of a royalty on ore or coal mined, has often been held to be constructively conditional on the existence of sufficient ore or coal.

Va.—Virginia Iron, Coal & Coke Co. v. Graham, 98 S.E. 659, 124 Va. 692 (1919).

Eng.—Lord Clifford v. Watts, L.R. 5 C.P. 577 (1870).

performance therein required is an impossible one, the parties are bound in accordance with their actual agreement; and reformation of the mistaken document is an available remedy, just as in other similar cases of mistake in which no impossibility is involved. In some cases, just as in those in which the impossibility is caused by some event after the contract is made, the particular performance that is impossible may constitute a small and nonessential part of the contract, as where the specified mode of attaining a result can not be performed but another and reasonable mode is available. In such a case, it may be proper to hold that the contract is not made unenforceable by the impossibility.

### § 1327. Interpretation of the Contract May Show That Performance is Not Impossible—Promises to Indemnify

In all cases alike, the problem of interpretation is ever before the court; and this process involves reading between the lines, as well as along them, using the light that may be made available by all the surrounding circumstances. By this process, it may be found that the performance actually undertaken is not impossible at all, or that the promise was to render one of two or more alternative performances, some one of which is neither impossible nor impracticable.

Thus, a man may warrant or promise that a certain machine is without flaw. If the flaw actually then exists, it might be thought that the warranty or promise is of an impossibility; instead, however, the undertaking is interpreted as one of indemnity. "If the machine is not flawless, I will indemnify you against all injury or loss." [32] But if one promises to sell and deliver his motor car, not knowing that it has just been destroyed by fire, his promise will not be interpreted as one of indemnity, although it could be so interpreted if such was the customary understanding in the community.

The cases just put are cases of impossibility existing when the contract was made; but the same problem of interpretation arises with respect to the risks of loss caused by subsequent events. Which party "assumed the risk," if either one did so? A contract may be so expressed as to indicate that the promisor assumes the risk of his own inability to perform—an interpretation that is commonly given to all contractual promises, or even assumes the risk that the performance will become objectively impossible—an interpretation the effect of which is to make the promisor's obligation one of indemnity.

One who warrants that sheep will be sound at the end of the year,[33] or that a ship will return safe to port, seems to promise what may turn out to be objectively impossible for the best of us; the only performance that is really promised is to indemnify against loss, the duty being conditional upon the event of unsoundness or destruction at sea. A promise to effect the cure of a person who is ill is not invalidated by the fact that the illness turns out to be fatal.[34]

A promise to induce action or forbearance by a third person involves the act and will of another. That his will turns out to be stubborn does not show that the performance is impossible; but, even if it did, indemnification is required. One who sells property to a buyer and promises him to find a subsequent purchaser thereof at a specified price must indemnify the promisee if it turns out that no one will pay the price.[35] A promise to sell and convey Blackacre is not invalidated by the fact that title to Blackacre is in a third person who has a will of his own.[36] A contract to sell specific goods is not invalidated by the fact that the seller has previously sold them to another, a fact that he now overlooks.[37]

Even though a contractor may have expected to perform in a particular manner or place, the subsequent impossibility or illegality of performing in that manner or place does not discharge him from duty, if the terms of his promise are such that the agreed performance is still possible and lawful in some other manner or place. A British embargo against shipment does not discharge one whose promise to ship can be performed by shipment from a non-British port.[38] A contract to send goods for transshipment at London is not discharged by an embargo against landing there, since the goods can be transshipped in the harbor.[39]

## § 1328.  When Does a Promisor Assume the Risk of Impossibility of Performance

What is meant by "assumption of risk" in dealing with contracts involving impossibility? Risk bearing may be determined by voluntary assent, or by custom, or by a rule of law based upon supposed social interest. Often, when a court says that a contractor "assumed the risk," we can not tell whether it means that the contractor expressed such an intention or that the court thinks on other grounds that he ought to carry the risk and bear the loss. He "assumed the risk" means only that the facts are such that he must carry it.

Cases holding that a promisor assumed the risk of certain types of impossibility and that he must pay damages in case of non-performance may sometimes be explained by process of reasonable interpretation; [40] but in other cases the same result may be reached even though the court is convinced that it never entered the minds of the parties that the performance might be impossible or that indemnity has to be paid. There has been reliance

39.   Eng.—Waugh v. Morris, L.R.
      8 Q.B. 202 (1873).

on the promise, a loss has occurred or an expected gain prevented; and it may be regarded as more just to make the promisor carry the risk and suffer the loss, instead of the promisee.  Some one must do this; and the court's action may well be governed by the custom of the community in such cases.  Do promisors in fact indemnify the promisee; or does the promisee bear his disappointment with patience and charge his injury to Providence? If custom is variable and uncertain, as it may well be, then there is no test of justice other than the fact that uniformity of decision will reduce strife and litigation and will enable contractors to adjust their affairs in accordance with the risk to be carried. It makes little difference to the community which party must bear the risk; but it makes much difference that we may know in advance which one must bear it.

Sometimes the purpose of one of the parties is to eliminate a particular risk of harm by getting a promise from another party to prevent that harm.  If an irrigation company promises to supply water for irrigation or other use in a dry country, it may be held to be its duty to anticipate natural shortages, even unusually severe ones, and to find the necessary water at the time and place that it exists.  Plenty of water is always available somewhere.[41] The promisor has assumed the risk, as all promisors must do, of his own inability to do what others could have done.

If A sells land to B and the latter promises that no building other than a dwelling house shall be erected thereon, what is the result if a railroad company takes the land by eminent domain and builds a station there?  Interpretation may show that B's undertaking was no more than a promise that he would not himself build or assent to the building of anything but a dwelling house.  On such interpretation, there has been no breach of B's promise; and the loss involved must be borne by A.[42]  On the other hand, interpretation may indicate that B clearly promised to indemnify A against such a loss; and he will be compelled to do so by the law.  A third possibility is to hold that B's promise does not indicate that any thought was given to the possibility of eminent domain proceedings, but that B must indemnify A anyway, reimbursing himself as best he can at the expense of the railroad company.[43]

As a general rule, every contractor must carry the risk of frustration of his hopes and expectations when subsequent events cause a decline in the value of that for which he bargained.  This is not a case in which the rendition of the specific performance for which he bargained has become impossible in any sense of that abused term; it is a case in which events have prevented

**42.** See Baily v. De Crispigny, L.R. 4 Q.B. 180 (1869), holding, whether on one ground or another, that B is not required to indemnify A.

the realization and enjoyment of expected values from a promised performance actually rendered.  In a comparatively small number of cases, it has been held that a contractor does not carry the risk of a catastrophic collapse of value.  In such cases it is found that the contractor did not in fact assume the risk and that the circumstances are so extraordinary that justice requires that he should not be compelled to carry it.

### § 1329.   Impossibility Which the Promisor could have Avoided —Burden of Proof

Whatever be the meaning given to the term impossibility, whether it be objective or subjective, and even though it be used to include varying degrees of difficulty and expense, the supervening situation that is so described does not excuse a promisor from his contractual duty if he himself wilfully brought it about, or if he could have foreseen and avoided it by the exercise of reasonable diligence and efficiency.[44]  In such a case, the promised performance was not impossible in any sense, either at the time the contract was made or for some time thereafter.  When one makes a contractual promise, the legal duty thereby created requires at least a reasonable degree of effort and diligence.  If the exercise of such degree as this would have resulted in performance, the promisor can not say that performance was prevented by supervening impossibility;  instead, it was prevented by his own wilful or negligent conduct.  Performance may have eventually become impossible;  but the promisor is himself the responsible cause of that impossibility.  The nature of the performance promised, and the character of the risks to be avoided, will tend to show the extent of diligence and the character of foresight that is required.

If one who has contracted to render a performance by a stated time puts off performance until the eleventh hour, he is not excused by the fact that performance has then become objectively impossible.[46]  On the other hand, one who contracts to repair a house by October first, the work being such that it could easily be performed within a single week, should be discharged from duty if the house is destroyed by lightning or hurricane on September 21.  Of course, fires and storms occur and will occur again;  but the contractor does not lack reasonable prudence by failing to foresee destruction between September 21 and October 1.  His leaving the performance until the last ten days is not such lack of diligence as to be held to be the responsible cause of

---

46.   Thus a mortgagor who promised to take out war risk insurance is not excused by the fact that after seven months of neglect in doing so it became impossible because the risk of war became so great that not even Lloyds would issue such a policy.  Moorgate Estate v. Trower, [1940] 1 All Eng. 195.

the impossibility that accrued. No doubt this result is made all the more certain by the fact that his repairs would have been destroyed along with the house, had they been made earlier, so that the delay is beneficial to the owner by saving him the cost of the repairs; but the decision is not dependent on this fact. One who contracts to supply water for irrigation knows that the purpose of the other party is to supply the deficiency in natural rainfall and that drought must be expected; his failure to procure water in time is the cause of his non-performance, not the drought that was unusually severe.[47]

In all the cases holding that the promisor was discharged from duty by impossibility of performance or frustration of purpose, it has been assumed that the promisor was not himself the responsible cause of the impossibility or frustration. In many such cases, the frustrating event is obviously one that he could not have brought about or prevented. In most such cases, no question has been raised as to which party must bear the burden of proof. Undoubtedly a promisor who is asserting his discharge must allege and prove the frustrating event and that after occurrence of the event it was impossible to render the promised performance or to attain the purpose for which the contract was made.[48]

## § 1330.  Alternative Performances, One of Which Becomes Impossible

If a contractor promises to render, at his own option, one of two alternative performances, and one of these becomes impossible, he is bound to perform the other.[52] The case might be different if the option is in the promisee. If he makes his choice while both alternatives are still possible, the contract ceases to be an alternative contract. If the chosen alternative then becomes impossible, it affects the promisor's duty just as it would if there never had been any alternative. After one of the alternatives has become impossible of performance, it would no doubt be held that the promisee no longer has an option; the contract is no longer an alternative one. An owner of goods who has an option of naming any one of several ports of delivery can not prevent the carrier from earning his freight by naming a port where delivery has become impossible; and if it becomes impossible at a port already named, he must name another.[53]

## § 1331.  Is Discharge by Impossibility Based on a Condition Implied in Fact?

In order to avoid the appearance of "making a contract for the parties," or of altering one that the parties have made, the courts have used the device of "implying a condition" in the contract.[55] Where the burning of a music hall made it impossible for the owner to deliver possession for its use by the hirer, the court held that the owner had committed no breach of contractual duty, for the reason that his promise was impliedly conditional on the continued existence of the building.[57]

Often, the parties insert expressions in the contract indicating that a promisor's duty shall be conditional upon the continued existence of person or thing. We are familiar with "strike clauses" and "excepted risks" and "causes beyond our control." Such expressions must be interpreted by the court; and interpretation is not always easy. In such cases, the condition is an "express" condition. If the interpretative process involves no more than factual inference of probable intention in the light of all relevant facts, the condition of a promisor's duty thus discovered may properly be called an "implied" condition. If, however, there are no expressions in the contract justifying a finding by the court that a promise is conditional, based upon interpretation as just described, then it is better not to talk in terms of "implied" conditions. Justice is more likely to be done if the court is conscious that it is filling a gap that the parties have left and uses language in its opinion that is not language of interpretation only.

In the music hall case cited above, we have little ground for supposing that the parties thought of the possibility of fire and so expressed their agreement as to make the owner's duty conditional on existence of the building.[58] In some instances, the court has recognized the fact that the parties did not give any thought to the possibility of death or destruction. Judges have held promises to be conditional expressly upon the ground that they believe that the parties would have made them conditional in express terms if they had thought about it.[59] They are aware that they are holding the promise to be conditional because they think that justice so requires, justice based upon custom, business practices, the mores of the community.[60]

Explanations of the judicial process in holding that a contractual duty is discharged by impossibility or frustration of

---

57. **Eng.**—Taylor v. Caldwell, 3 Best & S. 826 (1863).

58. Although Blackburn, J. said there was an "implied condition" and that his great purpose was to "fulfil the intention" of the parties, he also said: "The parties when framing their agreement evidently had not present to their minds the possibility of such a disaster, and have made no express stipulation with reference to it, so that the answer to the question must depend upon the general rules of law applicable to such a contract." By the aid of the fiction of an "implied condition" the courts have created an "applicable general rule;" but it is not the one stated in Paradine v. Jane, Aleyn 26 (1647), and continually repeated in numberless cases through three centuries.

60. The truth of this has been recognized by the House of Lords in Fibrosa Spolka Akcyjna v. Fairbairn L.C.B. Ltd. [1942] 2 All Eng. 122, [1943] A.C. 32, 167 L.T. 101, 111 L.J.K.B. 433.

purpose are best summed up by Lord Wright.[62] "The court has formulated the doctrine by virtue of its inherent jurisdiction, just as it has developed the rules of liability for negligence, or for the restitution or repayment of money where otherwise there would be unjust enrichment. I find the theory of the basis of the rule in Lord Sumner's pregnant statement that the doctrine of frustration is really a device by which the rules as to absolute contracts are reconciled with the special exceptions which justice demands.[63] Though it has been constantly said by high authority, including Lord Sumner, that the explanation of the rule is to be found in the theory that it depends on an implied condition of the contract, that is really no explanation. It only pushes back the problem a single stage. It leaves the question what is the reason for implying a term. Nor can I reconcile that theory with the view that the result does not depend on what the parties might, or would as hard bargainers, have agreed. The doctrine is invented by the court in order to supplement the defects of the actual contract. The parties did not anticipate fully and completely, if at all, or provide for what actually happened. It is not possible, to my mind, to say that if they had thought of it they would have said: 'Well, if that happens, all is over between is.' On the contrary, they would almost certainly on the one side or the other have sought to introduce reservations or qualifications or compensations. As to that the court cannot guess. What it can say is that the contract either binds or does not bind."

## § 1332. Subjective Inability of a Contractor to Perform His Promise

A distinction has been drawn between subjective and objective impossibility—between personal inability of a promisor to do what he promised and the objective impossibility that the promised performance can be rendered by anybody. The two terms call attention to a distinction between two kinds of facts that are very different in their legal operation.

Objective impossibility, heretofore discussed, may discharge a contractor from his duty, leaving no remedial right to compensation in his promisee. The risk of disappointment in not getting the profits of the bargained-for performance, by reason of the supervening events, is allocated to the promisee; the duty of the promisor to keep his promise is limited and conditional. The duty of a promisor is never discharged, however, by the mere fact that supervening events deprive him of the ability to perform, if they are not such as to deprive other persons, likewise, of ability to render such a performance.[64] The risk of such inabil-

---

62. Eng.—Denny, Mott & D. v. Fraser & Co. [1944] A.C. 265, [1944] 1 All Eng. 678, 171 L.T. 345, 113 L.J. P.C. 37.

64. Kan.—Western Drug Supply & Specialty Co. v. Board of Administration, 187 P. 701, 106 Kan. 256, 12 A.L.R. 1074 (1920).

ity as this rests on the promisor, in the absence of a provision in the contract indicating the contrary intention. Such is the allocation of risk that is made by our social and business mores, as well as by the law of contract that is based upon them. Such an allocation of risks is not a necessary or inevitable one. Many a promisee is willing to forgive his debtor by reason of hardship and misfortune. Distinctions are often made, in both law and morals, between the wilful transgressor and the unhappy, but inefficient, victim of circumstances. Thus far, however, it is common belief that to take away from contractors the societal pressure of legal sanction and remedy, in cases of mere personal inability and misfortune, would give too great encouragement and opportunity to the wilful, the lazy, and the inefficient.

Personal insolvency does not discharge a money debtor from his legal duty. It does not wholly deprive a debtor of ability to pay; but even if it did, it would be no defense in an action by his creditor. It is true that we have abolished imprisonment for debt—the legal sanctions have been modified and softened. Also, we have bankruptcy laws for the relief of the insolvent. But in bankruptcy, it is the court's decree that discharges, not the personal inability of the debtor; and the decree is entered only on compliance with supposedly rigid requirements.[65]

The fact that a contractor becomes insolvent,[66] or that a receiver has been appointed and put in charge of his business,[67] or that bankruptcy proceedings have been started and his assets put in charge of a trustee,[68] does not discharge the contractor from duty to perform. These facts merely evidence his personal inability to do those things that are necessary to his promised performance. Of course, the discharge eventually decreed by the court in the bankruptcy proceedings may operate as a discharge of the contractor; but this presupposes that the claim against the contractor was not previously discharged and that it was a provable claim in the bankruptcy proceedings.

## § 1333.  Effect of Unexpected Difficulties and Unprofitableness

A supervening discovery of facts that make the promised performance more difficult or expensive, or the occurrence of subsequent events having this effect, if they are such as are commonly foreseeable and in contemplation, has almost always been

---

Restatement, Contracts, § 455, reads: "Impossibility of performing a promise that is not due to the nature of the performance, but wholly to the inability of the individual promisor, neither prevents the formation of a contract nor discharges a duty created by a contract."

65. A discharge in bankruptcy does not include every kind of contractual duty; for example, a contract duty to convey land. Stewart v. Mann, 165 P. 590, 1169, 85 Or. 68, 75 (1917).

held not to discharge the contractor from his duty.[72]  No doubt, a contractor usually understands that, in the absence of express limitation, the risk of such difficulty and expense is for him to bear.[73]  So, one who contracts to make a foundation or a tunnel or other excavation usually investigates for himself the character of the location, whether it be sand or solid rock or swamp or frozen mixtures, before making his estimates and offers.  Therefore, the risk is usually borne by the contractor; he is not discharged from duty by actually unexpected difficulty or expense, and he has no right to extra pay for completing the job.[74]  One bound to keep a macadamized road in repair is not relieved by the fact that peacetime automobile traffic wears it out with unexpected rapidity.[75]  A contract to repair a machine and make it work is not discharged by discovery of unexpected defects or of faulty designing.[76]  One must perform his contract to care for another for life even though the latter becomes paralyzed and very difficult to care for.[77]  The fact that storms or unusual weather conditions make performance more difficult or expensive has generally been held to be no excuse.[78]  Financial difficulties growing out of general business depression may cause personal inability but do not constitute an excuse by impossibility of performance.[79]  The occurrence of strikes making performance difficult and expensive is not an excuse for not performing.[80]  The destruction, without fault, of necessary subject matter will operate as a discharge; and such destruction may occur by reason of storms or strikes.  They must also be considered in determining what is reasonable diligence or a reasonable time for performance.[81]  The fact that performance has been made more difficult and expensive by reason of an injunction or a receivership in a suit brought by a third party has been held to be no discharge.[82]

In every case of the kind now under discussion, the court must be alert to weigh any evidence to show a custom throwing the risk upon one party rather than the other, or to show that there was a mutual contemplation of its being borne by one of them. The owner, rather than the contractor, may be the one who has made preliminary investigations as to character of soil, foundation, or other factors; and the contractor may reasonably have relied upon representations as to such facts.[83]  Where neither custom nor agreement determines the allocation of a risk, the court must exercise its equity powers and pray for the wisdom of Solomon.[84]

A few cases can be found indicating that unexpected difficulty or expense may approach such an extreme that the court will

72.  U.S.—Day v. U. S., 38 S.Ct. 57, 245 U.S. 159, 62 L.Ed. 219 (1917), risk of unusual flood in building a bulkhead; Carnegie Steel Co. v. U. S., 36 S.Ct. 342, 240 U.S. 156, 60 L.Ed. 576 (1916), unforeseen difficulties in the new art of manufacturing armor plate.

hold them to amount to a practical impossibility and to operate as a discharge. "Business impracticability" may be treated as one kind of impossibility.[85] Also, even though performance itself may be neither difficult nor expensive, the purpose of the contractor may be so thoroughly frustrated by the cost of making use of material purchased as to operate as a discharge.[86] This must be an extreme and uncommon case, in the absence of proof of custom or actual understanding.

Attention may be called here to the fact that, although unexpected difficulty or expense may not discharge a contractor from his duty, there are cases holding that performance of a duty so impeded is a sufficient consideration for a promise of increased compensation by the other party.[87]

---

86. In Mineral Park Land Co. **v.** Howard, 156 P. 458, 172 Cal. 289 (1916), the defendant had a public contract to build a concrete bridge. The plaintiff owned land containing gravel and agreed to sell such gravel to defendant at 5¢ per cubic yard, the defendant promising to take all needed gravel from this land. After taking about 50,000 cubic yards, the defendant encountered the plane of water saturation, and got about 51,000 yards elsewhere. The plaintiff sued for damages. He pleaded that he took all gravel that was "available." The taking of the gravel was not impossible; and certainly the promised payment was not; but the defendant could have used the wet gravel only by drying it at a prohibitive cost. Thus his hope of profitable use was frustrated. The defendant was held to be discharged since the use of the wet gravel was "impracticable."

87. See § 184, Consideration, Unforeseen difficulties.

# CHAPTER 75

## DEATH—DESTRUCTION OF SPECIFIC THINGS OR CONDITIONS—PRO-RATING SUPPLY

### § 1334. Performance Rendered Impossible by Death or Disabling Illness

A promise may become physically impossible of performance by reason of the death or disabling illness of some person whose continued life and health are necessary by reason of the character of the performance to be rendered. It is now everywhere held that such impossibility discharges the contractual duty of the promisor.[1] The person may be either the promisor or the promisee, or he may be some third person.[2] If the promised performance is the rendition of some personal service by the promisor himself, his death or disabling illness operates to discharge his contractual duty; his non-performance so caused is not a breach; and no action for damages can be maintained against his personal representative.

Whether a performance promised is in fact to be rendered only by the promisor in person is a question that must be determined by interpretation of the contract in the light of the surrounding circumstances and customs of men in such cases.[3] It is merely putting the same question in another form to ask whether performance of the duty can be delegated to another and performed vicariously, or to ask whether the performance can and must be rendered by the promisor's executor. The words of the contract themselves may be such as to leave the matter free from any doubt. The promise may in terms provide for performance by the promisor or his "assigns";[4] on the other hand, it may provide for performance by the promisor in person and by no one else.[5] In many cases, however, there is no clear provision in words, and the answer must turn on the nature of the performance and on the custom of men in like cases. As a matter of course, a mere promise to pay money is not made impossible of performance by the death or illness of either the debtor or the creditor.[6]

The death or illness of one who is not a party to the contract at all operates as a discharge in those cases where his co-operation is necessary to the performance promised. A may contract with B that the latter shall act as tutor or valet or chauffeur for A's son. The death or extended illness of the son would here operate as a discharge of both parties to the contract.[7] The death of B would likewise discharge them; but the death of A would not. A contract that an artist, a third person, will render a performance is discharged by the incapacitating illness of the artist.[8] A contract to convey land with title approved and insured by a designated title company is discharged by the dissolution of the company.[9]

The duty of one who contracts to furnish personal care and support to another person for a stated period is discharged by the death of the person to be supported.[10] Death causes impossibility of performance. Illness of the person to be cared for will usually not operate as a discharge, since it is one of very risks that is ordinarily in contemplation when such a contract is made. The circumstances and the wording of the contract may lead to a different conclusion. Insanity of the person to be supported, resulting in a commitment to an institution, has been held to discharge a promisor who undertook to supply board, lodging, and stated sums of money.[11]

## § 1335. Contracts of Service—Effect of Death of Servant or of Employer

In a contract of employment, for rendering personal service, the death of the servant or employee makes further performance by him impossible. The servants executor can not perform; and the employer has no right to damages for the nonperformance.[12]

If the performance is one that requires artistic or mechanical skill, ability, or training, performance is ordinarily not delegable and the promisor's death would operate as a discharge.[13] The promise of Caruso to sing in grand opera or of Jenny Lind to sing in concert can be performed only by Caruso or Jenny Lind. Ordinarily, it is personal service that is promised by a ball player, an actor, an automobile mechanic, a travelling salesman, a school

---

**8.**    **N.Y.**—Spalding v. Rosa, 71 **N.Y.** 40 (1877), illness of a singer for     whose performance the defendant had contracted as manager.

teacher. Even though the promisor is not one of exceptional skill or training, the same result is reached if personal performance is promised. Differences in physical strength, in industry and trustworthiness, are of substantial importance.

The death of an employee who has contracted to render personal service also discharges the employer from further duty, except the duty of making compensation for services already received. He is not bound to receive or to pay for services offered by the employee's executor or other substitute.[14] This is not because performance of his own duty is impossible; it is because the condition precedent to his duty was the employee's personal performance, and this can not be rendered. For services already received, the employer must pay his debt. This is the amount fixed by the contract, if a definite compensation for such services was apportioned specifically; otherwise, it is their reasonable value.[15]

Illness may not be of a disabling character; or it may be so temporary as not to prevent substantial performance as agreed. In such cases there is no discharge except to the extent that performance is actually prevented. The promisor is discharged in so far as his performance is prevented by his illness.[16] Whether the other party is discharged from his reciprocal duties by the fact that the first party is ill and cannot perform in part or in whole is a question that is dealt with elsewhere under the headings of Conditions Precedent and Failure of Consideration.[17]

The death of the master or employer does not necessarily have the same effect as the death of the servant. If an essential part of the master's duty is to direct and supervise the work personally, his death makes this impossible. Likewise, it makes performance of the agreed work by the servant impossible, for the work was to be work specified and directed by the master. The master's duty to pay wages does not require his personal performance and has not become impossible; but it is nevertheless discharged, because its condition precedent—the rendition of the service—has become impossible. The servant's duty is discharged by impossibility of performance of it; the master's duty to direct is discharged by impossibility of performance of it; and the master's duty to pay wages is discharged by failure of consideration.[18]

The death of one of several employing partners has often been held to terminate an employment contract, leaving no claim for damages in the employee thus deprived of his job.[19] The con-

18. Ill.—Levy v. Wilmes, 239 Ill. App. 229 (1926), death of hotel proprietor terminated contract with his manager.

N.Y.—Kenny v. Doherty, 129 N.E. 201, 230 N.Y. 44 (1920), death of mistress employer of a cook; Lacy v. Getman, 23 N.E. 452, 119 N.Y. 109, 6 L.R.A. 728 (1890).

trary has been held, especially where the surviving partners proceed to carry on the business as before.[20]

The death of the employer does not have these effects if the service required by the contract was not to be specified and directed by the employer in person. His only duty is to pay the agreed wages, the performance of which is not affected by his death. In addition, his death does not make impossible the rendition of the agreed service by the employee; so there is no failure of consideration through impossibility of performance of the agreed equivalent.[21]

### § 1336. Performance Rendered Impracticable by Danger to Life, Health, or Property

The existing illness of a promisor or other party whose participation is necessary to the agreed performance may not be so severe or disabling as actually to prevent the rendition of that performance, and yet it may be of such a character as to make its rendition seriously dangerous to his life or subsequent health. The risk may be so great that courts will declare the contractual duty to be discharged. Without doubt some risks of this sort must be undertaken. There must be taken into consideration the imminence and degree of probability that life and health will be affected, the seriousness and extent of the injury to be feared, the importance of the promised performance, and the kind and extent of loss that breach will cause to others.

A contract of engagement to marry may be discharged by the acquisition by either party of such a disease as will make consummation of the marriage dangerous to life or seriously dangerous to the health of either party.[26] It is otherwise if the disease is only temporary and danger can be avoided.[27]

The rendering of performance may involve a like danger to life or health, wholly apart from any existing illness. An outbreak of plague in the neighborhood may discharge one's duty to render a performance there.[28] An employee is justified in quitting work within a building that is in serious danger of collapse. The danger from footpads, submarine destroyers, or wild animals may be such as to excuse one from performing.[29] The decision must turn on questions of fact and matters of degree. How serious a danger was threatening and how great was the probability that performance of the contract would result in the harm that was feared?

28. Me.—Lakeman v. Pollard, 43 Me. 463 (1857), workman excused by outbreak of cholera.

29. Sailors have been excused from performing when a supervening war has made the voyage dangerous to life or when they found they were on a boat laden with contraband destined to a belligerent port.

U.S.—The Epsom, 227 F. 158 (D.C. Wash.1915).

An acrobat or dancer who contracts to perform as directed is not bound to obey directions requiring a performance involving extraordinary risks of injury not reasonably in contemplation when the contract was made.[30]  This, however, is not a case of discharge of contractual duty. The contract created no duty to obey such directions.

Danger to the life and health of third persons may discharge a contractual duty even though they are not themselves participants in the performance.  A shipowner may be excused if performance will endanger the lives of his passengers.[31]  One who has contracted to conduct a baby show may be discharged by the outbreak of infantile paralysis such that performance would endanger the babies participating and also tend to spread the disease about the community.[32]

Danger to life, health, or property, known to exist when a contract is made, may be such as to make the contract contrary to public policy and illegal.  Otherwise, however, it would seem that the contractor means to assume the risks that are apparently involved.  Doctors and nurses are not discharged from their contractual duty to care for a smallpox patient, even though there may be danger to life.  The life of the patient also is at stake; and the danger is a part of their "business."  Even risks involved in supervening and unexpected conditions may be such as contractors customarily assume when they occur.  In such cases there is no discharge.  It may be said that the contractor has "assumed the risk," a phrase that may mean either that he expressed such an intention, to be found by actual interpretation, or that custom and the law require him to bear it even though he did not think of it at all and there is no expression to interpret.

## § 1337.  Destruction of Specific Subject Matter Necessary to Performance Discharges Duty

There are many contracts in which the performance of one of the promises will be absolutely impossible in case of the destruction or non-existence of some specific thing.  The parties both know this; but, in the happy-go-lucky fashion of mankind, they assume the thing's continued existence and express no intention as to what shall be done in case the thing is destroyed or nonexistent.  Either party may, of course, expressly or impliedly make himself an insurer, assume the risk, and promise indemnity in case of nonperformance.  Either party can expressly make his own promise conditional on the continued existence of the thing.  This is a matter of reasonable interpretation.  But the court must

32.  Hanford v. Connecticut Fair Ass'n, 103 A. 838, 92 Conn. 621 (1918).  Two judges dissented thinking that the danger did not discharge, although a prohibition by a board of health would have discharged.

find a solution, even in the cases where interpretation produces none.

Here is a case in which the much repeated dictum in the old case of Paradine v. Jane has been disregarded in actual decision. In the absence of some expression of contrary intention the risk of destruction of a necessary specific thing, there being no fault, is borne by both parties. One whose promised performance is rendered objectively impossible by such destruction is discharged from his duty.[34] Thus, the other party carries risk; he does not get the promised performance or the expected gain therefrom. On the other hand, he is discharged from his duty to pay the promised price of the performance that has become impossible; and if he has already paid it, in part or in full, he has a right to restitution. This is not because his own performance has been impossible; it is because of "failure of consideration," because requiring the payment of something for nothing is repugnant to our notions of justice. Thus, the first party also carries risk; he does not get his promised price or the expected gain therefrom. Both parties alike bear the risk of not getting the expected benefits of their bargain. The risk of property loss is on the owner of the thing destroyed; res perit domino. If one of the contracting parties is the owner, his misfortune is the greater.[35]

### § 1338.  Destruction of a Building in Course of Construction

One who has bound himself by contract to create a specified physical object or result is not discharged by the fact that during the course of performance the partly completed object is destroyed without his fault.[40] The risk is on the contractor; and he must start anew and perform to completion. This is the rule that is applied to contracts for the erection of buildings and bridges, the driving of tunnels, the building of dams, the manufacture of goods. It makes no difference that the destruction is by fire or flood, lightning or earthquake, or any other so-called "act of God." Performance is not made impossible thereby; it has merely been made more expensive. In these cases, the statement is often made that "impossibility of performance is no excuse"; but the statement is inapplicable. There is no specific physical object, the continued existence of which is necessary to perform-

---

34.    This general rule is now expressed in many cases.

U.S.—Israel v. Luckenbach S. S. Co., 6 F.2d 996 (C.C.A.2d, 1925); The Claveresk, 264 F. 276 (C.C.A.2d, 1920).

40.    U.S.—U. S. v. Lewis, 237 F. 80 (1916), levee.

Conn.—School Dist. v. Dauchy, 25 Conn. 530 (1857), destruction by lightning one day before completion.

Minn.—Stees v. Leonard, 20 Minn. 494 (1874).

N.J.—Superintendent & Trustees v. Bennett, 27 N.J.L. 513 (1859), building fell because of tornado and latent defect in soil.

ance. The same result is reached in case of a contract to "maintain" an existing structure or to keep one in "repair," provided that this language is interpreted to mean "reconstruct if necessary." [41]

Sometimes a construction contract is divisible, the work and the price being apportioned into pairs of equivalent parts.[42] In such a case, when the first section of the work is completed, there is a money debt for the agreed price thereof. The risk of destruction of the completed section may then be upon the owner. Building contracts are more commonly not apportioned in this manner, the risk of destruction, even after a part payment, being on the contractor. Care should be taken in wording the contract so as to prevent difficulty in interpretation.[43]

The destruction of an almost completed building may occur at so late a time as to make reconstruction on time an actual impossibility. When such is the case, the delay might well be held to be justifiable;[45] but the contractor is still bound to build the agreed structure.

If the destruction of the partly completed structure or the defects in it when completed are caused by the representations of the owner on which the contractor reasonably relied, or by defects in plans and specifications supplied by the owner which the contractor was required to follow, the contractor will not be liable in damages for nonperformance and will not be denied a judgment for compensation.[46] In such a case the nonperformance is caused by the owner and is not a breach of contract.

### § 1339. Destruction or Nonexistence of Contemplated Conditions or Means of Performance

One who contracts to sell and deliver a specific chattel is ordinarily discharged from duty by its destruction without his fault, in the absence of expressions allocating risk otherwise. The risk of property loss in such a case is on the seller; he has no right to the price when he cannot transfer the property. But the risk of losing the profits of the bargain rests on both parties alike.

Similarly, if one contracts to render a specified performance that requires the existence of definite physical conditions or means of performance, he will usually be discharged from duty by the destruction or non-existence of those necessary means or conditions.[47] Observe that this rule, as here stated, applies only where these means or conditions are "necessary" to the performance of one of the bargained-for equivalents. Many of the cases limiting thus strictly the operation of the rule in discharging a contractor were without doubt affected by the now wholly dis-

47. See Straus v. Kazemekas, 124 A. 234, 100 Conn. 581 (1924).

credited rule that a duty assumed by contract is never discharged by supervening impossibility of performing it except when so provided in the agreement.[48]

Thus one who contracts to produce goods at a specific factory, for sale and delivery to the plaintiff, is discharged by the destruction of the factory without his fault.[49] One who contracts to sell and deliver a crop of fruit, vegetables, grain, or hay then growing on a specific tract of land, or to be grown on such a tract within a specified growing season, is discharged from duty by the destruction of that crop without fault.[50] One who contracts to drive logs down a specific stream, in which the parties assume there will be sufficient water, will be discharged if the water dries up.[51] One who contracts to procure and deliver goods, from any one particular source of supply, is discharged if such procurement is made impossible by the government's requisitioning that entire source or by any entire destruction of it without fault.[52]

In all of the foregoing cases, the risk of not getting the profits of performance rests upon both parties alike, unless their expressions indicate a contrary intention. The seller can not get judgment for the price without delivering the goods; he does not get the hoped for economic gain. The buyer can not get judgment for damages for the seller's failure to deliver; he likewise is disappointed as to the expected gain. In any such case, however, the expressions of the parties, interpreted reasonably, may show that one party has assumed the whole risk, has warranted the possibility of performance or made himself an insurer. One who contracts to supply pasturage on specific land for a number of cattle may be found to have warranted that grass will grow and water run.[53] One who promises to supply water for irrigation must look out for droughts and find the water at the favorable time and place; [54] it is the risk of drought, usual and unusual, that the promisee expects to eliminate. The water company may, of course, protect itself by a clause respecting drought and other

50.    U.S.—Browne v. U. S., 30 Ct.Cl. 124 (1895), "Montana upland hay" all killed by drought; North American Oil Co. v. Globe Pipe Line Co., 6 F.2d 564 (C.C.A.8th, 1925).

Ark.—C. G. Davis & Co. v. Bishop, 213 S.W. 744, 139 Ark. 273 (1919), 300 bales of cotton from defendant's farm, actual production only 219.

51.    N.H.—Clarksville Land Co. v. Harriman, 44 A. 527, 68 N.H. 374 (1895), drought prevented the floating of logs down the river.

52.    U.S.—Moore & Tierney v. Roxford Knitting Co., 250 F. 278 (D.C. N.Y.1918), factory compelled to run solely for the government.

53.    U.S.—Berg v. Erickson, 234 F. 817 (C.C.A.8th, 1916).

causes beyond its control.[55]  One who promises to make delivery at a distant place may be held guilty of a breach, though his failure is due to a car shortage [56] or to the blocking of a canal by a landslide.[57]  Such events as these may not cause complete physical impossibility, although greatly adding to difficulty and expense, a fact that tends in the direction of leaving the entire risk on the seller.

If the contract does not require the delivery of goods made at one specified factory, the destruction of that factory does not create impossibility of performance and has been held not to discharge the seller from duty to procure and deliver.[58]  There are other sources of supply; and he must appeal to them though the cost be increased, and even though he had expected to rely upon the one factory or the one source.[59]  The same is true of crops to be grown; no discharge if they are not required to be the product of a particular tract of land during a particular season.[60]  The destruction of a building or other specific subject matter does not discharge a contractor or render performance impossible if the result that he promised to achieve can still be brought about by a commercially practicable alternative method, even though this method may be more expensive.[61]

### § 1340.  Effect of Refusal of Necessary Co-operation by a Third Party

One who contracts to render a performance or produce a result for which it is necessary to obtain the co-operation of third persons is not excused by the fact that they will not co-operate.[65]  This is a risk that is commonly understood to be on the promisor, in the absence of a provision to the contrary.  If workmen strike he must procure others, or induce the strikers to return by satisfying their demands.[66]  He is not discharged even though his difficulties are increased by the failure of police officers to enforce the law.[67]  One who contracts to deliver a quantity of goods manufactured by a specified company is not discharged by the fact that the company reduces its output and refuses to supply enough.[68]

If, instead of contracting to complete a performance by a specified date, the contractor promises to complete it within a reasonable time, the determination of what is a "reasonable time" requires the consideration of all the circumstances that exist at the

---

55.  **U.S.**—Souther v. San Diego Flume Co., 121 F. 347 (C.C.A.9th, 1903).

56.  **U.S.**—Madeirense do Brasil v. Stulman-Emrick Lbr. Co., 147 F.2d 399 (C.C.A.2d, 1945), shortage of ships was reasonably within contemplation.

time performance proceeds, not merely those that existed when the contract was made or that could have been foreseen. The occurrence of a strike is one of these circumstances.[69] The size and duration of the strike, the character of the demands of the workmen, the occurrence of violence, the action of the courts and the police—all these must be considered in answering that question of fact, was performance completed within a reasonable time.

Any contractor can, by proper expression, limit the risks that he must bear. His promise can be expressly conditional, as where he says that he shall not be liable in case of "strikes, fires, or other causes beyond his control," [70] or where a charter party lists certain "excepted risks." [71] Such provisions often raise difficult questions of interpretation—of inclusion and exclusion.[72]

### § 1342. Circumstances Justifying the Pro-Rating of Available Supply

As has been seen in the preceding section, the legal duty of a contractor may be suspended or discharged when without his fault the means of performance on which he relied have ceased to exist. This is true only when the existence of those means of performance was, as the other party had reason to know, a fundamental assumption on which the contract was made. Such a doctrine as this, growing out of the actual practices of men, reduces the contractor's risks and compels the other party to carry the risk of losing the benefits of an advantageous bargain. The late development of this doctrine, as well as the uncertainty of its application, led to the inclusion in many contracts, especially those of producers and suppliers and those requiring completion of a performance by a stated time, of an express provision making the duty of performance conditional on the absence of strikes, riots, fires, and other causes beyond the control of the contractor.[75] Such a provision of course includes the nonexistence of the contemplated means of performance.

The inclusion of such an express provision is of advantage to the contractor, and usually to the other party as well, since it makes for a reasonable allocation of risks and makes known in advance, with somewhat greater clarity, what that allocation is. Without doubt, such a provision reduces the contractor's risks somewhat more than does the doctrine as to means of performance. That doctrine has seldom, if ever, discharged a contractor

---

69. **U.S.**—The Richland Queen, 254 F. 668, 166 C.C.A. 166 (C.C.A.2d, 1918).

70. See § 642, Strike Clause.

75. For an analysis of conditional rights and duties, see Chapters 30–32, Conditions, and especially § 642, Express provisions as to strikes, fires, and causes beyond control.

from duty because of a strike. Probably it has not been used as such a discharge where the failure to make delivery is caused by a shortage of railroad cars, although it would be appropriate in some such cases. The express provision, besides covering much the same ground as the legal doctrine, has one other thing in common with it: the exact boundaries of its application are equally undefined. We can not always be sure what "causes are beyond the control" of the contractor. Many fires can be prevented by the use of foresight and sufficient expenditure. Most strikes can be avoided by a judicious yielding or by an abject surrender to demands. No contractor is excused under such an express provision unless he shows affirmatively that his failure to perform was proximately caused by a contingency within its terms; that, in spite of skill, diligence and good faith on his part, performance became impossible or unreasonably expensive.

In view of the very general practice of producers and suppliers to include in their contracts the express provision as to excuse by "causes beyond the control" of the contractor, there should be, and without doubt will be, a growing tendency to expand the legal doctrine of commercial impracticability so as to make it coextensive with the common express provision. The "fundamental assumptions" on the basis of which such contracts are made tend to become identical whether there is an express provision or not; and risks should be allocated according to those widely understood assumptions. By so doing, the requirements of justice, according to the prevailing mores of today, will be more effectively fulfilled. It is not justice to throw the risk of uncontemplated contingencies upon a contractor merely because it would have been so in older times and because he was not advised by counsel in preparing a written contract. If one party wishes the other to assume greater risks than those that are now commonly contemplated, it should be expressly so provided and compensation adjusted accordingly.

The doctrine of excuse by impossibility, including commercial impracticability, and the use of the express provision considered above, have brought up the problem of pro-rating deliveries among several customers. An excusing contingency may reduce supply without shutting it off altogether; so that the contractor can not supply all of his customers or perform all of his contracts, although he has enough for the full demands of a few of them. A jobber in coal or in the product of a special factory may be prevented from getting more than half of the amount necessary to perform his distribution contracts, because of a strike or fire at the mine or factory or because of a shortage in railroad cars. Assuming that he can show that the contingency is one that is within the terms of the contract provision and therefore excuses from performance, he remains bound by his distribution contracts insofar as supply is available and performance remains practicable. Under such circumstances he can discharge his contractual duties to his customers by a rationing process usually described as prorating the supply.[76]

76.　U.S.—Bliven v. New England Screw Co., 64 U.S. (23 How.) 420, 16 L.Ed. 510 (1859), defendant's custom to fill orders in the order received and to pro-rate; Consolidation Coal Co. v. Peninsular Portland Coal Co., 272 F. 625 (C.C.A. 6th, 1921); Nicoll v. Pittsvein Coal Co., 269 F. 968 (C.C.A.2d, 1920), custom to pro-rate; Luhrig Coal Co. v. Jones & Adams Co., 141 F. 617 (C.C.A.6th, 1905); McKeefrey v. Connellsville Coke & Iron Co. to Use of H. C. Frick Coke Co., 56 F. 212 (C.C.A.3d, 1893).

A detailed discussion of prorating may be found in the general treatise at this point.

# CHAPTER 76

## LEGAL PROHIBITION—EXIGENCIES OF WAR

## § 1343. Impossibility by Legal Prohibition or Act of State—Outbreak of War

The performance of a promise that was lawful and possible when made may become impossible by reason of subsequent legislation, the outbreak of war, or other action by government.[1] If the legislation prohibiting performance, or the action preventing it, is the legislation or action of domestic government, there is no question that the duty of the party whose performance is thus prevented is discharged.[2] The law does not require him to disobey the law; and the state does not penalize him for yielding to its own commands. Substantial failure to perform, because of such prevention by the state, discharges the duty of the other party to the contract, also; not because his performance is prohibited or prevented, but because he is not required to give something for nothing.[3] Unless his promise is of a kind that is held to be wholly independent, his duty is constructively conditional on substantial performance of the agreed equivalent.

We are all familiar with the many thousands of sealed bonds and other contracts for payment of money that expressly required the payment to be in gold coin of standard weight and fineness. Performance according to this promise was then prohibited by act of Congress; and the validity of the prohibition was sustained by the Supreme Court.[4] Thus was the duty of promisors

---

**2.** **U.S.**—Jackson & Co. v. Royal Norwegian Gov't, 177 F.2d 694 (C. A.2d, 1949); Borup v. Western Op. Corp., 130 F.2d 381 (C.C.A.2d, 1942).

One who has contracted to render personal service is discharged from duty by being drafted into the armed forces.

**N.Y.**—Havens v. Rochester Ropes, 46 N.Y.S.2d 534, 267 App.Div. 394 (1944).

**3.** **U.S.**—Jarrett v. Pittsburgh Plate Glass Co., 131 F.2d 674 (C.C.A.5th, 1942).

**4.** **U.S.**—Norman v. Baltimore & O. R. Co., 55 S.Ct. 407, 294 U.S. 240, 79 L.Ed. 885, 95 A.L.R. 1352 (1934), as to private domestic bonds; Holyoke Water Power Co. v. American Writing Paper Co., 57 S.Ct. 485, 300 U.S. 324, 81 L.Ed. 678 (1935).

effectively discharged, even though the consideration had been fully executed; the duty to pay in another medium was substituted.

Contracts of public carriers to give annual passes over their lines have been held nullified by statutes forbidding the giving of such passes.[5] Contracts by which one party is bound to construct a building, either new or in case of destruction, have been held to be discharged by subsequently passed laws and ordinances forbidding the construction of the materials or on the plans specified in the contract.[6] A contract to sell and deliver liquors is discharged by a statute prohibiting the performance of such contracts.[7] A contract by a public carrier to transport goods at a specific rate is discharged in case other rates are made compulsory by public authority.[8] Other illustrative cases are cited below.[9]

Just as the making of a contract by communication with a resident of an enemy country across the line of hostilities is illegal, so also the performance of a lawful contract already made may be made illegal by the subsequent outbreak of war. Insofar as performance is thus made illegal the duty to render it is discharged; and the entire contractual duty of a party is discharged just as soon as the purpose for which he entered into the contract is rendered apparently impossible by the legal prohibition against continuing performance.[10] Performance may be illegal either because it involves crossing the line of hostilities or because it would

N.Y.—Compania de Inv. Int. v. Industrial Mtge. Bank, 198 N.E. 617, 269 N.Y. 22, 101 A.L.R. 1313 (1935), foreign bonds payable in dollars, noted in 45 Yale L.J. 723 (1936).

The Court did, indeed, unanimously say that the Congressional repudiation of the promises of the United States to pay in gold was unconstitutional and invalid; but at the same time it held that Congress had effectively prevented the courts from giving any remedy. A legal duty with no legal remedy is an illusion. See Perry v. U. S., 55 S. Ct. 432, 294 U.S. 330, 79 L.Ed. 912, 95 A.L.R. 1335 (1934); Nortz v. U. S., 55 S.Ct. 428, 294 U.S. 317, 79 L.Ed. 907, 95 A.L.R. 1346 (1934). It is not impossible that the promise of the United States to pay in gold, without remedy though it be in the courts, may yet be given other juristic effects. The statute of frauds makes certain oral promises unenforceable by bringing suit; this is very far from depriving them of all legal effect.

5.　Ky.—Louisville & N. R. Co. v. Crowe, 160 S.W. 759, 156 Ky. 27 (1913).

9.　U.S.—Moller v. Herring, 255 F. 670, 3 A.L.R. 624 (C.C.A.5th, 1919), one who contracted to salvage cotton lost in a storm was discharged by taking of the cotton by a receiver for all claimants.

Ala.—Jersey Ice Cream Co. v. Banner Cone Co., 86 So. 382, 204 Ala. 532 (1920), wartime food regulations prevented manufacture of cones.

R.I.—Cinquegrano v. T. A. Clarke Motors, 30 A.2d 859, 69 R.I. 28 (1943), delivery of motor truck prevented by government "freezing order."

affect our country unfavorably by reducing our resources or increasing those of the enemy.[11]

If, before the outbreak of war, a contract with an enemy alien has been fully performed on one side, so that the only unperformed obligation is a money debt or the duty of making compensation for an already existing breach, an action to recover such debt or damages can be maintained after the end of the war.[12] Such a debt due from a citizen to an enemy alien may be made collectible by the Alien Property Custodian and the proceeds distributed according to statute or treaty provisions.

### § 1344.  Impossibility by Government Requisition of a Ship or Other Specific Subject Matter

A valid requisition, by the government, of the specific subject matter of a contract, makes performance unlawful if it conflicts with the government use.  Even an invalid requisition may make performance impossible.  Such requisitions usually occur in time of war.  They operate to discharge the contractor from any duty the performance of which conflicts with the requisition.[13]  The wartime requisition by the British government of vessels owned by British citizens but then under charter to Americans was held to discharge whatever duties the owners owed to the charterers with regard to the continued use of the vessels.[14]  The duty of the charterer to pay the hire is discharged, not by impossibility of performance of the duty but by failure of consideration.  The charterer's purpose has been "frustrated." [15]

Sometimes, however, the government makes requisition only for purposes of use during a limited period.  If, after this period ends, the purposes of the parties to the contract can still be substantially attained, there is no discharge.[16]  Thus, a ship that is under charter may be requisitioned for a period that is less than the time for which she is chartered.  Usually, however, the requisition is for an indefinite period; and the surrounding circumstances may be such as to make the charterer reasonably believe that the requisition will substantially frustrate the purpose for which he chartered the ship.  If, while under that reasonable belief, he charters another ship or otherwise materially

14.  **U.S.**—Texas Co. v. Hogarth Shipping Co., 41 S.Ct. 612, 256 U.S. 619, 65 L.Ed. 1123 (1921).

15.  This distinction between impossibility of performance and frustration of purpose as different grounds of defense for the two contracting parties is seldom seen by the courts; but it was specifically noted by L. Hand, J., in Earn Line S. S. Co. v. Sutherland S. S. Co., 254 F. 126 (D.C.N.Y., 1918).  Here, however, the *force majeure* clause ended with the words "mutually excepted," and the court thought this required interpretation in favor of the charterer as well as the owner. The decision was affirmed on appeal in The Claveresk, 264 F. 276 (C.C.A.2d, 1920).

changes his position, his duty as charterer is ended. So long as he has not changed his position materially, he is not discharged until it becomes too late to attain the substantial purpose for which he contracted. If the requisition is under such circumstances that a reasonable man would believe that the substantial attainment of the purpose of the transaction has been made impossible, the adventure is said to be "frustrated" and the owner is discharged from any further duty to the charterer [17] and the latter is discharged from duty to pay the hire.[18]

The duties of both owner and charterer are discharged if the government user lasts throughout the entire period covered by the contract.[19] And whenever performance strictly on time is of the essence of the contract, any delay by government requisition will operate as a discharge.

## § 1345.  Government Requisition of a Factory or Other Facilities or Specific Property Required for Performance

One who has contracted to manufacture goods may be prevented from performing by reason of government requisition. He may be required to deliver his entire output to the government for so long a period as to make it impracticable for him to perform his contracts with his private customers. To the extent that it is thus impracticable, he is discharged.[23] He is not required to enlarge his factory or to incur unreasonable expense in order to keep his promises.[24] The risk of governmental prevention must be borne in part by the party for whom the goods were to be made. Both bear the risk of loss of their bargain.[25]

23.  **U.S.**—Moore & Tierney v. Roxford Knitting Co., 250 F. 278 (D.C. N.Y.1918), affirmed 265 F. 177, 11 A.L.R. 1415 (C.C.A.2d 1920), judgment for the manufacturer for the part delivered.

25.  The following sections of the general treatise are omitted here: § 1346. Prevention by Order or Decree of a Court or Administrative Officer. § 1347. Effect of an Embargo, and of Refusal of a License or Permit. § 1348. Impossibility That is Temporary or of Uncertain Duration. § 1349. Effect of a Governmental Moratorium. § 1350. Outbreak of War May Make Performance Merely More Expensive. § 1351. Impossibility Caused by Foreign Law or Government. § 1352. Legal Impossibility Caused by Promisor's Own Act—Imprisonment.

# CHAPTER 77

## DISCHARGE BY FRUSTRATION OF PURPOSE

## § 1353. Frustration of Purpose as a Justification for Nonperformance

We have already discussed the distinction between "frustration of object" and impossibility of performance. A "contract" never has a purpose or object. Only the contracting persons have purposes; and the purpose of any one of these persons is different from the purpose of any other. The hopes and purposes and objects of one of the parties may be frustrated by supervening events, although the purposes of the other party may not be at all affected by those events. Of course, if the frustration of the one is held to justify his refusal to keep his promise, by such refusal he may successfully frustrate the purposes of the other party also; and so the frustration becomes mutual.[1]

Frustration of purpose is not identical with impossibility of performance. Frustration of one party's purpose is hardly ever caused by the impossibility of his own performance. His purpose may be frustrated by reason of the impossibility of the other party's performance; usually his purpose in making the contract

---

1. In Hirji Mulji v. Cheong Yue S. S. Co., [1926] A.C. 497, 507, the court said: "Evidently it is their common object that has to be frustrated, not merely the individual advantage which one party or the other might have gained from the contract." In this case the contract was one whereby the owner of a vessel chartered it to the defendant for a specified period at an agreed rental. Before delivery of the vessel it was requisitioned by the government for war purposes. It is difficult to see a "common object" of the two parties. The charterer's purpose was to procure the use of the ship. The owner's purpose was to get the rental. For each to attain his purpose, he had to render the performance desired by the other. The governmental requisition certainly defeated the purpose of the charterer. It did not in itself defeat the purpose of the shipowner; but the modern rule of law applicable in such a case did defeat his purpose. Of course, each one knew the purpose of the other.

1128

is to induce that performance and to secure the benefits thereof. But observe that his purpose is equally frustrated by the other's failure to perform, whatever was the cause. That failure is just as injurious and disappointing—just as great a frustration—if the other party's failure is due to his wilful repudiation, or to his unfortunate insolvency, as when it is due to act of state or to act of God.[2]

When the purpose of one party is substantially frustrated by the wilful breach of the other, no one doubts that such frustration ought to discharge him from further duty. There are cases in which mutual promises are wholly independent and unconditional; but they are not common. The same is true when the nonperformance by the other party, though not wilful, is caused by his subjective inability to perform. In such cases the frustrated party has an action for damages for breach; and we do not increase those damages by requiring him to proceed with his own uncompensated performance. The wrongful frustration of his purposes operates as his discharge from duty. Frustration of a contractor's purpose as a defense is debated only in those cases where he has no claim to compensation against the other party. The absence of such claim to compensation may be due to one of two things: (1) the other party's duty to perform was discharged by impossibility of performance; or (2) the other party has already performed, or is ready and able to perform, and the frustration of purpose is caused by collateral events.

It may be asked how can a contractor's purpose be frustrated by collateral events, when the agreed equivalent promised him in return for his own has been performed or is going to be. In such a case he gets that for which he bargained—his immediate object of desire. The answer to this is that a contractor has indirect and ultimate objects of desire; he bargains for the immediate object in order to attain more remote ends and in the confident belief that the attainment of the first will bring home the second one also. Thus a lessee promises to pay rent in order to induce the lessor to convey a limited estate in the land—the leasehold interest. He desires to be owner of this leasehold, with the manifold legal relations of which it is composed, in order to

2.    Fibrosa Spolka Akcyjna v. Fairbairn L. C. B. Ltd., [1943] A.C. 32, [1942] 2 All Eng. 122 (H.L.), was a case of this sort. The delivery of machines by a seller was made impossible by war. They were the agreed equivalent of the price, part of which had been paid in advance. The court gave judgment for restitution of the advance payment. The war prevented delivery by the seller and thus "frustrated" the purpose of the buyer. The court held that this justified the buyer's failure to pay, thus "frustrating" the purpose of the seller (the court even going so far as to require repayment of what the seller had already received). No court action was necessary to "frustrate" the purpose of the buyer.

enjoy the physical use and occupation and to realize the profits therefrom by operating it as a farm, a dwelling place, a movie theater, or a liquor saloon. The conveyance is made; and the lessee is in possession and owner of the leasehold interest. He has attained his immediate object. Yet he may be wholly ousted from possession by an invading army; the dwelling house may be burned down; a city ordinance may forbid the use of inflammable films; the legislature may prohibit the sale of liquor. In these cases, the ultimate purpose of the lessee is frustrated. It is what he now regards as his chief purpose; without it, he would not have promised to pay rent or, at least, so much rent. In great numbers of cases, this kind of frustration has caused the lessee to refuse to pay rent. He thinks that the lessor should bear part or all of the risk of the event; and the courts have had to make the law of such a case.

One who asserts frustration of purpose as a discharge from duty is seldom, if ever, asserting impossibility of performance of his own promise as a defense. The principal performance promised by the lessee, in the cases stated above is the payment of rent. Nothing has made that performance impossible. In setting up frustration of purpose, he is asserting a different sort of defense. Some kind of contemplated performance may have become impossible; but it is not that promised performance from which he asks to be excused.

## § 1354. Risks of Loss—The Assumption of Risk by Voluntary Assent, and the Allocation of Risks by the Law

Whenever a promise is made, there is always some degree of uncertainty that it will be performed, some degree of probability that the promisee will suffer disappointment. Life is full of risks, including the risk of not being able to convince a jury that a promise was made, the risk that the court will not render a favorable decree, and the risk that the sheriff will not be able to collect the amount that the court adjudges to be due. There is some risk that my house will be destroyed by fire. In return for a premium, an insurance company promises me that it will pay me the amount of the loss; it voluntarily assumes the risk that otherwise I would have had to carry, although I must still carry the risk of its unwillingness or inability to indemnify me.

The risks with which we are now dealing are not the risks of non-persuasion of a court or jury, or the risk of non-collection. They are the risks of the occurrence of supervening events that make some performance impossible or illegal or difficult or dangerous or expensive, or worthless, resulting in the frustration of purposes, in the destruction of values, and in the prevention of gains and the causing of losses.

In determining the effect of "supervening events" upon a contractor's legal duty, we must bear in mind that every act of man and every event in nature that occurs after the contract is made is a supervening event. By most of these events a contractor's ability, or even his willingness, to keep his promise is not affected in the least. Most of them do not "frustrate" his purposes in the smallest degree. Many of the events that do affect his ability and willingness, and to some extent frustrate his purposes by affecting the relative value of the agreed performances are the commonly recurring events of life, foreseen (or reasonably foreseeable) when the contract is made and discounted in the process of agreeing upon the bargain. Fruit is perishable, New England weather is variable, the stock market goes down and up, supply and demand are constant variables. Up to a point, such events as these do not cause contractors to ask or to expect relief. But there comes a "point" at which the request is regarded as reasonable and the expectation will not be disappointed. Where is that "point"? Unfortunately, it is a vanishing point; the line that it draws is an invisible line. In any specific case, its location depends upon customary business practice and commonly prevailing opinion. Is the frustration great or small, complete or partial? Is the "event" one that commonly recurs, one that "reasonable" men contemplate as possible and therefore discount in bargaining?

If a supervening event that causes material frustration of purposes is wilfully or negligently caused by one of the parties, he is the one on whom will be put the burden of the injury, including the burden of making compensation for the injuries of others. Often, however, such events occur without the fault of either party, causing losses and preventing gains. Who, then, must stand the loss or bear the disappointment? If a division of losses is to be made, in what proportion? Courts have had to answer these questions. The cases are numerous, various in character, and not wholly consistent in reasoning or in decision. In each case, the court has determined who must bear and who must pay. These cases must be classified; and tentative rules must be drawn, by means of which future decisions can be influenced, and therefore can be predicted. Thus we may judge which party must bear the risk of supervening events. As between lessor and lessee there are the risks of invading armies and of governmental seizures and prohibitions. As between buyer and seller, there is the risk of destruction of goods, the risk of governmental requisition, the risk of a market collapse. Master and servant have the risks of death and illness. There are the innumerable risks arising out of wars and rumors of wars, on sea and on land.

We can not hope to make all-inclusive rules, to foresee all such future events, or to allocate all the risks of life. Cases will still arise in which the court must blaze a new trail, modifying our tentative rules and adopting a new distribution of losses. But this is no reason for not making use of the extensive judicial experience already at hand. If, like an insurer, either party expresses an intention to assume and carry a particular risk, effect will be given to his expression and the loss distributed accordingly. We must know the processes of interpretation by which the courts have discovered such an assumption. If there is no such assumption, what other factors have influenced the courts in allocating the risks and in distributing the losses? [3]

The Uniform Commercial Code—Sales, § 2—615 (1950 draft), with the comment thereon, makes an excellent generalization applicable to contracts for the sale of goods. Those provisions may properly be used as a basis for decision, even in a jurisdiction in which the Code has not been adopted. Also, they may properly be used by analogy, with due allowance for differing conditions, in cases dealing with the performance of contracts other than for the sale of goods.

Where a contract for the carriage of goods by sea provides for payment of freight on shipment and that freight shall then be regarded as earned even though cargo is later lost or the voyage for any reason has to be abandoned, the risks have been allocated by the parties themselves. The outbreak of war or a governmental embargo after loading will not terminate the shipper's duty to pay freight, however much his purpose is frustrated.[4]

### § 1355. Frustration of Purpose by a Collateral Event That Affects the Value of a Performance without Making it Impossible—The Coronation Cases

At this point we may as well discuss the Coronation cases, as illustrations of frustration of a contractor's purpose by a collateral event that gravely affects relative values but does not make any of the promised performances either impossible or illegal

---

**3.** "When the scope of the undertaking is fixed, that is merely another way of saying that the contractor takes the risk of obstacles to that extent." Holmes, J., in Day v. U. S., 38 S.Ct. 57, 245 U.S. 159, 62 L.Ed. 219 (1917).

**4.** U.S.—Allanwilde Transp. Corp. v. Vacuum Oil Co., 39 S.Ct. 147, 248 U.S. 377, 63 L.Ed. 312, 3 A.L.R. 15 (1919).

A buyer who agreed to receive molasses either aboard his tankers or in the seller's tanks in Porto Rico was held to have "assumed the risk" of not being able to transport the molasses to the United States by reason of war conditions that existed when the contract was made. Baetjer v. New England Alcohol Co., 66 N.E.2d 798, 319 Mass. 592 (1946).

The promisor was held to have assumed the risk in Madeirense Do Brasil v. Stulman-Emrick Lumber Co., 147 F.2d 399 (C.C.A.2d, 1945), and Bolckow, V. & Co. v. Compania Minera, 115 L.T. 745, 33 T.L.R. 111 (1916, C.A.).

or dangerous or difficult or expensive.  In these cases, the English courts were faced with a new problem;  and they made decisions determining which party had to suffer the losses and bear the disappointments.  They laid down tentative rules for allocating the risks;  it can not be said that the American courts are strictly following these rules.

When Albert Edward succeeded his mother, Queen Victoria, as King Edward VII of England, great Coronation ceremonies were planned.  There were to be a review of the great battle fleet at sea and a magnificent processional pageant leading the king to the crowning at Westminster.  Ships were chartered for witnessing the review of the fleet; and, along the announced route of the procession, windows and porches and roofs were hired at high rates for the purpose of viewing it.  The king became ill.  The reviews and processions were indefinitely postponed.  Hamlet would not be Hamlet without the Prince of Denmark.  The supervening event, frustrating the hopes and purposes of thousands, was the illness of the king.  There were losses and there was prevention of expected gain.  How should the risks be allocated and who should bear loss and disappointment?

One defendant hired a steamship from its owner, at an agreed rental, for the purpose of a two day excursion to witness the Coronation naval review and to sail around the Isle of Wight.  This purpose of the defendant was stated in the contract; but nothing was said about the possible illness of the king.  Yet that illness prevented the naval review and prevented passengers from thronging to the ship and paying fares.  The illness of the king in no way affected the performances that were mutually promised other than by greatly reducing the value of one of them.  The plaintiff was still able and willing to deliver the steamship at the agreed time and place.  There was nothing to prevent the defendant from performing the agreed equivalent, the payment of the promised rental.  The court held that the defendant must pay the rent in full, even though his ultimate purpose was frustrated and his expected gains from passenger fares were totally prevented.[5]  So, the risk of the king's illness, with its resulting financial harm, was held to rest on the hirer of the ship.  The plaintiff, on the other hand did not risk even the loss of the profits of his bargain.  He did, indeed, have his ship available for the voyage as intended; but the rental that he received was out of proportion to the rental value of the ship on the two specified days.  He got his expected profit, although the play that made it possible was not given.

5. **Eng.**—Herne Bay S. S. Co. **v.** Hutton, [1903] 2 K.B. 683.

Had the rental or price of transportation been paid in advance, the **frustration of** purpose was held to create no quasi-contractual right to money back.  Civil Service Co-op. Soc. v. General Steam **Nav. Co.,** [1903] 2 K.B. 756.

Let us, at least, make the query whether it would not have been better to put both parties in statu quo, denying to the owner his inflated rental just as the events denied to the hirer his inflated fares. There is no one necessary answer to this question. A factor to be considered is that the hirer might have suffered a net loss even if the king had not been ill; also, he might have reaped a handsome profit.

In a second case, the plaintiff hired a room on Pall Mall, "to view the procession," expecting to erect seats for paying guests. The rental was £141, payable in advance; but only £100 was paid on account. The court held that the plaintiff had no right to money back, and gave judgment to the owner for the balance of £41 unpaid.[6] The court based this judgment on the fact that by the contract the entire rental was due and was collectible before the procession was called off. It thought that the law should leave the parties as they were at the moment when the procession was cancelled, but that the parties should be released from performances that were not due until after the happening of the frustrating event. The hirer should not be in a better position by reason of his not having paid when the money was due.

It should be observed that neither of the promised performances ever became impossible. All that the owner promised to do could still be done after the procession was cancelled; and the hirer of the window could and did pay the rental. The hirer bore the entire loss and made nothing of his expected gains. The owner received the whole of his inflated profit. But, according to the dictum of the court, the antecedent risks were divided to some extent. If the procession had been cancelled before any of the rent was due, the owner would have received nothing; the risk of such a relatively early cancellation was all his. If it had been cancelled before one part of the rent was due, the hirer would have been discharged from paying that part; the loss would be divided between the parties in such proportion as chance might prescribe. The risk that the events might be as they in fact turned out was all on the hirer. The court admitted that its stated rule was "to some extent arbitrary." It suggests, also, that the parties might well have agreed that the hirer should have his money back, with compensation to the owner to the extent of any change of position by reason of the contract. This suggestion seems reasonable. The court had power to adopt such a solution, in the absence of agreement by the parties. If this was justice and equity, the court was a court of justice and a court of equity.[7] There was no antecedent rule even tentatively con-

6.   Eng.—Chandler   v.   Webster, [1904] 1 K.B. 493 (C.A.).

7.   Since the above text was written, the House of Lords has disap-
proved the reasoning in Chandler v. Webster, and has decreed restitution of an advance payment for machines the delivery of which be-

trolling the case. The court stated its own rule; and it could have stated a different one.

In a third case, the defendant hired a flat on Pall Mall, to view the procession; he paid £25 down and promised to pay £50 more on June 24, prior to the day set for the procession. On the morning of June 24 the procession was cancelled. The hirer abandoned his claim to restitution of the £25 paid; and the court gave judgment that his duty to pay the balance of the rent was discharged.[8] The court said that "performance of the contract was prevented." As in the preceding case, this seems incorrect; and the other comments made above on that case are applicable here. The collateral event—illness of the king—frustrated the purposes of the hirer. It did not prevent performance, although it destroyed rental value.[9]

What effect should the king's illness have upon the thousands of other contracts made at that period? It should have no effect whatever unless the holding of the ceremonies as planned formed what is sometimes called the "basis of the contract," but is more accurately described as the basis on which one of the parties assented to the bargain. It is not such a "basis" unless it creates a major part—an essential part—of the value of one of the performances that the parties agree to exchange, inducing one of the parties and enabling the other to reach the agreement. If it is the planned ceremonies that give value to A's performance in the mind of B, that will enable B to realize a profitable purpose, and that enable A to charge an inflated price in excess of what would otherwise be possible, then they form the "basis of the contract." [10]

came impossible by outbreak of war. Fibrosa Spolka Akcyjna v. Fairbairn L. C. B. Ltd., [1943] A. C. 32, [1942] 2 All Eng. 122, 167 L.T. 101, 111 L.J.K.B. 433. Observe, however, that in this case the machines were the agreed equivalent of the money and that it was the performance of this equivalent that became impossible. In Chandler v. Webster, this was not the case. What the cancellation of the procession did was to cause a great depreciation in the value of the use of the rooms, a value that had been greatly inflated by the Coronation plans. That inflated value was instantly deflated.

8.　Eng.—Krell v. Henry, [1903] 2 K.B. 740 (C.A.).

9.　Alfred Marks Realty Co. v. Hotel Hermitage Co., 156 N.Y.S. 179, 170 App.Div. 484 (1915), is somewhat like the Coronation cases. A firm prepared a souvenir program for a yacht race and sold advertising space therein. The yacht race was cancelled, because of war, thus preventing the expected distribution and destroying the value of the advertising space. The court held that the advertisers did not have to pay the price agreed on. In a case like this, it would be rather difficult, although it might be equitable, to make the advertisers contribute a share of the expenditures incurred in printing their advertisements in the souvenir program.

A London resident contracts to buy a motor car; before delivery or full payment the king falls ill. The price must still be paid and the car delivered, because the Coronation plans do not affect the value of the car or the price that was agreed on. A ship is chartered for a voyage to India, the Coronation plans having no influence on values or terms; the king's illness frustrates nobody's purpose, and the contract stands.[11] A ship is chartered in France, to carry crowds of American tourists across the channel to see the procession; the king is ill, and the tourists remain on the Continent. If the agreed rental was at no more than the normal rate, there is no reason for relieving the charterer of the risk of getting few passengers. The king's illness may frustrate his purpose of making profits; but if the owner of the ship knew of this purpose it did not affect the terms of agreement.

If one contracts to buy property for the purpose of making a resale at a profit, his purpose is frustrated when he finds that no one will pay as much as he did or that no one will buy at all. But this fact is not a discharge of his duty to the seller. This is a risk that is customarily carried by the buyer without ever raising the question. His "frustration" is caused by no uncontemplated cataclysm.

The same result obtains even though the buyer's purpose is to export the goods, or to use them to build a house, and later his purpose is frustrated by an embargo against export or by a zoning ordinance preventing such building.[12] Here the "frustration" is caused by an unexpected event; but the value of the goods purchased is not directly dependent upon the buyer's particular purpose, and the seller was not enabled thereby to fix a price beyond the ordinary.

Many cases will be easy to decide. Differences in degree, small in some cases, are seen to be very great in others. No contract can be said to have only one "basis." Motivating reasons for an agreement are always complex. A writer can only respectfully follow the courts as they feel their way along lines so "wavering and blurred."

Variations in the value of a promised performance, caused by the constantly varying factors that affect the bargaining appetites of men, are the rule rather than the exception. Bargainers know this and swallow their losses and disappointments, meantime keeping their promises. Such being the business mores, court decisions that are not in harmony with them will not make for satisfaction or prosperity. Relief from duty, outside of the bankruptcy court, can safely be granted on the ground of frustration

12.   **Mass.**—Baetjer v. New England Alcohol Co., 66 N.E.2d 798, 319 Mass. 592 (1946).

of purpose by the rise or fall of values, only when the variation in value is very great and is caused by a supervening event that was not in fact contemplated by the parties and the risk of which was not allocated by them.

In a later section will be discussed the effect of fluctuations of the value of money in terms of other money or of commodities. At this point we are considering the effect of sudden and unexpected variation in the value of land, goods, rents, and services in terms of money or in terms of each other.

### § 1356.  Leases—Partial or Total Frustration of Lessee's Purpose

One who leases and takes possession of land and buildings, promising to pay rent therefor, always has some purpose in view. His immediate purpose is the acquisition of the leasehold interest in the land, with its manifold rights and privileges.  But such a property "interest" as this, as in the case of all legal relations of whatever sort, is a means to a more remote end, not the ultimate end and aim of the lessee.  He receives the conveyance and makes his contract in order to obtain the physical and pecuniary enjoyment of the premises, an enjoyment that he expects to realize in some particular way.  One who becomes the lessee of a farm may expect to occupy the house as his dwelling place, to use other farm buildings for his live stock, to cultivate the fields for the production of grain, and to gather in season the fruit from its orchards.  These purposes of the lessee may be fully known to the lessor; and it may be the usefulness of the land for these purposes that gives the land the rental value that the lessee promises to pay.

Suppose, now, that these purposes are frustrated by supervening events of which the lease says nothing.  Must the lessee continue to pay rent?  The frustration may be only in part, a large part or a small one;  or it may be total and include the entire period of the lease.  The house or the barn may be destroyed by fire, thus frustrating one of the major purposes of the lessee.  The buildings may be carried away and the fields destroyed by floods and hurricanes, frustrating all of the purposes of the lessee.  Yet there have been many cases holding that he must continue to pay the promised rent in spite of such frustration.[13]  This is true, even though the possibility of such destructive events was not within the actual contemplation of the parties.  Men are, indeed, aware of such possibilities;  and they sometimes make express provision for them.  In more cases, they overlook them and say nothing.

One of the early cases in this field has already been discussed herein at some length.  A lessee, when sued for three years' rent, pleaded that he had been ousted from possession for the three years by an invading army, "whereby he could not take the profits." The act of the invader did not invalidate the lease or make the lessee any the less an owner of the "property interest"; but it did prevent for three years the physical and pecuniary enjoyment thereof. It was held that the lessee must pay the rent.[14] Here the particular form of the expected use does not appear; and no doubt neither party anticipated an invasion or consciously "assumed the risk." This case contains the celebrated dictum that a promisor is not excused by impossibility of performance, a dictum that was long accepted and that has been repeated in great numbers of cases.

There are other cases of leases of land for a limited term in which the court has held that the destruction of the buildings discharged the lessee's duty to pay rent.[15] These may be distinguished on the ground that the tenant's property interest was small and his purposes were totally frustrated. The court treats the transaction as a contract for use and occupation rather than a conveyance; and, as in some of the liquor saloon cases that follow, throws a greater portion of risk upon the lessor, the risk of loss of rental value during the leasehold term as well as of the value of his reversionary property.

Contracts for the hiring of a building wholly apart from the land, or for the hiring of rooms or apartments in a building, are not regarded either by the parties or by the courts as conveyances of an estate in the land. The tenant does not have the rights and powers of ownership nor does he carry the risks of ownership; and his duty to pay rent ceases on destruction of the building or

---

14.  **Eng.**—Paradine v. Jane, Aleyn, 26 (1647, K.B.). See § 1322, ante.

This decision is followed in Robinson v. L'Engle, 13 Fla. 482 (1869).

The lessee of a tin mine in Johore was held not discharged from duty to pay by the fact that the Japanese army occupied the territory. Pelepah Valley R. Est. v. Sungei Besi Mines, 170 L.T. 338 (1944).

In Paradine v. Jane the court was quite aware that the risks of both gain and loss were involved. The defendant did not allege impossibility of performance as a defense; his words were "whereby he could not take the profits." As to this the report reads: "Another reason was added, that as the lessee is to have the advantage of casual profits, so he must run the hazard of casual losses, and not lay the whole burthen of them upon the lessor."

15.  **U.S.**—Waite v. O'Neil, 76 F. 408 (C.C.A.6th, 1896), lease of "river front and landing," all of which was destroyed by a flood.

It was held in Viterbo v. Friedlander, 7 S.Ct. 962, 120 U.S. 707, 30 L.Ed. 776 (1887), that by the civil and statutory law of Louisiana a lessee had a right to the annulment of the lease in case of destruction of the property by a Mississippi flood of a kind not contemplated by the parties. The court said that the common law is otherwise. In Cricklewood Prop. & Inv. Trust v. Leightons Inv. Trust, [1945] A.C. 221, [1945] 1 All Eng. 252, Lords Simon and Wright thought that a tenant's duty to pay rent would be discharged by total destruction of the land and its contents. The other two Lords thought not. In the case before them the frustration of the pur-

of the part occupied by him, no possession being retained. After the destruction, there is total failure of consideration, and a total frustration of the tenant's purpose known to be the basis of his contract.[16] The tenant, because his purpose is frustrated, does not have to pay rent; but neither can he make the landlord pay damages for not keeping the building intact or supplying him with other quarters.[17]

It was formerly thought to be a sufficient reason for making the lessee pay the agreed rent that he promised in general and unlimited terms, when he might have provided against such contingencies in his contract. He has "assumed the risk" by not having the foresight to exclude it in express terms. This reason has long since ceased to be convincing, as is shown by the multitude of cases holding that a promisor's duty is discharged by supervening events that make his performance impossible. Whether the frustration of the tenant's purposes operates in discharge of his duty depends upon all the circumstances, especially upon the extent of that frustration and the prevailing practices of men in like cases.

We should observe in these cases that the risk of loss is not wholly on the lessee. Res perit domino; but who is dominus? In this instance there are two owners. The lessee is an owner for the term; the lessor owns the reversion. When a building burns, neither party having promised to rebuild, the loss falls on both in proportion to their property interests. The lessee can not occupy it for the term; the lessor has no house thereafter. Each can insure his interest if he will.

Is it unjust that the lessee must continue to pay rent in spite of the frustration of his purpose? It is not, if he has received the agreed equivalent of that rent. According to the common understanding, that agreed equivalent is the conveyance of the leasehold property interest, with its risks and its values. This he has received. Of it he has not been deprived. If unforeseen events suddenly increase its value, the lessee profits thereby with no increase in the rent; should he not also carry the risk of losses and do his own insuring? The probability that this is the view that will still be taken increases with the length of the leasehold interest.

poses of a lessee was only partial, his lease having 90 years still to run. In Swift v. Macbean, [1942] 1 K.B. 375, the lessee of a furnished house had to pay rent in spite of requisition for war uses.

16.   **Ala.**—O'Byrne v. Henley, 50 So. 83, 161 Ala. 620 (1909), semble.

**Cal.**—Ainsworth v. Ritt, 38 Cal. 89

(1869), lease of half a building, not of the land.

**Pa.**—Moving Picture Co. v. Scottish Union & N. Ins. Co., 90 A. 642, 244 Pa. 358 (1914), lease of one floor in office building.

17.   This was the holding in the leading case Taylor v. Caldwell, 3 Best & S. 826 (1863), a decision that is everywhere approved.

Frequently, a lessee expects to use the premises for a very particular purpose. This fact may be not known to the lessor; and the usefulness of the premises for that specific purpose may have played no part in determining the amount of the rent. When such is the case, the risk of frustration and disappointment is left, as the old English decision left it, on the lessee, in so far as use and occupation during his own term are concerned.

In modern cases, there has been a tendency to treat a lease as a contract instead of a conveyance, although in fact it is both at once.[18] The older allocation of risks does not now always seem just. Many short term leases have been made, in which the purpose of the lessee was to conduct a liquor saloon, a purpose known to the lessor and one which gave to the premises a large part of its rental value. Then followed the enactment of a federal, state, or local prohibitory law preventing the use of the premises for the expected purpose. The prohibition law does not make it impossible or illegal for the lessee to keep his promise to pay the rent, or it may be to perform his other promises; [19] but it frustrates his purpose of using the premises for a liquor saloon in the reasonable hope of pecuniary profit. If the terms of the lease are such that the lessee is restricted to this one use, it has been held in a considerable number of cases that his duty to pay rent is discharged.[20] The risk of prohibition is on the lessor, at least in part. The lessor loses his contract right against the lessee and such part of the sale value of the premises as is dependent on the privilege of user for liquor selling. But he regains his possessory rights; so that his loss is thus mitigated. The lessee is relieved of the duty to pay rent, if he surrenders possession; but he still suffers the loss of his expected profits over and above the rental payments. In these cases, the law divides the risks by making

---

18. "A lease is in one sense a running rather than a completed contract. It is an agreement for a continuous interchange of values between landlord and tenant rather than a purchase single and completed of a term or estate in lands." Brewer, J., in Whitaker v. Hawley, 25 Kan. 674 (1881).

In Leonard v. Autocar S. & S. Co., 64 N.E.2d 477, 392 Ill. 182, 163 A.L.R. 670 (1946), the court accepted "for discussion the theory that in ascertaining the rights of the parties the lease should be treated solely as a contract and its aspects as a conveyance entirely disregarded."

20. Ala.—Greil Bros. Co. v. Mabson, 60 So. 876, 179 Ala. 444 (1913).

Cal.—Industrial Devel. & Land Co. v. Goldschmidt, 206 P. 134, 56 Cal. App. 507 (1922).

Ill.—Levy v. Johnston & Hunt, 224 Ill.App. 300 (1922).

Mich.—Hooper v. Mueller, 123 N.W. 24, 158 Mich. 595 (1909).

Cases contra, throwing the whole risk on the lessee and requiring him to pay the agreed rent:

Ga.—Goodrum Tobacco Co. v. Potts-Thompson Liquor Co., 66 S.E. 1081, 133 Ga. 776 (1910), lessee thought to have reason to foresee the prohibition law.

Mass.—Imbeschied v. Lerner, 135 N. E. 219, 241 Mass. 199, 22 A.L.R. 819 (1922).

each party bear the loss of his bargain, that is, the net profits that full performance would have given him.

In some saloon cases, the lease was so drawn that the lessee was not restricted to a single use.  In a saloon, the lessee may sell soft drinks, candies, tobaccos, food.  The prohibitory law does not wholly frustrate the lessee's purpose.  In such cases, the courts have often held that the lessee's duty to pay rent is not discharged, either in whole or in part.[21]  But these other uses may have played a very small part in the determination of rental value;  and the frustration of purpose may still clearly go "to the essence." [22]  If the case is one in which total frustration would discharge the lessee, he should not be held to the contract merely because he is still permitted to sell peanuts and give away free lunches.

22.    Other leasehold cases are here discussed in the general treatise. The following sections are here omitted: § 1357. Termination of Lease by a Taking of the Property by Eminent Domain Proceedings; § 1358. Contracts for Temporary Use and Occupation of Buildings;

§ 1359. School Teaching Contracts —Effect of Closing the School Because of Epidemic; § 1360. Frustration by the Inflationary Depreciation of Money; § 1361. Other Specific Illustrations of Frustration of Purpose.

# CHAPTER 78

## IMPOSSIBILITY OF PERFORMANCE OF A CONDITION—RESTITUTION IN CASES OF IMPOSSIBILITY

### § 1362. Impossibility of Performance of a Condition Precedent to the Defendant's Duty—Notices, Certificates, Appraisals

We have already considered the effect of impossibility of performance of a promise as a discharge of the duty of performing it. We have considered also the effect of frustration of the purpose of a promisor upon his duty to perform his promise, when such frustration is caused by supervening impossibility of attainment of the purpose. We are now to consider a different problem: What is the effect of supervening impossibility of performance of a condition precedent to the duty of a promisor? Here also a promisor is asserting that he is excused from performing his promise, but not because of any difficulty in performing it.

Instead, the situation is as follows: A contractor who is being sued defends on the ground that a condition precedent to his duty has not been performed. The plaintiff admits the fact; but he asserts that performance of the condition has been excused because supervening events have made it impossible to perform. The question is whether such impossibility eliminates the condition precedent, making the defendant's duty unconditional. It might be supposed that, when a promise is subject to a condition precedent, it can not be regarded as broken, and therefore can not be the basis of an action for breach, unless the condition has happened; but such is not always the case. That which was at first a condition of a promisor's duty may cease to be so. The legal relations of the parties to a contract are created by the law for purposes of justice. They are not dependent solely upon the will of the parties, or upon the express terms of their agreement. If subsequent events occur, not foreseen and provided for by the parties, the court will take them into account, and vary the legal relations of the parties as justice now requires.

Conditions precedent to duty are of various kinds. They may be such that their non-performance will do no substantial harm to the defendant; while at the same time, to let the defendant go scot free because of the non-performance of the relatively unimportant express condition will be gravely unjust to the plaintiff who has already performed his part of an agreed exchange. To allow the defendant to keep what he has received, and to pay nothing in return, causes what is often described as a forfeiture. Even though the parties have expressly agreed that a forfeiture shall take place, or that a penalty shall be paid, courts of equity have nullified the provision as abhorrent to justice. In the present instance, the parties have agreed that the defendant's duty shall be conditional upon a specified fact or event, not foreseeing, however, that other subsequent events would make it impossible. Here, it can not be said that they have agreed upon a forfeiture under the circumstances that now exist.[1]

The kind of condition precedent that is most often eliminated when subsequent events make it impossible of performance is the giving of a notice. Accident insurance policies often require that notice shall be given within a specified number of days after the accident or disability, as a condition precedent to the duty of the insurer. The death, insanity, or illness of the insured may make it impossible for him to cause such notice to be given; and, while some other person could give notice in his place, there may be no other person who knows of the existence of the policy or of its terms or who can reasonably be expected to think of giving any

1. In Bennett v. New York Life Ins. Co., 121 P.2d 551, 63 Idaho 427, 142 A.L.R. 841 (1942), the court denied that there was any "forfeiture," on the ground that the plaintiff had "lost" nothing to which he previously had a right. It is true that his right to the benefits promised was subject to a condition precedent that had never been performed, and that an immediately enforceable right was not being lost. But "forfeiture" should not be so narrowly limited as this. By reason of his insanity (as alleged), the insured lost the opportunity of turning his existing conditional contract right into an immediately enforceable one by giving a specified notice. Further, as a result of this, he made many payments for which no agreed equivalent was received. The court's decision may perhaps be justified by the long delay and the insured's death, making it difficult for the insurer to disprove the alleged total disability or insanity.

notice to the insurer. In cases like this, it has very generally been held that the performance of the condition—the giving of the notice within the specified number of days—is excused. The insurer must pay even though no notice was given.[2] Without doubt the court should take into consideration the length of the delay, the death of the insured, and the increased difficulty of the insurer's disproving the alleged accident or disability. It may be thought that these factors should be held to affect only the weight and credibility of the testimony; it is certain that the attention of the trial court should be specifically directed thereto. In this way justice will be better served than it is by a flat rule that an express condition precedent can not be eliminated by facts making its fulfilment impossible.

Often the impossibility of giving notice is caused by the very accident or disability insured against; but the elimination of the condition precedent does not depend upon this factor. The insured has paid his premiums and the insurer has them. The giving of the notice was no part of the compensatory equivalent for which the insurer bargained. It is true that the notice as specified is a matter of some importance, otherwise the policy would not have required it as a condition precedent. Prompt notice enables the insurer to protect himself against fraudulent claims. But such notice is not absolutely essential to that end, and its absence does not justify the discharge of the insurer from his promissory duty.

The rule that is applied as above, in cases where the condition that has become impossible is the giving of a notice, is equally applicable to other conditions precedent that do not constitute a substantial part of the compensatory equivalent for the defendant's promised performance. Thus, where a horse was sold for $800, the buyer promising to pay $100 additional if a test by M within 90 days showed that the horse could trot as fast as another specified horse, and the test was made impossible by the sickness of the horses, it was held that the buyer must pay the $100, if

2.   **U.S.**—Mutual Life Ins. Co. v. Johnson, 55 S.Ct. 154, 293 U.S. 335, 79 L.Ed. 398 (1934), following Virginia law; Magill v. Travelers Ins. Co., 133 F.2d 709 (C.C.A.8th, 1943); John Hancock Mut. Life Ins. Co. v. De Costa, 88 F.2d 479 (C.C.A.3d, 1937); Metropolitan Cas. Ins. Co. of New York v. Johnston, 247 F. 65, 7 A.L.R. 175 (C.C.A.3d, 1917).

**Mich.**—Reed v. Royal Prot. Ass'n, 117 N.W. 600, 154 Mich. 161 (1908).

**Wis.**—Schlintz v. Equitable Life Assur. Soc., 276 N.W. 336, 226 Wis. 255 (1937), follows Restatement, Contracts, § 301; Comstock v. Fraternal Acc. Ass'n, 93 N.W. 22, 116 Wis. 382 (1903).

In some states, the contrary rule is followed, holding that the condition of notice is not eliminated:

**N.Y.**—Hanna v. Commercial Trav. Mut. Acc. Ass'n, 197 N.Y.S. 395, 204 App.Div. 258 (1922), affirmed 142 N.E. 288, 236 N.Y. 571 (1923); Whiteside v. North Amer. Acc. Ins. Co., 93 N.E. 948, 200 N.Y. 320 (1911).

**Ohio**—W. & S. Life Ins. Co. v. Smith, 180 N.E. 749, 41 Ohio App. 197 (1932).

other evidence sufficiently established the speed of the horse.[3] Here the factor of major importance was the speed of the horse, not the manner of proving it. The test by M within 90 days was merely a mode of proof. Without doubt, when events eliminate that test by making it impossible, the court should make sure that the fact it was meant to establish has been proved by other means with an equal degree of certainty.

In innumerable building contracts, the certificate of a specified architect is in express terms made a condition precedent to the duty of the owner to pay instalments of the price. The performance of this condition by the architect may become impossible by reason of his death, insanity, or other disability. This does not prevent the builder from being entitled to the promised payment. The certificate is no part of the compensatory equivalent of the owner's money; that is the erection of the building according to plans and specifications. The certificate of the specified architect is merely evidential of the performance of the essential condition precedent to the duty to pay—the erection of the building or a part thereof. It is true that this particular mode of proof was a matter of great importance to the owner, but not as an end in itself. Justice requires rather that he should dispense with this mode of proof than that the builder should be deprived of the agreed payment for his work done. The court should make sure that the substituted proof is equally convincing to reasonable and competent men. When so assured, the builder has a right to the agreed price and is not limited to an action for quantum meruit.

In many cases property has been transferred or services rendered in return for a promise to pay the agreed compensation upon the occurrence of a specified event. If this event becomes impossible of occurrence and if reasonable interpretation shows that the contract was not aleatory, the event is eliminated as a condition of the duty of payment and the performance must be rendered within a reasonable time. Services rendered or repairs made on a ship, to be paid for on the return of the ship from a voyage or when the ship is sold, must be paid for at the agreed price if the ship is lost at sea.[8] One who promises to pay for land or other property or for services, as soon as a sale is made or a loan obtained, must pay the agreed amount if the sale becomes impossible by reason of destruction or otherwise, or if the loan can not be obtained.[9] A contractor may promise to pay a subcontractor as soon as payment is made by a third party on the principal contract,[10] or an owner may promise to pay a commission to a broker as soon as the owner receives payment from the purchaser;[11] the promise must generally be performed within a reasonable

3.    Mich.—Deyo v. Hammond, 60 N. W. 455, 102 Mich. 122 (1894).

9.    U.S.—Nunez v. Dautel, 86 U.S. (19 Wall.) 560, 22 L.Ed. 161 (1873).

time if the third party can not or will not pay.  It is otherwise if the contract is clearly worded to express an intention  that the promisee is to be paid out of the money that may be received from the third party and not otherwise;  in such case the promisee assumes the risk and the contract is aleatory.

In cases of this kind it is often said that one who promises to pay when a sale is made or a loan is obtained also impliedly promises that the sale or loan will be made within a reasonable time.[12] No such "implication" is necessary in order to hold that the condition has been eliminated;  and no such "implied" promise would be held to exist for the purpose of awarding additional damages for its breach.  The contract is not aleatory if the parties contemplate the specified event as one that is certain to occur in the near future and use it merely as a means of determining a convenient time for payment by the promisor.  The moderate delay involved would be regarded by the parties as not substantially material and would not affect the price to be paid—the agreed equivalency of the performances of the two parties.  The question is chiefly one of interpretation of the terms of agreement in the light of all the circumstances.  If the words used do not themselves answer it, a factor of great weight is the relation of the price promised to the prevailing market value.  If the price to be paid is greatly in excess of that value, it is not unfair to hold that the promisee bears the risk of getting nothing in case the event does not occur.

The occurrence of the event is eliminated as a condition if it is prevented by the fault of the promisor—either as the breach of an actually implied promise, by intentional action to avoid having to pay, or by wrongful negligence.  This is true even if the contract is aleatory;  the promisor must not wrongfully increase the risk carried by the promisee.

## § 1363.  Performance of the Agreed Exchange as a Condition— Effect of Its Impossibility

There is no doubt that the great majority of conditions precedent to the duty of a contractor to render his promised performance are very different in character and importance from those just discussed.  This becomes obvious when we contemplate that vast array of constructive conditions precedent, held to be such, not because so described in the express words of agreement, but because the prevailing notions of justice so require.  Of course, the parties themselves may be quite conscious of these requirements of justice and may use express words to turn such a condition precedent into an express condition.  It is the character of the performance and the part that it plays in the bargaining transaction that is of distinguishing importance, not the form of description as "express" or "constructive."

Where the condition of the promisor's duty is a performance by the promisee that constitutes the agreed equivalent for which the promise was given, the promisor can not justly be held bound to perform when the performance constituting the condition has become impossible. The reason for this is that a promisor ought not to be compelled to give something for nothing, when he did not promise to give something for nothing. He agreed upon an exchange of performances, an exchange that can not now take place. This result should be reached, even though the other party whose performance has become impossible is not guilty of a breach of contract, either for the reason that he made no promise to render the performance or because the impossibility excuses him from his duty to render it. Even though he is not in default, he should not demand something for nothing.[13]

If the contract that is proposed by an offeror is strictly unilateral in character—that is, if he offers his promise to pay for a specified return performance that is to be rendered without first making any promise to render it—it is obvious that the rendition of the requested return performance is a condition precedent to the legal duty of the promisor. Indeed, we say that until the return performance is performed or tendered no contract has yet been made. Such a condition of the promisor's duty is not eliminated by the fact that some unexpected event has made it impossible. If it has become impossible, the making of the contract has become impossible. Of course, the offeree has committed no breach of duty in failing to render the requested performance. He made no promise to render it; and therefore his failure to perform is no breach even though there is no impossibility or difficulty, and his refusal to perform is wilful.

If the offer that was made requested a return promise, the contract, when made, is bilateral. Each party has promised to render some performance; and, except in the case of an aleatory contract, these performances are agreed equivalents and the two promises are dependent. As has already been discussed, if one of these promises becomes impossible of performance, the party who made it may be excused from legal duty. His failure to perform is not a breach of contract. But the fact that the law excuses him from performance does not justify him in demanding performance by the other party. The other party is also discharged from

13.    Where the performance of a carrier's promise to render free service is made impossible by the order of a Public Utilities Commission, the other party's duty to permit free use of his land in exchange for such free service is likewise discharged. The carrier is not guilty of a breach; its duty is discharged by impossibility. The other party is discharged, not by impossibility, but by failure of consideration. Law v. Railroad Commission of Cal., 195 P. 423, 184 Cal. 737, 14 A.L.R. 249 (1921).

See many other cases, cited throughout the topic of Impossibility.

duty, not by impossibility but by failure of consideration. Even if not made so in express terms, that party's duty is constructively conditional, either upon the actual rendition of the agreed equivalent or upon readiness and willingness to render it. Except in aleatory contracts, a promisor does not intend to assume the risk of giving his performance for nothing, or for substantially less than the price agreed upon; and our system of justice does not require him to bear such a risk.

Suppose a bilateral contract for the painting of a house; the painting is a condition of the owner's duty to pay. If the house burns before painting, the performance of this condition is impossible; but it is not eliminated by the impossibility and the owner is discharged from duty to pay the agreed price.[14] Suppose a bilateral contract for the rendition of personal services for a salary. Death or disabling illness discharges the employee's duty to perform the services; but it does not eliminate the condition of the owner's duty to pay. No service, no pay.[15] One who has been prevented from rendering agreed service by the "restraint of princes" or by public authority can maintain no action for his employer's refusal to pay for unrendered service.[16] If the delivery of a ship by the owner to a charterer is prevented by a government requisition, the owner's duty is discharged; the charterer's duty to pay the hire is also discharged by failure of the consideration.[17]

## § 1364. Impossibility of Payment of Premiums on an Insurance Contract

There are conditions precedent that play a major role in a contractual transaction, even though they do not constitute the agreed equivalent for which the promisor assented to the contract, or any substantial part of such equivalent. In an aleatory contract there is no agreed exchange of equivalent performances; and yet it may be grave injustice to eliminate a condition on the ground of impossibility. In a life insurance policy, the duty of the insurer is generally made expressly conditional on the pay-

---

14. For a part performance before the destruction there is a right to reasonable compensation. Butterfield v. Byron, 27 N.E. 667, 153 Mass. 517 (1891); Carroll v. Bowersock, 164 P. 143, 100 Kan. 270 (1917).

See §§ 1367–1372, Restitution in cases involving impossibility.

One who contracts to repair a crevasse in a levee and fails because a great flood opens dozens of other crevasses, compelling total abandonment of the levee, can maintain no action for lost profits. Drown v. White River Levee Dist., 27 S.W.2d 793, 181 Ark. 629 (1930).

15. A singer who is prevented by disabling illness from singing, so that substantial performance is impossible, can maintain no action on the contract against the employer. Poussard v. Spiers & Pond, 1 Q.B. D. 410 (1876).

ment of the annual premiums. This is true even though the annual premium is far less than the sum promised by the insurer. Suppose that the payment of one or more of these premiums has been made impossible by the outbreak of war, putting insurer and insured on different sides of the line of hostilities. It has been held that such impossibility does not eliminate the condition; and the insurer does not have to pay the amount promised in the policy.[21] This seems to be just, even though the premiums unpaid are much less than the face of the policy; for the premiums are a part of the fund out of which must come the payments promised by the insurer. There are decisions to the contrary, holding that the express condition is nullified by war and that tender of the overdue premiums with interest is sufficient to reinstate the policy.[22] In any case, the insured has a right to the "equitable value" of the policy, measured by the premiums actually paid less the cost of carrying the risk prior to default.[23]

## § 1367.  Restitution as a Remedy in Cases of Impossibility

In a chapter dealing with the various types and degrees of so-called "impossibility," it seems desirable to include some discussion of the restitutionary remedy. As has been seen previously, the term "impossibility" is used in a variety of senses; and a careful analysis is always required before attempting to state the juristic result in any case. The remedy by way of restitution may be sought, First, against a defendant who has not performed his promise and who sets up some kind of impossibility as a defense; or, Secondly, by a plaintiff who has partly but not fully performed and who asserts some kind of impossibility as an excuse for his failure. In each of these two classes of cases the alleged impossibility may or may not be a good defense or a good excuse. We have, therefore, four general types of cases in which the availability of restitution as a remedy must be considered: (1) cases in which the defendant is guilty of breach of contract, the existing type of impossibility being such as not to operate as a discharge and not to be a good defense; (2) cases in which the asserted impossibility does operate as a discharge, so that the defendant is not guilty of a breach and is not under a liability in damages; (3) cases in which the plaintiff has failed, by reason of some type of impossibility, to perform a condition precedent to the defendant's promissory duty, but the impossibility is not legally operative as an excuse; and (4) cases in which the plaintiff's non-performance is legally justified by the existing impossibility of completing the performance.

---

23.  Omitted here are § 1365. Impossibility of Performance on Time, and § 1366. Impossibility of Bringing Suit Within a Time Limit—Inevitability of a Condition Subsequent.

In none of these classes of cases is the plaintiff entitled to a restitutionary remedy unless he has himself rendered a performance for which he has not received a just compensation and that performance has so far enriched the defendant that failure to make restitution would be unjust.

In the first of these four classes, we assume that the defendant is in default of duty and a contract breaker. Although the defendant's performance may have become impossible, he is not discharged. Against such a defendant, the plaintiff is entitled to the usual remedies. He will not be given a decree for specific performance, if such a decree would be impossible of enforcement; but he has a right to compensatory damages measured in accordance with the rules of law applicable to this remedy. The plaintiff's restitutionary remedy is an alternative remedy, one that has been dealt with elsewhere herein. These are merely ordinary cases in which an injured party seeks the usual remedies against a defendant who is guilty of a breach of contract.

## § 1368.   Restitution against a Defendant Whose Duty has been Discharged by Impossibility

Even though such a kind and degree of impossibility exists as to discharge a defendant from further legal duty, the law does not permit him to retain the benefits of a performance rendered by the plaintiff without making just compensation therefor. A defendant who has promised to deliver specific goods is discharged by their destruction without fault; yet if he has received part or all of the price from the buyer he must make full restitution thereof.[32] A defendant who has contracted to render personal services is discharged by death, incapacitating illness, or insanity; but restitution must be made of all money paid to him in advance for which the agreed service has not been rendered.[33] One who has contracted to manufacture and deliver goods and is discharged from his duty by the fact that the outbreak of war makes performance illegal, must pay back such part of the agreed price as was paid to him in advance.[34] The same is true wherever performance has been prevented by legislation or by a governmental order making performance illegal.[35]

If the defendant's promised performance is such that it is rendered impossible by the destruction of some specific building or of some other essential matter, the defendant may be discharged when such destruction occurs; but he must make restitution of

---

34.   Fibrosa Spolka Akcyjna v. Fairbairn L.C.B. Ltd., [1943] A.C. 32, [1942] 2 All Eng. 122; 167 L. T. 101, 111 L.J.K.B. 433, overruling cases that had for forty years supposedly settled the English law otherwise; Comptoir D'Achat v. Luis de Ridder [1949] 1 All Eng. 269 (H.L.); Cantiare San Rocco v. Clyde Shipping & Eng. Co., [1924] A.C. 226 (H.L.), applying Scots law.

compensation that has been paid to him in advance.[36]  The same result is reached when the defendant's promised performance has been made impossible by supervening change in the law or by the valid order of public officers.[37]

### § 1369.  Restitution in Favor of a Plaintiff in Default without Lawful Excuse

One who has contracted to erect a building, or to construct some other physical object, is not discharged from his duty by the fact that fire or flood destroys his partly completed work.  All the risks during performance are his, up to the time of completion and delivery of the result.  Even though at the time of destruction the work was almost finished, the contractor is not discharged.  This being so, there is no duty on the other party, either contractual or quasi contractual, to pay anything for the part performance that has been destroyed.[40]  The contractor can maintain no action for the agreed price by showing that he had rendered substantial performance before the destruction.[41]  Unfortunately for him, he has rendered no performance at all.  For the same reasons, he has no right to quantum meruit or to any restitutionary remedy.  This is true, even though the partly performed construction was attached to the land of the other party, and therefore had become a part of his property before destruction.  Here, the ordinary rule *res perit domino* does not help the contractor.[42]  Instead, the contractor is bound to reconstruct the destroyed work, and is bound to pay full compensatory damages if he refuses, with no deduction for the part performance now destroyed.[43]  Such is the rule unless there is some expression in the contract indicating an intention that the owner shall bear the risk of destruction in the course of performance.[44]

### § 1370.  Restitution in Favor of One Whose Failure of Performance is Excused by Impossibility

The rule of the foregoing section is not applicable as against a contractor whose duty of completing performance has been dis-

37.   **Cal.**—McGillycuddy v. Los Verjels Land and Water Co., 2 P.2d 19, 213 Cal. 145 (1931); Ogren v. Inner Harbor Land Co., 256 P. 607, 83 Cal.App. 197 (1927).

**N.Y.**—Jones v. Judd, 4 N.Y. 412 (1850); Tenner v. Retlaw Development Corp., 295 N.Y.S. 31, 163 Misc. 248 (1936); Panto v. Kentucky Distilleries & Warehouse Co., 214 N.Y.S. 19, 215 App.Div. 511 (1926).

Where a railroad company has contracted to pay for land by the giving of annual passes, and the giving of such passes is later forbidden by statute, the company must pay the reasonable value of the land, less the value of transportation actually received by the plaintiff.

**Ky.**—Louisville & N. R. Co. v. Crowe, 160 S.W. 759, 156 Ky. 27 (1913).

40.   **Conn.**—School District   v. Dauchy, 25 Conn. 530 (1857).

charged by supervening events causing impossibility. In these cases the risk of destruction is on the other party. This being so, the contractor may have either a right to the agreed contract price with some deduction, or a right to the reasonable value of the work actually done. For the former, he must show that his part performance so nearly approached completion as to constitute what is known as "substantial performance," actually received and owned by the other party. The contractor then has a right to the contract price, subtracting no more than the cost of completion that is saved. He would have had this remedy, even if his failure to complete the construction had been a breach of contract.

If, at the time that he is discharged by impossibility, he has not yet rendered "substantial performance" as that term is commonly used, but he has rendered a part performance of value, he has a right to compensation measured by the reasonable value thereof. For personal service rendered, completion being prevented by death of one party, the servant or his personal representative has a right to quantum meruit, the value of the service at market rates.[45] If the part performance includes goods and materials, as well as labor, the plaintiff has a right to the reasonable value of the goods and materials, in so far as they have become the property of the defendant. One who has contracted to make repairs and additions to an existing building, and is discharged by the destruction of the building after part performance, has a right to compensation for the repairs and additions made before the destruction.[46] The amount of this compensation is measured by the net addition to the value of the building just prior to its destruction. It is true that the repairs and additions have been destroyed, along with the original structure; but, like it, they had become the property of the owner of the building, by incorporation with it. The owner has lost them by destruction; but they were his for all purposes, including insurance, and the loss is his. Res perit domino.

For goods and materials never incorporated with the defendant's building and that have in no way ever enriched him by becoming his property, the contractor has no right to compensation.[47] This is true, even though they were specially adapted for this contract only. He is still the owner; and the risk of loss is his. They have not benefited the defendant.

46.    **Cal.**—Keeling v. Schastey & Vollmer, 124 P. 445, 18 Cal.App. 764 (1912).

Kan.—Carroll v. Bowersock, 164 P. 143, 100 Kan. 270 (1917), concrete floor.

Mass.—Young v. Chicopee, 72 N.E. 63, 186 Mass. 518 (1904); Butterfield v. Byron, 27 N.E. 667, 153 Mass. 517 (1891); Cleary v. Sohier, 120 Mass. 210 (1876).

## § 1371. Compensation for Services Rendered when Completion has become Impossible without Fault

Where a contract duty to render personal services has been discharged by the death or illness of one of the parties, the one rendering the service is entitled to payment of the reasonable value of the service that has actually been received.[60]  Here it is the service that is to be valued, and not the product or results of that service.  The recovery is often expressed in terms of "quantum meruit";  and generally this is measured by the market value of such service, not exceeding the contract rate if one was agreed upon by the parties.

## § 1372. Restitution Based upon Theory of "Unjust Enrichment"

The granting to the contractor of a right to reasonable compensation has been explained on the basis of the "unjust enrichment" theory.  The owner has been "enriched" by the part performance.  To some this explanation has not been convincing.  How can the owner be regarded as having been "enriched" by a part performance that was never completed and that was destroyed before it could be of any use?  It may well be that there have been other motivating reasons behind the decisions.  But this particular reason can be defended;  and it seems to bring these cases within the coverage of a rule that satisfies our notions of justice in many different kinds of cases.

If the contractor has partly performed his repairs and additions to an existing building or other structure belonging to the defendant, the latter's wealth increases just as fast as the work proceeds.  The goods, materials, and labor of the contractor are incorporated into the structure and become the defendant's property as fast as this incorporation occurs.  Step by step, the additions have increased the market value of that property, for purposes of sale, insurance, and taxation.[65]  It is true that this value has been destroyed along with that of the original structure.  With respect to both, res perit domino; there is no reason for distinguishing between the parts of the entire structure on the basis of date of origin or the length of defendant's ownership.

---

60.    **Ala.**—Dryer v. Lewis, 57 Ala. 551 (1877), death of servant.
**Me.**—Lakeman v. Pollard, 43 Me. 463 (1857), cholera epidemic prevented completion.
**Mass.**—Hathaway v. Cronin, 17 N.E. 2d 312, 301 Mass. 419 (1938), personal care prevented by illness.
**N.H.**—Stanley v. Kimball, 118 A. 636, 80 N.H. 431 (1922), proportionate part of agreed compensation of housekeeper.

# PART VIII

---

## ILLEGAL BARGAINS

### CHAPTER 79

#### INTRODUCTORY—CAUSES AND VARIETIES OF ILLEGALITY—PUBLIC POLICY

---

### § 1373. Varieties and Degrees of Illegality, with Variation in Legal Effect

At first thought it is sometimes supposed that an illegal bargain is necessarily void of legal effect, and that an "illegal contract" is self-contradictory. How can the illegal be also legal? The matter is not so simple. In the regulation of human conduct we know that it is not sufficient merely to classify acts as either criminal or not criminal. Criminal acts vary greatly in kind and quality. They are classified accordingly and the penalties and other legal effects are made to vary with the degree and the character of the act. Felony is worse than misdemeanor. Even in the case of homicide there are several degrees. And penalties range from death to a mild reprimand. Imprisonment may be long or short, harsh or mild; fines may be large or small. So it is with illegal bargains; their legal effect varies with the character of the factors that cause them to be called illegal.

A bargain may be illegal because the performance that is bargained for is illegal; and the performance may be illegal because governmental authority has declared it to be a "crime", in any one of the multiplicity of degrees, or because in like manner it has been declared to be a "tort". This is true whether the performance bargained for is one that is merely promised, to be rendered in the future, or is one that is rendered as the executed consideration for a return promise. On the other hand, a bargain may be illegal even though no illegal performance is either promised or executed as the consideration for a promise; it may be illegal because the making of such a bargain is itself forbidden and subjected to penalty. Thus, a bet on an election is an illegal bargain, even though the transfer of a sum of money for nothing in exchange from one to the other would be in no sense illegal. Again, there may be nothing illegal in a merchant's selling his goods at the same price as that of his competitor; but if the two competitors mutually agree to sell at the same price they may be guilty of a crime by statute.[1]

A bargain is an agreement between two parties for an exchange of performances, either executed or promised. Therefore, it takes two to make a bargain; and we must bear in mind that the illegality may be wholly restricted to one of these performances. Also, one of the two parties may be regarded by the law as entirely innocent, as where a man makes a bigamous agreement to marry a girl who knows nothing of his already being married; or one of the parties may be regarded as of lesser fault—not *in pari delicto,* and hence entitled to some legal remedy. Our legal system provides a good variety of legal remedies and they are applied by the courts with a high degree of flexibility.

Although it is convenient to entitle this chapter "Illegal Bargains", because it is usually in a bargaining transaction that illegality appears, we must remember that there are contracts that are not bargains at all and that a unilateral promise without any consideration may be illegal. A promise under seal to render a performance that is a crime or a tort is an illegal promise, without regard to whether any consideration is given for it or any action or forbearance is induced by it.

## § 1374.   What Makes a Bargain "Illegal"?

As will appear in the subsequent sections, "illegality" is not a simple concept. It has many forms and a great variety of effects. There is a zone within which even a well-meaning citizen can not determine whether a proposed bargain is or is not "illegal." The careful and the timorous may avoid worries and possible penalties by following such advice as "When the matter is doubtful, don't"; but such a practice may unnecessarily limit his own enterprise and the general prosperity as well. Moreover, there are many cases in which one may have no doubt whatever

---

1.   Other illustrations: A bargain consisting of a promise never to marry in return for a conveyance of property or for a promise of such conveyance is an "illegal" bargain, even though the forbearance to marry and the conveyance have no taint of illegality.
There are many statutes prohibiting the doing of business on Sunday, making illegal a bargain made on Sunday for the rendition of perfectly lawful performances on Monday.
An engagement to marry as soon as one party, being already married, shall have obtained a divorce is contrary to public policy and illegal, although the performance promised would be lawful.

and yet find himself in the toils of the law—that is, his supposedly innocent bargain turns out to be "illegal" in some one or more of its various senses.

It must not be supposed, however, that "legality" is always doubtful and that one must shiver with foreboding when assenting to any bargain. No question of "illegality" is ever raised as to the vast body of our business transactions. In the great majority of transactions the risk of "illegality" is nil, or at least negligible. And along the borders of legality there are plenty of warning signs that give reasonable protection to a man of probity and intelligence. The exact border line is, indeed, movable and there is a zone of uncertainty; but that zone is soon merged in the field where "illegality" becomes plain and clear, although its quality and degree and its effect on judicial remedies may for some distance still remain doubtful.

To what sources is the man of labor or business, or his legal adviser, to go in order to determine in which field a proposed bargain lies? What are the warning signs that indicate either certain or doubtful illegality, its degree and its penalty?

The first and most obvious source is legislation, by statute or constitution. That great difficulty may be encountered in interpreting and applying such legislation is well enough known, as witness such a phrase as "interstate commerce" and such a statute as the Sherman Anti-trust Act. But all of us know that legislation is a source of illegality that must be studied and understood as well as we can before entering into our bargaining transactions. The warning signs are ample, even though in their details they may be somewhat obscure or defaced.

In listing and discussing the bargains that are illegal because so declared by statute, it is impossible to be full and complete in any treatise on contract law. We need only point to the long shelves of huge statute books and to the thousands of administrative rules and regulations based upon the enactments that they record. This treatise can be no more than a warning sign pointing to the more numerous and detailed statutes themselves, classifying the bargains to which they are most commonly applicable, and indicating their juristic effects on remedies and legal relations.

Of course new statutes must be expected on almost every legislative day, sometimes enlarging the fields of the illegal and the doubtful. But there is another source of illegality to which we must resort, one that as compared with statute is perhaps greater in extent, is much more ancient in time, and is at times more doubtful in content. Bargains may be illegal because they are so declared by the Common Law, are against Public Policy, or are so treated in the prevailing mores of the community (contra bonos mores).

Bargains may be made illegal by the Common Law. But what is Common Law, and how may we know it? . As Holmes once said, it is not a "brooding omnipresence in the sky"; nor is it a bookful of definite and unchanging rules. With the vast number of judicial decisions now behind us, recorded in the books, it is to the records of those decisions, generally including a statement of the facts and issues and an opinion by the court in support of its decision, that we must go in order to know the Common Law. After one or more decisions that a transaction is illegal, we have a basis for predicting similar decisions in the future and a guide for our own future action. Careful interpretation and analysis of those decisions enable judges and lawyers and law writers to construct tentative generalizations that may be used as guides to future judicial and administrative action. These generalizations make up the Common Law. They constitute a vast and complicated source for determining the "legality" of a bargain.

The fact that these generalizations based on the cases can never be more than tentative working rules need not seriously disturb either the practicing lawyer or his bargaining client. All of our footsteps through life are guided by nothing better than tentative working rules. Following such a guide does, indeed, involve risks; but in the matter of "illegality" the risk is seldom greater than in other matters, and it is a risk to which life has accustomed us. Like it or not, it is as Justice Cardozo has told us "inevitable." [2] Here, as in the case of the statutory law, the risk of illegality is negligible in the vast majority of bargaining transactions. And in all cases it is a risk that men of probity and intelligence can greatly reduce by an unselfish use of conscience and common sense and, in the more difficult cases, by seeking counsel and advice.

There is still another source of "illegality," besides statute and judicial decision. That source is the great common background of life from which come both legislation and common law. It is the prevailing practices of the community of people and their notions as to what makes for the general welfare. Bargains are judged by the folkways and mores of the time. A bargain may be illegal because it is contrary to "Public Policy," as that is understood by the judges and administrative officers.

---

**2.** "As the years have gone by, and as I have reflected more and more upon the nature of the judicial process, I have become reconciled to the uncertainty, because I have grown to see it as inevitable. I have grown to see that the process in its highest reaches is not discovery, but creation; and that the doubts and misgivings, the hopes and fears, are part of the travail of mind, the pangs of death and the pangs of birth, in which principles that have served their day expire, and new principles are born." The Nature of the Judicial Process, p. 166 (1921).

A man of business can not escape feelings of uncertainty if the legality of his bargains is to be determined in this fashion. How can these officials know "public policy," a matter as to which there is often such violent disagreement? And how can a layman determine what the officials will decide? Here again, however, we shall advise that a man of probity and intelligence can avoid excessive risk without materially nullifying his enterprise. In most of his transactions the question of legality does not in fact arise. In most of those in which it does arise, the public policies involved have already been declared by statute or judicial decision. In the number remaining, some of which may be very important indeed, he knows that he will be judged by the practices and opinions of his fellow men, practices and opinions in the midst of which he was born and by which his own mind and conscience have been formed and educated. For a man of probity and intelligence, the risk involved in making a decision and acting on it need not be very great. But "probity" varies in degree, and intelligence may be lacking. Many men have believed that they were unjustly penalized for action wholly consistent with the public welfare. It is true that lack of probity and a minimum of intelligence may be found in the officials who decide as well as in the man who bargains. That is a risk that we can not wholly avoid, even in a democratic society. The best advice that can be given in this small residuum of cases is that risk of illegality can be avoided only by leaning over backwards and deciding against one's own interest. The bold and resolute may fight and win; but they should be prepared to take the medicine if they lose.

An additional source of uncertainty is to be found in the fact that there are many different systems of law by which the legality and legal operation of contracts are governed. It is not enough to say that legality and legal operation are determined by statute, by common law, and by the prevailing convictions as to public policy. Statutes vary among States and nations; the "common law" is not exactly common, since the common law of New York is not identical with the common law of California; and convictions as to public policy that are held in one State or community or judicial bench may not be held in a different one.

Most of the transactions of our daily lives do not cross State lines; but we must bear in mind that every one of them is within a nation as well as within a State. Under our Constitution, national law is also the law of every separate State; to this extent we do indeed have common law, although it is not what is generally intended by the phrase "the common law." [3] Inconsistencies

---

3. It was this quoted phrase that Brandeis was using when in Erie R. Co. v. Tompkins, 304 U.S. 64, 58 S.Ct. 817, 82 L.Ed. 1202 (1938), he said: "There is no federal general common law." His own opinion in Hinderlider v. La Plata, etc., Ditch Co., 58 S.Ct. 803, 304 U.

between national law and the law of a particular State are not instances of the "Conflict of Laws." If such inconsistency exists, the State "law" is not even the law of the State itself.[4]

But separate States within our Union, like separate nations, may have inconsistent statutes both of which are valid; and their judges as well as their legislatures may prescribe rules and policies whose validity does not depend on uniformity or consistency. By the statute or judicial rule of one State a bargain may be "illegal" or have a particular legal operation, while in another State a precisely similar bargain is not "illegal" or has a different legal operation. This is what is meant by the term "conflict of laws." Therefore, it is often necessary, in determining the "legality" and legal operation of a contract, for the court to make a choice between two equally valid even though inconsistent systems of law. Which one of them shall be applied by the court of the litigation to the specific transaction that is before it?

If all the acts of the contracting parties and every performance for which the agreement provides are within the boundaries of the State in which the court of litigation (the "forum") sits, it is the law of that State that will be applied. But a contract may be "made" in one State (or in no State), may provide for performances in another State (or in many States); and the litigation may be in a court sitting in a still different State. It is then that the choice of law may become troublesome. Fortunately, in multitudes of such cases no conflict in the systems of law that might be chosen is made to appear; the law of the State of the forum is applied without thought or question. In other cases, where the conflict appears and choice must be made, there is no rule that is uniformly and consistently followed in making the choice. The merits of the various rules and the reasons given for applying them must be sought in works on the Conflict of Laws.

S. 92, 82 L.Ed. 1202 (1938), and subsequent cases such as Clearfield Trust Co. v. U. S., 63 S.Ct. 573, 318 U.S. 363, 87 L.Ed. 838 (1943) and D'Oench, Duhme & Co. v. Federal Deposit Ins. Corp., 62 S.Ct. 676, 315 U.S. 447, 86 L.Ed. 956 (1942), clearly assert the supremacy of national law over inconsistent State rules. Some of this national law can not properly be described as "statutory," although all of it must find its justification in the Constitution, treaties, and statutes of the United States.

4. A bargain for a performance prohibited by a federal statute is illegal in any court. Sturges v. Bush, 5 Day (Conn.) 452 (1813), to export goods in violation of federal embargo; Pond v. Smith, 4 Conn. 297 (1822), to fit out a privateer; Lokes v. Kondrotas, 134 A. 246, 104 Conn. 703 (1926), note given for price of liquors. See the sections hereafter dealing with the Sherman Anti-Trust Act.

See Shelley v. Kraemer, 68 S.Ct. 816, 334 U.S. 1, 92 L.Ed. 1161, 3 A.L.R. 2d 441 (1948), holding that the 14th Amendment forbids enforcement by any State of a restrictive covenant in a contract or deed of conveyance the purpose of which is to prevent sale to or occupancy by persons of a race other than white.

All that will be said here is as follows: The legality of a contract *performance* is determined by the law of the place where it has been or is to be rendered; and a bargain or promise requiring a performance that is illegal by that law is ordinarily called an illegal bargain or promise, in any court. It may be the *making* of the bargain or promise that is illegal and forbidden, even though no performance that is required by it is unlawful; in such a case legality is determined by the law of the place where the bargain or promise is made.[5] Even though a contract may be lawful and enforceable where it is made and to be performed, the transaction may be one that is so abhorrent according to the mores and convictions of the community in which enforcement is sought that the court of litigation (the "forum") will deny all remedy; such a contract, however valid elsewhere, is "illegal" in the State of the forum.[6] Finally, when a court determines the legality and effect of a contract in accordance with the law of a State other than the forum, it is merely declaring the law of the forum itself as to the specific transaction that is before the court.

## § 1375. Public Policy as a Basis of Illegality

In thousands of cases contracts have been declared to be illegal on the ground that they are contrary to public policy; and those two alliterative words are often used as if they had a magic quality and were self-explanatory. What is "public policy" and who knows what it requires? Does a judge know this, merely by virtue of becoming a judge? Does an administrative officer or commission? Do the men constituting a legislature or a Congress? All of these persons have more or less power to make declarations of public policy and to make those declarations effective to the advantage or the detriment of their fellow men.

The loudest and most confident assertions as to what makes for the general welfare and happiness of mankind are made by the demagogue and the ignoramus. The wise man knows that he does not know and therefore speaks softly and less often. But even the wise man has opinions and of necessity must state them, vote for them, and occasionally fight for them. The soundness of an opinion on public policy depends upon experience and is in

5. In the case of a bargain, made by offer and acceptance, the place of making is usually held to be where the act of acceptance became operative. The problem is not always a simple one. If the contract is a unilateral documentary one, the place of making is the place of "delivery". This too has some complications.

6. See:
U.S.—Oscanyan v. Winchester Repeating Arms Co., 103 U.S. 261, 26 L.Ed. 539 (1880); May v. Mulligan, 36 F.Supp. 596 (D.C.Mich.1941), affirmed 117 F.2d 259 (C.C.A.6th); Holland Furnace Co. v. Connelley, 48 F.Supp. 543 (D.C.Mo.1943).
N.Y.—Roth v. Patino, 56 N.Y.S.2d 853, 185 Misc. 235, affirmed 62 N. Y.S.2d 820, 270 App.Div. 927 (1945).

proportion to the knowledge of the past and the intellectual power of the one who holds it. Wisdom consists in having the greatest knowledge and the best brains, with the result that the wise man's judgment is more often sustained by new experience and verified by his successors.

When the validity of a contract is in issue before a court, the judge is obliged to make decision whatever the degree of his ignorance or wisdom. Before decision there should be some debate and much evidence; afterwards the decision is subject to criticism, by litigant and lawyer, by juryman and jurist, by the learner and the scholar. It is thus that the mores, the considered notions as to what makes for human welfare and survival are formed, to be constantly verified or altered in new cases, forever hammered on the anvil of life experience.[7]

The court can not postpone decision until all possible evidence is in. Sometimes the judge may properly take "judicial notice" of what is common knowledge and generally held opinion.[8] But it is never wise to jump to a conclusion or to disregard experience; and it is never necessary to decide an issue as to public policy without expert briefing of former decisions and without listening to the testimony of those whose interests are at stake and of disinterested and experienced observers.[9]

7.　Courts are aware that opinions as to public policy differ in the several States. As to this the New York court said: "We are not so provincial as to say that every solution of a problem is wrong because we deal with it otherwise at home. . . . The courts are not free to refuse to enforce a foreign right at the pleasure of the judges, to suit the individual notion of expediency or fairness. They do not close their doors, unless help would violate some fundamental principle of justice, some prevalent conception of good morals, some deep-rooted tradition of the common weal." Loucks v. Standard Oil Co., 120 N.E. 198, 224 N.Y. 99 (1918), opinion by Cardozo. It is not inconsistent with this to say that the determination of whether a principle is "fundamental", a conception is "prevalent", and a tradition "deep-rooted" depends chiefly on the court's own depth of emotion and certainty of conviction.

8.　In Rodriguez v. Speyer Bros., 119 L.T. 409 (1918), Lord Haldane said: "I think there are many things of which the judges are bound to take judicial notice which lie outside the law properly so called, and among those things are what is called public policy and the changes which take place in it. The law itself may become modified by this obligation of the judges."

9.　" 'Public policy', said Burrough, J. (I believe quoting Hobart, C. J.), 'is an unruly horse and dangerous to ride.' I quote also another distinguished judge (more modern), Cave, J., 'Certain kinds of contracts have been held void at common law on the ground of public policy; a branch of the law, however, which certainly should not be extended, as judges are more to be trusted as interpreters of the law than as expounders of what is called public policy.' I think the present case is an illustration of

It must ever be borne in mind that times change, and that with them public policy must likewise change. A decision or a rule that is believed to be in accord with the general welfare today may not accord with it tomorrow. The mores of a people, those generally prevailing practices and opinions as to what promotes welfare and survival, also slowly change with time and circumstance. Especially is this true in times of stress and discomfort, like those of the two World Wars and the intervening severe business depression. Doubts arise as to the soundness of old practices and opinions. Experiment is demanded by the miserable and the discontented, always to the grief and dislike of those who are neither; and "wise" men arise to tell the multitude that old truth has become falsehood and to point out the shining new road to fortune.

Courts and administrative officers, as well as legislators, can not fail to be affected by these changes in times and opinions. Indeed, they can not properly perform their functions if they refuse to be affected by them.[10] Suffer they must from the charge

the wisdom of these remarks. I venture to make another. No evidence is given in these public policy cases. The tribunal is to say, as matter of law, that the thing is against public policy and void. How can the judge do that without any evidence as to its effect and consequences?" Bramwell, L. J., in Mogul S. S. Co. v. McGregor, [1892] A.C. 25.

There is every reason why judges should require "evidence" on the subject before making a decision. It may also be remarked that, however unruly the horse may be, it is not possible for the courts to refuse to ride. Justice (whether described as "natural" or artificial), public policy, general welfare, the settled convictions of mankind, community ideals, are all modes of describing substantially the same thing. It is this that the courts are established to administer, and upon which in the last analysis their judgments are based.

In Atty. Gen. of Australia v. Adelaide S. S. Co., [1913] A.C. 781 (P.C.), Lord Parker said: "the question whether a restraint of trade is reasonable either in the interest of the parties or in the interest of the public is a question for the Court, to be determined after construing the contract and considering the circumstances existing when it was made. It is really a question of public policy and not a question of fact upon which evidence of the actual or probable consequences, if the contract be carried into effect, is admissible." This involves an assumption of wisdom that can not properly be made by judges in the United States. "Public policy" is always a question of fact on which evidence of consequences is required.

10. In Wilson v. Carnley, [1908] 1 K.B. 729, 738, Vaughan Williams, L. J., partly quoting Lord Bowen, said: "The determination of what is contrary to the so-called 'policy of the law' necessarily varies from time to time. Many transactions are upheld now by our own courts which a former generation would have avoided as contrary to the supposed policy of the law. The rule remains, but its application varies with the principles which for the time being guide public opinion. I cannot myself in the least acquiesce in the suggestion that, as habits change and time goes on, we may not find new in-

of being mossbacks and reactionaries or demagogues and dreamers, their suffering being considerably mitigated when the charge is true. Supreme Courts are said to follow the election returns; but also their decisions are affected by the changes in climates of opinion on matters that have never been submitted to an election.

The art of generalization on the basis of past experience, judicial and otherwise, is always a difficult one; and old doctrine continually requires amendment and "restatement." It is doubly difficult when climates of opinion on political and economic welfare are in flux. The judge then deserves our sympathy who must make a decision on the basis of "public policy"; and he must expect our criticism after he makes it. *Fiat justitia ruat coelum* (let justice reign though the heavens fall) said the ancient jurists; but when the heavens are falling, justice must take off the bandage from her eyes—not to take a bribe from the wicked or to play toady to the strong, but to see the path of justice. The ancient jurists were right, although some of them may have erred

stances of contracts which cannot be enforced on the ground that they are contrary to public morality."

For conservative statements, see Baron Parke, in Egerton v. Brownlow, 4 H.L.C. 1, 122 (1853), and Halsbury, L. C., in Janson v. Driefontein Mines, [1902] A.C. 484, 491. See John B. Waite, "Public Policy and Personal Opinion" (1921) 19 Mich.L.Rev. 265; Percy H. Winfield, "Public Policy and the English Common Law," 42 Harv.L. Rev. 76.

In Veazey v. Allen, 66 N.E. 103, 173 N.Y. 359 (1903), the court said: "In many of its aspects the term public policy is but another name for public sentiment, and, as that is often transitory or shifting it lacks the permanency upon which fixed principles of law are, or should be based. There are, however, other phases of public policy which are as enduring and immutable as the law of gravity. One of them is that, as applied to the law of contracts, courts of justice will never recognize or uphold any transaction which in its object, operation or tendency is calculated to be prejudicial to the public welfare. That sound moral-

ity and civic honesty are cornerstones of the social edifice is a truism which needs no reinforcement by argument. It may therefore be taken for granted that whenever our courts are called upon to scrutinize a contract which is clearly repugnant to sound morality and civic honesty, they need not look long for a well-fitting definition of public policy, nor hesitate in its practical application to the law of contracts." The court's conclusion here stated is not at all invalidated by the fact that no social mores are as "immutable as the law of gravity."

Pollock (Cont. 9th ed. p. 383), discussing Egerton v. Earl Brownlow, said: "If this means only that the Court is to be guided by recognized principles, but will not and cannot bind itself by verbal definition, and in the application of constant principles must have due regard to any new or special facts, the proposition is correct and important, though by no means confined to this topic; but if it means to say that the Court may lay down new principles of public policy without any warrant even of analogy, it seems unwarranted."

as to the nature of justice.  Justice must indeed reign; but not a justice of fallacious absolutes in a realistic world of relativity, not a "Justice" who is herself one of the causes of the falling sky.[11]

The field of "legality of contract" is one of those most violently affected by the fluxing of opinion on "public policy"—on questions of political and economic welfare.  Out of the welter a mass of legislation is spawned, fathered by pressure groups, legislation for ends only dimly seen and expressed in words that are tumultuous and opaque.  A new welter of administrative regulation and judicial decision is produced, to the confusion of the man of business and to the despair of his legal adviser.  The writer on such a subject as restraint of trade must watch his step and his pen.  He can hope to state legal doctrine down to the period when the fluxing of opinion and legislation became violent; beyond that he can only discuss some of the numerous current decisions, point out trends and inconsistencies, and add his one small voice to the bedlam of criticism that surrounds him.

Constitutions and statutes are declarations of public policy by bodies of men authorized to legislate.  It is the function of the courts to interpret and apply these, so far as they go and so far as they are understandable.  Some judges have thought that they must look solely to constitutions and statutes and to earlier decisions interpreting and applying them as the sources from which they may determine what public policy requires.  This is far from true, even though these are the sources that are first to be considered and that often may be conclusive.[12]

In determining the constitutionality of legislation, state or federal, the decision does not turn primarily upon the social policy, economic, political, or otherwise, that the legislation effectuates.  The determination of such policy is almost wholly committed to

11.  Justice Cardozo wrote in 1921 (Nature of the Judicial Process, 166): "I was much troubled in spirit, in my first years upon the bench, to find how trackless was the ocean upon which I had embarked.  I sought for certainty. I was oppressed and disheartened when I found that the quest for it was futile.  I was trying to reach land, the solid land of fixed and settled rules, the paradise of a justice that would declare itself by tokens plainer and more commanding than its pale and glimmering reflections in my own vacillating mind and conscience.  I found 'with the voyagers in Browning's Paracelsus that the real heaven was always beyond.'  As the years have gone by, and I have reflected more and more upon the nature of the judicial process, I have become reconciled to the uncertainty, because I have grown to see it as inevitable.  I have grown to see that the process in its highest reaches is not discovery, but creation; and that the doubts and misgivings, the hopes and fears, are part of the travail of mind, the pangs of death and the pangs of birth, in which principles that have served their day expire, and new principles are born."

the legislative departments of government; and this is continually recognized in the opinions of the judges.[13]  In the interpretation of statutes, however, to determine what their legal operation shall be, and in the interpretation of a constitution, to determine the limits of the grant of legislative power, the court can not properly disregard economic considerations or the prevailing mores and social conditions.

In the absence of legislation, on the other hand, when the problem of the validity of a contract is in issue, the question of the social policy that is to be effectuated by the decision is committed directly to the court by our governmental system.  Our entire body of what is described as the "common law" is the resultant of innumerable court decisions, based upon the judicial notions of sound social policy and human welfare.  The truth of this has been realized at times only by a few of the judges and chancellors; and in huge numbers of cases the major premise on which the decision rested was an "inarticulate major premise."  But when a court holds that a contract is valid or invalid, because it is or is not "against public policy," the matter is plainly open to public view, and the question of what sound policy requires is plainly a judicial question.[14]

In determining what public policy requires, there is no limit whatever to the "sources" to which the court is permitted to go; and there is no limit to the "evidence" that the court may cause to be produced, other than that decision must be reasonably prompt and justice too long delayed becomes injustice.  In holding that a bargain by which a private corporation undertook to provide medical service for the county poor was against public policy, the supreme court of South Dakota has given us the excellent statement that is quoted in the general treatise.[15]

### § 1376.  Liberty of Contract—Progress from Status to Contract

Among the "Freedoms" for which World War II was said to be fought, we find no reference to Liberty of Contract.  In itself, this need not be taken as a conscious abandonment of this much-prized "liberty"; for slogans are drafted to rally support against dangerous foes, not to be subjected to a critical analysis that they can not bear.  "Liberty of Contract" is itself a concept requiring an analysis that it has seldom received and one which if made is at least mildly disillusioning.  No full analysis will be attempted here; but it may be pointed out that "liberty of contract" as that term is used by its admirers includes two very different elements. These are the privilege of doing the acts constituting the transaction and the power to make it legally operative.  One does not have "liberty of contract" unless organized society both forbears and enforces, forbears to penalize him for making his bargain and enforces it for him after it is made.

This is the "liberty of contract" that has so often been extolled as one of the great boons of modern democratic civilization, as one of the principal causes of prosperity and comfort. And yet the very fact that a chapter on "legality" of contract must be written shows that we have never had and never shall have unlimited liberty of contract, either in its phase of societal forbearance or in its phase of societal enforcement. There are many contract transactions that are definitely forbidden by the law, forbidden under pains and penalties assessed for crime and tort; and there are many more such transactions that are denied judicial enforcement, even though their makers are not subjected to affirmative pains and penalties.

Sir Henry Maine noted, it is believed correctly, that the evolution of civilization included a progress "from status to contract," that each individual has gradually acquired a greater "liberty of contract," an increasing forbearance by organized society to forbid his bargains and an increasing readiness to enforce them, thus making his condition in the world more dependent on his own free-willed action than on the action of his ancestors.[16] It is plain, however, that this "progress from status to contract," this increasing "liberty," is not uniform and constant. It goes by jerks. Like the storied frog trying to get out of the well, for every three feet that it jumps upward it slides two feet backward. Indeed, it has not been demonstrated that there may not be long periods of reverse "progress," sliding backward three feet toward "status" for every two feet upward toward "liberty of contract."

16.   "What public policy requires is often a vague and difficult inquiry. It is clear that public policy and the interests of society favor the utmost freedom of contract, within the law, and require that business transactions should not be trammelled by unnecessary restrictions. 'If,' said Sir George Jessel in Printing Co. v. Sampson, L. R. 19 Eq. 462, 'there is one thing more than any other which public policy requires, it is that men of full age and competent understanding shall have the utmost liberty of contracting, and that contracts, when entered into freely and voluntarily, shall be held good and shall be enforced by courts of justice.'" Diamond Match Co. v. Roeber, 13 N.E. 419, 106 N.Y. 473 (1887). Statements like these are not wholly without value, even though they do not tell us when a contract is "within the law" and when restriction is "unnecessary." Even though they "beg the question" as a matter of logic, they point the direction in which emphasis is intended.

In Dr. Miles Medical Co. v. John D. Park & Sons Co., 31 S.Ct. 376, 220 U.S. 373, 55 L.Ed. 502 (1911), Mr. Justice Holmes said: "I think that at least it is safe to say that the most enlightened judicial policy is to let people manage their own business in their own way, unless the ground for interference is very clear."

"It is an encouragement to industry and to enterprise in building up a trade that a man shall be allowed to sell the goodwill of the business and the fruits of his industry upon the best terms that he can obtain." Diamond Match Co. v. Roeber, supra.

The law with respect to contracts in restraint of trade and commerce, as it has been declared by both legislation and judicial decision since the close of World War I, may be demonstrating such a reverse progress. It seems clear that by both processes society is prohibiting the making of bargains that formerly were not prohibited and is refusing enforcement to bargains that formerly would have been enforced. These processes are determined by the changes in prevailing political and economic opinion or by the pressures of interested and influential groups.

No doubt there are also cases in which the courts are less likely to grant judicial enforcement than formerly, without prohibiting the making of the bargain or declaring it illegal in the more opprobrious sense. Standardized contracts such as insurance policies, drafted by powerful commercial units and put before individuals on the "accept this or get nothing" basis, are carefully scrutinized by the courts for the purpose of avoiding enforcement of "unconscionable" clauses. At times this avoidance is effected by a process of pseudo "interpretation;" at other times by refusing to permit successful "overreaching." [17]

### § 1377.   A Bargain may be Unenforceable without Being Illegal

Statutes sometimes declare certain agreements to be unenforceable by action without intending to prohibit their making, to make them illegal, or even to discourage their performance. Such statutes are the Statute of Frauds and the Statutes of Limitation.

The statute of frauds was passed "for the prevention of frauds and perjuries"; but the sections of this statute (sections 4 and 17) that have been so generally re-enacted in this country and that are now meant when we speak of "the Statute of Frauds" has no application whatever to agreements between two persons for the defrauding of a third or to those in which one party is induced to enter by the fraudulent representations of the other. The former of these is indeed illegal because of its purpose. The latter is voidable by the injured party, and the fraudulent conduct is a tort; but the bargain that was made is not an illegal bargain. The statute of frauds merely declares that certain kinds of contracts that are specifically named shall not be enforceable by action unless they are evidenced by some note or memorandum in writing, signed by the party to be charged. It does not forbid

---

17.   See the proposed Uniform Commercial Code—Sales, § 2—302 (1950 draft) which provides:

"If the court finds the contract or any clause of the contract to be unconscionable, it may refuse to enforce the contract or strike any

unconscionable clauses and enforce the contract as if the stricken clause had never existed."

This would apply to all contracts alike, whether in "standardized" form or not.

the making of these contracts orally or in any way discourage the parties from performing them. If a mortgage or pledge is delivered as security for performance, such security is as fully operative as if the contract had been in writing. All this has been fully set forth in the chapters dealing with the statute of frauds.

The first statute of limitations, in the 21st year of James I, provided only that no action of debt should be maintainable unless brought within six years from the accrual of the cause of action. The contracts to which this was applicable were not made illegal at the end of six years after maturity. Here, too, mortgages and pledges given as security were not invalidated by the statute. Payment of an old debt was not meant to be discouraged, nor was the debtor regarded as morally justified in his refusal to pay it. It was merely regarded as sound policy to discourage the litigation of stale claims, after witnesses may be dead or distant and some of the relevant facts forgotten. Modern statutes of limitation are made applicable to other transactions than debts and to other modes of enforcement at law; but their purpose and effect are otherwise the same.

There have been innumerable contracts and deeds of conveyance containing restrictive covenants against sale to or occupancy by Negroes, Japanese, or other persons not recognized as Caucasians. Prior to 1948 these covenants were held to be enforceable in nearly all the States. In that year, however, the Supreme Court held that the enforcement of such a covenant by any State court or other State officer is prohibited by the 14th Amendment to the Constitution as being a denial of equal protection of the laws.[18] Since that prohibition is directed against the States and not against individuals, the Court did not hold that the Constitution forbids either the making or the performance of such a restrictive covenant. However, the fact that the Constitution prohibits the enforcement of such covenants is based upon the belief that they are contrary to the public welfare.[19] They should therefore be described as "illegal" covenants, even though the only judicial sanction thus far established is non-enforceability. In this respect such covenants differ from oral contracts within the statute of frauds and contracts the enforcement of which is barred by a statute of limitations.

18.    **U.S.**—Shelley **v.** Kraemer, 68 S. Ct. 836, 334 U.S. 1, 92 L.Ed. 1161, 3 A.L.R.2d 441 (1948).

19.    Such covenants with respect to property in the District of Colum-

bia and the Territories are forbidden by Act of Congress, 8 U.S.C.A. § 42. See Hurd v. Hodge, 68 S.Ct. 847, 334 U.S. 24, 92 L.Ed. 1187 (1948).

## § 1378. Degrees of Illegality—Malum Prohibitum and Malum In Se

In very many court opinions a distinction has been drawn between that which is only "malum prohibitum" and that which is said to be "malum in se." This distinction involves a false assumption, one the falsity of which is the more successfully concealed by the use of Latin words. But in spite of the fact that many judges have said that the distinction has been "exploded," [20] it continues to be repeated; and it is in fact based upon differences in degree and in source and in extent of harm that often justify a variation in judicial remedies and other consequences. It is an interesting fact that doctrines have often survived an "explosion."

The falsity of the distinction, as expressed in the Latin phrases, rests in the assumption, made throughout so many centuries, that right and wrong are absolutes and that a mere human being can draw an absolute and unvarying line between good and evil.[21] In a human world where everything is relative and where judgments must rest upon human mores, nothing can be said to be evil "in itself." It is perfectly clear that neither the terms nor the notions that they express give to the courts any clear line of distinction by which court action can be determined, either as to the enforceability of a bargain or as to the availability of a particular remedy.

Nevertheless, even in this relative human world, some things are worse than others. Some things have been thought to be evil according to the mores of many tribes, nations and religions over long periods of time. Other things have been prohibited by legislation only because a small fraction of the community be-

**20.** In Gibbs v. Consolidated Gas Co., 9 S.Ct. 553, 130 U.S. 396, 32 L. Ed. 979 (1889), a Maryland statute prohibited consolidation of gas companies and declared contracts for such purpose to be "null and void." The court refused enforcement of such a contract, saying that a contract made in direct violation of a statutory prohibition can not be enforced, even though in absence of the statute it would not have been evil. The distinction between "malum in se" and "malum prohibitum," it was said, "has long been exploded."

"The distinction between an act *malum in se* and one merely *malum prohibitum* was never sound." Sharp v. Farmer, 20 N.C. 122 (1838), contract to divide up an estate without legally required administration held void.

"Where a statute designed for the protection of the public prescribes a penalty, that penalty is the equivalent of an express prohibition and a contract in violation of its terms is void. And with respect to such contracts . . . the distinction between *malum prohibitum* and *malum in se* has long since been exploded, both in this country and England." McManus v. Fulton, 278 P. 126, 85 Mont. 170, 67 A.L.R. 690 (1929).

**21.** The distinction between malum in se and malum prohibitum is considered in Y.B. 11 Hen. 7, 11, 35, that which is malum in se being regarded as forbidden by the "Ley de nature."

lieve them to be evil and have urged the legislation with great vociferation and voting threats. When a bargain involving the former of these is made, there may be more reason for a bargainer to know that he is doing wrong and more reason for attaching serious results to his conduct. It is generally when a bargain belongs in this class that it is described as "malum in se." When a bargain or other conduct is described as merely "malum prohibitum," a court usually means that it is now wrong and illegal only because it has been so declared by an act of legislation and that it was not so regarded under the prevailing mores prior to that legislation.[22]

Thus, it has not been thought wrong or harmful to import silks and spices from other countries; but after such importation is forbidden by statute as retaliation against the exporting nation, or is forbidden without payment of an import duty, such importation becomes illegal and wrong by statute. Though not "malum in se" it becomes "malum prohibitum." Many otherwise worthy citizens and church members have thought that "smuggling" is not "morally" wrong, even though it is prohibited by statute.[23]

22. The continued use of the Latin phrases, with their assumption of a distinction in kind, induces some curious distinctions. Thus in State v. Budge, 137 A. 244, 126 Me. 223 (1927), it is said to be "malum in se" to drive an automobile while "intoxicated," but merely "malum prohibitum" to drive one while "under the influence of liquor."

In People v. Townsend, 183 N.W. 177, 214 Mich. 267, 16 A.L.R. 902 (1921), voluntary intoxication was held to be "malum in se," citing ecclesiastical law and the Biblical attitude toward Noah's drunkenness and the conduct of Lot's daughters.

23. A long discussion of malum prohibitum as compared with malum in se is given us in Lewis v. Welch, 14 N.H. 294 (1843). Even though the court may have believed in the existence of some absolute standard separating good from evil and right from wrong, it was aware that it is not at hand for courts or litigants to apply. It said: "It is contended by the counsel for the plaintiff that there is a distinction between malum prohibitum and malum in se; between things intrinsically and morally wrong, and things which are made so merely by legislation. The inference he would make from this distinction is that when an act is merely malum prohibitum, it may conscientiously be done, provided only the party be willing to incur the penalty. He considers it optional with the party to do or to refrain from doing the act in question, and that the alternative is presented him by the legislature to abstain from the act or to do it and pay the penalty." The court disapproves this; because the test of conscience is too variable and uncertain. "Men differ in their views of right and wrong; the moral sense of one man is more obtuse than that of another . . . The subtle casuistry which self-interest teaches us is a most unsafe guide in questions of morals." The court then held that a bargain for the sale of liquor without a license was unenforceable, because the legislature intended to prohibit for protective purposes and not merely to collect a license tax for revenue purposes. The decision rightly turns on the purpose of

In the absence of statute there is nothing illegal or morally wrong in carrying on business as a real estate broker, a doctor or a teacher without getting somebody's permission. Yet such transactions are often prohibited by statute without first obtaining a license from public authority. Such a statute may say nothing as to the validity of a bargain for rendering such services by an unlicensed person; but the enforceability of the bargain can not be determined by observing that the transaction was merely "malum prohibitum." The words of the statute must be interpreted, the purposes of the legislature weighed, and the social effect of giving or refusing a remedy considered.

The fact that the courts continually recognize differences in degree of evil is made apparent throughout this chapter, especially in cases determining the availability of judicial remedies. Will the contract itself be enforced, either specifically or in damages for breach? Sometimes the answer is yes, if the plaintiff can be described as "innocent" or not "in pari delicto," and sometimes even in favor of a "guilty" party when the public welfare so requires. A party who has knowledge of the illegal purpose of the other but does not participate therein may be able to enforce the contract if the purpose was not too heinous, or as the court may say was not "malum in se." Again, although the court will not enforce the contract as made, it may be willing to give a restitutionary remedy, even to a "guilty" party, if the transaction is described as merely "malum prohibitum" or of some lesser degree of badness.[24] The discussion of these matters is reserved for succeeding sections.

the statute and on what sound policy requires, as a mode of enforcement.

24. One illustrative case is American-LaFrance & Foamite Industries v. Arlington County, 192 S.E. 758, 169 Va. 1 (1937).

The provision that "good moral character" is required for admission to citizenship has presented some knotty problems. On this ground, an alien who had performed euthanasia on his defective child was denied citizenship in Repouille v. U. S., 165 F.2d 152 (C.C.A.2d 1948), one judge dissenting. In the absence of a plebicite (or at least a "Gallup poll") the matter had to be determined by the moral feelings that the judges thought to be generally prevailing.

# CHAPTERS 80–90

The detailed treatment of many varieties of illegal bargains must be omitted from this one-volume edition. In order to indicate their subject-matter, the title headings of the various chapters are here given, as follows:

Chapter 80. Restraint of Trade—Development at Common Law.

Chapter 81. Restraint of Trade—The Sherman Anti-Trust Act and Later Developments.

Chapter 82. What Constitutes Restraint—Methods of Imposing It.

Chapter 83. Trade Associations—Mergers—Labor Unions.

Chapter 84. Bargains Harmful to the Administration of Justice.

Chapter 85. Bargains Harmful to the Public Service or to Performance of Fiduciary Duty.

Chapter 86. Bargains to Defraud or Otherwise Injure Third Persons.

Chapter 87. Bargains Harmful to Marriage, Family, or Morality—Sunday Laws.

Chapter 88. Wagering Bargains—Usury.

Chapter 89. Miscellaneous Illegal Bargains.

Chapter 90. Effects of Illegality—Restitution.

The first four of these chapters must generally be dealt with in special courses on Trade Regulation and Public Control of Business.

For a brief résumé of rules of law dealing with Illegality, see Restatement, Contracts.

# INDEX

This index is an abbreviation of the long index to the author's eight-volume general treatise on Contracts. Section numbers are identical with those in that treatise; but the sections herein are often greatly shortened. Consult the corresponding section in the treatise for matter that is omitted here and for the citation and analysis of the relevant court decisions.

**BURDEN OF PROOF—Cont'd**
Mode of describing a condition, effect, §§ 741, 749–751.
Negative, proof of, §§ 741, 1230, 1329.
Payment, § 1230.

**BUSINESS PURPOSE**
Subscriptions for, § 198.

**BUSINESS USAGE**
Acceptance by mail or telegram, §§ 67, 78, 81.
Gaps filled and uncertainty removed, §§ 95–102.
Not known to a contractor, § 557.
Terms added to a contract, § 556.
Time of delivery and payment, § 96.

**CANCELLATION**
As discharge or rescission, §§ 1229, 1236, 1250.
Power to cancel, §§ 160–170.

**CATALOG**
Price list, § 28.

**CAUSA**
Civil law, relation to consideration, §§ 111, 113, 115, 118, 196.
Louisiana law, § 149.
Nudum pactum, § 210.

**CAUSA MORTIS**
Gift assignment, §§ 912, 916.

**CAUSES BEYOND CONTROL**
Absence of, made an express condition, §§ 33, 642.
Express provisions limiting risk, §§ 1331, 1340, 1342.

**CAVEAT**
Emptor, vendor, grantor, § 605.

**CERTAINTY OF LAW**
Illegality, public policy, § 1375.
Tentative working rules, see Preface.

**CERTIFICATE OF APPROVAL,** §§ 649–652, 656.

**CHANGE OF POSITION**
Ground for refusing relief for mistake, §§ 599, 606.
Induced by other party's apparent inability, § 1260.
Induced by words of waiver or assurance, § 754.
Reliance on a promise, §§ 193–209, 441.

**CHARITABLE SUBSCRIPTIONS,** § 198.

**CHECK**
Cashing, as acceptance of offer, §§ 88, 1277, 1279.
Conditional payment, presumption, § 1284.
Death of drawer before presenting, § 880.
Gift assignment of another's, § 915.
Not an assignment, § 880.
Offered in full satisfaction, §§ 88, 1277, 1279, 1284.
Payment by, § 1235.

**CHOSE IN ACTION**
Assignment of, See Assignment.
Definition, §§ 859, 910.

**COLLATERAL SECURITY**
Assignments as, § 881.
Book accounts as, § 874.
Goes with an assignment, §§ 891, 907.

**COLLECTION**
Assignments for, § 882.
Gratuitous promise of, reliance thereon, § 207.
Promise to assign or to pay after, § 877.

**COLLECTIVE BARGAINS**
Employees as beneficiaries, §§ 781, 782, 814.
Employees as joint promisees, § 939.
Illusory, how far, § 1.
Joint and several contracts compared, § 923.
Power of bargaining agent to vary, § 814.

**COMMERCIAL IMPRACTICABILITY**
Effect on promisor's duty, §§ 642, 1325, 1333, 1342.

**COMMON COUNTS**
Assumpsit, forms of action, § 20.
Quasi contract, §§ 19, 20.

**COMMON LAW**
Consideration doctrine, early history, § 109.
Development of law of assignment, § 856.
Displacement by equity, joint and several contracts, §§ 924, 923–942.
Federal common law, § 1374.
Forms of action, abolition, § 117.
Sources and origins, §§ 109, 654, 1374.
Time of the essence, §§ 709, 713.
What and how known, § 1374.
See Joinder of Law and Equity.

END OF VOLUME